The Law of Journalism and Mass Communication

Third Edition

The Law of Journalism and Mass Communication

Third Edition

Robert Trager

University of Colorado

Joseph Russomanno

Arizona State University

Susan Dente Ross

Washington State University

Los Angeles | London | New Delhi
Singapore | Washington DC

CQ Press
2300 N Street, NW, Suite 800
Washington, DC 20037

Phone: 202-729-1900; toll-free, 1-866-4CQ-PRESS (1-866-427-7737)

Web: www.cqpress.com

Cover design: Anne C. Kerns, Anne Likes Red, Inc.
Composition: C&M Digitals (P) Ltd.

☺ The paper used in this publication exceeds the requirements of the American National Standard for Information Sciences—Permanence of Paper for Printed Library Materials, ANSI Z39.48-1992.

Printed and bound in the United States of America

15   14   13   12   11   1   2   3   4   5

Library of Congress Cataloging-in-Publication Data

Trager, Robert.
   The law of journalism and mass communication / Robert Trager, Joseph Russomanno, Susan Dente Ross. — 3rd ed.
      p. cm.
   Includes bibliographical references and index.
   ISBN 978-1-60871-669-2 (pbk. : alk. paper) 1. Mass media—Law and legislation—United States. 2. Press law—United States. 3. Freedom of the press—United States. I. Russomanno, Joseph. II. Ross, Susan Dente. III. Title.

   KF2750.T73 2011
   343.7309'9—dc23

                                                                          2011018892

For Our Families

About the Authors

Robert Trager is professor emeritus in journalism and mass communication at the University of Colorado at Boulder. He taught courses in communication law, freedom of expression and media institutions. He is the founding editor of the law journal "Communication Law and Policy." Before joining the University of Colorado faculty, he was an attorney with a major cable television company and practiced media law with a firm in Washington, D.C.

Joseph Russomanno is associate professor in the Walter Cronkite School of Journalism and Mass Communication at Arizona State University. He has worked as a news reporter in radio and television and as a television news writer, newscast producer and executive producer at stations in St. Louis and Denver. He has received several awards for his broadcast work. His teaching and research focus on media law and First Amendment issues.

Susan Dente Ross is professor of English at Washington State University where she teaches legal and creative writing and conducts research on how the freedoms of speech and press can improve global equity and justice. She is a creative writer and a leader in international initiatives to enhance media contributions to conflict transformation and resolution.

Brief Contents

Contents   x

Features   xx

Preface   xxvi

1. The Rule of Law
Law in a Changing Communication Environment   2

2. The First Amendment
Speech and Press Freedoms in Theory and Reality   48

3. Speech Distinctions
Dangers, Fights, Threats and Educational Needs   98

4. Libel
The Plaintiff's Case   138

5. Libel
Defenses and Privileges   186

6. Protecting Privacy
Conflicts between the Press and the Right to Privacy   222

7. Emotional Distress and Physical Harm
When Words and Pictures Hurt   278

8. **Newsgathering**
   Pitfalls and Protections   320

9. **Reporter's Privilege**
   Protecting the Watchdogs   380

10. **The Media and the Courts**
    Preserving Public Trials and Preventing Prejudice   420

11. **Electronic Media Regulation**
    From Radio to the Internet   474

12. **Obscenity, Indecency and Violence**
    Social Norms and Legal Standards   528

13. **Intellectual Property**
    Protecting and Using Intangible Creations   578

14. **Advertising**
    When Speech and Commerce Converge   640

   Endnotes   677
   Glossary   723
   Recommended Readings   733
   Photo Credits   739
   Text Credits   741
   Case Index   743
   Subject Index   755

Contents

Features   xx
Preface   xxvi

Chapter 1 The Rule of Law
Law in a Changing Communication Environment   2

The Court System   7
    Jurisdiction   7
    Trial Courts   9
    Courts of Appeal   10
    The U.S. Supreme Court   12
    Judicial Review   16
Sources of the Law   19
    Constitutions   20
    Statutes   21
    Equity Law   24
    Common Law   24
    Administrative Rules   26
    Executive Orders   26
The Case Process   27
    Civil Suits   28
    Summary Judgment   31
Finding the Law   32
    Useful Legal Research Resources   33
Reading Case Law   34
    Briefing Cases   35
    Analyzing *Marbury v. Madison*   36

CASES FOR STUDY   38

Citizens United v. Federal Election Commission   38

Marbury v. Madison   44

Chapter 2 The First Amendment
Speech and Press Freedoms in Theory and Reality   48

Interpreting the First Amendment   50

The Origins of the First Amendment   53

Foundations of First Amendment Theory   53

First Amendment Values   57

Contemporary Prior Restraints   61

Court Scrutiny of Laws That Affect First Amendment Rights   66

Content-Based Laws   67

Content-Neutral Laws   68

Political Speech   72

Elections and Campaign Finance   72

Anonymous Speech   75

Government Speakers   76

Public and Nonpublic Forums   78

Private Property as a Public Forum   81

Virtual Forums and Government Speakers   83

Compelled Speech   84

Media Emergence, Convergence and Consolidation   85

CASES FOR STUDY   89

New York Times Co. v. United States   89

United States v. O'Brien   92

Chapter 3 Speech Distinctions
Dangers, Fights, Threats and Educational Needs   98

National Security and Tranquility   100

Threats to National Security   101

Court Tests to Protect Disruptive Speech	**105**
The Clear and Present Danger Test	105
The *Brandenburg* (or Incitement) Test	108
Speech Assaults	**109**
Offensive Speech	109
Fighting Words	110
Hate Speech	111
Current Standard	112
Intimidation and Threats	112
Symbolic Speech	**116**
Burning Speech	116
Speech in the Schools	**118**
Protest in the Schools	119
Offensive or Inappropriate Conduct	121
Compelled Orthodoxy	124
Religion in the Schools	125
Campus Speech	125
Speech Codes	128
CASES FOR STUDY	**131**
Texas v. Johnson	131
Tinker v. Des Moines Independent Community School District	133

Chapter 4 Libel
The Plaintiff's Case

138

A Brief History	**140**
Contemporary Issues	**146**
The Elements of Libel: The Plaintiff's Case	**146**
Statement of Fact	147
Publication	147
Identification	152
Defamation	154
Falsity	157
Fault	160
Damages	175
Criminal Libel	176
CASES FOR STUDY	**178**
New York Times Co. v. Sullivan	178
Gertz v. Robert Welch, Inc.	180

Chapter 5 Libel
Defenses and Privileges

Defenses and Privileges — 186

Fair Report Privilege — 188
Fair Comment and Criticism — 191
Opinion — 193
  Innocent Construction — 195
  Letters to the Editor — 198
  Rhetorical Hyperbole, Parody and Satire — 198
Neutral Reportage — 201
Wire Service Defense — 202
Single-Publication Rule — 203
The Libel-Proof Plaintiff — 204
Single-Mistake Rule — 206
Other Defense Issues — 206
  Summary Judgment — 206
  Jurisdiction — 207
  Statute of Limitations — 209
  Length of Statutes of Limitation in Libel Actions — 209
  Retractions — 210
  Responsible Reporting — 211
CASES FOR STUDY — 213
  Ollman v. Evans — 213
  Milkovich v. Lorain Journal Co. — 218

Chapter 6 Protecting Privacy
Conflicts between the Press and the Right to Privacy

Conflicts between the Press and the Right to Privacy — 222

Sources of Privacy Protection — 227
Privacy Law's Development — 228
False Light — 229
  Plaintiff's Case — 231
  Defenses — 235

Appropriation   237
   Commercialization and Right of Publicity   238
   Plaintiff's Case   239
   Defenses   244
Intrusion   253
   Methods of Intruding   254
   Intrusion on Private Property   254
   Defenses   256
Private Facts   259
   Intimate Facts   260
   Legitimate Public Concern   262
   Publicity   265
   First Amendment Defense   266

CASES FOR STUDY   270
   Cox Broadcasting Corp. v. Cohn   270
   City of Ontario v. Quon   273

Chapter 7 Emotional Distress and Physical Harm
When Words and Pictures Hurt   278

Emotional Distress   280
   The Development of Emotional Distress Suits   280
Intentional Infliction of Emotional Distress   282
   Outrageousness   283
   Intentional or Reckless Action   288
Negligent Infliction of Emotional Distress   291
Physical Harm   293
   Negligence   294
   Foreseeability   295
Incitement   298
   Intending to Incite   299
Communications Decency Act   303
Other Dangers   305
   Breach of Contract   305
   Interference with Economic Advantage   306
   Fraudulent Misrepresentation   307
   Expanding Tort Law   307

CASES FOR STUDY   309
   Hustler Magazine Inc. v. Falwell   309
   Rice v. Paladin Enterprises, Inc.   311

Chapter 8 Newsgathering
Pitfalls and Protections

	320
Newsgathering Pitfalls	**323**
Trespass	325
Harassment	329
Fraud and Misrepresentation	330
Covert Recording	**335**
Face-to-Face Recording	335
Recording "Wire" Conversations	337
Noncovert Recording	341
Access to Military Operations	**343**
Denying Access to Records	345
Newsgathering Protections	**348**
Open Government Laws	348
Access to Federal Records	349
Access to Federal Meetings	**364**
State Open-Records Laws	365
State Open-Meetings Laws	368
CASES FOR STUDY	**370**
Wilson v. Layne	370
U.S. Department of Justice v. Reporters Committee for Freedom of the Press	374

Chapter 9 Reporter's Privilege
Protecting the Watchdogs

	380
Reporter's Privilege	**382**
After *Branzburg*	386
Shield Laws	**390**
Who Is Covered	393
What Is Covered	394

Other Shield Law Issues   395
Other Sources of Reporter's Privilege   397
Breaking Promises of Confidentiality   **398**
Search Warrants   **400**
Newsroom Searches   401
The Privacy Protection Act   402
CASES FOR STUDY   **405**
Branzburg v. Hayes   405
Cohen v. Cowles Media Co.   417

Chapter 10 The Media and the Courts

Preserving Public Trials and Preventing Prejudice   420

Fair Trials and Prejudicial Speech   **422**
Media Effects   423
Impartial Jurors   426
Anonymous Juries   428
Impartial Judges   428
Remedies to Prejudice   **429**
Selecting the Jury   429
Continuance   430
Juror Admonition   431
Juror Sequestration   431
Contempt   431
Access to Trials   **432**
Presumption of Open Trials   433
Justifying Court Closure   435
Closure to Protect Juveniles   439
Closure to Protect Sexual Assault Victims   441
Gags to Limit Extrajudicial Discussion   441
Challenging Closure   444
Electronic Access to Trials   **445**
Broadcasting and Recording   445
Cameras and Courtrooms   448
Newer Technologies   449
Bench-Bar-Press Guidelines   **451**
Access to Court Records   **452**
Constitutional and Statutory Access   452
Court Dockets   453
State Secrets   454

Court Access Rules   455
Electronic Access to Court Records   456
CASES FOR STUDY   **459**
Sheppard v. Maxwell   459
Richmond Newspapers Inc. v. Virginia   467

Chapter 11 Electronic Media Regulation
From Radio to the Internet   474

Federal Communications Commission   **478**
Broadcast Regulation   **481**
Reasons to Regulate Broadcasting   481
The Public Interest Standard   482
Program and Advertising Regulations   484
Broadcast Licensing   499
Noncommercial Broadcasting   501
Cable Television Regulation   **503**
Cable Regulation's Development   503
Cable Franchising   506
Cable Programming   509
Direct Broadcast Satellites   **514**
Internet Regulation   **515**
FCC Internet Regulation   515
The Internet's First Amendment Status   517
CASES FOR STUDY   **519**
Red Lion Broadcasting Co., Inc. v. Federal Communications Commission 519
Turner Broadcasting System, Inc. v. Federal Communications Commission 524

Chapter 12 Obscenity, Indecency and Violence
Social Norms and Legal Standards   528

Obscenity   **532**
Comstock and *Hicklin*   533
Current Obscenity Definition   535

Enforcing Obscenity Laws   **541**
Indecency   **546**
    Broadcast Indecency   547
    Television Program Ratings and the V-Chip   554
Cable Indecency   **555**
    Internet Indecency   557
Other Limits on Offensive Speech   **562**
    Public Funds for Pornographic Art   562
    Recording Labels   563
    Using Zoning to Restrict Adult Stores   563
    Dial-a-Porn: Telephone Indecency   565
Video Games and Media Violence   **566**

CASES FOR STUDY   **571**
    Miller v. California   571
    Fox Television Stations, Inc. v. Federal Communications Commission   575

Chapter 13 Intellectual Property
Protecting and Using Intangible Creations   578

Copyright   **580**
    The Development of U.S. Copyright Law   582
    The 1976 Copyright Act   583
    Proving Copyright Infringement   599
    Remedies for Copyright Infringement   602
    Copyright Infringement Defense: Fair Use   603
    Copyright, Computers and the Internet   607
    Music Licensing   609
    Music, the Internet and File Sharing   616
Trademarks   **618**
    Distinctiveness Requirement   619
    Registering a Trademark   622
    Domain Names   623
    Trademark Infringement   624
    Trademark Infringement Defenses   626

CASES FOR STUDY   **628**
    Eldred v. Ashcroft   628
    Metro-Goldwyn-Mayer Studios, Inc. v. Grokster, Ltd.   633

Chapter 14 Advertising

When Speech and Commerce Converge   640

The Evolution of the Commercial Speech Doctrine   642
   Putting the Doctrine to Work   646
   Corporate Speech Regulation   650
Legislative and Agency Advertising Regulation   652
   The Federal Trade Commission   654
Other Administrative Regulation   660
   Internet Advertising   660

CASES FOR STUDY   664
   *Central Hudson Gas & Electric Corp. v. Public Service
     Commission of New York*   664
   Lorillard v. Reilly   670

Endnotes   677
Glossary   723
Recommended Readings   733
Photo Credits   739
Text Credits   741
Case Index   743
Subject Index   755

Features

1. The Rule of Law

According to Aristotle (box)	5
Points of Law: What's in a Face?	**6**
Comparing State and Federal Courts (table)	8
Points of Law: A Test for Court Jurisdiction of Internet Disputes	**9**
The Federal Court System (figure)	10
The State Court System (figure)	10
U.S. Circuit Courts of Appeal (map)	11
Real World Law: Conservative Leanings	**13**
The U.S. Supreme Court at a Glance, Fall 2011 (box)	14
How an Appeal is Processed (figure)	15
Real World Law: Is Interpreting the Law a Bit Like Making Sausage?	**18**
Points of Law: Six Sources of Law	**20**
Points of Law: The Three Branches of Federal Government	**21**
The Bill of Rights to the U.S. Constitution (box)	22
How a Bill Becomes a Law (figure)	23
The Path of Civil Lawsuits (figure)	28
Real World Law: Blogger Bests "Bullying" Subpoena	**30**

2. The First Amendment

Is Journalism a "Conspiracy of Intellect"? (box)	52
Real World Law: True Treason?	**56**
Points of Law: What's the Value of Free Speech?	**58**
Real World Law: What, Exactly, Is "the Freedom of Speech"?	**60**
Points of Law: What Is a Prior Restraint?	**62**
Real World Law: The Pentagon Papers of Our Time?	**63**
Points of Law: When Are Prior Restraints Constitutional?	**65**
Points of Law: Strict Scrutiny	**67**
Points of Law: Intermediate-Level Scrutiny	**70**

Points of Law: Where Does Intermediate Scrutiny Apply? 71
Real World Law: The Politics of Election Finance 74
Real World Law: But Where Can I Speak? 80

3. Speech Distinctions

Real World Law: Terrorism or Efforts at Peace? 103
Real World Law: Are These "Troublous" Times? 104
Points of Law: The *Brandenburg* Test 108
Points of Law: Fighting Words 111
Points of Law: Is That a Threat? 114
Real World Law: Text Threats 115
Points of Law: Non-university Student Speech 119
Real World Law: You Can't Read This! 122
Real World Law: Is Shouting Always "Shouting Fire"? 127
Real World Law: A Conservative Take on Campus Speech? 129

4. Libel: The Plaintiff's Case

Points of Law: Slander vs. Libel 140
Reputation in History and Literature (box) 142
Libel (box) 142
Real World Law: "60 Minutes" and the Chilling Effect 143
The Star Chamber (box) 144
Points of Law: States with Anti-SLAPP Statutes 144
Real World Law: Is Libel Out of Fashion? 145
Points of Law: The Plaintiff's Libel Case 147
Real World Law: Libel and the Online Publisher 149
Real World Law: Online Libel 150
Real World Law: The Unknown Publisher 151
Points of Law: Libel Plaintiff's Case When Publisher Defendant Is Unknown 152
Libel in Fiction (box) 153
Real World Law: Oprah and the Cattlemen 156
Points of Law: The Burden of Proof as Deterrent 159
Real World Law: The Impact of *New York Times Co. v. Sullivan:* The "Central Meaning of the First Amendment" 163
Points of Law: Actual Malice 164
Real World Law: *Masson v. New Yorker Magazine, Inc.* and Journalistic Responsibility 165
Points of Law: "Reckless Disregard" Criteria 167
Points of Law: Limited Purpose Public Figure 170
Real World Law: On the Air: Talk Radio, Libel and Opinion 173

5. Libel: Defenses and Privileges

Points of Law: Fair Report Privilege 188
Real World Law: Fair Comment and Criticism: The Beginning 192
Points of Law: The *Ollman* Test for Opinion 194
Real World Law: Defining Opinion: *Ollman v. Evans* 196

Real World Law: Letters to the Editor: "A Special Type of Expression"   199

Points of Law: Neutral Reportage   201

Points of Law: The Wire Service Defense   202

Real World Law: *Edwards v. National Audubon Society:* The Origin of Neutral Reportage   202

Real World Law: The Libel-Proof Doctrine: Applied with Caution   205

Real World Law: Libel Tourism   208

Points of Law: A Test for Jurisdiction   209

Length of Statutes of Limitation in Libel Actions (map)   210

6. Protecting Privacy

Real World Law: What Others Know about You   226

Real World Law: Stolen Privacy?   227

Points of Law: The Four Privacy Torts   228

Real World Law: A False Tort   230

Points of Law: False Light   231

Real World Law: Lowest of the Low?   233

Real World Law: Why Have a False Light Tort?   236

Points of Law: Appropriation   237

Points of Law: Commercialization   241

Real World Law: Soldiers and Anti-war T-shirts   242

Real World Law: Is an Ad an Ad?   243

Real World Law: Football Players in Real Life and in Video Games   249

Points of Law: Intrusion by Trespass   255

Real World Law: Using False Pretenses?   257

Points of Law: Private Facts   260

Real World Law: Privacy in Public Records?   261

Real World Law: Privacy-Proof Plaintiff?   264

Real World Law: Public Is Not Private   269

7. Emotional Distress and Physical Harm

Points of Law: Intentional Infliction of Emotional Distress   283

Real World Law: Dateline, Texas: To Catch a Lawsuit?   284

Real World Law: Hurtful Speech and the First Amendment   287

Real World Law: The "Pornographer" and His Attorney   289

Points of Law: Parody or Satire?   289

Points of Law: Negligent Infliction of Emotional Distress   292

Points of Law: Proximate Cause   297

Real World Law: Cyberbullying   300

Real World Law: "Hit Man": Protected or Not?   302

Real World Law: Media Inspiring Violent Acts   303

Points of Law: What Is a Contract?   306

8. Newsgathering

Real World Law: A Question of Access   324

Points of Law: The Media and Search Warrants   327

Points of Law: *Wilson v. Layne:* The State of Ride-Alongs 328

The Propriety of Ride-Alongs (box) 329

Real World Law: "California v. Paparazzi" 331

Real World Law: *Food Lion:* Assessing the Impact 332

Points of Law: States That Forbid Unauthorized Use of Cameras in Private Places 335

Points of Law: Recording Calls 336

Recording Laws by State (map) 338

Real World Law: Video of Public Places 342

Points of Law: Freedom of Information Act: Some Basics 349

Real World Law: How Responsive Is the U.S. Government to FOIA Requests? 353

Points of Law: Freedom of Information Act: The Exemptions 354

Real World Law: NASA and FOIA 359

Real World Law: The Fight over Photos 362

Real World Law: E-Mail as a Public Record? 365

Real World Law: Access in the Digital Age 367

Points of Law: State Open-Meetings Laws: The New York Example 368

9. Reporter's Privilege

Points of Law: The *Branzburg* Test for Reporter's Privilege 384

Points of Law: Contempt of Court 385

Real World Law: "An Act of Conscience" 387

Real World Law: Examples of Reporters Fined for Refusing to Reveal Sources; Examples of Reporters Jailed for Refusing to Reveal Sources 388

Real World Law: Leakers and the Law 390

Points of Law: State Shield Laws: The U.S. Supreme Court's View 391

Points of Law: Shield Law States 392

Points of Law: Potential Options for Journalist Protection of Confidential Sources 393

Real World Law: Privilege Denied 394

Real World Law: Reporters, Subpoenas and Contempt 395

Real World Law: Blogging and Contempt of Court 396

Real World Law: Passing the First Test 397

Real World Law: Anonymous Posters on News Websites 398

Real World Law: *Cohen v. Cowles Media Co.:* A Reporter's Perspective 399

Real World Law: After *Stanford Daily:* A "Predictable Result" 403

10. The Media and the Courts

Real World Law: Crime Time News? 425

Real World Law: High Profile, Historic and Unsolved? The Marilyn Sheppard Murder 426

Real World Law: Publicity and Prosecutor Prejudice? 427

Real World Law: Fewer Newsrooms Fight for Open Courts 433

Points of Law: Open Courts 434

Points of Law: The *Press-Enterprise* Test for Court Closure 435

Does Publicity Bias Jurors? (box) 436

Real World Law: Jury Questionnaires in O.J. Simpson Robbery-Kidnapping Trial Should Be Open 438

Cameras in State and Federal Courtrooms (map) 440

Points of Law: Closing Media Mouths: The *Nebraska Press* Standard 442

Real World Law: Open Your Mouth and Open Courts 444

Real World Law: Lights, Cameras, Courts? 446

State by State Media Access to Juvenile Offender Identities (map) 447

Real World Law: Cameras or Coroners in the Court? 448

Real World Law: Managing New Media in Courts 450

Points of Law: What Is Fair Coverage of Criminal Trials? 451

11. Electronic Media Regulation

Real World Law: Congress Grounds the FCC 479

Real World Law: Obama's FCC Chair Choice 480

The Electromagnetic Spectrum (box) 483

Real World Law: Who Wins Political Campaigns? Broadcasters 485

Points of Law: How Section 315 Works 487

Real World Law: Can Children Be Protected from Media Content? 492

Real World Law: Wee/Wii Contest Leads to Death 494

Real World Law: Just a Joke 496

Real World Law: Australian-American 500

Points of Law: Local Radio Station Ownership 501

Real World Law: When More Providers Equals Less Access 510

Real World Law: Mailbox or Sandbox? 518

12. Obscenity, Indecency and Violence

Points of Law: Disgusting and Repugnant 530

Real World Law: Pornography's Harms 532

Real World Law: Pornography from a Different Viewpoint 533

Real World Law: Comstock in Action 534

Real World Law: Sex and the Restaurant 536

Real World Law: Sex and the Internet 537

Points of Law: The SLAPS Test 540

Real World Law: The Last Movie Censor 544

Real World Law: Comedian George Carlin 549

Real World Law: Pigs in Parlors 550

Television Program Ratings (box) 553

Points of Law: Censoring the Internet 557

Real World Law: Internet Indecency: ACLU v. Congress 559

Real World Law: Dickens v. The House of the Dead 567

Video Game Ratings (box) 569

13. Intellectual Property

Points of Law: The U.S. Constitution: Copyrights and Patents 580

Real World Law: Copyright: United States Ignored the World 582

Points of Law: An Original Creation 584

Real World Law: Happy Money...er, Birthday   587
Points of Law: Exclusive Rights in Copyrighted Works   591
Real World Law: The Sonny Bono Law   595
Points of Law: The Public Domain   596
Real World Law: Is Popeye Free?   597
Points of Law: Infringing Copyright   599
Points of Law: Fair Use Defense   603
2 Live Crew: Pretty or Hairy? (box)   605
Points of Law: What Does "Perform" Mean?   610
Real World Law: Music and Politics   615
Real World Law: We Own That Panther!   619
Points of Law: Confusing?   619
Real World Law: Diluting a Trademark   625

14. Advertising

Points of Law: The Free Flow of (Commercial) Information   644
Points of Law: The Commercial Speech Doctrine   645
Real World Law: *44 Liquormart:* The "Little Guy" Fights Back...and Wins   647
Real World Law: Smoke and Mirrors: A New Era for *Central Hudson*?   649
Real World Law: Advertising and Product Demand: Are They Linked?   653
Points of Law: FTC: False and Misleading Advertising   654
Points of Law: FTC Mechanisms   655
Real World Law: In the Amazon Jungle: Third Party Liability   661
Real World Law: CAN-SPAM: A Test Case   662

Preface

This third edition of "The Law of Journalism and Mass Communication" is the culmination of a decade of research, revision and interaction with students and faculty to create a truly readable textbook focused sharply on the most significant foundations and developments of the law situated within the social and political contexts that give them meaning. "The Law of Journalism and Mass Communication" embraces advertising and copyright, libel and news-gathering, privacy and zines. The fields of public relations, journalism, advertising and marketing are most centrally affected by the shifting ground of this field of law, but the impacts of new statutory and case law on the rights and freedoms of speech and intellectual property, the boundaries of obscenity, public access to information and protection against paparazzi are both far-reaching and profoundly individual. Here we offer a detailed overview of the continually changing reality of media law grounded in the past but moving forward with the stunning rapidity of evolving communications technologies and the innovative ways of using them. We have captured in the following pages the vital building blocks and most up-to-date developments to provide you with a solid grasp of this diverse and dynamic field.

Grounded in decades of teaching and attention to the distinct challenges and highly varied needs of both students and teachers of media law around the globe, we have developed this unique—interpretative, applied, transformative—approach to "The Law of Journalism and Mass Communication." The breadth and diversity of contemporary media law in the United States that you will discover in this volume is informed by cutting-edge research and inspired by our belief that study of the law can, and should, be both engaging and empowering. Accordingly, we hope this book embodies two overarching messages. First, we believe the law is exciting, interesting and fun, and learning it should be, too! And second, we see the law as a product of specific decisions at a particular time and place. As such, the law is best understood when we see and feel its effects on real people, as well as everyday conflicts and actions not only of our government but also of our friends, neighbors and family.

To those ends, we have fine-tuned a number of elements that you will not find in any other textbook on the law of journalism and mass communication. In each chapter, an initial quotation provides unique perspectives and real-life examples of the law at work by allowing legal participants and commentators to share their insights. These quotes often represent a colorful observation on an important topic or an enduring challenge related to the topic of the chapter. Timelines at the start of each chapter graphically introduce the evolution of that area of the law alongside the major historical events that often shaped both the black letter of the law and its development through court decisions. The **Suppose** . . . hypothetical situation that opens each chapter sets out case facts from a focal case to draw readers into and through a central issue of the law, which is resolved in one of the two excerpted cases at the chapter's end. Two excerpted **Cases for Study**—complete with case facts, an explanatory headnote and questions to guide reading—conclude every chapter, eliminating the need for a separate casebook. Cases new to this edition include *Marbury v. Madison, Citizens United v. Federal Election Commission,* and *City of Ontario v. Quon.*

Definitions to enhance comprehension and ease of reading of unfamiliar legal terminology are provided in the margins throughout the book as well as in a glossary at the back. **The realWorld Law** boxes in each chapter point readers to current controversies, unfolding issues and, sometimes, unexpected twists and turns as the law meets the people and problems of our day. Elements throughout every chapter, and included in the supplemental teaching and learning materials online, reinforce essential **Points of Law**, underscore significant shifts and highlight the text's goal of helping you identify the most important elements of this complex field. Our companion website, located at http://college.cqpress.com/medialaw, contains chapter summaries, learning objectives, practice quizzes, interactive flashcards and annotated Web links for further research. Instructor resources include test questions, PowerPoint lecture slides and sample classroom activities.

Just as Congress and the courts have altered the law in the two years since our last edition, updates and new information have reshaped every area of this edition of "The Law of Journalism and Mass Communication." Some of the changes in this edition offer new discussions of:

- The "hot news" doctrine
- "Sexting" as a form of child pornography
- The 2010 U.S. Supreme Court decision allowing corporations and unions to spend unlimited amounts on political ads
- The Obama administration and the Freedom of Information Act
- Emerging anti-cyberbullying statutes
- Appeals court rejection of the FCC's rule limiting national cable ownership to 30 percent of all subscribers
- The effect of WikiLeaks on a potential federal shield law
- Court damage awards for illegal downloads of recordings
- Shifting perspectives on free speech on campus
- Online privacy invasion

- The U.S. Supreme Court decision in 2010 that voir dire and jury selection should be open to the public and press, and lower court rulings allowing closures to protect trade and business secrets
- Reporting from courtrooms using new/social media, and
- An appeals court ruling that sexual material on the Internet should be judged by a national, not a community, standard.

Even with so many rich updates and revisions, this book still feels familiar. We have continued to employ the general organization of traditional media law texts and to sharpen the writing, replacing the common jargon-filled gray pages of most legal texts with bright, clear, concise writing and easy-to-navigate sections. We also continue to incorporate ample photographs, along with color and break-out boxes that not only make the book more attractive but also reinforce significant points, encourage close reading and aid critical evaluation of the quick-paced field of media law.

If you plan to be a journalist or media practitioner, this book is intended and designed primarily to serve your need to understand the protections and constraints imposed by the law upon the practice of your craft. At the same time, we suspect that some of our readers will be interested in a career in the law, and we would be very pleased indeed if this book not only fueled that interest but also helped start you on your way. Regardless of where you are headed or what brings you to this book, we hope you find this book in good order. As Aristotle said, "Good law is good order."

Acknowledgments

As with our previous editions, this book is a collaborative effort not only among its three authors but also between us and the community we serve. There is a large and expanding group of people whose knowledge, insights and comments have helped us update and improve this book. Although we cannot name you all here, we offer our sincere thanks to all those who have helped to shape our understanding of the field and to build the strengths of this edition of "The Law of Journalism and Mass Communication." We are grateful for your generous contributions, and we apologize for any errors or omissions this volume may contain. Beyond our friends, families, students and colleagues who have encouraged and supported us in uncounted ways, we would like to extend special thanks to Jane Thompson and other faculty and staff at the University of Colorado Law Library; Jack Goodman, Washington, D.C., attorney; and our reviewers who helped us identify important material to update: Courtney Barclay, Syracuse University; Ed Carter, Brigham Young University; Gary Mayer, Stephen F. Austin State; Kathleen Olson, Lehigh University; Christopher Sterling, The George Washington University; as well as the number of reviewers who favored our text among other books in the field. We also express our gratitude to the editors, designers and staff at CQ Press who believed in this work and have worked so steadfastly to bring this newest edition to print. We especially thank Charisse Kiino, Christina Mueller, Sarah Fell, Pam Suwinsky, and Kate Stern.

Finally, we thank you, our readers.

The Law of Journalism
and Mass Communication

Chapter 1

Living under a written constitution, no branch or department of the government is supreme; and it is the province and duty of the judicial department to determine in cases regularly brought before them, whether the powers of any branch of the government, and even those of the legislature in the enactment of laws, have been exercised in conformity to the Constitution; and if they have not, to treat their acts as null and void.

U.S. Supreme Court Chief Justice Earl Warren[1]

The U.S. Supreme Court's *Citizens United v. Federal Election Commission* decision in 2010 rejected some campaign finance regulations that had limited corporate campaign speech. Now corporations, such as AT&T, may spend freely on "electioneering communications." Shown is Randall Stephenson, AT& CEO, at a stockholders' meeting.

The Rule of Law

Law in a Changing Communication Environment

The Court System

Jurisdiction
Trial Courts
Courts of Appeal
The U.S. Supreme Court
Judicial Review

Sources of the Law

Constitutions
Statutes
Equity Law
Common Law
Administrative Rules
Executive Orders

The Case Process

Civil Suits
Summary Judgment

Finding the Law

Useful Legal Research
  Resources

Reading Case Law

Briefing Cases
Analyzing *Marbury v.
  Madison*

Cases for Study

➤ *Citizens United v.
  Federal Election
  Commission*
➤ *Marbury v. Madison*

Suppose . . .

. . . it now costs a lot to get elected, and people with money can distort elections. In response, the federal government adopts campaign finance laws that limit contributions to and spending by political candidates. The laws try to establish a balance between the right of individuals and groups to support candidates and the need to protect the integrity of elections from corruption. Big money challenges the campaign finance laws in court. In 1990 and 2003,[2] the U.S. Supreme Court upholds both state and federal restrictions on campaign funding by corporations and provides eloquent support for the need to regulate election spending. Then, in 2007, the Court finds a federal[3] ban on certain political advertisements unconstitutional. Writing in dissent, Justice David Souter argues that the Court's decision rejected more than a century of well-established law supporting limits on campaign spending and political advocacy. He writes, "The court (and, I think, the country) loses when important precedent is overruled without good reason."[4]

In the lead-up to the 2008 presidential election, a federal district court relied heavily on Supreme Court precedent to uphold campaign finance law and prohibit a nonprofit organization called Citizens United from running advertisements and airing a film about then-Sen. Hillary Clinton.[5] When appealed to the Supreme Court, one question posed by *Citizens United v. Federal Election Commission* was whether precedent bound the Court's ruling. In this chapter and the case excerpts that follow, we explore how the rule of law remains stable and how it changes.

S ome 2,500 years ago, the Greek philosopher Aristotle said people are basically self-interested; they pursue their own interests to the exclusion of the greater good or the cause of justice. However, self-interest is ultimately short-sighted and self-destructive. For example, a lumber company that seeks only to generate the greatest immediate profits ultimately deforests the timberlands it depends on, thereby eliminating its own future.[6] Far-sighted people therefore recognize that personal interests and short-term goals must sometimes give way to universal or long-term objectives. Aristotle observed that both individuals and the whole of society benefit when people adopt a mutually acceptable system of rules to promote a balance between gain and loss, cost and benefit, and between personal desires and universal concerns. Aristotle called this balance the "golden mean." Human interests are served and justice is achieved when a system of law applies equally and fairly to every individual—when people treat each other as they would like to be treated.

Belief in the power of laws to promote this balance and restrain human injustice is the foundation of the U.S. Constitution and the **rule of law**. The rule of law is intended to create a societal framework in which preestablished norms and procedures provide for consistent, neutral decision making. In essence, laws establish a contract that governs interactions among citizens, and between citizens and their government. The recognized system of laws binds both citizens and governors. A set of general, open and relatively stable legal rules determines the boundaries of acceptable individual and institutional behavior and empowers government to punish violations. The established rule of law limits the power of government because it prohibits government from infringing on the fundamental rights and liberties of the people. Another established set of procedures determines how government may enact, apply or alter the law. As a result, legal rules constrain the actions both of citizens and government to enhance liberty, freedom and justice for all.

The law functions best when citizens understand the boundary between legal and illegal behavior. Good laws must be sufficiently clear and precise to properly inform citizens of when and how the laws apply (as well as when they do not). **Vague laws** either fail to define their terms or use such general language that neither citizens nor judges know with certainty what the laws permit or punish. Vague laws relating to speech are unacceptable because they may chill or discourage speech by individuals who may choose not to speak rather than risk running afoul of a law that is unclear. Clear laws define their terms and detail their application in order to limit government officials' **discretion**. In this way, clear laws enhance justice by reducing the likelihood that officials will apply legal rules differently to their friends as opposed to their foes.

Good laws accomplish their objectives with minimum infringement on the freedoms and liberties of the people. Carefully tailored laws advance specific government interests or prevent particular harms without punishing activities that pose no conceivable risk to society. A law that sought to limit noisy disturbances of residential areas at night, for example, would be poorly drawn and **overbroad** if it prohibited all discussion out of doors at any time even in a

rule of law The framework of a society in which preestablished norms and procedures provide for consistent, neutral decision making.

vague laws Laws that either fail to define their terms or use such general language that neither citizens nor judges know with certainty what the laws permit or punish.

discretion The authority to determine the proper outcome.

overbroad law Violates the principles of precision and specificity in legislation.

stare decisis Literally, "stand by the previous decision."

precedent Case judgment that establishes binding authority and guiding principles for cases to follow on closely analogous questions of law within the court's jurisdiction.

facial challenges A broad legal claim based on the argument that the challenged law or government policy can never operate in compliance with the Constitution.

According to Aristotle

In 350 BCE, Aristotle wrote a foundational work on human ethics. In his Nicomachean Ethics, Aristotle observed that "justice exists only between men whose mutual relations are governed by law, and law exists for men between whom there is injustice." In other words, humans are inherently flawed and prone to injustice, prejudice and caprice. However, people also have a drive to improve the human condition. As a result, humans can and will freely adopt legal rules and ethical principles to govern their behavior, discourage injustice and enhance fairness.

commercial district far from any homes. Well-crafted laws also must be sufficiently stable to adequately inform people of the legal limitations they impose. People will not long support a system that punishes them for infractions they did not know existed. The rule of law thus requires the entire body of law to be internally consistent, logical and relatively stable. To ensure slow evolution rather than rapid revolution of legal rules, judges interpret and apply laws based upon the precedents established by other court rulings. Precedent, or **stare decisis,** is the legal principle that courts should stand by what has been decided. The principle holds that subsequent court decisions should adhere to the example and reasoning of earlier decisions on the same point. Reliance on **precedent** is the heart of the common law (discussed following) and encourages consistent, predictable application of the law. But precedent is not absolutely binding; it is not always followed; and sometimes precedents seem to conflict. As long-time Supreme Court reporter Linda Greenhouse wrote, "Continuity and change, the entwined spirals of a double helix, are the [law's] DNA."[7]

Laws are not inflexible. Even the U.S. Constitution—the foundational contract between the U.S. government and the citizens—can be changed through amendment. Other laws—the regulations, orders and rules that proliferate at the federal, state

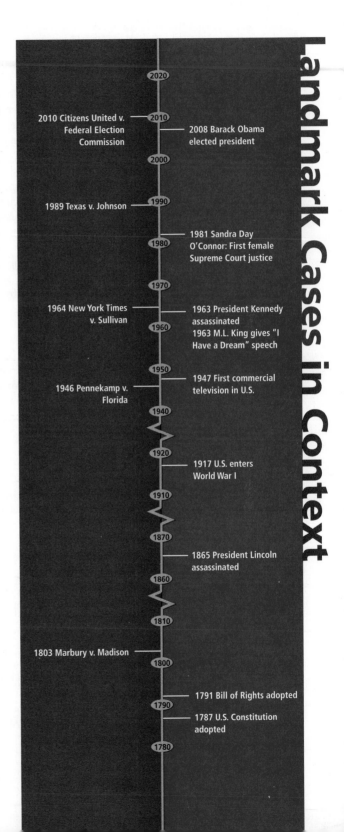

Landmark Cases in Context

- 2020
- 2010 Citizens United v. Federal Election Commission
- 2008 Barack Obama elected president
- 2000
- 1989 Texas v. Johnson
- 1981 Sandra Day O'Connor: First female Supreme Court justice
- 1970
- 1964 New York Times v. Sullivan
- 1963 President Kennedy assassinated
- 1963 M.L. King gives "I Have a Dream" speech
- 1947 First commercial television in U.S.
- 1946 Pennekamp v. Florida
- 1917 U.S. enters World War I
- 1865 President Lincoln assassinated
- 1803 Marbury v. Madison
- 1791 Bill of Rights adopted
- 1787 U.S. Constitution adopted

Points of Law

What's in a Face?

Some important constitutional challenges to laws are raised before a law is applied. Such challenges, called **facial challenges,** claim that the clear, plain and simple language of a law that "on its face" is constitutional nonetheless is unconstitutional. For example, challenges for vagueness and overbreadth generally arise as facial First Amendment challenges to laws related to speech.

Laws are unconstitutionally vague if they are expressed in a way that is too unclear for a person to reasonably know whether or not the law applies to specific conduct. Vague laws are objectionable because they do not provide fair notice to citizens about what actions are illegal, and they provide too much room for arbitrary or discriminatory enforcement. Vague laws also may have a "chilling" effect because, fearing legal punishment, individuals will avoid not only those activities the law was intended to proscribe but also anything that might possibly fit under the law. In such a case, the law's vagueness leads to overbreadth.

Concerns about overbroad laws generally come up with laws intended to regulate unprotected speech. The Supreme Court has ruled that certain types of speech (for example, obscenity and fighting words) may be regulated because such speech is not protected by the First Amendment. However, regulations of unprotected speech may not hamper protected speech. When a law designed to punish unprotected speech also infringes upon a substantial amount of protected speech, the law will be found unconstitutional under the overbreadth doctrine. Thus, in considering whether a law prohibiting the depiction of animal cruelty was unconstitutional, the Supreme Court in 2010 reiterated that "a law may be invalidated as overbroad if 'a substantial number of its applications are unconstitutional, judged in relation to the statute's plainly legitimate sweep.'"[1] Moreover, the Court said, the breadth of a statute is determined through a reasonable reading of its language. The government may not protect a law from being unconstitutionally overbroad either through "an unrealistically broad reading of the [statute's] exceptions"[2] or "because the Government promised to use [the law] responsibly."[3]

---

1. United States v. Stevens, 130 S. Ct. 1577, 1587 (2010).
2. *Id.* at 1590.
3. *Id.* at 1591.

and local levels—may be repealed or amended by the bodies that adopted them and interpreted or invalidated by the courts. As the Supreme Court wrote in its landmark 1803 ruling in *Marbury v. Madison,* "It is emphatically the province and duty of the judicial department to say what the law is. Those who apply the rule to particular cases, must of necessity expound and interpret that rule."[8] All legislatures from the local city council to the U.S. Congress, all executives from the mayor to the U.S. president, and many administrative agencies have the power to enact laws. Thousands of individuals and agencies across the country freely exercise the authority to pass legal rules that define and restrict the rights of people and organizations. These laws respond to the changing expectations of citizens and the evolving needs of the nation in a rapidly changing global environment.

THROUGH THE RULE OF LAW, citizens establish a system for dealing with the innate human tendency toward injustice. The rule of law is designed to promote justice and to provide a relatively clear, neutral and stable mechanism for resolving conflicts. Legal rules bind both government and citizens by defining the boundaries of acceptable behavior, establishing the power and range of punishment, and dictating procedures for creating, applying, interpreting and changing the law. Well-crafted laws are clear and well tailored to address identified harms or advance particular government or societal interests. Built-in procedures discourage rapid revolutionary change in the law while permitting legal flexibility in response to evolving needs and concerns. ■

The Court System

A basic understanding of the structure of the court system in the United States is fundamental to an appreciation of the functioning of the law. Trial courts, or federal district courts, do fact-finding, apply the law and adjudicate disputes. Courts of appeal, including federal circuit courts and supreme courts in each system, review the application of the law by the lower courts. The courts create equity and common law, and apply and interpret constitutions, statutes and orders. Through their judgments, courts can apply the law, reshape the law and even throw out a statute as unconstitutional.

Jurisdiction

An independent courts system operates in each of the states, the District of Columbia and the federal government. The military and the U.S. territories, such as Puerto Rico, also have separate court systems.

Each of these systems of courts operates under the authority of the relevant constitution. For example, the U.S. Constitution requires the establishment of the Supreme Court of the United States and authorizes Congress to establish other courts it deems necessary to the proper functioning of the federal judiciary. **Jurisdiction** refers to a court's authority to hear a case. Every court has its own jurisdiction—that is, its own geographic or topical area of responsibility and authority. In libel, for example, the traditional standard has been that any court in any locale where the statement in question could be seen or heard would have jurisdiction.[9]

Article III, Section 1, of the U.S. Constitution spells out the areas of authority of the federal courts. Within their geographic regions, federal courts exercise authority over cases that relate to interstate or international controversies

jurisdiction The geographic or topical area of responsibility and authority of a court.

TABLE 1.1 Comparing State and Federal Courts

The federal government and each state government has its own court system.

The Federal Court System	The State Court System
STRUCTURE	
• Article III of the Constitution invests the judicial power of the United States in the federal court system. Article III, Section 1 specifically creates the U.S. Supreme Court and gives Congress the authority to create the lower federal courts. • Congress has used this power to establish the 13 U.S. Courts of Appeals, the 94 U.S. District Courts, the U.S. Court of Claims, and the U.S. Court of International Trade. U.S. Bankruptcy Courts handle bankruptcy cases. Magistrate Judges handle some District Court matters. • Parties dissatisfied with a decision of a U.S. District Court, the U.S. Court of Claims, and/or the U.S. Court of International Trade may appeal to a U.S. Court of Appeals. • A party may ask the U.S. Supreme Court to review a decision of the U.S. Court of Appeals, but the Supreme Court usually is under no obligation to do so. The U.S. Supreme Court is the final arbiter of federal constitutional questions.	• The Constitution and laws of each state establish the state courts. A court of last resort, often known as a Supreme Court, is usually the highest court. Some states also have an intermediate Court of Appeals. Below these appeals courts are the state trial courts. Some are referred to as Circuit or District Courts. • States also usually have courts that handle specific legal matters, e.g., probate court (wills and estates); juvenile court; family court; etc. • Parties dissatisfied with the decision of the trial court may take their case to the intermediate Court of Appeals. • Parties have the option to ask the highest state court to hear the case. • Only certain cases are eligible for review by the U.S. Supreme Court.
SELECTION OF JUDGES	
The Constitution states that federal judges are to be nominated by the President and confirmed by the Senate. They hold office during good behavior, typically, for life. Through Congressional impeachment proceedings, federal judges may be removed from office for misbehavior.	**State court judges are selected in a variety of ways, including** • election, • appointment for a given number of years, • appointment for life, and • combinations of these methods, e.g., appointment followed by election.
TYPES OF CASES HEARD	
• Cases that deal with the constitutionality of a law; • Cases involving the laws and treaties of the U.S.; • Ambassadors and public ministers; • Disputes between two or more states; • Admiralty law, and • Bankruptcy.	• Most criminal cases, probate (involving wills and estates), • Most contract cases, tort cases (personal injuries), family law (marriages, divorces, adoptions), etc. State courts are the final arbiters of state laws and constitutions. Their interpretation of federal law or the U.S. Constitution may be appealed to the U.S. Supreme Court. The Supreme Court may choose to hear or not to hear such cases.
ARTICLE I COURTS	
Congress has created several Article I or legislative courts that do not have full judicial power. Judicial power is the authority to be the final decider in all questions of Constitutional law, all questions of federal law and to hear claims at the core of habeas corpus issues. • Article I courts are U.S. Court of Veterans' Appeals, the U.S. Court of Military Appeals, and the U.S. Tax Court.	

Source: United States Courts. http://www.uscourts.gov/EducationalResources/FederalCourtBasics/CourtStructure/ComparingFederal AndStateCourts.aspx

or that interpret and apply federal laws, treaties or the U.S. Constitution. Thus, federal courts hear cases involving copyright laws. The federal courts also decide cases in which the federal government is a party, such as when the news media ask the courts to require the Immigration and Naturalization Service to hold hearings open to the public when considering the deportation of aliens from the United States. Federal courts, therefore, would have jurisdiction over whether a U.S. citizen captured in a war zone has the right to face his accusers in court. Cases involving controversies between states, between citizens of different states or between a state and a citizen of another state also are heard in federal courts. Thus, a libel suit brought by a resident of Oregon against a newspaper in Washington would be heard in federal court.

New technologies present new challenges to the determination of jurisdiction. Consider online libel. Given that statements published online are potentially seen anywhere, any court could claim jurisdiction. More to the point, a plaintiff could initiate the lawsuit in any court, deciding to pursue the case in the court he or she thinks is most likely to render a favorable decision. Early in the 21st century, the U.S. Court of Appeals for the Fifth Circuit signaled significant limits to this practice, which is called **forum shopping.**[10]

In 2002, the court applied a three-pronged test to determine jurisdiction. The court said jurisdiction in a media libel case would be determined by whether (1) the media *purposefully conducted activities* in the locale of the court, (2) the alleged libelous *harm* arose out of the media's activities *in that locale,* and (3) the court's jurisdiction was constitutionally *reasonable.*[11] The test leaves open the question of what is constitutionally reasonable. It also establishes binding precedent only in the Fourth Circuit's mid-Atlantic region. However, the court's decision suggests a willingness to limit the ability of litigants to choose the court in which to pursue online disputes. A court may dismiss a lawsuit because it lacks jurisdiction.

Points of Law

A Test for Court Jurisdiction of Internet Disputes

To establish jurisdiction, the answer to all three of the following questions should be yes.

1. Did the defendant purposefully conduct activities in the jurisdiction of the court?

2. Did the plaintiff's claim arise out of the defendant's activities in this locale?

3. Is it constitutionally reasonable for the court to exercise jurisdiction?

forum shopping A plaintiff choosing a court in which to sue because he or she believes the court will rule in the plaintiff's favor.

Trial Courts

The separate court systems in the United States are organized similarly; most court systems have three tiers. Trial courts occupy the lowest level of courts. They are the only courts to use juries, and they are the courts where nearly all cases begin. Trial courts reach decisions by applying existing law to the specific facts of the case before them. They do not establish precedents. Each state contains at least one of the nation's 94 trial-level federal courts, which are called district courts. News reporters routinely cover legal actions taking place in trial courts, and some judges view media coverage as a threat to the fairness of trials (see Chapter 10). Some judges also fear media coverage will cast their court in disrepute and reduce public trust in the judicial system.

Courts of Appeal

Anyone who loses a case at trial may appeal the decision. However, courts of appeal generally do not make findings of fact or receive new evidence in the case. Instead, appellate courts defer to the factual assessment of the lower court and conduct an independent review of the legal process. In the main, courts of appeal examine the procedure of the lower court to determine whether **due process** was carried out— that is, whether the proper law was applied and whether the judicial process was fair and appropriate. In rare cases, courts of appeal may review the facts **de novo,** a phrase meaning "anew" or "over again." Decisions in appellate courts are based primarily on the written legal arguments, or briefs, of the parties and on short oral arguments from the attorneys representing each side of the case. Interested individuals and organizations who are not parties to the case may, with permission of the court, submit additional briefs for consideration. The interested person is called an **amicus curiae** ("friend of the court") and the filing is called an **amicus brief.**

Most court systems have two levels of appellate courts: the intermediate courts of appeal and the supreme court. In the federal court system, there are 13 intermediate-level appellate courts, called circuit courts. A panel of three judges hears all except the most important cases in the federal circuit courts of appeal. In rare cases, all the judges of the circuit court will sit **en banc** to hear an appeal. *En banc* literally means "on the bench" but now is used to mean "in full court." Twelve of the federal circuits represent geographic regions. For example, the U.S. Court of Appeals for the Ninth Circuit bears responsibility for the entire West

due process Fair legal proceedings. Due process is guaranteed by the Fifth and Fourteenth Amendments to the U.S. Constitution.

de novo Literally, "anew" or "over again." On appeal, the court may review the facts de novo rather than simply reviewing the legal posture and process of the case.

amicus brief A submission to the court from an **amicus curiae,** or "friend of the court," an interested individual or organization who is not a party in the case.

en banc Literally, "on the bench" but now meaning "in full court." The judges of a circuit court of appeals will sit en banc to decide important or controversial cases.

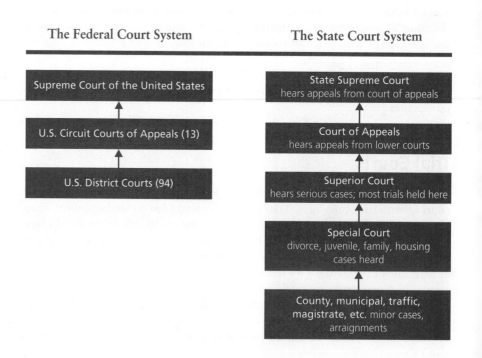

The Federal Court System

The State Court System

Supreme Court of the United States

State Supreme Court
hears appeals from court of appeals

U.S. Circuit Courts of Appeals (13)

Court of Appeals
hears appeals from lower courts

U.S. District Courts (94)

Superior Court
hears serious cases; most trials held here

Special Court
divorce, juvenile, family, housing cases heard

County, municipal, traffic, magistrate, etc. minor cases, arraignments

Coast, Hawaii and Alaska, and the U.S. Court of Appeals for the D.C. Circuit covers the District of Columbia. The 13th circuit, the U.S. Court of Appeals for the Federal Circuit, handles specialized appeals. In addition, separate, specialized federal courts handle cases dealing with the armed forces, international trade, or veterans' claims, among other things.

Courts of appeal may **affirm** the decision of the lower court with a majority opinion, which means they ratify or uphold the prior ruling and leave it intact. They may also **overrule** the lower court, reversing the previous decision. Any single judge or minority of the court may write a **concurring opinion** that agrees with the result reached in the majority opinion but that relies on different reasoning or legal principles or elaborates on significant issues not treated fully by the majority. When a judge disagrees with the opinion of the court, the judge may write a **dissenting opinion,** explaining the basis for the divergent conclusion. A dissenting opinion may challenge the majority's reasoning or the legal basis for its conclusion.

Majority decisions issued by courts of appeal establish precedent for lower courts within their jurisdiction. Their rulings also may be persuasive outside their jurisdiction. If a plurality rather than a majority of the judges hearing a case supports the opinion of the lower court, the decision does not establish binding

affirm To ratify, uphold or approve a lower court ruling.

overrule To reverse the ruling of a lower court.

concurring opinion A separate opinion of a minority of the court or a single justice agreeing with the majority opinion but applying different reasoning or legal principles.

dissenting opinion A separate opinion of a minority of the court or a single justice disagreeing with the result reached by the majority and challenging the majority's reasoning or the legal basis of the decision.

U.S. Circuit Courts of Appeal

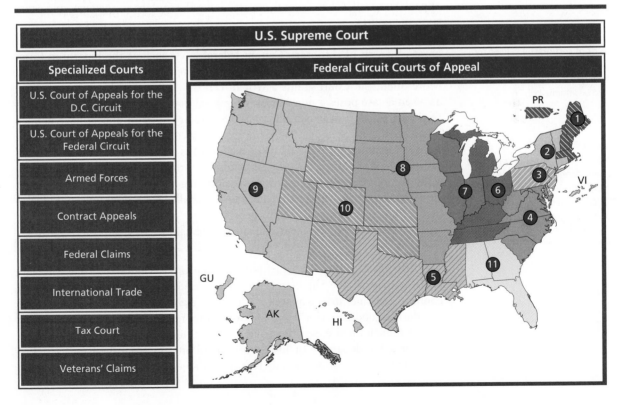

U.S. Supreme Court
Specialized Courts   **Federal Circuit Courts of Appeal**

Specialized Courts:
- U.S. Court of Appeals for the D.C. Circuit
- U.S. Court of Appeals for the Federal Circuit
- Armed Forces
- Contract Appeals
- Federal Claims
- International Trade
- Tax Court
- Veterans' Claims

precedent. Similarly, dissenting and concurring opinions do not have the force of law, but they often are highly influential to subsequent court decisions.

Courts of appeal also **remand,** or send back, decisions and require the lower court to reconsider the facts of the case. A decision to remand a case may not be appealed. Courts of appeal often remand cases when they believe that the lower court did not adequately explore the facts or issues in the case or that it needs to develop a more complete record of evidence as the basis for its decision.

A decision to affirm or reverse the lower court must be signed by at least two of the three sitting judges and is final. The losing party may ask the court to reconsider the case or may request a rehearing en banc. Such requests are rarely granted. The losing party also may appeal the verdict of an intermediate court of appeals to the highest court in the state or to the U.S. Supreme Court.

The U.S. Supreme Court

The Supreme Court of the United States was established in 1789. It functions primarily as an appellate court, although the Constitution establishes the Court's **original jurisdiction** in a few specific areas. In general, Congress has granted lower federal courts jurisdiction in these same areas, so almost no suits begin in the U.S. Supreme Court. Instead, the Court hears cases on appeal from all other federal courts, federal regulatory agencies and state supreme courts.

original jurisdiction The authority to consider a case at its inception, as contrasted with appellate jurisdiction.

Cases come before the Court either on direct appeal or through the Court's grant of a **writ of certiorari.** Certain federal laws, such as the Bipartisan Campaign Reform Act,[12] guarantee a direct right of appeal to the U.S. Supreme Court. More often, the Court grants a writ of certiorari for compelling reasons, such as when a case poses a novel or pressing legal question. The Court often grants certiorari to cases in which different U.S. circuit courts of appeal have handed down conflicting opinions. The Court also may consider whether an issue is ripe for consideration, meaning that the case presents a real and present controversy rather than a hypothetical concern. In addition, the Court may reject some petitions as **moot** because the controversy is no longer "live." Mootness may be an issue, for example, when a student who has challenged school policy graduates before the case is resolved. The Court sometimes accepts cases that appear to be moot if it believes the problem is likely to arise again.

writ of certiorari A petition for review by the Supreme Court of the United States; *certiorari* means "to be informed of."

moot Word used to describe a case in which the issues presented are no longer "live" or in which the matter in dispute has already been resolved; a case is not moot if it is susceptible to repetition but evading review.

The Court's Makeup The chief justice of the United States and eight associate justices comprise the Supreme Court. The president nominates and the Senate confirms the chief justice as well as the other eight members of the Court, who sit "during good behavior"[13] for life or until retirement. This gives the president considerable influence over the Court's political ideology.

The 2010 departure of Justice John Paul Stevens from the Court left Justice Sonia Sotomayor as the only true liberal among the sitting justices. Liberal

realWorld Law

Conservative Leanings

Four of the five most conservative justices to serve on the Supreme Court since 1937 and the presidency of Franklin D. Roosevelt are sitting on the bench today, according to a recent statistical study by Judge Richard Posner and law professor William Landes.[1] Clarence Thomas, appointed to the Court in 1991 and the Court's second African American justice, is ranked by the study as the most conservative justice of the past 70 years. Republican appointees Chief Justice John Roberts (ranked 4th) and Justice Samuel Alito (ranked 5th) join Justices Antonin Scalia (ranked 3rd) and Anthony Kennedy (ranked 10th) to build the conservative majority of the current Court. Democratic appointees Justices Ruth Bader Ginsburg and Stephen Breyer are the only sitting justices joining the ranks of the 15 least conservative justices.

Justices Sonia Sotomayor and Elena Kagan were not members of the Court at the time of the study. However, in her first year on the Supreme Court bench, Justice Sotamayor was perceived to be "a reliable liberal vote" but not necessarily a "liberal activist."[2] Justice Kagan is viewed by some as a "free speech devotee" who joins the conservatives in her dedication to "the importance of civil liberties as a bulwark against ideological orthodoxy."[3]

1. William M. Landes & Richard A. Posner, *Rational Judicial Behavior: A Statistical Study*, 1:2 J. OF LEGAL ANALYSIS 775 (2009).
2. David Savage, *Sotomayor Votes Reliably with Supreme Court's Liberal Wing*, L.A. TIMES, June 8, 2010, *available at* http://www.latimes.com/news/nationworld/nation/la-na-court-sotomayor-20100609,0,5116595.story.
3. Adam Liptak, *On First Amendment, Kagan Has Sympathized with Conservative Justices*, N.Y. TIMES, May 16, 2010, at A19.

justices tend to believe that government should play an active role in ensuring individual liberties. They also tend to support regulation of large businesses and corporations and to reduce emphasis on property rights. Justice Ruth Bader Ginsburg is sometimes viewed as the Court's only liberal-leaning moderate, but her voting patterns place her in the political center of the Court, along with Justice Stephen Breyer. Observers anticipate Justice Elena Kagan, who "might be best described as a center-left pragmatist," to join this highly influential group of swing voters.[14]

Justice Anthony Kennedy often joins Chief Justice John Roberts and Justices Antonin Scalia, Clarence Thomas and Samuel Alito to create a strong conservative bloc in the Roberts Court. Conservative justices, in general, want to reduce the role of the federal government, including the Supreme Court. They also tend to favor a narrow, or close, reading of the Constitution that relies more heavily on original intent than on contemporary realities or concerns. However, following the Roberts Court's second term, one legal scholar said: "The unifying element of the Court's conservative leanings is not a commitment to any particular conservative judicial doctrine (e.g. originalism), but a commitment to the political and ideological positions espoused by conservative Republicans in the 1980s. Further, the Court is not particularly 'minimalist' or restrained in its approach . . . [and] is quite willing to push a conservative agenda quite aggressively."[15]

The U.S. Supreme Court at a Glance, Fall 2011

Justice	Born	Nominating President	Year Appointed
Chief Justice John Roberts	1955	George W. Bush	2005
Associate Justice Antonin Scalia	1936	Ronald Reagan	1986
Associate Justice Anthony Kennedy	1936	Ronald Reagan	1988
Associate Justice Clarence Thomas	1948	George H. W. Bush	1991
Associate Justice Ruth Bader Ginsburg	1933	Bill Clinton	1993
Associate Justice Stephen Breyer	1938	Bill Clinton	1994
Associate Justice Samuel Alito	1950	George W. Bush	2006
Associate Justice Sonia Sotomayor	1954	Barack Obama	2009
Associate Justice Elena Kagan	1960	Barack Obama	2010

Granting Review Petitioners may ask the Supreme Court for a writ of certiorari if the court of appeals or the highest state court denies them a hearing or issues a verdict against them. Writs are granted at the discretion of the Court. All nine justices must consider a writ, which is granted only if at least four justices vote to hear the case. This is called the rule of four. There is a trend toward ever-increasing numbers of petitions for certiorari at the same time the Court is granting fewer petitions. The vast majority of petitions for certiorari are denied. Recently, approximately 2,000 petitions accompanied by the required fee of $150 have been filed each term and the Court rules in about 85 of them, or fewer than 4 percent. The Court consistently grants review to fewer than 5 percent of the paid petitions. Also, some 6,000 petitions are filed each term by those who cannot pay the required filing fee—often these are prisoners—and the court rules in only five or six of these. Officially, neither the decision to grant nor the decision to deny a writ of certiorari indicates anything about the Court's opinion regarding the merits of the lower court's ruling. Rather, denial of certiorari more likely means that the Court simply does not think the issue is sufficiently important or timely to decide.

Reaching Decisions Once the Court agrees to hear a case, the parties file written briefs outlining the facts and legal issues in the case and summarizing their legal arguments. The justices review the briefs prior to oral argument in the case, which generally lasts one hour. The justices may sit silent and implacable during oral argument, or, more often, they may pepper the attorneys with questions. Following oral argument, the justices meet in private in a closed conference session to discuss the case and to take an initial vote on the outcome. Discussion begins with the chief justice, who focuses on a few key issues. Discussion proceeds around the table with each associate justice speaking in turn, in order of descending seniority on the Court. When discussion is complete, voting begins with the most junior member of the Court and ends with the chief justice. A majority of the justices must agree on a point of law for the Court to establish binding precedent. The chief justice or the most senior justice in the majority determines who will draft the majority opinion. Draft opinions are circulated among the justices, and negotiations may attempt to shift votes. It may take months for the Court to achieve a final decision, which is then announced on decision day.

Two other options exist for the Supreme Court. It may issue a **per curiam opinion,** which is an unsigned opinion by the Court as a whole. Although a single justice may draft the opinion, that authorship is not made public. Per curiam opinions often do not include the same thorough discussion of the issues found in signed opinions. The Supreme Court also can resolve a case by issuing a **memorandum order.** A memorandum order simply announces the vote of the Court without providing an opinion. This quick and easy method to dispense with a case has become more common with the Court's tendency in the past decade to issue fewer and fewer signed opinions.

How an Appeal Is Processed

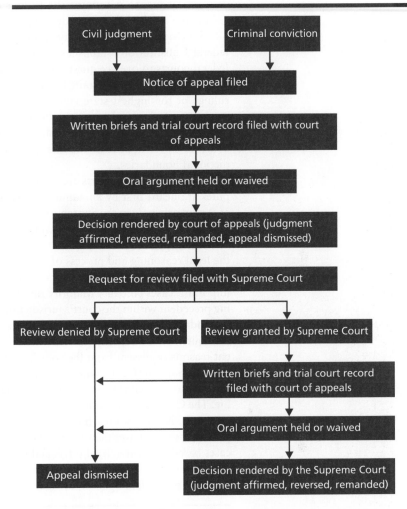

per curiam opinion An unsigned opinion by the court as a whole.

memorandum order An order announcing the vote of the Supreme Court without providing an opinion.

SUMMARY

A MULTITUDE OF COURT SYSTEMS exists in the United States: the federal system, one system for each state, the courts of the District of Columbia and the territories, and the military court system. There are three levels of courts: trial courts, intermediate appellate courts and supreme courts. Trial courts review the evidence, or facts, to determine the proper outcome of a case. Appellate courts review the legal basis for the decisions of lower courts.

State and federal courts function largely independently of each other. The federal Constitution establishes the U.S. Supreme Court and provides for other federal courts to oversee questions related to international, interstate and federal law. The U.S. Supreme Court has power to review the constitutionality of final rulings of the highest state courts. State courts are established by the relevant state constitution and have jurisdiction over issues arising within the state and relating to state law. New technologies raise challenges to the determination of court jurisdiction, because the Internet, for example, transcends traditional jurisdictional boundaries.

Trial, or district, courts are the entry level for most legal disputes. Some disputes are heard first by an administrative agency, and, on very rare occasions, a case may originate in the Supreme Court. Trial courts are fact-finding forums and are the only courts to use juries. Appeals courts, including the 13 federal circuit courts of appeal, generally defer to the trial court on matters of fact to review the legal reasoning and process of the lower court. Most federal court of appeals rulings are handed down by a three-judge panel, but courts sometimes review important cases en banc. Majority opinions of a court of appeals establish binding precedent within the court's jurisdiction. Appeals courts can affirm, reverse or remand the decision of the lower court. Individual judges may join the opinion of the court, write a separate concurrence reaching the same decision but for different reasons or dissent from the court's opinion.

The Supreme Court is the court of last resort, and in most cases it has discretion to determine which cases to review. The nine justices of the Court are appointed for life. The Court tends to review cases it believes are "ripe" and raise significant legal questions. Most cases reach the Court through a petition for certiorari. Typically the Court grants fewer than 5 percent of the writs of certiorari it receives. It reviews cases based on written legal briefs and oral argument by the attorneys for the two sides. Court decisions may be presented as relatively short memorandum orders, unsigned per curiam opinions or signed opinions of the Court. ■

Judicial Review

More than two centuries ago, in 1803, the U.S. Supreme Court essentially granted itself the power to strike down any laws it said conflicted with the U.S. Constitution. In *Marbury v. Madison,*[16] the Court said the Constitution's system of checks and balances provided the judicial branch with inherent authority to limit the power of the legislative branch and bar it from enacting unconstitutional laws. The Court decided that although the Constitution gave the legislative branch the power to make laws, the judicial branch was empowered to interpret laws and to discover what limits the Constitution placed on legislatures' law-making authority. In this controversial decision, the Court established its power of **judicial review.**

Judicial review allows all courts to examine government actions to determine whether they conform to the U.S. and state constitutions. However, courts other than the U.S. Supreme Court rarely use their power of judicial review. If a state supreme court determined that a statute was constitutional under its state constitution, the decision could be appealed to the U.S. Supreme Court, which could decide that the law did not meet the standards set by the U.S. Constitution. The Supreme Court tries to use its power of review sparingly and rarely strikes down laws as unconstitutional. As a general rule, the Court will defer to the law-making authority of the executive and legislative branches of government by interpreting laws in ways that do not conflict with the Constitution.

The ideological leanings of the individual justices, and of the Court as a whole, come into play in the choice of cases granted review and the ultimate decisions of the Court.[17] In 2010, for example, the Court was "bitterly divided" in its decision in *Citizens United v. Federal Elections Commission* (the case mentioned at the beginning and excerpted at the end of this chapter) that declared some campaign finance regulations unconstitutional. Many agreed that the decision's "sweeping changes in federal election law"[18] "represented a sharp doctrinal shift"[19] that split the Court "five-to-four along typical ideological lines." The majority in *Citizens United* "cavalierly tossed aside decades of judicial opinions upholding the constitutionality of campaign finance restrictions," wrote one lawyer and columnist. However, "the central principle which critics of this ruling find most offensive—that corporations possess 'personhood' and are thus entitled to Constitutional and First Amendment rights—has also been affirmed by decades of Supreme Court jurisprudence."[20] Thus, the ideological conflict at the core of the decision centered more on *which* precedents to follow than on whether to apply precedent at all.

In determining the meaning of the Constitution and in deciding the constitutionality of statutes, the U.S. Supreme Court relies on a wide range of sources. **Originalists** and **textualists,** such as Justice Antonin Scalia, find the meaning of the Constitution primarily in the explicit text, the historical context in which the document developed and the recorded history of its deliberation, ratification and originally intended meaning. Originalists and textualists are relatively unmoved by arguments that neither the intent nor the meaning of the Constitution is clear. Other justices look beyond the original intent and the text itself to discern the appropriate contemporary application of the Constitution. Their interpretation of the Constitution relies more expressly on deep-seated personal and societal values, well-established ethical and legal concepts and the evolving interests of a shifting society. The Court's reasoning at times also builds on international standards, treaties or conventions, such as the Universal Declaration of Human Rights, or the decisions of courts outside the United States as well as state and other federal courts. On occasion, such as when the Court discovered a right to privacy embedded in the First Amendment, the justices refer to the views and insights of legal scholars.[21]

judicial review The power of the courts to determine the meaning of the language of the Constitution and to assure that no laws violate constitutional dictates.

originalists Supreme Court justices who interpret the Constitution according to the perceived intent of its framers.

textualists Judges—in particular, Supreme Court justices—who rely exclusively on a careful reading of legal texts to determine the meaning of the law.

realWorld Law

Is Interpreting the Law a Bit Like Making Sausage?

Law professors and political scientists often disagree about how the Supreme Court makes decisions that shape the rule of law. Law professors generally say decision making follows an internal logic in which the Court adheres to legal rules, principles and precedents to reach its decisions. Political scientists emphasize the role of external factors and argue that the political ideologies and preferences of the individual justices determine votes and shape the law.

Speaking for the internal view, Justice Antonin Scalia wrote in 1991:

The judicial power of the United States conferred upon this Court ... must be deemed to be ... the power "to say what the law is," not the power to change it.... [Justices] make [the law] ... as though they were "finding" it—discerning what the law is, rather than decreeing what it is today changed to, or what it will tomorrow be.[1]

The difference between the internal and external views of legal decision making is largely one of degree: How often and why does the Court turn to sources *outside* the body of the law to guide its decisions? Justice Scalia and other advocates of internal determination of the law acknowledge that judges sometimes must look outside the law to reach decisions in difficult or ambiguous areas. They argue, though, that areas of legal uncertainty are few, and judges rarely need to turn to extra-legal considerations. Only when a case squarely addresses "gaps, or ... the edges of the law" will judges need to incorporate external sources of information into their decision making.[2]

Those who embrace the external view say that the law, like *all* texts, is inherently ambiguous and subject to multiple interpretations. Given that the meaning of every text is open and responsive to shifting traditions, communities and cultures, the interpretation of each text, including every law and its application, necessarily reflects the unique situation of the interpreter. From this perspective,

with legal interpretation, as with other types of interpretation, there is a potentially never-ending debate about the best reading of a text.... [T]he justices must *interpret* the First Amendment and relevant case precedents. As with other interpreters, the justices' expectations, interests and prejudices will shape their interpretive views.... Thus, the political preferences of the justices come into play.... Politics is always a part of the adjudicative process because legal interpretation is never mechanical.[3] (emphasis added)

Research suggests that the external view, which ties case outcomes to justices' ideologies, is fairly effective at predicting Supreme Court decisions. The predictive value of the external view does not mean, however, that politics rather than precedent are paramount in the reasoning of the Court.[4] The specific ingredients that comprise the justices' reasoning are obscured by a largely secret process of Supreme Court debate. Perhaps judicial reasoning is like sausage; the product is more appetizing when you don't see how it is made!

---

1. James B. Beam Distilling Co. v. Georgia, 501 U.S. 529, 549 (1991) (Scalia, J., concurring in judgment).
2. Stephen M. Feldman, *The Rule of Law or the Rule of Politics? Harmonizing the Internal and External Views of Supreme Court Decision Making*, 30 LAW & SOC. INQUIRY 89, 96 (2005).
3. *Id.* at 101, 108.
4. *Id.* at 129.

MORE THAN 200 YEARS AGO, the U.S. Supreme Court granted itself the power to review the constitutionality of laws and government actions. The Court said the power of judicial review was embedded in the Constitution's balance of power and was an essential means to maintain the rule of law and check abuse of power by the other two branches of government. Through judicial review, courts have the power to interpret constitutions and to determine when government actions are invalid because they fail to meet constitutional requirements. State courts rarely exercise their power of judicial review, and the U.S. Supreme Court prefers to use this power sparingly. Controversy surrounds the Court's exercise of judicial review because of the political appointment of justices and the argument that the justices' political philosophies inappropriately influence the Court's decisions. ■

Sources of the Law

The body of law in the United States has grown in size and complexity as American society has become increasingly diverse and complicated. As people's ways of interacting and communicating have changed, so have the laws. Many laws that govern communication today did not exist in the 1800s; neither did the technologies they regulate. Indeed, technology has been a driving force for change in the law of journalism and mass communication. U.S. law also has developed in response to social, political, philosophical and economic changes. Legislatures create new laws to reflect evolving understandings of individual rights, liberties and responsibilities. Employment and advertising laws, for example, emerged and multiplied as the nation's workforce shifted and the power of corporations grew. Even well-established legal concepts, such as defamation, have evolved to reflect new realities of the role of communication in society and the power of mass media to harm individuals.

The laws of journalism and mass communication generally originate from six sources. **Constitutional law** establishes the nature, functions and limits of government. The U.S. Constitution, the fundamental law of the United States, was framed in 1787 and ratified in 1789. Each of the states also has its own constitution. **Statutory law** is enacted by city, county, state and federal legislative bodies. Like constitutions, statutes are written down; both types of law are part of what is called **black-letter law.**

Judges create law in the form of both **equity law** and **common law.** Equity law arises when judges apply general principles of ethics and fairness rather than specific legal rules to determine the proper remedy for a legal harm. Thus, restraining orders that prevent reporters from intimidating child celebrities are a form of equity law. Judges also craft the common law, but judges rely on custom, or precedent, to guide their common law decisions. Common law often arises in novel situations not covered expressly by statutes and involves the extension of the legal **doctrines** (which, essentially, are the principles or

constitutional law The set of laws that establish the nature, functions and limits of government.

statutory law Written law formally enacted by city, county, state and federal legislative bodies.

black-letter law Formally enacted, written law that is available in legal reporters or other documents.

equity law Law created by judges to apply general principles of ethics and fairness, rather than specific legal rules, to determine the proper remedy for legal harm.

common law Unwritten, judge-made law consisting of rules and principles developed through custom and precedent.

doctrines Principles or theories of law (e.g., the doctrine of content neutrality).

Points of Law

Six Sources of Law

- Constitutions
- Statutes
- Equity law
- Common law
- Administrative law
- Executive orders

administrative law The orders, rules and regulations promulgated by executive branch administrative agencies to carry out their delegated duties.

executive orders Orders from a government executive, such as the president, a governor or a mayor, that have the force of law.

political questions Questions that the courts will not review because they are either outside the jurisdiction of the court or they are not capable of judicial resolution; an issue that can and should be handled more appropriately by another branch of government.

federalism A principle according to which the states are related to yet independent of each other, and related to yet independent of the federal government.

theories of law) that supported decisions in related areas. For example, under common law, publishers and distributors of indecent communications have been treated differently, a distinction that may no longer be relevant in the era of instant electronic dissemination among millions of interconnected individuals.[22]

Constitutions and legislatures grant authority to government executives and to specialized agencies to issue orders that form part of the law when published. Administrative agencies, such as the Federal Communications Commission (FCC) or the Federal Trade Commission (FTC), create the rules, regulations, orders and decisions that form **administrative law.** Government executives, such as the president, a governor or mayor can issue **executive orders,** another source of law. In 2002, for example, President George W. Bush issued an executive order that initiated the development of the U.S. Department of Homeland Security.

These sources of law form a hierarchy, with the Constitution standing at the pinnacle of the body of law. The following sections explore each source in turn.

Constitutions

Constitutions at both the federal and state levels establish the structure of government and allocate and limit government's authority. The U.S. Constitution organizes government into three separate and coequal branches—the executive, the legislative and the judicial—and designates the functions and responsibilities of each. The separate branches of the federal government each serve distinct functions. The executive branch oversees government and administers, or executes, laws. The legislative branch enacts laws, and the judicial branch interprets laws and resolves legal conflicts. Separation of government into branches provides internal checks and balances within government that limit the power of any branch. For example, "restrictions derived from the separation of powers doctrine prevent the judicial branch from deciding 'political questions,' controversies that revolve around policy choices and value determinations," because the Constitution delegates responsibility for such political decisions to the legislative and executive branches.[23]

Although many state constitutions closely mirror the U.S. Constitution, they are distinct and independent. The U.S. Constitution establishes the basic character, concepts and principles of government; organizes the federal government; and provides a minimum level of individual rights and privileges throughout the country. Under the principle of **federalism,** states are related to, yet independent of, the federal government and of each other. The independence of the state and federal constitutions is fundamental to federalism, which allows for and even encourages experimentation and variety in government. Each state, therefore, has the prerogative to structure its government in its own way and to craft state constitutional protections that exceed the rights granted by the U.S. Constitution. For example, the U.S. Constitution says nothing about municipalities; states create and determine the authority of cities or towns. Under this power, the Maine legislature amended the state constitution in 1970 to increase the independent authority of towns and to permit them to autonomously decide whether to abandon the traditional town meeting form of governance. In another example, Washington State's constitution contains an explicit privacy clause that protects individuals from disturbances of their private affairs. In contrast, the federal constitutional right to privacy exists only through the U.S. Supreme Court's interpretation of the protections afforded by the First Amendment.

The U.S. Constitution is the supreme law of the United States. It establishes the fundamental legal rules that dictate the proper actions of all divisions of government. As the foundation of government, the Constitution is relatively difficult to change. There are two ways to amend the Constitution. The first method, and the only one that actually has been used, is for a proposed constitutional amendment to pass both chambers of Congress by a two-thirds majority vote in each. The second method is for two-thirds of the state legislatures to vote for a Constitutional Convention, which then proposes one or more amendments. Regardless of the proposal method, all amendments to the Constitution also must be ratified by three-fourths of the state legislatures. State constitutions can be amended only by a direct vote of the people.

Congress has approved only 33 of the thousands of proposed amendments to the U.S. Constitution, and the states have ratified only 27 of these. The first 10 amendments to the Constitution—generally known as the Bill of Rights—are of primary interest to students of journalism and mass communication law. In fewer than 500 words, the Bill of Rights guarantees the fundamental rights and freedoms of Americans and limits the power of government. The First Amendment, which is the focus of Chapter 2, specifically protects the people's freedoms of speech, press, assembly and petition. It also provides for the free exercise of religion and prohibits government from establishing an official national religion.

Points of Law

The Three Branches of Federal Government
The Executive
  The president, the cabinet and the administrative agencies execute laws.
The Legislative
  The Senate and the House of Representatives pass laws.
The Judicial
  The three levels of courts review laws and adjudicate disputes.

Statutes

The U.S. Constitution explicitly delegates the power to enact statutory laws to the popularly elected legislative branch of government: the U.S. Congress and the state, county and city legislatures. Through their power to make laws, legislatures respond to—or predict and attempt to prevent—social problems. Thus, statutory law sometimes is extremely fact specific and defines the legal limits of particular types of activities. All criminal laws are statutes, for example. Statutes also establish the rules of copyright, broadcasting, advertising and access to government meetings and information. Statutes are formally adopted through a public process

The Bill of Rights to the U.S. Constitution

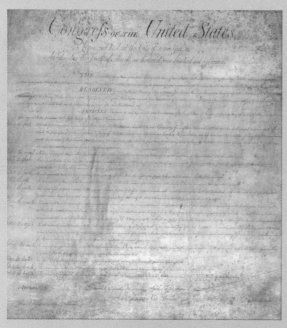

Amendment I

Congress shall make no law respecting an establishment of religion, or prohibiting the free exercise thereof; or abridging the freedom of speech, or of the press; or the right of the people peaceably to assemble, and to petition the government for a redress of grievances.

Amendment II

A well regulated militia, being necessary to the security of a free state, the right of the people to keep and bear arms, shall not be infringed.

Amendment III

No soldier shall, in time of peace be quartered in any house, without the consent of the owner, nor in time of war, but in a manner to be prescribed by law.

Amendment IV

The right of the people to be secure in their persons, houses, papers, and effects, against unreasonable searches and seizures, shall not be violated, and no warrants shall issue, but upon probable cause, supported by oath or affirmation, and particularly describing the place to be searched, and the persons or things to be seized.

Amendment V

No person shall be held to answer for a capital, or otherwise infamous crime, unless on a presentment or indictment of a grand jury, except in cases arising in the land or naval forces, or in the militia, when in actual service in time of war or public danger; nor shall any person be subject for the same offense to be twice put in jeopardy of life or limb; nor shall be compelled in any criminal case to be a witness against himself, nor be deprived of life, liberty, or property, without due process of law; nor shall private property be taken for public use, without just compensation.

Amendment VI

In all criminal prosecutions, the accused shall enjoy the right to a speedy and public trial, by an impartial jury of the state and district wherein the crime shall have been committed, which district shall have been previously ascertained by law, and to be informed of the nature and cause of the accusation; to be confronted with the witnesses against him; to have compulsory process for obtaining witnesses in his favor, and to have the assistance of counsel for his defense.

Amendment VII

In suits at common law, where the value in controversy shall exceed twenty dollars, the right of trial by jury shall be preserved, and no fact tried by a jury, shall be otherwise reexamined in any court of the United States, than according to the rules of the common law.

Amendment VIII

Excessive bail shall not be required, nor excessive fines imposed, nor cruel and unusual punishments inflicted.

Amendment IX

The enumeration in the Constitution, of certain rights, shall not be construed to deny or disparage others retained by the people.

Amendment X

The powers not delegated to the United States by the Constitution, nor prohibited by it to the states, are reserved to the states respectively, or to the people.

and are meant to be clear and stable. They are written down in statute books and codified or collected by codes into related topics, and anyone can find and read them in public repository libraries.

The language of statutes, however, can be unclear, imprecise or ambiguous. In cases where a statute suggests more than one meaning, courts determine the proper meaning and application of the statute through a review process called **statutory construction.** In general, courts attempt to interpret laws in the way the legislature intended. Courts look to the preambles, or statements of purpose, incorporated into many laws as an indication of legislative intent. Committee reports, legislative debates and the public statements of legislators and sponsors of the bills all guide court interpretation of a statute. Problems arise when, for example, some state statutes fail to define key terms, such as the word *meeting* under their open meetings law. As a consequence, it is unclear whether such laws apply to nonphysical meetings convened in electronic chat rooms, for example.[24]

Courts tend to interpret statutes narrowly and to confine a law's application to its clearly intended meaning. Courts prefer not to expand statutes by implication or inference beyond the statute's clear language. The effort to interpret laws according to the "plain meaning" of the words—the **facial meaning** of the law—limits any tendency courts might have to rewrite laws through creative or expansive interpretations. This policy reflects judicial awareness that the power to write laws rests with the publicly elected and responsible legislature. Moreover, because most judges are not elected, the power of courts to engage in judicial review is inherently nondemocratic.

In its own text, the U.S. Constitution establishes its supremacy over all other laws of the land.[25] The Constitution's Supremacy Clause resolves conflicts among laws by stating that all state laws must give way to federal law, and state or federal laws that conflict with the Constitution are invalid. Statutory laws also form

How a Bill Becomes a Law

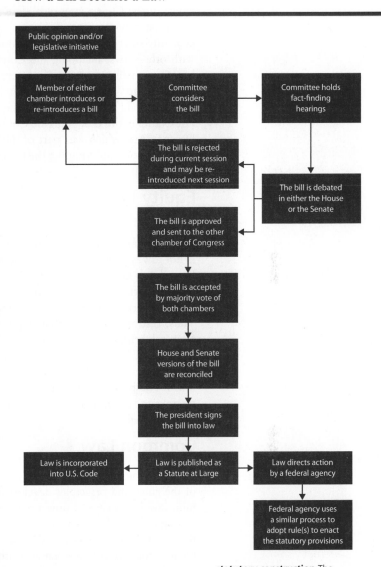

Public opinion and/or legislative initiative

Member of either chamber introduces or re-introduces a bill

Committee considers the bill

Committee holds fact-finding hearings

The bill is rejected during current session and may be re-introduced next session

The bill is debated in either the House or the Senate

The bill is approved and sent to the other chamber of Congress

The bill is accepted by majority vote of both chambers

House and Senate versions of the bill are reconciled

The president signs the bill into law

Law is incorporated into U.S. Code

Law is published as a Statute at Large

Law directs action by a federal agency

Federal agency uses a similar process to adopt rule(s) to enact the statutory provisions

statutory construction The review of statutes in which courts determine the meaning and application of statutes. Courts tend to engage in strict construction, which narrowly defines laws to their clear letter and intent.

facial meaning The surface, apparent or obvious meaning of a legal text.

a hierarchy; some federal laws preempt state laws, which in turn may preempt city statutes. Courts may invalidate state statutes that conflict with federal laws or city statutes that conflict with either state or federal law. However, courts generally interpret the plain meaning of a statute in a way that avoids conflict with other laws, including the Constitution, when possible. Courts review the constitutionality of a statute only as a last resort. When engaging in constitutional review, courts generally will attempt to preserve any provisions of the law that can be upheld without violating the general intent or functioning of the statute. For example, the U.S. Supreme Court in 1997 struck down the Communications Decency Act, which was part of the comprehensive Telecommunications Act of 1996, without undermining the balance of the new telecommunications law.

Equity Law

Judges, not legislatures, make equity law in order to provide fair remedies and relief for various harms. Equity law is based on the presumption that fairness is not always achieved through the rigid application of strict rules. No specific, black-letter laws dictate equity. Rather, equity law allows judges to require or to prohibit certain actions in order to achieve justice in individual cases. Essentially, judges determine what is fair and issue decrees to ensure that justice is achieved. Thus, restraining orders that require paparazzi to stay a certain distance away from celebrities are a form of equity law. An injunction in 1971 that temporarily prevented The New York Times and The Washington Post from publishing stories based on the Pentagon Papers was another form of equity relief. While the law of equity is closely related to common law, the rules of equity law are more flexible and are not governed by precedent.

Common Law

The common law is another body of judge-made law. The common law consists of the rules and principles developed through custom and precedent. The common law is a vast and unwritten body of legal rules and doctrines established through hundreds of years of dispute resolution that reaches past the founding of this country and across the Atlantic to England. For centuries prior to the settlement of the U.S. colonies, English courts "discovered" the doctrines people traditionally had used to resolve disagreements. Judges then applied these "common" laws to guide court decisions. The resulting judicial decisions, and the reasoning that supported them, came to be known as English common law, which became the foundation of U.S. common law.

Eventually, common law grew to reflect more than the problem-solving principles of the common people. Today, U.S. common law rests on the presumption that prior court rulings, or precedent, should guide future decisions. The essence of precedent, stare decisis, is that courts should follow each other's guidance. Once a higher court has established a principle relevant to a certain set of facts, fairness requires lower courts to try to apply the same principle to similar facts. This establishes consistency and stability in the law.

Under the rule of stare decisis, the decision of a higher court, such as the U.S. Supreme Court, establishes a precedent that is binding on lower courts. A binding precedent of the U.S. Supreme Court constrains all lower federal courts throughout the country, and the decisions of each circuit court of appeals bind the district courts in that circuit. Similarly, lower state courts must follow the precedents of their own state appellate courts and the state supreme court. However, courts from different and co-equal jurisdictions do not establish binding precedent upon their peers. Courts in Rhode Island are not bound to follow precedents established in Wyoming, and federal district courts are not bound to apply precedents established by appellate courts in other federal circuits. In fact, different federal appellate courts sometimes hand down directly conflicting decisions. Courts prefer to avoid such conflicts, however, and often will look to other courts and consider their decisions as a guide when facing a novel question.

Even when the power of stare decisis is at its greatest, lower courts may choose not to adhere to precedent. Courts may, at the risk of the judges' credibility, simply ignore precedent. After all, the common law is not written down in one easily accessible volume. Instead, the common law must be discovered through research in the thousands of court decisions collected into centuries of volumes, called court reporters. Courts also may depart from precedent with good reason. Courts examining a new but similar question may decide to **modify precedent**—that is, to change or revise the precedent to adapt to changed realities and perceptions. Thus, the U.S. Supreme Court might find that contemporary attitudes and practices no longer support a 20-year-old precedent permitting government to maintain the secrecy of computer compilations of public records. Given the rapid disappearance of paper records in government, the Court might modify its precedent on application of the federal Freedom of Information Act (FOIA) (see Chapter 8) to find that computer compilations, like paper records, must be available unless disclosure clearly violates personal privacy.[26]

> **modify precedent** To change or revise rather than follow or reject precedent.

Courts also may **distinguish from precedent** by asserting that differences between the current case and the precedent case outweigh any similarities. Thus, for example, the Supreme Court has distinguished between newspapers and broadcasters in terms of any right of public access.[27] The Court said the public has a right to demand that broadcasters provide diverse content on issues of public importance because broadcasters use the public airwaves. The Court did not apply that reasoning five years later when it considered virtually the same question as applied to newspapers. Newspaper owners, publishers and editors, the Court said, are private, independent members of the press who enjoy a virtually unabridgable right to control the content of their pages.

> **distinguish from precedent** To justify an outcome in a case by asserting that differences between that case and preceding cases outweigh any similarities.

Finally, courts will occasionally, but only occasionally, **overturn precedent** outright and reject the fundamental premise of that decision. This is a rare and radical step and generally occurs only to remedy past injustices or to reflect a fundamental rethinking of the law. In one such instance, the Supreme Court

> **overturn precedent** To reject the fundamental premise of a precedent.

in 1997 overruled a 12-year-old Court precedent that had prohibited public school teachers from providing remedial education in parochial schools.[28] The Court said the precedent had mistakenly confused government efforts to fulfill its mandate to educate all children with unconstitutional government establishment of religion.

Administrative Rules

The legislative branch of government often delegates authority to expert administrative agencies in the executive branch to interpret, enable and implement statutory laws. Administrative law may constitute the largest proportion of contemporary law in the United States. A wide range of state and federal administrative agencies with specific areas of responsibility and expertise, such as the FCC, which oversees interstate electronic communication, incorporate both legislative and judicial functions. An alphabet soup of administrative agencies adopts orders, rules and regulations to carry out the agencies' delegated duties. Administrative agencies also enforce administrative law; they conduct hearings in which they grant relief, resolve disputes and levy fines or penalties. This body of rules has the force of law.

Courts generally have the power to hear challenges or appeals to the rules enacted and the decisions reached by administrative agencies after appeal procedures within the agency have been exhausted. Courts engage in regulatory construction and judicial review of administrative agency rules and decisions in much the same way that they review statutory laws. However, the power of courts to void agency rules and actions is limited to situations in which the agency has exceeded its authority, violated its own rules and procedures, or provided no evidence to support its ruling. In other situations, courts are expected to show **deference** to the agency's decision, which means courts must give weight to the expert judgment of the agency.

deference An act in which courts give weight to the judgment of expert administrative agencies or legislative policies and strategies.

The authority of administrative agencies, or even their existence, can change. Legislatures may adopt new statutes or amend preexisting laws to revise the responsibilities and power of administrative agencies. Thus, when Congress adopted the Telecommunications Act of 1996, it substantially revised the responsibilities of the FCC, originally authorized by the Communications Act of 1934.

Executive Orders

Heads of the executive branch of government—the president, governors and mayors—have limited power to issue executive orders, which have the force of law. For example, each president of the United States issues orders that determine what types of records will be classified as secret, how long they will remain secret and who has access to them. Recent executive orders from the president also have limited media access to military zones, excluded the public from meetings of groups advising the president on energy policy, and redefined access to presidential records. Similarly, mayors and governors have issued orders—particularly under perceived emergency conditions—that limit public freedom of movement. For example, mayors across the country have imposed city curfews that prohibit teenagers from being on the streets after a certain hour and have established no-protest zones around major, controversial events.

SUMMARY

LAWS, OR LEGAL RULES, in the United States come from six sources. Federal and state constitutions establish government structure, responsibilities and power. Constitutions are the highest law of the land. Congress and the legislatures of every state, city and county enact statutes. All statutes are codified. Courts determine the meaning of statutes through the process of statutory construction. Equity and common law are judge-made law and are not compiled into books. Judges create equity law when they issue orders or injunctions to solve a specific problem. The common law has developed through the body of judicial decisions that rely on precedent and tradition to determine the outcome of disputes. The authority of administrative agencies is established by statute to oversee complex areas that require special expertise. Thousands of executive branch administrative agencies establish legal rules that determine everything from the definition of false advertising to the number of different media a given corporation can control. Executives at each level of government issue orders that have the force of law. ∎

The Case Process

Although each court and each case follows a somewhat idiosyncratic path, general patterns can be traced through the judicial process. In a criminal matter, the case starts when a government agency investigates a possible crime. After gathering evidence, the government arrests someone for a crime, such as distributing obscene material through the Internet. The standard of evidence needed for an arrest or to issue a search warrant is known as **probable cause.** Probable cause involves more than mere suspicion; it is a showing based on reliable information that a crime was committed and the accused individual is likely the person who committed it. The case then goes before a **grand jury** or a judge. Unlike trial juries (also called petit juries), grand juries do not determine guilt. Instead, grand juries are summoned on occasion to hear the state's evidence and determine whether that evidence establishes probable cause to believe that a crime has been committed. If the case proceeds without a grand jury, the judge is required to make a probable cause determination at a proceeding called a preliminary hearing. If the state fails to establish probable cause, the case may not proceed. If probable cause is found, the person is indicted.

probable cause The standard of evidence needed for an arrest or to issue a search warrant. More than mere suspicion, it is a showing through reasonably trustworthy information that a crime has been or is being committed.

grand jury A group summoned to hear the state's evidence in criminal cases and decide whether a crime was committed and whether charges should be filed; grand juries do not determine guilt. A grand jury may be convened on the county, state or federal level; with 12 to 23 members, grand juries are usually larger than trial juries.

Then the case moves to a court arraignment, where the defendant is formally charged and pleads guilty or not guilty. Often, a plea bargain may be arranged in which the defendant pleads guilty in exchange for a reduction in the charges or an agreed-upon sentence. In the absence of a guilty plea, the case ordinarily will proceed to trial. The judge may set bail. Proof beyond a reasonable doubt is required to establish guilt in a criminal trial. Upon a verdict of guilty, the judge normally requests a presentencing report from the probation department outlining the defendant's background and holds a sentencing hearing before pronouncing judgment. A criminal sentence may include time in a county jail, state or federal prison, and one or more fines.

Civil Suits

plaintiff The party who files a complaint; the one who sues.

defendant The party accused of violating a law, or the party being sued in a civil lawsuit.

The Path of Civil Lawsuits

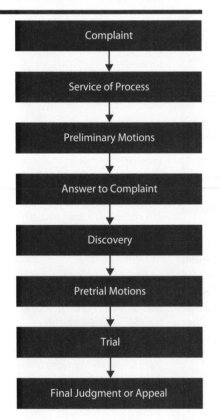

Complaint

Service of Process

Preliminary Motions

Answer to Complaint

Discovery

Pretrial Motions

Trial

Final Judgment or Appeal

Civil cases generally involve two private individuals or organizations that cannot resolve a dispute. The government provides a neutral process through its judicial system to help settle the conflict. In a civil suit, the person who files a complaint or sues because she believes she has been harmed by an intrusion on her privacy or the inaccuracy of a news report, for example, is the **plaintiff.** The person responding to the suit is the **defendant.** The civil harm involved is called a **tort.** A tort is a private or civil injury one person or organization inflicts on another, and tort law provides a mechanism for the injured party to identify the person at fault and receive compensation through an award of damages.

Many communication lawsuits are civil suits in which the plaintiff must prove his or her case by the preponderance of evidence. This standard of proof is lower than in criminal cases. Plaintiffs often may choose among several courts in which to file their civil suits because the court system in the hometown of either party and every court system in which the harm occurred has jurisdiction to hear the suit.

Civil suits begin when the plaintiff files a civil complaint with the clerk of court. The civil pleading outlines the complaint and the result desired and requires the defendant to appear in court. Most plaintiffs seek money damages. To receive a damage award, a plaintiff generally has to show that the harm occurred, that the defendant caused the harm and that the defendant was at fault, meaning the defendant acted either negligently or with malicious intent. Under a **strict liability** standard, the plaintiff does not need to demonstrate fault on the part of the defendant in order to win the suit. Under strict liability, the individual who produced a product or took an action is liable for any and all resulting harms.

Upon receiving a complaint, the court issues a summons to the defendant, notifying him or her of the complaint and requiring him or her to appear in court to respond. The court also schedules a hearing. The defendant may answer the complaint by filing a countersuit, by denying the charge, by filing a **motion to dismiss** or by filing a motion for summary judgment. A motion to dismiss, or **demurrer,** is a request to a court that a complaint be rejected because it is legally insufficient in some way. For example, a media defendant may admit that it published the news story that upset the plaintiff but argue that the story did not cause any legally actionable harm to the plaintiff. If the court grants the motion to dismiss, the plaintiff may appeal.

Before a case goes to trial, the disputing parties may agree to an out-of-court settlement. When this occurs, there is no public record of the outcome of the case. Out-of-court resolutions often prohibit the parties from discussing the terms of the settlement. Sometimes, as when Nike settled a lawsuit brought by attorney Mark Kasky in 2002,[29] some terms of the settlement are publicized. After a lengthy legal battle over Kasky's claim that Nike's statements about working conditions at its overseas factories amounted to false advertising, the parties settled out of court. Without admitting liability, Nike reported on its website that it had agreed to pay a total of $1.5 million toward independent oversight of its factories and additional worker training and development.[30]

If the issues in a civil suit are narrow or the parties are close to resolution, the judge may attempt to settle the case through a court conference. More often, the two sides do not agree on the facts and begin to gather evidence through a process called **discovery.** The discovery process can last for months, during which either side may file motions asking the court to take action on various issues or amend earlier complaints. In trying to build a case, one or both parties may issue a **subpoena,** which is a legal command for someone, sometimes a journalist, to testify in court. With few exceptions, citizens are legally obligated to comply with subpoenas. The judge may issue a contempt of court citation against individuals who refuse to comply with subpoenas. Contempt citations sometimes land journalists in jail. Throughout the pretrial period, both sides may attempt to "spin" their case in the media. Judges are sensitive to the potential harmful effects of pretrial publicity on the fairness of trials.

Finally, the dispute is heard in court. The majority of civil suits are resolved with a settlement between the parties before trial. If no settlement is reached, the case may then proceed to a jury trial, which is required if either party requests it. The court summons jurors to the courthouse from a local pool, usually from the voters' rolls. The locality of a lawsuit, where the original court hears the suit, is called the **venue.** The location from which a court draws its pool of jurors is the **venire.** The lawyers and judge select jurors through a process of questioning called **voir dire,** which literally means "to speak the truth." While the theoretical goal is to form an impartial jury to hear the evidence, attorneys on both sides hope to give themselves an advantage in the adversarial process. Today a large number of firms, such as Trial Behavior Consulting, provide expert consulting on jury selection, witness preparation, posttrial media interviews and the like. Either side's attorney may challenge potential jurors "for cause," such as when a prospective juror knows a party in the suit. Attorneys also may eliminate a limited number of potential jurors through **peremptory challenges,** in which they need not show a reason for the rejection.

tort A private or civil wrong for which a court can provide remedy in the form of damages.

strict liability Liability without fault; liability for any and all harms, foreseeable or unforeseen, which result from a product or an action.

motion to dismiss A request to a court for a complaint to be rejected because it does not state a claim that can be remedied by law or because it is legally lacking in some other way.

demurrer A request that a court dismiss a case on the grounds that although the claims are true they are insufficient to warrant a judgment against the defendant.

discovery The pretrial process of gathering evidence and facts. The word also may refer to the specific items of evidence that are uncovered.

subpoena A command for someone to testify in court.

venue The locality of a lawsuit and of the court hearing the suit. Thus, a change of venue means a relocation of a trial.

venire Literally, "to come" or "to appear"; the term used for the location from which a court draws its pool of potential jurors, who must then appear in court for voir dire; a change of venire means a change of the location from which potential jurors are drawn.

voir dire Literally, "to speak the truth"; the questioning of prospective jurors to assess their suitability.

peremptory challenge During jury selection, a challenge in which an attorney rejects a juror without showing a reason. Attorneys have the right to eliminate a limited number of jurors through peremptory challenges.

real**World** Law

Blogger Bests "Bullying" Subpoena

Blogger Chris Elliott

On New Year's Eve 2009, the federal Department of Homeland Security backed away from the subpoena it had issued two evenings earlier to a Florida-based travel blogger.

On Dec. 29, Transportation Security Administration (TSA) Special Agent Robert Flaherty hand-delivered a subpoena to Christopher Elliott in his home. The subpoena ordered Elliott to turn over to the agent no later than Dec. 31: "all documents, emails, and/or faxsimile transmissions in your control possession or control (sic) concerning your receipt of TSA Security Directive 1544-09-06 dated December 25, 2009."[1] Federal law makes failure to comply with a TSA subpoena punishable by up to a year in prison and a fine.

After Elliott's attorney said they would challenge the subpoena in federal court, DHS informed him the subpoena "is being withdrawn as no longer necessary."[2] TSA also withdrew its subpoena of another blogger, Steve Frischling.

Elliott and Frischling received the subpoenas two days after they posted a controversial TSA directive requiring physical pat-downs of all passengers boarding planes in the United States.[3] The directive was issued in the immediate wake of the failed bombing attempt of a Northwest Airlines flight on Christmas day.

Elliott gathered the TSA directive during reporting and posted it on his blog verbatim after he could not obtain TSA comment. The directive, dated Dec. 25, expired five days later.

"These are just, sort of, bullying subpoenas," said Lucy Dalglish, executive director of The Reporters Committee for Freedom of the Press (RCFP).[4] "I imagine TSA has never executed a subpoena on a journalist before so they probably think, 'What's the big deal?'"

The RCFP, the Electronic Frontier Foundation and others assisted Elliott in objecting to the subpoena on the grounds that it improperly sought to require a journalist to reveal his sources and materials.[5]

A TSA screening

In a public announcement in January 2010, TSA reported that it "takes any breach in security very seriously. In light of the posting of sensitive security information on the web, TSA sought to identify where the information came from. The investigation is nearing a successful conclusion and the subpoenas are no longer in effect."[6] In TSA's December note to Elliott's attorney, Deputy Chief Counsel John Drennan wrote, "Thank you for your assistance and have a happy and safe New Year."[7]

1. Christopher Elliott, *Full Text of My Subpoena from the Department of Homeland Security*, ELLIOTT BLOG, Dec. 29, 2009, *available at* http://www.elliott.org/blog/full-text-of-my-subpoena-from-the-department-of-homeland-security/.
2. Christopher Elliott, *Department of Homeland Security: Your Subpoena "Is No Longer Necessary"*, ELLIOTT BLOG, Dec. 31, 2009, *available at* http://www.elliott.org/blog/department-of-homeland-security-withdraws-subpoena/.
3. Christopher Elliott, *Full Text of SD 1544-09-06 Authorizing Pat-Downs, Physical Inspections*, ELLIOTT BLOG, Dec. 27, 2009, *available at* http://www.elliott.org/blog/full-text-of-sd-1544-09-06-authorizing-pat-downs-physical-inspection/.
4. Cindy Cohn, *EFF Helps Blogger Subpoenaed by TSA, TSA Backs Down*, ELECTRONIC FRONTIER FOUNDATION, Jan. 1, 2010, *available at* http://www.eff.org/deeplinks/2010/01/eff-helps-blogger-subpoenaed-tsa-tsa-backs-down.
5. *Id.*
6. Josh Gerstein, *TSA Subpoena Lifted*, POLITICO: UNDER THE RADAR, JOSH GERSTEIN ON THE COURTS, TRANSPARENCY & MORE, Dec. 31, 2009, *available at* http://www.politico.com/blogs/joshgerstein/1209/Journo_plans_challenge_to_TSA_subpoena.html.
7. Elliott, *supra*, note 2.

After all the evidence is presented at trial, the judge issues instructions to the jury on how the law should be applied to the facts of the case. Then the jury deliberates. If the jury cannot reach a verdict, it may be necessary to hold a new trial with a new jury. More typically, a jury deliberates until it reaches a verdict. The judge generally accepts the verdict and enters it as the judgment of the court. However, the judge has the authority to overturn the verdict if he or she believes it is contrary to the law. If the plaintiff is successful, he or she will usually be awarded damages. After the judgment of the court is entered, either the plaintiff or the defendant may appeal. For example, having the jury properly instructed on the law is part of the right of due process, and improper instructions sometimes form the basis for appeal. The person who appeals, called the petitioner or **appellant,** challenges the decision of the court. The respondent to the appeal, or the **appellee,** wants the verdict to be affirmed. It can take years and cost hundreds of thousands of dollars to appeal a case up to the Supreme Court. As noted previously, the chance the Court will agree to hear an appeal is slim.

appellant The party making the appeal; also called the petitioner.

appellee The party against whom an appeal is made.

Summary Judgment

When parties ask a court to dismiss a case, they file a motion for summary judgment. Parties moving for summary judgment seek to avoid the cost and risk of losing at trial by demonstrating to the judge that no material issues of fact remain in dispute. A motion for summary judgment must be filed with supporting evidence. A summary judgment is just what the name implies: a judge summarily decides the case and issues a judgment. Thus, a summary judgment results in a legal determination by a court *without* a full trial. A court's summary judgment may be issued based on the merits of the case as a whole or on specific issues critical to the case. If the judge determines there are no material issues of fact remaining for trial, the judge hands down a summary judgment in favor of one party. If there is no summary judgment or other form of pretrial dismissal, lawsuits generally proceed to trial.

summary judgment The quick resolution of a legal dispute in which a judge summarily decides certain points and issues a judgment dismissing the case.

A summary judgment can occur at any of several points in litigation, but usually prior to trial. In a libel case, this generally occurs when a plaintiff is clearly unable to meet one or more elements of the burden of proof (see Chapter 4). The U.S. Supreme Court has said that courts considering motions for summary judgment "must view the facts and inferences to be drawn from them in the light most favorable to the opposing party."[31] In libel cases, this means that courts must take into account the burden the plaintiff is required to meet at trial. The Court created this hurdle for individuals seeking summary judgment because the nonmoving party loses the opportunity to present his or her case when a judge grants summary judgment to the opposing side.[32]

Summary judgments can be important tools for protecting free expression, particularly in an environment in which plaintiffs have harassed the media by filing frivolous lawsuits. One federal judge wrote that summary judgments are especially important in the First Amendment area.[33] Societal interest in free and open debate can be jeopardized when frivolous lawsuits go forward because the high cost of defending against such suits may discourage people from robustly exercising their First Amendment rights in the future.

SUMMARY

LAWSUITS ARE EITHER CRIMINAL OR CIVIL. In criminal cases, the government brings an action against an individual for violating a criminal statute. Crimes may be punished by fines and/or jail time. In a civil lawsuit, a private individual (the plaintiff) initiates the process by filing a complaint alleging the defendant caused some harm for which he or she should be held legally responsible. Civil suits generally seek damages to compensate the plaintiff and to penalize the individual responsible. Both criminal and civil suits involve a variety of pretrial processes, and juries hear both types of cases. Jurors are called and questioned through voir dire, which provides an opportunity for attorneys to remove jurors for cause if the jurors are not able to render a decision based only on the facts presented in court. Attorneys may also remove potential jurors through peremptory challenges without showing cause. Cases are decided either when a jury reaches a verdict or, in the case of a bench trial, the judge issues a judgment. Either outcome may be appealed. Judges may dismiss cases that do not present a material issue or grant summary judgment when uncontested facts clearly support one side. ■

Finding the Law

This textbook provides an introduction and overview of key areas of the law of journalism and mass communication. Many students will wish, or their professors will require them, to supplement this text with research in primary legal sources. Primary sources are the actual documents that make up the law (e.g., statutes, case decisions and committee reports). Most students will want to begin legal research in secondary sources available in most government and academic libraries. Secondary sources analyze, interpret and discuss the primary documents. Perhaps the most useful secondary sources for beginning researchers in communication law are "American Jurisprudence 2d," "Corpus Juris Secundum" and "Media Law Reporter." The first two are legal encyclopedias. They provide summaries, indexed by subject, with citations to relevant cases and pertinent legal articles. "Media Law Reporter" provides both topical summaries and excerpts of key media law cases organized by subject. When using "Media Law Reporter," students must keep in mind that it is not comprehensive. It contains only the prominent cases selected by the editors to highlight central issues in media law.

To thoroughly research a topic in the law, students must turn to primary sources: the administrative, legislative and court documents that form the law. It is beyond the scope of this text to provide a detailed explanation of how to navigate through these complex and diverse legal materials. However, access to primary legal materials no longer requires extensive legal training and hours of research in intimidating legal libraries. Today a wealth of primary legal resources is available online and in databases such as Westlaw and LexisNexis. Law review articles provide invaluable scholarship and references to contemporary legal topics.

The notes at the end of this book contain the citations for many of the important cases in the law of journalism and mass communication. These legal citations provide the names of the parties in the case, the number of the volume in which the case is reported, the abbreviated name of the official legal reporter (or book) in which the case appears, the page of the reporter on which the case begins and the year in which the case was decided. For example, the citation in note 26 of this chapter looks like this: "Dept. of Justice v. Reporters Comm. for Freedom of the Press, 489 U.S. 749 (1989)." This citation shows that the first party, the U.S. Department of Justice, filed an appeal from a decision in favor of the second party, The Reporters Committee for Freedom of the Press. The decision in this case dealing with the application of the federal Freedom of Information Act can be found in the United States Reporter (U.S.), which contains U.S. Supreme Court opinions. The case appears in volume 489 (the number *before* the name of the reporter), beginning on page 749 (the number *after* the name of the reporter). The case was decided in 1989 (the number in parentheses).

Useful Legal Research Resources

A huge number and variety of indexes, research tools and interpretive aids help those seeking to find and understand U.S. law. The following short list identifies some of the most useful databases and online resources to offer a starting point for the enterprising student.

- *Online search engines* helpful in legal research include Findlaw (http://www.findlaw.com), LawCrawler (http://www.lawcrawler.com) and Meta-Index for U.S. Legal Research (https://gsulaw.gsu.edu/metaindex).
- *LegalTrac* is an online index of articles in nearly 2,000 legal and nonlegal periodicals since 1981, searchable by keyword or subject. Many of the articles in LegalTrac are not full text.
- *LEXIS-NEXIS,* available online at many universities through Academic Universe, is a full-text database of primary and secondary legal sources, business and financial information, and news. It has multiple search options, including quick, keyword, case name, citation, and detailed Boolean searches.
- *Websites* helpful in finding and interpreting the law include: the Reporters Committee for Freedom of the Press (http://www.rcfp.org), the Student Press Law Center (http://www.splc.org), the Freedom Forum (http://www.freedomforum.org), the First Amendment Center (http://www.firstamendmentcenter.org), the Electronic Frontier Foundation (http://www.eff.org), First Amendment Law Review (falr.unc.edu), Cornell Legal Information Institute (http://www.law.cornell.edu) and many more.

Reading Case Law

This chapter shows that the law of journalism and mass communication contains many terms and concepts that may be unfamiliar to the general reader. At the beginning, reading the law is a bit like reading a foreign language: so many of the words are unfamiliar that it is difficult to grasp the underlying meaning and importance of the case. The difficulty arises because opinions are written by judges (who tend to use legal words and complex syntax) for lawyers, who are already trained in legal terminology and doctrines. With practice, however, people who are not judges or lawyers or even law students can learn the language and read case law with relative ease. It's a skill that empowers you, as a citizen, to learn your own rights and responsibilities and to oversee the actions of your government.

The following steps will help you read the law more quickly and with better comprehension. You will understand the law far better and more easily if you give yourself sufficient time to use these three steps.

1. *Pre-read the case.* Do not underline or highlight during pre-reading because only after pre-reading will you really understand which elements are important to the case. Pre-reading is designed to identify the *structure* of the decision; the various *rules or doctrines* that underlie the court's reasoning; and the *outcome* of the case. These three elements provide a context to help you highlight the most important elements of the court's reasoning. To pre-read, quickly read:
    a. The topic sentence of each paragraph to get the gist of the case and identify the most important sections of the case
    b. The first few paragraphs of the case, which should establish the parties, the issues and the history of the case
    c. The last few paragraphs of the case to understand the **holding** (which is the legal principle taken from the decision of the court) or to get a summary of the outcome of the case
2. *Skim the entire case.* Skimming involves scanning lightly over the entire case. This provides more details to the pre-reading and further identifies the sections of the case that warrant careful reading. Again, do not highlight or underline. However, you will want to signal the start of key sections of the case for more careful reading.
3. *Read carefully the sections you have identified as important.* Underline or highlight as you go. You may want to identify different elements differently. In particular, take note of the following:
    a. *The issue.* Identifying the issue in the case helps you know which elements of the history and facts are significant. In this text, the chapter titles generally signal the issue on which the case excerpt will focus. The case itself also often includes language that identifies the issue. Such language includes, "The question before the Court is whether . . ." and "The issue in this case is . . ."
    b. *The facts.* Recognize that some facts are central to the issue whereas others are peripheral. To identify the important facts, ask yourself whether

the dispute in the case is about a question of fact (e.g., what happened) or a question of law (e.g., which test, doctrine or category of speech is relevant). A libel decision that turns on the identity of the individual whose reputation was harmed would represent a question of fact.[34]

c. *The case history.* The circumstances surrounding a decision often are pivotal to the issue before the Court. Sometimes the relevant history is one of shifting legal doctrine, as when the Court gradually affords commercial speech greater constitutional protection.[35] Sometimes the important context is factual, as when the Court protects defamatory comments situated within a generally accurate portrayal of the violent oppression of blacks during the civil rights movement.[36]

d. *The common law rule of law.* The rule is the heart of the decision; it is the common law developed in this case. To identify the rule, ask whether the Court has created a new test, engaged in balancing or applied an established doctrine in a new way. What are the elements of the rule and what are its exceptions? Under what conditions or to what type of communication does the rule apply?

e. *The analysis.* To analyze the decision, compare the facts to the rule. In libel law, for example, public officials must prove actual malice to win their suit. In analyzing the decision, ask whether the individual involved is a public official. If so, did he or she prove actual malice? If not, what elements of the actual malice standard did he or she fail to establish and why?

If you follow this step-by-step process, you will be well on your way toward reading the law. That's the first stage in conducting legal research. This detailed reasoning also positions you well to write a case brief in response to a course assignment or as an excellent study tool.

Briefing Cases

Case briefs are a focused summary of a court decision. They simplify and clarify the court's language by selecting the five most important components of the decision. They sort through the court's detailed and complicated discussions to set aside content and comments that do not directly inform the court's decision.

An acronym for the five components of a case brief is FIRAC. FIRAC stands for Facts, Issue, Rule of Law, Analysis and Conclusion. In brief, the five components of a case brief are

1. *The Facts.* The facts summary should include all the information needed to understand the issue and the decision of the court. The facts statement consists of a brief but inclusive discussion of what happened in the legal dispute before it reached this court. The statement of facts should include not only who the parties are and what happened in the trial court but also an explanation of the basis for appeal. What happened between the parties that gave rise to the case? Who initiated the lawsuit? What was the

substance of the complaint and what type of legal action was brought? What was the defense? What did other courts reviewing the case decide? What are the legal errors that provide the basis for the current appeal?

2. *The Issue.* Here, one sentence summarizes the specific question decided by the court in this case. The issue should be phrased as a single question that can be answered "yes" or "no."

3. *The Rule of Law.* The rule of law is the heart of the decision. It states, preferably in one sentence, the precedent established by this decision that will bind or guide lower courts.

4. *The Analysis.* This section, also called the *rationale,* details why the court reached its decision. In this section, it is important to discuss the details of the court's reasoning. What tests, logic, analysis, application of precedent, theory or evidence did the court use to justify and explain its decision? The analysis section needs to identify how and why the current decision creates new law. Consider whether it establishes a new test, clarifies existing legal distinctions, defines a new category or highlights changing realities that affect the law. A thorough analysis must describe the reasoning for all the opinions in the decision and highlight the specific points on which concurring and dissenting opinions diverge from the opinion of the court.

holding The decision or ruling of a court.

5. *The Conclusion.* This is a simple declarative statement of the **holding** reached by the present court. Did the court affirm, remand or reverse? Provide the vote of the court.

Analyzing *Marbury v. Madison*

The case brief below previews the second case excerpted at the end of this chapter.

FACTS: William Marbury was one of President John Adams' 42 "midnight appointments" on the eve of his departure from the White House. The necessary paperwork and procedures to secure his and several other appointments were completed, but Secretary of State John Marshall—himself a midnight appointee—failed to deliver Marbury's commission. Upon assuming the presidency, Thomas Jefferson ordered his secretary of state—James Madison—not to deliver the commission. Under authority of the Judiciary Act of 1789, Marbury sued to ask the Supreme Court to order Madison, through a writ of mandamus, to deliver the commission. A writ of mandamus is a court order requiring an individual or organization either to perform or to stop a particular action.

ISSUE: Does the Supreme Court have the power to review acts of Congress and declare them void if they violate the Constitution?

RULE: Under Article VI, Sec. 2 of the U.S. Constitution, the Supreme Court is implicitly given the power to review acts of Congress and to strike them down as void if they are "repugnant" to the Constitution.

ANALYSIS: A commission signed by the president and sealed by the secretary of state is complete and legally binding. Denial of Marbury's commission violates the law, creating a governmental obligation to remedy the violation. A writ of mandamus is such a remedy. The Constitution is the "supreme law of the land" (Art. VI). As such, it is "superior" and "fundamental and paramount." It establishes "certain limits" on the power of the government it creates, including the power of Congress. Accordingly, "a legislative act contrary to the Constitution is not law." The Constitution also establishes that "[it] is emphatically the province and duty of the judicial department to say what the law is." The Supreme Court, therefore, must determine the law that applies in a specific case and decide the case according to the law. If the Court finds that "ordinary" statutory law conflicts with the dictates of the Constitution, the "fundamental" constitutional law must govern. If Congress enacted legislation the Constitution forbids, the Court must strike it down to give the Constitution its due weight.

Under Article III of the Constitution, Congress has the power to regulate the appellate jurisdiction, but not the original jurisdiction, of the Supreme Court. The Court's original jurisdiction is defined completely and exclusively by Article III and cannot be altered except by amendment of the Constitution. Through the Judiciary Act of 1789, Congress *added* matters of mandamus to the original jurisdiction of the Court. Being outside the power given to Congress by the Constitution, this act is illegitimate. Neither was the power of mandamus granted to the Court by the Constitution. Following these principles, the Court does not have the power to order mandamus on behalf of Marbury.

The Court held the provision of the Judiciary Act unconstitutional and declared the mandamus void.

CONCLUSION: Marshall, C.J. 6–0. Yes. Relying heavily on the inherent "logical reasoning" of the Constitution, rather than on any explicit text, the Court dismissed the case for lack of jurisdiction but found that Congress' grant of original power of mandamus to the Court violated the division of power established in Article III of the Constitution.

SUMMARY

THE LAW IN ALL ITS FORMS is a rich topic for research. Many online sources and databases supplement and ease legal research once conducted exclusively in the numerous volumes held by legal, academic and government libraries. Law review articles are extremely valuable aids to legal research, as are legal encyclopedias. Legal researchers must be able to read and analyze case law. A three-step process of pre-reading, skimming and close reading helps those new to the law identify the important elements of case decisions. Creating case briefs, using the FIRAC method, helps clarify the key points of important court decisions. ∎

Cases for Study

Thinking About It

Critics of campaign finance regulations designed to prevent corruption in elections won several legal decisions in 2010 in the wake of the Supreme Court's ruling in *Citizens United v. Federal Elections Commission*.[37] As one legal scholar noted, "The relevance of Citizens United has become an issue in every new campaign finance case" since the decision was handed down in January 2010.[38] This aspect of the Court's decision is developed in Chapter 3 when the First Amendment implications of campaign finance laws are discussed. Here we look instead at what *Citizens United* demonstrates about precedent and the rule of law. The debate raised in the Court's opinions has spawned vibrant public discussion about whether the doctrine of stare decisis serves "as an agent of stability" or "to destabilize the rule of law."[39]

The following case excerpts begin with Chief Justice John Roberts' concurring opinion in *Citizens United,* in which he "elaborated on when it *is* acceptable for the Court to overturn precedent."[40] Justice John Paul Stevens' rather acerbic dissent forms the second part of this contemporary Court debate on the role of precedent. Then an excerpt from *Marbury v. Madison,*[41] the decision in which the Supreme Court established its own power of judicial review, follows. A central question resolved by the Supreme Court in *Marbury v. Madison* was whether, under the Constitution, the Court had authority to void duly enacted laws that it deemed to violate the U.S. Constitution.

As you read these case excerpts, keep the following questions in mind:

- How do the sitting justices differ in their interpretation of the binding nature of Supreme Court precedent?
- In the case of *Citizens United,* which justices are exercising "restraint" or "activism"? Why?
- What are the legal foundations for the different opinions?
- What do these decisions suggest about the stability or "transformation" of the rule of law under judicial review and stare decisis?

Citizens United v. Federal Election Commission
Supreme Court of the United States
130 S. Ct. 876 (2010)

JUSTICE ANTHONY KENNEDY delivered the Court's opinion.

CHIEF JUSTICE ROBERTS, with whom JUSTICE SAMUEL ALITO joined, concurring:

The Government urges us in this case to uphold a direct prohibition on political speech. It asks us to embrace a theory of the First Amendment that would allow censorship not only of television and radio broadcasts, but of pamphlets, posters, the Internet, and virtually any other medium that corporations and unions might find useful in expressing their views on matters of public concern. Its theory, if accepted, would empower the Government to prohibit newspapers from running editorials or opinion pieces supporting or opposing candidates for office, so long as the newspapers were owned by corporations—as the major ones are. First Amendment rights could be confined to individuals, subverting the vibrant public discourse that is at the foundation of our democracy.

The Court properly rejects that theory, and I join its opinion in full. The First Amendment protects more than just the individual on a soapbox and the lonely pamphleteer. I write separately to address the important principles of judicial restraint and *stare decisis* implicated in this case.

Judging the constitutionality of an Act of Congress is "the gravest and most delicate duty that this Court is called upon to perform." Because the stakes are so high, our standard practice is to refrain from addressing constitutional questions except when necessary to rule on particular claims before us. This policy underlies both our willingness to construe ambiguous statutes to avoid constitutional problems and our practice " 'never to formulate a rule of constitutional law broader than is required by the precise facts to which it is to be applied.' "

The majority and dissent are united in expressing allegiance to these principles. But I cannot agree with my dissenting colleagues on how these principles apply in this case.

The majority's step-by-step analysis accords with our standard practice of avoiding broad constitutional questions except when necessary to decide the case before us. The majority begins by addressing—and quite properly rejecting—Citizens United's statutory claim that [the Bipartisan Campaign Reform Act of 2002] does not actually cover its production and distribution of *Hillary: The Movie* (hereinafter *Hillary*). If there were a valid basis for deciding this statutory claim in Citizens United's favor (and thereby avoiding constitutional adjudication), it would be proper to do so. . . .

It is only because the majority rejects Citizens United's statutory claim that it proceeds to consider the group's various constitutional arguments, beginning with its narrowest claim (that *Hillary* is not the functional equivalent of express advocacy) and proceeding to its broadest claim (that *Austin v. Michigan Chamber of Commerce* (1990) should be overruled). . . .

The dissent advocates an approach to addressing Citizens United's claims that I find quite perplexing. It presumably agrees with the majority that Citizens United's narrower statutory and constitutional arguments lack merit—otherwise its conclusion that the group should lose this case would make no sense. Despite agreeing that these narrower arguments fail, however, the dissent argues that the majority should nonetheless latch on to one of them in order to avoid reaching the broader constitutional question of whether *Austin* remains good law. It even suggests that the Court's failure to adopt one of these concededly meritless arguments is a sign that the majority is not "serious about judicial restraint."

This approach is based on a false premise: that our practice of avoiding unnecessary (and unnecessarily broad) constitutional holdings somehow trumps our obligation faithfully to interpret the law. It should go without saying, however, that we cannot embrace a narrow ground of decision simply because it is narrow; it must also be right. Thus while it is true that "[i]f it is not necessary to decide more, it is necessary not to decide more," sometimes it is necessary to decide more. There is a difference between judicial restraint and judicial abdication. When constitutional questions are "indispensably necessary" to resolving the case at hand, "the court must meet and decide them.". . .

This is the first case in which we have been asked to overrule *Austin,* and thus it is also the first in which we have had reason to consider how much weight to give *stare decisis* in assessing its continued validity. The dissent erroneously declares that the Court "reaffirmed" *Austin*'s holding in subsequent cases. Not so. Not a single party in any of those cases asked us to overrule *Austin,* and as the dissent points out, the Court generally does not consider constitutional arguments that have not properly been raised. *Austin*'s validity was therefore not directly at issue in the cases the dissent cites. The Court's unwillingness to overturn *Austin* in those cases cannot be understood as a *reaffirmation* of that decision.

Fidelity to precedent—the policy of *stare decisis*—is vital to the proper exercise of the judicial function. "*Stare decisis* is the preferred course because it promotes the even-handed, predictable, and consistent development of legal principles, fosters reliance on judicial decisions, and contributes to the actual and perceived integrity of the judicial process." For these reasons, we have long recognized that departures from precedent are inappropriate in the absence of a "special justification."

At the same time, *stare decisis* is neither an "inexorable command," nor "a mechanical formula of adherence to the latest decision," especially in constitutional cases. If it were, segregation would be legal, minimum wage laws would be unconstitutional, and the Government could wiretap ordinary criminal suspects without first obtaining warrants. As the dissent properly notes, none of us has viewed *stare decisis* in such absolute terms.

Stare decisis is instead a "principle of policy." When considering whether to reexamine a prior erroneous holding, we must balance the importance of having constitutional questions *decided* against the importance of having them *decided right*. As Justice Jackson explained, this requires a "sober appraisal of the disadvantages of the innovation as well as those of the questioned case, a weighing of practical effects of one against the other."

In conducting this balancing, we must keep in mind that *stare decisis* is not an end in itself. It is instead "the means by which we ensure that the law will not merely change erratically, but will develop in a principled and intelligible fashion." Its greatest purpose is to serve a constitutional ideal—the rule of law. It follows that in the unusual circumstance when fidelity to any particular precedent does more to damage this constitutional ideal than to advance it, we must be more willing to depart from that precedent.

Thus, for example, if the precedent under consideration itself departed from the Court's jurisprudence, returning to the "'intrinsically sounder' doctrine established in prior cases" may "better serv[e] the values of *stare decisis* than would following [the] more recently decided case inconsistent with the decisions that came before it." Abrogating the errant precedent, rather than reaffirming or extending it, might better preserve the law's coherence and curtail the precedent's disruptive effects.

Likewise, if adherence to a precedent actually impedes the stable and orderly adjudication of future cases, its *stare decisis* effect is also diminished. This can happen in a number of circumstances, such as when the precedent's validity is so hotly contested that it cannot reliably function as a basis for decision in future cases, when its rationale threatens to upend our settled jurisprudence in related areas of law, and when the precedent's underlying reasoning has become so discredited that the Court cannot keep the precedent alive without jury-rigging new and different justifications to shore up the original mistake.

These considerations weigh against retaining our decision in *Austin*. First, as the majority explains, that decision was an "aberration" insofar as it departed from the robust protections we had granted political speech in our earlier cases . . . [and] does not explain why corporations may be subject to prohibitions on speech in candidate elections when individuals may not.

Second, the validity of *Austin*'s rationale—itself adopted over two "spirited dissents,"—has proved to be the consistent subject of dispute among Members of this Court ever since. The simple fact that one of our decisions remains controversial is, of course, insufficient to justify overruling it. But it does undermine the precedent's ability to contribute to the stable and orderly development of the law. In such circumstances, it is entirely appropriate for the Court—which in this case is squarely asked to reconsider *Austin*'s validity for the first time—to address the matter with a greater willingness to consider new approaches capable of restoring our doctrine to sounder footing.

Third, the *Austin* decision is uniquely destabilizing because it threatens to subvert our Court's decisions even outside the particular context of corporate express advocacy. The First Amendment theory underlying *Austin*'s holding is extraordinarily broad. *Austin*'s logic would authorize government prohibition of political speech by a category of speakers in the name of equality—a point that most scholars acknowledge (and many celebrate), but that the dissent denies.

It should not be surprising, then, that Members of the Court have relied on *Austin*'s expansive logic to justify greater incursions on the First Amendment, even outside the original context of corporate advocacy on behalf of candidates running for office. The dissent in this case succumbs to the same temptation, suggesting that *Austin* justifies prohibiting corporate speech because such speech might unduly influence "the market for legislation." The dissent reads *Austin* to permit restrictions on corporate speech based on nothing more than the fact that the corporate form may help individuals coordinate and present their views more effectively. A speaker's ability to persuade, however, provides no basis for government regulation of free and open public debate on what the laws should be.

If taken seriously, *Austin*'s logic would apply most directly to newspapers and other media corporations. They have a more profound impact on public discourse than most other speakers. These corporate entities are, for the time being, not subject to [the statute's] otherwise generally applicable prohibitions on corporate political speech. But this is simply a matter of legislative grace. The fact that the law currently grants a favored position to media corporations is no reason to overlook the danger inherent in accepting a theory that would allow government restrictions on their political speech.

These readings of *Austin* do no more than carry that decision's reasoning to its logical endpoint. In doing so, they highlight the threat *Austin* poses to First Amendment rights generally, even outside its specific factual context of corporate express advocacy. Because *Austin* is so difficult to confine to its facts—and because its logic threatens to undermine our First Amendment jurisprudence and the nature of public discourse more broadly—the costs of giving it *stare decisis* effect are unusually high.

Finally and most importantly, the Government's own effort to defend *Austin*—or, more accurately, to defend something that is not quite *Austin*—underscores its weakness as a precedent of the Court. The Government concedes that *Austin* "is not the most lucid opinion," yet asks us to reaffirm its holding. But while invoking *stare decisis* to support this position, the

Government never once even mentions the compelling interest that *Austin* relied upon in the first place: the need to diminish "the corrosive and distorting effects of immense aggregations of wealth that are accumulated with the help of the corporate form and that have little or no correlation to the public's support for the corporation's political ideas." *Austin*'s specific holding on the basis of two new and potentially expansive interests—the need to prevent actual or apparent quid pro quo corruption, and the need to protect corporate shareholders. Those interests may or may not support the result in *Austin*, but they were plainly not part of the reasoning on which *Austin* relied. . . .

To its credit, the Government forthrightly concedes that *Austin* did not embrace either of the new rationales it now urges upon us. To be clear: The Court in *Austin* nowhere relied upon the only arguments the Government now raises to support that decision. . . .

To the extent that the Government's case for reaffirming *Austin* depends on radically reconceptualizing its reasoning, that argument is at odds with itself. *Stare decisis* is a doctrine of preservation, not transformation. It counsels deference to past mistakes, but provides no justification for making new ones. There is therefore no basis for the Court to give precedential sway to reasoning that it has never accepted, simply because that reasoning happens to support a conclusion reached on different grounds that have since been abandoned or discredited.

Doing so would undermine the rule-of-law values that justify *stare decisis* in the first place. It would effectively license the Court to invent and adopt new principles of constitutional law solely for the purpose of rationalizing its past errors, without a proper analysis of whether those principles have merit on their own. This approach would allow the Court's past missteps to spawn future mistakes, undercutting the very rule-of-law values that *stare decisis* is designed to protect.

None of this is to say that the Government is barred from making new arguments to support the outcome in *Austin*. On the contrary, it is free to do so. And of course the Court is free to accept them. But the Government's new arguments must stand or fall on their own; they are not entitled to receive the special deference we accord to precedent. They are, as grounds to support *Austin,* literally unprecedented. Moreover, to the extent the Government relies on new arguments—and declines to defend *Austin* on its own terms—we may reasonably infer that it lacks confidence in that decision's original justification.

Because continued adherence to *Austin* threatens to subvert the "principled and intelligible" development of our First Amendment jurisprudence, I support the Court's determination to overrule that decision. . . .

JUSTICE JOHN PAUL STEVENS, with whom JUSTICE RUTH BADER GINSBURG, JUSTICE STEPHEN BREYER and JUSTICE SONIA SOTOMAYOR join, concurring in part and dissenting in part:

. . . The majority's approach to corporate electioneering marks a dramatic break from our past. Congress has placed special limitations on campaign spending by corporations ever since the passage of the Tillman Act in 1907. We have unanimously concluded that this "reflects a permissible assessment of the dangers posed by those entities to the electoral process," and have accepted the "legislative judgment that the special characteristics of the corporate structure require particularly careful regulation." The Court today rejects a century of history when it treats the distinction between corporate and individual campaign spending as an invidious novelty born of *Austin v. Michigan Chamber of Commerce.* Relying largely on individual dissenting opinions, the majority blazes through our precedents, overruling or disavowing a body of case law.

In his landmark concurrence in *Ashwander v. TVA* (1936), Justice Brandeis stressed the importance of adhering to rules the Court has "developed . . . for its own governance" when deciding constitutional questions. Because departures from those rules always enhance the risk of error, . . . I emphatically dissent from its principal holding.

The Court's ruling threatens to undermine the integrity of elected institutions across the Nation. The path it has taken to reach its outcome will, I fear, do damage to this institution. Before turning to the question whether to overrule *Austin* and part of *McConnell,* it is important to explain why the Court should not be deciding that question.

The first reason is that the question was not properly brought before us. . . . [T]he majority decides this case on a basis relinquished below, not included in the questions presented to us by the litigants, and argued here only in response to the Court's invitation. This procedure is unusual and inadvisable for a court. Our colleagues' suggestion that "we are asked to reconsider *Austin* and, in effect, *McConnell,*" would be more accurate if rephrased to state that "we have asked ourselves" to reconsider those cases. . . .

It is all the more distressing that our colleagues have manufactured a facial challenge, because the parties have advanced numerous ways to resolve the case that would facilitate electioneering by nonprofit advocacy corporations such as Citizens United, without toppling statutes and precedents. Which is to say, the majority has transgressed yet another "cardinal" principle of the judicial process: "[I]f it is not necessary to decide more, it is necessary not to decide more.". . .

The final principle of judicial process that the majority violates is the most transparent: *stare decisis.* I am not an absolutist when it comes to *stare decisis,* in the campaign finance area or in any other. No one is. But if this principle is to do any meaningful work in supporting the rule of law, it must at least demand a significant justification, beyond the preferences of five Justices, for overturning settled doctrine. "[A] decision to overrule should rest on some special reason over and above the belief that a prior case was wrongly decided." No such justification exists in this case, and to the contrary there are powerful prudential reasons to keep faith with our precedents.

The Court's central argument for why *stare decisis* ought to be trumped is that it does not like *Austin.* The opinion "was not well reasoned," our colleagues assert, and it conflicts with First Amendment principles. This, of course, is the Court's merits argument, the many defects in which we will soon consider. I am perfectly willing to concede that if one of our precedents were dead wrong in its reasoning or irreconcilable with the rest of our doctrine, there would be a compelling basis for revisiting it. But neither is true of *Austin*, and restating a merits argument with additional vigor does not give it extra weight in the *stare decisis* calculus.

Perhaps in recognition of this point, the Court supplements its merits case with a smattering of assertions. The Court proclaims that "*Austin* is undermined by experience since its announcement." This is a curious claim to make in a case that lacks a developed record. The majority has no empirical evidence with which to substantiate the claim; we just have its *ipse dixit* that the real world has not been kind to *Austin*. Nor does the majority bother to specify in what sense *Austin* has been "undermined." Instead it treats the reader to a string of non sequiturs: "Our Nation's speech dynamic is changing"; "[s]peakers have become adept at presenting citizens with sound bites, talking points, and scripted messages"; "[c]orporations . . . do not have monolithic views." How any of these ruminations weakens the force of *stare decisis*, escapes my comprehension.

The majority also contends that the Government's hesitation to rely on *Austin*'s antidistortion rationale "diminishe[s]" "the principle of adhering to that precedent." Why it diminishes the value of *stare decisis* is left unexplained. We have never thought fit to overrule a precedent because a litigant has taken any particular tack. Nor should we. Our decisions can often be defended on multiple grounds, and a litigant may have strategic or case-specific reasons for emphasizing only a subset of them. Members of the public, moreover, often rely on our bottom-line holdings far more than our precise legal arguments; surely this is true for the legislatures that have been regulating corporate electioneering since *Austin*. The task of evaluating the continued viability of precedents falls to this Court, not to the parties.

Although the majority opinion spends several pages making these surprising arguments, it says almost nothing about the standard considerations we have used to determine *stare decisis* value, such as the antiquity of the precedent, the workability of its legal rule, and the reliance interests at stake. It is also conspicuously silent about *McConnell*, even though the *McConnell* Court's decision to uphold

[the Bipartisan Campaign Reform Act (BCRA)] relied not only on the antidistortion logic of *Austin* but also on the statute's historical pedigree, and the need to preserve the integrity of federal campaigns.

We have recognized that "*[s]tare decisis* has special force when legislators or citizens 'have acted in reliance on a previous decision, for in this instance overruling the decision would dislodge settled rights and expectations or require an extensive legislative response.'" *Stare decisis* protects not only personal rights involving property or contract but also the ability of the elected branches to shape their laws in an effective and coherent fashion. Today's decision takes away a power that we have long permitted these branches to exercise. State legislatures have relied on their authority to regulate corporate electioneering, confirmed in *Austin*, for more than a century. The Federal Congress has relied on this authority for a comparable stretch of time, and it specifically relied on *Austin* throughout the years it spent developing and debating BCRA. The total record it compiled was *100,000 pages* long. Pulling out the rug beneath Congress after affirming the constitutionality of [the statutory provision] six years ago shows great disrespect for a coequal branch.

By removing one of its central components, today's ruling makes a hash out of BCRA's "delicate and interconnected regulatory scheme." . . .

Beyond the reliance interests at stake, the other *stare decisis* factors also cut against the Court. Considerations of antiquity are significant for similar reasons. *McConnell* is only six years old, but *Austin* has been on the books for two decades, and many of the statutes called into question by today's opinion have been on the books for a half-century or more. The Court points to no intervening change in circumstances that warrants revisiting *Austin*. Certainly nothing relevant has changed since we decided WRTL [*Federal Election Commission v. Wisconsin Right to Life, Inc.*] two Terms ago. And the Court gives no reason to think that *Austin* and *McConnell* are unworkable.

In fact, no one has argued to us that *Austin*'s rule has proved impracticable, and not a single for-profit corporation, union, or State has asked us to overrule it. Quite to the contrary, leading groups representing the business community, organized labor and the nonprofit sector, together with more than half of the States, urge that we preserve *Austin*. As for *McConnell*, the portions of BCRA it upheld may be prolix, but all three branches of Government have worked to make §203 as user-friendly as possible. For instance, Congress established a special mechanism for expedited review of constitutional challenges; the FEC has established a standardized process, with clearly defined safe harbors, for corporations to claim that a particular electioneering communication is permissible under WRTL; and, as noted above, THE CHIEF JUSTICE crafted his controlling opinion in WRTL with the express goal of maximizing clarity and administrability. The case for *stare decisis* may be bolstered, we have said, when subsequent rulings "have reduced the impact"

of a precedent "while reaffirming the decision's core ruling."

In the end, the Court's rejection of *Austin* and *McConnell* comes down to nothing more than its disagreement with their results. Virtually every one of its arguments was made and rejected in those cases, and the majority opinion is essentially an amalgamation of resuscitated dissents. The only relevant thing that has changed since *Austin* and *McConnell* is the composition of this Court. Today's ruling thus strikes at the vitals of *stare decisis*, "the means by which we ensure that the law will not merely change erratically, but will develop in a principled and intelligible fashion" that "permits society to presume that bedrock principles are founded in the law rather than in the proclivities of individuals.". . .

Marbury v. Madison
Supreme Court of the United States
5 U.S. 137 (1803)

CHIEF JUSTICE JOHN MARSHALL delivered the Court's opinion:

. . . The constitution vests the whole judicial power of the United States in one supreme court, and such inferior courts as congress shall, from time to time, ordain and establish. This power is expressly extended to all cases arising under the laws of the United States; and consequently, in some form, may be exercised over the present case; because the right claimed is given by a law of the United States.

In the distribution of this power it is declared that "the supreme court shall have original jurisdiction in all cases affecting ambassadors, other public ministers and consuls, and those in which a state shall be a party. In all other cases, the supreme court shall have appellate jurisdiction."

It has been insisted at the bar, that as the original grant of jurisdiction to the supreme and inferior courts is general, and the clause, assigning original jurisdiction to the supreme court, contains no negative or restrictive words; the power remains to the legislature, to assign original jurisdiction to that court in other cases than those specified in the article which has been

recited; provided those cases belong to the judicial power of the United States.

If it had been intended to leave it to the discretion of the legislature to apportion the judicial power between the supreme and inferior courts according to the will of that body, it would certainly have been useless to have proceeded further than to have defined the judicial power, and the tribunals in which it should be vested. The subsequent part of the section is . . . entirely without meaning, if such is to be the construction. If congress remains at liberty to give this court appellate jurisdiction, where the constitution has declared their jurisdiction shall be original; and original jurisdiction where the constitution has declared it shall be appellate; the distribution of jurisdiction, made in the constitution, is form without substance. . . .

It cannot be presumed that any clause in the constitution is intended to be without effect; and therefore such a construction is inadmissible, unless the words require it. . . .

When an instrument organizing fundamentally a judicial system, divides it into one supreme, and so many inferior courts as the legislature may ordain and establish; then enumerates its powers, and proceeds so far to distribute them, as to define the jurisdiction of the supreme court by declaring the cases in which it shall take original jurisdiction, and that in others it shall take appellate jurisdiction, the plain import of the words seems to be, that in one class of cases its jurisdiction is original, and not appellate; in the other it is appellate, and not original. If any other construction would render the clause inoperative, that is an additional reason for rejecting such other construction, and for adhering to their obvious meaning.

To enable this court then to issue a mandamus, it must be shown to be an exercise of appellate jurisdiction, or to be necessary to enable them to exercise appellate jurisdiction.

It has been stated at the bar that the appellate jurisdiction may be exercised in a variety of forms, and that if it be the will of the legislature that a mandamus should be used for that purpose, that will must be obeyed. This is true; yet the jurisdiction must be appellate, not original.

It is the essential criterion of appellate jurisdiction, that it revises and corrects the proceedings in a cause already instituted, and does not create that case. Although, therefore, a mandamus may be directed to courts, yet to issue such a writ to an officer for the delivery of a paper, is in effect the same as to sustain an original action for that paper, and therefore seems not to belong to appellate, but to original jurisdiction. Neither is it necessary in such a case as this, to enable the court to exercise its appellate jurisdiction.

The authority, therefore, given to the supreme court, by the act establishing the judicial courts of the United States, to issue writs of mandamus to public officers, appears not to be warranted by the constitution; and it becomes necessary to enquire whether a jurisdiction, so conferred, can be exercised.

The question, whether an act, repugnant to the constitution, can become the law of the land, is a question deeply interesting to the United States; but, happily, not of an intricacy proportioned to its interest. It seems only necessary to recognise certain principles, supposed to have been long and well established, to decide it.

That the people have an original right to establish, for their future government, such principles as, in their opinion, shall most conduce to their own happiness, is the basis, on which the whole American fabric has been erected. The exercise of this original right is a very great exertion; nor can it, nor ought it to be frequently repeated. The principles, therefore, so established, are deemed fundamental. And as the authority, from which they proceed, is supreme, and can seldom act, they are designed to be permanent.

This original and supreme will organizes the government, and assigns to different departments their respective powers. It may either stop here; or establish certain limits not to be transcended by those departments.

The government of the United States is of the latter description. The powers of the legislature are defined, and limited; and that those limits may not be mistaken, or forgotten, the constitution is written. To what purpose are powers limited, and to what purpose is that limitation committed to writing; if these limits may, at any time, be passed by those intended to be restrained? The distinction between a government with limited and unlimited powers is abolished, if those limits do not confine the persons on whom they are imposed, and if acts prohibited and acts allowed are of equal obligation. It is a proposition too plain to be contested, that the constitution controls any legislative act repugnant to it; or, that the legislature may alter the constitution by an ordinary act.

Between these alternatives there is no middle ground. The constitution is either a superior, paramount law, unchangeable by ordinary means, or it is on a level with ordinary legislative acts, and like other acts, is alterable when the legislature shall please to alter it.

If the former part of the alternative be true, then a legislative act contrary to the constitution is not law: if the latter part be true, then written constitutions are absurd attempts, on the part of the people, to limit a power in its own nature illimitable.

Certainly all those who have framed written constitutions contemplate them as forming the fundamental and paramount law of the nation, and consequently the theory of every such government must be, that an act of the legislature repugnant to the constitution is void.

This theory is essentially attached to a written constitution, and is consequently to be considered by this court as one of the fundamental principles of our society. It is not therefore to be lost sight of in the further consideration of this subject.

If an act of the legislature, repugnant to the constitution, is void, does it, notwithstanding its invalidity, bind the courts, and oblige them to give it effect? Or, in other words, though it be not law, does it constitute a rule as operative as if it was a law? This would be to overthrow in fact what was established in theory; and would seem, at first view, an absurdity too gross to be insisted on. It shall, however, receive a more attentive consideration.

It is emphatically the province and duty of the judicial department to say what the law is. Those who apply the rule to particular cases, must of necessity expound and interpret that rule. If two laws conflict with each other, the courts must decide on the operation of each. So if a law be in opposition to the constitution; if both the law and the constitution apply to a particular case, so that the court must either decide that case conformably to the law, disregarding the constitution; or conformably to the constitution, disregarding the law; the court must determine which of these conflicting rules governs the case. This is of the very essence of judicial duty.

If then the courts are to regard the constitution; and the constitution is superior to any ordinary act of the legislature; the constitution, and not such ordinary act, must govern the case to which they both apply.

Those then who controvert the principle that the constitution is to be considered, in court, as a paramount law, are reduced to the necessity of maintaining that courts must close their eyes on the constitution, and see only the law.

This doctrine would subvert the very foundation of all written constitutions. It would declare that an act, which, according to the principles and theory of our government, is entirely void, is yet, in practice, completely obligatory. It would declare, that if the legislature shall do what is expressly forbidden, such act, notwithstanding the express prohibition, is in reality effectual. It would be giving to the legislature a practical and real omnipotence with the same breath which professes to restrict their powers within narrow limits. It is prescribing limits, and declaring that those limits may be passed at pleasure.

That it thus reduces to nothing what we have deemed the greatest improvement on political institutions—a written constitution, would of itself be sufficient, in America where written constitutions have been viewed with so much reverence, for rejecting the construction. But the peculiar expressions of the constitution of the United States furnish additional arguments in favour of its rejection.

The judicial power of the United States is extended to all cases arising under the constitution. Could it be the intention of those who gave this power, to say that, in using it, the constitution should not be looked into? That a case arising under the constitution should be decided without examining the instrument under which it arises?

This is too extravagant to be maintained. . . .

. . . [I]t is apparent, that the framers of the constitution contemplated that instrument, as a rule for the government of courts, as well as of the legislature.

Why otherwise does it direct the judges to take an oath to support it? This oath certainly applies, in an especial manner, to their conduct in their official character. How immoral to impose it on them, if they were to be used as the instruments, and the knowing instruments, for violating what they swear to support!

The oath of office, too, imposed by the legislature, is completely demonstrative of the legislative opinion on the subject. It is in these words, "I do solemnly swear that I will administer justice without respect to persons, and do equal right to the poor and to the rich; and that I will faithfully and impartially discharge all the duties incumbent on me as according to the best of my abilities and understanding, agreeably to the constitution, and laws of the United States."

Why does a judge swear to discharge his duties agreeably to the constitution of the United States, if that constitution forms no rule for his government?

if it is closed upon him, and cannot be inspected by him?

If such be the real state of things, this is worse than solemn mockery. To prescribe, or to take this oath, becomes equally a crime.

It is also not entirely unworthy of observation, that in declaring what shall be the supreme law of the land, the constitution itself is first mentioned; and not the laws of the United States generally, but those only which shall be made in pursuance of the constitution, have that rank.

Thus, the particular phraseology of the constitution of the United States confirms and strengthens the principle, supposed to be essential to all written constitutions, that a law repugnant to the constitution is void; and that courts, as well as other departments, are bound by that instrument.

The rule must be discharged.

Chapter 2

Without freedom of thought, there can be no such thing as wisdom; and no such thing as publick liberty, without freedom of speech: Which is the right of every man, as far as by it he does not hurt and control the right of another. . . .

Cato's Letters[1]

Thousands of people daily use public spaces as a forum for free speech. Here, in 2007, "Reverend Billy" Talen sings in New York City's Union Square to protest his earlier arrest there for disorderly conduct after continually reciting the text of the First Amendment through a bullhorn while following police officers.

The First Amendment

Speech and Press Freedoms in Theory and Reality

Interpreting the First Amendment

The Origins of the First Amendment

Foundations of First Amendment Theory

First Amendment Values

Contemporary Prior Restraints

Court Scrutiny of Laws That Affect First Amendment Rights

Content-Based Laws
Content-Neutral Laws

Political Speech

Elections and Campaign Finance

Anonymous Speech

Government Speakers

Public and Nonpublic Forums

Private Property as a Public Forum
Virtual Forums and Government Speakers

Compelled Speech

Media Emergence, Convergence and Consolidation

Cases for Study

➤ *New York Times Co. v. United States*
➤ *United States v. O'Brien*

Suppose . . .

. . . that two leading national newspapers receive copies of classified federal government documents from an anonymous source. The 700-page report shows the government has been lying in public statements about the success of the U.S. war effort and the number of U.S. casualties. When the newspapers publish the first in a series of articles based on the documents, the federal government asks a court to prohibit publication of the remaining stories. The government claims that continued disclosure of the classified report will jeopardize the lives of U.S. soldiers, threaten ongoing military operations and undermine the security and foreign policy of the nation. The newspapers say they have a First Amendment right to publish the information and the public has a need to know the truth about the nation's war effort.

Does the First Amendment permit the government, through the courts, to prevent the media from accurately disclosing important information to the public? Does the government's authority to classify government records as secret also allow it to prevent public discussion of those records once legally obtained? Does it matter how the newspapers obtained the documents? Should the government be required to demonstrate the actual harm that will occur from continued publication? Look for the answers to these questions when the case of *New York Times Co. v. United States* is discussed later and the case is excerpted at the end of the chapter.

The First Amendment to the U.S. Constitution includes only 45 words. It says: "Congress shall make no law respecting an establishment of religion, or prohibiting the free exercise thereof; or abridging the freedom of speech, or of the press; or the right of the people peaceably to assemble, and to petition the government for a redress of grievances." Since the adoption of the Bill of Rights in 1791, thousands of articles, books and legal cases have tried to explain the meaning of the First Amendment and to define the boundaries of the six freedoms it protects. A literal interpretation of the First Amendment would completely ban Congress, and only Congress, from "abridging" the freedom of speech or of the press in any way. However, in 1925, the U.S. Supreme Court said the First Amendment applied to state legislatures as well as to Congress.[2] The Supreme Court since has struck down both federal and state laws, court rulings, administrative agency actions and executive decisions because they violate the First Amendment.

Through its decisions, the Supreme Court has clarified the meaning of the First Amendment. For example, although the amendment says government "shall make no law," no one seated on the Court argues that the First Amendment is an absolute ban.[3] Instead, the justices attempt to interpret the meaning of the amendment in various ways. Some members of the Court believe people can understand the law simply by reading the text of the First Amendment. These so-called textualists believe the Constitution's own words provide a full and clear explanation of the protections it guarantees to freedom of speech and press. But the text offers little guidance to justices who must decide whether, for example, cable companies are members of "the press" and whether a law that requires cable companies to carry local broadcast programming unconstitutionally "abridges" the freedom of speech or press of those cable companies.[4]

In most of its decisions, the Supreme Court has not distinguished between free speech and a free press. In fact, the Court often interchanges the two terms or even combines them under the label "free expression." Historians and Justice Potter Stewart, however, have argued that the free press clause was intended to provide special protections for journalists and the mass media in checking the power of government.[5]

Interpreting the First Amendment

Justice Stewart and others have looked to history or a variety of theories to help them decide what the First Amendment means. For example, members of the Court may try to discover the **original intent** of the framers of the Constitution to help them determine whether burning a flag to protest government actions is a form of speech protected by the First Amendment.[6] Unfortunately, intent is a slippery thing, and the authors of the First Amendment did not leave many records to indicate what they meant by "the freedom of speech, or of the press."

original intent The perceived intent of the framers of the First Amendment. The concept of original intent guides contemporary First Amendment application and interpretation.

ad hoc balancing Making decisions according to the specific facts of the case under review rather than more general principles.

Some justices argue that the Constitution should be a living document whose meaning evolves as society evolves. These members of the Court believe that even if they could determine with certainty what the words of the First Amendment meant in 1791, that meaning would not be helpful or relevant nearly 225 years later. They insist that the flexibility of constitutional language is its greatest strength, not its failing. Others complain that this fluidity of meaning gives the Court complete power to change the protections of the First Amendment at whim.

In practice, the Supreme Court tends to avoid broad statements about the First Amendment and generally decides what the First Amendment means on a case-by-case basis. This is an example of **ad hoc balancing,** in which courts make decisions according to the specific facts of the case under review rather than on the basis of more general principles. To reach a decision, the Court often weighs the constitutional interests on one side of a case against the competing interests on the other side. No clear rule dictates the Court's ad hoc balancing of interests. Instead, the justices carefully examine the competing rights and decide which side has the weightier constitutional merit. In 2004, when an attorney tried to use the federal Freedom of Information Act (FOIA) to obtain copies of photographs of the body of White House Counsel Vince Foster, for example, the Court weighed the public interest in access against the privacy interests of Foster's family and decided in favor of privacy.[7] In its reasoning, the Court considered the historical role of free speech and free press in America, and it concluded that neither the First Amendment nor the FOIA provided a right of access to private information. In 2010, the Supreme Court relied substantially on its own "historical and traditional" interpretation of the First Amendment to strike down a law prohibiting depictions of animal cruelty.[8]

Alternately, the Court will use a definitional or categorical approach to reach First Amendment decisions. Through decades of decisions, the Court has defined a variety of broad categories, such as political speech, and used them to determine the appropriate level of First Amendment protection.

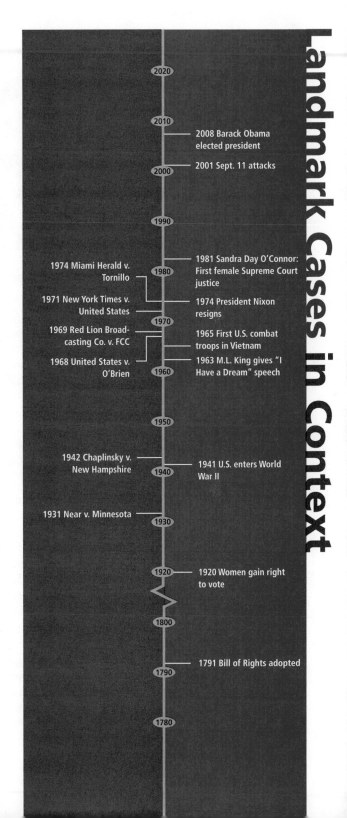

Landmark Cases in Context

- 2020
- 2010
- 2008 Barack Obama elected president
- 2001 Sept. 11 attacks
- 2000
- 1990
- 1974 Miami Herald v. Tornillo
- 1981 Sandra Day O'Connor: First female Supreme Court justice
- 1980
- 1971 New York Times v. United States
- 1974 President Nixon resigns
- 1970
- 1969 Red Lion Broadcasting Co. v. FCC
- 1965 First U.S. combat troops in Vietnam
- 1968 United States v. O'Brien
- 1963 M.L. King gives "I Have a Dream" speech
- 1960
- 1950
- 1942 Chaplinsky v. New Hampshire
- 1941 U.S. enters World War II
- 1940
- 1931 Near v. Minnesota
- 1930
- 1920 Women gain right to vote
- 1920
- 1800
- 1791 Bill of Rights adopted
- 1790
- 1780

Is Journalism a "Conspiracy of Intellect"?

Justice Potter Stewart believed the press had a particular, unique and special role under the Constitution. He said the framers of the Constitution intentionally singled out the press as the only business with a specific guarantee of freedom from government restraint because this protection was essential to the robust functioning of press criticism so vital to democracy. He wrote that, according to the framers:

U.S. Supreme Court Justice Potter Stewart

> [A] free press was not just a neutral vehicle for the balanced discussion of diverse ideas. Instead, the free press meant organized, expert scrutiny of government. The press was a conspiracy of the intellect, with the courage of numbers. This formidable check on official power was what the British Crown had feared—and what the American Founders decided to risk.[1]

1. Potter Stewart, *Or of the Press,* 26 HASTINGS L.J. 631, 634 (1975).

Simply put, the Court has decided that some types of speech deserve protection; others do not. In *Chaplinsky v. New Hampshire,*[9] the Court first noted that "certain well-defined and narrowly limited classes of speech . . . are no essential part of any exposition of ideas, and are of such slight social value as a step to truth" that government may prevent and punish this speech without violating the First Amendment.

Courts have used this approach to rule that entire categories of speech are unprotected by the First Amendment. When speech falls into one of these narrow classes, the courts do not balance the value of the speech against society's interests—the Supreme Court determined the proper balance long ago. Using the categorical approach, then, the only question today is whether a specific act of expression falls within an unprotected class.

In *Chaplinsky,* the Court did not fully develop the different "narrow" categories of speech, but subsequent rulings make clear that political speech enjoys full constitutional protection, while seditious speech, fighting words, obscenity and defamation are unprotected categories. The First Amendment also poses no barrier to laws that punish blackmail, extortion, perjury, false advertising and disruptive speech in the public school classroom, for example. In addition, recent Court opinions suggest that child pornography, cross-burning and true threats (particularly to national security) warrant little, if any, First Amendment protection.

Some categories of speech are neither well defined nor particularly narrow. But even loose categories serve as broad guidelines to the types of content that government may regulate with relative impunity. In addition, such categories assist courts seeking to resolve cases involving similar speech. In cases involving loosely defined categories, however, courts generally use **categorical balancing** to determine the outcome; they look beyond the speech itself to consider the particular circumstances and the extent of harm caused to determine whether the expression falls into a punishable category. If the harm is likely to be cataclysmic, society's interest in preventing the crisis is more likely to outweigh concerns about protection of speech. One problem, though, is that the gravity of harm caused by speech is very difficult to judge in advance or in the abstract.

categorical balancing A judge's or court's practice of developing rules by weighing different broad categories, such as political speech, against other categories of interests, such as privacy. The rules may be applied in later cases with similar facts.

SUMMARY

DESPITE THE ABSOLUTIST LANGUAGE of the Constitution's First Amendment, the Supreme Court consistently has said the Constitution does not prevent government from regulating speech and press freedoms. While Justice Stewart believed the First Amendment provided explicit and special protection for the media, many justices do not distinguish between the speech and press guarantees and do not recognize any distinct press rights.

The Court tends to avoid sweeping declarations of the meaning of speech and press freedoms and to interpret the First Amendment only as applied to a particular set of facts. Many First Amendment decisions rely on ad hoc balancing of the competing rights. In addition, the Court has used categorical definitions of speech to place some types of speech beyond constitutional protection. At other times, speech categories assist the Court in its balancing of interests. ∎

The Origins of the First Amendment

Historians of the First Amendment generally agree that it was never meant to be an absolute ban on all government actions involving freedom of speech or of the press. Instead, the First Amendment was intended to prevent the U.S. government from adopting the types of suppressive laws that flourished in England during the 300 years following the introduction of the printing press in 1450. Beginning in the early 1500s, the British crown licensed all presses in England. King Henry VIII and the Roman Catholic Church feared that broad public distribution of printed materials would erode their control of information and their authority. The Church and the Crown sought to suppress challenges to their power by outlawing critical views as heresy or sedition. They jointly imposed a strict system of licensing of printers and prior review of all texts. The king's officers banned books and censored disfavored ideas.

The Crown also provided favored printers with lucrative monopoly printing contracts for popular works like the Bible. In exchange, these printers became an extension of law enforcement, reporting suspicions of unlicensed publishing, punishing unlicensed printers and destroying their presses. Printers suspected of publishing or distributing unauthorized or outlawed texts faced fines, prison, torture or even execution. Despite the danger, unlicensed texts continued to appear in England.

Foundations of First Amendment Theory

In 1643, the power of prior review shifted from the king's officers to the British Parliament, but government censors continued to review all publications before they could be printed. Authors and publishers protested against government control of content and developed theories to justify freedom of the press. In 1644, for example, English poet John Milton's unlicensed "Areopagitica" argued that an open marketplace of ideas advanced the interests of society and mankind. Milton, who was angered by church and state condemnation and attempts to burn his earlier unlicensed pamphlet advocating divorce, said the free exchange of ideas was vital to the discovery of truth. He wrote, famously:

> Though all the winds of doctrine were let loose to play upon the earth, so Truth be in the field, we do injuriously by licensing and prohibiting to misdoubt her strength. Let her and Falsehood grapple; who ever knew Truth put to the worse in a free and open encounter?[10]

By the late 1600s, English philosopher and political theorist John Locke argued that government censorship was an improper exercise of power.[11] Locke first said that all people have fundamental natural rights, including life, personal liberty and self-fulfillment. Freedom of expression is central to these natural rights. In contrast, government does not have any innate rights or natural authority, Locke said. Government exists only through the grant of power from the people, and legitimate government may operate only within the sphere of its granted power. Because the people do not grant government the power to limit their natural human rights, government censorship is always illegitimate.

Locke's vision of government was revolutionary. Nearly three-quarters of a century later, Jean-Jacques Rousseau, a French political philosopher, advanced a similar view of a social contract between the people and their government.[12] Rousseau said all people are born free and equal but, unless constrained by morality and law, would become uncivilized and violent. People accordingly form a social contract in which they exchange some of their freedom for a limited government that advances the collective interest. Because the people remain sovereign and do not surrender their rights, government censorship violates the fundamental social contract and can never be justified. Many believe that Rousseau's ideas on the sovereignty of the people laid the foundation for the French Revolution.

prior restraint Action taken by the government to prohibit publication of a specific document or text before it is distributed to the public; a policy that requires government approval before publication.

defamation A false communication that harms another's reputation and subjects him or her to ridicule and scorn; incorporates both libel and slander.

In 1694, the British Parliament failed to renew the Licensing Act, which had authorized parliamentary **prior restraint** of publications. Still, for the next 100 years, the British government continued to enact and enforce laws that punished immoral, illegal or dangerous speech after the fact. Scholars, authors, publishers and the elite of the day generally accepted that punishment after the fact was a legitimate means of minimizing the harms of sedition (criticism of the government), **defamation** (criticism of individuals) and blasphemy (criticism of religion). Punishment after the fact was not defined as censorship because it allowed individuals to express themselves freely and citizens to receive a full range of information. Punishment after the fact merely held speakers responsible for their harmful or dangerous ideas. In 1769, Sir William Blackstone, a judge, professor and leading legal scholar, said that under English common law, freedom of speech meant only that government could not censor speech prior to publication.[13] He wrote:

> The liberty of the press is indeed essential to the nature of a free state, but this consists in laying no previous restraints upon publications, and not in freedom from censure for criminal matter when published. Every freeman has an undoubted right to lay what sentiments he pleases before the public: to forbid this is to destroy the freedom of the press: but if he publishes what is improper, mischievous, or illegal, he must take the consequences of his own temerity.[14]

Blackstone's view of freedom of the press moved across the Atlantic with the British troops. The shadows of British licensing, taxation and common law restraints on speech and press were evident in the early years of American colonization.[15] Presses in the colonies were licensed, and government censors previewed publications until the 1720s. The crime of **seditious libel,** for example, made it illegal to publish anything harmful to the reputation of a colonial governor. Truth was not a defense because truthful criticism still harmed the governor's reputation, and the governor had a legal right to exact punishment for that harm.

seditious libel Communication meant to incite people to change the government; criticism of the government.

As the colonies became more independent and chafed under British rule, the British common law traditions also came under attack. The most renowned case is that of John Peter Zenger, the publisher of one of two newspapers in the colony of New York. Zenger, a German immigrant, clearly had broken the sedition law by printing criticism of colonial Gov. William Cosby. Cosby jailed Zenger to stop the attacks. In Zenger's defense, attorney Andrew Hamilton argued that no one should be jailed for publishing truthful and fair criticism of government. The jury agreed and acquitted Zenger in 1734.

Very few trials for seditious libel occurred after that ruling. However, the struggle to define the acceptable limits of free speech and a free press in the colonies was not over. Colonial legislatures used their power of contempt to punish publishers with whom they were displeased. They had the power to question, convict, jail and fine publishers for breach of parliamentary privilege, which they defined broadly as virtually any criticism of their performance. Then, in 1765, the British Parliament set off the storm that would become the American Revolution. The British enacted a Stamp Act to collect taxes from the colonies to help finance the French and Indian War. Patrick Henry, among others, organized resistance to this taxation without representation and said, "If this be treason, make the most of it."[16]

The freedom of speech and of the press protected in the First Amendment grew out of this mixed history of suppression and resistance. The framers understood both the British tradition of punishment for sedition, blasphemy and libel, and the colonists' growing enthusiasm for increasingly wide-open debate. Certainly, it seems clear the authors of the First Amendment intended to provide a ban on prior restraints. It is less clear whether they intended to eliminate the common law regarding sedition, blasphemy and libel.[17]

True Treason?

In 2010, false reports of the arrest of 28-year-old Adam Gadahn[1] renewed interest in his four-year-old indictment on treason.[2] His was the first charge of treason in the United States in more than 50 years.[3] He could receive the death penalty if convicted.

Gadahn, an Oregon native raised in California, was indicted for treason and giving material support to the enemy, al-Qaida, for appearing in five al-Qaida videos in which he railed against the United States in English, praised the attacks of Sept. 11, 2001, and proclaimed al-Qaida's ability to attack again. One legal scholar said the indictment "follows the World War II treason cases in appearing to assert that propaganda amounts to treason under the 'aid and comfort' prong."[4]

This video image of Adam Gadahn was produced by al-Qaida and posted on the Internet in August 2007.

Speaking to the charges, Dep. Atty. Gen. Paul McNulty said he had no evidence that Gadahn had planned or participated in any terrorist attacks. However, he said:

> The significance of the propaganda part should not be underestimated.... This is a very significant piece of the way an enemy does business, to demoralize the troops, to encourage the spread of fear.[5] . . .

McNulty elsewhere explained:

> Gadahn is a U.S. citizen who made a choice to join and act as a propagandist for al-Qaeda, an enemy of this country responsible for the horrific deaths of thousands of innocent Americans on Sept. 11, 2001. The War on Terror is a fight for hearts and minds, and Gadahn gave himself to our enemies in al-Qaeda for the purpose of being a central part of their propaganda machine. By making this choice, we believe Gadahn committed treason—perhaps the most serious offense for which any person can be tried under our Constitution.[6] . . .

Willie Hulon, FBI Executive Assistant Director of the National Security Branch, said:

> Gadahn represents a new breed of home-grown extremist, who has chosen to betray the country of his birth, and align with the al-Qaeda terrorist network. Based on this indictment, Gadahn was added . . . to the FBI's Most Wanted Terrorists List.[7]

Some reports suggested Gadahn had been killed in a U.S. missile attack that destroyed a house in northern Pakistan in January 2008.[8] Government sources neither confirmed nor denied this and provided no information on his whereabouts.

Gadahn's alleged crime—participating in propaganda videos—is reminiscent of the wave of treason prosecutions during World War II in which the government used the "aid and comfort" theory of treason against American propagandists for Germany and Japan. But does that theory raise First Amendment questions? Does the speech in Gadahn's videos cross the line into an unprotected category? Is it treason?

---

1. Alex Rodriguez, *Pakistan Says U.S.-Born Suspect in Custody Is Not Gadahn,* L.A. TIMES, May 9, 2010, *available at* http://articles .latimes.com.
2. First Superseding Indictment P 8, United States v. Gadahn, SA CR 05-254(A) (C.D. Cal. Oct. 11, 2006), *available at* http://www .usdoj.gov/opa/documents/.
3. The National Terror Alert Response Center, *Adam Gadahn American Al-Qaeda Threatens Attacks on U.S.* (May 29, 2007), *available at* http://www.nationalterroralert.com.
4. Kristen Eichensehr, *Treason's Return,* 116 YALE L.J. Pocket Part 229, 230–31 (2007).
5. Paul McNulty, U.S. Deputy Attorney General, *Transcript of Press Conference Announcing Indictment of U.S. Citizen for Treason and Material Support Charges for Providing Aid and Comfort to al Qaeda* (Oct. 11, 2006).
6. U.S. Department of Justice, Press Release (Oct. 11, 2006), *available at* http://www.usdoj.gov.
7. *Id.*
8. B. Raman, *Mystery Surrounding Adam Gadahn,* International Terrorism Monitor Paper No. 401, South Asia Analysis Group (June 14, 2008), *available at* http://www.southasiaanalysis.org.

The passage of the Sedition Act seven years after the adoption of the First Amendment suggests that government leaders continued to support laws that punished criticism of government. The law imposed heavy fines and jail time on individuals who stirred up public emotions or expressed malicious views against the government. As the 18th century ended, more than a dozen prosecutions and convictions under the Alien and Sedition Acts targeted outspoken publishers, editors and political opponents of President John Adams' government.[18] The U.S. Supreme Court never reviewed the constitutionality of the federal Sedition Act, which expired in 1801. More than 150 years later, Justice William J. Brennan said "the court of history" had clearly decided that the Sedition Act had been unconstitutional.[19]

SUMMARY

IN THE 1500s, CHURCH AND STATE collaborated to license presses and strictly censor publications to limit the spread of information, retain power and suppress criticism of their power and authority. The following century outlined the philosophic argument against government censorship. Milton attacked government's prior review of publications as a form of thought control and lauded the value of a free and open marketplace of ideas. Locke argued that government's authority should be limited to assuring the full enjoyment of the people's natural rights of life, liberty and property. Rousseau said government was the result of a social contract under which the sovereign people do *not* grant government authority to censor their ideas or expression.

A century after British Parliament refused to renew the Licensing Act, Blackstone defined freedom of speech in England as freedom from prior restraint by government. Punishment for harmful speech such as seditious libel did not violate freedom of speech. Eventually, the American colonies largely rejected the British common law tradition of punishing truthful criticism of government. The American concept of freedom of speech and press developed from a mixture of government repression and public resistance. The framers of the First Amendment did not leave behind documents defining what they meant by "the freedom of speech and of the press." At a minimum, it stood for the assumption that government could not impose prior restraints on speech. Yet in the late 1700s, the U.S. Congress enacted laws that prohibited seditious expression. ∎

First Amendment Values

Where history has failed to provide a single, clear meaning for the First Amendment, the Supreme Court has interpreted it as a means to achieve specific social functions or advance certain fundamental values. When the First Amendment is understood as an instrument, freedom of speech and freedom of the press receive

Points of Law

What's the Value of Free Speech?

A morass of theories attempts to explain why we should care about speech. While some try to define the single core value of free speech, like some holy grail, most people agree that the freedom of speech protected by the First Amendment serves a number of important interests: individual and social, instrumental and inherent.[1] Some of the central values of free speech most frequently identified in Supreme Court decisions include:

- *Individual liberty.* The freedom of speech is deeply intertwined with basic concepts of fundamental natural rights: human liberty, self-expression and personhood; the freedom to think and believe; the right to realize one's own nature and to explore the expanse of one's own intellect and imagination. Freedom of speech enables each of us to develop our intellectual and spiritual capacity and to delimit the boundaries of self.[2] In this sense, free speech is an inalienable right.

- *Self-government.*[3] The freedom of speech enables each of us, as an autonomous individual, to join in collective discussion and participate in the public deliberations of "the people." Through free speech, we present ourselves to others, exchange ideas, influence attitudes, debate issues of public significance and "pursue the possibility of democratic self-determination."[4] To govern effectively, "we, the people" must be free to observe our government, discuss the relative merits and demerits of candidates and policy options, and render judgments. Free speech provides the essential instrument of this joint deliberation and decision making: the cornerstones of responsible self-governance.

- *Limited government power.* A closely related, and perhaps subsidiary, value of free speech is its role as an "invaluable bulwark against tyranny."[5] Here the freedoms of speech and press, and by extension the freedom of the vote, serve as a "check"[6] on authoritarian rule, a barrier to censorship or dictatorship, and a limit to the accumulation and abuse of power by the few. It is through free speech that "the people" exercise their right to judge the public officials whom they have entrusted to represent them.

protection only when they are necessary to advance such social benefits as the search for truth, an open marketplace of ideas or the process of self-governance.[20] This instrumental, or functional, concept of the First Amendment lies beneath many Court decisions favoring broadcast regulation to increase the diversity of ideas reaching U.S. voters. Speech also deserves protection because it provides a check on government abuse of power, a safety valve for social discontent or a means of personal self-realization.[21] The Court endorsed this first purpose in *New York Times v. Sullivan,* saying that robust criticism of government is so vital to democracy that the First Amendment protects news media from punishment for unintentional defamation of government officials (see Chapter 4).[22] Some scholars argue that the most significant value of the First Amendment is to improve the ability of minority groups in society to be heard effectively[23] or to encourage the development of a tolerant society.[24]

Those who value free speech in and of itself—as an end rather than a means—see free speech as a natural right of individuals. Accordingly, freedom of speech is worthy of constitutional protection because it is fundamental to individual natural liberty.[25] Free speech is essential to what it means to be human.

- *Attainment of truth.* Through its creation of the oft-cited "marketplace of ideas," free speech helps advance knowledge and the discovery of truth. Only by challenging "certain truth" and "received wisdom" through free and unfettered public discussion can a society test its accepted ideas and assure that they are not dead dogma.[7] The pursuit of truth, through free speech, contributes to both individual development and social well-being.

- *Safety valve.* Only through free speech do we acknowledge and attend to problems and grievances before they escalate into violence. Thus, the freedom of speech provides a necessary social means for "letting off steam" and diffusing individual and societal pressures. Free speech helps identify and achieve a social balance between stability and change, compromise and conflict, tolerance and hate.[8] This free speech value is most evident during "the worst of times," when societal tensions are high. One scholar called this the "pathological perspective" of free speech.[9]

- *Its own end.* Free speech may not be valued solely because of its beneficial functions for individuals and societies. Rather, free speech, like clean air, or beauty, or justice, may be an end in and of itself. It is, quite simply, a good that we should value and cherish.[10]

---

1. Thomas I. Emerson, *Toward a General Theory of the First Amendment,* 72 Yale L.J. 877 (1963).
2. *See* John Locke, Two Treatises of Government, II 4 (Peter Laslett, ed., Cambridge Univ. Press 1988) (1698).
3. For detailed discussion, *see* Alexander Meiklejohn, Free Speech and Its Relation to Self-Government (1948).
4. Robert Post, *Managing Deliberation: The Quandary of Democratic Dialogue,* 103 Ethics 654, 672 (1993).
5. James Madison, Report on the Virginia Resolutions (Jan. 1800), reprinted in 5 The Founders' Constitution (Philip B. Kurland & Ralph Lerner eds., 1987).
6. Vincent Blasi, *The Checking Value in First Amendment Theory,* Am. B. Found. Res. J. 523 (1977).
7. Zechariah Chafee, Jr., Freedom of Speech 37 (1920); Zechariah Chafee, Jr., *Freedom of Speech in War Time,* 32 Harv. L. Rev. 932 (1919).
8. C. Edwin Baker, *Scope of the First Amendment Freedom of Speech,* 25 UCLA L. Rev. 964 (1978).
9. Vincent Blasi, *The Pathological Perspective and the First Amendment,* 85 Colum. L. Rev. 449, 464 (1985).
10. Ronald Dworkin, A Moral Reading of the American Constitution (1996).

Both the functional and the inherent-value perspectives on free speech are useful to the extent that they help courts determine what types of speech should be protected and what types of speech should be punished. Neither approach does a very good job of this, however. For instance, the functional approach does not establish a clear boundary between speech that helps democratic self-governance and speech that does not. For example, does a pornographic caricature of the governor help create an engaged and informed electorate? Is a nonviolent march on the Capitol part of protected political expression? If speech is an essential element of what it means to be human, where is the logical limit to the right of self-expression? If individuals express themselves by shooting a gun in the middle of the city, by lying on the witness stand or by making harassing telephone calls, should all of these actions be protected? As the preceding questions suggest, both the functional and the inherent-value, or the natural rights, approaches are somewhat helpful, but neither provides strict guidelines or clear lines (what the law calls bright-line distinctions) to determine when speech deserves protection.

The dilemmas presented by value-based adjudication are made clear in the Court's apparently contradictory rulings in two landmark cases exploring the right of the public to use the mass media as a means to distribute its own free speech. In the first of these cases, *Red Lion Broadcasting Co. v. FCC*, decided in 1969, the Supreme Court ruled 7–0 that regulations requiring broadcasters to seek out and broadcast competing views on controversial public issues were constitutional.[26] Broadcasters posed a First Amendment challenge to Federal Communication Commission rules that required broadcasters to notify and provide free air time to political candidates to reply to station editorials endorsing their opponents and to people attacked on the air. They argued that the rules violated the core free speech right of broadcasters to choose the information they broadcast. But the Court disagreed. The Supreme Court said:

> The right of free speech of a broadcaster, the user of a sound truck, or any other individual does not embrace a right to snuff out the free speech of others. . . . [The broadcaster] has no constitutional right to . . . monopolize a radio frequency to the exclusion of his fellow citizens.[27]

Here the Court held that *public* speech was of paramount value, but five years later, with a new chief justice and two new members of the Court, the Supreme Court ruled in *Miami Herald v. Tornillo* that "compelling editors or publishers to publish that which 'reason tells them should not be published'" is unconstitutional.[28] The Court held in *Miami Herald* that the First Amendment barred government from requiring a newspaper to provide free reply space to political candidates attacked in the paper. Although the Court recognized the value of newspapers as a platform for broad and open public debate, it reasoned that "press responsibility

realWorld Law

What, Exactly, Is "the Freedom of Speech"?

It's hard to know how much to care about the freedom of speech when people can't even agree on what it is. People seem to think speech is virtually everything . . . or practically nothing. At one pole of the debate, folks argue that we understand reality and our place in it only through speech. Without free speech, we cannot know ourselves, operate autonomously, interact with others, develop shared understandings or participate in collective governance.

At the other pole, words are essentially meaningless. The malleability, ambiguity and indeterminacy of language open it to such sweeping imprecision and subjective interpretation that we can almost never convey what we mean or fully comprehend someone else. Worse yet, because language may be an implement of power, words don't necessarily serve to uncover or illuminate truth; speech can distort, misrepresent and manipulate the unwary. Add in the view that practically everything we do—how we dress (or refuse to wear clothing), what we burn in public, where we sit in protest, and so on—is a component of our self-expression, and the already fuzzy notion of speech seems to have limitless reach. Given this confusion and the fast-changing array of communication technologies, how can we begin to define what is "the press" protected by the First Amendment?

is not mandated by the Constitution, and like many other virtues it cannot be legislated."[29] In this case, the Court lauded the autonomy of the printed press:

> A newspaper is more than a passive receptacle or conduit for news, comment and advertising. The choice of material to go into a newspaper, and the decisions made as to limitations on the size and content of the paper, and treatment of public issues and public officials—whether fair or unfair—constitute the exercise of editorial control and judgment. It has yet to be demonstrated how governmental regulation of this crucial process can be exercised consistent with First Amendment guarantees of a free press.

SUMMARY

THE SUPREME COURT HAS INTERPRETED the First Amendment through decisions that rest in part on British common law precedents. At a minimum, the First Amendment stands as a bulwark against government prior restraints on speakers or the press. Court interpretation and application of the First Amendment also rely upon the justices' different understandings of the purposes and values of free expression in a democratic society. Some justices believe free expression warrants specific constitutional protection because it is a fundamental natural right outside the reach of government. Other justices believe freedom of expression is protected only to the extent that it advances other extremely important interests, such as self-governance, self-expression and self-fulfillment. As a consequence, the Court has not set down one clear, fixed description of the freedoms of speech and press. Instead, the Court allows the exact parameters of First Amendment freedoms to respond to social changes, such as emerging communication technologies. This leads to a system in which the Constitution provides different degrees of protection both to different speakers and to different types of speech. ∎

Contemporary Prior Restraints

Although the Supreme Court has not settled on a single interpretation of the First Amendment, the Court nevertheless has established one bedrock principle: freedom of the press cannot coexist with prior restraint. Prior restraint stops speech before it is expressed and halts presses before publication. It is the essence of censorship. The Court's modern understanding of prior restraint began with its 1931 decision in *Near v. Minnesota*.[30]

In *Near* the Court said prior restraint, especially any prior restraint that involves an outright ban on expression, is the least tolerable form of government intervention in the speech marketplace.[31] The case began after Jay Near, publisher of The Saturday Press in Minneapolis, printed eight issues of his paper filled with

Dr. Daniel Ellsberg (left), the RAND Corporation employee and U.S. Defense Department consultant who leaked the Pentagon Papers to the media, speaks to reporters after his 1971 arraignment on charges of illegal possession of the classified documents.

Points of Law

What Is a Prior Restraint?

A prior restraint is what we think of as good old garden-variety censorship. When government prohibits publication or suppresses particular material, this is prior restraint. Prior restraint occurs when

1. Any government body or representative

2. Reviews speech or press prior to distribution and

3. Stops the dissemination of ideas *before* they reach the public.

According to the Supreme Court, prior restraint is "the most serious and the least tolerable infringement on First Amendment rights."[1]

---

1. *Nebraska Press Ass'n v. Stuart*, 427 U.S. 539, 559 (1976).

injunction A court order prohibiting a person or organization from doing some specified act.

charges that city government and police officials were doing nothing to stop Jewish gangsters operating gambling, bootlegging and racketeering businesses all over the city. The paper was shut down under a state public nuisance law that allowed judges to stop publications that had published "scandalous or defamatory material," unless the publisher could convince a judge that the attacks were true and published with good intent.

When the Supreme Court reviewed the case, it ruled that the permanent ban on future issues of The Saturday Press was unconstitutional. The Court said the Minnesota law that allowed government to ban "nuisance" publications was a classic prior restraint, to which the First Amendment stands as a nearly absolute barrier. A classic prior restraint has three components: (1) It imposes government oversight of whole categories of speech, content or publication, (2) it allows the government to choose what content is acceptable, and (3) it empowers government censors to ban content before it is distributed to the public.

In 1971, the Supreme Court created a legal landmark when it ruled in *New York Times Co. v. United States* that a court order preventing publication of news stories based on the Pentagon Papers was an unconstitutional prior restraint.[32] The Pentagon Papers, as they were commonly known, were the top-secret Department of Defense study of U.S. involvement in Vietnam between 1945 and 1967. Using information obtained from classified documents leaked to the newspaper, The New York Times started a series of news stories about the reality and history of the Vietnam War. The Nixon administration said the publication threatened national security and the safety of U.S. troops and asked for a court **injunction**. The court agreed and stopped the stories.

Acting with unusual speed, the Supreme Court said the injunction violated the Constitution because the federal government had not met its burden of showing that the ban was essential to prevent a real and immediate risk of harm to a compelling government interest. The Court said, "[A]ny system of prior restraints of expression comes to this Court bearing a heavy presumption against its constitutional validity."[33] However, the Court's decision left open the possibility that prior restraints may be constitutional if the

The Pentagon Papers of Our Time?

Many compared WikiLeaks' 2010 posting of more than 90,000 classified U.S. military documents on the war in Afghanistan to the publication of the Pentagon Papers during the Vietnam War.[1]

Both leaks hinged on media providing greater transparency to an ongoing and controversial war involving U.S. troops. And both highlighted mainstream media's importance in establishing the credibility of the documents. "Transparency is moot without authority,"[2] according to one observer noting WikiLeaks' use of The New York Times to vet the documents prior to release. Another called the collaboration "a very sophisticated illustration of how newly evolving media continually change the way we get information but don't totally replace existing systems."[3]

The comparisons obscure significant differences between the WikiLeaks and Pentagon Papers situations. The government imposed a prior restraint on the Pentagon Papers but not on WikiLeaks.

WikiLeaks was not a "traditional" newspaper. It described itself as the world's "first stateless news organization," working "across the globe to obtain, publish and defend … sensitive materials" and post them on the Web for public access.[4]

While the 1971 release of the Pentagon Papers disclosed dramatic differences between the government's public statements and the truth about the war, the WikiLeaks archives revealed less truly startling information.

The documents involved in the Pentagon Papers were at least three years old and released as U.S. troops began to be withdrawn; some WikiLeaks material dated back seven months, when the Obama administration was developing strategy to ramp up the war in Afghanistan.

Although the Obama White House condemned the WikiLeaks release, it did not seek an injunction to stop their publication,[5] perhaps because "it is technology, even more than law, that makes it nearly futile to pursue injunctions against publication of leaked documents…. Injunctions [do] not work once the cat is out of the bag or the genie out of the bottle"[6] or the information is already available worldwide on the Web.

Forty years after the Supreme Court's Pentagon Papers[7] ruling that government could not prevent publication of newsworthy information based on vague assertions of national security, WikiLeaks' release raises profound questions about government's ability to protect secrets. In the age of the Internet, "the legal lesson of the Pentagon Papers regarding injunctions is almost beside the point," one observer said.[8]

1. Janie Lorber, *Early Word: WikiLeaked*, N.Y. TIMES, July 30, 2010, *available at* http://thecaucus.blogs.nytimes.com.
2. Adam Kirsch, *Why Wikileaks Still Needs the New York Times*, NEW REPUBLIC, July 26, 2010, *available at* http://www.tnr.com/.blog/foreign-policy/.
3. James Fallows, *On the AfPak/Wikileaks Documents*, ATLANTIC, July 26, 2010, *available at* http://www.theatlantic.com/politics/archive/.
4. WIKILEAKS, *available at* http://wikileaks.org/.
5. Alexandra Topping, *Wikileaks Condemned by White House over War Documents*, GUARDIAN , July 26, 2010, *available at* http://www.guardian.co.uk/world/.
6. Lyrissa Lidsky, *Pentagon Papers II?: Wikileaks and Information Control in the Internet Era*, PRAWFSBLAWG, July 26, 2010, *available at* http://prawfsblawg.blogs.com.
7. New York Times Co. v. United States, 403 U.S. 713 (1971).
8. Lidsky, *supra* note 6.

government can show they are necessary to prevent serious harm to extremely important government interests.

The Court repeatedly has reasoned that prior restraints are generally unconstitutional because they pose too great a risk that government will censor ideas it disfavors and distort the marketplace of ideas. In 1976, for example, the Court said that if "a threat of criminal or civil sanctions after publication 'chills' speech, prior restraint 'freezes' it."[34] The First Amendment poses its greatest obstacle to direct prior restraints on the news media because every moment of a ban on reporting causes direct harm to the First Amendment rights of both the media and the public.[35]

For the past 70 years, the Supreme Court has attempted to clarify what constitutes an impermissible prior restraint of speech. The term "prior restraint" is applied in a variety of different situations, and prior restraints take a variety of forms. Today, prior restraints often appear in the form of court orders that stop speech or publication. In 1994, Justice Harry A. Blackmun struck down a state court order preventing the scheduled broadcast of an investigative news report.[36] Justice Blackmun said indefinite delay of news broadcasts is unacceptable under the First Amendment. The case involved footage taken inside a South Dakota meatpacking plant by a plant employee wearing a hidden camera during his shift. Although CBS obtained the footage through "calculated misdeeds" that might cause significant harm to the meatpacking company, the injunction was unwarranted because the company had failed to show the prior restraint was essential. A prior restraint on the media "is a most extraordinary remedy" and can be justified only in exceptional situations. Prior restraints may be permitted either when there is clear and convincing evidence that the publication will cause great and certain harm that cannot be addressed by less intrusive measures or when the news media clearly engaged in criminal activity to obtain the information being restrained.[37]

Despite the Court's strong presumption that outright bans on expression are unconstitutional, the permissible boundaries of prior restraint may be redrawn by a case one observer called "ground zero of . . . the future of news online."[38] In *Barclays Capital v. TheFlyontheWall.com*, several Wall Street banking firms sued the online financial news service for copyright infringement (see Chapter 13 for related discussion) and misappropriation of "hot news."[39] In 2010, a federal district court imposed a fine and a permanent injunction requiring TheFlyontheWall to delay distribution of "hot news" facts gleaned from these firms.

The Supreme Court introduced the hot news doctrine in a 1918 decision, finding a news service liable for reuse of timely facts gathered at some expense by its rival, the Associated Press.[40] The Court relied on equity law to hold that reuse by a competing news distributor of information from AP's published news stories constituted unfair competition even if the competitor employed the "false pretense [of] rewriting the articles."[41] The Court's decision turned in no small part upon three features of commercial news production: (1) the "peculiar" value of "novelty and freshness" to its commercial worth, (2) the competitive commercial benefits of reuse without costly independent reporting and verification, and

(3) the extensive delays of production and distribution that make news "necessarily" susceptible to "piracy."

Twitter, Google and other online news and information aggregators as well as a number of free expression watchdogs objected to the injunction as a prior restraint and argued that application of the hot news doctrine in *Barclays Capital* threatened to stifle common newsgathering practices and popular new forms of information sharing.[42] While the Internet effectively erases the Court's concern that distribution delays encourage piracy, it makes the first two issues increasingly compelling, particularly given the financial crisis facing today's print news media. Yet in 1918, Justice Louis Brandeis wrote in dissent to warn that the Court's decision would lead to "curtailment of the free use of knowledge and of ideas."[43] "The general rule of law is that the noblest of human productions—knowledge, truths ascertained, conceptions, and ideas—become, after voluntary communication to others, free as the air to common use."[44] The Court of Appeals for the Second Circuit was scheduled in 2010 to determine whether the injunction imposed on TheFlyontheWall was an unconstitutional restraint that fettered this common use.[45]

State courts also struggled with the use of injunctions as a means to reduce the potentially severe and immediate harms of free speech on the Internet. In New Hampshire, for example, the state supreme court in 2010 ruled that a lower court injunction forcing the website removal of a leaked document was an unlawful prior restraint.[46] The case involved an article on a mortgage lender posted on Implode-O-Meter with a link to a document leaked anonymously from the state banking authority. A state superior court had granted a request from the mortgage company demanding removal of the document and disclosure of its source.[47] At roughly the same time, a New Jersey Superior Court ordered several websites shut down in response to allegations of hateful, racist and defamatory content.[48] The sweeping order also required Internet service providers to disclose immediately the identities of the sources of anonymous posts. The allegedly defamatory comments related to visas for foreign workers, work contracts and U.S. immigration policies. The restraining order ended six months later, when the court granted a defense motion to dismiss the case.[49]

Prior restraints on Internet content may not be effective because of the ability to publish anonymously via a multiplicity of foreign and mirror sites. In one case, the court-ordered shutdown of the WikiLeaks website, in response to a suit from a Cayman Islands bank, lasted only one week. The case was dismissed after the material appeared elsewhere.[50] Yet in each of these situations, website information or the entire website was blocked for days or months. In the eyes of some courts, "news delayed is news denied."[51]

Points of Law

When Are Prior Restraints Constitutional?

The Supreme Court suggested in *Near v. Minnesota*[1] that government prior restraints of speech may be found constitutional when they are necessary to prevent:

- Obstruction of military recruitment

- Publication of troop locations, numbers and movements in time of war

- Obscene publications

- Incitements to violence

- Forcible overthrow of government, or

- Fighting words likely to promote imminent violence.

1. 283 U.S. 697 (1931).

Despite this strong prohibition on prior restraints, many laws prevent or limit specific speakers from discussing particular topics. For instance, the government may prevent speech that threatens national security. Judges' orders prohibiting trial participants from discussing the ongoing trial also generally are acceptable. Laws that limit use of copyrighted material are mandated by the Constitution, and laws that criminalize the production and distribution of obscenity are accepted. Police also may legally prevent the speech involved when individuals conspire to commit a crime or to incite others to violence. In addition, some government actions that appear to restrain freedom of speech are permitted because the Court does not view them as prior restraints.

These laws generally are constitutional because they are content-neutral regulations of the time, place or manner of expression, which means they do not target or restrict particular messages because of their content. Accordingly, cities may require permits for parades in the streets or meetings in public parks, as long as the permit process does not give uncontrolled authority to officials. Laws restricting antiabortion protests and counseling outside family planning facilities are constitutional.[52] Laws that ban campaigning or distribution of election materials within a certain distance of the polls are acceptable, too.[53] More discussion of cases involving **content-neutral laws** follows.

content-neutral laws Laws that incidentally and unintentionally affect speech as they advance other important government interests.

SUMMARY

A FUNDAMENTAL PRINCIPLE OF THE First Amendment is that it stands as a nearly absolute barrier to government prior restraints on expression. A prior restraint involves government officials who review and either permit or prohibit certain content before it may be disseminated. In 1931, the Supreme Court said prior restraints may be constitutional under extremely narrow circumstances. Forty years later, in a famous case involving press publication of the classified Pentagon Papers, the Supreme Court said the Constitution presumes prior restraints are unconstitutional and places an extremely heavy burden on government to justify prior restraint of news media. State courts are struggling with issues of prior restraint related to Internet content. Parade and facilities permits that allow the efficient use of public spaces are not prior restraints. They generally are constitutional if they do not give government officials unlimited discretion or the ability to penalize users they disfavor. ■

Court Scrutiny of Laws That Affect First Amendment Rights

Some laws of journalism and mass communication do not involve speech at all. Minimum-wage regulations or laws that prevent monopolies are both laws that fall within the power of Congress to regulate commerce. Article I, Section 8,

Clause 3, of the U.S. Constitution gives Congress authority "to regulate Commerce with foreign nations, and among the several states, and with the Indian Tribes." The Court generally presumes that laws of general application, such as wage and hour regulations, are constitutional and may be applied to media businesses. They regulate commerce and do not infringe on protected constitutional rights. The Supreme Court reviews challenges to these laws under minimum or **rational review**. Rational review presumes the constitutionality of legislative or administrative enactments that have a rational purpose. Laws reviewed under minimum scrutiny must be reasonable and serve a legitimate government purpose to be constitutional.

> **rational review** A standard of judicial review that assumes the wisdom of reasonable legislative or administrative enactments and applies minimum scrutiny to their review.

However, many laws of journalism and mass communication do affect the freedom of speech and press protected by the Constitution. When asked to decide whether such laws violate the Constitution, the Supreme Court first determines whether the law targets the ideas expressed or aims at some goal unrelated to the content of the message. The Court calls the first type of law "content based" and the second "content neutral." **Content-based laws** regulate what is being said; they single out certain messages for punishment because of government disapproval of the ideas or subjects they present. Laws that prohibit the "desecration" of the U.S. flag are content based. Content-neutral laws restrict where, when and how ideas are expressed; they often advance public interests unrelated to speech. Laws that regulate the size and placement of billboards, and ordinances that limit noise in hospital zones are content neutral and, generally, constitutional if they restrict speech as little as necessary to provide quiet zones that encourage healing and recuperation.

> **content-based laws** Laws enacted because of the message, the subject matter or the ideas expressed in the regulated speech.

> **strict scrutiny** A test for determining the constitutionality of laws restricting speech, under which the government must show it has a compelling interest at stake that is advanced by the least restrictive means available.

Content-Based Laws

The Supreme Court generally views content-based laws as presumptively invalid. Like prior restraints, laws that punish the expression of specific ideas after the fact pose a direct and serious threat of government censorship. To stop government censorship of disfavored ideas, the Supreme Court applies a very rigorous test to determine when content-based laws are constitutional. Under its most rigorous test, called **strict scrutiny,** the Court strikes down laws that discriminate on the basis of content unless they use (1) the least restrictive means (2) to advance a compelling government interest. So few laws pass strict scrutiny review that people say strict scrutiny is strict in theory but fatal in fact.

The Court has found that laws employ the least restrictive means only when they are extremely well tailored to their goals and restrict the smallest possible amount of protected speech. The Court generally finds that a law is least restrictive if no other

Points of Law

Strict Scrutiny

The Supreme Court has said content-based laws are constitutional only if they pass strict scrutiny. To be constitutional, a content-based law must:

1. Be necessary
2. To advance a compelling government interest and
3. Go no further than necessary in harming First Amendment rights.

Strict scrutiny is the most rigorous test used by the Court to determine whether a law is constitutional.

compelling interest A
government interest of the highest
order, an interest the government
is required to protect.

methods available to the government would achieve its goals and be less harmful to free speech rights. To pass strict scrutiny, laws also must directly advance a compelling or paramount government interest. The Court has said a **compelling interest** is an interest of the highest order. Compelling government interests relate to core constitutional concerns and to the most significant functions of government. Frequently cited compelling government interests are national security, the electoral process and the public health and welfare.

A case illustrating this point is *Simon & Schuster v. Crime Victims Board*, in which the Supreme Court struck down a New York law that attempted to compensate crime victims and limit the rewards of crime. [54] Following a well-publicized series of killings by the notorious Son of Sam in the mid-1970s, New York state passed a law that required criminal authors earning money from works describing their crimes or their thoughts related to their crimes to turn over the related income to the state. The money would compensate crime victims, with only the remaining balance paid to the author. The law applied to any authors who made even passing comments about actual crimes. The state said the law was intended to increase victim compensation and decrease the "fruits" of crime.

Simon & Schuster, which had published an acclaimed true-crime autobiography of mafia figure Henry Hill, challenged the law as facially unconstitutional on the grounds that it targeted specific content for punitive treatment by the government. In *Simon & Schuster*, the Supreme Court applied strict scrutiny review to decide that the content-based law advanced a compelling government interest but punished a substantial quantity of literature fully protected by the First Amendment. [55] The Court found the law unconstitutional because it was overbroad.

Content-Neutral Laws

time/place/manner (TPM) laws
A First Amendment concept that
laws regulating the conditions of
speech are more acceptable than
those regulating content; also, the
laws that regulate these conditions.

The Supreme Court is much more willing to uphold the constitutionality of laws that affect speech but do not discriminate on the basis of content. Content-neutral laws generally regulate the non-speech elements of a message, such as the time, the place or the manner (size or volume) in which the speech occurs. Thus, some content-neutral laws are called **time/place/manner** (TPM) laws. In general, content-neutral laws, such as noise ordinances, that do not censor specific ideas and seek to achieve some legitimate government goal may, in fact, reduce the overall quantity and diversity of speech available in the marketplace of ideas or reduce the ability of a speaker to reach a large audience. In a case arising out of protests over the Vietnam War, the Court established its foundational First Amendment test for content-neutral laws. In 1968, when the Court reviewed the conviction of David O'Brien for burning his draft card on the steps of the South Boston Courthouse to protest the Vietnam War, it tried to establish boundaries to proper government action. O'Brien had been convicted for violating a federal law that prohibited the knowing destruction of draft cards. [56] The law required that 18-year-old males obtain and carry draft cards at all times to aid the smooth functioning of the draft and the U.S. military and to protect the national security. O'Brien argued that the law was unconstitutional both facially (see Chapter 1) and as applied to the facts in his case because it infringed on freedom of speech. In *United States v. O'Brien*, the Supreme Court disagreed and affirmed O'Brien's conviction, focusing on why the government enacted the law and how the law operated.[57]

The Court's decision hinged neither on the government's intent nor the effect of the speech but rather on the purposes of the federal law. Looking at the actual words of the law—a type of review called statutory construction (see Chapter 1)— the Supreme Court said Congress had enacted the statute to ensure the efficient and orderly operation of the military draft. Any infringement the law caused to O'Brien's speech was minimal and merely incidental to the government's compelling interest in protecting the proper functioning of the military. The law did not target disfavored viewpoints and left O'Brien free to express his opposition to the draft in any number of ways. In addition, the Court said that when speech and action are intimately intertwined into **symbolic expression,** such as the burning of a draft card, the government's legitimate regulation of the actions may constitutionally place a small, incidental and content-neutral burden on protected speech.

Finding the law content neutral, the Court applied **intermediate scrutiny** by crafting a new test, now known as the **O'Brien test.** The O'Brien test's three substantive parts hold that a content-neutral law will be constitutional if the law (1) is not related to the suppression of speech, (2) advances an important government interest, and (3) is narrowly tailored to achieve that interest with only an incidental restriction of free expression. Generally, the *O'Brien* test does not have many teeth. Most laws reviewed under intermediate scrutiny are upheld. If the Court says a law is content neutral because it does not target ideas disfavored by government, the law also generally is unrelated to suppression of speech. Laws said to serve government goals unrelated to content tend to meet this standard. Under the *O'Brien* test, a law also must serve an **important government interest.** A government interest is important when it is more than merely convenient or reasonable. Important interests are substantial, weighty or significant; they are not, however, compelling or of the highest order.

The third part of the *O'Brien* test, sometimes called the narrow-tailoring standard, requires a law to "fit" its purpose. A law "fits" when it advances the government interest without imposing an unnecessary burden on speech.[58] The calculation is not precise. The Supreme Court often defers to the expertise of administrative agencies and legislatures to decide the best means to achieve content-neutral objectives. However, complete bans are rarely constitutional because they are not well tailored; their harm to speech is more than incidental. The Court also says laws are not narrowly tailored when they grant unlimited discretion to officials. To be narrowly tailored, laws must be clear and specific and may not vest officials with vague or unfettered power.[59]

symbolic expression Action that warrants First Amendment protection because its primary purpose is to express ideas.

intermediate scrutiny A standard applied by the courts to the review of laws that implicate core constitutional values; also called heightened review.

O'Brien **test** A three-part test used to determine whether a content-neutral law is constitutional.

important government interest An interest of the government that is substantial or significant (i.e., more than merely convenient or reasonable) but not compelling.

Points of Law

Intermediate-Level Scrutiny

The Supreme Court generally applies some form of intermediate scrutiny to content-neutral laws that affect the freedom of speech. To be constitutional under intermediate scrutiny, a law must:

1. Fall within the power of government

2. Advance an important or substantial government interest

3. That is unrelated to suppression of speech and

4. Be narrowly tailored to impose only an incidental restriction on First Amendment freedoms.

Pro-choice and pro-life activists gathered outside the U.S. Supreme Court in 2009 to mark the anniversary of the Court's 1973 Roe v. Wade **decision. Their demonstration symbolizes ongoing legal challenges to laws limiting public protests outside abortion clinics.**

In a case in the late 1980s involving public concerts in New York City's Central Park, the Court applied the *O'Brien* test to uphold a regulation requiring city employees to control the volume and sound mix of performers.[1] Performers said the rule unconstitutionally allowed the city to control their expression even when the control served no important government interest because there was no threat of excess noise or public disturbance. The Court, however, said the city's complete control of sound was a narrowly tailored means for the city to assure that park users did not disturb people living nearby. *Ward v. Rock Against Racism* established that government need not explore all possible means of achieving its goal and adopt the least speech-intrusive method. Rather, a content-neutral law is narrowly tailored if it advances the government's interest reasonably well and the government interest would suffer in its absence.

Thus, when several states passed laws restricting access and speech around family planning clinics that were the sites of protests, bombings, assaults and murders of abortion providers, the Court said the protective zones generally were constitutional. In a representative decision, the Court ruled, in 2000, in *Hill v. Colorado* that a state law creating moving, non-protest zones around people entering abortion clinics was a valid, narrowly tailored, content-neutral, time, place and manner restriction that directly advanced the government's significant and legitimate interest in protecting the public from confrontational and harassing conduct.[2] The Court also applied intermediate scrutiny review in a range of cases related to election financing and advertising.

---

1. 491 U.S. 781 (1989).
2. 530 U.S. 703 (2000).

Points of Law

Where Does Intermediate Scrutiny Apply?

The Supreme Court applies intermediate scrutiny review to a wide array of laws with differing results. The scope of the Court's intermediate scrutiny review includes:

Symbolic conduct. Although the Court has held that activities as wide-ranging as the destruction of draft cards, the operation of adult bookstores and nude dancing are all forms of symbolic speech, it has applied intermediate scrutiny to uphold regulations that banned or severely constrained these activities. When applied to symbolic conduct, intermediate scrutiny of content-neutral regulations rarely protects speech activities that have undesirable "secondary effects."

Public forums. In general, the Supreme Court has applied intermediate scrutiny to find flat bans on speech activities in traditional public forums unconstitutional. However, if time, place and manner regulations leave open effective, alternate channels of speech or if they apply to speech on government or public property that is not a traditional public forum, they usually withstand intermediate scrutiny.

Government employees. While the Supreme Court has not explicitly applied intermediate scrutiny review to laws or government actions that sanction employee speech, its balancing of interests approach in these cases "manifestly resembles the Court's approach to content-neutral speech regulations."[1] Under this balancing, the Court has upheld restrictions of employee speech.

Private media and property. When the Court has applied intermediate scrutiny to content-neutral regulations of the content of electronic media,[2] the laws generally have been upheld. But the Court has employed a heightened version of intermediate scrutiny to strike down a ban on signs on private property,[3] limits on charitable solicitation,[4] and sanctions on media distribution of information received from another party's illegal interception of electronic communications.[5]

---

1. Ashutosh Bhagwat, *The Test That Ate Everything: Intermediate Scrutiny in First Amendment Jurisprudence,* 2007 U. Ill. L. Rev. 783 (2007).
2. *See, e.g.,* Turner Broad. Sys. Inc. v. FCC, 512 U.S. 622 (1994); 520 U.S. 180 (1997).
3. City of Ladue v. Gilleo, 512 U.S. 43 (1994).
4. *See, e.g.,* Riley v. Nat'l Fed'n of the Blind of NC, 487 U.S. 781 (1988).
5. Bartnicki v. Vopper, 532 U.S. 514 (2001).

SUMMARY

THE SUPREME COURT HAS DESIGNED A VARIETY of tests to help determine when government actions or laws infringe on rights protected by the Constitution. When a government action falls within the delegated power of government, such as the power to levy taxes, the Court assumes the law is constitutional and examines it under its most lenient test, called "minimum scrutiny" or "rational review." If a law affects constitutionally protected rights, such as speech and press, the Court uses a heightened form of review to assure that government is not overstepping its bounds. Many laws designed to achieve an important government interest unrelated to the suppression of speech affect speakers. They regulate the time, place and manner of expression and neither target particular messages nor are intended to limit speech that government disfavors. Such content-neutral laws, also called time, place and manner laws, must pass intermediate scrutiny, or the *O'Brien* test. Government actions that directly regulate or intentionally restrict particular messages are called content based. Such laws are constitutionally disfavored because they especially distort the marketplace of ideas. Consequently, the Court presumes these content-based laws are unconstitutional and reviews them under strict scrutiny, its most rigorous standard. ∎

Political Speech

Political speech—which consists of expression intended to generate or undermine public support for a particular issue, position or candidate—lies at the "core of what the First Amendment is designed to protect."[60] Two decades ago, the Supreme Court said political speech involves any "interactive communication concerning political change."[61] Political speech encompasses ballots and voting, electioneering speeches and lobbying, campaign contributions and yard signs, government speech and anonymous political advertisements, political cartoons and blogs, petitions and placards and buttons and more. Believing that political speech is integral to the functioning of the democratic government established by the Constitution, the Court generally has used strict scrutiny to review laws that seem to infringe on political speech.[62]

Elections and Campaign Finance

In recent decades, public debate and Court review have focused increasingly on the role of money in the political process. The central question is whether campaign spending by individuals, corporations, unions, lobbyists and special interest groups is a quintessential exercise of their political speech or whether massive contributions distort and corrupt the democratic process and subvert the will of the citizens. To protect federal elections from this corrupting influence, Congress passed the McCain-Feingold Act (the Bipartisan Campaign Reform Act [BCRA]) in 2002. The law banned "soft money" contributions to national political parties, requiring them to adhere to limits on the amount and source of funds they accept and spend. The law specifically prohibited corporate (including nonprofit and union) funding of political messages during a certain period prior to an election.

In its most recent ruling on the BCRA, the Supreme Court's 2010 decision in *Citizens United v. FEC* overturned a 2003 precedent to find restrictions on election spending by corporations and unions unconstitutional.[63] In *Citizens United,* the

Court struck down a key campaign finance limit, saying the government had failed to provide sufficient evidence to justify its claim that unrestricted corporate election spending led to political corruption. Directly reversing parts of its decision in *McConnell v. FEC*,[64] the Court in *Citizens United* ruled 5–4 that the provision restricting how corporations and unions could fund "electioneering communications" facially violated the First Amendment. In dissent, Justice John Paul Stevens argued that corporations are not citizens and government has a compelling interest to curb corporate influence on elections.

The Court in 2010 also issued a two-sentence order upholding the federal ban on national political party use of unregulated, soft money contributions to fund election activities.[65] Federal district courts, dealing with the application of the BCRA's campaign contributions limits to a nonprofit organization designed to advance First Amendment freedoms[66] and to a "hybrid" nonprofit organization that engaged in both candidate support and get-out-the-vote drives,[67] found the restrictions unconstitutional. The courts reasoned that individuals have a First Amendment right to band together and pool their resources to express their political ideas.

In 2007, the Court had ruled that the ban on corporate-funded electioneering was unconstitutionally overbroad as applied to a series of ads sponsored by the Wisconsin Right to Life (WRL) advocacy group during the run-up to the 2004 election. In its 5–4 decision in *Federal Election Commission v. Wisconsin Right to Life*,[68] the Court said the law's application to the specific WRL ads would harm protected political speech rather than limit improper electoral influence by large corporations. And in its splintered 2003 decision in *McConnell*, the Court had upheld the BCRA's ban on corporate funding of campaign ads and its restriction on "soft money" against a constitutional challenge for vagueness and overbreadth, among other things.

The earlier landmark ruling in the area was the Court's per curiam decision in 1976 in *Buckley v. Valeo*.[69] The complicated foundational opinion distinguished between promoters (campaign contributors) and speakers (candidate spenders), effectively permitting government to limit the former but not the latter. In its constitutional review of the federal Elections Campaign Act of 1971, the Court noted that both campaign spending and contribution limits directly implicate significant fundamental First Amendment concerns. The Court then ruled that the law's restrictions on campaign contributions constitutionally advanced the government's significant interest in reducing political influence peddling. In contrast, the Court found that limits on candidate spending were not well tailored and unconstitutionally burdened the candidate's right to free speech, while doing little to advance the government's interest in averting campaign corruption.

The Court also has ruled on the degree to which government (through employee payroll deductions) can become involved in political contributions.[70] Although the First Amendment is clearly implicated, the Court voted 6–3 to uphold an Idaho state ban on the use of government payroll deductions for political contributions. The majority reasoned that the Constitution imposed no affirmative obligation on government to facilitate such political activities.

Employing rational review, the Court said the ban reasonably advanced the state's interest in avoiding the appearance of partisan political activity.

The Supreme Court has also reviewed a number of constitutional challenges to state limits on campaign financing. In 2006, a plurality of the Court in *Randall v. Sorrell*[71] struck down a Virginia state law imposing expenditure limits to prevent corruption and reduce the amount of time candidates spent raising money. The Court said the government interests in the law were legitimate but the

realWorld Law

The Politics of Election Finance

The Supreme Court's 2010 decision in *Citizens United*[1] struck down limits on election spending by corporations and unions that the Court had upheld only seven years earlier in *McConnell*.[2] This quick reversal of precedent struck many observers as imprudent, at best.

"Gosh," said Justice Sandra Day O'Connor, who penned *McConnell* and was appointed to the Court by Ronald Reagan. "I step away for a couple of years and there's no telling what's going to happen." When asked to discuss the First Amendment implications of *Citizens United*, she said, "If you want my legal opinion, you can go read" *McConnell*.[3]

Justice O'Connor is well known for her cautious public comments, but legal observers suggest that the politics of the sitting justices could be a major factor in the Court's about-face.

"Supreme Court justices do not acknowledge that any of their decisions are influenced by ideology rather than by neutral legal analysis," according to a recent law journal article.[4] But knowing the political party of the president who appointed a given justice tells you a great deal about how the justice will vote in highly political cases such as those dealing with election finance.

The leading study[5] that ties voting by Supreme Court justices to their political ideology shows that the Rehnquist Court reached a liberal outcome 70 percent of the time when it struck down laws and 60 percent of the time in the 45 precedents it overruled during its 19 years. In contrast, during its first five years, the Roberts Court reached a conservative result in all but one of the eight precedents it overruled and 60 percent of the time overall. While both Chief Justice William Rehnquist and Chief Justice John Roberts were Republican appointees, the ideological positions of the sitting justices on their Courts differed dramatically.

In response to *Citizens United*, President Barack Obama ordered aides "to get to work immediately with Congress" to develop "a forceful response" to a ruling he said "has given a green light to a new stampede of special interest money in our politics."[6]

---

1. Citizens United v. Federal Election Commission, 558 U.S. 50 (2010).
2. McConnell v. Federal Election Commission, 540 U.S. 93 (2003).
3. Adam Liptak, *Former Justice O'Connor Sees Ill in Election Finance Ruling*, N.Y. Times, Jan. 26, 2010, *available at* http://www.nytimes.com.
4. Adam Liptak, *Court Under Roberts Is Most Conservative in Decades*, N.Y. Times, July 24, 2010, *available at.* http://www.nytimes.com.
5. Judicial Research Institute. *Supreme Court Data, available at* http://www.cas.sc.edu/poli/juri/sctdata.htm.
6. *Statement from the President on Today's Supreme Court Decision*, Jan. 21, 2010, *available at* http://www.whitehouse.gov.

law was not narrowly tailored and imposed unconstitutionally broad restrictions on the fundraising assistance of individuals and political parties as well as on the ability of candidates themselves to raise and spend the money necessary for a competitive campaign. The Court in *Nixon v. Shrink Missouri Government PAC*[72] upheld a Missouri law setting limits on campaign contributions to state political candidates. The Court found no evidence that the Missouri statute's contribution limitations adversely affected either the funding of campaigns or candidates' political associations. The Court said the law constitutionally furthered the government interest in fair elections without unduly inhibiting candidates' ability to gather the funds needed for effective advocacy.

The influence of lobbyists on elections and government decision making was the target of two recent legal developments. First, the Federal Election Commission in 2009 crafted new regulations requiring disclosure of the names of contributors to "bundled" political contributions of more than $15,000. The rules implemented provisions of the 2007 Honest Leadership and Open Government Act. Second, the Obama administration issued a memo that year prohibiting lobbyists from speaking with officials in the executive branch regarding specific projects or processes of the Recovery Act, the national economic stimulus package, although written comments were acceptable.[73]

Anonymous Speech

A decade ago, the Supreme Court said that anonymous political speech has an "honorable tradition" that "is a shield from the tyranny of the majority."[74] In *McIntyre v. Ohio Election Commission,* the Court found a state ban on anonymous campaign literature unconstitutional. While the state's interest in preventing fraud and informing the public about the source of the political information was sufficiently important, the law was not narrowly tailored to advance that government interest. *McIntyre* was part of a line of cases dating back half a century that protect anonymous political speech.[75]

However, in 2010 in *Doe v. Reed,* the Court suggested that citizens engaged in the political process do not have an absolute right to keep their identities secret.[76] The case involved a citizen referendum to repeal a Washington state law granting new rights to same-sex domestic partners. The state open records law (see more about these laws in Chapter 8) required release of the names of all those who had endorsed the referendum, but the referendum supporters, who feared harassment and reprisal, said disclosure violated the First Amendment. The Supreme Court applied strict scrutiny to find the ban constitutional on the grounds that public disclosure of referendum petitions as a general policy was substantially related to the important government interest in preserving the integrity of balloting and elections. The Court remanded on the question of whether the First Amendment protected anonymity in this case, where disclosure might facilitate harassment.

Government Speakers

The First Amendment limits government regulation of private speech but does not deal expressly with the issues raised when the government itself speaks. It is clear the government must sometimes communicate with the public. It is not always clear, though, when the government is speaking for itself and when it is curbing the speech of others. In recent years, the Supreme Court has been articulating a doctrine of government speech that supports the government's right to speak and, sometimes, to control or prevent the speech of others.

In its unanimous 2009 decision in *Pleasant Grove City v. Summum,* the Supreme Court established the power of government to select the monuments it chooses to display permanently in its public parks.[77] A religious group raised a First Amendment challenge to the city's decision not to display the group's "Seven Aphorisms" on a permanent monument in a city park alongside other monuments, including the Ten Commandments.[78] In reviewing the case, the Court declined to apply public forum doctrine (discussed below) on the grounds that space and other constraints implicit in public displays in parks make it impossible, or impractical, for government to accommodate a large number of speakers. Instead, the Court said, selection of monuments was a form of government speech subject to government control of content. Here, the city had effectively taken ownership of privately donated monuments selected to present the image the city wished to project. In an opinion written by Justice Samuel Alito, the Court concluded "that the City's decision to accept certain privately donated monuments while rejecting respondent's is best viewed as a form of government speech. As a result, the City's decision is not subject to the Free Speech Clause."[79]

In a concurring opinion, Justice David Souter wrote: "The interaction between the 'government speech doctrine' and Establishment Clause principles [that bar government from "establishing" an official religion] has not, however, begun to be worked out. . . . [T]here are circumstances in which government maintenance of monuments does not look like government speech at all."

While the Court recognizes government authority to speak through its selection process, it generally has not agreed with scholars that freedom of expression has particular significance as applied to government employees because "[it] is here that the state has a special incentive to repress opposition and often wields a more effective power of suppression."[80] To the contrary, the Court generally has ruled that government has greater power to control the speech of its own workers than the expression of a private citizen. Government employees clearly do not shed their personal right to freedom of speech when they accept government work.[81] However, when a government employee speaks for government, government may impose codes of silence and control the content of the speech and work product to advance government interests.[82] Thus, the Court has said laws prohibiting political campaigning by federal employees pose no constitutional problem.[83] In addition, government clearly has the authority to classify highly sensitive materials and control their distribution.

Many government employees are silenced and government documents kept secret to protect national security.

In *Garcetti v. Ceballos*,[84] in 2006, for example, the Supreme Court ruled that the First Amendment did not prohibit the government from punishing a public employee for expression related to his job. In his work as deputy district attorney, Richard Ceballos wrote a memo to his superiors in the Los Angeles County District Attorney's Office recommending they dismiss a criminal case because of alleged inaccuracies in a key affidavit from a sheriff. Ceballos said he later was reassigned, transferred and denied a promotion based on his opposition to the prosecution of the case. He filed a First Amendment suit asserting that these punishments violated his constitutional right of free speech. The government countered that the memo was not speech protected by the First Amendment because Ceballos was communicating in his role as a government employee, not "as a citizen upon matters of public concern."[85] In a 5–4 ruling, the Supreme Court said the Constitution does not ban sanctions against employees for speech that is part of their official duties. When a public employee speaks as a government employee, the government employer has authority "over what [expression] the employer itself has commissioned or created."[86] In fact, the power to evaluate, and if necessary sanction, an employee's "work product," as the Court judged the memo to be, is central to an employer's ability to direct employee activities to achieve desired goals.

In dissent, Justice John Paul Stevens wrote, "The proper answer to the question 'whether the First Amendment protects a government employee from discipline based on speech made pursuant to the employee's official duties,' is 'Sometimes,' not 'Never.'" One First Amendment scholar called the Court's decision "a break from past precedent—or at least a significant addition to the calculus. . . . [T]his new employer-friendly rule represented a dramatic shift . . . and would work against outspoken public employees in free-speech cases—and thereby work against the public's interest in good government, as well."[87]

SUMMARY

POLITICAL SPEECH LIES AT THE CORE of the First Amendment and is accorded the highest degree of protection from government intrusion. Thus, the Supreme Court reviews most political speech cases using strict scrutiny. In recent years, federal courts have found several campaign finance restrictions to be unconstitutional restraints on free speech, and in 2010 the Supreme Court reversed precedent to strike down bans on corporate funding of campaign advertising. Congress and the Federal Election Commission continue to try to craft rules that honor the First Amendment while protecting against the corrupting influence of big money.

The Court has generally recognized the right of individuals to speak anonymously about political issues and has identified an honorable tradition of anonymous political speech that protects a robust democracy. However, this right is not absolute. The government itself also enjoys a right, and often an obligation, to speak. Government control of the content of government speech, through direct supervision of employees or the discriminatory selection of monuments in a public park, is constitutional so long as it advances a central objective of the government program involved. Government may censor the speech of its workers when the workers speak for government or when employee speech presents a danger of real harm to the operation of government. ■

Public and Nonpublic Forums

At a rock concert in Central Park and at thousands of other daily events in the United States, private citizens gather on public property or in government buildings to exchange ideas and associate freely. Local musicians practice in a conference room in town hall. The kennel club meets in the high school gym after hours. The Young Republicans protest tuition hikes on the university mall. People for the Ethical Treatment of Animals march down the public streets. Political organizers, grassroots groups, garage musicians and soapbox speakers all use the public parks and walkways to organize and to share information.

public forum Government property held for use by the public, usually for purposes of exercising rights of speech and assembly.

Each of these gatherings occurs in what the Supreme Court calls a **public forum**. The legal concept of public forums recognizes the long and central role of public oratory in the United States. The basic idea is that a great deal of government property is essentially held in trust for use by the public; it is the public's space. In 1939, in a case involving a challenge to a city ordinance prohibiting the distribution of pamphlets on city streets and in city parks, the Supreme Court explained the idea as follows:

> Wherever the title of streets and parks may rest, they have immemorially been held in trust for the use of the public and, time out of mind, have been used for purposes of assembly, communicating thoughts between citizens, and discussing public questions. Such use of the streets and public places has, from ancient times, been a part of the privileges, immunities, rights, and liberties of citizens.[88]

From this perspective, the people have a First Amendment right to use public property to express themselves freely. Access to public spaces without fear of government censorship or punishment has been critical to open public debate and dissent in the United States.[89] In recent times, the Court has said the Constitution allows Nazis, Vietnam War protesters, civil rights activists and the homeless to march and assemble in public places.[90]

While people have a right to speak and assemble in public forums, this right is balanced against other considerations. Public use of public forums must be compatible with the normal activity in that place. For example, a 10 a.m. meeting of the Girl Scouts in an elementary school classroom would disrupt educational activities; an evening meeting would not. A meeting at any time in the Pentagon is unlikely; a weekday meeting in the city park is far less likely to cause any problems.

The Supreme Court has defined three categories of public forums according to the nature of the place, the pattern of its primary activities and the history of public access.[91] First, lands designed for public use and historically used for public gathering, discussion and association—such as parks, streets and sidewalks adjacent to many public buildings—are **traditional public forums**.[92] The public has a general and presumed right to use these places for expression.

Government may set up rules, hours and policies to facilitate use of traditional public forums. In fact, many cities close parks after dark and coordinate use of park facilities by issuing permits. Such regulations are constitutional if they are fairly applied and content neutral, meaning they do not discriminate because of the official's degree of approval of the group's ideas or politics. To deny all public access or ban all expressive activities in a traditional public forum, the government must meet the requirements of strict scrutiny. In particular, the city would have to demonstrate a compelling interest in denying public access to the park.

Some government spaces or buildings have never served primarily as places for public assembly or speech. Yet spaces such as public school and university classrooms, public libraries, pages of high school newspapers, state fairgrounds and statehouses may provide ideal settings for individuals to gather literally or virtually and share ideas. These spaces are not automatically or presumptively available for public use. However, in many cases, government chooses to allow public use of these spaces as **designated public forums**.[93] Essentially, a designated public forum is a place that sometimes is, and sometimes is not, a public forum. This happens, for example, when a city school board says the public may use school buildings outside of school hours for activities that are suitable for the space.

In a designated public forum, the government limits the times, places or manners of public use to ensure that public access does not conflict with the primary function of the property. Government may impose well-tailored, reasonable, content-neutral licensing and usage regulations. In general, the Supreme Court reviews regulations of limited public forums under intermediate scrutiny, balancing the citizen right of free expression against the primary role of the facility. Speech and access compatible with the location's primary function usually must be permitted. When the government facility is operating as a public forum, government may not make content-based discriminations among users. Public access cannot be denied entirely without a compelling reason.

Some types of government property simply are not available for public use. The public has no right to hold a meeting in the secure areas of a federal penitentiary, for example. **Nonpublic forums** exist where public access, assembly and speech would conflict with the proper functioning of the government service and where there is no history of public access. Courts generally defer to the government to determine when government property is off limits to the public. In nonpublic forums, government is not the trustee but the user of the property. Government behaves more like a private property owner and controls nonpublic forum space to achieve government objectives. Military bases, prisons, post office

traditional public forum
Lands designed for public use and historically used for public gathering, discussion and association (e.g., public streets, sidewalks and parks). Free speech is protected in these areas.

designated public forum
Government spaces or buildings that are available for public use (within limits).

nonpublic forum Government-held property that is not available for public speech and assembly purposes.

realWorld Law

But Where Can I Speak?

In 1940, the Supreme Court held that "the freedom of speech and of the press guaranteed by the Constitution embraces at least the liberty to discuss *publicly* and truthfully all matters of public concern without prior restraint or fear of subsequent punishment."[1] The concept that government property serves as a critical forum for the healthy public exchange of ideas and information on important issues has since developed into the Court's public forum doctrine.

While acknowledging the vital speech functions of public spaces, the Court has employed its public forum doctrine from the start to allow varying degrees of government restrictions on speech depending upon the *type* of public spaces involved. Recognizing that assembly and speech in public places may interfere with the significant primary use of government property, the Court has established three categories of public property and three tiers of judicial protection for public speech there.[2]

- *Traditional public forums.* In areas (such as public parks and sidewalks) specifically established for public gatherings or where expressive activity historically has occurred, the Court applies a heightened form of intermediate scrutiny to regulations.

- *Limited/designated public forum.* When government opens areas such as convention centers, theaters and off-hours public school rooms for public use, restrictions on their use also receive heightened intermediate scrutiny review. However, when government has *not* expressly provided public access to these spaces, the Court applies rational review to regulations on speech in them.

- *Nonpublic forum.* In other types of public property, where the government's primary purpose prevents or overshadows the rights of public access and speech (e.g., inside the Pentagon or a prison), the Court subjects speech regulations to rational review.

Even in the most quintessentially public spaces, traditional or all-purpose public forums, the Court generally upholds time, place and manner (TPM) restrictions on speech without constitutional problem.[3] Some argue that the increasing government imposition of a particular form of TPM restriction, the creation of "protest zones"[4] for speech, has reduced the visibility and impact of significant dissent about important public issues.[5]

walkways, utility poles, airport terminals and private mailboxes are all nonpublic forums.[94] Government may exclude the entire public or certain speakers or messages from nonpublic forums on the basis of a reasonable or rational, viewpoint-neutral interest.[95]

The three categories of forums establish a hierarchy of public access rights. However, the Supreme Court often balances the public right to use a forum against other interests. For example, the Supreme Court has said government may ban public picketing and protests from traditional public forums such as sidewalks and streets to protect core privacy, safety or health interests. Thus, the Court has upheld a ban on targeted picketing outside a doctor's residence and no-protest buffer zones outside abortion clinics.[96]

Some argue that new communication technologies, particularly the growth of the Internet, provide ample virtual space for public speech, reducing the need to protect the physical space for public debate. Justice Anthony Kennedy, for example, has said:

> Minds are not changed in the streets and parks as they once were. To an increasing degree, the more significant interchanges of ideas and shaping of public consciousness occur in mass and electronic media.[6]

Others disagree and decry the loss of the public sphere.[7] According to one law scholar, in the United States today "the simple regulation of place has made dissent effectively invisible, practically pointless, and criminally dangerous!"[8] As another scholar noted:

> Among the hallmarks of an open society, surely one must be that not every group of people on the streets is "a mob," and another that its streets, time out of mind, have been used for purposes of assembly, communicating thoughts between citizens and discussing public questions.[9]

1. Thornhill v. Alabama, 310 U.S. 88, 101–2 (1940).
2. See, e.g., Madsen v. Women's Health Ctr., 512 U.S. 753 (1994); United States v. Kokinda, 497 U.S. 720 (1990); Frisby v. Schultz, 487 U.S. 474 (1988); United States v. Grace, 461 U.S. 171 (1983); Cox v. Louisiana, 379 U.S. 536 (1965); Schneider v. New Jersey, 308 U.S. 147 (1939).
3. See, e.g., Cox v. New Hampshire, 312 U.S. 569 (1941) (emphasis added).
4. For discussion of protest-free zones around President George W. Bush and at his public appearances, see, e.g., Jonathan M. Katz, Thou Dost Protest Too Much: An Old Law Turns Protestors into Threats Against the President, Slate, available at http://www.slate.com; James Bovard, Quarantining Dissent: How the Secret Service Protects Bush from Free Speech, S.F. Chron., Jan. 4, 2004, at D1. For related cases, see, e.g., Coal. to Protest the Democratic Nat'l Convention v. City of Boston, 327 F. Supp. 2d 61 (D. Mass. 2004); Menotti v. City of Seattle, 409 F.3d 1113 (9th Cir. 2005).
5. See Thomas P. Crocker, Displacing Dissent: The Role of "Place" in First Amendment Jurisprudence, 75 Fordham L. Rev. 2587 (2007). See also, Carol L. Zeiner, Zoned Out! Examining Campus Speech Zones, 66 La. L. Rev. 1 (2005).
6. Denver Area Educ. Telecomms. Consortium v. FCC, 518 U.S. 727, 802–03 (1996) (Kennedy, J., dissenting).
7. See Jürgen Habermas, The Structural Transformation of the Public Sphere: An Inquiry into a Category of Bourgeois Society (T. Burger trans., 1991) (1962); Cass R. Sunstein, The Future of Free Speech, in Eternally Vigilant: Free Speech in the Modern Era, 285–87 (Lee C. Bollinger & Geofrey R. Stone eds., 2002).
8. Thomas P. Crocker, Displacing Dissent: The Role of "Place" in First Amendment Jurisprudence, 75 Fordham L. Rev. 2587 (2007).
9. Harry Kalven, Jr., The Concept of the Public Forum: Cox v. Louisiana, 1965 Sup. Ct. Rev. 1, 32.

Private Property as a Public Forum

Public forums do not exist only on government property. When private property replaces or functions as a traditional public space, it may be treated as a public forum. When the open area of an enclosed shopping mall or a large private parking lot is used widely for public assembly and expression, the Supreme Court has said the private property owner sometimes may be required to allow public gatherings and free expression.[97] The law in this area is unclear. For example, the general public unquestionably is invited into shopping malls during the normal hours of business. It is not clear, though, whether working journalists enjoy the same degree of access to shopping mall spaces as the public does. Moreover, a journalist with a pen and notepad may blend in with the public and not attract undue attention or disrupt shoppers. However, members of the electronic media—particularly television—may attract notice that prompts mall owners to exclude them. In such circumstances, television reporters may, or may not, have the same rights as citizens.

The U.S. Supreme Court has held that citizens' free speech and petition rights may remain intact in a privately owned shopping center.[98] The issue reached the Court after the owners of a California shopping center called Prune Yard attempted to exclude teenagers circulating a petition. The shopping center owners said mandatory access for the group would amount to illegal "taking" of their property without just compensation. In other words, the owners said that if the Court required the mall to permit the teens to use their space for First Amendment purposes, the government would effectively be seizing part of their property for public use without payment.

"It is true," the Court acknowledged, "that one of the essential sticks in the bundle of property rights is the right to exclude others. . . . But it is well established that not every destruction or injury to property by governmental action has been held to be a 'taking' in the constitutional sense."[99] Instead, the Court said, the determination hinges on whether the "taking" of property forces some individuals to bear burdens that should be the responsibility of the public as a whole—responsibilities usually shouldered by government.[100]

In a very narrow ruling based in part on the expansive speech protections of the California constitution, the Court in *Prune Yard Shopping Center v. Robins* reasoned that enforcing the free speech and petition rights of the teenagers did not unduly impose on the rights of the property owner. The large mall was a peculiarly public space, and the slight intrusion created by those circulating the petition did not infringe on the owner's own freedom of speech.

Courts have struggled with this precedent and have not applied it directly to the question of news media access to shopping malls. Some believe that the First Amendment freedom of press should provide a right for news media to enter private property to gather information.[101] By using *Prune Yard* as the benchmark, it may be argued that there is no "taking" of property when news media, even with cameras rolling, are in a space that is the functional equivalent of a public forum. After all, the images collected are of nothing more than what is available to the public eye, and the cameras do not infringe on the owners' own rights to speech.

The Supreme Court's *Prune Yard* ruling also suggests limits to the right of a property owner to exclude; all restrictions of the owner's rights are not automatically a "taking" of the property.[102] This may be especially true when the media's presence does not interfere with the property owner's opportunity for economic gain, when the news media presence on the property causes no harm. According to this reasoning, the press has a right equal to the teenagers to be present in a shopping mall.

Courts, however, have shied away from a broad reading of *Prune Yard*. Some U.S. Supreme Court justices have suggested that its precedent allowing government to "coerce [the] creation of a speaker's forum" only applies in California.[103] And most people agree that *Prune Yard* does not extend to newsgathering situations. Although mall owners open their property to the public, they do so for the purpose of shopping. While on the job, members of the media are not there for that purpose.

Virtual Forums and Government Speakers

Not all public forums exist in physical space. Sometimes government funds that subsidize expression create a virtual public forum. When government funds are designed to support general speech and associational activities, the government may not discriminate on the basis of the ideas expressed.[104] Selection criteria must be neutral in terms of message content. The ban on discrimination also applies generally when government imposes taxes or provides tax exemptions on expression. **Laws of general application** that distribute tax obligations or benefits may not, for example, disfavor large newspapers, general interest magazines or commercial publications.[105]

laws of general application Laws such as tax and equal employment laws that fall within the express power of government. Laws of general application are generally reviewed under minimum scrutiny.

Government collection and distribution of money does not always create a public forum. In fact, the Court has acknowledged that some government funding procedures can achieve their objectives only if they discriminate among applicants according to the ideas they express. The National Endowment for the Arts (NEA), for example, is a government agency that funds artists on the basis of its judgments about the value and quality of the artistic proposals it reviews. NEA grants are designed to fund the specific objectives of the NEA, not to create a public forum for art. So the NEA may choose not to fund art it disfavors or finds indecent or offensive.[106] The same is true of book purchases for public school libraries. School libraries are not public forums for all printed materials; they are funded specifically to provide curriculum- and age-appropriate materials to school students. Therefore, library discriminations based on the content of the books do not violate the Constitution; they are vital to the library's purpose.[107]

SUMMARY

THE SUPREME COURT RECOGNIZES that the right to speak freely means little if you cannot reach an audience. Accordingly, public property often provides a place for citizens to express themselves. Government spaces devoted to use by the public to accommodate free speech activities are called public forums. Traditional public forums are designed for public use and historically have been used by the people for the free exchange of ideas. Government has greater latitude to impose reasonable content-neutral rules in designated public forums to eliminate uses that are incompatible with the primary function of these places. Nonpublic forums exist on government property where public access would undermine or endanger the government service conducted there, such as high-security areas of prisons or the Pentagon. Neither journalists nor the public have a right of access to these places.

Property owners generally control access to their private property unless the property assumes a quasi-public function. Sometimes government distribution of funds creates a public forum that requires the government to provide nondiscriminatory access to users regardless of their message. ■

Compelled Speech

The First Amendment protects both the right to speak out publicly and to remain silent. In a case involving a New Hampshire law that made it a crime to remove or cover up the state slogan, "Live Free or Die," on a vehicle license plate, the Supreme Court protected an individual's right "to refrain from speaking."[108] George Maynard, a Jehovah's Witness, had been fined $50 and served six months in jail for covering up the slogan on his license plate. The Court ruled that Maynard had a constitutional right "not to be coerced by the state into advertising a slogan which [he found] morally, ethically, religiously, and politically abhorrent."

The Court also has ruled in a group of cases that private organizations cannot be forced to include individuals or to support messages with which they disagree.[109] In one case, organizers of the annual St. Patrick's Day parade in Boston, which includes a huge number and diversity of organizations, refused to allow an alliance of gay, lesbian and bisexual individuals to participate. The alliance sued, arguing that their exclusion from the parade violated their freedom of speech. The trial court agreed. Because the parade had no expressive purpose, the court said forced inclusion of alliance members in the event would cause no harm to the parade organizer's First Amendment rights.

A unanimous Supreme Court reversed. Significantly, the Court said it was unnecessary to the alliance's message that it participate in the organizer's event. The alliance could arrange its own parade or reach the desired audience in a number of ways that would not infringe on the organizer's freedom of association and speech. The Court said: "Whatever the reason [for excluding the group], it boils down to the choice of a speaker not to propound a particular point of view, and that choice is presumed to lie beyond the government's power of control."[110]

SUMMARY

IN ADDITION TO PROTECTING an individual's right of expression, the Supreme Court says the First Amendment also contains a right to refrain from speaking. Laws that create compelled speech in city streets generally are unconstitutional. ■

Media Emergence, Convergence and Consolidation

In 1791, when the First Amendment was adopted, speaking to crowds in town squares was an important way to distribute a message broadly to the public. Beyond that, individuals who wanted to share their ideas could print flyers, pamphlets, leaflets, posters, books and, of course, newspapers. The only media of the day were printed materials.

The first American newspapers were published in the early 1700s, and some 2,000 newspapers emerged during the next century. Few survived, though, and even the largest newspaper had a circulation of no more than two hundred or so readers. While the printed word was *the* medium of mass communication, newspapers were small and contained as much unsubstantiated rumor and out-of-date gossip as accurate news. British licensing of presses eliminated most controversial news, especially criticism of the crown. Gradually, however, revolutionary editors rejected the censors and replaced bland reports of the weather and stories of disasters abroad with direct and very caustic challenges to British control. These printed materials passed from hand to hand, and residents of small towns often read city newspapers weeks, or even months, after they were published. Still, word of mouth remained a primary means of spreading timely information, and reading clubs (the New World's equivalent of the renowned salons of Europe) became important venues for sharing news and discussing contemporary issues in the public sphere.

Today, the First Amendment faces a very different press. In the past century, in particular, mass communication has changed dramatically. The arrival of motion pictures, radio and then television in the first half of the 20th century provided new communication and entertainment options to the public. Citizens willingly turned away from the extended discussions that had been a major source of news and entertainment, spent less time reading their newspapers and devoted their evenings to listening to the radio or watching blurry black-and-white images on tiny television screens. Movies became a major social event, and broadcast television offered timely, active news from the local community and around the globe.

As new media emerged, so did their critics. Observers feared each new medium in turn would dissolve families and disintegrate communities. Critics said film would divert citizens' attention from important issues and, in turn, radio and television would transform active community members into isolated media consumers who interacted with media rather than with each other.[111] Newspaper owners feared the competition and warned that the new entertainment focus posed a threat to democracy. In response, spokesmen for the new media argued that radio and television offered new avenues for speech and press and provided important news alternatives. Some analysts believe that competition between broadcast networks and among the different media produced a golden age of news coverage in America in the mid-20th century.

In the 1970s and 1980s, cable television entered the mix, extending the reach of broadcast signals across mountains and other geographic barriers into remote valleys. Cable was originally an ally of broadcast television, but because it offered a clearer picture and greater programming capacity, it soon became a direct competitor for broadcast viewers. Before long, satellites and telephone lines also were feeding video images into homes across the country. Then the Internet evolved from a network that linked a select group of university and military computers into a World Wide Web of home computers offering a previously unimaginable amount and diversity of information and entertainment to hundreds of millions of individuals around the world. The advent of wireless digital communications merged all of these capabilities into the equivalent of personal mobile broadcast stations slightly larger than a business card that receive and transmit voice, text, photographs and moving images instantly around the globe.

Clearly, today's media are not "the press" experienced by the framers of the First Amendment. In the global economy of the 21st century, the printed word is no longer the only means of disseminating information broadly. In fact, many argue that print is no longer a dominant medium of mass communication. And in 2009, some analysts were foretelling the impending elimination of print newspapers in the United States. For several years, the number of newspapers published in the United States has declined despite a significant growth in the number of households. In addition, the traditional press represents a shrinking share of the media reaching the U.S. audience. The same is true of broadcast television, which has seen its viewership and revenue drop sharply as the audience turns increasingly to video games, film, music, sports and entertainment programming beamed or cabled into their homes, onto their laptops or into their palms.

For 75 years, the Supreme Court has struggled to decide when and how the First Amendment protects these diverse media.[112] Are they members of "the press"? Is all communication via any medium for any purpose "speech"? For half a century, the Court generally treated each medium of communication differently because each presented unique First Amendment strengths and problems. In 1949, for example, one justice expressed the view that "the moving picture screen, the radio, the newspaper, the handbill, the sound truck and the street corner orator have differing natures, values, abuses and dangers. Each, in my view, is a law unto itself."[113]

The Court has held, however, that regulatory differences must be "justified by some special characteristic of the press"[114] or by some specific distinctions among the media. Accordingly, the Constitution allows government to regulate broadcasters differently from newspapers because broadcasters act as trustees of the scarce public airwaves.[115] Similarly, unique regulations may be imposed on cable operators without violating the First Amendment because cable systems threaten the economic survival of broadcasters.[116] Significant changes and continuing developments in the ownership and operation of mass media challenge these carefully drawn distinctions. Ownership conglomerates blend newspapers, television, video, film, the Internet and wireless. In the past 20 years, the number of corporations dominating American media plummeted from 50 to 10.[117] In the five years following enactment of the Telecommunications Act of 1996, some 90 percent of the nation's 10,000 existing radio stations changed ownership.[118] Record labels and entertainment firms, book publishers and video game producers joined forces and extended their reach around the globe. Clear Channel Communications operated radio stations in nearly two-thirds of the country's 289 Arbitron-rated markets in 2005.[119] The 10 largest companies providing television programming served 85 percent of American households.[120]

Newspaper companies, once satisfied to converge into chains and groups, have evolved into multinational multimedia conglomerates. In 2005, fewer than two dozen newspaper companies provided daily news to three-fourths of the nation's readers.[121] The top eight news media firms in New York ranked among the 300 largest companies in the world,[122] and General Electric alone— which owned NBC, USA Network and Universal Pictures, among other media holdings—reported $134 billion in revenue in 2003.[123]

At the same time, two out of three professional journalists have said that increasing emphasis on media profits was seriously hurting the quality of news reporting in the United States.[124] Ownership consolidation creates economic efficiencies and increases profits but may produce a monotony, if not a monopoly, of content. Today's cable and television news programs increasingly cover entertainment instead of the economy, and pop culture instead of politics. Animated video game characters "star" in full-length films, advertise soft drinks and appear on the covers of news magazines. At the same time, Second Life avatars transform each of us into digital action figures.

Technology increasingly also makes historically discrete forms of communication virtually indistinguishable. Daily newspapers, broadcast programming and cable content all are beamed across the country via satellite. Television screens double as computer monitors and vice versa. Cell phones deliver calls from family, digitized songs and movies, cable programs, photographs and high-speed messaging services. Media hubs allow home users to integrate all of their computer-based information and entertainment with their televisions and stereos. One remote control connects broadcast television and radio shows, cable and satellite programming, video streams, and all the vast and varied data stored on computers throughout the network. Usage patterns also are shifting as corporate mergers, content sharing and technological convergence blur the lines between various media. Each year, citizens spend less time watching television or reading newspapers and other periodicals and more time playing video games and surfing the Internet.

The rapid transformations of the communication environment stretch the traditional definition of "the press." They also challenge established understanding and application of First Amendment guarantees. The Supreme Court may have reflected this befuddlement and uncertainty when in 2003 it reversed its decision to hear a case that would have required the Court to draw a clear distinction between advertising and nonadvertising content.[125] As the discrete characteristics of different content and distinct media continue to blur, consistent application of established First Amendment precedents becomes ever more difficult. As the decisions become increasingly difficult, citizens might do well to recall the adage that hard cases make bad law.

SUMMARY

ISSUES OF MEDIA CONVERGENCE AND CONSOLIDATION present new challenges to the Court's interpretation and application of the First Amendment. The proliferation of new media suggests a growing abundance of avenues for free expression. However, control of an increasing number of media outlets by a very few corporations may limit the diversity of content reaching the public and reduce opportunities for citizens to send their messages to large audiences. The increasing overlap of once-distinct media also blurs once-clear distinctions under the First Amendment, posing new and difficult questions for the courts. ∎

Cases for Study

The excerpts below of two cases related to the then-ongoing Vietnam War examine two limits imposed by the First Amendment. In *New York Times Co. v. United States,* the Supreme Court provided expedited review of a federal injunction against war reporting by the Times and the Washington Post based on leaked classified documents that came to be known as the Pentagon Papers. Through a careful delineation of the government's limited ability to exercise prior restraint on speech, the Court's Pentagon Papers decision underscored the importance of the separation of powers and reaffirmed that the government has very limited authority over the press. The second case shifts focus from the press to symbolic speech to identify the extent and limits of First Amendment protection for expressive actions. In *United States v. O'Brien,* the Court reviewed a war protestor's challenge to a federal law that prohibited the burning of draft cards, and in doing so established an enduring test for determining whether specific "speech acts" deserve the protection of the Constitution.

Thinking About It

The two case excerpts explore the extent and limits of the First Amendment's protection for the freedom of speech and of the press. As you read these case excerpts, keep the following questions in mind.

- What significant distinctions do the Court's two decisions craft between the freedom of symbolic speech and the freedom of the press?

- What do the decisions indicate about the power of government to restrain different types of free expression?

- What type or types of scrutiny do the justices use in each of the cases and why?

- Do the tests and rationales used by the Court provide clear and solid guidance to lower courts facing similar issues? How?

New York Times Co. v. United States
SUPREME COURT OF THE UNITED STATES
403 U.S. 713 (1971)

PER CURIAM OPINION:

We granted certiorari in these cases in which the United States seeks to enjoin the New York Times and the Washington Post from publishing the contents of a classified study entitled "History of U.S. Decision-Making Process on Viet Nam Policy."

"Any system of prior restraints of expression comes to this Court bearing a heavy presumption against its constitutional validity." The Government "thus carries a heavy burden of showing justification for the imposition of such a restraint." The District Court for the Southern District of New York in the New York Times case and the District Court for the District of Columbia and the Court of Appeals for the District of Columbia Circuit in the *Washington Post* case held that the Government had not met that burden. We agree.

The judgment of the Court of Appeals for the District of Columbia Circuit is therefore affirmed. The order of the Court of Appeals or the Second Circuit is reversed, and the case is remanded with directions to enter a judgment affirming the judgment of the District Court for the Southern District of New York. The stays entered June 25, 1971, by the Court are vacated. The judgments shall issue forthwith.

So ordered.

JUSTICE HUGO BLACK, with whom JUSTICE WILLIAM DOUGLAS joined, concurring:
I adhere to the view that the Government's case against the Washington Post should have been dismissed, and that the injunction against the New York Times should have been vacated without oral argument when the cases were first presented to this Court. I believe that every moment's continuance of the injunctions against these newspapers amounts to a flagrant, indefensible, and continuing violation of the First Amendment. . . .

In the First Amendment, the Founding Fathers gave the free press the protection it must have to fulfill its essential role in our democracy. The press was to serve the governed, not the governors. The Government's power to censor the press was abolished so that the press would remain forever free to censure the Government. The press was protected so that it could bare the secrets of government and inform the people. Only a free and unrestrained press can effectively expose deception in government. And paramount among the responsibilities of a free press is the duty to prevent any part of the government from deceiving the people and sending them off to distant lands to die of foreign fevers and foreign shot and shell. In my view, far from deserving condemnation for their courageous reporting, the New York Times, the Washington Post, and other newspapers should be commended for serving the purpose that the Founding Fathers saw so clearly. In revealing the workings of government that led to the Vietnam war, the newspapers nobly did precisely that which the Founders hoped and trusted they would do. . . .

The word "security" is a broad, vague generality whose contours should not be invoked to abrogate the fundamental law embodied in the First Amendment. The guarding of military and diplomatic secrets at the expense of informed representative government provides no real security for our Republic. The Framers of the First Amendment, fully aware of both the need to defend a new nation and the abuses of the English and Colonial governments, sought to give this new society strength and security by providing that freedom of speech, press, religion, and assembly should not be abridged. . . .

JUSTICE WILLIAM DOUGLAS, with whom JUSTICE HUGO BLACK joined, concurring:
. . . It should be noted at the outset that the First Amendment provides that "Congress shall make no law . . . abridging the freedom of speech, or of the press." That leaves, in my view, no room for governmental restraint on the press. . . .

The dominant purpose of the First Amendment was to prohibit the widespread practice of governmental suppression of embarrassing information. It is common knowledge that the First Amendment was adopted against the widespread use of the common law of seditious libel to punish the dissemination of material that is embarrassing to the powers-that-be. The present cases will, I think, go down in history as the most dramatic illustration of that principle. . . .

Secrecy in government is fundamentally anti-democratic, perpetuating bureaucratic errors. Open debate and discussion of public issues are vital to our national health. On public questions there should be "uninhibited, robust, and wide-open" debate. . . .

JUSTICE WILLIAM BRENNAN, concurring:

. . . The error that has pervaded these cases from the outset was the granting of any injunctive relief whatsoever, interim or otherwise. The entire thrust of the Government's claim throughout these cases has been that publication of the material sought to be enjoined "could," or "might," or "may" prejudice the national interest in various ways. But the First Amendment tolerates absolutely no prior judicial restraints of the press predicated upon surmise or conjecture that untoward consequences may result. Our cases, it is true, have indicated that there is a single, extremely narrow class of cases in which the First Amendment's ban on prior judicial restraint may be overridden. Our cases have thus far indicated that such cases may arise only when the Nation "is at war," during which times "[n]o one would question but that a government might prevent actual obstruction to its recruiting service or the publication of the dates of transports or the number and location of troops." Even if the present world situation were assumed to be tantamount to a time of war, or if the power of presently available armaments would justify even in peacetime the suppression of information that would set in motion a nuclear holocaust, in neither of these actions has the Government presented or even alleged that publication of items from or based upon the material at issue would cause the happening of an event of that nature. "[T]he chief purpose of [the First Amendment's] guaranty [is] to prevent previous restraints upon publication." Thus, only governmental allegation and proof that publication must inevitably, directly, and immediately cause the occurrence of an event kindred to imperiling the safety of a transport already at sea can support even the issuance of an interim restraining order. . . . Unless and until the Government has clearly made out its case, the First Amendment commands that no injunction may issue. . . .

JUSTICE POTTER STEWART, with whom JUSTICE BYRON WHITE joined, concurring:

. . . . If the Constitution gives the Executive a large degree of unshared power in the conduct of foreign affairs and the maintenance of our national defense, then, under the Constitution, the Executive must have the largely unshared duty to determine and preserve the degree of internal security necessary to exercise that power successfully. It is an awesome responsibility, requiring judgment and wisdom of a high order. I should suppose that moral, political, and practical considerations would dictate that a very first principle of that wisdom would be an insistence upon avoiding secrecy for its own sake. For when everything is classified, then nothing is classified, and the system becomes one to be disregarded by the cynical or the careless, and to be manipulated by those intent on self-protection or self-promotion. I should suppose, in short, that the hallmark of a truly effective internal security system would be the maximum possible disclosure, recognizing that secrecy can best be preserved only when credibility is truly maintained. . . .

JUSTICE BYRON WHITE, with whom JUSTICE POTTER STEWART joined, concurring:

I concur in today's judgments, but only because of the concededly extraordinary protection against prior restraints enjoyed by the press under our constitutional system. I do not say that in no circumstances would the First Amendment permit an injunction against publishing information about government plans or operations. . . . But I nevertheless agree that the United States has not satisfied the very heavy burden that it must meet to warrant an injunction against publication in these cases, at least in the absence of express and appropriately limited congressional authorization for prior restraints in circumstances such as these. . . .

CHIEF JUSTICE WARREN BURGER, dissenting:

. . . As I see it, we have been forced to deal with litigation concerning rights of great magnitude without an adequate record, and surely without time for adequate treatment either in the prior proceedings or in this Court. . . .

. . . I agree generally with Mr. Justice Harlan and Mr. Justice Blackmun, but I am not prepared to reach the merits.

JUSTICE JOHN HARLAN, with whom CHIEF JUSTICE WARREN BURGER and JUSTICE HARRY BLACKMUN join, dissenting:

. . . The power to evaluate the "pernicious influence" of premature disclosure is not, however, lodged in the Executive alone. I agree that, in performance of its duty to protect the values of the First Amendment against political pressures, the judiciary must review the initial Executive determination to the point of satisfying itself that the subject matter of the dispute does lie within the proper compass of the President's foreign relations power. . . . Moreover, the judiciary may properly insist that the determination that disclosure of the subject matter would irreparably impair the national security be made by the head of the Executive Department concerned. . . .

But, in my judgment, the judiciary may not properly go beyond these two inquiries and re-determine for itself the probable impact of disclosure on the national security. . . .

JUSTICE HARRY BLACKMUN, dissenting:

. . .The First Amendment, after all, is only one part of an entire Constitution. . . . Each provision of the Constitution is important, and I cannot subscribe to a doctrine of unlimited absolutism for the First Amendment at the cost of downgrading other provisions. First Amendment absolutism has never commanded a majority of this Court. What is needed here is a weighing, upon properly developed standards, of the broad right of the press to print and of the very narrow right of the Government to prevent. Such standards are not yet developed. . . .

United States v. O'Brien
SUPREME COURT OF THE UNITED STATES
391 U.S. 367 (1968)

CHIEF JUSTICE EARL WARREN delivered the Court's opinion:

. . . David Paul O'Brien and three companions burned their Selective Service registration certificates on the steps of the South Boston Courthouse. A sizable crowd, including several agents of the Federal Bureau of Investigation, witnessed the event.[i] Immediately after the burning, members of the crowd began attacking O'Brien and his companions. An FBI agent ushered O'Brien to safety inside the courthouse. After he was advised of his right to counsel and to silence, O'Brien stated to FBI agents that he had burned his registration certificate because of his beliefs, knowing that he was violating federal law. . . .

For this act, O'Brien was indicted, tried, convicted, and sentenced in the United States District Court for the District of Massachusetts.[ii] . . . He stated in argument to the jury that he burned the certificate publicly to influence others to adopt his antiwar beliefs, as he put it, "so that other people would reevaluate their positions with Selective Service, with the armed forces, and reevaluate their place in the culture of today, to hopefully consider my position."

The indictment upon which he was tried charged that he "willfully and knowingly did mutilate, destroy, and change by burning . . . [his] Registration Certificate . . . in violation of Title 50, App. United States Code, Section 462 (b)." Section 462 (b) is part of the

---

i. At the time of the burning, the agents knew only that O'Brien and his three companions had burned small white cards. They later discovered that the card O'Brien burned was his registration certificate, and the undisputed assumption is that the same is true of his companions.

ii. He was sentenced under the Youth Corrections Act to the custody of the attorney general for a maximum period of six years for supervision and treatment.

Universal Military Training and Service Act of 1948. Section 462 (b)(3) was amended by Congress in 1965 (adding the words italicized below), so that, at the time O'Brien burned his certificate, an offense was committed by any person, "who forges, alters, *knowingly destroys, knowingly mutilates,* or in any manner changes any such certificate. . . ." (Italics supplied.) In the District Court, O'Brien argued that the 1965 Amendment prohibiting the knowing destruction or mutilation of certificates was unconstitutional because it was enacted to abridge free speech, and because it served no legitimate legislative purpose. The District Court rejected these arguments, holding that the statute on its face did not abridge First Amendment rights, that the court was not competent to inquire into the motives of Congress in enacting the 1965 Amendment, and that the Amendment was a reasonable exercise of the power of Congress to raise armies.

On appeal, the Court of Appeals for the First Circuit held the 1965 Amendment unconstitutional as a law abridging freedom of speech. At the time the Amendment was enacted, a regulation of the Selective Service System required registrants to keep their registration certificates in their "personal possession at all times." Willful violations of regulations promulgated pursuant to the Universal Military Training and Service Act were made criminal by statute. The Court of Appeals, therefore, was of the opinion that conduct punishable under the 1965 Amendment was already punishable under the non-possession regulation, and consequently that the Amendment served no valid purpose; further, that in light of the prior regulation, the Amendment must have been "directed at public, as distinguished from private, destruction." On this basis, the court concluded that the 1965 Amendment ran afoul of the First Amendment by singling out persons engaged in protests for special treatment. . . .

The Government petitioned for certiorari . . . , arguing that the Court of Appeals erred in holding the statute unconstitutional, and that its decision conflicted with decisions by the Courts of Appeals for the Second and Eighth Circuits. . . . We granted the Government's petition to resolve the conflict in the circuits. . . . We hold that the 1965 Amendment is constitutional both as enacted and as applied. We therefore vacate the judgment of the Court of Appeals and reinstate the judgment and sentence of the District Court. . . .

When a male reaches the age of 18, he is required by the Universal Military Training and Service Act to register with a local draft board. . . .

Both the registration and classification certificates are small white cards, approximately 2 by 3 inches. . . .

Both the registration and classification certificates bear notices that the registrant must notify his local board in writing of every change in address, physical condition, and occupational, marital, family, dependency, and military status, and of any other fact which might change his classification. Both also contain a notice that the registrant's Selective Service number should appear on all communications to his local board.

Congress demonstrated its concern that certificates issued by the Selective Service System might be abused well before the 1965 Amendment here challenged. The 1948 Act itself prohibited many different abuses involving "any registration certificate. . . ."

By the 1965 Amendment, Congress added . . . the provision here at issue, subjecting to criminal liability not only one who "forges, alters, or in any manner changes" but also one who "knowingly destroys, [or] knowingly mutilates" a certificate. We note at the outset that the 1965 Amendment plainly does not abridge free speech on its face . . . [and rather] deals with conduct having no connection with speech. It prohibits the knowing destruction of certificates issued by the Selective Service System, and there is nothing necessarily expressive about such conduct. The Amendment does not distinguish between public and private destruction, and it does not punish only destruction engaged in for the purpose of expressing views. A law prohibiting destruction of Selective Service certificates no more abridges free speech on its face than a motor vehicle law prohibiting the destruction of drivers' licenses, or a tax law prohibiting the destruction of books and records.

O'Brien nonetheless argues that the 1965 Amendment is unconstitutional in its application to him, and is unconstitutional as enacted because what he calls the "purpose" of Congress was "to suppress freedom of speech." We consider these arguments separately.

O'Brien first argues that the 1965 Amendment is unconstitutional as applied to him because his act of burning his registration certificate was protected "symbolic speech" within the First Amendment. His argument is that the freedom of expression [that] the First Amendment guarantees includes all modes of "communication of ideas by conduct," and that his conduct is within this definition because he did it in "demonstration against the war and against the draft."

We cannot accept the view that an apparently limitless variety of conduct can be labeled "speech" whenever the person engaging in the conduct intends thereby to express an idea. However, even on the assumption that the alleged communicative element in O'Brien's conduct is sufficient to bring into play the First Amendment, it does not necessarily follow that the destruction of a registration certificate is constitutionally protected activity. This Court has held that, when "speech" and "nonspeech" elements are combined in the same course of conduct, a sufficiently important governmental interest in regulating the nonspeech element can justify incidental limitations on First Amendment freedoms. To characterize the quality of the governmental interest which must appear, the Court has employed a variety of descriptive terms: compelling; substantial; subordinating; paramount; cogent; strong. . . . [W]e think it clear that a government regulation is sufficiently justified if it is within the constitutional power of the Government; if it furthers an important or substantial governmental interest; if the governmental interest is unrelated to the suppression of free expression; and if the incidental restriction on alleged First Amendment freedoms is no greater than is essential to the furtherance of that interest. We find that the 1965 Amendment to the Universal Military Training and Service Act meets all of these requirements, and consequently that O'Brien can be constitutionally convicted for violating it.

The constitutional power of Congress to raise and support armies and to make all laws necessary and proper to that end is broad and sweeping. The power of Congress to classify and conscript manpower for military service is "beyond question." Pursuant to this power, Congress may establish a system of registration for individuals liable for training and service, and may require such individuals within reason to cooperate in the registration system. The issuance of certificates indicating the registration and eligibility classification of individuals is a legitimate and substantial administrative aid in the functioning of this system. And legislation to insure the continuing availability of issued certificates serves a legitimate and substantial purpose in the system's administration. . . .

The many functions performed by Selective Service certificates establish beyond doubt that Congress has a legitimate and substantial interest in preventing their wanton and unrestrained destruction and assuring their continuing availability by punishing people who knowingly and willfully destroy or mutilate them. And we are unpersuaded that the pre-existence of the non-possession regulations in any way negates this interest. . . .

. . . [I]t has never been suggested that there is anything improper in Congress' providing alternative statutory avenues of prosecution to assure the effective protection of one and the same interest. . . .

We think it apparent that the continuing availability to each registrant of his Selective Service certificates substantially furthers the smooth and proper functioning of the system that Congress has established to raise armies. We think it also apparent that the Nation has a vital interest in having a system for raising armies that functions with maximum efficiency and is capable of easily and quickly responding to continually changing circumstances. For these reasons, the Government has a substantial interest in assuring the continuing availability of issued Selective Service certificates.

It is equally clear that the 1965 Amendment specifically protects this substantial governmental interest. We perceive no alternative means that would more precisely and narrowly assure the continuing availability of issued Selective Service certificates than a law which prohibits their willful mutilation or destruction. . . . The 1965 Amendment prohibits such conduct and does nothing more. In other words, both the governmental interest and the operation of the 1965 Amendment are limited to the non-communicative aspect of O'Brien's conduct. The governmental interest and the scope of the 1965 Amendment are limited to preventing harm to the smooth and efficient functioning of the Selective Service System. When O'Brien deliberately rendered unavailable his registration certificate, he willfully frustrated this governmental interest. For this non-communicative impact of his conduct, and for nothing else, he was convicted.

The case at bar is therefore unlike one where the alleged governmental interest in regulating conduct arises in some measure because the communication allegedly integral to the conduct is itself thought to be harmful. . . .

In conclusion, we find that, because of the Government's substantial interest in assuring the continuing availability of issued Selective Service certificates, because amended § 462 (b) is an appropriately narrow means of protecting this interest and condemns only the independent non-communicative impact of conduct within its reach, and because the non-communicative impact of O'Brien's act of burning his registration certificate frustrated the Government's interest, a sufficient governmental interest has been shown to justify O'Brien's conviction.

O'Brien finally argues that the 1965 Amendment is unconstitutional as enacted because what he calls the "purpose" of Congress was "to suppress freedom of speech." We reject this argument because under settled principles the purpose of Congress, as O'Brien uses that term, is not a basis for declaring this legislation unconstitutional.

It is a familiar principle of constitutional law that this Court will not strike down an otherwise constitutional statute on the basis of an alleged illicit legislative motive. . . .

Inquiries into congressional motives or purposes are a hazardous matter. When the issue is simply the interpretation of legislation, the Court will look to statements by legislators for guidance as to the purpose of the legislature, because the benefit to sound decision-making in this circumstance is thought sufficient to risk the possibility of misreading Congress' purpose. It is entirely a different matter when we are asked to void a statute that is, under well settled criteria, constitutional on its face, on the basis of what fewer than a handful of Congressmen said about it. What motivates one legislator to make a speech about a statute is not necessarily what motivates scores of others to enact it, and the stakes are sufficiently high for us to eschew guesswork. . . .

. . . [While] the inevitable effect of a statute on its face may render it unconstitutional[,] . . . [t]he statute attacked in the instant case has no such inevitable unconstitutional effect, since the destruction of Selective Service certificates is in no respect inevitably or necessarily expressive. Accordingly, the statute itself is constitutional. . . .

Since the 1965 Amendment to the Universal Military Training and Service Act is constitutional as enacted and as applied, the Court of Appeals should have affirmed the judgment of conviction entered by the District Court. . . . It is so ordered.

JUSTICE JOHN MARSHALL took no part in the consideration or decision of these cases.
JUSTICE JOHN HARLAN, concurring:
The crux of the Court's opinion, which I join, is, of course, its general statement that:

> a government regulation is sufficiently justified if it is within the constitutional power of the government; if it furthers an important or substantial governmental interest; if the governmental interest is unrelated to the suppression of free expression; and if the incidental restriction on alleged First Amendment freedoms is no greater than is essential to the furtherance of that interest.

I wish to make explicit my understanding that this passage does not foreclose consideration of First Amendment claims in those rare instances when an "incidental" restriction upon expression, imposed by a regulation which furthers an "important or substantial" governmental interest and satisfies the Court's other criteria, in practice has the effect of entirely preventing a "speaker" from reaching a significant audience with whom he could not otherwise lawfully communicate. This is not such a case, since O'Brien manifestly could have conveyed his message in many ways other than by burning his draft card.

JUSTICE WILLIAM DOUGLAS, dissenting:
The Court states that the constitutional power of Congress to raise and support armies is "broad and sweeping," and that Congress' power "to classify and conscript manpower for military service is 'beyond question.'" This is undoubtedly true in times when, by declaration of Congress, the Nation is in a state of war. The underlying and basic problem in this case, however, is whether conscription is permissible in the absence of a declaration of war. That question has not been briefed nor was it presented in oral argument; but it is, I submit, a question upon which the litigants and the country are entitled to a ruling. . . . This case should be put down for reargument. . . .

Chapter 3

The character of every act depends upon the circumstance in which it is done. The most stringent protection of free speech would not protect a man in falsely shouting fire in a theatre and causing a panic. It does not even protect a man from an injunction against uttering words that may have all the effect of force. The question in every case is whether the words used are used in such circumstances and are of such a nature as to create a clear and present danger that they will bring about the substantive evils that Congress has a right to prevent. It is a question of proximity and degree.

U.S. Supreme Court Justice Oliver Wendell Holmes[1]

Police officers restrain Gregory Johnson after his flag-burning demonstration to express anger against Reagan administration policies during the Republican National Convention.

Speech Distinctions

Dangers, Fights, Threats and Educational Needs

National Security and Tranquility
Threats to National Security

Court Tests to Protect Disruptive Speech
The Clear and Present Danger Test
The *Brandenburg* (or Incitement) Test

Speech Assaults
Offensive Speech
Fighting Words
Hate Speech
Current Standard
Intimidation and Threats

Symbolic Speech
Burning Speech

Speech in the Schools
Protest in the Schools
Offensive or Inappropriate Content
Compelled Orthodoxy
Religion in the Schools
Campus Speech
Speech Codes

Cases for Study
➤ *Texas v. Johnson*
➤ *Tinker v. Des Moines Independent Community School District*

Suppose . . .

. . . that about 100 protesters outside the 1984 Republican National Convention in Dallas set an American flag they had removed from a nearby flagpole ablaze while chanting, "America, the red, white, and blue, we spit on you!" A Texas law prohibited the "desecration" or "physical mistreatment" of the state or national flag in a manner intended to offend observers. Several onlookers reported that they were offended by the flag burning, and the protester, Gregory "Joey" Johnson, was sentenced to a year in prison and a $2,000 fine. Johnson, a member of the Revolutionary Communist Youth Brigade, appealed, arguing that the law violated his freedom of speech. But is burning a flag part of free speech? Is the American flag a unique symbol of national unity whose intentional destruction threatens the fabric of this country? Does intentionally burning a flag as part of an antigovernment protest actually incite illegal violence? Look for the answers to these questions when the case of *Texas v. Johnson* is discussed later in this chapter and the Supreme Court's opinion in the case is excerpted at the chapter's end.

C hapter 2 established a foundation for First Amendment analysis. This chapter digs more deeply into the topic by looking at expression that resides at the fringes of constitutional protection, as well as expression that takes place in and around public educational institutions. It examines how courts determine the boundaries of protected speech.

Although the First Amendment says government may not abridge free speech, the prohibition is not absolute. Courts use a variety of methods to determine when expression is and is not protected—what speech the government is permitted to abridge. One method is for a court to balance the benefits of permitting the expression against the harm to competing values caused by the speech. As noted in Chapter 2, this method of determining whether speech is protected—weighing competing values case by case—is called ad hoc balancing. A drawback to ad hoc balancing is that it is difficult to generalize from such fact-specific decisions, and thus the courts and society have difficulty applying them as a precedent to decide other similar controversies.

More often, then, courts use a method called **categorical balancing**. Using this method, a judge or a court develops rules by weighing different broad categories, such as political speech, against other categories of interest, such as privacy. The rules crafted then may be applied in later cases involving similar categories of speech. Under categorical balancing, some categories of speech—blackmail, extortion, perjury, false advertising and obscenity, for example—are unprotected by the First Amendment. Categorical balancing comes into play frequently when disruptive speech or school audiences are central to a case. In such cases, the central question is whether the speech is so disruptive to national security or educational interests that the interests in silencing it outweigh the benefits of its expression. If so, lawmakers may prohibit the speech.

Some categories of speech are not very well defined. In cases involving such categories, courts look at the specific circumstances and the level of offense or disruption to determine whether the speech falls into a punishable category. Under this approach, government's power to punish or ban a student newspaper article or a vitriolic speech before an armed and hostile audience depends on how much harm the speech is likely to cause. If the harm is likely to be cataclysmic, society's interest in preventing the crisis is more likely to outweigh concerns about protection of speech. One problem, though, is that the gravity of harm caused by speech cannot be known in advance.

categorical balancing The process through which courts reach judgments by weighing different broad categories, such as political speech, against other categories of interests, such as privacy.

National Security and Tranquility

Determining what speech threatens national security or how best to promote public peace and tranquility tends to reflect the national outlook and to shift with the historical context. Historically, during times of political conservatism, war or national turmoil, radical speech and organized protests are perceived to be more dangerous than during times of calm. Courts tend to restrict speech more readily when there is national unrest or the public is fearful. When the country moves from peace to war and back again, the nation alternately experiences waves of relative speech and press freedom followed by heightened suppression. These vacillations undermine the promised stability of the rule of law.[2] Despite one and a quarter centuries of trial and error, the Court has not created legal rules that consistently protect core First Amendment freedoms and counter-balance the urge to stifle speech during times of instability.[3] As Ann Beeson of the American Civil Liberties Union noted: "Sadly, our government has an ugly history of using its investigative powers to squelch dissent. We saw it during the Japanese internments of World War II, the Red Scare of the 1950s and the civil rights movement of the 1960s, and now we see it in the post–9/11 investigations and detention of Arabs and Muslims."[4]

Threats to National Security

Government efforts to punish speech that threatens its authority or undermines the security and stability of the nation did not end in 1801 when the Sedition Act (discussed in Chapter 2) expired. In the more than two centuries since, both federal and state governments have enacted laws to ensure that speakers do not provoke discontent or incite overthrow of government. Laws that target the speech related to conspiracies to commit crimes, advocacy of terrorism, treason, protest and intimidation also abound; these laws place limits on the types of speech protected in the United States.

Throughout U.S. history, threats to freedom of speech and of the press have occurred both when the nation is at war and when the national security appears vulnerable. In 2010, the U.S. Supreme Court ruled 6–3 that a 1996 federal ban on "material support" of terrorist groups did not violate the First Amendment, even when the law prevented support of legal activities by a designated terrorist organization.[5] In *Holder v. Humanitarian Law Project,* a nonprofit organization established in 1985 to protect human rights and promote peaceful conflict resolution sought a court injunction to prevent application of the ban to their

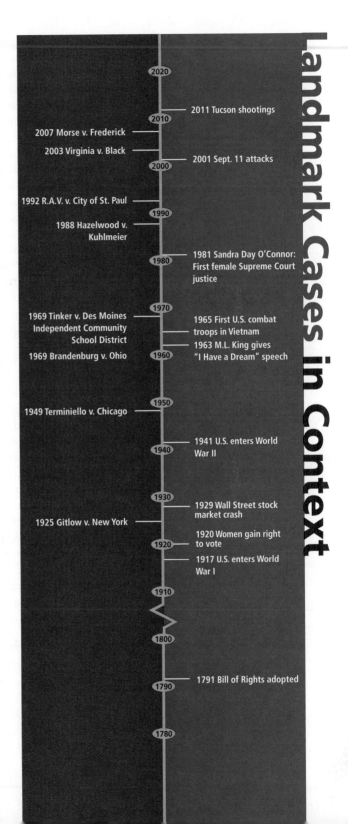

Landmark Cases in Context

- 2011 Tucson shootings
- 2007 Morse v. Frederick
- 2003 Virginia v. Black
- 2001 Sept. 11 attacks
- 1992 R.A.V. v. City of St. Paul
- 1988 Hazelwood v. Kuhlmeier
- 1981 Sandra Day O'Connor: First female Supreme Court justice
- 1969 Tinker v. Des Moines Independent Community School District
- 1965 First U.S. combat troops in Vietnam
- 1963 M.L. King gives "I Have a Dream" speech
- 1969 Brandenburg v. Ohio
- 1949 Terminiello v. Chicago
- 1941 U.S. enters World War II
- 1929 Wall Street stock market crash
- 1925 Gitlow v. New York
- 1920 Women gain right to vote
- 1917 U.S. enters World War I
- 1800
- 1791 Bill of Rights adopted

proposed training of members of the Kurdistan Workers Party, also known as the PKK, which was designated a terrorist organization. The group provided training on how to negotiate peace or seek help from the United Nations. Under the law, "prohibited material support" was defined to include any service, training, expert advice or assistance, among other things. The State Department strongly supported the ban, saying the identification and prevention of support to terrorist organizations played "a critical role in our fight against terrorism."[6]

The Court said the law as applied to the Humanitarian Law Project was neither vague nor overbroad because it did not unconstitutionally punish legal advocacy. Although "the scope of the material-support statute may not be clear in every application, . . . the dispositive point here is that the statutory terms are clear in their application to plaintiffs' proposed conduct," the Court wrote.[7] Ruling that the law's ban did not violate the group's freedom of speech, the Court said it applied strict scrutiny but gave due "respect for the government's conclusions . . . "given the sensitive interests in national security and foreign affairs at stake."[8] While the ban might not be constitutional in all its applications, and while not every "statute relating to speech and terrorism would satisfy the First Amendment," the law's prevention of training to the PKK constitutionally advanced the government's compelling interest in "provid[ing] for the common defense," the Court concluded.[9]

The terrorist attacks on the World Trade Center and the Pentagon on Sept. 11, 2001, revived citizens' concerns about the safety and stability of the United States. Government at all levels responded with new laws and strategies intended to better protect U.S. citizens and to punish terrorists and their supporters. One of the more visible and controversial actions of the federal government was the rapid enactment of the **USA Patriot Act** of 2001.[10] Five years later, behind a banner reading "Protecting the Homeland," President George W. Bush signed a "reauthorization and improvement" of the act.[11] The Patriot Act was designed to identify suspicious activity and speed the interception and prosecution of terrorists. The act also raised concerns among its critics that unclear definitions of "terrorism" and "support for terrorism" had a **chilling effect** on speech. A chilling effect arises from any practice that discourages the exercise of a constitutional right. In First Amendment law, it is brought about by any measure that deters freedom of expression.

By potentially placing a broad array of radical political organizing, activism and speech within the category of support for terrorism, and by granting expanded power to law enforcement authorities, the Patriot Act increased some people's fear that they might be investigated and punished. According to the Free Expression Policy Project (FEPP), the Patriot Act "contains more than 150 sections and amends over 15 federal statutes, including laws governing criminal procedure, computer fraud, foreign intelligence, wiretapping, and immigration."[12] Among its broad sweep are four provisions that have specific First Amendment implications: Section 206 permits roving wiretaps and secret court orders to monitor electronic communications of people in the United States suspected of involvement with terrorists; Sections 214 and 216 greatly expand authority for Internet monitoring in

USA Patriot Act The Uniting and Strengthening America by Providing Appropriate Tools Required to Intercept and Obstruct Terrorism Act of 2001. Passed in the wake of the Sept. 11, 2001, attacks, the act was designed to give law enforcement agencies greater authority to combat terrorism.

chilling effect The discouragement of a constitutional right, especially free speech, by any practice that creates uncertainty about the proper exercise of that right.

realWorld Law

Terrorism or Efforts at Peace?

In its 2010 ruling in *Holder v. Humanitarian Law Project,* the Supreme Court upheld a federal law that makes it a crime to support an organization labeled "terrorist," even if the support works toward peaceful resolution of conflict.[1]

"The bottom line is that the Court has now said that the First Amendment permits Congress to make human rights advocacy and peacemaking into a terrorist crime," said law professor David Cole, who argued the case before the Court.

Only three justices said that punishing advocacy of peaceful dispute resolution violated the First Amendment. The majority, led by Chief Justice John Roberts, upheld the ban on all charitable contributions to and support of terrorist organizations because money is fungible; donations to peacemaking activities free up funds for terrorist purposes.

The "material support" provision of the Anti-Terrorism and Effective Death Penalty Act makes it a crime to provide any assistance, advice, training or expertise to any group designated by the secretary of state as a terrorist organization. The Humanitarian Law Project, which challenged the law, has long worked toward peaceful resolution of international disputes. The group wanted to train members of the Kurdistan Workers Party (also known as the PKK) to present their grievances for resolution by the United Nations.

1. Nina Totenberg, *High Court Backs "Material Support" Anti-Terror Law,* June 21, 2010, *available at* http://www.scpr.org/news/2010/06/21/high-court-backs-material-support-anti-terror-law/.

all criminal investigations; and Section 215 relaxes oversight of search warrants on business, medical, educational, library and bookstore records that might be related to an ongoing terrorism investigation or intelligence activity. Section 215 also contains a gag order, making it illegal for anyone served with one of these search warrants to disclose what has taken place. "These enhanced surveillance powers license law enforcement officials to peer into Americans' most private reading, research and communications," according to FEPP.

Reporters said the law's secrecy provisions hampered their ability to inform the nation about the state of the country's security. The act's reauthorization in 2006 made some of the earlier provisions permanent and expanded the government's wiretapping powers but imposed judicial oversight on some law enforcement activity. In 2008, another law designed to enhance foreign intelligence gathering increased government surveillance of U.S. residents and provided legal immunity to telecommunication companies participating in secret government surveillance.[13]

Some observers have said laws enacted following the Sept. 11, 2001, attacks and since made permanent permitted government to persecute individuals who had spoken out against government policy or who were merely associated with members of unpopular groups or "suspect" religions. Dozens of lawsuits claimed that arrests and detentions undermined fundamental civil liberties, reflected prejudice and constituted guilt by association in violation of the First Amendment

realWorld Law

Are These "Troublous" Times?

During the Civil War, Lambden P. Milligan was sentenced to death for disloyalty by a military commission. Asked to determine whether the Constitution permitted civilians to be tried under military law, the Supreme Court held that military tribunals could not exist when the civil courts were operating. Justice David Davis, writing for the Court, noted:

> . . . Wicked men, ambitious of power, with hatred of liberty and contempt of law, may fill the place once occupied by Washington and Lincoln; and if this right [to open civilian trials] is conceded, and the calamities of war again befall us, the dangers to human liberty are frightful to contemplate.
>
> . . . Time has proven the discernment of our ancestors. . . . Those great and good men foresaw that troublous times would arise, when . . . the principles of constitutional liberty would be in peril. . . . The Constitution of the United States is a law . . . equally in war and in peace, and covers with the shield of its protection all classes of men, at all times, and under all circumstances. No doctrine, involving more pernicious consequences, was ever invented by the wit of man than that any of its provisions can be suspended during any of the great exigencies of government. Such a doctrine leads directly to anarchy or despotism.[1]

1. Ex parte Milligan, 71 U.S. (4 Wall.) 2 (1866).

right to freedom of expression.[14] In contrast, the Department of Justice said the actions were essential and some restriction of liberty was necessary to ensure national security. As Chief Justice William H. Rehnquist once said, "It is neither desirable nor is it remotely likely that civil liberty will occupy as favored a position in wartime as it does in peacetime."[15]

Some Supreme Court decisions support Rehnquist's view. For example, in 1950 the Court said the First Amendment did not stop government from requiring its employees to swear loyalty oaths and reject communism.[16] And in the early 1970s, the Court said the Constitution permitted the U.S. attorney general to exclude a foreign economist from visiting and speaking at U.S. universities simply because he was a Marxist.[17] Contemporary trials for espionage and treason, challenges to the secret proceedings of foreign intelligence courts and sweeping government authority to wiretap its own citizens raise new questions about the expanse and limits of government power under the ongoing "war on terror."

SUMMARY

FIRST AMENDMENT PROTECTIONS ARE NOT ABSOLUTE. History shows that expression tends to be more susceptible to government restraints during wartime. The government may restrict the freedom of expression when it establishes a sufficiently important interest in doing so. Protecting the national security is a sufficiently important concern to outweigh speech protection under certain conditions. The Court has said, however, that the First Amendment does not allow government to silence a speaker because the government or the general public prefers not to hear comments it finds unsettling. In evaluating laws that limit speech, courts tend to balance the interests at stake, usually categorically. ∎

Court Tests to Protect Disruptive Speech

The Supreme Court has developed several tests to help it decide when speech must be protected in order to encourage robust discussion and debate and when speech may be punished. The Court has said speech and press content are not protected if they would cause imminent harm or play "no essential part of any exposition of ideas, and are of such slight social value as a step to truth that any benefit that may be derived from them is clearly outweighed by the social interest in order and morality."[18] However, the lines drawn around this category are not clear. The boundary between protected and unprotected speech is not fixed. The Court's tests afford leeway for different interpretations in response to changing circumstances.

The Clear and Present Danger Test

In 1919, Justice Oliver Wendell Holmes wrote for a unanimous Supreme Court that government had a right and a duty to prevent speech that presented a "clear and present danger" to the nation.[19] The case of *Schenck v. United States* began when Charles Schenck, a member of the Socialist Party, mailed some 15,000 anti-draft pamphlets to men in Philadelphia. The pamphlets encouraged recipients to reject the pro-war philosophy of the U.S. government and oppose U.S. participation in World War I. Schenck was convicted of violating the Espionage Act of 1917, which was one of several federal laws enacted to unify the nation behind the war effort.

In affirming Schenck's conviction, the Court said the mailing had a "bad tendency" and posed a clear and present danger to national security. Justice Holmes said ordinarily harmless words can become criminal during times of war because of the heightened danger they pose: "It is a question of proximity and degree."[20] Common sense indicates that "the most stringent protection of free speech would not protect a man in falsely shouting fire in a theatre and causing a panic." Nor would it protect an individual in a military recruitment office falsely shouting, "I have a bomb."[21]

In other cases involving the Espionage Act, Justice Holmes continued to write for a unanimous Court and affirmed the conviction of anti-war protesters for speeches and pamphlets the Court said might tend to endanger the nation. In one case, the Court upheld Jacob Frohwerk's fine and ten-year prison sentence for published writings that questioned the constitutionality of the draft and the

clear and present danger
Doctrine establishing that restrictions on First Amendment rights will be upheld if they are necessary to prevent an extremely serious and imminent harm.

merits of the war.[22] The Court said the publications presented "a little breath [that] would be enough to kindle a flame" of unrest.[23] In another, Socialist leader Eugene Debs was convicted of an attempt to cause military insubordination and to obstruct the draft for giving a speech at a Socialist convention opposing the government's war policy.[24] Debs' most direct comment was to tell listeners, "You are fit for something better than slavery and cannon fodder." In court, Debs said he abhorred war, and the jury used this statement as evidence that there was both intent and likelihood that his speech would harm the war effort.

Yet that same year, when the Court used the so-called bad-tendency standard to uphold the Sedition Act conviction of Jacob Abrams and four friends for pamphlets critical of U.S. interference in the Russian revolution and encouraging strikes at U.S. munitions factories,[25] Justice Holmes dissented. The five men had dropped leaflets from a New York City high-rise building urging workers to unite to oppose "the hypocrisy of the United States and her allies." In dissent, Justice Holmes said the "surreptitious publishing of a silly leaflet by an unknown man" did not pose a sufficiently grave and imminent danger to permit punishment.[26] The First Amendment requires government to protect diverse and loathsome opinions, he wrote, "unless they so imminently threaten immediate interference with the lawful and pressing purposes of the law that an immediate check is required to save the country."[27] This 1919 dissent by Holmes in *Abrams v. United States* marked a transformation in his interpretation of the First Amendment.

Still, the Court relied on various forms of the clear and present danger test for 50 years to affirm punishment of communists during the Red scares of the 1920s and 1950s.[28] During the 1920s, the Court affirmed the conviction of an immigrant arrested as a threat to the U.S. government. Benjamin Gitlow, the business manager of a branch of the Socialist Party, oversaw publication and distribution of party literature urging class action to establish socialism in the United States.[29] Without evidence that the pamphlets caused any harm or disruption, the trial court convicted Gitlow of criminal anarchy and sentenced him to prison for advocating the overthrow of government. In *Gitlow v. New York*, the Supreme Court upheld the conviction, finding that the pamphlets "endanger[ed] the foundations of organized government and threaten[ed] its overthrow by unlawful means."[30] The Court said the writings constituted a "revolutionary spark" that might incite a "sweeping and destructive conflagration."[31] In dissent, Justice Holmes declared, "Every idea is an incitement."[32] He said most ideas "should be given their chance and have their way" in the dialogue of a free and democratic society, and radical political advocacy should be protected by the First Amendment because the mere dissemination of ideas would not endanger the nation.

incorporation The Fourteenth Amendment concept that most of the Bill of Rights applies equally to the states.

The Court did not embrace Holmes' view, but it used *Gitlow* to expand free speech protection by establishing the doctrine of **incorporation**. The incorporation doctrine applies the Fourteenth Amendment's due process clause to limit the power of state and local governments to abridge the guarantees of the Bill of Rights.[33] In other words, incorporation prevents the states, as well as the federal government, from abridging protected First Amendment rights.

In the years leading up to U.S. involvement in World War II, the Court continued to use the clear and present danger test. In 1927, it upheld the conviction of a 64-year-old female labor activist who participated in meetings of the Communist Labor Party.[34] The majority of the Court ruled that the First Amendment did not prevent California from making it a crime for Anita Whitney merely to belong to a group—the Communist Labor Party—that advocated violence as a means to bring about political change.

The Court accepted, without evidence, that the Communist Labor Party was violent. Whitney's membership in the party was sufficient to pose a danger that was imminent and constituted a threat that was "relatively serious."[35] In his concurrence in *Whitney v. California*, Justice Louis Brandeis said a clear and present danger existed and punishment was constitutional when previous conduct suggested a group *might contemplate* advocacy of immediate serious violence.[36]

Among the Hollywood personnel who were subpoenaed as witnesses for the House Un-American Activities Committee hearings are, front L-R: Robert Kenny and Bartley Crum, attorneys for the group; Robert Rossen, Director; Waldo Salt, writer; Larry Parks, actor; Edward Dymtryk and Irving Rachel, directors; Adrian Scott, producer. Back L-R: unidentified lady and man; spectators; Ring Lardner Jr., a writer; Lardner's wife; and Richard Collins, a writer.

During the wave of anti-communist frenzy in the 1950s, the Court upheld a federal law that required labor union officers to swear they were not communists. In dissent, Justice Hugo Black expressed concern that the clear and present danger test did not sufficiently protect unpopular or radical political speech and association: "Too often it is fear which inspires such passions, and nothing is more reckless or contagious. In the resulting hysteria, popular indignation tars with the same brush all those who have ever been associated with any member of the group under attack."[37] Members of the Court increasingly questioned the utility and appropriateness of the clear and present danger test. In 1951, only a plurality of justices agreed that the Constitution allowed punishment under the Smith Act—which made it a crime to advocate the violent overthrow of the government—simply for belonging to the Communist Party.[38] The Court then established that regulation of speech is unconstitutional if it is not narrowly tailored to avoid infringing on protected speech.[39] In 1957, the Court upheld the Smith Act only after declaring that the law did not punish mere expression of government overthrow as an abstract concept.[40] Accordingly, it is constitutional to regulate speech that advocates illegal action, but government may not punish speech that simply expresses a radical political idea. This doctrine is established fully by the Court in a case involving incitement.

The *Brandenburg* (or Incitement) Test

The 50-year history of the clear and present danger test demonstrates that the test did not consistently protect innocuous speech because it was too flexible, too subjective and too easily swayed by political realities or social concerns.[41] In 1969, the Court attempted to resolve this problem by adopting a new test that drew a bright-line distinction between advocating violence as an abstract concept and inciting imminent illegal or violent activity. In *Brandenburg v. Ohio*, the Supreme Court ruled that the First Amendment protects the right to advocate but not to incite violence.[42] Speech that incites, prompts or provokes immediate violence is not protected by the First Amendment.

The case involved Clarence Brandenburg, a television repairman and Ku Klux Klan (KKK) leader, who spoke to a rally of a dozen KKK members in the woods of rural Ohio. In his speech, Brandenburg made nonspecific threats to take "revengeance" against various leaders in government. The rally was covered by a television news crew. After Brandenburg's comments were broadcast, he was convicted under a state law that made it a crime to conspire to violently overthrow government. He appealed, arguing that the conviction violated his right of free speech.

The Supreme Court readily acknowledged that Brandenburg's anti-Semitic and racist comments were highly offensive. However, the Court ruled that the First Amendment protects people's right to advocate abhorrent ideas about social, political and economic change: "Mere advocacy of the use of force or

Points of Law

The *Brandenburg* Test

In 1969, the Supreme Court replaced its rather vague "clear and present danger" standard with the *Brandenburg* test to determine when speech is sufficiently likely to prompt illegal action that it no longer warrants First Amendment protection. The *Brandenburg* incitement test allows punishment of "advocacy of illegal action" if the speech is

1. Directed toward inciting

2. Immediate violence or illegal action and

3. Is likely to produce that action.

The *Brandenburg* decision established that government may punish criticism of government or advocacy of radical ideas only when speakers intentionally incite immediate illegal activity. That remains the rule today.

violence does not remove speech from the protection of the First Amendment."[43] The teaching and expression of abstract philosophies, even those that embrace or advise the necessity of violence, were protected free speech. To ensure that government did not intrude upon this protected speech, the Court said government could not forbid or punish the advocacy of force unless the advocacy were (1) directed to and (2) were likely to (3) incite or produce imminent lawless action.[44]

SUMMARY

FOR YEARS, COURTS USED THE "clear and present danger" test, first developed early in the 20th century, to determine the proper balance between freedom of speech and harmful incitement of lawless activity. Under this loose test, courts asked whether the words used had a tendency to create the kind of danger lawmakers might constitutionally prevent. In early 20th-century rulings, the Supreme Court used the test in several First Amendment cases and frequently upheld the constitutionality of laws that overtly constrained unpopular political speech. The test was fine-tuned over the years and eventually evolved into the current *Brandenburg* test. Under *Brandenburg,* the Constitution prohibits government punishment of advocacy of an idea unless the speech is meant to and likely to produce imminent illegal action. ■

Speech Assaults

Words can cause harm unrelated to the security or stability of government. Speakers—sometimes intentionally, sometimes not—insult, denigrate and degrade others. People call each other names; they throw hateful insults and hurtful epithets in each other's faces. They threaten, they harass and they offend. They fill the streets with dissent and discontent, disturbing the tranquility with messages and symbols that challenge society's mores and values. The words and images they use alienate others, cause fear and generate conflict.

Offensive Speech

In 1971, the Supreme Court ruled directly on whether obscenity was protected under the First Amendment. The case of *Cohen v. California*[45] involved an antiwar protest by Paul Robert Cohen, who wore a jacket in the Los Angeles Courthouse bearing the phrase "Fuck the Draft." Convicted of disturbing the peace for "offensive conduct," Cohen appealed on First Amendment grounds, arguing that the conviction targeted his pure political speech. The Supreme Court acknowledged that court officials, like school administrators, have broad authority to maintain order and decorum. Nevertheless, if the speech did not disturb the court's functioning, government could not ban particular words it found offensive unless the words fell into an unprotected category, such as obscenity, incitement or fighting words.

The Court went further. In *Cohen*, the Court said the First Amendment protected both the content and the emotional value of a message. Information would have been lost, and Cohen's message would have been diluted, if he were forced to express his opposition to the war by declaring, "Please do not support the war." Meaningful protection for free speech went beyond the "cognitive content" of expression to protect its "emotive function" as well, the Court said. In other words, it is not simply *what* you say but *how* you say it that enjoys constitutional protection.

Fighting Words

The First Amendment protects people's right to say offensive, unkind and even ugly things to each other. Some argue that the ability to vent anger in words rather than in physical violence is a primary value of free speech. Free speech serves as a societal safety valve; it helps maintain civility and social stability because it provides catharsis to discontented individuals and allows them to blow off steam.[46] But the Supreme Court also recognizes that words used to vent anger may inflame tempers and "set fire to reason."[47] They do not inform; they assail. They hurt like a slap in the face.

The Supreme Court's 1942 ruling in *Chaplinsky v. New Hampshire*[48] first articulated the logic that violent listener reaction may provide the basis for limits on the freedom of speech. In response to a complaint that Walter Chaplinsky was distributing Jehovah's Witness pamphlets on the streets of Rochester, N.H., a police officer warned him to stop because he was disturbing the peace and the residents. Later in the day, as a group of people became increasingly restless in response to Chaplinsky's continuing pamphlet distribution, another officer detained Chaplinsky. On the way to the police station, they encountered the first officer, who repeated his earlier warning. Angered, Chaplinsky called the officer a "goddamned racketeer" and a "damned Fascist," for which he was convicted under a state law that said calling someone "any offensive, derisive or annoying word . . . or name, [or] mak[ing] any noise or exclamation in his presence and hearing with intent to deride, offend or annoy" while in public was punishable as a disturbance of the peace.

On appeal, the U.S. Supreme Court upheld the conviction, reasoning that the First Amendment did not protect narrow categories of speech that made no contribution to the discussion of ideas or the search for truth. While today Chaplinsky's speech may seem routine or harmless, the Court said his comments were unprotected **fighting words** that "by their very utterance inflict injury or tend to incite immediate breach of peace."[49]

In 1949, the Supreme Court heard the case of a priest whose anti-Semitic and pro-Fascist comments to a sympathetic audience riled a group gathered outside the assembly hall. When the crowd outside became increasingly violent, the police

fighting words Words not protected by the First Amendment because they cause immediate harm or illegal acts.

arrested the speaker for breach of the peace or disorderly conduct. Illinois courts upheld his conviction, ruling that the law punished only fighting words, which it defined as any behavior that "stirs the public to anger, invites dispute, brings about a condition of unrest . . . creates a disturbance or . . . molests the inhabitants in the enjoyment of peace and quiet by arousing alarm."

But the Supreme Court reversed and reasoned that "a function of free speech under our system of government is to *invite* dispute."[50] The Court in *Terminiello v. Chicago* said speech "may indeed best serve its high purpose when it induces a condition of unrest, creates dissatisfaction with conditions as they are, or even stirs people to anger."[51] Such speech is protected by the First Amendment "unless shown likely to produce a clear and present danger of a serious substantive evil that rises far above public inconvenience, annoyance or unrest."[52] Subsequent Supreme Court rulings[53] have confirmed that the Constitution permits government to prohibit only those face-to-face comments—including hate speech—that are inherently likely to trigger a group reaction of disorder and violence.

Fighting Words

Under the Supreme Court's fighting words doctrine, the First Amendment does not protect words that:

... Are directed at an individual
... That automatically inflict emotional harm or trigger violence.

Hate Speech

More contemporary concerns about the harms caused by intolerance, racism and bigotry have generated state and local speech codes to regulate so-called **hate speech,** but these laws generally have been found unconstitutional. Courts have not defined hate speech, but it is commonly understood to involve name-calling and pointed criticism that demeans others on the basis of race, color, gender, ethnicity, sexual preference, religion, national origin, disability, intellect or the like. Few cases dealing squarely with hate speech have reached the Supreme Court, but lower courts consistently have found anti-bias and anti-hate speech laws unconstitutional.

The primary Supreme Court decision dealing with hate speech, *R.A.V. v. City of St. Paul,* involved several white teenage boys who, late one night, made a crude wooden cross from a broken chair and set it ablaze in the yard of a black family living in the neighborhood of one of the boys.[54] They were convicted of violating a St. Paul, Minn., statute that punished the display of symbols or objects—such as a burning cross—that arouse "anger, alarm or resentment in others on the basis of race, color, creed, religion or gender." The Minnesota Supreme Court upheld the conviction, reasoning that the bias-motivated crime statute punished only unprotected fighting words. The U.S. Supreme Court reversed.

While the members of the Court voted unanimously in *R.A.V.* that the ordinance was unconstitutional, the justices did not agree as to why. Five justices said the law was too narrow, or **underinclusive,** because it punished only a specific subset of fighting words that the government found particularly objectionable. Thus, the law imposed unconstitutional **viewpoint-based discrimination** because it censored expression on the basis of the message expressed. It punished certain

hate speech A category of speech that includes name-calling and pointed criticism that demeans others on the basis of race, color, gender, ethnicity, religion, national origin, disability, intellect or the like.

underinclusive A First Amendment doctrine that disfavors narrow laws that target a subset of a recognized category for discriminatory treatment.

viewpoint-based discrimination Government censorship or punishment of expression based on the ideas or attitudes expressed. Courts will apply a strict scrutiny test to determine whether the government acted constitutionally.

forms of racist speech (cross burnings) but not others, such as homophobic or sexist speech, for example. In contrast, the remaining four justices said the law was overbroad; it punished too much speech, not too little. They said the law unconstitutionally went beyond fighting words to punish speech that did not arise in face-to-face encounters and whose only harm was to prompt "generalized reactions" of hurt feelings, resentment or offense. Since *R.A.V.*, most efforts to tailor a constitutional hate speech ordinance have failed.

Current Standard

In the past 60 years, the Supreme Court has shied away from directly applying the fighting words category to determine the expanse of constitutional protection for free speech. Instead, the Court has tended to judge the constitutionality of laws that attempt to regulate highly volatile speech directed at specific individuals on the basis of the reach of the law. The Court has struck down a variety of laws that attempt to punish specific categories of extremely offensive speech on the grounds that the laws are not sufficiently narrowly tailored to prevent intrusion on protected speech. In one such ruling, the Court re-articulated the category of fighting words and said this type of speech sometimes does warrant protection by the First Amendment. In 1992, the Court wrote:

> Our cases [on fighting words] surely do not establish the proposition that the First Amendment imposes no obstacle whatsoever to regulation of particular instances of such proscribable expression, so that the government "may regulate [them] freely." . . . Such a simplistic, all-or-nothing-at-all approach to First Amendment protection is at odds with common sense and with our jurisprudence as well. It is not true that "fighting words" have at most a "di minimus" expressive content, or that their content is in all respects "worthless and undeserving of constitutional protection"; sometimes they are quite expressive indeed. We have not said that they constitute "no part of the expression of ideas," but only that they constitute "no essential part of any expression of ideas." . . . [T]he unprotected features of [fighting] words are, despite their verbal character, essentially a "nonspeech" element of communication.

Given this and other similar Supreme Court decisions, the precise level of protection the Constitution affords fighting words is unclear. The most relevant decisions suggest that speech loses its constitutional protection when the speaker intends to provoke violence or incite unrest.

Intimidation and Threats

But what happens when speech is more than merely offensive or intolerant? At what point can government punish speakers because the message they convey is sufficiently detrimental to important competing interests?

In 2003, the Supreme Court helped answer some of the questions regarding offensive speech in another case involving cross burning. In *Virginia v. Black,* the Court ruled that states may punish Ku Klux Klansmen and others who set crosses ablaze if the intent is to intimidate someone.[55] The Court said the First Amendment permits states to target a specific set of fighting words, such as cross burnings, when the speech constitutes a true threat because it is "inextricably intertwined" with a clear and pervasive history of violence. The Court said a burning cross is such a powerful and threatening instrument of racial terror and impending violence that its ability to intimidate overshadows free speech concerns. Justice Clarence Thomas dissented to argue that the law punished only illegal acts and therefore was unrelated to First Amendment concerns: "Those who hate cannot terrorize and intimidate to make their point."[56]

Former U.S. Supreme Court Justice Sandra Day O'Connor, who wrote the 2003 majority opinion in *Virginia v. Black,* works in her Supreme Court offices in 2007.

true threat Speech directed toward one or more specific individuals with the intent of causing listeners to fear for their safety.

Writing for a slim majority of the Court, Justice Sandra Day O'Connor reasoned that despite the inextricable connection between cross burnings and the KKK's "reign of terror in the South," history alone does not transform merely offensive speech into unprotected threats or intimidation. For speech to become punishable as a true threat, a speaker must (1) direct the threat toward one or more individuals (2) with the intent of causing the listener(s) (3) to fear bodily harm or death.[57] In this case, the majority reasoned that cross burning was constitutionally punishable because the virulent intimidation of a burning cross is intended to create pervasive fear of violence in the targeted individual or group. It is not clear whether *Black* redefines and reinvigorates the category of fighting words by tying this unprotected form of speech to historic oppression and violence or whether it establishes a new category of punishable expression: true threats that intimidate.

The concept of true threat had been tested previously in a federal trial court when a University of Michigan student posted an allegedly fictional story on the Internet in 1994. The story graphically described the torture, rape and murder of a woman. The woman had the same name as one of the author's female classmates. The student author was arrested and jailed for violating a federal law making it a crime to transmit any communication containing a threat to injure another person across a state line. The court dismissed the case, finding that the Internet message did not amount to a true threat.[58] The federal district court said a punishable threat must be unequivocal, unconditional, immediate and specific.

In this case, nothing suggested any imminent prospect that the author intended to carry out the "threat";[59] nothing in the story suggested the "threatened"

Points of Law

Is That a Threat?

In everyday life and common sense, we know what a threat is. A threat is a message a reasonable speaker would expect the listener to interpret as a sincere expression of the intent to do serious harm.

Although the Constitution does not explicitly exclude threats from First Amendment protection, some 60 years ago the U.S. Supreme Court defined a threat as an "utterance in a context of violence [that] can lose its significance as an appeal to reason and become part of an instrument of force ... [and that is] not meant to be sheltered by the Constitution."[1]

In *Virginia v. Black,* a decision one observer said "simply invented the category"[2] of true threats, the Court held that punishment of true threats is acceptable under the Constitution. The Court said a punishable threat exists if:

- The speaker intended the statement to be a threat; and

- The statement, taken in context, conveys the speaker's intention to do bodily harm to the target.

In a range of decisions,[3] the Court identified several rationales for government punishment of truly threatening speech. They include:

- Protecting individuals from the fear of violence

- Protecting society from the disruptive effects of violent threats

- Pre-empting the violence threatened by the speaker;[4] and

- Preventing coercion of the target of threats.

---

1. Milk Wagon Drivers Union of Chic. v. Meadowmoor Dairies, 312 U.S. 287, 293 (1941), emphasis added.
2. Kenneth Karst, *Threats and Meanings: How the Facts Govern First Amendment Doctrine,* 58 STAN. L. REV. 1337, 1346 (2006).
3. *See, e.g.,* Virginia v. Black, 538 U.S. 343 (2003); Schenck v. Pro-Choice Network of Western New York, 519 U.S. 357, 373 (1997); Madsen v. Women's Health Center, 512 U.S. 753, 773 (1994); R.A.V. v. St. Paul, 505 U.S. 377 (1992); NAACP v. Claiborne Hardware, 458 U.S. 886 (1982); Watts v. United States, 394 U.S. 705, 708 (1969). *See also* Chaplinsky v. New Hampshire, 315 U.S. 568 (1942) (providing the concept of words that "by their very utterance inflict injury").
4. R.A.V. v. St. Paul, 505 U.S. 377, 388 (1992).

violence would even occur.[60] The court said that while dissemination of a message over the Internet may communicate potentially harmful ideas to a vast and varied audience, "may complicate analysis, and may sometimes require new or modified laws, it does not in this instance qualitatively change the analysis under the statute or under the First Amendment."[61]

The Internet was involved in another court ruling on true threats that began after several abortion clinics in the United States were bombed and several doctors associated with clinics were murdered in the 1990s. At least three of the murdered doctors previously had been identified on "unWANTED" posters produced by the American Coalition of Life Activists (ACLA). The posters said the doctors were "extremely dangerous to women and children" and were "guilty" of "crimes against humanity." They offered $5,000 rewards to people who helped

realWorld Law

Text Threats

In 2010, a Maryland Court of Appeals ruled that comments posted by Walter C. Abbott, Jr., on a state website soliciting feedback to the governor might be punishable under a valid state law making it a crime to threaten state officials.[1] Convicted for "knowingly and willfully mak[ing] a threat to take the life of, kidnap, or cause physical injury to a State official or local official," Abbott appealed and argued that he "meant no harm" with a message he claimed was merely "political hyperbole."

In an e-mail laced with obscenities and typing errors, Abbott provided his real name and address and identified himself as "president" of an organization called "FUCKING SOLD OUT AMERICAN." After saying he was losing his wife, his home and his business due to wrong-headed government policies, Abbott wrote:

> If I ever get close enough to you, I will rap [sic] my hands around your throat and strangle the life from you. This will solve many problems for true AMERICANS. Maybe you can send your MEXICAN army after me, you no good AMERICAN SELL OUT PIECE OF SHIT. I HOPE YOU DROP DEAD BEFORE I GET TO YOU, I WOULD HATE TO LOSE MY LIFE BECAUSE OF A PIECE OF SHIT LIKE YOU.

Although Abbott's e-mail met the law's target of a "threat in any written form," the appeals court remanded the case because the trial court had failed to advise the jury "how to determine whether [Abbott's] communication amounted to a threat, or instruct that only a 'true threat' violates the statute."

---

1. Abbott v. State, 989 A.2d 795 (Md. App. 2010).

the doctors "leave" their professions. ACLA's printed materials suggested that a mafia-type "contract" should be taken out on abortion providers whose "crimes" were compared to the Nazi extermination of Jews during World War II. The ACLA website listed 200 "abortionists" and approximately 200 other supporters of abortion. Color coding identified these individuals as "working," "wounded" or "fatality." The three murdered doctors were listed, with their names struck through to identify them as fatalities.

Four doctors, whose names, addresses and family member information appeared on the website and the posters, sued under a federal law that made it a crime to intentionally intimidate abortion providers with a threat of force. They said they feared for their lives and were afraid to continue practicing medicine. A jury found the ACLA guilty of intentionally threatening to harm the doctors as a means to stop them from providing legal medical services. On appeal, a federal court of appeals initially upheld both the decision and a permanent injunction preventing ACLA from publishing or posting threats against abortion doctors.[62] The court remanded for review an award of more than $100 million in damages. Sitting en banc, the U.S. Court of Appeals for the Ninth Circuit held that true threats arise not from the use of specific words but from the meaning of a message interpreted in context. When speech such as this, taken in context, is intended and likely to convey a threat of serious harm to a reasonable person, it is not protected by the First Amendment.

SUMMARY

THE CONSTITUTION PROTECTS THE RIGHT TO express ideas in an offensive manner because effective speech has both cognitive and emotional content. While the First Amendment protects most forms of offensive speech, the Supreme Court has established fighting words as a disfavored category of speech. It has said that efforts to regulate such disfavored speech must be well tailored to the government's objectives. The Court has suggested that laws that target highly offensive speech are constitutional only if they are extremely narrowly tailored to address real and demonstrable harms. The Supreme Court has not established "hate speech" as a specific category of speech. The Court's most relevant decisions suggest that attempts to prohibit unpopular or racist speech as a subset of fighting words will rarely be constitutional. The Supreme Court generally has said the Constitution prohibits punishment for vague statements with distant or speculative harms, but in recent years the Court has developed the concept of "true threats." When speech becomes an overt act of threat or intimidation it may be regulated. ∎

Symbolic Speech

Much speech that could anger or upset people may not cross the line into hate speech, fighting words, threats or incitement. Sometimes it doesn't even take the form of words. Nonverbal expression, in the form of burning flags, wearing armbands or marching through the public streets, are all parts of what the Supreme Court has called "symbolic speech." The Court has said symbolic speech deserves First Amendment protection in some cases, but it has rejected "the view that an apparently limitless variety of conduct can be labeled speech whenever the person engaging in the conduct intends thereby to express his idea."[63] Only actions that are "closely akin to 'pure speech'" are viewed as symbolic speech.[64]

Some of the most vehement and heated debate in recent memory involved symbolic speech during the 1960s, at the height of the civil rights movement and protests against the Vietnam War. In general, the Constitution protected the right of members of protest groups to express the most radical and unpopular political ideas. However, there were limits, and the line between protected political protest and illegal activity, incitement or fighting words was not always obvious.

Burning Speech

In the first of these cases (which is discussed and excerpted in Chapter 2), the Supreme Court affirmed the power of government to punish David Paul O'Brien for burning his draft card in violation of a federal law intended to facilitate the military draft and the ongoing war effort. The *O'Brien* ruling established intermediate scrutiny as the proper review of content-neutral laws that incidentally infringe on protected speech. In affirming O'Brien's conviction, the Court focused on why the government enacted the law and how the law operated while acknowledging the expressive content of the public destruction of a draft card.[65]

Some 15 years later, the Court reviewed another case of political protest involving symbolic speech. Gregory Lee Johnson had been convicted, sentenced to a year in prison and fined $2,000 for desecration of a venerated object, for burning the American flag during a protest at the 1984 Republican National Convention in Dallas. In *Texas v. Johnson,* the Supreme Court employed strict scrutiny to strike down a Texas law that made it a crime to desecrate the flag.[66] The state of Texas said its ban on flag desecration preserved an important symbol of national unity and helped prevent breaches of the peace. Johnson challenged the law and argued that it violated his right to free speech. After determining that flag burning was a form of symbolic speech, the Supreme Court ruled that the Texas law prohibiting flag desecration was unconstitutional.

A sharply divided Supreme Court held that the law failed to pass strict scrutiny because it served no compelling interest. The state's interest was insufficient to justify the law's content-based suppression of speech. In fact, the government interest in preserving the sanctity of the flag represented an unconstitutional attempt to punish ideas the government disliked. The law's sole purpose was to prohibit expression the state found offensive. "If there is a bedrock principle underlying the First Amendment," Justice William Brennan wrote for the Court, "it is that the government may not prohibit the expression of an idea simply because society finds the idea itself offensive or disagreeable."[67] The law was unconstitutional because it failed to serve a compelling interest and it did not use the least intrusive means to advance its goals.

The Constitution also protects exaggeration, hyperbole and excess in speech by considering the context of the speech to determine whether government may punish protest. For example, the Court said an antiwar protester's comment to fellow marchers that "we'll take the fucking street later" did not present the clear and present danger of violence required under the *Brandenburg* test because it was unlikely to prompt any immediate action.[68]

SUMMARY

THE COURT HAS RECOGNIZED THAT CERTAIN symbolic acts are a form of speech that implicates the First Amendment. Rulings on speech acts suggest that nondisruptive political protest is generally protected from government regulation. One exception was a draft card-burning case in which the Supreme Court upheld criminal punishment on the grounds that the cards were vital to the efficient operation of the draft and the military. ∎

Speech in the Schools

There is nothing in the wording of the First Amendment itself to suggest that it protects the rights of minors, public-school students or campus media differently from the rights of other speakers and members of the press. However, society does have unique interests in protecting and educating its youth. Sometimes courts have accepted the idea that the nation's interest in raising its young people outweighs the free speech rights of public-school students.

Courts have struggled for nearly a century to determine both how and where to draw the line between advancing the important concerns of parents and educators and protecting the freedom of speech and association of children, students or others in the public educational system. In fact, the courts have not developed a consistent approach to decide when, or whether, student press and speech are protected. The Supreme Court generally has viewed public schools and universities—including school-sponsored events, publications, funding and physical spaces—as limited public forums. Under public forum doctrine, discussed in Chapter 2, schools may impose reasonable content-neutral time, place and manner regulations on student speech activities to advance educational objectives. What this means in practice is that schools and universities may adopt regulations to achieve their educational goals even if the rules incidentally limit the freedom of speech of students and teachers. However, school officials generally may not dictate the content of student speech except to prevent speech that would directly undermine the educational missions of the school.

The standards for what speech may and may not be regulated by schools depend upon the age, impressionability and maturity of the students; the place in which the expression occurs; and the specific educational goals of the institution. As a result, the standards applied to primary schools, high schools and universities differ. The standards also differ, for example, between a school-run high school newspaper and a university student's speech during an open public debate.

Court distinctions based on differences among student speakers and types of speech are not always clear-cut. The political unrest and security of the nation also play a part. As one Court observer noted: "The very concept of academic freedom is under fire. In the aftermath of the Sept. 11 attacks, public reaction to the dangers of international terrorism generated an atmosphere of intolerance for political dissent" inside the schools as well as outside.[69] Public schools may regulate, among other things, the clothing of students, the hours facilities may be used by outsiders, the school-related expression of teachers and the content of school-sponsored student speech and publications. Rules affecting expression in public schools generally are constitutional as long as the policies neither (1) limit expressive content that is compatible with the school's educational priorities nor (2) target specific content without a strong educational justification.

The Court tends to protect the free speech and free press rights of university students as an essential part of the educational experience. The university and, to a lesser degree, its faculty control the content of the curriculum. Otherwise, university policies and procedures generally must provide a neutral platform for

Points of Law

Non-university Student Speech

In an array of cases on student expression in the past century, the Court generally has approached non-university student speech cases in one of three ways:

1. Is the speech disruptive? If the speech disrupts the functioning of the public school or violates the rights and interests of other students, it may be regulated.[1]

2. Is the speech of low value? If the speech is lewd or if it conflicts with the school's pedagogical goals or public values, it may be regulated.[2]

3. Is the speech sponsored by the school and therefore perceived to reflect the school's official position and attitude? If the speech occurs in a school-sponsored forum or event, if it is part of the school's official curriculum, or if it appears to entangle the school with a particular religious viewpoint, it may be regulated.[3]

---

1. *See, e.g.,* Tinker v. Des Moines Independent Community School District, 393 U.S. 503, 509 (1969).
2. *See, e.g.,* Bethel School District v. Fraser, 478 U.S. 675 (1986); Hazelwood v. Kuhlmeier, 484 U.S. 260 (1988).
3. *See, e.g.,* Hazelwood v. Kuhlmeier, 484 U.S. 260 (1988); Lemon v. Kurtzman, 403 U.S. 602 (1971); Board of Regents of the Univ. of Wisc. v. Southworth, 529 U.S. 217 (2000).

broad student discussion of issues.[70] The Court has refused to grant university administrators "the same degree of deference" it grants to high school administrators to regulate student expression[71] because college students are "less impressionable than younger students"[72] and because the free speech rights of public school students are "not automatically coextensive with the rights of adults in other settings."[73] Although courts tend to defer to the expertise of school authorities to determine the proper boundaries of speech in the public school environment, they generally require universities to justify speech-intrusive rules.

Protest in the Schools

In 1969, the Court reviewed a case involving symbolic anti-war protest and handed down its foundational decision establishing the school classroom as a location that is "peculiarly the marketplace of ideas." The case of *Tinker v. Des Moines Independent Community School District*[74] began with junior and senior high school students silently wearing black armbands to school to protest the Vietnam War. The three students did not act out or disrupt classes, but the school suspended them for violating a new school policy prohibiting the wearing of black armbands, which was a common means of opposing the war. The students sued, claiming the suspensions violated their right to free speech.

In what has been called "the most important Supreme Court case in history protecting the constitutional rights of students,"[75] the Court in *Tinker* agreed with the students. The Court said the symbolic expression of the armbands was "akin to pure speech" and was protected under the First Amendment.[76] When novel or deviant issues are expressed, the First Amendment must weigh heavily in favor of the expression and against the bureaucratic urge to suppress. Without any evidence that the armbands disrupted education, the school did not have a sufficient interest to justify the rule. Officials could not suppress student expression simply to avoid unpleasantness or discomfort or because of some vague fear that disruption might occur. School administrators did not have authority to control the students' silent political expression unless that expression materially or substantially disrupted the school's educational activities, which it did not.[77]

In addition, the school's decision to ban only the armbands but not other potentially disruptive expressive symbols suggested that the administration was attempting to exclude disfavored viewpoints. This was patently unconstitutional, the Court said. Although school administrators have broad authority to establish rules of conduct, the Constitution prohibits them from limiting free speech to "only that which the State chooses to communicate."[78] The Constitution makes it "unmistakable" that individuals do not "shed their constitutional rights to freedom of speech or expression at the schoolhouse gate."[79]

Until 2007, the rule was clear: Only when protests inside or adjacent to the school during school hours disrupt school activities may they be punished. While the Supreme Court had upheld content-neutral regulations intended to prevent disruptive protests on school grounds during school hours,[80] it was the Court's 2007 ruling in *Morse v. Frederick* that crafted a new standard for student speech law. In *Morse,* the Court held that the "substantial disruption" rule established in *Tinker* was not the only acceptable basis for restricting student speech.[81]

The case began in 2002, when high school senior Joseph Frederick, with the assistance of several others, displayed a 14-foot-long banner reading "Bong Hits 4 Jesus" during a school field trip to watch the Olympic torch pass through Juneau, Alaska. Frederick said he did it for a laugh and to get himself on TV. The school's principal, Deborah Morse, apparently was not laughing when she told him to take the banner down. He refused. She tore down the sign and suspended him for 10 days, asserting that the banner violated a school policy banning the advocacy of illegal drug use. Frederick sued, alleging that the principal had violated his right to free speech. The district court sided with the principal, but the U.S. Court of Appeals for the Ninth Circuit reversed, ruling that school officials may not "punish and censor non-disruptive" speech by students at school-sponsored events simply because they object to the message.

In a 5–4 ruling, the Supreme Court again reversed. The Court held that school officials may prohibit messages that advocate illegal drug use without running afoul of the First Amendment. Writing for the majority, Chief Justice John Roberts confirmed that students do not lose their right to freedom of speech inside schools but said the freedom of student speech does not extend to speech that directly contravenes an important school anti-drug policy. The majority flatly rejected the dissent's contention that the case implicated political speech, noting that Frederick's banner played no role in any "political debate" over the national war on drugs. Instead, the Court reasoned that the "special environment" and the educational mandate of the schools permitted officials to prohibit student speech that raises a "palpable" danger to established school policy.

In this case, Justice Roberts wrote, "failing to act would send a powerful message to the students . . . about how serious the school was about the dangers of illegal drug use. The First Amendment does not require schools to tolerate at school events student expression that contributes to those dangers."[82] The dissent—concerned about a possible expansion of the majority's exception to student free speech rights—said the Court's ruling amounted to viewpoint discrimination. Justice John Paul Stevens also argued that "the Court's ham-handed, categorical approach is deaf to the constitutional imperative to permit unfettered debate, even among high-school students."[83]

Young people gather beneath 18-year-old Joseph Frederick's banner at a public, school-sponsored event in Juneau, Alaska. In *Morse v. Frederick,* the U.S. Supreme Court in 2007 upheld the right of the school officials to punish student speech that promotes illegal drug use.

Today, school officials have greater latitude than previously to sanction non-disruptive speech.

Offensive or Inappropriate Content

Some 30 years ago, the Court said students' free speech rights prevented schools from removing books from the school library simply because someone might find them offensive.[84] The school board of the Island Trees Union Free School District in New York state, on its own initiative, removed 10 books from the school libraries. The board removed the books despite the recommendation of a library review committee who said the volumes were appropriate and educationally suitable. Some of the board members said the books, which they had not reviewed, were "objectionable," "anti-American, anti-Christian, anti-[Semitic], and just plain filthy."[85] Several students sued.

The Supreme Court said the book removal violated the First Amendment. Although schools must exercise oversight of curriculum to assure an age-appropriate, quality education for students, school authority does not extend to the summary removal of books from the school library simply to placate a few hypersensitive individuals. The Court distinguished between required classroom reading and optional readings available in the school's library for selection by individual students. If students are compelled to read a specific book, schools

realWorld Law

You Can't Read This!

Each year the American Library Association and other groups sponsor Banned Books Week to encourage citizens to vigilantly protect their constitutional right to read.[1]

Banned Books Week focuses national attention on ongoing attempts by parents, students, residents and school faculty and administrators to ban hundreds of books each year from U.S. public schools. Those challenging particular books generally argue that their content is inappropriate for school-aged children.

A Radcliffe listing of the top 100 novels of the 20th century names 43 of its selected titles as books that have been challenged or banned in U.S. public schools.[2] Challenged titles include works ranging from the Bible to John Steinbeck's "Of Mice and Men." In recent years, the most frequent challenges have been leveled against the popular "Harry Potter" series of fantasy books by J.K. Rowling. Complaints assert that the books promote witchcraft and paganism. Other frequently challenged titles include Mark Twain's "The Adventures of Huckleberry Finn" for racist language; "It's Perfectly Normal," a sex education book by Robie Harris, for its explicit and graphic treatment of sex; "I Know Why the Caged Bird Sings" by Maya Angelou, for its depiction of her rape as a child; and "The Color Purple," by Alice Walker, for offensive language and its portrayal of homosexuality.

1. American Library Association, *Banned Books Week—Celebrating the Freedom to Read,* July 2006, *available at* http://www.ala.org/ala/pio/mediarelationsa/factsheets/bannedbooksweek.cfm.
2. American Library Association, *Banned and/or Challenged Books from the Radcliffe Publishing Course Top 100 Novels of the 20th Century,* n.d., *available at* http://www.ala.org/ala/oif/bannedbooksweek/bbwlinks/reasonsbanned.cfm.

may exercise greater sensitivity and responsiveness. However, when—as in this case—students voluntarily choose to read particular books, the Court said that "access [to controversial materials] prepares students for active and effective participation in the pluralistic, often contentious society in which they will soon be adult members."[86]

The Court did not suggest, however, that public schools must purchase highly controversial books for inclusion in their libraries. Nor did it say schools cannot remove books for good reason. Rather, the Court said decisions to remove books must not be made "in a narrowly partisan or political manner."[87] Such decisions were more likely to be constitutional if they advanced a curricular purpose, responded to a real educational disruption and did not unduly limit or bias student access to ideas.

The issue of mandatory exposure to offensive speech in public schools arose in 1986 in *Bethel School District v. Fraser.*[88] In 1983, Matthew Fraser gave a speech nominating one of his classmates for student government. Nearly 600 high school students, including some 14-year-olds, attended the assembly, which was a required, school-sponsored activity. Throughout his speech, Fraser somewhat cleverly used metaphors for male sexual virility to describe the candidate. The assistant principal said the speech violated a school policy forbidding profanity and obscenity that "materially and substantially interferes with the educational process." She suspended Fraser for three days and said he could not be a candidate for graduation speaker.

Fraser challenged the action as a violation of his First Amendment rights. On review, the Supreme Court affirmed the punishment. The Court said that when student speech occurs during a school-sponsored event, the student's liberty of speech may be curtailed to protect the school's educational purpose, especially when young students are in the audience. This was particularly true if the forum for the student speech suggested that the student were speaking for the school.

In *Fraser*, the Court said eliminating vulgarity and profanity from school events advanced the obligation of schools to "inculcate . . . habits and manners of civility."[89] Rather than view student First Amendment rights as paramount, the Court said it was "perfectly appropriate" for a school to impose student sanctions to disassociate the school from speech that threatened its core purpose.

Hazelwood East High School principal Robert Reynolds holds a copy of the school newspaper, Spectrum, after the Supreme Court ruled that school administrators did not violate the First Amendment when they censored the student publication.

A case involving students in the journalism class at Hazelwood East High School presented related issues. The class published a student newspaper, Spectrum, under the supervision of a faculty adviser, who reviewed the content. The principal also reviewed each issue before publication, but school policy said students enjoyed freedom of "responsible" speech.

In 1983, the principal removed two pages of the newspaper that contained a story about teen pregnancy at Hazelwood and another about the impact of divorce on students at the school. Pregnant students and children of divorced parents were interviewed for the stories. The principal said the stories invaded the privacy of the students and their parents, contained material inappropriate for younger students in the school and were biased and poorly researched. Other stories that appeared on the same pages as the articles in question were also cut from the paper to expedite printing of the newspaper before the school year ended.

Student staffers challenged the removal as an unconstitutional violation of their freedom of speech and press. The trial court rejected their challenge, but the court of appeals sided with the students, saying the school could edit the newspaper's content only to avoid legal liability, not to advance grammatical, journalistic or social values.

In *Hazelwood v. Kuhlmeier,* the Supreme Court reversed and said school administrators, not student reporters and editors, have authority to determine the appropriate content of a school-sponsored student newspaper.[90] When a school creates and supervises a forum for student speech, such as a student assembly or a teacher-supervised student newspaper, the school endorses that speech and is not only permitted but required to control the content to achieve educational goals, the Court said.[91] Schools are not only free from any obligation to "promote particular student speech"[92] but must exercise their supervisory function to promote a positive educational environment in all "school-sponsored publications, theatrical productions and other expressive activities that students, parents and members of the public might reasonably perceive to bear the imprimatur of the school."[93]

In a footnote, however, the Court said its decision did not address the freedoms enjoyed by the university student press.[94]

Compelled Orthodoxy

The U.S. Supreme Court has said, "The right to speak and the right to refrain from speaking are complementary components of the broader concept of individual freedom of mind."[95] Accordingly, government may not force citizens to express ideas with which they disagree.

More than 60 years ago, students who were Jehovah's Witnesses used this rationale to challenge a policy mandating the daily flag salute and pledge of allegiance in school as a violation of their religious beliefs. The Court agreed.[96] Despite the important role of public schools in teaching students civic values and responsibilities,[97] schools may not indoctrinate students into particular ideologies or silence teachers who wish to speak out on issues of public concern, the Court said.[98] Compulsory saluting of the American flag is unconstitutional because the requirement enables government to dictate a particular belief and a certain attitude of mind.[99]

"If there is any fixed star in our constitutional constellation," the Court wrote, "it is that no official, high or petty, can prescribe what shall be orthodox in politics, nationalism, religion or other matters of opinion or force citizens to confess by word or act their faith therein."[100] Unless schools demonstrate that failure to salute the flag (or to engage in other compelled speech) presents a grave threat to the functioning of the school, forced speech violates the students' First Amendment freedom of belief and association and "invade[s] the sphere of intellect and spirit" vital to self-expression and self-fulfillment.[101]

The ban on most government-enforced slogans and indoctrination applies both inside and outside the schools. Using reasoning similar to its analysis in establishment cases, the Supreme Court said that a "service charge" levied by a teacher's union upon its members to fund ideological activities that some members opposed was unconstitutional.[102]

Religion in the Schools

While some Americans would argue that teaching religion advances the interests of public education and helps inculcate important social values, others argue that any introduction of religion into schoolhouses violates the First Amendment's **establishment clause.** The establishment clause prohibits government from establishing an official religion or using its regulatory powers to advance specific religious beliefs. Sometimes it is difficult to distinguish the right of free speech from the related First Amendment right to the free exercise of religious choice. Because speech and religion can be intimately intertwined, some recent Supreme Court decisions attempting to protect students' right to exercise their personal religious preferences while prohibiting school endorsement of religion offer some guidance on the boundaries of protected student expression. In its student religious speech cases, the Court has made clear that schools may not indoctrinate religious beliefs through the curriculum but must provide a neutral platform that permits students to engage in private religious expression to the extent that it does not conflict with or disrupt effective functioning of the schools.[103]

A Texas case decided in 2000 is illustrative. A school policy allowed students to elect a student chaplain to deliver invocations before football games. The message was nonsectarian, nondenominational and written by the student. Nonetheless, the Court said a school policy to compel a religious message at school events was unconstitutional. The Court reasoned, "The delivery of [a student] message—over a school's public address system, by a speaker representing the student body, under the supervision of school faculty and pursuant to a school policy . . .—is not properly characterized as 'private' speech."[104] Instead, the Court said, the invocation was school speech for which the government was responsible.

As an official expression of the school, the invocation, or prayer, impermissibly advanced a religious activity at a school event and created an unconstitutional establishment of religion. In dissent, then-Chief Justice William Rehnquist said the majority of the Court had failed to understand the "crucial difference between government speech endorsing religion, which the establishment clause forbids, and private speech endorsing religion, which the free speech and free exercise clauses protect."[105] That distinction remains unclear.

establishment clause The portion of the First Amendment that prohibits government from setting up an official religion or passing laws that favor a specific religious doctrine.

Campus Speech

The Supreme Court has established that universities have a greater obligation to create and maintain forums for broad public discussion than do the public schools. Thus, as mentioned in Chapter 2, when a university's funding "program [is] designed to facilitate private speech," the funding creates a public forum that prohibits government control of the content of the speech.[106] Consequently, neither the students who contribute the fees nor the university administrators who oversee their allocation may discriminate among student groups because of the ideas they express.[107] Public universities must fund all student groups on the basis of the same content-neutral policies.

In 2000, the Court upheld a University of Wisconsin policy to use mandatory student fees to fund an array of student organizations, including organizations with political or ideological objectives opposed by some students who paid the fees. The Court said the fees established a public forum, and the university was obliged to support all student expression without consideration of content. Writing in concurrence, Justice David Souter said the power of school authorities "to limit expressive freedom of students . . . is confined to high schools, whose students and their schools' relation to them are different and at least arguably distinguishable from their counterparts in college education."[108]

More than a quarter-century ago, the Supreme Court held that the expulsion of a graduate student for distributing a campus newspaper containing what university officials labeled "indecent speech" violated her First Amendment rights.[109] University of Missouri School of Journalism student Barbara Papish, 32, distributed an issue of the Free Press Underground that contained a political cartoon depicting policemen raping the Statue of Liberty and the Goddess of Justice and an article under the title, "M—f—Acquitted." The student conduct board held that the newspaper violated the university's standards of conduct that prohibited "indecent conduct or speech." But in its per curiam decision in *Papish v. Board of Curators of the University of Missouri,* the U.S. Supreme Court established that "the mere dissemination of ideas—no matter how offensive to good taste—on a state university campus may not be shut off in the name alone of 'conventions of decency.'"[110]

While unpopular or inflammatory speech may disrupt the functioning of public schools, radical and unpopular speech on a university campus advances the institution's educational objectives. A university's "mission is well served if students have the means to engage in dynamic discussions of philosophical, religious, scientific, social and political subjects in their extracurricular campus life outside the lecture hall."[111] As a consequence, Justice Souter wrote, university "students are inevitably required to support the expression of personally offensive viewpoints in ways that cannot be thought constitutionally objectionable."[112] Public universities not only may but must support all messages without regard to content to enhance wide-open extracurricular debate and free speech interests.[113]

The Court reshaped this concept in 2010 when it ruled in *Christian Legal Society v. Martinez* that a California law school could deny funding and other benefits to an explicitly religious student group whose members were required to sign a statement of faith.[114] The Court said the law school's requirement that official student groups be open to "all comers" was a reasonable, viewpoint-neutral policy and advanced school interests in nondiscriminatory access for students. By denying Christian Legal Society (CLS) status as a recognized student group, the university refused to allow CLS to maintain tables at university recruitment fairs, to send bulk e-mails to all registered law students and to post messages on law school bulletin boards—benefits that clearly implicate First Amendment rights. Writing for the Court, Justice Ruth Bader Ginsburg said alternative, non-university means of

realWorld Law

Is Shouting Always "Shouting Fire"?

In 2010, members of a Muslim student association at the University of California, Irvine, disrupted a speech by shouting repeatedly, so the audience could not hear Israeli Ambassador to the United States Michael Oren's comments.

Nearly a dozen people were arrested in the incident, in which one person after another would shout until escorted out of the auditorium. Ensuing debate was polarized between those who argued that members of the "Irvine 11" were simply exercising their own right to speak and others who said the students should be expelled from the university.

"Both of these views are wrong," according to legal scholar and professor Erwin Chemerinsky.[1] "Freedom of speech never has been regarded as an absolute right to speak out at any time and in any manner." There also is no absolute right to falsely shout "Fire" in a crowded theater.

But the students did not shout anything false or incite panic or illegal activity. However, as Professor Chemerinsky observed, "[T]he government, including public universities, always can impose time, place and manner restrictions on speech." While the offense did not rise to the level justifying expulsion, the government can and should protect a speaker's rights by preventing a heckler's veto—audience reaction that silences the speaker.

---

1. Erwin Chemerinsky, *UC Irvine's Free Speech Debate*, L.A. Times, Feb. 18, 2010, *available at* http://articles.latimes.com/2010/feb/18/opinion/la-oe-chemerinsky18-2010feb18/2.

communication available to CLS "reduce[d] the importance of those [university] channels" for reaching law school students and adequately protected the group's speech interests.[115] The decision also blurred or erased the long-standing distinction between adult students and younger students by relying on *Tinker* to reason that the Court should defer to the judgment of law school administrators "in light of the special characteristics of the school environment."[116]

In dissent, Justice Samuel Alito wrote that the *Christian Legal Society* decision established that there is "no freedom for expression that offends prevailing standards of political correctness in our country's institutions of higher learning."[117] An attorney with the Student Press Law Center said the majority opinion in the Court's 5–4 ruling "could end up doing more violence to student expression rights than any decision in the last 22 years."[118]

Despite the fact that student fees, or even university allocations, support student newspapers and yearbooks, the Court generally has viewed campus publications as forums for student expression in which universities may not control content. For example, in one highly publicized case, the U.S. Court of Appeals for the Sixth Circuit said Kentucky State University could not constitutionally refuse to distribute the student yearbook because of content and aesthetic concerns.[119] Over the objections of the university, the court in *Kincaid v. Gibson* ruled that the yearbook constituted a limited public forum that must be free from university censorship. The court said the university had neither the need nor the authority to control the content of speech in this student publication.

Despite the Court's clear signals, some university administrators continue to try to influence the content of student media by pressuring faculty or staff advisers. Such efforts pose a threat to the freedom of the student press and to the diversity of viewpoints valued on university campuses. Even if courts eventually reject university authority to pressure student media to provide certain content, the university's short-term success may produce a long-term chill in student newsrooms.

In 2005, a federal appellate court said the *Hazelwood* decision could apply to college and university publications.[120] This would allow administrators to review school-sponsored publications before they were printed and distributed. The case began when the dean of student affairs at Governors State University, a public institution, said she would have to approve each issue of the student newspaper, the Innovator, before it could be published. Three students sued, claiming the dean and other administrators infringed upon the students' First Amendment rights. The court rejected that claim, saying the Supreme Court's *Hazelwood* ruling hinged on whether the paper was a designated public forum. If it is, students may make editorial decisions; if not, administrators may edit the paper. The appellate court said even if a newspaper is an extracurricular activity, as the Innovator was, and not published as a classroom exercise, the university may not be required to financially support publication of views that administrators reject.

In 2004, another fight over content of a university student newspaper involved the court-sanctioned reassignment of the paper's adviser. A federal district court reversed itself to rule that the First Amendment did not prohibit the removal of the Kansas State (University) Collegian's adviser.[121] The adviser was dismissed amid controversy over the newspaper's coverage of campus diversity issues and events, both court records and published reports show.[122] Complaints surfaced after the newspaper failed to cover the university-hosted annual Big 12 Conference on Black Student Government. Adviser Ron Johnson also had been removed from his advising post briefly in 1998 after he refused to exercise control over the newspaper's content.[123]

Editors of the Collegian joined Johnson's lawsuit claiming that the removal amounted to censorship. A letter from the head of both the journalism school and the university's publications board from 1997 to 2004 said a content analysis of the newspaper supported the recommendation to remove the adviser.[124] University administrators denied that the decision was based on displeasure with the paper's content, and members of the student publications board said the vote reflected budget concerns.[125] The Society of Professional Journalists and the Student Press Law Center both officially condemned Johnson's removal, criticized administrators who recommended the move and urged the university to reinstate the former newspaper adviser.[126]

Speech Codes

In what some considered to be a concession to political correctness[127] and others believed to be an important step toward a more tolerant and inclusive society,[128]

realWorld Law

A Conservative Take on Campus Speech?

Even before the Supreme Court's 2010 ruling in *Christian Legal Society v. Martinez*, observers argued that the Roberts Court has "moved the law sharply to the right on a number of constitutional fronts" and "limited free speech in ways that could adversely affect higher education."[1] Of particular concern, were

- The Supreme Court's 5–4 decision in *Morse v. Frederick* that affirmed the right of high school administrators to discipline an 18-year-old student for displaying a banner that read "Bong Hits 4 Jesus" at an off-campus school-supported event. Chief Justice Roberts reasoned that the school's obligation "to protect those entrusted to their care from . . . celebrating illegal drug use."[2]

- The decision in *Rumsfeld v. Forum for Academic and Institutional Rights, Inc.,* in which the Court rejected university claims that requiring campus access for U.S. military recruiters who engage in employment discrimination based on sexual orientation violated university freedoms of association and speech. The Court reasoned that recruitment is a form of conduct, not speech.[3]

An extension of these decisions "would support punishing student speech that conflicts with important institutional values, punishing faculty speech that occurs in the course of employment, and punishing the university itself if it fails to comply with external commands regarding the conduct of its auxiliary activities," according to one author.[4]

Although First Amendment pundits often make dire predictions in the wake of each new Supreme Court ruling, the Court's decision in *Christian Legal Society* may provide evidence that supports these fears.

---

1. *See* David Kairys, *Searching for the Rule of Law,* 36 SUFFOLK U. L. REV. 307, 325 (2003); Mark C. Rahdert, *Point of View: The Roberts Court and Academic Freedom,* CHRON. HIGHER EDUC., July 27, 2007,, *available at* http://chronicle.com/forums/index.
2. 127 S. Ct. 2618 (2007).
3. 547 U.S. 47 (2006).
4. Rahdert, *supra* note 1.

universities across the United States began adopting and strengthening campus speech codes in the 1980s.[129] While the codes varied widely from campus to campus, they generally prohibited verbal harassment of minorities, hate-filled invective, bigotry and offensive speech among members of the university community. Beginning in the 1990s, courts around the nation consistently and resoundingly found these codes unconstitutional because they targeted disfavored speech and reduced the flow of information and ideas.[130] As one federal district court wrote in 1989, "The Supreme Court has consistently held that statutes punishing speech or conduct solely on the grounds that they are unseemly or offensive are unconstitutionally overbroad."[131]

Despite these rulings, campus hate speech codes continue to be adopted.[132] A study conducted in 2001 found that nearly one-fifth of surveyed universities enforced some rules against hate speech on campus. The universities argue that the codes are essential to the protection of informed discourse and serve the core educational mission of universities. Courts have not found this justification sufficient to warrant abridging the First Amendment rights of those on campus. In other words, courts have not accepted the notion that limiting hateful speech enhances the diversity of ideas discussed in the university environment.

SUMMARY

SUPREME COURT PRECEDENTS ESTABLISHING the constitutional limits to regulation of threats and objectionable speech inside schools and universities are complicated, drawing fine distinctions and turning on specific facts. Case outcomes hinge on statutory language, the intensity of the threat or offense and the societal interest in either protecting vulnerable groups or permitting robust discussion. Few bright lines or broad precedents exist in this evolving area of First Amendment law. Government generally may curb the language reaching schoolchildren to advance educational goals, but universities have a greater obligation to afford forums for wide-ranging expression of opinion on campus. ∎

Cases for Study

Thinking About It

The two case excerpts that follow highlight the Supreme Court's attempts to balance the First Amendment freedom of speech with concerns for personal safety and educational goals. Both cases help identify the parameters of First Amendment protection: the first helps define when actions have sufficient expressive content and intent that they warrant constitutional protection; the second clarifies the extent to which important competing values—in this case, education of the young—may limit the freedom of speakers.

- Consider what each decision as well as the two taken together demonstrate about the different categories of speech in the Court's jurisprudence.

- In these two decisions defining the extent of First Amendment freedoms, does the Court focus on the nature of the speech, the intent of the law, the impact of the regulation or on something else to make it reach its conclusion?

- Does *Texas v. Johnson* provide a workable definition of symbolic speech and a clear test to determine when it is protected under the First Amendment?

- To what extent does the Court's decision in *Tinker* turn on the category of speech, the type of speaker, the location of speech or other factors involved?

Texas v. Johnson
SUPREME COURT OF THE UNITED STATES
491 U.S. 397 (1989)

JUSTICE WILLIAM BRENNAN delivered the Court's opinion:

. . . The First Amendment literally forbids the abridgment only of "speech," but we have long . . . acknowledged that conduct may be "sufficiently imbued with elements of communication to fall within the scope of the First and Fourteenth Amendments" . . . [when] "[a]n intent to convey a particularized message was present, and [whether] the likelihood was great that the message would be understood by those who viewed it.". . .

. . . Johnson burned an American flag as part—indeed, as the culmination—of a political demonstration. . . . The expressive, overtly political nature of this conduct was both intentional and overwhelmingly apparent. . . .

The government generally has a freer hand in restricting expressive conduct than it has in restricting the written or spoken word. . . .

[However,] the governmental interest in question [must] be unconnected to expression in order to come under *O'Brien*'s less demanding rule. . . .

. . . The State, apparently, is concerned that [flag desecration] will lead people to believe either that the flag does not stand for nationhood and national unity, but instead reflects other, less positive concepts, or that the concepts reflected in the flag do not in fact exist, that is, that we do not enjoy unity as a Nation. These concerns blossom only when a person's treatment of the flag communicates some message, and thus are related "to the suppression of free expression." . . .

. . . Johnson was not, we add, prosecuted for the expression of just any idea; he was prosecuted for his expression of dissatisfaction with the policies of this country, expression situated at the core of our First Amendment values.

Moreover, Johnson was prosecuted because he knew that his politically charged expression would cause "serious offense." . . . The Texas law is thus not aimed at protecting the physical integrity of the flag in all circumstances, but is designed instead to protect it only against impairments that would cause serious offense to others. . . .

. . . Johnson's political expression was restricted because of the content of the message he conveyed. We must therefore subject the State's asserted interest in preserving the special symbolic character of the flag to "the most exacting scrutiny.". . .

If there is a bedrock principle underlying the First Amendment, it is that the government may not prohibit the expression of an idea simply because society finds the idea itself offensive or disagreeable.

We have not recognized an exception to this principle even where our flag has been involved. . . .

. . . [N]othing in our precedents suggests that a State may foster its own view of the flag by prohibiting expressive conduct relating to it. . . .

. . . [T]heir enduring lesson, that the government may not prohibit expression simply because it disagrees with its message, is not dependent on the particular mode in which one chooses to express an idea. If we were to hold that a State may forbid flag burning wherever it is likely to endanger the flag's symbolic role, but allow it wherever burning a flag promotes that role . . . [w]e would be permitting a State to "prescribe what shall be orthodox" by saying that one may burn the flag to convey one's attitude toward it and its referents only if one does not endanger the flag's representation of nationhood and national unity. . . .

There is, moreover, no indication—either in the text of the Constitution or in our cases interpreting it—that a separate juridical category exists for the American flag alone. Indeed, we would not be surprised to learn that the persons who framed our Constitution and wrote the Amendment that we now construe were not known for their reverence for the Union Jack. The First Amendment does not guarantee that other concepts virtually sacred to our Nation as a whole—such as the principle that discrimination on the basis of race is odious and destructive—will go unquestioned in the marketplace of ideas. We decline, therefore, to create for the flag an exception to the joust of principles protected by the First Amendment.

. . . We are tempted to say, in fact, that the flag's deservedly cherished place in our community will be strengthened, not weakened, by our holding today. Our decision is a reaffirmation of the principles of freedom and inclusiveness that the flag best reflects, and of the conviction that our toleration of criticism such as Johnson's is a sign and source of our strength. . . . It is the Nation's resilience, not its rigidity, that Texas sees reflected in the flag—and it is that resilience that we reassert today.

The way to preserve the flag's special role is not to punish those who feel differently about these matters. It is to persuade them that they are wrong. . . .

. . . We do not consecrate the flag by punishing its desecration, for in doing so we dilute the freedom that this cherished emblem represents. . . . Affirmed.

JUSTICE ANTHONY KENNEDY, concurring:
. . . The hard fact is that sometimes we must make decisions we do not like. We make them because they are right, right in the sense that the law and the Constitution, as we see them, compel the result. And so great is our commitment to the process that, except in the rare case, we do not pause to express distaste for the result, perhaps for fear of undermining a valued principle that dictates the decision. This is one of those rare cases. . . .

. . . It is poignant but fundamental that the flag protects those who hold it in contempt. . . .

CHIEF JUSTICE WILLIAM REHNQUIST, with whom JUSTICE BYRON WHITE and JUSTICE SANDRA DAY O'CONNOR join, dissenting:
. . . The American flag, then, throughout more than 200 years of our history, has come to be the visible

symbol embodying our Nation. It does not represent the views of any particular political party, and it does not represent any particular political philosophy. The flag is not simply another "idea" or "point of view" competing for recognition in the marketplace of ideas. Millions and millions of Americans regard it with an almost mystical reverence regardless of what sort of social, political, or philosophical beliefs they may have. I cannot agree that the First Amendment invalidates the Act of Congress, and the laws of 48 of the 50 States, which make criminal the public burning of the flag. . . .

. . . As with "fighting words," so with flag burning, for purposes of the First Amendment: It is "no essential part of any exposition of ideas, and [is] of such slight social value as a step to truth that any benefit that may be derived from [it] is clearly outweighed" by the public interest in avoiding a probable breach of the peace. . . .

. . . The Texas statute deprived Johnson of only one rather inarticulate symbolic form of protest—a form of protest that was profoundly offensive to many—and left him with a full panoply of other symbols and every conceivable form of verbal expression to express his deep disapproval of national policy. Thus, in no way can it be said that Texas is punishing him because his hearers—or any other group of people—were profoundly opposed to the message that he sought to convey. Such opposition is no proper basis for restricting speech or expression under the First Amendment. It was Johnson's use of this particular symbol, and not the idea that he sought to convey by it or by his many other expressions, for which he was punished. . . .

. . . Surely one of the high purposes of a democratic society is to legislate against conduct that is regarded as evil and profoundly offensive to the majority of people—whether it be murder, embezzlement, pollution, or flag burning. . . .

. . . I would uphold the Texas statute as applied in this case.

JUSTICE JOHN PAUL STEVENS, dissenting:
. . . The value of the flag as a symbol cannot be measured. Even so, I have no doubt that the interest in preserving that value for the future is both significant and legitimate. . . . [S]anctioning the public desecration of the flag will tarnish its value—both for those who cherish the ideas for which it waves and for those who desire to don the robes of martyrdom by burning it. That tarnish is not justified by the trivial burden on free expression occasioned by requiring that an available, alternative mode of expression—including uttering words critical of the flag—be employed. . . .

The Court is . . . quite wrong in blandly asserting that respondent "was prosecuted for his expression of dissatisfaction with the policies of this country, expression situated at the core of our First Amendment values." Respondent was prosecuted because of the method he chose to express his dissatisfaction with those policies. Had he chosen to spray paint—or perhaps convey with a motion picture projector—his message of dissatisfaction on the facade of the Lincoln Memorial, there would be no question about the power of the Government to prohibit his means of expression. The prohibition would be supported by the legitimate interest in preserving the quality of an important national asset. Though the asset at stake in this case is intangible, given its unique value, the same interest supports a prohibition on the desecration of the American flag. . . .

I respectfully dissent.

Tinker v. Des Moines Independent Community School District
SUPREME COURT OF THE UNITED STATES
393 U.S. 503 (1969)

JUSTICE ABE FORTAS delivered the Court's opinion:
. . . The District Court recognized that the wearing of an armband for the purpose of expressing certain views is the type of symbolic act that is within the Free Speech Clause of the First Amendment. As we shall discuss, the wearing of armbands in the circumstances of this case was entirely divorced from actually or

potentially disruptive conduct by those participating in it. It was closely akin to "pure speech" which, we have repeatedly held, is entitled to comprehensive protection under the First Amendment.

First Amendment rights, applied in light of the special characteristics of the school environment, are available to teachers and students. It can hardly be argued that either students or teachers shed their constitutional rights to freedom of speech or expression at the schoolhouse gate. This has been the unmistakable holding of this Court for almost 50 years. . . .

. . . On the other hand, the Court has repeatedly emphasized the need for affirming the comprehensive authority of the States and of school officials, consistent with fundamental constitutional safeguards, to prescribe and control conduct in the schools. . . . Our problem lies in the area where students in the exercise of First Amendment rights collide with the rules of the school authorities.

The problem posed by the present case . . . does not concern aggressive, disruptive action or even group demonstrations. Our problem involves direct, primary First Amendment rights akin to "pure speech."

The school officials banned and sought to punish petitioners for a silent, passive expression of opinion, unaccompanied by any disorder or disturbance on the part of petitioners. There is here no evidence whatever of petitioners' interference, actual or nascent, with the school's work or of collision with the rights of other students to be secure and to be let alone. Accordingly, this case does not concern speech or action that intrudes upon the work of the schools or the rights of other students. . . .

. . . Outside the classrooms, a few students made hostile remarks to the children wearing armbands, but there were no threats or acts of violence on school premises.

The District Court concluded that the action of the school authorities was reasonable because it was based upon their fear of a disturbance from the wearing of the armbands. But, in our system, undifferentiated fear or apprehension of disturbance is not enough to overcome the right to freedom of expression. Any departure from absolute regimentation may cause trouble. Any variation from the majority's opinion may inspire fear. Any word spoken, in class, in the lunchroom, or on the campus, that deviates from the views of another person may start an argument or cause a disturbance. But our Constitution says we must take this risk; and our history says that it is this sort of hazardous freedom—this kind of openness—that is the basis of our national strength and of the independence and vigor of Americans who grow up and live in this relatively permissive, often disputatious, society.

In order for the State in the person of school officials to justify prohibition of a particular expression of opinion, it must be able to show that its action was caused by something more than a mere desire to avoid the discomfort and unpleasantness that always accompany an unpopular viewpoint. Certainly where there is no finding and no showing that engaging in the forbidden conduct would "materially and substantially interfere with the requirements of appropriate discipline in the operation of the school," the prohibition cannot be sustained.

. . . [T]he record fails to yield evidence that the school authorities had reason to anticipate that the wearing of the armbands would substantially interfere with the work of the school or impinge upon the rights of other students. . . .

On the contrary, the action of the school authorities appears to have been based upon an urgent wish to avoid the controversy which might result from the expression, even by the silent symbol of armbands, of opposition to this Nation's part in the conflagration in Vietnam. It is revealing, in this respect, that the meeting at which the school principals decided to issue the contested regulation was called in response to a student's statement to the journalism teacher in one of the schools that he wanted to write an article on Vietnam and have it published in the school paper. (The student was dissuaded.)

It is also relevant that the school authorities did not purport to prohibit the wearing of all symbols of political or controversial significance. The record shows that students in some of the schools wore buttons relating to national political campaigns, and some even wore the Iron Cross, traditionally a symbol of Nazism. . . . Instead, a particular symbol—black armbands worn to exhibit opposition to this Nation's involvement in Vietnam—was singled out for prohibition. Clearly, the prohibition of expression of one particular opinion, at least without evidence that it is necessary to avoid material and substantial interference with schoolwork or discipline, is not constitutionally permissible.

In our system, state-operated schools may not be enclaves of totalitarianism. School officials do not possess absolute authority over their students. Students in school as well as out of school are "persons" under our Constitution. They are possessed of fundamental rights, which the State must respect, just as they themselves must respect their obligations to the State. In our system, students may not be regarded as closed-circuit recipients of only that which the State chooses to communicate. They may not be confined to the expression of those sentiments that are officially approved. In the absence of a specific showing of constitutionally valid reasons to regulate their speech, students are entitled to freedom of expression of their views. . . .

. . . A student's rights, therefore, do not embrace merely the classroom hours. When he is in the cafeteria, or on the playing field, or on the campus during the authorized hours, he may express his opinions, even on controversial subjects like the conflict in Vietnam, if he does so without "materially and substantially interfer[ing] with the requirements of appropriate discipline in the operation of the school" and without colliding with the rights of others. But conduct by the student, in class or out of it, which for any reason—whether it stems from time, place, or type of behavior—materially disrupts class work or involves substantial disorder or invasion of the rights of others is, of course, not immunized by the constitutional guarantee of freedom of speech.

Under our Constitution, free speech is not a right that is given only to be so circumscribed that it exists in principle but not in fact. Freedom of expression would not truly exist if the right could be exercised only in an area that a benevolent government has provided as a safe haven for crackpots. . . . [W]e do not confine the permissible exercise of First Amendment rights to a telephone booth or the four corners of a pamphlet, or to supervised and ordained discussion in a school classroom.

If a regulation were adopted by school officials forbidding discussion of the Vietnam conflict, or the expression by any student of opposition to it anywhere on school property except as part of a prescribed classroom exercise, it would be obvious that the regulation would violate the constitutional rights of students, at least if it could not be justified by a showing that the students' activities would materially and substantially disrupt the work and discipline of the school. In the circumstances of the present case, the prohibition of the silent, passive "witness of the armbands," as one of the children called it, is no less offensive to the Constitution's guarantees. . . .

JUSTICE POTTER STEWART, concurring:
Although I agree with much of what is said in the Court's opinion, and with its judgment in this case, I cannot share the Court's uncritical assumption that, school discipline aside, the First Amendment rights of children are coextensive with those of adults. . . . I continue to hold the view [that] . . . "[A] State may permissibly determine that, at least in some precisely delineated areas, a child—like someone in a captive audience—is not possessed of that full capacity for individual choice which is the presupposition of First Amendment guarantees."

JUSTICE BYRON WHITE, concurring:
While I join the Court's opinion, I deem it appropriate to note, first, that the Court continues to recognize a distinction between communicating by words and communicating by acts or conduct which sufficiently impinges on some valid state interest. . . .

JUSTICE HUGO BLACK, dissenting:
The Court's holding in this case ushers in what I deem to be an entirely new era in which the power to control pupils by the elected "officials of state supported public schools . . ." in the United States is in ultimate effect transferred to the Supreme Court. The Court brought this particular case here on a petition for certiorari urging that the First and Fourteenth Amendments protect the right of school pupils to express their political

views all the way "from kindergarten through high school." Here, the constitutional right to "political expression" asserted was a right to wear black armbands during school hours and at classes in order to demonstrate to the other students that the petitioners were mourning because of the death of United States soldiers in Vietnam and to protest that war which they were against. . . .

. . . [T]he crucial . . . questions are whether students and teachers may use the schools at their whim as a platform for the exercise of free speech—"symbolic" or "pure"—and whether the courts will allocate to themselves the function of deciding how the pupils' school day will be spent. While I have always believed that, under the First and Fourteenth Amendments, neither the State nor the Federal Government has any authority to regulate or censor the content of speech, I have never believed that any person has a right to give speeches or engage in demonstrations where he pleases and when he pleases. . . .

While the record does not show that any of these armband students shouted, used profane language, or were violent in any manner, . . . [e]ven a casual reading of the record shows that this armband did divert students' minds from their regular lessons, and that talk, comments, etc., made John Tinker "self-conscious" in attending school with his armband. . . . I think the record overwhelmingly shows that the armbands did exactly what the elected school officials and principals foresaw they would, that is, took the students' minds off their class work and diverted them to thoughts about the highly emotional subject of the Vietnam War. And I repeat that, if the time has come when pupils of state-supported schools, kindergartens, grammar schools, or high schools, can defy and flout orders of school officials to keep their minds on their own schoolwork, it is the beginning of a new revolutionary era of permissiveness in this country fostered by the judiciary. . . .

. . . There was at one time a line of cases holding "reasonableness" as the court saw it to be the test of a "due process" violation. . . .

. . . [We] totally repudiated the old reasonableness-due process test, the doctrine that judges have the power to hold laws unconstitutional upon the belief of judges that they "shock the conscience" or that they are "unreasonable," "arbitrary," "irrational," "contrary to fundamental 'decency,'" or some other such flexible term without precise boundaries. I have many times expressed my opposition to that concept on the ground that it gives judges power to strike down any law they do not like. If the majority of the Court today, by agreeing to the opinion of my Brother Fortas, is resurrecting that old reasonableness-due process test, I think the constitutional change should be plainly, unequivocally, and forthrightly stated for the benefit of the bench and bar. It will be a sad day for the country, I believe. . . .

I deny, therefore, that it has been the "unmistakable holding of this Court for almost 50 years" that "students" and "teachers" take with them into the "schoolhouse gate" constitutional rights to "freedom of speech or expression." . . . The truth is that a teacher of kindergarten, grammar school, or high school pupils no more carries into a school with him a complete right to freedom of speech and expression than an anti-Catholic or anti-Semite carries with him a complete freedom of speech and religion into a Catholic church or Jewish synagogue. . . . It is a myth to say that any person has a constitutional right to say what he pleases, where he pleases, and when he pleases. Our Court has decided precisely the opposite.

In my view, teachers in state-controlled public schools are hired to teach there. . . . [C]ertainly a teacher is not paid to go into school and teach subjects the State does not hire him to teach as a part of its selected curriculum. Nor are public-school students sent to the schools at public expense to broadcast political or any other views to educate and inform the public. The original idea of schools, which I do not believe is yet abandoned as worthless or out of date, was that children had not yet reached the point of experience and wisdom which enabled them to teach all of their elders. It may be that the Nation has outworn the old-fashioned slogan that "children are to be seen, not heard," but one may, I hope, be permitted to harbor the thought that taxpayers send children to school on the premise that at their age they need to learn, not teach.

. . . Iowa's public schools . . . are operated to give students an opportunity to learn, not to talk politics by actual speech, or by "symbolic" speech. And, as I have pointed out before, the record amply shows that public protest in the school classes against the Vietnam War "distracted from that singleness of purpose which the State [here Iowa] desired to exist in its public educational institutions." . . . It was, of course, to distract the attention of other students that some students insisted up to the very point of their own suspension from school that they were determined to sit in school with their symbolic armbands.

Change has been said to be truly the law of life, but sometimes the old and the tried and true are worth holding. The schools of this Nation have undoubtedly contributed to giving us tranquility and to making us a more law-abiding people. Uncontrolled and uncontrollable liberty is an enemy to domestic peace. We cannot close our eyes to the fact that some of the country's greatest problems are crimes committed by the youth, too many of school age. School discipline, like parental discipline, is an integral and important part of training our children to be good citizens— to be better citizens. Here a very small number of students have crisply and summarily refused to obey a school order designed to give pupils who want to learn the opportunity to do so. One does not need to be a prophet or the son of a prophet to know that, after the Court's holding today, some students in Iowa schools and indeed in all schools will be ready, able, and willing to defy their teachers on practically all orders. This is the more unfortunate for the schools since groups of students all over the land are already running loose, conducting break-ins, sit-ins, lie-ins, and smash-ins. Many of these student groups, as is all too familiar to all who read the newspapers and watch the television news programs, have already engaged in rioting, property seizures, and destruction. They have picketed schools to force students not to cross their picket lines and have too often violently attacked earnest but frightened students who wanted

an education that the pickets did not want them to get. . . . Turned loose with lawsuits for damages and injunctions against their teachers as they are here, it is nothing but wishful thinking to imagine that young, immature students will not soon believe it is their right to control the schools, rather than the right of the States that collect the taxes to hire the teachers for the benefit of the pupils. This case, therefore, wholly without constitutional reasons, in my judgment, subjects all the public schools in the country to the whims and caprices of their loudest-mouthed, but maybe not their brightest, students. I, for one, am not fully persuaded that school pupils are wise enough. . . . I wish, therefore, wholly to disclaim any purpose on my part to hold that the Federal Constitution compels the teachers, parents, and elected school officials to surrender control of the American public school system to public school students. I dissent.

JUSTICE JOHN HARLAN, dissenting:
I certainly agree that state public school authorities in the discharge of their responsibilities are not wholly exempt from the requirements of the Fourteenth Amendment respecting the freedoms of expression and association. At the same time I am reluctant to believe that there is any disagreement between the majority and myself on the proposition that school officials should be accorded the widest authority in maintaining discipline and good order in their institutions. To translate that proposition into a workable constitutional rule, I would, in cases like this, cast upon those complaining the burden of showing that a particular school measure was motivated by other than legitimate school concerns—for example, a desire to prohibit the expression of an unpopular point of view, while permitting expression of the dominant opinion.

Finding nothing in this record which impugns the good faith of respondents in promulgating the armband regulation, I would affirm the judgment below.

Chapter 4

[D]ebate on public issues should be uninhibited, robust, and wide open, and [ ] it may well include vehement, caustic, and sometimes unpleasantly sharp attacks on government and public officials. . . . [E]rroneous statement is inevitable in free debate, and [ ] it must be protected if the freedoms of expression are to have the breathing space that they need to survive.

U.S. Supreme Court Justice William Brennan[1]

Montgomery, Ala., police commissioner L.B. Sullivan (second from left) celebrates with his attorneys after an Alabama jury found in his favor in his libel lawsuit against The New York Times. The verdict would eventually be appealed to the U.S. Supreme Court, resulting in a landmark case on libel law.

Libel
The Plaintiff's Case

A Brief History

Contemporary Issues

**The Elements of Libel:
   The Plaintiff's Case**

Statement of Fact
Publication
Identification
Defamation
Falsity
Fault
   Actual Malice
Damages
Criminal Libel

Cases for Study

➤ *New York Times Co. v.
   Sullivan*
➤ *Gertz v. Robert Welch,
   Inc.*

Suppose . . .

. . . that a civil rights group buys space in a major national newspaper. Within its full-page editorial, attention is called to the plight of many individuals who are engaged in nonviolent demonstrations. Some recent events are described. The overall thrust of the text is accurate, but it also contains some minor errors. In addition, it is critical of how some public officials—police officers, in particular—handled one demonstration. Several public officials, including the police commissioner, believe this piece has damaged their reputations; they sue for defamation of character. Especially given the false statements contained in the text, should the plaintiffs be able to win their lawsuit? Should it make any difference that they are public officials? Look for the answers to these questions when the case of *New York Times Co. v. Sullivan* is discussed later in this chapter and in an excerpt at the end of this chapter.

L ibel law is meant to protect an individual's reputation. It allows a person who believes his or her reputation has been injured to file a claim against the party responsible, asking for damages in an effort to obtain monetary compensation and to restore the person's reputation.

The idea that a person's reputation is something of value that is worth protecting is a centuries-old concept. Most, if not all, societies regard individual reputation as important. Throughout the course of Western civilization, reputation has been closely associated with the ability to participate in a community's social and economic life.[2] It is a concept rooted in civilized society: "The

Points of Law

Slander vs. Libel

Historically, "slander" has been associated with spoken words that damage reputation and "libel" with written defamation. The laws governing each were similar but distinct, with the damages awarded for libel usually being higher than for slander. The idea was that a written communication likely caused more harm because it lasted longer and its audience was larger. But with the development of mass communication technology, that distinction has been blurred. Defamatory motion picture content may be grounds for libel. Defamatory content in broadcasting is deemed libel in most states, slander in some others. Some states say that if broadcast defamation is from scripted (i.e., written) material, it is libel. Otherwise, it is slander.

Why does it matter? What the plaintiff must prove to win his or her case may vary depending on whether the defamation is categorized as slander or libel. Perhaps more than anything, however, the distinction is simply a leftover from another time.

right of a man to the protection of his own reputation from unjustified invasion and wrongful hurt reflects no more than our basic concept of the essential dignity and worth of every human being—a concept at the root of any decent system of ordered liberty."[3] Shakespeare was one among many writers who explored the importance of a man's or woman's good name.

As stated by the U.S. Supreme Court three and a half centuries after Shakespeare, the common law of slander and libel is designed to achieve society's "pervasive and strong interest in preventing and redressing attacks upon reputation."[4] The challenge becomes "balanc[ing] the State's interest in compensating private individuals for injury to their reputation against the First Amendment interest in protecting this type of expression."[5]

Of course, one who damages an individual's reputation through the spoken or written word has not necessarily committed libel. One important consideration is the truthfulness of the statement in question. Should one who makes a truthful statement that happens to damage a person's reputation be subject to penalty under the law? There was a time when truthful statements that damaged reputation were seen as more serious violations of the law. That is no longer the case.

The word "defamation" refers generally to false communications about another person that damage that person's "fame" or bring him into disrepute. Both slander and libel are forms of defamation. The general purpose of libel laws, as noted previously, is to allow people whose reputations have been defamed to restore their reputations. But those laws also serve as a deterrent to prevent similar defamation in the future. When a successful plaintiff—the party initiating the lawsuit—is awarded damages, three objectives are served: the plaintiff is compensated for his losses, the defendant is punished, and the defendant and others are discouraged from committing the same kind of libelous conduct in the future. Thus, a societal benefit may result, particularly if as much attention is given to setting the record straight as was given to the reputation-damaging remarks. Whether that occurs with any consistency, however, is another matter.

A Brief History

Western civilization's earliest recorded prosecution for reputation-damaging remarks is arguably the trial and execution of Socrates in 399 BCE. In response to charges of slandering Greek gods and corrupting the youth of Athens, the philosopher was brought before a Heliastic court (a public court unique to Ancient Athens). He admitted his "slanderous" teachings and, by a vote of 277 to 224, was found guilty. Socrates accepted his execution to dramatize the primacy of the life of the mind and the need for freedom of thought.[6]

While Ancient Greece may have contributed to the development of libel law in Western societies, it is the English common law—itself a descendant of Roman law—where American libel law finds its most significant roots. In a general sense, English defamation law tells us slander is a false accusation that results in the humiliation of its victims. The law tries to suppress such language, "which is seen to pose various threats to the social order."[7]

Many people believe that laws against defamation help to maintain the status quo, particularly when libel laws are enforced to punish criticism of those in positions of power.[8] Consequently, the development of libel law depends a great deal on the social and political forces at play in a given historical period.

In 15th-century England, complaints against defamation were heard in one of two courts: the court of common law or the infamous court of the Star Chamber. In the early 1600s, the court of the Star Chamber declared libel a criminal offense because it tended to cause breach of the peace. If the libel was "against a magistrate, or other public person, it [was] a greater offence."[9] The court of the Star Chamber tended to view written defamation as a more serious offense than the spoken version. Penalties for defamation included the possibility that the defamer "may be punished by fine and imprisonment, and if the case be exorbitant, by pillory and loss of his ears."[10] To the dismay of very few English citizens, the Star Chamber was disbanded in 1641, and common law courts resumed their jurisdiction over defamation cases. It was not until about 1660 that the common law courts consistently began to distinguish between libel and slander.[11]

As noted in Chapter 1, the role of Sir William Blackstone and his "Commentaries on the Law of England" played a major role in the development of

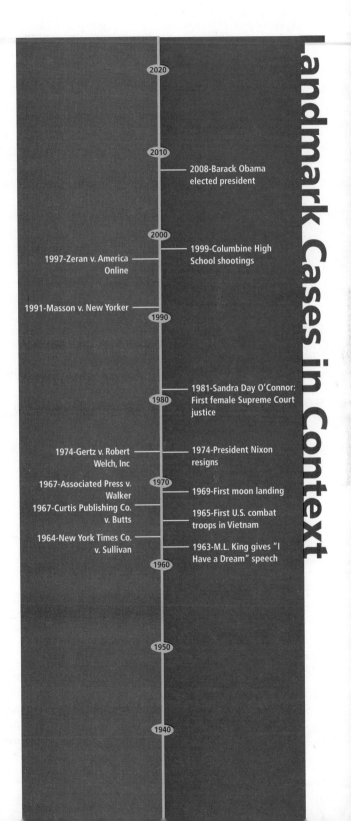

Landmark Cases in Context

- 2020
- 2010
- 2008-Barack Obama elected president
- 2000
- 1999-Columbine High School shootings
- 1997-Zeran v. America Online
- 1991-Masson v. New Yorker
- 1990
- 1981-Sandra Day O'Connor: First female Supreme Court justice
- 1980
- 1974-Gertz v. Robert Welch, Inc
- 1974-President Nixon resigns
- 1967-Associated Press v. Walker
- 1970
- 1969-First moon landing
- 1967-Curtis Publishing Co. v. Butts
- 1965-First U.S. combat troops in Vietnam
- 1964-New York Times Co. v. Sullivan
- 1963-M.L. King gives "I Have a Dream" speech
- 1960
- 1950
- 1940

Reputation in History and Literature

Many famous and infamous statements have been recorded that illustrate the significance of good name and reputation. A sampling:

A good name is rather to be chosen than great riches.

Proverbs 22:1

Good name in man and woman, dear my lord, Is the immediate jewel of their souls: Who steals my purse steals trash. . . . But he that filches from me my good name, Robs me of that which not enriches him, And makes me poor indeed.

William Shakespeare, "Othello," III. iii

A good reputation is more valuable than money.

Publilius Syrus, Roman writer, first century BCE

A reputation once broken may possibly be repaired, but the world will always keep their eyes on the spot where the crack was.

Joseph Hall, English cleric, 1574–1656

Who, for the sake of his good reputation, has never once sacrificed himself?

German philosopher Friedrich Nietzsche

When a leopard dies, it leaves its skin; when a person dies, he leaves his reputation.

Chinese proverb

Reputation is an idle and most false imposition; oft got without merit, and lost without deserving.

William Shakespeare, "Othello," II. iii

A single lie destroys a whole reputation of integrity.

Baltasar Gracian, Spanish cleric and writer, 1601–1658

No man will ever bring out of that office the reputation which carries him into it.

Thomas Jefferson, on the U.S. presidency

The most important thing for a young man is to establish credit—a reputation and character.

John D. Rockefeller, American industrialist, 1839–1937

Libel

The word "libel" comes from the Latin *libellus,* or "little book." The legal term derives from the practice in ancient Rome of publishing little books or booklets that were used by one Roman to defame another. The history of valuing and protecting reputation is centuries old.

law in the United States. Libel law is no exception. Punishment for defamation, Blackstone believed, was not inconsistent with the concept of freedom of the press. A free press, he wrote, "consists in laying no previous restraints upon publications, and not in freedom from censure for criminal matter when published."[12] Anyone can express his sentiments to the public, he added, "but if he publishes what is improper, mischievous, or illegal, he must take the consequences of his own temerity."[13]

realWorld Law

"60 Minutes" and the Chilling Effect

Jeffrey Wigand

One of the best examples of the chilling effect occurred when one of the most powerful media organizations in the United States succumbed to the effect's power. In the mid-1990s, Jeffrey Wigand, a former executive with the Brown & Williamson Tobacco Company, had reluctantly agreed to be interviewed by members of the CBS newsmagazine "60 Minutes." He was reluctant, in large part, because doing the interview would be in violation of a confidentiality agreement he had signed with B&W. Under its terms, he was not allowed to discuss his work, even after he had left the company.

But his conscience had gotten the best of him. He wanted to go public with what he believed to be unethical and unsafe practices in the making of cigarettes committed not just by B&W, but industrywide.

With the interview taped and a segment built around it ready for broadcast, CBS ordered "60 Minutes" to kill the story. The reasons centered on threats by B&W—already known for its willingness to engage in legal battles—to sue if the interview aired. The threat alleged wrongful interference with the confidentiality agreement. In other words, CBS would be accused of playing a major role in Wigand's violating his signed agreement with B&W and would be held responsible. The reported amount of the threatened lawsuit was $15 billion—never an appealing amount, and especially not so when the sale of a company is in the works, as it was with CBS at that time.

With the threat looming, CBS killed the story. Although it ultimately aired an abbreviated form of the Wigand interview after newspapers disclosed its contents, the damage had been done to the reputations of CBS and "60 Minutes" as unmitigated standard-bearers for journalistic integrity and courage. Possibly the world's most powerful media organization had fallen victim to the chilling effect.[1] This incident is portrayed in the motion picture "The Insider."

---

1. *See* Joseph A. Russomanno and Kyu Ho Youm, *The 60 Minutes Controversy: What Lawyers Are Telling the News Media* 65–91, Comm. & L. (Sept. 1996).

Those consequences were to take the form of monetary **damages** sought by a plaintiff in compensation for a tarnished reputation. As a chief justice of the United States later described its evolution, "Defamation law developed not only as a means of allowing an individual to vindicate his good name, but also for the purpose of obtaining redress for harm caused by such statements. As the common law developed in this country, apart from the issue of damages, one usually needed only allege an unprivileged publication of false and defamatory matter to state a cause of action for defamation."[14]

That legal principle was brought to the American colonies and later followed in the states after independence. But England also provided America with legal theories that were less desirable in a republic committed to individual freedoms. Among them was the concept of **seditious libel**. At various times throughout

damages Monetary compensation that may be recovered in court by any person who has suffered loss or injury. Damages may be compensatory for actual loss or punitive as punishment for outrageous conduct.

seditious libel Communication meant to incite people to change the government; criticism of the government.

The Star Chamber

The court of the Star Chamber evolved from the meetings of the king's royal council. It was established in 1487 and was named after the star painted on the ceiling of the room in which it met. Over time, its powers expanded to include issues of public disorder, land disputes and sedition against royal policies. It was disbanded in 1641 by Parliament, though its name survives still to designate arbitrary, secretive proceedings in opposition to personal rights and liberty.

Sedition Act of 1798 Federal legislation under which anyone "opposing or resisting any law of the United States, or any act of the President of the United States" could be imprisoned for up to two years. The act also made it illegal to "write, print, utter, or publish" anything that criticized the president or Congress. The act ultimately was seen as a direct violation of the First Amendment and expired in 1801.

Points of Law

States with Anti-SLAPP Statutes

Arkansas	Missouri
California	Nebraska
Delaware	Nevada
Florida	New Mexico
Georgia	New York
Hawaii	Oklahoma
Indiana	Oregon
Louisiana	Pennsylvania
Maine	Rhode Island
Maryland	Tennessee
Massachusetts	Utah
Minnesota	Washington

American history the authorities have been especially sensitive to criticism of the government. In response, laws have been passed criminalizing such expression. One of those eras was the post–Revolutionary War period. The **Sedition Act of 1798** made it a crime to write "any false, scandalous and malicious" statements against either the president or Congress.[15] While the act permitted a defendant to escape penalty by proving the truth of the writing, and juries were permitted to decide critical questions of law and fact, there was no doubt that it was intended to silence critics of the entrenched political powers.

Echoing Blackstone, John Marshall—a public official of the same era who would become Chief Justice of the United States—defended the Sedition Act as being consistent with the First Amendment because it did not impose a prior restraint.[16] "It is known to all," he wrote, that those who publish libels or who "libel the government of the state" may "be both sued and indicted."[17] Among the act's opponents was James Madison, the principal author of the First Amendment, who said, "It would seem a mockery to say that no laws should be passed preventing publications from being made, but that laws might be passed punishing them in case they should be made."[18] Madison and his supporters ultimately prevailed, with the act expiring in 1801.

In tracts opposing the Sedition Act, one finds the earliest musings on the notion of the "chilling effect," a form of prior restraint that recognizes that laws punishing behavior after it takes place will also likely deter, or chill, that behavior from occurring in the first place. While it is certainly desirable to deter people from committing crimes, discouraging relatively innocuous activities like speaking and writing because of the threat of a libel lawsuit threatens to make speakers and writers less inclined to communicate in the first place. Many people believe that is itself an infringement on the freedom of expression guaranteed by the First Amendment.

Chilling speech is precisely the goal of some defamation lawsuits. In those cases libel law is used not as a shield against threatened harms or as a means of correcting them, but as a weapon to prevent speech from occurring in the first place. These are called **SLAPP (strategic lawsuits against public participation)** suits.[19] They are meant to silence critics. The plaintiffs who file them are sometimes under investigation for possible wrongdoing or people whose questionable business motives are being probed. Plaintiffs rarely win these cases. Indeed, they often don't expect to. Instead, their purpose is to harass their critics into silence. Noting that SLAPPs are often used to suppress a party's First Amendment rights, some states have enacted anti-SLAPP legislation.[20] The constitutionality of these laws has been upheld.

realWorld Law

Is Libel Out of Fashion?

While libel remains an important element of the law of journalism and mass communication, the number of cases going to trial in U. S. courts has dropped significantly. According to the Media Law Resource Center, this is the picture of libel trials over the past few decades:

1980s	266
1990s	192
2000s	124

In 2009, only nine libel cases went to trial.

Why? There are several reasons, among them the severe economic downturn that began in the late 2000s. Media companies were seriously affected and thus are more inclined than ever to avoid being sued. Rather than incurring the often immense cost of defending libel claims, they may be more willing to soften stories or make changes to stories that address the concerns of would-be plaintiffs. The economic decline also means fewer news organizations are engaging in costly investigative journalism, probing investigations that can often include reputation-damaging assertions. Economics also contribute to another explanation for the decrease in libel trials: both plaintiffs and defendants often seek and reach out-of-court settlements before claims are even filed, or before trial.

Other reasons for the decline in libel trials include Internet growth. Because of the large amount of content, a single potentially libelous story has less impact than it would have had in previous eras. Moreover, websites not only allow the alleged libel victim to respond and set the record straight, but media organizations themselves have websites on which problem content can be changed quickly. "In print, maybe you'll get a correction, but in the plaintiff's view, the damage has already been done," says George Freeman, counsel to The New York Times. "On the other hand, if you complain about a mistake because you see it on the Internet, it's more likely a rapid change can be made and people don't feel the necessity to sue because they feel like their complaint has been dealt with."[1]

Last, libel claims against media organizations are often an uphill battle. They are very difficult to win, in large part because of what many characterize as the tilted playing field that favors libel defendants. This is especially true when the plaintiff is a public official or public figure—the kind of people usually the subject of news media reports. Potential plaintiffs are finding it advantageous to move outside the sphere of libel altogether. Instead, many potential plaintiffs are being advised to turn to areas in which the truth or falsity of the material is less critical. (Military field generals and football coaches employ similar strategies; it makes sense to attack where defenses are weakest, not strongest.)

1. John Koblin, *The End of Libel?* N. Y. Observer, June 8, 2010, *available at* http://www.observer.com/2010/media/end-libel?page=0.

As an example, in June 2010 a strengthened anti-SLAPP law took effect in the state of Washington. The enhanced law covered more kinds of speech and allowed judges both to dismiss meritless lawsuits more quickly and to award attorney's fees in cases that had been dismissed. A Seattle attorney who helped draft the new law, Bruce E.H. Johnson, said that after three decades of defamation defense, "I was tired of defending meritless libel lawsuits, and then telling clients that they

SLAPP (strategic lawsuits against public participation) Libel suits whose purpose is to harass critics into silence, often to suppress those critics' First Amendment rights.

had no basis for getting reimbursed for the expenses incurred in getting rid of the case."[21] Anti-SLAPP laws can address meritless claims of all kinds, not just libel.

Contemporary Issues

Many of the issues involving libel that existed in previous eras have surfaced again in the 20th and 21st centuries. Just as defamation of character was recognized first as a harm committed by the spoken word and later as one that could also be committed through writing, the opportunities for libelous speech have increased exponentially with the development of communications technology. Each new communicative medium increases the volume of communication in the world and, accordingly, the opportunities for defamatory statements increase. In the Internet age—complete with blogging and social networking—and because of the ease of communicating, the speed with which messages can be sent and received, the volume of messages and the greater distances they may travel, the possibilities for libel are on the rise. Add to this a seemingly always present media preoccupation with sensational events and a public fixation on celebrities and other renowned people, and the potential for libel has never been greater.

Libel law serves to check the power of the media by opening its newsgathering and decision-making processes to public scrutiny and accountability. While the best cure for bad speech may be more speech,[22] contemporary American society is often unwilling to rely only on corrective speech as a remedy for false and damaging statements to reputations. Libel law is one of the checks and balances in that process. The right of individuals to be secure in their reputations is weighed against the rights of others to be heard on issues of importance.

SUMMARY

THE VALUE OF INDIVIDUAL REPUTATION, the importance of protecting it and the ability to restore it once it is damaged are centuries-old concepts. Libel law is meant to help with those processes. As with much of law in the United States, libel stems in large part from the English common law. The threat of a libel suit can create a chilling effect in the media—a reluctance to publish freely and pursue stories aggressively. For those who either file or defend libel claims, it is an expensive process, taking a toll both financially and emotionally. Many claims are settled out of court. ∎

The Elements of Libel: The Plaintiff's Case

burden of proof The requirement for a party to a case to demonstrate one or more claims by the presentation of evidence. In libel law, for example, the plaintiff has the burden of proof.

Unlike in the era of common law libel, when the defendant was required to prove that a defamatory statement was true, the entire initial **burden of proof** is now on the plaintiff in libel cases. To win, the plaintiff must prove that all of the required elements apply to the allegedly libelous material. Each of these elements requires definition and explanation.

Statement of Fact

In order to be libelous, a statement must make an assertion of fact. An expression of opinion cannot be libelous. Legitimate opinion cannot be considered libelous because an opinion cannot be false—falsity being another requirement for libelous material. (The opinion defense is considered in detail in Chapter 5.) For now, it is enough to understand that whether material can be considered an expression of opinion requires a rigorous analysis.

Publication

In order for a statement to be libelous, the plaintiff must show that the statement was made public. To satisfy this standard, only one person in addition to the source and receiver of the material must have seen or heard the information in question. When information is presented through the mass media, publication is presumed. Under the law of libel, material is considered published any time it is printed in a periodical, broadcast over the airwaves or posted on the Internet. Again, publication simply means making material public.

Republication Repeating libelous information is as potentially harmful to someone's reputation as publishing it in the first place. Thus, the republisher can be held just as responsible as the originator. Republishing libelous information is seen as a new publication in the eyes of the law. This is true even when careful attribution occurs. The law's rationale here is to prevent individuals or the media from freely committing defamation simply by attributing the libelous material to another source.

Particularly in an age of advancing communications technology, the republication rule would seem at odds with the wish to promote the free flow of ideas—clearly a tenet of the First Amendment. In fact, even in a slightly less technological age, some courts began to allow for some degree of protection for publication of otherwise libelous information. The neutral reportage and wire service defenses, discussed in Chapter 5, confront this issue.

An online version of republication illustrates how new technologies open the door to refinements in the law. New comments made to older messages in order to return them to prominent positions on a website to keep a conversation alive—"bump messages"—do not count as republication in the libel context. A New York judge wrote, "One of the unique characteristics of the Internet is that it allows for the dissemination of information and ideas on a global scale," adding that considering bump messages as republication would have "a serious inhibitory effect" on this form of communication.[23]

Vendors and Distributors Publisher liability in libel is predicated on the notion that publishers are or should be aware of the material they disseminate, possibly including a presumption that they have read and edited the content. To prove publication, a libel plaintiff must show not just that libelous material was

Points of Law

The Plaintiff's Libel Case

1. A statement of fact
2. That is published,
3. That is of and concerning the plaintiff,
4. That is defamatory,
5. That is false and
6. For which the defendant is at fault.

published, the plaintiff must also identify a specific person, group or business responsible for the publication. Simply making information available to the public is not the same as publishing it. Among those who are granted a sort of republication exception are vendors and distributors of information. For example, bookstores, libraries and newsstands are not considered to be publishers of the works they stock. They cannot be sued for libel based on the works they make available because they do not control the content of those products, nor can they be expected to know what they contain.

Given this "vendor exception," how should the law treat information providers on the Internet? Information appears on the Internet in a variety of ways. One way is through an Internet service provider (ISP) that stores and facilitates access to material, for example, on a bulletin board or in a database. If the ISP originates any part of this information, then it is considered the publisher and can be held responsible for its content. More commonly, the ISP simply makes information posted by users available to subscribers. In that situation, the ISP is like the newsstand vendor—a provider of information but not a publisher and therefore not responsible for it. One court likened ISPs to a telephone company, "which one neither wants nor expects to superintend the content of its subscribers' conversations."[24]

Communications Decency Act (CDA) The part of the 1996 Telecommunications Act that largely attempted to regulate Internet content. The CDA was successfully challenged in *Reno v. ACLU* (1997).

This protection of ISPs did not exist until one section of the **Communications Decency Act (CDA)** was put to the test. Before Congress passed the CDA in 1996 as part of the Telecommunications Act, court rulings in this area had been mixed. Some judges ruled that ISPs should be regarded as publishers,[25] while others said that they were only distributors of information that others had published.[26] The discrepancy was resolved when Section 230 of the CDA was tested by a libel claim against America Online (AOL).[27]

Not all online defamation takes place in a liability-free zone, however. In fact, defamatory material posted on an ISP site can be the subject of a libel action, provided that the publisher is identified. For example, when a former aide to President Bill Clinton claimed he was defamed by statements of political columnist Matt Drudge about his alleged history of spousal abuse, the ex-aide tried to sue AOL, the ISP that posted "The Drudge Report" where the comments appeared. The court refused to allow the suit to go forward against AOL, saying that AOL was not responsible for information it had transmitted but not originated. However, the court permitted the lawsuit to proceed against "The Drudge Report."[28] That case was ultimately settled out of court.

Weblogs, or "blogs," which are websites usually maintained by individuals who periodically post content to the sites, provide another example of a "publisher." A blogger is responsible for the material he or she posts. Note, for example, part of the warning Google provides to users of its blogging service: "Google does not endorse, support, represent or guarantee the truthfulness, accuracy, or reliability of any communications posted via the Service or endorse any opinions expressed via the Service. You acknowledge that any reliance on material posted via the Service will be at your own risk."[29]

But is the blogger legally responsible for items others may post on his or her site? What if the postings are anonymous? In a ruling that also relied on Section

realWorld Law

Libel and the Online Publisher

Given that publishing is one element of the libel plaintiff's case, it becomes important to determine who or what entity published the material at issue. Those are the defendants in the suit. Moreover, particularly with the advent of online communication and its nuances, questions surfaced as to whether companies that provide individuals access to the Internet should necessarily be considered publishers and therefore subject to libel claims.

Congress addressed this when it passed the Communications Decency Act (CDA) in 1996. Section 230 of the law, sometimes referred to as the "Online Defamation Limited Liability Act," states, in part, "No provider or user of an interactive computer service shall be treated as the publisher or speaker of any information provided by another information content provider."[1] In short, the law was meant to give Internet service providers (ISPs) immunity from libel claims.

Not long afterward, the new law was tested when America Online (AOL) was sued by a Seattle man, Kenneth Zeran. Zeran claimed AOL's negligence in removing false information about him injured his reputation. His claim stemmed from a situation in which an anonymous AOL user posted an advertisement for T-shirts with images and a slogan glorifying the 1995 Oklahoma City bombing. Zeran's telephone number was part of the ad. He claimed no knowledge of the ad or anything to do with it. Ultimately, a federal appeals court ruled, "By its plain language, Section 230 creates a federal immunity to any cause of action that would make service providers liable for information originating with a third-party user of that service." Specifically, the court said, Section 230 prevents courts from even considering claims that place a computer service provider in the role of publisher.[2] The court reaffirmed Congress' recognition that if interactive computer service providers were forced to restrict or eliminate speech to avoid liability, it would create an "obvious chilling effect" on speech.[3]

More recently, a court clarified another aspect of this issue. The First Circuit affirmed that the definition of "provider of an interactive computer service" includes service providers who do not directly connect their users to the Internet.[4] Unlike AOL in the *Zeran* case, the defendant here did not provide users with access to the Internet; it operated a series of websites. To narrow the limitation to include only interactive computer service providers who provide Internet access would undermine the congressional intent and policy underlying the CDA.[5] The First Circuit said that Section 230 immunity should be broadly construed.[6]

1. Communications Decency Act, 47 U.S.C. § 230 (c)(1).
2. Zeran v. America Online, Inc., 129 F.3d 327, 330 (4th Cir. 1997).
3. *Id.* at 331.
4. Universal Communication Systems, Inc. v. Lycos, Inc., 478 F.3d 413 (1st Cir. 2007).
5. *Id.* at 418–19.
6. *Id.* at 419.

230, a federal judge dismissed a libel claim against a website operator whose site included anonymous postings that the plaintiff claimed damaged his reputation.[30] The judge relied on what he said was the intention of Section 230: to promote the free flow of information, a goal that was especially well served in a medium where citizens from all walks of life could have a voice. Otherwise, he wrote, the specter of liability "in an area of such prolific speech would have an obvious chilling effect."[31] On the other hand, in 2010 a website sustained an $11 million judgment after posting false accusations about a Cincinnati Bengals cheerleader.

realWorld Law

Online Libel

Libel law applies to material that is transmitted online just as it does to all other forms of communication. More specifically, this principle applies not merely to traditional media organizations, such as newspapers, that have an online presence; anyone who uses the Internet can be held responsible for libelous content that is transmitted. Moreover, while the Internet and social networking applications clearly enhance the free flow of information, as one law professor writes, they "pose threats to people's control over their reputations and their ability to be who they want to be."[1]

Information on the Internet can be just as libelous as anything on paper, film, tape or in a broadcast—perhaps even more so given the speed at which Internet messages travel and the distances they cover. Generally, the same principles apply in terms of the plaintiff's case and protections available to defendants.

In one case, two irate people posted numerous remarks on an Internet bulletin board about their former employer and two of its executives. After a jury found for the plaintiffs, the defendants appealed, partly on the premise that Internet message boards are so filled with outrageous postings that no reasonable person would interpret such a posting as a true statement of fact. A California appeals court rejected that notion:

> Even if the exchange that takes place on these message boards is typically freewheeling and irreverent, we do not agree that it is exempt from established legal and social norms. The Internet may be the "new marketplace of ideas," but it can never achieve its potential as such unless it is subject to the civilizing influence of the law like all other social discourse.[2]

Also consider the case of Sue Scheff. Scheff, who operates a referral service, was contacted by a client who wanted help in withdrawing her sons from a boarding school in Costa Rica. Scheff complied and referred a consultant to the client, Carey Bock.

Bock, however, later became critical of Scheff and posted messages about her on a website that included calling Scheff a "crook," a "con artist" and a "fraud." Scheff sued Bock for libel. After Bock could no longer afford a defense lawyer, she offered no defense. The judge found in favor of Scheff, and a jury awarded her $11.3 million in damages.

Scheff realized Bock would be unable to pay but pursued the case anyway. "People are using the Internet to destroy people they don't like, and you can't do that."[3]

Scheff's attorney, David Pollack, said the case "will make people think twice before they make defamatory statements on the Internet or anywhere else. You can destroy somebody with the click of a mouse. The ramifications of being able to say anything about anyone without any consequences are very serious."[4]

According to Michael Sanger, an adjunct professor at Georgetown University Law Center and a partner at a Washington, D.C., law firm, "This case sends a signal that if you were going to write blog entries, that you need to, like any other journalist, be aware of what you write. It could have a chilling effect when people have to sit down and worry about losing their house."[5]

---

1. Daniel J. Solove, The Future of Reputation 4 (2007).
2. Varian Medical Systems, Inc. v. Delfino, 113 Cal. App. 4th 273, 288 (Cal. Ct. App. 2003).
3. Laura Parker, *Jury Awards $11.3M over Defamatory Internet Posts*, USA Today, Oct. 11, 2006, at 4A.
4. Kara Rowland, *Lawsuit Award a Warning to Blogs: Woman Wins $11.3 Million*, Wash. Times, Oct. 12, 2006, at C8.
5. *Id.*

realWorld Law

The Unknown Publisher

Unknown publisher cases present unique challenges to courts. A California court once wrote that the traditional reluctance to permitting filings against John Doe defendants should be tempered by the need to provide injured parties with a forum in which they may seek redress for grievances. However, this need must be balanced against the legitimate and valuable right to participate in online forums anonymously or pseudonymously.[1]

These challenges were apparent when an Arizona appeals court handled an anonymous publisher case. The chief executive officer (CEO) of a company used his work e-mail account to send an intimate message to a personal friend. Six days later, a number of people, including members of the company's management team, received an e-mail from an anonymous sender with an e-mail address from an e-mail service provider called theanonymousemail.com. The e-mail contained the contents of the CEO's message and was entitled, "Is this a company you want to work for?"

The company then filed an action that demanded the e-mail service provider reveal the identity of the interceptor. In evaluating the case, the Arizona court noted U.S. Supreme Court precedents supporting the concepts that the First Amendment protects anonymous speech[2] and speech on the Internet.[3] Recognizing the Internet as a unique "democratic forum for communication," one court concluded, "the constitutional rights of Internet users, including the First Amendment right to speak anonymously, must be carefully safeguarded."[4] However, the Arizona court noted that the right to speak anonymously is not absolute: it does not protect obscenity, libel, or copyright infringement, for example. The court held that in order to compel discovery [information] of an anonymous Internet speaker's identity, the requesting party must show:

1. The speaker has been given adequate notice and a reasonable opportunity to respond to the discovery request.

2. The requesting party's cause of action could survive a motion for summary judgment on elements not dependent on the speaker's identity.

3. A balance of the parties' competing interests favors disclosure.[5]

The court was especially adamant about the third part, justifying its preference for disclosure by saying it "is necessary to achieve appropriate rulings in the vast array of factually distinct cases likely to involve anonymous speech."[6] In sum, an e-mail service provider is not required to disclose the identity of an anonymous e-mailer who allegedly breached a company's computer system and e-mail accounts unless the company demonstrates that competing interests outweighed the e-mailer's First Amendment rights.

1. Columbia Insurance Company v. Seescandy.com, 185 F.R.D. 573 (N.D. Cal. 1999).
2. Buckley v. American Constitutional Law Found., 525 U.S. 182, 199–200 (1999).
3. Reno v. American Civil Liberties Union, 521 U.S. 844, 870 (1997).
4. Doe v. 2THE MART.COM, 140 F. Supp. 2d 1088, 1097 (W.D. Wash. 2001).
5. Mobilisa, Inc. v. John Doe 1 and The Suggestion Box, Inc., 217 Ariz. 103, 112 (2007).
6. *Id.* at 111.

Points of Law

Thedirt.com refused to respond to the libel lawsuit, resulting in the judgment against its operator.[32]

Unknown Publisher Sometimes material is published, but the specific publisher is unknown. A hallmark of cyberspace is anonymous communication. The ability to speak anonymously serves several interests, including allowing ideas and viewpoints that otherwise might remain unexpressed to enter the marketplace of ideas because the fear of reprisal is reduced. U.S. Supreme Court Justice Antonin Scalia once noted the historical significance of anonymous speech. He wrote: "Under our constitution, anonymous pamphleteering is not a pernicious, fraudulent practice, but an honorable tradition of advocacy and of dissent. Anonymity is a shield from the tyranny of the majority."[33]

Thus, a dilemma presents itself: the wish to protect anonymous speech collides with the imperative of holding people accountable for libelous expression. One appeals court has said that in these situations trial courts should strike "a balance between the well-established First Amendment right to speak anonymously, and the right of the plaintiff to protect its proprietary interests and reputation through the assertion of recognizable claims based on the actionable conduct of the anonymous [or] fictitiously-named defendants."[34]

To resolve this dilemma some judges have allowed "John Doe" lawsuits to proceed in which the identity of the defendant is withheld by the court. Knowing that IP addresses and user names can be traced—with some providers, identities are readily accessible—plaintiffs file John Doe claims and then compel the ISP to disclose the identity of the "anonymous" poster to the presiding court. The person's identity, however, is shielded in the courtroom and kept out of court documents, thus preserving some measure of anonymity.

The plaintiff must meet several requirements: First, to identify the anonymous party with as much specificity as possible—enough so the court can determine whether the defendant is a real person or an entity that can be sued; second, to demonstrate what steps were taken to identify the anonymous defendant; third, to show that its case is strong enough to withstand a motion to dismiss. Finally, the plaintiff must file a request for discovery with the court. If the court finds that these requirements have been met, it may proceed to seek the identity of the anonymous message poster(s) from the applicable ISP, many of which have the capability to trace that information.

Identification

A libel plaintiff is required to show that he or she was specifically the person whose reputation was harmed or, possibly, was a member of a small group that was defamed. Early common law asked whether the statement was "of and concerning" the plaintiff—a standard still employed. This test asks whether the statement reasonably refers to the plaintiff. There are several ways a person can be identified. The most obvious is by name, but people can be identified in other ways—for instance, by title, through photographic images or within a context in which their identity can be inferred. As long as someone other than the plaintiff and the defendant recognize that the content is about the plaintiff, identification has taken place. In addition, the intention of the publisher is not critical to this determination; a publisher may not have intended to implicate the plaintiff, but identification could have occurred nonetheless.

Group Identification In some circumstances, libel law allows any member of a group to sue when the entire group has been libeled. The key is whether in libeling the group, the information is also "of and concerning" the specific individual bringing the lawsuit. In general, the smaller the group, the more likely it is that its individual members have been identified. For example, writing "all members of our town's city council are taking bribes" when there are only five members of the council would make it possible for any one of them to sue for libel. In effect, each one has been identified. On the other hand, a claim that "all politicians are on the take" would not allow any single politician to sue because the group being libeled is so large that no single politician has been identified. Where is the line drawn? How many members must a group include before it crosses the threshold from small enough to too big? Like so much in the law, there is no definitive answer. According to one authority, "It is not possible to set definite limits as to the size of the group or class, but the cases in which recovery [of damages] has been allowed usually have involved numbers of 25 or fewer."[35]

A court will evaluate each situation on its specific facts. Some rulings in this category indicate that if a group has fewer than 100 members, any one of them could file a successful libel claim, depending on the libelous material in question. As a group grows in size, the inclusiveness of the language that allegedly libeled its members becomes a factor. For example, a book entitled "USA: Confidential" disparaged various groups of employees of the Neiman-Marcus department store in Dallas, Tex., including "some" of the models, the saleswomen and "most" of the salesmen. All nine models, 30 of 382 saleswomen and 15 of the 25 salesmen filed lawsuits. The libel claims of the models and the salesmen were allowed to go forward, but the saleswomen's case was dismissed by a federal trial judge. The trial court said that the large size of the saleswomen group made it impossible for a reader to conclude anything about any of its individual members. But the court conceded that even with large groups, if a particular member is identified in some manner, that individual would have a legitimate complaint.[36]

Identification in Fiction A somewhat recent permutation of libel law has been libel claims based on works of fiction. One key to the sustainability of the claim is whether the work

---

Libel in Fiction

According to one commentator, "Authors who give their readers fiction as fact do so at their peril. A work may so effectively portray a fictional reality that a reader reasonably may mistake the writing for a factual representation of real persons and real events. In addition, the fictionist's success in depicting 'fact' may leave him unable, as a practical matter, to assert successfully that he accidentally portrayed the plaintiff."[1]

---

1. Comment, *Defamation by Fiction*, 42 Mᴅ. L. Rᴇᴠ. 387, 406 (1983).

identifies the plaintiff. Is it "of and concerning" him or her? Generally, the plaintiff must prove that a reasonable reader would perceive the writing as intending to portray a real person and that the plaintiff is that person. The level of recognition must rise to a portrayal of the fictional character as the plaintiff—a standard that is rarely met in fiction. A notable example revolves around "Primary Colors," a novel whose characters strongly resemble Bill Clinton and those around him. A libel lawsuit by a person who claimed that she was identified and defamed through a character in the book was dismissed. "For a depiction of a fictional character to constitute actionable defamation," the judge wrote, "the description of the fictional character must be so closely akin to the real person claiming to be defamed that a reader of the book, knowing the real person, would have no difficulty linking the two. Superficial similarities are insufficient."[37] In this case, the court said, any similarities between the plaintiff and the fictional character were insufficient for a reader, even one who knew the plaintiff, to reasonably believe the characterizations were about her.

Similarly, various forms of "new journalism" that blend fact and fiction to create compelling narratives about real-life events can present challenges when applying the rules of libel law. For example, the author of a nonfiction book may imagine conversations between various real-life people that convey the essence of what transpired but do so through largely invented dialogue. These unorthodox forms of journalistic storytelling straddle the line between fact and fiction—they are neither one nor the other, but both—and categorizing them for libel law purposes poses unique challenges.

Works of fiction also may be protected from defamation law for reasons other than nonidentification. Works of parody, satire and rhetorical hyperbole—in short, works that are unbelievable and could not be construed as statements of fact—generally are immune from libel suits. These are explored in Chapter 5.

Defamation

Another element in the plaintiff's case involves the allegedly libelous content itself. In order for the plaintiff to win, the material at issue must be defamatory. The challenge, of course, is defining and establishing a standard of defamation. The standard begins with the premise that when reputation is damaged, defamation occurs.

Some words by themselves may qualify as defamatory. Some kinds of statements convey such defamatory meaning that they are considered to be defamatory as a matter of law; on its face and without further proof, the content is defamatory. This is referred to as **libel per se**. Libel per se typically involves accusations of criminal activity. However, there is no list of "automatically" defamatory words. While "red flag" words are sometimes compiled, because so much depends on context, these lists are of little use.

libel per se A statement whose injurious nature is apparent and requires no further proof.

Distinguishing defamatory from nondefamatory statements is more art than science. Within various contexts, the following definitions of "defamatory" have been offered:

- Words that are false and injurious to another
- Words that expose another person to hatred, contempt or ridicule
- Words that tend to harm the reputation of another so as to lower him or her in the estimation of the community or deter third persons from associating or dealing with him[38]
- Words that subject a person to the loss of goodwill or confidence from others[39]
- Words that subject a person to scorn or ridicule
- Words that tend to expose a person to hatred, contempt or aversion, or tend to induce an evil or unsavory opinion of him or her in the minds of a substantial number in the community
- Words that tend to prejudice someone in the eyes of a substantial and respectable minority of the community[40]

Whatever the standard, courts have traditionally said that the matter must be viewed from the perspective of "right-thinking" people.[41]

In contrast with libel per se is **libel per quod**. It arises when the matter by itself does not appear to be defamatory, but knowledge of additional information would damage the plaintiff's reputation. An example of libel per quod would be a news report that the plaintiff was seen visiting 123 Main Street. By itself, that report would not seem defamatory. But if many readers are aware there is a drug-manufacturing lab at that address, then the report would have accused the plaintiff of involvement in illegal activity. Both kinds of libel lawsuits proceed along similar paths through the courts once it has been determined that the statement at issue was defamatory.

libel per quod A statement whose injurious nature requires proof.

Article headlines can occasionally be the source of successful libel claims. As with captions and teasers, their abbreviated nature and shortened message can be interpreted in a defamatory way, as with the published headline "Red Tape Holds Up Bridge." Courts often deny recovery, however, perhaps in deference to the space demands of journalism. Whether the headline is "of and concerning" the plaintiff becomes material—as, of course, do the other elements of the plaintiff's case. In a lawsuit spawned by the 1995 murder trial of O.J. Simpson, the National Examiner was found liable for the headline "Cops Think Kato Did It." The implication regarding Brian "Kato" Kaelin was clear: The "it" being referred to was the murder of Nicole Brown Simpson and Ronald Goldman. The article itself clarified that the "it" mentioned in the front page headline was actually perjury related to his trial testimony. Kaelin sued, claiming his reputation was damaged.[42] A defense witness who admitted that "the front page of the tabloid paper is what we sell the paper on, not what's inside it"[43] only served to strengthen the plaintiff's case.

Like libel, slander (spoken defamation) can also be categorized as per se or per quod. To understand the distinction first requires being aware of the four categories of **slander per se**. They clearly reflect an era when slander was first recognized as a harmful act: (1) an accusation of criminal conduct, (2) a charge of moral turpitude, (3) allegations tending to injure another in his or her trade, business, profession or office, and (4) suggestion of having a loathsome disease.

slander per se A spoken statement whose injurious nature is apparent and requires no further proof.

realWorld Law

Oprah and the Cattlemen

Oprah Winfrey

In an example of a defamation claim originating from criticism of a product, talk show host Oprah Winfrey was sued by a group of Texas cattlemen for remarks made about "Mad Cow" disease. Diseased beef was a topic explored on "The Oprah Winfrey Show" broadcast on April 16, 1996, and entitled "Dangerous Food."

Although neither Texas nor any of the plaintiffs was mentioned, the Texas Beef Group and several other Texas-based cattle companies filed suit. Among their claims was that the producers "intentionally edited from the taped show much of the factual and scientific information that would have calmed the hysteria it knew one guest's false exaggerations would create."[1] The plaintiffs added that this "malicious" treatment "caused markets to immediately" crash and that they suffered damages as a result.[2]

Adding to the plaintiffs' anguish was Winfrey's well-documented influence on her millions of viewers—she could turn a book into a best-seller merely by mentioning it or start a diet craze by extolling the virtues of dieting.[3] When Winfrey commented during the show that the information about tainted beef had "just stopped me cold from eating another burger. I'm stopped,"[4] the flames were fanned.

During the trial that followed in Amarillo, Texas, Winfrey established a temporary residence there. The plaintiffs who opposed her were seeking $100 million in damages through a variety of claims. Her integrity and ethics were being challenged. "Why me?" she asked herself. So in addition to consulting with her attorneys, Winfrey sought assistance from a company called Courtroom Sciences in Dallas. She hired its founder, psychologist Phil McGraw, to help. His clients had included Exxon and The New York Times.

McGraw advised Winfrey not only on how to keep her composure and remain positive but also on how to testify. "There's a huge difference between telling the truth and telling the truth effectively," McGraw said.[5] The federal trial court ruled for the defense, stating that the plaintiffs had not proven that knowingly false statements had been made.[6] A federal appeals court affirmed.[7] Winfrey gives much of the credit for her successful defense to "Dr. Phil." After the trial, she began inviting him to appear regularly on her show. His popularity led to his books becoming best-sellers and to his own daily television program.

1. Texas Beef Group v. Oprah Winfrey, 11 F. Supp. 2d 858, 862 (N.D. Tex. 1998). The program had been tape recorded on April 11, 1996.
2. Id.
3. See, e.g., Richard Roeper, *Oprah's Sheep Ready to Follow Every Whim,* CHI. SUN-TIMES, Jan. 22, 1998, at 11 ("If Oprah Winfrey appeared on her show tomorrow morning wearing a bucket on her head while extolling the virtues of yodeling, by this weekend you'd see millions of Americans walking around with buckets on their heads as they warbled to the sky: 'Yo-da-lay-dee-yo-da-lay-dee-yo-da-lay-hee-hoo....' Such is Winfrey's power to sway her flock to do her bidding. Sometimes I think she couldn't have any more influence on her viewers if she had them hypnotized. That's why there's a trial going on in Amarillo, Texas."). See also David McLemore, *Oprah's Talk Shows Why She's Daytime Queen,* DAILY TELEGRAPH, Feb. 5, 1998, at 20 ("On Tuesday, she acknowledged her show, seen by 20 million people daily, had the power to influence her viewers.").
4. Texas Beef Group v. Oprah Winfrey, 11 F. Supp. 2d at 869 (1998).
5. CNN Business Unusual, Sept. 10, 2000. *available at* http://transcripts.cnn.com TRANSCRIPTS/0009/10/bun.00.html.
6. Texas Beef Group v. Oprah Winfrey, 11 F. Supp. 2d 858. The ruling was also based on the failure of the plaintiffs to prove that cattle are perishable food, a requirement under the Texas False Disparagement of Perishable Food Products Act. The plaintiffs sued for the alleged violation of this provision of the act.
7. Texas Beef Group v. Oprah Winfrey, 201 F.3d 680 (9th Cir. 2000).

While the categories are "arbitrary and archaic,"[44] they remain valid today. With that, slander per se is slander that falls into one of the four categories; **slander per quod** is slander that falls outside the four categories.

slander per quod A spoken statement whose injurious nature requires proof.

Among the challenges for a court is deciding what the words or images at issue in a libel case mean and whether they can be considered defamatory. Whether they are actionable cannot simply be determined according to whether they harmed the plaintiff's reputation. The allegedly libelous matter may conceivably harm reputation without rising to the level of defamation. Thus, another element of defamation that plaintiffs must show is that the material "is reasonably capable of sustaining defamatory meaning."[45] A judge decides whether the words constituting the statement at issue are capable of conveying defamatory meaning. If so, the case may move to trial to determine whether, in fact, the words did convey a defamatory meaning.

Business Reputation While businesses and corporations do not have reputations in the same sense that individuals do, they can suffer a kind of reputational harm that can impair their ability to conduct business. Consequently, they may sue, particularly if their business depends on the goodwill of the public. In addition, individuals within businesses and corporations may have a legitimate libel claim when criticism of the business falsely implies wrongdoing on their part.

Trade Libel Trade libel pertains to criticism of products rather than criticism of people or businesses. For example, the Bose Corporation sued the publisher of Consumer Reports magazine for negative remarks in a review of audio speakers. In part, the review said: "[I]ndividual instruments heard through the Bose system seemed to grow to gigantic proportions and tended to wander about the room. . . . We think they might become annoying when listening to soloists."[46] The U.S. Supreme Court ultimately ruled that no libel had taken place because the review was not published knowing it contained false information or with reckless disregard for the truth.

Bose was no exception to the reality that plaintiffs who file trade libel claims find it difficult to win. Another example is the successful defense presented by CBS when its "60 Minutes" television news program was sued for product disparagement. A claim in a segment of the program suggested that apples grown in Washington state were unsafe because they were treated with the chemical Alar. The Washington apple growers, however, were unable to prove that the "60 Minutes" claims were false.[47] The case was dismissed, and the ruling was upheld on appeal.[48]

Falsity

For a statement to be libelous, it must be false. The plaintiff is responsible for demonstrating that the statement at issue is false rather than the defendant's being saddled with the burden of proving the statement is true.

Historically this scheme was reversed: the burden of proof was placed on the defendant. That is, the libel defendant was required to prove that the statement in question was true. This was the case in English common law. Moreover, when the English government used libel law in an effort to silence critics, truth was rejected as a defense. True but defamatory statements about the government, it was believed, were even more harmful than false criticism. Later, the common law recognized truth as a defense in civil libel cases.

Libel law in the United States now clearly places the burden of proof regarding falsity on the plaintiff. The U.S. Supreme Court has emphatically reinforced this aspect of libel law. Justice Sandra Day O'Connor, writing for the Court in a case involving a Philadelphia newspaper, emphasized the importance of protecting and encouraging the free flow of information and ideas:

> We believe that the Constitution requires us to tip [the scales] in favor of protecting free speech. . . . The burden of proving truth upon media defendants who publish speech of public concern deters such speech because of the fear that liability will unjustifiably result. . . . Because such a "chilling" effect would be antithetical to the First Amendment's protection of true speech on matters of public concern . . . a plaintiff must bear the burden of showing that the speech at issue is false before recovering damages for defamation from a media defendant. To do otherwise could only result in a deterrence of the speech which the Constitution makes free.[49]

Substantial Truth Libel law provides some latitude with regard to falsity. Minor error or discrepancy does not necessarily make a statement false. As long as the statement is substantially true, it cannot meet the standard for falsity and therefore cannot be libelous. As one federal trial court said, "Slight inaccuracies of expression are immaterial provided that the defamatory charge is true in substance."[50] The Supreme Court has agreed, saying that substantial truth "would absolve a defendant even if she cannot justify every word of the alleged defamatory matter; it is sufficient if the substance of the charge is proved true, irrespective of the slight inaccuracy in the details. . . . Minor inaccuracies do not amount to falsity so long as the substance, the gist, the sting of the libelous charge can be justified."[51]

One appellate court has used a test to determine whether a published statement is substantially true by considering both the gist of the statement and "whether the alleged defamatory statement was more damaging to the plaintiff's reputation, in the mind of the average listener, than a truthful statement would have been."[52] The nonlibelous nature of substantially true statements would mean, for example, that if a newspaper reports that an individual was in police custody when, in fact, the individual had been released on bail, the story would likely be substantially true because the individual had been in custody and it was only an error in timing that had caused the mistake. If, however, a newspaper publishes a story saying that a person has been charged with a crime when in fact she has only been investigated by the police, it is unlikely the story would be judged to be substantially true. In sum, if something is not at least substantially true, then it is false.

Implication and Innuendo Falsity is often clear-cut. Sometimes, however, it is not. While individual statements within an article or report may be factually accurate, taken together they may paint a different sort of picture. Through implication or innuendo, libelous messages may be created. In a case dismissed by a Washington state appeals court in 2010, for example, a crane operator sued a newspaper for what he said was implied in headlines. After an accident, Seattle Post-Intelligencer headlines read, "Operator in crane wreck has history of drug abuse" and "Man completed mandated rehab program after his last arrest in 2000." The crane operator's tests for drugs after the accident were negative. He filed several claims including libel, though he admitted that there were no false statements in the newspaper. Still, he claimed "defamation by implication" due to the juxtaposing of true statements in a way that created a false impression. While the Washington court said it did recognize libel by implication (some states do not), it is only when a false implication occurs through the omission of facts. There was nothing to indicate, the court ruled, that the Seattle newspaper omitted any facts.[53] This case followed a 2007 Iowa Supreme Court ruling that public plaintiffs there can sue for "defamation by implication." The court said that if a true fact is not properly and thoroughly explained, it can become defamatory if, when read in a particular way, it carries false implications.[54]

Those in the electronic media face another pitfall: the meaning of a story may be altered, sometimes dramatically, through voice inflections. Given the informal style that is a hallmark of broadcast writing, the effect can be devastating. Imagine, for example, a newscaster saying in a cynical tone, "Well, the mayor was at it again last night." The juxtaposition of visual images and accompanying "voice over," while each may be factually correct, can combine to create a false statement. As an example, a libel suit was filed against a Chicago television station claiming that one of its reporters gave a false impression of what had occurred and thereby defamed the plaintiffs with his skeptical tone of voice. That is, while his words themselves were innocent enough, the tone with which they were delivered was at the root of the libel claim. The judge, however, agreed with the defendant's position that in this case the tone alone could not support the defamation suit, and the claim was dismissed.[55]

Points of Law

The Burden of Proof as Deterrent

The burden of proof of falsity occasionally serves as a deterrent to potential plaintiffs. The requirement to delve deeply into the allegedly libelous statement and refute its veracity is sometimes so distasteful that would-be plaintiffs choose not to file libel claims in the first place. The information revealed in the process may be more embarrassing and damaging to reputation than the allegedly libelous statement. In addition, this proof of falsity requirement leads targets of some news media investigations to conclude that a libel claim is not their best course of action. That is, under some circumstances plaintiffs may not want the truth or falsity of a news report's claims analyzed. The possibility that the allegations could be proved true or substantially true can be discouraging to a potential plaintiff. (See, e.g., the examination of the *Food Lion* case in Chapter 8.)

SUMMARY

THE LIBEL PLAINTIFF'S CASE HAS SEVERAL ELEMENTS, all of which must be proved in court to win. The material in question must be (1) a statement of fact (2) that is published, (3) that is of and concerning the plaintiff, (4) that is defamatory, (5) that is false, and (6) that is the result of fault by the defendant. The first five elements are examined in the preceding sections. No matter where libel occurs or in what communicative medium, the plaintiff must prove the same elements. ■

Fault

negligence Generally, the failure to exercise reasonable or ordinary care. In libel law, negligence is usually the minimum level of fault a plaintiff must prove in order to receive damages.

To support a libel claim, a plaintiff must show that the defendant was at fault in making public the allegedly false and defamatory statement of fact. Whether the defendant was at fault was traditionally established by showing that the defendant had engaged in some form of negligence. **Negligence** is commonly defined as the failure to exercise reasonable or ordinary care. For a news media defendant, reasonable care would likely mean those attributes that are common to sound journalism: fact-checking, confirming information with multiple sources, ensuring balance and fairness and so on. By the middle of the 20th century, the idea began taking root that enforcing liability without fault was contrary to the First Amendment, improperly infringing on the free speech and press guarantees. Moreover, while some level of fault was required, questions remained regarding what standards of fault should be established and under what kind of circumstances each should be imposed. Some questioned whether a tougher standard than negligence should be established for a libel claim to stick, especially when considering the First Amendment.

New York Times Co. v. Sullivan One of the most important legal cases in the history of American constitutional law is a libel case, *New York Times Co. v. Sullivan*.[56] The U.S. Supreme Court's ruling in that case has had a monumental impact, not just on journalism but on society as a whole.

The circumstances of *New York Times Co. v. Sullivan* arose within the context of the civil rights movement of the 1960s. African-American groups seeking racial equality under the law frequently engaged in nonviolent marches in Southern states. These events tended to be minimized or ignored by the local press in those states but were covered elsewhere, including frequently in The New York Times. Many Southern leaders resented the Times and other Northern newspapers that covered the marches.

Against that backdrop, a coalition of civil rights leaders purchased space in The New York Times for a full-page statement. Carrying the headline "Heed Their Rising Voices," the "advertorial" made charges against officials in Southern states who, the statement claimed, had used violent and illegal methods to suppress the marches. While the gist of the statements was factually accurate, there were some errors of fact. Asserting he had been defamed, L.B. Sullivan, the police commissioner of Montgomery, Ala., filed a libel claim against the Times and some of the civil rights leaders who had purchased the newspaper space. He sought $500,000 in damages from the Times, which was at the time far from financially invulnerable.

Although Sullivan was not identified by name in the statement, he maintained that it was nevertheless "of and concerning" him. The ad criticized public officials who, it said, used illegal tactics and violence to counter peaceful demonstrations. Sullivan maintained that the statements implicated him. He and his attorneys were able to file a libel claim in Alabama because several copies of the paper had been circulated in Montgomery County. A trial court there quickly ruled in Sullivan's favor, awarding him $500,000 in damages. The Alabama Supreme Court upheld both the verdict and the award.

The New York Times appealed the case to the U.S. Supreme Court, arguing that because Sullivan was a public official, a higher standard should be applied to his claim that a news story had libeled him. The case came at a critical time both in the history of the civil rights movement and for The New York Times, which could have suffered crippling financial damage if the judgment against it was affirmed. In a landmark ruling that rewrote the law of libel in the United States, the Court ruled 9–0 in favor of the Times, reversing the judgment of the Alabama Supreme Court. Associate Justice William Brennan, who wrote the opinion for a unanimous Court, had labored to win the votes of all eight of his brethren on the Court so that the opinion would arrive with the resounding authority its subject matter deserved.

The Court's decision in *Sullivan* was based on the premise that to readily punish a media organization for publishing criticism of government officials was contrary to "the central meaning of the First Amendment," an argument that for the first time made the magisterial protections of the First Amendment apply to the law of libel. The Court's decision rested on the principle that media defendants did not have sufficient protection from libel suits. Awarding victories to libel plaintiffs too easily, the Court reasoned, threatened to choke off the free flow of information that is essential to the maintenance of a democratic society. Fear of making even minor errors would result in a chilling effect on the media, unduly restricting press freedom. Moreover, this freedom was especially important when it came to criticism of the government and government officials. This kind of "political speech" is a core First Amendment value.[57] To allow libel plaintiffs who are government officials to be successful without a showing of fault at a level higher than negligence would be tantamount to reinstituting seditious libel—prohibiting criticism of the government.

For Sullivan to win his case, Brennan wrote, the police commissioner would have to prove that The New York Times published the editorial-advertisement knowing it contained false information or with reckless disregard for its truth. This standard, Brennan wrote, was called "**actual malice.**" Media defendants must have some room for error—"breathing space," as Justice Brennan called it.[58] After this ruling, it was no longer enough for plaintiffs who are public officials to prove only that the defendant was negligent. They had to show that the content was published with actual malice—a new and more difficult to prove level of fault.

actual malice In libel law, a statement made knowing it is false or with reckless disregard for its truth.

Justice Brennan explained that the Court's ruling was based on the importance in a free society of unfettered debate on public issues: "We consider this case against the background of a profound national commitment to the principle that debate on public issues should be uninhibited, robust, and wide-open."[59] This debate should be open not just to members of the press but also to members of

> *"The growing movement of peaceful mass demonstrations by Negroes is something new in the South, something understandable. . . . Let Congress heed their rising voices, for they will be heard."*
>
> —*New York Times* editorial
> Saturday, March 19, 1960

Heed Their Rising Voices

As the whole world knows by now, thousands of Southern Negro students are engaged in widespread non-violent demonstrations in positive affirmation of the right to live in human dignity as guaranteed by the U. S. Constitution and the Bill of Rights. In their efforts to uphold these guarantees, they are being met by an unprecedented wave of terror by those who would deny and negate that document which the whole world looks upon as setting the pattern for modern freedom...

In Orangeburg, South Carolina, when 400 students peacefully sought to buy doughnuts and coffee at lunch counters in the business district, they were forcibly ejected, tear-gassed, soaked to the skin in freezing weather with fire hoses, arrested en masse and herded into an open barbed-wire stockade to stand for hours in the bitter cold.

In Montgomery, Alabama, after students sang "My Country, 'Tis of Thee" on the State Capitol steps, their leaders were expelled from school, and truckloads of police armed with shotguns and tear-gas ringed the Alabama State College Campus. When the entire student body protested to state authorities by refusing to re-register, their dining hall was padlocked in an attempt to starve them into submission.

In Tallahassee, Atlanta, Nashville, Savannah, Greensboro, Memphis, Richmond, Charlotte, and a host of other cities in the South, young American teenagers, in face of the entire weight of official state apparatus and police power, have boldly stepped forth as protagonists of democracy. Their courage and amazing restraint have inspired millions and given a new dignity to the cause of freedom.

Small wonder that the Southern violators of the Constitution fear this new, non-violent brand of freedom fighter... even as they fear the upswelling right-to-vote movement. Small wonder that they are determined to destroy the one man who, more than any other, symbolizes the new spirit now sweeping the South—the Rev. Dr. Martin Luther King, Jr., world-famous leader of the Montgomery Bus Protest. For it is his doctrine of non-violence which has inspired and guided the students in their widening wave of sit-ins; and it is this same Dr. King who founded and is president of the Southern Christian Leadership Conference—the organization which is spearheading the surging right-to-vote movement. Under Dr. King's direction the Leadership Conference conducts Student Workshops and Seminars in the philosophy and techniques of non-violent resistance.

Again and again the Southern violators have answered Dr. King's peaceful protests with intimidation and violence. They have bombed his home almost killing his wife and child. They have assaulted his person. They have arrested him seven times—for "speeding," "loitering" and similar "offenses." And now they have charged him with "perjury"—a *felony* under which they could imprison him for *ten years*. Obviously, their real purpose is to remove him physically as the leader to whom the students and millions of others—look for guidance and support, and thereby to intimidate *all* leaders who may rise in the South. Their strategy is to behead this affirmative movement, and thus to demoralize Negro Americans and weaken their will to struggle. The defense of Martin Luther King, spiritual leader of the student sit-in movement, clearly, therefore, is an integral part of the total struggle for freedom in the South.

Decent-minded Americans cannot help but applaud the creative daring of the students and the quiet heroism of Dr. King. But this is one of those moments in the stormy history of Freedom when men and women of good will must do more than applaud the rising-to-glory of others. The America whose good name hangs in the balance before a watchful world, the America whose heritage of Liberty these Southern Upholders of the Constitution are defending, is *our* America as well as theirs...

We must heed their rising voices—yes—but we must add our own.

We must extend ourselves above and beyond moral support and render the material help so urgently needed by those who are taking the risks, facing jail, and *even death* in a glorious re-affirmation of our Constitution and its Bill of Rights.

We urge you to join hands with our fellow Americans in the South by supporting, with your dollars, this combined appeal for all three needs—the defense of Martin Luther King—the support of the embattled students—and the struggle for the right-to-vote.

Your Help Is Urgently Needed . . . NOW!!

Stella Adler	Dr. Alan Knight Chalmers	Anthony Franciosa	John Killens	L. Joseph Overton	Maureen Stapleton
Raymond Pace Alexander	Richard Coe	Lorraine Hansbury	Eartha Kitt	Clarence Pickett	Frank Silvera
Harry Van Arsdale	Nat King Cole	Rev. Donald Harrington	Rabbi Edward Klein	Shad Polier	Hope Stevens
Harry Belafonte	Cheryl Crawford	Nat Hentoff	Hope Lange	Sidney Poitier	George Tabor
Julie Belafonte	Dorothy Dandridge	James Hicks	John Lewis	A. Philip Randolph	Rev. Gardner C.
Dr. Algernon Black	Ossie Davis	Mary Hinkson	Viveca Lindfors	John Raitt	Taylor
Marc Blitzstein	Sammy Davis, Jr.	Van Heflin	Carl Murphy	Elmer Rice	Norman Thomas
William Branch	Ruby Dee	Langston Hughes	Don Murray	Jackie Robinson	Kenneth Tynan
Marlon Brando	Dr. Philip Elliott	Morris Iushewitz	John Murray	Mrs. Eleanor Roosevelt	Charles White
Mrs. Ralph Bunche	Dr. Harry Emerson	Mahalia Jackson	A. J. Muste	Bayard Rustin	Shelley Winters
Diahann Carroll	Fosdick	Mordecai Johnson	Frederick O'Neal	Robert Ryan	Max Youngstein

We in the south who are struggling daily for dignity and freedom warmly endorse this appeal

Rev. Ralph D. Abernathy *(Montgomery, Ala.)*	Rev. Matthew D. McCollom *(Orangeburg, S.C.)*	Rev. Walter L. Hamilton *(Norfolk, Va.)*	Rev. A. L. Davis *(New Orleans, La.)*
Rev. Fred L. Shuttlesworth *(Birmingham, Ala.)*	Rev. William Holmes Borders	I. S. Levy *(Columbia, S.C.)*	Mrs. Katie E. Whickham *(New Orleans, La.)*
Rev. Kelley Miller Smith *(Nashville, Tenn.)*	*(Atlanta, Ga.)*	Rev. Martin Luther King, Sr. *(Atlanta, Ga.)*	Rev. W. H. Hall *(Hattiesburg, Miss.)*
Rev. W. A. Dennis *(Chattanooga, Tenn.)*	Rev. Douglas Moore *(Durham, N.C.)*	Rev. Henry C. Bunton *(Memphis, Tenn.)*	Rev. J. E. Lowery *(Mobile, Ala.)*
Rev. C. K. Steele *(Tallahassee, Fla.)*	Rev. Wyatt Tee Walker *(Petersburg, Va.)*	Rev. S.S. Seay, Sr. *(Montgomery, Ala.)* Rev. Samuel W. Williams *(Atlanta, Ga.)*	Rev. T. J. Jemison *(Baton Rouge, La.)*

COMMITTEE TO DEFEND MARTIN LUTHER KING AND THE STRUGGLE FOR FREEDOM IN THE SOUTH

312 West 125th Street, New York 27, N.Y. UNiversity 6-1700

Chairmen: A. Philip Randolph, Dr. Gardner C. Taylor; *Chairmen of Cultural Division:* Harry Belafonte, Sidney Poitier; *Treasurer:* Nat King Cole; *Executive Director:* Bayard Rustin; *Chairmen of Church Division:* Father George B. Ford, Rev. Harry Emerson Fosdick, Rev. Thomas Kilgore, Jr., Rabbi Edward E. Klein; *Chairman of Labor Division:* Morris Iushewitz

Please mail this coupon TODAY!

Committee To Defend Martin Luther King
and
The Struggle For Freedom in The South
312 West 125th Street, New York 27, N.Y.
UNiversity 6-1700

I am enclosing my contribution of $
for the work of the Committee.

Name _____

Address _____

City _____ Zone _____ State _____

☐ I want to help   ☐ Please send further information

Please make checks payable to:
Committee to Defend Martin Luther King

The New York Times' "advertorial" that prompted L. B. Sullivan's libel lawsuit against the newspaper.

realWorld Law

The Impact of *New York Times Co. v. Sullivan:* The "Central Meaning of the First Amendment"

New York Times Co. v. Sullivan "revolutionized the law of libel and, equally importantly, it signaled a critical shift in our general First Amendment jurisprudence."[1] The ruling went beyond determining whether particular material was protected or unprotected. It embraced principles that decry chilling effects and include a speech-protective approach, what one scholar suggested was the central meaning of the First Amendment. Harry Kalven, Jr., wrote that for the first time, the *Sullivan* ruling put seditious libel—criticism of government or government officials—in its proper place. "The concept of seditious libel strikes at the very heart of democracy," Kalven wrote. "Political freedom ends when government can use its powers and its courts to silence its critics."[2] Defamation of the government, he continued, is an impossible notion for a democracy.

Kalven believed that *New York Times Co. v. Sullivan* squarely addressed the concept of seditious libel, punishment for which was first legalized in the United States by the Sedition Act of 1798. In turn, that law made possible two early 20th-century laws that, in Kalven's words, "oddly echoed the idiom of seditious libel."[3] By doing so, the Supreme Court reaffirmed the core meaning of the First Amendment initially outlined by James Madison.

1. Kermit L. Hall (ed.), The Oxford Guide to United States Supreme Court Decisions 216 (1999).
2. Harry Kalven, Jr., *The New York Times Case: A Note on "The Central Meaning of the First Amendment,"* 1964 Sup. Ct. Rev. 191, 205.
3. *Id.* at 207.

the public, who otherwise may not have access to the press.[60] If libel plaintiffs were not required to show actual malice by news organizations before they could win libel suits, he wrote, such debate would be unduly limited, because of self-censorship by both public and press.[61] His opinion for the Court emphasized that when people enter government service, they assume roles in which their job performance is rightly scrutinized and often criticized by the public and press. Thus, the open debate the Court sought to protect, he acknowledged, "may well include vehement, caustic, and sometimes unpleasantly sharp attacks on government and public officials."[62]

Furthermore, because public officials have easy access to the news media, the Court reasoned, they have an avenue by which to correct any reputational harm they may have suffered. Thus, the level of fault they must show should be a higher, more difficult standard to prove than negligence.

One major impact of the Court's decision in *New York Times Co. v. Sullivan* was to embolden the U.S. news media. The opinion emphasized that the First Amendment permitted—even encouraged—an aggressive press. This was especially true with regard to the media's role as a "watchdog" in democratic society, keeping an eye on those in government. Allowing libel suits to proceed too easily against this vital organ of democratic society would be damaging to our form of government. Referring to the consequences of large damage awards against

Points of Law

Actual Malice

- Knowledge of falsity or
- Reckless disregard for the truth

newspapers, Brennan wrote, "Whether or not a newspaper can survive a succession of such judgments, the pall of fear and timidity imposed upon those who would give voice to public criticism is an atmosphere in which the First Amendment freedoms cannot survive."[63]

Enjoying added protection from lawsuits in public official libel cases, the news media were more aggressive in the wake of the *Sullivan* case. Whether one views this favorably or unfavorably, it is hardly a coincidence that, in the years immediately following the ruling, aggressive coverage of events such as the civil rights movement, the Vietnam War and the Watergate scandal followed. That same protection was later used by the media in public figure cases. Some argue that a revival or increase of tabloid journalism during the last two or three decades of the 20th century is attributable to the application of the actual malice standard.[64]

Thus, with *New York Times Co. v. Sullivan*, libel law was "constitutionalized." The phrase "freedom of the press" was given new meaning. Restricting the flow of information, as the Court observed was possible under prior libel standards, is antithetical to the philosophy and spirit of the First Amendment.

Actual Malice

As noted previously, "actual malice" is defined as knowledge of falsity or reckless disregard for the truth. Though the examination of this concept began within the discussion of *New York Times Co. v. Sullivan*, additional scrutiny is required given the developments that followed that ruling.

Knowledge of Falsity Knowledge of falsity is nothing more than lying—publishing information knowing it is false. Knowledge of falsity tends to be uncommon in the news media, where truth and accuracy are virtually universal standards. Nonetheless, a news report in which the publisher "stacks the deck" to produce an intentionally distorted representation may rise to the level of knowledge of falsity. During the 1964 presidential campaign, for example, some people questioned the fitness for office of the Republican Party nominee, Senator Barry Goldwater. The publisher of Fact magazine, Ralph Ginsburg, sent a questionnaire to hundreds of psychiatrists that asked them to analyze Goldwater's mental condition. He received a variety of responses but, in a "psychobiographical" article, published only those that reflected poorly on the senator. When Goldwater sued for libel, the court concluded Ginsburg's conduct qualified as knowledge of falsity.[65]

Does knowingly changing the statements of an interview subject also qualify as knowledge of falsity, especially when those words are enclosed by quotation marks in print? Not necessarily. Reporter Janet Malcolm did just that in articles published in The New Yorker in 1983. The articles were based on more than 40 hours of taped interviews with psychoanalyst Jeffrey Masson. When Masson

Masson v. New Yorker Magazine, Inc. and Journalistic Responsibility

The U.S. Supreme Court's handling of *Masson v. New Yorker Magazine, Inc.* led to disillusionment in some circles over a ruling that some say is inconsistent with any semblance of journalistic responsibility. Given that public trust is at the foundation of journalistic ethics—and that deliberately altering the words of someone who has granted an interview violates that trust—the approval of a practice that undermines that trust has attracted criticism.[1] In fact, Justice Byron White's dissenting opinion expressed the idea that because reporter Janet Malcolm wrote that Jeffrey Masson said certain things she knew Masson did not say, she acted with "knowing falsehood,"[2] thus satisfying the actual malice standard. According to this view, the sort of quotation alteration in which Malcolm engaged would not be permitted, and Masson's libel suit ultimately could have been successful.

Jeffrey Masson

Masson also raises questions about whether the deliberate alteration of quotations satisfies the definition of either prong of actual malice (knowledge of falsity or reckless disregard for the truth). The U.S. Supreme Court considered whether Malcolm's action could be considered knowledge of falsity. In this case, the reporter's act was purposeful and therefore with her knowledge. However, the Court ruled, the alteration did not result in converting the quotation to a false statement. That is, quotations cannot be considered false unless their material meaning is changed.[3] The application of this part of the actual malice standard also rests on the judgment that Malcolm did not change the meaning of Masson's actual words. As long as the meaning is not materially changed—and thus the quotation remains true—she could not have exhibited reckless disregard for the truth.

Janet Malcolm

In the end, *Masson* may serve as a classic example of a case that represents a clash between legal and ethical standards.

---

1. *See, e.g.*, Neil J. Kinkopf, *Malice in Wonderland: Fictionalized Quotations and the Constitutionally Compelled Substantial Truth Doctrine*, 41 Case W. Res. 1271 (1991).
2. Masson v. New Yorker Magazine, Inc., 501 U.S. 496, 526 (1991) ("By any definition of the term, this was "knowing falsehood").
3. *Id.* at 517. "We conclude that a deliberate alteration of the words uttered by a plaintiff does not equate with knowledge of falsity for purposes of New York Times . . . unless the alteration results in a material change in the meaning conveyed by the statement."

sued for libel, a decade-long journey through the courts began. At one stop along the way, the U.S. Supreme Court noted that in those hours of recorded interviews, no statements identical to the challenged passages appeared. In its decision, the Court ruled that while readers presume that words within quotation marks are verbatim reproductions of what the interviewee said, it would be unrealistic for the law to require the press to meet such a standard. Justice Anthony Kennedy wrote, "A deliberate alteration of the words uttered by a plaintiff does not equate with knowledge of falsity . . . unless the alteration results in a material change in the meaning conveyed by the statement."[66] Absent an alteration that changes the meaning, the words remain substantially true.

Reckless Disregard for the Truth Reckless disregard for the truth may be thought of as sloppy journalism—very sloppy. The sloppiness must be both careless and irresponsible. In its *New York Times Co. v. Sullivan* ruling, the U.S. Supreme Court made it clear that the failure by the newspaper in that case to check the advertisement against its own records did not rise to the level of reckless disregard. A few years later, the Court considered two cases simultaneously that began to add to the understanding of this prong of actual malice. In the first, a weekly magazine, The Saturday Evening Post, published an article in 1963 about an attempt to fix a 1962 college football game. The magazine's source claimed he had been "patched" into a telephone conversation between the athletic director at the University of Georgia, Wally Butts, and the head football coach at the University of Alabama, Paul "Bear" Bryant. Moreover, the source claimed that in the call he heard the two men arranging the fix. The source, George Burnett, said he took careful notes of the conversation. The Saturday Evening Post based its article on Burnett's recollection but never asked to see his notes. No effort was made by the magazine to corroborate the information with other sources, nor were other potential sources of information consulted, such as football experts, game films or witnesses. Burnett's credibility also went unchecked. It turned out he had a criminal record. The magazine's editors—and Burnett—failed to do their jobs adequately. As Justice John Harlan wrote in his opinion for the Court, "In short, the evidence is ample to support a finding of highly unreasonable conduct constituting an extreme departure from the standards of investigation and reporting ordinarily adhered to by responsible publishers."[67] The Court indicated that the omissions of responsibility by The Saturday Evening Post clearly qualified as the kind of conduct that rises to the level of reckless disregard for the truth.

In the second case, a retired major general, Edwin Walker, sued the Associated Press (AP) for its reports on his role in incidents surrounding efforts to keep the peace at the University of Mississippi when that institution was attempting to enroll its first African-American student in 1962. The AP reported that Walker had taken command of a violent crowd of protestors and had personally led a charge against federal marshals sent there to enforce a court decree and to assist in preserving order. The report also described Walker as encouraging rioters to use violence and giving them technical advice on combating the effects of tear gas.[68] These false statements were distributed to several other media outlets.

In distinguishing the two cases, the Court cited one significant factor:

The evidence showed that the Butts story was in no sense "hot news" and the editors of the magazine recognized the need for a thorough investigation of the serious charges. . . . In contrast to the Butts article, the dispatch which concerns us in Walker was news which required immediate dissemination. The Associated Press received the information from a correspondent who was present at the scene of the events and gave every indication of being trustworthy and competent. His dispatches in this instance, with one minor exception, were internally consistent and would not have seemed unreasonable to one familiar with General Walker's prior publicized statements on the underlying controversy. Considering the necessity for rapid dissemination, nothing in this series of events gives the slightest hint of a severe departure from accepted publishing standards. We therefore conclude that General Walker should not be entitled to damages from the Associated Press.[69]

Thus, the urgency of a story has a significant bearing on whether the methods used by the news media defendant exhibit reckless disregard for the truth. The Court is willing to allow the news media some "wiggle room" when there is deadline pressure. In addition, the reliability of a story's source and the believability of the information are also factors in the judgment.

The following year, the Supreme Court further developed its reckless disregard standard. First, the Court admitted that "reckless disregard" cannot be summarized in a single, infallible definition. But it went on to say that reckless conduct is not measured merely by whether a reasonably prudent person would have published or would have investigated before publishing. "There must be sufficient evidence to permit the conclusion that the defendant in fact entertained serious doubts as to the truth of his publication. Publishing with such doubts shows reckless disregard for the truth or falsity and demonstrates actual malice."[70] Thus, the Supreme Court had now infused the reckless disregard standard with an element of subjectivity. It was no longer enough to merely examine the evidence related to the publisher's actions; now it was also necessary to determine the publisher's state of mind. But does this standard place a premium on ignorance? Does it reward a publisher who has doubts about the information but does nothing prior to publication to investigate? Evidence of investigation could be used against the publisher in court. The Supreme Court admitted that this possibility existed but said the purpose of the entire actual malice standard was to emphasize free expression. It seems the Court was saying that if it was going to err in its definition of reckless disregard, it would do so on the side that tends to enhance rather than chill expression.

More than a decade later, the Supreme Court considered whether evidence could be used to help make judgments about a libel

Points of Law

"Reckless Disregard" Criteria

- *Urgency of the story.* Is there time to check the information?

- *Source reliability.* Is the source trustworthy?

- *Story believability.* Is further examination necessary?

deposition Testimony by a witness conducted outside a courtroom and intended to be used in preparation for trial.

defendant's state of mind. During a **deposition** (testimony by a witness conducted outside a courtroom and intended to be used in preparation for a trial), a "60 Minutes" segment producer had refused to answer certain questions related to his editorial decisions concerning a 1973 broadcast about a government cover-up of atrocities during the Vietnam War, claiming the First Amendment protected them from being disclosed. The Supreme Court disagreed and ruled that the plaintiff could look into the defendant's mental processes.[71]

A decade later, in 1989, the Court further indicated that a judgment concerning reckless disregard need not necessarily focus on any single lapse by the defendant but may rest on an evaluation of the record as a whole. In other words, the more mistakes are made, the more readily a court may conclude that a defendant acted with reckless disregard.

The Court ruled that an Ohio newspaper had acted with actual malice when it failed to interview the one witness who could have verified its story about alleged corruption in a local election for a judgeship; the newspaper did not listen to a tape it had been told would exonerate the plaintiff, a tape that the plaintiff delivered to the newspaper at the newspaper's request; an editorial the newspaper published prior to the libelous report indicated the editor had already decided to publish the allegations at issue regardless of evidence to the contrary; and discrepancies in the testimony of the defendant's own witnesses that supported the idea that the defendant had failed to conduct a complete investigation with the deliberate intent of avoiding the truth.[72]

Public Officials *New York Times Co. v. Sullivan* also established that not only is the content of the allegedly libelous material important, so is the nature of the plaintiff. The ruling said in attempting to prove their case, public official plaintiffs must show that fault on the part of the defendant is at the level of actual malice. Private figures, on the other hand, are usually required to show some lesser, easier-to-prove level of fault, typically negligence. As one authority has written, "Paradoxically, holding public office simultaneously raised and put in jeopardy one's reputation."[73] Justice Brennan believed this paradox was justified.

But who qualifies as a public official? There is a temptation to answer by saying, "All government employees." But this is not quite accurate. The U.S. Supreme Court, again through Justice Brennan, has said, "It is clear that the 'public official' designation applies at the very least to those among the hierarchy of government employees who have or appear to have to the public substantial responsibility for or control over the conduct of governmental affairs."[74] The idea is that people who meet that definition are people whom the public is justified in wanting to know about because they serve the public. Information about them may relate to the officials' qualifications, conduct and character. But not all those paid by government for their work meet the criteria.

Conversely, one can meet the public official standard without being a government employee. For example, a libel plaintiff in New Hampshire who was hired by three elected county commissioners to supervise a public recreation facility owned by the county was deemed to be a public official by the Supreme Court in 1966. The Court explained the standard as follows: "Where a position in government has such apparent importance that the public has an independent interest in the qualifications and performance of the person who holds it, beyond the general public interest in the qualifications, conduct and performance of all government employees, both elements we identified in New York Times are present and the New York Times malice standards apply."[75]

A person usually remains a public official even after leaving a position that includes substantial responsibility for or control over the conduct of governmental affairs as long as the allegedly libelous material pertains to the person's conduct while in that post. However, the U.S. Supreme Court has said that it is possible, though rare, for the passage of time to erode the public's interest in the official's conduct in office so much that the actual malice standard would no longer apply.[76]

Public Figures After *New York Times Co. v. Sullivan*, the question arose whether the actual malice standard should be limited only to public officials. Is there another category of people whose public status ought to require them to also prove the defendant acted with actual malice when they sue for libel? The U.S. Supreme Court answered this question in the affirmative in *Curtis Publishing Co. v. Butts* and *Associated Press v. Walker*, the two cases described previously and considered simultaneously by the Court. Chief Justice Earl Warren wrote: "To me, differentiation between 'public figures' and 'public officials' and the adoption of separate standards of proof for each has no basis in law, logic, or First Amendment policy. Increasingly in this country, the distinctions between governmental and private sectors are blurred."[77] As Chief Justice Warren noted, one reason that a higher level of fault is required of public officials is that they typically have access to the media to correct damage to their reputation. **Public figures,** he claimed, are no different:

> "Public figures," like "public officials," often play an influential role in ordering society. And surely as a class these "public figures" have as ready access as "public officials" to the mass media of communication, both to influence policy and to counter criticism of their views and activities. Our citizenry has a legitimate and substantial interest in the conduct of such persons, and freedom of the press to engage in uninhibited debate about their involvement in public issues and events is as crucial as it is in the case of "public officials." The fact that they are not amenable to the restraints of the political process only underscores the legitimate and substantial nature of the interest, since it means that public opinion may be the only instrument by which society can attempt to influence their conduct.[78]

public figure In libel law, a plaintiff who is in the public spotlight, usually voluntarily, and must prove the defendant acted with actual malice in order to win damages.

Thus, the opportunity to "set the record straight" because of access to the media justified expanding the actual malice standard to any public figure. Private figures typically have no such access to the media. One question remained, however: Who qualifies as a public figure?

All-Purpose Public Figures The U.S. Supreme Court has defined two categories of public figures. Both must prove that a defendant acted with actual malice. In *Gertz v. Robert Welch, Inc.* (excerpted at the end of this chapter), the Court said that some people "occupy positions of such persuasive power and influence that they are deemed public figures for all purposes."[79] An **all-purpose public figure** is anyone whom a court labels to be "public" under all circumstances. That is, no matter the context, the individual's name is widely recognizable to at least some segments of the public. However, some courts demand that an additional requirement be met for all-purpose public figure status: The person must also have written or spoken about a broad range of issues. These are people who have acquired some degree of fame outside the public official sphere—"celebrities," if you will. This could include not only those in the entertainment field but also some athletes, activists, religious leaders and business leaders.

all-purpose public figure In libel law, a person who occupies a position of such persuasive power and influence as to be deemed a public figure for all purposes. Public figure libel plaintiffs are required to prove actual malice.

Limited-Purpose Public Figures More common than all-purpose public figures are those people who have attained public status but only within a narrow set of circumstances. These people, in the words of the Court, "have thrust themselves to the forefront of particular public controversies in order to influence the resolution of the issues involved."[80] Like an all-purpose public figure, a **limited-purpose public figure** invites attention and comment. An individual may be a limited-purpose public figure within a particular community or a particular field. In the *Gertz* ruling, Justice Lewis Powell echoed Justice Brennan's *New York Times Co. v. Sullivan* rationale, noting that an individual who seeks government office must accept "certain necessary consequences of that involvement in public affairs. He runs the risk of closer public scrutiny than might otherwise be the case."[81] He then added the key declaration: "Those classed as public figures stand in a similar position."[82]

limited-purpose public figure In libel law, those plaintiffs who have attained public figure status within a narrow set of circumstances by thrusting themselves to the forefront of particular public controversies in order to influence the resolution of the issues involved; this kind of public figure is more common than the all-purpose public figure.

Points of Law

Limited-Purpose Public Figure

- A public controversy must exist before the publication of the allegedly libelous statement.
- The plaintiff must have in some way participated voluntarily in trying to resolve this controversy.
- The plaintiff's participation actively sought to influence public opinion regarding the controversy.

While the groundwork had already been established,[83] another series of rulings by the Court more precisely articulated a definition of who qualifies as a public figure. In one case, a man had been in the news 16 years prior to a false characterization in a book, but he had not voluntarily thrust himself into the public eye. The Supreme Court there ruled he was not a public figure.[84] In another case, when a wealthy and well-known socialite sued for libel over a report about her behavior that led to divorce, the Court said she was private because her involvement in the divorce was not voluntary.[85] In yet another case, the Court held that a scientist who had received federal grants and who had published papers in scientific journals in his field was nevertheless a private figure. The defendant tried to claim the scientist had become a public figure through the notoriety of his libel suit. The Court ruled that libel defendants cannot, in effect, create a public figure through the defamation itself or media coverage of it.[86]

This and similar cases illustrate what is described as **bootstrapping**. Bootstrapping occurs when media defendants "attach" themselves to the protection of the actual malice standard by citing media coverage—including the very media coverage they generate—of the plaintiff as evidence that the plaintiff is a public figure. Courts have noted that the public controversy at issue must have existed prior to the publication upon which the defamation claim is based in order for the plaintiff to be categorized as a public figure. As the Supreme Court said, "Clearly, those charged with defamation cannot, by their own conduct, create their own defense by making the claimant a public figure."[87] However, a possible side effect can occur when a court rigidly applies the pre-existing controversy requirement. Such an approach may punish legitimate reporting that uncovers specific acts of wrongdoing. Courts therefore attempt to carefully decide which came first: the controversy or the allegedly libelous story about the controversy.

Just as media are not permitted to bootstrap themselves onto their own material to strengthen their defense, a plaintiff may not avoid the actual malice standard by claiming that the attention was unwanted. The proper question for a court is not whether the plaintiff volunteered for the publicity but whether the plaintiff volunteered for an activity from which publicity would foreseeably arise.

Even if an individual is not active in a particular field of endeavor, mere presence within that field may satisfy a court's public figure requirements. One court explains that where a person has "chosen to engage in a profession which draws him regularly into regional and national view and leads to fame and notoriety in the community, even if he has no ideological thesis to promulgate, he invites general public discussion. . . . If society chooses to direct massive public attention to a particular sphere of activity, those who enter that sphere inviting such attention overcome the *Times* standard."[88] Thus, voluntary entry into a sphere of activity, a federal trial court reasoned, is sufficient to satisfy this element of the public figure inquiry.

Because the Supreme Court has said that a public figure is someone with widespread fame or notoriety, the individual's prominence is important in determining public figure status. Moreover, that prominence may apply to a narrowly drawn context. Merely being an executive within a prominent and influential company does not by itself make one a public figure. Professionals are typically not public figures, but under certain circumstances they can be. For example, voluntary use of controversial or unorthodox techniques may be enough to confer public figure status. Publicly defending such methods or adopting other controversial stands also tends to bring about public figure status. Thus, a doctor who had written extensively on health issues as a newspaper columnist, who had authored several journal articles on the subject and who had appeared on at

bootstrapping In libel law, the forbidden practice of a defendant claiming that the plaintiff is a public figure solely on the basis of the statement that is the reason for the lawsuit.

least one nationally broadcast television program discussing health and nutrition issues was held to be a public figure for a limited range of issues—those pertaining to health and nutrition.[89]

An individual may assume public figure status within small publics but may revert to being a private figure in larger spheres. For example, a university professor may be a public figure on campus and in the adjacent academic community but a private person beyond those boundaries. The professor therefore may be a public figure for purposes of an article in the university newspaper but not if featured in a regional newspaper or a national magazine. Thus, the professor's public figure status is limited. Similarly, an individual may attain the status of an all-purpose public figure within a particular geographical area.[90]

Involuntary Public Figures In the same ruling that categorized public figures as all-purpose and limited-purpose, the U.S. Supreme Court also suggested that there may be a third category: **involuntary public figures.** These are people, the Supreme Court said, who do not necessarily thrust themselves into public controversies voluntarily but who are drawn into specific issues.[91] An individual could be drawn into a matter of public controversy through unforeseen or unintended circumstances, becoming a public figure through no purposeful action. The Court added, however, that the occurrence of such public figures is "exceedingly rare."[92]

Nevertheless, cases surface occasionally where plaintiffs are declared involuntarily public figures. For example, a Connecticut court in 2008 ruled that a plaintiff who had served time in prison for a crime he did not commit was just such an involuntary public figure. "There are . . . individuals who have not sought publicity or consented to it," the court ruled, "but through their own conduct or otherwise have become a legitimate subject of public interest. They have, in other words, become 'news.'"[93]

Losing Public-Figure Status It is theoretically possible for one-time public figures to revert to private status with the passage of time. However, the courts have been inconsistent in their application of any standard to this phenomenon. How much time must pass before a person loses his public status is difficult to pin down. One consideration is whether the person's role in a particular matter remains in the public consciousness or is of public concern. To return to private figure status, it is likely that a plaintiff would need to demonstrate not only that she is no longer a subject of public concern but also that her libel claim is not connected to events or controversies of which the public remains aware.

Private Figures A libel plaintiff who does not qualify as a public official or public figure is considered a **private figure.** Private figures usually do not have to prove actual malice as the level of fault in their cases. Instead, they need to show only that the libel defendant acted with negligence. While the definition of

involuntary public figure In libel law, a person who does not necessarily thrust himself or herself into public controversies voluntarily but is drawn into a given issue.

private figure In libel law, a plaintiff who cannot be categorized as either a public figure or public official. Generally, in order to recover damages a private figure is not required to prove actual malice but merely negligence on the part of the defendant.

realWorld Law

On the Air: Talk Radio, Libel and Opinion

When a libel case against a nationally syndicated radio talk show host was dismissed, it illustrated many of the dynamics of libel cases and the extent to which the burden of proof is on the plaintiff. A military contractor, CACI International, sued Randi Rhodes, then of Air America Radio, for criticizing the contractor's actions in Iraq, including at the Abu Ghraib detention facility. CACI cited 13 separate statements by Rhodes in which she said contractors committed rape, torture and murder. CACI claimed the statements were made with actual malice. But a district court judge disagreed, saying that the statements were neither demonstrably false nor made with reckless disregard for the truth.[1] In fact, Rhodes had repeatedly cited military reports and other documentation within the context of her accusations. She had no reason to doubt the validity of those reports.

The Court of Appeals (Fourth Circuit) concurred with the lower court ruling, saying each of the 13 statements in question was protected by the First Amendment. Citing *New York Times Co. v. Sullivan,* the court noted that defamation cases involving issues of public concern are considered "against the background of a profound national commitment to the principle that debate on public issues should be uninhibited, robust, and wide-open, and that it may well include vehement, caustic, and sometimes unpleasantly sharp attacks on government[,] public officials, and public figures."[2] Talk radio is an especially appropriate forum for such debate.

Both the district and appeals courts noted that Rhodes frequently expressed herself not using actual facts but through hyperbole, a protection for speech. The appeals court noted that while frequently caustic, "[t]he medium of talk radio is one in which hyperbole and diatribe reign as the preferred tools of discourse."[3] Such expression, the court said, enjoys robust First Amendment protection.[4]

1. CACI v. Rhodes, 2006 U.S. Dist. LEXIS 96057 (E.D. Va., Sept. 21, 2006).
2. CACI v. Rhodes, 536 F.3d 280, 293 (4th Cir. 2008) (quoting New York Times Co. v. Sullivan, 376 U.S. 254, 270 (1964)).
3. *Id.* at 304.
4. *Id.*

negligence varies from state to state, it is in all cases easier to prove than actual malice. As noted earlier in this chapter, negligence is the failure to exercise reasonable or ordinary care. What constitutes negligence, however, can vary from one professional setting to another. When establishing what constitutes negligence in the field of journalism, it can be difficult to arrive at a single definition, since news media operate according to a variety of professional standards. What is "acceptable" in television news reporting may not be so in a daily newspaper or online. In other words, unlike professions such as medicine and law, journalism has no single authoritative code of conduct.

That said, some common examples of negligent behavior in the news media have emerged. These include, but are not limited to, the following:

- Relying on a single or anonymous source
- Relying on other media reports without independent investigation

- Careless misstatements of the contents of documents
- Possessing ill will toward the plaintiff
- Conclusions or inferences unreasonably deduced
- Failure to follow established internal practices and policies
- Errors in taking notes and quoting sources

In sum, journalistic negligence may be viewed as the failure to take reasonable care to ensure that a report is accurate and that its subjects are treated fairly.

The Nature of the Statement Whether a plaintiff is considered a public figure for purposes of a libel suit can depend on the nature of the material being published—specifically whether it relates to a matter of public concern. In one case that reached the U.S. Supreme Court, a credit reporting agency issued a credit report that erroneously reported the bankruptcy filing of a Vermont construction contractor. The credit report had been sent to five subscribers who, by agreement, could not repeat the information. The contractor sued for libel. The U.S. Supreme Court upheld a lower court ruling that the contractor was a private figure, making it easier for the company to make a case that it had been libeled. The reason: the statement about its supposed bankruptcy was not a matter of public concern.[94] The Court's opinion stated that the purpose of the speaker and the nature and size of the audience are relevant in determining when speech involves matters of public concern.[95] In determining whether a statement is libelous, therefore, the Court identified the importance of both the status of the plaintiff and the nature of the statement in question.

There was some concern in the media that this ruling might dilute libel protections if plaintiffs were no longer required to prove fault on the part of media outlets who reported on matters that were not of public concern. But that has not occurred. In this same case, the question surfaced as to whether plaintiffs could be required to prove actual malice even when suing a non-media defendant. The Court stated that since its inception, the standard had been applied to non-media defendants.[96] That application, however, is facilitated when the statement is a matter of public concern.

SUMMARY

THE LAST ELEMENT OF THE LIBEL PLAINTIFF'S CASE is to show that the defendant is at fault for publishing the defamatory material. The level of fault that must be proved varies according to the status of the plaintiff. Public officials and public figures must show the defendant acted with actual malice, meaning with knowledge of falsity or reckless disregard for the truth. Private figures usually must prove negligence on the part of the defendant, a much less difficult standard to meet. This distinction in fault standards began with the landmark 1964 U.S. Supreme Court ruling in *New York Times Co. v. Sullivan.* Justice Brennan's opinion for the Court transformed the law and journalism. By affording the media more "breathing space" for error, the ruling reduces the possible chilling effect of libel suits and encourages the journalistic tradition of close scrutiny and criticism of government. ∎

Damages

In addition to restoring a damaged reputation, a typical goal of libel plaintiffs is to extract financial damages from the defendant. Damages in libel have generated controversy, particularly when excessive awards produce a chilling effect in the news media.[97] While not an element of the libel plaintiff's case specifically, it is useful in understanding libel law to have a basic understanding of the different kinds of civil damages a plaintiff may seek and the distinctions among them.

Actual Actual damages are the most common kind of libel damages. They represent the quantity of the harm actually suffered by the plaintiff due to the libel. The plaintiff is required to produce evidence showing the monetary loss attributable to the harm suffered. This may include compensation for loss of standing in the community, humiliation and mental suffering—all harms for which it is admittedly difficult to assign a specific dollar amount. Thus, the awarding of actual damages, whether by the court or a jury, tends to be imprecise.

Special Special damages are those for which there is an exact monetary figure specifically related to the material loss suffered because of the libel. These could include extra costs incurred by the plaintiff, lost earnings and other economic losses resulting from the libelous statement. This may lead one to wonder if the names of actual and special damages should be reversed. Plaintiffs typically do not seek special damages, although there are some circumstances in which they are the only kind of damages a plaintiff may seek.

Presumed Unlike actual or special damages, presumed damages do not require the plaintiff to produce evidence of harm. Some degree of harm is presumed even absent proof. There are limitations, however, with regard to the kind of plaintiff who is entitled to presumed damages and under what circumstances. Public officials, public figures and private figures suing over matters of public concern can be awarded presumed damages only where the defendant acted with actual malice.[98] Private figures suing over matters not of public concern are required to prove the defendant's negligence to obtain presumed damages.

Punitive Punitive damages are intended to punish libel defendants with a monetary penalty and to make an example of them as a means of discouraging both the defendant and others from committing similar acts in the future. A survey of libel plaintiffs showed that nearly one-third were motivated to bring lawsuits in order to punish the defendants who defamed them.[99] When they are awarded, punitive damages are often the biggest monetary part of a judgment. Punitive damages (also sometimes called "exemplary damages") are also controversial, and efforts to eliminate or reduce them through legal reforms—both in libel and other areas of law—have proliferated.[100] Especially in an era when news media organizations tend to be owned by multibillion-dollar corporations, plaintiffs typically target these "deep pockets," or what defense attorneys sometimes refer to as the "smart money." In this environment, the plaintiff's attorney may benefit from portraying the case as a David-versus-Goliath battle. Jurors may be sympathetic to such rhetorical appeals and are frequently willing to grant large damage requests. Many believe this to be an unfair situation, leading several states to prohibit punitive damages altogether, while others have limited them.

The courts themselves have also addressed excessive punitive damage awards. In some cases the trial judge has authority to reduce punitive damages awarded by a jury. Appeals courts may also reduce the monetary amount of a punitive damages award. Courts sometimes weigh a punitive damages award against the defendant's ability to pay, as judged by net worth.[101] Under this model, wealthy corporations are more likely to have large punitive damage awards assessed against them. Does this mean their libelous conduct was more egregious than one committed by a small media organization with fewer resources? Not necessarily; hence, another rationale for reform.

Criminal Libel

Everything discussed thus far in this chapter is within the context of civil law. In other words, libel as explained up to this point involves one private (i.e., nongovernment) party filing a claim against another private party. But in some states, libel may also be a criminal offense. That is, the state may file criminal libel charges against a defendant seeking criminal penalties such as fines and imprisonment. This happens not because the government was defamed (in a democracy there is no such thing; the government is supposed to be open to criticism), but because it has seen fit to file criminal charges to protect individuals in the society who have been victimized by the defendant's criminal behavior.

Fewer than half the states have criminal libel statutes. Even in those states, prosecutions are relatively rare. Because of the protection provided by the First Amendment, it may seem counterintuitive that a state would charge a journalist with libel. But according to the Reporters Committee for Freedom of the Press, criminal libel laws are used against journalists occasionally, especially when reports are politically charged.[102]

Criminal libel laws are subject to the same constitutional requirements as civil law. Thus, for example, if the person allegedly libeled is a public figure or public official, the state prosecutor must prove actual malice. Furthermore, the burden of proof is higher than in a civil libel suit, since to establish guilt the alleged libel must be proved beyond a reasonable doubt, not merely by a preponderance of the evidence.

SUMMARY

LIBEL PLAINTIFFS TYPICALLY SEEK FINANCIAL COMPENSATION. This comes in the form of monetary damages. There are four categories of damages: actual, special, presumed and punitive. Excessive awards, especially in the latter category, have prompted some critics to call for reform of the laws and standards that govern damages. In some states, the government may file criminal libel charges that could expose defendants to the punishment of a fine or imprisonment. ■

Cases for Study

Thinking About It

The two case excerpts that follow are considered landmark libel cases. The U.S. Supreme Court issued its rulings in these cases at a time when libel law was being dramatically transformed. As you read these case excerpts, keep the following questions in mind:

- How do the two decisions help define the meaning of libel and the contours of libel law?

- How do these rulings balance the freedoms of speech and press protected by the First Amendment against the right of individuals to protect their reputations?

- What are the important concepts that each of these decisions adds to libel law?

- How, according to the Supreme Court in *New York Times Co. v. Sullivan*, does libel law implicate the First Amendment?

New York Times Co. v. Sullivan
SUPREME COURT OF THE UNITED STATES
376 U.S. 254 (1964)

JUSTICE WILLIAM BRENNAN delivered the Court's opinion:

We are required in this case to determine for the first time the extent to which the constitutional protections for speech and press limit a State's power to award damages in a libel action brought by a public official against critics of his official conduct.

Respondent L.B. Sullivan is one of the three elected Commissioners of the City of Montgomery, Alabama. He testified that he was "Commissioner of Public Affairs and the duties are supervision of the Police Department, Fire Department, Department of Cemetery and Department of Scales." He brought this civil libel action against the four individual petitioners, who are Negroes and Alabama clergymen, and against petitioner the New York Times Company, a New York corporation which publishes the New York Times, a daily newspaper. A jury in the Circuit Court of Montgomery County awarded him damages of $500,000, the full amount claimed, against all

the petitioners, and the Supreme Court of Alabama affirmed. . . .

Of the 10 paragraphs of text in the advertisement, the third and a portion of the sixth were the basis of respondent's claim of libel. . . .

It is uncontroverted that some of the statements contained in the two paragraphs were not accurate descriptions of events which occurred in Montgomery. Although Negro students staged a demonstration on the State Capitol steps, they sang the National Anthem and not "My Country, 'Tis of Thee." Although nine students were expelled by the State Board of Education, this was not for leading the demonstration at the Capitol, but for demanding service at a lunch counter in the Montgomery County Courthouse on another day. Not the entire student body, but most of it, had protested the expulsion, not by refusing to register, but by boycotting classes on a single day; virtually all the students did register for the ensuing semester. . . .

Because of the importance of the constitutional issues involved, we granted the separate petitions for certiorari of the individual petitioners and of the Times. We reverse the judgment. We hold that the rule of law applied by the Alabama courts is constitutionally deficient for failure to provide the safeguards for freedom of speech and of the press that are required by the First and Fourteenth Amendments in a libel action brought by a public official against critics of his official conduct. We further hold that under the proper safeguards the evidence presented in this case is constitutionally insufficient to support the judgment for respondent. . . .

The publication here was not a "commercial" advertisement in the sense in which the word was used in Chrestensen. It communicated information, expressed opinion, recited grievances, protested claimed abuses, and sought financial support on behalf of a movement whose existence and objectives are matters of the highest public interest and concern. That the Times was paid for publishing the advertisement is as immaterial in this connection as is the fact that newspapers and books are sold. . . . Any other conclusion would discourage newspapers from carrying "editorial advertisements" of this type, and so might shut off an important outlet for the promulgation of information and ideas by persons who do not themselves have access to publishing facilities—who wish to exercise their freedom of speech even though they are not members of the press. . . . To avoid placing such a handicap upon the freedoms of expression, we hold that, if the allegedly libelous statements would otherwise be constitutionally protected from the present judgment, they do not forfeit that protection because they were published in the form of a paid advertisement. . . .

The general proposition that freedom of expression upon public questions is secured by the First Amendment has long been settled by our decisions. The constitutional safeguard, we have said, "was fashioned to assure unfettered interchange of ideas for the bringing about of political and social changes desired by the people. . . ."

. . . The First Amendment, said Judge Learned Hand, "presupposes that right conclusions are more likely to be gathered out of a multitude of tongues, than through any kind of authoritative selection. To many this is, and always will be, folly; but we have staked upon it our all.". . .

Thus we consider this case against the background of a profound national commitment to the principle that debate on public issues should be uninhibited, robust, and wide-open, and that it may well include vehement, caustic, and sometimes unpleasantly sharp attacks on government and public officials. The present advertisement, as an expression of grievance and protest on one of the major public issues of our time, would seem clearly to qualify for the constitutional protection. The question is whether it forfeits that protection by the falsity of some of its factual statements and by its alleged defamation of respondent. . . .

That erroneous statement is inevitable in free debate, and that it must be protected if the freedoms of expression are to have the "breathing space" that they "need . . . to survive. . . ."

Injury to official reputation affords no more warrant for repressing speech that would otherwise be free than does factual error. . . .

If neither factual error nor defamatory content suffices to remove the constitutional shield from criticism of official conduct, the combination of the two elements is no less inadequate. . . .

. . . A rule compelling the critic of official conduct to guarantee the truth of all his factual assertions—and to do so on pain of libel judgments virtually unlimited in amount—leads to a comparable "self-censorship." Allowance of the defense of truth, with the burden of proving it on the defendant, does not mean that only false speech will be deterred. . . . The constitutional guarantees require, we think, a federal rule that prohibits a public official from recovering damages for a defamatory falsehood relating to his official conduct unless he proves that the statement was made with "actual malice"—that is, with knowledge that it was false or with reckless disregard of whether it was false or not. . . .

. . . As Madison said, "the censorial power is in the people over the Government, and not in the Government over the people." It would give public servants an unjustified preference over the public they serve, if critics of official conduct did not have a fair equivalent of the immunity granted to the officials themselves. . . .

We hold today that the Constitution delimits a State's power to award damages for libel in actions brought by public officials against critics of their official conduct. Since this is such an action, the rule requiring proof of actual malice is applicable. . . .

Applying these standards, we consider that the proof presented to show actual malice lacks the convincing clarity which the constitutional standard demands, and hence that it would not constitutionally sustain the judgment for respondent under the proper rule of law. . . .

Finally, there is evidence that the Times published the advertisement without checking its accuracy against the news stories in the Times' own files. The mere presence of the stories in the files does not, of course, establish that the Times "knew" the advertisement was false, since the state of mind required for actual malice would have to be brought home to the persons in the Times' organization having responsibility for the publication of the advertisement. . . .

The judgment of the Supreme Court of Alabama is reversed and the case is remanded to that court for further proceedings not inconsistent with this opinion.

Reversed and remanded.

Gertz v. Robert Welch, Inc.
SUPREME COURT OF THE UNITED STATES
418 U.S. 323 (1974)

JUSTICE LEWIS POWELL delivered the Court's opinion:
This Court has struggled for nearly a decade to define the proper accommodation between the law of defamation and the freedoms of speech and press protected by the First Amendment. With this decision we return to that effort. We granted certiorari to reconsider the extent of a publisher's constitutional privilege against liability for defamation of a private citizen.

I

In 1968, a Chicago policeman named Nuccio shot and killed a youth named Nelson. The state authorities prosecuted Nuccio for the homicide and ultimately obtained a conviction for murder in the second degree. The Nelson family retained petitioner Elmer Gertz, a reputable attorney, to represent them in civil litigation against Nuccio.

Respondent publishes American Opinion, a monthly outlet for the views of the John Birch Society. Early in the 1960's, the magazine began to warn of a nationwide conspiracy to discredit local law enforcement agencies and create in their stead a national police force capable of supporting a Communist dictatorship. As part of the continuing effort to alert the public to this assumed danger, the managing editor of American Opinion commissioned an article on the murder trial of Officer Nuccio. For this purpose, he engaged a regular contributor to the magazine. In March, 1969, respondent published the resulting article under the title "FRAME-UP: Richard Nuccio And The War On Police." The article purports to demonstrate that the testimony against Nuccio at his criminal trial was false, and that his prosecution was part of the Communist campaign against the police.

In his capacity as counsel for the Nelson family in the civil litigation, petitioner attended the coroner's inquest into the boy's death and initiated actions for damages, but he neither discussed Officer Nuccio with the press nor played any part in the criminal proceeding. Notwithstanding petitioner's remote connection with the prosecution of Nuccio, respondent's magazine portrayed him as an architect of the "frame-up." According to the article, the police file on petitioner took "a big, Irish cop to lift." The article stated that petitioner had been an official of the "Marxist League for Industrial Democracy, originally known as the Intercollegiate Socialist Society, which has advocated the violent seizure of our government." It labeled Gertz a "Leninist" and a "Communist-fronter." It also stated that Gertz had been an officer of the National Lawyers Guild, described as a Communist organization that "probably did more than any other outfit to plan the Communist attack on the Chicago police during the 1968 Democratic Convention."

These statements contained serious inaccuracies. The implication that petitioner had a criminal record was false. Petitioner had been a member and officer of the National Lawyers Guild some 15 years earlier, but there was no evidence that he or that organization had taken any part in planning the 1968 demonstrations in Chicago. There was also no basis for the charge that petitioner was a "Leninist" or a "Communist-fronter." And he had never been a member of the "Marxist League for Industrial Democracy" or the "Intercollegiate Socialist Society."

The managing editor of American Opinion made no effort to verify or substantiate the charges against petitioner. Instead, he appended an editorial introduction stating that the author had "conducted extensive research into the Richard Nuccio Case." And he included in the article a photograph of petitioner and wrote the caption that appeared under it: "Elmer Gertz of Red Guild harasses Nuccio." Respondent placed the issue of American Opinion containing the article on sale at newsstands throughout the country and distributed reprints of the article on the streets of Chicago.

Petitioner filed a diversity action for libel in the United States District Court for the Northern District of Illinois. He claimed that the falsehoods published by respondent injured his reputation as a lawyer and a citizen. Before filing an answer, respondent moved to dismiss the complaint for failure to state a claim upon which relief could be granted, apparently on the ground that petitioner failed to allege special damages. But the court ruled that statements contained in the article constituted libel *per se* under Illinois law, and that consequently petitioner need not plead special damages. . . .

After answering the complaint, respondent filed a pretrial motion for summary judgment, claiming a constitutional privilege against liability for defamation.

It asserted that petitioner was a public official or a public figure, and that the article concerned an issue of public interest and concern. For these reasons, respondent argued, it was entitled to invoke the privilege enunciated in *New York Times Co. v. Sullivan*. Under this rule, respondent would escape liability unless petitioner could prove publication of defamatory falsehood "with 'actual malice'—that is, with knowledge that it was false or with reckless disregard of whether it was false or not." Respondent claimed that petitioner could not make such a showing, and submitted a supporting affidavit by the magazine's managing editor. The editor denied any knowledge of the falsity of the statements concerning petitioner, and stated that he had relied on the author's reputation and on his prior experience with the accuracy and authenticity of the author's contributions to American Opinion.

The District Court denied respondent's motion for summary judgment in a memorandum opinion of September 16, 1970. The court did not dispute respondent's claim to the protection of the *New York Times* standard. Rather, it concluded that petitioner might overcome the constitutional privilege by making a factual showing sufficient to prove publication of defamatory falsehood in reckless disregard of the truth. During the course of the trial, however, it became clear that the trial court had not accepted all of respondent's asserted grounds for applying the *New York Times* rule to this case. It thought that respondent's claim to the protection of the constitutional privilege depended on the contention that petitioner was either a public official under the *New York Times* decision or a public figure under *Curtis Publishing Co. v. Butts* (1967), apparently discounting the argument that a privilege would arise from the presence of a public issue. After all the evidence had been presented but before submission of the case to the jury, the court ruled in effect that petitioner was neither a public official nor a public figure. It added that, if he were, the resulting application of the *New York Times* standard would require a directed verdict for respondent. Because some statements in the article constituted libel *per se* under Illinois law, the court submitted the case to the jury under instructions that withdrew from its consideration all issues save the measure of damages. The jury awarded $50,000 to petitioner.

Following the jury verdict and on further reflection, the District Court concluded that the *New York Times* standard should govern this case even though petitioner was not a public official or public figure. It accepted respondent's contention that that privilege protected discussion of any public issue without regard to the status of a person defamed therein. Accordingly, the court entered judgment for respondent notwithstanding the jury's verdict. . . .

Petitioner appealed to contest the applicability of the *New York Times* standard to this case. . . . After reviewing the record, the Court of Appeals endorsed the District Court's conclusion that petitioner had failed to show by clear and convincing evidence that respondent had acted with "actual malice" as defined by *New York Times.* There was no evidence that the managing editor of American Opinion knew of the falsity of the accusations made in the article. In fact, he knew nothing about petitioner except what he learned from the article. The court correctly noted that mere proof of failure to investigate, without more, cannot establish reckless disregard for the truth. Rather, the publisher must act with a " 'high degree of awareness of . . . probable falsity.' " The evidence in this case did not reveal that respondent had cause for such an awareness. The Court of Appeals therefore affirmed. For the reasons stated below, we reverse.

II

The principal issue in this case is whether a newspaper or broadcaster that publishes defamatory falsehoods about an individual who is neither a public official nor a public figure may claim a constitutional privilege against liability for the injury inflicted by those statements. . . .

Three years after *New York Times,* a majority of the Court agreed to extend the constitutional privilege to defamatory criticism of "public figures." This extension was announced in *Curtis Publishing Co. v. Butts* and its companion, *Associated Press v. Walker* (1967). . . .

III

We begin with the common ground. Under the First Amendment, there is no such thing as a false idea. However pernicious an opinion may seem, we depend for its correction not on the conscience of judges and juries but on the competition of other ideas. But there is no constitutional value in false statements of fact. Neither the intentional lie nor the careless error materially advances society's interest in "uninhibited, robust, and wide-open" debate on public issues. They belong to that category of utterances which "are no essential part of any exposition of ideas, and are of such slight social value as a step to truth that any benefit that may be derived from them is clearly outweighed by the social interest in order and morality."

Although the erroneous statement of fact is not worthy of constitutional protection, it is nevertheless inevitable in free debate. As James Madison pointed out in the Report on the Virginia Resolutions of 1798: "Some degree of abuse is inseparable from the proper use of every thing; and in no instance is this more true than in that of the press." And punishment of error runs the risk of inducing a cautious and restrictive exercise of the constitutionally guaranteed freedoms of speech and press. Our decisions recognize that a rule of strict liability that compels a publisher or broadcaster to guarantee the accuracy of his factual assertions may lead to intolerable self-censorship. Allowing the media to avoid liability only by proving the truth of all injurious statements does not accord adequate protection to First Amendment liberties. As the Court stated in *New York Times Co. v. Sullivan:* "Allowance of the defense of truth, with the burden of proving it on the defendant, does not mean that only false speech will be deterred." The First Amendment requires that we protect some falsehood in order to protect speech that matters.

The need to avoid self-censorship by the news media is, however, not the only societal value at issue. If it were, this Court would have embraced long ago the view that publishers and broadcasters enjoy an unconditional and indefeasible immunity from liability for defamation. Such a rule would, indeed, obviate the fear that the prospect of civil liability for injurious falsehood might dissuade a timorous press from the effective exercise of First Amendment freedoms. Yet absolute protection for the communications media requires a total sacrifice of the competing value served by the law of defamation.

The legitimate state interest underlying the law of libel is the compensation of individuals for the harm inflicted on them by defamatory falsehood. . . .

Some tension necessarily exists between the need for a vigorous and uninhibited press and the legitimate interest in redressing wrongful injury. . . . In our continuing effort to define the proper accommodation between these competing concerns, we have been especially anxious to assure to the freedoms of speech and press that "breathing space" essential to their fruitful exercise. To that end, this Court has extended a measure of strategic protection to defamatory falsehood.

The *New York Times* standard defines the level of constitutional protection appropriate to the context of defamation of a public person. Those who, by reason of the notoriety of their achievements or the vigor and success with which they seek the public's attention, are properly classed as public figures and those who hold governmental office may recover for injury to reputation only on clear and convincing proof that the defamatory falsehood was made with knowledge of its falsity or with reckless disregard for the truth. This standard administers an extremely powerful antidote to the inducement to media self-censorship of the common-law rule of strict liability for libel and slander. And it exacts a correspondingly high price from the victims of defamatory falsehood. . . .

Theoretically, of course, the balance between the needs of the press and the individual's claim to compensation for wrongful injury might be struck on a case-by-case basis. . . . But this approach would lead to unpredictable results and uncertain expectations, and it could render our duty to supervise the lower courts unmanageable. Because an *ad hoc* resolution of the competing interests at stake in each particular case is not feasible, we must lay down broad rules of general application . . . .

With that caveat, we have no difficulty in distinguishing among defamation plaintiffs. The first remedy of any victim of defamation is self-help—using available opportunities to contradict the lie or correct the error and thereby to minimize its adverse impact on reputation. Public officials and public figures usually enjoy significantly greater access to the channels of effective communication, and hence have a more realistic opportunity to counteract false statements than private individuals normally enjoy. Private individuals are therefore more vulnerable to injury, and the state interest in protecting them is correspondingly greater.

More important than the likelihood that private individuals will lack effective opportunities for rebuttal, there is a compelling normative consideration underlying the distinction between public and private defamation plaintiffs. An individual who decides to seek governmental office must accept certain necessary consequences of that involvement in public affairs. He runs the risk of closer public scrutiny than might otherwise be the case. And society's interest in the officers of government is not strictly limited to the formal discharge of official duties. . . .

Those classed as public figures stand in a similar position. Hypothetically, it may be possible for someone to become a public figure through no purposeful action of his own, but the instances of truly involuntary public figures must be exceedingly rare. For the most part those who attain this status have assumed roles of special prominence in the affairs of society. Some occupy positions of such persuasive power and influence that they are deemed public figures for all purposes. More commonly, those classed as public figures have thrust themselves to the forefront of particular public controversies in order to influence the resolution of the issues involved. In either event, they invite attention and comment.

Even if the foregoing generalities do not obtain in every instance, the communications media are entitled to act on the assumption that public officials and public figures have voluntarily exposed themselves to increased risk of injury from defamatory falsehood concerning them. No such assumption is justified with respect to a private individual. . . .

For these reasons, we conclude that the States should retain substantial latitude in their efforts to enforce a legal remedy for defamatory falsehood injurious to the reputation of a private individual. . . .

We hold that, so long as they do not impose liability without fault, the States may define for themselves the appropriate standard of liability for a publisher or broadcaster of defamatory falsehood injurious to a private individual. This approach provides a more equitable boundary between the competing concerns involved here. It recognizes the strength of the legitimate state interest in compensating private individuals for wrongful injury to reputation, yet shields the press and broadcast media from the rigors of strict liability for defamation. . . .

IV

Our accommodation of the competing values at stake in defamation suits by private individuals allows the States to impose liability on the publisher or broadcaster of defamatory falsehood on a less demanding showing than that required by *New York Times*. This conclusion is not based on a belief that the considerations which prompted the adoption of the *New York Times* privilege for defamation of public officials and its extension to public figures are wholly inapplicable to the context of private individuals. Rather, we endorse this approach in recognition of the strong and legitimate state interest in compensating private individuals for injury to reputation. . . . [T]he States may not permit recovery of presumed or punitive damages, at least when liability is not based on a showing of knowledge of falsity or reckless disregard for the truth. . . .

We would not, of course, invalidate state law simply because we doubt its wisdom, but here we are attempting to reconcile state law with a competing interest grounded in the constitutional command of the First Amendment. It is therefore appropriate to require that state remedies for defamatory falsehood reach no farther than is necessary to protect the legitimate interest involved. It is necessary to restrict defamation plaintiffs who do not prove knowledge of falsity or reckless disregard for the truth to compensation for actual injury. . . .

We also find no justification for allowing awards of punitive damages against publishers and broadcasters

held liable under state-defined standards of liability for defamation. In most jurisdictions jury discretion over the amounts awarded is limited only by the gentle rule that they not be excessive. Consequently, juries assess punitive damages in wholly unpredictable amounts bearing no necessary relation to the actual harm caused. . . .

V

Notwithstanding our refusal to extend the *New York Times* privilege to defamation of private individuals, respondent contends that we should affirm the judgment below on the ground that petitioner is either a public official or a public figure. There is little basis for the former assertion. Several years prior to the present incident, petitioner had served briefly on housing committees appointed by the mayor of Chicago, but at the time of publication, he had never held any remunerative governmental position. Respondent admits this, but argues that petitioner's appearance at the coroner's inquest rendered him a "*de facto* public official." Our cases recognize no such concept. Respondent's suggestion would sweep all lawyers under the *New York Times* rule as officers of the court, and distort the plain meaning of the "public official" category beyond all recognition. We decline to follow it.

Respondent's characterization of petitioner as a public figure raises a different question. That designation may rest on either of two alternative bases. In some instances an individual may achieve such pervasive fame or notoriety that he becomes a public figure for all purposes and in all contexts. More commonly, an individual voluntarily injects himself or is drawn into a particular public controversy, and thereby becomes a public figure for a limited range of issues. In either case such persons assume special prominence in the resolution of public questions.

Petitioner has long been active in community and professional affairs. He has served as an officer of local civic groups and of various professional organizations, and he has published several books and articles on legal subjects. Although petitioner was consequently well known in some circles, he had achieved no general fame or notoriety in the community. None of the prospective jurors called at the trial had ever heard of petitioner prior to this litigation, and respondent offered no proof that this response was atypical of the local population. We would not lightly assume that a citizen's participation in community and professional affairs rendered him a public figure for all purposes. Absent clear evidence of general fame or notoriety in the community, and pervasive involvement in the affairs of society, an individual should not be deemed a public personality for all aspects of his life. It is preferable to reduce the public-figure question to a more meaningful context by looking to the nature and extent of an individual's participation in the particular controversy giving rise to the defamation.

In this context it is plain that petitioner was not a public figure. He played a minimal role at the coroner's inquest, and his participation related solely to his representation of a private client. He took no part in the criminal prosecution of Officer Nuccio. Moreover, he never discussed either the criminal or civil litigation with the press and was never quoted as having done so. He plainly did not thrust himself into the vortex of this public issue, nor did he engage the public's attention in an attempt to influence its outcome. We are persuaded that the trial court did not err in refusing to characterize petitioner as a public figure for the purpose of this litigation.

We therefore conclude that the *New York Times* standard is inapplicable to this case, and that the trial court erred in entering judgment for respondent. Because the jury was allowed to impose liability without fault and was permitted to presume damages without proof of injury, a new trial is necessary. We reverse and remand for further proceedings in accord with this opinion.

It is so ordered.

Chapter 5

Under the First Amendment there is no such thing as a false idea. However pernicious an opinion may seem, we depend for its correction not on the conscience of judges and juries but on the competition of other ideas. But there is no constitutional value in false statements of fact.

U.S. Supreme Court Justice Lewis Powell[1]

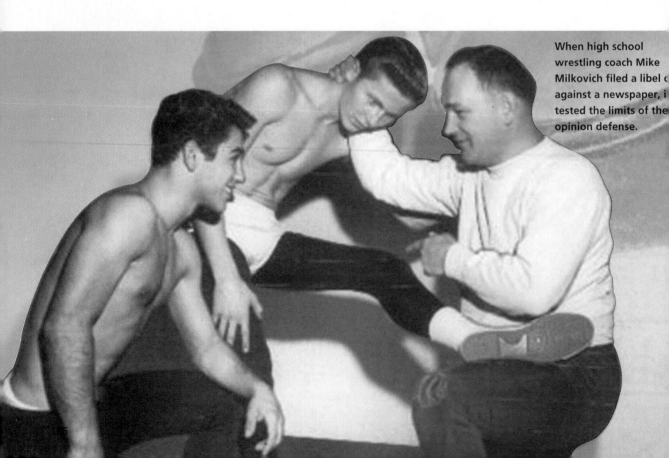

When high school wrestling coach Mike Milkovich filed a libel [...] against a newspaper, i[...] tested the limits of the[...] opinion defense.

Libel
Defenses and Privileges

Fair Report Privilege

Fair Comment and Criticism

Opinion

Innocent Construction
Letters to the Editor
Rhetorical Hyperbole, Parody and Satire

Neutral Reportage

Wire Service Defense

Single-Publication Rule

The Libel-Proof Plaintiff

Single-Mistake Rule

Other Defense Issues

Summary Judgment
Jurisdiction
Statute of Limitations
Retractions
Responsible Reporting

Cases for Study

➤ *Ollman v. Evans*
➤ *Milkovich v. Lorain Journal Co.*

Suppose . . .

. . . that a newspaper columnist writes about a school board hearing that is investigating possible neglect or wrongdoing on the part of school employees. The column contains accusations that some people lied at the hearing. One of the accused, believing that the statement was false and damaged his reputation, sues the columnist and his newspaper for libel. The defendants claim the column is an expression of opinion and they are therefore protected by the First Amendment. These were the circumstances in *Milkovich v. Lorain Journal Co.,* discussed in this chapter and excerpted at the end.

Parties sued for libel are by no means defenseless. They can use many defenses, any of which has the potential to be successful, depending on the circumstances of the case. There is one vitally important difference between the plaintiff's case and the defendant's challenges: While the plaintiff must prove every element of her case, a successful defendant needs only one suitable defense. An analogy may be useful here. The libel defense attorney is like a carpenter who must choose the right tool for a given job. A carpenter has many tools to choose from, yet it is crucial to choose the proper one to get the job done. The libel defense attorney is no different.

On the one hand, defending a libel suit may consist of merely turning the plaintiff's case inside out. That is, by taking those elements of the plaintiff's case explained in Chapter 4 and proving their inverse, a libel defendant may be able to demonstrate that there is no liability for publishing the statement at issue. For example, truth or substantial truth is the appropriate counterargument to the plaintiff's claim that the material at issue is false. In fact, truth is sometimes viewed as the most basic and ironclad of all libel defenses. On the other hand, those accused of libel have several defenses at their disposal that may not directly correspond with any element of the plaintiff's case.

Fair Report Privilege

Imagine that you, a journalist, get a telephone call from someone who says that a fight involving two local celebrities is taking place at a nearby watering hole. By the time you get there, order has been restored and the celebrities are gone. But you interview witnesses, and some of them tell you the fight began when one man made some disparaging remarks about the other's girlfriend. You write the story, including details about the accusations that started the dispute, and it is published in the next day's newspaper.

You are distressed to see that the competing newspaper in town also has a story about the fight that includes the same details you used in your story, even though it had no reporter on the scene. The writer of that story cobbled together some facts strictly from the official police report. Then, a week later, you are shocked to learn that the celebrity's girlfriend is suing you and your newspaper for libel, accurately claiming the accusations reported about her are false. On top of that, her attorney knows libel law well enough not to sue the other reporter and his paper.

The other paper's reporter is protected by the **fair report privilege** because its story is based on a police report, but it is unlikely that you have that same defense. Why? The fair report privilege is based on the idea that keeping citizens informed about matters of public concern is sometimes more important than avoiding occasional damage to individual reputations. It gives reporters some breathing room to report on official governmental conduct without having to first prove the truth of what the government says. How does the privilege apply to this situation? By relying only on the police report, the other reporter satisfied the conditions to maintain the privilege. Your story came from sources that were not official government records or proceedings. Even if a contributor to an official proceeding makes a statement that is false and defamatory—or if an official government record does the same—a news organization whose report is based exclusively on the statement will not be liable for defamation as long as the story accurately and fairly reflects the content of the report or proceeding.

In addition, some question has been raised about whether a reporter's intent to harm a person's reputation may terminate the fair report privilege. This

fair report privilege A privilege claimed by journalists who report events on the basis of official records. The report must fairly and accurately reflect the content of the records; this is the condition that sometimes leads to this privilege being called "conditional privilege."

Points of Law

Fair Report Privilege

1. The information must be obtained from a record or proceeding recognized as "official."

2. The news report must fairly and accurately reflect what is in the public record or what was said during the official proceeding.

3. The source of the statement should be clearly noted in the news report.

question surfaced in a Minnesota case in which a citizen mentioned the name of a police officer during a city council meeting. The citizen accused the officer of dealing drugs. The reporter who covered the meeting did not report the accusation immediately but instead investigated the situation. When the reporter published several articles, the officer sued, claiming not only that the articles were inaccurate but also that they were written with malice, or ill will. (This is not the same as actual malice, discussed in Chapter 4.) First, lower courts said the fair report privilege could be lost if the defendants are motivated by ill will. But ultimately courts ruled that the reporter in this case had no intent to injure the plaintiff.[2] Nevertheless, the question of whether malice could possibly eliminate the privilege in some jurisdictions remains.

The fair report privilege covers officials and proceedings in the executive, judicial and legislative branches of state, local and federal governments and, often, private individuals communicating with the government. Law enforcement agencies are included as part of the executive branch of government, so official reports of police activity are included. One case illustrates how the fair report privilege can work. A former Belleville, Ill., police chief sued the News-Democrat there for libel after the newspaper reported that the chief had been the subject of a rape investigation. A three-judge panel of the state appellate court unanimously dismissed the case, ruling that the newspaper was protected by the fair report privilege because its article was a fair and accurate report based on a local prosecutor's comments.[3]

Not every statement by a police officer is privileged, however. One state supreme court, for example, refused to apply the fair report privilege to statements made by a police officer to a reporter during an interview.[4] The court ruled that the officer's participation in the interview and his remarks were not considered to be part of his official duties—a key determinant in deciding whether the privilege applies.

The justification for the fair report privilege is that it stems from another kind of privileged situation. Within some spheres of society, it is so vitally important that people be allowed to speak and

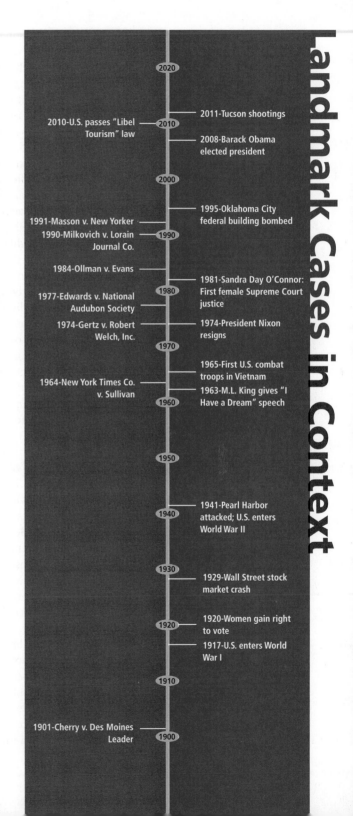

Landmark Cases in Context

2020

2011-Tucson shootings

2010-U.S. passes "Libel Tourism" law — 2010

2008-Barack Obama elected president

2000

1995-Oklahoma City federal building bombed

1991-Masson v. New Yorker

1990-Milkovich v. Lorain Journal Co. — 1990

1984-Ollman v. Evans

1981-Sandra Day O'Connor: First female Supreme Court justice

1977-Edwards v. National Audubon Society — 1980

1974-Gertz v. Robert Welch, Inc.

1974-President Nixon resigns

1970

1965-First U.S. combat troops in Vietnam

1964-New York Times Co. v. Sullivan

1963-M.L. King gives "I Have a Dream" speech — 1960

1950

1941-Pearl Harbor attacked; U.S. enters World War II — 1940

1930

1929-Wall Street stock market crash

1920-Women gain right to vote — 1920

1917-U.S. enters World War I

1910

1901-Cherry v. Des Moines Leader — 1900

communicate information without fear of being sued for libel that they are granted immunity from liability. The rationale is that citizens in a participatory democracy are entitled to such information.[5] As a Massachusetts judge, Oliver Wendell Holmes, Jr., was among those who reasoned that the public should be provided with information about judicial proceedings because "those who administer justice should act under a sense of public responsibility."[6] Nearly a century later, another Massachusetts court echoed Holmes and held that the value of granting privilege to media reports about the courts is "the security which publicity gives for the proper administration of justice."[7]

This privilege—called **absolute privilege**—typically occurs within the context of carrying out the business of government. An open society demands that members of the public have access to information relating to government proceedings. It logically follows that people reporting on these proceedings or information related to these proceedings also have some protection. That protection, though, is only available when the news report is fair and accurate. Thus, in addition to this protection sometimes being referred to as the fair report privilege, it also is called **conditional privilege** or **qualified privilege**.

Reports about judicial activities—the courts—are conditionally privileged. Therefore, media accounts of testimony, depositions, attorney arguments, trials, verdicts, opinions and orders—those aspects that are typically open or available to the public—are among the proceedings covered. Also, documents that relate to the judicial branch are typically privileged. In a 2010 ruling, the New Jersey Supreme Court ruled that journalists who report accurately from court filings, including pretrial documents, are protected from libel claims. The ruling said, "It is critical for the press to be able to report fairly and accurately on every aspect of the administration of justice, including the complaint and answer, without fear of having to defend a defamation case."[8]

The fair report privilege is critically important to the news media given that much of what they do is to report on the activities of the various levels of government, the people who work within those governments and the volumes of records and documents these people produce. The privilege can be forfeited if the allegedly defamatory material is published with inaccuracies or if reported unfairly. This unfair reporting can include ill will toward the plaintiff, if the gist of the article is not substantially true or if the author draws conclusions or adds comments to the official report. The fair report privilege protects media reports of official government actions, regardless of possible defamatory elements within those reports and proceedings.

The Detroit News, for example, successfully used the fair report privilege when it was sued for libel for printing the names of convicted felons working in Detroit public schools. The newspaper had obtained the names from state records. One of the people named sued for libel, claiming the felony charges against her would soon be dismissed. "The privilege precludes damages in a libel suit," the Michigan Court of Appeals ruled, "where a defendant engages in the publication of the contents of a public record, provided the defendant presents a 'fair and true' report of the public record."[9]

absolute privilege A complete exemption from liability for the speaking or publishing of defamatory words of and concerning another because the statement was made within the performance of duty such as in judicial or political contexts.

conditional (or qualified) privilege An exemption from liability for repeating defamatory words of and concerning another because the original statement was made within the performance of duty such as in judicial or political contexts; usually claimed by journalists who report statements made in absolutely privileged situations; this privilege is conditional (or qualified) on the premise that the reporting is fair and accurate.

Fair Comment and Criticism

Reviews of books and other works subject to public scrutiny are at the root of another libel defense: fair comment and criticism. **Fair comment and criticism** is a common law privilege that protects critics from lawsuits brought by individuals in the public eye. A "critic" can be anyone who comments on these individuals and their work. Being "in the public eye" is not the same as being a public figure for purposes of actual malice. A person in the public eye is anyone who enters a public sphere: artists, entertainers, dramatists, writers, members of the clergy, teachers—anyone who moves in and out of the public eye, either professionally or as an amateur. By placing their work products or services into the public sphere, they invite criticism. The privilege also protects commentary on institutions whose activities are of interest to the public or where matters of public interest are concerned. Thus, not only are written works subject to fair comment and criticism, but so are works of art and other products of businesses such as restaurants that implicitly invite reviews of their offerings.

A libel suit involving a book review is instructive: An author sued The New York Times for a reviewer's criticisms of his book. Among other things, the reviewer wrote that the book contained "too much sloppy journalism to trust the bulk of [its] 512 pages including its whopping 64 pages of footnotes."[10] Ultimately, a federal appeals court held that the review was not defamatory, ruling that the genre of the writing and the context within which it appeared must be considered:

> [This] case involves a context, a book review, in which the allegedly libelous statements were evaluations quintessentially of a type readers expect to find in that genre. . . . There is a long and rich history in our cultural and legal traditions of affording reviewers latitude to comment on literary and other works. The statements at issue in the instant case are assessments of a book, rather than direct assaults on [the author's] character, reputation, or competence as a journalist. . . . While a critic's latitude is not unlimited, he or she must be given the constitutional "breathing space" appropriate to the genre.[11]

Historically, the fair comment and criticism privilege was incorporated into the common law to afford legal immunity for the honest expression of opinion on matters of legitimate public interest based on a true or privileged statement of fact.[12] Comment was generally privileged when it concerned a matter of public concern, was based on true or privileged facts, represented the actual opinion of the speaker and was not made solely for the purpose of causing harm.[13] The privilege of fair comment applied only to an expression of opinion and not to a false statement of fact, whether it was expressly stated or implied from an expression of opinion.[14] As the U.S. Supreme Court has stated, "The privilege of 'fair comment' was the device employed to strike the appropriate balance between the need for vigorous public discourse and the need to redress injury to citizens wrought by invidious or irresponsible speech."[15]

fair comment and criticism A common law privilege that protects critics from lawsuits brought by individuals in the public eye.

Fair Comment and Criticism: The Beginning

In 1898, a well-known stage act, the Cherry Sisters, was touring Iowa towns such as Davenport, Cedar Rapids, Dubuque and Des Moines. A local newspaper editor wrote a review of one of their performances, calling the youngest of the three sisters a "capering monstrosity." He continued:

The Cherry Sisters

> Their long, skinny arms, equipped with talons at the extremities, swung mechanically, and anon were waved frantically at the suffering audience. The mouths of their rancid features opened like caverns, and sounds like the wailing of damned souls issued there from. They pranced around the stage . . . strange creatures with painted features and hideous mien. Effie is spavined, Addie is knock-kneed and string-halt, and Jessie, the only one who showed her stockings, has legs without calves, as classic in their outlines as the curves of a broom handle.[1]

After the review was republished by the Des Moines Leader, the sisters were less than amused. They sued that newspaper for libel. They lost in trial court, according to some accounts because the judge had seen their act and agreed it was pretty bad. The sisters then appealed to the Iowa Supreme Court, which also held for the newspaper. "One who goes upon the stage to exhibit himself to the public, or who gives any kind of a performance to which the public is invited, may be freely criticized," the opinion stated. It continues:

> [A performer] may be held up to ridicule, and entire freedom of expression is guarantied [sic] dramatic critics, provided they are not actuated by malice or evil purpose in what they write. Fitting strictures, sarcasm, or ridicule, even, may be used, if based on facts, without liability, in the absence of malice or wicked purpose. The comments, however, must be based on truth, or on what in good faith and upon probable cause is believed to be true, and the matter must be pertinent to the conduct that is made the subject of criticism. Freedom of discussion is guarantied by our fundamental law and a long line of judicial decisions.[2]

The court added that as long as the publisher harbored no ill will toward the plaintiff, "the editor of a newspaper has the right to freely criticise any and every kind of public performance."[3] This ruling is regarded as being partly responsible for the acceptance of the fair comment and criticism privilege. To this day, the privilege stands as a valid shield for criticism of work that is placed before the public.

---

1. Cherry v. Des Moines Leader, 114 Iowa, 298, 299 (1901).
2. *Id.* at 304.
3. *Id.* at 300.

Opinion

Although similar to fair comment and criticism, the libel defense of opinion is distinct. The primary difference is that fair comment and criticism is rooted in the common law. Opinion, on the other hand, stems from the First Amendment and is therefore a constitutional defense and thus stronger and more effective. It is considered to be an unqualified defense in that once proved, it cannot be lost. The question, however, becomes whether specific case circumstances permit the application of the opinion defense.

Holding opinions and being able to express them is a right indisputably and unequivocally guaranteed by the First Amendment. U.S. Supreme Court Justice Lewis Powell laid this out explicitly: "Under the First Amendment there is no such thing as a false idea. However pernicious an opinion may seem, we depend for its correction not on the conscience of judges and juries but on the competition of other ideas."[16] The First Amendment "rests on the assumption that the widest possible dissemination of information from diverse and antagonistic sources is essential to the welfare of the public."[17] Moreover, as Justice Louis Brandeis wrote early in the 20th century, "[F]reedom to think as you will and speak as you think are means indispensable to the discovery and spread of political truth."[18] Thus, a libel defendant may put forth an argument that, in part, echoes Justice William Brennan's opinion in *New York Times Co. v. Sullivan.*[19] The question becomes, "Does the speech contribute to the 'profound national commitment to the principle that debate on public issues should be uninhibited, robust, and wide-open'?"[20] At a very fundamental level, a libel defense may be constructed on constitutional grounds—a claim that limiting ability to convey information is an abridgment of the First Amendment guarantees of free speech and press. Denying an individual the opportunity to express an opinion would be such an abridgment.

The challenge comes in attempting to distinguish statements of fact from statements of opinion. To attempt to separate statements of fact from statements of opinion is to venture onto one of the law's slipperiest of slopes. Yet to do so is vital in establishing the boundaries of the opinion defense's protection. Stating an opinion involves far more than attaching "In my opinion," "I believe" or similar qualifiers to a statement.

The distinguishing attributes of opinion were developed and ultimately solidified by a federal appeals court. That court articulated a four-part test to determine whether a statement was one of fact or an expression of opinion.[21] Not all of the test's elements need to be satisfied; rather, the answers to its questions are to be evaluated in total.

The *Ollman* test (named for the case from which it stems, *Ollman v. Evans*[22]) appeared to provide a sound and relatively straightforward instrument to assess opinion. The four parts are as follows:

1. Is the statement verifiable—objectively capable of proof or disproof? In other words, can the statement be proved either true or false? Opinion is indirectly linked to the falsity/truth element of libel. That is, if a statement

cannot be proved true or false, then it may satisfy the legal definition of an expression of opinion.

2. What is the common usage or meaning of the words?

3. What is the journalistic context in which the statement occurs? This element can be especially important for the media. It provides added weight for an opinion defense when the material in question appears in a part of a publication (or, e.g., a broadcast or Web page) traditionally reserved for opinions—for example, the op-ed pages or personal columns. The entire article or column must be considered as a whole. The language of the entire column may signal that a specific statement, standing alone, which would appear to be factual, is in fact an expression of opinion.

4. What is the broader social context into which the statement fits? For example, was the statement at issue made within a context or in a place where the expression of opinions is not only common but expected? Or was it made within a context in which opinion is not commonplace and, instead, statements are presumed to be statements of fact?

Over time, opinion came to be granted a wide berth of protection. Newsweek magazine, for example, was vindicated in publishing a reference to a false accusation that a former South Dakota governor had sexually assaulted a teenage girl. The words appeared to some people to constitute a statement of fact, but the court found them to be "imprecise, unverifiable" and "presented in a forum where spirited writing is expected and involves criticism of the motives and intentions of a public official."[23] Other plaintiffs who sued because they were called unscrupulous charlatans, neo-Nazis, sleazebags and ignorant and spineless politicians lost their cases because these charges were determined to be expressions of opinion rather than statements of fact.[24]

The latitude afforded to opinion was extensive, but then came a case that put the "no such thing as a false idea"[25] doctrine to the test. Six years after the *Ollman* test was created, the U.S. Supreme Court reframed what had appeared to be close to an absolute opinion defense. The case involved a high school wrestling team that brawled with a competing team during a match. Several people were injured. After a hearing, the coach of one team was censured and his team was placed on probation. A lawsuit was filed in an attempt to prevent the team probation. At a hearing regarding that suit, the coach, Michael Milkovich, denied that he had incited the brawl. In the next day's newspaper, a local sports columnist wrote that Milkovich, along with a school superintendent, misrepresented the truth in an effort to keep the team from being placed on probation. "Anyone who attended the meet . . . knows in his heart that [they] lied at the hearing after each having given his solemn oath to tell the truth," the column read. "But they got away with it." The columnist added that the entire episode provided a lesson for the student body: "If you get in a jam, lie your way out."[26]

Points of Law

The *Ollman* Test for Opinion

1. Verifiability
2. Common meaning
3. Journalistic context
4. Social context

The coach sued for libel. After 15 years and several appeals, the Ohio Court of Appeals held that the column was constitutionally protected opinion, but the U.S. Supreme Court reversed.[27] The Court rejected the broad application of the concept that there is "no such thing as a false idea." "[T]his passage has become the opening salvo in all arguments for protection from defamation actions on the ground of opinion," wrote Chief Justice William Rehnquist, "even though [the original] case did not remotely concern the question."[28] The passage was not intended to create a wholesale defamation exemption for anything that might be labeled "opinion," he continued. "Not only would such an interpretation be contrary to the tenor and context of the passage, but it would also ignore the fact that expressions of 'opinion' may often imply an assertion of objective fact."[29] Rehnquist wrote that facts can disguise themselves as opinions, and, when they do, they imply knowledge of hidden facts that led to the opinion. Merely embedding statements of fact in a column does not transform those statements into expressions of opinion. They remain statements of fact and, if false, may be the basis of a libel suit. Whether the material is verifiable—whether it can be proved true or false—is paramount. The Supreme Court said the key question in this case was whether a reasonable reader could conclude that the statements in the column implied that Milkovich had lied in the judicial proceeding. The Court believed that such an implication had been made and ruled for Milkovich. Even though the material was in a column and thus satisfied the "journalistic context" part of the *Ollman* test, the Court said it was not opinion.[30]

Innocent Construction

Libel cases often hinge on what words mean. Determining meaning in a specific circumstance, in turn, may depend on context. In most states, if a statement has two possible meanings—and one is defamatory and one is not—a jury decides how the words are understood for that case. But this situation is treated differently in Illinois. Under the **innocent construction** rule, as long as the words at issue have one non-defamatory (or innocent) meaning, the defendant wins. In establishing the rule, the Illinois Supreme Court said that allegedly libelous words capable of being read innocently "must be so read and declared nonactionable as a matter of law."[31]

A federal appeals court recently affirmed the ruling of a lower federal court in Illinois that deferred to the innocent construction rule. The case centered on a book written by a former police officer. In it, she mentions a man who had advised her after she left the police department. The two had disagreements and later parted ways. The book was nonfiction but contained "fantasy sequences" in which the author created fictional scenes to symbolically describe her experiences. This included a story that she had been beaten. Though her former adviser was mentioned in the book, it was never by name within these sequences. Still, he believed he had been identified in the sequences and sued for libel. The Seventh Circuit ruled that these sequences could be read in a way that did not call into question the plaintiff's integrity or reputation. The court added that "statements

innocent construction Allegedly libelous words that are capable of being interpreted, or construed, to have an innocent meaning are not libelous, so long as that interpretation is a reasonable one.

realWorld Law

Defining Opinion:
Ollman v. Evans

The University of Maryland was trying to fill a vacancy for chair of its Department of Government and Politics. A political science professor at New York University (NYU), Bertell Ollman, was contacted and invited to apply. Initially reluctant to do so, he ultimately relented. After the typical interviews and give-and-take, Ollman was offered the position, and he accepted.

The news that Ollman was a Marxist began to spread, in his words, "like wildfire," first across the University of Maryland campus and into the community at large, then to nearby

Rowland Evans, Jr.   Robert Novak

Washington, D.C. Maryland's acting governor was among those who denounced Ollman's appointment. The news media took an interest, and columnists began expressing their views. Among those were Rowland Evans, Jr., and Robert Novak, whose jointly written syndicated column was published in newspapers nationwide. In particular, Novak had his interest piqued by this situation. "I'd gotten close to the University," he says. "I knew a lot of the administrative people—the president of the University, the chancellor of the College Park campus. It struck me as an interesting column of why in the world this state university would hire a Marxist, and what kind of Marxist he was. I didn't know anything about him until I started doing some research on him."[1]

The column—included as the Appendix to the court opinion at the end of this chapter—was authored primarily by Novak and was published by a number of newspapers, including The Washington Post, on May 4, 1978. It was entitled "The Marxist Professor's Intentions." It questioned whether Ollman was qualified to assume his

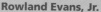

that cannot reasonably be interpreted as stating actual facts are protected under the First Amendment."[32]

Courts can be tough, however, in deciding whether to apply the rule. In another case originating in Illinois, a court ruled that a press release that accused the plaintiff of filing false documents was not eligible for innocent construction protection. In other words, the court believed that the statement at issue could be read only in a way that damaged the plaintiff's reputation.[33]

There is also some evidence that the innocent construction rule exists in Ohio, Missouri, New Mexico and Montana. In addition, a few states hold that

new role at the University of Maryland. But Ollman thought the column did more than that. He believed it damaged his reputation and contributed to the ultimate withdrawal of the job offer. In February 1979, Ollman filed a $6 million libel suit against Evans and Novak, charging that their column contained statements "false both on their face and in their intended innuendo."

The case began what proved to be a circuitous path in which a battle was waged over what constitutes a statement of fact as opposed to an expression of opinion. The case is also noteworthy for those judges at the U.S. Court of Appeals in Washington, D.C., who participated in the ruling. The D.C. Circuit Court of Appeals ruled 6–5 against Ollman.

The court's majority opinion in favor of Evans and Novak was written by Judge Kenneth Starr (who acquired perhaps his greatest notoriety in the late 1990s as the independent counsel in the Whitewater investigation of the Clinton administration). It was in that majority opinion that Starr outlined the most noteworthy element to stem from this case: the *Ollman* test, a four-part test to distinguish fact from opinion. A concurring opinion was written by Judge Robert Bork, whose 1987 nomination to the U.S. Supreme Court was rejected by the Senate amid a storm of political controversy.

A dissenting opinion in *Ollman* was authored by a judge who was, two years later, appointed to the Supreme Court, Antonin Scalia. He referred to the Evans and Novak column as "classic and cooly crafted libel."[2]

"I think what was really at issue was whether a columnist could give a fair opinion, using sources and giving justification, on someone who is a private citizen or a public figure,"[3] said Novak. "Certainly a columnist has a wide berth of freedom to render judgments about public people who are in controversial positions. I think that there is no dividing line between the column and the news story."[4]

An appeal to the U.S. Supreme Court was denied. Ollman believes the decision was a product of a system that protects the powerful: "I start by thinking these people were quite happy that this Marxist who's terribly advocating all these outrageous things, that he got his comeuppance. Now, they also have to find legal reasons to justify what they want because of their personal biases."[5] Ollman returned to NYU.

---

1. JOSEPH RUSSOMANNO, SPEAKING OUR MINDS: CONVERSATIONS WITH THE PEOPLE BEHIND LANDMARK FIRST AMENDMENT CASES 92 (Mahwah, N.J.: Lawrence Erlbaum Associates/Taylor & Francis, 2002).
2. Ollman v. Evans, 750 F.2d 970, 1036 (D.C. Cir. 1984).
3. RUSSOMANNO, *supra* note 1, at 115.
4. *Id.* at 112.
5. *Id.* at 108–9.

statements susceptible to the application of the rule are actionable only when special damages can be proved. They are Alabama, Mississippi, Iowa, Montana and Oklahoma.[34]

The mention of this rule brings up the matter of state libel law. As noted in Chapter 4, the federal Constitution affects libel law. *New York Times Co. v. Sullivan* recognized that the First Amendment affords some protection to libel defendants. Most libel lawsuits are brought in state, not federal, courts. Many nuances of libel law vary from state to state. As long as states are consistent with the First Amendment, they may structure libel laws as they choose.

Letters to the Editor

Letters to the editor are typically viewed as expressions of opinions rather than statements of fact. For that reason, newspapers and magazines have won most cases based on the publication of such letters. Courts have sought to provide protection for the publication of letters, often viewing them as part of an open forum for the general public.

Where a letter appears within a publication is likely to have a significant bearing in determining whether it qualifies as opinion. This stems directly from the "journalistic context" element of the *Ollman* test. That is, by appearing within a section of a publication that is clearly set aside for the expression of opinions—including opinions from readers—a letter (versus an article) is much more likely to be viewed by a court as an expression of opinion.

In those cases in which letters were not protected as opinion, courts have held that those letters combined opinion and facts. Often cases based on such expressions are resolved in favor of libel plaintiffs. For example, a Florida appellate court ruled that a letter questioning a child psychologist's qualifications was defamatory because it was just such a mixed expression and therefore not privileged.[35]

An example of the idea that authors of letters to the editor enjoy the same constitutional protection for their opinions as newspaper reporters was provided by an early 21st-century case. In the ruling on this case, a state court said, "The robust exchange of ideas that occurs each day on the editorial pages of our state's newspapers could indeed suffer if the nonmedia authors of letters to the editor published in these forums were denied the same constitutional protections enjoyed by the editors themselves."[36] Thus, the authors of letters that the news media publish are as shielded as the media themselves.

Rhetorical Hyperbole, Parody and Satire

It has been noted that "the very problem with defamation is its ability to be believed and thus inflict damage on its victims." In turn, if a statement is not believable, it loses its sting and thus its ability to defame. The history of successful libel defenses includes just that premise: that if the material on which a libel claim is based is so outrageous that no reasonable person could believe it, damage to the plaintiff's reputation could not have happened. The most infamous example lies within the circumstances of *Hustler Magazine v. Falwell*,[37] discussed in Chapter 7.

As with other libel defenses, context can be a critical element when it comes to the defense of rhetorical hyperbole, parody and satire. The context of the material in question can play a big role in determining if a reasonable person would believe it to be a statement of fact.

The U.S. Supreme Court first recognized rhetorical hyperbole as protected speech—and therefore a libel defense—when a developer sued the publisher of a newspaper after the newspaper printed articles reporting that some people characterized the developer's negotiating tactics as blackmail.[38] The developer argued

realWorld Law

Letters to the Editor: "A Special Type of Expression"

An analysis of some rulings involving letters to the editor helps to illustrate how state courts tend to view them. In one, the New York Court of Appeals said letters to the editor were "a special type of expression" and that because such letters are generally not published on the authority of a newspaper or journal, "any damage to reputation done by a letter to the editor generally depends on its inherent persuasiveness and the credibility of the writer, not on the belief that it is true because it appears in a particular publication."[1]

In another case, a former police officer sued a newspaper for libel (and several other claims) when it printed a letter to the editor that included accusations he believed falsely damaged his reputation. The newspaper asked the case to be dismissed, and a lower court granted that motion. In affirming, the Georgia Court of Appeals said the former police officer would have to show the statements were made with actual malice. The newspaper's president swore that neither he nor any employee knew of any falsity in the letter and that the letter contained opinions in addition to facts.[2]

In analyzing a letter to the editor that called for retaliation against Muslims in the United States for events in the Iraq War, the Arizona Supreme Court looked through the lens of the First Amendment. Speech on matters of public concern goes to the heart of the First Amendment, the court said. Rejecting arguments that the letter incited lawless action or contained true threats, the court ruled that claims against the Tucson Citizen, the newspaper that published the letter, should be dismissed.[3]

1. Immuno AG v. Moor-Jankowski, 549 N.E.2d 129, 133 (N.Y. 1989).
2. Evans v. The Sandersville Georgian, Inc., 675 S.E.2d 574 (Ct. App. Ga. 2009).
3. Citizen Publishing Co. v. Miller, 115 P.3d 107 (Ariz. 2005). In part, the letter stated, "We can stop the murders of American soldiers in Iraq by those who seek revenge or to regain their power. Whenever there is an assassination or another atrocity we should proceed to the closest mosque and execute five of the first Muslims we encounter." *Id.* at 515.

that the word "blackmail" implied that the developer had committed the crime of blackmail. The Supreme Court rejected the developer's argument, holding that the word "blackmail" was not slander when spoken and not libel when reported because "even the most careless reader must have perceived that the word was no more than rhetorical hyperbole, a vigorous epithet used by those who considered [the developer's] negotiating position extremely unreasonable."[39]

That case was mentioned in another ruling a few years later, this one involving a labor dispute.[40] In its monthly newsletter a local union published, under the headline "List of Scabs," the names of those who had not joined the union. This was followed up by union literature that contained writer Jack London's definition of "scab," which read in part: "After God had finished the rattlesnake, the toad, and the vampire, He had some awful substance left with which He made a scab. A scab is a two-legged animal with a corkscrew soul, a water brain, a combination backbone of jelly and glue. Where others have hearts, he carries a tumor of rotten principles."[41] The definition also described a scab as a "traitor."

The Court noted that the use of "scab" is common in labor disputes and is entitled to protection, and that words such as "traitor" cannot be construed as representations of fact: "It is similarly impossible to believe that any reader of the [newsletter] would have understood [it] to be charging [those listed] with committing the criminal offense of treason. . . . Jack London's 'definition of a scab' is merely rhetorical hyperbole, a lusty and imaginative expression of the contempt felt by union members towards those who refuse to join."[42] As one court has said: "The specific context of a statement shades its meaning. Language that is 'loose, figurative and hyperbolic . . . tends to negate the impression that a statement contains an assertion of verifiable fact.'"[43] One of those contexts can be within labor disputes.

Similar to rhetorical hyperbole, satire or parody meant to be humorous or offer social commentary is often not libelous. For example, an artist was sued for libel because one of his paintings portrayed the plaintiffs holding knives and attacking a young woman. The artist knew the plaintiffs, also artists, but had become embroiled in a spat with them over their views on art. The painting was meant to satirize the views of those depicted. An appellate court considered the context and identified it as symbolic expression with no accusation of criminal conduct.[44]

However, compare that to a situation in which a newspaper published a fictional article describing a Texas juvenile court judge who ordered the detention of a first grader for making a threat in a book report. The fictional student was described as appearing before the judge in handcuffs and ankle shackles.[45] The problem arose because the judge used in this otherwise made-up story was real. The satirical article came out after a real court case in which that same judge had ordered the detention of a 13-year-old student who wrote a Halloween horror story depicting the shooting death of a teacher and two students. The newspaper did not dispute that its article on the first grader was completely made up. It was meant to be a commentary on the judge and his heavy-handed justice. But the judge and a district attorney sued for libel, claiming that the article could be understood by a reasonable reader as making false statements of fact about them and that they were made with actual malice. The newspaper defended itself by claiming the article was satire and parody and therefore protected by the First Amendment. Ultimately, the Texas Supreme Court ruled for the newspaper.[46] The court cited clues in the article that would alert a reasonable reader that the article was not a statement of fact but instead a criticism or opinion. Though the article did have a superficial degree of plausibility, the court said, that is the hallmark of satire.

SUMMARY

THOSE SUED FOR LIBEL HAVE SEVERAL OPTIONS from which to choose, any one of which can lead to a successful defense. Truth is often regarded as the most straightforward defense, given that material must be false to be libelous. Even material that is less than completely accurate may be regarded as substantially true.

Journalists are able to report on certain events without fear of libel as long as their reporting is fair and accurate. The fair report privilege generally applies to reporting on official government proceedings (e.g., hearings, trials) or records. Another defense, fair comment and criticism, pertains to honest evaluation of works or series of legitimate public interest.

Expressing an opinion is regarded as a basic First Amendment right. Opinion is protected speech, not susceptible to a libel claim. However, for material to qualify as protected opinion, it must satisfy the four-part *Ollman* test. Published letters to the editor are typically viewed as protected opinion. If a statement is unbelievable, then it cannot be libelous. Thus, parody, satire and rhetorical hyperbole can be used as libel defenses when it is clear to a reasonable person that their use is not to be taken seriously. ■

Neutral Reportage

As explained in Chapter 4, someone who repeats libelous information is as potentially responsible as the originator of that same information. In other words, republication is not a valid libel defense. But that longtime rule of libel law was loosened somewhat by the doctrine of neutral reportage. **Neutral reportage** recognizes that the First Amendment principle of the free flow of information and ideas is important. Among the kinds of information that should be free to reach people, the doctrine suggests, are accusations made by one party about another. In some circumstances, the news value lies not in whether the accusation is true but simply in the fact that the accusation was made or who made it. According to neutral reportage, the news media should not be restrained from merely reporting an accusation, as long as the reporting is done in a fair, objective and balanced (i.e., neutral) manner. Even if the publisher of the reported accusations has serious doubts about their veracity, the neutral reportage doctrine could provide a successful defense.

The neutral reportage defense was established in 1977,[47] restricting its application to cases involving public figures. While since then the scope of that application has sometimes expanded beyond public figures, the nation's courts have not embraced neutral reportage. Its recognition, in fact, has been spotty. One obstacle to more widespread acceptance is the fact that the U.S. Supreme Court has had virtually nothing to say about the neutral reportage theory. As the writer of a 2010 article says, protections under the neutral reportage defense "remain elusive for most publishers," and because it has been left to individual state and federal districts how to handle it, the legal landscape is uncertain.[48] Thus, while neutral reportage remains an option in the libel defendant's arsenal, the inconsistent manner in which courts have accepted it makes its application in a specific case questionable. Much depends on how a court in a given jurisdiction may have ruled on neutral reportage previously.

neutral reportage In libel law, a defense accepted in some jurisdictions that says that when an accusation is made by a responsible and prominent organization, reporting that accusation is protected by the First Amendment even when it turns out the accusation was false and libelous.

Points of Law

Neutral Reportage

The First Amendment is a defense in a libel case if

- The story is newsworthy and related to a public controversy.
- The accusation is made by a responsible person or group.
- The charge is about a public official, public figure or public organization.
- The story is accurate, containing denials or other views.
- The reporting is neutral.

Points of Law

The Wire Service Defense

The wire service defense may be applied as long as

1. The defendant received material containing the defamatory statements from a reputable news-gathering agency.

2. The defendant did not know the story was false.

3. Nothing on the face of the story reasonably could have alerted the defendant that it may have been incorrect.

4. The original wire service story was republished without substantial change.

Wire Service Defense

Somewhat related to the neutral reportage doctrine is the wire service defense. It is similar to neutral reportage in that it provides a defense for republication on the condition that the reporting meets certain standards. The wire service defense reflects and acknowledges the extent to which news media are dependent on news services, particularly for non-local news. To expect verification of every report is unreasonable. This defense holds that the accurate republication of a story provided by a reputable news agency does not constitute fault as a matter of law. The wire defense is available to libel defendants if four factors are met: (1) the defendant received material containing the defamatory

realWorld Law

Edwards v. National Audubon Society: The Origin of Neutral Reportage

Envision a situation in which a journalist discovers that a famous former college athlete has made serious accusations about his former coach that could be false and defamatory—that is, libelous. In addition, suppose there is a reasonable argument that news about the accusations is in the public interest. The accusations include that the coach arranged for cash payments, free cars and other rewards—all in violation of National Collegiate Athletics Association (NCAA) rules—while the player was enrolled.[1] Should the journalist be able to publish the accusations without fearing a libel lawsuit?

This question is at the heart of the neutral reportage libel defense. It stems from a case that concluded with a ruling by a federal appeals court.[2] A group of scientists sued the National Audubon Society and The New York Times for libel. An article in the Times had reported that the scientists were paid liars for their support of DDT as a chemical pesticide. The National Audubon Society was among those who had opposed DDT because the chemical was linked to endangering birds. An Audubon Society publication, "American Birds," contained an article critical of DDT and claiming that bird counts were actually down. "Any time you hear a 'scientist' say the opposite, you are in the presence of someone who is being paid to lie."

The accusation came to the attention of The New York Times' nature reporter. He contacted the writer of the article in "American Birds" to ask for names of people who qualified as the "paid liars" for DDT. After some research, the "American Birds" writer provided the names of five scientists who had distorted Audubon statistics. The Times reporter then attempted to contact each of the five individuals. He succeeded in reaching three of them. All denied the charges, with one of them referring to the charges as "almost libelous."

The reporter then wrote an article, published by The New York Times, in which it was reported that the five scientists—identified by name—were accused of being paid liars by the Audubon publication. Three of the scientists sued the National Audubon Society, The New York Times and both writers—the Times reporter and the "American Birds" writer.

statements from a reputable news-gathering agency, (2) the defendant did not know the story was false, (3) nothing on the face of the story reasonably could have alerted the defendant that it may have been incorrect, and (4) the original wire service story was republished without substantial change.

The wire service defense has succeeded even when a newspaper published a story that relied on past wire service articles[49] and when a network affiliate broadcast news reports of its parent network.[50] Also, like the neutral reportage privilege, the wire service defense has been accepted in a limited number of jurisdictions.

Single-Publication Rule

Another issue related to republication revolves around the availability of an article subsequent to its initial publication. In other words, does the republication of a work weeks, months or years after its original publication constitute a new publication, therefore making it susceptible to additional, separate libel claims?

After a federal trial court jury found for the scientists, the ruling was reversed on appeal. The opening remarks of that ruling are revealing:

In a society which takes seriously the principle that government rests upon the consent of the governed, freedom of the press must be the most cherished tenet. It is elementary that a democracy cannot long survive unless the people are provided the information needed to form judgments on issues that affect their ability to intelligently govern themselves.[3]

The court emphasized that The New York Times article accurately reported the facts of the story, and thus a libel judgment against the newspaper would be constitutionally impermissible:

When a responsible, prominent organization like the National Audubon Society makes serious charges against a public figure, the First Amendment protects the accurate and disinterested reporting of those charges, regardless of the reporter's private views regarding their validity. . . . What is newsworthy about such accusations is that they were made. We do not believe that the press may be required under the First Amendment to suppress newsworthy statements merely because it has serious doubts regarding their truth.[4]

The court's rationale for its finding was the public interest in being fully informed about controversial and sometimes sensitive issues. Literal accuracy is not a prerequisite, the court said, for the press' right of neutral reportage, especially when the journalist believes reasonably and in good faith that the report accurately conveys the charges made.

---

1. *See, e.g.,* Pete Thamel, *Clarett Accuses Ohio State of N.C.A.A. Violations*, N.Y. Times, Nov. 10, 2004, at C17.
2. Edwards v. National Audubon Society, 556 F.2d 113 (2d Cir. 1977).
3. *Id.* at 115.
4. *Id.* at 120.

single publication rule A rule that limits libel victims to only one cause of action even with multiple publications of the libel, common in the mass media and on websites.

According to the **single-publication rule,** no. According to the rule, the entire edition of a newspaper or magazine is a single publication. Subsequent sales or reissues are not new publications. Thus, a new libel suit is not possible in such circumstances. However, if in the republication process, content changes in a way that creates a new libel, the single-publication rule is unlikely to apply.

The Libel-Proof Plaintiff

When an individual's reputation is already so bad that additional false accusations could not harm it further, the individual may be without the ability to win a defamation suit. In other words, it may be argued that the individual's reputation cannot be harmed any further by a new, libelous publication. Under these circumstances, a libel defendant may be able to invoke the concept of the **libel-proof plaintiff.** Since the concept was first articulated as a libel defense,[51] two different ways to implement it have emerged.

libel-proof plaintiff A plaintiff whose reputation is deemed to be so damaged already that additional false statements of and concerning him or her cannot cause further harm.

One way stipulates that any reputational harm to the plaintiff caused by a false accusation only incrementally injures the reputation beyond its already damaged condition. Suppose, for example, that an individual is identified in an article as a thief, child molester and tax evader. If all of those charges are true, does it make any difference if the article also falsely identifies the individual as a kidnapper? According to the libel-proof plaintiff concept, no. In such a case, the publisher could probably win, arguing that the single false statement causes harm that is negligible (or incremental) beyond what already exists and therefore is not grounds for a libel suit. In short, under these kinds of circumstances the false statement causes very little harm to the reputation beyond where the plaintiff's reputation stood prior to the most recent publication.

Like other common law libel privileges, the acceptance of this part of the doctrine has not been universal. For example, a federal appeals court issued an outright rejection of the libel-proof plaintiff doctrine in 1984.[52] A journalist had described the founder of an organization as a racist, fascist, anti-Semitic neo-Nazi, and wrote that he had founded the organization to pursue his goals. The defense argued that previous publications had already so irreparably tarnished the plaintiff's reputation that the libel-proof doctrine should apply. In an opinion written by then-judge Antonin Scalia, an appellate court rejected the claim, ruling that "we cannot envision how a court would go about determining that someone's reputation had already been 'irreparably' damaged—i.e., that no new reader could be reached by the freshest libel."[53] In writing that no matter how bad one's reputation is, it can always be worsened, Scalia offered an analogy: "It is shameful that Benedict Arnold was a traitor; but he was not a shoplifter to boot, and one should not have been able to make that charge while knowing its falsity with impunity."[54]

Courts may also recognize the second aspect of the libel-proof doctrine, which says that libel plaintiffs with tarnished reputations with regard to a particular issue are libel-proof only with respect to that topic area. Libel claims pursued in this context present the question of whether previous publicity and the issue before the court are within the same framework.

realWorld Law

The Libel-Proof Doctrine: Applied with Caution

The libel-proof doctrine was central to a preliminary stage of a 2009 case involving a book about the late Anna Nicole Smith, a model and celebrity who died in 2007 at the age of 39. Her former lawyer and companion, Howard K. Stern, sued the author and publisher for libel. He claimed the book libeled him by falsely stating or suggesting, among other things, that he had engaged in a homosexual relationship with the father of Smith's child, "pimped" Smith to as many as 50 men a year and played a role in Smith's death.

Howard K. Stern and Anna Nicole Smith

The defendants claimed that Stern was libel-proof.[1] The basis of the defendants' claim was that Stern had been a frequent subject on tabloid television and in celebrity gossip magazines. Those stories, the defendants said, had already damaged Stern's reputation beyond repair. A U.S. District Court rejected this claim.

First, the court said, Stern should not be precluded from suing for libel just because his story had been a subject in other media. For starters, Stern denied the accusations made in those. If those accusations were false, being falsely accused again did not mean his reputation could not be damaged further. "That someone has been falsely called a thief in the past does not mean that he is immune from further injury if he is falsely called a thief again."[2]

Second, the court indicated it would hold the book in question to a higher standard than tabloid television. The judge noted that the book purported to be a work of investigative journalism by an award-winning journalist. By that standard, the book did not seem to measure up to its own claims in the eyes of the judge.

Last, the court was clearly reluctant to apply the libel-proof doctrine at all. Citing precedent, it said the doctrine "is to be applied with caution, since few plaintiffs will have so bad a reputation that they are not entitled to obtain redress for defamatory statements, even if their damages cannot be quantified and they receive only nominal damages."[3] The judge ruled that the libel-proof doctrine did not apply and allowed the case to go to trial against the book's author.

1. Stern v. Cosby, 645 F. Supp. 2d 258 (S.D.N.Y 2009).
2. *Id.* at 270–71.
3. *Id.* at 270.

A couple of examples may be helpful. In the first, the plaintiff challenged a newspaper report that he had tested positive for drug use. The court found that while the report was incorrect, the plaintiff was libel-proof regarding this specific issue because he had previously admitted using drugs.[55] Had the new report falsely damaged his reputation regarding a topic unrelated to drug use, the libel-proof plaintiff doctrine could not have been invoked. The plaintiff still had a positive reputation to protect in those other areas.

Second, a defendant periodical had published an article stating that the plaintiff had used his relationship with actress Elizabeth Taylor for financial gain.[56] The court ruled that the plaintiff had a "reputation for taking advantage of women generally, and of Miss Taylor specifically." The ruling went on to say, "An individual who engages in certain antisocial or criminal behavior and suffers a diminished reputation may be 'libel-proof' as a matter of law, as it *relates to that specific behavior*."[57] Thus, the doctrine of the libel-proof plaintiff may serve a defendant who has published otherwise defamatory statements about an individual whose reputation is already so sullied as to render additional accusations moot, regardless of their falsity. Depending on the circumstances, the doctrine may apply to accusations of any nature or to those that relate only to a specific issue.

The libel-proof plaintiff doctrine remains a valuable defense weapon, particularly against frivolous libel suits and especially given the U.S. Supreme Court's opinion that states are free to adopt the doctrine as they see fit.[58]

Single-Mistake Rule

Falsely reporting that a professional person has made a mistake within the context of his or her profession may not necessarily be libelous. The single-mistake rule excuses such reporting by reasoning that the public understands that some kinds of professionals occasionally make mistakes. Similarly, according to this rule, to mistakenly report that someone such as a doctor, lawyer or financial adviser made an error does not necessarily damage the professional's reputation. Accordingly, the single-mistake rule can serve as a libel defense.[59]

SUMMARY

SOME LIBEL DEFENSES ALLOW FOR A KIND OF REPUBLICATION. These include neutral reportage and the wire service defense. Multiple issues of the same publication, however, do not make the defendant vulnerable to multiple libel claims, under the single-publication rule.

Sometimes false, defamatory material is published about someone whose reputation cannot be lowered beyond its current level. Under those circumstances, a defendant may argue the plaintiff is libel-proof.

The single-mistake rule can work to defend otherwise libelous material when the inaccurate reporting of a professional making an error would not damage his or her reputation. ■

Other Defense Issues

Summary Judgment

A libel defendant can ask a court to dismiss a lawsuit by filing a motion for summary judgment. As noted in Chapter 1, a summary judgment is just what the name implies: A judge promptly decides certain points of a case and grants the motion to dismiss the case. It can occur at any of several points in litigation but usually occurs prior to trial.

A judge may issue a summary judgment on grounds that there is no genuine dispute about any material fact. With libel, this generally means a plaintiff is clearly unable to meet at least one element in his or her burden of proof. On numerous occasions, the U.S. Supreme Court said that when considering motions for summary judgment, courts "must view the facts and inferences to be drawn from them in the light most favorable to the opposing party."[60] Particularly in libel cases, this means that courts must take into account the burden the plaintiff must meet at trial. The rationale behind this view is that if the summary judgment is granted, the plaintiff's opportunity to prove a case ends; but if a defendant's motion for summary judgment is denied, the defendant still has an opportunity to prove his or her case at trial.[61]

Summary judgments can be important tools for protecting free expression, particularly in an environment in which plaintiffs have harassed the media by filing frivolous lawsuits (e.g., see Chapter 4's description of SLAPPs). One federal judge wrote that in the First Amendment area, summary procedures are even more essential. Free debate is at stake if the harassment succeeds. One purpose of the *New York Times Co. v. Sullivan* actual malice principle, the judge wrote, is to prevent people from being discouraged in the full and free exercise of First Amendment rights with respect to the conduct of their government.[62]

Until 1979, summary judgment was a preferred method of dealing with libel cases involving actual malice. When the defense submitted a motion for summary judgment—based on the contention that the plaintiff could not prove actual malice—the judge would either grant or deny it. If granted, the case was over; if denied, the case would go forward and possibly result in a trial.

In 1979, the U.S. Supreme Court cast doubt on the appropriateness of summary judgment in libel cases because any examination of actual malice "calls a defendant's state of mind into question." Such a circumstance "does not readily lend itself to summary disposition."[63] While some lower courts took the admonition to heart—using it as a basis for denying summary judgment—motions for summary judgment are still granted more often than not. Then in 1986, the Court ruled that in deciding whether to grant motions for summary judgment, trial judges should decide whether public plaintiffs who file lawsuits claiming they have been libeled can meet the actual malice standard by "clear and convincing evidence." If not, summary judgment for the party they have sued should be granted.[64] This tempered the impact of the Court's 1979 ruling that curtailed summary judgments in libel cases, suggesting that summary judgment remains a viable option.

Jurisdiction

A court may dismiss a lawsuit on the ground that the court lacks jurisdiction. Traditionally in libel, the standard has been that wherever the material in question could be seen or heard, a court in any of those locales would have jurisdiction.[65] Thus, a plaintiff could go "forum shopping" in an attempt to find a jurisdiction most favorable to his or her case.

realWorld Law

Libel Tourism

Because U.S. libel law is more weighted to protecting defendants than are the laws in other countries, U.S. citizens have historically been more susceptible to libel verdicts against them in foreign courts. In fact, international plaintiffs have been known to engage in "libel tourism," shopping for a country other than the United States in which to file a libel claim. Their claims are often filed in England, where libel laws are especially plaintiff friendly.

Rachel Ehrenfeld

In 2010, the U.S. Congress passed a libel tourism bill designed to address this problem. The new law prevents federal courts from enforcing a foreign libel judgment against an American journalist, author or publisher if it is inconsistent with the protections afforded by the First Amendment. It also allows individuals who have a foreign judgment levied against them to demonstrate that it is not enforceable in the United States. One of the law's co-sponsors, Sen. Patrick Leahy, said: "The freedoms of speech and the press are cornerstones of our democracy. They enable vigorous debate, and an exchange of ideas that shapes our political process. Foreign libel lawsuits are undermining this informational exchange.[1]

Rachel Ehrenfeld, now director of the American Center for Democracy, was instrumental in bringing attention to the phenomenon of libel tourism. She was sued for libel in England by a Saudi Arabian who claimed to be defamed by her book, "Funding Evil." Though the book was marketed and sold exclusively in the United States, he showed that 23 copies had entered England through online sales. As Ehrenfeld wrote in 2010, "English libel law originated to protect thin-skinned lords from 19th-century gossips. Today it makes London the libel capital of the world, an international destination of 'libel tourists' who, because of the Internet, can sue anyone for spreading alleged mistruths in England."[2]

Ehrenfeld did not defend the claim, and the English court issued a default judgment against her. In turn, she sued the original plaintiff in a federal court in New York, asking that the libel verdict not be enforceable against her. New York's highest court ultimately said state law as it then stood would not allow it to rule for her, but it noted that the state legislature could change the law.[3] In 2008 New York became the first state to pass a law designed to remedy this situation. The New York law now prevents libel rulings like the one against Ehrenfeld by the English court from being enforced. Similar legislation has been passed in Illinois and Florida. The 2010 federal law will provide similar protection in federal courts.

---

1. U.S. Passes Historic SPEECH Act, Europe News, July 28, 2010, *available at* http://europenews.dk en/node/34081.
2. Rachel Ehrenfeld, *A Legal Thriller in London*, Newsweek, June 7, 2010, at 12.
3. Ehrenfeld v. Mahfouz, 881 N.E.2d 83 (N.Y. 2007), *aff'd*, 518 F.3d 102 (2d. Cir. 2008).

Consider, however, online libel. Given that statements published on the Internet are potentially seen anywhere, any court could claim jurisdiction. More to the point, a plaintiff could initiate the lawsuit in any court, including those that might be most favorable. But early in the 21st century, significant restrictions were placed on this practice. The U.S. Court of Appeals for the Fourth Circuit applied a three-pronged test for determining the exercise of jurisdiction: (1) whether the defendant purposefully conducted activities in the state, (2) whether the plaintiff's claim arises out of the defendant's activities there, and (3) whether the exercise of jurisdiction would be constitutionally reasonable.[66]

To understand the test, it may be helpful to examine the circumstances surrounding the case in which it was first applied. Two Connecticut newspapers were investigating conditions of confinement at a Virginia prison. The story was relevant in Connecticut because some of the overflow prison population in Connecticut was being transferred to a Virginia facility. Articles that included content critical of the Virginia prison and its management appeared in the newspaper in both its print and online editions. The Virginia prison warden sued in federal court in Virginia, claiming that the online content was seen in Virginia and had defamed him there. The appeals court ultimately ruled that because the newspapers did not intend to direct their website content to a Virginia audience, courts there had no jurisdiction. The court carefully reviewed the articles and determined they were aimed at a local (Connecticut) audience.[67] Placing content online, the court ruled, is not sufficient by itself to subject a person to the jurisdiction in another state just because the information could be accessed there.[68] Otherwise, a person who places information on the Internet could be sued anywhere the information could be accessed. The bottom line, according to this ruling, is that jurisdiction rests where the publication's intended audience is located.

Statute of Limitations

For virtually all crimes and civil actions, a statute of limitations applies. Charges of most criminal activity and civil actions can be filed only during a limited time after the alleged violation of the law. Courts do not like old claims. While not a defense per se, delay in filing a libel lawsuit can work to the benefit of a defendant, sometimes requiring dismissal where the lawsuit is barred by the statute of limitations.

Length of Statutes of Limitation in Libel Actions

In libel, the length of the statue of limitations is one, two or three years, depending on the state. The clock begins ticking on the date the material was made available to the public. With some printed publications, this can be prior to the date of publication on the cover. Many monthly magazines, for example, are mailed to subscribers and appear on newsstands well before the official publication date.

On a related note, the single-publication rule also applies to statutes of limitation. The reissue of a publication does not restart the statute of limitation calendar as a truly new publication would. This standard now also applies to Internet publications. A modification to a website—when the modification is unrelated to the allegedly defamatory statement—does not amount to a new publication.

Length of Statutes of Limitation in Libel Actions

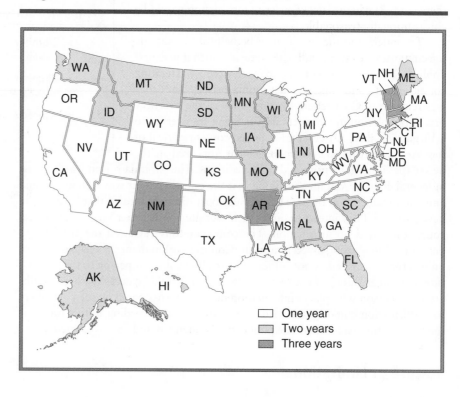

For purposes of libel claims and the statute of limitations, the date of publication remains the date on which the site was originally posted.

Retractions

While not a libel defense per se, retractions and corrections published to correct content can play a role in helping libel defendants by mitigating the damage to the plaintiff that resulted from the libelous publication. The degree to which a retraction is offered promptly, is displayed prominently and is plainly stated will likely help the defendant's cause. The rationale for this is that a retraction can help reduce the damage to the plaintiff's reputation; the defendant therefore should be required to pay less in damages.

Note one pitfall of issuing retractions or apologies: While issuing one is certainly the responsible action to undertake, doing so may actually work against the defendant if the offended party files a lawsuit. Depending on their wording, retractions may be viewed as an admission of guilt. Consequently, libel defense attorneys may advise against issuing them in the first place. In part as a response to this paradox, a majority of states have adopted **retraction statutes.** Increasingly, these laws prevent plaintiffs from recovering entire categories of damages after publication of a retraction.[69] Retraction statutes vary in their strength and coverage.[70] The protection they offer differs in many ways, from prohibitions on punitive damages to restricting damages to out-of-pocket losses.[71] Most of these statutes look favorably on media defendants who issue retractions. Rather than penalizing media organizations that indirectly acknowledge some degree of negligence, these statutes offer a kind of compensation by reducing their obligation to pay damages.

Considering a specific retraction statute may be instructive. California's law is regarded as one of the more intricate statutes. It stipulates that the plaintiff in a libel action may recover only special damages unless a correction is demanded and not published or broadcast. The demand must be in writing, it must specify the statements claimed to be libelous and it must be submitted within 20 days of the plaintiff's learning of the publication. If the defendant fails to publish or broadcast the retraction within three weeks "in substantially as conspicuous a manner" as the original material was placed, the plaintiff may recover general, special and exemplary damages.

Retraction statutes do not always fare well under judicial review in their respective states. Some, in fact, have been ruled unconstitutional. The Arizona Supreme Court, for example, ruled that the retraction statute in that state violated the state constitution.[72] The law limited plaintiffs to recovering only special damages when retractions were published.[73] But the Arizona Constitution holds that "[t]he right of action to recover damages for injuries shall never be abrogated, and the amount recovered shall not be subject to any statutory limitation."[74] Because the law conflicted with the Arizona constitution, it did not survive judicial scrutiny. However, while a retraction or correction of a news report in Arizona may no longer immunize a libel defendant from all punitive damage claims, it may serve to reduce those damages.

Responsible Reporting

As part of a defense strategy, a libel defendant may attempt to demonstrate to a court that it conducted itself in a responsible way in gathering and reporting the news. The defendant is then more likely to garner support for its argument that it should not be found legally responsible for committing libel. The media defendant, for example, may need to disprove the plaintiff's claim that its employees acted with reckless disregard for the truth or that they were negligent.

In attempting to prove that a libel defendant acted with reckless disregard, a plaintiff is likely to attempt to build a case bit by bit, demonstrating a series of irresponsible or careless acts in the news-gathering and publishing process. Courts have said that no single element is sufficient to prove clearly and convincingly that a defendant acted with reckless disregard, but each can be used as evidence to build a case. A libel defendant wants to strengthen its position by showing as many of the following as possible:

retraction statutes In libel law, state laws that limit the damages a plaintiff may receive if the defendant had issued a retraction of the material at issue. Retraction statutes are meant to discourage the punishment of any good-faith effort of admitting a mistake.

- The story was investigated thoroughly.
- Interviews were conducted with people who had knowledge of facts related to the story, including the subject of the report.
- Previously published material was not relied on.
- Biased stories were not relied on.
- The reporting was careful, systematic and painstaking.
- Multiple viewpoints were sought and, when possible, included in the report.
- There was a willingness to retract or correct if facts warranted such action.
- If applicable, there was a demonstrable deadline.
- There was no ill will or hatred toward the plaintiff.

Even if media defendants are unable to escape liability altogether, they are likely to mitigate damages by substantiating these points and demonstrating responsible reporting.

Two situations illustrate how courts may consider one or more of the elements of responsible reporting. Within the context of a libel suit, a state appellate court once concluded that a reporter's failure to interview one of the police officers accused of brutality in a series of reports could be regarded as negligent behavior. The court ruled, however, that such irresponsibility alone did not support the officer's claim that the reporter had acted with actual malice.[75] In another case, a television journalist argued that his reporting methods were responsible by maintaining that he spent four days interviewing 30 people and reviewing 500 pages of court records in preparing the story. This argument contributed to an appellate court decision overturning a libel judgment against him.[76]

SUMMARY

A LIBEL DEFENDANT OFTEN FILES A MOTION to dismiss the lawsuit when it is clear that the plaintiff cannot prove his case. Courts granting such a motion issue a summary judgment.

Questions about jurisdiction can also work in the defendant's favor. Whether the court has authority over a certain defendant and whether the applicable statute of limitations has expired can affect the court's authority to act at all in a particular case.

Libel defendants should know about retractions, corrections and apologies. These may help to reduce damage awards. Media defendants want to be viewed as reliable and trustworthy organizations that conduct themselves responsibly. While it is not technically a defense, demonstrating basic journalistic responsibility can enhance the defendant's standing with the court and provide either a defense in the lawsuit or a solid basis for the court to minimize monetary damages assessed against a media defendant. Moreover, journalistic integrity is simply the proper way to conduct business and often tends to be the best way to avoid libel suits in the first place. ■

Cases for Study

Thinking About It

The two case excerpts that follow are very important libel cases. Note that only one of them is from the U.S. Supreme Court. The other is from the D.C. Circuit Court of Appeals. At the center of each is the libel defense of opinion. As you read these case excerpts, keep the following questions in mind:

- How do the two decisions help define the meaning of opinion?

- Does either ruling outline any kind of test or standard to help judge opinion? If so, what is that?

- Do these rulings expand or narrow the definition of opinion?

Ollman v. Evans
UNITED STATES COURT OF APPEALS FOR THE DISTRICT OF COLUMBIA CIRCUIT
750 F.2d 970 (1984)

JUDGE KENNETH STARR delivered the court's opinion:

This defamation action arises out of the publication of a syndicated column by Rowland Evans and Robert Novak in May 1978. The question before us is whether the allegedly defamatory statements set forth in the column are constitutionally protected expressions of opinion or, as appellant contends, actionable assertions of fact. We conclude, as did the District Court, that the challenged statements are entitled to absolute First Amendment protection as expressions of opinion. . . .

The plaintiff, Bertell Ollman, is a professor of political science at New York University. . . . In March 1978, Mr. Ollman was nominated by a departmental search committee to head the Department of Government and Politics at the University of Maryland. The committee's recommendation was "duly approved by the Provost of the University and the Chancellor of the College Park campus."

With this professional move from Washington Square to College Park, Maryland thus in the offing, the Evans and Novak article appeared. . . .

This case presents us with the delicate and sensitive task of accommodating the First Amendment's protection of free expression of ideas with the common law's protection of an individual's interest in reputation. It is a truism that the free flow of ideas and opinions is integral to our democratic system of government. Thomas Jefferson well expressed this principle in his First Inaugural Address, when the Nation's memory was fresh with the passage of the notorious Alien and Sedition Acts:

> If there be any among us who would wish to dissolve this Union or to change its republican form, let them stand undisturbed as monuments of the safety with which error of opinion may be tolerated where reason is left free to combat it.

At the same time, an individual's interest in his or her reputation is of the highest order. Its protection is an eloquent expression of the respect historically afforded the dignity of the individual in Anglo-American legal culture. A defamatory statement may destroy an individual's livelihood, wreck his standing in the

213

community, and seriously impair his sense of dignity and self-esteem. . . .

. . . In *Gertz,* the Supreme Court in *dicta* seemed to provide absolute immunity from defamation actions for all opinions and to discern the basis for this immunity in the First Amendment. The Court began its analysis of the case by stating:

Under the First Amendment there is no such thing as a false idea. However pernicious an opinion may seem, we depend for its correction not on the conscience of judges and juries but on the competition of other ideas. But there is no constitutional value in false statements of fact. Neither the intentional lie nor the careless error materially advances society's interest in "uninhibited, robust, and wide-open debate on the public issues." . . .

. . . *Gertz*'s implicit command thus imposes upon both state and federal courts the duty as a matter of constitutional adjudication to distinguish facts from opinions in order to provide opinions with the requisite, absolute First Amendment protection. At the same time, however, the Supreme Court provided little guidance in *Gertz* itself as to the manner in which the distinction between fact and opinion is to be discerned. . . .

. . . With largely uncharted seas having been left in *Gertz*'s wake, the lower federal courts and state courts have, not surprisingly, fashioned various approaches in attempting to articulate the *Gertz*-mandated distinction between fact and opinion. . . .

In formulating a test to distinguish between fact and opinion, courts are admittedly faced with a dilemma. Because of the richness and diversity of language, as evidenced by the capacity of the same words to convey different meanings in different contexts, it is quite impossible to lay down a bright-line or mechanical distinction. . . . While this dilemma admits of no easy resolution, we think it obliges us to state plainly the factors that guide us in distinguishing fact from opinion and to demonstrate how these factors lead to a proper accommodation between the competing interests in free expression of opinion and in an individual's reputation. . . .

While courts are divided in their methods of distinguishing between assertions of fact and expressions of opinion, they are universally agreed that the task is a difficult one. . . .

The degree to which such kinds of statements have real factual content can, of course, vary greatly. We believe, in consequence, that courts should analyze the totality of the circumstances in which the statements are made to decide whether they merit the absolute First Amendment protection enjoyed by opinion. To evaluate the totality of the circumstances of an allegedly defamatory statement, we will consider four factors in assessing whether the average reader would view the statement as fact or, conversely, opinion. . . .

First, we will analyze the common usage or meaning of the specific language of the challenged statement itself. Our analysis of the specific language under scrutiny will be aimed at determining whether the statement has a precise core of meaning for which a consensus of understanding exists or, conversely, whether the statement is indefinite and ambiguous. . . . Second, we will consider the statement's verifiability—is the statement capable of being objectively characterized as true or false? . . . Third, moving from the challenged language itself, we will consider the full context of the statement—the entire article or column, for example—inasmuch as other, unchallenged language surrounding the allegedly defamatory statement will influence the average reader's readiness to infer that a particular statement has factual content. . . . Finally, we will consider the broader context or setting in which the statement appears. Different types of writing have, as we shall more fully see, widely varying social conventions which signal to the reader the likelihood of a statement's being either fact or opinion. . . .

. . . [O]nce our inquiry into whether the statement is an assertion of fact or expression of opinion has concluded, the factors militating either in favor of or against the drawing of factual implications from any statement have already been identified. A separate inquiry into whether a statement, already classified in this painstaking way as opinion, implies allegedly defamatory facts would, in our view, be superfluous. In short, we believe that the application of the four-factor analysis set forth above, and drawn from the considerable judicial teaching on the subject, will identify those statements so "factually laden" that they should not receive the benefit of the opinion privilege. . . .

Now we turn to the case at hand to apply the foregoing analysis. As we have seen, Mr. Ollman alleges various instances of defamation in the Evans and Novak column. Before analyzing each such instance, we will first examine the context (the third and fourth factors in our approach) in which the alleged defamations arise. We will then assess the manner in which this context would influence the average reader in interpreting the alleged defamations as an assertion of fact or an expression of opinion.

From the earliest days of the Republic, individuals have published and circulated short, frequently sharp and biting writings on issues of social and political interest. From the pamphleteers urging revolution to abolitionists condemning the evils of slavery, American authors have sought through pamphlets and tracts both to stimulate debate and to persuade. Today among the inheritors of this lively tradition are the columnists and opinion writers whose works appear on the editorial and Op-Ed pages of the Nation's newspapers. The column at issue here is plainly part and parcel of this tradition of social and political criticism.

The reasonable reader who peruses an Evans and Novak column on the editorial or Op-Ed page is fully aware that the statements found there are not "hard" news like those printed on the front page or elsewhere in the news sections of the newspaper. Readers expect that columnists will make strong statements, sometimes phrased in a polemical manner that would hardly be considered balanced or fair elsewhere in the newspaper. That proposition is inherent in the very notion of an "Op-Ed page." Because of obvious space limitations, it is also manifest that columnists or commentators will express themselves in condensed fashion without providing what might be considered the full picture. Columnists are, after all, writing a column, not a full-length scholarly article or a book. This broad understanding of the traditional function of a column like Evans and Novak will therefore predispose the average reader to regard what is found there to be opinion. . . .

. . . Evans and Novak made it clear that they were not purporting to set forth definitive conclusions, but instead meant to ventilate what in their view constituted the central questions raised by Mr. Ollman's prospective appointment. . . . Prominently displayed

in the Evans and Novak column, therefore, is interrogatory or cautionary language that militates in favor of treating statements as opinion. . . .

Nor is the statement that "[Mr. Ollman] is widely viewed in his profession as a political activist" a representation or assertion of fact. . . . While Mr. Ollman argues that this assertion is defamatory since it *implies* that he has no reputation as a scholar, we are rather skeptical of the strength of that implication, particularly in the context of this column. . . .

Next we turn to Mr. Ollman's complaints about the column's quotations from and remarks about his writings . . . . When a critic is commenting about a book, the reader is on notice that the critic is engaging in interpretation, an inherently subjective enterprise, and therefore realizes that others, including the author, may utterly disagree with the critic's interpretation. . . . The reader is thus predisposed to view what the critic writes as opinion . . . .

Evans' and Novak's statements about Mr. Ollman's article clearly do not fall into the category of misquotation or misrepresentation. . . .

Professor Ollman also objects to the column's posing the question, prompted in Evans' and Novak's view by Mr. Ollman's article, of whether he intended to use the classroom for indoctrination. As we noted previously, the column in no wise affirmatively stated that Mr. Ollman was indoctrinating his students. Moreover, indoctrination is not, at least as used here in the setting of academia, a word with a well-defined meaning. . . .

Finally, we turn to the most troublesome statement in the column. In the third-to-last paragraph, an anonymous political science professor is quoted as saying: "Ollman has no status within the profession but is a pure and simple activist." . . .

Certainly a scholar's academic reputation among his peers is crucial to his or her career. . . .

We are of the view, however, that under the constitutionally based opinion privilege announced in *Gertz*, this quotation, under the circumstances before us, is protected. . . . [H]ere we deal with statements by well-known, nationally syndicated columnists on the Op-Ed page of a newspaper, the well-recognized home of opinion and comment. In addition, the thrust of the column, taken as a whole, is to raise questions about Mr. Ollman's scholarship and intentions, not to state conclusively from Evans' and Novak's first-hand knowledge that Professor Ollman is not a scholar or that his colleagues do not regard him as such. . . .

. . . [W]e are reminded that in the accommodation of the conflicting concerns reflected in the First Amendment and the law of defamation, the deep-seated constitutional values embodied in the Bill of Rights require that we not engage, without bearing clearly in mind the context before us, in a Talmudic parsing of a single sentence or two, as if we were occupied with a philosophical enterprise or linguistic analysis. Ours is a practical task, with elemental constitutional values of freedom looming large as we go about our work. And in that undertaking, we are reminded by *Gertz* itself of our duty "to assure to the freedoms of speech and press that 'breathing space' essential to their fruitful exercise." For the contraction of liberty's "breathing space" can only mean inhibition of the scope of public discussion on matters of general interest and concern. The provision of breathing space counsels strongly against straining to squeeze factual content from a single sentence in a column that is otherwise clearly opinion. . . .

The judgment of the District Court is therefore *Affirmed*

Judge Robert Bork, concurring:

. . . [T]he statement challenged in this lawsuit, in terms of the policies of the first amendment, is functionally more like an "opinion" than a "fact" and should not be actionable. It thus falls within the category the Supreme Court calls "rhetorical hyperbole." . . .

. . . Ollman, by his own actions, entered a political arena in which heated discourse was to be expected and must be protected; the "fact" proposed to be tried is in truth wholly unsuitable for trial, which further imperils free discussion; the statement is not of the kind that would usually be accepted as one of hard fact and appeared in a context that further indicated it was rhetorical hyperbole.

Plaintiff Ollman, as will be shown, placed himself in the political arena and became the subject of heated political debate. . . .

. . . [I]n order to protect a vigorous marketplace in political ideas and contentions, we ought to accept the proposition that those who place themselves in a political arena must accept a degree of derogation that others need not. . . .

. . . [T]he core function of the first amendment is the preservation of that freedom to think and speak as one please which is the "means indispensable to the discovery and spread of political truth." Necessary to the preservation of that freedom, of course, is the willingness of those who would speak to be spoken to and, as in this case, to be spoken about. . . .

. . . Ollman has, as is his undoubted right, gone well beyond the role of the cloistered scholar, and he did so before Evans and Novak wrote about him. . . . Professor Ollman was an active proponent not just of Marxist scholarship but of Marxist politics. . . . It was plain that Ollman was a political activist and that he saw his academic post as, among other things, a means of advancing his political goals. . . .

. . . Ollman was not simply a scholar who was suddenly singled out by the press or by Evans and Novak. . . . He had entered the political arena before he put himself forward for the department chairmanship. . . . [H]e must accept the banging and jostling of political debate, in ways that a private person need not, in order to keep the political arena free and vital. . . .

. . . Ollman entered a first amendment arena and had to accept the rough treatment that arena affords. . . .

. . . [I]t is indisputable that this swirling public debate provided a strong context in which charges and countercharges should be assessed. In my view, that context made it much less likely that what Evans and Novak said would be regarded as an assertion of plain fact rather than as part of the judgments expressed by each side on the merits of the proposed appointment. . . .

When we come to the context in which this statement occurred, it becomes even more apparent that few people were likely to perceive it as a direct assertion of fact, to be taken at face value. That context was one of controversy and opinion, and it is known to be such by readers. It is significant, in the first place, that the column appeared on the Op-Ed pages of newspapers. These are pages reserved for the expression of opinion, much of it highly controversial opinion.

That does not convert every assertion of fact on the Op-Ed pages into an expression of opinion merely by its placement there. It does alert the reader that he is in the context of controversy and politics, and that what he reads does not even purport to be as balanced, objective, and fair-minded as he has a right to hope to be the case with what is contained in the news columns of the paper. . . .

. . . I am persuaded that Ollman may not rest a libel action on the statement contained in the Evans and Novak column.

Judge Antonin Scalia, dissenting:

More plaintiffs should bear in mind that it is a normal human reaction, after painstakingly examining and rejecting thirty invalid and almost absurd contentions, to reject the thirty-first contention as well, and make a clean sweep of the matter. I have no other explanation for the majority's affirmance of summary judgment dismissing what seems to me a classic and coolly crafted libel, Evans and Novak's disparagement of Ollman's professional reputation. . . .

. . . [T]o say, as the concurrence does, that hyperbole excuses not merely the exaggeration but *the fact sought to be vividly conveyed by the exaggeration* is to mistake a freedom to enliven discourse for a freedom to destroy reputation. The libel that "Smith is an incompetent carpenter" is not converted into harmless and nonactionable word-play by merely embellishing it into the statement that "Smith is the worst carpenter this side of the Mississippi." . . .

APPENDIX

"The Marxist Professor's Intentions"
by Rowland Evans & Robert Novak

The Washington Post
May 4, 1978

What is in danger of becoming a frivolous public debate over the appointment of a Marxist to head the University of Maryland's department of politics and government has so far ignored this unspoken concern within the academic community: the avowed desire of many political activists to use higher education for indoctrination.

The proposal to name Bertell Ollman, professor at New York University, as department head has generated wrong-headed debate. Politicians who jumped in to oppose Ollman simply for his Marxist philosophy have received a justifiable going-over from defenders of academic freedom in the press and the university. Academic Prince Valiants seem arrayed against McCarythite [sic] know-nothings.

But neither side approaches the central question: not Ollman's beliefs, but his intentions. His candid writings avow his desire to use the classroom as an instrument for preparing what he calls "the revolution." Whether this is a form of indoctrination that could transform the real function of a university and transcend limits of academic freedom is a concern to academicians who are neither McCarthyite nor know-nothing.

To protect academic freedom, that question should be posed not by politicians but by professors. But professors throughout the country troubled by the nomination, clearly a minority, dare not say a word in today's campus climate.

While Ollman is described in news accounts as a "respected Marxist scholar," he is widely viewed in his profession as a political activist. Amid the increasingly popular Marxist movement in university life, he is distinct from philosophical Marxists. Rather, he is an outspoken proponent of "political Marxism."

He twice sought election to the council of the American Political Science Association as a candidate of the "Caucus for a New Political Science" and finished last out of 16 candidates each time. Whether or not that represents a professional judgment by his colleagues, as some critics contend, the verdict clearly rejected his campaign pledge: "If elected . . . I shall use every means at my disposal to promote the study of Marxism and Marxist approaches to politics throughout the profession."

Ollman's intentions become explicit in "On Teaching Marxism and Building the Movement," his article in the Winter 1978 issue of New Political Science. Most students, he claims, conclude his course with a "Marxist outlook." Ollman concedes that will be seen "as an admission that the purpose of my course is to convert students to socialism."

That bothers him not at all because "a correct understanding of Marxism (as indeed of any body of scientific truths) lead automatically to its acceptance." Non-Marxists students are defined as those "who do not yet understand Marxism." The "classroom" is a place where the students' "bourgeois ideology is being dismantled." "Our prior task" before the revolution, he writes, "is to make more revolutionaries. The revolution will only occur when there are enough of us to make it."

He concludes by stressing the importance to "the movement" of "radical professors." If approved for his new post, Ollman will have a major voice in filling a new professorship promised him. A leading prospect is fellow Marxist Alan Wolfe; he is notorious for his book "The Seamy Side of Democracy," whose celebration of communist China extols the beneficial nature of "brainwashing."

Ollman's principal scholarly work, "Alienation: Marx's Conception of Man in Capitalist Society," is a ponderous tome in adoration of the master (Marxism "is like a magnificently rich tapestry"). Published in 1971, it does not abandon hope for the revolution forecast by Karl Marx in 1848. "The present youth rebellion," he writes, by "helping to change the workers of tomorrow" will, along with other factors, make possible "a socialist revolution."

Such pamphleteering is hooted at by one political scientist in a major eastern university, whose scholarship and reputation as a liberal are well known. "Ollman has no status within the profession, but is a pure and simple activist," he said. Would he say that publicly? "No chance of it. Our academic culture does not permit the raising of such questions."

"Such questions" would include these: What is the true measurement of Ollman's scholarship? Does he intend to use the classroom for indoctrination? Will he indeed be followed by other Marxist professors? Could the department in time be closed to non-Marxists, following the tendency at several English universities?

Even if "such questions" cannot be raised by the faculty, they certainly should not be raised by politicians. While dissatisfaction with pragmatism by many liberal professors has renewed interest in the comprehensive dogma of the Marxists, there is little tolerance for confronting the value of that dogma. Here are the makings of a crisis that, to protect its integrity and true academic freedom, academia itself must resolve.

Milkovich v. Lorain Journal Co.
SUPREME COURT OF THE UNITED STATES
497 U.S. 1 (1990)

CHIEF JUSTICE WILLIAM REHNQUIST delivered the Court's opinion:

Respondent J. Theodore Diadiun authored an article in an Ohio newspaper implying that petitioner Michael Milkovich, a local high school wrestling coach, lied under oath in a judicial proceeding about an incident involving petitioner and his team which occurred at a wrestling match. Petitioner sued Diadiun and the newspaper for libel, and the Ohio Court of Appeals affirmed a lower court entry of summary judgment against petitioner. This judgment was based in part on the grounds that the article constituted an "opinion" protected from the reach of state defamation law by the First Amendment to the United States Constitution. We hold that the First Amendment does not prohibit the application of Ohio's libel laws to the alleged defamations contained in the article.

This case is before us for the third time in an odyssey of litigation spanning nearly 15 years. Petitioner Milkovich, now retired, was the wrestling coach at Maple Heights High School in Maple Heights, Ohio. In 1974, his team was involved in an altercation at a home wrestling match with a team from Mentor High School. Several people were injured. In response to the incident, the Ohio High School Athletic Association (OHSAA) held a hearing at which Milkovich and H. Don Scott, the Superintendent of Maple Heights Public Schools, testified. Following the hearing, OHSAA placed the Maple Heights team on probation for a year and declared the team ineligible for the 1975 state tournament. OHSAA also censured Milkovich for his actions during the altercation. Thereafter, several parents and wrestlers sued OHSAA in the Court of Common Pleas of Franklin County, Ohio, seeking a restraining order against OHSAA's ruling on the grounds that they had been denied due process in the OHSAA proceeding. Both Milkovich and Scott testified in that proceeding. The court overturned OHSAA's probation and ineligibility orders on due process grounds.

The day after the court rendered its decision, respondent Diadiun's column appeared in the News-Herald, a newspaper which circulates in Lake County, Ohio, and is owned by respondent Lorain Journal Co. The column bore the heading "Maple beat the law with the 'big lie,'" beneath which appeared Diadiun's photograph and the words "TD Says." The carryover page headline announced " . . . Diadiun says Maple told a lie." The column contained the following passages:

. . . [A] lesson was learned (or relearned) yesterday by the student body of Maple Heights High School, and by anyone who attended the Maple-Mentor wrestling meet of last Feb. 8.

A lesson which, sadly, in view of the events of the past year, is well they learned early.

It is simply this: If you get in a jam, lie your way out.

If you're successful enough, and powerful enough, and can sound sincere enough, you stand an excellent chance of making the lie stand up, regardless of what really happened.

The teachers responsible were mainly head Maple wrestling coach, Mike Milkovich, and former superintendent of schools H. Donald Scott.

. . . .

Anyone who attended the meet, whether he be from Maple Heights, Mentor, or impartial observer, knows in his heart that Milkovich and Scott lied at the hearing after each having given his solemn oath to tell the truth.

But they got away with it.

Is that the kind of lesson we want our young people learning from their high school administrators and coaches?

I think not.[77]

Petitioner commenced a defamation action against respondents in the Court of Common Pleas of Lake County, Ohio, alleging that the headline of Diadiun's article and the nine passages quoted above "accused plaintiff of committing the crime of perjury, an indictable offense in the State of Ohio, and damaged plaintiff directly in his life-time occupation of coach and teacher, and constituted libel *per se*." The action proceeded to trial, and the court granted a directed verdict to respondents on the ground that the evidence failed to establish the article was published with "actual malice" as required by *New York Times Co. v. Sullivan*. The Ohio Court of Appeals for the Eleventh Appellate District reversed and remanded, holding that there was sufficient evidence of actual malice to go to the jury. The Ohio Supreme Court dismissed the ensuing appeal for want of a substantial constitutional question, and this Court denied certiorari.

On remand, relying in part on our decision in *Gertz v. Robert Welch, Inc.*, (1974), the trial court granted summary judgment to respondents on the grounds that the article was an opinion protected from a libel action by "constitutional law," and alternatively, as a public figure, petitioner had failed to make out a *prima facie* case of actual malice. The Ohio Court of Appeals affirmed both determinations. On appeal, the Supreme Court of Ohio reversed and remanded. The court first decided that petitioner was neither a public figure nor a public official under the relevant decisions of this Court. The court then found that "the statements in issue are factual assertions as a matter of law, and are not constitutionally protected as the opinions of the writer. . . . The plain import of the author's assertions is that Milkovich, *inter alia*, committed the crime of perjury in a court of law." This Court again denied certiorari.

Meanwhile, Superintendent Scott had been pursuing a separate defamation action through the Ohio courts. Two years after its Milkovich decision, in considering Scott's appeal, the Ohio Supreme Court reversed its position on Diadiun's article, concluding that the column was "constitutionally protected opinion." Consequently, the court upheld a lower court's grant of summary judgment against Scott.

The *Scott* court decided that the proper analysis for determining whether utterances are fact or opinion was set forth in the decision of the United States Court of Appeals for the District of Columbia Circuit in *Ollman v. Evans* (1984). Under that analysis, four factors are considered to ascertain whether, under the "totality of circumstances," a statement is fact or opinion. These factors are: (1) "the specific language used"; (2) "whether the statement is verifiable"; (3) "the general context of the statement"; and (4) "the broader context in which the statement appeared." The court found that application of the first two factors to the column militated in favor of deeming the challenged passages actionable assertions of fact. That potential outcome was trumped, however, by the court's consideration of the third and fourth factors. With respect to the third factor, the general context, the court explained that "the large caption 'TD Says' . . . would indicate to even the most gullible reader that the article was, in fact, opinion." As for the fourth factor, the "broader context," the court reasoned that because the article appeared on a sports page—"a traditional haven for cajoling, invective, and hyperbole"—the article would probably be construed as opinion.

Subsequently, considering itself bound by the Ohio Supreme Court's decision in *Scott*, the Ohio Court of Appeals in the instant proceedings affirmed a trial court's grant of summary judgment in favor of respondents, concluding that "it has been decided, as a matter of law, that the article in question was constitutionally protected opinion." The Supreme Court of Ohio dismissed petitioner's ensuing appeal for want of a substantial constitutional question. We granted certiorari, to consider the important questions raised by the Ohio courts' recognition of a constitutionally required "opinion" exception to the application of its defamation laws. We now reverse. . . .

Respondents would have us recognize, in addition to the established safeguards discussed above, still another First-Amendment-based protection for defamatory statements which are categorized as "opinion" as opposed to "fact." For this proposition they rely principally on the following dictum from our opinion in *Gertz*:

"Under the First Amendment there is no such thing as a false idea. However pernicious an opinion may seem, we depend for its correction not on the conscience of judges and juries but on the competition of other ideas. But there is no constitutional value in false statements of fact." Judge Friendly appropriately observed that this passage "has become the opening salvo in all arguments for protection from defamation actions on the ground of opinion, even though the case did not remotely concern the question." Read in context, though, the fair meaning of the passage is to equate the word "opinion" in the second sentence with the word "idea" in the first sentence. Under this view, the language was merely a reiteration of Justice Holmes' classic "marketplace of ideas" concept. ("[T]he ultimate good desired is better reached by free trade in ideas . . . the best test of truth is the power of the thought to get itself accepted in the competition of the market"). Thus, we do not think this passage from *Gertz* was intended to create a wholesale defamation exemption for anything that might be labeled "opinion." (The "marketplace of ideas" origin of this passage "points strongly to the view that the 'opinions' held to be constitutionally protected were the sort of thing that could be corrected by discussion"). Not only would such an interpretation be contrary to the tenor and context of the passage, but it would also ignore the fact that expressions of "opinion" may often imply an assertion of objective fact.

If a speaker says, "In my opinion John Jones is a liar," he implies a knowledge of facts which lead to the conclusion that Jones told an untruth. Even if the speaker states the facts upon which he bases his opinion, if those facts are either incorrect or incomplete, or if his assessment of them is erroneous, the statement may still imply a false assertion of fact. Simply couching such statements in terms of opinion does not dispel these implications; and the statement, "In my opinion Jones is a liar," can cause as much damage to reputation as the statement, "Jones is a liar." As Judge Friendly aptly stated: "[It] would be destructive of the law of libel if a writer could escape liability for accusations of [defamatory conduct] simply by using, explicitly or implicitly, the words 'I think.'" It is worthy of note that, at common law, even the privilege of fair comment did not extend to "a false statement of fact, whether it was expressly stated or implied from an expression of opinion."

. . . [R]espondents do not really contend that a statement such as, "In my opinion John Jones is a liar," should be protected by a separate privilege for "opinion" under the First Amendment. But they do contend that in every defamation case the First Amendment mandates an inquiry into whether a statement is "opinion" or "fact," and that only the latter statements may be actionable. They propose that a number of factors developed by the lower courts (in what we hold was a mistaken reliance on the *Gertz* dictum) be considered in deciding which is which. But we think the " 'breathing space' " which " 'freedoms of expression require in order to survive,' " is adequately secured by existing constitutional doctrine without the creation of an artificial dichotomy between "opinion" and fact.

Foremost, we think [precedent] stands for the proposition that a statement on matters of public concern must be provable as false before there can be liability under state defamation law, at least in situations, like the present, where a media defendant is involved. Thus, unlike the statement, "In my opinion Mayor Jones is a liar," the statement, "In my opinion Mayor Jones shows his abysmal ignorance by accepting the teachings of Marx and Lenin," would not be actionable. [Precedent] ensures that a statement of opinion relating to matters of public concern which does not contain a provably false factual connotation will receive full constitutional protection. . . .

We are not persuaded that, in addition to these protections, an additional separate constitutional privilege for "opinion" is required to ensure the freedom of expression guaranteed by the First Amendment. The

dispositive question in the present case then becomes whether a reasonable factfinder could conclude that the statements in the Diadiun column imply an assertion that petitioner Milkovich perjured himself in a judicial proceeding. We think this question must be answered in the affirmative. As the Ohio Supreme Court itself observed, "The clear impact in some nine sentences and a caption is that [Milkovich] 'lied at the hearing after . . . having given his solemn oath to tell the truth.'" This is not the sort of loose, figurative, or hyperbolic language which would negate the impression that the writer was seriously maintaining that petitioner committed the crime of perjury. Nor does the general tenor of the article negate this impression.

We also think the connotation that petitioner committed perjury is sufficiently factual to be susceptible of being proved true or false. A determination whether petitioner lied in this instance can be made on a core of objective evidence by comparing, *inter alia,* petitioner's testimony before the OHSAA board with his subsequent testimony before the trial court. As the *Scott* court noted regarding the plaintiff in that case, "Whether or not H. Don Scott did indeed perjure himself is certainly verifiable by a perjury action with evidence adduced from the transcripts and witnesses present at the hearing. Unlike a subjective assertion, the averred defamatory language is an articulation of an objectively verifiable event." So too with petitioner Milkovich.

[Previous] decisions [ ] establishing First Amendment protection for defendants in defamation actions surely demonstrate the Court's recognition of the Amendment's vital guarantee of free and uninhibited discussion of public issues. But there is also another side to the equation; we have regularly acknowledged the "important social values which underlie the law of defamation," and recognized that "[s]ociety has a pervasive and strong interest in preventing and redressing attacks upon reputation.". . .

We believe our decision in the present case holds the balance true. The judgment of the Ohio Court of Appeals is reversed, and the case is remanded for further proceedings not inconsistent with this opinion.

Reversed.

Chapter 6

There is a huge disconnect between what consumers think happens to their data [online] and what really happens.

Jonathan Leibowitz, chair, Federal Trade Commission[1]

You have zero privacy anyway. Get over it.

Scott McNealy, former chief executive, Sun Microsystems[2]

Smartphones, computers, and other digital media store and transmit private and personal information.

Protecting Privacy

Conflicts between the Press and the Right to Privacy

Sources of Privacy Protection

Privacy Law's Development

False Light
Plaintiff's Case
Defenses

Appropriation
Commercialization and
    Right of Publicity
Plaintiff's Case
Defenses

Intrusion
Methods of Intruding
Intrusion on Private
    Property
Defenses

Private Facts
Intimate Facts
Legitimate Public Concern
Publicity
First Amendment Defense

Cases for Study
➤ *Cox Broadcasting
    Corp. v. Cohn*
➤ *City of Ontario v.
    Quon*

Suppose . . .

. . . that a reporter learns the name of a rape-murder victim who is a minor. The reporter learns the name because it is in a public document made available to journalists in a courtroom. The reporter broadcasts the minor's name during a local television news program. However, the state where the crime took place and the story was broadcast has a law making it a misdemeanor to publish or broadcast the name or identity of a rape victim. The victim's father sues the television station, relying on the state law, claiming his right to privacy has been invaded by the television broadcast's giving the name of his deceased daughter. Should the father win the lawsuit? Does the station have a First Amendment right to report the victim's name? Does it matter that the name was revealed in a public document? Look for the answers to these questions when the case of *Cox Broadcasting Corp. v. Cohn* is discussed later in this chapter and the case is excerpted at the end of the chapter.

Americans have been concerned about their privacy since the United States' inception. The U.S. Constitution reflects this, as the framers, for example, adopted the Fourth Amendment, protecting "the right of the people to be secure in their persons, houses, papers, and effects, against unreasonable searches and seizures."[3] The Third Amendment ensures that the government cannot force residents to have soldiers living in their homes, except perhaps during wartime.[4] More than a century later, in 1890, reporters prying into private affairs of the rich and elite prompted two prominent Boston lawyers to write a law review article arguing that the courts should protect people's privacy.

In the 21st century, people are less concerned with soldiers in their homes and snooping reporters asking personal questions than with technology allowing other individuals, the government, the press and corporations to learn about their innermost secrets. There is substantial reason for these concerns.

Today, Google, Microsoft and many popular websites install tracking devices on users' computers, some able to "record a person's keystrokes online and then transmit the text to a data-gathering company that analyzes it for content, tone and clues to a person's social connections." A 2010 Wall Street Journal study found the devices "enabled data-gathering companies to build personal profiles that could include age, gender, race, zip code, income, marital status and health concerns, along with recent purchases and favorite TV shows and movies." One company alone sells more than 50 million pieces of this information each day to advertisers and others.[5] Courts have allowed websites and advertisers to put cookies—technology that tracks what websites people visit—on computers.[6]

Many smart phone applications send users' sensitive information to advertisers and companies compiling data about individuals.[7] Google's Street View feature collected and retained information from Wi-Fi networks, and an AT&T website flaw disclosed iPad users' e-mail addresses.[8] A hacker gained access to several Twitter accounts, including President Barack Obama's, and sent fake messages that seemed to come from those Twitter users.[9] A hacker released a file with 100 million Facebook users' names, profile addresses and unique identification numbers.[10]

Digital privacy invasions are serious matters when they lead to identity theft, a possibility if someone discovers another person's Social Security number, bank account number or passwords for various websites. For example, counties in the state of Virginia have more than 200 million land records, such as home sales and home foreclosures, online. Many of these records have individuals' Social Security numbers attached despite state laws requiring that the numbers be removed. A woman advocating that counties be certain Social Security numbers are removed from land records posted some of those numbers on her own website to show how easily accessible they are. Virginia then adopted a law making it illegal to post other people's Social Security numbers. In 2010 the U.S. Court of Appeals for the Fourth Circuit held that the law violated the woman's First Amendment rights.[11] The state argued posting Social Security numbers did not express ideas so should not have First Amendment protection. The court said posting the numbers was "integral to her message."

Another important privacy concern is protecting minors. The Federal Trade Commission (FTC) says 90 percent of U.S. minors between 12 and 17 years old spend time online. Although they consider themselves skilled at online activities, the FTC says young people often inadvertently or deliberately disclose personal information and other sensitive details that could lead to identity theft, online stalking and more serious attacks.[12]

Current federal and state privacy laws do not sufficiently protect American consumers, according to the FTC. Rather, today the burden of understanding websites' privacy policies is with online users who must affirmatively try to ensure their own privacy.[13] Is it possible for individuals to do that? In mid-2010, the social networking site Facebook's privacy policy was 5,830 words long, nearly 1,300 words longer than the U.S. Constitution. Facebook's policy requires users to opt out if they want privacy. That is, users' posted information is publicly available and becomes private only if a user clicks through more than 50 privacy buttons that are included among 170 options.[14] How many of Facebook's more than 500 million members who share 25 billion postings each month read the policy and opt for privacy?

As law professor Jeffrey Rosen wrote, "We've known for years that the Web allows for unprecedented voyeurism, exhibitionism and inadvertent indiscretion . . . [that] goes into our permanent— and public—digital files." And the "Internet never seems to forget," meaning that what users post on the Internet is there forever, whether they want it to be or not.[15]

There is little privacy in the workplace and only somewhat more privacy protection for personal health information. Despite a federal law protecting the privacy of health care information possessed by health care providers and health plans, the law does not cover health information in school records, employment files or financial records. Courts allow an employer to inspect employees' e-mail, including personal messages, and listen to their telephone conversations.

The U.S. Supreme Court in 2010 held that government employers may see public employees' text messages sent and received on government-issued equipment if the searches have a legitimate work-related purpose and the public employees have been told not to expect privacy.[16] The case, *City of Ontario v. Quon,* involved an Ontario, Calif., police officer who used a department-issued pager to communicate with fellow officers. The city gave permission to use the pagers for a limited number of personal messages. When the city audited officers' pagers, it found one

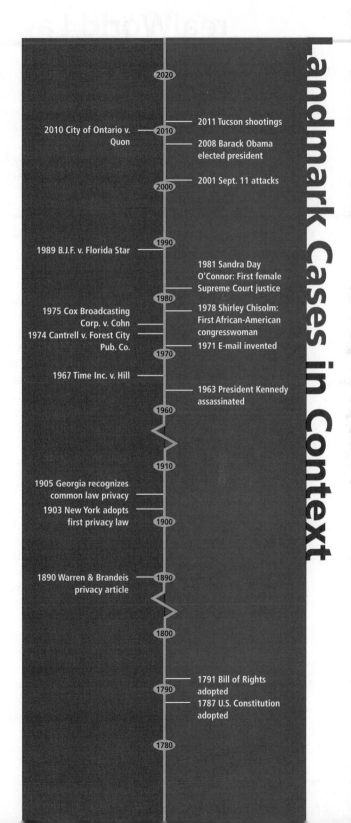

Landmark Cases in Context

- 2011 Tucson shootings
- 2010 City of Ontario v. Quon
- 2008 Barack Obama elected president
- 2001 Sept. 11 attacks
- 1989 B.J.F. v. Florida Star
- 1981 Sandra Day O'Connor: First female Supreme Court justice
- 1978 Shirley Chisolm: First African-American congresswoman
- 1975 Cox Broadcasting Corp. v. Cohn
- 1974 Cantrell v. Forest City Pub. Co.
- 1971 E-mail invented
- 1967 Time Inc. v. Hill
- 1963 President Kennedy assassinated
- 1905 Georgia recognizes common law privacy
- 1903 New York adopts first privacy law
- 1890 Warren & Brandeis privacy article
- 1791 Bill of Rights adopted
- 1787 U.S. Constitution adopted

realWorld Law

What Others Know about You

If you are on the street and someone takes your picture with a cell phone, "through tagging of your photo on the Internet and the use of facial recognition software, the person who has taken the photo now knows your name, your political affiliation, religious organizations, as well as what blogs you read, and a list of your 'friends' on Facebook."[1]

1. Brian Kane, *Balancing Anonymity, Popularity, & Micro-Celebrity: The Crossroads of Social Networking & Privacy,* 20 ALB. L.J. SCI. & TECH. 327, 339 (2010).

officer had sent text messages to and received them from both his wife and mistress. The Court said the messages were sexually explicit. The officer claimed the city violated his reasonable expectation of privacy. The Court said even if the office did have a reasonable expectation of privacy, the city's search of his pager did not violate it. The Court cited the city's written policy that public employees had no privacy expectation when using city equipment. Also, the city had a reasonable purpose in auditing police officers' pagers. The city wanted to know if it needed to increase the limit it had set on pager messages. Although the Court stressed its ruling was narrowly applied to the case facts, it could relate to government-issued cell phones, computers and other communication technologies. The decision affects the country's more than 20 million public employees.

The *Quon* decision is not the first time the Supreme Court ruled that employees have limited privacy rights. The Court in 1987 said a search of a public employee's desk and filing cabinet did not violate his Fourth Amendment rights.[17] May a private employer look at an e-mail message on an employee's computer? Courts have said the First Amendment does not bar companies from doing so.[18] "By intercepting [e-mail] communications, the company is not . . . requiring the employee to disclose any personal information about himself or invading the employee's person or personal effects. Moreover, the company's interest in preventing inappropriate and unprofessional comments or even illegal activity over its e-mail system outweighs any privacy interest the employee may have . . . ," one federal court said.[19]

Privacy protection diminished after Sept. 11, 2001. At airports, employees of the Transportation Safety Administration, a federal government agency, may open and look through travelers' luggage. The USA Patriot Act allows the government to obtain information about anyone from public libraries, businesses, hospitals and Internet service providers. The government only has to say the information is being sought for a terrorism investigation. The person revealing the information is not allowed to tell anyone else that the government asked for it.[20]

Is personal privacy more at risk from the press than from the government? Journalists often are accused of delving into people's private lives, using new

realWorld Law

Stolen Privacy?

Would it be fun to see aerial pictures of Steve Jobs', Kobe Bryant's or other celebrities' estates? Maybe, though Apple boss Jobs and basketball star Bryant likely would consider those pictures an invasion of their privacy. And if you were a burglar, the pictures might allow you to enter the houses more easily. The website celebrityaddressaerial. com listed addresses and showed aerial pictures of hundreds of celebrities' houses. Authorities learned that at least one member of an alleged burglary ring used the site to learn about Hollywood stars' homes. A skilled Web surfer might find the information and pictures without using the site. But celebrityaddressaerial.com accumulated everything in one place. Access was free until mid-2009 when the site began charging—and the burglary ring stopped using it. A privacy attorney said the site amounted to "a how-to handbook for stalkers and burglars." He said the site is "bad, it's immoral and, for right now, probably legal." The attorney may have been referring to a 2003 Los Angeles Superior Court decision dismissing Barbra Streisand's intrusion suit against a person posting an aerial picture of her Malibu home, together with 12,000 other photographs of the California coast.[1]

1. Andrew Blankstein, *Not Star Gazing, but Casing?*, L.A. Times, Nov. 10, 2009, at A3.

technologies to uncover their deepest secrets. Of course, journalists need access to information, sometimes including private facts, to write their stories, as discussed in Chapter 8. This chapter treats the privacy torts for which the media often are sued.

Sources of Privacy Protection

The U.S. Constitution, state and federal laws and court decisions offer some limited privacy protection. Although the word "privacy" is not in the federal Constitution, the U.S. Supreme Court has said the Constitution protects certain privacy rights.[21] The Court said the word "liberty" in the Fourteenth Amendment—"nor shall any State deprive any person of life, liberty, or property, without due process of law"—includes personal privacy.[22] Additionally, the Constitution includes the Third and Fourth Amendments, mentioned earlier in this chapter, and the Fifth Amendment protecting people from having to incriminate themselves.[23] Based on these constitutional provisions, the Court has overturned laws prohibiting use of contraceptives,[24] distributing contraceptives to unmarried couples,[25] providing abortions,[26] and same-sex intimate contact.[27] Beyond the bedroom, however, the U.S. Constitution does not protect against government, media or private snooping into people's personal lives.

State and federal governments have adopted statutes protecting privacy. Most of these laws stop government agencies from giving out confidential information without the individual's permission. As discussed in Chapter 8, state public records laws make certain government documents obtainable for

Points of Law

The Four Privacy Torts

1. *False light:* Intentionally or recklessly publicizing false information a reasonable person would find highly offensive

2. *Appropriation:* Using another's name or likeness for advertising or other commercial purposes without permission

3. *Intrusion:* Intentionally intruding on another's solitude or seclusion

4. *Private facts:* Publicizing private, embarrassing information

distribution but categorize others—usually those containing private information—as not accessible to the public.

There are federal laws attempting to protect privacy, such as the anti-spam and telemarketing regulations discussed in Chapter 14. For example, after a U.S. Supreme Court nominee's videotape rental records were given to a reporter, Congress adopted the Video Privacy Protection Act.[28] The law prohibits stores from revealing information about what videos or DVDs an individual rents or buys without the customer's prior written permission. Several states have adopted similar laws.[29] The Video Privacy Protection Act recently has been used successfully to challenge Facebook's privacy policies.[30]

Privacy Law's Development

Using tort law—in civil law, a tort is an injury one person or entity inflicts on another—to sue the media for invading privacy is a relatively new idea. Although libel has been recognized for four centuries, the notion that courts or legislatures should protect privacy rights is only about 120 years old. Concerns about the press delving into individuals' private lives date back at least to the 19th century in the United States, but it took two Boston lawyers to put privacy on the legal map.[31] Samuel Warren and his law partner, future Supreme Court justice Louis Brandeis, wrote an article for the Harvard Law Review—perhaps the country's most prestigious academic law journal—entitled "The Right to Privacy."[32] Published in 1890, the article argued that human dignity required protecting individual privacy. Warren and Brandeis knew that no statutes shielded people's private lives from prying journalists, but the lawyers contended that the common law should recognize privacy rights.[33] The article elaborated for the first time a legal theory as to why the courts should recognize a right to privacy, and it proved influential when the Supreme Court eventually recognized a right to privacy based in the U.S. Constitution and its underlying principles.

During the seven decades after Warren and Brandeis' article, courts in a few states accepted a common law right of privacy, and several other states adopted laws protecting privacy.[34] But courts were unclear about what was being protected. Some decisions conflicted with others, state statutes differed from each other and privacy law became a jumble. In 1960, William Prosser, a torts expert and law school dean, published an article trying to clarify matters.[35] Prosser suggested privacy law be divided into four categories: false light, appropriation, intrusion and private facts.

Courts and state legislatures adopted and continue to use Prosser's categories, but not all states allow plaintiffs to sue for each of the four privacy torts.

The New York state legislature, for instance, adopted a law allowing suits for appropriation but not for any other privacy tort.[36] Several states do not permit plaintiffs to sue for false light.

Only living individuals may sue for three of the privacy torts: intrusion, private facts and false light.[37] Like a person's reputation in a libel case, privacy is considered a personal right. The dead do not have personal rights. Also, businesses, associations, unions and other groups do not have personal rights and most often cannot sue for a privacy tort.[38] Only individuals may sue for appropriation in many states. But a few states allow businesses, nonprofit organizations and associations to bring appropriation lawsuits.

SUMMARY

PROTECTING PERSONAL PRIVACY HAS BEEN a concern since the country's founding. There is some protection found in the U.S. Constitution and in federal and state laws. However, for the media, privacy questions usually arise in tort suits. Legal attention to privacy began with Samuel Warren and Louis Brandeis' 1890 Harvard Law Review article suggesting the law recognize the right to be let alone as a way to recognize human dignity. In 1960, Prosser divided privacy law into four torts: false light, appropriation, intrusion and private facts.

Privacy law among states is inconsistent; some states even refuse to recognize one or more of the privacy torts. Only living individuals may bring privacy lawsuits, though a few suits allow businesses to sue for appropriation. ∎

False Light

False light is a first cousin to libel. It is so close to libel, some state courts say, that it should not exist as a separate tort. If someone publishes a false statement, sue that person for libel, not false light, such courts maintain. But not all false statements are defamatory, other courts say. Some false statements make a person appear better than they really are . . . but the statement still is false. The false light tort, then, includes statements both disparaging and flattering.

False light and libel both punish publishing false information. Libel protects reputation—a person's good name. In contrast, false light compensates for the emotional distress a false report causes. An article making a person appear to be someone he or she is not but not injuring the person's reputation may be grounds for a false light suit, but not libel. For example, a poetry magazine publishes a poem and attributes it to a famous poet, but the poet did not write it. The poem is not so bad that it injures the poet's reputation; however, the magazine says the poet wrote something the poet did not, putting the poet in a false light. If the poem was very badly written, the poet might sue for libel because her reputation would be injured.[39]

false light A privacy tort that involves making a person seem in the public eye to be someone he or she is not. Several states do not allow false light suits.

For example, an unauthorized biography said that a former baseball player was a war hero, but he was not. The book said the player won a medal for outstanding heroism, but he did not. If the player sued the author and publisher, would he sue for libel? To win a libel suit, the player must prove the book injured his reputation. But the community likely would not be contemptuous of a person called a war hero, making a successful libel suit impossible. Instead, the player might sue for a privacy tort called false light, based on making a person appear to be someone he or she is not. Warren Spahn, a Hall of Fame pitcher, did just that and won the case.[40] The book's author did not speak to Spahn but instead obtained information from news reports. The author also invented conversations and events. Winning a lawsuit because you were called a war hero? Confusing? Foolish? Some state courts say the false light tort is both, and therefore they refuse to recognize it. Courts in these states argue that false light should not be a separate tort because it is similar to defamation. They also say false light is so vague it encroaches on First Amendment rights. Some courts do not want to consider lawsuits based on articles that make people appear better than they really are. Although 30 states allow false light suits, 13 states explicitly reject them.[41] California sees false light and libel as such close relatives that a false light plaintiff must prove reputational injury.[42] A number of courts allow a plaintiff to sue for both defamation and false light based on the same facts. Several law professors have written that no state should allow false light suits, saying that the tort causes media self-censorship.[43]

realWorld Law

A False Tort

Florida became a recent convert to the don't-bother-us-with-false-light-cases approach. One of the cases in which the Florida Supreme Court rejected the false light tort began in 2003 when the Pensacola News-Journal published a story saying in part:

In 1988, while still on probation and before his conviction was reversed, [Joe] Anderson [Jr.] shot and killed his wife, Ira Anderson, with a 12-gauge shotgun.

The death occurred in Dixie County just north of Suwannee, where days before the shooting Joe Anderson had filed for divorce but then had the case dismissed.

Law enforcement officials determined the shooting was a hunting accident.

Anderson claimed the words "shot and killed his wife" falsely suggested he murdered his wife. He sued the paper for false light. At trial, a jury agreed with Anderson and awarded him $18 million in damages.

The Florida Supreme Court said most cases involving false statements should be brought as libel claims; in only a few unusual situations is the false light tort appropriate. Also, the danger of inhibiting protected speech outweighs the benefits of recognizing the false light tort, the court held.[1]

---

1. Anderson v. Gannett Co., Inc., 994 So. 2d 1048 (Fla. 2008); *see also* Jews for Jesus v. Rapp, 997 So. 2d 1098 (Fla. 2008).

Plaintiff's Case

Most states recognizing false light require a plaintiff to prove (1) the material was published, (2) the plaintiff was identified, (3) the published material was false or created a false impression, (4) the statements or pictures put the plaintiff in a false light that would be highly offensive to a reasonable person and (5) the defendant knew the material was false or recklessly disregarded its falsity.[44] Corporations, other businesses, unions, associations and other groups cannot sue for false light. Only individuals can bring a false light suit because only individuals can be highly offended.[45]

Publication Like the private facts tort, false light requires material to have been widely distributed to the public generally or to a large segment of the community.[46] An oral comment to a few people does not amount to publicity for the false light tort. Courts in a few states disagree and allow publication to be proved by dissemination to just one person or a few people.[47] For these courts, that smaller group must have a special relationship with the plaintiff so the plaintiff would be highly offended if the group saw or heard the publication.[48] Anything published in a mass medium likely will meet the publicity test.

Identification The plaintiff must prove the offensive material was about her or him. The courts of some states, such as California, define identification for false light as they do for libel. It is sufficient if one or more persons say the article identified the plaintiff.[49] Most courts hold that because the publication requirement means many people must be exposed to the story, a large segment of the public must reasonably believe the offensive material refers to the plaintiff. For example, a young boy's photograph accompanied an article about retarded children. The boy was not retarded. The boy's face was not visible because of the angle from which the picture was taken. Only a few people were able to recognize the boy. Although that might prove identification in a libel case, it was not sufficient for a false light claim.[50]

Falsity The tort's name makes it clear: Published material supporting a false light suit must be false or imply false information. If the publication is true, it cannot be grounds for a false light suit even if the material emotionally upset the plaintiff. Minor errors ordinarily do not make a story sufficiently incorrect to meet the falsity standard.

Some courts hold that true facts can lead to false implications if the defendant intended that result. For example, The New York Times published a story implying that a businessman named Robert Howard

Points of Law

False Light

Plaintiff's Case

- Publicizing
- False facts
- About someone who is identified
- That would be highly offensive to a reasonable person
- Acting intentionally or recklessly (according to the Supreme Court), or negligently if the plaintiff is a private person (according to some courts)

Defense

- Libel defenses

John Grisham

might be using an alias and really was another person, Howard Finkelstein, a convicted felon. The story included only true statements: Records showed that Finkelstein used the name Robert Howard; Howard denied he was Finkelstein, yet rumors circulated saying he might be. A jury found that the reporter did not libel Howard because the story did not absolutely say he was Finkelstein. A federal appellate court said the story's implication that the businessman might be the felon could sustain a false light suit.[51]

However, there must be a clear connection between the statements leading to a false light suit and the implied falsehood the plaintiff claims. For example, best-selling author John Grisham's book, "The Innocent Man," described two men who were wrongly convicted of rape and murder, jailed for more than a decade and then exonerated. Several people involved with the conviction sued Grisham for false light. In 2010, the U.S. Court of Appeals for the Tenth Circuit held that nothing in Grisham's book accused the plaintiffs of a crime or, despite the plaintiff's contentions, could be construed as implying a crime.[52]

fact finder In a trial, a judge or the jury determining which facts presented in evidence are accurate.

Highly Offensive At a false light trial, the **fact finder**—the jury, if there is one, or the judge—must determine whether the published material would be highly offensive to a reasonable person. There are no definite standards. Defining "highly offensive" is a very subjective task. It is made even more difficult because a publication may be highly offensive although it is positive, such as making a person appear to be a superhero, as did the unauthorized biography of pitcher Warren Spahn.

Some legal scholars try to clarify the term "highly offensive" by putting false light cases into three categories: embellishment, distortion and fictionalization. Categorizing may highlight the false statements' offensive nature.

A story is embellished when false material is added to otherwise true facts. For example, a series of newspaper columns told a true story of a mother giving up a baby for adoption, the baby being adopted, a court giving the natural father custody four years later and the father hiring a psychologist to help the child adjust to a new home. One column falsely said the psychologist "has readily admitted that she sees her job as doing whatever the natural parents instruct her to do." A jury could find it highly offensive to a reasonable person to suggest a psychologist would ignore her professional commitments, a court ruled.[53]

Distortion occurs when facts are omitted or the context in which material is published makes an otherwise accurate story appear false. In one case, police arrested four people at a chop shop, a garage where, authorities alleged, stolen

realWorld Law

Lowest of the Low?

The Arizona Supreme Court said:

A good example of a false light cause of action based on implication is *Douglass v. Hustler Magazine, Inc.* In *Douglass,* the plaintiff posed nude, consenting to the publication of her photographs in Playboy magazine. Her photographer subsequently left the employ of Playboy for Hustler magazine, a publication of lower standing in the journalistic community. He sold her photographs to Hustler, which published them. The plaintiff sued. . . . Plaintiff had no cause of action for defamation because essentially, there was nothing untrue about the photographs. She posed for them and, as published, they did not misrepresent her. . . . However, the court upheld her recovery for false light invasion of privacy. The jury may have focused on the differences between Playboy and Hustler and concluded that to be published in Hustler, as if she had posed for that magazine and consented to publication of the photos, falsely placed her in a different light than the Playboy publication.[1]

1. Godbehere v. Phoenix Newspapers, 783 P.2d 781, 787 n.2 (Ariz. 1989) (citing Douglass v. Hustler Magazine, Inc., 769 F.2d 1128 (7th Cir. 1985), *cert. denied,* 475 U.S. (1986).

cars were reduced to parts and then sold. The local newspaper ran a story about the arrest. Three of those arrested were convicted, but the fourth was found not guilty. Police located the chop shop by using a LoJack, a device attached to a car that emits a signal when the car is stolen. The LoJack Corporation used the newspaper story in its advertising but did not include information that one of those arrested was acquitted. A federal district court allowed a suit for defamation and false light to continue. The court said a jury could conclude that the advertising material implied the plaintiff was a car thief.[54]

Context, as well as omitted facts, can cause distortion and lead to a false light suit. For example, a young woman consented to having a photographer take her picture. The photographer said it was for his portfolio. A magazine later used the picture to illustrate a story headlined, "In Cold Blood—An Exposé of the Baltimore Teen Murders." The accompanying article said the high murder rate among the city's African-American teenagers was due to drug abuse and poor economic conditions. Used in other circumstances, the photo might not have led to a lawsuit. This context, however, implied that the young woman was poor, abused drugs or perhaps even was connected with a murder. A federal district court allowed the young woman's false light suit against the photographer and magazine to go to a jury.[55]

Fictionalization in false light occurs when some truth, such as a person's name or identifying characteristics, is part of a largely fictional piece. In one case, The Sun, a supermarket tabloid newspaper, published a picture of 97-year-old Arkansas resident Nellie Mitchell to illustrate a story carrying the headline, "Pregnancy Forced Granny to Quit Work at Age 101." The story was a fictional account of an Australian woman who left her paper route at the age of 101 because she became pregnant during an extramarital affair with a rich client on her route. Mitchell, in fact, delivered newspapers in her hometown for nearly 50 years. Mitchell won her false light suit and, after the newspaper's appeals, was awarded $1 million in damages.[56]

Fault   The U.S. Supreme Court has decided only two false light cases: *Time, Inc. v. Hill* in 1967, and *Cantrell v. Forest City Publishing Co.* in 1974. Despite the plaintiffs in both cases being private individuals, not public officials or public figures, the Court held that they had to prove actual malice to win their false light cases.

The seven Hill family members sued Time, Inc., publisher of Life magazine, for a story based on the family's experience of being held hostage by escaped convicts. News stories across the country had reported that three prison escapees had held the Hills hostage for 19 hours. The Hills were not harmed, and the family later said they were treated with respect. The family moved from their Philadelphia suburban home to Connecticut, trying to return to a private life. But within a year of the incident, a novel appeared: "The Desperate Hours" was about the fictional Hilliard family of four held hostage by escaped convicts. In the novel, the convicts beat the fictional father and son and subjected the daughter to verbal sexual insults. The novel was turned into a play of the same name, portraying the same fictional family and violent convicts. Life published an article about the play, including pictures of actors staging scenes in the Hills' Philadelphia house. The Hills claimed that the text and accompanying photographs suggested the convicts had treated the real Hill family as ruthlessly as the convicts treated the fictional hostages. The Hills said that did not happen; the convicts had treated them well. Implying they had been treated badly put the family in a false light. The Hills sued and won in the New York state courts. Richard Nixon, who was elected U.S. president in 1968, represented Time, Inc., in its appeal to the U.S. Supreme Court.

The Court reversed, saying the jury should have been told that the Hills could win only if they proved actual malice.[57] The First Amendment protects the press from being sued for negligent misstatements when reporting stories of public interest, the Court reasoned. After pursuing their case for more than 10 years, the Hills decided not to return to trial court. At trial, they would have to show that Life either knew the article and photographs were false or recklessly disregarded whether they were false.

In the *Cantrell* case, decided seven years after *Hill*, the Court again said a private plaintiff had to prove actual malice to win a false light case. A bridge in West Virginia collapsed, killing 43 people, including Margaret Cantrell's husband, Melvin. Five months later, Cleveland Plain Dealer reporter Joe Eszterhas went with a photographer to the Cantrell home. Eszterhas talked with the Cantrell children, and the photographer took dozens of pictures. Margaret Cantrell was not at home while Eszterhas was at her residence. According to the Supreme

Court, Eszterhas' article in the Plain Dealer stressed the family's abject poverty. The children's old, ill-fitting clothes and the deteriorating condition of their home were detailed in both the text and the accompanying photographs. As he had done in his original, prize-winning article on the Silver Bridge disaster, Eszterhas used the Cantrell family to illustrate the impact of the bridge collapse on the lives of the people in the Point Pleasant area. According to the Supreme Court:

> It is conceded that the story contained a number of inaccuracies and false statements. Most conspicuously, although Mrs. Cantrell was not present at any time during the reporter's visit to her home, Eszterhas wrote, "Margaret Cantrell will talk neither about what happened nor about how they are doing. She wears the same mask of non-expression she wore at the funeral. She is a proud woman. Her world has changed. She says that after it happened, the people in town offered to help them out with money and they refused to take it." Other significant misrepresentations were contained in details of Eszterhas' descriptions of the poverty in which the Cantrells were living and the dirty and dilapidated conditions of the Cantrell home.[58]

The Supreme Court upheld a jury verdict in the Cantrells' favor because the trial judge had told the jury actual malice was part of the plaintiff's false light case. The Court said there was sufficient evidence to show that portions of the article were false and published with knowing falsity or reckless disregard for the truth.

Cantrell and the Hills were not public officials, limited-purpose public figures or universal public figures. They were private people who, the Court said, had to prove in their false light suits that the media defendants had acted with actual malice.

Lower courts are supposed to follow U.S. Supreme Court rulings. But when requiring private persons to prove actual malice in false light cases, some courts do not agree with the Supreme Court. State courts are divided regarding this question. Courts in at least five states and the District of Columbia have applied *Gertz v. Robert Welch, Inc.* to false light cases, as they suggest the Supreme Court would if it heard another false light appeal.[59] These courts would require only that a private individual prove negligence in a false light suit, not malice. Courts in at least 11 other states follow the Supreme Court dictates in *Hill* and *Cantrell*, requiring all false light plaintiffs to show actual malice.[60]

Defenses

Because false light is a relatively new tort—Dean Prosser essentially invented it in his 1960 law review article[61]—and not all courts recognize it, parts of it remain in flux. However, many courts say that if a false light plaintiff proves all elements of his case, a media defendant may use the libel defenses to defeat the claim.[62]

realWorld Law

Why Have a False Light Tort?

If a person is said to be something that in many people's eyes would be positive—a war hero, for example—but it is not true, should there be a legal remedy? If the statement does not harm the person's reputation, so she cannot win a libel suit, should she be able to sue for false light? Why should there be a lawsuit if the person is made to appear better than she is? In Eric Ambler's classic spy story, "Judgment on Deltchev," an English playwright is sent to an Eastern European country to report on a treason trial. While there, he is falsely accused of being a spy himself. Ambler explained one reason this bothered the playwright:

Eric Ambler

> With [English] friends and acquaintances it [is] extraordinarily embarrassing to be described in print as a member of the British secret service. The trouble is that you cannot . . . convince people that you are not. They reason that if you are a member you will still presumably have to say that you are not. You are suspect. If you say nothing, of course, you admit all. Your denials become peevish. It is very tiresome. Probably the only really effective denial would be a solemn, knowing acknowledgment that there *might* be some truth in the rumor. But I can never bring myself to it.[1]

1. Eric Ambler, Judgment on Deltchev 114 (Bantam Books 1964) (1951).

People with an absolute privilege if sued for libel—those involved in judicial proceedings or government meetings, certain public officials and others discussed in Chapter 5—also are absolutely privileged in false light suits. The press has a conditional privilege to report what people with absolute privilege and in absolutely privileged documents say. It also is likely in false light cases that the media may use a privilege of fair and accurate reporting about government meetings and activities.[63]

Truth is a defense to a false light suit. A defendant can prove truth by showing that the story is substantially true. If a person agrees to an interview in which she reveals highly offensive false facts or agrees to an article containing those false facts being published, consent will be an effective defense. The few courts deciding the issue disagree about whether opinion is a defense for a false light suit.[64]

States disagree about the appropriate statute of limitations for false light suits. A state may apply the general statute of limitations for torts, the same one used for battery or trespass, for example. Or the statute of limitations for privacy suits may be based on the time period for filing a libel suit. The statute of limitations period for libel suits usually is shorter than the general torts limitation period.[65]

Not all states allow false light suits. Most that do require a plaintiff to prove (1) publicity, (2) identification, (3) the published material was false or created a false impression, (4) the statements or pictures put the plaintiff in a false light that would be highly offensive to a reasonable person, and (5) the defendant knew the material was false or recklessly disregarded its falsity. A story need not be derogatory to put a person in a false light. Publishing false information praising a person may be grounds for a false light suit. In the only two false light cases the U.S. Supreme Court has decided, it said all plaintiffs must prove actual malice. Some lower courts also require all false light plaintiffs to prove actual malice. Other courts require public officials and public figures, but not private persons, to prove actual malice.

Courts recognize most libel defenses as defenses in false light cases, including conditional privilege, fair reporting and truth. States may use the shorter statute of limitations applied to libel cases, or the longer limitations period used for other torts, in false light cases. ■

Appropriation

If a celebrity's picture is used on a greeting card without her permission, can the celebrity sue the greeting card company? Yes, a court said. This is **appropriation**—generally, using a person's name, picture or voice without permission for commercial or trade purposes. Hallmark Cards used Paris Hilton's "picture above a caption that reads, 'Paris's First Day as a Waitress.' The picture depicts a cartoon waitress, complete with apron, serving a plate of food to a restaurant patron. An oversized photograph of Hilton's head is super-imposed on the cartoon waitress's body."[66] Hilton said the card was based on an episode of Fox Television's "The Simple Life," in which she starred with celebrity Nicole Ritchie. In a program called "Sonic Burger Shenanigans," Hilton works in a fast food restaurant. In 2010 the U.S. Court of Appeals for the Ninth Circuit said, "[W]e see Paris Hilton, born to privilege, working as a waitress." The program and card were similar, the court said, and Hilton could sue for right of publicity, a celebrity's version of appropriation.

appropriation Using a person's name, picture, likeness, voice or identity for commercial or trade purposes without permission.

Points of Law

Appropriation

The appropriation tort may be divided into two torts:

1. *Commercialization:* Applying to someone who wants to remain private and unknown except to family and friends. Using this person's name, picture, likeness or voice for advertising or other commercial purposes without permission is commercialization. It is invading this person's privacy, causing emotional distress.

2. *Right of publicity:* Applying to someone who wants to be known far and wide, to be a celebrity—a musician, athlete, movie star, television personality. Using this person's name, picture, likeness, voice, identity—or a look-alike or sound-alike—for advertising or other commercial purposes without permission invades this person's right of publicity. It diminishes the person's economic value.

Commercialization and Right of Publicity

Appropriation includes two different torts: **commercialization** and the **right of publicity.** Most people do not want their names or pictures to be in advertisements because they want to remain private. Despite all the contestants clamoring to be on televised reality programs, most people prefer to remain anonymous. The appropriation tort used to protect people who want privacy is called "commercialization" or "misappropriation." Commercialization, the word this chapter uses, prohibits using another person's name or likeness for advertising purposes without permission. No state has refused to allow appropriation suits, though courts in some have not yet ruled on the issue.[67]

Some people, however, want their names and pictures to be publicized. They make their living by being famous. Movie stars, television personalities, recording artists and professional athletes, for example, would be disappointed if they were not well known. But they want to control when and where their names and pictures will be used for advertising and other commercial purposes. They also want to be paid for giving their permission. Courts often refer to this part of the appropriation tort as the "right of publicity."[68]

Although both commercialization and the right of publicity prevent the use of someone's name, picture, likeness, voice or identity for advertising or other commercial purposes without permission, they differ in two important ways. One difference is that commercialization protects an individual's dignity connected with personal privacy, while the right of publicity protects the monetary value of using well-known individuals' names and pictures.

A second difference is that courts generally consider commercialization to be a personal right, one that does not survive a person's death. However, the right of publicity may be considered a property right, not a personal right. Just as a person may say who gets her car after she dies—through a will or by state law—she may choose who will control her right of publicity after death.[69] In a majority of states the right of publicity survives after a person's death.[70] The right may last for a specific number of years (from 20 to 100 years, depending on the state), as long as the right is used or, in at least one state, forever.[71]

New York state adopted the country's first appropriation law.[72] Without obtaining permission, a milling company put Abigail Roberson's picture on posters advertising its flour. Below the young woman's picture were the words "Flour of the Family." The company put the poster in warehouses, saloons and other places where people gathered. Roberson sued, using the Warren and Brandeis article as support. But in 1902 a New York court said the state did not have a privacy statute, so Roberson could not win her lawsuit.[73] Recognizing a privacy right might limit the press' right to comment on people's private affairs, the court said.[74] The court's ruling outraged the public. Newspaper articles and lawyers railed against the decision. In 1903, the New York legislature enacted a law forbidding the use of people's names and pictures for commercial purposes without their consent.

Two years later, Georgia became the first state to recognize appropriation as a common law tort. An Atlanta newspaper published a life insurance company advertisement. The ad showed Paulo Pavesich's picture. He appeared to be saying that his life was healthy and productive because he bought the company's insurance. Next to Pavesich was a picture of an ill-dressed, sickly person who had not bought insurance and now recognized his error. The life insurance company had not obtained Pavesich's permission to use his picture. Pavesich sued. In 1905, the Georgia Supreme Court said a right to privacy is an important component of human dignity.[75] The court held that despite the lack of a state privacy statute in Georgia, Pavesich could win his case based on the common law.

A federal appeals court judge, Jerome Frank, first used the phrase "right of publicity" nearly 60 years ago.[76] The court ruled that professional baseball players had a right to earn money when their names were used on baseball cards. Unlike Roberson and Pavesich, who wanted to retain their privacy, the ball players already were well known. Their goal was to control when their names were used publicly—and to be paid when that happened. Courts generally find that everyone has both a right to protect their privacy and a right to decide when his or her name or picture may or may not be used commercially by others.[77] The commercial value of a celebrity's name or picture, though, will be much greater than that of a relatively unknown individual. Also, the court said a right of publicity could be transferred, as a car can be sold. But the right of privacy cannot be transferred.

Plaintiff's Case

To win a commercialization or right-of-publicity case, a plaintiff must prove her or his name or likeness was used in an advertisement without permission. The plaintiff also must show the ad was of and concerning her and was widely distributed.

Name or Likeness Appropriation occurs most obviously when a person's name, picture or likeness—clearly identifying the person—is used in an advertisement without permission. Having the same name that is used in an advertisement is not enough to show identification. Something in the ad must show the ad was of and concerning that plaintiff. However, identification may be proved despite the defendant's not intending to identify the plaintiff. For example, a name and hometown used in an ad may have been meant to be fictitious. But if a real person with that name living in that town can show a number of people assumed the ad referred to that person, identification may be established.[78]

There can be appropriation even if identification is not immediately obvious. When a beauty product ad used a picture taken from behind a woman and her child, both nude after bathing in a pond, a court said faces and names are not needed for identification.[79] The husband and father's recognition was sufficient, the court said. Although individual faces of the 1969 New York Mets World Series–winning team were very small when printed on jerseys without the players' permission, a court said "legions of baseball fans" could recognize them.[80] However, it is not sufficient that the ad only hints at the plaintiff's identity or may remind some people of the plaintiff.[81] Rather, there must be reasonable grounds for identifying the plaintiff as the person in the advertisement.

Kareem Abdul-Jabbar successfully sued for appropriation when an Oldsmobile advertisement used his birth name, Lew Alcindor, without his permission.

What if the name used is not a person's real name? Could Norma Jeane Baker have sued if the name Marilyn Monroe was used in an advertisement without permission? Likely yes, because Baker was widely known as Monroe. In one case, an Oldsmobile commercial used the name Lew Alcindor. Kareem Abdul-Jabbar sued because he had not given permission. Oldsmobile said Alcindor no longer was Abdul-Jabbar's name, so he had no right to protect it. A federal appellate court disagreed. Abdul-Jabbar was named Ferdinand Lewis ("Lew") Alcindor at birth. He played college and several years of professional basketball under that name. When he converted to Islam, he took the name Kareem Abdul-Jabbar, later legally adopting that as his name. The court said the name Lew Alcindor still identified Abdul-Jabbar.[82]

When an advertisement uses a person who looks like a celebrity, can the celebrity prove identification? An actor looking very much like New Orleans chef Paul Prudhomme urged television viewers to buy Folgers coffee. A federal district court said people could be confused, justifiably believing the real Prudhomme endorsed Folgers.[83] In another case, three singers who looked like members of a rap group called The Fat Boys appeared in a Miller beer commercial. A federal court allowed members of the group to sue, in part because they had declined to appear in the commercial when asked.[84] Similarly, an ad for Christian Dior clothing used a model looking like Jacqueline Kennedy Onassis. Onassis had not given permission to Dior. Onassis sued. A court said Dior improperly exploited Onassis' image for commercial purposes, even though it was not Onassis herself in the advertisement.[85]

Look-alike actors are not out of business, however. If an advertisement includes a prominent disclaimer that the look-alike is not the actual celebrity, a court likely will not find appropriation. For example, the comedian and filmmaker Woody Allen sued a video rental store that used a Woody Allen look-alike in a magazine advertisement without Allen's permission. A federal district court held that, without a disclaimer in the advertisement, consumers could reasonably believe Allen endorsed the video rental company.[86] A different advertisement, using the same Allen look-alike in an ad for a clothing store, also violated Allen's rights. The court in that case said a disclaimer must be in large, bold-faced type and make clear that the impersonated celebrity—Allen, in this instance—does not endorse the product or service being advertised.[87]

sound-alike Someone whose voice sounds like another person's voice. Sound-alikes may not be used ʔr commercial or trade purposes ʔout permission or a disclaimer.

Voice Individuals' voices are protected against use for commercial or trade purposes. Further, advertisers may not use **sound-alikes,** just as they may not use look-alikes, without permission or a disclaimer. Singer and actress Bette Midler refused to allow Ford Motor Co. to use her hit recording "Do You Want to Dance?" in a commercial. Ford's advertising agency then hired a member of Midler's backup singing group. The singer was told to imitate Midler's rendition of the song. After the radio commercial aired, a number of people told Midler they thought she had performed in the ad. The commercial failed to say Midler was not the singer. Midler sued Ford and its advertising agency. The defendants had appropriated part of Midler's identity, a federal appellate court said.[88] Ford and its advertising agency "used an imitation to convey the impression that Midler was singing for them. Why did the defendants ask Midler to sing if her voice was not of value to them? Why did they studiously acquire the services of a sound-alike and instruct her to imitate Midler if Midler's voice was not of value to them[?]," the court asked.[89] The court said a "voice is as distinctive and personal as a face" and "is one of the most palpable ways identity is manifested."

What applies to well-known singers like Midler also applies to not-so-famous performers. Shortly after the Midler case, Frito-Lay's advertising agency devised a radio commercial for SalsaRio Doritos. The commercial's script imitated the rhyming word pattern of a Tom Waits song, "Step Right Up"—a strange choice because the song satirically condemns advertising. The agency did not bother to ask Waits to sing in the advertisement, knowing he consistently had refused to perform in commercials. The ad agency found a singer known to imitate Waits and hired him to sing the Doritos jingle. Waits heard the commercial and, according to the court, "was shocked." He was sure people would think he had agreed to make the commercial. A federal appellate court found that the defendants intentionally created the commercial using Waits' distinctive voice and singing style. The court said: "Waits is a professional singer, songwriter, and actor of some renown. Waits has a raspy, gravelly singing voice, described by one fan as 'like how you'd sound if you drank a quart of bourbon, smoked a pack of cigarettes, and swallowed a pack of razor blades. . . . Late at night. After not sleeping for three days.'"[90] The jury was justified in believing listeners would think Waits performed in the advertisement, the court said. The appellate court upheld the jury's $2.4 million award to Waits.

Identity Do people have characteristics—beyond Woody Allen's face or Bette Midler's voice—that the appropriation tort should protect? A robot wearing a blond wig standing in front of a letterboard may bring to mind a well-known person as quickly as a raspy voice recalls Tom Waits. Game-show hostess Vanna White thought so and sued Samsung Electronics for appropriation. The company ran a series of magazine ads showing its products in futuristic settings. The ads intended to show that the products were stylish and long lasting. One ad pictured a Samsung videocassette recorder in a game show set. A robot standing by

realWorld Law

Soldiers and Anti-war T-shirts

Arizona, Florida, Louisiana, Oklahoma and Texas have adopted statutes making it illegal to use the name, picture or likeness of a member of the U.S. armed forces for commercial purposes without permission.[1] The Arizona legislature adopted that state's law in response to complaints from family members whose relatives' names were on an anti-war T-shirt. Dan Frazier, an anti-war activist, manufactured and sold the shirts containing the names of 3,461 soldiers who died in Iraq as well as an anti-war message. The soldiers' names were in small print, difficult to read without holding the shirt close to one's eyes. Frazier challenged the Arizona law in federal court.

Anti-war activist Dan Frazier

A federal district court in Arizona said the T-shirts were political speech.[2] The soldiers' appropriation rights were not more important than Frazier's First Amendment rights, the court said. Although the T-shirts suggested the soldiers may have died for no good purpose, that did not allow Arizona to limit Frazier's free speech. Further, the court said, Frazier did not commercially benefit from using any particular soldier's name.

---

1. Ariz. Rev. Stat. §§ 12-761; 13-3726; Fla. Stat. Ann. § 540.08(3); La. Rev. Stat. Ann. § 14:102.21; Okla. Stat. Ann. tit. 21, § 839.1A; Tex. Bus. & Com. Code Ann. § 35.64.
2. Frazier v. Boomsma, 2007 U.S. Dist. LEXIS 72427 (D. Ariz., Sept. 27, 2007); 2008 U.S. Dist. LEXIS 63896 (D. Ariz., Aug. 20, 2008).

a letterboard wore an evening gown, jewelry and a long blond wig. The advertising agency wanted the scene to look like the set from "Wheel of Fortune."

A federal appellate court agreed that it did, and said the ad appropriated White's identity.[91] Although the ad did not use White's name, picture, likeness or voice, it nonetheless used White, the court said. The court cited Dean Prosser's 1960 law review article suggesting that invasion of privacy be thought of as four individual torts. In discussing appropriation, Prosser said, "It is not impossible that there might be appropriation of the plaintiff's identity, as by impersonation, without the use of either [the plaintiff's] name or . . . likeness."[92]

Two actors from the television show "Cheers" brought a lawsuit that extended the rule from the Vanna White court decision even further. A company wanted to install in airport bars a set looking like the scene from the television program "Cheers." Two animatronic figures named Hank and Bob were to sit at the bar, and customers could have a drink sitting next to the figures. Paramount, which owned the "Cheers" copyright, granted permission. However, George Wendt, who played Norm on "Cheers," and John Ratzenberger, who played Cliff, refused to give consent. Wendt and Ratzenberger sued, claiming the company would appropriate their identities without permission.

realWorld Law

Is an Ad an Ad?

Not all advertisements are for commercial purposes, so using a person's name or picture might not lead to an appropriation lawsuit. For example, when John McCain's presidential campaign ran ads in 2008 calling Barack Obama a celebrity on a par with Paris Hilton, neither Obama nor Hilton could bring a successful appropriation suit. Although Obama's and Hilton's names and pictures were used in McCain's ads, the ads were political speech. Despite being in the form of and paid for as television commercials, they were not advertisements meant to convince consumers to buy products or services. Therefore, Obama and Hilton were not used for a commercial purpose without their consent.

Paris Hilton responded to the McCain campaign ad with a video posted on http://www.funnyordie.com.

The animatronic figures resembled Wendt's and Ratzenberger's characters in their size, clothing and sitting positions at the bar. But the figures' faces were different from the actors.' That difference, however, was not enough. Ruling in Wendt's and Ratzenberger's favor, a federal appellate court said the figures sufficiently resembled the actors that Wendt and Ratzenberger could bring a suit claiming appropriation of their identities.[93] It would be for a jury to decide if the figures looked sufficiently like the actors, the court said. The parties settled the case out of court before a trial was held.[94]

Vanna White was able to sue because the robot in the Samsung advertisement looked like Vanna White. Wendt and Ratzenberger were able to sue because the robots might look like characters the actors played. Actors do not lose the right to exploit their likenesses, or to prevent others from such exploitation, just because they portrayed fictional characters, the court said in the "Cheers" case.

Actors impersonating celebrities in nonadvertising situations, such as in a satire or parody, are not appropriating the celebrities' likenesses or voices. The First Amendment protects such expression.[95] But the Vanna White case shows that protection does not extend to impersonations in advertisements or other commercial situations. The appellate court specifically rejected Samsung's contention that the robot ad was meant as a satire.

Although a celebrity himself is not in an advertisement, that person's identity may be implied in a number of ways. The public may think of the well-known person based on "a unique vocal style, body movement, costume, makeup or distinguishing setting."[96] One or more of these elements could lead to a right-of-publicity lawsuit based on using someone's identity for commercial purposes without permission. Some courts do not so easily find a plaintiff's identity when the plaintiff is not identified. A singing group, the Romantics, claimed "What I Like About You" so reminded listeners of that group that the video game, "Guitar Hero Encore: Rock the '80s," abridged the group's right of publicity by using the song in the game. The Romantics did not claim a copyright in the song (see Chapter 13 for a discussion of music licensing), but they said the song and the group's identity were intertwined. A federal district court disagreed. The court held that because the game did not refer to the Romantics in its advertising and said the Romantics made the song famous but were not performing the song in the game, the group could not show the game used the Romantics' identity for commercial purposes.[97]

Damages Plaintiffs may be awarded monetary damages based on two injuries. First, they may be compensated for injured feelings caused by their names or pictures being distributed widely in connection with a commercial product or service. Second, they may receive damages for unwillingly helping another gain financially.[98] The value of this latter injury naturally will be greater for well-known individuals than for others.

SUMMARY

APPROPRIATION IS ONE OF THE FOUR PRIVACY TORTS, together with intrusion, private facts and false light. Appropriation is divided into commercialization and right of publicity. Commercialization protects individuals from having their names, pictures, likenesses, voices and identities used for commercial or trade purposes without their permission. Commercialization applies to famous and ordinary people alike. Courts recently have recognized a right of publicity that protects celebrities from being exploited for commercial or trade reasons.

A successful appropriation plaintiff must prove her name, picture, likeness, voice or identity was used for commercial or trade purposes without her permission. Even a pseudonym or stage name is protected. An advertisement may use a model who looks like another person only if a disclaimer explains the person not pictured in the ad is not endorsing the product or service. Similarly, a person who sounds like another when talking or singing may be used in an advertisement if accompanied by a disclaimer. Some courts also allow a plaintiff to sue for appropriation if his identity is used for commercial or trade purposes without permission. Some individuals are so well known for what they do—a game show hostess, in one case—they are identified with that role. An advertisement showing someone with those characteristics might be grounds for an appropriation suit. ∎

Defenses

Even if a plaintiff can prove that his or her name or likeness was used for commercial purposes without permission, there may be a defense to the appropriation allegation.

Newsworthiness Newsworthiness is the defense most often used against appropriation suits. If a newspaper article about an automobile accident used the driver's name, the driver cannot successfully bring an appropriation suit. The article is newsworthy. Newspapers and other media publish newsworthy material despite having a commercial purpose. As one federal court said, "Speech is protected even though it is carried in a form that is sold for profit."[99]

Courts have defined the word "newsworthy" broadly. Courts see a bright line between commercial use (advertising) and trade use on one side of the line, and nearly everything else on the other side of the line. Judges do not carefully analyze an article to determine if it is newsworthy. Rather, if it is not on the commercial/trade use side of the bright line, it will be found newsworthy.

For example, a magazine, Young and Modern, took pictures of a 14-year-old girl who hoped to be a model. The girl's mother had not consented to the photo session. The magazine used the photos to illustrate a "Love Crisis" column that printed a letter from an underage girl identified only as "Mortified." The letter said the girl had attended a party, had too much to drink and had sex with her boyfriend and two of his friends. Responding to the letter, the magazine advised the writer to avoid similar situations in the future and to be tested for pregnancy and sexually transmitted diseases. Neither the girl nor her mother had approved using the pictures with the letter. The girl sued, saying the magazine used her pictures for commercial purposes without permission. Basing its decision on New York's appropriation statute, the state's highest court said articles about matters of public interest are newsworthy.[100] A story remains newsworthy even if it includes a person's name or picture used to boost the mass medium's audience. The court ruled that "the 'Love Crisis' column was newsworthy, since it is informative and educational regarding teenage sex, alcohol abuse and pregnancy—plainly matters of public concern." The magazine's newsworthiness defense defeated the girl's appropriation claim.

Some courts find the line between newsworthy material and advertising not so bright. Hustler magazine could not use the newsworthiness defense when publishing 20-year-old nude photographs of a murdered woman, the U.S. Court of Appeals for the 11th Circuit held. The victim was a model and female wrestler. Her husband, also a professional wrestler, murdered his wife and child and committed suicide. Hustler published a brief story about the events but surrounded the article with nude pictures of the victim taken 20 years before her death. When the victim's family sued Hustler for violating the woman's right of publicity, the appellate court held that Hustler used the pictures for economic gain—increasing magazine sales—and not news reporting. The pictures did not accompany the article, the court said; rather the article accompanied the pictures. The nude pictures were not newsworthy, the court said.[101]

The U.S. Supreme Court has heard only one appropriation case. The Court's decision, applied to a unique set of facts, rejected a television station's claim that it had a newsworthy defense to a right- of-publicity suit. Hugo Zacchini was a human cannonball. He made his living being shot from a cannon into a net at fairs and other events. A television station recorded 15 seconds of Zacchini's act, including his flight from the cannon to the net, and showed the recording on its news program. A public event shown on a news program would seem to be newsworthy.

The U.S. Supreme Court said human cannonball Hugo Zacchini could win an appropriation lawsuit against a television station that aired only 15 seconds of his performance. The station claimed the newsworthiness defense, but the Court rejected it. The station showed Zacchini's entire act, the Court said, threatening the performance's economic value.[102]

People seeing the entire act on television are less likely to attend the performance in person, according to the Court. *Zacchini* is a right-of-publicity case. The Court focused on the economic value of his act, not on his desire to be private. The television station's First Amendment rights were not more important than protecting Zacchini's financial interest in his performance, the Court said.

Public Domain Courts have held that names and associated information may be widely available to the public and therefore cannot be protected by right of publicity. An online fantasy baseball league operator could use Major League Baseball (MLB) players' names and statistics without MLB's permission, the U.S. Court of Appeals for the Eighth Circuit ruled.[103] The court said that information is widely available in the public domain. That is, many print, electronic and digital sources provide players' names and statistics, making that information factual rather than personal to the players.

First Amendment Does the First Amendment protect using a celebrity's name or picture if the use is not in an advertisement? What if the use is for parody or satirical purposes or is in a fictional or artistic work? Or if the use is for a commercial product such as a poster or bobble-head doll?

Courts have considered whether the merchandise—such as posters, dolls, T-shirts and games—that is the focus of many right-of-publicity cases has First Amendment protection.[104] The first case in which a court used the term "right-of-publicity" involved baseball cards included in bubble gum packages. Players could give a company an exclusive right to use their pictures because a baseball player has a right to exploit the value of his name or likeness, a federal appellate court said.[105]

The First Amendment may protect the satirical use of personal information. The Major League Baseball Players Association sued a company selling baseball cards with recognizable caricatures of baseball players accompanied by satiric comments. For example, the player on one card is named Treasury Bonds, a spoof of Barry Bonds' name. The card includes such statements as "Having Bonds on your team is like having money in the bank" and "He plays so hard he gives 110 percent, compounded daily."[106] A federal appellate court said the First Amendment fully protects the baseball cards. The cards "provide social commentary on public figures, major league baseball players, who are involved in a significant commercial enterprise, major league baseball," the court said.[107] The cards are "an important form of entertainment and social commentary that deserve First Amendment protection," the court concluded.[108]

Posters are not like satirical baseball cards. Courts most often have decided posters do not have First Amendment protection. Courts found appropriation when posters of singer Elvis Presley, model Christy Brinkley and professional wrestlers were distributed without permission.[109]

But courts have said the First Amendment protects selling posters with pictures of newsworthy individuals or events, such as a poster with a picture of comedian Pat Paulson when he ran for president and one showing former San Francisco 49ers quarterback Joe Montana celebrating the team's 1990 Super Bowl victory.[110] Courts drew a distinction between merchandise exploiting celebrities' names or likenesses and posters conveying newsworthy information of public interest.

The question of First Amendment protection versus right of publicity arises when a well-known person is used in an artistic work. One approach to this conflict is the artistic relevance test. This test asks whether using a celebrity's name or picture is relevant to a work's artistic purpose. If it is, the First Amendment, which applies to artistic as well as journalistic works, may allow using the celebrity's name without permission. However, consent is needed if the name or a celebrity's likeness is used primarily to give the work commercial appeal. For example, Italian movie director Federico Fellini made a film titled "Ginger and Fred." To movie fans, the obvious reference is to the Fred Astaire and Ginger Rogers films. The Fellini movie was about two cabaret dancers who were given the nicknames Ginger and Fred because they imitated Rogers and Astaire. Ginger Rogers sued, claiming the movie title infringed on her right to use her name for commercial purposes. In *Rogers v. Grimaldi,* a federal appellate court applied the **artistic relevance test.**[111] The court said Rogers could not win unless the movie title had no artistic relevance to the film itself or misled consumers about the film's contents. The movie's title and contents were artistically related, the court held.

Similarly, Mattel, the manufacturer of Barbie dolls, sued the band Aqua. The group's song "Barbie Girl" parodied Barbie dolls and the lifestyle the band said Barbie represented. Using the *Rogers* test, a federal appellate court held that the song title had an artistic relevance to the song lyrics.[112]

Not all song titles clearly relate to the song's lyrics. For example, the rap duo Outkast recorded a song titled "Rosa Parks." Parks was a major figure during the civil rights struggles of the 1950s and 1960s. In 1955, riding in the middle of a racially segregated Montgomery, Ala., bus, Parks refused to give her seat to a white person and move to the back of the bus, as city law required. Her defiant act spurred a 381-day bus boycott by Montgomery blacks and touched off other boycotts, sit-ins and demonstrations throughout the South.[113]

artistic relevance test A test to determine whether the use of a celebrity's name, picture, likeness, voice or identity is relevant to a disputed work's artistic purpose. It is used in cases regarding the infringement of a celebrity's right of publicity.

Rosa Parks won a right-of-publicity suit against the rap group Outkast when she convinced a court that a song's title, "Rosa Parks," was not artistically relevant to the song's lyrics.

transformativeness test A test to determine whether a creator has transformed a person's name, picture, likeness, voice or identity for artistic purposes. If so, the person cannot win a right-of-publicity suit against the creator.

Applying the *Rogers* test, a federal appellate court concluded that a jury could find the title "Rosa Parks" had no artistic relevance to the lyrics, despite the phrase "move to the back of the bus" being used repeatedly in the chorus. The court considered interviews in which the Outkast members said the song had nothing to do with Rosa Parks. The court also used online rap dictionaries to decipher the song's lyrics. The lyrics, containing profanity and explicit sexual references, only meant that Outkast had recorded a new album, the court concluded. The lyrics said that all other rap groups' work was inferior to Outkast's new recording. Using Rosa Parks' name in the title also was misleading, the court held. It could make potential consumers believe the song in fact was about Parks, although the lyrics in no way referred to her.

Instead of the *Rogers* artistic relevance test, some courts have used a **transformative test** to decide whether a challenged work has First Amendment protection against a right-of-publicity suit.[114] These courts ask if the new work only copies the original—an artist makes an exact drawing of a celebrity and sells copies of that picture—or instead transforms the original by adding new creative elements. If an artist drawing a caricature exaggerates a person's facial or body features, perhaps for comic effect, the caricature transforms the original, that is—changes the person's actual physical features. The First Amendment protects caricatures that have enough originality.

The California Supreme Court developed the **transformative test** in a case involving the Three Stooges.[115] An artist created a charcoal sketch of the Three Stooges, transferred the sketch to T-shirts and lithographs and sold thousands of the items. A company owning the Three Stooges' publicity rights sued.[116] The California court acknowledged the conflict between the artist's First Amendment right to express himself, particularly about public personalities, and the right of celebrities to protect their property and financial interests in their images. The sketch was an expressive work, the court said. Commentary about celebrities is part of a public discussion about public matters. The court also said that a right-of-publicity suit could stifle discourse about a celebrity even if a libel or privacy action would not be successful.

But many celebrities work hard to achieve their fame, the California court said. These efforts justify protecting celebrities' rights to exploit their renown. The court proposed the transformative test to distinguish protected artistic expression about celebrities from expression that encroaches on a personality's right of publicity. The First Amendment protects a work that adds enough new elements to the original to transform it. Changing the original by giving it a new

realWorld Law

Football Players in Real Life and in Video Games

Video football games using players who look like and are dressed in uniforms of real collegiate players and are pictured playing in stadiums where those players performed cannot pass the transformative test, a federal district court ruled in 2010. Sam Keller, a starting quarterback for Arizona State University and then University of Nebraska during his college football career, sued Electronic Arts (EA) for using Keller's and other college football players' virtual identities in EA's "NCAA Football" video games. The court said that in the video game "the virtual player wears the same jersey number, is the same height and weight and hails from the same state [as Keller].... EA does not depict Plaintiff in a different form; he is represented as what he was: the starting quarterback for Arizona State University." A jury could find EA did not sufficiently transform Keller's character to avoid the player's right of publicity claim, the court said.[1]

Sam Keller

1. Keller v. Electronic Arts, Inc., 2010 U.S. Dist. LEXIS 10719 (N.D. Calif., Feb. 8, 2010).

meaning or a different message justifies First Amendment protection. Transformative works may be satires, news reports, or works of fiction or social criticism, the court said. However, the court concluded, "When artistic expression takes the form of a literal depiction or imitation of a celebrity for commercial gain, directly trespassing on the right of publicity without adding significant expression beyond that trespass," the celebrity's rights outweigh First Amendment protections.[117] The court found that the Three Stooges' drawing was a "literal, conventional" depiction of the three men, with no discernible transformative elements. Because the drawing did not transform the Three Stooges' pictures, it had no First Amendment protection.

The transformative test may result in First Amendment protection for artists. The California Supreme Court used the test to rule that a comic book artist transformed images of two musicians, Johnny and Edgar Winter.[118] One issue of the Jonah Hex series showed the Winter brothers as half-human, half-worm creatures named Edgar and Johnny Autumn. But the characters had the Winters' long white hair and albino skin. The court said the drawings were not "conventional depictions" but rather had "significant expressive content." That is, the comic book artist has transformed the brothers into cartoon characters as part of a story that itself had expressive content.

A court found Rick Rush's painting, "The Masters of Augusta," transformed Tiger Woods' image into an artistic work, preventing Woods from winning his right-of-publicity lawsuit.

Image reprinted by permission of Jireh Publishing and Rick Rush, www.RickRushArt.com

When does an artist transform someone's image into art? The California Supreme Court said "an artist depicting a celebrity must contribute something more than a 'merely trivial' variation" of the celebrity's image. The artist "must create something recognizably 'his own'" for a court to find "significant transformative elements" in the artist's work.[119]

Similarly, the artist Rick Rush sold prints of his painting portraying the golfer Tiger Woods' win at the Professional Golfers' Association's 1997 Masters Tournament. The painting shows Woods in several poses and includes his caddy and six other famous golfers. Woods sued, claiming that the artist's sales of the prints violated Woods' right of publicity. Applying the transformative test, a federal appellate court held for the artist.[120] The work was more than a literal picture of Woods, the court said. It placed the golfer in the context of the Masters golf course, with his caddy and other Masters winners. The painting and prints used Woods' image to comment on sports' place in American culture, according to the court. The court also used the *Rogers* test and said that Woods' picture had artistic relevance to the painting.

A California court also held that a video game creator sufficiently transformed a game character, although it had some resemblance to the lead singer of a retro-funk group. The court said the singer and the video game character shared some similarities, but the computer-generated character's physique was different, as were the character's hairstyle and costume. Further, the court said, the character's role as a 25th-century reporter put it in a very different context than that in which the singer appeared.[121]

predominant use test In a right-of-publicity lawsuit, a test to determine whether the defendant used the plaintiff's name or picture more for commercial purposes or protected expression.

Another way to balance the First Amendment and the right of publicity is the **predominant use test.** The question is whether a person's name or picture is used more for commercial purposes or substantive expression. The Missouri Supreme Court applied this test in ruling that a comic book creator named a character "Anthony 'Tony Twist' Twistelli" more to sell the comics than for free speech purposes. In the comic, Twistelli was portrayed as an organized crime leader. A real Tony Twist, a former professional hockey player, sued for misuse of his name. A jury awarded $15 million in damages.[122]

Courts long have held that the First Amendment protects using celebrities' names in biographies and fiction, including movies and television programs.

Although this was part of appropriation law long before the California Supreme Court used the transformative test, the reasons are similar. Books, news stories, movies and television programs add transformative elements by putting the names in a context. For example, a movie called "Panther," combining fact and fiction, portrayed several members of the Black Panther Party, a political group active in the 1960s and '70s that promoted black power and social activism. Bobby Seale, a prominent member of the Black Panthers, sued. A federal district court rejected Seale's appropriation claim, saying the First Amendment protected using his name in the film.[123]

Some celebrities, such as the wealthy recluse Howard Hughes, have tried to limit who may write their biographies.[124] But no person, or deceased person's relative, has the right to prevent anyone from writing about another's life.[125]

The First Amendment usually protects even fictionalized biographies from right-of-publicity suits. Courts found that somewhat fictionalized televised biographies of the silent screen star Rudolph Valentino and the actress Elizabeth Taylor were as protected as factual biographies.[126] Even fiction including the names of real people is protected.

However, if an author claims that a work is a biography, but the work is much more fiction than fact, the First Amendment may not protect it. Warren Spahn, the Baseball Hall of Fame pitcher discussed earlier in this chapter, won his lawsuit over an unauthorized, largely invented biography that did not present a factual account of his life.[127] The highest court in New York agreed with Spahn that the book violated the state's appropriation law.

Ads for the Media Another First Amendment-based appropriation defense says mass media may run advertisements for themselves that use names and likenesses they have included in their coverage. They may do this without being granted permission by those whose names and likenesses were used. Courts recognized this defense when a magazine, Holiday, ran ads for itself in two other publications. One ad urged people to subscribe to Holiday. The other ad suggested advertising agencies place their clients' ads in Holiday. Both ads included pictures Holiday had published in one of its issues. The pictures were of Shirley Booth, a well-known actress during the mid-20th century. Booth sued under New York's appropriation law. The state's highest court said that in order to stay in business and to use its First Amendment rights, the magazine had to attract subscribers and advertisers. Illustrating the magazine's contents and quality by showing what it publishes does not violate Booth's rights, the court concluded.[128]

Holiday magazine won the suit in part because it did not suggest Booth endorsed the magazine. However, a men's magazine's advertisement for itself used a picture of the actress and singer Cher. The picture accompanied an interview with Cher that the magazine had published. A cartoon balloon over Cher's head included the words, "So join Cher and FORUM's hundreds of thousands of other adventurous readers today." Cher sued, saying the magazine had used her name in its promotion and implied her endorsement of the magazine without permission, which is impermissible under the California appropriation statute. A federal appellate court agreed with her.[129]

Consent The best appropriation defense is having the person's consent to use his or her name or likeness. That is why professional photographers use model releases—contracts prepared by lawyers and signed by all parties involved—when taking pictures for advertisements. Oral consent can be a defense, but proving it can be difficult if the plaintiff claims she or he did not give permission. Also, the law does not allow certain people to give consent, such as minors and those who are not mentally or emotionally capable of agreeing. And consent is limited to the agreement's terms. Consent to use a picture in an ad during 2009, for example, does not allow its use in 2011. Similarly, if a person gives consent to use a picture in a shampoo ad, the picture cannot be used to advertise bed sheets. If a person gives sweeping consent—to use a picture at any time in the future in any advertisement—a court likely will hold that the agreement is more limited than its words, or lack of words, indicate.

Consent most often is explicit. A person agrees to allow his or her name to be used in an advertisement. But consent may be implied. In one case, two people sat on a bench at a dog-racing track. Track personnel announced that a picture would be taken of the area where the people sat, and the camera was within their view. The two people did not move from the bench. When the track used the picture in an advertising brochure, the two people sued for appropriation. A court ruled that the plaintiffs gave implied consent by not moving when they knew their picture would be taken.[130]

Incidental Use The use of a person's name or likeness may be incidental to a work's primary purpose. A court could rule that a person's name or likeness was used so briefly that the purpose was not to make a profit or gain commercial benefit. For example, a name applied to a fictional terrorist in a comic book appeared in 1 of 116 panels spanning 24 pages. A person who said the comic book applied his name to the terrorist sued under New York's appropriation law. A federal district court said the name's use was incidental to the comic book's primary purpose and could not sustain a privacy suit.[131] Similarly, if a photograph of a large crowd of people is used in an advertisement, it is unlikely one person in the group could claim successfully that her picture is being used for commercial purposes.

Incidental use is not measured in time or space only. An organization sponsored a hole-in-one contest. Dan Pooley, a professional golfer, made a hole-in-one to win $1 million, half going to a charity. The organization made an eight-minute promotional videotape to help sell its products and promote the contest. Six seconds of the tape included Pooley's name and his winning shot. Pooley, who had not given his permission, sued. A federal district court did not accept the incidental use defense. Pooley's name and picture, although a very small part of the tape, were significantly related to the tape's purpose, the court said, and the organization needed Pooley's permission.[132]

COURTS RECOGNIZE SEVERAL DEFENSES TO an appropriation suit. The press most often uses the newsworthiness defense. Courts consider media content to be newsworthy if it is not used in an advertisement. The Supreme Court has held that the media lose the newsworthiness defense if they show a performer's entire act in a news program.

Courts recognize a First Amendment defense in cases celebrities bring for right of publicity. Courts use several tests in balancing celebrities' rights to earn money from their names and likenesses against the media's free speech rights. One is to determine whether a celebrity's name or likeness is used in conveying information of public concern. Another is to assess whether using a celebrity's name or likeness is artistically relevant to the work. A third is to decide whether the disputed work transformed the celebrity's likeness, making it into something new.

Courts allow the media to use someone's name or likeness in an advertisement for the mass medium itself if the ad does not suggest the person is endorsing the mass medium. Also, if a person consents to a commercial use of her name or likeness, the person cannot sue successfully for appropriation unless the use goes beyond the consent given. Finally, an incidental use of a person's name or likeness is not appropriation. ■

Intrusion

Critics say the press is obsessed with publishing the sensational, the lurid, the most confidential secrets. Some argue this obsession prompts journalists to intrude into personal privacy through whatever means necessary—planting microphones (bugs), using telescopic camera lenses and infrared heat-sensing film, trespassing on private property, lying. Nonsense, the media say. Simply, the media must inform the public. Unconventional newsgathering techniques may be necessary in order to provide information about the targets of investigative reporting, who often have the most to hide, journalists claim. Whose rights should be dominant: those who want privacy or journalists who want to report on matters of public interest?

Invasive newsgathering techniques may amount to intrusion or, as courts say, **intrusion upon seclusion**.[133] A journalist may be sued for intrusion if he intentionally interferes with another person's solitude or meddles in the person's private concerns, and if the intrusion would highly offend a **reasonable person** (the law's version of an average person). The intrusion may be physical, such as entering someone's house without permission, or technological, such as using a miniature camera. The intrusion tort is intended to ensure people retain their dignity by preventing unwanted encroachment into their physical space and their private affairs. Only New York state and Virginia have refused to recognize the intrusion tort.[134] (Newsgathering techniques that may be classified as intrusion are discussed further in Chapter 8.)

intrusion upon seclusion Physically or technologically disturbing another's reasonable expectation of privacy.

reasonable person The law's version of an average person.

Methods of Intruding

The more technology develops, the more ways intrusion can occur. The Internet in particular presents many opportunities to delve into another's private affairs. But even older technology, such as a camera's telephoto lens, can be a means of intruding. In one case, a woman mysteriously disappeared from her home. The woman's sister-in-law, husband and children visited the woman's home. They were in bathing suits at the home's swimming pool, surrounded by a seven-foot high fence, when a CBS television network cameraman stood on a neighbor's porch and, using a telephoto lens, videotaped the family. A federal district court permitted the family to sue CBS for intrusion, saying, "We find that the plaintiffs' allegations that they were swimming in the backyard pool of a private home surrounded by a seven foot privacy fence are sufficient to allege both that they believed they were in a secluded place and that the activity was private."[135]

Intrusion suits have been brought based on news reporters finding information in public records. Courts hold that there is no reasonable expectation of privacy in public records.[136]

Intrusion on Private Property

Journalists might obtain information by intentionally entering private property without permission. A reporter who does so has committed intrusion, an act similar to trespass (discussed in Chapter 8). Trespass is both a crime and a tort. A trespasser may be fined or jailed and also may be sued for civil damages. The trespasser also may be sued for the tort of intrusion.

A plaintiff suing for intrusion must prove that the defendant acted intentionally to intrude into private matters in a way a reasonable person would find highly offensive. A highly offensive and intrusive act is one the community thinks is beyond the limits of decency.

Intrusion may occur only if a person has a reasonable expectation of privacy. For instance, there is a reasonable expectation others will not enter into private property, such as a house or apartment, without consent. A person who controls the property, such as the homeowner or renter, must give permission for entry. Without the owner's or occupant's consent, a journalist entering a private residence is intruding. Simply entering private land, however, may not be intruding. In a lawsuit involving Google's Street View feature, which provides panoramic views of streets in metropolitan areas, a couple sued Google for intrusion. Street View showed the couple's house and swimming pool. The couple claimed the pictures could be obtained only by driving up the private street on which their home is located, a street marked as "Private Road, No Trespassing." However, no reasonable person would be highly offended by Google's entry onto the road, the U.S. Court of Appeals for the Third Circuit said, because guests and delivery trucks entered the road and see what Street View's pictures showed.[137]Ordinarily, there is not a reasonable expectation of privacy on public streets and sidewalks and in public parks. People should realize they can be seen or overheard in these places. However, there may be circumstances when people do have a reasonable expectation of privacy in public places.

For example, the U.S. Supreme Court upheld a Colorado law that created an eight-foot bubble around individuals entering a health care facility.[138] The statute made it illegal to approach within eight feet of a person going into an abortion clinic—the law's primary focus—to hand her a leaflet, show her a sign or talk with her without her consent. The law applied within a 100-foot radius around a health care facility's entrance. In *Hill v. Colorado,* the Court said the law was neither content based nor viewpoint based. Therefore, the Court did not apply a strict-scrutiny standard. The state needed to show only a substantial interest. The Court said Colorado's interests in public health and in protecting the rights of individuals to avoid unwanted communication met the intermediate scrutiny test. Although the Court did not specifically say so, apparently Colorado considered people entering health clinics to have a reasonable expectation of privacy.

Courts may not permit journalists to exceed acceptable means of obtaining information. The press engaged in a "moronic photographic frenzy that preceded and memorialized the dying moments of Britain's Princess Diana (and perhaps contributed to the accident that killed her)."[139] Following Princess Diana's death, California passed an anti-paparazzi law.[140] The California law says that offensively trespassing to photograph or record a person's personal or family activities is an invasion of privacy. A plaintiff may receive three times the damages a jury awards and may receive punitive damages under the California statute.

These cases show that reporters are wrong if they assume people involved in a news event occurring on public property do not have a reasonable expectation of privacy. In another example, an automobile accident victim reasonably expected discussions with emergency personnel to be private even if medical treatment took place on the side of a public road, a court held.[141]

It is not always easy to determine if property is private or public. Taxpayers own government land, but they may not always be permitted on the property. Reporters entering a naval base without permission to cover protests could be arrested, a federal district court ruled.[142] Businesses invite the public to enter to buy their products or services. However, reporters entering for other reasons may be intruding. A television news crew burst into a New York City restaurant with cameras on and bright lights blazing to report on a health code violation at the establishment, which specialized in French cuisine. The court said the journalists had trespassed in this instance, because the restaurant only allowed the public to enter for the purpose of dining, not to take pictures and generate news reports.[143]

Points of Law

Intrusion by Trespass

Plaintiff's Case

- A reasonable expectation of privacy
- Intentional intrusion on the privacy
- The intrusion would be highly offensive to a reasonable person

Defense

- Consent

Defenses

Consent is the only defense for an intrusion suit based on trespass in nearly all cases. Newsworthiness is not a defense because publishing is not an element of the tort. The intrusion happens in the news-gathering process, not when the material is published. However, the U.S. Court of Appeals for the Ninth Circuit said a story's newsworthiness may reduce the intrusion's offensiveness.[144] This is important because a plaintiff must prove the intrusion was highly offensive.

Consent A person cannot claim a reasonable expectation of privacy if he or she gave consent for someone to be on his or her private property. For example, a restaurant owner allowed a television news crew to videotape a health inspector evaluating the restaurant. After the station ran an unflattering story, the restaurant sued for intrusion. Because a trial jury found that the restaurant owner had given the television crew consent to enter the premises, an appeals court rejected the restaurant's claim.[145]

Consent can be implied. For example, if a journalist enters private property and the property owner responds to the reporter's questions, there is implied consent to remain and continue the interview.[146]

False Pretenses A journalist who cannot get permission to be on private property might lie to obtain consent. Using false pretenses to enter private property is a long-standing reporting technique. For example, Nelly Bly, a New York World reporter in the late 19th century, pretended to be a patient so she could expose the horrible conditions in New York's mental institutions. In the early 20th century, Upton Sinclair took a job in a meatpacking plant and wrote about the unsanitary way meat was processed. Sinclair's novel "The Jungle" and magazine articles he wrote led Congress to create the Food and Drug Administration.[147]

If consent to enter private premises is obtained through false pretenses—lying—is the consent an effective defense to an intrusion suit? Courts are not in agreement, but generally they say reporters may use deceit to gain entry. At least two federal courts have reached that conclusion. In one case, a producer for the ABC television network program "Primetime Live" sent seven people to eye clinics owned by Dr. J.H. Desnick. The seven posed as patients, each equipped with hidden cameras used to record the eye surgeons who examined them. "Primetime Live" aired a story, using portions of the video, that said the Desnick clinics "may be doing unnecessary cataract surgery for the money." Desnick sued ABC for intrusion and other torts. The clinics were open to anyone who wanted an eye examination, a federal appellate court said. The people posing as patients were allowed into the clinics, just as anyone else would have been. That the "patients" meant to deceive did not invalidate the consent to enter, the court held.[148]

The U.S. Court of Appeals for the Seventh Circuit observed that many people use deception to enter private or semi-private premises. For example, a restaurant owner might refuse entry to a food critic known to write harsh reviews. But restaurant critics usually do not identify themselves to the owner. They enter and

realWorld Law

Using False Pretenses?

Jon Entine, "Primetime Live" producer of the Dr. Desnick story, said:

In terms of trespass and being on private property uninvited, we *were* invited. The public was invited. It was a walk-in clinic. So there's no "uninvited" there. I don't see there's trespassing. He invited people in to get looked at as prospective patients. So there's no trespassing there. The real issue is did we violate some patient-doctor privacy relationship. But the reality of it is, that's a two-part relationship in which the patient grants to the doctor that right. I don't see any violation in that sense. If the patient leaves a doctor's office and spills the beans about what went on in a discussion, there's nothing illegal about that. All we did was record that rather than just the person representing that orally. These were prospective patients. They could have gotten surgery if they wanted. I wouldn't have stopped them. What I did was actually recruit people who were of age and could go in and might or might not need surgery. I didn't see any advertisement that said, "Only people who definitely need surgery are allowed to come into this office." Instead it said, "Come to the Desnick office. We're offering surgery and we'll give you a free exam." We fit—by any measure if you read their advertising—the patients went in fit every single qualification that was offered in their advertising. There was no fine print that said, "You can come in here unless you're accompanied by a hidden camera, or you have motivations other than getting surgery." It just said, "Come in for a free exam." We went in for a free exam.[1]

---

1. Joseph Russomanno, Speaking Our Minds: Conversations with People Behind Landmark First Amendment Cases 146 (Mahwah, N.J.: Lawrence Erlbaum Associates, 2002).

eat anonymously. That is, they deceive the restaurant owner by pretending to be ordinary patrons. The court said this deception does not negate the restaurant owner's consent that the unknown critic enter. The court indicated, however, that this analysis might not apply to someone using false pretenses to enter with no substantive reason to be there, citing as an example someone who pretends to be a utilities meter reader to enter a private home. In contrast, the hypothetical restaurant critic—and the eye clinic "patients"—did have valid reasons to be on private property, the court said.

After a domestic violence victim realized she had allowed into her house a television cameraman along with a crisis intervention team and that her story would be broadcast, she sued for intrusion, among other torts. A federal district court said her permission to enter prevented a successful intrusion suit.[149]

Some courts disagree with these decisions, particularly when the context is medical treatment. In one case, a photographer recorded video of emergency room personnel treating a man who had a bad reaction to a drug. The photographer, dressed in hospital apparel, asked the man to sign a release form allowing the recording. The photographer said the video would be used to help train hospital personnel. The patient signed the form, thinking the photographer was a doctor. After a portion of the video ran on a cable program, "Trauma: Life in the ER," the patient sued for intrusion and other claims. A court agreed with the patient's argument that he was in a "zone of physical and sensory privacy and he had a reasonable expectation of seclusion" in a hospital emergency room. The court said the photographer's deception invalidated the patient's consent.[150]

The fact that someone gained entry to a home using false pretenses may not provide grounds for an intrusion suit in most circumstances. But at least one court said that combining false pretenses with surreptitious image and audio recording after entering the home was intrusive. To investigate a person practicing medicine without a license, a Life magazine reporter and a photographer claimed to be patients and were admitted to the man's home. The reporter had a microphone in her purse, and the photographer used a small, concealed camera to take pictures. A federal appellate court ignored the false pretenses question and focused on the surreptitious reporting. The court said people have a reasonable expectation of privacy in their homes. Even though a person might expect a visitor to repeat what is said in the house and describe the scene, it is not expected that "what is heard and seen will be transmitted by photograph or recording, or in our modern world, in full living color and [high fidelity] to the public at large or to any segment of it that the visitor may select."[151] The court said that "the First Amendment has never been construed to accord newsmen immunity from torts or crimes committed during the course of newsgathering. The First Amendment is not a license to trespass, to steal, or to intrude by electronic means into the precincts of another's home or office."[152]

Most states have laws making it illegal to pretend to be a law enforcement officer. In some states it is unlawful to pretend to be any public official.

Newsworthiness Newsworthiness rarely is a defense to an intrusion suit based on trespass or surreptitious surveillance. The story's newsworthiness is irrelevant to the harm that occurs when information is gathered for the story.[153] This is because a plaintiff can win an intrusion lawsuit without proving that the defendant published the information or pictures obtained through the intrusion. Publication is not part of the plaintiff's burden of proof in an intrusion case. Whether a journalist has committed intrusion is determined on the basis of the techniques used to gather information. Publishing that information may lead to other torts, such as libel. But publication alone does not prove that the journalist committed intrusion. Therefore, the story's newsworthiness is not an intrusion defense.

For example, in the case of a car accident victim airlifted to a hospital, a court said the story's newsworthiness did not make recording in the aircraft or secret audio recording permissible.[154]

Newsworthiness may be a defense in rare circumstances, however. One court held that reporters using false pretenses to enter a medical laboratory and then secretly recording activities in that lab was not highly offensive because the journalists were investigating laboratory errors in testing for certain cancers. The public's interest in important health issues prevailed over privacy interests, the court said.[155] Another court said that "the legitimate motive of gathering the news" could "negate the offensiveness element of the intrusion tort."[156] That is, the plaintiff could not prove the intrusion was highly offensive to a reasonable person and therefore could not win an intrusion suit.

SUMMARY

INTRUSION OCCURS IF A PERSON INTENTIONALLY interferes with another's solitude or private concerns through physical or technological means. Physical intrusion is also trespass. Trespass is both a crime and a tort.

To win an intrusion suit, a plaintiff must prove the defendant acted intentionally to intrude into private matters in a way a reasonable person would find highly offensive. A highly offensive and intrusive act is one the community thinks is beyond the limits of decency. If highly offensive intrusion occurs, a plaintiff is able to show he had a reasonable expectation of privacy that the defendant violated.

Intrusion concerns how information is gathered. Publication is not part of the intrusion tort.

Intrusion by trespass occurs when entering private property where a person has a reasonable expectation of privacy. Generally, people on public property have no reasonable expectation of privacy, but particularly aggressive news gathering even on public property can be considered intrusion. Also, some publicly owned property, such as military bases, is not open to the public. Consent is the defense for intrusion by trespass. The person who owns or is using the property must give consent. Courts have ruled that law enforcement officials may not give journalists consent to enter private property. Courts generally, but not unanimously, hold that consent is valid even if obtained by using false pretenses.

Journalists may use visible equipment to photograph or record on public property. However, secret recording is intrusion if the circumstances suggest a person should have a reasonable expectation of privacy in public, such as during a medical emergency. People talking so passersby can hear do not have a reasonable expectation of privacy in the workplace or other private locations. Secretly videotaping on private property is intrusion.

Consent is a defense in an intrusion suit. Newsworthiness rarely is an effective defense against an intrusion suit. ■

Private Facts

Journalists are supposed to report accurate, factual information. They understand that if they publish false stories they can be sued for libel and other torts. They do not expect to be sued for publishing the truth—but they can be. Journalists can be sued for a tort called **private facts** if they publish truthful private information that is not of legitimate public concern and if publicizing the facts would be highly offensive to a reasonable person.[157] The private facts tort is intended to protect

private facts The tort under which media are sued for publishing highly embarrassing private information that is not newsworthy or lawfully obtained from a public record.

Points of Law

Private Facts

Plaintiff's Case

- Publicizing

- Private, intimate facts

- That would be highly embarrassing to a reasonable person

- And are not of legitimate concern to the public

Defenses

- First Amendment: Truthful information lawfully obtained from public records

a person's dignity and peace of mind by discouraging the publication of intimate facts. If intimate private facts are publicized, a jury may award monetary damages to compensate for the resulting emotional injury.[158] Of course, the egg cannot be put back into the shell: Once intimate facts are revealed to the public, money cannot make the facts private again.

A court first recognized the private facts tort in 1927, holding that placing a large sign in the window of a car repair business correctly stating that a local veterinarian owed $49.67 could violate the veterinarian's right of privacy.[159] Today, a plaintiff must show that the facts were private, dealt with intimate or highly personal matters, were not of legitimate public concern and were published. Courts recognize a First Amendment defense to a private facts lawsuit. Forty-one states and the District of Columbia allow private facts lawsuits.[160]

Intimate Facts

Private facts cases involve a person's most intimate or personal information. Intimate facts are those that a person would not want the community to know. This information must be more than just embarrassing. A plaintiff will not win a private facts case if the media reveal she or he chews bubble gum or slipped on a patch of ice. But intimate facts do not have to concern illegal or reprehensible matters. There are many facts a person might want to keep private simply because they are not for public knowledge. Private facts suits can relate to a person's financial condition,[161] medical information,[162] domestic difficulties[163] and similar intimate facts.

Often, private facts suits concern sexual activities.[164] For example, a newspaper asked readers to submit stories about unique love situations. A woman's former husband responded by telling of his relationship with the woman. The paper, which published the story using only first names and no other identifying information, said that "Denise" had several abortions and had swapped partners with another couple. The story also reported that Denise had a surrogate parenting relationship with her former husband and with the woman who had been the maid of honor at her wedding. Denise sued the paper, saying that close relatives and friends and her employer had recognized her in the story and had not known these intimate details of her life. A court ruled that a jury could find the published information to be "embarrassing private facts."[165]

It is not always clear why a court does or does not find publishing a fact offensive. In 2002 a federal court said showing on television a woman kissing drummer Dominic Weir in a women's bathroom stall in a bar was not offensive and objectionable.[166] However, a state court in 2004 ruled that it was reasonable

realWorld Law

Privacy in Public Records?

The Supreme Court said:

> We do not hold that truthful publication is automatically constitutionally protected, or that there is no zone of personal privacy within which the State may protect the individual from intrusion by the press, or even that a State may never punish publication of the name of a victim of a sexual offense. We hold only that where a newspaper publishes truthful information which it has lawfully obtained, punishment may lawfully be imposed, if at all, only when narrowly tailored to a state interest of the highest order. . . .[1]

1. Florida Star v. B.J.F., 491 U.S. 524, 540 (1989).

for a jury to find objectionable television commercials showing a man having hair replacement treatments.[167]

Private facts cases focus on the community's reaction to disseminating the intimate information.[168] If without permission a newspaper published a picture of a woman nursing her child, the community might be outraged.[169] The community would not be outraged that a woman nursed her child; rather, it might be highly offended that the paper printed a picture of the woman and her child. That is the question before a court hearing a private facts case: Would it outrage the community's notions of decency if the intimate information were published?[170]

Not all facts about a person are private; not even all intimate facts about a person are private. Information in a public record, such as a court filing or an arrest record, by definition is public information, not private. Nor are facts private if the person himself or herself made them public. Courts hold that information told to a few close relatives or friends remains private. A person may define her or his own circle of intimacy.[171] But if a person reveals intimate facts publicly, the private facts tort does not limit the media from also publishing the information.

One illustrative case involves a friendship between two high school girls that deteriorated into a bitter feud. The first girl accused the second of being pregnant, and that girl teased the first about her Jewish heritage, seeking psychological counseling and having plastic surgery. The feud also involved swastikas painted on road signs and culminated in the second girl's family self-publishing a book about the feud. The book included school, police and legal documents connected with the situation. The first girl sued for private facts, among other torts. She claimed the book included "1) excerpts and summaries from her myspace.com webpage; 2) three statements related to her Jewish ancestry; 3) her enrolment at [a university]; 4) two statements regarding Plaintiff's decision to seek professional psychological care or counselling; 5) Plaintiff's transfer from one high school to another under a superintendent's agreement; and 6) two statements regarding plastic surgery on Plaintiff's nose."[172] The court held categories 1, 2, 3 and 5 were not private, noting the plaintiff agreed she could not conceal what she posted on her MySpace Web page. She also wrote on her MySpace page that she sought psychological help. As to plastic surgery, the court said it "questions whether this matter is truly private: cosmetic surgery on one's face is by its nature exposed to the public eye."

A well-known case in which facts were not private before a newspaper published them arose when a former U.S. Marine, Oliver Sipple, may have saved President Gerald Ford's life. As Ford was walking out of a hotel near a crowd in San Francisco in 1975, a woman named Sara Jane Moore pointed a gun at Ford. Sipple, who was standing nearby, hit Moore's arm just as the gun fired, and the bullet missed Ford. As national media attention focused on Sipple, he asked the press not to report that he was gay because his family was unaware of his sexual orientation. But two days later, a San Francisco newspaper columnist correctly implied that Sipple was gay. A court threw out Sipple's private facts suit in part because gay communities in several cities already knew of Sipple's sexual orientation. He had marched in gay pride parades and frequented gay bars, and his name had been published in several gay magazines, according to the court. Because the newspaper only gave more publicity to information already publicly known, Sipple could not show the facts were private, the court ruled.[173]

SUMMARY

A PRIVATE FACTS PLAINTIFF MUST SHOW THE WIDELY disseminated facts were private, dealt with intimate or highly personal matters, and were not of legitimate public concern. A plaintiff also must prove that publication would be highly offensive to a reasonable person. It is not the published facts that must be highly offensive, but that the facts were published. Facts are not private if they are from public records or generally known. ■

Legitimate Public Concern

Even if intimate facts were private before being published, a plaintiff cannot win a private facts lawsuit if the information is newsworthy or of legitimate public concern. The mass media help determine what is newsworthy by reporting on some stories and not others, partly by considering community standards. The media often publish reports including intimate facts. Stories about crimes, suicides, divorces, catastrophes, diseases and other topics may include intimate information the people involved do not want published. Also, once people are part of a newsworthy event, their lives are open books. The media often reveal intimate facts about them.[174] If newsworthy, these private facts cannot be the basis of a successful private facts suit. Can so much intimate information be newsworthy? Should the media be permitted to reveal nearly anything about anyone who happens to be connected with a news event?

Courts give the media considerable freedom to determine what is newsworthy. Judges do not want to infringe on journalists' First Amendment rights to report the news. Nor do judges want to become journalists by deciding what is of public concern. But courts do draw lines, finding that very intimate facts are not newsworthy if publishing the information would outrage the community.

Many courts have adopted a test to determine newsworthiness, first used by a federal appeals court in a case in which a Southern California surfer sued Sports Illustrated magazine.[175] A Sports Illustrated story included information about Mike Virgil, who bodysurfed at the Wedge, a public beach near Newport Beach, Calif. The Wedge is reputed to be the world's most dangerous place to bodysurf. To illustrate the surfers' daredevil attitudes, the story said Virgil put out a cigarette on his tongue, burned holes through a dollar bill that rested on the back of his hand, dove headfirst down a flight of stairs to impress women, ate spiders and jumped off billboards. Virgil spoke with the Sports Illustrated reporter but withdrew his consent to the story before publication. The surfer sued the magazine for publishing private facts.

The court said the First Amendment did not protect publicity of highly intimate facts unless they were of public concern. Defining newsworthiness, the court distinguished between information the public is entitled to know and facts published for a morbid and sensational reason, prying into private lives for no justifiable purpose. If a reasonable person would have no interest in knowing the information, a court could find it was published for morbid and sensational reasons, the court said. Surfing at the Wedge could be of public concern, the court grudgingly admitted. But did that justify revealing intimate details of Mike Virgil's life? The court sent the case back to the trial court to decide that question.[176] The trial court held that the information in the article about eating spiders, diving down stairs and other private facts in the article was embarrassing but not morbid and sensational. The facts helped describe people who bodysurfed at the Wedge, the court said in ruling for Sports Illustrated.[177]

Several courts have taken a slightly different approach to defining what is newsworthy when stories concern people involuntarily put in the public eye. These courts determine whether there is a logical connection between the news event and the private facts revealed. If there is not a clear connection, the intimate information is not newsworthy, these courts say. For example, a television crew recorded conversations between a woman and a rescue crew nurse after the woman was injured in an automobile accident. The woman, who was not known to the public before a television program broadcast her comments, sued for disseminating private facts. A court said that broadcasting the audio and video showing the woman in a dazed state after her accident was relevant to a news program about emergency care workers.[178] Well-known persons such as actors, athletes, politicians and musicians are inherently more newsworthy than others. The public wants to know about them and they have chosen to be in the public

realWorld Law

Privacy-Proof Plaintiff?

Libel-proof plaintiffs, discussed in Chapter 5, cannot successfully sue for defamation because their reputations already are so bad that nothing else published about them could lower their esteem in the community any further.

Is it possible now to have privacy-proof plaintiffs? These would be people who have shown they do not want privacy. They have pages on MySpace, Facebook, Photobucket and Flickr. They post videos on YouTube. They Twitter. They blog. They talk loudly in public on cell phones. Anyone with the slightest familiarity with the Internet can find out nearly anything they want about these people.[1]

How could these people sue for, say, embarrassing facts? What remains private in their lives? Or have they shown they do not care if anything remains private? Should a person be able to reveal nearly everything about herself or himself yet then claim publication of one private item would be highly embarrassing to a reasonable person? Or should the law not allow such publicity hounds to claim privacy?[2]

---

1. Eric Auchard, *Virtual Me,* Courier Mail (Australia), July 18, 2007, at 41.
2. *See* Nicholas Gerbis, The Birth of the Privacy-Proof Person? (Walter Cronkite School of Journalism and Mass Communication, Arizona State University, Sept. 2008) (on file with textbook authors).

eye. Even celebrities, though, have a right to keep private those facts that would be highly embarrassing if publicized. For example, in part based on a private facts claim, actress Pamela Anderson Lee and rock musician Bret Michaels successfully prevented distribution of a videotape showing them having sex.[179]

At one time, newsworthiness was a defense to a private facts suit. A media defendant had the burden of showing that the facts were of legitimate public interest. Some courts continue to put the newsworthiness burden on the defendant. Many courts instead now require the plaintiff in a private facts suit to prove the intimate facts were not newsworthy. This change came when a newspaper reported that a student body president was a transsexual.[180] Toni Diaz, born Antonio Diaz, underwent sex reassignment surgery before entering a community college. Elected student body president, she charged school administrators with mishandling student funds. A local newspaper columnist wrote of Diaz, "Now I realize, that in these times, such a matter is no big deal, but I suspect his female classmates in P.E. 97 may wish to make other showering arrangements." Diaz, who had told only close relatives and friends of her operation, sued the paper and columnist.

A court ruled that Diaz, as plaintiff, had to prove the private facts were not newsworthy. The special role of the press in society must be protected, the court said. Putting the burden on the media could lead to self-censorship. The press might be concerned that it could not prove newsworthiness no matter how much in the public interest it thought the story to be. The court ruled that Diaz could show it was not newsworthy to publish remarks about her gender and that her gender had no connection with her ability to be student body president. Nor, the court said, did her being the college's first female student body president open her entire life to examination.

Publicity

A private facts plaintiff must prove that the defendant gave publicity to the intimate information. Publicity in the private facts tort is not the same as publication in a libel suit. In libel, publication to a third party, someone other than the plaintiff and defendant, is sufficient. For the private facts tort, most courts require widespread publicity[181] These courts hold that telling one other person or a small group of people will not show publicity in a private facts suit. The mass media, of course, communicate with large numbers of people. Revealing intimate information in the mass media will meet the definition of giving publicity to private facts.[182]

Some courts hold that revealing private facts to small groups of people who have a special relationship with the plaintiff is sufficient to show there was publicity. This could include the plaintiff's fellow workers, church members, colleagues in a social organization or neighbors.[183] For instance, Kmart hired private investigators to pose as employees in the company's distribution warehouse to check on reports of theft and drug sales. Through the undercover investigators' reports, Kmart managers learned private facts about their employees, including facts regarding family matters, sexual conduct and health. Several employees sued Kmart for revealing private facts. A court said that telling private facts to a few people with whom a plaintiff has close ties may prove the publicity element.[184]

Some courts take a middle position between telling the general public and telling only a few people. For example, a lawyer's domestic partner was diagnosed with AIDS. The lawyer asked the head of his firm to arrange to cover some of the lawyer's responsibilities over the next few days so he could be tested for HIV. The head of the firm told his wife and two secretaries about the lawyer's situation. Soon everyone in the law firm knew. The lawyer sued the head of his firm for revealing private facts. The publicity requirement means the disclosure must be made to the general public or to a large group of people, a court said. The court held that there is no certain number that makes a group "large," and a jury could make that decision.[185]

Publishing private facts is permissible if the information is newsworthy or of legitimate public concern. Judges or juries determine newsworthiness in private facts cases. The criteria many courts use is that private facts are newsworthy if the publication was not intended to be sensational and morbid. Courts also consider whether there is a logical connection between the news event and the published private facts. Most courts require a private facts plaintiff to prove the article was not newsworthy. Some courts regard newsworthiness as a defense to a private facts lawsuit. Most courts require a private facts plaintiff to prove the information was widely published.

First Amendment Defense

When the press faces a private facts lawsuit, it often argues the First Amendment protects publishing truthful information. It is not surprising that a tort allowing suits for disseminating the truth would conflict with the First Amendment. One way to balance privacy interests against free speech interests is to focus on the source of the information. Should the press lose a private facts suit if the intimate information came from a **public record**—that is, a government document, particularly one publicly available?

public record A government record, particularly one that is publicly available.

The U.S. Supreme Court has said the First Amendment protects publishing truthful information of public significance lawfully obtained from public records, unless punishing the media would serve a compelling state interest. Court decisions have not held that the First Amendment always will protect publishing truthful information taken from public records.[186] However, in each of the cases it has decided involving private facts obtained from public records, the Supreme Court has ruled for the press. The Court has not yet found a compelling state interest that overrides the press's First Amendment rights.

Public Significance In determining whether a publication is about a matter of public significance, the Supreme Court focuses on the story's subject, not on individuals named in the article.[187] Whether a person mentioned in the story is of public interest is not the important factor. Rather, the question is whether the story's topic is of public importance.

In *B.J.F. v. Florida Star,* for example, the Supreme Court held that the First Amendment protected a newspaper that published the name of a rape victim, reasoning that violent crime is a publicly significant topic.[188] In October 1983, a woman identified as B.J.F. reported to a Florida sheriff's department that she had been robbed and sexually assaulted by an unknown assailant. The sheriff's department prepared a report on the incident that identified B.J.F. by her full name and placed the report in its pressroom. There were no restrictions on the public entering or looking at reports in the pressroom. A beginning reporter for the Florida Star, a weekly newspaper, saw the report and the paper published a story on the case in a section containing brief articles describing local criminal incidents, including B.J.F.'s full name. This was contrary to the paper's policy of not naming rape victims. B.J.F. sued the sheriff's department and the Florida Star under a state law making it illegal for media to publish the name of a sexual assault victim. The sheriff's department settled before trial, and B.J.F. won her case against the newspaper, a result that was upheld by a Florida appellate court.

The newspaper, however, appealed the case to the U.S. Supreme Court, which reversed, holding that the First Amendment protects a newspaper that publishes truthful information lawfully obtained from public records, provided no compelling state interest requires otherwise. If the government had wanted to shield B.J.F.'s identity, it should not have put the report where a journalist could see it, the Court suggested. Because the government made the information available, it could not punish the press for publishing it. If the media could be punished for publishing truthful information, the court said, "timidity and self-censorship" might result, and such "excessive media self suppression" is not consistent with the press freedoms guaranteed by the First Amendment.

Although protecting the identity of a sexual assault victim could in principle be a compelling state interest, the Court said, three factors worked against that conclusion in this case: First, the government itself supplied the information. Second, the state law forbidding names from being published had no exceptions, not even if the community already knew the victim's name. Third, the state law applied only to the media, allowing individuals or non-media groups to disseminate a victim's name. Under these circumstances, the Court said, the right to a free press outweighed the state's interest in preventing publication of B.J.F.'s name.

This case remains good law. In 2005, a federal appeals court relied on the Court's holding in *B.J.F. v. Florida Star* in deciding that the First Amendment protected a Pennsylvania newspaper that reported on a minor being arrested for rape.[189] The paper had obtained information from a police officer that the minor had been arrested for allegedly raping a 7-year-old girl he had been babysitting. The court rejected the minor's private facts lawsuit, holding that the paper published information lawfully obtained from a public record.

Lawfully Obtained In three other decisions underscoring the primacy of press freedoms over individual privacy, the Court ruled that where the press had legally obtained truthful information from public records it was not liable for publishing private facts. In *Cox Broadcasting Corp. v. Cohn,* the Court said for the first time that truthful information lawfully obtained from a public record could not be the basis of a private facts lawsuit.[190] The case had its genesis in a 1971 rape and murder of a 17-year-old female in Georgia. Although there was substantial press coverage of the crime, the identity of the victim was not disclosed pending trial. At a court proceeding some months later, though, a reporter covering the incident learned the name of the victim from an examination of indictments filed against six defendants that were made available for inspection in the courtroom. Her name was published in a television newscast later that day. The victim's father sued the television station for broadcasting the name of his daughter. He won at trial and again on the television station's appeal to the Georgia Supreme Court. But the U.S. Supreme Court reversed, holding in favor of the television station that the First Amendment protects the press against a private facts tort if the information is obtained from generally available public records. It would impinge on the press's obligation to accurately report judicial proceedings, the Court said, if reporters had access to information but were not allowed to publish it.

In a separate case originating in Oklahoma in 1976, news media violated a juvenile court judge's order by publishing the name and picture of an 11-year-old boy who was charged with second-degree murder for shooting a railroad employee. Reporters were in the courtroom when the juvenile appeared, and the court put his name on the public record. Photographers took pictures as the minor left the courthouse. The Supreme Court said the press had lawfully obtained information available to the public and held that the First Amendment prohibits punishing the press for revealing information taken from public records.[191]

In a third case affirming the importance of press freedoms, newspaper reporters who had been monitoring a police scanner in West Virginia in 1978 responded
to a crime scene and learned from witnesses and investigators the name of a
14-year-old boy charged with killing a classmate at a junior high school. State
prosecutors obtained an indictment against the press for publishing the boy's
name in violation of a state law making it illegal to publish, without prior court
approval, the name of a juvenile offender. The Supreme Court, however, disagreed
with the government. It ruled in favor of the newspaper, reasoning that the First
Amendment protects news reports where journalists have lawfully obtained truthful information from publicly available sources. The Court said protecting the
minor's privacy was not a compelling reason to restrict the freedom of the press.[192]

These cases show that sensitive personal information legally obtained from
law enforcement officials, from generally available records, or by what a journalist sees or hears will not support a private facts lawsuit. The Supreme Court has
also held that the First Amendment sometimes protects publication of private
information even where it was not lawfully obtained—so long as the media were
not involved in illegally acquiring the information. In *Bartnicki v. Vopper* (discussed further in Chapter 8), the Court said the media were not liable for intercepting a cell phone conversation between two labor negotiators. Punishing the
media for publishing information they obtained without acting illegally would
not further a compelling government interest, the Court said.[193]

Public Record Publicly available facts are not private. Names, addresses and
telephone numbers are available in phone books, so they are not confidential.[194]
Information in government records available to the public cannot be considered
private. Facts presented in public meetings also are not secret. Unless a judge
seals a record, making it unavailable, court records are public. A private facts suit
cannot be based on intimate information contained in publicly accessible records.

In one case, the CBS program "48 Hours" aired a segment about lottery winners, including charges that one lottery winner had sexually abused his daughter.
A federal appellate court rejected a private facts claim brought by the daughter.
The court said the accusations were discussed in the divorce proceedings between
the lottery winner and the daughter's mother. CBS lawfully obtained the information from a public record, the court ruled.[195]

Some government records are not publicly accessible and may not be considered public records in a private facts lawsuit. For example, grand jury proceedings are closed and not available to the public or press.[196] Also, information about
individuals' medical conditions, tax filings and other personal data may not be
considered a public record.[197]

Similarly, not all publicly accessible places are "public." Publishing a picture
and a conversation obtained by entering a private hospital room may not be protected even if the hospital generally is open to the public.[198]

Passage of Time Some private facts plaintiffs have argued that the passage of
time may mean that information is no longer of legitimate concern to the public.
Either the plaintiff was newsworthy many years before the media published the

realWorld Law

Public Is Not Private

A television program included information about a lottery winner's wife and daughter, including assertions that the daughter had been sexually abused. A federal district court rejected a claim of revelation of private facts because the information had been discussed in open court during the couple's divorce hearing. The court said:

> Notwithstanding the public nature of the sexual assault allegations, Plaintiffs argue that it is immaterial whether all 600 residents of Roby knew of the sexual assault charges because others outside of Roby were not aware of the charges until the "Lotto Town" broadcast aired. Plaintiffs' argument is untenable because it assumes a critical, but missing element of their cause of action, namely, that the published information is private. Where the Court determines that the information is not private, it need not proceed to the "publication" element of the cause of action. Thus, whether the information is published globally or to a single individual is immaterial if it is not of a private nature.[1]

1. Green v. CBS Broadcasting, Inc., 2000 U.S. Dist. LEXIS 19962, 33 (N.D. Tex., Dec. 19, 2000).

intimate information, or the private facts relate to events that happened long ago. Courts have rejected this contention, saying that newsworthiness does not disappear over time. In a well-known case, a child prodigy who, at age 11, lectured on complex mathematical concepts and graduated from Harvard at age 16 dropped out of the public eye. Many years later, a magazine published a "Where are they now?" feature about him. The story accurately said the former prodigy worked as a store clerk and lived in a small apartment. He sued the magazine, in part claiming that his public fame had disappeared long ago. A federal appellate court said he remained newsworthy, the public being interested in what he did after he was no longer well-known.[199]

SUMMARY

THE FIRST AMENDMENT PROTECTS PUBLISHING truthful information of public significance lawfully obtained from public records. However, this would not be a defense to a private facts lawsuit if a court determined that punishing the media would serve a compelling state interest. The U.S. Supreme Court, though, has never found a state interest compelling enough to allow such punishment, even where the media has revealed the name of a rape victim.

The topic of a news story, rather than the individual people discussed in the story, determines whether the story is of public significance. Information is lawfully obtained so long as a journalist does nothing illegal to obtain it. Information is public if it is in government records or otherwise available to the public.

Newsworthiness does not diminish over time. Facts and people once newsworthy remain newsworthy. ∎

Cases for Study

Thinking About It

The two case excerpts that follow are considered landmark privacy cases. As you read these case excerpts, keep the following questions in mind:

- Did the passage of 35 years between the two decisions change the Court's view of personal privacy?

- How do the decisions try to balance right to privacy against other important rights?

- A minor is raped and murdered, and the Court allows her name to be broadcast without protecting her family's privacy. Cell phone calls an individual thought private are heard by public officials. Do you agree with the Court's reasons for deciding the cases in these ways?

Cox Broadcasting Corp. v. Cohn
SUPREME COURT OF THE UNITED STATES
420 U.S. 469 (1975)

JUSTICE BYRON WHITE delivered the Court's opinion:

The issue before us in this case is whether, consistently with the First and Fourteenth Amendments, a State may extend a cause of action for damages for invasion of privacy caused by the publication of the name of a deceased rape victim which was publicly revealed in connection with the prosecution of the crime.

I

In August 1971, appellee's 17-year-old daughter was the victim of a rape and did not survive the incident. Six youths were soon indicted for murder and rape. Although there was substantial press coverage of the crime and of subsequent developments, the identity of the victim was not disclosed pending trial, perhaps because of Ga. Code Ann. sec. 26–9901 (1972), which makes it a misdemeanor to publish or broadcast the name or identity of a rape victim. In April 1972, some eight months later, the six defendants appeared in court. Five pleaded guilty to rape or attempted rape, the charge of murder having been dropped. The guilty

pleas were accepted by the court, and the trial of the defendant pleading not guilty was set for a later date.

In the course of the proceedings that day, appellant Wassell, a reporter covering the incident for his employer, learned the name of the victim from an examination of the indictments which were made available for his inspection in the courtroom. That the name of the victim appears in the indictments and that the indictments were public records available for inspection are not disputed. Later that day, Wassell broadcast over the facilities of station WSB-TV, a television station owned by appellant Cox Broadcasting Corp., a news report concerning the court proceedings. The report named the victim of the crime and was repeated the following day.

In May 1972, appellee brought an action for money damages against appellants, relying on sec. 26–9901 and claiming that his right to privacy had been invaded by the television broadcasts giving the name of his deceased daughter. Appellants admitted the broadcasts but claimed that they were privileged under both state law and the First and Fourteenth

Amendments. The trial court, rejecting appellants' constitutional claims and holding that the Georgia statute gave a civil remedy to those injured by its violation, granted summary judgment to appellee as to liability, with the determination of damages to await trial by jury.

. . .

III

Georgia stoutly defends . . . the State's common-law privacy action challenged here. Its claims are not without force, for powerful arguments can be made, and have been made, that however it may be ultimately defined, there *is* a zone of privacy surrounding every individual, a zone within which the State may protect him from intrusion by the press, with all its attendant publicity. Indeed, the central thesis of the [1890] root article [in Harvard Law Review] by Warren and Brandeis was that the press was overstepping its prerogatives by publishing essentially private information and that there should be a remedy for the alleged abuses.

More compellingly, the century has experienced a strong tide running in favor of the so-called right of privacy. In 1967, we noted that "[i]t has been said that a 'right of privacy' has been recognized at common law in 30 States plus the District of Columbia and by statute in four States." . . . [By 1971] "[i]n one form or another, the right of privacy [was] . . . recognized and accepted in all but a very few jurisdictions." Nor is it irrelevant here that the right of privacy is no recent arrival in the jurisprudence of Georgia, which has embraced the right in some form since 1905 when the Georgia Supreme Court decided the leading case of *Pavesich v. New England Life Ins. Co.*

These are impressive credentials for a right of privacy, but we should recognize that we do not have at issue here an action for the invasion of privacy involving the appropriation of one's name or photograph, a physical or other tangible intrusion into a private area, or a publication of otherwise private information that is also false although perhaps not defamatory. The version of the privacy tort now before us—termed in Georgia "the tort of public disclosure"—is that in which the plaintiff claims the right to be free from unwanted publicity about his private affairs, which, although wholly true, would be offensive to a person of ordinary sensibilities. Because the gravamen of the claimed injury is the publication of information, whether true or not, the dissemination of which is embarrassing or otherwise painful to an individual, it is here that claims of privacy most directly confront the constitutional freedoms of speech and press. The face-off is apparent, and the appellants urge upon us the broad holding that the press may not be made criminally or civilly liable for publishing information that is neither false nor misleading but absolutely accurate, however damaging it may be to reputation or individual sensibilities.

. . . . Rather than address the broader question whether truthful publications may ever be subjected to civil or criminal liability consistently with the First and Fourteenth Amendments, or to put it another way, whether the State may ever define and protect an area of privacy free from unwanted publicity in the press, it is appropriate to focus on the narrower interface between press and privacy that this case presents, namely, whether the State may impose sanctions on the accurate publication of the name of a rape victim obtained from public records—more specifically, from judicial records which are maintained in connection with a public prosecution and which themselves are open to public inspection. We are convinced that the State may not do so.

In the first place, in a society in which each individual has but limited time and resources with which to observe at first hand the operations of his government, he relies necessarily upon the press to bring to him in convenient form the facts of those operations. Great responsibility is accordingly placed upon the news media to report fully and accurately the proceedings of government, and official records and documents open to the public are the basic data of governmental operations. Without the information provided by the press most of us and many of our representatives would be unable to vote intelligently or to register opinions on the administration of government generally. With respect to judicial proceedings in particular, the function of the press serves to guarantee the fairness of trials and to bring to bear the beneficial effects of public scrutiny upon the administration of justice.

Appellee has claimed in this litigation that the efforts of the press have infringed his right to privacy by broadcasting to the world the fact that his daughter was a rape victim. The commission of crime, prosecutions resulting from it, and judicial proceedings arising from the prosecutions, however, are without question events of legitimate concern to the public and consequently fall within the responsibility of the press to report the operations of government.

The special protected nature of accurate reports of judicial proceedings has repeatedly been recognized. This Court, in an opinion written by MR. JUSTICE DOUGLAS, has said:

"A trial is a public event. What transpires in the court room is public property. If a transcript of the court proceedings had been published, we suppose none would claim that the judge could punish the publisher for contempt. And we can see no difference though the conduct of the attorneys, of the jury, or even of the judge himself, may have reflected on the court. *Those who see and hear what transpired can report it with impunity.* There is no special perquisite of the judiciary which enables it, as distinguished from other institutions of democratic government, to suppress, edit, or censor events which transpire in proceedings before it" (emphasis added).

The developing law surrounding the tort of invasion of privacy recognizes a privilege in the press to report the events of judicial proceedings. The Warren and Brandeis article noted that the proposed new right would be limited in the same manner as actions for libel and slander where such a publication was a privileged communication: "the right to privacy is not invaded by any publication made in a court of justice . . . and (at least in many jurisdictions) reports of any such proceedings would in some measure be accorded a like privilege.". . .

Thus even the prevailing law of invasion of privacy generally recognizes that the interests in privacy fade when the information involved already appears on the public record. The conclusion is compelling when viewed in terms of the First and Fourteenth Amendments and in light of the public interest in a vigorous press. The Georgia cause of action for invasion of privacy through public disclosure of the name of a rape victim imposes sanctions on pure expression—the content of a publication—and not conduct or a combination of speech and nonspeech elements that might otherwise be open to regulation or prohibition. The publication of truthful information available on the public record contains none of the indicia of those limited categories of expression, such as "fighting" words, which "are no essential part of any exposition of ideas, and are of such slight social value as a step to truth that any benefit that may be derived from them is clearly outweighed by the social interest in order and morality."

By placing the information in the public domain on official court records, the State must be presumed to have concluded that the public interest was thereby being served. Public records by their very nature are of interest to those concerned with the administration of government, and a public benefit is performed by the reporting of the true contents of the records by the media. The freedom of the press to publish that information appears to us to be of critical importance to our type of government in which the citizenry is the final judge of the proper conduct of public business. In preserving that form of government the First and Fourteenth Amendments command nothing less than that the States may not impose sanctions on the publication of truthful information contained in official court records open to public inspection.

We are reluctant to embark on a course that would make public records generally available to the media but forbid their publication if offensive to the sensibilities of the supposed reasonable man. Such a rule would make it very difficult for the media to inform citizens about the public business and yet stay within the law. The rule would invite timidity and self-censorship and very likely lead to the suppression of many items that would otherwise be published and that should be made available to the public. At the very least, the First and Fourteenth Amendments will not allow exposing the press to liability for truthfully publishing information released to the public in official court records. If there are privacy interests to be protected in judicial proceedings, the States must respond by means which avoid public documentation or other exposure of private information. Their political institutions must weigh the interests in privacy with the interests of the public to know and of the press to publish. Once true information is disclosed in public court documents open to public inspection, the press cannot be sanctioned for publishing it. In this instance as in others reliance must rest upon the judgment of those who decide what to publish or broadcast.

Appellant Wassell based his televised report upon notes taken during the court proceedings and obtained the name of the victim from the indictments handed to him at his request during a recess in the hearing. Appellee has not contended that the name was obtained in an improper fashion or that it was not on an official court document open to public inspection. Under these circumstances, the protection of freedom of the press provided by the First and Fourteenth Amendments bars the State of Georgia from making appellants' broadcast the basis of civil liability.

Reversed.

City of Ontario v. Quon
SUPREME COURT OF THE UNITED STATES
130 S. Ct. 2619 (2010)

JUSTICE KENNEDY delivered the Court's opinion:

This case involves the assertion by a government employer of the right, in circumstances to be described, to read text messages sent and received on a pager the employer owned and issued to an employee. The employee contends that the privacy of the messages is protected by the ban on "unreasonable searches and seizures" found in the Fourth Amendment to the United States Constitution, made applicable to the States by the Due Process Clause of the Fourteenth Amendment. Though the case touches issues of far-reaching significance, the Court concludes it can be resolved by settled principles determining when a search is reasonable.

I

A

The City of Ontario (City) is a political subdivision of the State of California. The case arose out of incidents in 2001 and 2002 when respondent Jeff Quon was employed by the Ontario Police Department (OPD). He was a police sergeant and member of OPD's Special Weapons and Tactics (SWAT) Team. The City, OPD, and OPD's Chief, Lloyd Scharf, are petitioners here. As will be discussed, two respondents share the last name Quon. In this opinion "Quon" refers to Jeff Quon, for the relevant events mostly revolve around him.

In October 2001, the City acquired 20 alphanumeric pagers capable of sending and receiving text messages. Arch Wireless Operating Company provided wireless service for the pagers. Under the City's service contract with Arch Wireless, each pager was allotted a limited number of characters sent or received each month. Usage in excess of that amount would result in an additional fee. The City issued pagers to Quon and other SWAT Team members in order to help the SWAT Team mobilize and respond to emergency situations.

Before acquiring the pagers, the City announced a "Computer Usage, Internet and E-Mail Policy" (Computer Policy) that applied to all employees. Among other provisions, it specified that the City "reserves the right to monitor and log all network activity including e-mail and Internet use, with or without notice. Users should have no expectation of privacy or confidentiality when using these resources." In March 2000, Quon signed a statement acknowledging that he had read and understood the Computer Policy.

The Computer Policy did not apply, on its face, to text messaging. Text messages share similarities with e-mails, but the two differ in an important way. In this case, for instance, an e-mail sent on a City computer was transmitted through the City's own data servers, but a text message sent on one of the City's pagers was transmitted using wireless radio frequencies from an individual pager to a receiving station owned by Arch Wireless. It was routed through Arch Wireless' computer network, where it remained until the recipient's pager or cellular telephone was ready to receive the message, at which point Arch Wireless transmitted the message from the transmitting station nearest to the recipient. After delivery, Arch Wireless retained a copy on its computer servers. The message did not pass through computers owned by the City.

Although the Computer Policy did not cover text messages by its explicit terms, the City made clear to employees, including Quon, that the City would treat text messages the same way as it treated e-mails. At an April 18, 2002, staff meeting at which Quon was present, Lieutenant Steven Duke, the OPD officer responsible for the City's contract with Arch Wireless, told officers that messages sent on the pagers "are considered e-mail messages. This means that [text] messages would fall under the City's policy as public information and [would be] eligible for auditing." Duke's comments were put in writing in a memorandum sent on April 29, 2002, by Chief Scharf to Quon and other City personnel.

Within the first or second billing cycle after the pagers were distributed, Quon exceeded his monthly text message character allotment. Duke told Quon about the overage, and reminded him that messages sent on the pagers were "considered e-mail and could be audited." Duke said, however, that "it was not his intent to audit [an] employee's text messages to see if the overage [was] due to work related transmissions." Duke suggested that Quon could reimburse the City for the overage fee rather than have Duke audit the messages. Quon wrote a check to the City for the overage. Duke offered the same arrangement to other employees who incurred overage fees.

Over the next few months, Quon exceeded his character limit three or four times. Each time he reimbursed the City. Quon and another officer again incurred overage fees for their pager usage in August 2002. At a meeting in October, Duke told Scharf that he had become "'tired of being a bill collector.'" Scharf decided to determine whether the existing character limit was too low—that is, whether officers such

as Quon were having to pay fees for sending work-related messages—or if the overages were for personal messages. Scharf told Duke to request transcripts of text messages sent in August and September by Quon and the other employee who had exceeded the character allowance.

At Duke's request, an administrative assistant employed by OPD contacted Arch Wireless. After verifying that the City was the subscriber on the accounts, Arch Wireless provided the desired transcripts. Duke reviewed the transcripts and discovered that many of the messages sent and received on Quon's pager were not work related, and some were sexually explicit. Duke reported his findings to Scharf, who, along with Quon's immediate supervisor, reviewed the transcripts himself. After his review, Scharf referred the matter to OPD's internal affairs division for an investigation into whether Quon was violating OPD rules by pursuing personal matters while on duty.

The officer in charge of the internal affairs review was Sergeant Patrick McMahon. Before conducting a review, McMahon used Quon's work schedule to redact the transcripts in order to eliminate any messages Quon sent while off duty. He then reviewed the content of the messages Quon sent during work hours. McMahon's report noted that Quon sent or received 456 messages during work hours in the month of August 2002, of which no more than 57 were work related; he sent as many as 80 messages during a single day at work; and on an average workday, Quon sent or received 28 messages, of which only 3 were related to police business. The report concluded that Quon had violated OPD rules. Quon was allegedly disciplined.

. . .

II

The Fourth Amendment states: "The right of the people to be secure in their persons, houses, papers, and effects, against unreasonable searches and seizures, shall not be violated. . . . ." It is well settled that the Fourth Amendment's protection extends beyond the sphere of criminal investigations. "The Amendment guarantees the privacy, dignity, and security of persons against certain arbitrary and invasive acts by officers of the Government," without regard to whether the government actor is investigating crime or performing another function. The Fourth Amendment applies as well when the Government acts in its capacity as an employer.

The Court discussed this principle in *O'Connor v. Ortega* (1987). There a physician employed by a state hospital alleged that hospital officials investigating workplace misconduct had violated his Fourth Amendment rights by searching his office and seizing personal items from his desk and filing cabinet. All Members of the Court agreed with the general principle that "[i]ndividuals do not lose Fourth Amendment rights merely because they work for the government instead of a private employer." A majority of the Court further agreed that "'special needs, beyond the normal need for law enforcement,'" make the warrant and probable-cause requirement impracticable for government employers.

[In *O'Connor* a] . . . four-Justice plurality concluded that the correct analysis has two steps. First, because "some government offices may be so open to fellow employees or the public that no expectation of privacy is reasonable," a court must consider "[t]he operational realities of the workplace" in order to determine whether an employee's Fourth Amendment rights are implicated. On this view, "the question whether an employee has a reasonable expectation of privacy must be addressed on a case-by-case basis." Next, where an employee has a legitimate privacy expectation, an employer's intrusion on that expectation "for noninvestigatory, work-related purposes, as well as for investigations of work-related misconduct, should be judged by the standard of reasonableness under all the circumstances."

. . .

Later, in the [*Treasury Employees* v.] *Von Raab* (1985) decision, the Court explained that "operational realities" could diminish an employee's privacy expectations, and that this diminution could be taken into consideration when assessing the reasonableness of a workplace search. In the two decades since *O'Connor*, however, the threshold test for determining the scope of an employee's Fourth Amendment rights has not been clarified further. . . .

III

A

Before turning to the reasonableness of the search, it is instructive to note the parties' disagreement over whether Quon had a reasonable expectation of privacy. The record does establish that OPD, at the outset, made it clear that pager messages were not considered private. The City's Computer Policy stated that "[u]sers should have no expectation of privacy or confidentiality when using" City computers. Chief Scharf's memo and Duke's statements made clear that this official policy extended to text messaging. The disagreement, at least as respondents see the case, is over whether Duke's later statements overrode the official policy. Respondents contend that because Duke told Quon that an audit would be unnecessary if Quon paid for the overage, Quon reasonably could expect that the contents of his messages would remain private.

At this point, were we to assume that inquiry into "operational realities" were called for, it would be necessary to ask whether Duke's statements could be taken as announcing a change in OPD policy, and if so, whether he had, in fact or appearance, the authority to make such a change and to guarantee the privacy of text messaging. It would also be necessary to consider whether a review of messages sent on police pagers, particularly those sent while officers are on duty, might be justified for other reasons, including performance evaluations, litigation concerning the lawfulness of police actions, and perhaps compliance with state open records laws. These matters would all bear on the legitimacy of an employee's privacy expectation.

The Court must proceed with care when considering the whole concept of privacy expectations in communications made on electronic equipment owned by a government employer. The judiciary risks error by elaborating too fully on the Fourth Amendment implications of emerging technology before its role in society has become clear. In *Katz* [*v. United States* (1967)], the Court relied on its own knowledge and experience to conclude that there is a reasonable expectation of privacy in a telephone booth. It is not so clear that courts at present are on so sure a ground. Prudence counsels caution before the facts in the instant case are used to establish far-reaching premises that define the existence, and extent, of privacy expectations enjoyed by employees when using employer-provided communication devices.

Rapid changes in the dynamics of communication and information transmission are evident not just in the technology itself but in what society accepts as proper behavior. As one *amici* brief notes, many employers expect or at least tolerate personal use of such equipment by employees because it often increases worker efficiency. Another *amicus* points out that the law is beginning to respond to these developments, as some States have recently passed statutes requiring employers to notify employees when monitoring their electronic communications. At present, it is uncertain how workplace norms, and the law's treatment of them, will evolve.

Even if the Court were certain that the *O'Connor* plurality's approach were the right one, the Court would have difficulty predicting how employees' privacy expectations will be shaped by those changes or the degree to which society will be prepared to recognize those expectations as reasonable. Cell phone and text message communications are so pervasive that some persons may consider them to be essential means or necessary instruments for self-expression, even self-identification. That might strengthen the case for an expectation of privacy. On the other hand, the ubiquity of those devices has made them generally affordable, so one could counter that employees who need cell phones or similar devices for personal matters can purchase and pay for their own. And employer policies concerning communications will of course shape the reasonable expectations of their employees, especially to the extent that such policies are clearly communicated.

A broad holding concerning employees' privacy expectations vis-à-vis employer-provided technological equipment might have implications for future cases that cannot be predicted. It is preferable to dispose of this case on narrower grounds. For present purposes we assume several propositions *arguendo*: First, Quon had a reasonable expectation of privacy in the text messages sent on the pager provided to him by

the City; second, petitioners' review of the transcript constituted a search within the meaning of the Fourth Amendment; and third, the principles applicable to a government employer's search of an employee's physical office apply with at least the same force when the employer intrudes on the employee's privacy in the electronic sphere.

B

Even if Quon had a reasonable expectation of privacy in his text messages, petitioners did not necessarily violate the Fourth Amendment by obtaining and reviewing the transcripts. Although as a general matter, warrantless searches "are *per se* unreasonable under the Fourth Amendment," there are "a few specifically established and well-delineated exceptions" to that general rule. The Court has held that the "'special needs'" of the workplace justify one such exception.

Under the approach of the *O'Connor* plurality, when conducted for a "noninvestigatory, work-related purpos[e]" or for the "investigatio[n] of work-related misconduct," a government employer's warrantless search is reasonable if it is "'justified at its inception'" and if "'the measures adopted are reasonably related to the objectives of the search and not excessively intrusive in light of'" the circumstances giving rise to the search. The search here satisfied the standard of the *O'Connor* plurality and was reasonable under that approach.

The search was justified at its inception because there were "reasonable grounds for suspecting that the search [was] necessary for a noninvestigatory work-related purpose." As a jury found, Chief Scharf ordered the search in order to determine whether the character limit on the City's contract with Arch Wireless was sufficient to meet the City's needs. This was, as the Ninth Circuit noted, a "legitimate work-related rationale." The City and OPD had a legitimate interest in ensuring that employees were not being forced to pay out of their own pockets for work-related expenses, or on the other hand that the City was not paying for extensive personal communications.

As for the scope of the search, reviewing the transcripts was reasonable because it was an efficient and expedient way to determine whether Quon's overages were the result of work-related messaging or personal use. The review was also not "'excessively intrusive.'" Although Quon had gone over his monthly allotment a number of times, OPD requested transcripts for only the months of August and September 2002. While it may have been reasonable as well for OPD to review transcripts of all the months in which Quon exceeded his allowance, it was certainly reasonable for OPD to review messages for just two months in order to obtain a large enough sample to decide whether the character limits were efficacious. And it is worth noting that during his internal affairs investigation, McMahon redacted all messages Quon sent while off duty, a measure which reduced the intrusiveness of any further review of the transcripts.

Furthermore, and again on the assumption that Quon had a reasonable expectation of privacy in the contents of his messages, the extent of an expectation is relevant to assessing whether the search was too intrusive. Even if he could assume some level of privacy would inhere in his messages, it would not have been reasonable for Quon to conclude that his messages were in all circumstances immune from scrutiny. Quon was told that his messages were subject to auditing. As a law enforcement officer, he would or should have known that his actions were likely to come under legal scrutiny, and that this might entail an analysis of his on-the-job communications. Under the circumstances, a reasonable employee would be aware that sound management principles might require the audit of messages to determine whether the pager was being appropriately used. Given that the City issued the pagers to Quon and other SWAT Team members in order to help them more quickly respond to crises—and given that Quon had received no assurances of privacy—Quon could have anticipated that it might be necessary for the City to audit pager messages to assess the SWAT Team's performance in particular emergency situations.

From OPD's perspective, the fact that Quon likely had only a limited privacy expectation, with boundaries that we need not here explore, lessened the risk that the review would intrude on highly private details of Quon's life. OPD's audit of messages on Quon's employer-provided pager was not nearly as intrusive as a search of his personal e-mail account or pager, or a wiretap on his home phone line, would have been. That the search did reveal intimate details of Quon's life does not make it unreasonable, for under the circumstances a reasonable employer would not expect that such a review would intrude on such matters. The search was permissible in its scope.

. . .

Because the search was motivated by a legitimate work-related purpose, and because it was not excessive in scope, the search was reasonable under the approach of the *O'Connor* plurality. For these same reasons—that the employer had a legitimate reason for the search, and that the search was not excessively intrusive in light of that justification—the Court also concludes that the search would be "regarded as reasonable and normal in the private-employer context." . . . The search was reasonable, and the Court of Appeals erred by holding to the contrary. Petitioners did not violate Quon's Fourth Amendment rights.

. . .

It is so ordered.

Chapter 7

When school shootings and other random acts of terror occasionally invade our communities, the media look like a pretty good target, for lawmakers and litigants alike. . . .

Bruce Sanford, First Amendment lawyer[1]

Hustler magazine publisher Larry Flynt printed an ad parody skewering Moral Majority leader Rev. Jerry Falwell. Falwell sued Flynt in a case that reached the U.S. Supreme Court. The Court ruled that Falwell, as a public figure, had to prove actual malice to win a lawsuit for intentional infliction of emotional distress.

Emotional Distress and Physical Harm

When Words and Pictures Hurt

Emotional Distress

The Development of
    Emotional Distress Suits
Intentional Infliction of
    Emotional Distress
Negligent Infliction of
    Emotional Distress

Physical Harm

Negligence
Incitement
Communications Decency
    Act

Other Dangers

Breach of Contract
Interference with Economic
    Advantage
Fraudulent
    Misrepresentation
Expanding Tort Law

Cases for Study

➤ *Hustler Magazine
    Inc. v. Falwell*
➤ *Rice v. Paladin
    Enterprises, Inc.*

Suppose . . .

. . . that a particularly raunchy men's magazine publishes what is supposed to be a satirical ad, a parody of a liquor advertisement that has celebrities discussing their "first time" to taste the liquor and also implying their first sexual experience. The satirical ad really is meant to skewer a well-known religious leader who long has advocated public morality. The ad, labeled "parody, not to be taken seriously," says the religious leader's "first time" was with his mother in an outhouse. Should the religious leader win a lawsuit against the magazine for libel, invasion of privacy and intentional infliction of emotional distress? Look for the answer to this question when the case of *Hustler Magazine v. Falwell* is discussed later in this chapter and the case is excerpted at the end of the chapter.

America is a litigious society. Americans sue for imagined slights to real harms, from spilling McDonald's hot coffee on themselves to medical malpractice.[2] They sue neighbors, businesses, lawyers, doctors and the media. News sources, people named in stories, people who believe articles or entertainment programs harmed them sue the media. Although libel and invasion of privacy claims are the most commonly filed suits based on media content and news gathering, the media are sued for a variety of other legal claims as well.

Emotional Distress

emotional distress Serious mental anguish.

Mass media content might harm a plaintiff in several ways. For example, a story could cause **emotional distress** even though it is not defamatory. Or a libelous story injuring a plaintiff's reputation also will upset him or her emotionally. Plaintiffs increasingly have difficulty winning libel and privacy suits. First Amendment principles—such as public plaintiffs having to prove actual malice, as discussed in Chapter 4—mean fewer plaintiffs will prevail in defamation suits. Plaintiffs usually do not win embarrassing facts and false light privacy cases. Several states have refused to allow plaintiffs to sue for false light, as noted in Chapter 6. Plaintiffs' lawyers searching for alternatives to libel and privacy claims may turn to the emotional distress tort.

intentional infliction of emotional distress Extreme and outrageous intentional or reckless conduct causing plaintiff severe emotional harm; public official and public figure plaintiff also must show actual malice on defendant's part.

negligent infliction of emotional distress Owing a duty to a plaintiff, breaching that duty and causing the plaintiff severe emotional harm.

reckless Word used to describe actions taken with no consideration of the legal harms that might result.

There are two categories of emotional distress suits: **intentional infliction of emotional distress** and **negligent infliction of emotional distress**. Just as a libel defendant may act with actual malice—that is, intentionally or recklessly publishing false material—so may an intentional or **reckless** act or statement cause emotional distress. Acting recklessly is not caring what the result of an action will be. Also, being negligent—an act or statement made by mistake or without anticipating the possible harm the act or statement could cause—may inflict emotional distress, just as a negligently published article may defame someone. Emotional distress cases sometimes are called "emotional injury" or "mental distress" suits.

The law defines "emotional distress" as being frightened or extremely anxious. A plaintiff must show the emotional injury is very serious or severe, that she or he experienced considerable mental pain or anguish.[3] Merely being upset, angry, embarrassed or resentful is not enough to win a lawsuit based on infliction of emotional distress.[4] However, emotions such as severe disappointment or an intense feeling of shame or humiliation may cause the extreme mental pain that the emotional distress tort requires.[5]

The Development of Emotional Distress Suits

The media can emotionally upset people in many ways, but only rarely will a person be able to sue successfully for emotional distress.[6] For example, a man saw a newspaper article that mentioned the funeral home that buried his wife. Looking at the accompanying photograph, he recognized his deceased wife lying in an open casket. He became emotionally upset because he had told the funeral home not to open his wife's casket for any reason. In another case, the head of a police and military training company claimed to be emotionally injured when a newspaper headline called him a militant. The widower and the company manager both sued, claiming the media caused them mental distress. Neither suit was successful. One court said the widower did not have a special relationship with the newspaper, which was required in that state to win a negligent infliction of emotional distress case. The other court said it was not outrageous to use the word "militant" in a headline.[7] In fact, that court said it would be nearly impossible for a plaintiff to win an intentional infliction of emotional distress case in New York state, where the plaintiff filed suit.

Courts denied all mental suffering claims when plaintiffs began bringing emotional distress cases a century ago. Today American law still severely limits a plaintiff's chances of winning damages for emotional injury. Plaintiffs do not often win emotional distress suits because mental suffering is difficult to prove. Tort law traditionally compensated plaintiffs for physical injuries to themselves or damage to their property caused by another person. A judge can see a broken arm caused by a traffic accident, but it is more difficult to measure the emotional trauma the accident caused. Judges feared plaintiffs would pretend to have emotional pain or would concoct emotional injuries. Because internal anguish cannot be seen, judges were concerned juries could be fooled into awarding damages for fictitious grievances. Even if a plaintiff could prove emotional injury, courts did not know what it was worth. How could a jury put a monetary value on emotional suffering? Judges also believed people should be able to overcome mental pain, not be compensated for having mental pain inflicted.

It is understandable that early 20th-century courts had doubts about compensating mental distress. Medical science then knew little about diagnosing or treating emotional injury.[8] In the 1920s and '30s, some jurisdictions began allowing plaintiffs to recover for emotional distress, but only if the mental pain directly resulted from a physical injury. A jury could find a defendant had to pay damages for hitting the plaintiff and could add more for the plaintiff's emotional suffering caused by being hit. As emotional distress law progressed, a few jurisdictions allowed compensation for emotional injuries even if the accompanying physical harm was slight,

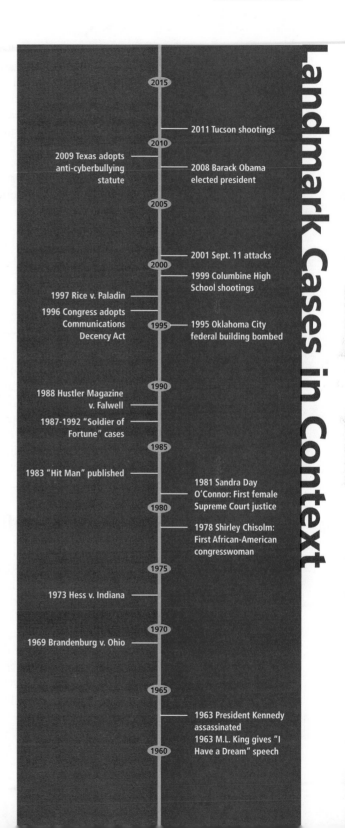

Landmark Cases in Context

2015

2011 Tucson shootings

2010

2009 Texas adopts anti-cyberbullying statute

2008 Barack Obama elected president

2005

2001 Sept. 11 attacks

2000

1999 Columbine High School shootings

1997 Rice v. Paladin

1996 Congress adopts Communications Decency Act

1995

1995 Oklahoma City federal building bombed

1990

1988 Hustler Magazine v. Falwell

1987-1992 "Soldier of Fortune" cases

1985

1983 "Hit Man" published

1981 Sandra Day O'Connor: First female Supreme Court justice

1980

1978 Shirley Chisolm: First African-American congresswoman

1975

1973 Hess v. Indiana

1970

1969 Brandenburg v. Ohio

1965

1963 President Kennedy assassinated
1963 M.L. King gives "I Have a Dream" speech

1960

such as the defendant brushing against the plaintiff. By the 1950s, courts realized advances in psychiatry's understanding of emotional injuries allowed mental distress to be identified and treated. An increasing number of state courts began allowing plaintiffs to recover for emotional distress and its physical manifestations, such as severe headaches or stomach disorders.[9]

In the last few decades, some jurisdictions have stopped requiring emotional distress to be connected with physical harm.[10] Currently, some jurisdictions recognize legal actions for intentional infliction of emotional distress alone—without accompanying physical injury or other offensive conduct—if the defendant's actions causing the emotional injury were outrageous and deliberate or reckless.

Some states also now permit negligent infliction of emotional distress suits if the defendant violates a plaintiff's legal rights, such as defaming the plaintiff or invading his privacy.[11] In these cases, the plaintiff must show the defendant acted negligently rather than intentionally or recklessly. However, some states, such as Mississippi, do not to allow negligent infliction of emotional distress lawsuits based on news coverage.[12]

SUMMARY

AT ONE TIME COURTS DID NOT ALLOW RECOVERY for emotional distress. Over time, courts began requiring physical injury to accompany emotional distress. Then judges allowed emotional distress suits if they arose from an invasion of a person's legal rights, such as libel or privacy. However, the requirements for a successful emotional distress lawsuit continue to differ among the states. There are two categories of emotional distress tort claims: intentional and negligent. Emotional distress is defined as severe mental anguish. ∎

Intentional Infliction of Emotional Distress

Intentional or reckless conduct that is extreme and outrageous and causes severe emotional harm can be grounds for a successful lawsuit.[13] The key to intentional infliction of emotional distress (IIED) is that the defendant's actions must have been outrageous—that is, actions a civilized society considers intolerable and beyond all bounds of decency.[14] Because this element of the tort is so important, some courts call the tort "outrage" instead of intentional infliction of emotional distress.

Usually insults do not amount to outrageous conduct, nor do words that annoy, or even statements that are mild threats. Courts understand the verbal jousting people experience in 21st-century America can cause hurt feelings. People are not always polite and considerate. The law expects people to ignore unpleasant comments. The high standard plaintiffs must meet—the defendant's conduct must be beyond all possible bounds of decency—is meant to prevent lawsuits being filed over mere insults, annoying comments and other remarks that are aggravating but not outrageous.[15] That some harms suffered in life do not rise to the level of legally actionable claims is captured in the Latin phrase *de minimus non curat lex*, "the law does not concern itself with trifles."

Outrageousness

Media defendants win most intentional infliction of emotional distress cases, primarily because courts do not find the media acted in an outrageous manner. As one federal district judge put it, "In order to make out an IIED claim the 'recitation of the facts to an average member of the community [should] arouse his resentment against the [defendant], and lead him to exclaim, 'Outrageous!'"[16] For example, there was nothing extreme or outrageous when a photographer on assignment for Harper's magazine took a picture of a soldier's body lying in an open casket at the soldier's funeral. The soldier, who died while serving in Iraq, was the first member of the Oklahoma National Guard to be killed in action in more than 50 years. Harper's published the photograph along with others showing Americans and Iraqis mourning those killed in the war. A federal appellate court rejected a lawsuit for intentional infliction of emotional distress brought by the soldier's family, ruling that the photograph was not "so extreme and outrageous as to go beyond all possible bounds of decency."[17]

Nor was it extreme and outrageous to say a person continually lied about a serious environmental offense. A book described a lawsuit in which a number of companies were accused of dumping toxic solvents into city water wells, causing several fatal cases of leukemia. The author wrote that one of the companies' owners "committed perjury," "lied" under oath, "lied about" dumping a toxic chemical and "covered up" by "destroying records." A federal appellate court held that the plaintiff had not met the high standard of proving it was "atrocious, and utterly intolerable in a civilized community" to publish the statements.[18] The book merely expressed the author's belief that the company owner "had not given truthful testimony."[19]

Broadcasting the identity of undercover narcotics police officers has not been found outrageous. A federal appellate court said publishing "upsetting but true news reports" is not "so extreme and outrageous as to permit recovery" in an intentional infliction of emotional distress lawsuit.[20]

Not even incorrectly suggesting a scientist sent anthrax-laced letters was deemed outrageous. In a series of newspaper columns, New York Times columnist Nicholas Kristof wrote that the Federal Bureau of Investigation (FBI) should focus on a Mr. Z in the investigation into the mailing of letters containing anthrax, which caused five deaths. The columnist later identified Mr. Z as

Points of Law

Intentional Infliction of Emotional Distress

Plaintiff's Case

Defendant's intentional or reckless conduct

1. Was extreme and outrageous—beyond the bounds of decency tolerated in civilized society,
2. Involved actual malice, if plaintiff is a public official or public figure, and
3. Caused plaintiff's severe emotional distress.

Defenses

There is no defense if plaintiff proves his or her case.

realWorld Law

Dateline, Texas: To Catch a Lawsuit?

A 2008 case shows that altering or creating events to generate a story may result in an intentional infliction of emotional distress lawsuit. The case began with the NBC "Dateline" series, "To Catch a Predator," a show that works with local police departments and an online watchdog group called Perverted Justice to identify and arrest sexual predators. "Dateline" uses decoys posing as teenagers online to lure individuals suspected of being sexual predators to a "sting house."[1]

Chris Hansen

One target was an assistant district attorney in Texas, Louis Conradt. Conradt had been in contact with a decoy and agreed to appear at a house. But when he did not show up, the host of the television series, Chris Hansen, insisted the local police obtain arrest and search warrants on Conradt's home.[2] The police chief agreed and the warrants were ready the next day.

When the warrants were ready to be served, ten members of the "To Catch a Predator" crew were at the home, including some who trespassed onto Conradt's property.[3] At least a dozen police officers were also present, including a SWAT team. They entered the home and announced their presence. Conradt emerged from a room holding a handgun, said he was not going to hurt anyone, then shot himself in the head. He died an hour later in a hospital.

A former detective with the local police department said, "I understand he took his own life, but I have a feeling that he took his own life when he looked out the door and saw there was a bunch of television cameras outside."[4]

Conradt's sister filed several claims against NBC, maintaining the network was responsible for her brother's death. NBC filed a motion requesting that all claims be dismissed. A U.S. district court judge granted the request in part. But given his description earlier in his opinion that "Dateline" "seeks to sensationalize and enhance the entertainment value" of confrontations with its targets,[5] and that the "mainstay of the show is public humiliation,"[6] it was not surprising that he ruled that some claims—those for intentional infliction of emotional distress and civil rights violations—would not be dismissed and that a trial based on those should proceed.[7] That led NBC to reach a settlement of the $105 million lawsuit. Terms were undisclosed.

1. Conradt v. NBC Universal, 536 F. Supp. 2d 380, 384 (S.D.N.Y. 2008).
2. *Id.* at 386.
3. *Id.*
4. Brian Stelter, *NBC Settles with Family That Blamed a TV Investigation for a Man's Suicide*, N.Y. TIMES, June 26, 2008, at C3.
5. Conradt v. NBC Universal, 536 F. Supp. 2d 380, 385 (S.D.N.Y. 2008).
6. *Id.*
7. *Id.* at 400.

Dr. Steven J. Hatfill, a research scientist employed by the U.S. Department of Defense. Hatfill sued the Times for intentional infliction of emotional distress and other torts. A federal appellate court found Hatfill could not show that publishing the columns constituted extreme and outrageous conduct.[21] The U.S. government exonerated Hatfill in 2008 and awarded him $4.6 million to settle a lawsuit he brought against the government.[22]

However, plaintiffs have proved outrageousness in several intentional inflic-tion of emotional distress cases brought against the media. In a 2010 case, Eran Best sued for intentional infliction of emotional distress based on an episode of the A&E network reality program, "Female Forces." The program follows female police officers through their workday. An episode focused on the Naper-ville, Ill., police department. A male Naperville officer stopped Best and called for a female officer, who arrived with a "Female Forces" camera crew. The officers gave Best a field sobriety test and arrested her for driving on a suspended driver's license. They handcuffed Best, searched her car and took her to the police sta-tion, all recorded by the camera crew. In the police car, the male officer told Best her arrest would not be on "Female Forces" if she did not sign a consent form. At the police station, a "Female Forces" producer urged Best to sign. Best repeatedly refused and did not sign a consent form. Despite that, footage of her arrest appeared on "Female Forces," including the sobriety test and her being handcuffed. Best's face is visible and her voice heard. The program also included a scene in which the two officers kidded about Best's "expensive taste" while searching her car. One officer said Best "likes Coach purses, bags, and shoes." The other commented on Best's driving a Jaguar. The court held Best could show outrageousness based on the program's airing footage that included the mocking comments, knowing Best objected and ignoring the assurances given her that the footage would not be televised.[23]

Also, a Florida court ruled that showing a murdered child's skull on televi-sion was outrageous.[24] Police in Florida had determined that an unearthed skull and dress belonged to a 6-year-old child abducted three years earlier. The police chief agreed to show the skull to a television news reporter, who videotaped the chief lifting the skull from a box. Some station personnel objected to airing the tape, but the news director overruled them. The child's unsuspecting family, who had attended the child's memorial service that day, happened to be watching when the tape aired. "The close-up of the skull was intentionally included to cre-ate sensationalism for the report. The close-up was gruesome and macabre," the court said.[25] No doubt the station's conduct "was outrageous in character and exceeded the bounds of decency so as to be intolerable in a civilized community," the court said.[26] Indeed, if these facts "do not constitute the tort of outrage, then there is no such tort," the court concluded.[27]

Courts have ruled that some newsgathering techniques by themselves are outrageous. For instance, a television news reporter and cameraman approached a house next door to one where earlier in the day a woman had murdered her two small children and then committed suicide. The reporter talked with a 5-year-old child, her 7-year-old sister and their 11-year-old babysitter, who were home without an adult present. The reporter asked the children what had happened next door. After the children said they knew nothing about it, the reporter said, "Well, the mom has killed the two little kids and herself." With the camera continuing to film, the reporter asked about the family next door. Although the station did not show the videotape, the children's parents sued for intentional infliction of emotional distress. Ruling in favor of the plaintiff,

Nancy Grace, television host and former prosecutor, is known for her victim's rights advocacy and outspoken style.

a California appellate court noted that the reporter approached the children suddenly and with no warning; a cameraman pointed bright lights at the children; the reporter pushed the door open; the reporter blurted out "information with emotionally devastating potential"; the children were not allowed to object to being interviewed on videotape and were too young to understand they could refuse.[28] The court said these actions could be seen as extreme and outrageous, especially because they involved children under 12 years old.

Entertainment programs as well as news reports may be the basis of intentional infliction of emotional distress cases. For example, a visitor to Howard Stern's radio program brought to the studio the cremated remains of a woman who had been a regular guest on Stern's show. Stern held up bone fragments, guessing aloud whether they came from the deceased's skull or ribs. Stern also told the guest to "chew on it," said he would "glue her together," remarked that one of the larger pieces of bone "looks like a piece of her head" and said another bone piece "looks like her ribs." The videotaped program also ran on Stern's cable television show. The woman's family sued Stern for intentional infliction of emotional distress. A New York state appellate court said the remarks were "crude" and ruled that a jury could decide that Stern's comments, combined with his handling the woman's remains for entertainment purposes, went beyond the bounds of decent behavior.[29]

In another case, two radio personalities named a woman the winner of "the ugliest bride" contest.[30] A New York state appellate court allowed the woman to sue for intentional infliction of emotional distress. The woman's bridal picture, along with others, appeared in the local paper the morning of the broadcast. The disc jockeys made belittling remarks about the woman and stated her full name, where she worked and the name of her supervisor. The court said the plaintiff was a private, not public, individual and that the disc jockeys' comments did not involve a matter of public interest. The court also suggested the disc jockeys deliberately chose to belittle the plaintiff because she and her supervisor worked for a company operating several competing radio stations in the area.

A court may find remarks are extreme and outrageous if the person who made the statements knew or should have known that the plaintiff was particularly susceptible to emotional distress. For example, after Melinda Duckett's 2-year-old son disappeared, CNN's Nancy Grace recorded a telephone conversation with Duckett. The recording was for Grace's show the following day. Just before the program aired, Duckett committed suicide. CNN ran the recording as

realWorld Law

Hurtful Speech and the First Amendment

In 2011 the U.S. Supreme Court rejected a claim of intentional infliction of emotional distress (and invasion of privacy) in a case involving pickets at the funeral of a Marine killed in Iraq.[1] The Marine's father, Albert Snyder, filed the claims against members of the Westboro Baptist Church. The church is led by Rev. Fred Phelps, who believes it is the church's duty to point out the public's sins. At the Snyder funeral, the church's signs included "Thank God for Dead Soldiers" and "You're Going to Hell." Writing for an eight-member majority, Chief Justice John G. Roberts noted the picketing was peaceful, was on public land 1,000 feet from the funeral site and ended before the service began. Another key factor for the Court was its conclusion that Westboro's speech was about matters of public concern: the political and moral conduct of the nation and its citizens. The Court cited precedent that "debate on public issues should be uninhibited, robust, and wide-open."[2] Speech on public issues, the Court said, occupies the highest rung of the hierarchy of First Amendment values and is entitled to special protection. "As a Nation we have chosen … to protect even hurtful speech on public debate to ensure that we do not stifle public debate."[3] Citing *Hustler v. Falwell,* the Court said the First Amendment is a defense against an intentional infliction of emotional distress claim.[4]

Members of the Westboro Baptist Church stand outside the U.S. Supreme Court building with signs typical of those they carry at military funerals.

1. Snyder v. Phelps, 131 S. Ct. 1207 (2011).
2. *Id.* at 1215 (citing New York Times Co. v. Sullivan, 376 U.S. 254, 270 (1964)).
3. *Id.* at 1220.
4. *Id.* at 1215 (citing Hustler Magazine, Inc. v. Falwell, 485 U.S. 46, 50–51 (1988)).

scheduled and several times after that. Duckett's estate, her parents and her sister sued CNN and Grace for intentional infliction of emotional distress. A federal district court allowed the suit to go forward. The court said if the defendants knew Duckett already suffered emotional and psychological stress because her son had disappeared, as the plaintiffs alleged, "'the potential for severe emotional distress is enormously increased.'"[31]

Not all untrue or exaggerated entertainment program content will lead to successful intentional infliction of emotional distress lawsuits. In one case, a federal appellate court ruled that inaccuracies in a television miniseries based on a novel about the Temptations, a singing group, were not extreme and outrageous.[32] The miniseries depicted the beaten body of David Ruffin, the group's lead singer, being thrown from a moving car in front of a hospital, where he died. The program also said no one claimed Ruffin's body at the morgue for a week after his death. Ruffin's family members said a limousine brought Ruffin to the hospital, the driver escorted Ruffin to the waiting area and one of Ruffin's children claimed his body within a few days after his death. The miniseries also incorrectly depicted Ruffin as an unmarried ruffian who was childless. Ruffin's relatives sued the series producers and others. The court held that even if the series included each of the inaccuracies the family cited, the producers did not act in a way that went beyond all bounds of decency.

Intentional or Reckless Action

In addition to proving that the defendant's actions or statements were outrageous, a plaintiff suing for intentional infliction of emotional distress must prove the defendant acted intentionally or recklessly.[33] If the defendant knew his or her actions or speech would cause emotional harm, a plaintiff can show the defendant acted intentionally. But the plaintiff does not have to show the plaintiff acted intentionally. A defendant only needed to act in a reckless way—a way that a reasonable person should have known could cause severe emotional distress.

For example, an 18-year-old girl was decapitated in an automobile accident. On Halloween, two California Highway Patrol (CHP) officers e-mailed to their friends and family nine pictures of the victim. Subsequently, the pictures went viral on the Internet. The family sued the CHP for intentional infliction of emotional distress. A California appellate court said that because the girl's father identified himself to officers at the accident scene and some people who saw the pictures on the Internet sent them, along with hateful comments, to the girl's family, the officers must have included information about the family with the photos. The plaintiffs could show, then, that the officers intentionally "directed their conduct toward" the family, causing them "severe emotional distress."[34]

Actual Malice Public officials and public figures have an additional hurdle to overcome to win an intentional infliction of emotional distress case. The U.S. Supreme Court requires public people to prove actual malice in addition to the tort's other elements. As discussed in Chapter 4, in *New York Times Co. v. Sullivan* the Court defined "actual malice" as publishing with knowledge of falsity or a reckless disregard for the truth.[35] The Court's intentional infliction of emotional distress decision, in *Hustler Magazine v. Falwell*, prevented the Rev. Jerry Falwell from winning his suit against Hustler magazine's publisher, Larry Flynt.[36] Flynt published what he claimed was a parody of a Campari advertising campaign. Campari, a liquor manufacturer, published ads in which celebrities discussed their "first time," an obvious double entendre about tasting Campari and having sex.

In Flynt's satire, Falwell, the leader of a national organization named the Moral Majority, described his "first time" as being with his mother in an outhouse. The magazine portrayed Falwell, who was known for speaking out against immorality, as a hypocrite for engaging in immoral activities. Hustler included a

realWorld Law

The "Pornographer" and His Attorney

Allan Isaacman (the attorney representing Hustler at the Supreme Court in *Hustler Magazine v. Falwell*):

Losing the intentional infliction of emotional distress [at trial] was easy to explain because Flynt, in his deposition, said he intended to assassinate the character of Falwell—tried to hurt him in his profession and that was his whole purpose. He also said in his deposition testimony that he meant it as a factual statement, and it wasn't intended to be a parody. He said he had witnesses to Falwell having sex with his mother in an outhouse. [Flynt] did everything he could to make it tough for us to win the case.

Larry Flynt (Hustler publisher):

I actually thought I was going to lose the case, and I'm not just saying that. I saw it was the preacher versus the pornographer, and I felt that there was no way I would win that case. But after being able to analyze it since, I realized what happened. First of all, had they come down on the side of Jerry Falwell, the mainstream press would have been in chaos. That means that in order to collect damages, you didn't have to prove libel, you only had to prove intentional infliction of emotional distress. So what would that do to Jay Leno's monologue or David Letterman or "Saturday Night Live"? I think that the justices could see far enough ahead to realize what a ruling the other way would have meant.[1]

---

1. Joseph Russomanno, Speaking Our Minds: Conversations with People Behind Landmark First Amendment Cases 179, 188 (Mahwah, N.J.: Lawrence Erlbaum Associates, 2002).

disclaimer saying "ad parody—not to be taken seriously," and the magazine's table of contents cited the page as "Fiction—Ad and Personality Parody."

Falwell sued Flynt for libel, appropriation and intentional infliction of emotional distress. A federal district court jury rejected the libel claim because the satire was so outlandish no one would believe it was a statement of fact. And while the court also ruled that Falwell could not win on the appropriation part of his lawsuit, it allowed the emotional distress claim to proceed. At trial on that issue, a jury said Flynt intentionally inflicted emotional distress, and it awarded Falwell $100,000 in compensatory damages and $100,000 in punitive damages.[37] A federal appellate court affirmed, saying the satire was outrageous and intentionally published.[38]

But the Supreme Court reversed that decision, holding that as a public figure Falwell had to present proof of actual malice.[39] The Court found that, as satire, the

Points of Law

Parody or Satire?

The Supreme Court has explained that there is a difference between "parody" (in which the copyrighted work is the target) and "satire" (in which the copyrighted work is merely used to poke fun at another target): "Parody needs to mimic an original to make its point, and so has some claim to use the creation of its victim's (or collective victims') imagination, whereas satire can stand on its own two feet and so requires justification for the very act of borrowing."[1]

---

1. Campbell v. Acuff-Rose Music, 510 U.S. 569, 580–81 (1994).

Jerry Falwell talks about his first time.*

FALWELL: My first time was in an outhouse outside Lynchburg, Virginia.

INTERVIEWER: Wasn't it a little cramped?

FALWELL: Not after I kicked the goat out.

INTERVIEWER: I see. You must tell me all about it.

FALWELL: I never really expected to make it with Mom, but then after she showed all the other guys in town such a good time, I figured, "What the hell!"

INTERVIEWER: But your mom? Isn't that a bit odd?

FALWELL: I don't think so. Looks don't mean that much to me in a woman.

INTERVIEWER: Go on.

FALWELL: Well, we were drunk off our God-fearing asses on Campari, ginger ale and soda—that's called a Fire and Brimstone—at the time. And Mom looked better than a Baptist whore with a $100 donation.

INTERVIEWER: Campari in the crapper with Mom . . . how interesting. Well, how was it?

FALWELL: The Campari was great, but Mom passed out before I could come.

INTERVIEWER: Did you ever try it again?

FALWELL: Sure . . .

lots of times. But not in the outhouse. Between Mom and the shit, the flies were too much to bear.

INTERVIEWER: We meant the Campari.

FALWELL: Oh, yeah. I always get sloshed before I go out to the pulpit. You don't think I could lay down all that bullshit sober, do you?

© 1983—Imported by Campari U.S.A., New York, NY 48° proof Spirit Aperitif (Liqueur)

Campari, like all liquor, was made to mix you up. It's a light, 48-proof, refreshing spirit, just mild enough to make you drink too much before you know you're schnockered. For your first time, mix it with orange juice. Or maybe some white wine. Then you won't remember anything the next morning. **Campari. The mixable that smarts.**

CAMPARI **You'll never forget your first time.**

*AD PARODY—NOT TO BE TAKEN SERIOUSLY

The parody that prompted Jerry Falwell to sue Larry Flynt and Hustler magazine.

magazine's Campari ad was protected by the First Amendment, just as political cartoons are. Biting, even hurtful, humor is the stock-in-trade of satirical works, the Court found, and it was simply not possible to create a constitutionally valid distinction between political cartoons and satires and the arguably tasteless Campari ad spoof. If juries were permitted to award damages for such satires, the Court warned, jurors could decide what was outrageous based on their political leanings, which would violate the First Amendment.

However, not all parodies and satires were protected, the *Falwell* Court said. A public figure or public official who could prove that a satire included a false statement of fact published with actual malice could win a lawsuit for intentional infliction of emotional distress. Because the jury in this case had found there were no factual statements in the piece—it was just a parody—Falwell could not successfully sue for intentional infliction of emotional distress.

The Court also suggested Falwell may have used intentional infliction of emotional distress as an expedient replacement for his rejected libel claim. If public figures had to prove actual malice to win libel cases, they should carry that burden for intentional infliction as well, the Court implied. In both torts, actual malice served to protect the press's First Amendment right to make caustic comments about public people.

EXTREME OR OUTRAGEOUS CONDUCT THAT IS DONE either intentionally or recklessly and results in severe emotional harm may amount to intentional infliction of emotional distress. The most important element is the defendant's actions. Outrageous actions, defined as being beyond all bounds of decency, may lead to successful intentional infliction of emotional distress suits. A plaintiff who is especially susceptible to emotional harm may successfully sue if the defendant knew of the plaintiff's vulnerability. In addition to proving outrageous intentional or reckless conduct and severe emotional harm, public officials and public figures must show the defendant acted with actual malice to win an intentional infliction of emotional distress case. The First Amendment likely will not allow successful intentional infliction of emotional distress based on satires and parodies. In a few instances, journalists and media personalities have lost intentional infliction of emotional distress lawsuits in cases not involving public plaintiffs. ■

Negligent Infliction of Emotional Distress

If one person accidentally causes another emotional harm, the injured person may sue using a tort called negligent infliction of emotional distress, or negligence. The law asks whether the defendant should have anticipated that her or his careless action would injure the plaintiff. More formally, a plaintiff suing for negligent infliction of emotional distress must prove (1) the defendant had a duty to use due care, (2) the defendant negligently breached that duty, (3) the breach caused the plaintiff's injury, and (4) the breach was the proximate cause of the plaintiff's severe emotional distress.[40]

A "duty of due care" means the defendant should have foreseen that negligence could cause harm to the person or people to whom he or she owed a duty. Breaching the duty means the defendant did not act as a reasonable person would. Causing the plaintiff's emotional distress means the defendant's actions were the direct reason the plaintiff was emotionally harmed. This may be called "cause-in-fact." Proximate cause is the law's way of asking if it is reasonable to conclude the defendant caused the plaintiff's injury. Negligent infliction of emotional distress suits against the media often turn on the proximate cause question. Courts usually find that actions taken by a media organization are only tangentially related to the plaintiff's injury. If the connection between what the organization did and how the plaintiff was injured is too indirect to find the mass medium responsible, the plaintiff cannot prove proximate cause.

Courts in some states also require plaintiffs to show a degree of physical harm. The harm may be that the defendant physically injured (or even just touched) the plaintiff, causing emotional harm, or that the defendant caused emotional harm resulting in physical symptoms.[41] The plaintiff's problem is convincing courts that

Points of Law

Negligent Infliction of Emotional Distress

Plaintiff's Case

- The defendant had a duty to use due care,

- Negligently breached that duty,

- Causing the plaintiff's severe emotional distress, and

- The breach was the proximate cause of the plaintiff's emotional distress.

Defense

There is no defense if plaintiff proves the case.

an emotional distress claim is real. Courts agree the negligent infliction of emotional distress tort is caught between two important concerns. First, the law wants to compensate people whose emotional injuries are caused by others' negligence. But second, judges want to avoid suits for trivial, de minimus, harms or fraudulent emotional harm claims.[42] These competing interests have "caused inconsistency and incoherence in the law," one court said.[43]

The competing interests are reflected in two approaches applicable to suits against the media for negligent infliction of emotional distress. Some jurisdictions require proof that physical harm caused emotional injury, or vice versa. Examples include not being able to sleep, having an upset stomach, experiencing weight loss or not being able to work.[44] Either way, to be sure the emotional injury is real, courts in these jurisdictions want proof of a physical injury connected with emotional distress.

Other jurisdictions require proof that the defendant acted negligently and that it was reasonably foreseeable such conduct would cause the plaintiff severe emotional distress. These courts do not require a physical injury or a subsequent physical manifestation of emotional distress.[45] Under this scheme, plaintiffs can allege negligent infliction of emotional distress if it accompanies another tort, such as defamation or invasion of privacy.[46]

Negligent infliction of emotional distress suits against the media usually fail. However, two cases show plaintiffs can be successful if the court does not require a physical injury to be connected with emotional harm. In one instance, a television station produced a report about rape. Station employees asked two rape victims if they would consent to interviews, promising to disguise the women's faces and voices. The women agreed to participate, but after seeing a promotional ad about the program the employer of one of the rape victims recognized her face and voice. After the first interview ran, friends of the second rape victim said they recognized her, particularly through her voice. One of the women complained to the station and the producers assured her that future broadcasts would better disguise the interviewees. Nevertheless, both women were again recognized in the next program, which failed to disguise their voices and included a brief shot of one victim's face. The women said they were emotionally distraught. A New York state appellate court allowed them to sue for negligent infliction of emotional distress.[47]

In a second case, in preparing a directory for the 15-year reunion of the class of 1975, Yale University's Alumni Records Office mailed questionnaires to the graduates. One returned questionnaire included a graduate's name along with the statement, "I have come to terms with my homosexuality and the reality of AIDS in my life. I am at peace." The questionnaire response was a hoax; it was not completed by the person named on the questionnaire. However, the directory mailed to the 1975 graduates included the plaintiff's name along with the incorrect information. The person named on the hoax questionnaire sued Yale for negligent infliction of emotional distress. A federal district court held that a jury could find Yale had a duty to carefully review personal statements and to confirm whether unusual statements were valid.[48] A jury could find Yale acted negligently by not checking the questionnaires, the court said. A reasonable person could foresee that someone might submit a false questionnaire that would cause severe emotional injury. The court allowed the graduate to proceed with a suit for negligent infliction of emotional distress.

Plaintiffs also have successfully sued for negligent infliction of emotional distress when the media have put them in harm's way. For example, after a woman had been physically attacked, but before the assailant was apprehended by police, a newspaper published the woman's name and address. After the newspaper published the article, the assailant terrorized his victim several more times. A Missouri appellate court upheld the victim's negligent infliction of emotional distress suit.[49]

Similarly, a woman witnessed a murder. A newspaper published her name while the murderer remained at large. A California appellate court ruled that the First Amendment did not protect the newspaper against the witness' negligent infliction of emotional distress lawsuit.[50]

SUMMARY

A plaintiff may successfully sue for infliction of emotional distress, even if caused accidentally, if the defendant acted negligently. A plaintiff suing for negligent infliction of emotional distress must prove the defendant had a duty of due care and breached that duty, causing the plaintiff's severe emotional distress, and that there is proximate cause to find the defendant liable for the tort. Some states require that physical harm accompany emotional trauma. In some jurisdictions even slight touching of the plaintiff will be enough. In some other states it is sufficient that another tort, such as libel or privacy, cause the emotional harm. Most jurisdictions find the media do not owe a duty to individuals because the media cannot know what particular individuals will hear or see the mass medium. ■

Physical Harm

Americans have been concerned for nearly eight decades about media violence causing real-life violence. Movies were the focus in the 1920s, comic books in the 1950s, music lyrics in the 1990s and video games in the early 21st century. A Federal Trade Commission (FTC) report concluded that the products with violent content were marketed and advertised to children by the video game, music recording and movie industries. The FTC report said researchers "generally have agreed that exposure to violence in entertainment media alone does not cause a child to commit a violent act and that it is not the sole, or even necessarily the most important, factor contributing to youth aggression." But the report recognized that studies show "a high correlation between exposure to media violence and aggressive and, at times, violent behavior."[51]

Despite inconclusive research results, courts continually are asked to make a connection between media content and physical violence. The media have been blamed—and sued—for encouraging people to injure or kill others.[52] For example, a mother claimed a role-playing game had caused a young person to kill her son, and a family contended a movie had inspired two young people to engage in a killing spree. Lawsuits also claim people injure or kill themselves because of media content. Media violence cases may arise from copycat situations—the plaintiff arguing that injury resulted from imitating media content such as that in the movies "Natural Born Killers" and "The Basketball Diaries," and video games such as "Doom" and "Mortal Kombat."

This pattern of lawsuits began three decades ago. When he was 13 years old, Ronny Zamora shot and killed his 83-year-old neighbor. Zamora's parents sued the major television networks—ABC, CBS and NBC. The parents claimed their son "became involuntarily addicted to and 'completely subliminally intoxicated' by the extensive viewing of television violence." They said the networks failed to exercise "ordinary care to prevent Ronny Zamora from being 'impermissibly stimulated, incited and instigated' to duplicate the atrocities he viewed on television."[53] In 1979 a federal district court said the networks could not be held responsible for Zamora's actions.

Media violence lawsuits often are not successful. Courts usually find the media did not act negligently or did not intend to cause harm. However, recently some jurisdictions have refused to dismiss suits alleging that the media caused injury or death.

Negligence

Plaintiffs suing the media for causing physical harm most often argue the defendants negligently distributed material leading to injury or death. These suits are based on the tort of negligence, discussed earlier in this chapter. The plaintiff must show the media defendant had a duty of due care, negligently breached that duty, caused the plaintiff's physical injury and proximately caused the injury.

For example, the *Zamora* court rejected the argument that television networks had a duty to stop making violent programs available to the public. The court said it would be against public policy to require networks to determine what would be too violent and against the networks' First Amendment rights to limit their ability to provide their audiences a breadth of programming.[54]

Similarly, a court did not find a television network negligent when a young girl was raped after a television film showed a rape scene. NBC aired the film "Born Innocent." Set in a girl's reformatory, the film implied that four inmates used a toilet plunger to rape another girl. Four days later a 9-year-old girl suffered a similar attack, being raped with a bottle, at a San Francisco beach. The girl's parents sued NBC and the San Francisco station that broadcast the movie, claiming the defendants were negligent in showing the movie when children could watch it. A state appellate court said the First Amendment did not allow the argument that NBC had a duty to the raped girl.[55] Finding NBC negligent would cause television networks to engage in self-censorship, the court said.

Foreseeability

To determine whether a defendant had a duty to the plaintiff, courts often ask whether the defendant should have foreseen the plaintiff's injury. This means that if the person should have anticipated an action would cause harm, the person had a duty to protect others. But if a reasonable person could not have foreseen the harm, there is no duty. In a case arising from the 1999 shooting deaths of 12 students and one teacher at Columbine High School in Littleton, Colo., the family of the murdered teacher, William Sanders, sued video game and movie producers. The Sanders family said the student shooters, Eric Harris and Dylan Klebold, copied what they had seen in the movie "The Basketball Diaries," which includes a dream sequence of a high school student killing his teacher and several classmates. The family said Harris and Klebold also played a number of video games, such as "Mortal Kombat," "Mech Warrior," "Nightmare Creatures," "Doom," "Quake" and "Redneck Rampage." A federal district court rejected the suit, saying the media defendants did not have an obligation to protect Sanders.[56] The movie producers and game manufacturers could not have foreseen Harris and Klebold would commit illegal acts, the court ruled. The movie and video game producers, then, did not have a duty and so were not negligent.

In a similar case, a federal appellate court held there was insufficient proof that video game, movie production and Internet companies should have foreseen that their products could lead a 14-year-old boy to shoot several of his fellow high school students.[57] After arresting Michael Carneal for killing three people and wounding several more, police found that Carneal regularly had played violent interactive computer games, visited pornographic Internet sites and owned a videotape of the movie "The Basketball Diaries." The dead students' families and the wounded students sued the media companies, contending that Carneal's actions were a reaction to the violent media representations. The court said even if the contention were true, the defendants could not have foreseen

Leonardo DiCaprio starred as Jim Carroll in "The Basketball Diaries," a movie alleged to have inspired illegal acts. Lawsuits against the movie's producers have not been successful.

Carneal's response to the violent images. It is "simply too far a leap from shooting characters on a video screen . . . to shooting people in a classroom," the court said.[58] The defendants did not owe the students a duty of care because Carneal's actions were unforeseeable.

Three cases, all tied to classified advertisements in the magazine Soldier of Fortune, show how courts use the foreseeability element to determine whether the defendant had a duty. Soldier of Fortune publishes stories about hunting, war and guns. The magazine appeals to "a male who owns camouflage clothing and more than one gun."[59] In each decision, a court considered whether it was foreseeable that the ad would lead to physical injury. The magazine won the case in which a judge ruled criminal activity was not foreseeable. Plaintiffs won the two cases in which courts said physical harm was foreseeable.

In the first case, *Norwood v. Soldier of Fortune Magazine,* two people each published an advertisement. Michael Savage's ad said, "GUN FOR HIRE: 37 year old professional mercenary desires jobs. Vietnam Veteran. Discreet and very private. Bodyguard, courier, and other special skills. All jobs considered." The second ad said, "GUN FOR HIRE. NAM sniper instructor. SWAT. Pistol, rifle, security specialist, body guard, courier plus. All jobs considered, Privacy guaranteed." Norman Norwood claimed Larry Gray, and others Gray contacted through Savage's ad, conspired to kill Norwood. Several unsuccessful attempts on Norwood's life resulted in physical injuries, he said. A federal district court rejected the magazine's argument that its First Amendment rights protected publishing the ads.[60] The court said free speech is not absolute. Plaintiffs may recover damages if speech causes injuries. In refusing to throw out Norwood's suit, as Soldier of Fortune requested, the court said a jury could find the ads "had a substantial probability of ultimately causing harm to some individuals."[61] The magazine had a duty of due care because it was foreseeable that the ads could lead to physical injury.

In the second case, *Eimann v. Soldier of Fortune Magazine,* a federal appellate court took a different view of an advertisement.[62] John Wayne Hearn's Soldier of Fortune ad said, "EX-MARINES—67–69 'Nam Vets, Ex-DI, weapons specialist—jungle warfare, pilot, M.E., high risk assignments, U.S. or overseas." Hearn testified that he hoped the ad would bring an offer to train troops in South America. However, when Robert Black saw the ad and offered Hearn $10,000 to kill Black's wife, Hearn accepted and murdered Sandra Black. Sandra Black's mother and son sued the magazine. A jury found that Soldier of Fortune breached its duty, resulting in Sandra Black's death. The jury awarded $9.4 million in damages. The appellate court reversed. The magazine had "no duty to refrain from publishing a facially innocuous classified advertisement when the ad's context— at most—made its message ambiguous," the court held.[63] The magazine's burden in investigating all its advertisers and their ads to prevent criminal solicitation would be much greater than the unlikely possibility that an ad may result in physical harm. A reasonable person would not have foreseen that the ad might cause physical harm, the court ruled.

Finally, *Braun v. Soldier of Fortune* involved another Michael Savage ad, one identical to the ad in the *Norwood* case.[64] In this instance, a man contacted Savage through the ad and arranged to have Savage kill the man's business partner. Savage and others committed the murder. The murdered man's family sued the magazine. A jury awarded $12.4 million, which the trial judge reduced to $4.4 million. The jury properly found that "the advertisement on its face would have alerted a reasonably prudent publisher to the clearly identifiable risk of harm to the public" the ad posed, a federal appellate court held.[65] The court said that while Soldier of Fortune did not have a duty to investigate every ad submitted for publication, it was obligated to determine whether, based on the ad's language, publishing the ad would create an unreasonable risk of causing violent crime.

Plaintiffs rarely are successful when suing the media for injury caused by false information. For example, a book publisher had no obligation to confirm the accuracy of all information in a book about mushrooms, a federal appellate court held, although people became seriously ill after eating mushrooms the book said were edible.[66]

Proximate Cause A plaintiff bringing a negligence suit must prove it is reasonable to find that the defendant caused the plaintiff's harm. A court decides if there is a direct relationship between the defendant's action and the plaintiff's injury. This direct relationship is called **proximate cause.** In one case, a teenager committed suicide while listening to an Ozzy Osbourne album that includes the song "Suicide Solution." The song's lyrics say in part, "Suicide is the only way out." The teenager's parents sued Osbourne and his record company. A California appellate court said there was not a close connection between the recording and the suicide.[67] The court noted that Osbourne had composed and recorded the song years before the teenager's death. That made the connection between the recording and the suicide too tenuous to show proximate cause.[68] It was not reasonable to blame Osbourne for the teenager's death.

A connection between a defendant's actions and a plaintiff's injuries can be broken by unanticipated incidents. Courts often refuse to find proximate cause if there is an unforeseeable event intervening between the defendant's act and the plaintiff's later physical injury. In one case a mother whose son committed suicide sued the manufacturer of "Dungeons and Dragons," a game in which players assume roles in adventures illustrated in booklets.[69] The mother said her son lost touch with reality because of his devotion to the game. However, the child's suicide was an independent action, a federal appellate court said, not caused by playing the game. That is, the child's decision to commit suicide was an intervening cause between playing the games and the child's taking his life.

proximate cause Determining whether it is reasonable to conclude the defendant's actions led to the plaintiff's injury.

Points of Law

Proximate Cause

In a negligence case, the plaintiff must prove both "cause" and "proximate cause." Cause is straightforward. If the defendant's actions led to the plaintiff's injury, the defendant caused the injury. But courts do not say every defendant who caused an injury is liable. That is because the plaintiff may not be able to prove the second element: proximate cause.

SUMMARY

PLAINTIFFS SUING THE MEDIA FOR CAUSING PHYSICAL injury or death may claim the media were negligent. To establish liability, the plaintiff must prove the defendant had a duty of care that was breached and that the breach was the proximate cause of physical harm. Courts may decide whether the defendant had a duty of care by determining whether a reasonable person would have foreseen the resulting harm. Courts also must be convinced the defendant caused the plaintiff's harm. Proximate cause is the most difficult element to prove. Proximate cause means it is reasonable to find the defendant responsible for causing the plaintiff's harm. ∎

Incitement

An alternative to showing that a media defendant acted negligently is to prove the defendant incited harm. First Amendment scholar David Anderson suggests that the two legal concepts—negligence and incitement—are related rather than separate.[70] Anderson says courts first should determine whether a plaintiff is able to prove that a mass medium's negligence caused physical injury. If the plaintiff cannot prove negligence, the defendant wins and the case is over. But if the plaintiff can prove all elements of the negligence tort, the defendant then will claim First Amendment protection. To counter the defendant's argument, the plaintiff will insist that the incitement test removes the First Amendment shield, Anderson says. That is, the First Amendment does not protect communication that incites harm.

However, jurisdictions using the incitement test often skip the negligence analysis. Many courts go straight to deciding if the mass medium intentionally meant for harm to happen and whether imminent harm likely would result from the defendant's actions.

As discussed in Chapter 3, the U.S. Supreme Court established the incitement test in its *Brandenburg v. Ohio* and *Hess v. Indiana* decisions. In *Brandenburg*, a Ku Klux Klan leader was arrested and convicted for declaring at a Klan rally that "revengeance" might have to be taken against politicians and for making a number of derogatory remarks about African-Americans and Jews. The U.S. Supreme Court overturned the conviction. The Court said the government may not punish advocacy unless it is "directed to inciting or producing imminent lawless action and is likely to incite or produce such action."[71]

In the second case, at an anti–Vietnam War rally Gregory Hess used profane language in saying that the crowd should wait until a later time to take over a public street. Hess made his remark after sheriff's officers moved demonstrators from the street to the sidewalks. The sheriff overheard Hess, who was not talking to the gathering generally or to anyone in particular, and arrested him for disorderly conduct. A jury convicted Hess. The U.S. Supreme Court overturned the verdict, holding that the First Amendment protected Hess' comments because his words were not intended to, and not likely to, provoke an imminent violation of the law.[72]

If a court uses the incitement test when a mass medium is sued for causing physical harm, a plaintiff likely will not win. With rare exceptions, such as the "Hit Man" case discussed later in this chapter, courts have not found that a mass media defendant incited physical injury.[73] Plaintiffs generally have not convinced courts that media companies intentionally encourage people to harm themselves or others after being exposed to media content.

The movie "Natural Born Killers," starring Woody Harrelson (right) and directed by Oliver Stone (left), did not incite violence, a state appellate court ruled.

Intending to Incite

The *Brandenburg/Hess* incitement test requires a plaintiff to show that the media defendant intentionally meant to cause harm. Courts consistently reject this notion. For example, two people robbed a convenience store. During the robbery the store clerk was shot and seriously wounded. The clerk claimed the movie "Natural Born Killers" inspired her assailants. The woman who shot the store clerk admitted the movie motivated her and her boyfriend to commit violence. The film portrays a man and a woman engaging in a crime spree, killing people they do not know, and being glorified by the media after they are apprehended. The film's characters then foment a prison riot during which they escape from prison.[74] A state appellate court dismissed the store clerk's lawsuit.[75] The movie may exalt and glamorize violence, the court said, but the movie's fantasy violence did not urge or encourage viewers to engage in unlawful or violent activity. Nor did the movie order or command anyone to immediately commit a crime. The incitement test cannot be met without proving that the movie producers intentionally urged immediate unlawful activity, the court held.

In another case, Hustler magazine published an article titled "Orgasm of Death," describing autoerotic asphyxiation. A 14-year-old boy accidentally hanged himself in his closet with a copy of Hustler on the floor open to the story. The boy's parents sued Hustler, but a federal appellate court held that the article did not incite the boy's actions.[76] The court said not only did the magazine not urge readers to perform the act described but repeatedly warned not to attempt autoerotic asphyxiation.

Courts have not found incitement even when the media knew criminal activity might be related to media content. For example, Paramount Pictures continued distributing the movie "The Warriors" despite knowing about two killings

realWorld Law

Cyberbullying

Megan Meier, 13 years old, and Sarah Drew were classmates in 2006. Sarah's mother, Lori, used MySpace to establish a profile for a nonexistent 16-year-old boy Lori Drew called Josh Evans. The profile included a photograph of a boy posted without that boy's knowledge or approval. Using Josh's MySpace, Drew contacted Megan, flirted with her, then said he was moving away, no longer liked her and that "the world would be a better place without her in it." The day those comments were posted, Megan committed suicide by hanging herself with a belt. Federal prosecutors charged Drew with violating the Computer Fraud and Abuse Act (CFAA)[1] that makes it illegal to use a computer in excess of authorization to commit a crime or tort. The prosecutors said Drew violated MySpace's rules prohibiting posting of anything that "harasses or advocates harassment of another person, solicits personal information from anyone under 18, provides information that you know is false or misleading, or includes a photograph of another person that you have posted without that person's consent." At trial, the jury cleared Drew of the most serious charges but found her guilty of three misdemeanors. The trial judge, however, found the CFAA vague and dismissed all charges against Drew.[2]

In response to Megan's suicide, several states considered anti-cyberbullying statutes. Texas' 2009 statute makes it illegal (1) to use another's name without permission, (2) to create a Webpage, open a profile on a social networking site or send a digital communication, such as an e-mail message, (3) intending to harm, defraud, intimidate or threaten another person. The law also forbids sending a digital communication that includes, without permission, another's name, domain address, phone number or other identifying information.[3]

---

1. 18 U.S.C. § 1030.
2. United States v. Drew, 259 F.R.D. 449 (C.D. Calif. 2009).
3. Tex. Penal Code § 33.07.

near California theaters that showed the film. The movie includes many scenes of young people fighting with guns, knives and other weapons. Two days after the California murders, a teenager was stabbed and killed by another youth after leaving a showing of "The Warriors" in Boston. The murdered boy's father sued Paramount, claiming the movie producer incited violence by keeping the movie in circulation despite knowing it caused criminal activity. Massachusetts' highest court held that the film's fictional portrayal of gang warfare did not constitute incitement.[77] The movie did not advocate violent or unlawful acts, the court said, and therefore it retained its First Amendment protection.

In the only decision of its kind, a court said a book publisher encouraged a murderer.[78] The publisher said it intended for criminals to purchase and use a book, "Hit Man: A Technical Manual for Independent Contractors," to plan and carry out real murders. When a contract killer did just that, a federal appellate court said the book publisher had aided and abetted murder. The court said the First Amendment did not protect media that aid in the commission of a crime. In this case, after Paladin Press published "Hit Man," James Perry bought and read it. Acting as a contract killer, Perry mimicked the book's detailed, graphic instructions almost to the letter in brutally murdering a woman, her 8-year-old quadriplegic son and the son's nurse. The victims' relatives sued Paladin Press.

Paladin Press argued that because the First Amendment completely protected it, the publisher could not be responsible for any crimes connected to "Hit Man." The appellate court rejected Paladin's argument, saying that "every court that has addressed the issue" agrees the First Amendment does not necessarily prevent finding a mass medium liable for assisting a crime, even if that aid "takes the form of the spoken or written word."[79] After the court's ruling and before the trial began, Paladin Press settled the case for $5 million.[80]

Imminent Lawless Action The incitement test requires a plaintiff to show that media content would result in violent or unlawful activity immediately after the criminal was exposed to it. That is nearly impossible to prove in court. The *Brandenburg* and *Hess* decisions were meant to protect speech unless a speaker so inflamed a crowd that people responded to their emotions and immediately committed illegal acts. Media content does not ordinarily provoke such a rapid response. After seeing, reading or hearing media material, there is time to think before taking action, even time to have someone else prevent a person from committing violent acts.

For example, after a young friend stabbed to death a 13-year-old boy, the murdered child's mother sued the manufacturers of "Mortal Kombat," a video game. The mother claimed the murderer's addiction to the game made him believe he was one of the game's characters, causing him to stab her son. Using the incitement test, a federal district court said even if the game caused the boy's death, the game's advocacy of violence was no more than urging illegal action at some indefinite future time.[81] The incitement test requires that the media content cause "imminent" lawless action—a crime directly and immediately connected with the content. The court said the murdered boy's mother could not show a connection between "Mortal Kombat" and her son's death, so she could not win her case.

Likelihood of Lawless Acts The incitement test also requires proof that it is likely media content would cause violence. This is not the same as foreseeability. For example, it may be foreseeable that a movie with violent scenes would cause a deranged person to commit unlawful acts. But courts say the determining factor is whether the movie is likely to cause a reasonable person to act illegally. Rarely will a court find it likely that a reasonable person would commit violence in response to media content.

One court held that a radio station advertising campaign did inspire reasonable people to commit illegal acts. A Los Angeles Top 40 station with a large teenage audience devised a promotional campaign. It gave a bright red car to one of its well-known disc jockeys. The DJ drove to several locations in the Los Angeles area, periodically calling the station and broadcasting his intended destination. Anyone finding the DJ would win a cash prize and be interviewed on the air. Two teenagers independently saw the DJ's car on a Los Angeles freeway

realWorld Law

"Hit Man": Protected or Not?

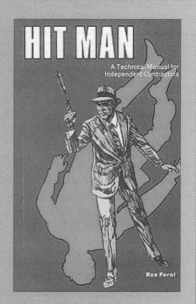

James Edward Perry forced his way into Mildred Horn's home and killed her, her 8-year-old quadriplegic son and the son's nurse. Horn's former husband, Lawrence, had hired Perry to commit the murders so that Lawrence Horn would inherit the $1.7 million the son had received to settle a medical malpractice lawsuit. Perry, sentenced to death for committing the murders, said he followed instructions in a book, "Hit Man: A Technical Manual for Independent Contractors." The book clearly explains how to commit a murder. The U.S. Court of Appeals for the Fourth Circuit said the First Amendment did not protect the book's publisher from a lawsuit for aiding and abetting the murders.[1]

One view is that the Fourth Circuit's decision was wrong. The court should have applied the *Brandenburg v. Ohio* test—speech that advocates committing an unlawful act is protected unless it is "directed to inciting or producing imminent lawless action and was likely to incite or produce such action."[2] As one law review article noted, "Hit Man" was published in 1983 and sold 13,000 copies. Out of that number sold, only Perry is known to have used the book's instructions to kill someone. "This correlates to less than a one-ten-thousandth of a percent (.0001%) chance that the book actually incited imminent lawless activity and strongly suggests that such activity was not likely to occur from reading this book."[3] Also, Perry committed the murders a year after reading the book, hardly the "*imminent* lawless activity" required by the *Brandenburg* test.[4]

Alternatively, "Hit Man" may be called a recipe book with clearly defined instructions that provide "otherwise missing information needed to commit a crime," combining "description with details that amount to instructions" with "a detailed road map for violence."[5] How could such a book be anything but incitement to commit imminent violence? The Fourth Circuit was correct, according to this view.

Which is the better analysis? The decision is excerpted at the end of this chapter.

---

1. *See* Gregory Akselrun, Note: *Hit Man: The Fourth Circuit's Mistake in* Rice v. Paladin Enters., Inc., 19 Loy. L.A. Ent. L.J. 375, 375 (1999).
2. 395 U.S. 444, 447 (1969) (per curiam).
3. Akselrun, *supra* note 1.
4. *Id.*
5. David Crump, *Camouflaged Incitement: Freedom of Speech, Communicative Torts, and the Borderland of the Brandenburg Test,* 29 Ga. L. Rev. 1, 33–37 (1994); see also Lise Vansen, Comment: *Incitement by Any Other Name: Dodging a First Amendment Misfire in* Rice v. Paladin Enters., Inc., 25 Hastings Const. L.Q. 605 (1998).

and raced to catch him. As the DJ took an off-ramp to exit the freeway, the two cars followed. One of the teenagers forced a third car off the highway, killing the driver. The dead driver's relatives sued the station. The family won at trial, and the jury awarded $300,000 in damages.

On appeal, the California Supreme Court ruled that it was foreseeable the station's promotion could lead to physical injury or death.[82] The station staged

realWorld Law

Media Inspiring Violent Acts

Zazi Pope, Warner Brothers' senior vice president and deputy general counsel, commenting on the effects of media content, said the Book of Revelations inspired the Branch Davidians in Waco, Texas; the Beatles inspired Charles Manson, convicted of organizing Sharon Tate's murder; the novel "The Catcher in the Rye" inspired Mark David Chapman, John Lennon's killer; the movie "Taxi Driver" inspired John W. Hinckley, who shot President Ronald Reagan. Pope said, "If you're going to say that anything that could inspire some crazy person to commit a violent act is going to be subject to liability, our culture would cease to have any meaning." Rather, Pope said, courts have ruled that these "random violent acts, even if somehow linked to a movie, song, or other work of art" do not justify holding responsible those who create and distribute mass media content.[1]

---

1. F. Jay Dougherty et al., *Potential Liability Arising from the Dissemination of Violent Music*, 22 Loyola L.A. Ent. L. Rev. 237, 249 (2002).

---

the promotion in the summer, when many teenagers with cars were at home and bored. The promotion offered money and a bit of fame. The disc jockey testified he had seen certain cars following him from one location to another. The court took this admission to mean the station should have foreseen that a teenager who missed winning the money at one location would speed to the next. It is foreseeable that speeding and reckless driving are likely to result in death or serious injury. The station is not relieved of liability because a third party, the teenagers, caused the harm, the court said. The station's action in broadcasting the promotion created the circumstances leading to the harm.

SUMMARY

THE INCITEMENT TEST IS AN ALTERNATIVE to the negligence test when a plaintiff contends a media defendant caused physical harm: Did the defendant intentionally or recklessly intend to cause harm, and was imminent harm likely to result from the defendant's actions? There is no free speech protection if the media defendant intended harm to result. ■

Communications Decency Act

The Communications Decency Act (CDA) shields Web-based service providers from legal claims based on their carriage of material that third parties create.[83] For example, this protects Internet service providers against libel, as discussed in Chapter 4, privacy and emotional distress suits, as long as the provider did not create the disputed content. Congress adopted the CDA as part of the Tele-communications Act of 1996 primarily to limit minors' access to indecent and obscene material on the Internet. As discussed in Chapter 11, the U.S. Supreme Court found most of the CDA abridged Internet users' First Amendment rights. However, courts have upheld the part of the CDA protecting Web-based service providers. This allows interactive computer service providers, when sued for allegedly causing physical harm, to defend themselves by asserting protection under the CDA.

The CDA applied, for example, when a 13-year-old girl created a MySpace profile and chose to represent herself as 18 years old. A year later she met a 19-year-old man through her MySpace profile. The two spoke by phone. He then sexually assaulted her when they met in person. The girl and her mother sued MySpace, claiming it failed to institute reasonable safety measures that would prevent older users from communicating with minors. The U.S. Court of Appeals for the Fifth Circuit read the CDA as giving broad immunity to Web services that carry information third parties provide and rejected the suit against MySpace.[84] The court said MySpace did not publish the material on the girl's profile; it merely transmitted information the girl placed there. The CDA protects Web services that transmit but do not create material, the court said.

When other girls aged 13 to 15 years old were assaulted by adults they met through MySpace, the minors and their families sued the social networking site. A California appellate court said the CDA protects Web service provid-ers against civil suits when the providers do not create the disputed material.[85] Similarly, a federal district court held that the CDA protected MySpace when a minor, not MySpace, provided the information that led to an assault.[86] Plaintiffs in these suits argue the social networking sites do not merely transmit material, they create it because they process users' information. For example, after a user entered her date of birth, MySpace automatically displayed the user's zodiac sign. MySpace also prompted the user to enter additional information about background and lifestyle, schools and preferred music. Courts have determined when a site requires users to provide specific information, as did a site allowing users to search for a roommate, it could be an information content provider, not just an information transmitter, and would not come under the CDA's pro-tection.[87] But courts have determined sites only prompting a user to provide information, such as MySpace, do not create content and therefore enjoy CDA's safeguards.[88]

Craigslist is a Web service that does not create content itself. A person bought a gun though a Craigslist ad and shot and wounded Calvin Gibson. Gibson sued Craigslist for not ensuring that "inherently hazardous objects, such as handguns, did not come into the hands of individuals" who would use them to physically injure others. A federal district court said Craigslist provided an interactive com-puter service, did not itself post the handgun ad and acted only as a transmitter of third-party content. Those three factors, the court held, meant the CDA protected Craigslist.[89]

Although some courts have interpreted the CDA broadly to cover many claims against Web service providers, others have not. For example, Cynthia Barnes' ex-boyfriend posted profiles on Yahoo that included nude pictures of Barnes and implications that she was seeking casual sex with men. The profiles contained Barnes' work contact information. Men began contacting Barnes, even coming to her workplace. Several times she unsuccessfully asked Yahoo to remove the profiles. A local television reporter learned of Barnes' situation and contacted Yahoo. A Yahoo employee contacted Barnes and said the profiles would be removed. Barnes conveyed that information to the reporter, but the profiles remained on Yahoo. Barnes sued Yahoo, claiming she relied on its promise to take down the profiles, yet Yahoo did not comply with its promise, a legal concept called "promissory estoppel." That is, Yahoo promised to remove the profiles, did not do so, and Barnes continued to hear from men who wanted to have sex with her. Federal courts ruled the CDA did not prevent Barnes from suing Yahoo for promissory estoppel.[90]

SUMMARY

THE COMMUNICATIONS DECENCY ACT protects interactive computer service providers that did not create the disputed content from liability when plaintiffs seek damages for information originating with a third-party user of the computer service. Courts generally, though not always, read the CDA broadly, shielding interactive computer service providers from defamation, privacy, emotional distress and physical harm civil lawsuits. ■

Other Dangers

Reporters, editors, photographers, newspapers, television stations, Internet sites—any person and company involved with preparing and publishing news, entertainment and advertising—may be sued for any number of legal claims. In addition to those already discussed in this and previous chapters, the following are samples of other lawsuits media have faced.

Breach of Contract

Media personnel often make contractual agreements. They sign employment contracts, contracts to buy new computers for the newsroom and contracts to buy advertising time on a television station. They also may contract with a news source—agreeing to keep a source's name secret in exchange for the source's information.

Points of Law

What Is a Contract?

A contract is an agreement, an exchange of promises between the contracting parties. A court can enforce a legal contract against a party who has breached—violated in some way—the terms or conditions of the agreement. Most contracts are written documents. However, an oral agreement may be as legally binding as a contract. To form a contract, there must be both a valid offer and a valid acceptance. There also must be "consideration," or payment for the obligation. "I want to buy your car." "OK, I agree to sell it to you." The first statement is an offer. The second is an acceptance. But there is no contract because there is no consideration. "I want to buy your car for $5,000." "OK, I agree to sell it to you for $5,000." This constitutes a contract—offer, acceptance and consideration of $5,000 to pay for the obligation to sell the car.

Media personnel may be sued for breaching a contract. For example, a British documentary producer planned a film about American censorship of art. A British television channel financially supported the production and would air the film when completed. The producer wanted to include an interview with Donald Wildmon, a prominent critic of government arts funding. Wildmon agreed, but only if the producer signed a contract stating that the interview would not be made available to any other media outlet besides the British channel without Wildmon's permission. The producer agreed. The film, "Damned in the U.S.A.," won many awards after it aired in Britain. When Wildmon learned that the film was selected to open a prestigious documentary festival in New York City, he sued. Wildmon objected to his picture and words being juxtaposed in the film with images of art Wildmon considered obscene. Wildmon asked a federal district court to declare that the contract prevented showing the film in America. The film producers argued that the contract referred only to the complete interview, not the brief portions used in the film.

The court said neither the contract's wording nor the parties' intentions were clear.[91] However, the court read the contract to mean that the raw interview footage could not be used by the British producer or anyone else to make a new film. The original documentary, including the interview excerpts, could be exhibited wherever the producer wanted, the court held.

The *Cohen v. Cowles Media Co.* decision, discussed in Chapter 9, in which newspapers revealed the name of a source to whom confidentiality was promised, also is a breach of contract case.

Interference with Economic Advantage

A person who has an opportunity to gain financially but believes another person interfered with that opportunity may file a tort suit. The tort goes by different names in different states. No matter what the tort is called, the complaint remains the same: The defendant interfered with the plaintiff's prospective business relationship that promised economic rewards. For example, a utility company executive pressured a newspaper that reported on energy matters not to use articles by a freelance writer whom the executive thought was biased. The writer sued the utility company for interfering with her economic relationship with the paper. A California appellate court said the utility executive might have acted improperly in influencing the paper.[92] The writer could pursue her economic interference claim, the court ruled.

The First Amendment can be a defense against an economic interference claim. A software company owner wrote a letter to the editor disagreeing with certain statements in an article a computer magazine published. The magazine printed the letter together with a response from the article's author. The company owner thought the response made him appear uninformed about important aspects of computer software. He complained that the response caused his company to lose business and he sued for interference with prospective economic gain. A federal district court said the First Amendment protected the article author's response.[93] Because the response was constitutionally protected, it could not be the basis of any tort suit, the court said.

Fraudulent Misrepresentation

Some relationships require full disclosure. A **fiduciary relationship** is a legal duty or responsibility one party owes to another when the parties are in certain relationships with each other. For example, when a person agrees to act primarily for another's benefit, he or she must reveal pertinent facts to the other person. A financial consultant investing a person's savings is in a fiduciary relationship with the client and must give the client important information about the investments. It is fraudulent misrepresentation if the fiduciary fails to disclose information. What does this have to do with the media? In one case, a teacher was convicted of sexually molesting some of his former students. One of those students appeared at the teacher's sentencing hearing. The judge ordered reporters in the courtroom not to identify any of the sexual assault victims who testified. Thinking the media would not reveal his name, the former student testified. An Associated Press (AP) reporter wrote a story using the victim's name, the only journalist to do so. The victim sued the AP for fraudulent misrepresentation. A federal appellate court said the AP did not have a fiduciary relationship with the victim.[94] In fact, the court said, the AP and the victim had no relationship at all. Without a fiduciary relationship, the AP was not required to tell the victim it planned to ignore the judge's order and publish his name, the court ruled.

fiduciary relationship A legal duty or responsibility one party owes to another when the parties are in certain relationships with each other.

Expanding Tort Law

If plaintiffs think no existing tort will be successful in suing the media, they may consider tort law flexible enough to invent a new tort. Judges usually do not go along with this, but plaintiffs continue trying. For example, two men went to sea on a fishing boat. Severe weather conditions caused one man to be thrown overboard and drowned. Using a novel tort approach, the man's widow sued The Weather Channel, a cable television network. She said her husband had watched The Weather Channel before boarding the boat. She claimed The Weather Channel had not issued a small craft warning for that day and had not forecast bad weather. The judge wrote:

The plaintiff seeks an unprecedented expansion of the scope of tort law: to impose on a television broadcaster of weather forecasts a general duty to viewers who watch a forecast and take action in reliance on that forecast. As the Defendant points out, if the court were to impose such a duty under either a breach of contract or tort theory, the duty could extend to farmers who plant their crops based on a forecast of no rain, construction workers who pour concrete or lay foundation based on the forecast of dry weather, or families who go to the beach for a weekend based on a forecast of sunny weather. The court further notes that if it were to impose a duty upon a weather broadcaster for a faulty broadcast, such a duty could be extended to non–weather related broadcasts such as traffic reports upon which individuals rely to arrive timely to scheduled events. It is clear that to impose such a duty would be to chill the well established First Amendment rights of the broadcasters.[95]

SUMMARY

PLAINTIFFS SUE THE MASS MEDIA FOR MANY DIFFERENT TORTS. For example, breach of contract means media personnel agree to do something but fail to meet their commitment. A contract may be an oral as well as written agreement. Interfering with prospective economic gain may occur when an advertiser, for example, pressures a mass medium to fire a journalist. The journalist may sue her former employer. ∎

Cases for Study

Thinking About It

The two case excerpts that follow deal with unusual sets of facts. As you read these case excerpts, keep the following questions in mind:

- Do the decisions do more to protect individuals or the press?
- How do the decisions try to balance the media's First Amendment rights against individuals' rights?
- Do the two cases show that sometimes judges know in advance what decisions they want to reach and then go about finding justifications for those decisions?

Hustler Magazine Inc. v. Falwell
SUPREME COURT OF THE UNITED STATES
485 U.S. 46 (1988)

CHIEF JUSTICE WILLIAM REHNQUIST delivered the Court's opinion:
Petitioner Hustler Magazine, Inc., is a magazine of nationwide circulation. Respondent Jerry Falwell, a nationally known minister who has been active as a commentator on politics and public affairs, sued petitioner and its publisher, petitioner Larry Flynt, to recover damages for invasion of privacy, libel, and intentional infliction of emotional distress. . . .

The inside front cover of the November 1983 issue of Hustler Magazine featured a "parody" of an advertisement for Campari Liqueur that contained the name and picture of respondent and was entitled "Jerry Falwell talks about his first time." This parody was modeled after actual Campari ads that included interviews with various celebrities about their "first times." Although it was apparent by the end of each interview that this meant the first time they sampled Campari, the ads clearly played on the sexual double entendre of the general subject of "first times." Copying the form and layout of these Campari ads, Hustler's editors chose respondent as the featured celebrity and drafted an alleged "interview" with him in which he states that his "first time" was during a drunken incestuous rendezvous with his mother in an outhouse. The

Hustler parody portrays respondent and his mother as drunk and immoral, and suggests that respondent is a hypocrite who preaches only when he is drunk. In small print at the bottom of the page, the ad contains the disclaimer, "ad parody—not to be taken seriously." The magazine's table of contents also lists the ad as "Fiction; Ad and Personality Parody."

[Falwell sued. He failed on the libel and privacy claims.] The jury ruled for respondent on the intentional infliction of emotional distress claim, however, and stated that he should be awarded $100,000 in compensatory damages, as well as $50,000 each in punitive damages. . . .

On appeal, the United States Court of Appeals for the Fourth Circuit affirmed the judgment against petitioners. . . .

At the heart of the First Amendment is the recognition of the fundamental importance of the free flow of ideas and opinions on matters of public interest and concern. . . . We have therefore been particularly vigilant to ensure that individual expressions of ideas remain free from governmentally imposed sanctions. . . .

The sort of robust political debate encouraged by the First Amendment is bound to produce speech that is critical of those who hold public office or those public figures who are "intimately involved in the resolution of important public questions or, by reason of their fame, shape events in areas of concern to society at large." . . . Such criticism, inevitably, will not always be reasoned or moderate; public figures as well as public officials will be subject to "vehement, caustic, and sometimes unpleasantly sharp attacks." . . .

Of course, this does not mean that any speech about a public figure is immune from sanction in the form of damages. Since *New York Times Co. v. Sullivan,* we have consistently ruled that a public figure may hold a speaker liable for the damage to reputation caused by publication of a defamatory falsehood, but only if the statement was made "with knowledge that it was false or with reckless disregard of whether it was false or not." False statements of fact are particularly valueless; they interfere with the truth-seeking function of the marketplace of ideas, and they cause damage to an individual's reputation that cannot easily be repaired by counterspeech, however persuasive or effective. But even though falsehoods have little value in and of themselves, they are "nevertheless inevitable in free debate," and a rule that would impose strict liability on a publisher for false factual assertions would have an undoubted "chilling" effect on speech relating to public figures that does have constitutional value. "Freedoms of expression require 'breathing space.'" This breathing space is provided by a constitutional rule that allows public figures to recover for libel or defamation only when they can prove both that the statement was false and that the statement was made with the requisite level of culpability. . . .

Generally speaking, the law does not regard the intent to inflict emotional distress as one which should receive much solicitude, and it is quite understandable that most if not all jurisdictions have chosen to make it civilly culpable where the conduct in question is sufficiently "outrageous." But in the world of debate about public affairs, many things done with motives that are less than admirable are protected by the First Amendment. . . .

[Although] a bad motive may be deemed controlling for purposes of tort liability in other areas of the law, we think the First Amendment prohibits such a result in the area of public debate about public figures.

Were we to hold otherwise, there can be little doubt that political cartoonists and satirists would be subjected to damages awards without any showing that their work falsely defamed its subject. . . .

. . . Several famous examples of this type of intentionally injurious speech were drawn by Thomas Nast, probably the greatest American cartoonist to date, who was associated for many years during the post–Civil War era with Harper's Weekly. In the pages of that publication Nast conducted a graphic vendetta against William M. "Boss" Tweed and his corrupt associates in New York City's "Tweed Ring." It has been described by one historian of the subject as "a sustained attack which in its passion and effectiveness stands alone in the history of American graphic art." . . .

Despite their sometimes caustic nature, from the early cartoon portraying George Washington as an ass down to the present day, graphic depictions and satirical cartoons have played a prominent role in public and political debate. . . .

Respondent contends, however, that the caricature in question here was so "outrageous" as to distinguish it from more traditional political cartoons. There is no doubt that the caricature of respondent and his mother published in Hustler is at best a distant cousin of the political cartoons described above, and a rather poor relation at that. If it were possible by laying down a principled standard to separate the one from the other, public discourse would probably suffer little or no harm. But we doubt that there is any such standard, and we are quite sure that the pejorative description "outrageous" does not supply one. "Outrageousness" in the area of political and social discourse has an inherent subjectiveness about it which would allow a jury to impose liability on the basis of the jurors' tastes or views, or perhaps on the basis of their dislike of a particular expression. An "outrageousness" standard thus runs afoul of our longstanding refusal to allow damages to be awarded because the speech in question may have an adverse emotional impact on the audience. . . .

We conclude that public figures and public officials may not recover for the tort of intentional infliction of emotional distress by reason of publications such as the one here at issue without showing in addition that the publication contains a false statement of fact which was made with "actual malice," *i.e.*, with knowledge that the statement was false or with reckless disregard as to whether or not it was true. This is not merely a "blind application" of the *New York Times* standard, it reflects our considered judgment that such a standard is necessary to give adequate "breathing space" to the freedoms protected by the First Amendment.

Here it is clear that respondent Falwell is a "public figure" for purposes of First Amendment law. The jury found against respondent on his libel claim when it decided that the Hustler ad parody could not "reasonably be understood as describing actual facts about [respondent] or actual events in which [he] participated." The Court of Appeals interpreted the jury's finding to be that the ad parody "was not reasonably believable," and in accordance with our custom we accept this finding. Respondent is thus relegated to his claim for damages awarded by the jury for the intentional infliction of emotional distress by "outrageous" conduct. But, for reasons heretofore stated, this claim cannot, consistently with the First Amendment, form a basis for the award of damages when the conduct in question is the publication of a caricature such as the ad parody involved here. The judgment of the Court of Appeals is accordingly

Reversed.

Rice v. Paladin Enterprises, Inc.
128 F.3d 233 (4th Cir. 1997), cert. denied 523 U.S. 1074 (1998)

Circuit Judge J. Michael Luttig delivered the court's opinion:

[The court begins by excerpting passages from the 130-page book, some very explicit in explaining how to prepare for and carry out the killing of someone. The opinion said the court "has even felt it necessary to omit portions of these few illustrative passages in order to minimize the danger to the public from" repeating them in the court's opinion.]

I.

On the night of March 3, 1993, readied by these instructions and steeled by these seductive adjurations from *Hit Man: A Technical Manual for Independent Contractors*, a copy of which was subsequently found in his apartment, James Perry brutally murdered Mildred Horn, her eight-year-old quadriplegic son Trevor, and Trevor's nurse, Janice Saunders, by shooting Mildred Horn and Saunders through the eyes and by strangling Trevor Horn. Perry's despicable crime was not one of vengeance; he did not know any of his victims. Nor did he commit the murders in the course of another offense. Perry acted instead as a contract killer, a "hit man," hired by Mildred Horn's ex-husband, Lawrence Horn, to murder Horn's family so that Horn would receive the $2 million that his eight-year-old son had received in settlement for injuries that had previously left him paralyzed for life. At the time of the murders, this money was held in trust for the benefit of Trevor, and, under the terms of the trust instrument, the trust money was to be distributed tax-free to Lawrence in the event of Mildred's and Trevor's deaths.

In soliciting, preparing for, and committing these murders, Perry meticulously followed countless of *Hit Man*'s 130 pages of detailed factual instructions on how to murder and to become a professional killer. . . .

In this civil, state-law wrongful death action against defendant Paladin Enterprises—the publisher of *Hit Man*—the relatives and representatives of Mildred and Trevor Horn and Janice Saunders allege that Paladin aided and abetted Perry in the commission of his murders through its publication of *Hit Man*'s killing instructions. For reasons that are here of no concern to the court, Paladin has stipulated to a set of facts which establish as a matter of law that the publisher is civilly liable for aiding and abetting James Perry in his triple murder, unless the First Amendment absolutely bars the imposition of liability upon a publisher for assisting in the commission of criminal acts. As the parties stipulate: "The parties agree that the sole issue to be decided by the Court . . . is whether the

First Amendment is a complete defense, as a matter of law, to the civil action set forth in the plaintiffs' Complaint. All other issues of law and fact are specifically reserved for subsequent proceedings."

Paladin, for example, has stipulated for purposes of summary judgment that Perry followed the above-enumerated instructions from *Hit Man,* as well as instructions from another Paladin publication, *How to Make a Disposable Silencer, Vol. II,* in planning, executing, and attempting to cover up the murders of Mildred and Trevor Horn and Janice Saunders. Paladin has stipulated not only that, in marketing *Hit Man,* Paladin "intended to attract and assist criminals and would-be criminals who desire information and instructions on how to commit crimes," but also that it "intended *and* had knowledge" that *Hit Man* actually "would be used, *upon receipt,* by criminals and would-be criminals to plan and execute the crime of murder for hire." Indeed, the publisher has even stipulated that, through publishing and selling *Hit Man,* it assisted Perry in particular in the perpetration of the very murders for which the victims' families now attempt to hold Paladin civilly liable.

Notwithstanding Paladin's extraordinary stipulations that it not only knew that its instructions might be used by murderers, but that it actually *intended* to provide assistance to murderers and would-be murderers which would be used by them "upon receipt," and that it in fact assisted Perry in particular in the commission of the murders of Mildred and Trevor Horn and Janice Saunders, the district court granted Paladin's motion for summary judgment and dismissed plaintiffs' claims that Paladin aided and abetted Perry, holding that these claims were barred by the First Amendment as a matter of law.

Because long-established case law provides that speech—even speech by the press—that constitutes criminal aiding and abetting does not enjoy the protection of the First Amendment, and because we are convinced that such case law is both correct and equally applicable to speech that constitutes civil aiding and abetting of criminal conduct (at least where, as here, the defendant has the specific purpose of assisting and encouraging commission of such conduct and the alleged assistance and encouragement

takes a form other than abstract advocacy), we hold, as urged by the Attorney General and the Department of Justice, that the First Amendment does not pose a bar to a finding that Paladin is civilly liable as an aider and abetter of Perry's triple contract murder. We also hold that the plaintiffs have stated against Paladin a civil aiding and abetting claim under Maryland law sufficient to withstand Paladin's motion for summary judgment. For these reasons, which we fully explain below, the district court's grant of summary judgment in Paladin's favor is reversed and the case is remanded for trial.

II.

A.

In the seminal case of *Brandenburg v. Ohio* (1969), the Supreme Court held that abstract advocacy of lawlessness is protected speech under the First Amendment. Although the Court provided little explanation for this holding in its brief *per curiam* opinion, it is evident the Court recognized from our own history that such a right to advocate lawlessness is, almost paradoxically, one of the ultimate safeguards of liberty. Even in a society of laws, one of the most indispensable freedoms is that to express in the most impassioned terms the most passionate disagreement with the laws themselves, the institutions of, and created by, law, and the individual officials with whom the laws and institutions are entrusted. Without the freedom to criticize that which constrains, there is no freedom at all.

However, while even speech advocating lawlessness has long enjoyed protections under the First Amendment, it is equally well established that speech, which, in its effect, is tantamount to legitimately proscribable nonexpressive conduct, may itself be legitimately proscribed, punished, or regulated incidentally to the constitutional enforcement of generally applicable statutes. . . .

Were the First Amendment to bar or to limit government regulation of such "speech brigaded with action," the government would be powerless to protect the public from countless of even the most pernicious criminal acts and civil wrongs. . . .

In particular as it concerns the instant case, the speech-act doctrine has long been invoked to sustain convictions for aiding and abetting the commission of criminal offenses. Indeed, every court that has addressed the issue, including this court, has held that the First Amendment does not necessarily pose a bar to liability for aiding and abetting a crime, even when such aiding and abetting takes the form of the spoken or written word. . . .

Indeed, as the Department of Justice recently advised Congress, the law is now well established that the First Amendment, and *Brandenburg*'s "imminence" requirement in particular, generally poses little obstacle to the punishment of speech that constitutes criminal aiding and abetting, because "culpability in such cases is premised, not on defendants' 'advocacy' of criminal conduct, but on defendants' successful efforts to assist others by detailing to them the means of accomplishing the crimes." . . .

B.

We can envision only two possible qualifications to these general rules, neither of which, for reasons that we discuss more extensively below, is of special moment in the context of the particular aiding and abetting case before us.

1.

The first, which obviously would have practical import principally in the civil context, is that the First Amendment may, at least in certain circumstances, superimpose upon the speech-act doctrine a heightened intent requirement in order that preeminent values underlying that constitutional provision not be imperiled. . . . That is, in order to prevent the punishment or even the chilling of entirely innocent, lawfully useful speech, the First Amendment may in some contexts stand as a bar to the imposition of liability on the basis of mere foreseeability or knowledge that the information one imparts could be misused for an impermissible purpose. Where it is necessary, such a limitation would meet the quite legitimate, if not compelling, concern of those who publish, broadcast, or distribute to large, undifferentiated audiences, that the exposure to suit under lesser standards would be intolerable. At the same time, it would not relieve from liability those who would, for profit or other motive, intentionally assist and encourage crime and then shamelessly seek refuge in the sanctuary of the First Amendment. Like our sister circuits, at the very least where a speaker—individual or media—acts with the purpose of assisting in the commission of crime, we do not believe that the First Amendment insulates that speaker from responsibility for his actions simply because he may have disseminated his message to a wide audience. . . . This is certainly so, we are satisfied, where not only the speaker's dissemination or marketing strategy, but the nature of the speech itself, strongly suggest that the audience both targeted and actually reached is, in actuality, very narrowly confined, as in the case before us. Were the First Amendment to offer protection even in these circumstances, one could publish, by traditional means or even on the internet, the necessary plans and instructions for assassinating the President, for poisoning a city's water supply, for blowing up a skyscraper or public building, or for similar acts of terror and mass destruction, with the specific, indeed even the admitted, purpose of assisting such crimes—all with impunity. . . .

2.

The second qualification is that the First Amendment might well (and presumably would) interpose the same or similar limitations upon the imposition of civil liability for abstract advocacy, without more, that it interposes upon the imposition of criminal punishment for such advocacy. In other words, the First Amendment might well circumscribe the power of the state to create and enforce a cause of action that would permit the imposition of civil liability, such as aiding and abetting civil liability, for speech that would constitute pure abstract advocacy, at least if that speech were not "directed to inciting or producing imminent lawless action, and . . . likely to incite or produce such action. The instances in which such advocacy might give rise to civil liability under state statute would seem rare, but they are not inconceivable. Again, however, an exhaustive analysis of this likely limitation is not required in this case.

Here, it is alleged, and a jury could reasonably find that Paladin aided and abetted the murders at issue through the quintessential speech act of providing step-by-step instructions for murder (replete with photographs, diagrams, and narration) so comprehensive and detailed that it is as if the instructor were literally present with the would-be murderer not only in the preparation and planning, but in the actual commission of, and follow-up to, the murder; there is not even a hint that the aid was provided in the form of speech that might constitute abstract advocacy. . . . Moreover, although we do not believe such would be necessary, we are satisfied a jury could readily find that the provided instructions not only have no, or virtually no, noninstructional communicative value, but also that their only instructional communicative "value" is the indisputably illegitimate one of training persons how to murder and to engage in the business of murder for hire.

Aid and assistance in the form of this kind of speech bears no resemblance to the "theoretical advocacy," the advocacy of "principles divorced from action," "the mere abstract teaching [of] the moral propriety or even moral necessity for a resort to force and violence," or any of the other forms of discourse critical of government, its policies, and its leaders, which have always animated, and to this day continue to animate, the First Amendment. Indeed, this detailed, focused instructional assistance to those contemplating or in the throes of planning murder is the antithesis of speech protected under *Brandenburg*. It is the teaching of the "techniques" of violence, the "advocacy and teaching of concrete action," the "preparation . . . for violent action and [the] steeling . . . to such action." . . . As such, the murder instructions in *Hit Man* are, collectively, a textbook example of the type of speech that the Supreme Court has quite purposely left unprotected, and the prosecution of which, criminally or civilly, has historically been thought subject to few, if any, First Amendment constraints. Accordingly, we hold that the First Amendment does not pose a bar to the plaintiffs' civil aiding and abetting cause of action against Paladin Press. If, as precedent uniformly confirms, the states have the power to regulate speech that aids and abets crime,

then certainly they have the power to regulate the speech at issue here.

III.

. . .

A. . . .

Paladin itself has stipulated that "Perry followed a number of instructions outlined in *Hit Man*" in preparing for and in murdering Mildred and Trevor Horn and Janice Saunders. In fact, as noted, the publisher has actually stipulated that it assisted Perry in the "perpetration of the murders."

Even without these express stipulations of assistance, however, a reasonable jury could conclude that Paladin assisted Perry in those murders, from the facts that Perry purchased and possessed *Hit Man* and that the methods and tactics he employed in his murders of Mildred and Trevor Horn and Janice Saunders so closely paralleled those prescribed in the book. . . . Perry followed, in painstaking detail, countless of the book's instructions in soliciting, preparing for, and carrying out his murders. Without repeating these in detail here, Perry faithfully followed the book's instructions in making a home-made silencer, using a rental car with stolen out-of-state tags, murdering the victims in their own home, using an AR-7 rifle to shoot the victims in the eyes from point blank range, and concealing his involvement in the murders. The number and extent of these parallels to the instructions in *Hit Man* cannot be consigned, as a matter of law, to mere coincidence; the correspondence of techniques at least creates a jury issue as to whether the book provided substantial assistance, if it does not conclusively establish such assistance.

A jury likewise could reasonably find that Perry was encouraged in his murderous acts by Paladin's book. *Hit Man* does not merely detail how to commit murder and murder for hire; through powerful prose in the second person and imperative voice, it encourages its readers in their specific acts of murder. It reassures those contemplating the crime that they may proceed with their plans without fear of either personal failure or punishment. And at every point where the would-be murderer might yield either to reason or to reservations, *Hit Man* emboldens the killer, confirming not only that he should proceed, but that he must proceed, if he is to establish his manhood. The book is so effectively written that its protagonist seems actually to be present at the planning, commission, and cover-up of the murders the book inspires. . . .

. . . Wholly apart from Paladin's stipulations, there are four bases upon which, collectively, if perhaps not individually, a reasonable jury could find that Paladin possessed the intent required . . . under any heightened First Amendment standard.

First, the declared purpose of *Hit Man* itself is to facilitate murder. Consistent with its declared purpose, the book is subtitled "A Technical Manual for Independent Contractors," and it unabashedly describes itself as "an instruction book on murder." A jury need not, but plainly could, conclude from such prominent and unequivocal statements of criminal purpose that the publisher who disseminated the book intended to assist in the achievement of that purpose.

Second, the book's extensive, decided, and pointed promotion of murder is highly probative of the publisher's intent, and may be considered as such, whether or not that promotion, standing alone, could serve as the basis for liability consistent with the First Amendment. After carefully and repeatedly reading *Hit Man* in its entirety, we are of the view that the book so overtly promotes murder in concrete, nonabstract terms that we regard as disturbingly disingenuous . . . Paladin's cavalier suggestion that the book is essentially a comic book whose "fantastical" promotion of murder no one could take seriously. . . . The unique text of *Hit Man* alone, boldly proselytizing and glamorizing the crime of murder and the "profession" of murder as it dispassionately instructs on its commission, is more than sufficient to create a triable issue of fact as to Paladin's intent in publishing and selling the manual.

Third, Paladin's marketing strategy would more than support a finding of the requisite intent. It is known through Paladin's stipulations that it "engaged in a marketing strategy intended to attract and assist criminals and would be criminals who desire information and instructions on how to commit crimes." But an inference as to such a strategy would be permitted from Paladin's catalogue advertisement of *Hit Man*.

The publisher markets the book as follows, invoking a disclaimer which, the district court's characterization notwithstanding, a jury could readily find to be transparent sarcasm designed to intrigue and entice:

> Learn how a pro gets assignments, creates a false identity, makes a disposable silencer, leaves the scene without a trace, watches his mark unobserved and more. Feral reveals how to get in, do the job and get out without getting caught. *For academic study only!*

From this statement by the publisher in its own promotional sales catalogue, a jury could conclude that Paladin marketed *Hit Man* directly and even primarily to murderers and would-be criminals, and, from this permissible conclusion, in turn conclude that Paladin possessed the requisite intent necessary to support liability. . . .

In summary, a reasonable jury clearly could conclude from the stipulations of the parties, and, apart from the stipulations, from the text of *Hit Man* itself and the other facts of record, that Paladin aided and abetted in Perry's triple murder by providing detailed instructions on the techniques of murder and murder for hire with the specific intent of aiding and abetting the commission of these violent crimes.

B.

Any argument that *Hit Man* is abstract advocacy entitling the book, and therefore Paladin, to heightened First Amendment protection under *Brandenburg* is, on its face, untenable. Although the district court erred in its alternative conclusion that the speech of *Hit Man* is protected advocacy, even that court expressly found that "the book merely teaches what must be done to implement a professional hit." Indeed, Paladin's protests notwithstanding, this book constitutes the archetypal example of speech which, because it methodically and comprehensively prepares and steels its audience to specific criminal conduct through exhaustively detailed instructions on the planning, commission, and concealment of criminal conduct, finds no preserve in the First Amendment. To the extent that confirmation of this is even needed, given the book's content and declared purpose to be "an instruction book on murder," that confirmation is found in the stark contrast between this assassination manual and the speech heretofore held to be deserving of constitutional protection.

1.

Through its stipulation that it intended *Hit Man* to be used by criminals and would-be criminals to commit murder for hire in accordance with the book's instructions, Paladin all but concedes that, through those instructions, *Hit Man* prepares and steels its readers to commit the crime of murder for hire. But even absent the publisher's stipulations, it is evident from even a casual examination of the book that the prose of *Hit Man* is at the other end of the continuum from the ideation at the core of the advocacy protected by the First Amendment.

The cover of *Hit Man* states that readers of the book will "learn how a pro makes a living at this craft [of murder] without landing behind bars" and, "how he gets hit assignments, creates a false working identity, makes a disposable silencer, leaves the scene without a trace of evidence, watches his mark unobserved, and more . . . how to get in, do the job, and get out—without getting caught."

In the first pages of its text, *Hit Man* promises, consistent with its title as "A Technical Manual for Independent Contractors," that the book will prepare the reader, step by step, to commit murder for hire:

> Within the pages of this book you will learn one of the most successful methods of operation used by an independent contractor. You will follow the procedures of a man who works alone, without backing of organized crime or on a personal vendetta. Step by step you will be taken from research to equipment selection to job preparation to successful job completion. You will learn where to find employment, how much to charge, and what you can, and cannot, do with the money you earn.

> But deny your urge to skip about, looking for the "good" parts. Start where any amateur

who is serious about turning professional will start—at the beginning.

And, faithful to these promises, in the successive chapters of the 130 pages that follow, *Hit Man* systematically and in meticulous detail instructs on the gruesome particulars of every possible aspect of murder and murder for hire. The manual instructs step-by-step on building and using fertilizer bombs, constructing silencers, picking locks, selecting and using poisons, sinking corpses, and torturing victims. It teaches would-be assassins how to arrive at, and conduct surveillance of, a potential victim's house, and it instructs on the use of a fake driver's license and registration at a motel, the placement of stolen out-of-state license plates on rental cars, and the deception of the postal service into delivering weapons to the murder scene. The book instructs the reader in murder methods, explaining in dispassionate and excruciatingly graphic detail how to shoot, stab, poison, and incinerate people, and in gory detail it expounds on which methods of murder will best ensure the death of the victims. The book schools the reader on how to escape the crime scene without detection, and how to foil police investigations by disassembling and discarding the murder weapon, altering the ballistics markings of that weapon, stealing and switching license plates, and disguising the reader's physical appearance. And it counsels on how to manipulate the legal system, if caught. . . .

2.

In concluding that *Hit Man* is protected "advocacy," the district court appears to have misperceived the nature of the speech that the Supreme Court held in *Brandenburg* is protected under the First Amendment. In particular, the district court seems to have misunderstood the Court in *Brandenburg* as having distinguished between "advocating or teaching" lawlessness on the one hand, and "inciting or encouraging" lawlessness on the other, any and all of the former being entitled to protection. The district court thus framed the issue before it as "whether *Hit Man* merely advocates or teaches murder or whether it incites or encourages murder." And, finding that *Hit*

Man "merely teaches" in technical fashion the fundamentals of murder, it concluded that "the book does not cross that line between permissible advocacy and impermissible incitation to crime or violence."

The Court in *Brandenburg,* however, did not hold that "mere teaching" is protected; the Court never even used this phrase. And it certainly did not hold, as the district court apparently believed, that *all* teaching is protected. Rather, however inartfully it may have done so, the Court fairly clearly held only that the "mere *abstract* teaching" of principles are protected. In the final analysis, it appears the district court simply failed to fully appreciate the import of the qualification to the kind of "teaching" that the Supreme Court held to be protected in *Brandenburg.* . . .

Although we believe the district court's specific misreading of *Brandenburg* was plainly in error, we cannot fault the district court for its confusion over the opinion in that case. The short *per curiam* opinion in *Brandenburg* is, by any measure, elliptical.

In particular, the Court unmistakably draws the distinction discussed above, between "the mere abstract teaching . . . of the moral propriety or even moral necessity for a resort to force and violence" on one hand, and the "preparation [of] a group for violent action and steeling it to such action" on the other. And it then recites in the very next sentence that "[a] statute which fails to draw *this* distinction" (emphasis added)—a seeming reference to the distinction between "mere abstract teaching" and "preparing and steeling"—is unconstitutional under the First Amendment. In the succeeding paragraph and a later footnote, however, the Court distinguishes between "mere advocacy" and "incitement to imminent lawless action," a distinction which, as a matter of common sense and common parlance, appears different from the first distinction drawn, because "preparation and steeling" can occur without "incitement," and vice-versa.

It would have been natural, based upon its prior cases, for the Court actually to have contemplated and intended both distinctions, and to have developed the latter only, because the case before it turned exclusively on that distinction. It is more likely, however, that the Court did not focus at all on the seeming facial incongruity between the first and the latter two

of these distinctions. The Court, therefore, may well have intended to equate the preparation and steeling of a group to violent action with speech that is directed to inciting imminent lawless action and likely to produce such action. In other words, the Court may well have meant to imply that one prepares and steels another or others for violent action only when he does so through speech that is "directed to inciting or producing imminent lawless action and . . . [that is] likely to incite or produce such action," and thus that preparation and steeling is not per se unprotected. Assuming that it did so mean to imply, however, we are confident it meant to do so only in the context of advocacy—speech that is part and parcel of political and social discourse—which was the only type of speech at issue in *Brandenburg.* . . . For, as this case reveals, and as the Court itself has always seemed to recognize, one obviously can prepare, and even steel, another to violent action not only through the dissident "call to violence," but also through speech, such as instruction in the methods of terror or other crime, that does not even remotely resemble advocacy, in either form or purpose. And, of course, to understand the Court as addressing itself to speech other than advocacy would be to ascribe to it an intent to revolutionize the criminal law . . . by subjecting prosecutions to the demands of *Brandenburg's* "imminence" and "likelihood" requirements whenever the predicate conduct takes, in whole or in part, the form of speech—an intent that no lower court has discerned and that, this late in the day, we would hesitate to impute to the Supreme Court.

Accordingly, we hold that plaintiffs have stated, sufficient to withstand summary judgment, a civil cause of action against Paladin Enterprises for aiding and abetting the murders of Mildred and Trevor Horn and Janice Saunders on the night of March 3, 1993, and that this cause of action is not barred by the First Amendment to the United States Constitution.

IV.

Paladin, joined by a spate of media *amici,* including many of the major networks, newspapers, and publishers, contends that any decision recognizing even a potential cause of action against Paladin will have far-reaching chilling effects on the rights of free speech and press. That the national media organizations would feel obliged to vigorously defend Paladin's assertion of a constitutional right to intentionally and knowingly assist murderers with technical information which Paladin admits it intended and knew would be used immediately in the commission of murder and other crimes against society is, to say the least, breath-taking. But be that as it may, it should be apparent from the foregoing that the indisputably important First Amendment values that Paladin and *amici* argue would be imperiled by a decision recognizing potential liability under the peculiar facts of this case will not even arguably be adversely affected by allowing plain-tiffs' action against Paladin to proceed. . . .

Paladin and *amici* insist that recognizing the exis-tence of a cause of action against Paladin predicated on aiding and abetting will subject broadcasters and publishers to liability whenever someone imitates or "copies" conduct that is either described or depicted in their broadcasts, publications, or movies. This is simply not true. In the "copycat" context, it will presumably never be the case that the broadcaster or publisher actually intends, through its description or depiction, to assist another or others in the com-mission of violent crime; rather, the information for the dissemination of which liability is sought to be imposed will actually have been misused vis-a-vis the use intended, not, as here, used precisely as intended. It would be difficult to overstate the significance of this difference insofar as the potential liability to which the media might be exposed by our decision herein is concerned.

And, perhaps most importantly, there will almost never be evidence proffered from which a jury even could reasonably conclude that the producer or pub-lisher possessed the actual intent to assist criminal activity. In only the rarest case, as here where the pub-lisher has stipulated in almost taunting defiance that it intended to assist murderers and other criminals, will there be evidence extraneous to the speech itself which would support a finding of the requisite intent; surely few will, as Paladin has, "stand up and proclaim to the world that because they are publishers they have a unique constitutional right to aid and abet murder."

Moreover, in contrast to the case before us, in vir-tually every "copycat" case, there will be lacking in the speech itself any basis for a permissible inference that the "speaker" intended to assist and facilitate the criminal conduct described or depicted. Of course, with few, if any, exceptions, the speech which gives rise to the copycat crime will not directly and affirma-tively promote the criminal conduct, even if, in some circumstances, it incidentally glamorizes and thereby indirectly promotes such conduct.

Additionally, not only will a political, informa-tional, educational, entertainment, or other wholly legitimate purpose for the description or depiction be demonstrably apparent; but the description or depic-tion of the criminality will be of such a character that an inference of impermissible intent on the part of the producer or publisher would be unwarranted as a matter of law. So, for example, for almost any broadcast, book, movie, or song that one can imagine, an inference of unlawful motive from the description or depiction of particular criminal conduct therein would almost never be reasonable, for not only will there be (and demonstrably so) a legitimate and lawful purpose for these communications, but the contexts in which the descriptions or depictions appear will them-selves negate a purpose on the part of the producer or publisher to assist others in their undertaking of the described or depicted conduct.

Paladin contends that exposing it to liability under the circumstances presented here will necessar-ily expose broadcasters and publishers of the news, in particular, to liability when persons mimic activ-ity either reported on or captured on film footage and disseminated in the form of broadcast news. This con-tention, as well, is categorically wrong. News report-ing, we can assume, no matter how explicit it is in its description or depiction of criminal activity, could never serve as a basis for aiding and abetting liability consistent with the First Amendment. It will be self-evident in the context of news reporting, if nowhere else, that neither the intent of the reporter nor the pur-pose of the report is to facilitate repetition of the crime or other conduct reported upon, but, rather, merely to report on the particular event, and thereby to inform the public.

A decision that Paladin may be liable under the circumstances of this case is not even tantamount to a holding that all publishers of instructional manuals may be liable for the misconduct that ensues when one follows the instructions which appear in those manuals. Admittedly, a holding that Paladin is not entitled to an absolute defense to the plaintiffs' claims here may not bode well for those publishers, if any, of factually detailed instructional books, similar to *Hit Man,* which are devoted exclusively to teaching the techniques of violent activities that are criminal per se. But, in holding that a defense to liability may not inure to publishers for their dissemination of such manuals of criminal conduct, we do not address ourselves to the potential liability of a publisher for the criminal use of published instructions on activity that is either entirely lawful, or lawful or not depending upon the circumstances of its occurrence. Assuming, as we do, that liability could not be imposed in these circumstances on a finding of mere foreseeability or knowledge that the instructions might be misused for a criminal purpose, the chances that claims arising from the publication of instructional manuals like these can withstand motions for summary judgment directed to the issue of intent seem to us remote indeed, at least absent some substantial confirmation of specific intent like that that exists in this case.

Thus, while the "horribles" paraded before us by Paladin . . . have quite properly prompted us to examine and reexamine the established authorities on which plaintiffs' case firmly rests, we regard them ultimately as but anticipatory of cases wholly unlike the one we must decide today.

Paladin Press in this case has stipulated that it specifically targeted the market of murderers, would-be murderers, and other criminals for sale of its murder manual. Paladin has stipulated both that it had knowledge and that it intended that *Hit Man* would immediately be used by criminals and would-be criminals in the solicitation, planning, and commission of murder and murder for hire. And Paladin has stipulated that, through publishing and selling *Hit Man,* it "assisted" Perry in particular in the perpetration of the brutal triple murders for which plaintiffs now seek to hold the publisher liable. Beyond these startling stipulations, it is alleged, and the record would support, that Paladin assisted Perry through the quintessential speech act of providing Perry with detailed factual instructions on how to prepare for, commit, and cover up his murders, instructions which themselves embody not so much as a hint of the theoretical advocacy of principles divorced from action that is the hallmark of protected speech. And it is alleged, and a jury could find, that Paladin's assistance assumed the form of speech with little, if any, purpose beyond the unlawful one of facilitating murder.

Paladin's astonishing stipulations, coupled with the extraordinary comprehensiveness, detail, and clarity of *Hit Man*'s instructions for criminal activity and murder in particular, the boldness of its palpable exhortation to murder, the alarming power and effectiveness of its peculiar form of instruction, the notable absence from its text of the kind of ideas for the protection of which the First Amendment exists, and the book's evident lack of any even arguably legitimate purpose beyond the promotion and teaching of murder, render this case unique in the law. In at least these circumstances, we are confident that the First Amendment does not erect the absolute bar to the imposition of civil liability for which Paladin Press and *amici* contend. Indeed, to hold that the First Amendment forbids liability in such circumstances as a matter of law would fly in the face of all precedent of which we are aware, not only from the courts of appeals but from the Supreme Court of the United States itself. *Hit Man* is, we are convinced, the speech that even Justice Douglas, with his unrivaled devotion to the First Amendment, counseled without any equivocation "should be beyond the pale" under a Constitution that reserves to the people the ultimate and necessary authority to adjudge some conduct—and even some speech—fundamentally incompatible with the liberties they have secured unto themselves.

The judgment of the district court is hereby reversed, and the case remanded for trial.

It is so ordered.

Chapter 8

News must not be unnecessarily cut off at its source, for without freedom to acquire information the right to publish would be impermissibly compromised. Accordingly, a right to gather news, of some dimensions, must exist.

U.S. Supreme Court Justice Lewis Powell[1]

When The New York Times sought cockpit voice recordings after the space shuttle Challenger exploded, a court ruled against the Times, holding that privacy rights outweighed the public interest in hearing the recordings.

Newsgathering
Pitfalls and Protections

Newsgathering Pitfalls

Trespass
Harassment
Fraud and
    Misrepresentation

Covert Recording

Face-to-Face Recording
Recording "Wire"
    Conversations
Noncovert Recording

**Access to Military
   Operations**

Denying Access to Records

**Newsgathering
   Protections**

Open Government Laws
Access to Federal Records

**Access to Federal
   Meetings**

State Open-Records Laws
State Open-Meetings Laws

Cases for Study

➤ *Wilson v. Layne*
➤ *U.S. Department of
   Justice v. Reporters
   Committee for
   Freedom of the Press*

Suppose . . .

. . . that a team of law enforcement officers executes a search warrant on what they believe is the home of a suspect. With them are a reporter and photographer from a newspaper. The officers forcibly enter the home in the early morning hours, awakening the home's two residents. The couple is the suspect's parents, who assure the officers their son is not there. The photographer takes several pictures, though none are published. After a search of the home to confirm, the officers and journalists leave. Was the presence of the journalists illegal? If so, who is responsible—the journalists or the law enforcement agency? Look for the answers to these questions when the case of *Wilson v. Layne* is discussed later in this chapter. The case is also excerpted at the end of the chapter.

This chapter deals with how journalists obtain information. (Chapter 9 is about whether and how journalists can keep from having to reveal information already in their possession.) In discussing newsgathering, the issue largely revolves around access—whether the journalist has access to information—to documents, records, people and places where newsworthy information potentially resides.

As Justice Powell's statement at the beginning of the chapter about the importance of newsgathering clearly asserts, unless journalists have some ability to obtain information, the First Amendment freedom of the press clause would seem toothless. After all, what purpose does the freedom to distribute news serve unless there is also some protection to acquire that news in the first place? As logical as that argument may seem, however, it largely falls on deaf ears within the judiciary. In the same ruling in which the Court said that some newsgathering protection may exist, it also stated that "the First Amendment does not guarantee the press a constitutional right of special access to information not available to the public generally."[2] On the whole, the courts have said that journalists have the same amount of access as any person. No more. No less. The news media are not without newsgathering protection. What they have, however, is no different than the rights and privileges that can be exercised by any citizen. This is one area where the concept of general applicability comes into play. Laws are not unconstitutional merely because they may incidentally or unintentionally infringe on the news media's First Amendment rights. As long as the laws do not specifically target or single out the press, they may be applied to the press. Claims that they violate the First Amendment will not prevail.[3]

Perhaps the clearest articulation of the judicial perspective on whether any special newsgathering privilege exists for journalists under the First Amendment came in 1975 from U.S. Supreme Court Justice Potter Stewart:

> So far as the Constitution goes, the autonomous press may publish what it knows, and may seek to learn what it can. But this autonomy cuts both ways. The press is free to do battle against secrecy and deception in government. But the press cannot expect from the Constitution any guarantee that it will succeed. There is no constitutional right to have access to particular government information, or to require openness from the bureaucracy. The public's interest in knowing about its government is protected by the guarantee of a Free Press, but the protection is indirect. The Constitution itself is neither a Freedom of Information Act nor an Official Secrets Act.[4]

Nevertheless, many people have diligently argued that because of the logic in the contention that providing a freedom to publish information matters little without the protection to obtain it in the first place, an explicit newsgathering privilege is required.[5] Given that information is the lifeblood of the news media, the ability to obtain it should not only be valued but also should be an integral element of freedom of the press. If the First Amendment protects only distribution, a journalist may ask, "The freedom to distribute what?" The Supreme Court has proclaimed that "without some protection for seeking out the news, freedom of the press could be eviscerated."[6] Yet one source calls this proclamation "empty rhetoric"[7] and claims that because newsgathering serves core purposes of the First Amendment, it should be regarded as a First Amendment–protected activity.[8] Another says the "simplistic 'general law' approach is not so much a solution as a judicial abdication of responsibility in this area of the law."[9]

But those core purposes of the First Amendment also provide support for the contention that there neither is, nor should be, specific protection for newsgathering. That argument—one that the courts seem to accept—relies, in part, on an "originalist" interpretation of the Constitution and, specifically, the First Amendment. In other words, according to this approach, the original intent of the framers governs how constitutional provisions should be applied today. Newsgathering was not a major function of the press during the era when the Bill of Rights was debated and ultimately adopted. Press outlets largely printed information that they were provided. News reporting, as we know it today—including the pursuit of government-held information—was virtually nonexistent. Thus, according to this argument, the freedom of press clause in the First Amendment could not have been intended for newsgathering. It merely protected the publication of information once it was obtained.

Newsgathering Pitfalls

The First Amendment rights afforded the media are sometimes characterized as "shield" or "sword." They can be used as a defense (shield) when the press is attacked (i.e., sued) for what it has done. That usually means what it has published. First Amendment rights can also be used as a weapon (sword) in the news media's efforts to conduct business—namely, acquiring information. The fact is, however, that the First Amendment is not always effective as a sword. The courts generally do not accept the First Amendment as a basis for a right to gather news.

The First Amendment is, in fact, much stronger as a shield than as a sword. A good example is the development of libel law, as described in Chapters 4 and 5. That shield is so solid, in fact, that parties who feel they have been wronged by the press are becoming more likely to confront the media on a legal battlefield where media shields are weakest.[10] Frequently, the wrongs and the legal responses arise in the area of newsgathering. This became especially true during the late 20th and early 21st centuries. The methods of newsgathering often attracted more criticism than the publications themselves. As the definition of "investigative reporting" was stretched, as newsgathering technologies evolved to make surveillance and the recording of it easier and more covert, and as television news magazines and "reality" programs multiplied, so did the legal complaints in the newsgathering area. Legal claims related to

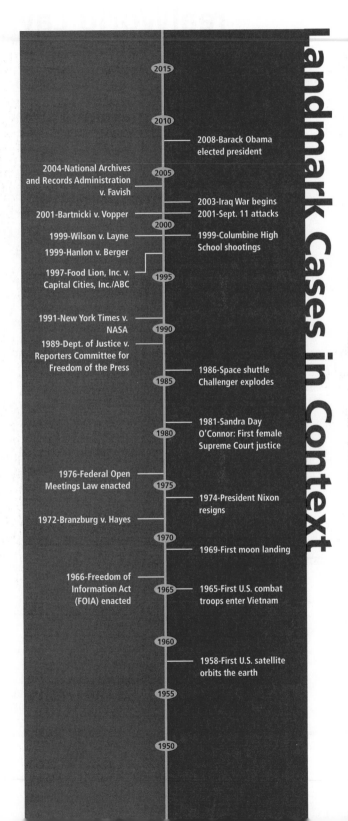

Landmark Cases in Context

- 2015
- 2010
- 2008-Barack Obama elected president
- 2005
- 2004-National Archives and Records Administration v. Favish
- 2003-Iraq War begins
- 2001-Bartnicki v. Vopper
- 2001-Sept. 11 attacks
- 2000
- 1999-Wilson v. Layne
- 1999-Columbine High School shootings
- 1999-Hanlon v. Berger
- 1997-Food Lion, Inc. v. Capital Cities, Inc./ABC
- 1995
- 1991-New York Times v. NASA
- 1990
- 1989-Dept. of Justice v. Reporters Committee for Freedom of the Press
- 1986-Space shuttle Challenger explodes
- 1985
- 1981-Sandra Day O'Connor: First female Supreme Court justice
- 1980
- 1976-Federal Open Meetings Law enacted
- 1975
- 1974-President Nixon resigns
- 1972-Branzburg v. Hayes
- 1970
- 1969-First moon landing
- 1966-Freedom of Information Act (FOIA) enacted
- 1965
- 1965-First U.S. combat troops enter Vietnam
- 1960
- 1958-First U.S. satellite orbits the earth
- 1955
- 1950

A Question of Access

The issue of access to locations with potential news and information value surfaced amid the 2010 BP oil spill in the Gulf of Mexico. Members of the news media and others who wanted to observe and document what they saw in the area were often denied access. Many cried "Foul!," particularly when the Federal Aviation Administration (FAA) granted a request to restrict flights over the affected area. It seemed as if the federal government was assisting BP's efforts to limit not just the flow of the oil, but also the flow of information.

Oil floats on the surface of the Gulf of Mexico after the 2010 BP oil spill.

The New York Times was among the news organizations that reported journalists repeatedly being denied access to public areas in the Gulf region.[1] An Associated Press senior managing editor likened the situation to embedding reporters in Afghanistan, where, he said, "there is a continued effort to keep control over the access."[2] Rep. Edward Markey said he believed access was being limited. When Sen. Bill Nelson wanted to take a small group of journalists with him on a Coast Guard vessel trip into the Gulf, he was told by the Department of Homeland Security that no journalists would be allowed. CBS News reported that one of its news crews was threatened with arrest for trying to shoot video of a public beach where oil had washed ashore.[3] A piloting business was questioned about a permission request to fly over the Gulf. "We were questioned extensively," says the co-owner. "Who was on the aircraft? Who did they work for? The minute we mentioned media, the answer was: 'Not allowed.'"

These incidents illustrate the tension inherent in many newsworthy situations: journalists' desire to gather and record information versus government officials' need to conduct their work. For example, an FAA spokesperson said flight restrictions were necessary to prevent civilian air traffic from interfering with aircraft working on the disaster. Alarming many critics, however, was that the way some government agencies and officials seemed to operate helped insulate BP, a private (i.e., nongovernment) company from media and public scrutiny.[4] That is, some were concerned that the restrictions were an example of the government itself playing an active role in denying public access to important information, thereby keeping people uninformed. When a commission investigated the BP spill, it was told by Thad Allen, the retired Coast Guard admiral who commanded the federal response in the Gulf, that an independent third party should be created to oversee future spills rather than leaving the job to the government. An independent expert, he said, would reduce concerns about a conflict of interest given the public mistrust of BP and the government.

1. Jeremy W. Peters, *Efforts to Limit the Flow of Spill News,* N.Y. Times, June 10, 2010, at A20.
2. Lynn Hermann, *Air Space over Oil Disaster Restricted, Media Access Restricted,* Digital Journal, June 12, 2010, *available at* http://www.digitaljournal.com/article/293304.
3. Jeremy W. Peters, *As Oil Disaster Unfolds, BP and Officials Keep Journalists at Arm's Length: Critics Call Restrictions on Access Part of Attempt to Filter What Public Sees,* N.Y. Times, June 11, 2010, at 5.
4. *See, e.g.,* David Carr, *The Oil Slick Is in Plain Sight; The Facts Are a BP Secret and a Daily Riddle; Corporation Keeping Lid on Spill Information—with Government Help,* Int'l Herald Trib., June 15, 2010, at 18.

newsgathering often involve the electronic media, particularly television. The newsgathering tools of television are more obtrusive, are more noticeable and seem to cause more alarm and apprehension in many settings than the pen and notepad of the newspaper reporter.

The doctrine that news media have no more or less access than other citizens was reinforced by a series of U.S. Supreme Court rulings involving the right to gather news in jails and prisons. In each of three cases, the media claims were rejected. The Court ruled that "[n]ewsmen have no constitutional right of access to prisons or their inmates *beyond that afforded the general public.*"[11] This doctrine was highlighted when a San Francisco television station challenged limitations placed on its crew. The crew was advised it could view parts of a county jail by taking part in one of the regular tours of the facility but could not have unregulated access to the jail. The station challenged the jail policy in court and lost.[12] Similar challenges brought by the press against policies barring interviews with selected inmates were also rejected.[13]

Trespass

Trespassing is simply going onto the property of another without permission.[14] The opportunity to provide that permission is not restricted to the property owner. The resident of a dwelling, even if he or she is not the owner, has the authority to grant or deny others the permission to enter. An exception is when law enforcement officials obtain a search warrant or have emergency control of property; they then have the legal authority to enter without permission.

Trespassing is similar to the concept of intrusion discussed in Chapter 6. Both involve people being where they legally may not be. But while intrusion claims are based on an invasion of privacy according to whether the plaintiff has a reasonable expectation of privacy, trespass is not directly linked to privacy issues.

As is the situation with other strategies for newsgathering, journalists have no more right than any other citizen to enter the property of others. This includes entering property in the course of newsgathering, no matter how important or how much in the public interest the resulting information would be. The prohibition against trespassing is generally applicable; no one, journalists included, may trespass.

Trespass problems in the course of newsgathering often occur in settings that are privately owned but generally accessible to the public. A restaurant, for example, was the site of an instructive case. A reporter and camera crew from a New York City television station entered restaurants that had been cited for health code violations. The journalists were specifically instructed by their managers not to schedule an appointment or ask for permission but to catch the occupants by surprise "with cameras rolling."[15] Following these instructions, the crew members entered the restaurant, turned on their lights and began photographing patrons who were dining, Restaurant management asked the crew to leave. Instead, it was patrons who left, many without paying. As the court said,

"Patronizing a restaurant does not carry with it an obligation to appear on television."[16] The restaurant was successful in its trespassing lawsuit.

Notably, the journalists in this case were asked to leave the restaurant. The absence of a request to leave can be crucial as a court considers a case. In one instance, members of the news media were invited by a local fire marshal into a home that was badly damaged by a fire that had killed a 17-year-old girl. When the fire marshal ran out of film in a camera he was using to document the fire, he asked a newspaper photographer to take a picture of the floor where the victim's body had been. While a copy was provided to police and fire officials, the photo was also one of several published in the next day's newspaper. In part because the victim's mother was out of town, she first learned of her daughter's death from the newspaper story and photos. She filed several claims against the newspaper. Her claim of trespass was ultimately rejected by the Florida Supreme Court on the basis of long-standing custom and practice. Evidence had been presented at trial that it had been customary for members of the news media to enter private residences where a disaster of public importance occurred as long as they did so at the invitation of law enforcement officials and caused no further damage. The court also applied a broad rule stipulating that in Florida there is no trespass when the consent of the owner may be implied.[17]

ride-along A term given to the practice of journalists and other private citizens accompanying government officials—usually those in law enforcement or other emergency response personnel—as they carry out their duties.

The tradition of the **ride-along**—in which journalists accompany law enforcement or emergency personnel, often by invitation, to rescues, raids or other scenes—was deep-seated in the cultures of both journalism and law enforcement. The practice tended to serve parties on both sides, particularly the media representatives who were provided with the material for stories or, in some cases, program segments. The custom, however, began to be questioned when homes and other private property were visited. In these situations, the media's First Amendment rights were weighed against the resident's Fourth Amendment protection against unreasonable searches of their dwellings. A series of rulings has significantly limited news media access in these ride-along situations.

The tide began to turn against media participation in ride-alongs—particularly when they involved entering private residences—in the 1980s in state court cases. In one of those, a television crew accompanied a paramedic unit from the Los Angeles Fire Department into the home of a heart attack victim. The resuscitation efforts, ultimately unsuccessful, were videotaped and broadcast on a local newscast that night and later as part of a documentary on paramedics. The victim's widow and daughter sued. Among their claims was trespassing. A California appeals court ruled for the plaintiffs. Its analysis included the following points:

- There was no evidence the crew considered entering the home to be improper.
- Because entering the home was intentional, the crew members were liable in spite of acting in good faith and being of the belief that they had committed no wrong.

- The defendants claimed that by calling for paramedics the plaintiffs gave implied consent for the television crew to enter the home. The court called this claim "devoid of merit."[18]
- "Personal security in a society saturated daily with publicity about its members requires protection not only from governmental intrusion, but some basic bulwark of defense against private commercial enterprises which derive profits from gathering and disseminating information."[19]

The court acknowledged the importance of newsgathering as part of news dissemination but noted that the "First Amendment has never been construed to accord newsmen immunity from torts or crimes committed during the course of newsgathering. The First Amendment is not a license to trespass, to steal, or to intrude by electronic means into the precincts of another's home or office."[20] To hold the television crew liable for trespass, the court ruled, does not place an impermissible burden on newsgatherers or their First Amendment rights. "To hold otherwise," the court said, "might have extraordinarily chilling implications for all of us."[21] What began emerging from this and similar rulings was the doctrine that government permission for media to enter a private residence is not equivalent to obtaining the consent of the resident, nor is it adequate for legal entry.

The U.S. Supreme Court reinforced that doctrine. In one case a CNN crew accompanied federal agents to a Montana ranch. U.S. Fish and Wildlife Service (FWS) agents obtained a warrant to search the 75,000-acre ranch. Officials suspected the residents, the Berger family, had shot or poisoned eagles, violating federal wildlife laws.[22] The Bergers did not know until later that CNN and the FWS had struck a deal in which the lead FWS officer would wear a CNN microphone and the officers would use CNN video cameras. CNN agreed to air the videotape only if the government did not press charges against the family, until a jury had been chosen if charges were brought or if the case against the Bergers was resolved some other way.[23] When they learned of the FWS–CNN agreement, the Bergers claimed the FWS officers violated their Fourth Amendment rights to be free from unreasonable searches and seizures. In *Hanlon v. Berger* the Supreme Court said a jury could consider whether the Bergers' Fourth Amendment rights were violated.[24] The Court's decision in *Berger* sidestepped any sort of First Amendment analysis, choosing instead to analyze the case through the lens of the Fourth Amendment as a search matter, not a free speech matter. The nature of the raid violated the Fourth Amendment largely because it was intended to serve a purpose other than law enforcement. The Court characterized the taping as being for "entertainment purposes."[25] Before the trial began, CNN and the Bergers settled the case out of court.[26]

On the same day that it announced its decision in *Berger,* the Supreme Court dealt another blow to ride-alongs in *Wilson v. Layne.* This important decision is excerpted at the end of this chapter. Wilson involved the search of a private home. Armed with a search warrant, deputy federal marshals and

Points of Law

The Media and Search Warrants

We hold that police violate the Fourth Amendment rights of homeowners when they allow members of the media to accompany them during the execution of a warrant in their home.[1]

1. Hanlon v. Berger, 526 U.S. 808, 810 (1999).

Points of Law

Wilson v. Layne: The State of Ride-Alongs

- A search warrant entitles officers, but not reporters, to enter a home.

- Presence of reporters is not related to the authorized intrusion.

- Presence of reporters serves no legitimate law enforcement purposes.

- Inviting reporters for the execution of a search warrant violates the Fourth Amendment.

local police officers had invited a Washington Post reporter and photographer to accompany them when they conducted a raid to arrest a fugitive. The raid began at 6:45 a.m. Once inside, officers were confronted by a man who had been asleep but who now demanded an explanation. Police wrestled him to the floor as his wife emerged from the bedroom. The photographer took pictures throughout the ordeal, although none of the photos was published. It turned out the couple in the home were the parents of the fugitive, who was not in the home. Believing that their Fourth Amendment rights prohibiting unreasonable searches had been violated, the couple sued the law enforcement officials. What was unreasonable, they thought, was the presence of the journalists.[27]

Ruling in favor of the couple in its 1999 decision, the U.S. Supreme Court in *Wilson v. Layne* cited a number of reasons why the news media were not lawfully in the home. In doing so the Court established a number of legal points that have enduring application in the day-to-day lives of working journalists.

First, because the officers had a warrant, they were clearly entitled to enter the home to serve the arrest warrant. But it does not necessarily follow that they could invite a newspaper reporter and a photographer to accompany them.[28] Second, the presence of reporters inside the home was not related to the objectives of the authorized entry. The law enforcement defendants conceded that the reporters did not engage in the execution of the warrant and did not assist the police in their task. The reporters, therefore, were not there for any reason related to the presence of law enforcement.[29]

The defendants argued that the presence of the journalists served a number of legitimate law enforcement purposes. But the Court said any such benefits did not outweigh the residential privacy rights protected by the Fourth Amendment. Even if media ride-alongs further police objectives in a general sense, that is not the same as furthering the purposes of the search. The law enforcement officials also argued that the presence of third parties helped publicize the government's efforts to combat crime and facilitated accurate reporting on law enforcement activities. However worthy those objectives, said the Court, they are similarly insufficient to overcome the Fourth Amendment, which concerns itself with fundamental individual rights, and it is in terms of those rights that media ride-alongs must be evaluated.[30] Neither good public relations for the police nor the need for accurate reporting on police activities furnishes an adequate constitutional justification for media to accompany police into a home during execution of an arrest warrant.[31]

The Court also rejected the argument that third parties could help minimize police abuses and protect suspects. But while the police may well take videos to preserve evidence and document an arrest, the intent of the Washington Post journalists in this case was to gather news, not to serve officers or residents. Although the presence of third parties during the execution of a warrant in some circumstances may be constitutionally permissible, the Court said, in this case it was not.[32] The rule that emerged, then, is that it is generally a violation of the Fourth Amendment for police to bring members of the media or other third parties into a home during the execution of a warrant unless that third party is there to help execute the warrant.[33] It should be emphasized that in the two U.S. Supreme Court rulings just discussed, neither media organizations nor journalists were named as defendants. Instead, law enforcement officials were held accountable. Nevertheless, the implications for news media are clear.

The law is now clearly on the side of residents in this area. Media ride-alongs that remain on public property are safer territory for journalists, but reporters are not immune from liability even in those circumstances.[34]

Many believed that the Supreme Court's ruling in *Wilson v. Layne* would mean the end of television programs, such as Fox's "COPS," that depend on cameras accompanying law enforcement officers onto private property, including inside homes. Instead, "COPS" continued to be financially successful. "While we do not necessarily agree with that decision," said "COPS" executive producer John Langley, "we are obligated to point out that, as a so-called 'ride-along' show, we are unaffected by the decision because we obtain releases from everyone involved in our program."[35]

The Propriety of Ride-Alongs

From the news media's perspective, the benefits of ride-alongs are apparent: the opportunity to observe and record law enforcement or emergency personnel at work. But the practice is also highly questionable. Among those who have commented on the custom is First Amendment scholar Rodney Smolla. Journalists, he says, should be careful about ride-alongs. If nothing else, ride-alongs place the media and government officials "dangerously close" to working together. While that may seem innocent, it endangers press autonomy from government and the adversarial relationship necessary to hold those in government accountable. At the very least, Smolla says, journalists should make the distinction between public and private spaces. Cruising neighborhoods is one thing; being part of warrant execution, especially on private property, is another. Granted, in public spheres, journalists may be provided unique and valuable access. It is vital, however, to maintain independence and stay away from a quid pro quo relationship. For law enforcement officials to have to defend themselves by claiming journalists were working with them, as in *Wilson v. Layne,* is an embarrassment, Smolla says.[1]

1. Rodney A. Smolla, *Privacy and the Law: The Media's Intrusion on Privacy: Privacy and the First Amendment Right to Gather News,* 67 Geo. Wash. L. Rev. 1097 (1999).

Harassment

Another by-product of the adoption of aggressive newsgathering efforts by some in the media occurs when those tactics cross a line and become harassment. Perhaps the most notable examples occur when celebrities are pursued by photographers known as "paparazzi." One of the most infamous cases developed when one of these photographers repeatedly stalked former First Lady Jacqueline Kennedy Onassis and her children.[36] The photographer, Ron Galella, was sued not only by Onassis but also by the Secret Service, which claimed that Galella continually interfered with agents assigned to protect Onassis and her children. Galella had asserted that the First Amendment was a complete defense to his behavior. The court flatly rejected that contention and ordered Galella to remain 150 feet from Mrs. Onassis, 225 feet from her children, and 300 feet from their homes and schools. The distances were significantly reduced on appeal.[37]

Jacqueline Kennedy Onassis in 1968 with her children, Caroline and John, Jr.

tortious newsgathering The use of reporting techniques that are wrongful and unlawful and for which the victim may obtain damages in court.

The sort of "ambush-and-surveillance" journalism practiced by Galella became even more commonplace in the late 20th century, prompting the label **tortious newsgathering** to be invoked. Tortious newsgathering encompasses the various pitfalls examined in this chapter. One case particularly symbolizes the evolution of the law—and the media—in this area. Employees of the syndicated television program "Inside Edition" were working on a story on the insurance firm U.S. Health-care. Their interview request with the CEO was denied, so they targeted his daughter and son-in-law, also executives in the company. The "Inside Edition" tactics included staking out the executives' home, following them to and from work and following their 3-year-old to preschool. Hidden cameras, powerful microphones and cameras with telephoto lenses were also used. To escape, the family vacationed in Florida. The "Inside Edition" crew followed them, rented a boat and set up shop offshore, about 50 yards from the family beach house.

Upon return to their Philadelphia home, the family sought an injunction. A federal district court granted the request.[38] In doing so, the judge noted that the efforts of the "Inside Edition" crew members would not be "irreparably harmed by an injunction narrowly tailored to preclude them from continuing their harassing conduct"[39] toward the family, nor would the injunction impair their "*legal* newsgathering activities."[40] This seemed to be an indication of concern in the judiciary about newsgathering tactics that are not only illegal but breach ethical standards as well.

After incidents like these—and especially after the 1997 car accident that killed England's Princess Diana as photographers pursued her—the idea of anti-paparazzi legislation grew in popularity. Such a statute was passed and signed into law in celebrity-populated California. The law establishes liability for trespass with the intent to capture any kind of visual image or sound recording.[41] A similar measure was proposed on the federal level. Interest in it, however, could not be sustained, and it has not been enacted.[42]

Fraud and Misrepresentation

In the effort to obtain and report a story of significant public interest, how far can journalists go? Does the importance of the story warrant breaking the law? Bending the law? In the early 1990s, producers working for an ABC News television magazine program decided to investigate accusations of unsanitary practices at

realWorld Law

"California v. Paparazzi"

Newsgathering practices typically associated with paparazzi were targeted in a law passed by California lawmakers in 2010. The new law is directed at photographers who drive recklessly in pursuit of celebrity photos or who block sidewalks to create a sort of "false imprisonment."[1] The bill adds a misdemeanor charge to those stopped on suspicion of reckless driving when a celebrity pursuit is in play. Extra penalties are added if it is determined that children have been endangered as a result. Those who trespass or invade a celebrity's privacy to obtain a good picture will face triple the normal penalties and up to three times the damages they would have faced before the bill passed.[2] Critics of the bill, which include the California Newspaper Publishers Association, say laws against reckless driving and trespassing already address these concerns and do so without implicating the First Amendment.

This law follows an effort two years prior by Malibu and other Los Angeles-area cities to regulate paparazzi conduct, thereby making their celebrity residents and guests more comfortable. That undertaking was also criticized by First Amendment advocates.[3]

1. Patrick McGreevy & Jack Dolan, *Pay Reforms Inspired by Bell OKd*, L.A. Times, Sept. 1, 2010, at AA1.
2. Dennis Romero, *Stiff Penalties for Aggressive Paparazzi in California Likely*, L.A. Weekly, Sept. 1, 2010, *available at* http://blogs.laweekly.com informer/hollywood/paparazzi-bill-passes/.
3. Harriet Ryan, *Plan Would Protect Stars from Paparazzi*, L.A. Times, Nov. 20, 2008, at B4.

the Food Lion grocery chain. With the approval of many within ABC, producers decided that the best way to investigate the store's practices was to have reporters infiltrate the store as employees. Two female news reporters applied for jobs at Food Lion using false names and invented work histories. The plan worked. Both women were hired, one in North Carolina and the other in South Carolina. To document their findings, the producers used hidden miniature cameras and microphones.[43] Their story, complete with video recordings, aired on Nov. 5, 1992, on ABC's "Primetime Live." The report documented allegedly unsanitary meat-handling practices at the stores and was sharply critical of Food Lion.

Food Lion denied the accusations and then filed a lawsuit against ABC. The high-profile case, *Food Lion, Inc. v. Capital Cities, Inc./ABC*, initially went well for the plaintiff grocery chain and sent a chill through the media industry. Although a federal appellate court eventually reversed the verdict against ABC, the case remains a cautionary tale for the press and is important on several levels.[44] First, it was a milestone in the developing trend of plaintiffs veering away from libel claims. Rather than suing ABC for libel, where the truth or falsity of ABC's claims would be examined, Food Lion waged its legal battle on the newsgathering front, alleging fraud, trespass, unfair trade practices and breach of duty of loyalty.[45] In fact, the trial court's published opinion on the case asserted that because Food Lion chose not to sue for libel, it could be assumed the content of the story was true.[46] Rather than claim its reputation had been unfairly damaged, the court said, "Food Lion attacked the methods used by Defendants to gather the information ultimately aired on 'PrimeTime Live.'"[47] At trial, the

realWorld Law

Food Lion: Assessing the Impact

Because of the many issues that *Food Lion* raised, numerous analysts have commented on the case and its impact. The following are brief excerpts of some of those:

> This case brings up the almost impossible balance that must be achieved between the press' rights, the public's need to know, and a business' right to privacy.[1]

> Despite its reversal, *Food Lion* looms over journalists as a warning that even when significant wrongs are uncovered, an elaborate scheme of deception to obtain a story can lead to costly legal battles. . . . [I]t shows a growing mistrust of the media among judges and jurors.[2]

> By focusing on the substance of the newsgathering techniques used rather than the procedure followed in the investigation, the *Food Lion* court . . . was led to condemn the use of modern technology in newsgathering, particularly when used in the context of a trespass. The *Food Lion* court was greatly troubled, in particular, by the journalists' use of hidden cameras to record their experiences within the private spheres of their subjects.[3]

> What may well be driving successful plaintiffs' outcomes in these situations is not so much sympathy for the plaintiff as outrage at the perceived misconduct of journalists, who are often caricatured as arrogant and driven entirely by the glory that comes from a juicy scoop or sting, and the profits that come from highly-rated programming featuring investigative reports that are not particularly expensive to produce. The journalists are seen as presumptuously claiming a right to take the law into their own hands, thumbing their noses at civil and criminal limitations that apply to everyone else.[4]

> The line of cases . . . make clear that plaintiffs will have an easier time attacking the methods by which a story is reported than the veracity of the story itself. . . . As costs grow, so grow the potentially chilling effects from the liability threat posed when newsgathering techniques possibly violate laws of general applicability that have merely "incidental effects" on First Amendment rights.[5]

> Driven by competition, the need for profits, and demands for higher ratings or circulations, and provided with technological marvels such as ever-smaller video cameras and tape machines, the media have shown an increasing willingness to engage in unlawful methods of newsgathering.[6]

---

1. Lori Keeton, *What Is Really Rotten in the Food Lion Case: Chilling the Media's Unethical Newsgathering Techniques,* 49 FLA. L. REV. 111, 115 (1997).
2. Jennifer L. Marmon, *Intrusion and the Media: An Old Tort Learns New Tricks,* 34 IND. L. REV. 155, 173 (2002).
3. Ethan E. Litwin, *The Investigative Reporter's Freedom and Responsibility: Reconciling Freedom of the Press with Privacy Rights,* 86 GEO. L.J. 1093, 1115 (1998).
4. Rodney A. Smolla, *Qualified Intimacy, Celebrity, and the Case for a Newsgathering Privilege,* 33 U. RICH. L. REV. 1233, 1248 (2000).
5. Michael W. Richards, *Tort Vision for the New Millennium: Strengthening News Industry Standards as a Defense Tool in Law Suits over Newsgathering Techniques,* 10 FORDHAM INTELL. PROP. MEDIA & ENT. L.J. 501, 518 (2000).
6. John J. Walsh, et al, *Undercover Newsgathering Techniques: Issues and Concerns: Media Misbehavior and the Wages of Sin: The Constitutionality of Consequential Damages for Publication of Ill-Gotten Information,* 4 WM. & MARY BILL RTS. J. 1111, 1144 (1996).

jury found for Food Lion, awarding the grocery chain negligible amounts of money for its actual damages but more than $5.5 million in punitive damages. However, the trial court judge ruled that the punitive damages award was excessive and reduced it to $315,000. ABC appealed.

By a vote of 2–1, a three-judge panel of the federal appeals court reversed the verdict for Food Lion on all but the trespass and breach of loyalty claims. In the end, Food Lion was awarded a total of two dollars. But the ripple effects of this case remained. Between the jury verdict and the appeal, some segments of the journalism community were uneasy.[48] Not only were some newsgathering techniques being called illegal, the offending party had initially been hit hard with a punitive damages award, even though it was later reduced and then all but eliminated. In addition, the dissenting judge on the federal appeals court would have sustained the fraud claim against ABC as well as the punitive damages award.[49] At least one federal appeals court judge, in other words, believes that the conduct of the ABC producers constitutes fraud and merits stiff punishment.

This case also forced the media to justify their newsgathering methods. One organization was required to explain at length why the behavior of some of its employees was not criminal. While the news organization was ultimately required to pay less than pocket change in damages, a few factors should not be overlooked:

- First, the attorney fees alone were costly.[50]
- Second, those costs led to a chilling effect on the sort of newsgathering techniques used in producing the Food Lion story.
- Third, although the jury's verdict was overturned, its decision and subsequent interviews of jury members revealed a deep-seated animosity toward the news media, particularly toward an organization perceived as big, powerful, and possessing an above-the-law attitude and deep pockets. In interviews with the media following the trial, several jurors seemed to have delighted in reaching into those pockets with their punitive damage award.[51]

The success of ABC's appeal hinged to a large extent on interpretations of the state laws in North and South Carolina, where the alleged transgressions took place. Had the case arisen in another state it is conceivable that a different result could have occurred. In fact, that did happen about a year after the *Food Lion* ruling. In circumstances very similar to those in *Food Lion*, an employee of a local television station in Minneapolis applied for volunteer work at a ministry's care facility for the mentally disabled. She did not disclose that she was a station employee, saying she was unemployed. In the course of her volunteer work, she was armed with a hidden camera that recorded video later used in broadcasts critical of the facility. The ministry claimed that it was forced to relocate as a result of the reports. Its lawsuit against the station included claims of fraud and trespass. A Minnesota appeals court ruled against the station's effort to dismiss the suit, saying that the station misrepresented itself and entered private property without the consent of its owner—that is, it had trespassed.[52] The parties eventually reached a confidential settlement.

Misrepresentation can take other forms as well. Rather than completely masking their identities and intent, as occurred in the cases just discussed, journalists may be honest about who they are while misrepresenting the nature of the story they are seeking. For example, an NBC newsmagazine wanted to produce a story on the trucking industry. Truckers, however, were generally unwilling to cooperate. Ultimately, producers were referred to Peter Kennedy, a truck driver with a Maine trucking company. Although reluctant at first, Kennedy was persuaded when he was promised that the report would be positive and that it would contain no comments from anyone from Parents Against Tired Truckers (PATT). The driver agreed but still wanted the approval of his boss, Raymond Veilleux. Although skeptical initially, Veilleux was made the same promises and eventually agreed. The "Dateline" segment that ultimately aired was not positive about the trucking industry or Kennedy. Typical of its tone was the statement within the segment, "American highways are a trucker's killing field."[53] The report also contained interviews with PATT members.

The claims that Veilleux and Kennedy filed against NBC included fraud and misrepresentation. On the one hand, a federal appeals court ruled that the network's promises to produce a "positive portrayal" were too vague to sustain a claim against it.[54] On the other hand, although the court ruled in favor of NBC on nearly every point, it decided NBC's promise that no one from PATT would appear in the report was specific and unequivocal. Thus, damages could be awarded based on that misrepresentation. The parties settled for an undisclosed amount.[55] Media defendants may agree to such settlements in part because the U.S. Supreme Court has held that media promises—at least promises of source confidentiality—are legally binding.[56] In a 1991 decision, the Supreme Court said that media organizations could be responsible for damages after they published the name of a source to whom they had promised confidentiality. On remand, the Minnesota Supreme Court affirmed a judgment of $200,000 against the media for breaking that promise.[57] (This case is explained further in Chapter 9.)

SUMMARY

REPORTERS' EXUBERANCE IN PURSUING A STORY MAY be legally punishable when it constitutes harassment. Precisely when zealous reporting crosses the line into tortious interference is a factual determination that courts make case by case. However, persistence that resembles stalking or that frightens the subjects may result in court restraining orders or fines. Assault, with or without a reporter's pad, is illegal.

When reporters use deceit to gather news, they clearly violate ethical standards. They sometimes also violate the law. Courts generally look carefully at the specific facts of each case to determine when fraud or misrepresentation is legally punishable. Reporters should realize that their promises may be legally binding. ■

Covert Recording

The information gathering inherent in journalism and other professions often means its practitioners record conversations and behavior. Sometimes this is done without the knowledge of those being recorded. News organizations may defend this practice by claiming that it is often the only way to gather evidence of possible wrongdoing. Without images or sound recordings, they say, disputes about what happened or what was said can come down to one person's word against another's.

Ethical questions surround such a practice. Some degree of deception is necessarily involved since, by definition, the use of hidden recording devices is secretive. Many media organizations recognize the need to carefully consider whether hidden recording is necessary. Some regard it as a last resort. In addition to ethical considerations, there is the law—or more accurately, there are the laws, since various state and federal laws come into play. Laws and court decisions may or may not permit surreptitious recording. Recording may be acceptable in one state but not another.[58] Covert recording also may violate federal laws.

Technological developments increase the ability to record communication without the knowledge of one or more of the parties. First, miniaturized recording devices make secret audio and video recording easier for a participant in a face-to-face conversation. Second, the evolution of communications technology—from telephone to e-mail to computer-based voice messaging systems—permits new platforms from which conversations can be recorded. In these situations, recording can be done not only by one of the participants in the conversation but also by someone who is eavesdropping on the chat.

The use of hidden cameras by the news media does not typically in and of itself constitute an intrusion. Recall, for example, that the use of hidden cameras was not central to the lawsuit and ruling in the *Food Lion* case. The focus was the fraudulent means by which the producers gained entry into the stores.[59] In 13 states, laws specifically prohibit the unauthorized use or installation of cameras in private places.

Face-to-Face Recording

Reporters often record interviews. Recording audio or video in an interview with plainly visible equipment does not violate any state or federal law. There is nothing secret about recording this way. An interviewee knows recording is taking place and may stop the interview if she objects to its being recorded.

Points of Law

States That Forbid Unauthorized Use of Cameras in Private Places[1]

- Alabama*
- Arkansas
- California
- Delaware*
- Georgia*
- Hawaii*
- Kansas*
- Maine*
- Michigan*
- Minnesota*
- New Hampshire
- South Dakota*
- Utah*

---

1. Reporters Committee for Freedom of the Press, *The First Amendment Handbook,* n.d., *available at* http://www.rcfp.org/handbook/c03p02.html/.

*States that also prohibit trespassing on private property to conduct surveillance of people.

If a reporter records an interview without the interviewee's knowledge, circumstances change and laws may be triggered. A recorder hidden in a reporter's jacket pocket, for example, does not allow the interviewee to know about the recording. Thirty-seven states and the District of Columbia allow using a hidden recorder for a face-to-face interview. These are called "one-party" states. Only one party to the interview must know the recording is happening—and that party can be the reporter. While the one-party approach may seem frivolous, it protects against an electronic eavesdropper or illegal wiretapper recording when no one in the conversation is aware of the recording.

Twelve states, however, are not so lenient. These "all-party" states have laws requiring all participants in an interview or conversation to give consent or recording is not permitted. (Vermont remains the one state without a law specifically addressing audio recording of interviews.) California is one of these "all-party" states.[60] Its law provides punishment for recording a "confidential communication" unless all parties in the conversation give consent.[61] This was central to an incident in the aftermath of a high-profile murder case. A producer for an ABC television newsmagazine went to the front door of a flight attendant's home. He had learned that the flight attendant had worked the flight that O.J. Simpson had taken from Los Angeles to Chicago on the same night of the murders of Simpson's ex-wife and her friend, Ronald Goldman. The producer identified himself with an ABC picture ID. A conversation ensued in which the flight attendant said she was not interested in appearing on any program. But the flight attendant did mention being frustrated over inaccurate reports about Simpson's behavior on the flight, saying that Simpson did not keep his hand in a bag of ice. As the producer was leaving, she said she would think about appearing on the program. When he telephoned her the next day, she again declined his invitation to appear on the program. He then told her that he had tape recorded their conversation and that a camera operator had videotaped them talking from a public street.[62]

After ABC broadcast a five-second clip of the video with an announcer voice-over about Simpson's not using an ice bag on the plane, the flight attendant sued ABC. A federal district court dismissed the case. On appeal, the district court's decision for ABC was affirmed. The key was the "confidential communication" clause of the California law. The court said that the flight attendant could not have reasonably expected the conversation to be confidential. The reasons: The producer had revealed he worked for ABC and wanted her to appear on the air to discuss the flight; she did not say her statements were in confidence; she did not ask that the information not be shared; and no promise was made to keep the conversation in confidence.[63] The court also rejected claims of intrusion, violating the federal eavesdropping statute, fraud and conspiracy to commit fraud and unfair business practices against ABC.

Points of Law

Recording Calls

State Laws

- Thirty-seven states require one-party consent.

- Twelve states require all-party consent.

Federal Laws

- Federal laws allow one-party consent but not if to commit a crime or tort.

- FCC rules require all-party consent, notification to all parties or repeating beep.

- FCC rules require notifying all parties if a phone conversation will be recorded and broadcast or if it will be aired live.

Recording "Wire" Conversations

One category of communication that laws cover is what is referred to as "wire communication" (the category includes technology that is not necessarily wired but that transfers the human voice between a point of origin and a point of reception).[64] It includes traditional telephones, cell phones and computer-based voice messaging services, sometimes called "Voice over Internet Protocol" (VoIP). There are several VoIPs that share certain characteristics. They record the user's voice, then convert it into data packets that are transmitted over the Internet. The receiver's computer converts the packets into an audio format.[65] These VoIPs include Skype, Google Talk and iChat.

Until recently, laws covering wire communication applied to telephones only. But with the development of VoIPs and their inclusion as another form of wire communication, they have fallen under the same regulatory umbrella. Language within the federal **Wiretap Act**[66] suggests that because VoIPs operate similarly to telephones as a form of wire communication, the law applying to the interception (and recording) of a VoIP call as it occurs would be handled in the same manner as a traditional telephone call.

One limitation of the Wiretap Act is that it only protects communications that are intercepted in transit, not those that are stored after transmission. VoIP calls create data packets that are stored after transmission. Those packets are subject to the Stored Communications Act,[67] a law that offers "considerably less protection" than the Wiretap Act.[68] The data are accessible through warrants and subpoenas.

Recording In-State Calls Problems may arise when reporters want to record an interview (or other conversation) conducted over wire communication (telephone or VoIP). Each state has authority over telephone calls that originate and end within the state. For example, Texas law governs a call from Dallas to Houston. Some state courts will insist on applying that state's laws even if the case involves an interstate phone call.[69] The Reporters Committee for Freedom of the Press is among the organizations that urge journalists to err on the side of caution when recording calls, due in part to the varying state laws. The safest strategy is to assume that the stricter law will apply and request permission to record from all parties.[70]

As with face-to-face recording, 12 states' laws make it illegal to record a telephone conversation without all parties consenting, and it is the same 12 states.[71] Some of these "all-party" state laws apply only to confidential conversations. Thirty-seven states, the District of Columbia, and federal law allow recording a phone call if only one party to the conversation agrees. That one party could be the reporter conducting a phone interview. In these states, the reporter would not need to ask the other person's permission to record the call.

Recording Interstate Calls The authority over calls that cross state lines comes from both federal law and a federal agency. Federal law allows recording if only one party consents.[72] At the same time, the FCC has jurisdiction over calls that

Wiretap Act A federal law initially passed in 1968 to protect the privacy of phone calls and other oral conversations. It has been amended and updated several times, largely to keep up with the changing communications landscape. The law makes it illegal to intercept, record, disseminate or use a private communication without one party's permission. The consenting person has to be a party to the conversation. Tapping into other people's phone calls violates the wiretap law. The federal wiretap law allows the government to bring criminal charges and those whose privacy was violated to sue for civil damages.

Recording Laws by State

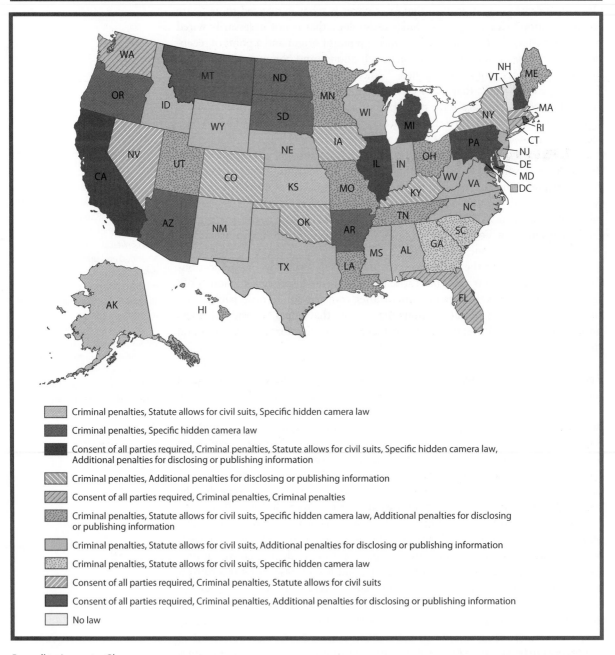

Recording Laws at a Glance

Source: Reporters Committee for Freedom of the Press, *Can We Tape?*, n.d., available at http://rcfp.org/taping/quick.html.

cross state lines. An FCC rule requires notifying all parties at the beginning of a call that it will be recorded, or using a regularly repeating beep tone so all parties will be aware the call is being recorded, and obtaining all parties' consent to recording.[73] The FCC rule and the federal law conflict, but the commission explains that away. The FCC says the federal law is meant to help law enforcement officers listen to calls as part of their duties but that the commission rule is meant to dissuade the public from recording calls without permission.[74] As mentioned earlier regarding intra-state calls, several organizations recommend playing it safe and obtaining permission to record from all parties.

Broadcasting Recorded Calls The FCC requires radio and television stations to notify parties to a phone conversation that the station will broadcast the call live or intends to record and broadcast the call. Consent is not necessary, only notification. The FCC refers to this as "The Phone Rule." There is an exception for programs that customarily air calls live or broadcast recorded calls, such as radio call-in shows. Callers are expected to realize that their conversations may be aired live or recorded and broadcast.[75]

The federal Electronic Communications Privacy Act (ECPA) also addresses eavesdropping, wiretapping and intercepting electronic communication. This law prohibits the unauthorized interception of electronic communication while the communication is in transit or in electronic storage. Consent of either the sender or the recipient of this kind of communication is considered authorization for interception. However, in *Bartnicki v. Vopper*, the U.S. Supreme Court ruled the First Amendment allows the use of a recording—so long as the person who uses the recording is not the one who made it. In this case, an unknown person intercepted and recorded a cell phone conversation between two teachers' union negotiators. The union and school board were in heated negotiations over a collective bargaining agreement. On the tape, one negotiator says to the other, "[W]e're gonna have to go to their, their homes . . . [t]o blow off their front porches, we'll have to do some work on some of those guys."[76] Local media received copies of the tape. Two radio stations played it on the air, and local newspapers printed its contents.

The negotiator who made the remarks sued media representatives. He acknowledged the media did not illegally intercept the conversation. However, they did intentionally "disclose" the exchange by playing the tape or reporting on its content when they had reason to know it was obtained illegally. That violates the federal wiretap law, the negotiator charged.[77] The media argued the First Amendment allowed using the tape as long as they did not engage in wiretapping.

The First Amendment protects a journalist who reports illegally intercepted private conversations, the U.S. Supreme Court ruled. But the journalist is protected only if the conversation is newsworthy and the journalist was not involved in the interception. The Court reached this conclusion because it found the federal wiretap statute to be content neutral, meaning the law applied no matter what the private conversation was about. But instead of using the standard of intermediate scrutiny, as courts usually do in deciding whether a content-neutral statute is constitutional (see Chapter 2), the Court applied the higher strict-scrutiny standard because the ban on disclosing illegally intercepted communications is a prohibition on speech content. The Court did not focus on the act of intercepting the conversation but rather on disseminating the conversation's contents.

Under the strict-scrutiny test, the government may apply the wiretap statute to the media only to serve a compelling state interest. In *Bartnicki*, the government said there were two compelling interests. First, the law dissuaded people from intercepting private communications. But the Court said there was little evidence that the law convinced people not to wiretap. More important, the media in this case did not intercept the conversation. The second compelling interest was to minimize harm to the people whose conversations were intercepted by discouraging distribution of illegally obtained information. The Court said privacy is important, but informing people about matters of public interest can be more important. The union negotiator heard on the recording, then, could not win a suit against the media for disclosing the conversation's contents. Justice Stephen Breyer, concurring in the result, said the Court's decision should be limited to instances concerning personal safety, as in this case. The Court's rationale in ruling for the broadcaster was threefold: (1) Radio station personnel played no part in the illegal interception; (2) their access to the information on the tapes was obtained lawfully, even though the information itself was intercepted unlawfully by someone else; and (3) the subject matter of the conversation was a matter of public concern.[78]

Included in the Court's analysis was reference to the 1971 Pentagon Papers case in which "the Court upheld the right of the press to publish information of great public concern obtained from documents stolen by a third party."[79] To restrain the publication of important information prior to its broadcast bears a heavy burden. Noting that publication of information of public interest is one of the "core purposes of the First Amendment," the Court concluded that "a stranger's illegal conduct does not suffice to remove the First Amendment shield from speech about a matter of public concern."[80]

The ECPA also prohibits accessing an electronic information computer facility without permission to obtain and disclose information. Thus, Internet messages intended for private use are not legally accessible.

Alleged violation of the ECPA has been among the claims in suits against Internet service providers (ISPs) when they reveal the identity of a message poster. Courts generally agree the ECPA applies to ISPs, yet they have favored ISPs that disclose identities according to the standards outlined in the act. In one case, for example, the plaintiff had posted a message on America Online (AOL) that harassed the soon-to-be ex-wife of the plaintiff's lover. AOL had already been made aware of the posting, investigated it and terminated the poster's contract for violating AOL's "Rules of the Road." The subject of the posting asked her attorney to subpoena AOL for the identity of the poster. In compliance with a provision in ECPA that permits disclosure when a subpoena is issued, AOL provided the information. When the poster of the message sued AOL, a federal court ruled that AOL had not violated the ECPA.[81]

Under federal law and many state laws, if a recording is made to commit a crime or a tort, recording is illegal regardless of who consents. For example, rap artists Andre Young, Snoop Dogg, Ice Cube and Eminem were scheduled to perform in Detroit as part of a nationwide tour. In each of 10 cities before Detroit, a short video introduced Andre Young and Snoop Dogg. Just before the Detroit show began, police and other city officials met with tour producers and told them the video violated obscenity laws and could not be shown. People connected with the tour used secret cameras and microphones to record the meeting. Parts of the secretly recorded meeting were included in a music video called "Gangster Rap Concert DVD" that was marketed and sold internationally. The city officials sued under the federal wiretap law that makes it impermissible to record, disclose or use any private conversation.[82] However, it is not illegal if one party to the conversation gives consent. The tour representatives told a federal district court they gave themselves permission to record, disclose and use the conversation. The court said one-party consent is ineffective if recording is for an illegal purpose or to commit a tort.[83] If the tour representatives made the video intending to use it to commit the tort of appropriation—taking the material without consent for commercial purposes (see Chapter 6)—by using an excerpt in a DVD, the court said, one-party consent would not be effective.

Noncovert Recording

Even in situations in which public access is permitted, noncovert recording of certain events as a newsgathering technique may be restricted. The Maryland legislature, for example, prohibits reporters with recording devices from attending its sessions. The exclusion was challenged by reporters who claimed the speed and accuracy of recording justifies the practice. A Maryland appeals court disagreed, saying that while newsgathering is entitled to some First Amendment protection, banning recorders does not infringe on that right.[84] It called the ban "a mere inconvenience."[85] Similar reasoning guides the federal court system and the few state judiciaries that continue to limit cameras in courtrooms, as explained in Chapter 10.[86]

Noncovert recording may also be limited simply by preventing access to news events altogether. Obtaining access through trespass, harassment, or fraud and misrepresentation is illegal. Generally, a distinction is made according to the kind of property onto which access is desired. Even then, however, there may be exceptions.

Access to public property is generally permitted to any member of the public. Moreover, whatever can be seen from public property can generally be recorded. If access to a specific area of public property is restricted by law enforcement officials, however, individuals must comply. This could apply to disaster sites. For example, when an airliner crashed at a publicly owned airport, the crash site was secured with officers positioned to keep unauthorized people away. When a television photojournalist followed an emergency vehicle through a roadblock, a city detective pursued. When the photographer stopped, he was ordered to leave. As

realWorld Law

Video of Public Places

In late 2009, a New Jersey man was arrested for recording video outside of a federal courthouse in New York City. Antonio Musumeci shot video of a man handing out pamphlets in a plaza area, then interviewed that man. During the interview, the interviewee was approached and arrested by a member of the Federal Protective Service. After that, Musumeci was also arrested, the memory card from his camera was confiscated and he was charged with violating a federal regulation that governs photography on federal property.[1]

The regulation requires advance permission for taking photographs in certain agency-occupied areas. The regulation also identifies specific areas that are exempt from this requirement, provided the photography is for a news purpose. An accompanying regulation states that notice of the restriction must be posted at the entrance to each facility to which it applies. Musumeci filed a complaint in 2010 in U.S. District Court alleging that his First and Fourteenth Amendment rights were violated.[2]

In a settlement, the federal government agreed that no federal statutes or regulations bar photography of federal courthouses from publicly accessible property. In addition, the settlement required a nationwide directive to be issued to all federal employees who monitor federal buildings about the rights of photographers.[3]

1. 41 C.F.R. § 102-74.420.
2. Musumeci v. U.S. Dep't of Homeland Security, S.D.N.Y., Index No. 10 CIV 3370 (2010).
3. *Id., available at* http://www.nyclu.org/files/releases/Final_Stip_and_Order_10.18.10.pdf.

he walked back to the roadblock, he jumped a fence that separated the street from the airport, ran to the top of a hill and began taking pictures of the crash site. The officer again followed and ordered the photojournalist to leave the restricted area. The photojournalist said he would not stop taking pictures unless he was arrested. The officer arrested him. After being convicted of disorderly conduct, the photojournalist appealed. The Wisconsin Supreme Court upheld the conviction. It rejected the argument that the First Amendment demands news media access to emergency sites. It also pointed out that, in fact, media access was not denied in this situation. While the photojournalist was arguing with the detective, other journalists who had followed the airport's media guidelines were meeting with the airport director, who took them directly to the crash site.[87]

An airport is an example of what is sometimes called "quasi-public property." As explained in Chapter 2, this is property that serves a public purpose but is not generally available for public use. In the case just described, the airport tarmac qualifies. As that case illustrates, public and press access to such areas is much more restricted than with explicitly public property. At the other extreme is private property, where public access is extremely limited. Highly restricted media access applies to emergency scenes even when law enforcement or firefighting officials invite members of the media to accompany them. Accepting such invitations still leaves the journalist exposed to trespass claims.

REPORTERS' USE OF HIDDEN AUDIO AND VIDEO recording equipment can raise serious legal and ethical questions. Many states have specific laws forbidding covert recording. These laws often require informed consent from the parties being recorded. In addition, federal law prohibits electronic eavesdropping and wiretapping and protects the privacy of electronic communications via telephone or the Internet. The U.S. Supreme Court, however, ruled that journalists who do not know the material was illegally recorded are not liable for broadcasting an illegally intercepted newsworthy telephone conversation. Under some conditions, Internet service providers may also disclose the identity of senders and the content of private Internet communications without liability.

It is not always true that simply because reporters are allowed into a particular place they may record there. While print journalists without cameras often report without limitation, some government proceedings may ban recordings. Overt recording to document news events also may be limited by constraints on physical access to emergency scenes and private property. ■

Access to Military Operations

In 2010, Defense Secretary Robert Gates issued a memo to all of those under his command. Its subject: "Interaction with the Media." It began by stressing the importance of news media access to many aspects of Department of Defense activities and operations. "[W]e are obliged to ensure that the information provided to them is timely, accurate, credible and consistent," Gates wrote. "I have said many times that we must strive to be as open, accessible and transparent as possible."[88] In the next paragraph, however, Gates expressed concern that his department had grown lax in how the media were engaged, possibly in violation of rules and procedures. Far too may people were talking to the media outside of channels, he continued, sometimes providing unauthorized information. It was important to deal with the media so integrity of government decision-making processes was maintained. Gates reminded that all media activities were to be coordinated through proper channels. This memo was issued on the heels of a Rolling Stone article that profiled Gen. Stanley McChrystal. The general's candor and feelings revealed by the article led to his forced resignation. The article may have also led to the military's reassessing its relationship with the news media.[89]

News media coverage from the battlefield has a long history, dating to the U.S. Civil War in the mid-19th century. As the media and technology evolved, so did the coverage in both scope and immediacy. A reporter with a notepad and pencil, or even a radio microphone, has usually been of less concern to the U.S. government than reporters with cameras. Television coverage was blamed by many for the demise of public support for the U.S. effort in Vietnam. At the time, the Vietnam War was sometimes referred to as "the living room war" because of the vivid television images that were broadcast into American homes. As a result, government officials resolved to assume greater control over the media presence in future military operations, so while the technological ease with which those images could be made and transmitted increased over the years, the struggle over access to the battlefield and control of those images grew.

This struggle was illustrated in post–Vietnam era U.S. military operations. The absence of media during the 1983 invasion of the Caribbean nation of Grenada and the media protests that followed led to the establishment of a congressional commission to study the situation. The commission recommended "pool reporting"—reporting by small groups of journalists who would accompany operations onto the battlefield. The chosen reporters would represent all media and share their information and video with other members of the media upon their return. This plan was used in Panama in 1989 and in the Persian Gulf War in 1991. In the invasion of Panama, Defense Secretary Richard Cheney ordered delays in the formation, transportation and deployment of the reporting pool that kept pool reporters confined to a military base during most of the fighting. In the Gulf War, military personnel reviewed and selected the members of the press pool, dictated terms of coverage (including a requirement that the media not violate the stringent press standards of the Saudi Arabian government), required full-time military escorts of pool reporters and reviewed material before it could be transmitted.

While the media accepted standard military restrictions, such as barring the reporting of troop locations and movements, the media protested the pool plan as restricting their access. In one lawsuit, veterans joined news photographers to protest U.S. Department of Defense (DOD) rules prohibiting pictures of flag-draped caskets at Dover Air Force Base, the main military mortuary for American soldiers killed abroad. In 2009, the federal government reversed policy, allowing news media to photograph those coffins, but only with the consent of the families of the fallen troops.

Courts dismissed media lawsuits challenging military censorship practices as moot or ruled that the First Amendment did not require media access to sources of government information, especially during times of combat.[90] Officials representing the DOD and major news organizations then met in an attempt to resolve their differences. Among the areas of common ground was the conclusion that pool reporting was a restriction and that it should not be the norm. During the 2002 military operation in Afghanistan, journalists were given access to ships in the Arabian Sea but not to ground operations. Hustler magazine publisher Larry Flynt filed suit in federal district court claiming that this policy and the exclusion of Hustler reporters from the pool denied the media their right to gather information.[91] The court refused to issue an injunction requiring the military to provide broader media access because broader access was available by the time its ruling was handed down.

Leading up to the 2003 invasion of Iraq, the DOD developed a plan in conjunction with news media organizations. The idea was to allow journalists to be embedded within military units. To participate, journalists had to undergo extensive training and sign a contract agreeing to comply with military directions and a set of ground rules. The rules largely focused on preventing reporting that would reveal locations, tactics, strategies and numbers of U.S. forces. Once the invasion began, so did the reports from these embedded journalists. On the one hand, the rules provided reporters greater access and some of the most immediate and direct war coverage ever. On the other hand, criticism centered on the potential lack of objectivity of reporters who identified too closely with the military units they were covering and on the limited coverage of American casualties. One journalist noted, "Whether reporters and photographers in Iraq could maintain their

Embedded journalist Jill Carroll of the Christian Science Monitor (right) drives through Iraq with the U.S. Marines. She later was kidnapped and held hostage for 82 days before being released unharmed.

independence while accompanying the troops has been the subject of ongoing debate."[92] Do reporters develop a devotion to their military hosts and provide a sanitized version of reality in exchange for security?

Another concern centers on perspective. While the public was being provided with many pieces of a puzzle, there were questions about whether those pieces had ever been adequately assembled to provide a clear and unvarnished picture of the whole. Finally, as the military occupation of Iraq continued, criticism surfaced about full disclosure of American casualties, especially after a nonmilitary contract worker was fired for releasing photographs of military coffins in Seattle.[93]

Denying Access to Records

Later in this chapter, obtaining access to records is examined under "News-gathering Protections." However, there are some federal laws that allow or mandate agencies to withhold records, usually in an effort to protect individual privacy. While the four areas of privacy analyzed in Chapter 6 are torts whose violation may result in civil lawsuits, those described here stem from legislation. Violation of them may result in criminal prosecution. These laws are meant to protect privacy, but from the media's perspective they limit the ability to gather news.

One is the Privacy Act. Passed in 1974, it gives individuals the right to examine government files that contain information about themselves. Just as important, the act also allows government agencies to use the information in these files only for the reason it was collected. In other words, agencies cannot disclose such information—at least not without the written consent of the person involved. A 1984 amendment to the Privacy Act stated that the law could not be used to deny access to information that should be available under the Freedom of Information Act (FOIA). Whenever the two were in opposition to one another, the FOIA was to prevail. In reality, federal agencies have been very careful about violating personal privacy. Some observers, however, are concerned about invasions of privacy that may result from increased sharing of information among government agencies. The USA Patriot Act allows agencies to swap information that they previously were required to keep only for internal use.

Family Educational Rights and Privacy Act (FERPA) A federal law that protects the privacy of student education records. The law applies to all schools that receive funds under an applicable program of the U.S. Department of Education; FERPA gives parents certain rights with respect to their children's school records; these rights transfer to the student when he or she reaches the age of 18 or attends a school beyond the high school level.

Student Records Another federal statute that limits access to information is the **Family Educational Rights and Privacy Act (FERPA)**, passed in 1974 and sometimes referred to as the Buckley Act.[94] This act forbids federally funded institutions of education from releasing school records of students unless they, as adults, or their parents provide consent. The parents themselves are permitted access to the records of their children as minors. State-supported schools are also forbidden from releasing grades or information related to a student's health, although they can disclose "directory" information such as a student's name, address, telephone number, date and place of birth, major field of study, dates of attendance, and degrees and awards received. Violating the law puts an institution's government funding at risk.

The protected records are those containing personally identifiable information. The U.S. Department of Education (DOE) defines "personally identifiable information" as including the student's name, a family member's name, the student's or family member's address, personal information such as the student's Social Security number or student number, and personal characteristics or other information that would make it easy to determine the student's identity.[95]

Professional and student journalists often are told that FERPA prevents schools from releasing information about disciplinary actions involving students. The act has sometimes been a source of controversy. University officials have cited it as preventing them from releasing information such as campus police records or student disciplinary records. While nondisclosure may protect individuals, the news media argue that the public has a right to know information related to possible crimes and justice systems on the campuses of public institutions. The federal Campus Security Act, or the Clery Act as it is now known, requires universities to compile and publish statistics on campus crime each year. Enterprising reporting that used these statistics has unveiled significant problems on campuses. For example, excesses in fraternity hazing and gay bashing at the University of Georgia came to light when student journalists obtained records of university disciplinary hearings.[96] The Georgia Supreme Court held that universities could release student disciplinary records without violating FERPA.[97] The Georgia court said disciplinary records were not student records under FERPA because they were not concerned with student academic performance, financial aid or academic probation.

Such campus information is more difficult to obtain in the wake of a federal district court ruling, however. A student newspaper at Miami University of Ohio sought discipline records to look at crime trends on the campus. Also, the Chronicle of Higher Education, a weekly newspaper, asked Miami University and The Ohio State University for student disciplinary records. Both newspapers wanted records of the universities' internal discipline committees. The U.S. DOE asked a federal court to rule that disciplinary records were student records and could not be released under FERPA without permission. A federal appellate court supported the DOE's interpretation.[98] The court said the law's language made clear that disciplinary proceedings were part of student records and could not be released without a student's consent.

In sum, the university environment poses some particular challenges to journalists. While student media enjoy the same First Amendment rights as non-campus media to publish legally obtained information and a full range of ideas, privacy and campus security laws permit a variety of campus records to be kept confidential. Legal as well as institutional barriers impede journalists' access to information about individual university students. Laws that protect interests in personal privacy and the integrity of educational files pose obstacles to campus reporters.

Medical Records In addition to the protection provided by other measures, the Health Insurance Portability and Accountability Act (HIPAA) shields medical records. When Congress passed HIPAA in 1996, it started efforts to fashion rules designed to protect the medical privacy of patients. The act eventually led the Department of Health and Human Services to offer the first federal medical privacy regulations, called the Standards for Privacy of Individually Identifiable Health Information. These rules were designed to give patients more control over their health information and to limit the use and release of health records to third parties. Generally, the privacy standards established a federal requirement that most doctors, hospitals and other health care providers obtain a patient's written consent before using or disclosing the patient's personal health information. The rules restrict the use of such records for marketing and research purposes.

Driver's Information The federal **Driver's Privacy Protection Act** of 1994 prohibits states from releasing information obtained from driver's license and vehicle registration records without permission.[99] The law allows disclosure under certain circumstances. Driver's license and motor vehicle records may include an individual's name, address, picture, telephone number, vehicle description, Social Security number, medical information and other personal data. At one time, many states sold this information to individuals and companies, earning millions of dollars annually. Congress stopped this practice in part to prevent stalkers from obtaining information about potential targets. However, the law also prevents journalists from using these records to find information for stories. The U.S. Supreme Court upheld the law against a constitutional challenge, finding that Congress' power over interstate commerce allowed it to adopt the statute.[100]

Driver's Privacy Protection Act
Federal legislation that prohibits states from disclosing personal information that drivers submit in order to obtain drivers' licenses.

Video Voyeurism Advancements in technology often drive developments in the law. Miniaturized cameras and cellular phones equipped with cameras were the catalyst for laws meant to protect against video voyeurism. Described in various ways, video voyeurism includes photography in private areas and the practice of "upskirting"—covertly taking low-angle photos up a woman's skirt, often with the intent of posting them online. The federal Video Voyeurism Prevention Act[101] prohibits unauthorized photography of an individual's private areas. In addition, 23 states have laws that specifically address this issue, while another 26 states have general "anti-voyeurism" or "peeping" laws. (As of this writing, New Mexico is the only state without either a specific or general law in the area.)

SUMMARY

LIKE ACCESS TO FEDERAL RECORDS, OBTAINING ACCESS to U.S. military operations can be challenging. The history in this area is one of give-and-take, with the government attempting to exert more control in recent decades.

Many federal and state laws limit access to records held by government that contain individually identifiable information. The federal Privacy Act permits individuals to access their own records—but not the records of others—to verify their accuracy. Federal laws protect the privacy of educational, medical and driver's license records from disclosure. ∎

Newsgathering Protections

While courts have repeatedly and consistently ruled that no explicit newsgathering right exists under the First Amendment, there are various protections that can enhance access to information. Some of these protections take the form of statutes or other enacted legislation; others stem from court rulings. Either way, it was only in the latter part of the 20th century that the concept of a truly open government—open to all citizens—was codified to any meaningful extent.

Open Government Laws

"Knowledge will forever govern ignorance; and a people who mean to be their own governors must arm themselves with the power which knowledge gives."[102] The words are James Madison's. They epitomize both the spirit of, and the need for, openness in a democratic government. Absent information, the electorate is blind. Liberal democratic theory maintains that an obligation exists on the part of those in authority to open the blinds and allow in the sunshine by providing access to the information necessary to self-govern. Fulfillment of the obligation results in accountability. The governed—that is, the people—cannot maintain control of their government absent knowledge of its inner workings. This responsibility of government to open its processes to citizens, however, did not emerge in a significant and material way until almost a century and a half after Madison's proclamation.

Access to Federal Records

The ability of citizens to hold their governments accountable, as Madison noted, depends on knowledge. That knowledge stems from two primary sources to which laws can enhance access: government records and government meetings. The section that follows focuses on the law that helps to provide access to records kept by the federal government. (Access to court records is addressed in Chapter 10.)

The Freedom of Information Act Growing secrecy in the federal government during and after World War II led to a movement for greater transparency. The press, along with some congressional support, pushed for creating a law to allow greater access to information. Organizations such as the American Society of Newspaper Editors and the Society of Professional Journalists played key roles in the late 1940s.[103] Still, momentum was slow to build.

Freedom of Information Act (FOIA) The 1966 act that requires records held by federal government agencies to be made available to the public, provided that the information sought does not fall within one of nine exempted categories.

The growth of the federal government through the mid-20th century saw the creation of agency after agency. This added to the criticism that government was a closed system. The sheer size and complexity of the rapidly expanding government gave rise to concerns about the ability of citizens to understand it and oversee its workings. The Congressional Record was no longer enough to report on federal government business because government business was being conducted on multiple levels outside the U.S. Capitol. After much debate, Congress responded to critics by passing the **Freedom of Information Act (FOIA)** in 1966. It was intended to permit any person access to records held by federal executive branch agencies. The act was amended in 1974, with additional revisions in 1976, 1986, and 1996 and, with the Open Government Act, in 2007.

The U.S. Supreme Court has stated that the basic policy is that "disclosure, not secrecy, is the dominant objective of the act."[104] Under the FOIA, government records are presumed to be open. Exemptions that enable government to withhold information from citizens must be interpreted narrowly to afford the greatest possibility of a fully informed citizenry. To that end, the FOIA is available to anyone, not just to members of the news media. In fact, some argue that journalists do not use the act's provisions enough. Still, it has been a valuable tool in the pursuit of information for many reporters, including journalists seeking and obtaining information related to NASA

Points of Law

Freedom of Information Act: Some Basics

- It applies to all executive federal government agencies but not to the U.S. Congress, federal courts and courts-martial or the military during wartime.

- It requires each federal agency to publish in the Federal Register a description of its organization and a list of its personnel who can be contacted for records.

- It requires each agency to publish the procedures by which records can be obtained.

- It requires that all records be segregated so that an entire record cannot be classified as exempt, only part(s) of it.

mishaps,[105] design deficiencies in both the Ford Pinto's gas tank and the Hubble space telescope, dangers to local communities from nuclear weapons plants and hazardous lead levels in imported wine.

The FOIA specifies that records held by federal agencies may be requested. That raises two questions:

1. *What is an agency?* "Agency" is defined as "any executive department, military department, Government corporation, Government controlled corporation, or other establishment in the executive branch of the Government, including the Executive Office of the President, or any independent regulatory agency."[106] By specifically including the "Executive Office of the President," which encompasses offices such as the Office of Management and Budget, the Office of Policy Development and the Office of Science and Technology Policy, Congress implicitly excluded the White House Office, which includes the president's closest advisers and their staffs.[107] Also excluded are Congress and the federal courts. Organizations that receive federal funding but are not under the direct control of the federal government—for example, the Corporation for Public Broadcasting—are also outside the FOIA's coverage.

   Among the covered agencies are federal agencies, departments, commissions, and government-controlled corporations at the federal level only. This includes cabinet-level departments such as Defense, Homeland Security, State, Treasury, and Justice. Regulatory agencies such as the Federal Communications Commission, the Securities and Exchange Commission, and the Federal Trade Commission are also included under the FOIA, as are NASA and the U.S. Postal Service.

2. *What is a record?* The FOIA does not define a record, but the act has been interpreted to apply to all tangible or fixed items that (a) document government actions and (b) may be reproduced. Thus, computer files, paper reports, films, videotapes, photographs and audio recordings are considered to be records under the law. A record is something that already exists, not something that government could compile from the diverse information it holds.

But are all records in the possession of a federal government agency records under the law? There is no precise answer to that question. Neither the text of the FOIA nor its legislative history defines "agency record."[108] While Congress has largely resolved the question of what an agency is, and courts have generally agreed on the necessary properties of a record, what satisfies the link between an agency and a record necessary to make the document an agency record remains in dispute.

The U.S. Supreme Court, while noting that "Congress has supplied no definition of 'agency records in the FOIA,'"[109] observed that "[t]he use of the word 'agency' as a modifier demonstrates that Congress contemplated some relationship between an 'agency' and the 'record' requested."[110] In that same ruling, the

Court noted that during the FOIA Senate hearings, the term "agency record" was assumed to include "all papers which an agency preserves in the performance of its functions."[111]

A federal appeals court noted the congressional failure to identify the link between an agency and a record: "[T]he Freedom of Information Act, for all its attention to the treatment of 'agency records,' never defines that crucial phrase."[112] Some observers believe that such "statutory silence"[113] permits courts to construe the phrase too narrowly, diminishing the FOIA's policy of broad disclosure.[114]

One of the first judicial interpretations of the term was provided in 1978 by a federal appellate court.[115] A party requesting an agency record sought a congressional hearing transcript that was located in Central Intelligence Agency (CIA) files. The CIA argued that the transcript was not an agency record but was instead a congressional document exempt from FOIA coverage. The court agreed with the CIA and held that the agency's possession of a document, by itself, was not sufficient to create an agency record. Under the circumstances, the court concluded, the decision to disclose should be made by the originating body—in this case, Congress—not the recipient agency.[116]

In spite of the ambiguity in establishing what an agency record is under the FOIA, the following criteria have developed:

- A record is anything in documentary form. This now includes computer-stored records, and the Electronic Freedom of Information Act of 1996 mandates disclosure of records in the format chosen by the requester if that format is available as part of the agency's normal business procedures.
- An agency record likely includes any document created and possessed by the agency.
- A record possessed but not created by an agency may not qualify as an agency record.
- An agency is not required either to create a record if the record does not exist or obtain the requested record if it is not in the control of the agency at the time the request is made.
- The requested record must be part of the legitimate conduct of the agency's official duties.

Using the FOIA to Obtain Records Requesting a record from a federal government agency is relatively easy. (Obtaining the record may be another matter.) Familiarity with the FOIA and the preferred procedures is extremely helpful and enhances the likelihood that the request will be granted. Useful information is provided by the Reporters Committee for Freedom of the Press and its online guide, "How to Use the Federal FOI Act."[117] This includes an online FOIA letter generator[118] that provides step-by-step guidance on letter preparation. Contacting the agency is the next step. This can be done by telephone, e-mail or mail. It is sometimes best to begin with a friendly telephone call to clarify the nature of your request, identify the record holder and perhaps obtain the records without further ado. However, a written request allows keeping track of the date of the request, the records requested and the agency's responses, all of which are essential if the agency must be taken to court for noncompliance with the law.

Because agencies exert a certain amount of discretion on whether they release records, understanding the elements of human interaction is also helpful in the records request process. Sometimes agencies will ignore friendly requests, so reminders of the law can be useful in getting their attention. Two studies conducted by a FOIA researcher show that a threatening letter resulted in faster responses, lower copy fees and more compliance with the law than a friendly or neutral letter.[119] That same researcher, together with another FOIA expert, has outlined strategies for working with record custodians to acquire records without having to go to court. They suggest that the records request process is not like barging through a door to get information; rather, it's like winding through a maze, turning different corners, going around roadblocks and eventually getting where you need to be.[120]

Federal agencies now have links within their own websites that guide the FOIA user. Federal agencies and departments have websites that include instructions on how to file FOIA requests to that specific agency or department. It is important that requests be as detailed and specific as possible. Otherwise, the exchange needed to clarify the request wastes valuable time. Sweeping searches for all the records related to a given property transaction, for example, also increase response time. The FOIA permits agencies to charge search and/or duplicating fees at cost, but fee waivers may be granted upon request. In fact, there is a specific FOIA provision that allows news media members to obtain fee waivers. Fee reductions are also available to nonprofit organizations. But other users of the FOIA have sometimes found that requests for fee waivers can trigger lengthy delays as agency personnel attempt to classify the requester's appropriate fee status. If the budget permits, a record requester may simply want to pay the costs.

Agencies have 20 working days to respond to FOIA requests. This does not mean comply; it just means respond. In other words, it is possible for the agency to respond by saying the record being sought is not readily available, for example, or that there is a backlog of requests and the record will be provided as soon as possible or that there will be a certain cost for the records. If a wait seems unreasonable, written appeals may be made. If the agency refuses the request, a claim may be filed in a federal district court. The burden of proof lies with the government; it must show why the delay or nondisclosure is valid. The agency must cite the specific exemption that justifies nondisclosure and must withhold only those portions of the requested records that qualify for the exemption. In 2008, for example, a federal judge ruled the National Nuclear Security Administration (NNSA) unnecessarily delayed responding to numerous records requests from a citizens' group regarding documents on nuclear waste sites in New Mexico. The judge said NNSA's reliance on the complexity and sensitive

realWorld Law

How Responsive Is the U.S. Government to FOIA Requests?

The Coalition of Journalists for Open Government (CJOG) released its most recent study in 2008 showing how 25 federal departments and agencies responded to Freedom of Information Act (FOIA) Requests.[1] The report was not encouraging for those who believe their government should be open and responsive to its citizens' requests for information. These are some excerpts from that report:

[F]ederal departments and agencies have made little if any progress in responding to Freedom of Information Act requests, despite a two-year-old presidential order to improve service. . . .

The CJOG review of performance reports shows agencies did cut their record backlog but more because of a steep decline in requests than stepped up processing of requests. It also indicated scant improvement and some regression in traditional measures of response, including the amount of time requesters have to wait for an answer and whether a request or an appeal is granted. . . .

The CJOG study looked at 25 departments and agencies that handle the bulk of the third-party information requests. . . .

The 25 agencies blew an opportunity to make a significant dent in their huge backlog of requests. Those agencies received the fewest requests since reporting began in 1998—63,000 fewer than 2006. But they processed only 2,100 more requests than they did in 2006 when the backlog soared to a record 39%. . . .

Agencies got even stingier in granting requests. Fewer people got all the information they sought than at any time since agency reporting began in 1998. The percent of requesters getting either a full or a partial grant fell to 60%, also a record low.

Those who did get information still had to endure lengthy delays. Fifteen of the agencies reported slower processing times than the year before in the handling of "Simple" requests, and 13 showed slower times in dealing with "Complex" requests. And all 21 agencies that processed requests in the "Complex" category said they missed the 20-day statutory response deadline for at least half of the requests processed.

Those who file administrative appeals are usually out of luck—even more so in 2007. However, a majority of the agencies did say "no" more quickly. In 2007, the percentage of appeals granted dropped to the lowest level in 10 years. Only 13% of those who appealed got any satisfaction. Of those who appealed, only 3% got all the records requested; another 10% received a partial grant. . . .

---

1. Coalition of Journalists for Open Government, *An Opportunity Lost: An In-Depth Analysis of FOIA Performance from 1998 to 2007,* July 3, 2008, *available at* http://www.cjog.net/documents//Part_1_2007_FOIA_Report.pdf.

nature of the records being sought was inconsistent with the agency's obligations under the FOIA.[121]

FOIA Exemptions Federal agencies are not compelled to hand over any and every record requested. There are nine specifically enumerated FOIA exemptions to disclosure. Information within requested records that falls into one or more of those categories does not have to be provided. It is important to note, however,

Points of Law

Freedom of Information Act: The Exemptions

1. National security

2. Internal agency rules and procedures

3. Disclosures forbidden by other statutes

4. Trade secrets

5. Agency memoranda

6. Personal privacy

7. Law enforcement records

8. Financial records

9. Geological information

that the wording of the FOIA permits agencies to reject a request for information. The law does not make nondisclosure mandatory; the decision is at the agency's discretion. Nevertheless, that discretion is often exercised in favor of nondisclosure.

If an agency chooses to deny all or part of a FOIA request, the law requires that the agency show that the request falls under one of the nine exemptions. The exemptions to disclosure are permissive, and the law requires agencies to interpret the exemptions narrowly. Thus, record keepers are required to cover up, or redact, only the specific portions of records covered by the law's exemptions. The physical process of redacting records line by line is painstaking, and delays in accomplishing the task can result in backlogs of weeks, months or even years. In addition, even if a portion of a record may be exempted, the agency may still choose to release it. Agency administrators, though, may take a dim view of such a practice.

Among the major sticking points of the FOIA since its enactment have been agency interpretations of its nine exemptions. A very narrow reading of them results in agencies releasing more information more often; a broad interpretation reduces the likelihood of disclosure. In the aftermath of the Sept. 11, 2001, terrorist attacks, for example, then-U.S. Atty. Gen. John Ashcroft issued a memorandum to the heads of all federal departments and agencies urging restraint with any discretionary granting of records when it could fall under one or more exemptions.[122] The memo instructed federal agencies to withhold information sought through FOIA requests whenever a "sound legal basis" might justify secrecy. It also required record keepers to review all applicable FOIA exemptions and disclose information "only after full and deliberate consideration of the institutional, commercial and personal privacy interests that could be implicated."[123] This represented an about-face to established policy that had advised agencies to grant more liberal public access to federal government records in response to FOIA requests. An audit of federal agencies that receive the vast majority of FOIA requests found that, after the Ashcroft memo, the system was in "extreme disarray," with slow response times, lackadaisical document searches, lost requests and no accountability.[124]

Another post–Sept. 11 development was the passage of the Homeland Security Act of 2002. Many regard it as weakening the Freedom of Information Act by providing broad exemptions under the FOIA for information related to the security of critical infrastructure or protected systems, including computer systems and information.[125] Thus, a broad interpretation of the Homeland Security Act expands the categories under which records may be withheld. As a result, fewer FOIA requests were granted after Sept. 11, 2001, than before.

Many believed that trend would likely change under the administration of President Barack Obama. On his first day in office, President Obama issued a

confinement box. The other inquiry involved claims that the SERE training caused two individuals to engage in criminal behavior, namely, felony shoplifting and downloading child pornography onto a military computer. According to this official, these claims were found to be baseless. Moreover, he has indicated that during the three and a half years he spent as ████████ ████████ of the SERE program, he trained 10,000 students. Of those students, only two dropped out of the training following the use of these techniques. Although on rare occasions some students temporarily postponed the remainder of their training and received psychological counseling, those students were able to finish the program without any indication of subsequent mental health effects.

You have informed us that you have consulted with ████████████ who has ten years of experience with SERE training ██ ██ He stated that, during those ten years, insofar as he is aware, none of the individuals who completed the program suffered any adverse mental health effects. He informed you that there was one person who did not complete the training. That person experienced an adverse mental health reaction that lasted only two hours. After those two hours, the individual's symptoms spontaneously dissipated without requiring treatment or counseling and no other symptoms were ever reported by this individual. According to the information you have provided to us, this assessment of the use of these procedures includes the use of the waterboard.

Additionally, you received a memorandum from the ████████████████████ ████████████████████████████ which you supplied to us. ████████████ has experience with the use of all of these procedures in a course of conduct, with the exception of the insect in the confinement box and the waterboard. This memorandum confirms that the use of these procedures has not resulted in any reported instances of prolonged mental harm, and very few instances of immediate and temporary adverse psychological responses to the training. ████████████ reported that a small minority of students have had temporary adverse psychological reactions during training. Of the 26,829 students trained from 1992 through 2001 in the Air Force SERE training, 4.3 percent of those students had contact with psychology services. Of those 4.3 percent, only 3.2 percent were pulled from the program for psychological reasons. Thus, out of the students trained overall, only 0.14 percent were pulled from the program for psychological reasons. Furthermore, although ████████████ indicated that surveys of students having completed this training are not done, he expressed confidence that the training did not cause any long-term psychological impact. He based his conclusion on the debriefing of students that is done after the training. More importantly, he based this assessment on the fact that although training is required to be extremely stressful in order to be effective, very few complaints have been made regarding the training. During his tenure, in which 10,000 students were trained, no congressional complaints have been made. While there was one Inspector General complaint, it was not due to psychological concerns. Moreover, he was aware of only one letter inquiring about the long-term impact of these techniques from an individual trained

An example of a redacted document that was released under FOIA. This is one page from a memo to the CIA's general counsel written by the Assistant Attorney General in 2002.

Despite announcing a commitment to FOIA and transparency in government, President Barack Obama and his administration have disappointed many.

memo to the heads of federal agencies. In words that echoed Madison, he noted that a "democracy requires accountability, and accountability requires transparency." In our democracy, he continued, the Freedom of Information Act "is the most prominent expression of a profound national commitment to ensuring an open Government."[126] While the principle may stand in theory, some government watchdog groups believe that, in practice, the record is unquestionably mixed. Some say the Obama administration took as many steps to shield government information as it did to make it accessible. In part, this perception may have been driven by high expectations. Moreover, many critics acknowledge that openness is a matter of degree, with the Obama administration being transparent in ways that previous presidencies were not. In fact, a 2010 study found that some of the problem lies in agencies that are not following President Obama's directive: that is, to release any information whose disclosure was not prohibited by law or would not cause foreseeable harm. The study by the National Security Archive concludes that the Obama administration "clearly stated a new policy direction for open government but has not conquered the challenge of communicating and enforcing that message throughout the executive branch."[127] A point remains that open government laws and policies are subject to interpretation, including by the officials who decide during any given period how to implement them. This especially applies to FOIA and its exemptions. When there is disagreement between a requester and an agency over whether one or more of the exemptions applies to a particular request, a federal court may ultimately settle the dispute.

Exemption 1: National Security Records fall under the exemption of national security if they are classified as confidential, secret or top secret. Each classification reflects a greater sensitivity of the information and its potential for harm if released. The authority to classify information, and thus use the national security exemption, is ripe for abuse. Members of the executive branch reinterpret the standards for classification of government secrets in ways that may radically increase or decrease the amount of information unavailable to the public.[128] A 1974 FOIA amendment addressed this by empowering judges to assess whether information was properly classified. Federal judges have the authority to privately examine the requested materials to determine whether they could damage national security or foreign policy if released. Records requests denied on the basis of this exemption have proved to be the most difficult to overturn. Typically, judges rule in favor of classification. The U.S. Supreme Court, for example, in suggesting that Exemption 1 should have been used by the CIA to prevent disclosure of records related to research about brainwashing techniques, referred to the exemption as the "keystone of a congressional scheme that balances deference to the Executive's interest in maintaining secrecy with continued judicial and congressional oversight."[129] The CIA's refusal to disclose the names of some institutions and all individual researchers related to the project was affirmed.

Exemption 2: Internal Agency Rules and Procedures The exemption related to internal agency rules and procedures is sometimes known as the "housekeeping" exemption. It pertains to matters related exclusively to the practices of the agency itself: vacation policies, lunch break rules, parking space assignments and so on. The rationale is not so much that any harm could result in the disclosure of such information but that keeping the records and then retrieving them when requests are made is not worth the expense. An exception to this no-harm aspect—but still justifying nondisclosure—is any internal policy that could be used inappropriately. For example, break or shift change procedures used by federal prison guards could conceivably be used to breach the security of a particular facility.

It is generally accepted that the spirit of open government is not violated by the enforcement of this exemption. Nevertheless, the exemption cannot be used to conceal all agency practices. If a matter is of public concern and its disclosure would not circumvent agency regulations or statutes, a court could rule that related records do not qualify for Exemption 2 and order their release. The U.S. Supreme Court addressed this issue in a case in which the records related to Air Force Academy honor and ethics hearings were sought. Where the situation is not one where disclosure would compromise agency regulation, Exemption 2 is not applicable to subjects that are genuinely in the public interest, the Court ruled. "The exemption was not designed to authorize withholding of all matters except otherwise secret law bearing directly on the propriety of actions of members of the public. Rather, the general thrust of the exemption is simply to relieve agencies of the burden of assembling and maintaining for public inspection matter in which the public could not reasonably be expected to have an interest."[130]

Exemption 3: Statutory Exemptions The FOIA provision regarding statutory exemptions stipulates that the act cannot override other laws that forbid the disclosure of certain information. This exemption increasingly comes into play as Congress continues to enact laws that prohibit disclosure of information. Still, litigation surfaces related to this exemption. Courts usually require the government to show that (1) the information being sought falls within the scope of the statute being cited, and (2) the statute grants no discretionary authority to the government agency holding the information (i.e., the nondisclosure is mandatory). If those standards are met, the decision of nondisclosure is generally upheld.

Exemption 4: Trade Secrets In compliance with federal law, the Chrysler Corporation had turned over to a government agency documents related to its affirmative action program and the general composition of its workforce. Afterward, the agency received a FOIA request that targeted those records. The agency was inclined to grant the request, but Chrysler objected and challenged it on the basis of Exemption 4.

This situation illustrates that private businesses generate a lot of information that is provided to various government agencies. That includes profit and loss statements, market share information and secret formulas. No government agency or its personnel has created the information; agencies merely collect and keep it to assist other government objectives, such as enforcement of copyright law or regulation of broadcasters. Often, other businesses could use to their competitive advantage information that government requires businesses to disclose. And that is why the FOIA exempts such information from mandatory disclosure. When an agency's nondisclosure decision under Exemption 4 is challenged, the agency is expected to show that the information sought is, in fact, a trade secret. In other words, it has to prove that the information is confidential and that its release would cause considerable competitive harm or loss to a business or make it more difficult to collect similar information in the future.

As for the *Chrysler* case, the U.S. Supreme Court ruled that the automaker had no claim to prevent disclosure. The FOIA, it said, "is an attempt to meet the demand for open government while preserving workable confidentiality in governmental decisionmaking."[131]

Exemption 5: Agency Memos Sometimes referred to as the "working papers" or "discovery" exemption, the exemption regarding agency memos protects two kinds of information from disclosure. First, internal agency memoranda, studies or drafts that are prepared and used to create final reports or policies are exempted from disclosure. One court ruled that this exemption helps both to protect the integrity of the decision-making process and to avoid confusing the public if preliminary policy decisions were to be disclosed.[132] Opponents argue that this exemption hides the processes that lead up to final policies and obscures the true decision-making process.

In one situation, Exemption 5 was at the center of a request to disclose documents related to water allocation that had been transmitted by various Native American tribes to the Department of the Interior and the Bureau of Indian Affairs. The association seeking those documents challenged the rejection of its FOIA request. Ultimately, the Supreme Court ruled in favor of full disclosure. The Court emphasized that Exemption 5 is not intended to protect government secrets, noting that the exemptions collectively "do not obscure the basic policy that disclosure, not secrecy, is the dominant objective of the Act."[133] The key here was whether the transmission of the documents from tribes to the Interior Department qualified as "inter-agency or intra-agency memoranda or letters." The Court said they did not.

Second, this exemption protects information exchanged between an agency and its attorney(s). This is directly related to the traditional attorney-client privilege. Exemption 5 recognizes that the privilege is not waived merely because the client is a federal agency. Nothing that is considered discovery material—the evidence gathered by both sides in a civil trial that both sides may examine—must be disclosed under FOIA.

realWorld Law

NASA and FOIA

An illustration of FOIA Exemption 6 at work occurred when The New York Times sued NASA. Several months after the 1986 explosion of the space shuttle Challenger that killed all seven astronauts aboard, The New York Times filed a FOIA request with NASA for cockpit voice recordings and their accompanying transcripts. NASA provided the transcripts but refused to release any recordings, citing Exemption 6. After unsuccessfully appealing to the Office of the Administrator of NASA, the Times sued.

The newspaper claimed there was a public interest in the cockpit recording because there was substantial interest in the disaster and in NASA's conduct before, during and after the tragedy. NASA, on the other hand, maintained that the privacy that Exemption 6 protects extends to the families of the astronauts. Moreover, NASA claimed that voice recordings would shed no additional light on the tragedy and the space administration's conduct beyond what was revealed in the transcript.

After an appeal and re-hearing, the U.S. District Court for the District of Columbia provided the final word. It determined that the privacy interests clearly outweighed the public interest and ruled against The New York Times.[1]

1. New York Times Co. v. National Aeronautics and Space Administration, 783 F. Supp. 628 (D. D.C. 1991).

Exemption 6: Personal Privacy Privacy is at the heart of Exemptions 6 and 7. Under Exemption 6, "personnel and medical files and similar files the disclosure of which would constitute a clearly unwarranted invasion of personal privacy" may be withheld. The phrase "similar files" has been the source of much dispute. It has generally been interpreted broadly to include lists, files, records and letters.

Courts attempt to balance privacy concerns against the purpose of the FOIA—informing the public about government activities. It is a delicate balance. Sometimes courts consider the purpose of the request. How will the information be used? Is there a legitimate public interest in its disclosure? If so, the scales of justice sometimes tip in favor of disclosure. "Exemption Six overwhelmingly favors the disclosure of information relating to a violation of the public trust by a government official," a federal appeals court once ruled.[134] However, the balance sometimes tilts toward privacy interests. The U.S. Supreme Court recognized that the FOIA's purpose is allowing government activity—not that of private citizens—to be open for public scrutiny.[135]

Exemption 7: Law Enforcement Records Records compiled within the context of law enforcement investigations may be exempt from FOIA disclosure. There are limits, however, to the exemption. For the government to deny disclosure, release of a record must reasonably be expected to

a. Interfere with enforcement proceedings, or
b. Deprive a person of the right to a fair trial with an impartial jury, or
c. Constitute an unwarranted invasion of privacy, or
d. Disclose the identity of a confidential source, or

e. Disclose law enforcement techniques and procedures, or

f. Endanger the life or physical safety of any individual.

The government needs to show only that one of these circumstances would occur if the requested record is released.

At one time, items such as rap sheets, arrest records, convictions records and department manuals were not exempt. More recently, however, nondisclosure is the norm. One of the more noteworthy FOIA-related cases is *U.S. Department of Justice v. Reporters Committee for Freedom of the Press,* excerpted at the end of this chapter. A journalist filed a FOIA request with the FBI for its criminal records on four members of a family suspected of criminal activity. The FBI complied with the requests pertaining to the three family members who were deceased but not to the remaining living member of the family. That decision was challenged but upheld on the basis of Exemption 7. With regard to the surviving family member, the journalist and the Reporters Committee argued that there was a public interest in learning about his past arrests or convictions. First, he allegedly had improper dealings with a corrupt congressman and, second, he was an officer of a corporation with defense contracts. But as is clear in its ruling, the Supreme Court was of a mind to safeguard personal privacy. "Disclosure of records regarding private citizens, identifiable by name, is not what the framers of the FOIA had in mind,"[136] wrote Justice John Paul Stevens, upholding the FBI's decision against disclosure.

There has been a tendency toward nondisclosure when personal privacy is at stake. In 2004, the U.S. Supreme Court affirmed the authority of several federal agencies and organizations to withhold death scene photographs of Vincent Foster. At the time of his death, Foster was legal counsel to President Bill Clinton.[137] The U.S. Park Police conducted an investigation into Foster's death and took color photographs of the death scene, including 10 pictures of Foster's body. The investigation concluded that Foster committed suicide by shooting himself with a revolver. Subsequent investigations by the FBI, Congress and independent counsels reached the same conclusion. Still, several people remained skeptical, among them attorney Allan Favish. He believed disclosure of the pictures was vital to public understanding about whether Foster was a victim of a murder that had been

Skepticism about the 1993 death of Vincent Foster, Jr. (left), former deputy counsel to President Bill Clinton, led to a FOIA request for photos. Foster is seen here in 1988 with his wife, Lisa, and Hillary and Bill Clinton.

disguised as a suicide. Favish filed FOIA requests with two different federal agencies. Both were denied. Lawsuits followed, with appeals culminating at the U.S Supreme Court.

In ruling against Favish, the Court explicitly recognized that surviving family members enjoy a right of privacy under FOIA regarding pictures of their deceased relative. In addition, the Supreme Court refused to accept Favish's conspiracy theory as sufficient grounds to overcome the family's right to privacy. The Court said that when people seek information that implicates personal privacy interests, they must demonstrate a clear connection between the information sought and a significant public interest. More important, the Court said when

the public interest being asserted is to show that responsible officials acted negligently or otherwise improperly in the performance of their duties, the requester must establish more than a bare suspicion in order to obtain disclosure. Rather, the requester must produce evidence that would warrant a belief by a reasonable person that the alleged Government impropriety might have occurred.[138]

Thus, rather than requiring broad disclosure of records that might shed some light on possible government malfeasance, the Court said Favish could overcome the family's privacy interest only if he provided substantial evidence to demonstrate the public interest in the records. The Court relied on an earlier decision in which it had said the FOIA is intended to provide access to "official information that sheds light on an agency's performance of its statutory duties. . . . That purpose, however, is not fostered by disclosure of information about private citizens that is accumulated in various governmental files but that reveals little or nothing about an agency's own conduct."[139]

In 2011, the U.S. Supreme Court narrowed and clarified this privacy exemption. AT&T's records revealed it overbilled the federal government for telephone and other services. The company said exemption 7 should keep those records secret. A group had submitted a FOIA request for records that AT&T had forwarded to the FCC. The FCC thought the records could be released, believing that AT&T did not qualify for the personal privacy exemption. Ultimately, the Supreme Court agreed that the exemption is for individuals, not corporations. Chief Justice John Roberts concluded the Court's opinion by writing, "We trust that AT&T will not take it personally."[140]

Exemption 8: Financial Records This exemption is meant to deny disclosure of sensitive financial reports or audits. The burden on the government agency is to show that the disclosure of certain reports would undermine public confidence in banks and other financial institutions. While seldom used, this exemption assumes greater significance during periods when financial scandals take place. Information about institutions that federal agencies possess is in greater demand. This is a sweeping exemption that left many questions unanswered during the massive financial crisis of savings and loan organizations during the 1980s.

realWorld Law

The Fight over Photos

Freedom of Information Act (FOIA) Exemptions 6 and 7 were at the heart of a battle over whether the Defense Department should release photos of U.S. detainees in Afghanistan and Iraq, including the Abu Ghraib prison. The Defense Department initially claimed the FOIA exemptions protecting privacy applied—claiming the privacy of those in the pictures was at stake—relieving the department of any obligation to release the photos. Later, the Pentagon added another part of Exemption 7 to its argument, claiming that disclosure of the photos could reasonably endanger the life or physical safety of any individual. It was referring to U.S. troops abroad.

The Second Circuit Court of Appeals said that "FOIA's purpose is to encourage public disclosure of information in the possession of federal agencies so that the people may know what their government is up to," adding that the release of information of this sort represents FOIA's basic purpose: to ensure an informed citizenry, vital to the functioning of a democratic society, needed to check against corruption and to hold the governors accountable to the governed."[1] In its ruling in favor of releasing the photos, the court concluded that the exemption required a specific anticipated danger to a particular individual rather than diffuse risks to "any" members of the U.S. forces.

The case was far from over, however. A new law was passed allowing the secretary of defense to block the pictures' release. At the urging of his national security advisers, President Obama was convinced that releasing the photos would inflame anti-American sentiment abroad and endanger U.S. troops. The Justice Department brought the case to the U.S. Supreme Court. Without comment, the Court vacated the lower court ruling in light of the new law.[2]

1. ACLU v. Dep't of Defense, 543 F.3d 59, 66 (2nd Cir. 2008) (internal quotations omitted).
2. Dep't of Defense v. ACLU, 130 S. Ct. 777 (2009).

Exemption 9: Geological Data Like Exemption 8, Exemption 9 rarely comes into play within a news media context and is equally broad. It is designed to prevent oil and gas exploration companies from obtaining information from federal agencies that can provide them a competitive advantage. In other words, because those companies must file information about their exploration and the location of discovered natural gas or oil deposits with federal agencies, profitable information could be obtained through the FOIA were it not for this exemption.

Computer Records As more government records and information are kept and transferred to electronic storage, the demand for access to computerized formats grows. Access advocates wanted to make sure that records were not concealed or buried merely because of their nonpaper format. The FOIA now applies to computer records. Congress passed an amendment to the FOIA in 1996 known as the **Electronic Freedom of Information Act (EFOIA)**.[141] It provides access to electronic federal records. Among other things, the law clearly established that records in electronic format are records subject to disclosure under the FOIA. The law also stipulates that computer searches to retrieve records do not constitute creation of a new record, a justification some agency record keepers had used previously to deny access to electronic records.

Electronic Freedom of Information Act (EFOIA) A 1996 amendment to the Freedom of Information Act that updates the act by including electronically stored information and subjecting it to the FOIA's provisions.

To aid public access to government records, the EFOIA mandates that publicly accessible electronic records be posted in a readily reproducible format, generally in the format of choice of the requester. The law also requires federal agencies to create a FOIA section on their websites and to provide "electronic reading rooms" filled with online copies of records, policy statements, administrative opinions and indexes of frequently sought documents. This provision applies only to records created after Nov. 1, 1996.

When Congress examined the effects of the law in 2000, it found that the number of public records requests had been stable or even declined at most agencies. Nonetheless, most agencies reported an increasing number of unprocessed requests for records.[142] The law does not permit agencies to extend the response deadline of 20 days simply because of routine backlogs. Moreover, the EFOIA encourages agencies to provide expedited access to records when the requester can demonstrate a compelling need for rapid access based on personal safety or heightened public concern.

Despite the promise of electronic access, the General Accounting Office (GAO), which monitors compliance with the law, reported in 2002 that agencies had not put enough resources into providing and maintaining electronic access to public records. The report concluded, in part, that many agencies had not begun to implement electronic access options. The GAO recommended that noncompliant agencies be held accountable for their failure to improve citizen access to government records.

Because federal agencies are not obligated to create records that do not already exist, that provision sometimes creates a way out for agencies reluctant to part with electronic-based information. They may claim that the computer programming required to retrieve a record amounts to record "creation," thereby relieving them of any duty to disclose. The EFOIA is designed to prevent such evasion. It requires agencies to deliver documents in "any form or format requested" that is "readily reproducible by the agency." In 2003, a federal appeals court said this required the Department of Defense to provide files in zipped format because the agency used such files as part of its "business as usual."[143] Another obstacle for seekers of computer-based records can be agencies that subcontract with private companies to computerize their hard-copy records. During those periods, because a record is not in the agency's possession, access likely is difficult.

While the EFOIA applies only to federal records, many states followed the federal example and adopted specific provisions to ensure and improve electronic access to state records.[144]

Following Sept. 11, 2001, and the start of the war on terrorism, government agencies hesitated to release defense-related data and a wide array of other information potentially related to national security. Some government agencies also argued that they must move slowly in providing public online access to their records for fear that such access would violate personal privacy rights. In 2003, the GAO also reported that the huge proliferation of electronic records was creating an increasing nightmare for archivists and record keepers.[145] The sheer volume of records, some record keepers argue, was impeding electronic access.

SUMMARY

The federal Freedom of Information Act was intended to shed light on the inner workings of government. Its goals were to better inform citizens about the actions of their governors and to protect against government malfeasance. The FOIA applies to federal executive branch agencies and departments. It does not regulate access to federal courts or Congress. The act mandates public access to agency records in any format. Although the law presumes the public should have access to most agency records, courts have struggled to determine which records are covered by the act. Requests under the FOIA may be written or oral, and requesters do not need to provide information about themselves or the purpose of their request.

The FOIA includes nine categories of exemptions that permit government to maintain the secrecy of records. Some of the exemptions are narrow and pose little difficulty for reporters. Others, including the protection of investigative records, statutory exemptions or personal privacy rights, are more sweeping and often pose barriers to newsgathering. Statutes specifically exempting federal records from disclosure have multiplied since the adoption of the FOIA. Concerns over privacy have swelled. Nevertheless, the language of the act makes clear that exemptions should be read narrowly to permit the greatest level of access. The exemptions are permissive; they allow but do not require government to withhold the identified records. ■

Access to Federal Meetings

The protections and limits described so far in this chapter relate largely to access to records. Another source of valuable information to journalists and other members of the public is meetings. Important information about topics of great public interest arises and is discussed in a myriad of meetings held by various governing and policymaking bodies at all levels of government. Moreover, because the public's business is being conducted, the processes involved and not merely the results are of legitimate interest. This philosophy was adopted into law when the **Government in the Sunshine Act**—also known as the "Federal Open Meetings Law"— was passed in 1976. It applies to the 50 or so federal agencies, commissions and boards whose members are appointed by the president and that have some independent authority. These groups are required to conduct their business in public and to give public notice of their meetings. Ten exemptions allow the closing of these meetings. Exemptions 1–9 are similar to those of the FOIA. Exemption 10 applies to agency litigation or arbitration. An often-invoked reason for closing meetings is that the board will discuss matters related to personnel, and closure is needed to protect the privacy of those involved.

Government in the Sunshine Act Sometimes referred to as the Federal Open Meetings Law, an act passed in 1976 that mandates that meetings of federal government agencies be open to the public unless all or some part of a meeting is exempted according to exceptions outlined in the law.

realWorld Law

E-Mail as a Public Record?

Whether the e-mail of public employees is a public record was an issue handled by the Wisconsin Supreme Court in 2010. Using that state's open-records law, a citizen had requested records of school teachers' e-mail, both work-related and private. The teachers did not object to revealing their work-related e-mail, but they resisted releasing their personal e-mails, even those that had been sent and received on their work computers.

A circuit court first ruled that all the e-mails should be released. But the state supreme court reversed, ruling that because the teachers' personal e-mail could not be considered "records" under Wisconsin law, it was not subject to the public records request. "To be a record . . . the content of the document must have a connection to a government function. In the instant case, the contents of the teachers' personal e-mails have no connection to a government function and therefore are not records," the court held. The Wisconsin law exempts "materials which are purely the personal property of the custodian and have no relation to his or her office."[1] The court also cited the intent of lawmakers who passed the open-records bill. They said to be considered a record, a document must have a connection to a government function.[2]

The Wisconsin ruling followed similar decisions made by courts in West Virginia,[3] Michigan[4] and the District of Columbia[5] in which private e-mails, even those sent or received on government workplace computers, were determined not to be subject to open records or FOIA requests. Like other state and District of Columbia rulings, these rulings are not binding in other states.

1. Wis. Stat. §§ 19.31–19.39.
2. Schill v. Wisconsin Rapids School Dist., 786 N.W.2d 177 (Wisc. 2010).
3. Associated Press v. Canterbury, 688 S.E.2d 317 (W. Va. 2009).
4. Howell Education Association v. Howell Board of Education, 789 N.W.2d 495 (Mich. App. 2010).
5. Convertino v. United States Dept. of Justice, 674 F. Supp. 2d 97 (D.D.C. 2009).

Some observers estimate that nearly 1,000 advisory boards provide expert guidance to the federal government. These boards are not covered by either the FOIA or the Government in the Sunshine Act because they have no independent decision-making authority. Yet they play a major, and often definitive, role in the development of government policy. In 1972, the Federal Advisory Committee Act (FACA) opened the meetings and records of these advisory groups to the public unless the committee is "composed wholly of full-time officers or employees of the federal government."

State Open-Records Laws

As important as the federal Freedom of Information Act is, most journalists' work occurs on the local level. As a result, they are more likely to rely on the open-records laws in the state in which they live.[146] Every state and the District of Columbia have some version of an access-to-information statute. Some follow the model of the FOIA, while others look very different. Those differences may be in the form of requiring more or less disclosure than the FOIA or in the enforcement mechanisms. In Texas, for example, a state agency has 10 days either to comply with a request or seek the state attorney general's judgment on whether access can be denied.

State laws that facilitate access to records have a tradition whose roots are much deeper than the federal version. In 1849, Wisconsin provided for inspection of public records. Only eight states—Arkansas, Delaware, Maryland, Mississippi, New Hampshire, New York, South Carolina and Virginia—did not have some kind of open-records law when the FOIA was passed in 1966. The explicit purposes of state open-records laws tend to be consistent: government accountability. Some go further. Hawaii's statute, for example, echoing James Madison, says that opening government to public scrutiny "is the only viable and reasonable method of protecting the public's interest."[147] The Delaware law asserts, "It is vital that citizens have easy access to public records in order that the society remain free and democratic."[148] Illinois links the right of access with enabling "people to fulfill their duties of discussing public issues fully and freely" and making "informed political judgments."[149]

Because there is so much state-to-state variation in these laws, characterizing them broadly is virtually impossible. Even those that appear similar may, in reality, differ in how states implement and interpret them. Generally speaking, however, some observations are helpful:

- Like federal agencies, those on the state level are not required to create or acquire records in response to a request.
- Some state open-records laws cover the legislature, executive branch and courts.
- Few states require record indexes to be produced by agencies.
- Some states require that requesters be state residents.
- Many states have exemptions similar to those of the FOIA.
- Most states' open-records laws cover electronic and computer-stored records, but some states do not require that these records be transformed into a user-friendly format. Some charge extra for electronic manipulation.
- Some states' open-records laws do not specify response time limits. Delays can be lengthy.
- Some states do not specify penalties for agencies violating the law.

State open-records laws apply to not only state government agencies and departments, but also to cities, school districts and other governing authorities within a given state. These laws are utilized frequently—much more than the U.S. FOIA. Like the FOIA, state laws have been amended to apply to the digital age. The law in Tennessee, for example, covers "all documents, papers, letters, maps, books, photographs, microfilms, electronic data processing files and output, sound recordings, or other materials regardless of physical form made or

realWorld Law

Access in the Digital Age

As with FOIA on the federal level, states grapple with how to apply open-records laws to computerized records, including information that appears in social media. In one recent case, the issue was whether metadata was part of a public record or separate from it. Metadata was information that is embedded in an electronic record that may not be readily readable. This embedded data may include the creation and edit dates of a file, its authorship and edit history. In the case, as part of an administrative complaint, a Phoenix police officer filed a public records request. After examining the records, he suspected that some information had been altered, such as backdating when the files had been created. His request for the metadata to confirm his suspicions was denied. The city claimed the metadata was not part of the record, but something

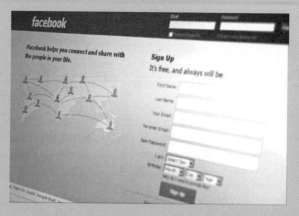

Social media websites such as Facebook allow government officials to post and exchange information in ways not considered when most open records and open meetings laws were adopted.

separate, and therefore not subject to the state open-records law. The Arizona Supreme Court disagreed, ruling that metadata in an electronic document is "part of the underlying document; it does not stand on its own."[1] In 2010, the Washington Supreme Court ruled similarly, holding that metadata is subject to disclosure because it may contain information that relates to the conduct of government and is important for the public to know.[2]

Electronic mail and social media websites such as Facebook represent not only a shift in how people communicate and share information but also in how records are created and meetings held. It makes sense for lawmakers and other officials to use technology and its platforms and applications to communicate with citizens and one another. In doing so, records are created that are often subject to state access laws. Just because some people can view some information online does not relieve a government entity from the obligation to provide the information to other citizens on request.[3] Moreover, "Internet exchanges that create virtual records can also create virtual meetings," write two lawyers who analyzed how to apply open records and open-meeting laws in their native Texas.[4] That is, while technology permits online meetings, it is also forcing an expanded definition of "meeting" and how laws permitting access may apply.

---

1. Lake v. City of Phoenix, 218 P.3d 1004, 1007 (Ariz. 2009).
2. O'Neill v. City of Shoreline, 240 P.3d 1149 (Wash. 2010).
3. *See* Alan J. Bojorquez and Damien Shores, *Open Government and the Net: Bringing Social Media into the Light,* 11 TEX. TECH. ADMIN. L. J. 45, 59 (2009).
4. *Id.*

received pursuant to law or ordinance or in connection with the transaction of official business by a governmental agency."[150] Like many states and the federal government, Tennessee emphasizes that only records are covered by its law. A requester cannot demand that a government agency provide information.[151]

Points of Law

State Open-Meetings Laws: The New York Example

The following is excerpted from the New York State Opening Meeting Law's section on opening meetings and executive sessions:

(a) Every meeting of a public body shall be open to the general public, except that an executive session of such body may be called and business transacted thereat in accordance with section one hundred five of this article. (b) Public bodies shall make or cause to be made all reasonable efforts to ensure that meetings are held in facilities that permit barrier-free physical access to the physically handicapped, as defined in subdivision five of section fifty of the public buildings law. (c) A public body that uses videoconferencing to conduct its meetings shall provide an opportunity to attend, listen and observe at any site at which a member participates. (d) Public bodies shall make or cause to be made all reasonable efforts to ensure that meetings are held in an appropriate facility which can adequately accommodate members of the public who wish to attend such meetings.[1]

---

1. Committee on Open Government, New York State Dept. of State, n.d, *available at* http://www.dos.state.ny.us/coog/openmeetlaw.html.

Enforcement is an issue within the context of newsgathering access. That is, while laws demand compliance, what happens when government agencies refuse to cooperate as laws require? Thirty-four states and the District of Columbia have civil and/or criminal sanctions for first-time government official violators who do not properly comply with records requests.[152] In fact, several states have recently revised enforcement provisions in their open-records laws. For example, in 2009 Illinois added a provision to its law stating "that it is the public policy of the State of Illinois that access by all persons to public records promotes the transparency and accountability of public bodies at all levels of government," adding that openness is a "fundamental obligation of government to operate openly."[153]

State Open-Meetings Laws

While seven states combine public records and open meetings access into one law,[154] the vast majority of states—and the federal government—find it best to address these areas of access separately. All states and the District of Columbia have open-meetings laws or constitutional provisions ensuring some degree of access to public meetings. These laws vary widely from state to state, as do the penalties for violating them. In general, open-meetings laws trigger public access whenever a quorum of a decision-making body deliberates public business. By law, a meeting generally means either a physical gathering or videoconferencing that allows members to interact in real time. Applying this same logic, some observers believe open-meetings laws should apply to online chat rooms. Boards may accommodate citizens' right to attend meetings either by providing space in their meeting room or by providing electronic access. Most state laws require agencies to provide public notice in advance of meetings and to keep minutes of their business. A few states also require boards to keep minutes of their executive sessions, which become available to the public if closure is improper or once the need for closure has passed.

Several states outline those provisions for the enforcement of open-meetings laws. In Michigan, for example, any citizen may challenge in court a decision made by a public body to deny access. If it is determined by the court that the decision was in violation of the law, the court can invalidate that decision. In addition, a public official who intentionally breaks the law is subject to a fine up to $1,000. A second deliberate violation can result in a fine up to $2,000, being jailed up to one year, or both.[155]

SUMMARY

THE COMPUTER AGE HAS NOT CIRCUMVENTED freedom of information. The Electronic Freedom of Information Act provides access to digitally recorded and stored information in the hands of the federal government.

Just as federal records laws help provide access to federal records, similar laws exist on the state level. In fact, the states have overwhelmingly been ahead of the federal government in advancing the idea of open records. Similarly, access to meetings is provided for by law on both the federal and state levels. ∎

Cases for Study

Thinking About It

The two case excerpts that follow cover different subsets in the broad area of news gathering. The first case addresses the concept of the ride-along. The second is a case related to the Freedom of Information Act. As you read these case excerpts, keep the following questions in mind:

- Note that in the *Wilson* ride-along case, a media organization is not a party to the case. Nevertheless, it is a ruling that affects the media significantly. How and why?

- In *Wilson*, why were members of the news media on the scene? Did their presence help in the execution of the warrant?

- Just how much information does the Freedom of Information Act provide? Are the limits that have been established fair?

- In the *Reporters Committee* case, what factor does the Supreme Court identify as critical in deciding whether to disclose a private document?

- The *Reporters Committee* case was decided in 1989. Has the nature of privacy changed in such a way that the ruling would be different today?

Wilson v. Layne
SUPREME COURT OF THE UNITED STATES
526 U.S. 603 (1999)

CHIEF JUSTICE WILLIAM REHNQUIST delivered the Court's opinion:

While executing an arrest warrant in a private home, police officers invited representatives of the media to accompany them. We hold that such a "media ride along" does violate the Fourth Amendment, but that because the state of the law was not clearly established at the time the search in this case took place, the officers are entitled to the defense of qualified immunity.

I

In early 1992, the Attorney General of the United States approved "Operation Gunsmoke," a special national fugitive apprehension program in which United States Marshals worked with state and local police to apprehend dangerous criminals. The "Operation

Gunsmoke" policy statement explained that the operation was to concentrate on "armed individuals wanted on federal and/or state and local warrants for serious drug and other violent felonies." This effective program ultimately resulted in over 3,000 arrests in 40 metropolitan areas.

One of the dangerous fugitives identified as a target of "Operation Gunsmoke" was Dominic Wilson, the son of petitioners Charles and Geraldine Wilson. Dominic Wilson had violated his probation on previous felony charges of robbery, theft, and assault with intent to rob, and the police computer listed "caution indicators" that he was likely to be armed, to resist arrest, and to "assault police." The computer also listed his address as 909 North Stone Street Avenue in Rockville, Maryland. Unknown to the police, this was actually the home of petitioners, Dominic Wilson's parents. Thus, in April 1992, the Circuit Court for Montgomery County issued three arrest warrants for Dominic Wilson, one for each of his probation violations. The warrants were each addressed to "any duly authorized peace officer," and commanded such officers to arrest him and bring him "immediately" before the Circuit Court to answer an indictment as to his probation violation. The warrants made no mention of media presence or assistance.

In the early morning hours of April 16, 1992, a Gunsmoke team of Deputy United States Marshals and Montgomery County Police officers assembled to execute the Dominic Wilson warrants. The team was accompanied by a reporter and a photographer from the Washington Post, who had been invited by the Marshals to accompany them on their mission as part of a Marshal's Service ride-along policy.

At around 6:45 a.m., the officers, with media representatives in tow, entered the dwelling at 909 North Stone Street Avenue in the Lincoln Park neighborhood of Rockville. Petitioners Charles and Geraldine Wilson were still in bed when they heard the officers enter the home. Petitioner Charles Wilson, dressed only in a pair of briefs, ran into the living room to investigate. Discovering at least five men in street clothes with guns in his living room, he angrily demanded that they state their business, and repeatedly cursed the officers. Believing him to be an angry Dominic Wilson, the officers quickly subdued him on the floor. Geraldine Wilson next entered the living room to investigate, wearing only a nightgown. She observed her husband being restrained by the armed officers.

When their protective sweep was completed, the officers learned that Dominic Wilson was not in the house, and they departed. During the time that the officers were in the home, the Washington Post photographer took numerous pictures. The print reporter was also apparently in the living room observing the confrontation between the police and Charles Wilson. At no time, however, were the reporters involved in the execution of the arrest warrant. The Washington Post never published its photographs of the incident.

Petitioners sued the law enforcement officials in their personal capacities for money damages . . . . They contended that the officers' actions in bringing members of the media to observe and record the attempted execution of the arrest warrant violated their Fourth Amendment rights . . . .

II

. . . [G]overnment officials performing discretionary functions generally are granted a qualified immunity and are "shielded from liability for civil damages insofar as their conduct does not violate clearly established statutory or constitutional rights of which a reasonable person would have known."

. . . A court evaluating a claim of qualified immunity "must first determine whether the plaintiff has alleged the deprivation of an actual constitutional right at all, and if so, proceed to determine whether that right was clearly established at the time of the alleged violation." This order of procedure is designed to "spare a defendant not only unwarranted liability, but unwarranted demands customarily imposed upon those defending a long drawn-out lawsuit." Deciding the constitutional question before addressing the qualified immunity question also promotes clarity in the legal standards for official conduct, to the benefit of both the officers and the general public. We now turn to the Fourth Amendment question.

In 1604, an English court made the now-famous observation that "the house of every one is to him as his castle and fortress, as well for his defence against injury and violence, as for his repose." In his Commentaries on the Laws of England, William Blackstone noted that

> the law of England has so particular and tender a regard to the immunity of a man's house, that it stiles it his castle, and will never suffer it to be violated with impunity: agreeing herein with the sentiments of antient Rome . . . . For this reason no doors can in general be broken open to execute any civil process; though, in criminal causes, the public safety supersedes the private.

The Fourth Amendment embodies this centuries-old principle of respect for the privacy of the home:

"The right of the people to be secure in their persons, houses, papers, and effects, against unreasonable searches and seizures, shall not be violated, and no Warrants shall issue, but upon probable cause, supported by Oath or affirmation, and particularly describing the place to be searched, and the persons or things to be seized."

Our decisions have applied these basic principles of the Fourth Amendment to situations, like those in this case, in which police enter a home under the authority of an arrest warrant in order to take into custody the suspect named in the warrant. In *Payton v. New York* (1980), we noted that although clear in its protection of the home, the common-law tradition at the time of the drafting of the Fourth Amendment was ambivalent on the question of whether police could enter a home without a warrant. We were ultimately persuaded that the "overriding respect for the sanctity of the home that has been embedded in our traditions since the origins of the Republic" meant that absent a warrant or exigent circumstances, police could not enter a home to make an arrest. We decided that "an arrest warrant founded on probable cause implicitly carries with it the limited authority to enter a dwelling in which the suspect lives when there is reason to believe the suspect is within."

Here, of course, the officers had such a warrant, and they were undoubtedly entitled to enter the Wilson home in order to execute the arrest warrant for Dominic Wilson. But it does not necessarily follow that they were entitled to bring a newspaper reporter and a photographer with them. . . .

Certainly the presence of reporters inside the home was not related to the objectives of the authorized intrusion. Respondents concede that the reporters did not engage in the execution of the warrant, and did not assist the police in their task. The reporters therefore were not present for any reason related to the justification for police entry into the home—the apprehension of Dominic Wilson.

This is not a case in which the presence of the third parties directly aided in the execution of the warrant. Where the police enter a home under the authority of a warrant to search for stolen property, the presence of third parties for the purpose of identifying the stolen property has long been approved by this Court and our common-law tradition.

Respondents argue that the presence of the Washington Post reporters in the Wilsons' home nonetheless served a number of legitimate law enforcement purposes. They first assert that officers should be able to exercise reasonable discretion about when it would "further their law enforcement mission to permit members of the news media to accompany them in executing a warrant." But this claim ignores the importance of the right of residential privacy at the core of the Fourth Amendment. It may well be that media ride-alongs further the law enforcement objectives of the police in a general sense, but that is not the same as furthering the purposes of the search. Were such generalized "law enforcement objectives" themselves sufficient to trump the Fourth Amendment, the protections guaranteed by that Amendment's text would be significantly watered down.

Respondents next argue that the presence of third parties could serve the law enforcement purpose of publicizing the government's efforts to combat crime, and facilitate accurate reporting on law enforcement activities. There is certainly language in our opinions interpreting the First Amendment which points to the importance of "the press" in informing the general public about the administration of criminal justice . . . . But the Fourth Amendment also protects a very important right, and in the present case it is in terms of that right that the media ride-alongs must be judged.

Surely the possibility of good public relations for the police is simply not enough, standing alone, to justify the ride-along intrusion into a private home. And even the need for accurate reporting on police issues in general bears no direct relation to the constitutional justification for the police intrusion into a home in order to execute a felony arrest warrant.

Finally, respondents argue that the presence of third parties could serve in some situations to minimize police abuses and protect suspects, and also to protect the safety of the officers. While it might be reasonable for police officers to themselves videotape home entries as part of a "quality control" effort to ensure that the rights of homeowners are being respected, or even to preserve evidence, such a situation is significantly different from the media presence in this case. The Washington Post reporters in the Wilsons' home were working on a story for their own purposes. They were not present for the purpose of protecting the officers, much less the Wilsons. A private photographer was acting for private purposes, as evidenced in part by the fact that the newspaper and not the police retained the photographs. Thus, although the presence of third parties during the execution of a warrant may in some circumstances be constitutionally permissible, the presence of these third parties was not.

The reasons advanced by respondents, taken in their entirety, fall short of justifying the presence of media inside a home. We hold that it is a violation of the Fourth Amendment for police to bring members of the media or other third parties into a home during the execution of a warrant when the presence of the third parties in the home was not in aid of the execution of the warrant.

III

Since the police action in this case violated the petitioners' Fourth Amendment right, we now must decide whether this right was clearly established at the time of the search. As noted above, government officials performing discretionary functions generally are granted a qualified immunity and are "shielded from liability for civil damages insofar as their conduct does not violate clearly established statutory or constitutional rights of which a reasonable person would have known." What this means in practice is that "whether an official protected by qualified immunity may be held personally liable for an allegedly unlawful official action generally turns on the 'objective legal reasonableness' of the action, assessed in light of the legal rules that were 'clearly established' at the time it was taken.". . .

We hold that it was not unreasonable for a police officer in April 1992 to have believed that bringing media observers along during the execution of an arrest warrant (even in a home) was lawful. First, the constitutional question presented by this case is by no means open and shut. The Fourth Amendment protects the rights of homeowners from entry without a warrant, but there was a warrant here. The question is whether the invitation to the media exceeded the scope of the search authorized by the warrant. Accurate media coverage of police activities serves an important public purpose, and it is not obvious from the general principles of the Fourth Amendment that the conduct of the officers in this case violated the Amendment.

Second, although media ride-alongs of one sort or another had apparently become a common police practice, in 1992 there were no judicial opinions holding that this practice became unlawful when it entered a home. . . .

Finally, important to our conclusion was the reliance by the United States marshals in this case on a Marshal's Service ride-along policy which explicitly contemplated that media who engaged in ride-alongs might enter private homes with their cameras as part of fugitive apprehension arrests. The Montgomery County Sheriff's Department also at this time had a ride-along program that did not expressly prohibit media entry into private homes. Such a policy, of course, could not make reasonable a belief that was contrary to a decided body of case law. But here the state of the law as to third parties accompanying police on home entries was at best undeveloped, and it was not unreasonable for law enforcement officers to look and rely on their formal ride-along policies.

Given such an undeveloped state of the law, the officers in this case cannot have been "expected to predict the future course of constitutional law." Between the time of the events of this case and today's decision, a split among the Federal Circuits in fact developed on the question whether media ride-alongs that enter homes subject the police to money damages. If judges thus disagree on a constitutional question, it is unfair to subject police to money damages for picking the losing side of the controversy.

For the foregoing reasons, the judgment of the Court of Appeals is affirmed.

It is so ordered.

U.S. Department of Justice v. Reporters Committee for Freedom of the Press
SUPREME COURT OF THE UNITED STATES
489 U.S. 749 (1989)

JUSTICE JOHN PAUL STEVENS delivered the Court's opinion:

The Federal Bureau of Investigation (FBI) has accumulated and maintains criminal identification records, sometimes referred to as "rap sheets," on over 24 million persons. The question presented by this case is whether the disclosure of the contents of such a file to a third party "could reasonably be expected to constitute an unwarranted invasion of personal privacy" within the meaning of the Freedom of Information Act (FOIA).

I

In 1924 Congress appropriated funds to enable the Department of Justice (Department) to establish a program to collect and preserve fingerprints and other criminal identification records. That statute authorized the Department to exchange such information with "officials of States, cities and other institutions.". . . Congress created the FBI's identification division, and gave it responsibility for "acquiring, collecting, classifying, and preserving criminal identification and other crime records and the exchanging of said criminal identification records with the duly authorized officials of governmental agencies, of States, cities, and penal institutions." Rap sheets compiled pursuant to such authority contain certain descriptive information, such as date of birth and physical characteristics, as well as a history of arrests, charges, convictions, and incarcerations of the subject. Normally a rap sheet is preserved until its subject attains age 80. Because of the volume of rap sheets, they are sometimes incorrect or incomplete and sometimes contain information about other persons with similar names.

The local, state, and federal law enforcement agencies throughout the Nation that exchange rap-sheet data with the FBI do so on a voluntary basis. The principal use of the information is to assist in the detection and prosecution of offenders; it is also used by courts and corrections officials in connection with sentencing and parole decisions. As a matter of executive policy, the Department has generally treated rap sheets as confidential and, with certain exceptions, has restricted their use to governmental purposes. Consistent with the Department's basic policy of treating these records as confidential, Congress in 1957 amended the basic statute to provide that the FBI's exchange of rap-sheet information with any other agency is subject to cancellation "if dissemination is made outside the receiving departments or related agencies."

As a matter of Department policy, the FBI has made two exceptions to its general practice of prohibiting unofficial access to rap sheets. First, it allows the subject of a rap sheet to obtain a copy, and second, it occasionally allows rap sheets to be used in the preparation of press releases and publicity designed to assist in the apprehension of wanted persons or fugitives. . . .

Although much rap-sheet information is a matter of public record, the availability and dissemination of the actual rap sheet to the public is limited. Arrests, indictments, convictions, and sentences are public events that are usually documented in court records. In addition, if a person's entire criminal history transpired in a single jurisdiction, all of the contents of his or her rap sheet may be available upon request in that jurisdiction. That possibility, however, is present in only three States. All of the other 47 States place substantial restrictions on the availability of criminal-history summaries even though individual events in those summaries are matters of public record. Moreover, even in Florida, Wisconsin, and Oklahoma, the publicly available summaries may not include information about out-of-state arrests or convictions.

II

The statute known as the FOIA is actually a part of the Administrative Procedure Act (APA). Section 3 of the APA as enacted in 1946 gave agencies broad discretion concerning the publication of governmental records. In 1966 Congress amended that section to implement "'a general philosophy of full agency disclosure.'" The amendment required agencies to publish their rules of procedure in the Federal Register, and to make available for public inspection and copying their opinions, statements of policy, interpretations, and staff manuals and instructions that are not published in the Federal Register . . . requires every agency "upon any request for records which . . . reasonably describes such records" to make such records "promptly available to any person." If an agency improperly withholds any documents, the district court has jurisdiction to order their production. Unlike the review of other agency action that must be upheld if supported by substantial evidence and not arbitrary or capricious, the FOIA expressly places the burden "on the agency to sustain its action" and directs the district courts to "determine the matter de novo."

Congress exempted nine categories of documents from the FOIA's broad disclosure requirements. Three of those exemptions are arguably relevant to this case. Exemption 3 applies to documents that are specifically exempted from disclosure by another statute. Exemption 6 protects "personnel and medical files and similar files the disclosure of which would constitute a clearly unwarranted invasion of personal privacy." Exemption 7(C) excludes records or information compiled for law enforcement purposes, "but only to the extent that the production of such [materials] . . . could reasonably be expected to constitute an unwarranted invasion of personal privacy."

Exemption 7(C)'s privacy language is broader than the comparable language in Exemption 6 in two respects. First, whereas Exemption 6 requires that the invasion of privacy be "clearly unwarranted," the adverb "clearly" is omitted from Exemption 7(C). This omission is the product of a 1974 amendment adopted in response to concerns expressed by the President. Second, whereas Exemption 6 refers to disclosures that "would constitute" an invasion of privacy, Exemption 7(C) encompasses any disclosure that "could reasonably be expected to constitute" such an invasion. This difference is also the product of a specific amendment. Thus, the standard for evaluating a threatened invasion of privacy interests resulting from the disclosure of records compiled for law enforcement purposes is

somewhat broader than the standard applicable to personnel, medical, and similar files.

III

This case arises out of requests made by a CBS news correspondent and the Reporters Committee for Freedom of the Press (respondents) for information concerning the criminal records of four members of the Medico family. The Pennsylvania Crime Commission had identified the family's company, Medico Industries, as a legitimate business dominated by organized crime figures. Moreover, the company allegedly had obtained a number of defense contracts as a result of an improper arrangement with a corrupt Congressman.

The FOIA requests sought disclosure of any arrests, indictments, acquittals, convictions, and sentences of any of the four Medicos. Although the FBI originally denied the requests, it provided the requested data concerning three of the Medicos after their deaths. In their complaint in the District Court, respondents sought the rap sheet for the fourth, Charles Medico (Medico), insofar as it contained "matters of public record.". . .

IV

Exemption 7(C) requires us to balance the privacy interest in maintaining, as the government puts it, the "practical obscurity" of the rap sheets against the public interest in their release.

The preliminary question is whether Medico's interest in the nondisclosure of any rap sheet the FBI might have on him is the sort of "personal privacy" interest that Congress intended Exemption 7(C) to protect. As we have pointed out before, "[t]he cases sometimes characterized as protecting 'privacy' have in fact involved at least two different kinds of interests. One is the individual interest in avoiding disclosure of personal matters, and another is the interest in independence in making certain kinds of important decisions." Here, the former interest, "in avoiding disclosure of personal matters," is implicated. Because events summarized in a rap sheet have been previously disclosed to the public, respondents contend that Medico's privacy interest in avoiding disclosure of a federal compilation of these events approaches zero. We reject respondents' cramped notion of personal privacy.

To begin with, both the common law and the literal understandings of privacy encompass the individual's control of information concerning his or her person. In an organized society, there are few facts that are not at one time or another divulged to another. Thus the extent of the protection accorded a privacy right at common law rested in part on the degree of dissemination of the allegedly private fact and the extent to which the passage of time rendered it private. According to Webster's initial definition, information may be classified as "private" if it is "intended for or restricted to the use of a particular person or group or class of persons: not freely available to the public." Recognition of this attribute of a privacy interest supports the distinction, in terms of personal privacy, between scattered disclosure of the bits of information contained in a rap sheet and revelation of the rap sheet as a whole. The very fact that federal funds have been spent to prepare, index, and maintain these criminal-history files demonstrates that the individual items of information in the summaries would not otherwise be "freely available" either to the officials who have access to the underlying files or to the general public. Indeed, if the summaries were "freely available," there would be no reason to invoke the FOIA to obtain access to the information they contain. Granted, in many contexts the fact that information is not freely available is no reason to exempt that information from a statute generally requiring its dissemination. But the issue here is whether the compilation of otherwise hard-to-obtain information alters the privacy interest implicated by disclosure of that information. Plainly there is a vast difference between the public records that might be found after a diligent search of courthouse files, county archives, and local police stations throughout the country and a computerized summary located in a single clearinghouse of information.

This conclusion is supported by the web of federal statutory and regulatory provisions that limits the disclosure of rap-sheet information. That is, Congress has authorized rap-sheet dissemination to banks, local licensing officials, the securities industry, the nuclear-power industry, and other law enforcement agencies. Further, the FBI has permitted such disclosure to the subject of the rap sheet and, more generally, to assist in the apprehension of wanted persons or fugitives. Finally, the FBI's exchange of rap-sheet information "is subject to cancellation if dissemination is made outside the receiving departments or related agencies." This careful and limited pattern of authorized rap-sheet disclosure fits the dictionary definition of privacy as involving a restriction of information "to the use of a particular person or group or class of persons." Moreover, although perhaps not specific enough to constitute a statutory exemption under FOIA Exemption 3, these statutes and regulations, taken as a whole, evidence a congressional intent to protect the privacy of rap-sheet subjects, and a concomitant recognition of the power of compilations to affect personal privacy that outstrips the combined power of the bits of information contained within.

Other portions of the FOIA itself bolster the conclusion that disclosure of records regarding private citizens, identifiable by name, is not what the framers of the FOIA had in mind. Specifically, the FOIA provides that "[t]o the extent required to prevent a clearly unwarranted invasion of personal privacy, an agency may delete identifying details when it makes available or publishes an opinion, statement of policy, interpretation, or staff manual or instruction." Additionally, the FOIA assures that "[a]ny reasonably segregable portion of a record shall be provided to any person requesting such record after deletion of the portions which are exempt under Section (b)." These provisions, for deletion of identifying references and disclosure of segregable portions of records with exempt information deleted, reflect a congressional understanding that disclosure of records containing personal details about private citizens can infringe significant privacy interests.

Also supporting our conclusion that a strong privacy interest inheres in the nondisclosure of compiled computerized information is the Privacy Act of 1974. The Privacy Act was passed largely out of concern over "the impact of computer data banks on individual privacy." The Privacy Act provides generally that "[n]o agency shall disclose any record which is contained in a system of records . . . except pursuant to a written request by, or with the prior written consent of, the individual to whom the record pertains." Although the Privacy Act contains a variety of exceptions to this rule, including an exemption for information required to be disclosed under the FOIA, Congress' basic policy concern regarding the implications of computerized data banks for personal privacy is certainly relevant in our consideration of the privacy interest affected by dissemination of rap sheets from the FBI computer.

Given this level of federal concern over centralized data bases, the fact that most States deny the general public access to their criminal-history summaries should not be surprising. As we have pointed out, in 47 States nonconviction data from criminal-history summaries are not available at all, and even conviction data are "generally unavailable to the public." State policies, of course, do not determine the meaning of a federal statute, but they provide evidence that the law enforcement profession generally assumes—as has the Department of Justice—that individual subjects have a significant privacy interest in their criminal histories. It is reasonable to presume that Congress legislated with an understanding of this professional point of view.

In addition to the common-law and dictionary understandings, the basic difference between scattered bits of criminal history and a federal compilation, federal statutory provisions, and state policies, our cases have also recognized the privacy interest inherent in the nondisclosure of certain information even where the information may have been at one time public . . . .

In sum, the fact that "an event is not wholly 'private' does not mean that an individual has no interest in limiting disclosure or dissemination of the information." The privacy interest in a rap sheet is substantial. The substantial character of that interest is affected by the fact that in today's society the computer can accumulate and store information that would otherwise have surely been forgotten long before a person attains age 80, when the FBI's rap sheets are discarded.

V

Exemption 7(C), by its terms, permits an agency to withhold a document only when revelation "could reasonably be expected to constitute an unwarranted invasion of personal privacy." We must next address what factors might warrant an invasion of the interest described in Part IV.

Our previous decisions establish that whether an invasion of privacy is warranted cannot turn on the purposes for which the request for information is made. Except for cases in which the objection to disclosure is based on a claim of privilege and the person requesting disclosure is the party protected by the privilege, the identity of the requesting party has no bearing on the merits of his or her FOIA request. Thus, although the subject of a presentence report can waive a privilege that might defeat a third party's access to that report, and although the FBI's policy of granting the subject of a rap sheet access to his own criminal history is consistent with its policy of denying access to all other members of the general public, the rights of the two press respondents in this case are no different from those that might be asserted by any other third party, such as a neighbor or prospective employer. As we have repeatedly stated, Congress "clearly intended" the FOIA "to give any member of the public as much right to disclosure as one with a special interest [in a particular document]." . . . "The Act's sole concern is with what must be made public or not made public."

Thus whether disclosure of a private document under Exemption 7(C) is warranted must turn on the nature of the requested document and its relationship to "the basic purpose of the Freedom of Information Act 'to open agency action to the light of public scrutiny'" . . . rather than on the particular purpose for which the document is being requested. In our leading case on the FOIA, we declared that the Act was designed to create a broad right of access to "official information ." . . .

This basic policy of "'full agency disclosure unless information is exempted under clearly delineated statutory language'" . . . Official information that sheds light on an agency's performance of its statutory duties falls squarely within that statutory purpose. That purpose, however, is not fostered by disclosure of information about private citizens that is accumulated in various governmental files but that reveals little or nothing about an agency's own conduct. In this case—and presumably in the typical case in which one private citizen is seeking information about another—the requester does not intend to discover anything about the conduct of the agency that has possession of the requested records. Indeed, response to this request would not shed any light on the conduct of any Government agency or official. . . .

Respondents argue that there is a twofold public interest in learning about Medico's past arrests or convictions: He allegedly had improper dealings with a corrupt Congressman, and he is an officer of a corporation with defense contracts. But if Medico has, in fact, been arrested or convicted of certain crimes, that information would neither aggravate nor mitigate his allegedly improper relationship with the Congressman; more specifically, it would tell us nothing directly about the character of the Congressman's behavior. Nor would it tell us anything about the conduct of the Department of Defense (DOD) in awarding one or more contracts to the Medico Company. Arguably a FOIA request to the DOD for records relating to those contracts, or for documents describing the agency's procedures, if any, for determining whether officers of a prospective contractor have criminal records, would constitute an appropriate request for "official information." Conceivably Medico's rap sheet would provide details to include in a news story, but, in itself, this is not the kind of public interest for which Congress enacted the FOIA. In other words, although there is undoubtedly some public interest in anyone's criminal history, especially if the history is in some way related to the subject's dealing with a public official or agency, the FOIA's central purpose is to ensure that the Government's activities be opened to the sharp eye of public scrutiny, not that information about private citizens that happens to be in the warehouse of the Government be so disclosed. Thus, it should come as no surprise that in none of our cases construing the FOIA have we found it appropriate to order a Government agency to honor a FOIA request for information about a particular private citizen.

What we have said should make clear that the public interest in the release of any rap sheet on Medico that may exist is not the type of interest protected by the FOIA. Medico may or may not be one of the 24 million persons for whom the FBI has a rap sheet. If respondents are entitled to have the FBI tell them what it knows about Medico's criminal history, any other member of the public is entitled to the same disclosure—whether for writing a news story, for deciding whether to employ Medico, to rent a house to him, to extend credit to him, or simply to confirm or deny a suspicion. There is, unquestionably, some public interest in providing interested citizens with answers to their questions about Medico. But that interest falls outside the ambit of the public interest that the FOIA was enacted to serve.

Finally, we note that Congress has provided that the standard fees for production of documents under the FOIA shall be waived or reduced "if disclosure of the information is in the public interest because it is likely to contribute significantly to public understanding of the operations or activities of the government and is not primarily in the commercial interest of the requester." Although such a provision obviously implies that there will be requests that do not meet such a "public interest" standard, we think it relevant to today's inquiry regarding the public interest in release of rap sheets on private citizens that Congress once again expressed the core purpose of the FOIA as "contribut[ing] significantly to public understanding of the operations or activities of the government."

VI

Both the general requirement that a court "shall determine the matter de novo" and the specific reference to an "unwarranted" invasion of privacy in Exemption 7(C) indicate that a court must balance the public interest in disclosure against the interest Congress intended the Exemption to protect. Although both sides agree that such a balance must be undertaken, how such a balance should be done is in dispute. The Court of Appeals majority expressed concern about assigning federal judges the task of striking a proper case-by-case, or ad hoc, balance between individual privacy interests and the public interest in the disclosure of criminal-history information without providing those judges standards to assist in performing that task. Our cases provide support for the proposition that categorical decisions may be appropriate and individual circumstances disregarded when a case fits into a genus in which the balance characteristically tips in one direction. . . .

. . . [W]e hold as a categorical matter that a third party's request for law enforcement records or information about a private citizen can reasonably be expected to invade that citizen's privacy, and that when the request seeks no "official information" about a Government agency, but merely records that the Government happens to be storing, the invasion of privacy is "unwarranted." The judgment of the Court of Appeals is reversed.

It is so ordered.

Chapter 9

[N]o harassment of newsmen will be tolerated. . . . [I]f the newsman is called upon to give information bearing only a remote and tenuous relationship to the subject of the investigation, or if he has some other reason to believe that his testimony implicates confidential source relationships without a legitimate need of law enforcement, he will have access to the court on a motion to quash and an appropriate protective order may be entered. The asserted claim to privilege should be judged on its facts by the striking of a proper balance between freedom of the press and the obligation of all citizens to give relevant testimony with respect to criminal conduct.

U.S. Supreme Court Justice Lewis Powell[1]

Former New York Times reporter Judith Miller leaves U.S. District Court after a hearing. She was later jailed for refusing to reveal the identity of a source.

Reporter's Privilege
Protecting the Watchdogs

Reporter's Privilege

After *Branzburg*

Shield Laws

Who Is Covered
What Is Covered
Other Shield Law Issues
Other Sources of Reporter's
   Privilege

**Breaking Promises of
  Confidentiality**

Search Warrants

Newsroom Searches
The Privacy Protection Act

Cases for Study

➤ *Branzburg v. Hayes*
➤ *Cohen v. Cowles
   Media Co.*

Suppose . . .

. . . that a reporter promises a source anonymity in exchange for sensitive information that relates to criminal activity. When the article is published, law enforcement officials are alerted to the fact that the reporter has information that could help their investigation. The reporter receives a subpoena to appear before a grand jury. When asked questions that would force him to reveal his source's identity, he refuses. He says to do so would infringe on his and his newspaper's First Amendment rights.

Is refusing to disclose a source a First Amendment right for journalists, even when it involves an investigation of criminal activity? Why or why not?

Should a journalist who refuses to cooperate with criminal investigations be forced to go to jail? Look for the answers to these questions when the case of *Branzburg v. Hayes* is discussed later in this chapter and is excerpted at the end of the chapter.

In the course of doing their work, journalists can come across a lot of information. Some of that information may be sensitive and potentially useful to criminal investigations. That same information may have been revealed to a reporter on the condition that its source or specific elements of it not be revealed. The reporter may agree, granting the source confidentiality in exchange for information that will contribute to a story.

This chapter explores whether reporters can be forced to reveal information in their possession, particularly the identities of confidential sources. No issue in media law has generated more controversy over the past several years. The use of confidential sources is a long-standing practice in journalism.[2] One estimate claims that at least 33 percent of newspaper stories and up to 85 percent of all newsmagazine sources contain veiled attribution.[3] The use of confidential sources has been referred to as "one form of currency that journalists use to get something they want and need, which is information."[4]

A promise of anonymity may be the only way a reporter can convince a source to talk. In return, reporters and their news organizations typically keep those promises, except when compelled by courts to break them. Keeping such promises is not only ethical but also practical. "Burned" sources tend to become former sources. Moreover, reporters and news organizations that break promises develop a reputation for being untrustworthy. Sources vanish. A chilling effect ensues. A source may successfully sue a reporter.

For these reasons, many argue that a reporter's privilege that protects journalists from being forced to reveal source identity should exist. If the First Amendment guarantees freedom of the press, according to this rationale, it also must protect against any infringement on the free flow of ideas. Divulging information can act as just such an infringement. But balanced against reporter's privilege is the deep-rooted judicial philosophy that justice is best served by requiring anyone who has information related to a crime to reveal it. More than 60 years ago, the U.S. Supreme Court wrote, "For more than three centuries it has now been recognized as a fundamental maxim that the public has a right to every man's evidence."[5] Later, the Court noted, "the obligation of all citizens [is] to give relevant testimony with respect to criminal conduct."[6]

Anyone may be subpoenaed. As professional recorders of news and information, journalists have an enhanced possibility of being subpoenaed. As noted in Chapter 1, a subpoena is a court order that a person appear in court on a specific date and time to answer questions. Often that means revealing information and/or producing evidence. Those who receive subpoenas are expected to comply. However, recipients may file a motion to quash the subpoena. A motion to **quash** is simply a request to a court to annul or vacate the order to appear; it may be based on any number of factors, including that the information being sought is available elsewhere.

quash To nullify or annul, as in quashing a subpoena.

Reporter's Privilege

Whether reporters can keep the identities of their sources confidential, even when that information is sought through a court order, revolves around the concept of **reporter's privilege**. This concept is also sometimes called "journalist's privilege." The privilege is tenuous and depends on several conditions being met. Thus, it is a qualified privilege.

reporter's privilege The concept that reporters can keep information such as source identity confidential. The idea is that the reporter–source relationship is similar to doctor–patient and lawyer–client relationships.

The concept of privilege within the courts is not unusual. It has long been accepted that people have a right not to testify against those with whom they have a special relationship—lawyer–client, doctor–patient, husband–wife or clergy–parishioner, for example. Journalists maintain that they have similar relationships with their sources and should not be forced to testify against them by revealing their identities. Moreover, they believe reporter's privilege has the protection of the First Amendment. Compelling a journalist to violate an agreement with a source for confidentiality, according to this view, impinges on freedom of the press by interfering with the free flow of information. While arguments drawing parallels between lawyer–client and reporter–source privileges have been made,[7] some maintain there is a vital distinction: Whereas a client may release his attorney from their agreement—thus removing the lawyer's privilege against testifying—even if a source releases a journalist, the journalist may still maintain the confidentiality. According to this view, reporter's privilege belongs to the reporter, someone who is protecting not only a source, but also the integrity of the process.[8]

The conditions that may trigger reporter's privilege can be complex. They can best be discovered through an examination of how the courts have handled the issue. The starting point is the landmark U.S. Supreme Court case *Branzburg v. Hayes*.[9]

Branzburg v. Hayes involved four consolidated cases heard together in the U.S. Supreme Court, two of them involving Paul Branzburg, a reporter with the Louisville Courier-Journal. In the course of his reporting, Branzburg had uncovered and written about illegal drug use and sales in the Louisville, Ky., area. He promised his sources that he would not identify them. When he was issued a subpoena to appear before a grand jury to answer questions about the published stories and his sources, he kept his promises. The other two cases decided at the same time also involved journalists who refused to provide information to grand juries. Both of those reporters had observed activities of militant organizations.

All three reporters made arguments similar to those outlined. The First Amendment and its free

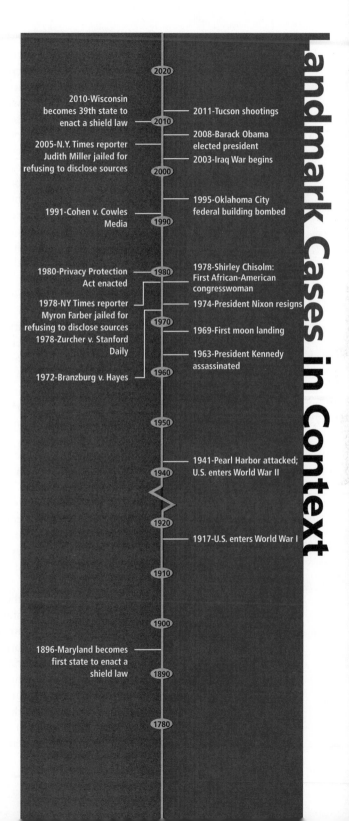

Landmark Cases in Context

- 2020
- 2011-Tucson shootings
- 2010-Wisconsin becomes 39th state to enact a shield law
- 2010
- 2008-Barack Obama elected president
- 2005-N.Y. Times reporter Judith Miller jailed for refusing to disclose sources
- 2003-Iraq War begins
- 2000
- 1995-Oklahoma City federal building bombed
- 1991-Cohen v. Cowles Media
- 1990
- 1980-Privacy Protection Act enacted
- 1980
- 1978-Shirley Chisolm: First African-American congresswoman
- 1978-NY Times reporter Myron Farber jailed for refusing to disclose sources
- 1974-President Nixon resigns
- 1970
- 1978-Zurcher v. Stanford Daily
- 1969-First moon landing
- 1963-President Kennedy assassinated
- 1972-Branzburg v. Hayes
- 1960
- 1950
- 1941-Pearl Harbor attacked; U.S. enters World War II
- 1940
- 1920
- 1917-U.S. enters World War I
- 1910
- 1900
- 1896-Maryland becomes first state to enact a shield law
- 1890
- 1780

The dissenting opinion by Justice Potter Stewart in *Branzburg v. Hayes* proposed a qualified reporter's privilege.

Points of Law

The *Branzburg* Test for Reporter's Privilege

A reporter's privilege to withhold information may exist unless the government can demonstrate:

1. Probable cause to believe that the reporter has information clearly relevant to a specific violation of law

2. That the information sought cannot be obtained by alternative means less destructive of First Amendment values and

3. That there is a compelling and overriding interest in the information.

press clause, they claimed, meant that they should not be required to reveal confidential information given the circumstances of their cases. If forced to do so, their ability to report news would be irreparably harmed. Not only would those specific sources be betrayed and less likely to cooperate with the news media in the future, but many potential future sources would also go silent. The reporters argued that even if they refused to name sources, their mere appearance before a grand jury could cause this harm because their sources would never know what the reporter had revealed during the closed grand jury process. As a result, less information would be available, both to the public and the press. The reporters maintained this disruption of the journalistic process constituted a violation of the First Amendment's guarantee of press freedom.

A 5–4 majority of the Supreme Court rejected the idea that there is a First Amendment privilege for journalists under these circumstances. In balancing the possibility of such a privilege against the public interest in law enforcement, the Court favored the latter. The importance of obtaining evidence is critical to that effort. That it is a reporter who may be in possession of the evidence is immaterial. Grand juries, Justice Byron White wrote for the Court, are entitled to "every man's evidence."[10] Journalists are not exempted.

The concurring and dissenting opinions written in the case were also significant. Writing in concurrence, Justice Lewis Powell emphasized "the limited nature"[11] of the Court's holding. He suggested that any journalist's privilege to withhold information should be evaluated case by case. In addition, he wrote that a refusal to provide information might be permitted if the information was not relevant to an investigation or failed to serve "a legitimate need of law enforcement."[12]

Justice Potter Stewart led the dissenters, criticizing the "Court's crabbed view of the First Amendment."[13] He stated that reporters have a limited First Amendment right to refuse to reveal sources, a right that stems from "the broad societal interest in a full and free flow of information to the public."[14] That basic concern, he wrote, underlies the First Amendment's protection for a free press—a guarantee "not for the benefit of the press so much as for the benefit of all of us."[15]

Justice Stewart did not minimize the importance of either the grand jury process or the need for "every man's

Points of Law

Contempt of Court

Judges have broad power to issue contempt of court orders. In general, any willful disobedience of a court order, any misconduct in court or any action that interferes with the judge's administration of justice might be cited for contempt of court and may be punishable by a fine, imprisonment or both. Each judge has discretion to determine what types of conduct constitute contempt, to cite someone for contempt, to find the person guilty and to decide the penalty. The judge's decision to issue a contempt citation most often cannot be reviewed by another judge. Contempt citations must be obeyed even if they may be found unconstitutional upon appeal. There is both civil and criminal contempt, and the distinction between the two often is unclear.

Civil Contempt

Civil contempt citations usually compel an individual to do something, such as name a source or turn over interview notes or outtakes of a broadcast program. They also arise when someone intentionally disobeys a court order. For example, if attorneys speak to the media in violation of a court order not to discuss the trial in public, they may be cited for contempt. Civil contempt sometimes is called "indirect contempt" because the action that prompts the citation generally occurs outside the direct supervision of the judge. Civil contempt orders most often are lifted as soon as the individual performs the required action or the trial ends.

Criminal Contempt

Criminal contempt is any conduct in or near the court that willfully disobeys a court order or obstructs court proceedings. Because much criminal contempt directly interferes with the proceedings of the court, some forms of criminal contempt are also called "direct contempt." It is often unclear whether a particular action is a form of criminal or civil contempt or both. For example, if journalists under oath refuse to answer questions about confidential sources, they may be cited for both civil and criminal contempt.

While judges enjoy sweeping authority to issue contempt citations, their power is not unlimited. Some states limit judges' contempt power to punishment of actions committed by the officers of the court, actions in the court or acts that directly disobey court mandates, orders or rules. The First Amendment prevents judges from using their contempt power to silence criticism of themselves or court proceedings unless the criticism poses a clear and present danger to justice.[1] Thus, even when newspapers publish caustic attacks on the court that are, at best, partially accurate, judges may not cite them for contempt unless the comments reach the level of intimidating jurors or undermining the fairness of the trial. The Supreme Court has ruled that individuals charged with contempt who could be sentenced to more than six months in jail if convicted have a right to a jury trial.

---

1. Pennekamp v. Florida, 328 U.S. 331 (1946).

---

evidence." However, he believed those interests ought to be balanced against the critical role of the press. A First Amendment privilege to withhold information should exist, he said, unless officials could meet "a heavy burden of justification" to overcome the privilege.[16] He outlined the conditions under which that burden could be met: (1) There is probable cause to believe the reporter has information clearly relevant to a specific violation of law, (2) the information being sought cannot be obtained by other means that are less intrusive of First Amendment values, and (3) there is a compelling and overriding interest in the information.[17] This was adopted by courts nationwide and is now commonly referred to as the *Branzburg* test.

After *Branzburg*

In the wake of *Branzburg,* questions surfaced. Most notably, there was uncertainty about whether and to what degree reporter's privilege existed. Part of the ambiguity lay in Justice Powell's opinion. Although listed as a concurrence and therefore placing Justice White's opinion in the majority, Powell's concurrence seemed to have more in common with the dissenters. That included his willingness to consider a reporter's privilege under certain conditions. Thus, a sort of "unofficial majority" of the Court said that a qualified reporter's privilege should at least be contemplated. In fact, in the years since *Branzburg,* many jurisdictions have recognized something akin to the privilege called for in that ruling's dissent.

Because the ruling in *Branzburg* was narrow, speaking only to circumstances in which a journalist is issued a subpoena by a grand jury, its direct application has been relatively limited. The Court was unequivocal when it came to one venue: There was no reporter's privilege with regard to grand juries. In cases not pertaining to grand juries, however, lower courts often adopted the three-part *Branzburg* test in determining whether the privilege survives. It is therefore most accurate to characterize reporter's privilege as limited or qualified. That is, its survival depends on the three-part test. If a prosecutor can satisfy the three conditions, the journalist loses the privilege, but only for that case.

So does reporter's privilege exist? The answer: a definite maybe. The meaning of *Branzburg* has been interpreted in almost as many ways as there are lower courts that have considered it. The privilege, in the abstract, has permeated the jurisprudence of both state and federal courts. It remains considered largely case by case. On a practical level, if investigators can obtain the information being sought in ways other than by demanding the testimony of a journalist, as required by the second element of the *Branzburg* test, the chances that the privilege would be recognized are enhanced. Also, a journalist's ability to protect information, including source identity, within state proceedings may be protected by shield laws or through a state's constitution. These are explained below.

TV reporter Jim Taricani was found in contempt of court for refusing to reveal a source.

realWorld Law

"An Act of Conscience"

The most recent and well-known situation of a journalist refusing to disclose a source and going to prison involved New York Times reporter Judith Miller. Miller was a target of a probe into a White House leak that led to the outing of a CIA agent. She refused to comply with a court order to reveal what she knew, including the identity of her source. She was ultimately cited for contempt of court by a federal appellate judge.[1] Any possible sentence was delayed until all possible appeals were exhausted.

The U.S. Supreme Court rejected her appeal,[2] allowing the lower appeals court decision to stand and leaving it to the judge there whether Miller would be sentenced to prison. The New York Times did not waver in its support of Judith Miller, who claimed never to have published anything based on information she received from the undisclosed source.

The prosecutor in the case maintained that testimony from Miller was necessary, writing that "journalists are not entitled to promised complete confidentiality—no one in America is.[3] "Special treatment" for journalists, in the prosecutor's words, may counteract the coercive effect of jail and enable, rather than deter, defiance of the court's authority.

Miller chose to protect her source's identify and refused to testify. The judge ordered Miller to prison until she agreed to testify or until October 2005, when the grand jury's term expired. In response, New York Times Company chairman Arthur Sulzberger, Jr., said: "There are times when the greater good of democracy demands an act of conscience. Judy has chosen such an act in honoring her promise of confidentiality to her sources. She believes, as do we, that the free flow of information is critical to an informed citizenry."[4]

In announcing his decision to jail Miller, however, the judge disputed Miller's claims that jailing her would bring good reporting to an end. "*Branzburg* has been the law for 33 years," he said, "and it hasn't stopped anything."[5] After spending 85 days in jail, Miller testified before the federal grand jury in late September 2005 when her source relieved her of any confidentiality obligation. She had spent more time in jail than any reporter in American history for refusing to identify a source.

In November 2005, Miller and The New York Times reached an agreement for her to leave the newspaper.

---

1. *In re* Grand Jury Subpoena, (Miller), 397 F.3d 964 (D.C. Cir. 2005).
2. Miller v. U.S., 545 U.S. 1150 (2005).
3. *New York Times Reporter Jailed,* Oct. 28, 2005, *available at* http://www.cnn.com/2005/LAW/07/06/reporters.contempt/.
4. Adam Liptak, *Reporter Jailed After Refusing to Name Source,* N.Y. Times, July 7, 2005, at A1.
5. Carol D. Leonnig, *N.Y. Times Reporter Jailed,* Wash. Post, July 7, 2005, at A1.

Even when required to relinquish the privilege and comply with a subpoena, some journalists still refuse to testify. They remain steadfast in their belief that upholding a journalist's creed not to expose sources when promises of confidentiality are made is their primary obligation. Allegiance to this doctrine, however, comes with a price. Anyone who refuses to comply with a court order risks being found in contempt of court, with penalties of jail, a fine or both as possibilities. Occasionally journalists cling to their principled, First Amendment-based arguments and accept the penalties.[18] A finding of criminal contempt results in a specific jail term and/or fine. More common is a sanction of civil contempt, in which

Examples of Reporters Fined for Refusing to Reveal Sources

- 1978, $1,000 against Myron Farber, $100,000 against The New York Times (criminal contempt), plus $5,000 per day against the Times while Farber was in jail. He eventually served 40 days of a six-month sentence for refusing to reveal sources in a criminal trial, and the Times paid $185,000 in civil contempt fines. Contempt convictions stood until Farber was pardoned by Gov. Brendan Byrne of New Jersey, and the Times got back the $101,000 in criminal contempt fines.

- 1983, $500 against James Wright of the Daily Idahonian for refusing to reveal a confidential source in a criminal trial. Later, the judge imposed a $500 per day fine, stayed pending appeal. In May 1985, the state supreme court ruled the Idaho Constitution gives reporters a qualified privilege.

- 1985, $1,000 against freelancer Christopher Van Ness, who refused to release a tape of conversation with Cathy Smith about John Belushi's death. Van Ness was also sentenced to 10 days in jail but turned over the tape after serving a day.

- 1992, $2,000 per day, plus $4,000 in government legal fees, against Susan Smallheer and the Rutland, Vt., Herald. Smallheer had sought an interview with a prison escapee. The state high court ruled the prospective contempt fines and attorney fees were improper.

- 1996, $500 ($250 per day for two days) against the Minnesota Daily, a university newspaper, for refusing to turn over photos.

Examples of Reporters Jailed for Refusing to Reveal Sources[1]

- 2000, Timothy Crews, Red Bluff, Calif. Sacramento Valley Mirror editor and publisher served a five-day sentence for refusing to reveal his confidential sources in a story involving the sale of an allegedly stolen firearm by a state patrol officer.

- 2003, Vanessa Leggett, Houston, Tex. Book author, jailed 168 days.

- 2004, Jim Taricani, Providence, R.I. WJAR-TV reporter, jailed for refusing to reveal the source of a tape showing a city official accepting a bribe.

- 2005, Judith Miller, The New York Times reporter, jailed for refusing to testify before a grand jury in the Valerie Plame matter.

- 2006, Joshua Wolf, San Francisco, Calif. Freelance video blogger initially jailed for a month when he refused to turn over a video recording that federal officials suspected of showing protesters damaging a police car.

---

1. Reporters Committee for Freedom of the Press, *Paying the Price*, n.d., *available at* http://www.rcfp.org/jail.html.

the journalist is jailed until he or she complies with the order to disclose. Some journalists have remained in jail until a judge allows their release, usually when their information is no longer necessary in the resolution of the case at hand.

In the early 21st century, journalists and news organizations witnessed renewed government efforts to demand source information, with courts increasingly holding uncooperative reporters in contempt. The situation that attracted the most attention ended with the incarceration in 2005 of Judith Miller, then a New York Times reporter. (See "An Act of Conscience," p. 387, for more details on this case.)

In another case, Providence, R.I., television reporter Jim Taricani was convicted of contempt for refusing to reveal who illegally gave him an FBI surveillance tape that showed a city official accepting a bribe. "When I became a reporter 30 years ago," Taricani said, "I never imagined that I would be put on trial and face the prospect of going to jail for doing my job."[19] In 2004 he was sentenced. The judge said Taricani deserved to go to prison but instead sentenced the 55-year-old heart-transplant recipient to six months of home confinement. The judge said that the belief that refusal to name a source is protected by the First Amendment is a myth.[20]

A case concerning a freelance writer resulted in her being jailed for 168 days. English teacher Vanessa Leggett had conducted numerous interviews while investigating a murder case, with the hopes of publishing a book about the incident.[21] A federal grand jury had investigated possible illegal activities of a millionaire bookie from Houston, Tex. When Leggett was subpoenaed by the grand jury, she failed to comply with the demand to turn over her notes. The court cited her for civil contempt and ordered her jailed until she furnished the sought-after materials. These consisted of tape recordings, notes of interviews and photographs.[22] The statute under which she was cited allows a court to jail people held in contempt until the requested materials are relinquished, or a maximum of 18 months. A federal appeals court concluded that "the journalist's privilege is ineffectual against a grand jury subpoena absent evidence of governmental harassment or oppression."[23] Finding no governmental harassment or oppression, the appeals court held that the district court did not abuse its discretion in ordering Leggett incarcerated.[24] In 2002 Leggett was released from jail after 168 days—but only after the grand jury's term expired.

SUMMARY

JOURNALISTS MAY RECEIVE SUBPOENAS THAT REQUIRE them to reveal information in judicial proceedings. That information may include divulging sources of information. A qualified reporter's privilege to keep that information confidential may be invoked if the proceeding is something other than a grand jury inquiry. Courts typically use the three-part *Branzburg* test to determine whether the privilege stands. That standard demands that the information being sought is essential to an investigation and that there is no other way of obtaining it. Anyone who does not comply with a subpoena, including journalists who are denied reporter's privilege, are subject to contempt-of-court citations, which can result in time in jail and/or fines. ∎

Shield Laws

The U.S. Supreme Court's opinion in *Branzburg* more or less invited legislatures—both federal and state—to address whether "a statutory newsman's privilege is necessary and desirable."[25] Although 17 states had already dealt with the

realWorld Law

Leakers and the Law

An illustration of how real-world events can influence laws and lawmaking occurred in 2010 when attempts to pass a federal shield law hit a snag in the U.S. Senate. Shortly after the website WikiLeaks published tens of thousands of Afghanistan war documents, some senators concluded that any shield law should exclude from protection websites like WikiLeaks that are based outside the United States. There is doubt, however, whether a non-U.S. entity could even be subject to a subpoena.

Julian Assange, WikiLeaks Editor-in-Chief

Some senators had repeatedly expressed reservations about the legislation and how its provisions applied to leakers of classified information. The WikiLeaks situation played into their hands. Sen. Charles Schumer was among those seeking to amend the bill "to remove even a scintilla of doubt"[1] that a shield law would not protect a site like WikiLeaks from prosecution. "WikiLeaks should not be spared in any way from the fullest prosecution possible under the law," Sen. Schumer added.[2] A particular concern was publishing raw data without editorial oversight.

While some people claimed that the WikiLeaks situation pointed to the dangers of a federal shield law, others claimed just the opposite. Paul Boyle, senior vice president of the Newspaper Association of America, believed the WikiLeaks situation highlighted the need for the law. Absent the bill's protections, journalists would become "the first stop rather than the last" in efforts to obtain information in legal cases. This could create a potential chilling effect on investigative reporting, he said, as whistleblowers would stay silent rather than risk exposure and news organizations would pull back in fear of protracted legal costs.[3]

The reason lies in Boyle's belief that without a shield law, would-be leakers would take more material to groups like WikiLeaks because they cannot be forced to give up their sources. A shield law, however, would give whistleblowers greater confidence that their identities would not become public, making it more likely they would work with news organizations that exercise editorial control.

1. Charlie Savage, *After Afghan War Leaks, Revisions in a Shield Bill*, N.Y. TIMES, Aug. 3, 2010, at A12.
2. *Id.*
3. Paul Farhi, *WikiLeaks Is Barrier to Shiled Arguments*, WASH. POST, Aug. 21, 2010, at C1.

State Shield Laws: The U.S. Supreme Court's View

There is . . . merit in leaving state legislatures free, within First Amendment limits, to fashion their own standards in light of the conditions and problems with respect to the relations between law enforcement officials and press in their own areas. It goes without saying, of course, that we are powerless to bar state courts from responding in their own way and construing their own constitutions so as to recognize a newsman's privilege, either qualified or absolute.[1]

A Shield Law Example

The following excerpts are from one of the newest state shield laws, Wisconsin's, enacted in 2010:

Disclosure of information and sources by news person. "News person" means any of the following:

(a) Any business or organization that, by means of print, broadcast, photographic, mechanical, electronic, or other medium, disseminates on a regular and consistent basis news or information to the public, including a newspaper, magazine, or other periodical; book publisher; news agency; wire service; radio or television station or network; cable or satellite network, service, or carrier; or audio or audiovisual production company; and a parent, subsidiary, division, or affiliate of any of these businesses or organizations.

(b) Any person who is or has been engaged in gathering, receiving, preparing, or disseminating news or information to the public for an entity described in paragraph (a), including any person supervising or assisting the person in gathering, receiving, preparing, or disseminating such news or information.

SUBPOENAS ISSUED TO NEWS PERSON. No person having the power to issue a subpoena may issue a subpoena compelling a news person to testify about or produce or disclose any of the following that is obtained or prepared by the news person in the news person's capacity in gathering, receiving, or preparing news or information for potential dissemination to the public:

1. The identity of a confidential source of any news or information.
2. Any information that would tend to identify the confidential source of any news or information.
3. Any news or information obtained or prepared in confidence by the news person.
4. Any news, information, or identity of any source of any news or information that is not described in 1, 2, or 3.

A circuit court may issue a subpoena only if all of the following conditions are met:

1. The news, information, or identity of the source is highly relevant to the investigation, prosecution, action, or proceeding.
2. The news, information, or identity of the source is necessary to the maintenance of a party's claim, defense, or to the proof of an issue material to the investigation, prosecution, action, or proceeding.
3. The news, information, or identity of the source is not obtainable from any alternative source for the investigation, prosecution, action, or proceeding.
4. There is an overriding public interest in the disclosure of the news, information, or identity of the source.

---

1. Branzburg v. Hayes, 408 U.S. 665, 706 (1972).

shield laws State laws that protect journalists from being found in contempt of court for refusing to reveal sources.

issue by enacting laws prior to *Branzburg*, many other state legislatures answered in the affirmative by passing **shield laws,** which protect journalists from being found in contempt of court for refusing to reveal a source. To date, 38 states and the District of Columbia have laws that recognize and protect reporter's privilege to one extent or another. There is no federal shield law, though the U.S. House of Representatives did pass a version, the Free Flow of Information Act, in 2007. A Senate version of the bill was approved in late 2009 by the Judiciary Committee but has not been heard on the floor of the full Senate. Thus, journalists involved in federal court cases are left to use only the qualified reporter's privilege in situations where it is warranted. In state court proceedings, journalists may use shield laws in those states that have them, and in states without such laws journalists may attempt to invoke the reporter's privilege. Every state but one, Wyoming, has either a shield law or its courts have recognized some kind of reporter's privilege.

Reasons vary for the absence of shield laws in those states without such laws. In Massachusetts, for example, the Supreme Judicial Court has ruled that the First Amendment interests of journalists do not warrant any kind of comprehensive privilege: "News reporters do not have a constitutionally based testimonial privilege that other citizens do not have. There is no such statutory privilege, nor is there any rule of court providing such a privilege."[26] That court, though, did acknowledge that courts may refuse to enforce a subpoena based on common law principles—in other words, on a case-by-case basis.

The details of shield laws vary from state to state, sometimes widely. To one extent or another, these laws grant some degree of reporter's privilege, and some people believe they are preferable to relying on the privilege in the abstract. With a concrete law on the books, a journalist does not have to rely on the subjective judgment of a court in evaluating whether a constitutionally based privilege exists within a given case. The shortcoming, however, may lie in the wording of a state shield law and just what and whom it protects. That is, some journalists and certain material are excluded from protection.

Historically, any suggestion that a shield law offered journalists protection from grand jury subpoenas was rejected. In part, courts took their cue from the *Branzburg* Court in its affirmation of the importance of the grand jury process, in turn rejecting the notion that any qualified reporter's privilege would apply. But in 2008, the Pennsylvania Supreme Court modified

Points of Law

Shield Law States[1]

- Alabama
- Alaska
- Arizona
- Arkansas
- California
- Colorado
- Connecticut
- Delaware
- Florida
- Georgia
- Hawaii
- Illinois
- Indiana
- Kansas
- Kentucky
- Louisiana
- Maine
- Maryland
- Michigan
- Minnesota
- Montana
- Nebraska
- Nevada
- New Jersey
- New Mexico
- New York
- North Carolina
- North Dakota
- Ohio
- Oklahoma
- Oregon
- Pennsylvania
- Rhode Island
- South Carolina
- Tennessee
- Utah
- Washington
- Wisconsin

1. The District of Columbia also has a shield law.

a decades-long practice, at least in that state. A newspaper reporter used a confidential source to report about a grand jury proceeding. The high court ruled that the state shield law grants an absolute privilege to journalists and protects their source's identities from compelled disclosure in all cases—civil, criminal and grand jury proceedings.[27] It is worth noting that the reporter was not the subject of a grand jury subpoena but merely reported on a grand jury. Nevertheless, based on her articles, she and her newspaper employer were named as defendants in a libel lawsuit and within that context were issued subpoenas seeking the identity of her confidential source.[28]

Points of Law

Potential Options for Journalist Protection of Confidential Sources

Federal Court Situations	State Court Situations
1. Qualified reporter's privilege*	1. Shield law but if none, then
	2. State Constitution, either explicitly stated or a court-recognized implication but if none, then
	3. Qualified reporter's privilege*
*But never in grand jury situations.	*But not in most grand jury situations. Pennsylvania is the exception.

Who Is Covered

U.S. Supreme Court Justice Byron White was among those who recognized the challenge in creating a privilege and determining precisely who would be protected. Indeed, this challenge has materialized. How can the words "journalist" or "reporter" be defined, especially when the First Amendment freedom of the press implicitly allows anyone to assume those roles? Unlike doctors and lawyers, for example, journalists are not licensed and do not have to meet any particular qualifications to practice their trade.

Some shield law statutes recognize this difficulty by applying protection to several categories of people. For example, the Minnesota shield law broadly defines those eligible for protection. Many other shield laws define "journalist" in ways that protect only those who work full-time for a newspaper or broadcast station. Others use the term "news media" to specify those who are covered. A few states even shield those engaged in reporting or editorial activities for motion picture news. Freelance writers, book authors, Internet journalists and many others are left out. Some states also exclude magazine writers.

Reporter's privilege is not necessarily limited to traditional media. For example, in a case involving online reporter Matt Drudge, a district judge ruled that Drudge could invoke a qualified reporter's privilege. In addition, scholars whose research may require confidentiality may be able to claim the privilege. On at least two occasions, one federal appellate court upheld this argument.

Like other privileges, reporter's privilege can be waived—another way in which it is qualified. Particularly when a journalist is on the verge of going to court, the source who had been granted anonymity may waive the reporter's obligation of confidentiality. In other words, the source may grant permission to the reporter

realWorld Law

Privilege Denied

Book author Dary Matera was conducting research for a book detailing how an ex-mobster exposed political corruption in Arizona. Matera was provided information intended to be confidential, some of it by sources who wanted anonymity. When an indicted state lawmaker learned of this, she subpoenaed Matera with the expectation that his notes could help with her criminal defense.

Matera asked a trial court to quash the subpoena, relying in part on the Arizona shield law. A trial court denied his motion. An appeal to a county superior court was also unsuccessful. The superior court said Matera did not qualify for reporter's privilege. Book authors do not meet the definition of "news media," the court said. The law "was intended to apply to persons who gather and disseminate news on an ongoing basis as part of the organized, traditional, mass media."[1] Book authors do not report news, the court said, nor do they report information regularly.

The superior court said *Branzburg* precluded Matera from invoking the privilege: "The heart of the claim is that the burden on news gathering resulting from compelling reporters to disclose confidential information outweighs any public interest in obtaining the information."[2] "Matera has not, and cannot, claim that the subpoena in this case would cause him to reveal confidential sources or information, nor would the subpoena impede the gathering of information."[3]

---

1. Matera v. Superior Court, 825 P.2d 971 (Ariz. 1992).
2. *Id.* at 975, *quoting* Branzburg v. Hayes, 408 U.S. 665, 682 (1972).
3. *Id.*

to disclose his identity. While the reporter may then feel comfortable disclosing the source, it is still not necessary for him to do so. The privilege of not disclosing the source belongs to the journalist. By the same token, a court is likely to consider the privilege weak under those circumstances and thus to order disclosure.

What Is Covered

The specific kind of information protected by shield laws also varies from state to state. At stake are not only sources of information but also items such as notes and outtakes. While a shield law such as Tennessee's is broad in scope, applying to any information and the source of information obtained for publication or broadcast, others are not so generous. When testifying about witnessed events such as crimes, most statutes do not protect journalists. The Kentucky shield law explicitly protected Paul Branzburg from having to reveal his source. However, Branzburg's source was also involved in criminal activity. Branzburg was subpoenaed to testify about that activity, not specifically about his source. The law did not protect him from fulfilling that obligation.

Though not specifically a shield law case, the *Branzburg* ruling suggests a continuum of circumstances within which reporters may or may not be able to protect sources. First, protection is least likely to occur when a journalist has

realWorld Law

Reporters, Subpoenas and Contempt

When a former USA Today reporter became embroiled in a source confidentiality situation, she risked having to pay $5,000 per day out of her own pocket. Toni Locy covered the investigation into the 2001 anthrax mailings that killed five people. Former Army scientist Stephen Hatfill was identified as a "person of interest." When Hatfill sought the identities of reporters' sources, a federal judge ordered six journalists, including Locy, to reveal their sources. Locy declined, and the judge found her in contempt of court, ruling that until she disclosed all of her sources, she would face fines starting at $500 per day for the first seven days, $1,000 per day for the next seven days, and $5,000 a day for the next seven. In addition, the judge decided not to stay (i.e., suspend) those fines pending Locy's appeal because he decided she was unlikely to prevail and held that Locy could not receive any assistance in paying the fines from her former employer or from any person.[1]

Eventually, a federal appeals court stayed Locy's contempt fines pending her appeal. Several months later, Hatfill reached a settlement with the government. That was expected to result in the dismissal of Locy's case, but Hatfill then sought to collect attorney's fees from her—fees that could have totaled hundreds of thousands of dollars. In Nov. 2008, a federal appeals court vacated (i.e., set aside) the contempt order on the grounds that Hatfill's settlement left the order moot. In effect, that dismissed the request for fees. "To go after someone for attorney fees you have to have substantially prevailed in litigation," said Gregg Leslie, legal defense director at the Reporters Committee for Freedom of the Press, "and there's no order finding [Hatfill] prevailed. If every time reporters stood up for constitutional rights they're hit with huge attorneys' fees, that would be a huge chilling effect. It would be a novel way of harassing reporters."[2] Many experts claimed this situation was further evidence of the need for a federal shield law.

1. *See. e.g.*, Kevin Johnson, *Anthrax Settlement Doesn't Address Reporters' Issue,* USA TODAY, June 30, 2008, at 6A; Kevin Johnson, *Reporter's Fines Blocked in Anthrax Case,* USA TODAY, Mar. 12, 2008, at 3A.
2. *Judge Tosses Contempt Order Against ex-USA Today Reporter,* USA TODAY, Nov. 17, 2008, *available at* http://www.usatoday.com/news/washington/2008-11-17-locy-contempt_N.htm.

witnessed a crime or has knowledge that is tantamount to a criminal confession. Second, when journalists and/or news organizations are defendants—for example, in a libel case—protecting source identity is likely to be rejected. To prove that the defendant acted with negligence or actual malice, the plaintiff may require access to the reporter's knowledge, notes and other work materials. Finally, protecting source confidentiality in civil cases in which journalists are third parties are much easier to sustain. Not only are such cases usually less serious than in criminal cases, but there are often alternative sources for the information that do not implicate the First Amendment.

Other Shield Law Issues

Another issue concerning shield laws is whether they protect information regardless of whether it was published or broadcast. States are divided. Some states, such as Maryland, provide protection only for published information; for them, unpublished information is fair game. Others protect the reporter from having to

realWorld Law

Blogging and Contempt of Court

Like other media, blogging is susceptible to subpoenas and contempt citations. An ongoing question is whether bloggers are journalists. In 2010, a New Jersey appeals court said "no" in one case because the blogger was not engaged in journalism. The ruling affirmed a lower court ruling that said the blogger was neither a professional journalist nor affiliated with any legitimate media publication. But the appeals court left open the possibility that some bloggers could be considered journalists and perhaps be covered by the state's shield law.[1]

Josh Wolf

This ruling came a few years after freelance video blogger Josh Wolf received a subpoena ordering him to provide video he recorded. He had recorded a protest in San Francisco and posted excerpts on the Internet. Federal officials suspected that portions of video Wolf shot but had not posted showed protesters damaging a San Francisco police car. The subpoena sought the unposted portions.

Because the subpoena came from a federal court, Wolf could not claim the protection of California's state shield law. He refused to comply with the subpoena and was held in contempt of court. He went to jail on Aug. 1, 2006, but was released one month later pending a review. One week later, an appeals court affirmed the lower court's contempt order. Wolf returned to jail on Sept. 22. The following April, Wolf reached an agreement with prosecutors. They agreed to provide him with the questions they wanted to ask him in court—whether he witnessed or had any knowledge of an assault on a police officer or damage to a police car. In his testimony, Wolf answered no. In addition, Wolf agreed to post all of his video from the protest on his blog, thus giving prosecutors access to all his video without giving it to them directly. He was released after spending more than seven months in jail.

1. Too Much Media v. Hale, 413 N.J. Super 135 (2010).

testify about any information, even if it was not published or broadcast.[29] Some states incorporate into their statutes a sort of recognition of the philosophical roots of the privilege and the values that are being shielded by the laws.[30]

Another question surrounds the kind of venue in which a shield law is triggered. Some statutes shield information that is sought by any legal authority. Others are more limiting, covering only civil proceedings, for example, or criminal proceedings.

In sum, shield laws can be helpful to journalists in the 38 states and the District of Columbia that have them. However, the who, what and where of the laws' protective properties fluctuate, and in some cases widely. In states where protection is narrow, journalists are urged to resist the inclination toward overconfidence. Information they have could very well be the kind that is legally

realWorld Law

Passing the First Test

In 2010, just five months after being enacted, the Kansas shield law passed its first test. The Wichita Eagle had reported on a 5-year-old boy who had fallen to his death from a ride at an indoor playground. Two former employees of the playground were quoted anonymously in an article, saying the way they had been taught to operate the ride caused the boy's death. The boy's mother subpoenaed the reporter for the sources' names. A county judge ruled the new state shield law protected the reporter because no effort had been made to seek that information elsewhere. The judge said all other means must be exhausted before going to the media. Even then, the law requires that the information being sought is relevant to a case and that a compelling interest exists in providing it.[1]

1. *See* Daniel Skallman, *Judge Upholds Reporter's Right in First Test of Kansas Shield Law,* Reporter's Committee for Freedom of the Press, Oct. 27, 2010, *available at* http://www.rcfp.org/newsitems/index.php?i=11614.

unprotected from disclosure to one authority or another, particularly when that information is relevant to a criminal investigation.

Other Sources of Reporter's Privilege

The courts generally agree that a reporter's privilege is not embedded within the U.S. Constitution's First Amendment, but that a qualified privilege may exist. The privilege is qualified on whether specific circumstances exist that would eliminate the privilege's protection. State shield laws provide some protection under some circumstances. Thus, many holes exist when it comes to reporter's privilege. But other sources of protection exist.

When the U.S. Supreme Court challenged states to deal with the question of reporter's privilege, lower federal courts also took up the Court's invitation. All but one of the circuits of the U.S. Courts of Appeals have recognized a journalist's privilege to protect confidential sources at least once since 1972.[31]

Some state courts have found a reporter's privilege in their state's constitution regardless of whether that state also has a shield law. New York, for example, recognizes a qualified privilege under its constitution in addition to its shield law. In some states, courts have recognized a constitution-based privilege seemingly in an effort to bridge the gap left by their shield laws[32] or when shield laws do not exist at all.

SUMMARY

BECAUSE JOURNALISTS ARE OFTEN GOOD RECORDERS of information, they and their notes are sometimes subject to subpoenas that require them to reveal what they know. This is usually information regarding criminal conduct. But journalists sometimes

realWorld Law

Anonymous Posters on News Websites

Can a shield law protect a newspaper from having to reveal the identity of someone who made comments anonymously on a newspaper's website? Yes, according to one North Carolina judge. In a 2010 case, an attorney for an accused murderer wanted to force the Gaston Gazette to unmask the anonymous poster. The comments included information that had not yet been made public, raising suspicion about the poster's identity. But the judge said the information was protected by the First Amendment and the state shield law.[1]

This ruling followed one in 2008 where a Montana district court said the shield law there protects anonymous bloggers. The Billings Gazette had been issued a subpoena demanding the identities of two bloggers who had posted comments anonymously on the newspaper's website. Although Montana's shield law does not specifically protect bloggers or online commenters, the judge agreed with the Gazette that online commenters are sufficiently connected to the newspaper to warrant protection.[2]

1. Kevin Ellis, *Judge Gives Online Commenters First Amendment Protection,* Gaston Gazette, July 28, 2010, *available at* http://www.gastongazette.com/waptest/news/judge-49409-online-amendment.html.
2. Reporters Committee for Freedom of the Press, *Anonymous Bloggers Protected by Shield Law, Judge Finds,* n.d., *available at* http://www.rcfp.org/newsitems/index.php?i=6964.

claim they have reporter's privilege—a right to keep information confidential. Courts have not ruled clearly whether such a privilege exists and, if so, under what circumstances. The U.S. Supreme Court has established a three-part test to determine under what circumstances the qualified privilege may exist. In addition, 38 states and the District of Columbia have shield laws that grant some journalists some degree of privilege. State constitutions may also establish reporter's privilege. In all, 49 states and Washington, D.C., recognize the privilege in one way or another. Wyoming is the exception. ■

Breaking Promises of Confidentiality

Reporter's privilege protects journalists who do not want to reveal sources of information. But what happens when a news organization voluntarily decides to reveal the identity of a source after making a promise of confidentiality? Can the source successfully sue for damages? Or does the First Amendment protect a news organization's freedom to include its sources in its reports even when it promised not to do so?

These questions were answered by the U.S. Supreme Court in its 1991 ruling in *Cohen v. Cowles Media Co.*, excerpted at the conclusion of this chapter. Dan Cohen had been associated with the campaign of a Minnesota gubernatorial candidate. As Election Day neared, he contacted four Twin Cities news

realWorld Law

Cohen v. Cowles Media Co.: A Reporter's Perspective

One of the two reporters who agreed to accept Dan Cohen's information in exchange for his anonymity was Bill Salisbury of the St. Paul Pioneer Press. Cohen's offer, Salisbury felt, was not out of the ordinary: "That happens occasionally in this business. It's fairly widely used in politics and in covering government." After closing the deal, Salisbury contacted the subject of the information, a political candidate. She confirmed what the documents revealed: an arrest and conviction for theft several years earlier.

Salisbury then received a call from the newspaper's top editor, who ordered that Cohen's name be included in the article. "We had an argument about that," Salisbury said. "I told him that I made a promise and that I strenuously objected to breaking the promise."

When Cohen's case went to trial, Salisbury testified against the Pioneer Press. "I'm not a lawyer—I'm not that familiar with the law," he said. "But it seemed to me that I had made a contract with Dan Cohen and we broke that contract."

Many of Salisbury's colleagues agreed: "No matter whether we broke the law or not, they thought that morally it was wrong for us to break our promise. It was a bad practice because it raised suspicion about the newspaper by our sources. By burning a source we made a lot of potential sources worried about coming to us and giving us information. We may have lost some of our subsequent stories because of our actions."

Salisbury agreed with the U.S. Supreme Court's ruling. "I think it was important for us in journalism to learn the lesson from this case," he said. "Our credibility was really at stake. I think the bottom line is that we've learned that we can't burn our sources. We have to keep our promises. If we don't, we're liable."

Perhaps most significant is the impact the ruling has had on journalism. "I think perhaps the most important ramification is that our sources are aware of it," says Salisbury. "I think they feel more confident about dealing with us—that if we do make a promise, for example to go off the record, that we will keep that promise. I think the decision has helped us in the practice of journalism. I think sources trust us more knowing that we have to keep our promises or we risk being sued."[1]

---

1. Joseph Russomanno, Speaking Our Minds: Conversations with the People Behind Landmark First Amendment Cases 204–05, 220, 239 (Mahwah, N.J.: Lawrence Erlbaum Associates/Taylor & Francis, 2002).

reporters and offered them information about a political opponent, informing them that she had been arrested for unlawful assembly and for petty theft more than 10 years earlier. Cohen stipulated, however, that the information could be used only if he were not identified as its source. Two newspaper reporters accepted the offer.

Before publication, debate ensued in both newsrooms whether to keep the promises to Cohen. Editors believed that Cohen had engaged in "dirty tricks" politics. They concluded that identifying him was essential so readers could completely evaluate the stories. In spite of the promises made to the contrary, the articles were published with Cohen clearly identified.

As a result, Cohen was fired from his job. He sued the newspapers, claiming breach of a contractual agreement. A trial court agreed, awarding Cohen

promissory estoppel A legal doctrine requiring liability when a clear and unambiguous promise is made and is relied on and injury results from the breaking of the promise.

$200,000 in compensatory damages and $500,000 in punitive damages. An appeals court threw out the punitive damages award, and the Minnesota Supreme Court reversed the ruling against the newspapers entirely. At the Minnesota Supreme Court, an alternative to breach of contract arose, a concept called **promissory estoppel.** The doctrine of promissory estoppel requires courts to enforce a promise if it is relied on and its breach creates an injustice that should be remedied by law. The state supreme court, however, said it was unnecessary to consider this concept because enforcing it against the press would violate the First Amendment. Cohen appealed to the U.S. Supreme Court. The Court ruled in Cohen's favor that the First Amendment did not shield the press from the requirements of promissory estoppel.

generally applicable law A law that is enforced evenly, across the board. Within First Amendment contexts, it is the idea that the freedom of the press clause does not exempt journalists and news organizations from obeying laws.

Promissory estoppel is a **generally applicable law,** meaning that it is one of many that are enforced evenly, across the board. The First Amendment does not insulate news organizations or those employed by them from the law. "Generally applicable laws do not offend the First Amendment simply because their enforcement against the press has incidental effects on its ability to gather and report the news," wrote Justice White in *Cohen.* The case was sent back to Minnesota, and the Minnesota Supreme Court awarded Cohen $200,000 (plus interest) in damages. The ruling means promises of confidentiality must be kept. It has also resulted in news organizations instituting and clarifying policies that address whether and how to grant sources anonymity.

Search Warrants

search warrant A written order issued by a judge, directed to a law enforcement officer, authorizing the search and seizure of any property for which there is reason to believe it will serve as evidence in a criminal investigation.

No matter the source of reporter's privilege—the common law, a court decree, a state constitution or a shield law—the privilege can, in effect, be wiped out by a search warrant. A **search warrant** is a court order directing law enforcement officers to conduct a search of specified premises for particular items or people. The Fourth Amendment to the U.S. Constitution requires that searches be conducted reasonably. Warrants are issued by judges only when there is probable cause to believe that items or people vital to a criminal investigation are on the premises to be searched. Some believe that an exception to the search warrant requirement exists when national security is at stake—that is, that such searches do not need to be approved by a court. The U.S. Supreme Court has never recognized such an exception.

Although search warrants have some similarity to subpoenas in that both are court orders requiring cooperation with the justice system, they differ in very important ways. Search warrants demand immediate cooperation and compliance. When law enforcement officials arrive with a search warrant, they are fully authorized to immediately enter and conduct a search of the premises. There is no legal way to delay, resist or prevent the search. Subpoenas, on the other hand, do not require on-the-spot compliance. They order the named person to appear on some future date for a judicial proceeding. In the interim, the recipient can file a motion to quash the subpoena. For journalists, that motion may contain a request to invoke reporter's privilege. A search warrant implies greater urgency and may be justified where evidence could imminently be lost or destroyed. In fact, concern that important evidence could be destroyed during the period between serving a subpoena and the date of the required court appearance is one of the justifications for search warrants.

Newsroom Searches

What happens when a newsroom is the location targeted by a search warrant? Does the First Amendment protect news organizations from government searches? Should freedom of the press protections bar execution of search warrants that might reveal confidential sources or otherwise infringe on press freedoms?

These questions were put to the test in a case that was ultimately decided by the U.S. Supreme Court in 1978. After a demonstration on the campus of Stanford University, investigators wanted to look at unpublished photographs taken by staff members of the campus newspaper, the Stanford Daily. Police hoped that the photos would help identify people who took part in the demonstration, including some who assaulted police officers. A search warrant was obtained and served on the Daily. There was no specific indication as to why the situation required the warrant rather than a subpoena.

After the search, the Daily brought action against the chief of police and other local officials claiming the search violated the newspaper's First, Fourth and Fourteenth Amendment rights. A district judge concluded that because no one at the Daily was suspected of a crime, a search warrant should not have been issued unless it could be shown that a subpoena was impractical. In addition, the judge said that when a newspaper is the object of a search, a warrant may be issued only when there is a clear showing that important materials would be destroyed or removed and that a restraining order would be useless. An intermediate appellate court upheld this decision, but the police chief appealed to the U.S. Supreme Court.

In reversing, the Supreme Court overturned the lower court decision and delivered a blow to media organizations across the country, ruling that newsrooms are entitled to no special treatment beyond that afforded any citizen by the Fourth Amendment's prohibition of unreasonable searches and seizures. The Daily had argued that searches of newspaper offices for crime evidence threatens the ability of the press to gather, analyze and disseminate news. As summarized by Justice White, the argument was based on five points:

1. Searches will be physically disruptive to such an extent that timely publication will be impeded.

2. Confidential sources of information will dry up, and the press will also lose opportunities to cover various events because of the fears of participants that press files will be readily available to authorities.

3. Reporters will be deterred from recording and preserving their recollections for future use if such information is subject to seizure.

4. The processing and dissemination of news will be chilled by the prospect of searches that would disclose internal editorial deliberations.

5. The press will resort to self-censorship to conceal its possession of information of potential interest to the police.[33]

The Court rejected these arguments, saying that the identified harms were already sufficiently guarded against by the Fourth Amendment's prohibition of unreasonable searches and seizures. Perhaps most important, the Court ruled that nothing in the Fourth Amendment restricted searches of newsrooms. Implicitly, the ruling also suggested that there is nothing in the First Amendment that prevented newsroom searches.

Criticism, particularly from the news media, followed swiftly in the wake of the *Stanford Daily* ruling. Compared with search warrants, subpoenas suddenly appeared a rather mild intrusion. At least reporters could see them coming and challenge them legally. Not surprisingly, another result of the ruling was an increase in search warrant applications by law enforcement organizations targeting newsrooms. As one report of a search noted, police swept through the desks and files of a newsroom "with the authority of the Supreme Court."[34]

The Privacy Protection Act

After the *Stanford Daily* case, the media lobbied for legislative relief. Incidents in which law enforcement officials were accused of abusing the search warrant right underscored their arguments. Congress ultimately obliged, passing a law that applies to both state and federal searches. The Privacy Protection Act of 1980 significantly limits the use of search warrants against public communicators. The act states that, "notwithstanding any other law," federal and state officers and employees are prohibited from searching or seizing a journalist's work product or documentary materials in the journalist's possession, as part of a criminal investigation. A journalist's work product includes notes and drafts of news stories. Documentary materials include videotapes, audiotapes and computer disks.[35] The law provides much more protection for outtakes—the raw materials of the journalistic process that are not included in the final published or broadcast product.

Some limited exceptions under the Privacy Protection Act allow the government to search for or seize certain types of national security information, child pornography, evidence that a journalist has committed a crime or documentary materials that must be immediately seized to prevent death or serious bodily injury. Documentary materials also may be seized if there is reason to believe that they would be destroyed in the time it took government officers to seek a subpoena. Those materials also can be seized if a court has ordered disclosure, the news organization has refused and all other remedies have been exhausted. The Privacy Protection Act gives journalists the right to sue the United States or a state government, or federal and state employees, for

realWorld Law

After *Stanford Daily:* A "Predictable Result"

In the immediate aftermath of the *Stanford Daily* ruling, the frequency of newsroom searches increased, a predictable result of the *Stanford Daily* ruling according to First Amendment attorney Floyd Abrams.[1] One search occurred at a Boise, Idaho, television station.

During a riot at a state prison, two journalists from the station, at the request of inmates, entered the prison and videotaped a variety of images. After peace was restored, a county prosecutor wanted to see the tapes in an effort to identify leaders of the riot. The station's news director said he would let authorities subpoena parts of the tape after it was broadcast, but he resisted the request for segments and other information not presented on the air. Not satisfied with that offer, the prosecutor obtained a search warrant and arrived at the station with five armed deputy sheriffs. After being read the warrant, the news director responded: "I feel like this is a clear infringement of our First Amendment rights. Seeing as how we have no legal recourse, I suppose I have to let you in."[2]

The officials spent 90 minutes looking through desk drawers, cabinets and the station's video library. Station employees neither helped nor hindered the officials during their search. That included refusing to point out either where the tapes were or how to operate playback equipment that would have allowed the officials to view the tapes. Eventually, they found the tapes they sought.[3]

The station later sued the prosecutor claiming that the search was "precipitous" and "unwarranted."[4] But the prosecutor believed that the station gave up its rights when its reporter was invited into the prison by inmates to listen to grievances. That made him an "agent" for the inmates, reasoned the attorney, and it made the station "not a news-gathering source but a news-*generating* source."[5] About a year and a half later, the matter was resolved in favor of the prosecutor. An Idaho judge ordered the release of two cartons of tapes he had been holding, saying that the search warrant had been obtained and executed properly.[6]

Newsweek magazine described this and another police search as "underscor[ing] the need to curb surprise searches of news rooms."[7] The Christian Science Monitor wrote, "Freedom of the press has never been under more serious attacks."[8] Others, including the American Society of Newspaper Editors, said the search demonstrated the need for congressional action on legislation to protect news organizations from such actions.[9] That congressional action came in the form of the Privacy Protection Act.

---

1. Arlie Schardt, *Raiding the News Room,* NEWSWEEK, Aug. 11, 1980, at 52.
2. Wayne King, *TV Tapes Are Seized in an Idaho Inquiry on Prison Uprising,* N.Y. TIMES, July 27, 1980, at 1.
3. *Invading the Newsroom,* N.Y. TIMES, July 29 1980, at A14.
4. *Prosecutor Sued on Raid of Boise TV Room,* N.Y. TIMES, Aug. 2, 1980, at A6.
5. Arlie Schardt, *Raiding the News Room,* NEWSWEEK, Aug. 11, 1980, at 52 (emphasis added).
6. *TV Tapes of Prison Riot Go to Idaho Prosecutor,* N.Y. TIMES, Jan. 8, 1982, at A10.
7. Arlie Schardt, *Raiding the News Room,* NEWSWEEK, Aug. 11, 1980, at 52.
8. Ward Morehouse III, *Bill Seeking Tighter Reins on Police Searches of Newsroom Hits Snag,* CHRISTIAN SCIENCE MONITOR, Aug. 1, 1980, at 5.
9. *Publisher's Group Urges Ban on Surprise Newsroom Searches,* N.Y. TIMES, July 31, 1980, at B13.

damages for violating the law. The law also allows journalists to recover attorney's fees and court costs.

In short, the Privacy Protection Act significantly mitigates the effect of the *Stanford Daily* ruling by restricting the use of search warrants on newsrooms, forcing law enforcement officials to rely on subpoenas instead.

SUMMARY

WHEN JOURNALISTS PROMISE SOURCES that their identities will be kept confidential in exchange for information, the journalists and their employers are legally bound to keep their word. Freedom of the press is not freedom to break the law. Laws that are generally applicable pertain to the media.

The concept of general applicability also applies to legally issued search warrants on newsrooms. The First Amendment does not grant freedom from such searches. ∎

Cases for Study

Thinking About It

The two case excerpts that follow address very different aspects of source confidentiality. The first is the U.S. Supreme Court ruling that established a test for a qualified reporter's privilege. The second ruling, also from the U.S. Supreme Court, dealt with news organizations that not only did not want to protect a source but consciously decided to expose him. As you read these case excerpts, keep the following questions in mind:

- How did the reporters in each case behave? What actions did they take to precipitate the lawsuits that eventually reached the Supreme Court?

- Does the Court seem to understand the purpose of journalism and the inner workings of a newsroom in each case?

- In *Branzburg*, from whose opinion does the *Branzburg* test emerge? What kind of opinion is that?

- In *Cohen*, the Court mentions "generally applicable laws." What does it say about them and the First Amendment? Do you agree with the Court's position?

- Aside from the ruling in *Cohen*, do you agree with how the newspapers handled their source's identity? If not, what should they have done differently?

Branzburg v. Hayes
SUPREME COURT OF THE UNITED STATES
408 U.S. 665 (1972)

JUSTICE BYRON WHITE delivered the Court's opinion:

The issue in these cases is whether requiring newsmen to appear and testify before state or federal grand juries abridges the freedom of speech and press guaranteed by the First Amendment. We hold that it does not. . . .

I

On November 15, 1969, the Courier-Journal carried a story under petitioner's by-line describing in detail his observations of two young residents of Jefferson County synthesizing hashish from marihuana, an activity which, they asserted, earned them about $5,000 in three weeks. The article included a photograph of a pair of hands working above a laboratory table on which was a substance identified by the caption as hashish. The article stated that petitioner had promised not to reveal the identity of the two hashish makers. Petitioner was shortly subpoenaed by the Jefferson County grand jury; he appeared but refused to identify the individuals he had seen possessing marihuana or the persons he had seen making hashish from marihuana. A state trial court judge ordered petitioner to answer these questions and rejected his contention that the Kentucky reporters' privilege statute, Ky.

Rev. Stat. § 421.100 (1962), the First Amendment of the United States Constitution, or §§ 1, 2, and 8 of the Kentucky Constitution authorized his refusal to answer. Petitioner then sought prohibition and mandamus in the Kentucky Court of Appeals on the same grounds, but the Court of Appeals denied the petition. It held that petitioner had abandoned his First Amendment argument in a supplemental memorandum he had filed and tacitly rejected his argument based on the Kentucky Constitution. It also construed Ky. Rev. Stat. § 421.100 as affording a newsman the privilege of refusing to divulge the identity of an informant who supplied him with information, but held that the statute did not permit a reporter to refuse to testify about events he had observed personally, including the identities of those persons he had observed.

The second case involving petitioner Branzburg arose out of his later story published on January 10, 1971, which described in detail the use of drugs in Frankfort, Kentucky. The article reported that in order to provide a comprehensive survey of the "drug scene" in Frankfort, petitioner had "spent two weeks interviewing several dozen drug users in the capital city" and had seen some of them smoking marihuana. A number of conversations with and observations of several unnamed drug users were recounted. Subpoenaed to appear before a Franklin County grand jury "to testify in the matter of violation of statutes concerning use and sale of drugs," petitioner Branzburg moved to quash the summons; the motion was denied, although an order was issued protecting Branzburg from revealing "confidential associations, sources or information" but requiring that he "answer any questions which concern or pertain to any criminal act, the commission of which was actually observed by [him]." Prior to the time he was slated to appear before the grand jury, petitioner sought mandamus and prohibition from the Kentucky Court of Appeals, arguing that if he were forced to go before the grand jury or to answer questions regarding the identity of informants or disclose information given to him in confidence, his effectiveness as a reporter would be greatly damaged. The Court of Appeals once again denied the requested writs, reaffirming its construction of Ky. Rev. Stat. § 421.100, and rejecting petitioner's claim of a First Amendment privilege. It distinguished *Caldwell v. United States*, 434 F.2d 1081 (1970), and it also announced its "misgivings" about that decision, asserting that it represented "a drastic departure from the generally recognized rule that the sources of information of a newspaper reporter are not privileged under the First Amendment." It characterized petitioner's fear that his ability to obtain news would be destroyed as "so tenuous that it does not, in the opinion of this court, present an issue of abridgement of the freedom of the press within the meaning of that term as used in the Constitution of the United States.". . .

II

Petitioners Branzburg and Pappas and respondent Caldwell press First Amendment claims that may be simply put: that to gather news it is often necessary to agree either not to identify the source of information published or to publish only part of the facts revealed, or both; that if the reporter is nevertheless forced to reveal these confidences to a grand jury, the source so identified and other confidential sources of other reporters will be measurably deterred from furnishing publishable information, all to the detriment of the free flow of information protected by the First Amendment. Although the newsmen in these cases do not claim an absolute privilege against official interrogation in all circumstances, they assert that the reporter should not be forced either to appear or to testify before a grand jury or at trial until and unless sufficient grounds are shown for believing that the reporter possesses information relevant to a crime the grand jury is investigating, that the information the reporter has is unavailable from other sources, and that the need for the information is sufficiently compelling to override the claimed invasion of First Amendment interests occasioned by the disclosure. Principally relied upon are prior cases emphasizing the importance of the First Amendment guarantees to individual development and to our system of representative government, decisions requiring that official action with adverse impact on First Amendment rights be justified by a public interest that is "compelling" or "paramount," and those precedents establishing the principle that justifiable governmental goals may not be achieved by unduly broad means having an unnecessary impact on protected rights of speech, press, or association. The heart of the claim is that the burden on news gathering resulting from compelling reporters to disclose confidential information outweighs any public interest in obtaining the information.

We do not question the significance of free speech, press, or assembly to the country's welfare. Nor is it suggested that news gathering does not qualify for First Amendment protection; without some protection for seeking out the news, freedom of the press could be eviscerated. But these cases involve no intrusions upon speech or assembly, no prior restraint or restriction on what the press may publish, and no express or implied command that the press publish what it prefers to withhold. No exaction or tax for the privilege of publishing, and no penalty, civil or criminal, related to the content of published material is at issue here. The use of confidential sources by the press is not forbidden or restricted; reporters remain free to seek news from any source by means within the law. No attempt is made to require the press to publish its sources of information or indiscriminately to disclose them on request.

The sole issue before us is the obligation of reporters to respond to grand jury subpoenas as other citizens do and to answer questions relevant to an investigation into the commission of crime. Citizens generally are not constitutionally immune from grand jury subpoenas; and neither the First Amendment nor any other constitutional provision protects the average citizen from disclosing to a grand jury information that he has received in confidence. The claim is, however, that reporters are exempt from these obligations because if forced to respond to subpoenas and identify their sources or disclose other confidences, their informants will refuse or be reluctant to furnish newsworthy information in the future. This asserted burden on news gathering is said to make compelled testimony from newsmen constitutionally suspect and to require a privileged position for them.

It is clear that the First Amendment does not invalidate every incidental burdening of the press that may result from the enforcement of civil or criminal statutes of general applicability. Under prior cases, otherwise valid laws serving substantial public interests may be enforced against the press as against others, despite the possible burden that may be imposed. The Court has emphasized that "the publisher of a newspaper has no special immunity from the application of general laws. He has no special privilege to invade the rights and liberties of others." It was there held that the Associated Press, a news-gathering and disseminating organization, was not exempt from the requirements of the National Labor Relations Act. . . .

The prevailing view is that the press is not free to publish with impunity everything and anything it desires to publish. Although it may deter or regulate what is said or published, the press may not circulate knowing or reckless falsehoods damaging to private reputation without subjecting itself to liability for damages, including punitive damages, or even criminal prosecution.

It has generally been held that the First Amendment does not guarantee the press a constitutional right of special access to information not available to the public generally. . . .

Despite the fact that news gathering may be hampered, the press is regularly excluded from grand jury proceedings, our own conferences, the meetings of other official bodies gathered in executive session, and the meetings of private organizations. Newsmen have no constitutional right of access to the scenes of crime or disaster when the general public is excluded, and they may be prohibited from attending or publishing information about trials if such restrictions are necessary to assure a defendant a fair trial before an impartial tribunal. . . .

It is thus not surprising that the great weight of authority is that newsmen are not exempt from the normal duty of appearing before a grand jury and answering questions relevant to a criminal investigation. At common law, courts consistently refused to recognize the existence of any privilege authorizing a newsman to refuse to reveal confidential information to a grand jury. . . .

The prevailing constitutional view of the newsman's privilege is very much rooted in the ancient role of the grand jury that has the dual function of determining if there is probable cause to believe that a crime has been committed and of protecting citizens against unfounded criminal prosecutions. Grand jury proceedings are constitutionally mandated for the institution of federal criminal prosecutions for capital or other serious crimes, and "its constitutional prerogatives are rooted in long centuries of Anglo-American history." The Fifth Amendment provides that "no person shall be held to answer for a capital, or otherwise infamous crime, unless on a resentment or indictment of a Grand Jury." The adoption of the grand jury "in our Constitution as the sole method for preferring charges in serious criminal cases shows the high place it held as an instrument of justice." Although state systems of criminal procedure differ greatly among themselves, the grand jury is similarly guaranteed by many state constitutions and plays an important role in fair and effective law enforcement in the overwhelming majority of the States. Because its task is to inquire into the existence of possible criminal conduct and to return only well-founded indictments, its investigative powers are necessarily broad. "It is a grand inquest, a body with powers of investigation and inquisition, the scope of whose inquiries is not to be limited narrowly by questions of propriety or forecasts of the probable result of the investigation, or by doubts whether any particular individual will be found properly subject to an accusation of crime." Hence, the grand jury's authority to subpoena witnesses is not only historic, but essential to its task. Although the powers of the grand jury are not unlimited and are subject to the supervision of a judge, the longstanding principle that "the public . . . has a right to every man's evidence," except for those persons protected by a constitutional, common-law, or statutory privilege. . . .

A number of States have provided newsmen a statutory privilege of varying breadth, but the majority have not done so, and none has been provided by federal statute. Until now the only testimonial privilege for unofficial witnesses that is rooted in the Federal Constitution is the Fifth Amendment privilege against compelled self-incrimination. We are asked to create another by interpreting the First Amendment to grant newsmen a testimonial privilege that other citizens do not enjoy. This we decline to do. . . .

This conclusion itself involves no restraint on what newspapers may publish or on the type or quality of information reporters may seek to acquire, nor does it threaten the vast bulk of confidential relationships between reporters and their sources. Grand juries address themselves to the issues of whether crimes have been committed and who committed them. Only where news sources themselves are implicated in crime or possess information relevant to the grand jury's task need they or the reporter be concerned about grand jury subpoenas. Nothing before us indicates that a large number or percentage of all confidential news sources falls into either category and would in any way be deterred by our holding that the Constitution does not, as it never has, exempt the newsman from performing the citizen's normal duty of appearing and furnishing information relevant to the grand jury's task.

The preference for anonymity of those confidential informants involved in actual criminal conduct is presumably a product of their desire to escape criminal prosecution, and this preference, while understandable, is hardly deserving of constitutional protection. It would be frivolous to assert—and no one does in these cases—that the First Amendment, in the interest of securing news or otherwise, confers a license on either the reporter or his news sources to violate valid criminal laws. Although stealing documents or private wiretapping could provide newsworthy information, neither reporter nor source is immune from conviction for such conduct, whatever the impact on the flow of news. Neither is immune, on First Amendment grounds, from testifying against the other, before the grand jury or at a criminal trial. The Amendment does not reach so far as to override the interest of the public in ensuring that neither reporter nor source is invading the rights of other citizens through reprehensible conduct forbidden to all other persons. To assert the contrary proposition "is to answer it, since it involves in its very statement the contention that the freedom of the press is the freedom to do wrong with impunity and implies the right to frustrate and defeat the discharge of those governmental duties upon the performance of which the freedom of all, including that of the press, depends. . . . It suffices to say that, however complete is the right of the press to state public things and discuss them, that right, as every other right enjoyed in human society, is subject to the restraints which separate right from wrong-doing." Thus, we cannot seriously entertain the notion that the First Amendment protects a newsman's agreement to conceal the criminal conduct of his source, or evidence thereof, on the theory that it is better to write about crime than to do something about it. Insofar as any reporter in these cases undertook not to reveal or testify about the crime he witnessed, his claim of privilege under the First Amendment presents no substantial question. The crimes of news sources are no less reprehensible and threatening to the public interest when witnessed by a reporter than when they are not.

There remain those situations where a source is not engaged in criminal conduct but has information suggesting illegal conduct by others. Newsmen frequently receive information from such sources pursuant to a tacit or express agreement to withhold the source's name and suppress any information that the source wishes not published. Such informants presumably desire anonymity in order to avoid being entangled as a witness in a criminal trial or grand jury investigation. They may fear that disclosure will threaten their job security or personal safety or that it will simply result in dishonor or embarrassment.

The argument that the flow of news will be diminished by compelling reporters to aid the grand jury in a criminal investigation is not irrational, nor are the records before us silent on the matter. But we remain unclear how often and to what extent informers are actually deterred from furnishing information when newsmen are forced to testify before a grand jury. The available data indicate that some newsmen rely a great deal on confidential sources and that some informants are particularly sensitive to the threat of exposure and may be silenced if it is held by this Court that, ordinarily, newsmen must testify pursuant to subpoenas, but the evidence fails to demonstrate that there would be a significant constriction of the flow of news to the public if this Court reaffirms the prior common-law and constitutional rule regarding the testimonial obligations of newsmen. Estimates of the inhibiting effect of such subpoenas on the willingness of informants

to make disclosures to newsmen are widely divergent and to a great extent speculative. It would be difficult to canvass the views of the informants themselves; surveys of reporters on this topic are chiefly opinions of predicted informant behavior and must be viewed in the light of the professional self-interest of the interviewees. Reliance by the press on confidential informants does not mean that all such sources will in fact dry up because of the later possible appearance of the newsman before a grand jury. The reporter may never be called and if he objects to testifying, the prosecution may not insist. Also, the relationship of many informants to the press is a symbiotic one which is unlikely to be greatly inhibited by the threat of subpoena: quite often, such informants are members of a minority political or cultural group that relies heavily on the media to propagate its views, publicize its aims, and magnify its exposure to the public. Moreover, grand juries characteristically conduct secret proceedings, and law enforcement officers are themselves experienced in dealing with informers, and have their own methods for protecting them without interference with the effective administration of justice. There is little before us indicating that informants whose interest in avoiding exposure is that it may threaten job security, personal safety, or peace of mind, would in fact be in a worse position, or would think they would be, if they risked placing their trust in public officials as well as reporters. We doubt if the informer who prefers anonymity but is sincerely interested in furnishing evidence of crime will always or very often be deterred by the prospect of dealing with those public authorities characteristically charged with the duty to protect the public interest as well as his. . . .

We note first that the privilege claimed is that of the reporter, not the informant, and that if the authorities independently identify the informant, neither his own reluctance to testify nor the objection of the newsman would shield him from grand jury inquiry, whatever the impact on the flow of news or on his future usefulness as a secret source of information. More important, it is obvious that agreements to conceal information relevant to commission of crime have very little to recommend them from the standpoint of public policy. . . .

Of course, the press has the right to abide by its agreement not to publish all the information it has, but the right to withhold news is not equivalent to a First Amendment exemption from the ordinary duty of all other citizens to furnish relevant information to a grand jury performing an important public function. Private restraints on the flow of information are not so favored by the First Amendment that they override all other public interests. . . .

Neither are we now convinced that a virtually impenetrable constitutional shield, beyond legislative or judicial control, should be forged to protect a private system of informers operated by the press to report on criminal conduct, a system that would be unaccountable to the public, would pose a threat to the citizen's justifiable expectations of privacy, and would equally protect well-intentioned informants and those who for pay or otherwise betray their trust to their employer or associates. . . .

We are admonished that refusal to provide a First Amendment reporter's privilege will undermine the freedom of the press to collect and disseminate news. But this is not the lesson history teaches us. As noted previously, the common law recognized no such privilege, and the constitutional argument was not even asserted until 1958. From the beginning of our country the press has operated without constitutional protection for press informants, and the press has flourished. The existing constitutional rules have not been a serious obstacle to either the development or retention of confidential news sources by the press.

It is said that currently press subpoenas have multiplied, that mutual distrust and tension between press and officialdom have increased, that reporting styles have changed, and that there is now more need for confidential sources, particularly where the press seeks news about minority cultural and political groups or dissident organizations suspicious of the law and public officials. These developments, even if true, are treacherous grounds for a far-reaching interpretation of the First Amendment fastening a nationwide rule on courts, grand juries, and prosecuting officials everywhere. The obligation to testify in response to grand jury subpoenas will not threaten these sources not involved with criminal conduct and without information relevant to grand jury investigations, and we cannot hold that the Constitution places the sources in these two categories either above the law or beyond its reach.

The argument for such a constitutional privilege rests heavily on those cases holding that the infringement of protected First Amendment rights must be no broader than necessary to achieve a permissible governmental purpose. We do not deal, however, with a governmental institution that has abused its proper function, as a legislative committee does when it "expose[s] for the sake of exposure." Nothing in the record indicates that these grand juries were "prob[ing] at will and without relation to existing need." Nor did the grand juries attempt to invade protected First Amendment rights by forcing wholesale disclosure of names and organizational affiliations for a purpose that was not germane to the determination of whether crime has been committed. . . . The investigative power of the grand jury is necessarily broad if its public responsibility is to be adequately discharged. . . .

Similar considerations dispose of the reporters' claims that preliminary to requiring their grand jury appearance, the State must show that a crime has been committed and that they possess relevant information not available from other sources, for only the grand jury itself can make this determination. The role of the grand jury as an important instrument of effective law enforcement necessarily includes an investigatory function with respect to determining whether a crime has been committed and who committed it. To this end it must call witnesses, in the manner best suited to perform its task. "When the grand jury is performing its investigatory function into a general problem area . . . society's interest is best served by a thorough and extensive investigation." A grand jury investigation "is not fully carried out until every available clue has been run down and all witnesses examined in every proper way to find if a crime has been committed." Such an investigation may be triggered by tips, rumors, evidence proffered by the prosecutor, or the personal knowledge of the grand jurors. It is only after the grand jury has examined the evidence that a determination of whether the proceeding will result in an indictment can be made. . . .

The privilege claimed here is conditional, not absolute; given the suggested preliminary showings and compelling need, the reporter would be required to testify. Presumably, such a rule would reduce the instances in which reporters could be required to appear, but predicting in advance when and in what circumstances they could be compelled to do so would be difficult. Such a rule would also have implications for the issuance of compulsory process to reporters at civil and criminal trials and at legislative hearings. If newsmen's confidential sources are as sensitive as they are claimed to be, the prospect of being unmasked whenever a judge determines the situation justifies it is hardly a satisfactory solution to the problem. For them, it would appear that only an absolute privilege would suffice.

We are unwilling to embark the judiciary on a long and difficult journey to such an uncertain destination. The administration of a constitutional newsman's privilege would present practical and conceptual difficulties of a high order. Sooner or later, it would be necessary to define those categories of newsmen who qualified for the privilege, a questionable procedure in light of the traditional doctrine that liberty of the press is the right of the lonely pamphleteer who uses carbon paper or a mimeograph just as much as of the large metropolitan publisher who utilizes the latest photocomposition methods. Freedom of the press is a "fundamental personal right" which "is not confined to newspapers and periodicals. It necessarily embraces pamphlets and leaflets. . . . The press in its historic connotation comprehends every sort of publication which affords a vehicle of information and opinion." The informative function asserted by representatives of the organized press in the present cases is also performed by lecturers, political pollsters, novelists, academic researchers, and dramatists. Almost any author may quite accurately assert that he is contributing to the flow of information to the public, that he relies on confidential sources of information, and that these sources will be silenced if he is forced to make disclosures before a grand jury.

In each instance where a reporter is subpoenaed to testify, the courts would also be embroiled in preliminary factual and legal determinations with respect to whether the proper predicate had been laid for the reporter's appearance: Is there probable cause to believe a crime has been committed? Is it likely that the reporter has useful information gained in confidence? Could the grand jury obtain the information elsewhere? Is the official interest sufficient to outweigh the claimed privilege?

Thus, in the end, by considering whether enforcement of a particular law served a "compelling" governmental interest, the courts would be inextricably involved in distinguishing between the value of enforcing different criminal laws. By requiring testimony from a reporter in investigations involving some crimes but not in others, they would be making a value judgment that a legislature had declined to make, since in each case the criminal law involved would represent a considered legislative judgment, not constitutionally suspect, of what conduct is liable to criminal prosecution. The task of judges, like other officials outside the legislative branch, is not to make the law but to uphold it in accordance with their oaths.

At the federal level, Congress has freedom to determine whether a statutory newsman's privilege is necessary and desirable and to fashion standards and rules as narrow or broad as deemed necessary to deal with the evil discerned and, equally important, to refashion those rules as experience from time to time may dictate. There is also merit in leaving state legislatures free, within First Amendment limits, to fashion their own standards in light of the conditions and problems with respect to the relations between law enforcement officials and press in their own areas. It goes without saying, of course, that we are powerless to bar state courts from responding in their own way and construing their own constitutions so as to recognize a newsman's privilege, either qualified or absolute.

In addition, there is much force in the pragmatic view that the press has at its disposal powerful mechanisms of communication, and is far from helpless to protect itself from harassment or substantial harm.

Furthermore, if what the newsmen urged in these cases is true—that law enforcement cannot hope to gain and may suffer from subpoenaing newsmen before grand juries—prosecutors will be loath to risk so much for so little. Thus, at the federal level the Attorney General has already fashioned a set of rules for federal officials in connection with subpoenaing members of the press to testify before grand juries or at criminal trials. These rules are a major step in the direction the reporters herein desire to move. They may prove wholly sufficient to resolve the bulk of disagreements and controversies between press and federal officials.

Finally, as we have earlier indicated, news gathering is not without its First Amendment protections, and grand jury investigations if instituted or conducted other than in good faith, would pose wholly different issues for resolution under the First Amendment. Official harassment of the press undertaken not for purposes of law enforcement but to disrupt a reporter's relationship with his news sources would have no justification. Grand juries are subject to judicial control and subpoenas to motions to quash. We do not expect courts will forget that grand juries must operate within the limits of the First Amendment as well as the Fifth. . . .

Justice Lewis Powell, concurring:

I add this brief statement to emphasize what seems to me to be the limited nature of the Court's holding. The Court does not hold that newsmen, subpoenaed to testify before a grand jury, are without constitutional rights with respect to the gathering of news or in safeguarding their sources. . . .

As indicated in the concluding portion of the opinion, the Court states that no harassment of newsmen will be tolerated. If a newsman believes that the grand jury investigation is not being conducted in good faith, he is not without remedy. Indeed, if the newsman is called upon to give information bearing only a remote and tenuous relationship to the subject of the investigation, or if he has some other reason to believe that his testimony implicates confidential source relationships without a legitimate need of law enforcement, he will have access to the court on a motion to quash, and an appropriate protective order may be entered. The

asserted claim to privilege should be judged on its facts by the striking of a proper balance between freedom of the press and the obligation of all citizens to give relevant testimony with respect to criminal conduct. The balance of these vital constitutional and societal interests on a case-by-case basis accords with the tried and traditional way of adjudicating such questions.

In short, the courts will be available to newsmen under circumstances where legitimate First Amendment interests require protection.

Justice Potter Stewart, with whom Justice William Brennan and Justice Thurgood Marshall join, dissenting:

The Court's crabbed view of the First Amendment reflects a disturbing insensitivity to the critical role of an independent press in our society. The question whether a reporter has a constitutional right to a confidential relationship with his source is of first impression here, but the principles that should guide our decision are as basic as any to be found in the Constitution. While Mr. Justice Powell's enigmatic concurring opinion gives some hope of a more flexible view in the future, the Court in these cases holds that a newsman has no First Amendment right to protect his sources when called before a grand jury. The Court thus invites state and federal authorities to undermine the historic independence of the press by attempting to annex the journalistic profession as an investigative arm of government. Not only will this decision impair performance of the press' constitutionally protected functions, but it will, I am convinced, in the long run harm rather than help the administration of justice.

I respectfully dissent.

I

The reporter's constitutional right to a confidential relationship with his source stems from the broad societal interest in a full and free flow of information to the public. It is this basic concern that underlies the Constitution's protection of a free press, because the guarantee is "not for the benefit of the press so much as for the benefit of all of us." Enlightened choice by an informed citizenry is the basic ideal upon which an open society is premised, and a free press is thus indispensable to a free society. Not only does the press enhance personal self-fulfillment by providing the people with the widest possible range of fact and opinion, but it also is an incontestable precondition of self-government. The press "has been a mighty catalyst in awakening public interest in governmental affairs, exposing corruption among public officers and employees and generally informing the citizenry of public events and occurrences. . . ." As private and public aggregations of power burgeon in size and the pressures for conformity necessarily mount, there is obviously a continuing need for an independent press to disseminate a robust variety of information and opinion through reportage, investigation, and criticism, if we are to preserve our constitutional tradition of maximizing freedom of choice by encouraging diversity of expression.

A

In keeping with this tradition, we have held that the right to publish is central to the First Amendment and basic to the existence of constitutional democracy.

A corollary of the right to publish must be the right to gather news. The full flow of information to the public protected by the free-press guarantee would be severely curtailed if no protection whatever were afforded to the process by which news is assembled and disseminated. We have, therefore, recognized that there is a right to publish without prior governmental approval, a right to distribute information, and a right to receive printed matter.

No less important to the news dissemination process is the gathering of information. News must not be unnecessarily cut off at its source, for without freedom to acquire information the right to publish would be impermissibly compromised. Accordingly, a right to gather news, of some dimensions, must exist. As Madison wrote: "A popular Government, without popular information, or the means of acquiring it, is but a Prologue to a Farce or a Tragedy, or perhaps both."

B

The right to gather news implies, in turn, a right to a confidential relationship between a reporter and his source. This proposition follows as a matter of simple logic once three factual predicates are recognized: (1) newsmen require informants to gather news; (2) confidentiality—the promise or understanding that names or certain aspects of communications will be kept off the record—is essential to the creation and maintenance of a news gathering relationship with informants; and (3) an unbridled subpoena power— the absence of a constitutional right protecting, in any way, a confidential relationship from compulsory process—will either deter sources from divulging information or deter reporters from gathering and publishing information.

It is obvious that informants are necessary to the news-gathering process as we know it today. If it is to perform its constitutional mission, the press must do far more than merely print public statements or publish prepared handouts. Familiarity with the people and circumstances involved in the myriad background activities that result in the final product called "news" is vital to complete and responsible journalism, unless the press is to be a captive mouthpiece of "newsmakers."

It is equally obvious that the promise of confidentiality may be a necessary prerequisite to a productive relationship between a newsman and his informants. An officeholder may fear his superior; a member of the bureaucracy, his associates; a dissident, the scorn of majority opinion. All may have information valuable to the public discourse, yet each may be willing to relate that information only in confidence to a reporter whom he trusts, either because of excessive caution or because of a reasonable fear of reprisals or censure for unorthodox views. The First Amendment concern must not be with the motives of any particular news source, but rather with the conditions in which informants of all shades of the spectrum may make information available through the press to the public. . . .

Finally, and most important, when governmental officials possess an unchecked power to compel newsmen to disclose information received in confidence, sources will clearly be deterred from giving information, and reporters will clearly be deterred from publishing it, because uncertainty about exercise of the power will lead to "self-censorship." The uncertainty arises, of course, because the judiciary has traditionally imposed virtually no limitations on the grand jury's broad investigatory powers.

After today's decision, the potential informant can never be sure that his identity or off-the-record communications will not subsequently be revealed through the compelled testimony of a newsman. A public-spirited person inside government, who is not implicated in any crime, will now be fearful of revealing corruption or other governmental wrongdoing, because he will now know he can subsequently be identified by use of compulsory process. The potential source must, therefore, choose between risking exposure by giving information or avoiding the risk by remaining silent.

The reporter must speculate about whether contact with a controversial source or publication of controversial material will lead to a subpoena. In the event of a subpoena, under today's decision, the newsman will know that he must choose between being punished for contempt if he refuses to testify, or violating his profession's ethics and impairing his resourcefulness as a reporter if he discloses confidential information.

Again, the commonsense understanding that such deterrence will occur is buttressed by concrete evidence. The existence of deterrent effects through fear and self-censorship was impressively developed in the District Court in *Caldwell*. Individual reporters and commentators have noted such effects. Surveys have verified that an unbridled subpoena power will substantially impair the flow of news to the public, especially in sensitive areas involving governmental officials, financial affairs, political figures, dissidents, or minority groups that require in-depth, investigative reporting. And the Justice Department has recognized that "compulsory process in some circumstances may have a limiting effect on the exercise of First Amendment rights." No evidence contradicting the existence of such deterrent effects was offered at the trials or in the briefs here by the petitioner in *Caldwell* or by the respondents in *Branzburg* and *Pappas*.

The impairment of the flow of news cannot, of course, be proved with scientific precision, as the Court seems to demand. Obviously, not every news-gathering relationship requires confidentiality. And it is difficult to pinpoint precisely how many relationships do require a promise or understanding of nondisclosure. But we have never before demanded that First Amendment rights rest on elaborate empirical studies demonstrating beyond any conceivable doubt that deterrent effects exist; we have never before required proof of the exact number of people potentially affected by governmental action, who would actually be dissuaded from engaging in First Amendment activity.

Rather, on the basis of common sense and available information, we have asked, often implicitly, (1) whether there was a rational connection between the cause (the governmental action) and the effect (the deterrence or impairment of First Amendment activity), and (2) whether the effect would occur with some regularity, *i.e.,* would not be *de minimis*. And, in making this determination, we have shown a special solicitude towards the "indispensable liberties" protected by the First Amendment, for "[f]reedoms such as these are protected not only against heavy-handed frontal attack, but also from being stifled by more subtle governmental interference." Once this threshold inquiry has been satisfied, we have then examined the competing interests in determining whether there is an unconstitutional infringement of First Amendment freedoms. . . .

. . . We cannot await an unequivocal—and therefore unattainable—imprimatur from empirical studies. We can and must accept the evidence developed in the record, and elsewhere, that overwhelmingly supports the premise that deterrence will occur with regularity in important types of news-gathering relationships.

Thus, we cannot escape the conclusion that when neither the reporter nor his source can rely on the shield of confidentiality against unrestrained use of the grand jury's subpoena power, valuable information will not be published and the public dialogue will inevitably be impoverished.

II

Posed against the First Amendment's protection of the newsman's confidential relationships in these cases is society's interest in the use of the grand jury to administer justice fairly and effectively. The grand jury serves two important functions: "to examine into the commission of crimes" and "to stand between the prosecutor and the accused, and to determine whether the charge was founded upon credible testimony or was dictated by malice or personal ill will." And to perform these functions, the grand jury must have available to it every man's relevant evidence.

Yet the longstanding rule making every person's evidence available to the grand jury is not absolute. The rule has been limited by the Fifth Amendment, the Fourth Amendment, and the evidentiary privileges of the common law. So it was that in *Blair, supra,* after recognizing that the right against compulsory self-incrimination prohibited certain inquiries, the Court noted that "some confidential matters are shielded from considerations of policy, and perhaps in other cases for special reasons a witness may be excused from telling all that he knows." And in *United States v. Bryan,* the Court observed that any exemption from the duty to testify before the grand jury "presupposes a very real interest to be protected."

Such an interest must surely be the First Amendment protection of a confidential relationship that I have discussed above in Part I. As noted there, this protection does not exist for the purely private interests of the newsman or his informant, nor even, at bottom, for the First Amendment interests of either partner in the newsgathering relationship. Rather, it functions to insure nothing less than democratic decisionmaking through the free flow of information to the public, and it serves, thereby, to honor the "profound national commitment to the principle that debate on public issues should be uninhibited, robust, and wide-open."

In striking the proper balance between the public interest in the efficient administration of justice and the First Amendment guarantee of the fullest flow of information, we must begin with the basic proposition that because of their "delicate and vulnerable" nature, and their transcendent importance for the just functioning of our society, First Amendment rights require special safeguards.

A

This Court has erected such safeguards when government, by legislative investigation or other investigative

means, has attempted to pierce the shield of privacy inherent in freedom of association. In no previous case have we considered the extent to which the First Amendment limits the grand jury subpoena power. But the Court has said that "the Bill of Rights is applicable to investigations as to all forms of governmental action. Witnesses cannot be compelled to give evidence against themselves. They cannot be subjected to unreasonable search and seizure. Nor can the First Amendment freedoms of speech, press . . . or political belief and association be abridged." And, in *Sweezy v. New Hampshire,* it was stated: "It is particularly important that the exercise of the power of compulsory process be carefully circumscribed when the investigative process tends to impinge upon such highly sensitive areas as freedom of speech or press, freedom of political association, and freedom of communication of ideas."

The established method of "carefully" circumscribing investigative powers is to place a heavy burden of justification on government officials when First Amendment rights are impaired. The decisions of this Court have "consistently held that only a compelling state interest in the regulation of a subject within the State's constitutional power to regulate can justify limiting First Amendment freedoms." And "it is an essential prerequisite to the validity of an investigation which intrudes into the area of constitutionally protected rights of speech, press, association and petition that the State convincingly show a substantial relation between the information sought and a subject of overriding and compelling state interest."

Thus, when an investigation impinges on First Amendment rights, the government must not only show that the inquiry is of "compelling and overriding importance," but it must also "convincingly" demonstrate that the investigation is "substantially related" to the information sought.

Governmental officials must, therefore, demonstrate that the information sought is clearly relevant to a precisely defined subject of governmental inquiry. They must demonstrate that it is reasonable to think the witness in question has that information. And they must show that there is not any means of obtaining the information less destructive of First Amendment liberties.

These requirements, which we have recognized in decisions involving legislative and executive investigations, serve established policies reflected in numerous First Amendment decisions arising in other contexts. The requirements militate against vague investigations that, like vague laws, create uncertainty and needlessly discourage First Amendment activity. They also insure that a legitimate governmental purpose will not be pursued by means that "broadly stifle fundamental personal liberties when the end can be more narrowly achieved.". . .

I believe the safeguards developed in our decisions involving governmental investigations must apply to the grand jury inquiries in these cases. Surely the function of the grand jury to aid in the enforcement of the law is no more important than the function of the legislature, and its committees, to make the law. We have long recognized the value of the role played by legislative investigations, for the "power of the Congress to conduct investigations is inherent . . . [encompassing] surveys of defects in our social, economic or political system for the purpose of enabling the Congress to remedy them." Similarly, the associational rights of private individuals, which have been the prime focus of our First Amendment decisions in the investigative sphere, are hardly more important than the First Amendment rights of mass circulation newspapers and electronic media to disseminate ideas and information, and of the general public to receive them. Moreover, the vices of vagueness and overbreadth that legislative investigations may manifest are also exhibited by grand jury inquiries, since grand jury investigations are not limited in scope to specific criminal acts, and since standards of materiality and relevance are greatly relaxed. For, as the United States notes in its brief in *Caldwell,* the grand jury "need establish no factual basis for commencing an investigation, and can pursue rumors which further investigation may prove groundless."

Accordingly, when a reporter is asked to appear before a grand jury and reveal confidences, I would hold that the government must (1) show that there is probable cause to believe that the newsman has information that is clearly relevant to a specific probable violation of law; (2) demonstrate that the information sought cannot be obtained by alternative means less destructive of First Amendment rights; and (3) demonstrate a compelling and overriding interest in the information.

This is not to say that a grand jury could not issue a subpoena until such a showing were made, and it is not to say that a newsman would be in any way privileged to ignore any subpoena that was issued. Obviously, before the government's burden to make such a showing were triggered, the reporter would have to move to quash the subpoena, asserting the basis on which he considered the particular relationship a confidential one.

B

The crux of the Court's rejection of any newsman's privilege is its observation that only "where news sources themselves are implicated in crime or possess information relevant to the grand jury's task need they or the reporter be concerned about grand jury subpoenas." But this is a most misleading construct. For it is obviously not true that the only persons about whom reporters will be forced to testify will be those "confidential informants involved in actual criminal conduct" and those having "information suggesting illegal conduct by others." As noted above, given the grand jury's extraordinarily broad investigative powers and the weak standards of relevance and materiality that apply during such inquiries, reporters, if they have no testimonial privilege, will be called to give information about informants who have neither committed crimes nor have information about crime. It is to avoid deterrence of such sources and thus to prevent needless injury to First Amendment values that I think the government must be required to show probable cause that the newsman has information that is clearly relevant to a specific probable violation of criminal law.

Similarly, a reporter may have information from a confidential source that is "related" to the commission of crime, but the government may be able to obtain an indictment or otherwise achieve its purposes by subpoenaing persons other than the reporter. It is an obvious but important truism that when government aims have been fully served, there can be no legitimate reason to disrupt a confidential relationship between a reporter and his source. To do so would not aid the administration of justice and would only impair the flow of information to the public. Thus, it is to avoid deterrence of such sources that I think the government must show that there are no alternative means for the grand jury to obtain the information sought. . . .

The error in the Court's absolute rejection of First Amendment interests in these cases seems to me to be most profound. For in the name of advancing the administration of justice, the Court's decision, I think, will only impair the achievement of that goal. People entrusted with law enforcement responsibility, no less than private citizens, need general information

relating to controversial social problems. Obviously, press reports have great value to government, even when the newsman cannot be compelled to testify before a grand jury. The sad paradox of the Court's position is that when a grand jury may exercise an unbridled subpoena power, and sources involved in sensitive matters become fearful of disclosing information, the newsman will not only cease to be a useful grand jury witness; he will cease to investigate and publish information about issues of public import. I cannot subscribe to such an anomalous result, for, in my view, the interests protected by the First Amendment are not antagonistic to the administration of justice. Rather, they can, in the long run, only be complementary, and for that reason must be given great "breathing space.". . .

Cohen v. Cowles Media Co.
SUPREME COURT OF THE UNITED STATES
501 U.S. 663 (1991)

JUSTICE BYRON WHITE delivered the Court's opinion:

The question before us is whether the First Amendment prohibits a plaintiff from recovering damages, under state promissory estoppel law, for a newspaper's breach of a promise of confidentiality given to the plaintiff in exchange for information. We hold that it does not.

During the closing days of the 1982 Minnesota gubernatorial race, Dan Cohen, an active Republican associated with Wheelock Whitney's Independent-Republican gubernatorial campaign, approached reporters from the St. Paul Pioneer Press Dispatch (Pioneer Press) and the Minneapolis Star and Tribune (Star Tribune) and offered to provide documents relating to a candidate in the upcoming election. Cohen made clear to the reporters that he would provide the information only if he was given a promise of confidentiality. Reporters from both papers promised to keep Cohen's identity anonymous and Cohen turned over copies of two public court records concerning Marlene Johnson, the Democratic-Farmer-Labor

candidate for Lieutenant Governor. The first record indicated that Johnson had been charged in 1969 with three counts of unlawful assembly, and the second that she had been convicted in 1970 of petit theft. Both newspapers interviewed Johnson for her explanation, and one reporter tracked down the person who had found the records for Cohen. As it turned out, the unlawful assembly charges arose out of Johnson's participation in a protest of an alleged failure to hire minority workers on municipal construction projects, and the charges were eventually dismissed. The petit theft conviction was for leaving a store without paying for $6 worth of sewing materials. The incident apparently occurred at a time during which Johnson was emotionally distraught, and the conviction was later vacated.

After consultation and debate, the editorial staffs of the two newspapers independently decided to publish Cohen's name as part of their stories concerning Johnson. In their stories, both papers identified Cohen as the source of the court records, indicated his connection to the Whitney campaign, and included denials by Whitney campaign officials of any role in the matter. The same day the stories appeared, Cohen was fired by his employer.

Cohen sued respondents, the publishers of the Pioneer Press and Star Tribune, in Minnesota state court, alleging fraudulent misrepresentation and breach of contract. The trial court rejected respondents' argument that the First Amendment barred Cohen's lawsuit. A jury returned a verdict in Cohen's favor, awarding him $200,000 in compensatory damages. . . .

A divided Minnesota Supreme Court reversed the compensatory damages award. . . . The court then went on to address the question whether Cohen could establish a cause of action under Minnesota law on a promissory estoppel theory. Apparently, a promissory estoppel theory was never tried to the jury, nor briefed nor argued by the parties; it first arose during oral argument in the Minnesota Supreme Court when one of the justices asked a question about equitable estoppel. . . .

We granted certiorari to consider the First Amendment implications of this case. . . .

. . . We proceed to consider whether that Amendment bars a promissory estoppel cause of action against respondents. . . .

Respondents rely on the proposition that, "if a newspaper lawfully obtains truthful information about a matter of public significance, then state officials may not constitutionally punish publication of the information, absent a need to further a state interest of the highest order." That proposition is unexceptionable, and it has been applied in various cases that have found insufficient the asserted state interests in preventing publication of truthful, lawfully obtained information.

This case, however, is not controlled by this line of cases but rather by the equally well-established line of decisions holding that generally applicable laws do not offend the First Amendment simply because their enforcement against the press has incidental effects on its ability to gather and report the news. As the cases relied on by respondents recognize, the truthful information sought to be published must have been lawfully acquired. The press may not with impunity break and enter an office or dwelling to gather news. Neither does the First Amendment relieve a newspaper reporter of the obligation shared by all citizens to respond to a grand jury subpoena and answer questions relevant to a criminal investigation, even though the reporter might be required to reveal a confidential source. The press, like others interested in publishing, may not publish copyrighted material without obeying the copyright laws. . . .

There can be little doubt that the Minnesota doctrine of promissory estoppel is a law of general applicability. It does not target or single out the press. Rather, insofar as we are advised, the doctrine is generally applicable to the daily transactions of all the citizens of Minnesota. The First Amendment does not forbid its application to the press. . . .

Also, it is not at all clear that Respondents obtained Cohen's name "lawfully" in this case, at least for purposes of publishing it. . . . [R]espondents obtained Cohen's name only by making a promise that they did not honor. The dissenting opinions suggest that the press should not be subject to any law, including copyright law for example, which in any fashion or to any degree limits or restricts the press' right to report truthful information. The First Amendment does not grant the press such limitless protection.

Nor is Cohen attempting to use a promissory estoppel cause of action to avoid the strict requirements for establishing a libel or defamation claim. As the Minnesota Supreme Court observed here, "Cohen could not sue for defamation because the information disclosed [his name] was true." Cohen is not seeking damages for injury to his reputation or his state of mind. He sought damages in excess of $50,000 for breach of a promise that caused him to lose his job and lowered his earning capacity. . . .

Respondents and *amici* argue that permitting Cohen to maintain a cause of action for promissory estoppel will inhibit truthful reporting because news organizations will have legal incentives not to disclose a confidential source's identity even when that person's identity is itself newsworthy. . . . But if this is the case, it is no more than the incidental, and constitutionally insignificant, consequence of applying to the press a generally applicable law that requires those who make certain kinds of promises to keep them. . . . The Minnesota Supreme Court's incorrect conclusion that the First Amendment barred Cohen's claim may well have truncated its consideration of whether a promissory estoppel claim had otherwise been established under Minnesota law, and whether Cohen's jury verdict could be upheld on a promissory estoppel basis. Or perhaps the State Constitution may be construed to shield the press from a promissory estoppel cause of action such as this one. These are matters for the Minnesota Supreme Court to address and resolve in the first instance on remand. Accordingly, the judgment of the Minnesota Supreme Court is reversed, and the case is remanded for further proceedings not inconsistent with this opinion.

Chapter 10

From the cases coming [before the Supreme Court] we note that unfair and prejudicial news comment on pending trials has become increasingly prevalent. Due process requires that the accused receive a trial by an impartial jury free from outside influences. Given the pervasiveness of modern communications and the difficulty of effacing prejudicial publicity from the minds of the jurors, the trial courts must take strong measures to ensure that the balance is never weighed against the accused. . . . The cure lies in those remedial measures that will prevent the prejudice at its inception.

U.S. Supreme Court Justice Tom Clark[1]

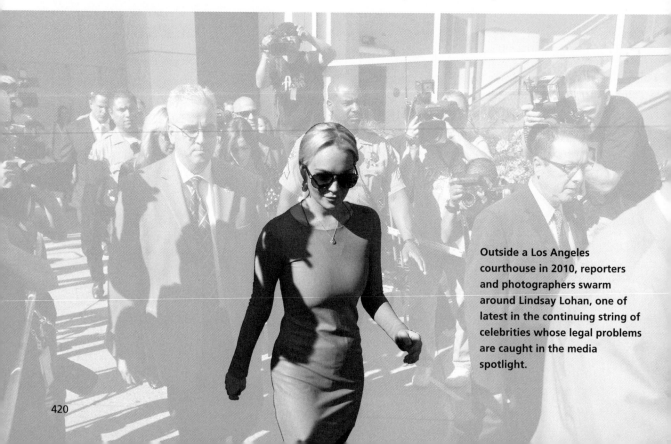

Outside a Los Angeles courthouse in 2010, reporters and photographers swarm around Lindsay Lohan, one of latest in the continuing string of celebrities whose legal problems are caught in the media spotlight.

The Media and the Courts

Preserving Public Trials and Preventing Prejudice

Fair Trials and Prejudicial Speech

Media Effects
Impartial Jurors
Anonymous Juries
Impartial Judges

Remedies to Prejudice

Selecting the Jury
Continuance
Juror Admonition
Juror Sequestration
Contempt

Access to Trials

Presumption of Open Trials
Justifying Court Closure
Closure to Protect Juveniles
Closure to Protect Sexual
    Assault Victims
Gags to Limit Extrajudicial
    Discussion
Challenging Closure

**Electronic Access to
    Trials**

Broadcasting and Recording
Cameras and Courtrooms
Newer Technologies

**Bench-Bar-Press
    Guidelines**

**Access to Court
    Records**

Constitutional and Statutory
    Access
Court Dockets
State Secrets
Court Access Rules
Electronic Access to Court
    Records

Cases for Study

➤ *Sheppard v. Maxwell*
➤ *Richmond
    Newspapers Inc. v.
    Virginia*

Suppose . . .

. . . that a well-known local professional in a quiet suburban community is accused of bludgeoning his wife to death in their home while she and their son slept. Local and national media swarm to the town, converging on the home, the police and every aspect of the investigation. Investigative and pretrial proceedings are open to the media, with one grand jury process held in a raucous, public session in the school gym. Daily headlines and broadcasts relentlessly scream the husband's guilt, castigate investigators for not moving more swiftly to put him behind bars and publish rumors and inaccuracies about the defendant and the crime.

The husband is formally charged with second-degree murder about a month later. During the trial, the media dominate the court, filling the hallways and all available rooms, sitting inside the bar and occupying the majority of seats in the courtroom. They are so close to the defendant that he and his attorney cannot converse privately.

The jurors, drawn from the local community where the trial is held, are allowed to follow the inflammatory coverage; they literally rub elbows with the press before, during and after each day's trial proceedings. Their names, photos and personal details are widely publicized, making them and their families media celebrities. Although sequestered, at night jurors are allowed to make unsupervised telephone calls.

The husband is convicted, but, on appeal, the courts are asked to determine whether the media coverage damaged his constitutional right to a fair trial. Did media coverage before and throughout the trial undermine the defendant's due process rights? If so, if media coverage harms a defendant's right to a fair trial, what steps must a judge take to prevent or remedy media's adverse impact? What restrictions can courts impose on press coverage of trials without running afoul of the public's right to open proceedings or the First Amendment right of a free press? Look for the answers to these questions when the case of *Sheppard v. Maxwell* is discussed later and excerpted at the end of the chapter.

Many people likely would argue that very little has changed for the better in the nearly 45 years since U.S. Supreme Court Justice Tom Clark suggested that it was the responsibility of the courts to remedy the inherent conflict between a free and robust press and fair trials. Today, news media cover crimes when they occur, often in lurid detail and with exuberant fascination. Reporters seek access to crime scenes and provide the public with descriptions of the evidence. Interviews with neighbors, police and victims follow the progress of the investigations, shedding light on the nature of any threat to public safety but also disclosing both accurate and inaccurate information about suspects, methods and victims. Gory photographs appear in tabloid newspapers and on the evening news. The media subject high-profile suspects, such as basketball star Kobe Bryant or California fertilizer salesman Scott Peterson, to intensive scrutiny even before any charges are filed.[2]

The audience responds to the media barrage of crime coverage. First, those who rely on media for a portrait of crime—a majority of people—misunderstand the frequency and nature of criminal activity.[3] For example, people who spend a lot of time with news media mistakenly believed that crime in schools skyrocketed following the shootings at Columbine High School in Littleton, Colo. Second, people increasingly view crimes and trials as entertainment. True crime TV shows have high ratings, and voyeuristic citizens flock to high-publicity trials. When Michael Jackson entered a plea of not guilty to charges of child molestation in 2004, a charge for which he was found not guilty in 2005, police were forced to erect barricades to keep thousands of fans and media from mobbing the California courthouse.

Fair Trials and Prejudicial Speech

The Sixth Amendment to the U.S. Constitution gives criminal defendants the right to a speedy public trial by an impartial jury of his or her peers. But what is an impartial juror? Is an impartial juror someone who has no information about the defendant or the crime before he or she steps into the courtroom? The answer is no. An impartial juror is anyone who will give the facts full and unbiased consideration and render a verdict solely on the basis of evidence presented in court. The problem is, as the news makes clear daily, criminal trials do not exist in a vacuum.

Media Effects

Some of the citizens engrossed by media coverage of crime may be called to sit on a jury. Nearly five decades ago, in the early days of America's romance with television, the U.S. Supreme Court handed down two decisions recognizing the potential harms media publicity might cause to fair trials. In *Estes v. Texas,* the Court in 1965 ruled that televised coverage of the criminal trial of Texas financier Billie Sol Estes was inherently prejudicial.[4]

The defendant was charged with a multimillion-dollar con involving government officials, improper federal loans, a phony storage business and fraudulent fertilizer sales to Texas farmers. Congress launched a high-profile investigation of Estes, more than six dozen FBI agents dug into the case and the press across the country covered developments almost daily. The May 25, 1962, cover of Time magazine bore his image beneath the banner "The Billie Sol Estes Scandal," and Oscar Griffin, Jr., editor of the Pecos (Texas) Independent and Enterprise, won the 1963 Pulitzer Prize for local reporting for bringing the fraud "to national attention with resultant investigation, prosecution and conviction of Estes."[5] Estes was convicted on federal charges of conspiracy and fraud as his trial in state court was proceeding. Prior to the state trial, defense lawyers requested that the judge ban photographs and broadcasts, but dozens of reporters with yards of cable snaking through the courtroom were allowed to disrupt the proceedings.

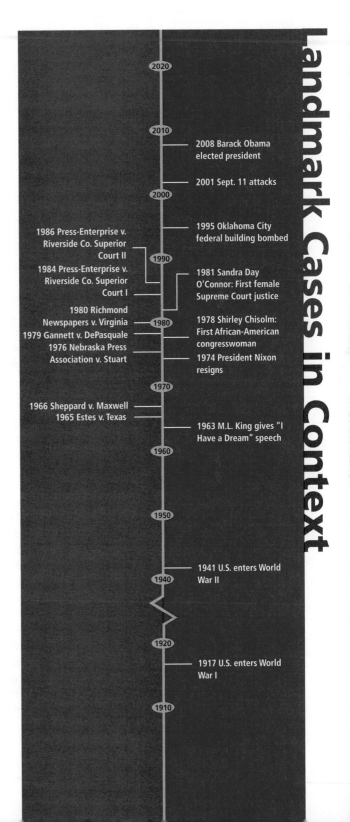

Landmark Cases in Context

- 2020
- 2010
- 2008 Barack Obama elected president
- 2001 Sept. 11 attacks
- 2000
- 1995 Oklahoma City federal building bombed
- 1986 Press-Enterprise v. Riverside Co. Superior Court II
- 1990
- 1984 Press-Enterprise v. Riverside Co. Superior Court I
- 1981 Sandra Day O'Connor: First female Supreme Court justice
- 1980 Richmond Newspapers v. Virginia
- 1978 Shirley Chisolm: First African-American congresswoman
- 1980
- 1979 Gannett v. DePasquale
- 1976 Nebraska Press Association v. Stuart
- 1974 President Nixon resigns
- 1970
- 1966 Sheppard v. Maxwell
- 1965 Estes v. Texas
- 1963 M.L. King gives "I Have a Dream" speech
- 1960
- 1950
- 1941 U.S. enters World War II
- 1940
- 1920
- 1917 U.S. enters World War I
- 1910

Financier Billy Sol Estes sits in a Texas courtroom in 1962. The U.S. Supreme Court later overturned his embezzlement conviction, saying the presence of television cameras deprived Estes of a fair trial.

In reviewing Estes' state conviction, the U.S. Supreme Court held that intensive pretrial broadcast coverage automatically altered juror perceptions of the case and constituted a form of harassment of the defendant. Given the significant potential harms of publicity, the Court required judges to take steps to reduce the impact of media on trials. The Court later rejected the assumption that all broadcast coverage of trials is inherently prejudicial.[6] Nonetheless, media coverage creates additional burdens on judges, who are required to maintain fairness and decorum in their courts. The Court has said judges must protect trials from the effects of publicity that saturates a community, increases the uneasiness of witnesses and may alter the opinions of jurors.

In the second case, *Sheppard v. Maxwell,* the Supreme Court severely criticized a judge who had allowed extensive pretrial and trial publicity to turn the high-profile murder trial mentioned in the "Suppose . . ." section at the beginning of the chapter into a "Roman holiday."[7] The Court said some press coverage may be consistent with a fair trial, but "massive and pervasive" media coverage that reaches the jurors and permeates the trial may be presumed to prejudice the fairness of the process.

The *Sheppard* case involved the 1954 beating death of the wife of a well-respected physician in Bay Village, Ohio, a wealthy suburb of Cleveland. Dr. Sam Sheppard said he struggled with and was knocked unconscious by a "bushy-haired stranger" who entered the family home the night of the murder. The doctor said he woke to find his wife, Marilyn, dead. He called the police.

The media frenzy began the day of the crime and pervaded every aspect of what was called "the trial of the century." Media swarmed the coroner's inquest into the cause of death and "emphasized evidence that tended to incriminate Sheppard."[8] Although no hard evidence tied him to crime, Sheppard was arrested for second-degree murder. During the trial, media filled the courtroom, broadcast live coverage and printed verbatim transcripts of the proceedings almost every day. Sheppard was convicted, sentenced to life imprisonment and spent 10 years in prison before the U.S. Supreme Court overturned his conviction on the grounds that the intense and prejudicial press coverage prevented a fair trial. Retried in 1966, Sheppard was found not guilty.

In overturning his conviction, the Supreme Court said judges must protect the fair trial rights of a defendant by controlling the participants and the process of the trial, including the media. In an 8–1 decision, the Court acknowledged

realWorld Law

Crime Time News?

For at least a decade, researchers have said skewed crime reporting may lead Americans to believe incorrectly that crime rates are soaring and anti-crime efforts are failing because the quantity of crime coverage is not tied to real rates of crime. One study found that more than three-fourths of network television news stories about rural America focused on crime.[1]

Surveys suggest some viewers are concerned about the nature of televised crime reporting. They fear that sensational, repetitive coverage of crimes makes it more difficult to catch criminals, harms a suspect's right to a fair trial, neglects victims and may prompt "copycat" crimes. These viewers want more "meaningful" crime reporting that focuses more on the apprehension of criminals than on the crimes they commit, coverage that emphasizes punishment rather than crime.[2]

Given the nature of TV crime reporting, blogger Don Campagna coined the phrase "crime time news."

---

1. The Center for Media and Public Affairs (results based on analysis of all morning and evening newscasts on ABC, NBC and CBS). See summary of the 2002 study at 17 Media Monitor (Jan./Feb. 2003), available at http://www.cmpa.com/files/media_monitor/03janfeb.pdf.
2. *The Right to More Meaningful Crime Coverage*, Insite Media Research (2000), *available at* http:www.tvsurveys.com/billofrites/crime.htm.

---

the importance of free press in a democracy and its role in the administration of justice. However, the Court said the press does not have the right to inflame the minds of jurors, jeopardize the fairness of trials or make a mockery of the solemn judicial process. The Court said judges should use any of a variety of narrowly tailored measures to preserve the fairness of criminal trials. These measures, which are discussed in more detail later in the chapter, include the following:

1. **Continuance,** or delay, of the trial until publicity has subsided

2. Change of the trial venue, or location, to relocate it outside the area of intense media attention

3. **Sequestration,** or isolation, of the jury from the public

4. Extensive voir dire, or questioning, to identify juror prejudice

5. **Gag orders** on participants to limit discussion of the case outside the courtroom

6. Protection of potential witnesses from outside influences

7. Instructions, or **admonitions,** to the jury to avoid media coverage of the trial and to set aside any prejudices or preconceptions they may have

continuance Postponement of a trial to a later time.

sequestration The isolation of jurors to avoid prejudice from publicity in a sensational trial.

gag orders A nonlegal term used to describe court orders that prohibit publication or discussion of specific materials.

admonitions Judges' instructions to jurors warning them to avoid potentially prejudicial communications.

realWorld Law

High Profile, Historic and Unsolved? The Marilyn Sheppard Murder

The Sheppard murder case at issue in the Supreme Court's landmark ruling in *Sheppard v. Maxwell* inspired a 1960s TV series and a 1993 film called "The Fugitive," which followed Dr. Richard Kimble, a respected doctor wrongly accused of his wife's murder. In both, Kimble is a fugitive trying to clear his name by capturing the mysterious one-armed man he says broke into his home and killed his wife.

In reality, the murder of Dr. Sam Sheppard's pregnant wife, Marilyn, in their lakeside Ohio home remains unsolved today, almost 60 years later.

Shortly after the murder, Dr. Sheppard was convicted of second-degree murder and spent 10 years in prison before the U.S. Supreme Court overturned his

Thirteen years after his murder conviction and one year after a retrial found him not guilty of that crime, Sam Sheppard drew media attention when he sought the restoration of his medical license, which had been rescinded after his conviction.

conviction. Retried in 1966, Sheppard was found not guilty. In 2000, a Ohio jury rejected Sheppard's son's effort to prove his father's innocence and receive $2 million in damages from the state for his father's wrongful imprisonment.[1] The son said genetic tests provided "conclusive evidence" that blood found on Dr. Sam Sheppard's pants and in his home was not his father's. Earlier DNA tests established the blood also was not from Sheppard's wife.

1. Fox Butterfield, *Jury Rejects Innocence of Sheppard in '54 Murder,* N.Y. Times, April 13, 2000, *available at* http://www.nytimes.com/2000/04/13/us/jury-rejects-innocence-of-sheppard-in-54-murder.html?ref=marilyn_sheppard.

8. Retrial if the jury or the judicial process has been contaminated by media coverage

9. Limitations on press attendance, through measures such as pool reporting, to reduce the impact of their presence on jurors and witnesses

While the *Sheppard v. Maxwell* ruling has been applauded as a watershed in protecting the rights of defendants, it also has been criticized for prompting judges to move away from open judicial proceedings.[9]

Impartial Jurors

An impartial juror is not ignorant of the case. Rather impartial jurors must have no fixed opinion of the guilt or innocence of the defendant.[10] And they must be capable of rendering a verdict based purely on the evidence presented in court. A potential juror is not disqualified simply because he or she has seen or read

realWorld Law

Publicity and Prosecutor Prejudice?

In 2006, the small town of Jena, La., made national news when white students hung nooses from a tree on the high school grounds. As publicity increased, the high school was damaged by fire, and violent fights and assaults occurred at the school, with sides drawn along racial lines. In one incident, a group of six African-American students, later called the Jena Six, beat a white student and were charged with attempted murder and conspiracy. The district attorney called the students' tennis shoes murder weapons, as grounds for the murder charge.

Protesters outside the U.S. Justice Department demanding charges be dropped against the Jena Six.

In the first prosecution, the defendant was tried as an adult and convicted of attempted murder by an all-white jury. When his conviction was overturned, he was tried as a juvenile and found guilty of aggravated assault. In 2009, the remaining five defendants pled guilty to misdemeanor simple battery and received $500 fines and seven days probation.

But was justice done? Two years earlier, the Louisiana Supreme Court required the district attorney who had prosecuted the Jena Six to recuse himself from related proceedings. The court said the prosecutor's publicly stated "intent to charge [the six] co-defendants with the harshest crimes and to seek the maximum penalty allowed by law, while characterizing efforts to intimidate African-Americans as a 'prank,' and bringing only misdemeanor charges against the whites" raised serious concerns about fairness and provided sufficient grounds for the district attorney to withdraw from the case.[1]

---

1. State v. Bailey, 969 So. 2d 610, 613 (La. 2007).

news accounts about the crime or the defendant. Similarly, prejudice may not be assumed simply because of a juror's race or gender.[11] Instead courts are required to engage in close questioning of the jury pool during voir dire to determine when media exposure results in prejudice against the defendant.

Courts generally do not rely on social science research to determine when, or whether, news coverage affects jurors. If they did, however, they would find conflicting evidence about the impact of news coverage. Instead, courts generally accept the commonsense notion that media coverage has an effect on the fairness of a trial.[12] Members of the legal community tend to believe that when officials of the court—police and attorneys, for example—publicly discuss ongoing trials, their speech influences jurors' perceptions of witnesses and may potentially alter their determination of guilt or innocence. Courts also believe other government officials may affect the impartiality of jurors. During the George W. Bush administration, for example, a federal judge rebuked then-U.S. Atty. Gen. John Ashcroft after he violated a federal district court order not to discuss the details of the first public terrorism prosecution in the United States following the Sept. 11, 2001, attacks. The court said the attorney general's highly publicized comments about the progress of the trial and the credibility of key witnesses "exhibited a distressing lack of care [about] potentially prejudicial statements about this case."[13]

Anonymous Juries

Criminal defense attorneys often argue that shielding a juror's identity increases his or her anxiety and perception that the crime is especially severe and the defendant is guilty. Courts, however, have said anonymous juries are not inherently prejudicial to defendants. Some courts refuse to release the names and identities of jurors in high-profile cases or in cases where jurors may legitimately be concerned for their personal safety.[14] In fact, the Texas criminal code requires anonymous juries unless there is a showing that access serves the public good.[15] Elsewhere courts justify their refusal to release information about jurors by claiming that the release would violate the jurors' personal privacy interests. Court bans on press photographs of jurors outside the courtroom generally must pass strict scrutiny of their constitutionality because they constitute a form of prior restraint on a free press.

Impartial Judges

Sometimes the fairness of the judge is also cast into doubt. Many judges run for election. In enumerating its concerns about the enormous number of prejudicial influences on the trial in *Sheppard v. Maxwell,* the U.S. Supreme Court noted that the judge was running for reelection and the lead prosecutor was a candidate for a judgeship in an election that took place two weeks after the trial began.[16] In 2009, the Court ruled that the due process clause of the Constitution requires judges to disqualify themselves from hearing a "pending or imminent" case in which "a risk of actual bias or prejudgment" arises because "a person with a personal stake . . . had a significant and disproportionate influence" in getting the judge elected or appointed to the bench.[17] When spending on the election campaign of a judge by one of the parties presents "a serious, objective risk of actual bias," the judge must step off the case, according to the 5–4 majority in *Caperton v. Massey Coal Co.*[18]

In some states where judges stand for election, laws have been passed to protect the appearance of judicial fairness and impartiality by prohibiting judges from campaigning on disputed issues that might come before them in court. But in 2002 the U.S. Supreme Court ruled that such laws violate the First Amendment rights of judicial candidates.[19] The Court said the laws directly limit speech vital to elections, "place . . . most subjects of interest to voters off limits" and undermine the ability of citizens to inform themselves effectively about the candidates.[20]

MEDIA COVERAGE OF CRIME OFTEN INCLUDES details about the crime scene, evidence, arrests, the character and criminal history of the defendant, and the charges. Some of the information presented in the news may be incorrect or may not be admissible in court. Although the media have a First Amendment right to publish this information, such pretrial publicity may undermine the defendant's Sixth Amendment right to a fair trial. A fair trial requires impartial jurors and an impartial judge. Media exposure may cause potential jurors to form fixed ideas about the guilt or innocence of the defendant before a trial begins. While studies disagree on whether publicity harms juror deliberations and verdicts, courts struggle with the effect of media on court processes. The U.S. Supreme Court ruled that judges must withdraw from proceedings when there is substantial likelihood of a risk of bias. State laws designed to protect the appearance of judicial impartiality by prohibiting judges from taking public stands on issues that may come before them in court are unconstitutional. ■

Remedies to Prejudice

Media are involved in numerous ways—including disclosing details of the crime before a verdict has been reached, covering ongoing trials, seeking interviews with and reporting comments by trial participants—that courts have ruled may prejudice a fair trial. Courts apply the guidelines set out by the U.S. Supreme Court in *Sheppard v. Maxwell* through a number of conventional and extraordinary measures to prevent or correct prejudice in the jury. Judges determine where and how the jury is chosen, where and when the trial takes place and the amount of speech freedom jury members and other trial participants will have during the presentation of evidence and during deliberations. These decisions, as well as the defendant's right to appeal an unfair process, are designed to ensure fairness.

Selecting the Jury

When a court needs to select a jury for a trial, the clerk of court chooses names at random from a list of adult licensed drivers, registered voters or another source in the county where the trial will be held. The location from which the pool of jurors is drawn is known as the "venire." Each potential juror receives a **summons,** a notice asking him or her to appear at the court. Attorneys for each side and/or the judge question those in the jury pool about their backgrounds, life experiences and opinions to determine whether each individual will be able to weigh the evidence presented during trial objectively. As noted in Chapter 1, this process is called "voir dire," which literally means "to speak the truth."

summons A notice asking an individual to appear at a court. Potential jurors receive such a summons.

for-cause challenge In the context of jury selection, the ability of attorneys to remove a potential juror for a reason the law finds sufficient, as opposed to a peremptory challenge.

Using the information gathered during voir dire, either the defense or the prosecution in a criminal trial may bring a **for-cause challenge** against a potential juror if the individual's responses to questioning suggest a prejudice relevant to the case. The person's life experiences, attitudes, employment or association with the defendant may justify for-cause challenges. Each attorney also has a limited number of peremptory challenges with which to remove potential jurors without stating a cause, or reason, why the person is not qualified to sit as a juror. The process is designed to ensure that overtly biased individuals do not sit on a jury.

The defense and the prosecution both work hard to eliminate jurors they believe will be hostile to their sides of the case. In major criminal or civil cases, a party with sufficient financial resources may hire consultants on jury selection to identify a model juror who will be most sympathetic to their case. These consultants rely on trial experience, psychology, expertise in nonverbal cues, computer modeling and private investigations of potential jurors to improve the chances of obtaining a sympathetic jury. Once both sides accept the jury, jurors are **impaneled** (selected and seated). Then the jury is sworn in.

impanel To select and seat a jury.

Changing Venue A trial may be transferred from one venue, or location, to another to protect fairness if pretrial publicity, the political atmosphere or other conditions in the initial location likely would prevent a fair trial. Either side in a criminal trial may request a change of venue, which requires the relocation of the trial and all its participants. A change of venue means that the jury pool will be selected from the new location, where jurors' attitudes theoretically are not tainted by the publicity that permeated the original site. Sometimes this evasive maneuver fails because media coverage follows the trial. Besides, it is expensive to move a trial.

New Venire Another means to avoid prejudicial publicity is to bring in a pool of jurors from a different, adjoining county. With a change of venire, the trial stays in its original location, which provides easier access to witnesses but requires transporting a jury back and forth each day of the trial or housing them in the town where the trial is held. Like changes of venue, changes of venire are expensive, and some defense attorneys believe that the inconveniences they impose on jurors make them hostile to the defendant.

Continuance

The Sixth Amendment protects the right of criminal defendants to a speedy trial. However, defendants sometimes will waive this right if they, and their attorneys, believe that a delay, or continuance, will reduce the prejudicial impact of publicity. Parties to the trial may oppose a continuance because postponements often reduce the availability and recall of witnesses. In extraordinary situations, a judge may call for a retrial to ensure that the defendant receives a trial free from prejudice.

Juror Admonition

Judges routinely issue admonitions, or warnings, to jurors, telling them to avoid potentially prejudicial communications, including media coverage of the trial. Judges also instruct jurors not to discuss the case among themselves or with others or to express any opinion about the case until they begin deliberations. Experts disagree on whether such admonitions are effective. Judges also give instructions on the law to the jury prior to deliberation. These instructions generally advise jurors about the applicable law and inform them of their duty to reach a verdict in the case on the basis only of the evidence presented in court, not on speculation, sympathy or prejudice.

Juror Sequestration

Sometimes, though rarely, a judge will sequester, or isolate, a jury during a trial. Members of a sequestered jury generally are housed in a hotel near the courthouse and prohibited from having contact with people outside of court. Sequestered jurors generally have only limited and supervised opportunities to communicate with their families. Sequestration may be used to protect jurors in response to threats to their safety or to keep them away from media during highly publicized cases. Jurors do not like to be sequestered, and some people believe that sequestration affects juror attitudes, the quality of their deliberations and the outcome of the trial.

Contempt

Judges have broad discretion to find witnesses, parties or even lawyers in a case in **contempt of court.** Disobeying a court order, misconduct in the courtroom or other actions that interfere with the administration of justice can form the basis of a contempt order, which may be punishable by a fine, imprisonment or both. Direct contempt occurs when the misconduct occurs in front of the judge, usually in the courtroom. Curiously, the judge who believes that contempt has been committed in his or her courtroom functions as the victim, witness, prosecutor and judge in the contempt proceeding. Contempt citations issued in trial courts often are overturned on appeal by judges who have no personal involvement in the alleged contempt.

Both civil and criminal contempt exist, but it is often unclear how to distinguish the two. Judges typically use **civil contempt** citations to force someone to perform a specific act, such as disclosing the identity of a source or turning over interview notes or outtakes of a broadcast program to the court. Civil contempt citations also may arise when attorneys violate a gag order not to discuss a pending lawsuit in public. Civil contempt sometimes is called "indirect contempt" because the act involved generally occurs outside the court beyond the presence of the judge. Civil contempt orders most often are lifted as soon as the individual performs the required action or the trial ends.

contempt of court Any act that is judged to hinder or obstruct a court in its administration of justice. For example, journalists may be cited for contempt of court for refusing to disclose information.

civil contempt Acts, generally outside the courtroom, that defy court orders or obstruct court proceedings, such as failure to comply with a subpoena to appear in court; sometimes called "indirect contempt."

criminal contempt Conduct in or near a court that willfully disregards, disobeys or interferes with the court's authority; sometimes called "direct contempt."

Criminal contempt is used to punish a person who clearly will not comply with a court order, such as when a journalist refuses to disclose his or her source when ordered to do so by the court. Criminal contempt orders may also be used to deter others who might be tempted to defy court orders in the future. Because criminal contempt is normally committed in the direct presence of the judge, it is sometimes referred to as "direct contempt." A journalist who refuses under oath to answer questions about confidential sources could be charged with civil or criminal contempt.

Some states limit the discretion judges have to issue contempt citations. For example, Pennsylvania judges may issue only direct contempt citations. Judges also may not abuse their power of contempt citations to suppress criticism of court proceedings, unless the criticism poses a clear and present danger to justice. Anyone charged with contempt where the potential penalty is more than six months in jail has a right to a jury trial.

SUMMARY

THE SIXTH AMENDMENT TO THE CONSTITUTION guarantees criminal defendants the right to a speedy and public trial before an impartial jury to be held in the district where the crime was committed. The Supreme Court has determined that the right to an open public trial belongs to the public as well as the defendant. To protect these important components of justice, courts take care in composing juries and in protecting the court's fair process from external influences, including media. The careful selection of jurors includes both the drawing of a fair cross-section of the community and the detailed questioning of potential jurors through voir dire. Judges also use admonitions, instructions and sequestration to encourage jurors to consider only the evidence presented in court in rendering a verdict. Judges use both civil and criminal contempt citations to force participants in the trial to comply with their orders. On occasion, judges will delay or relocate a trial to overcome impediments to fairness. These remedies are rare because they are expensive and interfere with the right to a speedy trial. ∎

Access to Trials

Although the Sixth Amendment to the U.S. Constitution provides a right to public trials in criminal cases, the U.S. Supreme Court has had to consider whether a defendant may waive his right to a public trial and exclude the public. The Court also considered the question from an alternative perspective: Does the public, including the media, have a Sixth Amendment right of access to criminal court proceedings? According to that theory, the defendant would not have a right to a private trial because it would infringe on the right of the public to participate in and oversee the process of the courts.

Presumption of Open Trials

For more than 30 years, the U.S. Supreme Court has said the Sixth Amendment creates a personal right for criminal defendants to be tried in an open court by their peers to ensure they receive a fair trial and due process.[21] However, the public also enjoys a long-standing common law right to view public trials. The Court said the two rights must be balanced. The ruling in *Gannett v. DePasquale* arose after Judge Daniel DePasquale granted pretrial motions to exclude the public and the press from the trial of three individuals charged with the murder of an off-duty police officer. At the same hearing, he also granted pretrial motions to suppress evidence and confessions by the defendants. No one present during the pretrial hearing, including a Gannett reporter, objected to the motions or the court's rulings.

After Gannett reporter Carol Ritter later objected to the closure, the judge reviewed the pretrial motions and said the defendant's right to a fair trial outweighed the right of the press to cover the pretrial suppression hearing. On subsequent review, Justice Potter Stewart, writing for the Supreme Court, agreed that publicity could prejudice the defendant's right to a fair trial and affirmed the right of a judge to use means that "are not strictly and inescapably necessary" to protect a fair trial.[22] Justice Stewart observed:

> There can be no blinking the fact that there is a strong societal interest in public trials. Openness in court proceedings may improve the quality of testimony, induce unknown witnesses to come forward with relevant

realWorld Law

Fewer Newsrooms Fight for Open Courts

The traditional role of the media as champions of open courts appears to be waning. "The days of powerful newspapers with ample legal budgets appear to be numbered," according to one Georgia public defender, who questions whether "underfunded bloggers [will] be able to carry the financial burdens of opening our courtrooms."[1]

The shrinking number of media-spearheaded battles for access to courtrooms and court records sometimes allows controversial rulings to go unchallenged. For example, as part of a settlement in a lawsuit against Amtrak, a federal district court judge vacated several of his prior decisions in the case and instructed the legal databases Westlaw and LexisNexis to remove the decisions from their files as well. The two companies complied.

Given their financial straits, news media have "shifted our emphasis from principle to survival," according to access advocate Jane Kirtley.

1. Adam Liptak, *Shrinking Newsrooms Wage Fewer Battles for Public Access to Courtrooms*, N.Y. Times, Aug. 31, 2009, at 10.

testimony, cause all trial participants to perform their duties more conscientiously, and generally give the public an opportunity to observe the judicial system. But there is a strong societal interest in other constitutional guarantees extended to the accused as well.[23]

In a concurring opinion joined by three other justices, however, Justice Harry Blackmun suggested that court closure "may implicate interests beyond those of the accused . . . [including] important social interests relating to the integrity of the trial process."[24] He said judges must weigh those competing interests fully even if neither the prosecution nor the defense objects to closure. To do so, judges should presume that court processes should be open and require the party seeking closure to demonstrate (1) the probability that publicity would infringe on the right to a fair trial, (2) the inadequacy of alternatives to closure, and (3) the effectiveness of closure.

In 1980, a majority of the U.S. Supreme Court moved toward Justice Blackmun's position and found that the Sixth Amendment right to a public trial does not belong exclusively to the defendant. In *Richmond Newspapers, Inc. v. Virginia*,[25] the Court held that criminal trials are presumptively open and that the First Amendment prohibits judges from closing courtrooms without a full exploration of the alternatives. The First Amendment protects the people's right to assemble and petition government for redress of grievances through the courts. It also provides some presumptive right for the press, as members of the public, to cover criminal trials because court processes have been open to the public throughout history.[26] Chief Justice Warren Burger wrote that "absent an overriding interest articulated in findings, the trial of a criminal case must be open to the public."[27]

The Court said open criminal trials serve the public interest in a variety of ways, including advancement of the core First Amendment goal of protecting "freedom of communications on matters relating to the functioning of government."[28] Information about the criminal process enables citizens to evaluate government performance, to maintain faith in the judicial system and to seek catharsis for the trauma of crimes.

Points of Law

Open Courts

According to the U.S. Supreme Court's rulings in the two *Press-Enterprise* cases, court proceedings are presumptively open to the public and the press if logic and experience dictate openness. Accordingly, court processes are presumed to be open if:

1. This type of proceeding has a largely uninterrupted history of openness, and

2. Openness contributes to the proper functioning of the proceeding itself.

In a separate ruling that followed fast on the heels of *Richmond Newspapers, Inc.*, the Supreme Court said that because courts are presumptively open, states may not require closure of certain portions of criminal trials.[29] The *Globe Newspaper Co. v. Superior Court* decision struck down a Virginia law that closed courtrooms during all testimony of any minor who was a victim of sexual assault. The Court said some parts of a trial might need to be closed, but the Constitution requires judges to demonstrate the need for such closures: "The institutional value of the open criminal trial is recognized in both logic and experience."[30]

In the mid-1980s, a pair of cases involving the Press-Enterprise company allowed the Supreme Court to make clear that the public enjoys a right of access to both jury selection and preliminary hearings, since these are an integral part of the judicial process.[31] Preliminary hearings generally determine whether there is sufficient evidence to proceed to trial. The Court first said that two interrelated factors—experience and logic—determine whether a court proceeding is presumptively open.[32] According to the **experience and logic test,** if the proceeding has historically been open and if openness contributes to the proper functioning of the process itself, the proceeding is presumptively open. In the second of these rulings, *Press Enterprise II v. Superior Court,* the Supreme Court said access to the hearings themselves, not merely to a transcript of the proceeding released after the fact, is vital to assure the public that the process is functioning properly.

Although the Court in *Press-Enterprise* emphasized that jury selection historically had been open to the public, it acknowledged that the responses of some jurors to some particularly sensitive questions during voir dire could raise legitimate privacy concerns and might warrant protection from public disclosure. Thus, courts may develop narrowly tailored measures to close only those portions of voir dire that raise serious concerns without running afoul of the Constitution. Some courts have expanded beyond this recognition of an individual juror's right to personal privacy to rule that juror privacy in general justifies closed voir dire and anonymous juries. They reason that access to jury selection and juror identity erodes the willingness of potential jurors to speak candidly and harms effective juror selection.

experience and logic test A doctrine that determines the presumptive openness of judicial proceedings on the basis of their history and the role openness plays in assuring the credibility of the process.

Justifying Court Closure

The two *Press-Enterprise* decisions should make clear that generalized privacy interests are insufficient to justify closing a courtroom. Anyone seeking to close a presumptively public judicial hearing must meet a high standard, which the court articulated through a two-part test. First, the individual seeking to close records or proceedings must show that openness has a "substantial probability" of significantly threatening the fair trial process. Second, the evidence must prove that closure is a last resort and is "essential" in order to preserve fair trial rights.

Generally, courts must demonstrate that the interests of justice require withholding information from the public, including the names and addresses of jurors.[33] A request to close a courtroom should be granted only if closure meets the standards of strict scrutiny and if the party seeking closure makes a specific showing of serious harm that would result from an open proceeding. "The presumption of openness may be overcome only by an overriding interest based on findings that closure is essential to preserve higher values and is narrowly tailored to serve that interest," the Court said.[34] Thus, before closing a courtroom, judges are required to determine that facts demonstrate *all* of the following:

- Openness poses a substantial threat to the fair trial rights of the defendant.
- No alternative exists that would effectively eliminate the threat to a fair trial.
- Closure will effectively eliminate the threat to a fair trial.
- Closure will be narrowly tailored to eliminate the threat while protecting the greatest public access to the court.

The Court also has said judges may not close any part of a trial unless they first allow interested parties and the public to raise objections to the proposed closure.

Despite this high standard, courts continue to close their doors and seal their records. When in 2003–04, Martha Stewart was tried for securities fraud, for example, the trial court barred the media from attending jury selection and from contacting potential jurors. Voir dire was conducted in the judge's robing room with transcripts of the proceedings released the following day without the names of the potential jurors. But in response to a media challenge to the judge's closure order, the federal court of appeals found the trial judge's actions unconstitutional, writing:

> No right is more sacred in our constitutional firmament than that of the accused to a fair trial. Our national experience instructs us that except in rare circumstances openness preserves, indeed, is essential to, the realization of that right and to public confidence in the administration of justice. The burden is heavy on those who seek to restrict access to the media, a vital means to open justice. Here, the government has failed to overcome the presumption of openness. The mere fact of intense media coverage of a celebrity defendant, without further compelling justification, is simply not enough to justify closure.[35]

In 2010, the U.S. Supreme Court issued two rulings on access to courts. In a largely procedural ruling, the Court issued an emergency stay to prevent the broadcast of a

---

Does Publicity Bias Jurors?

Some experts argue that court strategies to ensure the fairness of trials are more than adequate to counteract any harmful effects of media coverage on the fair trial rights of defendants. They say pretrial publicity alters the outcome of a trial only in very narrow and rare circumstances. Pretrial publicity may create prejudice only when:

- Jurors are exposed to pretrial publicity.

- The evidence in court does not point convincingly to a clear verdict.

- The information provided by the media seems better—more convincing, more likely or more reliable—than the evidence presented in court.

- The media consistently lean toward one verdict.

- All the remedies available to the court fail at the same time.

The final point "is perhaps one of the most crucial conclusions. . . . We believe pretrial publicity does not usually bias decisions in actual cases because of the care courts take to apply remedies," two legal scholars concluded.[1]

---

1. Jon Bruschke & William E. Loges, Free Press vs. Fair Trials: Examining Publicity's Role in Trial Outcomes 134-37 (2004).

federal district court trial on California's ballot measure banning same-sex marriage.[36] The Court barred cameras on the grounds that the lower court failed to "follow the appropriate procedures set forth in federal law" for allowing broadcasts and because camera coverage might increase the potential harassment of trial participants. The trial judge subsequently ruled that the ban violated the civil rights of gay Californians, and the state declined to pursue an appeal to defend the ballot measure.[37]

In the second case, *Presley v. Georgia,* the Supreme Court ruled that the defendant, as well as the public and the press, had a Sixth Amendment right to have voir dire and jury selection conducted in public.[38] Eric Presley appealed his conviction of cocaine trafficking, claiming that the exclusion of his uncle, the only member of the public seeking to attend the jury questioning in his trial, violated his constitutional rights. In excluding the public from voir dire, the judge had said, "It's totally up to my discretion whether or not I want family members in the courtroom."[39] In overturning the Georgia Supreme Court's affirmation of the courtroom closure, the U.S. Supreme Court said that "there are no doubt circumstances" in which a judge could constitutionally exclude the public from jury selection, but before excluding the public the court must "consider all reasonable alternatives to closure."[40]

In 2008, The New York Times, The Washington Post, The Reporters Committee for Freedom of the Press and a virtual who's who of the elite media in the United States filed a second motion to unseal records in the high-profile antitrust case between computer industry giant Intel and its chief competitor, Advanced Micro Devices (AMD).[41] In 2006, District Court Judge Joseph Farnan, Jr., approved a protective order in *AMD v. Intel* that sealed "hundreds of millions of pages of documentation" to safeguard the companies' trade secrets and facilitate discovery between the litigants.[42] The media coalition argued that records had been sealed too sweepingly and too readily without a proper showing that confidentiality was necessary to preserve the judicial process or the legitimate interest in protecting trade secrets. Reporters asserted that the protective order improperly shielded Intel business practices from scrutiny by its customers, investors and the broader public.

In an earlier related case brought before the European Union's antitrust tribunal, AMD had sought some 600,000 pages of discovery records through the U.S. courts. After the district court rejected the request, the Ninth Circuit Court of Appeals, and ultimately the U.S. Supreme Court, agreed that nothing in the relevant federal statute limited disclosure of discovery records to proceedings in U.S. courts. The Court ordered that the documents be produced.[43]

When the social networking sites Facebook and ConnectU faced off in court over claims of misappropriation and unfair business practices, among other things, the federal judge closed the courtroom and sealed related documents to protect business secrets. In 2009 another federal judge sealed the courtroom and records to shield confidential trade secrets that might otherwise be divulged in a lawsuit brought by the Motion Picture Association of America to prevent RealDVD from selling descrambling software that allowed copying of encrypted DVDs.[44]

realWorld Law

Jury Questionnaires in O.J. Simpson Robbery-Kidnapping Trial Should Be Open

Late in 2009, the Nevada Supreme Court ordered the release of both blank and completed questionnaires used in the selection of jurors for the robbery-kidnapping trial of O.J. Simpson that ended a year earlier with Simpson convicted and sentenced to 9 to 33 years in prison.

The court said juror questionnaires are presumptively open, and judges must enumerate specific findings of a "countervailing interest to public access" prior to closing these records. The lower court improperly issued "a blanket promise of confidentiality" to the jurors without allowing the media to intervene to protect the public interest in access to criminal proceedings.[1]

O.J. Simpson (C) appears in court with attorneys Gabriel Grasso (L) and Yale Galanter prior to sentencing at the Clark County Regional Justice Center December 5, 2008, in Las Vegas, Nevada. Simpson and co-defendant Clarence "C.J." Stewart were sentenced on 12 charges, including felony kidnapping, armed robbery and conspiracy related to a 2007 confrontation with sports memorabilia dealers in a Las Vegas hotel.

1. Associated Press, *Nevada High Court: O.J. Jury Questions Should Have Been Public*, Dec. 28, 2009, *available at* http://www.firstamendmentcenter.org/news.aspx?id=22442.

The Supreme Court has not ruled directly on whether hearings to consider the suppression of evidence or plea bargains must be open. The American Bar Association suggests that these hearings also are presumptively open. In contrast, at least one federal appeals court has affirmed the traditional authority of judges to hold conferences in closed chambers or conduct whispered bench conferences in the courtroom with the lawyers during the trial. Courts also recognize and protect the secrecy of jury deliberations. Narrowly drawn orders to protect jury deliberation by preventing jurors from discussing key aspects of other jurors' comments in a specific case—particularly when the case may be appealed or reheard—may be constitutional.

Although the broad right of public access extends to virtually all criminal trial proceedings, some related procedures generally are closed. Thus, grand jury hearings, which determine whether an individual should be indicted and prosecuted for a crime, generally are closed. The long-standing tradition of secret grand jury proceedings also generally seals all grand jury documents. However, the Supreme Court said a state may not punish grand jury witnesses who discuss their own testimony after the conclusion of a grand jury investigation.[45]

Closure to Protect Juveniles

Courts generally recognize that different public interests may apply to legal proceedings involving juveniles. On one hand, the public has a legitimate interest in access to juvenile proceedings, and open proceedings may provide all the benefits that accrue in open judicial processes for adults. On the other, government also has a substantial interest in restricting exposure of juvenile defendants and witnesses to reduce potential trauma and stigma to the juvenile and to facilitate his or her rehabilitation.

As far back as 1966, the Supreme Court expressed concern that individuals in the juvenile justice system may receive neither the due process protections provided to adults nor the care and rehabilitation intended for children. The Court said procedures in juvenile courts intended to protect minors also must assure that minors receive the full "reach of constitutional guarantees applicable to adults."[46] The next year, the Supreme Court decided that the rights of juvenile defendants include the right to counsel and notice, but the Court failed to determine whether juvenile proceedings must be open to the public.[47] A decade later, Justice William Rehnquist noted that the confidentiality of juvenile processes, particularly the ability to shield them from the media, had played an important historical role in order to reduce stigma of minors.[48]

Today, most federal courts do not consider juvenile proceedings to be presumptively open criminal prosecutions. Instead, federal law permits but does not require closure of juvenile proceedings. As a result, federal judges may close juvenile proceedings on a case-by-case basis. The judge also decides which juvenile court records and what identifying information will be released to the public. This is true in some states as well, where judges enjoy a great deal of discretion in deciding which juvenile proceedings should be open. Many states ask judges to weigh the age of the minor and the seriousness of the offense in deciding whether to expose the juvenile to public scrutiny.

Laws in about a third of the states, including Alaska and South Carolina, presume that juvenile proceedings are closed,[49] but confidentiality has given way to significant openness in juvenile proceedings in many states.[50] Some states provide a broad right of public access to juvenile courts.[51] In Washington, for example, state law presumes that juvenile proceedings will be open: "The general public and press shall be permitted to attend any hearing unless the court, for good cause, orders a particular hearing to be closed."[52] Juvenile courts in Colorado, Florida and New Mexico also operate with a presumption of openness, but in 2000 the Ohio Supreme Court ruled that juvenile proceedings are neither presumptively open nor closed.[53] Decisions on openness depend on a weighing of the public and private interests involved. California and Virginia require that juvenile proceedings related to certain violent crimes be open. In Illinois the media, but not the public, may attend juvenile proceedings. Some states impose more narrow restrictions. In Alabama, for example, state law prohibits anyone attending juvenile proceedings from releasing the identity of the child. However, only two

Cameras in State and Federal Courtrooms

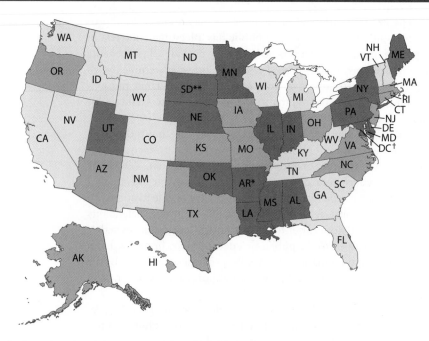

†The District of Columbia is the only jurisdiction that prohibits trial and appellate coverage entirely.

19 states allow coverage in most courts, generally at the discretion of the presiding judge

California
Colorado
Florida
Georgia
Idaho
Kentucky
Michigan

Montana
Nevada
New Hampshire
New Mexico
North Dakota
South Carolina
Tennessee (no minors)

Vermont
Washington
West Virginia
Wisconsin
Wyoming

15 states prohibit coverage of certain types of proceedings, or some or all witnesses (especially those who object)

Alaska
Arizona
Connecticut
Hawaii
Iowa

Kansas
Massachusetts
Missouri
North Carolina
New Jersey
Ohio

Oregon
Rhode Island
Texas
Virginia

16 states that effectively prevent coverage or allow coverage only of appellate courts

Alabama
Arkansas*
Delaware
Illinois
Indiana
Louisiana

Maine
Maryland
Minnesota
Mississippi
Nebraska

New York
Oklahoma
Pennsylvania
South Dakota**
Utah

Only two U.S. Circuit Courts of Appeals broadly allow cameras, i.e. the Second and Ninth Circuits.

*The Arkansas Supreme Court in 2010 ruled that media would be permitted to broadcast oral arguments before the state's appellate courts, including the supreme court.
**In 2010, the South Dakota Supreme Court planned to consider rules to allow cameras in trial courts.

states prohibit media access to the identity of juvenile offenders, and 35 states allow media to obtain basic information and identity on youths in delinquency proceedings.[54]

Traditionally, most states have maintained the confidentiality of juvenile court records, but these too are increasingly being made available. Many states allow schools and youth agencies some access to juvenile records. All states allow the courts to grant individuals with a legitimate interest some access to juvenile court records and allow certain juveniles to be treated as adults within the justice system, but Maryland, New Jersey and Wisconsin may prohibit the media from revealing the identity of a juvenile.[55] In Washington, however, juvenile court files are presumptively open, but the more detailed records contained in personal history and probation files are confidential. News reporters who legally obtain information about the juvenile or the proceeding from sources outside the juvenile court process generally may publish the information without fear of punishment.

States have moved to open both juvenile proceedings and records in response to increased public concern about juvenile violence. This is particularly true when juveniles are charged with felonies, especially those involving handguns. Public or media access to juvenile proceedings does not raise concerns about prejudicial publicity because juvenile courts do not involve juries. However, judges may want to avoid publicity when a case may be transferred to adult court, where the juvenile would have the right to a jury trial.

Closure to Protect Sexual Assault Victims

Related issues arise frequently in cases of sexual assault, where open courts and press coverage are widely perceived to aggravate the injury to the victim. Every state has a rape shield law intended to protect the alleged victim from questions about sexual history and other topics likely to prejudice jurors against the victim. With the exception of Mississippi, every state has a statute making evidence of the complaining witness's past sexual activity generally inadmissible in court.[56] A few states also exclude opinion or evidence of the complainant's chastity, past relations with the defendant and manner of dress. Some of these laws also shield the victim's identity and other personal information in much the same way courts protect children's legal rights to privacy.[57] Most states enacted the statutes in the 1970s in order to encourage women to report and support the prosecution of sexual assaults, but Arizona enacted its law in 2010.[58]

Gags to Limit Extrajudicial Discussion

Because the Supreme Court has found it generally unconstitutional to close courtrooms to protect the fairness of a trial, many judges attempt to limit prejudicial publicity by using **restraining orders** to prevent trial participants from disclosing information to the press. A restraining order is a court order forbidding an individual from doing a specified act until a hearing can be conducted. In *Sheppard v.*

restraining order A court order forbidding the defendant from doing a specified act until a hearing can be conducted.

Points of Law

Closing Media Mouths: The *Nebraska Press* Standard

In the wake of *Nebraska Press Association v. Stuart,* a judge must justify orders that prevent media disclosure of information produced in court with convincing evidence of the following:

1. Disclosure of the protected information would present a substantial threat to a fair trial.

2. There is no effective alternative to a gag on the press.

3. The gag will effectively eliminate the danger to the fair trial, and

4. The gag is narrowly tailored to restrict only the information that must be kept secret.

Maxwell, the Supreme Court suggested that judges use their authority over participants in the trial to prevent them from discussing potentially prejudicial information outside the courtroom. Such orders are a logical extension of the judge's duty to protect the trial process inside the courtroom.

Gag orders, as journalists prefer to call restraining orders, control information at its source. Gag order is a nonlegal phrase that describes court orders that prohibit publication or discussion of specific materials. In 1991, the Supreme Court said court-ordered speech restrictions on attorneys during a trial are not subject to the First Amendment's nearly complete ban on prior restraints of speech.[59] The Court reasoned that the lawyers, and quite possibly jurors, witnesses and other trial participants, are insiders to a vital government process. They have special access to sensitive information. They have unique power to derail justice. Accordingly, their speech may be subject to control when it poses a "substantial likelihood" of jeopardizing a fair trial.

Court orders, or gags, may ban some or all of the participants in a trial from talking with the media about the trial. They also may target specific individuals or limit discussion of particular topics or information. Gag orders on trial participants generally are upheld on appeal if the judge has considered alternatives and made the restrictions as narrow as possible, and evidence demonstrates that media coverage poses a substantial likelihood of denying the defendant a fair trial. Narrowly drawn restraining orders generally end as soon as the threat to the trial process passes. Thus, in 1990, the Supreme Court struck down a state ban on grand jury witnesses discussing their testimony even after the grand jury proceeding was completed.[60]

In contrast, court orders barring media from publicizing legally obtained information about ongoing trials are prior restraints on speech and are therefore rarely constitutional.[61] In 1976, in *Nebraska Press Association v. Stuart,* the Court called press gags an extraordinary remedy and found that such gags are presumptively unconstitutional.[62] The case involved the murders of six family members in a tiny rural town in Nebraska. The day after the murders, a 30-year-old neighbor turned himself in to police and confessed to the crime. National news media converged on the town of 850 residents, and the judge ordered the media not to publish information obtained during the pretrial proceedings.

The county judge then issued an order barring publication of the confession or of lab test results relating to a sexual assault of one of the victims. Moreover, the judge required the media to observe the voluntary Nebraska Bar/Press Guidelines. The guidelines, endorsed by members of the state bar and media, suggested that the press should not publish information about confessions, opinions of guilt or innocence, the results of lab tests, comments on witness credibility or other statements that reasonably would be expected to influence the outcome of the trial. The state press association appealed the order, which the Nebraska Supreme Court upheld.

The U.S. Supreme Court reversed. The Court viewed gag orders on the media as the type of prior restraint that is the most serious and least tolerable infringement on First Amendment freedoms. Judges who impose restraining orders directly on the press bear a heavy burden of showing that pervasive media coverage is likely to pose a substantial threat to the fair trial. Courts must consider three things when determining whether a press gag may be constitutional: (1) the quantity and content of media coverage, (2) the potential effectiveness of alternatives to a gag, and (3) the likelihood that a gag would remedy the harmful publicity.

Before issuing an order that prohibits media from disclosing information obtained in open court, judges must show that the gag targets information that represents a clear and present danger to a fair trial. The gag must also be a last resort and be designed to protect the fair trial. Only the most narrowly tailored gags on media are constitutional. This test is very difficult to meet, and so constitutionally valid gag orders against news media are rare.

In one such rare example, a federal appeals court upheld a temporary gag order after Panamanian ruler Gen. Manuel Noriega was overthrown, seized, and transferred to the United States to face trial on federal trafficking and racketeering charges.[63] CNN had obtained copies of tape recordings of conversations between Noriega and his defense attorneys and intended to broadcast them. CNN contacted the lawyers to confirm the authenticity of the tapes and aired portions of the tapes during a broadcast of that interview.

The lawyers immediately asked a federal district court to impose a restraining order on CNN to prevent further broadcast of the tapes. The trial judge complied and demanded that the tapes be turned over for review by the court to determine whether they threatened the right of the defendant to confer privately with his attorneys (what's generally referred to as "attorney/client privilege"). A federal appellate court upheld the gag and told CNN it had to turn the tapes over to the trial judge.[64] After reviewing the tapes, the trial court said the tapes were not prejudicial.[65] The judge later found CNN guilty of contempt for violating the original restraining order.[66] Rather than pay an undetermined but hefty fine, CNN agreed to the trial judge's alternative sentence and broadcast an admission of guilt and apology for violating the court's order.[67]

In 1984 the Supreme Court upheld a restraining order that prevented two newspapers from publicizing a confidential membership and donor list of a religious group that they had received in discovery during the course of a libel lawsuit.[68] After the lawsuit, the newspapers sought to use the donor and membership information in news reports. But the Court refused to allow that, ruling that because the information was made available to the newspapers through a trial proceeding, it could not be used in a news story. The Court unanimously ruled that the restraining order was constitutional, in part because it did not prohibit

realWorld Law

Open Your Mouth and Open Courts

The Society of Professional Journalists (SPJ) encourages citizens and reporters alike to help maintain the openness of judicial proceedings by attending court processes and objecting to any improper attempts at closure.[1] If you wish to object to the closing of records or court processes, the SPJ recommends you stand, receive the judge's recognition and permission to speak, and say the following:

> I respectfully protest closure of [this record or this proceeding]. The U.S. Supreme Court has ruled that the First Amendment forbids exclusion of the public from pretrial and trial proceedings without findings of fact identifying the overriding interest to be protected and the necessity of closure to protect that interest.
>
> The Court has also ruled openness is a constitutional presumption. More than speculation or conclusory assertion of harm is required to justify closure. I ask the court to follow the rulings of the U.S. Supreme Court.

Or, if you plan to involve an attorney, then you might say:

> I request that the court delay further proceedings to allow time for counsel to appear and file a motion in opposition to closure.

Finally, if you actually are barred from entering the courtroom, you may write a note using one of the two statements above and give it to the bailiff or clerk to provide to the judge. As a reporter, you likely will want to file a story on the closure as well!

---

1. A POCKET GUIDE TO ACCESS TO COURTS AND COURT RECORDS, Apr. 1, 1994, *available at* http://www.journalism.sfsu.edu/www/internet/pocket1.txt.

the newspapers from publishing the same information if they could obtain it in another way. The order simply prevented the newspapers from improperly using the legal discovery process as a reporting tool.

Challenging Closure

The media, like all members of the public, have a right to challenge court closures. They may ask a judge not to seal records or not to close any proceeding during the criminal process. Such requests should be made in open court. The Society for Professional Journalists long has published a pocket reference to instruct both journalists and citizens on how to protest when courtrooms are closed. In general, individuals should stand and request recognition by the presiding judge and then simply state an objection to the closure. As an alternative, anyone may request that the court delay proceedings so they can seek the advice of an attorney in order to file an objection to the closure.

STARTING IN THE 1980s, THE SUPREME COURT established that the First Amendment and common law provide a public right to attend criminal trials and many of the hearings associated with trials. The presumption of open proceedings extends to pretrial hearings and voir dire. It may also include other historically open proceedings integral to the trial process. Criminal trials are presumptively open unless the individual seeking to close the trial can show with clear evidence that closure is vital to serve a compelling government interest, such as the fairness of the trial. Closures must be limited in scope and duration to provide the broadest possible public access. Grand jury proceedings are closed as are some juvenile proceedings. Laws that automatically close parts of trials are not constitutional. Rather than close trials, court restraining orders that limit public discussion of trials may reduce prejudicial publicity. Gags on trial participants are constitutional if a substantial likelihood exists that publicity would harm the fair trial rights of the defendants. Direct gags on the media rarely are constitutional. Trial observers can challenge the closure of court sessions as individuals or through attorneys. ∎

Electronic Access to Trials

The Supreme Court has said the Sixth Amendment prevents judges from imposing outright bans on media coverage of trials because the media, like the public, have a right to access and scrutinize the judicial system. Open courtrooms are essential to the fairness of the courts and to the public's faith in the judicial system. But openness and access are not absolute. Judges may limit the number of media representatives in the courtroom, and they may exclude cameras and recording devices to prevent disruptions and distractions, protect the fairness of the trial and ensure the solemnity of the proceedings.

Broadcasting and Recording

In 1981, the U.S. Supreme Court said the right of access to public trials did not include a promise of access for cameras.[69] In *Chandler v. Florida,* the Court recognized that technological advances had decreased (and likely would continue to decrease) the intrusiveness of cameras so they were no longer inherently prejudicial but said individual states could determine whether to permit cameras in courtrooms. The Court reasoned that coverage by print alone sufficiently protected the interests of the media and the public in open trials. The Court expressed concern that electronic media subtly transformed the trial process and influenced its participants in unpredictable ways.

Debate over the costs and benefits of using cameras and other new technologies to cover the courts was still raging a quarter-century later. In 2008, a group of

realWorld Law

Lights, Cameras, Courts?

"Justices' objections to cameras range from the personal (they enjoy their anonymity) to the philosophical (resisting the spotlight sends the message that the Court is above the rough and tumble of politics and the media)," according to Supreme Court watcher Tony Mauro.[1]

But in 2010 a groundswell was forming to increase broadcast of federal courts. The Judiciary Committee of the U.S. Senate urged the U.S. Supreme Court to open its doors and those of lower federal courts to cameras and presented three bills to the full Senate encouraging cameras in the federal courts.[2] At the same time, a New York Times editorial favored "reality TV" in the nation's highest court,[3] and a majority of U.S. voters said televising the Supreme Court would be "good for democracy."[4]

It is unclear, however, that Congress has the power to order the courts to permit camera coverage of the proceedings. The Supreme Court establishes its own policies, and the Judicial Conference determines rules for televising lower federal courts. Few of the sitting justices on the U.S. Supreme Court have publicly supported the idea of cameras inside the Court.[5]

1. Tony Mauro, *Poll Shows Public Support for Cameras at the High Court*, Nat'l Law J., March 9, 2010, *available at* http://www.law.com/jsp/article.jsp?id=1202445941834.
2. Associated Press, *Senate Panel Endorses Televising Supreme Court Proceedings*, May 2, 2010, *available at* http://www.firstamendmentcenter.org/news.aspx?id=22904.
3. Peter Hardin, *Editorial Urges "Reality TV" at Supreme Court*, Mar. 15, 2010, *available at* http://www.gavelgrab.org/?p=8945.
4. Mauro, *supra*, note 1.
5. Associated Press, *On Cameras in Supreme Court, Souter Says, "Over My Dead Body,"* N.Y. Times, Mar. 30, 1996, *available at* http://www.nytimes.com/1996/03/30/us/on-cameras-in-supreme-court-souter-says-over-my-dead-body.html.

prominent judicial experts examined how accelerating news cycles, 24-hour news coverage, citizen blogs and other "new media" were affecting coverage of the courts. U.S. Supreme Court Justice Stephen G. Breyer said increased media coverage could be "helpful" and offered "tremendous potential in getting across the message [about the justice system] that might be oppressed."[70] But some studies have found that media do not fulfill their potential to serve the public. One study in 2002, for example, reported that rather than inform and educate the public, cameras in courts sensationalize, focus selectively and present fleeting, dramatic images of the most accessible portions of trials with little or no context.[71]

In most state courts and federal courts of appeals, judges generally do permit cameras in the courtroom at least some of the time. Camera access to state courts generally is determined at the discretion of the presiding judge, with court rules determining the conditions under which cameras may be allowed. Many states limit the number and location of cameras. Florida courts, however, for years have assumed that access for recording equipment is essential to reporting by television and radio journalists and serves both the courts and the public.

Federal Rule of Criminal Procedure 53 generally prohibits cameras in federal criminal trial courts, and federal policy bans televised civil proceedings. However, the 13 federal circuit courts of appeal each may decide whether to allow

State by State Media Access to Juvenile Offender Identities

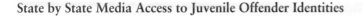

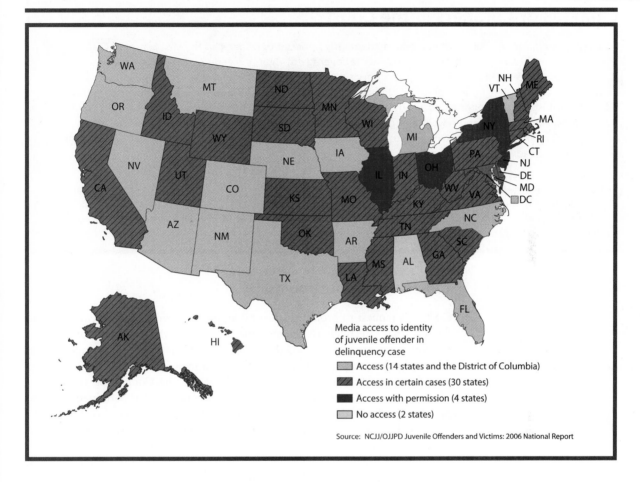

Media access to identity
of juvenile offender in
delinquency case

▨ Access (14 states and the District of Columbia)
▨ Access in certain cases (30 states)
■ Access with permission (4 states)
☐ No access (2 states)

Source: NCJJ/OJJPD Juvenile Offenders and Victims: 2006 National Report

televised or other news media coverage of oral arguments. The circuits vary in their policies, with the Fifth Circuit Court of Appeals forbidding broadcasts and the Second Circuit Court of Appeals allowing cameras during oral arguments that do not involve criminal matters. Congress has considered, but not passed, bills that would give judges in federal courts discretion to permit the photographing, electronic recording, broadcasting or televising of court proceedings.

Despite experience and studies indicating that unobtrusive cameras in courtrooms have only a minimal effect upon jurors, some judges believe that cameras influence the testimony of witnesses, discourage some witnesses from testifying, encourage theatrics in the courtroom and change the attitudes and behavior of jurors and other trial participants. The U.S. Supreme Court is famous for its dislike of cameras. Neither still nor video cameras are permitted in the U.S. Supreme Court.

realWorld Law

Cameras or Coroners in the Court?

As long as one or more sitting justices remain adamantly opposed to cameras in the U.S. Supreme Court, lower court judges feel secure in banning electronic media coverage of their proceedings. Former Justice David Souter is famous for his 1996 statement to Congress opposing cameras in the high court: "The day you see a camera coming into our courtroom, it's going to roll over my dead body."[1] A decade later, after his first term on the Court, Chief Justice John Roberts told a conference of judges that the Supreme Court might never allow cameras into its proceedings. "We don't have oral arguments to show people, the public, how we function," he said. We are "trustees of an extremely valuable institution,. . . [and] we're going to be very careful before we do anything that will have an adverse impact on that."[2]

---

1. Marcia Coyle, *Justices Voice Extralegal Musings*, Nat'l L.J., Apr. 22, 1996, at A16; *see also* Tim O'Brien, *High Court TV*, N.Y. Times, Jan. 6, 1997, at A17.
2. Associated Press, *Chief Justice Says Court Not Interested in Allowing Cameras*, July 16, 2006, available at http://www.first amendmentcenter.org/news.aspx?id=17161.

Cameras and Courtrooms

C-SPAN's request to broadcast the oral arguments before the Supreme Court in the case that effectively determined the outcome of the 2000 U.S. presidential election was denied. In rejecting the request, then-Chief Justice William Rehnquist said the ban on cameras reflected the view of a majority of the Court's nine justices. Immediately after oral arguments, however, the Court took the unprecedented step of releasing an audiotape of the arguments that permitted media to broadcast audio of the hearings the same day they occurred. During its 2010–11 term, the U.S. Supreme Court began releasing audio recordings of the oral arguments for every case heard the previous week on each Friday of the term.

Cameras are allowed in some courtrooms some of the time in all 50 states. Some of this access is long-standing, some is experimental, some is broad and some is extremely limited. Roughly 20 states are extremely permissive when it comes to television cameras in the courtroom. In Florida, for example, a judicially created presumption permits camera coverage of virtually all cases.[72] In Mississippi, the law generally allows cameras that do not disrupt the proceedings. Applying this standard in a 2005 case, the Mississippi Supreme Court overturned a circuit judge's ruling prohibiting television coverage of the sentencing phase of a conspiracy case.

In overturning the ban, Mississippi's highest court noted that exclusion of cameras restricts public access and should be a last resort. The Court wrote:

> The proper standard for restricting press coverage is that there is a "substantial probability" that the accused will be deprived of a fair trial. . . . The decision to restrict press access, whether by closing proceedings or by eliminating the use of the tools of the trade must be supported by specific, on the record findings of fact which show in what manner the coverage will cause a party to lose the right to a fair trial.[73]

In contrast, California has no presumption of camera access to courts. Instead, judges have broad discretion as to whether to allow electronic coverage in their courtrooms.[74] States from Alaska to Virginia limit camera coverage of trials based on the type of case or the ages of the witnesses involved. Judges who permit cameras in the courtroom sometimes limit their number and location, prohibit recording of jurors or especially vulnerable witnesses such as children or require broadcast reporters to pool cameras. Pool reporting may be used in extremely high-profile cases to limit the media swarm in the courtroom.

Some states prohibit some, but not all, camera coverage of trials. Rhode Island, for example, prohibits cameras in criminal trials. In another 15 states, courts are virtually closed to cameras. Because state laws vary widely on their standards for cameras in courtrooms, reporters must be familiar with the details of the laws in the states where they report.

In addition to their variety, state laws on cameras in courtrooms are a moving target. Several state legislatures have formed judicial committees to review the effects of current state laws on access and to recommend modifications if needed. In 2008, a Maryland committee recommended that the state retain its ban on cameras in criminal trials. The committee reported that "the putative benefits of electronic media coverage are illusory, while the adverse impacts on the criminal justice process are real."[75] A decade earlier, New York had allowed its law permitting cameras in the courts to lapse.

Newer Technologies

While the executive and legislative branches of government have run willingly toward new technologies to transform their ways of doing business as usual, the courts have lagged behind. Claims that "social media is the new norm" in courts still struggling to adapt to cameras overstates the slow evolution of U.S. courts.[76] However, new media are making inroads and offering both new opportunities and new challenges to the administration of justice, and a variety of judicial and extra-judicial groups, including journalists, have begun exploring how to leverage the opportunities and minimize the risks of new media in the courts.

In 2010, courts across the country, led by California and Massachusetts, were developing unique strategies to integrate new communication technologies into their administrative offices and courtrooms and beginning to establish a presence on Facebook, Twitter, YouTube and other social media sites as a component of their efforts in public education and outreach. Courts were using blogs, embedded video, image sharing and other multimedia technologies to connect directly with a public whose concepts of access and openness were shifting rapidly within the new media environment. In 2009, a federal district judge allowed a reporter to use Twitter to provide play-by-play coverage of a racketeering trial in Kansas,[77] and another in Massachusetts permitted live Internet streaming coverage of a hearing in an illegal file-sharing case involving the recording industry. Agreeing to a defense request, the judge in Massachusetts said she found nothing in local rules or in "life or logic" to prevent the new form of access in a case that

realWorld Law

Managing New Media in Courts

In response to broad disagreement and growing trends both in favor of and against the use of new media in courts, the Media Law Resource Center in 2010 proposed a model policy for court use of electronic media. The first portion of the policy deals with new technologies in the administrative and public areas of the courts. The second section dealing with new media in courtrooms reads:

1. Inside courtrooms, persons may use an electronic device to silently take notes and/or transmit and receive data communications in the form of text, only, without need for obtaining prior authorization from the presiding judge or judicial officer.

2. A judge or other judicial officer may prohibit or further restrict use of electronic devices if they interfere with the administration of justice, pose any threat to safety or security, or compromise the integrity of the proceeding.

3. It should be anticipated that reporters, bloggers and other observers seated in the courtroom may use electronic devices to prepare and post online news accounts and commentary during the proceedings. Absent any of the circumstances identified above in paragraph [2], such use is presumptively permitted.[1]

---

1. Media Law Resource Center, Newsgathering Committee Defense Counsel Section (2010) *available at* http://www.medialaw .org/Content/NavigationMenu/Member_Resources/Litigation_Resources/Litigation_Resources.htm.

had special implications in this digital age, particularly for young people who rely heavily on the Internet for their news. The hearing was part of a copyright infringement suit brought by the Recording Industry Association of America against Joel Tenenbaum, a Boston University student, who faced a $1 million penalty if convicted of intentionally illegally downloading and sharing copyrighted songs over the Web service KaZaA.[78] When the U.S. Court of Appeals for the First Circuit heard Tenenbaum's appeal of a jury verdict of $675,000 copyright infringement on 30 songs, that court refused to allow the appeal to be webcast.[79] Tenenbaum's fine later was reduced to $67,500.[80]

At the same time, the "oversharing" of personal information on social networks had propelled Facebook to become a leading source of online evidence in divorce cases,[81] and courts were struggling to determine the boundaries of appropriate use of new media in the courts. In 2009, responding to worries that texting and "tweets" threatened the sanctity of the judicial process, the Michigan Supreme Court became the first to ban all electronic communication by jurors during trials, and a number of courts declared mistrials because of juror use of new media during trial.[82] By 2010, such bans were spreading across the country.[83]

WHILE THE SUPREME COURT HAS RULED THAT CAMERAS are not inherently prejudicial to fair trials, judges generally have discretion to determine whether, when and how cameras and other electronic technologies are permitted to cover court proceedings. Electronic access to courts varies widely based on distinct court rules and policies established by the federal and state judiciaries. Most courts allow some electronic coverage during some of their proceedings, but federal trial courts generally are closed to cameras. Judges, attorneys and scholars continue to debate the costs and benefits of real-time coverage of trials, with some jurisdictions expanding experiments with cameras and Web coverage and others moving away from electronic access. ■

Bench-Bar-Press Guidelines

In the wake of *Sheppard v. Maxwell,* starting in the early 1960s, many state media groups, bar associations and members of the judiciary met together to craft cooperative agreements to provide guidance to reporters covering the courts. The goals of these groups varied, but in general they aimed at limiting the prejudicial impact of media coverage of the courts by restricting both the content and the tone of media coverage of upcoming and ongoing trials. The guidelines represent an attempt at balancing the sometimes competing interests of the media and the courts by recognizing the needs of both privacy and openness, robust debate and solemn deliberation. Some of these agreements include voluntary adjudication boards that review media practices and issue statements of disapproval when media transgress appropriate coverage rules.

By 1980, some courts tried to impose the voluntary bench-bar-press guidelines designed to balance fair trial and free press principles as enforceable contracts on media practice. In Washington, for example, one state court excluded the press from a suppression hearing.[84] The court ruled that pretrial publication of incriminating ballistics information violated the guidelines and justified exclusion of reporters. The media had always considered the guidelines completely voluntary and had adhered to them strictly as a matter of ethics.

Points of Law

What Is Fair Coverage of Criminal Trials?

Agreements between media and the judiciary—as well as independent media standards of professional and ethical performance—provide guidelines for fair reporting on ongoing criminal proceedings. Many of the guidelines say that without some overwhelming justification to do otherwise, media coverage should not include any of the following:

- The existence of a confession
- The content of a confession
- Statements or opinions of guilt or innocence
- The results of lab tests
- Statements or opinions on witness credibility
- Statements or opinions on the credibility of the evidence or the investigative process or personnel, and
- Other information or statements reasonably likely to affect the trial verdict.

Another trial judge made press adherence to the guidelines a necessary condition for media to attend a pretrial hearing, even though the general public was admitted without limitation. The Washington Supreme Court upheld this procedure,[85] and the U.S. Supreme Court denied review. However, the U.S. Supreme Court has never adopted the position of the Washington state court: that the guidelines are legally binding on media. Although Justice Harry Blackmun implicitly accepted the guidelines endorsed by Nebraska's bar-press guidelines when he granted a temporary injunction in the case of *Nebraska Press Association v. Stuart,* the full Court said decisions about appropriate news content were the domain of editors, not judges. While that remains the law today, some media organizations are reluctant to officially endorse bench-bar-press agreements for fear the courts may subsequently use the guidelines to punish press practices.

SUMMARY

MANY STATES HAVE ADOPTED VOLUNTARY bench-bar-press guidelines to delimit the appropriate bounds of media coverage of courts and the proper conduct of trial participants in interactions with the media. Some media organizations choose not to endorse the guidelines out of fear that courts will attempt to enforce them as binding contracts, limiting their editorial discretion in covering judicial proceedings. ∎

Access to Court Records

The public and the media have a right to access court records that is grounded in common law, the U.S. and state constitutions and numerous public records laws. This right is not unlimited; it must be balanced against competing interests within the judicial system as well as external interests, such as national security, privacy and trade secrets. Court rules that vary by jurisdiction also shape the specific character of access to records.

Constitutional and Statutory Access

The Supreme Court made clear in 1978 that the common law right of access to court records is not unlimited and must be balanced against other competing rights, such as the right to privacy. The decision stemmed from the criminal trial of some of the people involved in the Watergate conspiracy in which tape recordings of former President Richard Nixon were used as evidence. A federal law establishes procedures to retain and provide public access to presidential records of historic interest, including the Nixon tapes. Finding that public rebroadcast of the tapes might prejudice the appeals of the defendants, the district court denied media requests to make copies of the tapes. In *Nixon v. Warner Communications,* the court of appeals reversed, but the U.S. Supreme Court held that courts are not required to release all records in their custody, particularly when—as in this case—the records are available through alternative means.[86] In addition, the Court rejected the idea that the press had a First Amendment right to inspect and copy the tapes, holding instead that the media have no rights of access superior to those of the general public.[87]

At present, some 40 percent of state open records laws (see Chapter 8 for more information about state access laws) apply to court and judicial records, at least to some extent. The Indiana Open Records Law, for example, covers all court records unless there is a specific exemption or a protective order to constrain their release.[88] The Kansas Open Records Act also applies to courts but explicitly excludes judges from its definition of "public agency."[89] Other states generally provide more limited rights of access. In Washington, state courts have interpreted the broad provisions of the Public Disclosure Act to exclude the courts.[90]

The Ohio State Supreme Court ruled in 2004 that neither the constitutional right to open courts nor the state's open records law prevented a judge from sealing the entire court record five weeks after the conclusion of a criminal trial in which the defendant was acquitted of all charges.[91] The Court found that "limit[ing] the life of a particular record" did not harm the public's right to know about criminal proceedings because it did not diminish the ability of the press or the public to attend or report on the trial.

In contrast, a 2007 ruling from the Louisiana Supreme Court struck down a judge's order to seal the entire record of a divorce proceeding. The Court said the blanket order sealing the record violated the state constitution's strong presumption in favor of open public access to court proceedings.[92]

State open records laws and the federal Freedom of Information Act (also discussed in Chapter 8) recognize the strong public interest in information about law enforcement investigations of crime and criminal prosecutions. These laws also recognize, however, that law enforcement would be rendered ineffectual unless some investigative details remain secret. Thus, while most states require that the public be given access to arrest reports, jail logs and general information about crimes, more detailed information about pending investigations generally may be withheld. In addition, the federal and more than half of the state laws do not apply to court records.

Court Dockets

For the past decade, growing concerns over global terrorism have produced new issues and strategies for prosecuting criminal conspirators and terrorists while protecting the secrecy of national counter-terrorism practices and personnel. Virtually all of the actions of the Foreign Intelligence Surveillance Court are kept secret, for example. But within hours of his inauguration, President Barack Obama signed an executive order that promised to reduce the secrecy surrounding the apprehension, detention and prosecution of accused terrorists.[93] Some observers argue that he has failed to make good on this promise.

Particularly since Sept. 11, 2001, courts across the United States have cited national security and other concerns and taken cases off the docket or "super-sealed" them to remove the proceedings from the public eye. Super-sealed cases are never listed on the public dockets, or schedules, of cases appearing in the courts. In comparison, sealed cases generally appear in court records but are referenced only by docket numbers. Because super-sealed cases never appear in the filing systems of the courts, the public—and the media—have virtually no way to learn that the cases exist as a necessary prerequisite to challenging their secrecy. Some observers fear that the use of super-sealed and secret dockets is spreading.

In Oklahoma, the Tulsa World newspaper conducted an extensive search and reported that judges sealed all or part of more than 2,300 court cases in Oklahoma between 2003 and 2007, including divorce documents, wrongful death settlements, name changes and probate cases involving the deceased person's will.[94] Mark Thomas, executive vice president of the Oklahoma Press Association, expressed dismay. He said: "It gives the appearance that justice is for sale in Oklahoma, like it was 50 years ago. On occasion, there is a valid reason to seal a court record, but it should be an extreme rarity. If the public pays for our court system, then we ought to know who it's being used for. If you want privacy, settle your affairs in private."

In 2008, the Court of Appeals for the Third Circuit reviewed a motion to unseal a case that raised neither state secrets nor national security issues and refused to open the sealed docket or files in the underlying abortion case.[95] In *Doe v. C.A.R.S. Protection Plus, Inc.*, a woman suing anonymously claimed she was wrongfully fired for ending her pregnancy. The case had been super-sealed, and it first emerged into public view when the Third Circuit reversed the lower court's dismissal of the case but upheld the court's discretion to seal the entire case file and docket. The court of appeals said, "The issue of the propriety of the continued sealing of the case . . . is an important one,"[96] but it rejected a motion from media attorneys to unseal the docket and files.[97] The Supreme Court declined to review the ruling of the Third Circuit.

A recent study by the Federal Judicial Center cited a lack of judicial standards as the foundation for wide disparities in court practices of sealing cases.[98] The study found that despite requirements that access restrictions be narrowly tailored to meet a compelling interest, few courts provided a public record of evidence justifying closure. Public access is further jeopardized by failure of some courts to include sealed cases in their electronic case management systems, making the cases effectively invisible to the public and preventing public challenges to closure.

State Secrets

A 2008 report on government secrecy suggests that the executive branch of government is increasingly using its power to declare "state secrets" to thwart open judicial proceedings.[99] In 1953, the Supreme Court gave the executive branch the power to keep secret—with little judicial review—information that it said would present a "reasonable danger" to national security.[100] According to the organization Open the Government, "The trend is toward the government claiming this privilege earlier in civil litigation, to block discovery. The end result is often the complete dismissal of cases."

In 2010, a narrow majority of the U.S. Court of Appeals for the Ninth Circuit upheld the Obama administration's claim that details of the Bush administration's rendition program should be protected as "state secrets" and therefore kept outside the authority of the courts.[101] The case, which sought criminal punishment of the Boeing subsidiary that removed alleged terrorists from the country, was initiated by rendition/torture victim Binyam Mohamed. Media observers criticized the court's ruling for "hand[ing] a major victory to the Obama administration in its effort to advance a sweeping view of executive secrecy power."[102]

In one non-terrorism-related case brought before the U.S. Court of Appeals for the D.C. Circuit, however, the court reinstated a lawsuit that had been dismissed after the government had claimed state secrets privilege.[103] The lawsuit was filed in 1994 by former Drug Enforcement Administration official Richard Horn, who claimed the State Department and the CIA had illegally wiretapped his communications while he was overseas. In 2000, the government invoked its state secrets privilege, and the federal district court dismissed the case in 2004. In reversing the dismissal, the circuit court of appeals did not challenge the government's use of the state secrets privilege. Nonetheless, it said sufficient unprivileged evidence existed on the record to allow the case to proceed.

Court Access Rules

In most states, court rules dictate the handling and release of court records. Access to records of the courts raises concerns about invasion of privacy and fair trial because many court files contain information litigants are required to disclose under filing requirements or rules of discovery (such as personal financial information), and some of this information will not become public until and unless it is presented in the open courtroom. To protect these interests, states generally limit the release of information from the courts and impose penalties on state employees who violate these rules.

During the past decade, many courts around the country have reviewed and upgraded their records access rules and implemented new forms of electronic access. Two court organizations—the Conference of Chief Justices and the Conference of State Court Administrators—led a nationwide group examining access issues and providing guidelines to facilitate policies that would assure public access to court records while protecting personal privacy, among other interests.[104] In addition to providing an accounting of existing access policies and practices, the report and its follow-up recommendations called for generous, remote electronic access to civil case files as well as electronic access to criminal case files on the same terms as is provided in the courthouse.[105]

While spawning nationwide reconsideration of judicial rules for access to court records, the committee's report also "touched a nerve in the field of judicial administration."[106] Some observers suggested that the resulting examination and transformation of court access policies paralleled the revolution in public access to government that occurred during the 1970s and resulted in an explosion of freedom of information laws (see Chapter 8). To date, however, state and federal court systems have responded to the guidelines in a variety of ways unique to their individual cultures, contexts and histories. It is too soon to say whether this process will lead to new openness in the courts or instead will reinvigorate efforts to diminish public access in favor of such competing concerns as personal privacy.

While state courts control many aspects of access to their records, the Supreme Court has ruled that states may not punish media for publishing legally obtained truthful information obtained from court files.[107] In *Florida Star v. B.J.F.*, the Supreme Court said states may not impose penalties on the press for the publication of legally obtained truthful information unless they demonstrate that the penalty is "narrowly tailored to a state interest of the highest order."[108] (See Chapter 6 for a discussion of this case.)

In general, decisions to seal court records are subject to the same constitutional limits as court closure, are strongly disfavored under the First Amendment and must pass the stringent *Press-Enterprise* test.

Electronic Access to Court Records

Although court clerks, judges and public officials generally have little difficulty allowing a citizen or reporter to see a divorce file or murder case at the courthouse, some records keepers are very concerned about what will happen if and when millions of people view the same records online from the comfort of their homes.

Electronic access to public records—either online or as compiled databases used by journalists or commercial information providers—has prompted fears and challenges that alter the amount of access in different states or courts. As mentioned earlier in this chapter, access to court records in many states is not dictated by the legislature. Instead, state courts generally develop their own rules and policies for handling court information.

In many jurisdictions, scanned court documents are now available online or on a CD, but other jurisdictions are resisting digitization of records due to concerns about personal privacy, identity theft and nosy neighbors. In 2008, the New Jersey Supreme Court was considering allowing Internet access to most records that had previously been available only at the courthouse. A two-year study of the judicial system in New Jersey prompted the revision when it concluded that increased judicial transparency would enhance public confidence in the courts. Around the same time, by contrast, the Oklahoma Supreme Court reversed that state's online records policy and pulled that state's court records off the Internet, reasoning that access via hard copies in courthouse files struck a better balance between individual privacy rights and public access.

Access advocates and journalists who argue the benefits of electronic access to court records must grapple with studies suggesting that media fail to deliver on their promises to the public. One study, for example, found that the electronic media sensationalize rather than educate, fail to provide adequate context in reporting on courtroom proceedings and generally seek to entertain rather than inform.[109] Some privacy advocates also argue that online access increases the likelihood that identity thieves will find Social Security numbers in court records. They point out that Internet distribution of court records also propels worldwide dissemination of false allegations made in divorce and civil disputes.[110]

Such concerns do not represent the first time in history that new technology has led to fears of privacy invasion and calls for restricted access to information. The emergence of newspaper photography and printing technology led to the famous 1890 Harvard Law Review article by Louis Brandeis and Samuel Warren in which they argued that people have a "right to be let alone."[111] With the advent of the Internet more than 100 years later, a variety of models have begun to emerge to balance privacy and online access to court documents.

A Minnesota court committee recommended recently that some information, such as Social Security numbers, financial account numbers and street addresses of litigants, be deleted from court records before they are posted online.[112] The National Center for State Courts and the Justice Management Institute earlier had advocated that online records be presumptively open. The state committee, however, recommended that some information accessible in paper records, such as health data or identification of people involved in some family law cases, not be put online.[113]

Courts sometimes use differential fee systems to discourage nefarious online access to court records. For example, in some jurisdictions attorneys, media and other bulk users must subscribe to online court access for hundreds or thousands of dollars a year. Such subscriptions generally are not available to non-bulk users, and the high fees designed to prevent identity thieves from fishing through online records also inhibit the access of law-abiding citizens with legitimate needs for information.

Courts also are trying to decide how best to handle requests for databases of aggregated information that can help journalists examine societal trends. For example, some journalists have combined databases of court conviction records with databases of school bus drivers, finding drivers who have extensive drunken driving records. Yet government agencies and the courts have been reluctant to provide aggregated information to the public, fearful of people piecing together personal information. In 1989, the Supreme Court ruled in *Department of Justice v. Reporters Committee for Freedom of the Press* that federal law did not allow journalists to have access to an FBI electronic compilation of rap sheets.[114] The reporter intended to piece together the background of a suspected mobster, but the Court said access to the compiled information represented an unacceptable threat to individual privacy.

The *Reporters Committee* case involved the federal Freedom of Information Act, not court rules, but courts have applied similar reasoning to electronic access. For example, a court rule approved in Washington in 2004 requires people who request criminal conviction data to sign a contract agreeing to allow court officials to examine the person's computer that houses the data—even in the newsroom—to make sure the information is being used responsibly.[115] The Minnesota court records committee suggests that large fees be charged for court databases in order to make money. Such revenue comes at the expense of providing access only to those wealthy groups that can afford it.

With the continuing development of the Internet, electronic access to court records is likely to evolve. The courts and legislatures will continue their efforts to achieve the correct balance between personal privacy and public access.

SUMMARY

NEARLY 35 YEARS AGO, THE U.S. SUPREME COURT recognized a common law right of public access to court records. This right is not unlimited, and it is shaped by the specific access rules established in each court jurisdiction. State constitutions and public records laws vary widely on whether and how they treat public access to court records. The restrictions that apply to some information held in courthouse files may be overcome when records are presented in an open courtroom. Once presented in court, most records are presumptively open. However, they may not remain open permanently. Some jurisdictions are enhancing public access by making court records available online, but court clerks and others are concerned that such easy access may increase identity theft, invasion of privacy and other possible crimes.

Courts generally must exhaust all reasonable alternatives before sealing presumptively open court records. National security concerns and state secrets privilege are being used to close court records, including any mention of some cases in progress. The U.S. Supreme Court has said media cannot be punished for accurately publishing information legally obtained from court records even when state law prohibits dissemination of the information. However, the media have no extraordinary right of access to court records that exceeds the right of the public. ∎

Cases for Study

Thinking About It

The two case excerpts that follow examine the constitutional right of public—and media—access to criminal trials as well as the limits to press freedoms within the confines of the courtroom. The two cases exemplify the threats that exist to the U.S. justice system from media running amok and from closed proceedings that eliminate public checks and balances on the courts. When reading these excerpts, keep these questions in mind:

- What are the assumptions and evidence used by the Supreme Court in assessing the prejudicial impact of media coverage?

- In *Sheppard v. Maxwell,* does the Court distinguish between the media and trial participants when it establishes judicial remedies to threats to fair trials? If so, why?

- What are the foundations the Court draws upon in *Richmond Newspapers v. Virginia* to conclude that the public has a right of access to criminal trials?

- To what extent do these two cases provide a judicial foundation for a right of electronic access to trials and court records?

Sheppard v. Maxwell
SUPREME COURT OF THE UNITED STATES
384 U.S. 333 (1966)

JUSTICE TOM CLARK delivered the Court's opinion:

This federal habeas corpus application involves the question whether Sheppard was deprived of a fair trial in his state conviction for the second-degree murder of his wife because of the trial judge's failure to protect Sheppard sufficiently from the massive, pervasive and prejudicial publicity that attended his prosecution. The United States District Court held that he was not afforded a fair trial. . . . The Court of Appeals for the Sixth Circuit reversed. . . . We granted certiorari [and] have concluded that Sheppard did not receive a fair trial consistent with the Due Process Clause of the Fourteenth Amendment and, therefore, reverse the judgment.

Marilyn Sheppard, petitioner's pregnant wife, was bludgeoned to death in the upstairs bedroom of their lakeshore home in Bay Village, Ohio, a suburb of Cleveland. . . .

From the outset officials focused suspicion on Sheppard. After a search of the house and premises on the morning of the tragedy, Dr. Gerber, the Coroner, is reported—and it is undenied—to have told his men, "Well, it is evident the doctor did this, so let's go get the confession out of him." He proceeded to interrogate and examine Sheppard while the latter was under sedation in his hospital room. On the same occasion, the Coroner was given the clothes Sheppard wore at the time of the tragedy together with the personal items in them. Later that afternoon Chief

Eaton and two Cleveland police officers interrogated Sheppard at some length, confronting him with evidence and demanding explanations. Asked by Officer Shotke to take a lie detector test, Sheppard said he would if it were reliable. Shotke replied that it was "infallible" and "you might as well tell us all about it now." At the end of the interrogation, Shotke told Sheppard: "I think you killed your wife." Still later in the same afternoon, a physician sent by the Coroner was permitted to make a detailed examination of Sheppard. Until the Coroner's inquest on July 22, at which time he was subpoenaed, Sheppard made himself available for frequent and extended questioning without the presence of an attorney.

On July 7, the day of Marilyn Sheppard's funeral, a newspaper story appeared in which Assistant County Attorney Mahon—later the chief prosecutor of Sheppard—sharply criticized the refusal of the Sheppard family to permit his immediate questioning. From there on headline stories repeatedly stressed Sheppard's lack of cooperation with the police and other officials. Under the headline "Testify Now In Death, Bay Doctor Is Ordered," one story described a visit by Coroner Gerber and four police officers to the hospital on July 8. When Sheppard insisted that his lawyer be present, the Coroner wrote out a subpoena and served it on him. Sheppard then agreed to submit to questioning without counsel and the subpoena was torn up. The officers questioned him for several hours. On July 9, Sheppard, at the request of the Coroner, re-enacted the tragedy at his home before the Coroner, police officers, and a group of newsmen, who apparently were invited by the Coroner. The home was locked so that Sheppard was obliged to wait outside until the Coroner arrived. Sheppard's performance was reported in detail by the news media along with photographs.

The newspapers also played up Sheppard's refusal to take a lie detector test and "the protective ring" thrown up by his family. Front-page newspaper headlines announced on the same day that "Doctor Balks At Lie Test; Retells Story." A column opposite that story contained an "exclusive" interview with Sheppard headlined: "'Loved My Wife, She Loved Me,' Sheppard Tells News Reporter." The next day,

another headline story disclosed that Sheppard had "again late yesterday refused to take a lie detector test" and quoted an Assistant County Attorney as saying that "at the end of a nine hour questioning of Dr. Sheppard, I felt he was now ruling [a test] out completely." But subsequent newspaper articles reported that the Coroner was still pushing Sheppard for a lie detector test. More stories appeared when Sheppard would not allow authorities to inject him with "truth serum."

On the 20th, the "editorial artillery" opened fire with a front-page charge that somebody is "getting away with murder." The editorial attributed the ineptness of the investigation to "friendships, relationships, hired lawyers, a husband who ought to have been subjected instantly to the same third-degree to which any other person under similar circumstances is subjected. . . ." The following day, July 21, another page-one editorial was headed: "Why No Inquest? Do It Now, Dr. Gerber." The Coroner called an inquest the same day and subpoenaed Sheppard. It was staged the next day in a school gymnasium; the Coroner presided with the County Prosecutor as his advisor and two detectives as bailiffs. In the front of the room was a long table occupied by reporters, television and radio personnel, and broadcasting equipment. The hearing was broadcast with live microphones placed at the Coroner's seat and the witness stand. A swarm of reporters and photographers attended. Sheppard was brought into the room by police who searched him in full view of several hundred spectators. Sheppard's counsel were present during the three-day inquest but were not permitted to participate. When Sheppard's chief counsel attempted to place some documents in the record, he was forcibly ejected from the room by the Coroner, who received cheers, hugs, and kisses from ladies in the audience. Sheppard was questioned for five and one-half hours about his actions on the night of the murder, his married life, and a love affair with Susan Hayes. At the end of the hearing the Coroner announced that he "could" order Sheppard held for the grand jury, but did not do so.

Throughout this period the newspapers emphasized evidence that tended to incriminate Sheppard and pointed out discrepancies in his statements to authorities. At the same time, Sheppard made many public statements to the press and wrote feature articles asserting his innocence. During the inquest on July 26, a headline in large type stated: "Kerr [Captain of the Cleveland Police] Urges Sheppard's Arrest." In the story, Detective McArthur "disclosed that scientific tests at the Sheppard home have definitely established that the killer washed off a trail of blood from the murder bedroom to the downstairs section," a circumstance casting doubt on Sheppard's accounts of the murder. No such evidence was produced at trial. The newspapers also delved into Sheppard's personal life. Articles stressed his extramarital love affairs as a motive for the crime. The newspapers portrayed Sheppard as a Lothario, fully explored his relationship with Susan Hayes, and named a number of other women who were allegedly involved with him. The testimony at trial never showed that Sheppard had any illicit relationships besides the one with Susan Hayes.

On July 28, an editorial entitled "Why Don't Police Quiz Top Suspect" demanded that Sheppard be taken to police headquarters. It described him in the following language: "Now proved under oath to be a liar, still free to go about his business, shielded by his family, protected by a smart lawyer who has made monkeys of the police and authorities, carrying a gun part of the time, left free to do whatever he pleases. . . ."

A front-page editorial on July 30 asked: "Why Isn't Sam Sheppard in Jail?" It was later titled "Quit Stalling—Bring Him In." After calling Sheppard "the most unusual murder suspect ever seen around these parts," the article said that "except for some superficial questioning during Coroner Sam Gerber's inquest, he has been scot-free of any official grilling. . . ." It asserted that he was "surrounded by an iron curtain of protection [and] concealment."

That night at 10 o'clock, Sheppard was arrested at his father's home on a charge of murder. He was taken to the Bay Village City Hall, where hundreds of people, newscasters, photographers and reporters were awaiting his arrival. He was immediately arraigned—having been denied a temporary delay to secure the presence of counsel—and bound over to the grand jury.

The publicity then grew in intensity until his indictment on August 17. Typical of the coverage during this period is a front-page interview entitled: "DR. SAM: 'I Wish There Was Something I Could Get Off My Chest—but There Isn't.'" Unfavorable publicity included items such as a cartoon of the body of a sphinx with Sheppard's head and the legend below: "'I Will Do Everything In My Power to Help Solve This Terrible Murder.'—Dr. Sam Sheppard." Headlines announced, *inter alia,* that: "Doctor Evidence is Ready for Jury," "Corrigan Tactics Stall Quizzing," "Sheppard 'Gay Set' Is Revealed By Houk," "Blood Is Found In Garage," "New Murder Evidence Is Found, Police Claim," "Dr. Sam Faces Quiz At Jail On Marilyn's Fear Of Him." On August 18, an article appeared under the headline "Dr. Sam Writes His Own Story." And reproduced across the entire front page was a portion of the typed statement signed by Sheppard: "I am not guilty of the murder of my wife, Marilyn. How could I, who have been trained to help people and devoted my life to saving life, commit such a terrible and revolting crime?"

We do not detail the coverage further. There are five volumes filled with similar clippings from each of the three Cleveland newspapers covering the period from the murder until Sheppard's conviction in December 1954. The record includes no excerpts from newscasts on radio and television, but, since space was reserved in the courtroom for these media, we assume that their coverage was equally large.

With this background the case came on for trial two weeks before the November general election at which the chief prosecutor was a candidate for common pleas judge and the trial judge, Judge Blythin, was a candidate to succeed himself. Twenty-five days before the case was set, 75 veniremen were called as prospective jurors. All three Cleveland newspapers published the names and addresses of the veniremen. As a consequence, anonymous letters and telephone calls, as well as calls from friends, regarding the impending prosecution were received by all of the prospective jurors. . . .

The courtroom in which the trial was held measured 26 by 48 feet. A long temporary table was set up inside the bar, in back of the single counsel table. It ran the width of the courtroom, parallel to the bar railing, with one end less than three feet from the jury box. Approximately 20 representatives of newspapers and wire services were assigned seats at this table by the court. Behind the bar railing there were four rows of benches. These seats were likewise assigned by the court for the entire trial. The first row was occupied by representatives of television and radio stations, and the second and third rows by reporters from out-of-town newspapers and magazines. One side of the last row, which accommodated 14 people, was assigned to Sheppard's family, and the other to Marilyn's. The public was permitted to fill vacancies in this row on special passes only. Representatives of the news media also used all the rooms on the courtroom floor, including the room where cases were ordinarily called and assigned for trial. Private telephone lines and telegraphic equipment were installed in these rooms so that reports from the trial could be speeded to the papers. Station WSRS was permitted to set up broadcasting facilities on the third floor of the courthouse next door to the jury room, where the jury rested during recesses in the trial and deliberated. Newscasts were made from this room throughout the trial, and while the jury reached its verdict.

On the sidewalk and steps in front of the courthouse, television and newsreel cameras were occasionally used to take motion pictures of the participants in the trial, including the jury and the judge. Indeed, one television broadcast carried a staged interview of the judge as he entered the courthouse. In the corridors outside the courtroom, there was a host of photographers and television personnel with flash cameras, portable lights and motion picture cameras. This group photographed the prospective jurors during selection of the jury. After the trial opened, the witnesses, counsel, and jurors were photographed and televised whenever they entered or left the courtroom. Sheppard was brought to the courtroom about 10 minutes before each session began; he was surrounded by reporters and extensively photographed for the newspapers and television. A rule of court prohibited picture-taking in the courtroom during the actual sessions of the court, but no restraints were put on photographers during recesses, which were taken once each morning and afternoon, with a longer period for lunch.

All of these arrangements with the news media and their massive coverage of the trial continued during the entire nine weeks of the trial. The courtroom remained crowded to capacity with representatives of news media. Their movement in and out of the courtroom often caused so much confusion that, despite the loud-speaker system installed in the courtroom, it was difficult for the witnesses and counsel to be heard. Furthermore, the reporters clustered within the bar of the small courtroom made confidential talk among Sheppard and his counsel almost impossible during the proceedings. . . .

The daily record of the proceedings was made available to the newspapers, and the testimony of each witness was printed verbatim in the local editions, along with objections of counsel, and rulings by the judge. Pictures of Sheppard, the judge, counsel, pertinent witnesses, and the jury often accompanied the daily newspaper and television accounts. At times the newspapers published photographs of exhibits introduced at the trial, and the rooms of Sheppard's house were featured along with relevant testimony.

The jurors themselves were constantly exposed to the news media. Every juror, except one, testified at *voir dire* to reading about the case in the Cleveland papers or to having heard broadcasts about it. Seven of the 12 jurors who rendered the verdict had one or more Cleveland papers delivered in their home; the remaining jurors were not interrogated on the point. Nor were there questions as to radios or television sets in the jurors' homes, but we must assume that most of them owned such conveniences. . . .

. . . While the intense publicity continued unabated, it is sufficient to relate only the more flagrant episodes:

On October 9, 1954, nine days before the case went to trial, an editorial in one of the newspapers criticized defense counsel's random poll of people on the streets as to their opinion of Sheppard's guilt or innocence in an effort to use the resulting statistics to show the necessity for change of venue. The article said the survey "smacks of mass jury tampering," . . . The article was called to the attention of the court but no action was taken.

On the second day of *voir dire* examination, a debate was staged and broadcast live over WHK radio. The participants, newspaper reporters, accused Sheppard's counsel of throwing roadblocks in the way of the prosecution and asserted that Sheppard conceded his guilt by hiring a prominent criminal lawyer. Sheppard's counsel objected to this broadcast and requested a continuance, but the judge denied the motion. . . .

On November 19, a Cleveland police officer gave testimony that tended to contradict details in the written statement Sheppard made to the Cleveland police. Two days later, in a broadcast heard over Station WHK in Cleveland, Robert Considine likened Sheppard to a perjurer and compared the episode to Alger Hiss' confrontation with Whittaker Chambers. Though defense counsel asked the judge to question the jury to ascertain how many heard the broadcast, the court refused to do so. The judge also overruled the motion for continuance based on the same ground, saying:

"Well, I don't know, we can't stop people, in any event, listening to it. It is a matter of free speech, and the court can't control everybody. . . . We are not going to harass the jury every morning. . . . It is getting to the point where if we do it every morning, we are suspecting the jury. I have confidence in this jury. . . ."

On November 24, a story appeared under an eight-column headline: "Sam Called A 'Jekyll-Hyde' By Marilyn, Cousin To Testify." It related that Marilyn had recently told friends that Sheppard was a "Dr. Jekyll and Mr. Hyde" character. No such testimony was ever produced at the trial. . . . Defense counsel made motions for change of venue, continuance and mistrial, but they were denied. No action was taken by the court.

When the trial was in its seventh week, Walter Winchell broadcast over WXEL television and WJW radio that Carole Beasley, who was under arrest in New York City for robbery, had stated that, as Sheppard's mistress, she had borne him a child. The defense asked that the jury be queried on the broadcast. Two jurors admitted in open court that they had heard it. The judge asked each: "Would that have any effect upon your judgment?" Both replied, "No." This was accepted by the judge as sufficient; he merely asked the jury to "pay no attention whatever to that type of scavenging. . . . Let's confine ourselves to this courtroom, if you please." . . .

On December 9, while Sheppard was on the witness stand, he testified that he had been mistreated by Cleveland detectives after his arrest. Although he was not at the trial, Captain Kerr of the Homicide Bureau issued a press statement denying Sheppard's allegations which appeared under the headline: "'Bare-faced Liar,' Kerr Says of Sam." Captain Kerr never appeared as a witness at the trial. . . .

. . . After the verdict, defense counsel ascertained that the jurors had been allowed to make telephone calls to their homes every day while they were sequestered at the hotel. . . . By a subsequent motion, defense counsel urged that this ground alone warranted a new trial, but the motion was overruled and no evidence was taken on the question.

The principle that justice cannot survive behind walls of silence has long been reflected in the "Anglo-American distrust for secret trials." A responsible press has always been regarded as the handmaiden of effective judicial administration, especially in the criminal field. . . . The press does not simply publish information about trials, but guards against the miscarriage of justice by subjecting the police, prosecutors, and judicial processes to extensive public scrutiny and criticism. This Court has, therefore, been unwilling to place any direct limitations on the freedom traditionally exercised by the news media for "[w]hat transpires in the court room is public property." . . . And where there was "no threat or menace to the integrity of the trial," we have consistently required that the press have a free hand, even though we sometimes deplored its sensationalism.

But the Court has also pointed out that "legal trials are not like elections, to be won through the use of the meeting-hall, the radio, and the newspaper." And the Court has insisted that no one be punished for a crime without "a charge fairly made and fairly tried in a public tribunal free of prejudice, passion, excitement, and tyrannical power." "Freedom of discussion should be given the widest range compatible with the essential requirement of the fair and orderly administration of justice." But it must not be allowed to divert the trial from the "very purpose of a court system . . . to adjudicate controversies, both criminal and civil, in the calmness and solemnity of the courtroom according to legal procedures." Among these "legal procedures" is the requirement that the jury's verdict be based on evidence received in open court, not from outside sources. Thus, we set aside a federal conviction where the jurors were exposed "through news accounts" to information that was not admitted at trial. . . . At the same time, we did not consider dispositive the statement of each juror "that he would not be influenced by the news articles, that he could decide the case only on the evidence of record, and that he felt no prejudice against petitioner as a result of the articles." Likewise, even though each juror indicated that he could render an impartial verdict despite exposure to prejudicial newspaper articles, we set aside the conviction holding: "With his life at stake, it is not requiring too much that petitioner be tried in an atmosphere undisturbed by so huge a wave of public passion. . . ."

The undeviating rule of this Court was expressed by Mr. Justice Holmes over half a century ago . . . : "The theory of our system is that the conclusions to be reached in a case will be induced only by evidence and argument in open court, and not by any outside influence, whether of private talk or public print." Moreover, "the burden of showing essential unfairness . . . as a demonstrable reality," need not be undertaken when television has exposed the community "repeatedly and in depth to the spectacle of [the accused] personally confessing in detail to the crimes with which he was later to be charged." . . .

Only last Term we set aside a conviction despite the absence of any showing of prejudice. We said there: "It is true that in most cases involving claims of due process deprivations, we require a showing of identifiable prejudice to the accused. Nevertheless, at times a procedure employed by the State involves such a probability that prejudice will result that it is deemed inherently lacking in due process." . . .

It is clear that the totality of circumstances in this case also warrants such an approach. . . . Sheppard was not granted a change of venue to a locale away from where the publicity originated; nor was his jury sequestered. . . . [T]he Sheppard jurors were subjected to newspaper, radio, and television coverage of the trial while not taking part in the proceedings. They were allowed to go their separate ways outside of the courtroom, without adequate directions not to read or listen to anything concerning the case. The judge's "admonitions" at the beginning of the trial are representative:

"I would suggest to you and caution you that you do not read any newspapers during the progress of this trial, that you do not listen to radio comments nor watch or listen to television comments, insofar as this case is concerned. You will feel very much better as the trial proceeds. . . . I am sure that we shall all feel very much better if we do not indulge in any newspaper reading or listening to any comments whatever about the matter while the case is in progress. After it is all over, you can read it all to your heart's content. . . ."

At intervals during the trial, the judge simply repeated his "suggestions" and "requests" that the jurors not expose themselves to comment upon the case. Moreover, the jurors were thrust into the role of celebrities by the judge's failure to insulate them from reporters and photographers. . . . For months, the virulent publicity about Sheppard and the murder had made the case notorious. Charges and countercharges were aired in the news media besides those for which Sheppard was called to trial. In addition, only three months before trial, Sheppard was examined for more than five hours without counsel during a three-day inquest which ended in a public brawl. The inquest was televised live from a high school gymnasium seating hundreds of people. . . .

While we cannot say that Sheppard was denied due process by the judge's refusal to take precautions against the influence of pretrial publicity alone, the court's later rulings must be considered against the setting in which the trial was held. In light of this background, we believe that the arrangements made by the judge with the news media caused Sheppard to be deprived of that "judicial serenity and calm to which [he] was entitled." The fact is that bedlam reigned at the courthouse during the trial and newsmen took over practically the entire courtroom, hounding most of the participants in the trial, especially Sheppard.... Having assigned almost all of the available seats in the courtroom to the news media, the judge lost his ability to supervise that environment. The movement of the reporters in and out of the courtroom caused frequent confusion and disruption of the trial. And the record reveals constant commotion within the bar. Moreover, the judge gave the throng of newsmen gathered in the corridors of the courthouse absolute free rein. Participants in the trial, including the jury, were forced to run a gantlet of reporters and photographers each time they entered or left the courtroom....

There can be no question about the nature of the publicity which surrounded Sheppard's trial. We agree, as did the Court of Appeals, with the findings in Judge Bell's opinion for the Ohio Supreme Court: "Murder and mystery, society, sex and suspense were combined in this case in such a manner as to intrigue and captivate the public fancy to a degree perhaps unparalleled in recent annals. Throughout the pre-indictment investigation, the subsequent legal skirmishes and the nine-week trial, circulation-conscious editors catered to the insatiable interest of the American public in the bizarre.... In this atmosphere of a 'Roman holiday' for the news media, Sam Sheppard stood trial for his life." Indeed, every court that has considered this case, save the court that tried it, has deplored the manner in which the news media inflamed and prejudiced the public.

Much of the material printed or broadcast during the trial was never heard from the witness stand, such as the charges that Sheppard had purposely impeded the murder investigation and must be guilty since he had hired a prominent criminal lawyer; that Sheppard was a perjurer; that he had sexual relations with numerous women; that his slain wife had characterized him as a "Jekyll-Hyde"; that he was "a bare-faced liar" because of his testimony as to police treatment; and, finally, that a woman convict claimed Sheppard to be the father of her illegitimate child. As the trial progressed, the newspapers summarized and interpreted the evidence, devoting particular attention to the material that incriminated Sheppard, and often drew unwarranted inferences from testimony. At one point, a front-page picture of Mrs. Sheppard's blood-stained pillow was published after being "doctored" to show more clearly an alleged imprint of a surgical instrument.

Nor is there doubt that this deluge of publicity reached at least some of the jury. On the only occasion that the jury was queried, two jurors admitted in open court to hearing the highly inflammatory charge that a prison inmate claimed Sheppard as the father of her illegitimate child....

The court's fundamental error is compounded by the holding that it lacked power to control the publicity about the trial. From the very inception of the proceedings, the judge announced that neither he nor anyone else could restrict prejudicial news accounts. And he reiterated this view on numerous occasions. Since he viewed the news media as his target, the judge never considered other means that are often utilized to reduce the appearance of prejudicial material and to protect the jury from outside influence. We conclude that these procedures would have been sufficient to guarantee Sheppard a fair trial, and so do not consider what sanctions might be available against a recalcitrant press, nor the charges of bias now made against the state trial judge.

The carnival atmosphere at trial could easily have been avoided, since the courtroom and courthouse premises are subject to the control of the court.... [T]he presence of the press at judicial proceedings must be limited when it is apparent that the accused might otherwise be prejudiced or disadvantaged. Bearing in mind the massive pretrial publicity, the judge should have adopted stricter rules governing the use of the courtroom by newsmen.... They certainly should not have been placed inside the bar. Furthermore, the judge should have more closely regulated the conduct of newsmen in the courtroom....

Secondly, the court should have insulated the witnesses. All of the newspapers and radio stations apparently interviewed prospective witnesses at will, and in many instances disclosed their testimony....

Although the witnesses were barred from the courtroom during the trial, the full verbatim testimony was available to them in the press. This completely nullified the judge's imposition of the rule.

Thirdly, the court should have made some effort to control the release of leads, information, and gossip to the press by police officers, witnesses, and the counsel for both sides. Much of the information thus disclosed was inaccurate, leading to groundless rumors and confusion. . . .

Defense counsel immediately brought to the court's attention the tremendous amount of publicity in the Cleveland press that "misrepresented entirely the testimony" in the case. Under such circumstances, the judge should have at least warned the newspapers to check the accuracy of their accounts. And it is obvious that the judge should have further sought to alleviate this problem by imposing control over the statements made to the news media by counsel, witnesses, and especially the Coroner and police officers. The prosecution repeatedly made evidence available to the news media which was never offered in the trial. Much of the "evidence" disseminated in this fashion was clearly inadmissible. The exclusion of such evidence in court is rendered meaningless when news media make it available to the public. . . .

The fact that many of the prejudicial news items can be traced to the prosecution as well as the defense aggravates the judge's failure to take any action. Effective control of these sources—concededly within the court's power—might well have prevented the divulgence of inaccurate information, rumors, and accusations that made up much of the inflammatory publicity, at least after Sheppard's indictment.

More specifically, the trial court might well have proscribed extrajudicial statements by any lawyer, party, witness, or court official which divulged prejudicial matters, such as the refusal of Sheppard to submit to interrogation or take any lie detector tests; any statement made by Sheppard to officials; the identity of prospective witnesses or their probable testimony; any belief in guilt or innocence; or like statements concerning the merits of the case.

Being advised of the great public interest in the case, the mass coverage of the press, and the potential prejudicial impact of publicity, the court could

also have requested the appropriate city and county officials to promulgate a regulation with respect to dissemination of information about the case by their employees. In addition, reporters who wrote or broadcast prejudicial stories could have been warned as to the impropriety of publishing material not introduced in the proceedings. . . . Had the judge, the other officers of the court, and the police placed the interest of justice first, the news media would have soon learned to be content with the task of reporting the case as it unfolded in the courtroom—not pieced together from extrajudicial statements.

. . . Due process requires that the accused receive a trial by an impartial jury free from outside influences. Given the pervasiveness of modern communications and the difficulty of effacing prejudicial publicity from the minds of the jurors, the trial courts must take strong measures to ensure that the balance is never weighed against the accused. . . . Of course, there is nothing that proscribes the press from reporting events that transpire in the courtroom. But where there is a reasonable likelihood that prejudicial news prior to trial will prevent a fair trial, the judge should continue the case until the threat abates, or transfer it to another county not so permeated with publicity. In addition, sequestration of the jury was something the judge should have raised *sua sponte* with counsel. If publicity during the proceedings threatens the fairness of the trial, a new trial should be ordered. But we must remember that reversals are but palliatives; the cure lies in those remedial measures that will prevent the prejudice at its inception. The courts must take such steps by rule and regulation that will protect their processes from prejudicial outside interferences. Neither prosecutors, counsel for defense, the accused, witnesses, court staff nor enforcement officers coming under the jurisdiction of the court should be permitted to frustrate its function. Collaboration between counsel and the press as to information affecting the fairness of a criminal trial is not only subject to regulation, but is highly censurable and worthy of disciplinary measures.

Since the state trial judge did not fulfill his duty to protect Sheppard from the inherently prejudicial publicity which saturated the community and to control disruptive influences in the courtroom, we must reverse the denial of the habeas petition. . . .

Richmond Newspapers Inc. v. Virginia
SUPREME COURT OF THE UNITED STATES
448 U.S. 555 (1980)

CHIEF JUSTICE WARREN BURGER delivered the Court's opinion:

The narrow question presented in this case is whether the right of the public and press to attend criminal trials is guaranteed under the United States Constitution.

In March, 1976, one Stevenson was indicted for the murder of a hotel manager who had been found stabbed to death on December 2, 1975. Tried promptly in July, 1976, Stevenson was convicted of second-degree murder in the Circuit Court of Hanover County, Va. The Virginia Supreme Court reversed the conviction in October, 1977, holding that a blood-stained shirt purportedly belonging to Stevenson had been improperly admitted into evidence.

Stevenson was retried in the same court. This second trial ended in a mistrial on May 30, 1978, when a juror asked to be excused after trial had begun and no alternate was available.

A third trial, which began in the same court on June 6, 1978, also ended in a mistrial. It appears that the mistrial may have been declared because a prospective juror had read about Stevenson's previous trials in a newspaper and had told other prospective jurors about the case before the retrial began.

Stevenson was tried in the same court for a fourth time beginning on September 11, 1978. Present in the courtroom when the case was called were . . . reporters for appellant Richmond Newspapers, Inc. Before the trial began, counsel for the defendant moved that it be closed to the public:

"[T]here was this woman that was with the family of the deceased when we were here before. She had sat in the Courtroom. I would like to ask that everybody be excluded from the Courtroom because I don't want any information being shuffled back and forth when we have a recess as to what—who testified to what."

The trial judge, who had presided over two of the three previous trials, asked if the prosecution had any objection to clearing the courtroom. The prosecutor stated he had no objection and . . . the trial judge . . . ordered "that the Courtroom be kept clear of all parties except the witnesses when they testify." The record does not show that any objections to the closure order were made by anyone present at the time. . . .

Later that same day, however, appellants sought a hearing on a motion to vacate the closure order. The trial judge granted the request and scheduled a hearing to follow the close of the day's proceedings. When the hearing began, the court ruled that the hearing was to be treated as part of the trial; accordingly, he again ordered the reporters to leave the courtroom, and they complied.

At the closed hearing, counsel for appellants observed that no evidentiary findings had been made by the court prior to the entry of its closure order, and pointed out that the court had failed to consider any other, less drastic measures within its power to ensure a fair trial. Counsel for appellants argued that constitutional considerations mandated that before ordering closure, the court should first decide that the rights of the defendant could be protected in no other way.

Counsel for defendant Stevenson pointed out that this was the fourth time he was standing trial. He also referred to "difficulty with information between the jurors," and stated that he "didn't want information to leak out," be published by the media, perhaps inaccurately, and then be seen by the jurors. Defense counsel argued that these things, plus the fact that "this is a small community," made this a proper case for closure.

The trial judge noted that counsel for the defendant had made similar statements at the morning hearing. The court also stated: "One of the other points that we take into consideration in this particular Courtroom is layout of the Courtroom. I think that having people in the Courtroom is distracting to the jury. Now, we have to have certain people in here and maybe that's not a very good reason. When we get into our new Court Building, people can sit in the audience so the jury can't see them. The rule of the Court may be different under those circumstances. . . ."

The prosecutor again declined comment, and the court summed up by saying: "I'm inclined to agree with [defense counsel] that, if I feel that the rights of the defendant are infringed in any way, [when] he makes the motion to do something and it doesn't completely override all rights of everyone else, then I'm inclined to go along with the defendant's motion."

The court denied the motion to vacate and ordered the trial to continue the following morning "with the press and public excluded."

What transpired when the closed trial resumed the next day was disclosed in the following manner by an order of the court entered September 12, 1978: "[In] the absence of the jury, the defendant, by counsel, made a Motion that a mistrial be declared, which motion was taken under advisement.

"At the conclusion of the Commonwealth's evidence, the attorney for the defendant moved the Court to strike the Commonwealth's evidence on grounds stated to the record, which Motion was sustained by the Court.

"And the jury having been excused, the Court doth find the accused NOT GUILTY of Murder, as charged in the Indictment, and he was allowed to depart." . . .

. . . The Virginia Supreme Court . . . finding no reversible error, denied the petition for appeal. . . .

The criminal trial which appellants sought to attend has long since ended, and there is thus some suggestion that the case is moot. This Court has frequently recognized, however, that its jurisdiction is not necessarily defeated by the practical termination of a contest which is short-lived by nature. If the underlying dispute is "capable of repetition, yet evading review," it is not moot. . . .

. . . More often than not, criminal trials will be of sufficiently short duration that a closure order will evade review. . . . Accordingly, we turn to the merits. . . .

In prior cases the Court has treated questions involving conflicts between publicity and a defendant's right to a fair trial. . . . But here for the first time the Court is asked to decide whether a criminal trial itself may be closed to the public upon the unopposed request of a defendant, without any demonstration that closure is required to protect the defendant's superior right to a fair trial, or that some other overriding consideration requires closure.

The origins of the proceeding which has become the modern criminal trial in Anglo-American justice can be traced back beyond reliable historical records. . . . What is significant for present purposes is that, throughout its evolution, the trial has been open to all who cared to observe. . . .

From these early times, although great changes in courts and procedure took place, one thing remained constant: the public character of the trial at which guilt or innocence was decided. . . .

We have found nothing to suggest that the presumptive openness of the trial, which English courts were later to call "one of the essential qualities of a court of justice," was not also an attribute of the judicial systems of colonial America. . . .

In some instances, the openness of trials was explicitly recognized as part of the fundamental law of the Colony. . . .

Other contemporary writings confirm the recognition that part of the very nature of a criminal trial was its openness to those who wished to attend. . . .

As we have shown, . . . the historical evidence demonstrates conclusively that, at the time when our organic laws were adopted, criminal trials both here and in England had long been presumptively open. This is no quirk of history; rather, it has long been recognized as an indispensable attribute of an Anglo-American trial. . . . Jeremy Bentham not only recognized the therapeutic value of open justice but regarded it as the keystone:

"Without publicity, all other checks are insufficient: in comparison of publicity, all other checks are of small account. Recordation, appeal, whatever other institutions might present themselves in the character of checks, would be found to operate rather as cloaks than checks; as cloaks in reality, as checks only in appearance." . . .

. . . The early history of open trials in part reflects the widespread acknowledgment, long before there were behavioral scientists, that public trials had significant community therapeutic value. Even without such experts to frame the concent in words, people sensed from experience and observation that, especially in the administration of criminal justice, the means used to achieve justice must have the support derived from public acceptance of both the process and its results.

When a shocking crime occurs, a community reaction of outrage and public protest often follows. Thereafter the open processes of justice serve an important prophylactic purpose, providing an outlet for community concern, hostility, and emotion. Without an awareness that society's responses to criminal conduct are underway, natural human reactions of outrage and protest are frustrated and may manifest themselves in some form of vengeful "self-help," as indeed they did regularly in the activities of vigilante "committees" on our frontiers. . . .

Civilized societies withdraw both from the victim and the vigilante the enforcement of criminal laws, but they cannot erase from people's consciousness the fundamental, natural yearning to see justice done—or even the urge for retribution. The crucial prophylactic aspects of the administration of justice cannot function in the dark; no community catharsis can occur if justice is "done in a corner [or] in any covert manner." It is not enough to say that results alone will satiate the natural community desire for "satisfaction." A result considered untoward may undermine public confidence, and where the trial has been concealed from public view, an unexpected outcome can cause a reaction that the system at best has failed and at worst has been corrupted. To work effectively, it is important that society's criminal process "satisfy the appearance of justice," and the appearance of justice can best be provided by allowing people to observe it. . . .

People in an open society do not demand infallibility from their institutions, but it is difficult for them to accept what they are prohibited from observing. When a criminal trial is conducted in the open, there is at least an opportunity both for understanding the system in general and its workings in a particular case: "The educative effect of public attendance is a material advantage. Not only is respect for the law increased and intelligent acquaintance acquired with the methods of government, but a strong confidence in judicial remedies is secured which could never be inspired by a system of secrecy." . . .

. . . Instead of acquiring information about trials by firsthand observation or by word of mouth from those who attended, people now acquire it chiefly through the print and electronic media. In a sense, this validates the media claim of functioning as surrogates for the public. While media representatives enjoy the same right of access as the public, they often are provided special seating and priority of entry so that they may report what people in attendance have seen and heard. This "[contributes] to public understanding of the rule of law and to comprehension of the functioning of the entire criminal justice system. . . ."

From this unbroken, uncontradicted history, supported by reasons as valid today as in centuries past, we are bound to conclude that a presumption of openness inheres in the very nature of a criminal trial under our system of justice. . . .

Despite the history of criminal trials being presumptively open since long before the Constitution, the State presses its contention that neither the Constitution nor the Bill of Rights contains any provision which, by its terms, guarantees to the public the right to attend criminal trials. Standing alone, this is correct, but there remains the question whether, absent an explicit provision, the Constitution affords protection against exclusion of the public from criminal trials.

The First Amendment, in conjunction with the fourteenth, prohibits governments from "abridging the freedom of speech, or of the press; or the right of the people peaceably to assemble, and to petition the Government for a redress of grievances." These expressly guaranteed freedoms share a common core purpose of assuring freedom of communication on matters relating to the functioning of government. Plainly it would be difficult to single out any aspect of government of higher concern and importance to the people than the manner in which criminal trials are conducted; as we have shown, recognition of this pervades the centuries-old history of open trials and the opinions of this Court.

The Bill of Rights was enacted against the backdrop of the long history of trials being presumptively open. Public access to trials was then regarded as an important aspect of the process itself; . . . In guaranteeing freedoms such as those of speech and press, the First Amendment can be read as protecting the right of everyone to attend trials so as to give meaning to those explicit guarantees. "The First Amendment goes beyond protection of the press and the self-expression of individuals to prohibit government from limiting the stock of information from which members of the public may draw." Free speech carries with it some freedom to listen. . . . What this means in the context of trials is that the First Amendment guarantees of speech and press, standing alone, prohibit government from summarily closing courtroom doors which had long been open to the public at the time that Amendment was adopted. . . .

. . . It is not crucial whether we describe this right to attend criminal trials to hear, see, and communicate observations concerning them as a "right of access," or a "right to gather information," for we have recognized that "without some protection for seeking out the news, freedom of the press could be eviscerated." The explicit, guaranteed rights to speak and to publish concerning what takes place at a trial would lose much meaning if access to observe the trial could, as it was here, be foreclosed arbitrarily.

The right of access to places traditionally open to the public, as criminal trials have long been, may be seen as assured by the amalgam of the First Amendment guarantees of speech and press; and their affinity to the right of assembly is not without relevance. . . . [A] trial courtroom also is a public place where the people generally—and representatives of the media—have a right to be present, and where their presence historically has been thought to enhance the integrity and quality of what takes place.

The State argues that the Constitution nowhere spells out a guarantee for the right of the public to attend trials, and that, accordingly, no such right is protected. . . .

But arguments such as the State makes have not precluded recognition of important rights not enumerated. . . .

We hold that the right to attend criminal trials is implicit in the guarantees of the First Amendment; without the freedom to attend such trials, which people have exercised for centuries, important aspects of freedom of speech and "of the press could be eviscerated."

Having concluded there was a guaranteed right of the public under the First and Fourteenth Amendments to attend the trial of Stevenson's case, we return to the closure order challenged by appellants. . . . Despite the fact that this was the fourth trial of the accused, the trial judge made no findings to support closure; no inquiry was made as to whether alternative solutions would have met the need to ensure fairness; there was no recognition of any right under the Constitution for the public or press to attend the trial. There exist in the context of the trial itself various tested alternatives to satisfy the constitutional demands of fairness. . . . There was no suggestion that any problems with witnesses could not have been dealt with by their exclusion from the courtroom or their sequestration during the trial. Nor is there anything to indicate that sequestration of the jurors would not have guarded against their being subjected to any improper information. All of the alternatives admittedly present difficulties for trial courts, but none of the factors relied on here was beyond the realm of the manageable. Absent an overriding interest articulated in findings, the trial of a criminal case must be open to the public. Accordingly, the judgment under review is

Reversed. . . .

JUSTICE JOHN PAUL STEVENS concurring:
This is a watershed case. Until today, the Court has accorded virtually absolute protection to the dissemination of information or ideas, but never before has it squarely held that the acquisition of newsworthy matter is entitled to any constitutional protection whatsoever. . . .

Today, however, for the first time, the Court unequivocally holds that an arbitrary interference with access to important information is an abridgment of the freedoms of speech and of the press protected by the First Amendment. . . .

. . . I agree that the First Amendment protects the public and the press from abridgment of their rights of access to information about the operation of their government, including the Judicial Branch; given the total absence of any record justification for the closure order entered in this case, that order violated the First Amendment.

JUSTICE WILLIAM BRENNAN, with whom
JUSTICE THURGOOD MARSHALL joined,
concurring:

. . . I agree with those of my Brethren who hold that, without more, agreement of the trial judge and the parties cannot constitutionally close a trial to the public.

While freedom of expression is made inviolate by the First Amendment, and, with only rare and stringent exceptions, may not be suppressed, the First Amendment has not been viewed by the Court in all settings as providing an equally categorical assurance of the correlative freedom of access to information. Yet the Court has not ruled out a public access component to the First Amendment in every circumstance. Read with care and in context, our decisions must therefore be understood as holding only that any privilege of access to governmental information is subject to a degree of restraint dictated by the nature of the information and countervailing interests in security or confidentiality. These cases neither comprehensively nor absolutely deny that public access to information may at times be implied by the First Amendment and the principles which animate it.

The Court's approach in right-of-access cases simply reflects the special nature of a claim of First Amendment right to gather information. . . . [T]he First Amendment . . . has a structural role to play in securing and fostering our republican system of self-government. Implicit in this structural role is not only "the principle that debate on public issues should be uninhibited, robust, and wide-open," but also the antecedent assumption that valuable public debate—as well as other civic behavior—must be informed. The structural model links the First Amendment to that process of communication necessary for a democracy to survive, and thus entails solicitude not only for communication itself, but also for the indispensable conditions of meaningful communication. . . .

This judicial task is as much a matter of sensitivity to practical necessities as it is of abstract reasoning. But at least two helpful principles may be sketched. First, the case for a right of access has special force when drawn from an enduring and vital tradition of public entree to particular proceedings or information. Such a tradition commands respect, in part, because the Constitution carries the gloss of history. More importantly, a tradition of accessibility implies the favorable judgment of experience. Second, the value of access must be measured in specifics. Analysis is not advanced by rhetorical statements that all information bears upon public issues; what is crucial in individual cases is whether access to a particular government process is important in terms of that very process.

To resolve the case before us, therefore, we must consult historical and current practice with respect to open trials, and weigh the importance of public access to the trial process itself. . . .

. . . [S]ignificantly for our present purpose, [the Court has] recognized that open trials are bulwarks of our free and democratic government: public access to court proceedings is one of the numerous "checks and balances" of our system, because "contemporaneous review in the forum of public opinion is an effective restraint on possible abuse of judicial power." Indeed, the Court focused with particularity upon the public trial guarantee "as a safeguard against any attempt to employ our courts as instruments of persecution," or "for the suppression of political and religious heresies." Thus, . . . open trials are indispensable to First Amendment political and religious freedoms. . . .

Publicity serves to advance several of the particular purposes of the trial (and, indeed, the judicial) process. . . . But, as a feature of our governing system of justice, the trial process serves other, broadly political, interests, and public access advances these objectives as well. To that extent, trial access possesses specific structural significance. . . .

Secrecy is profoundly inimical to this demonstrative purpose of the trial process. . . .

But the trial is more than a demonstrably just method of adjudicating disputes and protecting rights. It plays a pivotal role in the entire judicial process, and, by extension, in our form of government. Under our system, judges are not mere umpires, but, in their own sphere, lawmakers—a coordinate branch of government. While individual cases turn upon the controversies between parties, or involve particular prosecutions, court rulings impose official and practical consequences upon members of society at large. Moreover, judges bear responsibility for the vitally important task of construing and securing constitutional rights. Thus, so far as the trial is the mechanism for judicial fact finding, as well as the initial forum for legal decision making, it is a genuine governmental proceeding.

It follows that the conduct of the trial is preeminently a matter of public interest. . . .

. . . [R]esolution of First Amendment public access claims in individual cases must be strongly influenced by the weight of historical practice and by an assessment of the specific structural value of public access in the circumstances. With regard to the case at hand, our ingrained tradition of public trials and the importance of public access to the broader purposes of the trial process, tip the balance strongly toward the rule that trials be open. What countervailing interests might be sufficiently compelling to reverse this presumption of openness need not concern us now, for the statute at stake here authorizes trial closures at the unfettered discretion of the judge and parties. Accordingly, [the law] violates the First and Fourteenth Amendments, and the decision of the Virginia Supreme Court to the contrary should be reversed.

JUSTICE POTTER STEWART concurring:

. . . [The presumption of open criminal proceedings] does not mean that the First Amendment fight of members of the public and representatives of the press to attend civil and criminal trials is absolute. Just as a legislature may impose reasonable time, place, and manner restrictions upon the exercise of First Amendment freedoms, so may a trial judge impose reasonable limitations upon the unrestricted occupation of a courtroom by representatives of the press and members of the public. Much more than a city street, a trial courtroom must be a quiet and orderly place. Moreover, every courtroom has a finite physical capacity, and there may be occasions when not all who wish to attend a trial may do so. And while there exist many alternative ways to satisfy the constitutional demands of a fair trial, those demands may also sometimes justify limitations upon the unrestricted presence of spectators in the courtroom.

Since, in the present case, the trial judge appears to have given no recognition to the right of representatives of the press and members of the public to be present at the Virginia murder trial over which he was presiding, the judgment under review must be reversed.

JUSTICE HARRY BLACKMUN concurring:

. . . I remain convinced that the right to a public trial is to be found where the Constitution explicitly placed it—in the Sixth Amendment.

The Court, however, has eschewed the Sixth Amendment route. The plurality turns to other possible constitutional sources and invokes a veritable potpourri of them—the Speech Clause of the First Amendment, the Press Clause, the Assembly Clause, the Ninth Amendment, and a cluster of penumbral guarantees recognized in past decisions. This course is troublesome, but it is the route that has been selected and, at least for now, we must live with it. . . .

. . . [W]ith the Sixth Amendment set to one side in this case, I am driven to conclude, as a secondary position, that the First Amendment must provide some measure of protection for public access to the trial. . . . It is clear and obvious to me, on the approach the Court has chosen to take, that, by closing this criminal trial, the trial judge abridged these First Amendment interests of the public.

I also would reverse, and I join the judgment of the Court.

JUSTICE WILLIAM REHNQUIST dissenting:

. . . I do not believe that either the First or Sixth Amendment, as made applicable to the States by the Fourteenth, requires that a State's reasons for denying public access to a trial, where both the prosecuting attorney and the defendant have consented to an order of closure approved by the judge, are subject to any additional constitutional review at our hands. . . .

. . . [T]o gradually rein in, as this Court has done over the past generation, all of the ultimate decision making power over how justice shall be administered, not merely in the federal system but in each of the 50 States, is a task that no Court consisting of nine persons, however gifted, is equal to. Nor is it desirable that such authority be exercised by such a tiny numerical fragment of the 220 million people who compose the population of this country. . . .

. . . [I]t is basically unhealthy to have so much authority concentrated in a small group of lawyers who have been appointed to the Supreme Court and enjoy virtual life tenure. . . .

The issue here is not whether the "right" to freedom of the press conferred by the First Amendment to the Constitution overrides the defendant's "right" to a fair trial conferred by other Amendments to the Constitution; it is, instead, whether any provision in the Constitution may fairly be read to prohibit what the trial judge in the Virginia state-court system did in this case. Being unable to find any such prohibition in the First, Sixth, Ninth, or any other Amendment to the United States Constitution, or in the Constitution itself, I dissent.

Chapter 11

Television is just another appliance. It's a toaster with pictures.

Then-FCC chair Mark Fowler[1]

Electronic media have moved from broadcast radio and television to satellite radio, cable and satellite television, the Internet, online newspapers and Web-transmitted television programs. Beginning in 1920s, the government required a radio, and later a television, station license to communicate with a large audience. The Internet, the newest mass medium, allows people to disseminate information and opinion widely without FCC permission.

Electronic Media Regulation

From Radio to the Internet

Federal Communications Commission

Broadcast Regulation

Reasons to Regulate
    Broadcasting
The Public Interest Standard
Program and Advertising
    Regulations
Broadcast Licensing
Noncommercial
    Broadcasting

Cable Television Regulation

Cable Regulation's
    Development
Cable Franchising
Cable Programming

Direct Broadcast Satellites

Internet Regulation

FCC Internet Regulation
The Internet's First
    Amendment Status

Cases for Study

➤ *Red Lion Broadcasting
    Co., Inc. v. Federal
    Communications
    Commission*
➤ *Turner Broadcasting
    System, Inc., v. Federal
    Communications
    Commission*

Suppose . . .

. . . an author publishes a book that criticizes a politically conservative presidential candidate. In reviewing the book, a newspaper columnist says the author must be sympathetic to terrorist groups. Could the newspaper be forced to give the author space to reply to the columnist? No, the First Amendment protects the paper from being required to grant a reply. But if a radio or television station airs similar criticism of the author, could the author force the station to allow a reply? If so, what would the rationale be for the courts to uphold that requirement despite the First Amendment? What differentiates broadcast stations from print media? Look for a discussion of these questions when the case of *Red Lion Broadcasting Co., Inc. v. Federal Communications Commission* is discussed later in this chapter and the case is excerpted at the end of the chapter.

Broadcasters can be sued for libel, invasion of privacy, intentional infliction of emotional distress and other torts discussed in previous chapters. So can Internet bloggers and producers of programs transmitted by satellite and cable. A judge may order a television reporter to reveal his story's sources, just as a judge may demand sources from a newspaper journalist. Legal issues discussed in this book apply to the electronic media just as they apply to the

Guglielmo Marconi, an Italian physicist, shared a Nobel Prize in 1909 for developing wireless telegraphy, one of the inventions leading to broadcast radio and television and ultimately to new technologies like the Internet.

print media. However, the electronic media, particularly radio and television, must comply with regulations that are not applicable to print. For example, it is illegal to broadcast without first obtaining a license from the Federal Communications Commission (FCC), a federal government agency. Newspaper, magazine and book publishers do not need a government license to print and distribute materials.

Of course, electronic media developed long after the United States adopted the First Amendment. Guglielmo Marconi is credited with inventing the means of sending radio signals without using wires. Many ships used Marconi's equipment for ship-to-shore communication. To protect his patents, Marconi ordered his employees not to accept messages from ships using other manufacturers' radios. Fearing that ships' distress signals would be ignored, Congress passed the Wireless Ship Act of 1910, requiring oceangoing vessels to carry radio equipment and radio operators.[2] The law also made it illegal for companies to disregard ships' radio transmissions.

Because all large ships had radios, countless radio messages went from ships to shore and ship to ship. Also, amateur radio fans sent many transmissions. All these messages clogged the spectrum, the range of electromagnetic radio frequencies used to transmit radio and television signals and data. Congress had not considered the law's impact on the spectrum. Congress required ships to have radios but had not specified what ships could use which portions of the spectrum. Signals carrying ships' messages interfered with each other, preventing messages from reaching their destinations.

Not only American ships but ships all over the world were affected. Countries pressured Congress to establish standards allowing messages to reach their destinations without other messages interfering. Many nations said they would cooperate in setting international norms.

Then tragedy struck. In 1912 the Titanic hit an Atlantic Ocean iceberg, plunging thousands to their deaths. Many passengers could have been saved if a rescue ship had arrived. The Titanic sent a distress signal, but there were two problems. The signal, received in Newfoundland, Canada, could not be sent to authorities because ordinary messages from other ships and amateur radio users' messages interfered with the Titanic's signal.[3] Also, the radio operator on the ship closest to the Titanic was off duty and did not hear the message.

The Titanic disaster prompted Congress to regulate wireless communication. This led to the Radio Act of 1912, the first statute directly regulating commercial radio.[4] The 1912 law required oceangoing ships to have radio operators on duty around the clock. It also gave the U.S. secretary of commerce power to grant radio station licenses, stipulating what frequency each licensee would use. The intent was to prevent message interference by allowing only one station operator to broadcast on a single frequency in one area.

However, the law did not give the secretary power to refuse a license or to regulate radio in any substantial way. Any person applying for a license would get one, as long as no two licenses were for the same frequency. The commerce secretary also had no authority to limit the power stations used to broadcast. A powerful station could drown out stations broadcasting at lower power even though they were not on the same frequency. Amateur radio operators began ignoring the law, changing the frequencies they used and even relocating to other cities without the secretary's permission. A federal court tied the secretary's hands, saying the 1912 law allowed moving a station without approval.[5]

During the early and mid-1920s a number of commercial radio stations went on the air. These stations experienced signal degradation from other commercial stations and amateur users who clogged the spectrum with their broadcasts. A federal appellate court said the secretary of commerce could not refuse to grant a radio license even when there was no frequency space available.[6] The decision also said the secretary could not limit the power level stations used to broadcast their signals, allowing some stations to drown out other stations' signals. The situation was chaotic. The secretary held several conferences during the mid-1920s trying to persuade radio station operators to reach agreement in the absence of laws requiring cooperation.

Congress finally realized that many Americans listened to radio and that radio was playing an increasingly important role in American commerce. Companies and individuals trying to make radio a commercial medium, instead of one dominated by naval and amateur users, implored the federal government to stop spectrum anarchy. Understanding that if it did not regulate the industry radio could not develop as a viable business, Congress adopted the

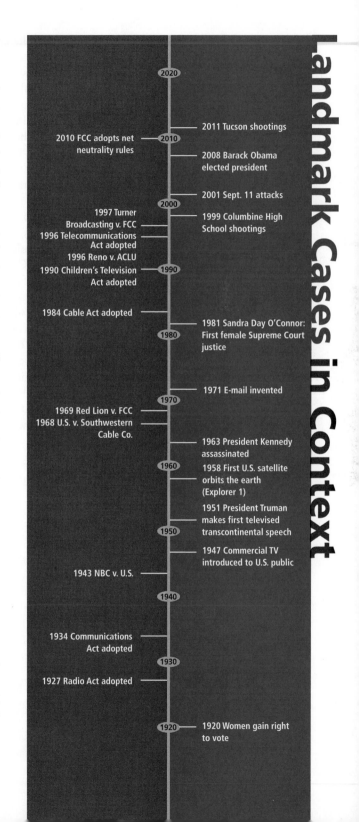

Landmark Cases in Context

2020

2010 FCC adopts net neutrality rules — 2010 — 2011 Tucson shootings

2008 Barack Obama elected president

2001 Sept. 11 attacks

2000

1997 Turner Broadcasting v. FCC

1996 Telecommunications Act adopted

1996 Reno v. ACLU

1990 Children's Television Act adopted — 1990

1999 Columbine High School shootings

1984 Cable Act adopted

1981 Sandra Day O'Connor: First female Supreme Court justice

1980

1971 E-mail invented

1970

1969 Red Lion v. FCC

1968 U.S. v. Southwestern Cable Co.

1963 President Kennedy assassinated

1960

1958 First U.S. satellite orbits the earth (Explorer 1)

1951 President Truman makes first televised transcontinental speech

1950

1947 Commercial TV introduced to U.S. public

1943 NBC v. U.S.

1940

1934 Communications Act adopted

1930

1927 Radio Act adopted

1920 — 1920 Women gain right to vote

Federal Radio Commission (FRC)
A federal agency established by the Federal Radio Act in 1927 to oversee radio broadcasting. The FRC was succeeded by the Federal Communications Commission in 1934.

Radio Act of 1927.[7] The law established the **Federal Radio Commission (FRC)**, a federal agency charged with issuing or denying radio licenses and assigning frequencies to prevent stations from interfering with each other. The law gave the FRC the power to regulate stations as necessary to allow radio's development.

The 1927 law included several provisions that are in effect today. First, the act specifically said the FRC could not censor radio content. Second, it said the public, not station licensees, owned the spectrum. Third, the law required the FRC to make decisions based on the "public interest, convenience and necessity." Also, a federal court interpreted the 1927 act to say the federal government had exclusive control over radio broadcasting, and states were not to make their own broadcasting laws.[8]

Congress intended the FRC to put the radio industry on firm footing and then have the secretary of commerce oversee radio stations. But Congress soon realized that plan would not work. Radio needed continued oversight. Also, in addition to the FRC, a number of different federal agencies had authority over various aspects of the radio industry. To resolve these problems, Congress rescinded the 1927 act and adopted the Communications Act of 1934.[9] Although often amended, the 1934 law still is in place, giving the **Federal Communications Commission (FCC)** authority to regulate over-the-air radio and television. States still may not regulate broadcasting. The 1934 act also allows the commission to oversee long-distance telephone companies and other industries providing interstate communication services by wire. In 1984, Congress gave the FCC power to regulate cable television.[10] The FCC also has jurisdiction over direct broadcast satellites.[11] The Internet is largely unregulated by either the FCC or other government agencies.

Federal Communications Commission (FCC) An independent U.S. government agency, directly responsible to Congress, charged with regulating interstate and international communications by radio, television, wire, satellite and cable. The FCC was established by the Communications Act of 1934; its jurisdiction covers the 50 states, the District of Columbia and U.S. possessions.

Federal Communications Commission

The 1934 act established the FCC as an independent federal agency; however, it is not completely independent. Politics envelop the commission. The U.S. president selects the five commissioners, who are appointed to five-year terms. The president also designates one of the commissioners to be FCC chair. The chair is the commission's chief executive officer. The U.S. Senate must approve the people nominated to be commissioners, including the chair. No more than three commissioners may be from the same political party at any one time. Commissioners may not have financial interests in any company or industry the FCC oversees and must be U.S. citizens. The FCC operates under the Administrative Procedure Act, a law telling federal agencies how they may propose and adopt regulations and giving federal courts power to rule on challenges to those decisions. Congress gives the FCC its funding, increasing or decreasing the budget each year as Congress chooses.

The commission's responsibilities include regulating all technologies using the electromagnetic spectrum, such as radio, television, cable and satellite communications. The FCC also regulates wireline and wireless telephone companies

realWorld Law

Congress Grounds the FCC

Because Congress created and funds the FCC, it may reward or punish the agency depending on whether members of Congress like or dislike the commission's decisions. For example, in 1934 Congress eliminated the five federal radio commissioners and replaced them with seven federal communications commissioners. In 1982, President Ronald Reagan and the U.S. Senate needed to appoint someone to fill a vacant seat on the commission. FCC Chair Mark Fowler supported someone who shared his antiregulation, pro-marketplace views. Many members of Congress disagreed with Fowler. Having had enough of the FCC ignoring its policy preferences, Congress not only did not appoint a new commissioner to the vacant seat, it voted to reduce the number of commissioners from seven to five and their terms from seven years to five years.[1]

---

1. *See* Christopher H. Sterling & John Michael Kittross, Stay Tuned: A History of American Broadcasting 565 (3d ed. 2002).

---

offering long-distance services. The FCC has about 2,000 employees in its various bureaus and offices. Day-to-day commission work includes enforcing the Communications Act of 1934 and the FCC's rules, granting licenses for various communications services, resolving disputes and ensuring that spectrum users comply with the commission's regulations.

The commissioners adopt rules and regulations affecting entire industries—every radio station or every television station, for example. The process starts when commissioners identify an issue they want to examine. FCC staff members prepare a **Notice of Proposed Rule Making** explaining what the commissioners plan to do—adopt a certain regulation, for example—and why. Members of the public and companies that will be affected by the regulations if they are adopted submit comments to the commission, saying why they like or dislike the proposal. There is an opportunity to submit reply comments responding to the original submissions. The FCC staff considers all the submissions and drafts a Report and Order. The commissioners discuss the draft, suggest changes and vote on a final version in a public meeting. Companies and individuals who object to the commission's final decision may ask the commissioners to reconsider. Sometimes the FCC will reconsider its decision, but usually it does not. The final regulations then become part of the FCC's rules.

A company, an industry association or an individual affected by a commission decision may challenge it in a federal appellate court. Usually the appeal is to the U.S. Court of Appeals for the District of Columbia Circuit, although other circuits also may hear an appeal of a commission decision. A federal court ruling takes precedence over an FCC decision. The FCC cannot enforce a regulation that a court rejected.

Companies, industries and individuals must comply with the FCC's rules or face sanctions. The commission's rules have the effect of a law. The commission has a range of possible punishments, from a letter of reprimand in a licensee's file,

Notice of Proposed Rule Making
A notice issued by the FCC announcing that the commission is considering changing certain of its regulations or adopting new rules.

realWorld Law

Obama's FCC Chair Choice

President Barack Obama appointed Julius Genachowski as FCC chair in 2009. Genachowski served as chief attorney for a previous FCC chair, Reed Hundt, and worked in private industry. Genachowski and Obama both graduated from Harvard Law School—and played basketball together.[1]

In mid-2011 other FCC commissioners were Democrat Mignon Clyburn and Republican Robert McDowell. Republican Meredith Baker and Democrat Michael Copps completed their terms as commissioners in 2011. It is the U.S. Senate's responsibility to appoint new commissioners.

Julius Genachowski

1. *See* Stephen Labaton, *Julius Genachowski to Be Nominee for F.C.C. Chairman*, N.Y. Times, Jan. 14, 2009, at B2.

to a fine, to revoking or not renewing a license. Commonly, the FCC punishes by issuing a fine, which the commission calls a "forfeiture."

The commission also may control industries by raising an eyebrow. If the FCC merely considers regulating, an industry may take action on its own. When the FCC suggested in 1971 that radio stations played songs glorifying and encouraging drug use, a number of stations self-censored their playlists. In 2004, the FCC and Congress expressed outrage after 80 million viewers saw singer Janet Jackson's breast for less than a second during a Super Bowl halftime program. Within a month, the country's largest radio station owner, Clear Channel Broadcasting, removed the Howard Stern show from its stations. The FCC earlier had found some Howard Stern programs indecent, and Stern switched his program to satellite radio. (Chapter 12 discusses the FCC's power to limit the airing of indecent material.)

SUMMARY

FEDERAL LAW FIRST REGULATED ELECTRONIC MEDIA—radio—in 1910, requiring oceangoing ships to have radios and radio operators. The 1912 law, prompted by the Titanic's sinking, gave the U.S. secretary of commerce power to license radio stations. Despite licensing, amateur and commercial radio stations continually interfered with each other's signals. National conferences urging cooperation among radio broadcasters were unsuccessful. In 1927, Congress established the Federal Radio Commission and gave it extensive power over radio broadcasting. The Federal Communications Commission replaced the FRC in 1934. Today, the FCC uses its powers to adopt regulations affecting large segments of the electronic media, as well as licensing spectrum users and enforcing the commission's regulations. ■

Broadcast Regulation

Over-the-air radio and television broadcasters use the electromagnetic spectrum to send signals to many listeners and viewers simultaneously. This is the Communication Act's definition of "broadcasting."[12] It is not a broadcast when the CBS television network sends a signal to the CBS station in Des Moines, Iowa. That is a private transmission from the network to the station, and it is illegal for anyone else to intercept the signal.[13] It is a broadcast when the Des Moines station sends the signal through its transmitter to thousands of television sets and to the local cable system. CBS, then, does not broadcast; rather, the stations owned by or affiliated with CBS broadcast. The FCC's broadcast regulations apply to radio and television stations.

Reasons to Regulate Broadcasting

Radio and television station licensees often tell courts there is no valid reason to regulate broadcasting. Stations are mass media, just like print media and the Internet, they say. The First Amendment should apply equally to all mass media, so broadcast stations should not be regulated any more than newspapers or magazines.

The U.S. Supreme Court has rejected this argument in two ways. First, the Court's decisions say all mass media need not be treated the same way under the First Amendment. The court has held that movies, for example, do not have the same First Amendment rights that print media have.[14] Each mass medium has its own peculiarities, although each has basic free speech protection, the Court said.

Second, broadcasting uses the spectrum, a publicly owned natural resource only a select few companies may use. Unlike the print media—anyone with enough money can start a newspaper—the spectrum limits the number of stations in a geographical area. In 1943, the Supreme Court for the first time said this is the principal reason broadcasters can be regulated.[15] In that case, the Court upheld the FCC's jurisdiction of broadcast networks. After the Communications Act of 1934 created the commission, radio station owners expected the FCC to prevent interference by carefully choosing licensees and controlling the power that stations used to broadcast. Owners wanted the FCC to do no more than that. But the commission took more control over the radio industry than expected. Among other decisions, the FCC adopted rules regulating the relationship between the emerging radio networks and local stations. The commission was concerned that networks exerted too much control over stations, requiring the stations to carry all network programs, for example. The networks sued the FCC, claiming that it overstepped its statutory responsibilities.

The U.S. Supreme Court supported the commission. The Court said radio's "facilities are limited; they are not available to all who may wish to use them; the radio spectrum simply is not large enough to accommodate everybody. There is a fixed natural limitation upon the number of stations that can operate without interfering with one another." The few companies using the spectrum have a special privilege, making it reasonable to regulate them, the Court said.

Twenty-six years later the Court reinforced this rationale for regulating the broadcast media. In *Red Lion Broadcasting Co. v. FCC,* the Court upheld the FCC's rule requiring that a station offer free time to an individual personally attacked by comments made on the station.[16] The audience's right to hear both sides of the issue was more important than the licensee's First Amendment rights, according to the Court. The Court justified this conclusion by saying the spectrum prevents everyone who wants to broadcast from doing so. Print media do not have the same right-of-reply requirement, the Court said. In fact, in *Miami Herald Publishing Co. v. Tornillo,* discussed in Chapter 1, the Court said a Florida statute requiring a newspaper that had printed a critical editorial about a candidate for public office to allow the candidate to publish a reply was unconstitutional.[17] The First Amendment prohibited government from forcing newspapers to publish anything, the Court said.

spectrum scarcity The limitation that arises because only a certain number of broadcast radio and television stations in a geographical area may use the spectrum without causing interference with other stations' signals. Spectrum scarcity is the primary reason courts give for allowing Congress and the FCC to regulate broadcasters.

Spectrum scarcity remains the reason courts most often give for allowing broadcast regulation. Not everyone who wants a license to operate a television or radio station may have one, because there is only enough room in the spectrum to accommodate a limited number of stations. The U.S. Supreme Court used this rationale in *National Broadcasting Co. v. FCC* in 1943 to justify the Federal Communications Commission adopting regulations affecting the broadcast industry.[18] Again, in the *Red Lion* case the Court emphasized that spectrum scarcity justifies limiting broadcasters' First Amendment rights.

In taking this position, courts seem to ignore the development of direct broadcast satellite (DBS) service, satellite radio, low-power radio and television stations (broadcasting signals available within a few miles of the transmitter), the Internet and other new technologies. The Supreme Court has recognized the advent of cable and satellite television technology and the Internet but said it would not alter its spectrum scarcity rationale "without some signal from Congress or the FCC that technological developments have advanced so far that some revision of the system of broadcast regulation may be required."[19]

In addition to spectrum scarcity, courts use two other rationales to justify regulating radio and television. One is that the broadcast media are pervasive. Radio and television sets are turned on and available nearly everywhere. Without regulation, children in particular could be exposed to inappropriate content.[20] A second reason is that broadcast media have a greater influence on audiences—a "special impact"—than do print media.[21] Again, this rationale is especially concerned with children.

Although broadcasting remains the most regulated mass medium, during the past two decades the FCC, with the courts' approval, has rescinded many broadcasting regulations. However, the Supreme Court has yet clearly to state that spectrum scarcity no longer is a valid rationale for regulating over-the-air radio and television.

The Public Interest Standard

In the 1927 Radio Act and again in the 1934 Communications Act, Congress said it wanted the public interest to come before the stations' interests. Both laws say

The Electromagnetic Spectrum

Radio stations, over-the-air television stations, and direct broadcast satellites (DBS) transmit signals using radio frequencies, a part of the electromagnetic spectrum. The "electromagnetic spectrum" is the name for the range of radiation making up what may be thought of as a seamless band. Electromagnetic radiation is a stream of photons, massless particles traveling at the speed of light in a pattern looking like a wave. Each photon contains energy, the amount of energy determining whether the wave is longer or shorter. Think of longer waves passing an imaginary point less frequently, and therefore at a lower frequency, than the shorter waves pass that point.

Electromagnetic radiation is identified by frequency (or by wavelength, which is equivalent to frequency). For example, gamma rays are very energetic photons, with very high energy and frequency and very short wavelengths. X-rays are slightly less energetic than gamma rays and therefore have slightly longer wavelengths and lower frequency. The light our eyes usually see—optical or visible light—consists of short wavelength (about one five-thousandths of a millimeter!) photons with a moderate amount of energy and moderate frequency. Radio waves are long (a centimeter to a meter) wavelength, low-energy photons with much lower frequencies.

Radio waves are just a slice of the spectrum, but a large enough slice that they can be further classified by giving them numbers. For example, 92.5 on the FM radio dial is a way of naming the photons having a frequency of 92.5 million cycles—passing that imaginary point 92.5 million times per second. Another part of the spectrum passes the point 101.2 million times a second and is 101.2 on the FM dial. For convenience, these radio frequencies are identified in millions of hertz (megahertz, or MHz), named after German physicist Heinrich Hertz. An FM station, then, may be at 92.5 MHz on the dial (a wavelength of 3.24 meters, or about 11 feet). Similarly, 550 on the AM dial is at 550 kHz (kilohertz) or 550 thousand cycles per second. Broadcast television stations also use portions of the spectrum's radio waves to transmit both their pictures and sound, as do direct broadcast satellites to send their signals to Earth.

Until recently technology allowed only one signal to be sent via a particular frequency to one geographical location at one time to avoid signals interfering with each other and listeners hearing intermingled broadcasts. Because the spectrum must be divided among different uses—ship-to-shore, television, public safety, the military, cell phones—only a limited number of users can be accommodated. Digital communication has increased how many signals the spectrum may accommodate, but the number remains finite. The Federal Communications Commission allocates parts of the spectrum to users, from microwave oven manufacturers to aeronautical uses. A global organization, the International Telecommunications Union, divides the spectrum among nations.

federal regulation is to be guided by the "public interest, convenience and necessity."[22] But the law does not define the term "public interest," allowing the FCC to interpret and apply the phrase as the commission prefers. The FCC can say it is in the public interest to adopt a specific regulation, and a different group of commissioners later can say the public interest requires rescinding the regulation. Courts over the years have not agreed how to define "public interest."

Through its first 50 years overseeing broadcasters, the FCC justified adopting regulations by citing the public interest. Then in the 1980s, the commission said the public interest required deregulating the broadcast industry. The FCC's focus turned more to letting the market rather than the commission regulate broadcasting. This became the commission's definition of regulating in the public interest. Mark Fowler, FCC chairman from 1981 to 1987, led the charge against regulation. He thought the marketplace could substitute for government regulation. His statement that television is only a toaster with pictures suggested that his focus was on television as a commercial medium rather than as a communication medium. Under Fowler and subsequent commission chairs, the FCC eliminated many program requirements, including rules obliging stations to survey their communities to determine programming preferences and limits on how many minutes per hour could be used for commercials and other regulations.

Program and Advertising Regulations

The FCC is not allowed to censor broadcast content, the 1934 law says.[23] This means the commission may not forbid airing a news story about the president catching a cold or tell CBS to take the television crime drama "CSI" off the air. But the FCC may set certain general programming rules, such as prohibiting hoaxes, requiring children's programming and regulating politicians' radio and television appearances.

Political Broadcasting Politicians want to be certain of reelection. It is not surprising, then, that in both the 1927 and 1934 laws Congress ensured that broadcasters could not favor one candidate for an elective office over another. The law and the commission's implementing rules say that when one legally qualified candidate for an elective office uses a radio or television station, the station must provide any other legally qualified candidate for the same office with an equal opportunity to use the station if the candidate asks for an opportunity. The law and commission's rules also apply to cable television systems. Section 315 of the 1934 act controls political broadcasting and is in effect any time there are two or more legally qualified candidates for the same office.[24]

Section 315 guarantees equal opportunity rather than equal time. "Equal opportunity" means being given the opportunity to reach approximately the same number and type of people as a candidate's opponent did. Being allowed to purchase a minute of time at midnight is not equal opportunity if the candidate's opponent purchased a minute at 9 p.m. Nor is being given one minute an equal opportunity if the candidate's opponent has been given 30 minutes. Also, equal opportunity means getting free time if a candidate's opponent appeared on a station or cable system without paying, or paying for time if a candidate's opponent pays.

Legally Qualified Candidate A legally qualified candidate can be voted for and elected under applicable rules. FCC regulations explain more thoroughly that a legally qualified candidate is someone who has publicly announced a bid for office, has her or his name on the ballot or is a serious write-in candidate. The candidate also must be legally qualified to hold the office.[25] For example, a 25-year-old cannot be a legally qualified candidate for president, because the Constitution requires the president to be at least 35 years old. Independent candidates and those running on a third-party ticket are legally qualified candidates if they meet the criteria.

realWorld Law

Who Wins Political Campaigns? Broadcasters

Political advertising in 2010 enriched television broadcasters by at least $3 billion. That amount is more than the $2.7 billion spent in the 2008 campaign when the presidency was at stake. In part, the 2010 expenditures resulted from U.S. Supreme Court decisions allowing corporations and unions the right to spend unlimited amounts on political ads, as discussed in Chapter 2.[1] In October 2010 alone, United States television viewers were exposed to nearly 1.5 million political commercials. [2]

1. *See Drowning in Campaign Cash*, N.Y. TIMES, Oct. 31, 2010, at WK7; Meg James, *For Ads, Campaigns Play It Old-Media Safe; Candidates Raise Cash on the Internet, but They Spend It on TV*, L.A. TIMES, Oct. 29, 2010, at A1.
2. COMM. DAILY, Nov. 8, 2010.

Candidates in a primary election for, say, mayor would seem to be running against each other. But that is not the case in applying Section 315. In a primary, Democrats oppose other Democrats for their party's nomination and Republicans oppose other Republicans. But neither party's candidates oppose the other's, nor do they oppose independents or third-party candidates. Therefore, if a Democrat buys 60 seconds of advertising time on a radio station during a primary election period, a Republican running in the primary cannot invoke Section 315 to require the station to sell him or her a minute. Not until the general election does a Democrat oppose a Republican as well as all other legally qualified candidates for the office. During the general election every legally qualified candidate may use the equal opportunity rule if another candidate for the office uses a broadcast station or cable system.

Use of a Station or Cable System Section 315's equal opportunity requirement applies when a legally qualified candidate uses a broadcast station or cable system. "Use" is defined as the candidate or the candidate's picture being seen or the candidate's voice being heard on a broadcast station or cable system. The broadcasting of a candidate's name without the candidate's picture or voice is not a use.

Whenever a candidate, her picture or her voice is on a station or cable system, there is a use. This does not apply only to a candidate's commercials. If a candidate appears on a television station's outdoor recreation program to give a fly-fishing demonstration, the candidate has used the station. This is true even if the candidate does not mention that she is a candidate, discuss her platform or refer to politics in any way. Potential voters might have a more favorable impression of the candidate when she proves herself a fly-fishing expert instead of discussing her political platform in a commercial. Her legally qualified opponents, then, may request equal opportunity.

Exceptions to the Use Rule Many years ago, independent and minor party candidates saw a loophole in the law. If a local news program interviews the

Republican and Democratic candidates for mayor, those candidates have used the station. Numerous mayoral candidates could demand equal opportunity, even if the station did not want to interview them. Realizing this, the station could decide to interview none of the candidates.

Not wanting to discourage broadcast reporting, Congress in 1959 adopted four exceptions to the use rule. First, regularly scheduled news programs are exempt. A candidate's appearance on these programs will not trigger Section 315 for opposing candidates. This exemption was meant for the 11 p.m. news and similar local news programs. But when the commission defined this category as including "programs reporting about some area of current events, in a manner similar to more traditional newscasts,"[26] it also included such programs as "Entertainment Tonight"[27] and "Celebrity Justice."[28] If an anchor or reporter on a regularly scheduled news program is a legally qualified candidate for an elective office, equal opportunity will apply. Why doesn't the news program qualify as an exception to the use rule? It is because the reporter, for example, is not the subject of a news report giving voters more information about the reporter's candidacy, the reason Congress adopted the news program exception. Rather, the employee is conveying news about others. If the reporter stays on the air in that role while running for office, all her opponents would be entitled to free air time.

Second, regularly scheduled news interview programs are exempt. These must have been regularly scheduled for some time before the election. For example, scheduling four interview shows, one each week for a month before an election, does not qualify a program as "regularly scheduled." Although this exemption initially was for programs such as "Meet the Press" and "Face the Nation," the FCC has included "Jerry Springer"[29] and even "The Howard Stern Show."[30]

Third, live coverage of bona fide news events is exempt. If a candidate's campaign speech is covered live, the candidate's on-air appearance will not be considered a use. Nor is it a use if candidates participate in a televised debate, no matter who sponsors the debate. Because debates are exempt from the use rule, the debate organizers may include and exclude any candidates they want. Even debates on noncommercial stations are exempt from the Section 315 use rule.[31]

Fourth, candidates' appearances on documentaries do not trigger Section 315 if the appearance is incidental to the program's topic. For example, if a mayoral candidate is an expert on the state's tourist industry and appears in a documentary about that topic, it will not be considered a use. Of course, if the documentary is about the candidate's childhood in a housing project, his appearance would not be incidental to the program's topic and would be a use.

Invoking Section 315 A candidate wanting equal opportunity must request time from the station or cable system within seven days of his opponent's appearance. The candidate need not use the station or system within seven days but must request time within a week. If the candidate fails to make a request within the seven-day period, the station or system need not honor a request for equal opportunity. The station or cable system is under no obligation to notify opponents of a political candidate who uses the station.

Points of Law

How Section 315 Works

If two or more legally qualified candidates are competing for the same elective office and one of the candidates uses a broadcast station or cable system, the station or system, if asked, must provide the candidate's opponents equal opportunity at the lowest unit rate or a comparable rate and without editing or censoring the opposing candidate's message.

1. If two or more legally qualified candidates

   o A legally qualified candidate has publicly announced her candidacy and has secured a place on the ballot or is a serious write-in candidate.

2. Are competing for the same elective office and

   o In a primary election, the test is whether they are running for the same nomination—the same office, and the same political party.

3. One candidate uses a broadcast station or cable system

   o A use is the candidate, the candidate's picture or likeness or the candidate's voice (but not the candidate's name only) being on the station or system—regardless of whether the candidate discusses the election.

   o But it is not a use if the appearance is

   - On a regularly scheduled newscast

   - On a regularly scheduled news interview program

   - In on-the-spot news coverage

   - In a documentary (if the candidate's appearance is not the documentary's primary focus)

4. The station or system, if asked,

   o A candidate must make a request within seven days of his opponent's use.

5. Must provide equal opportunity to the other candidate(s)

   o Equal opportunity is the opportunity to reach approximately the same audience for approximately the same amount of time.

6. At the lowest unit rate or a comparable rate

   o Free if the first candidate did not pay for the time

   o At the lowest unit rate if the ad runs 45 days before a primary or 60 days before a general election

   o At a rate comparable to other advertisers if the ad runs outside the lowest unit rate periods

7. And without editing or censoring the candidate's message.

Lowest Unit Rate If one candidate uses the station or system without paying—for example, making a pot roast as a guest on the station's cooking program—his opponents do not have to pay for their uses. Making one candidate pay while another gets free time is not equal opportunity. But if the first candidate pays for time—buying a minute to show a commercial, for instance—opponents also have to pay.

Congress ensured that politicians had to pay as little as possible to buy advertising time on broadcast stations and cable systems. Section 315 requires a station or system to charge politicians the **lowest unit rate,** equivalent to the rate the very best commercial advertiser pays. The advertiser buying the most time on the station gets the lowest per-minute advertising rate; a political candidate will pay no more than that. It does not matter if a candidate purchases only one minute of time during a campaign or 1,000 minutes of time. Each minute will cost what the station's biggest advertiser pays per minute. Of course, the biggest advertiser will pay less for a minute at 3 a.m. than at 8 p.m. So will political candidates.

lowest unit rate The maximum rate a broadcaster or cable system may charge a politician for advertising time during the 45 days before primary elections and the 60 days before general elections.

To reduce negative political advertising, a 2002 federal law requires candidates to promise stations they will not refer to their opponents in a commercial. A candidate may refer to an opponent only under certain conditions: For a radio commercial, the ad must include the candidate's voice approving the commercial's contents. For a television commercial, the ad must show the candidate or the candidate's picture with a printed statement approving the commercial. If a candidate mentions an opponent and these requirements are not met, the lowest unit rate will not apply.[32]

The lowest unit rate is in effect during the 45 days before any primary election and the 60 days before any general election. Outside those periods, political candidates are charged a rate comparable to other advertisers. If a candidate and a car dealer both buy 50 minutes of advertising time, they will pay the same per-minute amount when the lowest unit rate requirement does not apply.

Sponsorship Identification FCC regulations require any commercial on a broadcast station to identify who paid for the ad.[33] This rule applies to political advertisements as well. A candidate's ad, then, must say on radio or show in print for a televised ad something like, "This advertisement paid for by the Pat Smith for Congress Committee."

Censoring Not Permitted Broadcast stations and cable systems may not edit or censor political appearances. For example, if one candidate appears for 30 minutes showing how to fly-fish, the candidate's opponent must be given 30 minutes if he asks the station for that time. During his 30 minutes, he need not show his fly-fishing technique. He may discuss his candidacy and platform, say why voters should favor him and not his opponent or do anything else he wants with his time. Even if a station knows that a candidate will make racist or homophobic remarks, or say anything else the community does not want to hear, the station may not censor the candidate's presentation or refuse to put the candidate on the air. Similarly, if a station manager believes that a political ad is inappropriate for children, the manager may not air the commercial late at night, for example.[34] The ad must be broadcast when the candidate paid for it to be aired.

Because stations are not permitted to edit or censor, they also are not responsible for what candidates say. If a candidate libels his opponent, the opponent may sue the candidate but not the station.[35]

Reasonable Time for Federal Candidates It is possible for a station to avoid all the complications of political broadcasting by never putting candidates on the air. If the first legally qualified candidate running for an office does not appear on a station, Section 315 would not be triggered for other candidates. Although this is legal under Section 315, the FCC has suggested stations should not refuse candidates air time. The commission believes a station that does not allow its listeners to hear from candidates is not acting in the public interest.

However, Congress recognized this Section 315 loophole and decided to close it—at least for itself. Section 312(a)(7) of the Communications Act requires radio and television stations to provide federal candidates with reasonable access.[36] This means even the first candidate for a federal office asking to buy commercial time must be sold the advertising spot.[37] The federal elective offices are senator, representative and president. Although the law does not specifically state that it applies to cable systems, the FCC assumes it does. Section 312(a)(7) exempts noncommercial stations from complying with the section's requirements.

Section 312(a)(7)'s requirement that commercial stations provide candidates for federal office with "reasonable access" is not clear. The U.S. Supreme Court, rejecting CBS Television Network's decision not to sell President Jimmy Carter 30 minutes of prime time, gave only limited direction in interpreting the statute. The Court said Congress "did not give guidance on how the Commission should implement the statute's access requirement. Essentially, Congress adopted a 'rule of reason' and charged the Commission with its enforcement." Broadcasters must consider each federal candidate's request "on an individualized basis, and broadcasters are required to tailor their responses to accommodate, as much as reasonably possible, a candidate's stated purposes in seeking air time." However, broadcasters also may "give weight to such factors as the amount of time previously sold to the candidate, the disruptive impact on regular programming, and the likelihood of requests for time by rival candidates." But broadcasters may not use these criteria as an excuse to deny federal candidates the time requested. Rather, "broadcasters must cite a realistic danger of substantial program disruption" or the likelihood of too many requests. The Court concluded: "If broadcasters take the appropriate factors into account and act reasonably and in good faith, their decisions will be entitled to deference even if the Commission's analysis would have differed in the first instance. But if broadcasters adopt 'across-the-board policies' and do not attempt to respond to the individualized situation of a particular candidate, the Commission is not compelled to sustain their denial of access."[38]

Aside from being assured they can get on the air, federal candidates are treated under Section 315 just as candidates for state and local offices are.

Candidates' Supporters If a candidate's campaign manager appears in an ad saying, "Vote for my person," is Section 315 in effect? Not unless the candidate, the candidate's picture or the candidate's voice is in the ad. Realizing that this situation would be unfair to others running for the same office, the FCC said opposing candidates' supporters could ask for equal opportunity under the same standards that Section 315 requires. This means the candidate herself cannot ask for equal opportunity if her opponent's supporters use a station, but the candidate's supporters can ask for time. This is called the **Zapple rule**, named after a congressional staff attorney who first asked the FCC about these circumstances.

Broadcast Editorials If a station airs an editorial supporting one candidate, opposing candidates cannot request equal opportunity under Section 315. A federal appellate court said commercial radio and television stations have a First Amendment right to support candidates.[39] A federal law forbids noncommercial stations from supporting political candidates.[40] However, noncommercial stations may air editorials supporting or opposing public issues.[41]

Ballot Issues Section 315 does not apply to ballot issues, such as referendums, state constitutional amendments, initiatives and recalls of elected officials. These may be very controversial questions and broadcast stations may carry many commercials on both sides of these issues, but the equal opportunity rules are not applicable to ballot issues. Section 315 and Section 312(a)(7) apply only to legally qualified candidates for elective offices.

Recordkeeping Radio and television stations must keep records of requests they receive to broadcast political messages by or about candidates or to broadcast messages about "national legislative issues of public importance" or "a political matter of national importance."[42] The records must be available to the public upon request. The Supreme Court upheld the constitutionality of these requirements, adopted as part of the Bipartisan Campaign Reform Act of 2002.[43]

527 Groups A 527 group may purchase advertisements focusing on political issues but may not support or oppose individual candidates for elective office. It could urge people to vote, for example. The term "527 group" comes from a section of the federal tax code exempting the organizations from paying taxes on contributions they receive.[44] There are no limits on the amount of contributions an individual or business may give to a 527 group, unlike political action committees, which are subject to limits. The Federal Election Commission (FEC) and state election commissions do not oversee 527 groups unless a group supports or opposes a candidate. In 2006 and 2007, the FEC fined several 527 groups for violating the tax code rules during the 2004 presidential election. For example, Swift Boat Veterans for Truth spent $22.6 million on television ads opposing John Kerry, the Democratic presidential candidate, and MoveOn.org, a politically liberal group, opposed Republican George W. Bush's reelection. The FEC said that, as 527 groups, neither should have attempted to influence the presidential election.[45]

Children's Programming Despite several decades of deregulating radio and television, the political broadcast rules demonstrate that Congress and the FCC still are concerned about stations operating in the public interest. Children's programming rules also show that broadcasters must respond to the public's concern about radio and television content.

The clash over children's programming on broadcast television has continued for more than half a century. Parents and public advocacy groups representing children demand more and better quality programming meant for young people. Broadcast networks and stations say they carry good quality children's programming responsive to audience preferences. There have been congressional hearings, court cases and FCC proceedings about this issue. But there was little agreement or resolution until Congress acted in 1990, adopting the Children's Television Act.[46] The law sets general requirements for children's programming on broadcast television stations. This portion of the law does not apply to noncommercial stations or cable networks. The law also limits commercial time before, during and after children's programs on broadcast and cable television.

FCC rules require commercial television stations to broadcast programs meeting children's intellectual/cognitive and social/emotional needs. The commission has ruled that "telenovelas" on Spanish-language stations, such as "Cuidado con el Angel," shown here, and "The Jetsons" cartoon program do not meet these requirements.

The statute requires broadcast television stations to provide programming intended for children up to 17 years old that meets their "educational and informational needs."[47] Programming suitable for both children and adults is acceptable. Stations also may promote public television's children's programs and support children's programming in other ways.

Before, during and after programming specifically meant for children 12 years old and younger, advertising is limited to 12 minutes per hour during the week and 10 1/2 minutes per hour on the weekends. These limits are prorated—a half-hour program may have six minutes of commercials on a weekday afternoon, for example. The FCC also has ruled that characters in children's programs cannot appear in commercials before, during or after those programs.[48]

Two cable networks agreed to pay large fines in 2004 for violating the children's programming ad rules. Nickelodeon paid $1 million for not complying with the commercial time limitation and for carrying ads for products associated with the program in which the commercial ran.[49] ABC Family Channel paid $500,000 for carrying commercials for a product related to a program's content.[50]

realWorld Law

Can Children Be Protected from Media Content?

Congress adopted the Children's Television Act before the use of cable and satellite television, wireless services, non-networked devices such as videocassette recorders and DVD players and the Internet became widespread. Reacting to parental concerns about content available to children through these newer media and about the V-chip's effectiveness, Congress passed the Child Safe Viewing Act of 2007.[1] Among other provisions, the law required the FCC to encourage the development and use of advanced program-blocking technologies. In its initial report to Congress, the commission said:

> As a result of a number of technological innovations and the growing convergence of media, children today can access the same content sources from a variety of media platforms, many of which are portable. This increasingly complex media environment carries both risks and opportunities for the nation's children. Among other things, children are able to use the various platforms to discover new opportunities for education. . . . At the same time, however, they can be and often are exposed to harmful material that is inappropriate and unsuitable for minors. . . .

> Noting wide disparities in cost, accessibility, ease of use, range of parental controls, monitoring and children's ability to override controls, among other variables, the commission concluded both "that no single parental control technology available today works across all media platforms" and that "greater education and media literacy for parents, and more effective diffusion of information about the tools available to them" are needed to adequately protect minors.[2]

---

1. Child Safe Viewing Act of 2007, Pub. L. 110-452, 122 Stat. 5025.
2. Implementation of the Child Safe Viewing Act; Examination of Parental Control Technologies for Video or Audio Programming, 24 F.C.C.R. 11413, 11414–15 (2009).

The 1990 law does not state how much children's programming stations must carry. The FCC allowed individual stations to decide.[51] The broadcasting industry's attempts to comply with the law did not please the commission. For example, one industry executive said the cartoon "The Jetsons" was an educational program because it taught children about the future.

By 1996, the FCC lost patience and adopted standards for complying with the 1990 law.[52] The commission ruled that broadcast television stations must carry three hours per week, averaged over a six-month period, of programming specifically intended to meet children's intellectual/cognitive and social/emotional needs. The programs must be at least 30 minutes long, regularly scheduled weekly and broadcast between 7 a.m. and 10 p.m. local time. The commission identifies this as "core programming." A station not meeting the core programming standard may substitute shorter programs, public service announcements for children and programs not scheduled weekly. The FCC may choose not to renew a station's license if the station does not use one of these two methods to meet the requirements or otherwise convince the commission the station's programming meets the law's intent.

The commission's rule clarification did not solve the problem completely. For example, in 2007 the FCC and Univision, a company owning television and radio stations and broadcast and cable networks, agreed that Univision would pay $24 million for failing to comply with the Children's Television Act. For more than two years on 24 television stations, Univision counted telenovelas as children's programming. The FCC described these telenovelas as "similar to teen soap operas and not educational."[53]

The commission requires all television broadcasters to include an on-screen symbol, E/I (for programming designed to educate and inform children), throughout all core programming.[54]

The commission updated the children's television rules as television stations shifted to digital transmission, a transition discussed later in this chapter.[55] Stations using their spectrum allocation to provide several signals have to offer three hours of core programming on each of their channels.

Internet website addresses may be displayed during children's programming only if the website (1) offers a substantial amount of program-related or other noncommercial content, (2) is not primarily intended for commercial purposes, (3) has pages clearly labeled to distinguish noncommercial from commercial sections, and (4) does not immediately display a page used for commercial purposes. This restriction applies to cable television operators as well as all commercial television stations.

The FCC prohibits cartoon or live action characters in children's programs or children's program hosts from selling products in commercials during or adjacent to shows in which the character or host appears.[56] In the context of digital television, the commission's rules prevent displaying a Web address during a children's show if the website uses the show's characters to sell products or the site offers products featuring the show's characters.

It might seem the law forbidding FCC broadcast censorship would preclude the commission's children's programming regulations. However, the FCC said the rules are "reasonable, viewpoint-neutral" requirements for licensees who must operate in the public interest. Because the commission does not "tell licensees what topics they must address," the FCC is not acting as a censor, the commission said.[57]

Lotteries and Contests Broadcast stations may carry information about some, but not all, lotteries.[58] A lottery is a contest with a prize won by chance and requiring a person to purchase a ticket or otherwise give something of value— even buying a box of cereal—to enter the contest. A station located in a state that has a state-sponsored lottery may broadcast information about that lottery.[59] For example, the FCC fined an Arkansas radio station for broadcasting that listeners could go to a Missouri liquor store to purchase "a whole Lotto luck," referring to the Missouri state lottery. Although the liquor store was just across

realWorld Law

Wee/Wii Contest Leads to Death

Contests may boost a station's ratings, but stations must be very careful in devising audience competitions. A Sacramento, Calif., FM radio station ran a promotion in which contestants drank many bottles of water and tried to be the last person to use the bathroom. The winner would receive a Nintendo Wii video game console. The contest was called "Hold Your Wee for a Wii." One contestant died from water intoxication, a condition caused by consuming too much water, leading to a person's electrolytes, particularly sodium, becoming imbalanced. A jury awarded the contestant's family $16.57 million in a wrongful death lawsuit against the station. The station claimed it could not

A Nintendo Wii video game console was central to a radio station's contest leading to a contestant's death. A jury awarded the contestant's family $16.57 million in a wrongful death suit against the station.

have reasonably expected a contestant to suffer water intoxication. The plaintiff refuted this argument by using testimony from other contestants who experienced symptoms and calls to the station warning of such consequences.[1] Although the FCC did not fine the station, it has penalized other stations for not complying with the commission's contest regulations. For example, in 2010 the commission fined a station for posting rules saying a contest winner would be selected on June 13, when the winner was selected the evening of June 12.[2] The commission also fined a station for advertising that a contest winner would win one of three new cars. Rather, the winner received a two-year lease and would not win even that if the car dealership did not approve the winner's credit rating.[3]

---

1. Andy Furillo, *Sacramento Jury Awards $16.6 Million for Mom's Death in Wii Radio Contest*, SACRAMENTO BEE, Oct. 30, 2009, at A1.
2. Nassau Broadcasting III, L.L.C., 25 F.C.C.R. 12347 (2010).
3. Greater Boston Radio, Inc., 24 F.C.C.R. 8661 (2009).

the Arkansas state line in Missouri, the station was licensed in Arkansas, a state without a lottery.[60]

Stations also may carry information about contests sponsored by nonprofit groups or a company that does not sponsor lotteries as its primary business, if state law allows these contests. Stations may carry casino advertisements if casino gambling is legal in the state.[61] Also, stations may air information about contests that federal law allows Native American tribes to sponsor.

Stations may carry advertisements for their own promotional contests. The FCC defines these contests as "a scheme in which a prize is offered or awarded, based upon chance, diligence, knowledge or skill."[62] Advertisements must be honest and accurate, and the contest must be carried out as the ads describe.

Hoaxes FCC rules forbid stations to broadcast a hoax. Under current commission regulations a hoax occurs when a licensee knowingly broadcasts false reports of crimes or catastrophes that "directly cause" foreseeable, "immediate, substantial and actual public harm."[63] However, the definition of "hoax" has changed during the last 95 years. The Radio Act of 1912 made it illegal to transmit a false distress signal or fraudulent signal of any kind.[64] The Radio Act of 1927[65] and the Communications Act of 1934[66] were more limited, prohibiting false distress signals. Although that regulation remains in place today, the FCC adopted the current ban on broadcast hoaxes in 1992.

The most famous broadcast hoax was not a false distress signal, nor was it intended to be a hoax, merely a radio drama. Orson Welles directed and starred in a radio broadcast based on H.G. Wells' novel "The War of the Worlds." The drama aired nationwide on Oct. 30, 1938—the night before Halloween—and depicted Martian monsters emerging from a meteor that landed in New Jersey. Despite Welles breaking in four times to say the broadcast was fictional, the program sounded very real to many listeners. People ran from their homes, cars jammed streets, hospitals treated hysterical listeners and police station telephones were clogged with calls.[67] Some writers argue that newspaper stories exaggerated the public panic,[68] yet the FCC was sufficiently concerned to promise an inquiry. However, because the drama was not a false signal, the commissioners had no grounds to take any action other than making public statements that broadcasters should consider the public interest in choosing their programs.[69]

Almost 45 years after the "War of the Worlds" broadcast, the FCC adopted a regulation attempting to prohibit false broadcasts. During those four decades, the commission chastised stations for airing false weather predictions, reporting a disc jockey's kidnapping that the station staged, claiming a radio personality was lost in the Bermuda Triangle, using sound effects and other techniques while saying the country was under nuclear attack and pretending a murderer called the station to confess on the air.[70]

In 1992 the commission adopted a rule prohibiting the broadcast of false information concerning a crime or catastrophe if the station knows the story is false, it is foreseeable the broadcast will cause substantial public harm and harm does result. Public harm includes police and other public safety officials being diverted from their duties in reaction to a false broadcast.[71]

The FCC has heard of very few incidents since 1992 that could be considered hoaxes and has not punished a single station under the new rule. For example, a San Diego radio station falsely reported the Discovery space shuttle would be diverted from its usual landing area to set down at an airfield surrounded by houses and industry. More than a thousand people showed up, blocking roads

realWorld Law

Just a Joke

The news director for WALE-AM in Providence, R.I., announced over the air that a WALE talk show host had been "shot in the head" while outside the studios. Approximately 10 minutes later, the station stated that the "shooting" had been a dramatization. In the time between the two announcements, several police officers rushed to the scene, as did reporters.

The station management did not have prior knowledge of the hoax. After becoming aware of the circumstances, WALE's program director shut off the station's transmitter until the program's producer agreed to stop the broadcast. When the transmitter was turned back on, the program director aired a disclaimer, broadcast every half-hour for the next 30 hours. The station management fired the talk show host, the station's news director and the program producer. WALE apologized to the public and offered to repay the Providence Police Department for any costs resulting from the hoax. The FCC admonished North American Broadcasting Co., Inc., the licensee of WALE, citing the commission's policy "requiring licensees to program their stations in the public interest."[1]

1. Radio Station WALE (AM), 7 F.C.C.R. 2345 (1992).

and causing police to direct traffic. The commission said the false story was not about a crime or catastrophe, so the station had not violated the rule.[72]

Fairness Doctrine Eighty years ago the Federal Radio Commission, the FCC's predecessor, said radio stations should broadcast various views about public issues.[73] The FCC adopted regulations in 1949 stating how that policy, called the "fairness doctrine," should be put into effect. Forty years later, in 1989, a federal appellate court allowed the doctrine to expire.

The FCC's 1949 rule said that television and radio stations had to (1) air programs discussing public issues, and (2) include a variety of views about controversial issues of public importance.[74] Different views did not have to be presented in one program, but rather the station's overall programming had to reflect important opinions about controversial topics. The commission justified the fairness doctrine by pointing to licensees' responsibilities to the public.[75] The U.S. Supreme Court upheld the doctrine in the 1969 *Red Lion* decision, saying that spectrum scarcity allowed the FCC to require broadcasters to present a variety of opinions.[76] However, the Court has held that the First Amendment protects the print media from being subjected to rules similar to the fairness doctrine.[77]

The FCC changed its rules in 1987, finding that the fairness doctrine violated broadcasters' First Amendment rights.[78] The commission said that broadcasters censored themselves under the fairness doctrine, choosing not to present discussions about important public issues rather than be forced to air a variety of opinions about those issues. In 1989, a federal appellate court upheld challenges to the FCC's decision to eliminate the fairness doctrine.[79]

Recently, some members of Congress have suggested requiring the FCC to adopt fairness doctrine rules again. This proposal, largely based on the number of right-wing rather than left-wing radio talk shows on the air, has not yet been approved.[80]

Two features of the fairness doctrine remained even after 1989. First, the commission's personal attack rule, the *Red Lion* decision's focus, required broadcast stations to provide free reply time to any person or group whose integrity, honesty or character was attacked on the air. The rule did not apply to public officials. Second, the political editorial rule required broadcasters to give free time for a legally qualified candidate to respond to an editorial opposing the candidate or promoting any of the candidate's rivals. But in 2000, a federal appellate court said the FCC had not justified keeping these two rules after it eliminated the fairness doctrine.[81] Public stations still may not endorse or oppose a political candidate, although they may air editorials about public issues.[82]

Sponsorship Identification The FCC requires broadcasters to disclose when they are paid to air material, whether a car advertisement, stories in news programs or a recording.[83] Product placement in programs comes under this regulation, as do video news releases. If the furnished program is political or involves discussion of a controversial issue, broadcasters must tell the material's source even if there was little or no payment. This seemingly innocent rule caused many radio stations enormous problems when the so-called payola scandal broke in the 1960s and once more recently when some stations again were found to have accepted payola. And some television stations ran afoul of the rule recently when they broadcast video news releases (VNR).

Paying a radio station or station employees to play recordings—payola—spread through the industry in the 1950s and '60s. On-air personalities took money and other gifts from recording companies to play rock records and promote artists. Congress investigated and adopted an anti-payola law in 1960.[84] The commission's own rules require stations to inform listeners when someone pays to air programming.[85] Although the law made clear that a station's employees taking money to play records violated FCC regulations and could lead to criminal punishment, payola did not stop.[86] Recording companies used intermediaries to pay radio stations, putting the stations one step removed from the record companies. By the 1990s, some larger station owners were directly paid by recording companies, no longer using intermediaries. For example, in 2000 the FCC fined Clear Channel Communications $8,000. A company Clear Channel purchased had not revealed it received money to play a Bryan Adams recording.[87] That slap-on-the-wrist punishment paled compared with the $36 million in fines the state of New York imposed on four major record companies—Universal Music, Warner, EMI and Sony BMG—for offering radio station personnel trips, concert tickets and other gifts if they would air certain recordings.[88] The New York investigation spurred the FCC to undertake its own payola inquiry, resulting in four large radio station owners—CBS Radio, Citadel Broadcasting, Clear Channel and Entercom—paying fines of $12.5 million in 2007.[89] The FCC, together with the

U.S. Department of Justice and Univision Radio agreed to a $1 million fine to settle a payola investigation in 2010.[90]

Video news releases, essentially public relations stories used to promote a product or even a political agenda, are not new, having been produced since the early 1980s.[91] They first attracted public attention when the newspaper USA Today broke a story in 2005. USA Today reported that commentator Armstrong Williams took $240,000 from the U.S. Department of Education to advance the agency's plans on Williams' syndicated television show. In 2007 the FCC fined 10 stations for playing Williams' programs pushing the No Child Left Behind initiative in 2003. The stations did not tell viewers that Williams had been paid to offer positive commentary.[92] That same year the commission twice fined Comcast Corporation for showing VNRs on its cable channel without disclosing sponsorship identification.[93] The FCC said that although neither the television stations nor the cable channel received money to play the VNRs, the commission's rules require identifying a sponsor when a story contains "too much focus on a product or brand name in the programming." The commission reminded broadcast stations and cable systems that government-sponsored VNRs must state their source.[94]

The FCC also is concerned with product placement and what it calls "product integration." Product placement occurs when a program producer is paid to use as a prop, for example, a can of a particular brand of cola shown on a kitchen counter. Product integration occurs when a program's dialogue or plot focuses on a product.[95]

SUMMARY

THE FIRST AMENDMENT RIGHTS OF BROADCASTERS are not equal to those enjoyed by the print media. Spectrum scarcity limits broadcasting to a select few who obtain FCC licenses. Courts say this justifies limiting broadcasters' free speech rights. Courts also point to broadcasting's pervasiveness and impact on audiences, particularly children. The FCC regulates broadcasting to ensure it operates in the public interest, but the FCC is not allowed to censor broadcasting content.

Section 315 of the Communications Act of 1934 requires broadcasters and cable systems to give equal opportunity to use the airwaves to legally qualified candidates running for the same office. Federal candidates may obtain time even if their opponents have not appeared in a broadcast. A political "candidate" is someone who has announced he or she is running for office and has his or her name on the ballot or is a write-in candidate. "Use" of a station or cable system occurs whenever a candidate's image or voice appears on radio or television. A candidate appearing on a regularly scheduled news or interview program, however, is not deemed to have engaged in use, and the same goes for his or her appearance at a news event or in a documentary. Candidates must ask for equal opportunity within seven days of their opponents' broadcast appearances. Starting 45 days before a primary election and 60 days before a general election, stations and systems may charge candidates no more than the lowest unit rate to purchase time.

A federal law and FCC rules require broadcast television stations to show at least three hours per week of programming that meets children's intellectual/cognitive and social/emotional needs. Broadcasters may carry information about certain, but not all, lotteries and contests. FCC rules prohibit broadcasting hoaxes.

The FCC rescinded the Fairness Doctrine, requiring stations to cover all major views of important public issues. Some members of Congress have suggested the doctrine be adopted again.

FCC rules require that sponsorship identification accompany all material a station did not create itself. ■

Broadcast Licensing

Although pirate (unlicensed) radio stations sometimes can be heard, it is unlawful to operate any broadcast station in the United States without an FCC license. A license allows the station to use part of the broadcast spectrum.[96] A broadcast license is granted for an eight-year period and may be renewed for subsequent eight-year periods. Renewal is assured unless the licensee has not operated in the public interest, has regularly violated FCC rules or has shown a pattern of abusing the law. There is no limit on the number of renewals a station owner may receive; a corporate owner can retain a station license as long as the corporation exists. An FCC license is not transferable: A licensee wanting to sell a broadcast station may sell the building, equipment, transmitter and trucks—but not the license. Licensees do not own the licenses because licensees do not own the spectrum. The FCC acts for the public in allowing a licensee to use the spectrum for the license period.

If a frequency is not already used for broadcasting and two or more competing applicants want a license for the frequency, the FCC holds an auction.[97] The bidder offering to pay the government the most money is awarded the station license. Auctions are not used for noncommercial stations.

To obtain a license, a company or individual must meet certain criteria specified in the 1934 law and the FCC regulations.[98] The criteria apply to a company or an individual purchasing a station. One requirement is that a broadcast licensee must be an American citizen. A foreign corporation may not hold a license, nor may a corporation with more than 20 percent foreign ownership. A foreign government may not be a licensee, nor may a corporation controlled by another corporation with more than 25 percent foreign ownership.[99] These foreign ownership restrictions, first adopted in the 1927 law and continued in the 1934 act, were justified by national security concerns. Congress did not want American media used for foreign propaganda.

A licensee must have good character.[100] The commission does not want licensees who are convicted felons, have committed antitrust violations or have defrauded the FCC.[101] A licensee also must show that she or he has technical expertise and sufficient funds available to operate a station.[102]

realWorld Law

Australian-American

Rupert Murdoch controls newspapers from Australia to England to America, including the Wall Street Journal, the Fox broadcast television network, several Fox news and entertainment cable networks, a direct broadcast satellite company and many other media businesses throughout the world. Murdoch was born in Australia. Before purchasing several American television stations, Murdoch renounced his Australian citizenship and became a U.S. citizen. However, that did not meet the rule requiring licensees to be American citizens because Murdoch's Australian company, News Corporation, owned the stations. Murdoch asked the FCC to waive its rule so that a foreign company could own television

Rupert Murdoch

stations in the United States. The FCC ruled that a waiver would be in the public interest. The commission said forcing News Corporation to sell the stations might have prevented the Fox network from effectively competing with ABC, CBS and NBC. The FCC also said Murdoch controlled News Corporation. Effectively, then, an American citizen owned the company.[1]

---

1. Fox Television Stations, Inc., 78 Rad. Reg. 2d (P & F) 1294 (1995).

For decades, the commission also limited the number of stations a single licensee could own, both in one metropolitan area and nationally. Over time, the FCC removed some and changed other ownership restrictions. For example, there now is no limit on how many radio stations one licensee may own nationally. A single company may own from five to eight radio stations in one metropolitan area, depending on the number of radio stations in that area.[103] One company may own television stations reaching a maximum of 39 percent of the country's television households[104] and may own two television stations in the same community if (1) no more than one of the stations is among the four highest-rated stations in the city, and (2) at least eight independently owned commercial or noncommercial television stations remain in the community.[105] Also, one owner may have licenses for up to two television stations in a community and, at the same time, from one to six radio stations in the same area, depending on how many independent media voices (primarily local broadcast stations and local newspapers) remain in the community.[106] FCC rules forbid a company from owning more than one of the top four broadcast television networks—that is, ABC, CBS, Fox and NBC.[107]

A commission rule applying only to the country's 20 largest metropolitan areas allows a radio station licensee also to own a newspaper in the same city.[108] The rule also permits one owner to have a television station license and a newspaper in the same community if (1) the station is not one of the four most popular television stations in the city, and (2) at least eight independent "major media voices" remain in the metropolitan area after the television station and newspaper are joined under one owner. Major media voices include commercial and public full-power television stations and major newspapers. Before this rule was adopted, one owner could not control both a newspaper and a broadcast station in the same city.

The FCC has attempted to increase the number of minority- and female-owned broadcast stations.[109] Courts struck down the commission's rules specifically favoring these groups.[110] The commission then decided to give special consideration in awarding new broadcast licenses to those who own few or no other radio or television stations or daily newspapers. This is done by giving such applicants a financial discount in bidding for station licenses through the FCC's auction process.[111]

FCC rules also encourage stations to recruit members of minority groups and women as employees, particularly in positions of responsibility.[112] The rules require careful recordkeeping to show the FCC how well stations are doing with such recruiting efforts.[113]

Points of Law

Local Radio Station Ownership

The FCC's rules say a licensee may control a maximum number of radio station licenses in a community, depending on the number of local radio stations.

- *Communities with up to 14 radio stations:* Up to five stations, but no more than three AM or three FM stations, and no more than half the total number of stations in the community

- *Communities with 15–29 stations:* Up to six stations, but no more than four AM or four FM stations

- *Communities with 30–44 stations:* Up to seven stations, but no more than four AM or four FM stations

- *Communities with 45 or more stations:* Up to eight stations, but no more than five AM or five FM stations[1]

1. 47 C.F.R. § 73.3555(a).

Noncommercial Broadcasting

The FCC oversees public broadcasting stations, which must comply with most of the same rules commercial broadcasters follow. Public stations do not carry advertising.[114] However, corporations and individuals make financial contributions to noncommercial stations and may receive on-air acknowledgments of those contributions. The Communications Act bans advertisements on noncommercial stations that "promote any service, facility, or product" of a for-profit company.[115] The FCC interprets this as prohibiting announcements containing comparative or qualitative descriptions; price information; or exhortations to buy, rent or lease products or services.[116] The commission fines noncommercial stations violating this rule when they broadcast announcements more like an advertisement than an acknowledgment that a company gave the station a contribution.[117]

Public stations receive funding from the Corporation for Public Broadcasting (CPB). Congress allocates money to the CPB, which also receives funds from other sources. The CPB helps support National Public Radio (NPR) and the Public Broadcasting Service (PBS), which provides programming to public television stations.

The Public Broadcasting Act established the CPB. The act says public stations must strictly adhere to "objectivity and balance in all programs or series of programs of a controversial nature."[118] The Public Broadcasting Act did not give the FCC specific powers to enforce that requirement.[119] Despite the Public Broadcasting Act's "objectivity" language, the Supreme Court has allowed public stations to air editorials favoring or opposing public and political issues.[120] Public stations have "important journalistic freedoms which the First Amendment jealously protects," the Court said.[121]

Public station personnel may use their best judgments in selecting programming, courts have held. For example, several viewers sued two public stations that refused to show a program, "Death of a Princess," describing "the motivations and circumstances which were said to have led to the . . . execution for adultery of a Saudi Arabian princess and her commoner lover."[122] FCC regulations giving licensees the power to accept or reject any programming apply to public stations as well, a federal appellate court said.

Noncommercial stations may identify businesses and individuals contributing to the stations but may not air commercials. The difference is not always clear, but the FCC says announcements "may not contain comparative or qualitative descriptions, price information . . . or inducements to buy, sell, rent or lease."[123]

The FCC awards licenses to operate noncommercial stations by using a point system. The commission gives two points for ownership diversity, favoring license applicants without other stations near the community for which the license is being awarded. One to two points are awarded to applicants with technical proposals allowing the station's signal to cover large parts of the metropolitan area. Three points may be awarded if the applicant is based within the community for which the license is being awarded. The applicant with the highest number of points is awarded the license.[124]

SUMMARY

Every broadcast station must have an FCC license. If there is an available frequency, or if a station is being sold, the commission grants licenses to applicants who meet certain criteria. An applicant must be an American citizen or a corporation not controlled by foreign interests. An applicant also must be of good character and have the technical and financial ability to operate a station. The commission has a complex, ever-changing set of rules limiting broadcast ownership. The FCC recently changed some of these rules, but a federal appellate court stopped the new rules' enforcement.

Although the Public Broadcasting Act requires noncommercial stations to be objective, the FCC has no power to enforce the law, and the Supreme Court allowed public stations to air editorials supporting political candidates. ∎

Cable Television Regulation

Turn on a television set and a picture appears. Viewers do not care if the picture comes from an over-the-air signal sent by a broadcast station or a signal sent through a wire by a cable system. But to regulators there is a world of difference. Broadcast television stations use the spectrum to transmit signals. The Communications Act of 1934 gives the FCC jurisdiction over spectrum users. The FCC—not states, not cities—regulates broadcasting. Cable systems send signals through a wire—coaxial cable or fiber optic lines—and do not use the spectrum. However, cable systems do use public land, running their wires over or under city streets, sidewalks, alleys and other property. Does this mean local governments regulate cable systems and the FCC does not? The answer is not that simple.

Cable Regulation's Development

Cable television began because some people could not use the spectrum—they could not get a television signal. Programs began coming into television-owning homes in the late 1940s, but rural area residents could not receive them. Either they were too far away from the station's transmitter or the signal could not get through mountains or other barriers. Seeing an opportunity, a power company employee built a large antenna in the Appalachian Mountains of Pennsylvania. The antenna received signals from Philadelphia television stations. A wire ran from the antenna to a building, and other wires from there to houses with television sets, giving birth to cable television.[125] For decades, it was called "community antenna television" (CATV).

During the 1950s the FCC considered whether it had jurisdiction over CATV and decided not to become involved.[126] But broadcast television station owners became wary of CATV. They thought CATV could take away broadcast viewers and stations' advertisers. Station owners urged the FCC to look again at cable.

In 1962, the FCC said some CATV operators used microwave transmissions to get signals from stations' transmitters to the cable systems' antennas. Microwave transmissions use the spectrum. That was enough for the FCC to say it had jurisdiction over at least part of the CATV business.[127] With that jurisdiction, the commission adopted several CATV rules. Cable operators challenged the commission's authority to control CATV, but the U.S. Supreme Court upheld the FCC's cable jurisdiction.[128] The Court said CATV had the potential to affect broadcast television. Because the commission was responsible for protecting the public's interest in broadcasting, it had the right to oversee CATV as ancillary to its responsibility toward broadcasting, the Court held.

Broadcasters initially were wrong. Cable had little impact on broadcast television, except to allow viewing in homes that could not receive stations' signals over the air. But commission rule changes in the mid-1970s allowed cable systems to carry signals of stations not in the local community. For example, cable systems picked up Channel 17 in Atlanta, making WTBS the first superstation. Significantly, Home Box Office (HBO) began a pay cable service in 1975. With distant station signals and HBO, cable television could offer programming not available on local television stations.

Pole Rules Cable's wires started to attract considerable attention. Cable systems needed to string their wires across public streets, sidewalks and alleys. These are called public rights-of-way, and local governments control them. Telephone companies and power companies controlled poles that cable systems needed to use to string their wires down the streets. Cable was becoming a major factor in the home entertainment business, and others wanted to benefit. Cities charged high fees for cable to use rights-of-way. Pole owners charged high rents to allow cable systems to attach their wires. Trying to resolve disputes surrounding the industry, Congress allowed the FCC to take control of pole attachment agreements, limiting the rates pole owners could charge cable companies.[129]

Federal Cable Laws Controversy surrounded cable television by the early 1980s. Communities wanted to regulate cable, arguing that systems' wires ran over public streets and sidewalks. Telephone companies wanted to offer cable services throughout the country. Cable operators did not want their monthly customer charges regulated. Trying to strike a compromise among these and other competing interests, Congress adopted the Cable Communications Policy Act of 1984.[130] Somewhat deregulating the cable industry, the law gave local and state governments and the federal government shared authority over cable.

Only a few years later, critics said the 1984 law gave the cable industry monopoly power in communities and allowed cable companies to raise rates without limit, offer poor customer service and prevent any competition. Congress responded by re-regulating cable in the Cable Television Consumer Protection and Competition Act of 1992.[131] The 1992 law responded to cable customer complaints by allowing the government to regulate rates cable systems charged subscribers. Congress also thought competition would keep down cable rates and improve customer service. To foster competition, Congress required the cable industry to offer competitors, such as direct broadcast satellite companies, the programming cable companies had developed, such as ESPN and MTV. The 1992 law also barred local governments from letting only one cable system provide service if others wanted to compete and required cable systems to carry local broadcast television stations.

Congressional views about regulation seem to change with each election. Just four years after the 1992 law took effect, Congress adopted the Telecommunications Act of 1996, loosening many of the cable regulations imposed in 1992.[132] Designed primarily to foster competition in the telephone industry, the 1996 law also affected cable. It deregulated cable subscriber rates, again allowing cable companies to raise most prices without government permission. The basic, lowest-level programming package remains rate regulated for most cable systems. The law also allows cable companies to offer local telephone service.

Cable's First Amendment Rights The 1984, 1992 and 1996 laws did not define cable's First Amendment status. Should content-based regulations imposed on cable television be subject to strict scrutiny analysis of their constitutionality, as required for print media? Or should an intermediate scrutiny standard of judicial review be used, giving cable limited First Amendment rights similar to broadcasting's restricted First Amendment protection? The Supreme Court has vacillated. It once decided the cable industry had protection similar to the print media,[133] then suggested it was not certain what First Amendment analysis applied to cable television[134] and finally applied strict scrutiny to cable content regulations.[135]

In ruling on cable's challenge to must-carry rules—regulations requiring cable systems to transmit local broadcast television stations—the Supreme Court said cable sends signals by wire, not through the air. Therefore, the spectrum scarcity rationale does not apply to cable. In 1994 in *Turner Broadcasting System, Inc. v. FCC,* the Court applied to cable the First Amendment test it uses for print media: If the regulation affects speech because of its content, apply strict scrutiny; if the regulation is content neutral, apply an intermediate standard.[136] (Strict scrutiny and intermediate scrutiny are discussed in Chapter 2.) The 1994 *Turner* decision is excerpted at the end of this chapter. In the 1997 *Turner* decision the Court upheld the must-carry rules, saying they are content neutral, further a substantial governmental interest that is not related to suppressing speech and are no more restrictive than necessary.[137] These rules are discussed more fully later in this chapter.

However, two years later in *Denver Area Educational Telecommunications Consortium, Inc. v. FCC,* the Supreme Court overturned a law allowing cable companies to reject sexually offensive material on certain channels.[138] The justices could not agree on what First Amendment test to use for cable, despite having the *Turner* decision as precedent. Justice Stephen Breyer, writing only for himself and three other justices, said technology changed too fast to definitively apply a single standard to cable television. Instead, the four justices applied "close judicial scrutiny," a standard the Court never had used before for any mass medium. Justice Breyer said the test meant the statute was constitutional if "it properly addresses an extremely important problem, without imposing, in light of the relevant interests, an unnecessarily great restriction on speech."[139]

In its next try, the Court seemed to get it right. In 2000, the Court said that content-specific cable regulations are to be judged by the strict scrutiny test. The *United States v. Playboy Entertainment Enterprises, Inc.* case involved Congress' concern about adult programming on cable.[140] Even if a cable customer does not subscribe to an adult

U.S. Supreme Court Justice Stephen Breyer said fast-changing technology made it difficult to determine what cable television's First Amendment rights should be.

channel, the channel's signal could bleed into an adjacent channel and be seen. To protect children from seeing adult programming, Congress said cable systems had to take one of two steps. First, they could fully scramble adult channels' signals so programming could not be seen even if the signals bled. Alternatively, they could choose to carry adult programming only late at night when most children were not watching.[141] Hearing a challenge to the law, all nine Supreme Court justices said the restriction was content based, not content neutral, because it applied only to certain programming. To be constitutional, a content-based regulation must pass the strict scrutiny test, meeting two criteria. First, the regulation has to be narrowly tailored to further a compelling governmental interest. Second, there can be no alternative means of achieving Congress' goal that restricts First Amendment rights less than the adopted law does. The Court said although shielding children from adult programming is a compelling governmental interest, an alternative exists: subscribers can tell their cable company to block the adult channel's signal before it reaches their home. On that basis, the Court overturned the law.

The Court, then, held that strict scrutiny is the proper test for content-based regulations applied to cable television, and the intermediate test is to be used for content-neutral regulations. This approach still leaves much room for regulating cable, and cable does face much regulation.

Cable Franchising

Just as broadcast stations may not operate without an FCC license, cable systems may not provide service without permission from a local government. Usually, permission is obtained from the city where service will be offered. Alternatively, a few state governments, such as Hawaii and Connecticut, regulate cable companies. Some states, such as New York, give authority over cable to both the state and local governments. In areas not incorporated as cities, a county government oversees cable. The FCC requires cable systems to register with the commission before providing service, but the commission does not license cable systems.

franchise A contract or agreement between a government, usually a city, and a cable system operator.

franchising authority The governmental unit granting a franchise to a cable system operator; usually a city, but may also be a state or county.

A **franchise** is a contract or agreement between a government, usually a city, and a cable system operator. A cable system must obtain a franchise from the **franchising authority** where the system will offer service. Because franchises are contracts, they are negotiated between the cable company and the franchising authority—the city, county or state. The 1984, 1992 and 1996 federal laws establish certain franchise limits and requirements. Beyond that, the two sides must reach agreement. In general, the franchising authority is offering permission to use public rights-of-way for the system's wires to be placed over (on telephone and power poles) and under (in underground conduits) the city's streets and sidewalks. In return the cable company is offering to provide service to the community.

Franchises contain many provisions. For example, franchises are for definite periods of time. Once granted for as long as 20 or 25 years, franchises now usually are granted for 10 or fewer years. They may be renewed if the cable company and franchising authority agree. Franchise documents may be long and complex or short and simple, largely depending on the community's size—the bigger the city, the more detailed and complex the franchise will be.

Franchise fees—the charges cable system companies pay to franchising authorities to use public rights-of-way—once were a contentious point in negotiating a franchise. Early in cable's history, authorities charged as much as 35 percent of a cable system's income for the right to provide cable service in the community. The 1984 act set a maximum of 5 percent of a system's gross annual revenues.[142] Cable systems pass the franchise fees on to subscribers. If a cable system pays a 5 percent franchise fee, its subscribers will be charged 5 percent more than the rate for services.

The 1984 cable act limits franchising authorities' control of programming.[143] A franchise may require the cable system to offer subscribers certain categories of programming, such as children's programming, news and public affairs and sports. But the franchise may not require or prevent carrying particular cable networks, such as Nickelodeon, CNN or ESPN. Congress saw this provision as allowing communities to insist that certain kinds of programming be available without giving cities the right to censor cable operators' programming choices.

A cable company and its franchising authority can agree to renew the franchise, negotiating terms as they did for the initial franchise. However, if the franchising authority is unwilling to negotiate a renewal, the 1984 law specifies the process a cable operator may use to require the franchising authority to consider renewal.[144] Thirty to 36 months before the franchise expiration date, the cable operator notifies the city that the process will begin. The franchising authority must start a study of, first, how well the cable operator has served the city and, second, what the community will need from its cable system in the future. The cable system gives the city a proposal for a renewed franchise, taking into consideration the city's study. The franchising authority then may negotiate a franchise renewal. But if it tentatively decides not to renew, the city must hold a hearing—with lawyers, witnesses, public comment and evidence—to make a final decision. Finally, the franchising authority may deny renewal only if the cable operator (1) did not meet important franchise obligations, (2) provided poor customer service and inadequate programming, (3) does not have the financial, legal and technical ability to operate the system, or (4) did not promise to meet the community's future cable needs. The cable operator may appeal a final denial to the courts.

A cable operator may sell a system. Selling a cable system is similar to selling a broadcast station. The cable operator sells the equipment, the subscriber list, the trucks—everything but the franchise. The franchise belongs to the franchising authority, just as a broadcast license belongs to the FCC. A franchising authority may agree to allow the transfer of a franchise from one cable operator to another or may refuse to allow the transfer. A franchising authority also may ask to renegotiate the franchise before approving a transfer. If a franchising authority does not decide to approve or refuse a transfer request within three months of being asked, the 1992 act says, then approval is assumed.[145]

franchise fees The charges cable companies pay to franchising authorities for the right to use public rights-of-way.

Franchising authorities may not grant an exclusive cable franchise. If they request one, other qualified cable operators, including telephone companies, must be given a franchise to compete with an existing cable system in a community.[146] Similarly, the FCC in 2007 ruled that cable and satellite systems may not have exclusive contracts with owners of apartment buildings and other multiple-dwelling units. Building owners must allow their residents a choice of video service providers, whether the local cable system, a satellite system or other programming supplier.[147]

In 2007 the FCC stepped into the franchising process to ensure existing cable companies faced competition, particularly from telephone companies.[148] The commission required franchising authorities to speed up franchise negotiations with companies seeking to offer cable service, restricted cities' requests for certain payments and limited franchising authorities' demands for how quickly new cable providers have to offer service to the entire city. The FCC said it adopted these regulations to prevent franchising authorities from unreasonably preventing new cable providers from offering service.

Cable System Ownership Attempting to prevent any cable system operator from monopolizing cable service or programming, Congress in the 1992 cable act allowed the FCC to limit the number of subscribers one cable operator could serve. The commission twice set the maximum at 30 percent of all cable subscribers and twice, most recently in 2009, the U.S. Court of Appeals for the D.C. Circuit said the FCC did not justify that cap.[149] In the 2009 decision the court said the commission had not considered the growth of other multichannel video services (MVS), particularly direct broadcast satellites, as alternatives to cable. Other MVS could prevent a cable operator from dominating the field, the court said. In an earlier case the D.C. Circuit ruled the commission could set a subscriber limit,[150] but the FCC has not yet convinced the court that a 30 percent cap is justifiable.

Federal statutes additionally prevent the owner of a cable system from also controlling any other MVS in the city or country where the cable system provides service.[151] This restriction is waived when a cable system faces effective competition from, for example, a telephone company offering service comparable to that which the cable system provides.

Although once telephone companies were not allowed to own cable systems due to fears they simply would swallow the cable industry, today telephone companies may be cable system owners. They may operate cable systems under four different regulatory schemes, some requiring a franchise, others not.[152]

SUMMARY

THE FCC INITIALLY DECLINED TO REGULATE CABLE TELEVISION. In 1984, a federal law spread cable television jurisdiction between local governments and the FCC. After some vacillating, the Supreme Court said the strict scrutiny test should be applied to regulations affecting cable content, and the intermediate scrutiny test should be applied to content-neutral regulations imposed on cable.

Cable systems must have a franchise to offer service. Franchising authorities and cable operators negotiate terms of franchises. Franchises include provisions, for example, specifying the franchise fee and categories of programming the system will provide. Franchises may be renewed. If the franchising authority balks at renewing, the cable system may initiate a formal renewal process. Franchising authorities must approve sales of cable systems to new owners.

Congress has allowed the FCC to impose certain limits on cable system ownership, but courts have rejected the commission's cap forbidding any cable system owner to reach more than 30 percent of households that receive television programming by cable or satellite. ■

Cable Programming

Congress has tried to balance several factors in regulating cable programming. Congress knows that the First Amendment protects operators' choice of cable networks and other programs. But Congress also wants to ensure competition, such as from direct broadcast satellite systems, to help hold down customer rates. And Congress believes that cable systems have sufficient numbers of channels to allow the public, schools and local governments to use some cable system capacity as well as permit individuals or companies to purchase time on cable channels. Congress also wants cable systems to carry most local broadcasting stations to protect over-the-air television's future.

Cable Must-Carry and Retransmission Consent Rules Currently, nearly 90 percent of television viewers do not receive programming through antennas.[153] Most subscribe to cable, and others subscribe to direct broadcast satellite or other delivery systems. Broadcast television stations, then, must be on cable systems or most viewers will not watch them. Congress knew that subscribers would demand their cable systems carry the most popular local stations, but Congress was concerned about less popular stations. Cable systems would have no reason to use channel capacity for these marginal stations. The great majority of viewers, then, would not—could not—watch these stations. Congress argued that stations not carried would go out of business because they would have no audience and therefore no advertisers. To prevent this problem, Congress adopted the must-carry rules.

The number of local stations a cable system must carry depends on how many channels the system has. The largest systems must devote up to one-third of their channels to local stations plus carry all local noncommercial stations that do not duplicate another station's programming. A cable system must carry all of a station's programming, not just a few hours per day. A system is required to carry the station on the cable channel number that is the same as a station's

realWorld Law

When More Providers Equals Less Access

Broadcast television stations may demand or negotiate for carriage on cable and satellite television systems. Negotiating for carriage is called "retransmission consent." Usually, a retransmission agreement involves the cable or satellite system paying money to the station. However, large corporations now own many stations and also own cable programming networks. For example, Walt Disney Co. owns a number of television stations, the ABC television network, the several ESPN networks, ABC Family and others. When Disney negotiated with Time Warner Cable, the corporate owner of many cable systems throughout the United States, to carry the Disney-owned television stations, it asked Time Warner to pay to carry the cable networks and Disney-owned websites as well as paying to carry the stations. Time Warner agreed.

When an agreement cannot be reached, television stations—including those carrying broadcast networks—and cable networks are blacked out, preventing cable and satellite subscribers from seeing programming. In 2010, News Corp., which owns the Fox broadcasting stations and Fox broadcasting and cable networks, could not reach a deal with Cablevision, the cable system for 3 million New York City-area customers. Cablevision's subscribers were cut off from the World Series and other sports telecasts and even, for a time, Fox's online video. Satellite providers face similar problems. Dish Network, the second-largest satellite television service, faced a dispute about contract terms, including payments, with News Corp. in 2010, finally settling the conflict just before the World Series and election coverage. Fox and Dish reached an agreement before blackouts occurred, but Cablevision subscribers faced blackouts on Fox television stations and cable networks for two weeks before Fox and Cablevision signed a contract.

on-air channel number—broadcast channel 4 is carried on cable channel 4—unless the station agrees otherwise. The must-carry rules were applied to digital television signals beginning in 2009, when stations switched from analog to digital transmission.

A local station does not have to require carriage on a cable system. Instead, the station may choose to negotiate with the system for carriage.[154] The law calls this **retransmission consent.** Cable operators need to carry network-affiliated and popular independent television stations. These remain among the most watched programming on cable systems. Because they are so popular, these stations have negotiating power. The stations may demand that cable systems pay to carry the stations under the retransmission consent provision. Also, television networks such as ABC, CBS, NBC and Fox own many television stations. These station groups use the retransmission consent provision to negotiate carriage with large cable system owners such as Comcast and Time Warner. Unless a television station has chosen must-carry status, it will be dropped from a cable system's channel lineup if the station and system cannot agree on retransmission compensation.

The 1992 law said cable systems could carry broadcast television stations only with the stations' consent or under the law's must-carry provision. Every three years commercial television stations choose between must-carry and

retransmission consent Part of the federal cable television law allowing broadcast television stations to negotiate.

retransmission consent. Noncommercial stations may not choose retransmission consent; they are carried under the must-carry provision.

The cable industry fought the must-carry rule in court. Cable companies argued that a system can carry only a limited number of networks. Finding room to carry a local station's signal could force a cable system to eliminate programming it already was carrying—the Food Channel, for example. Cable companies also argued the must-carry rules therefore were content-specific regulations, forcing cable to choose a local station over some other programming. Congress would have to show it had a compelling interest to justify imposing a content-specific rule, cable companies argued, and no such compelling interest existed.

In the second *Turner Broadcasting System, Inc. v. FCC decision,* in 1997, the Supreme Court refused to accept the cable industry's argument that the must-carry rules were content specific.[155] The must-carry rules are content neutral because they do not dictate specific programming, the Court said. To determine the rules' constitutionality, the Court applied the test it established in *United States v. O'Brien,* discussed in Chapter 2.[156] The *O'Brien* test applies to regulations incidentally affecting speech when that is not the regulation's primary purpose. Protecting broadcast stations is an important objective, the Court said, and in doing so Congress did not intend to directly affect cable systems' speech. Rather, Congress needed to adopt the rules to achieve its purpose of ensuring that local stations could be seen on cable television, which approximately two-thirds of viewers use to watch television.

The cable industry again challenged the must-carry rules in 2009. The FCC ruled that Cablevision Systems, the New York City cable provider, must carry a Kingston, N.Y., television station. Kingston is 80 miles from New York City. The U.S. Court of Appeals for the Second Circuit rejected Cablevision's argument that must-carry rules violate cable operators' First Amendment rights.[157] In 2010 the U.S. Supreme Court refused to hear the case.

Cable Access Requirements By the time Congress adopted the Cable Communications Policy Act of 1984, most cable franchises already included provisions for public, educational or governmental (PEG) access channels. The 1984 statute made that reality into law. Congress saw **PEG access channels** as a way to allow the public, various educational institutions and local governments to have access to cable systems in ways they do not have for newspapers, magazines, radio and television stations, and other mass media. The 1984 law permits a franchising authority and cable company to negotiate, as part of the franchising process, to set aside channels for public, educational or governmental use.[158] Although the law does not require cable system operators to agree, they usually do.

PEG access channels Channels that cable systems set aside for public, educational and government use.

Public access channels generally allow local citizens, on a first-come basis, to put on programming they choose. Many municipalities have a government official or nonprofit organization oversee public channel programming.[159] Local school boards and colleges use educational channels. Government channels often carry city council and county board meetings.

A federal appellate court applying intermediate scrutiny found the law's PEG provisions constitutional.[160] However, the court said a cable system's First Amendment rights might be infringed upon if a franchising authority demanded a very large number of PEG channels.

The 1984 law also requires cable systems to make channels available for lease.[161] Congress originally may have meant these commercial leased access channels for cable networks the cable system chose not to carry. Now they more often are used by companies wanting to sell products or services to cable viewers. Medium-sized cable systems must set aside 10 percent of their channels for leased access, and larger systems must make 15 percent of their channels available. Cable operators may use these channels for other purposes, such as carrying cable networks, if no one wants to lease them. The FCC has devised a formula for setting the maximum price systems may charge to lease channels.[162] A federal appellate court upheld the formula and other commission rules applying to commercial leased access channels.[163]

The 1984 cable act prohibits cable system operators from exercising any editorial control over PEG or leased access programming.[164]

Nonduplication Rules To protect local broadcasters, the FCC's rules require a cable system to delete certain programming on distant stations the system carries. The network **nonduplication rules** allow a station carrying network programming to insist that a cable system block duplicate network programs on another station the system carries—even if the programs do not run at the same time.[165] The FCC adopted the rule when there were only three networks—ABC, CBS and NBC. The rule still applies only to those networks' programs.[166]

nonduplication rules FCC regulations requiring cable systems not to carry certain programming that is available through local broadcast stations.

Syndicated exclusivity rules apply to specific programs stations purchase on a market-by-market basis rather than programs provided by a network. A local station that has a contract to show a syndicated program may require a cable system to delete that program from any other station the system carries.[167]

Another FCC rule benefits professional sports team owners. A team may prohibit a local cable system from carrying the team's home game.[168] The blackout rule does not apply if a local television station is broadcasting the game. National Football League team owners have an internal agreement not to prohibit carriage if a home game is sold out at least 72 hours before it is to be played.

Sharing Programs and Channel Capacity To prevent cable companies from developing programming and keeping it to themselves, the 1992 law requires them to sell the programs to competitors.[169] For example, Time Warner owns cable systems throughout the United States. It also owns HBO. The 1992 statute and FCC rules require Time Warner to sell HBO programming, for reasonable rates, to direct broadcast satellite services and other cable competitors.[170] More generally, the FCC says companies owning cable systems and cable networks cannot unreasonably refuse to sell programming to competitors.[171] This provision was to expire in 2002 but the FCC has extended it twice, allowing it to be effective until at least 2012.[172]

The 1992 law also limits the number of channels a cable system may use to show programming that the system's owner controls.[173] By adopting this provision, Congress tried to increase the number of different programmers cable systems would carry. Commission rules say a cable operator may not use more than 40 percent of its channels or 30 channels, whichever is fewer, to carry programming in which the operator's owner has a financial interest. This limit applies to a cable system's first 75 channels.[174]

Cable Subscribers' Privacy When Congress adopted the first federal law regulating cable television, it was concerned about subscribers' privacy because cable operators would have access to bank-from-home and shop-from-home records as well as customers' programming choices. That was 1984. More than 25 years later, these concerns may have some basis in reality. Cable systems offer Internet connections that their customers use for banking and shopping from home. In 1984 Congress did not envision the Internet. Nonetheless, to protect cable subscribers Congress limited the information cable systems were allowed to collect and distribute.[175]

A cable company may obtain information such as a customer's name, address, phone number and programming services without the subscriber's permission, but it may use the information only to provide programming and to ensure that subscribers pay for the services they order. Also, a cable company may not share that information with others without the customer's permission, unless the sharing is necessary to provide requested programming and other services or for the cable operator's own business reasons. Cable companies may distribute aggregate information without their subscribers' permission if the information does not identify individual customers.

Cable systems are required to give customers an annual written notice explaining their privacy rights. The notice must say what subscriber information the company is collecting, what use the system makes of it, to whom it is disclosed and for what purpose. It also must explain how long the company will retain the information and that customers may sue if the cable system does not follow the privacy rules.

SUMMARY

CABLE SYSTEMS ARE REQUIRED TO USE A PORTION of their channels to carry local broadcast television stations. Every three years, stations choose to require their carriage or to negotiate with cable systems for carriage. The Supreme Court ruled the must-carry rules are constitutional. A cable operator and franchising authority may negotiate to include public, educational and governmental access channels on the system. Federal law requires cable systems to set aside several channels for lease.

Broadcasters may require cable systems to delete duplicative network and syndicated programming. Professional sports team owners may require blacking out home games, unless a local television station is carrying the game. Federal law prohibits the cable industry from unreasonably refusing to sell programming to competitors, such as direct broadcast satellite operators. The law also limits the number of channels a cable system may devote to programming in which the system's owner has a financial interest. ∎

Direct Broadcast Satellites

More than 20 million American households receive their television programming by subscribing to a direct broadcast satellite (DBS) service.[176] DBS was not entirely successful in the mid-1980s, when several companies offering the service failed financially. For many years, DBS used a large backyard antenna, called a dish, for receiving satellite signals. Currently, a small dish attached to a roof or the side of a house can receive signals from a high-powered satellite.

To encourage DBS service as a cable competitor, the FCC did not classify satellite service as broadcasting. The commission's decision relieved DBS of the regulatory burdens that broadcasters face. The commission instead categorized DBS as a point-to-multipoint nonbroadcast service, a ruling upheld in court.[177] Dissatisfied with the FCC's decision not to impose regulations on DBS, Congress, in the Cable Television Consumer Protection and Competition Act of 1992, required DBS providers to abide by the political broadcasting rules in Sections 315 and 312(a)(7). The law also required DBS operators to offer leased access channels for noncommercial educational purposes.[178] A federal appellate court rejected the PEG and leased access requirements as infringing on DBS providers' First Amendment rights.[179]

As DBS became a more prominent multichannel video provider, the FCC imposed additional regulations. The commission said DBS operators must abide by the syndicated exclusivity, network nonduplication and sports blackout rules.[180] In 1998, the FCC returned to its objective of having DBS operators use some of their capacity for educational programming. The commission required satellite operators to set aside 4 percent of their channel capacity for educational or informational programming.[181] The commission said carrying noncommercial broadcast stations would not satisfy this requirement. The FCC also required DBS systems to comply with the same advertising limits during children's programming the commission applied to broadcast television stations.[182]

Sirius, which combined with XM Radio in 2008, offers subscription satellite radio services. The FCC has regulatory power over Sirius because the company uses radio frequencies to transmit its programming.

DBS emerged as a challenger to cable's dominance when Congress allowed satellite services to offer subscribers their local television stations as well as satellite programming.[183] In 2010 Congress renewed legislation requiring a DBS operator to offer all local stations if the operator offers one or more local stations to subscribers.[184] If the satellite service offers one or more local stations carried in high definition, by no later than 2012 it must offer all high-definition signals from all stations in that city, the FCC ruled in 2008.[185] The commission also said commercial television stations may choose must-carry status or retransmission consent, as the stations may do for cable carriage.[186]

Internet Regulation

The Internet began as a computer network ensuring there would be a military communications network in the event of a nuclear attack. The goal was to set up a series of computers that could continue to receive and relay data even if one or more links in the communication chain were broken.[187] This network grew into the Internet, a series of computers linked together almost randomly. The Internet is redundant, meaning there are many ways for a message to get from its origin to its intended recipient. The computers comprising this network are in universities, government installations, public and private companies and other locations. There is no central focus, no international regulating agency. The Internet Corporation for Assigned Names and Numbers (ICANN) is a nonprofit organization responsible for standardizing the technology and computer codes needed to allow the simultaneous, instantaneous exchange of billions of messages. In particular, ICANN oversees the domain name system. Domain names are World Wide Web site names, such as www.fcc.gov. But ICANN does not regulate the Internet as, say, the FCC regulates broadcasting.[188]

FCC Internet Regulation

The FCC has considered its role in Internet regulation since 2005. Acknowledging Congress had not given the commission statutory authority over the Internet, the FCC said it had ancillary jurisdiction.[189] The notion of ancillary jurisdiction comes from the 1934 Communications Act. That law provides the FCC with the power to act "as may be necessary in the execution of its functions."[190] Years before Congress adopted the first cable television law in 1984, the U.S. Supreme Court held that the 1934 act's language gave the FCC jurisdiction over cable as "ancillary" to its statutory right to regulate broadcasting.[191] Because cable could have an adverse effect on broadcasters' business, the FCC said, the commission could regulate cable to protect local broadcast stations.

Although initially the FCC took a "hands off the Internet" approach, more recently it claimed it has ancillary jurisdiction over broadband. The FCC's claimed ancillary jurisdiction over the Internet has been upheld and rejected by courts. For example, one way to gain high-speed Internet access is through a cable modem offered by a cable television system. An Internet service provider (ISP) provides the Internet connection. In mid-2005 the Supreme Court held that cable television systems do not have to give their customers a choice of ISPs.[192] Many cable systems wanted their customers to use only an ISP the system owned or with which the system had an agreement. But other ISPs might want to use a cable system to provide high-speed Internet access through cable modems. Must cable systems allow these other ISPs to offer access?

The case turned on deciding into what legal category cable Internet access falls. The Telecommunications Act of 1996 says providers of telecommunications service can be regulated, which includes requiring them to sell access to their networks to anyone wanting it.[193] However, information service providers are not regulated and therefore can prevent anyone they want from using their networks. The FCC had decided each cable Internet access is an information service, not a telecommunications service.[194] The Supreme Court said the 1996 law was ambiguous on this point. Therefore, the FCC had a right to interpret that part of the law and courts should abide by the commission's decision, the Court said. The Court's ruling, allowing the FCC to categorize cable modem service as an information service, permits cable system operators to choose what ISPs may offer high-speed Internet access through cable modems. The ruling also prevents local cable television franchising authorities from regulating high-speed Internet access through cable modems.

As the volume of Internet traffic increased, particularly with the exchange of video files, some ISPs blocked or delayed certain Internet transmissions, allowing other messages to be sent more quickly. The FCC attempted to deal with this issue, called "network (or net) neutrality," but the U.S. Court of Appeals for the D.C. Circuit ruled the commission had no authority over the matter. Pitting the Internet's traditional free nature against ISPs' business interests, net neutrality would treat all Internet traffic equally. Alternatively, may an ISP favor certain messages over others? Perhaps the ISP charges more to carry some messages or the ISP needs to treat messages differently to allow its network to function most efficiently. In 2008, the FCC ruled that Comcast, a cable company also providing broadband Internet access, could not "selectively target and interfere with connections of peer-to-peer (P2P) applications." Comcast claimed it needed to divert and delay some Internet traffic that used particular peer-to-peer applications so Comcast could prevent network congestion. The commission said "the company's discriminatory and arbitrary practice unduly squelches the dynamic benefits of an open and accessible Internet."[195] However, the D.C. Circuit ruled that Congress had not given the FCC explicit statutory "authority to regulate an Internet service provider's network management practices."[196]

A few months after that court defeat, the commission made another attempt to regulate net neutrality. In December 2010 the FCC adopted rules forbidding Internet providers from blocking lawful content and applications that computers use. Nor may these providers unreasonably discriminate in transmitting content. The FCC could interpret this to prevent Internet providers from charging more to speed transmission of certain content while moving other content more slowly. Providers of mobile Internet services, such as for cell phones, may not block lawful websites or voice or video applications that compete with the provider's services. The commission based these rules on its ancillary jurisdiction over the Internet and on various other communications act provisions.[197] Judicial and congressional challenges to the FCC's net neutrality decision have begun.

The Internet's First Amendment Status

In overturning a congressional attempt to limit online sexual expression, the Supreme Court held in *Reno v. ACLU* that the Internet has complete First Amendment protection.[198] *Reno v. ACLU* decided a challenge to the Communications Decency Act (CDA), a provision of the Telecommunications Act of 1996.[199] The CDA prohibited using the Internet to transmit indecent, patently offensive or obscene material to minors.

To determine the CDA's constitutionality, the Court had to decide what First Amendment protections apply to the Internet. The starting assumption is that the First Amendment protects expression communicated by any means. But the Court has said each mass medium has its own peculiarities, so there may need to be adjustments to a medium's First Amendment rights. Broadcasting, for example, uses a scarce spectrum, justifying its limited First Amendment protection. The Internet does not use the spectrum. Nor is the Internet as invasive as broadcasting, the Court said in *Reno*. Families not wanting their children to have Internet access do not need to subscribe to an Internet service. There are reasons to regulate broadcasting, the Court said, but the Internet has not been "subject to the type of government supervision and regulation that has attended the broadcast industry."[200] Unlike broadcasting, the Internet does not have any special characteristics that require decreasing its First Amendment rights, the *Reno* Court held.

Justice John Paul Stevens, writing for the Court majority, emphasized the "wide variety of communication" taking place on the Internet and the number of places—homes and universities and cafés—where Internet access is available. Stevens characterized the Internet as "a unique medium" that is "located in no particular geographical location but available to anyone, anywhere in the world." The Internet is "a vast platform from which to address and hear from a worldwide audience of millions of readers, viewers, researchers, and buyers. Any person or organization with a computer connected to the Internet can 'publish' information," the Court said.[201]

Further emphasizing its unique nature as a communications medium, Justice Stevens said the Internet

includes not only traditional print and news services, but also audio, video, and still images, as well as interactive, real-time dialogue. Through the use of chat rooms, any person with a phone line can become a town crier with a voice that resonates farther than it could from any soapbox.

realWorld Law

Mailbox or Sandbox?

Justice John Paul Stevens, writing for the U.S. Supreme Court, said: "It is true that we have repeatedly recognized the governmental interest in protecting children from harmful materials. But that interest does not justify an unnecessarily broad suppression of speech addressed to adults. As we have explained, the Government may not 'reduce the adult population [to] only what is fit for children.'" Justice Stevens also said, "Regardless of the strength of the government's interest" in protecting children, "the level of discourse reaching a mailbox simply cannot be limited to that which would be suitable for a sandbox."[1]

---

1. Reno v. ACLU, 521 U.S. 844, 875 (1997) (citations omitted).

Through the use of Web pages, mail exploders, and newsgroups, the same individual can become a pamphleteer. . . . [O]ur cases provide no basis for qualifying the level of First Amendment scrutiny that should be applied to this medium.[202]

Having held that Internet content has full First Amendment protection, the Court overturned congressional restrictions on transmitting indecent and patently offensive material through the Internet. The Court did uphold the ban on obscene content sent over the Internet. The First Amendment does not protect obscene material on the Internet or in any medium. Courts define "obscenity" narrowly: material that appeals to the prurient interest, is patently offensive and has no serious literary, artistic, political or scientific value.[203] The *Reno* Court rejected the Communications Decency Act's limit on patently offensive material. Patent offensiveness is only one of the three factors defining obscenity. Patently offensive material may be protected if the other two obscenity elements are not present. (Additional Supreme Court decisions about indecency and the Internet are discussed in Chapter 12.)

SUMMARY

AT FIRST, THE FCC CHOSE TO REGULATE DIRECT broadcast satellites minimally. As DBS developed into a cable competitor, Congress required the commission to impose on satellite operators some cable and broadcast regulations. Congress allowed DBS to provide its subscribers their local television stations.

The Supreme Court said the Internet has full First Amendment protection. Although Congress has not given the FCC complete authorization to regulate the Internet, the commission has claimed it has ancillary jurisdiction over broadband providers. ∎

Cases for Study

Thinking About It

The two case excerpts that follow deal with an older mass medium, broadcasting, and a newer one, cable television. As you read these case excerpts, keep the following questions in mind:

- How does the U.S. Supreme Court treat each medium under the First Amendment?
- What reasons does the Court give for the way it applies the First Amendment to broadcasting and cable?
- Do these two decisions logically lead to the Court's ruling in *Reno v. ACLU* that the Internet should have full First Amendment protection?

Red Lion Broadcasting Co., Inc. v. Federal Communications Commission
SUPREME COURT OF THE UNITED STATES
395 U.S. 367 (1969)

[In the years after the U.S. Supreme Court ruled in *Red Lion*, the fairness doctrine and its corollary regulations, the personal attack and political editorial rules, have been found unconstitutional by the courts or rescinded by the FCC. However, the *Red Lion* decision remains important precedent for the spectrum scarcity rationale that still underlies broadcast regulation.]

JUSTICE BYRON WHITE delivered the Court's opinion:

The Federal Communications Commission has for many years imposed on radio and television broadcasters the requirement that discussion of public issues be presented on broadcast stations, and that each side of those issues must be given fair coverage. This is known as the fairness doctrine, which originated very early in the history of broadcasting and has maintained its present outlines for some time. It is an obligation whose content has been defined in a long series of FCC rulings in particular cases, and which is distinct from the statutory requirement of Section 315 of the Communications Act that equal time be allotted all qualified candidates for public office. Two aspects

of the fairness doctrine, relating to personal attacks in the context of controversial public issues and to political editorializing, were codified more precisely in the form of FCC regulations in 1967. The two cases before us now, which were decided separately below, challenge the constitutional and statutory bases of the doctrine and component rules. *Red Lion* involves the application of the fairness doctrine to a particular broadcast, and *RTNDA* arises as an action to review the FCC's 1967 promulgation of the personal attack and political editorializing regulations, which were laid down after the *Red Lion* litigation had begun.

I.

A.

The Red Lion Broadcasting Company is licensed to operate a Pennsylvania radio station, WGCB. On November 27, 1964, WGCB carried a 15-minute broadcast by the Reverend Billy James Hargis as part of a "Christian Crusade" series. A book by Fred J. Cook entitled "Goldwater—Extremist on the Right" was discussed by Hargis, who said that Cook had been fired by a newspaper for making false charges against city officials; that Cook had then worked for a Communist-affiliated publication; that he had defended Alger Hiss and attacked J. Edgar Hoover and the Central Intelligence Agency; and that he had now written a "book to smear and destroy Barry Goldwater." When Cook heard of the broadcast he concluded that he had been personally attacked and demanded free reply time, which the station refused. After an exchange of letters among Cook, Red Lion, and the FCC, the FCC declared that the Hargis broadcast constituted a personal attack on Cook; that Red Lion had failed to meet its obligation under the fairness doctrine . . . to send a tape, transcript, or summary of the broadcast to Cook and offer him reply time; and that the station must provide reply time whether or not Cook would pay for it. On review in the Court of Appeals for the District of Columbia Circuit, the FCC's position was upheld as constitutional and otherwise proper. . . .

C.

Believing that the specific application of the fairness doctrine in *Red Lion,* and the promulgation of the regulations in *RTNDA,* are both authorized by Congress and enhance rather than abridge the freedoms of speech and press protected by the First Amendment, we hold them valid and constitutional, reversing the judgment below in *RTNDA* and affirming the judgment below in *Red Lion.*

II.

The history of the emergence of the fairness doctrine and of the related legislation shows that the Commission's action in the *Red Lion* case did not exceed its authority, and that in adopting the new regulations the Commission was implementing congressional policy rather than embarking on a frolic of its own.

A.

Before 1927, the allocation of frequencies was left entirely to the private sector, and the result was chaos. It quickly became apparent that broadcast frequencies constituted a scarce resource whose use could be regulated and rationalized only by the Government.

Without government control, the medium would be of little use because of the cacophony of competing voices, none of which could be clearly and predictably heard. Consequently, the Federal Radio Commission was established to allocate frequencies among competing applicants in a manner responsive to the public "convenience, interest, or necessity."

Very shortly thereafter the Commission expressed its view that the "public interest requires ample play for the free and fair competition of opposing views, and the commission believes that the principle applies . . . to all discussions of issues of importance to the public." This doctrine was applied through denial of license renewals or construction permits, both by the FRC, and its successor FCC. After an extended period during which the licensee was obliged not only to cover and to cover fairly the views of others, but also to refrain from expressing his own personal views, the latter limitation on the licensee was abandoned and the doctrine developed into its present form.

There is a twofold duty laid down by the FCC's decisions and described by the 1949 Report on Editorializing by Broadcast Licensees. The broadcaster must give adequate coverage to public issues, and coverage must be fair in that it accurately reflects the opposing views. This must be done at the broadcaster's own expense if sponsorship is unavailable. Moreover, the duty must be met by programming obtained at the licensee's own initiative if available from no other source. . . .

When a personal attack has been made on a figure involved in a public issue, . . . [it is required] that the individual attacked himself be offered an opportunity to respond. Likewise, where one candidate is endorsed in a political editorial, the other candidates must themselves be offered reply time to use personally or through a spokesman. These obligations differ from the general fairness requirement that issues be presented, and presented with coverage of competing views, in that the broadcaster does not have the option of presenting the attacked party's side himself or choosing a third party to represent that side. But insofar as there is an obligation of the broadcaster to see that both sides are presented, and insofar as that is an affirmative obligation, the personal attack doctrine and regulations do not differ from the preceding fairness doctrine. The simple fact that the attacked men or unendorsed candidates may respond themselves or through agents is not a critical distinction, and indeed, it is not unreasonable for the FCC to conclude that the objective of adequate presentation of all sides may best be served by allowing those most closely affected to make the response, rather than leaving the response in the hands of the station which has attacked their candidacies, endorsed their opponents, or carried a personal attack upon them. . . .

III.

The broadcasters challenge the fairness doctrine and its specific manifestations in the personal attack and political editorial rules on conventional First Amendment grounds, alleging that the rules abridge their freedom of speech and press. Their contention is that the First Amendment protects their desire to use their allotted frequencies continuously to broadcast whatever they choose, and to exclude whomever they choose from ever using that frequency. No man may be prevented from saying or publishing what he thinks, or from refusing in his speech or other utterances to give equal weight to the views of his opponents. This right, they say, applies equally to broadcasters.

A.

Although broadcasting is clearly a medium affected by a First Amendment interest, differences in the characteristics of new media justify differences in the standards applied to them. For example, the ability of new technology to produce sounds more raucous than those of the human voice justifies restrictions on the sound level, and on the hours and places of use, of sound trucks so long as the restrictions are reasonable and applied without discrimination.

Just as the Government may limit the use of sound-amplifying equipment potentially so noisy that it drowns out civilized private speech, so may the Government limit the use of broadcast equipment. The right of free speech of a broadcaster, the user of a sound truck, or any other individual does not embrace a right to snuff out the free speech of others. . . .

It was . . . the chaos which ensued from permitting anyone to use any frequency at whatever power level he wished, which made necessary the enactment of the Radio Act of 1927 and the Communications Act of 1934. It was this reality which at the very least necessitated first the division of the radio spectrum into portions reserved respectively for public broadcasting and for other important radio uses such as amateur operation, aircraft, police, defense, and navigation; and then the subdivision of each portion, and assignment of specific frequencies to individual users or groups of users. Beyond this, however, because the frequencies reserved for public broadcasting were limited in number, it was essential for the Government to tell some applicants that they could not broadcast at all because there was room for only a few.

Where there are substantially more individuals who want to broadcast than there are frequencies to allocate, it is idle to posit an unabridgeable First Amendment right to broadcast comparable to the right of every individual to speak, write, or publish. If 100 persons want broadcast licenses but there are only 10 frequencies to allocate, all of them may have the same "right" to a license; but if there is to be any effective communication by radio, only a few can be licensed and the rest must be barred from the airwaves. It would be strange if the First Amendment, aimed at protecting and furthering communications, prevented the Government from making radio communication possible by requiring licenses to broadcast and by limiting the number of licenses so as not to overcrowd the spectrum.

This has been the consistent view of the Court. Congress unquestionably has the power to grant and deny licenses and to eliminate existing stations. No one has a First Amendment right to a license or to monopolize a radio frequency; to deny a station license because "the public interest" requires it "is not a denial of free speech."

By the same token, as far as the First Amendment is concerned those who are licensed stand no better than those to whom licenses are refused. A license permits broadcasting, but the licensee has no constitutional right to be the one who holds the license or to monopolize a radio frequency to the exclusion of his fellow citizens. There is nothing in the First Amendment which prevents the Government from requiring a licensee to share his frequency with others and to conduct himself as a proxy or fiduciary with obligations to present those views and voices which are representative of his community and which would otherwise, by necessity, be barred from the airwaves.

This is not to say that the First Amendment is irrelevant to public broadcasting. On the contrary, it has a major role to play as the Congress itself recognized in forbidding FCC interference with "the right of free speech by means of radio communication." Because of the scarcity of radio frequencies, the Government is permitted to put restraints on licensees in favor of others whose views should be expressed on this unique medium. But the people as a whole retain their interest in free speech by radio and their collective right to have the medium function consistently with the ends and purposes of the First Amendment. It is the right of the viewers and listeners, not the right of the broadcasters, which is paramount. It is the purpose of the First Amendment to preserve an uninhibited marketplace of ideas in which truth will ultimately prevail, rather than to countenance monopolization of that market, whether it be by the Government itself or a private licensee. "Speech concerning public affairs is more than self-expression; it is the essence of self-government." It is the right of the public to receive suitable access to social, political, esthetic, moral, and other ideas and experiences which is crucial here. That right may not constitutionally be abridged either by Congress or by the FCC.

B.

Rather than confer frequency monopolies on a relatively small number of licensees, in a Nation of 200,000,000, the Government could surely have decreed that each frequency should be shared among all or some of those who wish to use it, each being assigned a portion of the broadcast day or the broadcast week. The ruling and regulations at issue here do not go quite so far. They assert that under specified circumstances, a licensee must offer to make available a reasonable amount of broadcast time to those who have a view different from that which has already been expressed on his station. The expression of a political endorsement, or of a personal attack while dealing with a controversial public issue, simply triggers this time sharing. As we have said, the *First Amendment* confers no right

on licensees to prevent others from broadcasting on "their" frequencies and no right to an unconditional monopoly of a scarce resource which the Government has denied others the right to use.

In terms of constitutional principle, and as enforced sharing of a scarce resource, the personal attack and political editorial rules are indistinguishable from the equal-time provision of Section 315, a specific enactment of Congress requiring stations to set aside reply time under specified circumstances and to which the fairness doctrine and these constituent regulations are important complements. That provision, which has been part of the law since 1927, has been held valid by this Court as an obligation of the licensee relieving him of any power in any way to prevent or censor the broadcast, and thus insulating him from liability for defamation. The constitutionality of the statute under the First Amendment was unquestioned.

Nor can we say that it is inconsistent with the First Amendment goal of producing an informed public capable of conducting its own affairs to require a broadcaster to permit answers to personal attacks occurring in the course of discussing controversial issues, or to require that the political opponents of those endorsed by the station be given a chance to communicate with the public. Otherwise, station owners and a few networks would have unfettered power to make time available only to the highest bidders, to communicate only their own views on public issues, people and candidates, and to permit on the air only those with whom they agreed. There is no sanctuary in the First Amendment for unlimited private censorship operating in a medium not open to all. "Freedom of the press from governmental interference under the First Amendment does not sanction repression of that freedom by private interests."

C.

It is strenuously argued, however, that if political editorials or personal attacks will trigger an obligation in broadcasters to afford the opportunity for expression to speakers who need not pay for time and whose views are unpalatable to the licensees, then broadcasters will be irresistibly forced to self-censorship and their coverage of controversial public issues will be eliminated or at least rendered wholly ineffective. Such a result would indeed be a serious matter, for should licensees actually eliminate their coverage of controversial issues, the purposes of the doctrine would be stifled.

At this point, however, as the Federal Communications Commission has indicated, that possibility is at best speculative. The communications industry, and in particular the networks, have taken pains to present controversial issues in the past, and even now they do not assert that they intend to abandon their efforts in this regard. It would be better if the FCC's encouragement were never necessary to induce the broadcasters to meet their responsibility. And if experience with the administration of these doctrines indicates that they have the net effect of reducing rather than enhancing the volume and quality of coverage, there will be time enough to reconsider the constitutional implications. The fairness doctrine in the past has had no such overall effect.

That this will occur now seems unlikely, however, since if present licensees should suddenly prove timorous, the Commission is not powerless to insist that they give adequate and fair attention to public issues. It does not violate the First Amendment to treat licensees given the privilege of using scarce radio frequencies as proxies for the entire community, obligated to give suitable time and attention to matters of great public concern. To condition the granting or renewal of licenses on a willingness to present representative community views on controversial issues is consistent with the ends and purposes of those constitutional provisions forbidding the abridgment of freedom of speech and freedom of the press. Congress need not stand idly by and permit those with licenses to ignore the problems which beset the people or to exclude from the airways anything but their own views of fundamental questions. The statute, long administrative practice, and cases are to this effect.

Licenses to broadcast do not confer ownership of designated frequencies, but only the temporary privilege of using them. . . . The statute mandates the issuance of licenses if the "public convenience, interest, or necessity will be served thereby." . . . [In 1943] the Court considered the validity of the Commission's chain broadcasting regulations, which among other things forbade stations from devoting too much time to network programs in order that there be suitable opportunity for local programs serving local needs. The Court upheld the regulations, unequivocally recognizing that the Commission was more than a traffic policeman concerned with the technical aspects of broadcasting and that it neither exceeded its powers under the statute nor transgressed the First Amendment in interesting itself in general program format and the kinds of programs broadcast by licensees. . . .

E.

It is argued that even if at one time the lack of available frequencies for all who wished to use them justified the Government's choice of those who would best serve the public interest by acting as proxy for those who would present differing views, or by giving the latter access directly to broadcast facilities, this condition no longer prevails so that continuing control is not justified. To this there are several answers.

Scarcity is not entirely a thing of the past. Advances in technology . . . have led to more efficient utilization of the frequency spectrum, but uses for that spectrum have also grown apace. Portions of the spectrum must be reserved for vital uses unconnected with human communication, such as radio-navigational aids used by aircraft and vessels. Conflicts have even emerged between such vital functions as defense preparedness and experimentation in methods of averting midair collisions through radio warning devices. . . .

The rapidity with which technological advances succeed one another to create more efficient use of spectrum space on the one hand, and to create new uses for that space by ever growing numbers of people on the other, makes it unwise to speculate on the future allocation of that space. It is enough to say that the resource is one of considerable and growing importance whose scarcity impelled its regulation by an agency authorized by Congress. . . .

Even where there are gaps in spectrum utilization, the fact remains that existing broadcasters have often attained their present position because of their initial government selection in competition with others before new technological advances opened new opportunities for further uses. Long experience in broadcasting, confirmed habits of listeners and viewers, network affiliation, and other advantages in program procurement give existing broadcasters a substantial advantage over new entrants, even where new entry is technologically possible. These advantages are the fruit of a preferred position conferred by the Government. Some present possibility for new entry by competing stations is not enough, in itself, to render unconstitutional the Government's effort to assure that a broadcaster's programming ranges widely enough to serve the public interest.

In view of the scarcity of broadcast frequencies, the Government's role in allocating those frequencies, and the legitimate claims of those unable without governmental assistance to gain access to those frequencies for expression of their views, we hold the regulations and ruling at issue here are both authorized by statute and constitutional. . . .

Turner Broadcasting System, Inc., v. Federal Communications Commission
SUPREME COURT OF THE UNITED STATES
512 U.S. 622 (1994)

JUSTICE ANTHONY KENNEDY delivered the opinion of the Court:
. . . [T]he Cable Television Consumer Protection and Competition Act of 1992 requires cable television systems to devote a portion of their channels to the transmission of local broadcast television stations. This case presents the question whether these provisions abridge the freedom of speech or of the press, in violation of the First Amendment. . . .

The role of cable television in the Nation's communications system has undergone dramatic change over the past 45 years. Given the pace of technological advancement and the increasing convergence between cable and other electronic media, the cable industry today stands at the center of an ongoing telecommunications revolution with still undefined potential to affect the way we communicate and develop our intellectual resources.

The earliest cable systems were built in the late 1940's to bring clear broadcast television signals to remote or mountainous communities. The purpose was not to replace broadcast television but to enhance it. Modern cable systems do much more than enhance the reception of nearby broadcast television stations. With the capacity to carry dozens of channels and import distant programming signals via satellite or microwave relay, today's cable systems are in direct competition with over-the-air broadcasters as an independent source of television programming.

Broadcast and cable television are distinguished by the different technologies through which they reach viewers. Broadcast stations radiate electromagnetic signals from a central transmitting antenna. These signals can be captured, in turn, by any television set within the antenna's range. Cable systems, by contrast, rely upon a physical, point-to-point connection between a transmission facility and the television sets of individual subscribers. Cable systems make this connection much like telephone companies, using cable or optical fibers strung above ground or buried in ducts to reach the homes or businesses of subscribers. The construction of this physical infrastructure entails the use of public rights-of-way and easements and often results in the disruption of traffic on streets and other public property. As a result, the cable medium may depend for its very existence upon express permission from local governing authorities.

Cable technology affords two principal benefits over broadcast. First, it eliminates the signal interference sometimes encountered in over-the-air broadcasting and thus gives viewers undistorted reception of broadcast stations. Second, it is capable of transmitting many more channels than are available through broadcasting, giving subscribers access to far greater programming variety. . . .

The cable television industry includes both cable operators (those who own the physical cable network and transmit the cable signal to the viewer) and cable programmers (those who produce television programs and sell or license them to cable operators). In some cases, cable operators have acquired ownership of cable programmers, and vice versa. Although cable operators may create some of their own programming, most of their programming is drawn from outside sources. These outside sources include not only local or distant broadcast stations, but also the many national and regional cable programming networks that have emerged in recent years, such as CNN, MTV, ESPN, TNT, C-SPAN, The Family Channel, Nickelodeon, Arts and Entertainment, Black Entertainment Television, CourtTV, The Discovery Channel, American Movie Classics, Comedy Central, The Learning Channel, and The Weather Channel. Once the cable operator has selected the programming sources, the cable system functions, in essence, as a conduit for the speech of others, transmitting it on a continuous and unedited basis to subscribers.

In contrast to commercial broadcast stations, which transmit signals at no charge to viewers and generate revenues by selling time to advertisers, cable systems charge subscribers a monthly fee for the right to receive cable programming and rely to a lesser extent on advertising. In most instances, cable subscribers choose the stations they will receive by selecting among various plans, or "tiers," of cable service. In a typical offering, the basic tier consists of local broadcast stations plus a number of cable programming networks selected by the cable operator. For an additional cost, subscribers can obtain channels devoted to particular subjects or interests, such as recent-release feature movies, sports, children's programming, sexually explicit programming, and the like. Many cable systems also offer pay-per-view service, which allows an individual subscriber to order and pay a one-time fee to see a single movie or program at a set time of the day.

On October 5, 1992, Congress overrode a Presidential veto to enact the Cable Television Consumer Protection and Competition Act of 1992. Among other things, the Act subjects the cable industry to rate regulation by the Federal Communications Commission (FCC) and by municipal franchising authorities; prohibits municipalities from awarding exclusive franchises to cable operators; imposes various restrictions on cable programmers that are affiliated with cable operators; and directs the FCC to develop and promulgate regulations imposing minimum technical standards for cable operators. At issue in this case is the constitutionality of the so-called must-carry provisions, which require cable operators to carry the signals of a specified number of local broadcast television stations. . . .

Congress enacted the 1992 Cable Act after conducting three years of hearings on the structure and operation of the cable television industry. . . . Congress found that the physical characteristics of cable transmission, compounded by the increasing concentration of economic power in the cable industry, are endangering the ability of over-the-air broadcast television stations to compete for a viewing audience and thus for necessary operating revenues. Congress determined that regulation of the market for video programming was necessary to correct this competitive imbalance.

In particular, Congress found that over 60 percent of the households with television sets subscribe to cable, and for these households cable has replaced over-the-air broadcast television as the primary provider of video programming. This is so, Congress found, because "most subscribers to cable television systems do not or cannot maintain antennas to receive broadcast television services, do not have input selector switches to convert from a cable to antenna reception system, or cannot otherwise receive broadcast television services." In addition, Congress concluded that due to "local franchising requirements and the extraordinary expense of constructing more than one cable television system to serve a particular geographic area," the overwhelming majority of cable operators exercise a monopoly over cable service. "The result," Congress determined, "is undue market power for the cable operator as compared to that of consumers and video programmers."

According to Congress, this market position gives cable operators the power and the incentive to harm broadcast competitors. The power derives from the cable operator's ability, as owner of the transmission facility, to "terminate the retransmission of the broadcast signal, refuse to carry new signals, or reposition a broadcast signal to a disadvantageous channel position." The incentive derives from the economic reality that "cable television systems and broadcast television stations increasingly compete for television advertising revenues." By refusing carriage of broadcasters' signals, cable operators, as a practical matter, can reduce the number of households that have access to the broadcasters' programming, and thereby capture advertising dollars that would otherwise go to broadcast stations. . . .

In light of these technological and economic conditions, Congress concluded that unless cable operators are required to carry local broadcast stations, "[t]here is a substantial likelihood that . . . additional local broadcast signals will be deleted, repositioned, or not carried"; the "marked shift in market share" from broadcast to cable will continue to erode the advertising revenue base which sustains free local broadcast television; and that, as a consequence, "the economic viability of free local broadcast television and its ability to originate quality local programming will be seriously jeopardized.". . .

There can be no disagreement on an initial premise: Cable programmers and cable operators engage in and transmit speech, and they are entitled to the protection of the speech and press provisions of the First Amendment. Through "original programming or by exercising editorial discretion over which stations or programs to include in its repertoire," cable programmers and operators "seek to communicate messages on a wide variety of topics and in a wide variety of formats." By requiring cable systems to set aside a portion of their channels for local broadcasters, the must-carry rules regulate cable speech in two respects: The rules reduce the number of channels over which cable operators exercise unfettered control, and they render it more difficult for cable programmers to compete for carriage on the limited channels remaining. Nevertheless, because not every interference with speech triggers the same degree of scrutiny under the First Amendment, we must decide at the outset the level of scrutiny applicable to the must-carry provisions.

We address first the Government's contention that regulation of cable television should be analyzed under the same First Amendment standard that applies to regulation of broadcast television. It is true that our cases have permitted more intrusive regulation of broadcast speakers than of speakers in other media. . . . But the rationale for applying a less rigorous standard of First Amendment scrutiny to broadcast regulation, whatever its validity in the cases elaborating it, does not apply in the context of cable regulation.

The justification for our distinct approach to broadcast regulation rests upon the unique physical limitations of the broadcast medium. As a general matter, there are more would-be broadcasters than frequencies available in the electromagnetic spectrum. And if two broadcasters were to attempt to transmit over the same frequency in the same locale, they would interfere with one another's signals, so that neither could be heard at all. The scarcity of broadcast frequencies thus required the establishment of some regulatory mechanism to divide the electromagnetic spectrum and assign specific frequencies to particular broadcasters. In addition, the inherent physical limitation on the number of speakers who may use the broadcast medium has been thought to require some adjustment in traditional First Amendment analysis to permit the Government to place limited content restraints, and impose certain affirmative obligations, on broadcast licensees. As we said in *Red Lion*, "where there are substantially more individuals who want to broadcast than there are frequencies to allocate, it is idle to posit an unabridgeable First Amendment right to broadcast comparable to the right of every individual to speak, write, or publish." . . .

. . . The broadcast cases are inapposite in the present context because cable television does not suffer from the inherent limitations that characterize the broadcast medium. Indeed, given the rapid advances in fiber optics and digital compression technology, soon there may be no practical limitation on the number of speakers who may use the cable medium. Nor is there any danger of physical interference between two cable speakers attempting to share the same channel. . . .

This is not to say that the unique physical characteristics of cable transmission should be ignored when determining the constitutionality of regulations affecting cable speech. They should not. But whatever relevance these physical characteristics may have in the evaluation of particular cable regulations, they do not require the alteration of settled principles of our First Amendment jurisprudence. . . .

. . . Our precedents thus apply the most exacting scrutiny to regulations that suppress, disadvantage, or impose differential burdens upon speech because of its content. Laws that compel speakers to utter or distribute speech bearing a particular message are subject to the same rigorous scrutiny. In contrast, regulations that are unrelated to the content of speech are subject to an intermediate level of scrutiny, because in most cases they pose a less substantial risk of excising certain ideas or viewpoints from the public dialogue. . . .

As a general rule, laws that by their terms distinguish favored speech from disfavored speech on the basis of the ideas or views expressed are content-based. By contrast, laws that confer benefits or impose burdens on speech without reference to the ideas or views expressed are in most instances content-neutral.

Insofar as they pertain to the carriage of full-power broadcasters, the must-carry rules, on their face, impose burdens and confer benefits without reference to the content of speech. Although the provisions interfere with cable operators' editorial discretion by compelling them to offer carriage to a certain minimum number of broadcast stations, the extent of the interference does not depend upon the content of the cable operators' programming. The rules impose obligations upon all operators, save those with fewer than 300 subscribers, regardless of the programs or stations they now offer or have offered in the past. Nothing in the Act imposes a restriction, penalty, or burden by reason of the views, programs, or stations the cable operator has selected or will select. The number of channels a cable operator must set aside depends only on the operator's channel capacity; hence, an operator cannot avoid or mitigate its obligations under the Act by altering the programming it offers to subscribers.

The must-carry provisions also burden cable programmers by reducing the number of channels for which they can compete. But, again, this burden is unrelated to content, for it extends to all cable programmers irrespective of the programming they choose to offer viewers. And finally, the privileges conferred by the must-carry provisions are also unrelated to content. The rules benefit all full power broadcasters who request carriage—be they commercial or noncommercial, independent or network-affiliated, English or Spanish language, religious or secular. The aggregate effect of the rules is thus to make every full power commercial and noncommercial broadcaster eligible for must-carry, provided only that the broadcaster operates within the same television market as a cable system. . . .

That the must-carry provisions, on their face, do not burden or benefit speech of a particular content does not end the inquiry. Our cases have recognized that even a regulation neutral on its face may be content-based if its manifest purpose is to regulate speech because of the message it conveys.

Appellants contend, in this regard, that the must-carry regulations are content-based because Congress' purpose in enacting them was to promote speech of a favored content. We do not agree. Our review of the Act and its various findings persuades us that Congress' overriding objective in enacting must-carry was not to favor programming of a particular subject matter, viewpoint, or format, but rather to preserve access to free television programming for the 40 percent of Americans without cable. . . .

In short, Congress' acknowledgment that broadcast television stations make a valuable contribution to the Nation's communications system does not render the must-carry scheme content-based. The scope and operation of the challenged provisions make clear, in our view, that Congress designed the must-carry provisions not to promote speech of a particular content, but to prevent cable operators from exploiting their economic power to the detriment of broadcasters, and thereby to ensure that all Americans, especially those unable to subscribe to cable, have access to free television programming—whatever its content. . . .

Chapter 12

I have reached the conclusion . . . that under the First and Fourteenth Amendments criminal laws in this area are constitutionally limited to hard-core pornography. I shall not today attempt further to define the kinds of material I understand to be embraced within that shorthand description; and perhaps I could never succeed in intelligibly doing so. But I know it when I see it.

U.S. Supreme Court Justice Potter Stewart[1]

Janet Jackson's Super Bowl half-time appearance with Justin Timberlake caused the FCC to receive a flood of indecency complaints.

Obscenity, Indecency and Violence

Social Norms and Legal Standards

Obscenity

Comstock and *Hicklin*
Current Obscenity Definition

Enforcing Obscenity Laws

Indecency

Broadcast Indecency
Television Program Ratings
and the V-Chip

Cable Indecency

Internet Indecency

Other Limits on Offensive Speech

Public Funds for
Pornographic Art
Recording Labels
Using Zoning to Restrict
Adult Stores
Dial-a-Porn: Telephone
Indecency

Video Games and Media Violence

Cases for Study

➤ *Miller v. California*
➤ *Fox Television Stations, Inc. v. Federal Communications Commission*

Suppose . . .

. . . that a singer, a singer-actress and a television personality say four-letter words on live television broadcasts. On the one hand, these are words most people have heard from the time they were small children on the playground. On the other hand, for 85 years federal law has banned broadcasting such words. Should the FCC find the words indecent? Should the FCC punish stations for airing them? Look for the answers to these questions when the case of *Fox Television Stations, Inc. v. Federal Communications Commission* is discussed later in this chapter and the case is excerpted at the end of the chapter.

Michelangelo's "David"—a 13-foot statue on display at the Galleria dell'Accademia in Florence, Italy—depicts a fully nude young man. The "Venus de Milo," a sculpture in Paris' Louvre Museum, is a bare-breasted woman. Would Justice Potter Stewart, quoted in the introduction to this chapter, call these famous artistic creations "hard-core pornography"? Or to use the word courts apply today, would he call them "obscene"? Likely, he

The famous "Venus de Milo" statue is not obscene—is it?

would not, and neither would the Supreme Court. If the depiction of nudity is not obscene, what is? Who decides? Using what definition? (A note: There are words in this chapter that may be offensive to some, but part of everyday conversation to others. The words are taken from court and FCC decisions.)

Sexual expression is ubiquitous in contemporary societies—as it has been for centuries. It can be found in art, in beer commercials, on Internet sites and in television programs and movies. There is little agreement—aside from the Supreme Court's definition of "obscenity"—about what sexual expression should be protected and what should be illegal. The argument has two sides, each based on a different set of moral values. Some believe sexually explicit material does not deserve First Amendment protection. Others argue sexual expression is just that—expression. The First Amendment protects depictions of violence because the depictions are not real. Why not protect sexual expression that is not real sex but is only expression?

Current federal and state laws have stripped obscene material of all First Amendment protection. Making, selling, distributing and exhibiting obscene material, and possessing child pornography, are illegal activities. People can be jailed and fined for violating federal and state obscenity statutes.

Sex and "dirty" words that may refer to sex upset many people. For example, when passersby could see a bare buttock on a Jacksonville, Fla., outdoor movie screen, authorities prosecuted the theater owner. A local ordinance prohibited nudity on screens visible from outside the theater area. However, the U.S. Supreme Court said the image on the screen was not obscene.[2] The law abridged the First Amendment, the Court said, because it prohibited all nudity, obscene or not. Those offended by nudity on the screen could choose not to look, the Court said. Similarly, a Vietnam War protester walked into the Los Angeles

Points of Law

Disgusting and Repugnant

The U.S. Supreme Court wrote:

Derived from the Latin *obscaenus*, *ob* to, plus *caenum*, filth, "obscene" is defined in the Webster's Third New International Dictionary as "1a: disgusting to the senses . . . b: grossly repugnant to the generally accepted notions of what is appropriate . . . 2: offensive or revolting as countering or violating some ideal or principle."

The material we are discussing in [Miller v. California] is more accurately defined as "pornography" or "pornographic material." "Pornography" derives from the Greek (*porne*, harlot, and *graphos*, writing). The word now means ". . . a depiction (as in writing or painting) of licentiousness or lewdness: a portrayal of erotic behavior designed to cause sexual excitement." . . . The words "obscene material," as used in this case, have a specific judicial meaning . . ., i.e., obscene material "which deals with sex."[1]

1. Miller v. California, 413 U.S. 15, 19 n.2 (1973).

County courthouse, where women and children were present, with the words "Fuck the draft" printed on the back of his jacket.[3] As discussed in Chapter 3, he was arrested for disturbing the peace. The words may have been offensive, the Supreme Court said in overturning his conviction, but the words were not obscene. People not wanting to see the words may "avert their eyes," the Court said.

There is not even agreement on what word to use in describing offensive sexual expression. The word **pornography** is vague—not legally precise—because it encompasses both protected and unprotected sexual material. The term **indecency** has only a narrow legal meaning, referring to sexual expression inappropriate for children on broadcast radio and television. The obscenity definition the Supreme Court adopted more than three decades ago still is in use and is discussed later in this chapter.

No matter the label applied to sexual expression, heterosexual or homosexual intercourse recorded on videotape or film is a billion-dollar business.[4] Are the participants in these movies willing performers or are they victims of sexual exploitation? What effect do these movies have on women and men generally? Some people opposing sexually explicit content believe the material especially harms women.[5] They contend sexually explicit content in films and magazines and on Internet sites causes violence to women, including rape. They also argue that sexual material may lead to women's subjugation, to their being objectified as sexual objects. Further, these critics are concerned that movies and other materials combining sex and violence may cause some men to mimic what they see, harming their sexual partners.[6] The films' female actors may be physically and emotionally harmed as well, according to this view.[7]

Law professor Catharine MacKinnon has been the most prominent critic arguing that sexually explicit material harms women. In the early 1980s, MacKinnon and others persuaded the Minneapolis and Indianapolis city councils to adopt ordinances declaring that pornography discriminates against women. The ordinances defined "pornography" as material showing "graphic sexually explicit subordination of women" combined with pain, violence or

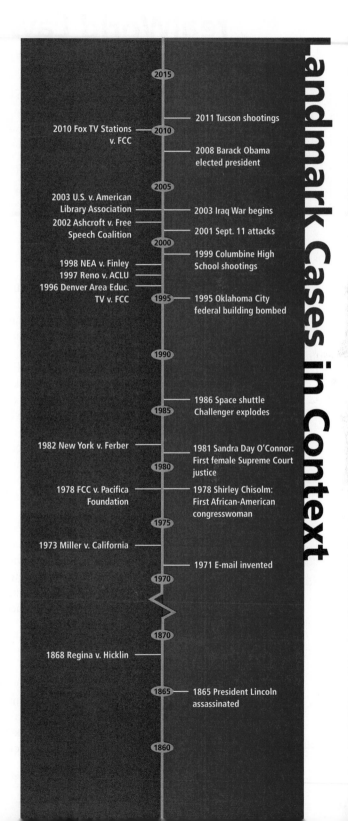

Landmark Cases in Context

- 2015
- 2011 Tucson shootings
- 2010 Fox TV Stations v. FCC — 2010
- 2008 Barack Obama elected president
- 2005
- 2003 U.S. v. American Library Association
- 2003 Iraq War begins
- 2002 Ashcroft v. Free Speech Coalition
- 2001 Sept. 11 attacks
- 2000
- 1998 NEA v. Finley
- 1999 Columbine High School shootings
- 1997 Reno v. ACLU
- 1996 Denver Area Educ. TV v. FCC — 1995
- 1995 Oklahoma City federal building bombed
- 1990
- 1986 Space shuttle Challenger explodes
- 1985
- 1982 New York v. Ferber
- 1981 Sandra Day O'Connor: First female Supreme Court justice
- 1980
- 1978 FCC v. Pacifica Foundation
- 1978 Shirley Chisolm: First African-American congresswoman
- 1975
- 1973 Miller v. California
- 1971 E-mail invented
- 1970
- 1870
- 1868 Regina v. Hicklin
- 1865 — 1865 President Lincoln assassinated
- 1860

realWorld Law

Pornography's Harms

Professor Cass Sunstein says pornography can be harmful to women in three ways. First, many women are forced into being models or actresses in pornographic pictures or films. These usually very young women may be abused and mistreated. Second, Sunstein sees a causal connection between pornography and men committing violence against women. Third, viewing pornography leads to degrading and dehumanizing behavior toward women, including sexual harassment.[1]

---

1. Cass R. Sunstein, Democracy and the Problem of Free Speech 216, 217, 219 (1993).

---

pornography A vague—not legally precise—term for sexually oriented material.

indecency A narrow legal term referring to sexual expression inappropriate for children on broadcast radio and television.

male domination. The Minneapolis mayor vetoed the law. A federal appellate court struck down the Indianapolis ordinance as violating the First Amendment.[8] Although agreeing that pornography plays a role in causing sexual discrimination, the court said nonobscene sexually explicit material is protected speech. Ironically, the court said pornography does cause harm, which demonstrates its power as speech.

The Canadian Parliament adopted a law similar to the Indianapolis statute. The Canadian law makes obscenity illegal and defines "obscenity" as material that unduly exploits sex or combines sex with crime, horror, cruelty or violence. The Canadian Supreme Court upheld the statute despite its apparent conflict with the Canadian Charter of Rights and Freedoms. The charter, Canada's guiding legal document, protects "freedom of thought, belief, opinion and expression, including freedom of the press." The Court said Parliament was justified in limiting this right because obscenity "reinforces male-female stereotypes to the detriment of both sexes. It attempts to make degradation, humiliation, victimization and violence in human relationships appear normal and acceptable."[9]

Pornography's presence on the Internet has renewed attempts to banish it. Pornography largely has moved from stores and theaters on the back streets, where people could ignore it unless they chose otherwise, to computers where people access it in their homes and offices, to portable devices such as smart phones where pornography is available anytime and anywhere but only to the person holding the device and those looking over her or his shoulder.[10]

Obscenity

In the late 18th century and through most of the 19th century, Americans paid no attention to regulating sexual expression. During those years American society considered religious blasphemy and heresy to be more troublesome than sexual expression. With few exceptions, governments—state and federal—did not adopt laws or bring criminal charges concerning sexual material.

realWorld Law

Pornography from a Different Viewpoint

Nadine Strossen, American Civil Liberties Union national president and a law professor at New York Law School, says there are important reasons for women that pornography not be censored. These are some of her reasons:

- Censoring pornography perpetuates the myth that sex is bad.
- Censoring pornography perpetuates the myth that women are victims and need help to protect themselves.
- Censoring pornography hinders the use of constructive approaches to counter discrimination and violence against women.
- Women who voluntarily work in the sex industry would be harmed by censoring pornography.
- Sexual freedom and freedom to publish sexually explicit material are important aspects of a free society.[1]

---

1. Nadine Strossen, *A Feminist Critique of "The" Feminist Critique of Pornography,* 79 Va. L. Rev. 1099, 1111–12 (1993).

Comstock and *Hicklin*

After the Civil War some people claimed that U.S. citizens, particularly indigent men, lacked morality. Anthony Comstock, a store clerk, became the unlikely champion of young men's decency.[11] In 1872, Comstock convinced the Young Men's Christian Association (YMCA) to support his campaign against sexual content in art, newspapers, books, magazines and other media. Comstock became secretary of the Society for the Suppression of Vice, funded in part by financier J.P. Morgan, mining tycoon William Dodge, Jr., and business magnate Samuel Colgate. Although federal laws already banned importing and mailing obscene material, Comstock vigorously lobbied Congress to further tighten mailing restrictions. His campaign culminated in the Comstock Act, a federal law adopted in 1873 prohibiting the mailing of "obscene, lewd, or lascivious" material.[12] Initially used only to stop mailings concerning contraception and abortion, the law was amended in 1876 to ensure that it banned mailing pornographic materials.[13] After the law's adoption, Congress appointed Comstock as a special postal inspector to help enforce the statute bearing his name. He held the post for 42 years. The law remains in effect today, although now it applies only to obscene content.

When courts in post–Civil War America began hearing cases involving sexually explicit material, it became clear that any publication found obscene would not have First Amendment protection. The question simply was how to define obscenity. Beginning in the late 19th century and continuing for more than 60 years, federal courts applied the *Hicklin* rule in deciding obscenity cases. The

Hicklin rule A rule taken from a mid-19th-century English case and used in the United States until the mid-20th century that defines material as obscene if it tends to corrupt children.

realWorld Law

Comstock in Action

Former grocer Anthony Comstock became a prominent crusader against all he considered immoral. He believed that "anything remotely touching upon sex was . . . obscene."[1] His Society for the Suppression of Vice, starting as an anti-obscenity movement in the late 1800s, lasted for more than 60 years. During that time, the society convinced schools and libraries to ban works by such prominent authors as D.H. Lawrence, Theodore Dreiser, Edmund Wilson, James Joyce, Leo Tolstoy and Honore de Balzac.[2] During the last three decades of the 19th century, Comstock and his society were involved in destroying more than 36 tons of books they said were obscene.[3] As a U.S. postal service special agent, Comstock prosecuted many people for selling and mailing material he considered obscene. He would order through the mail material he said was obscene. With the illicit item as evidence, he took the seller to court.[4] He successfully used these prosecutions to urge that courts adopt the *Hicklin* definition of obscenity.[5] He also effectively pushed all states to pass obscenity laws.

Anthony Comstock

1. Heywood Broun & Margaret Leech, ANTHONY COMSTOCK 265 (1927).
2. Robert Corn-Revere, *New Age Comstockery,* 4 COMMLAW CONSPECTUS 173, 173 (1996).
3. Donna I. Dennis, *Obscenity Law and Its Consequences in Mid-Nineteenth-Century America,* 16 COLUM. J. GENDER & L. 43, 53 (2007).
4. Margaret A. Blanchard, *The American Urge to Censor,* 33 WM. & MARY L. REV. 741, 749 (1992).
5. David Greene, Book Review: *Not in Front of the Children: "Indecency," Censorship, and the Innocence of Youth,* 10 B.U. PUB. INT. L.J. 360, 362 (2001).

rule came from an 1868 English case, *Regina v. Hicklin,* stating that "the test of obscenity is this, whether the tendency of the matter charged as obscenity is to deprave and corrupt those whose minds are open to such immoral influences and into whose hands a publication of this sort may fall."[14] Whose minds are open to immoral influences? Children's minds. The *Hicklin* rule meant adults could be exposed only to material acceptable for the young. U.S. courts commonly held that if even a portion of a publication met the *Hicklin* test, the entire publication was obscene. The *Hicklin* rule remained dominant in America into the 1930s.

Deciding whether U.S. customs officials could prevent James Joyce's novel "Ulysses" from being imported, a federal district court in 1933 rejected the *Hicklin* test. The court said the test for obscenity should be the entire work's impact on an "average person." The court said "Ulysses" was literary art and was not obscene.[15] Some federal and state courts continued to apply *Hicklin* into the 1950s. However, the "Ulysses" decision effectively showed courts they should determine what is obscene by reviewing the material in its entirety instead of assessing isolated passages or pictures. The decision also suggested the test should ascertain a work's effect on an average person instead of on children.

Federal laws prohibit mailing or importing obscene material and producing, transporting and selling obscene material across state lines.[16] Additionally, the U.S. Congress has adopted criminal laws prohibiting Internet obscenity, particularly addressed to minors.[17] States also have adopted obscenity laws.

SUMMARY

SEXUAL EXPRESSION IS FOUND THROUGHOUT American society, as it has been in many countries for centuries. Obscene material has no First Amendment protection. But not all sexually oriented content is obscene. The First Amendment protects most merely offensive sexual expression. The Supreme Court suggests those who are offended can turn their heads and refuse to look at offensive material. Even if sexual portrayals are protected, however, are they harmful to society, particularly to women? Sexual expression did not concern most Americans until the late 19th century when Anthony Comstock made it a public issue. Congress adopted the Comstock Act making it illegal to mail obscene or lewd material. That and other federal laws ban obscenity production and distribution, including on the Internet. States also have obscenity laws. Until the mid-20th century, American courts used a broad definition of obscenity, allowing government officials to ban a wide range of materials. ∎

Current Obscenity Definition

The U.S. Supreme Court handed down its first major obscenity decision in 1957, 167 years after the First Amendment took effect. In *Roth v. United States*, the Court said the First Amendment does not protect obscene material. At the same time it definitively rejected *Hicklin* and narrowed the obscenity definition to give sexual expression more freedom. The Court said material was obscene if, first, an "average person, applying contemporary community standards" found the work taken as a whole appealed to **prurient interest,** meaning that it "excites lustful thoughts." Second, obscene material was "utterly without redeeming social importance." Third, even if a work did appeal to the prurient interest, the *Roth* test said it was not obscene if it had even a small amount of social value.[18]

prurient interests Lustful thoughts or sexual desires.

The Court refined the *Roth* test several times between 1957 and 1973. The test remained difficult for government prosecutors to meet, however, and there were relatively few obscenity convictions after *Roth*.

Finally, the Court decided it needed to reconsider obscenity law. In 1973, the Court in *Miller v. California* set down a definition of obscenity unchanged to this day.[19] A defendant convicted under California's obscenity statute appealed to the Supreme Court. The justices used the case to establish a complex, three-part definition of obscenity. Under the *Miller* test, to find material obscene a court must consider whether (1) "the average person, applying contemporary

realWorld Law

Sex and the Restaurant

Marvin Miller sent brochures in a mass mailing to advertise four "adult" books and a film. The brochures included pictures, drawings and text "very explicitly depicting men and women in groups of two or more engaging in a variety of sexual activities, with genitals often prominently displayed," the Supreme Court said. Many of the brochures were mailed to people who had not requested the information. The manager of a Newport Beach, Calif., restaurant opened the mail one morning with his mother standing at his side. Five brochures slipped out of an unmarked envelope for all to see. The manager called the police. A jury convicted Miller of violating a California statute forbidding knowingly distributing obscene materials. Miller appealed to the U.S. Supreme Court. Before the Court could decide if Miller's brochures were obscene, it had to define obscenity.[1]

---

1. Miller v. California, 413 U.S. 15, 18 (1973).

community standards" would find that the work, taken as a whole, appeals to prurient interests, (2) the work depicts or describes, in a patently offensive way, sexual conduct specifically defined by the applicable state law, and (3) the work, taken as a whole, lacks serious literary, artistic, political or scientific value.[20]

A work must meet each part of the test to be obscene. That is, the government must show a work, considered in its entirety, (1) arouses sexual lust, (2) is hard-core pornography, and (3) has no serious social value. If the government cannot prove any part of this test, the work is not obscene and the First Amendment protects it.

Prurient Interest and Local Standards The first part of the Miller test to determine whether material is obscene requires showing that an average person would find the work, taken in its entirety, appeals to prurient interests, in other words, "lustful thoughts." The Court said prurient refers to "morbid or lascivious longings."[21] Material arousing morbid or shameful sexual thoughts meets this part of the *Miller* test.

The *Miller* case confirmed what the U.S. Supreme Court held in earlier cases: To determine whether material appeals to prurient interests, the content must be considered as a whole, not as discrete pictures or words. A photograph that might be found obscene on its own may be protected in a magazine by surrounding it with fiction and nonfiction articles by leading authors.

An assessment of whether the material appeals to prurient interests must be based on conclusions drawn by an average person, not a child or a particularly sensitive person. Jurors are not to use their own standards but instead those of an average person in the community.[22] The Court has not explained how a juror can know the standards of an average person. Some courts allow survey results to help jurors understand community attitudes, but not all courts permit social science data as evidence.

realWorld Law

Sex and the Internet

The U.S. Court of Appeals for the Ninth Circuit held that applying "contemporary community standards" to the Internet requires defining "community" as the entire country:

> Because persons utilizing email to distribute possibly obscene works cannot control which geographic community their works will enter, [defendants argue the] definition of contemporary community standards to works distributed via email unavoidably subjects such works to the standards of the least tolerant community in the country. . . . To avoid this constitutional problem, defendants argue, obscenity disseminated via email must be defined according to a national community standard. [The U.S. Court of Appeals for the Ninth Circuit] agree[s] with defendants that the district court should have instructed the jury to apply a national community standard. . . . [The court holds] that application of local community standards [when allegedly obscene material is sent via the Internet] raises grave constitutional doubts on its face and application of a national community standard does not, thereby persuading us to adopt a national community standard to alleviate the former doubts.[1]

---

1. United States v. Kilbride, 584 F.3d 1240, 1250, 1254 n.8 (9th Cir. 2009).

The standards are to be community-wide. Legislatures and courts decide what geographic area will be the community for setting obscenity standards. Although the Court once approved using the entire country as the community,[23] in *Miller* it ruled that jurors may not use national standards. The Supreme Court has said the community may be the city or county where the jurors live. In the *Miller* decision, the Court allowed California to use statewide standards. Other states, such as Illinois, also have permitted statewide obscenity standards.[24] Even a "deviant sexual group, rather than the public at large," may be a community for determining appropriate standards, the Court has said.[25]

It is easy to apply local, not national, standards when a movie theater shows a film. Local authorities charge the theater owner with showing an obscene film, and a local jury decides if the film meets the *Miller* obscenity definition. It is far more difficult to apply local standards when an Internet site in San Jose, Calif., sends sexually explicit photographs to Memphis, Tenn. Which is the local community—San Jose or Memphis or one of the hundreds of cities the Internet images passed through on their way to Tennessee?

In one case, a U.S. postal inspector in Memphis using an assumed name gained access to a bulletin board operating on a website physically located in Milpitas, Calif., a San Jose suburb. The postal inspector downloaded sexually explicit images and ordered videotapes delivered to him in Memphis by a freight service. Robert and Carleen Thomas, the bulletin board operators, were charged with sending obscene material across state lines and other obscenity-related crimes. The charges were filed in Memphis, and a Memphis jury convicted the defendants. Appealing their conviction, the bulletin board operators said a local community standard cannot apply to the Internet, a geographically limitless communication medium. The U.S. Court of Appeals for the Sixth Circuit disagreed, declining to use a national standard for determining obscenity.[26] The court also rejected the defendants' suggestion to use an "Internet community." The court said it was appropriate to use the local Memphis standards. Sellers of sexually explicit material should make certain they do not have customers in communities with inhospitable standards, the court said.

The Thomases' proposed Internet community would be the entire country. Websites may be viewed and their material downloaded in any U.S. city. Even an e-mail message sent to one person can be read wherever the recipient is, not necessarily in the person's home community. Under the *Miller* standard, then, which community's standard determines whether the material appeals to prurient interests—where the message was sent, where it was received, any community it passed through or a national standard? How can an online publisher avoid sending content to communities that would find the material appeals to prurient interests while also sending it to communities that would not? U.S. Supreme Court Justice Anthony Kennedy, joined by Justices Ruth Bader Ginsburg and David Souter, recognized that the "national variation in community standards constitutes a particular burden on Internet speech."[27] Similarly, Justice Stephen Breyer said applying "the community standards of every locality in the United States would provide the most puritan of communities with a heckler's Internet veto affecting the rest of the Nation."[28] Former Justice Sandra Day O'Connor also favored a national community for judging Internet communications.[29]

Despite several current and former Supreme Court justices suggesting a nationwide standard be used in Internet obscenity cases, the Court has not yet chosen to adopt that approach. That leaves lower courts to decide, and courts disagree about whether an Internet community is local or national. For example, in 2009 the U.S. Court of Appeals for the Ninth Circuit ruled that a jury must use a national community standard when deciding if material transmitted on the Internet is obscene.[30] However, in 2010 the U.S. Court of Appeals for the 11th Circuit disagreed. Paul Little, also known as Max Hardcore, was convicted of using the Internet to market obscene videos. Hearing Little's appeal, the 11th Circuit held that the *Miller* contemporary community requirement means a local or statewide standard "on the Internet or elsewhere."[31]

patently offensive Term describing material with hard-core sexual conduct.

Patently Offensive The second part of the Miller test requires the government to show the material is **patently offensive** according to state law. In Miller the U.S. Supreme Court provided examples of patent offensiveness: (1) "patently offensive representations or descriptions of ultimate sexual acts, normal or perverted, actual or simulated," or (2) "patently offensive representations or descriptions of masturbation, excretory functions and lewd exhibition of the genitals."[32] As in the first part of the *Miller* test, patent offensiveness is to be determined by contemporary community standards, the Court said.

The Supreme Court's examples of patent offensiveness mean that state definitions must meet a certain standard. Patently offensive material at least has to include hard-core sexual conduct, as the Court said. The Court made this clear when it rejected a jury's finding that the movie "Carnal Knowledge" was obscene.[33] The movie, directed by a leading Broadway and Hollywood director, Mike Nichols, contained some partial nudity but had no sex scenes. Starring Candice Bergen, Jack Nicholson and Ann-Margret, who received an Oscar nomination for her role, it had made several critics' Top 10 lists. An Albany, Ga., jury convicted a theater operator for showing the film, finding the movie to be obscene. The Supreme Court said the jury had the right

An Albany, Ga., jury found the 1971 movie "Carnal Knowledge" obscene, but the U.S. Supreme Court disagreed. Candice Bergen and Jack Nicholson starred in the film.

to use local community standards in deciding whether the film appealed to prurient interests. However, the jury could not find the movie was patently offensive unless at a minimum it met the Court's understanding of that term, as illustrated by the Court's examples.

Deciding if material appeals to prurient interests, then, largely is in a jury's hands. But the Supreme Court has established a minimum standard for finding patent offensiveness. The Court said "it would be a serious misreading of *Miller* to conclude that juries have unbridled discretion in determining what is 'patently offensive.'"[34] However, a jury could decide that local community standards set a higher level for patent offensiveness than the Court required. Jurors in San Francisco or New York, for example, might determine that in those communities patently offensive material depicts scenes even more offensive than the Court's examples. However, jurors in Albany, Ga., cannot decide that scenes of partly nude actors make a film patently offensive. Partial nudity is not the equivalent of the Court's criteria for finding patent offensiveness. The Court also has said the *Miller* examples of patently offensive material were just examples, not an exhaustive list. Sexually explicit material not included in the Court's list of sexual acts also could be patently offensive.[35]

The second part of the *Miller* obscenity test requires states to specifically define the sexual acts forbidden by state law. Courts require criminal laws to be clear and specific, allowing people to know what they must do or not do in order to obey the laws. The Supreme Court's language in *Miller* says that is how states must write obscenity laws—clearly and definitively. In practice, the court has not held to that standard. For example, the Court upheld a conviction under Illinois' very broad obscenity statute.[36] Illinois defined obscenity as material predominantly appealing to prurient interest "if it goes substantially beyond customary

Points of Law

serious social value Material cannot be found obscene if it has serious literary, artistic, political or scientific value determined using national, not local, standards.

limits of candor in description or representation" of sexual matters. The Supreme Court said it was sufficient that Illinois courts interpreted the state law to include the *Miller* examples of patently offensive material.

Serious Social Value The third part of the *Miller* obscenity test says material cannot be found obscene if it has serious literary, artistic, political or social value. In the *Roth* decision, the Court had said a work could be found obscene only if it were "utterly without redeeming social value."[37] This meant material with any redeeming social value at all could not be obscene. The *Miller* test is not so restrictive. Under *Miller*, the work has to lack serious social value to be considered obscene. There is a wide gap between any social value and serious social value. Material falling in the space between "any social value" and "serious social value" could be found obscene if it also meets the first two parts of the *Miller* test. *Miller*, then, does not protect as much sexual expression as some earlier Court decisions did.

In *Pope v. Illinois*, decided after *Miller*, the Court said serious social value should be decided using national standards, not local criteria.[38] The *Pope* decision also said a determination of **serious social value** should be based on what a reasonable person would decide. Because this suggests an objective, rather than a subjective, analysis of a work's social value, juries may consider testimony of expert witnesses who express their opinions about a work's social value. For example, at the request of a county sheriff in Florida, a federal district court found a 2 Live Crew album, "As Nasty as They Wanna Be," to be obscene. However, a federal appellate court observed that 2 Live Crew presented several expert witnesses at trial who testified the album had serious social value. The sheriff played the album at trial but offered no expert witnesses to support his contention that the recording was obscene. The appellate court said simply listening to a recording was not enough to determine if the recording possessed serious social value. Expert witnesses' testimony was required.[39]

SUMMARY

THE U.S. SUPREME COURT IN 1973 ADOPTED the definition of "obscenity" courts still use today. For the government to prove material is obscene and therefore without First Amendment protection, it must show the work considered in its entirety (1) arouses sexual lust, (2) is "hard-core pornography," and (3) has no serious social value. If the government is unable to prove any one of these elements, the material cannot be found obscene. Prurient interest, or arousing sexual lust, is determined using contemporary community standards. These may be citywide or statewide standards. The Supreme Court has provided examples of the kind of content that would be patently offensive, or be "hard-core pornography." Jurors may not find material patently offensive if it does not at least meet the Court's standards. Whether material has serious literary, artistic, political or scientific value is determined using national criteria based on expert testimony. ■

Enforcing Obscenity Laws

The *Miller v. California* decision did not answer all questions about obscenity. For example, is *Miller* the correct test to determine whether sexual material should be made available to minors? Even if it is illegal to produce, distribute, sell and exhibit obscene material, is it illegal to possess it? What is child pornography? The Supreme Court has worked its way through these and other matters concerning obscene material.

Variable Obscenity Long ago, the Supreme Court held that government officials may not limit adults to seeing only material acceptable for children. In 1957 the Court struck down a Michigan law making it illegal to distribute sexual material "tending to incite minors to violent or depraved or immoral acts."[40] The Court said the law violated the First Amendment because its effect "is to reduce the adult population of Michigan to reading only what is fit for children."[41]

However, the opposite is not true. That is, the First Amendment does not protect giving minors sexually explicit material that is protected for adults. For example, a restaurant owner appealed his conviction for selling minors magazines containing pictures of nude women. State law prohibited distributing to young people sexual material that would be harmful to minors. The magazines' content did not meet the Supreme Court's obscenity definition. However, in *Ginsberg v. New York* the Court said minors do not have a First Amendment right to sexual material acceptable for adults. Under its power to protect minors' well-being, the Court said, a state may "adjust the definition of obscenity to social realities" by considering minors' sexual interests.[42] Restricting minors' access to sexual material has been called **variable obscenity**: Material not obscene for adults may be obscene if the same material is given to minors.

variable obscenity The concept that sexually oriented material would not meet the definition of obscenity if distributed to adults but would be found obscene if distributed to minors.

Child Pornography Selling or possessing "sexually explicit visual portrayals that feature children" in movies or photographs is illegal under state and federal laws, some of which first were adopted in the 1970s.[43] By the beginning of the 21st century every state had **child pornography** laws, and Congress had tightened the federal law.[44] These laws say it is illegal to video, film or photograph minors in any sexual situation. The question is not whether children are appearing in videos, films or photographs that would be obscene under the *Miller v. California* test. Rather, the question is whether minors are being sexually exploited.

child pornography Any image showing children in sexual or sexually explicit situations.

In *Ferber v. New York* the Supreme Court upheld New York's child pornography law, one of the nation's strictest.[45] Ferber sold pornographic films of young boys to an undercover officer. Hearing Ferber's appeal of his conviction, the Court said child pornography laws are essential to protecting minors. Using children in sexual material harms minors' "physiological, emotional, and mental health" in several ways, the Court said.[46] First, there is the psychological harm the child endures, knowing there is a permanent record of his participation in sexual activity. Second, making, selling and obtaining pornography showing children in sexual situations helps to perpetuate the sexual exploitation of children and encourages pedophilia.

Federal law is applied to visual depictions and defines child pornography as any image showing minors in "sexually explicit conduct."[47] The conduct may be actual or simulated "sexual intercourse," "masturbation" or lewd "exhibition of the genitals or pubic area."[48]

Courts strictly interpret child pornography laws. "Unlike the Court's obscenity standards, child pornography laws involve no fuzzy facts like 'community standards' or 'artistic value,' and prosecutors can make a case with little more than proof that the defendant possessed or made a visual depiction of sexual conduct by a minor," wrote a First Amendment scholar.[49] For example, a film showed preteen and teenaged girls younger than 17 years old wearing bikinis, leotards or underwear (but not nude) and gyrating to music. The "photographer would zoom in on the children's pubic and genital area and display a close-up view for an extended period of time," a federal appellate court said.[50] The film was child pornography, the court found. The federal child pornography law does not require nudity, the court said. Non-nude child models in pictures and films "can qualify as lascivious exhibitions."[51] This broad interpretation of the federal law does not make the law unconstitutionally overbroad, the court held.

An award-winning radio and television journalist could not convince courts that the First Amendment allowed him to violate the federal child pornography law. The journalist attempted to create his own chat room; logged on to other chat rooms; used the Internet to be in touch with persons he thought were female minors, some of whom were FBI agents pretending to be minors; and sent or received 160 photographs that law enforcement officials said showed child pornography. All this was done to research a story he planned to write and sell, the journalist claimed. He entered a guilty plea based on sending or receiving 15 pictures but reserved the right to appeal. A federal appellate court would not accept the journalist's First Amendment argument, saying that "any literary, artistic, political, scientific (or journalistic) value of child pornography does nothing to ameliorate its harm to children."[52] The Supreme Court emphasized the importance of protecting children from being involved in the sex trade, the appellate court said. Reporting about child pornography is not more important than prohibiting it, according to the court.

Congress adopted the Child Pornography Protection Act (CPPA) in 1996, criminalizing the sending or possessing of digital images of children in sexual poses or activities, even if the images were not of real children or were of adults who looked young. The Supreme Court found the law unconstitutional.[53] (The topic of sexual material transmitted digitally is examined later in this chapter in the discussion of pornography and the Internet.)

Sexting is a new aspect of child pornography. Using cell phones, computers or other digital technologies, minors take pictures of themselves or others scantily dressed, nude or semi-nude, or engaging in sexual activities. The pictures then are transmitted to others, with or without permission of those pictured, and are perhaps posted on sites such as Facebook or MySpace. One survey found 20 percent of those between 13 and 19 years old have sent or posted nude or semi-nude pictures of themselves.[54] Also called "autopornography"[55] or "self-produced child pornography,"[56] sexting is classified as child pornography by some prosecutors. For example, two Florida teens took more than 100 pictures of themselves engaging in what a state appellate court did not deny was "legal sexual behavior." The 16-year-old girl and 17-year-old boy did not show the pictures to anyone else, although they did send the pictures from the girl's computer to the boy's computer. They were charged as juveniles with violating Florida's child pornography laws. The court upheld the girl's conviction, ruling that the state had a right to prevent sexual exploitation of children.[57]

In another sexting case, a 15-year-old girl sent nude pictures of herself using her cell phone. A prosecutor charged her under a state law the U.S. Supreme Court had previously upheld.[58] The

SEX AND TECH

RESULTS FROM A SURVEY OF TEENS AND YOUNG ADULTS

This report includes a survey that found 20 percent of those between 13 and 19 years old have used cellphones or other means to send or post nude or semi-nude pictures of themselves.

Court ruled the state law was constitutional only if limited to "lewd exhibition or graphic focus on a minor's genitals," a standard the girl's pictures did not meet. The girl could have been required to register as a sex offender for 20 years. Instead, she pleaded guilty to a lesser felony but violated a plea bargain condition (she was forbidden from using a cell phone) and was sentenced.[59]

If sexting pictures are child pornography, those who receive and retain those pictures can be charged with possessing child pornography, a felony under state and federal laws. Pictures of two teenage girls wearing opaque bras and another of a teenage girl with a towel wrapped around her bare breasts appeared on confiscated student cell phones in a Pennsylvania school district. Claiming the pictures showed provocative poses, the district attorney threatened to bring child pornography charges against the pictured girls and students whose phones contained the photographs. Alternatively, the district attorney said, the students could complete a months-long counseling and education class, including writing an essay about what they did wrong. In 2010 the U.S. Court of Appeals for the Third Circuit held that the district attorney's compelling a student to write an essay to avoid prosecution violated the student's First Amendment rights.[60]

realWorld Law

The Last Movie Censor

The last person to head a movie censorship committee—the last movie censor—was Mary Avara, who died at age 90 in 2000. She was head of the Maryland State Board of Censors and a board member for 21 years, from 1960 to 1981, when the state disbanded the board, which had existed for 65 years.

When the Maryland State Board was active, a black frame appeared before the start of every film saying the board had approved the movie. Avara's signature was at the bottom of that frame. Avara reviewed every film shown in Maryland, whether a Walt Disney movie or pornography.

Avara said she used her own rating system: G for garbage and R for rotten. The board's secretary said Avara "would become extremely upset at obscene and dirty scenes," having no hesitation in pronouncing a movie "trash." And Avara had the power to insist that a movie producer eliminate a scene or ban a film altogether.[1]

---

1. See Jacques Kelly & Frederick N. Rasmussen, *Film Censor Mary Avara, 90, Dies,* BALTIMORE SUN, Aug. 10, 2000, at 1A.

Some state legislatures—including those in Arizona, Connecticut, Louisiana and Illinois—have adopted laws imposing lighter sentences on teenage sexters than on adults convicted of making or possessing child pornography. In Louisiana, for example, a first offense for sexting warrants 10 days in jail and a second offense could lead to 30 days in jail. The Arizona law categorizes sexting by those 8 to 18 years old as a petty offense if pictures are sent to only one other person.[61]

Possessing Obscene Material Although courts have upheld laws against making, distributing, selling and exhibiting obscene material, the Supreme Court said the First Amendment protects having obscene material in the privacy of one's home. This does not apply to child pornography, however.

In the case establishing protection for possessing obscene material at home, police officers searched a suspected bookmaker's house for gambling evidence. Police found three films in a desk drawer, viewed the movies, decided they were obscene and arrested the suspect. Overturning a conviction for possessing obscene films, the Supreme Court in *Stanley v. Georgia* said merely categorizing the films as obscene did not justify "such a drastic invasion of personal liberties guaranteed by the First Amendment."[62] The Court said there are reasons to have obscenity statutes, but the reasons do not allow authorities to "reach into the privacy of one's own home."[63] Government may not tell people what books they may read or films they may watch, the Court said.

But the government may limit possession of child pornography.[64] The U.S. Supreme Court has said the underlying interests prohibiting the possession of child pornography are so vital that they support a ban on possession.[65] The justifications for punishing possession of child pornography—protecting children's physical and psychological well-being and ending the sexual exploitation of children—are sufficiently important to overcome First Amendment rights, the Court said.

Procedural Protections The First Amendment protects filmmakers, according to the Supreme Court.[66] Nonetheless, the Court has allowed government censorship boards to license films for exhibition. That is, in some states and communities a theater had to obtain board approval before it could show a film.[67] When they were active, some censorship boards assumed a given film was obscene and required the movie producer to prove it was not. This violated the movie producer's rights, the Supreme Court said.[68] Additionally, a censorship board had to follow careful procedures complying with First Amendment standards, the Court held, including making a quick decision as to whether a movie met the board's standards.

There are no more government movie censors. The last movie censorship board, the Maryland State Board of Censors, stopped functioning in 1981. But the procedural safeguards the Supreme Court required of those committees set the standard for all obscenity prosecutions. For example, government officials must prove in court that a work is obscene. Officials cannot merely claim material is obscene and then ban it. Also, any prior restraint on allegedly obscene material must be for as short a time as possible until a court decides whether the work meets the obscenity definition.

Authorities have tried to control obscenity using a law with more bite than censorship boards had. In 1970 Congress adopted the Racketeer Influenced and Corrupt Organizations Act, popularly known as RICO.[69] Thirty-two states also have RICO acts, many similar to the federal statute. The RICO laws forbid using money earned from illegal activities—racketeering—to finance legal or illegal businesses or nonprofit enterprises engaged in interstate commerce. Violators can be imprisoned and fined.[70]

RICO prosecutions implicate the First Amendment because the laws allow the government to seize all assets acquired through racketeering activity. This means the government may try to seize an adult bookstore's contents, for example. In one case, the owner of a dozen adult theaters and bookstores was convicted of violating obscenity laws. Under the state's RICO law, authorities seized the contents of the defendant's theaters and bookstores. The defendant claimed the seizure violated his First Amendment rights. In part, he said the seizure amounted to a prior restraint because not all his store's books and his theater's films were obscene. Nevertheless, he was not allowed to sell the store's books or show films in his theaters. The seizure was for past criminal acts—selling obscene material, the Supreme Court said.[71] If the defendant wanted to open a new adult bookstore that sold sexually explicit but not obscene material, he could do so in the future. Therefore, there was no prior restraint. The theater and bookstore owner also argued the seizure chilled his First Amendment rights, since he would be hesitant to operate another adult theater or bookstore. The Court said the RICO seizure penalty no more chilled free speech rights than does the possibility of a fine or imprisonment for racketeering activities.

SUMMARY

IT IS ILLEGAL TO PROVIDE MINORS WITH SEXUALLY explicit material that would not be obscene if given to an adult. Courts call this "variable obscenity." The federal government and all states have laws making it illegal to make, distribute or possess material showing children in sexual situations. This is child pornography. However, the First Amendment protects possessing obscene material if it is not child pornography. The government must act expeditiously if it wants to censor material on the basis that it is obscene. The government may use laws originally aimed at organized crime to seize the assets of people found guilty of creating or distributing obscene material. ∎

Indecency

Consider obscene sexual expression on one side of an imaginary line and non-obscene sexual expression on the other side. Take the non-obscene sexual expression, add excretory functions and filthy words, and it all adds up to indecent speech. The Supreme Court has made clear that the First Amendment does not protect obscenity. Does the First Amendment protect indecency? The answer is both yes and no. Indecent speech is protected in print media, movies, recordings and the Internet. It is protected on most cable television programming. Indecent speech is not protected if broadcast by radio or television during most hours of the day or if directed to children over the telephone.[72] As with obscenity, the problem is defining "indecency."

Arguments about how to define indecency, when, if ever, it should be protected in broadcasting and what penalties should be imposed for broadcasting indecent material have raged for years among the courts, Congress, broadcasters and the public. One example is that the Communications Act of 1934 makes it illegal to broadcast indecent material.[73] However, the courts and the FCC allow broadcast radio and television stations to air indecent material when it is likely that few children will be in the audience.

Many individuals and members of federal administrative agencies and Congress want to limit children's exposure to indecency. The anti-indecency campaign has become more fervent as courts have reduced the range of material found to be obscene. If sexually oriented material cannot be banned as obscene, perhaps it can be limited as indecent, critics contend.

What is indecent speech? According to the U.S. Supreme Court, "The normal definition of 'indecent' merely refers to nonconformance with accepted standards of morality."[74] Indecency is not a synonym for obscenity, the Court said.[75] Material that is patently offensive but does not have prurient appeal is not obscene but may be indecent.[76] Also, material may be indecent even if it has serious social value. The FCC once defined "indecency" as "language or material that, in context, depicts or describes in terms patently offensive as measured by contemporary community standards for the broadcast medium, sexual or excretory activities or organs."[77] However, this definition is flexible. During the past 35 years the commission variously has expanded, contracted and again expanded its interpretation of indecency.

Broadcast Indecency

The Federal Communications Commission, the courts and Congress agree and disagree about indecent material on broadcast radio and television. They agree the law forbids it. They disagree whether broadcasters may air indecent programming during certain times of the day. And they disagree about how to define indecency. In 2010 the courts won. The U.S. Court of Appeals for the Second Circuit held that the FCC's indecency policy, including its definition of indecency, was so vague that broadcasters could not know what would violate the commission's regulations.[78]

What is indecency? Is it the repetition of certain four-letter and other unacceptable words? Is it patently offensive material that describes or shows sexual or excretory organs or activities? Is it the single utterance of an expletive? At various times the FCC has said one or all of these definitions describe indecency.

In both the 1927 Federal Radio Act and the Communications Act of 1934, Congress prohibited broadcasting "any obscene, indecent, or profane language."[79] Congress later eliminated the 1934 act's provision but inserted the ban on indecent broadcasts into the federal criminal code.[80] In 1960 Congress gave the FCC power to impose civil fines on broadcasters who violate the commission's indecency regulations.[81]

The law seems clear: no indecent material on broadcast radio or television. But the First Amendment protects indecent speech unless the government has a compelling interest in regulating it and chooses the least restrictive regulatory method.[82] Also, the law forbids the FCC from censoring radio or television broadcasts.[83] And among all media, only broadcasting is forbidden from carrying indecent material. How, then, can banning broadcast indecency be justified?

The FCC and the courts, with Congress' acquiescence, found the answer to this conundrum by saying the reason for limiting indecent programs is to protect children.[84] For example, in fining a radio station for discussing oral sex during an afternoon program, the commission emphasized "the presence of children in the broadcast audience."[85] Also, the First Amendment protects indecent material in nonbroadcast media because these media can separate children from adults in their audiences. Minors can be prevented from having access to indecent books, magazines and movies, for example. But broadcast radio and television are too pervasive; they are available everywhere and children continually are exposed to them. Banning indecency, then, had to balance concerns for children against broadcasters' First Amendment rights.

Defining Broadcast Indecency The commission's statutory duty to limit indecent broadcasts lay dormant for many years. Despite the 1934 Communications Act's forbidding broadcast indecency, the FCC did not act against indecency until 1975. The commission responded to a father's complaint that in 1973 he and his young son heard a New York City radio station playing comedian George Carlin's "Filthy Words" monologue at 2 p.m. The 12-minute live performance on the recording "George Carlin, Occupation: FOOLE" contained the seven "words you couldn't say on the public airwaves" according to Carlin. He then said them repeatedly.[86] Defining indecency as "language that describes, in terms patently offensive as measured by contemporary community standards for the broadcast medium, sexual or excretory activities and organs, at times of the day when there is a reasonable risk that children may be in the audience," the FCC fined the station's operator, Pacifica Foundation.[87]

The case reached the U.S. Supreme Court. The Court said indecent broadcast speech is material in "nonconformance with accepted standards of morality." Broadcasters have First Amendment protection, the Court noted, but the protection is limited because of spectrum scarcity. This allows courts to restrict indecency in broadcasting but not other media, the Court said.

In determining whether the Carlin recording was indecent, the Court said the context of the challenged material is "all-important" and that an "occasional expletive" need not lead to sanctioning a broadcaster.[88] The Court focused on the "repetitive, deliberate use" of words that refer to "excretory or sexual activities or organs" in a "patently offensive" but non-obscene manner.[89] This suggested that indecency applied only to a Carlin-like monologue—defining indecency as "filthy words." Double-entendre and sly suggestions about sex seemed not to be included in the Court's definition of indecent speech. The Court stressed radio and television's "uniquely pervasive presence in the lives of all Americans" but focused on children. The nature of broadcasting made it "uniquely accessible to children, even those too young to read." That concern and the unique facts of the case—Carlin's repeatedly saying the seven words—justified the FCC's fining the radio station, the Court said.[90]

For a decade after *Pacifica* the FCC defined indecency as it did in that case—repeated dirty words—and took no action against broadcasters for violating the commission's indecency standard. In 1987 the commission decided to return to the indecency definition it offered in *Pacifica*. However, words not describing sexual activities or organs, and therefore not patently offensive, were not indecent unless they were Carlin-type words constantly repeated. When the words were only expletives, the commission said, "deliberate and repetitive use in a patently offensive manner is a requisite to a finding of indecency."[91] At that time, a single expletive was not indecent.

The calm ended in 1987. The FCC expressed a concern that the "filthy words" indecency definition did not sufficiently protect children. Instead, the commission adopted a broader generic standard to define indecency.[92] The commission said it would consider a broadcast's context and tone as well as its language. This allowed the FCC to expand its indecency definition beyond Carlin's

realWorld Law

Comedian George Carlin

George Carlin died in 2008 at the age of 71. Carlin's comedy routine, "Seven Words You Can Never Say on Television," from his third album, "Class Clown," was the focus of the U.S. Supreme Court's *FCC v. Pacifica Foundation* broadcast indecency decision. Carlin performed on stage, recordings, radio and television for 50 years, until a few weeks before his death. He also wrote three books.

Carlin grew up in New York City, did not finish high school and joined the Air Force. After his military service he worked as a disc jockey. He teamed with Jack Burns, another comedian, as a comedy act, appearing on radio, in nightclubs and on "The Tonight Show." Carlin and Burns split in the 1960s. Carlin continued television appearances but became best known for his comedy albums. His second album, "FM & AM," won a Grammy Award, one of four awarded to Carlin, and three albums sold more than a million copies each.

In the 1970s, Carlin used the "Seven Words" routine in his stage and nightclub appearances and was arrested several times on charges of public obscenity, though he was never convicted. He was host of the first "Saturday Night Live" show. But cable television, without indecency restrictions, was a better forum for Carlin. He did 14 HBO comedy shows in 30 years.[1]

George Carlin

1. See Mel Watkins & Bruce Weber, *George Carlin, Comic Who Chafed at Society and Its Constraints, Dies at 71*, N.Y. Times, June 24, 2008, at C12.

seven words. The FCC justified this change by referring to the Supreme Court's *Pacifica* decision.[93] The Court had said indecency includes all "language or material that depicts or describes, in terms patently offensive as measured by contemporary community standards for the broadcast medium, sexual or excretory activities or organs."[94] The *Pacifica* Court did not say what it meant by "patently offensive" as measured by "community standards for the broadcast medium," leaving broadcasters with little guidance beyond knowing what seven words George Carlin used in his monologue.

The FCC tried to clarify its standards in 2001 by adopting broadcast industry indecency guidelines. Revisiting its indecency definition, the commission again said material is indecent if it meets the generic *Pacifica* test. That is, the material must (1) describe or depict sexual or excretory organs or activities, and (2) be patently offensive as measured by contemporary community standards for broadcasting. The commission said it would consider several factors in determining whether broadcast material were patently offensive: (1) how explicitly or graphically the material describes sexual activities, (2) whether the material dwells on sexual activities, and (3) whether the material is meant to shock or sexually excite the audience. The FCC said it would consider the full context in which the material appeared.[95]

realWorld Law

Pigs in Parlors

The FCC's decision finding George Carlin's monologue was indecent for the broadcast media involved

a host of variables. The time of day was emphasized by the Commission. The content of the program in which the language is used will also affect the composition of the audience, and differences between radio, television, and perhaps closed-circuit transmissions, may also be relevant. As Mr. Justice Sutherland wrote, a "nuisance may be merely a right thing in the wrong place—like a pig in the parlor instead of the barnyard." We simply hold that when the Commission finds that a pig has entered the parlor, the exercise of its regulatory power does not depend on proof that the pig is obscene.[1]

---

1. FCC v. Pacific Foundation, 438 U.S. 726, 750–51 (1978), quoting Euclid v. Ambler Realty Co., 272 U.S. 365, 388 (1926).

Then U2 band member Bono received a Golden Globe award and, during the 2003 telecast, said, "This is really, really, fucking brilliant. Really, really, great." The FCC seemingly ignored its 2001 standards and asserted for the first time that a "fleeting expletive"—a single, nonliteral use of a curse word—could be indecent.[96] The "'F-Word' is one of the most vulgar, graphic, and explicit descriptions of sexual activity in the English language," and therefore "inherently has a sexual connotation," the commission said. This conclusion overruled previous FCC decisions finding a fleeting expletive not indecent. The commission also found Bono's comment "profane," discarding its earlier definitions of that word to mean blasphemy.

Similarly, the FCC found singer and actress Cher's unscripted exclamation on the 2002 Billboard Music Awards program—"People have been telling me I'm on the way out every year, right? So fuck em,"—and television personality Nicole Richie's remark on the 2003 Billboard Music Awards program—"Have you ever tried to get cow shit out of a Prada purse? It's not so fucking simple"—to be indecent and profane.[97] The FCC also said the two programs were patently offensive because the material was explicit, shocking and gratuitous. The U.S. Court of Appeals for the Second Circuit rejected the FCC's decision, saying the commission "failed to adequately explain why it had changed its nearly-30-year policy on fleeting expletives . . . [and] that the FCC's justification for the policy—that children could be harmed by hearing even one fleeting expletive . . .—bore 'no rational connection to the Commission's actual policy,' because the FCC had not instituted a blanket ban on expletives."[98]

Add to Bono, Cher and Richie's language, Justin Timberlake's ever-so-briefly exposing Janet Jackson's breast during the 2004 Super Bowl half-time show, and an anti-indecency frenzy ensued. Congress increased the maximum fine the FCC could impose for broadcasting indecent material "by a factor of 10—from $32,500 to $325,000—meaning that the fine for a single expletive uttered during a broadcast could easily run into the tens of millions of dollars."[99] Reacting to public and congressional outrage, the FCC said Jackson's partial nudity violated the indecency standard and imposed $550,000 in fines against Viacom-owned television stations that aired the Super Bowl.[100] Viacom Inc. owns CBS, the network carrying the Super Bowl. The U.S. Court of Appeals for the Third Circuit overturned the Commission's decision, saying that for three decades the FCC punished broadcasters for indecent programming only when the material was "so pervasive as to amount to 'shock treatment' for the audience. . . . [T]he Commission consistently explained that isolated or fleeting material did not fall within the scope of actionable indecency."[101] The U.S. Supreme Court told the Third Circuit to reconsider its decision.[102] The Court said its 2009 *FCC v. Fox Television Stations* ruling, discussed following, could mean the FCC did not act arbitrarily and capriciously in finding that CBS aired indecent material. The Third Circuit has not yet issued a new ruling.

After the Third Circuit's ruling in the Janet Jackson case, the U.S. Supreme Court overturned the Second Circuit's Cher and Nicole Richie decision. The Court disagreed with the Second Circuit's holding, saying the FCC did not act arbitrarily or capriciously when it ruled that a single use of an expletive is indecent. The FCC sufficiently supported its new policy, the Court said. The FCC admitted it overturned a long-standing regulation that a single use was not indecent. But the commission said the "F-word" has a sexual meaning no matter how it is used, a meaning that insults and offends. That was enough reason for the Court, in a 5–4 decision, to uphold the FCC's new rule.[103]

The FCC ruled indecent U2 lead singer Bono's uttering the "F-word" on broadcast television. The U.S. Court of Appeals for the Second Circuit held the FCC's indecency rule to be unconstitutionally vague.

The Supreme Court did not determine the constitutional issue but instructed the Second Circuit to consider whether the FCC's fleeting-obscenity rule abridged broadcasters' First Amendment rights. In 2010, the Second Court said the rule did infringe on broadcasters' free speech. The appellate court held that the commission's fleeting-expletive policy violated the First Amendment because it was vague, not allowing broadcasters to know what content would be found indecent and thus creating a chilling effect. The court said the chilling effect went beyond the fleeting-expletive regulation, forcing broadcasters not to take risks but rather self-censor content that might not meet the FCC's indecency definition. One reason the Second Circuit found the policy vague is that it was uncertain what words the commission would classify as indecent. For example, the FCC found "bullshit" in a "NYPD Blue" episode was indecent, but not the words "dick" and "dickhead."[104] Also, some words might be indecent in certain shows, but not necessarily in a news program or if used for educational or artistic purposes. The commission rejected complaints that swear words in the movie "Saving Private Ryan" were indecent when a television network carried the film.[105]

The FCC argued that not having fixed criteria for indecency protects broadcasters' First Amendment rights and gives the commission flexibility. The court rejected those arguments because they amount to a "standard that even the FCC cannot articulate or apply consistently," and the commission's discretion could be "enforced in a discriminatory manner." The Second Circuit decided to "strike down the FCC's indecency policy." The court did say the FCC might be able to "create a constitutional policy," but "the FCC's current policy fails constitutional scrutiny." The Supreme Court granted the FCC's appeal of the Second Circuit's decision to consider only whether the Commission's "current indecency-enforcement regime" is constitutional.

The Second Circuit noted the FCC's partial exemption for indecency in news broadcasts. The FCC has said there is not an absolute exemption from the indecency rules for news programs, but the commission has been very careful in dealing with these complaints. The FCC says it uses caution and restraint when an indecency complaint implicates a station's news judgment.[106] It has been two decades since the commission found indecency in a news or public affairs program.[107]

The Second Circuit in 2011 also held the FCC's indecency rules unconstitutionally vague when applied to televised nudity. The court overturned the commission's $1.2 million fine against television stations that carried ABC's "NYPD Blue" program showing a woman's bare buttocks.[108]

Channeling Broadcast Indecency Balancing the U.S. Supreme Court's expressed concern for children against broadcasters' free speech rights, and complying with a congressional mandate, the FCC adopted a **safe harbor policy** in 1993. The commission would not punish any station that broadcasts indecent programming in a certain time period, a scheduling practice called "channeling." An FCC rule says stations may air indecent—but not obscene—material from 10 p.m. to 6 a.m. local time.[109] Strictly speaking, broadcasting indecent material at any time violates federal law. But the commission, with court approval, agreed not to take action against indecent broadcasts aired at times when few children are expected to be in the audience.[110] The 10 p.m. to 6 a.m. period is a safe harbor, a time when stations safely may broadcast material that does not fully comply with the law's indecency ban.

Congress, the courts and the FCC took a circuitous route to reaching the current 10 p.m. to 6 a.m. safe harbor. As part of its 1987 decision to use a generic indecency definition, the commission suggested that broadcasters could air indecent material between midnight and 6 a.m.[111] But a federal appellate court found the rule arbitrary.[112] The court said the FCC could not justify picking midnight rather than 10 p.m., for example. However, two months after the appellate court's decision, Congress adopted a law ordering the FCC to enforce the law as written—no obscene, indecent or profane broadcasts anytime.[113] The commission did as it was told. At the same time, the FCC defined the children who should not be exposed to indecent material as those 17 years old and younger.[114] The appellate court rejected the FCC's ruling.[115] The court held that the First Amendment does not allow broadcast indecency to be banned completely. The court told the FCC to try again.

safe harbor policy An FCC policy designating 10 p.m. to 6 a.m. as a time when broadcast radio and television stations may air indecent material without violating federal law or FCC regulations.

Congress once more stepped in, telling the FCC to allow indecent broadcasts only between midnight and 6 a.m.[116] However, public radio and television stations going off the air at midnight or earlier also could broadcast indecent material between 10 p.m. and midnight. The FCC adopted that regulation.[117] The appellate court said Congress offered no justification for establishing two categories of broadcasters.[118] A 10 p.m. to 6 a.m. safe harbor for all stations met constitutional standards, the court ruled.

Television Program Ratings

Following is a list of television parental guidelines. The first two ratings are for programs designed solely for children. The rest are for programs designed for general audiences.

- TV-Y (All children—This program is designed to be appropriate for all children.) Whether animated or live-action, the themes and elements in this program are specifically designed for a very young audience, including children from ages 2–6. This program is not expected to frighten younger children.

- TV-Y7 (Directed to older children—This program is designed for children age 7 and older.) It may be more appropriate for children who have acquired the developmental skills needed to distinguish between make-believe and reality. Themes and elements in this program may include mild fantasy or comedic violence, or may frighten children under the age of 7. Therefore, parents may wish to consider the suitability of this program for their very young children. Note: For those programs where fantasy violence may be more intense or more combative than other programs in this category, such programs will be designated TV-Y7-FV.

- TV-G (General audience—Most parents would find this program suitable for all ages.) Although this rating does not signify a program designed specifically for children, most parents may let younger children watch this program unattended. It contains little or no violence, no strong language and little or no sexual dialogue or situations.

- TV-PG (Parental guidance suggested—This program contains material that parents may find unsuitable for younger children.) Many parents may want to watch it with their younger children. The theme itself may call for parental guidance and/or the program contains one or more of the following: moderate violence (V), some sexual situations (S), infrequent coarse language (L), or some suggestive dialogue (D).

- TV-14 (Parents strongly cautioned—This program contains some material that many parents would find unsuitable for children under 14 years of age.) Parents are strongly urged to exercise greater care in monitoring this program and are cautioned against letting children under the age of 14 watch unattended. This program contains one or more of the following: intense violence (V), intense sexual situations (S), strong coarse language (L), or intensely suggestive dialogue (D).

- TV-MA (Mature audience only—This program is specifically designed to be viewed by adults and therefore may be unsuitable for children under 17.) This program contains one or more of the following: graphic violence (V), explicit sexual activity (S), or crude indecent language (L).[1]

1. Federal Communications Commission, *V-Chip: Viewing Television Responsibly*, n.d., *available at* http://www.fcc.gov/vchip/.

Television Program Ratings and the V-Chip

In the mid-1990s some members of Congress expressed a concern about the impact on children of not only televised sexual content but also violent programming. Realizing that the First Amendment prevented government censorship of television programs, Congress considered other alternatives. After an acrimonious fight, Congress required television set manufacturers to include an electronic chip, the V-chip, enabling parents to block reception of certain programs. Congress also encouraged the FCC or the television industry to establish a program rating system.

Preferring to adopt its own program ratings system rather than have the FCC recommend or require one, the National Association of Broadcasters, representing broadcast stations and networks; the National Cable Television Association, representing cable system owners; and the Motion Picture Association of America, representing television program producers, created the TV Parental Guidelines. The guidelines are a voluntary ratings system. All broadcast and basic cable networks have chosen to rate their programs, as have premium cable networks such as Home Box Office (HBO) and the major distributors of syndicated television programs such as "Oprah" and "Wheel of Fortune."[119]

The broadcast television, cable and program production industries also established an Oversight Monitoring Board to review ratings applied to television programs.[120] The board has no legal authority. It can only encourage the television, cable and production industries to apply the ratings accurately and consistently. Neither the V-chip requirement nor the ratings system has been challenged in court.

The television rating system is similar to that adopted by the Motion Picture Association of America (MPAA) for movies. The MPAA system, also supported by the National Association of Theater Owners, is voluntary for film producers and movie theaters, but the film industry generally follows it.[121]

SUMMARY

THE FIRST AMENDMENT PROTECTS INDECENT material—except on broadcast television and radio. The FCC and the Supreme Court define broadcast indecency as patently offensive material describing or depicting sexual or excretory activities and organs. The FCC's rules considered whether the material explicitly or graphically describes and dwells on sexual activities, and whether the material is meant to shock or sexually excite the audience. However, a federal appellate court held the FCC's indecency regulations to be unconstitutionally vague. When indecency regulations are constitutionally acceptable, the courts allow broadcasters to air indecent material between 10 p.m. and 6 a.m.

Attempting to give parents control over the television programming their children watch, Congress required set manufacturers to include V-chips. The chips read ratings information television stations, networks and cable systems provide with their programming. ∎

Cable Indecency

Cable and broadcast television are very different media in the courts' and the FCC's eyes. Cable comes into a home only if the residents invite it in by paying a monthly fee. Even then, cable customers generally may select the cable networks they want to receive and not subscribe to others. For example, a cable customer might pay for HBO and Showtime or decide not to pay for any premium cable programming. However, radio and broadcast television programs are ubiquitous. They are everywhere—cars, stores, homes, restaurants. Broadcast indecency is channeled into the safe harbor period because children otherwise inadvertently could be exposed to it. The same rationale does not apply to cable television. At least, that is the courts' and the FCC's reasoning for not limiting indecent material on cable networks.

Not everyone agrees cable should be able to carry indecent material. HBO's development in 1975 spurred cable's popularity. Certain movies that HBO showed, and various other cable network content, so offended some state legislators and local officials that by the early 1980s they adopted laws forbidding cable indecency. Courts uniformly rejected these restrictions. For example, a Miami, Fla., ordinance prohibited cable systems from distributing "obscene or indecent" material.[122] A federal appellate court said the restrictions on broadcasting indecent material upheld in the *FCC v. Pacifica* decision did not apply to cable television. Parents may prevent their children from watching cable television by not subscribing. The court also said the Miami law was overbroad because it did not allow any time period when a cable system could transmit indecent material. Courts struck down several similar laws the Utah legislature, and many Utah cities adopted to ban indecent material on cable television.[123] Congress adopted the first federal law regulating cable in 1984 but did not use the statute to limit indecent content on cable television. Rather, the law only said the obvious: Cable systems could not transmit obscene material.[124] The 1984 Cable Act's one concession to those concerned about indecent material on cable networks was to require cable system operators to provide lockboxes to customers who requested them. Lockboxes allowed subscribers to block receipt of individual cable channels.[125]

The FCC has not attempted to extend its broadcast indecency regulations to cable television. Responding to complaints about the cable network FX show "Nip/Tuck," the commission stated clearly: "The Commission does not regulate cable indecency. In this regard, the Commission recently stated: 'Indecency regulation is only applied to broadcast services,' not cable."[126]

However, in 1992 Congress decided that indecent cable content required its attention. Legislation adopted that year included three provisions limiting indecent content on cable television. In *Denver Area Educational Telecommunications Consortium, Inc. v. FCC*, the Supreme Court found two of the provisions unconstitutional.[127] The law dealt only with two kinds of cable channels. First, community members, local schools and government agencies may use a cable system's public, educational and government (PEG) access channels. Congress allowed cable operators—though not the government—to ban indecent programming on PEG access channels. Second, cable systems' leased access channels can be rented by individuals and companies to show programming they want cable subscribers to see. (Both types of access channels are discussed in Chapter 11.) The law also said cable systems—again, not the government—could ban any leased access programming a cable operator believes "describes or depicts sexual or excretory activities or organs in a patently offensive manner." The Supreme Court upheld the leased access provision. But the Court said cable systems could not prohibit indecent programming on PEG access channels. Nor would the Court allow a requirement that cable systems put all patently offensive—that is, indecent—leased access programming on one channel and deliver that channel only to subscribers who request it.

The Court's *Denver Area* decision was fractious. Even when a group of justices agreed on a result, they could not agree on a reason for the outcome. Five justices voted to strike down the provision allowing cable operators to ban PEG indecent programming; six justices found the "segregate and block" provision unconstitutional; and seven justices voted to allow bans on leased access indecent programming. Justice Stephen Breyer wrote the Court's opinion, but five other justices wrote separate opinions.

Breyer questioned Congress' intent to control content. He acknowledged the important reason to control content: protecting children from sexually oriented programming. But even when the purpose of limiting content is extremely important, doing so is rarely constitutionally permitted. Permitting, rather than requiring, cable operators to ban indecent leased access programming is a narrowly drawn way to accomplish Congress' goal, Breyer said. That is not true for PEG programming, however. Cable operators historically have not controlled PEG content, Breyer said. Rather, government officials or nonprofit organizations oversee PEG programming. Congress gave cable operators a right they did not have—namely, the power to censor PEG content. This could eliminate, for example, sex education programming, content meant for marginal political groups or experimental artistic programs, Breyer said.

Breyer said it is unconstitutional to require cable operators to put all indecent leased access programming onto one channel and then deliver that channel only to subscribers who specifically request it. This is not a narrowly tailored way to protect children from sexually oriented content, Breyer said.

Congress continued its efforts to limit programming indecency on PEG access channels. In the Telecommunications Act of 1996, Congress said cable operators could not exercise editorial control over PEG content, but they "may refuse to transmit any public access program or portion of a public access program which contains obscenity, indecency, or nudity."[128] This provision has yet to be challenged in court.

However, the Supreme Court overturned other sections of the 1996 act dealing with sexually explicit cable programming. Congress required cable operators to scramble the signal of any indecent programming on adult-oriented channels.[129] In part, Congress said, this was to prevent adult programming signals from bleeding into channels that children could see even in homes that did not subscribe to adult channels. Alternatively, Congress said, cable programmers could offer adult programming only during hours when children are unlikely to be watching. The FCC said the time period would be 10 p.m. to 6 a.m.[130]

A unanimous Supreme Court said those provisions of the 1996 act were content-based regulations requiring a strict scrutiny analysis.[131] Protecting children from exposure to sexually explicit programming is a compelling state interest, the Court agreed. However, Congress' method was not the least restrictive approach. Instead, the Court said, cable subscribers may ask cable companies to block channels and may request lockboxes. The availability of these alternatives make the 1996 act's provisions unconstitutional, the Court ruled.

Internet Indecency

Many websites contain sexually explicit images. It has been estimated that 40 million Americans regularly look at pornographic Internet content.[132] It is not surprising that Congress' concern about cable indecency paled next to Congress' attempts to prevent children from seeing sexually explicit material on the Internet. Congress has used two approaches in trying to separate children from indecent Internet content.[133] First, it has limited content, making it illegal to provide children indecent material through the Internet. Courts have found these attempts unconstitutional because, in part, material they prohibit from being sent to children also cannot be seen by adults. There is no technologically feasible way to allow adults but not children to receive Internet transmissions. Second, Congress and some local governments have limited children's access to content by, for example, requiring public and school libraries to block indecent material. The Supreme Court approved this method of preventing children's exposure to sexually explicit Internet content.

Many parents told members of Congress they were angry their children could see indecent material on the Internet—sometimes deliberately, often not. Congress responded by including the Communications Decency Act (CDA) in the Telecommunications Act of 1996.[134] The CDA made it illegal to knowingly transmit "obscene or indecent messages to any recipient under 18 years of age" or to make available "patently offensive messages" to anyone under 18 years old. People could not be convicted of violating the CDA if they either took "good faith" actions to prevent minors from seeing those materials or used procedures the law specified (such as a verified credit card) to confirm a recipient's age.

The Supreme Court rejected the CDA, finding it unconstitutionally overbroad in *Reno v. ACLU*.[135] The Court first said that, unlike broadcasting, the Internet had full First Amendment protection. The

Points of Law

Censoring the Internet

The U.S. Supreme Court said:

> The record demonstrates that the growth of the Internet has been and continues to be phenomenal. As a matter of constitutional tradition, in the absence of evidence to the contrary, we presume that governmental regulation of the content of speech is more likely to interfere with the free exchange of ideas than to encourage it. The interest in encouraging freedom of expression in a democratic society outweighs any theoretical but unproven benefit of censorship.[1]

1. Reno v. ACLU, 521 U.S. 844, 875 (1997).

Internet is not limited by spectrum scarcity, as is broadcasting, because millions of people are able to use the Internet simultaneously. Also, the Internet is not as intrusive as broadcasting. Families not wanting children to access the Internet at home need not subscribe to an Internet service, the Court said. For these reasons, the Court refused to find the Internet bound by the *Pacifica* case, which involved George Carlin's seven dirty words. Also, *Pacifica* at least allowed indecent material on the air at times children likely were not in the audience. But the CDA completely banned indecent Internet content.

Because the CDA directly restricted speech, the Court used a strict scrutiny analysis. The Court did not deny that Congress had a compelling interest in protecting children from sexually explicit content. But the Court decided the law was too sweeping, not the least restrictive way to achieve the government's goal. The CDA denied adults access to protected speech as a way to prevent minors from being exposed to potentially harmful content, the Court said. The Court noted that there was no technology allowing adults to see Internet material while preventing children from doing so. The Court also said the CDA was overbroad because Congress had not carefully defined the words "indecent" and "offensive." The law made it illegal to provide children with "large amounts of nonpornographic material with serious educational or other value," the Court said.[136]

The Court's decision did not include the CDA's restriction on sending obscene material over the Internet. This limitation remains part of the federal law.

Congress enacted the Child Online Protection Act (COPA) in 1998, intending to correct the CDA's constitutional problems.[137] Courts consistently have found the COPA unconstitutional. The COPA differed from the CDA in two important ways. First, the COPA banned Internet distribution to children of material "harmful to minors," defined in part as being designed to pander to prurient interest, determined by applying contemporary community standards. The CDA more broadly limited obscene, indecent or offensive content. Second, the COPA's restriction on transmitting harmful content applied only to people intending to profit from using the Internet. The law also defined minors as 16 years old and younger, not 17 years old and younger as the CDA did.

Congress' definition of harmful to minors resembled the *Miller v. California* obscenity definition. This meant the COPA affected a narrower range of materials than did the CDA. But the definition focused on materials inappropriate for minors. For instance, the COPA restricted material that "depicts, describes, or represents in a manner patently offensive with respect to minors." This meant the COPA limited adults to accessing materials appropriate for children—just as the CDA did.

Challenges to the COPA stayed in the courts for a decade. First, a federal district court preliminarily stopped the government from enforcing the law.[138] The U.S. Court of Appeals for the Third Circuit affirmed that decision, concluding that the community standards language was overbroad.[139] The U.S. Supreme Court disagreed with the Third Circuit and vacated the decision.[140] In 2003, reviewing the case again, the Third Circuit issued an injunction blocking the COPA's enforcement. The court said there were technological methods of limiting

realWorld Law

Internet Indecency: ACLU v. Congress

When the ACLU and its attorneys decided to contest the constitutionality of the Communications Decency Act, they knew from the beginning the challenge lay in distinguishing the Internet from broadcasting, and their case from *Pacifica*. "A huge amount of the case was designed to distinguish us from *Pacifica*," says ACLU senior counsel Chris Hansen. "That's the whole fight. If we were television, then we were *Pacifica*. And if we were *Pacifica*, we lose."

Hansen's colleagues agree. "A lot of attention went into explaining how narrow *Pacifica* was, how distinguishable it was in terms of the medium that was being regulated, and *Pacifica* being an enforcement mechanism that didn't involve criminal prosecution," says Marjorie Heins, an ACLU attorney at the time of the case.

Because the courts had upheld the ruling in *Pacifica* that allowed the FCC to fine stations broadcasting indecent speech, the ACLU had a significant challenge. "The CDA's language used the same kind of indecency language that had been upheld specifically with respect to broadcast," says the ACLU's Ann Beeson. "In the opinion itself, that's exactly the analysis that the Supreme Court went through—to distinguish very clearly the *Pacifica* decision from this one."

In the end, the ACLU had to make the case that the Internet is neither a scarce resource nor is it pervasive. In short, the Internet is a much different medium than is broadcasting. Successfully making that case in the mid-1990s, when the Internet was still in its infancy, was not easy, but the ACLU succeeded.[1]

1. JOSEPH RUSSOMANNO, SPEAKING OUR MINDS: CONVERSATIONS WITH THE PEOPLE BEHIND LANDMARK FIRST AMENDMENT CASES 423, 434 (Mahwah, N.J.: Lawrence Erlbaum Associates, 2002).

children's access to websites containing inappropriate material and that therefore a sweeping ban on "material harmful to children" was not the least restrictive way to achieve Congress' purpose of preventing minors from being exposed to sexual material on the Internet.[141]

The Supreme Court left the preliminary injunction in place in 2004, saying that blocking and filtering software could effectively limit children's access to harmful material. However, the Court sent the case back to the trial court to update information about Internet technology. Courts must have current information to decide if the COPA limits more speech than necessary to protect children, the Court said. When a content-based speech regulation, such as the COPA, is challenged, the government must show there are no alternatives less restrictive of First Amendment rights. Less restrictive means do exist to limit children's access to Internet pornography, according to the Court. Filters could prevent children from seeing harmful material while allowing adults access to Internet content, the Court said. Also, filters would not chill speech. Websites could include content unacceptable for children but constitutionally protected for adults. Additionally, filters are able to prevent children's access to pornography sent via e-mail and available on websites located in other countries. The COPA applies only to websites located in the United States. A congressionally appointed commission found filtering software to be the most effective means of preventing children from seeing harmful material. For these reasons, it would be difficult for the government to show that the COPA would be more effective and less restrictive than filters, the Supreme Court concluded.[142]

A federal district court in 2007 found that the COPA was not narrowly tailored and not the least restrictive nor most effective way to achieve Congress' compelling interest in protecting children.[143] The government once again appealed the decision.

Hearing the case one more time, the Third Circuit affirmed the district court's decision.[144] Applying strict scrutiny, the appellate court agreed the government had a compelling interest in protecting children from exposure to harmful material on the Internet. But the court said the COPA was not narrowly tailored to achieve that goal. The government failed to show the COPA was a better, less restrictive method of protecting children than using filters that could prevent a computer from receiving certain Internet sites. The court also held that several words and phrases in the law, such as "minor," were vague and not clearly defined. The court referred to its earlier decision, in which it said:

> The type of material that might be considered harmful to a younger minor is vastly different—and encompasses a much greater universe of speech—than material that is harmful to a minor just shy of seventeen years old. Thus, for example, sex education materials may have "serious value" for, and not be "patently offensive" as to, sixteen-year-olds. The same material, however, might well be considered "patently offensive" as to . . . children aged, say, ten to thirteen, and thus meet COPA's standard for material harmful to minors.[145]

In 2009, the Supreme Court refused to hear the government's appeal of the Third Circuit's decision.[146] Eleven years after the COPA's adoption, courts definitively ruled it unconstitutional.

Even before Congress adopted the Child Online Protection Act, it took an indirect route to keeping sexual material off the Internet. The Child Pornography Protection Act (CPPA), adopted in 1996, made it illegal to send or possess digital images of child pornography (children in sexually suggestive or sexually explicit situations).[147] The CPPA applied whether the image was created by computer—"virtual kiddy porn"—or was an actual photograph or film. The law also applied if the image was of a real person who looked like a minor but in fact was 18 years old or older. The law said it is illegal to send or possess an image that "is, or appears to be, of a minor engaging in sexually explicit conduct," or if the image is advertised or distributed in a way "that conveys the impression" that a minor is "engaging in sexually explicit conduct."[148]

The Supreme Court said the CPPA abridged First Amendment rights.[149] In *Ashcroft v. Free Speech Coalition*, the Court said the language "appears to be" and "conveys the impression" was overbroad. The language made it illegal to send or possess images that were not obscene. This would prevent adults from seeing protected content in order to prevent children from being exposed to it. Because the CPPA was a content-based regulation, the Court applied strict scrutiny. It said Congress had a compelling interest in protecting children from being involved in the sex trade. However, the Court said, since computer-generated pictures are outlawed, the CPPA would prohibit child pornography that does not harm an actual child. That also would be true when adults who appear to be children are pictured.

In response, Congress adopted the Prosecutorial Remedies and Other Tools to End the Exploitation of Children Today Act (the Protect Act) of 2003.[150] The Protect Act makes it illegal to provide someone with or request from someone an image that "is indistinguishable from that of a minor" in a sexual situation. This wording differs from the "appears to be" and "conveys the impression" language in the CPPA. In 2008 the Supreme Court found the Protect Act constitutional. The Court said the act did not focus on the material but on the speech—offering or requesting child pornography—that could put the material into distribution. The First Amendment does not protect offers to engage in illegal transactions, the Court said, because offering to give or receive unlawful material has no social value.[151]

The Supreme Court found constitutional at least one congressional attempt to deal with online content. Congress enacted the Children's Internet Protection Act (CIPA) in 2000. This law focused on schools and libraries that receive money from a federal program helping to fund Internet connections and computer equipment purchases. The CIPA would stop money from going to schools and libraries that do not install "technology protection measures" on their computers accessing the Internet. Those schools and libraries wanting to continue receiving federal funds would have to install filtering software that blocks obscenity, child pornography or material "harmful to minors."[152] The Supreme Court held in *United States v. American Library Association* that Congress has the right to set conditions for receipt of federal money.[153] The Court said public libraries already choose to purchase or not purchase certain books and other materials. For example, most libraries exclude pornographic material from their print collections, the Court said. Limiting what Internet sites are available on the computers that libraries provide to the public is an equivalent decision. The Court also said requiring adults to ask a librarian to unblock a computer does not infringe on adults' First Amendment rights.

SUMMARY

BECAUSE PARENTS MAY CHOOSE NOT TO SUBSCRIBE to cable television, courts have not allowed the government to ban indecent material from cable. The one exception is that cable system operators may reject public access programs that are obscene or indecent or contain nudity.

The Supreme Court has rejected several congressional attempts to prevent children from seeing sexually oriented material on the Internet. The Court did allow Congress to withhold government funds for computers and Internet connections from public libraries and schools that do not install blocking software on computers available to the public. ∎

Other Limits on Offensive Speech

Legislators, courts, parents and administrative agencies have long debated how to define, limit and protect offensive speech. These debates usually center on sexually explicit content but also may involve media violence. Concerns about comic book, movie, radio and television content go back to the 1930s. More recently, other communication media have come under scrutiny, including recordings, art and telephones. Sometimes industries regulate themselves, as do music recording companies and the motion picture industry. Other industries—such as broadcasting—face government regulations.

Public Funds for Pornographic Art

As a method of limiting children's access to content considered inappropriate for minors, Congress used its power of the purse to require libraries and schools to install filtering software on computers the public or students use. The Supreme Court said the law meets First Amendment standards.[154] Similarly, Congress used its funding powers to limit the ability of the National Endowment for the Arts (NEA) to give artists grants. The Supreme Court upheld this action as well.

Congress created the National Foundation on the Arts and Humanities, under which the NEA operates, in 1965. The NEA experienced little controversy until the late 1980s, when it used government funds to give art grants to Robert Mapplethorpe and Andres Serrano. Some of Mapplethorpe's photographs were of men engaged in homosexual activities. Serrano's works included a photograph he titled "Piss Christ," showing a plastic crucifix suspended in a jar of Serrano's urine. A public outcry prompted some congressional members to insist the NEA's art grant program be stopped or at least limited.[155] Ultimately, Congress adopted a law preventing the NEA from granting funds for art that, in the NEA's judgment, "may be considered obscene, including depictions of sadomasochism, homo-eroticism, the sexual exploitation of children or individuals engaged in sex acts."[156] Later, Congress also required the NEA to use "artistic excellence and artistic merit [as] the criteria by which grant applications are judged, taking into consideration general standards of decency and respect for the diverse beliefs and values of the American public."[157] This became popularly known as the "decency clause." Four artists denied NEA funding, including the performance artist Karen Finley, challenged the decency clause. The Supreme Court upheld the clause.[158]

The Court said Congress required the NEA to consider decency as one factor in giving art grants. Because the NEA could give the clause as much or as little weight as the agency chose, the clause was not a bar to getting an NEA grant. Also, the clause was not content specific, the Court said. It merely was a criterion applied to all grant applications regardless of their content and therefore did not violate artists' First Amendment rights. But even if it was seen as a content-specific regulation, the Court said, Congress could place conditions on giving funds to artists. In essence, the Court said, the NEA was acting as a patron of the arts. The NEA was deciding what artists or organizations should receive the limited amount of government money available for such a purpose. This is no different from an individual deciding to give money to a local ballet company but not to the community orchestra, according to the Court. The Court also said the decency clause was not vague. An individual makes a decision to give money based on artistic excellence. The NEA could make a choice based on decency and respect, these two words being no more vague than "excellence," the Court said.

Recording Labels

In the early 1980s Tipper Gore, then Al Gore's wife (Gore was a U.S. senator in the 1980s and then served as vice president in the 1990s), urged Congress to hold hearings about music lyrics and the possibility of regulating recordings.[159] Rather than allow Congress to adopt a law regulating recordings, the Recording Industry Association of America (RIAA), the National Parent Teacher Association and a public interest group, the Parents Music Resource Center, agreed in 1985 to have recording companies voluntarily apply a Parental Advisory label on certain music recordings. Recordings containing "explicit lyrics, including explicit depictions of violence and sex," and references to drug use would carry the advisory label.[160] Advertisements for these recordings also should display the advisory label. The RIAA says the label is intended to notify parents that the recording might be inappropriate for certain children. A recording also may be issued in an edited version not containing certain lyrics that are in the original. The RIAA suggests these recordings contain an Edited Version label. Some retailers will not sell recordings with a Parental Advisory label to customers younger than 18 years old, and some other retailers will not stock labeled recordings at all.

Recording companies and artists are not required to comply with the RIAA system. The RIAA, in fact, does not oversee the labeling process other than establishing guidelines and creating the labels. The RIAA says fewer than 5 percent of recordings should be and are labeled.[161] The labeling system's critics say the Parental Advisory label provides insufficient information to allow parents to decide whether a recording is appropriate for their children.

Using Zoning to Restrict Adult Stores

Most cities would prefer that adult establishments—theaters, magazine and book stores, topless clubs—be in some other municipality, if they have to exist at all. But they do exist. If the film, printed material or other entertainment being sold is not obscene, the First Amendment protects it. Courts have said cities cannot adopt laws eliminating all adult theaters, stores and clubs.[162] But may a city use its zoning power to limit and geographically segregate adult establishments? Zoning allows a city to decide whether a convenience store may open in a residential neighborhood, whether an apartment house may be built in an industrial area or whether a big-box retail store may come into town at all. Does this same power permit a city to restrict adult establishments to one area of town or, instead, to prevent them from being close to one another? Or does a city's use of its zoning powers in this way infringe on the First Amendment rights of an adult establishment's owner?

The Supreme Court has allowed cities to zone adult establishments into confined areas or to disperse them in the city. The Court justifies these decisions on the basis that government may curb the secondary effects resulting from the presence of an adult establishment.[163] By "secondary effects," the Court means illegal activities such as prostitution and illicit drug sales that may occur around adult bookstores, theaters and clubs. This is not a justification the Court would use to uphold laws affecting other protected speech. But the Court has said nude and sexually explicit entertainment is "expressive conduct within the outer perimeters of the First Amendment, though . . . only marginally so."[164] (The Court has ruled that mere public nudity may be banned if it does not have an expressive component. A law making it illegal to appear in public totally nude is constitutional, the Court held.)[165]

Although the protection of adult establishments may be marginal, it is First Amendment protection nonetheless. When an adult theater owner is told he can operate in only one area of the city, he may claim his free speech is constrained because he wants to communicate with residents in another part of town. An adult bookstore owner may object when she is told she cannot do business next door to an adult theater, where she thinks movie patrons will become her customers, because the zoning law requires adult establishments to be at least 1,000 feet apart. Nonetheless, the Supreme Court allowed the City of Los Angeles to disperse adult establishments based on a 20-year-old study showing considerable crime in areas where several adult stores operated in close proximity.[166]

Because there is the possibility of infringing on First Amendment rights by clumping together or dispersing adult establishments, the Court has stipulated a test for assessing a zoning decision's constitutionality.[167] First, the zoning regulation must be content neutral. It seems a zoning restriction affecting adult content would be content based. But the restrictions do not apply to certain videos or specific books. Rather, they are time, place and manner restrictions (see Chapter 2). Second, the zoning decision must serve a substantial government interest, such as limiting illegal secondary effects. Finally, the zoning restriction must not limit alternative methods of communicating. That is, a city must allow an adult establishment to operate somewhere in the city limits; it cannot completely ban adult bookstores, theaters and clubs.[168] If a city meets this test, the Court will permit zoning restrictions on adult establishments.

Dial-a-Porn: Telephone Indecency

Congress has attempted to prevent children from having access to so-called dial-a-porn—telephone services that allow a caller to pay to hear a prerecorded sexually explicit message or to have a sexually oriented live talk with someone. In 1983, Congress adopted a law criminalizing the use of telephones to transmit obscene or indecent material to minors. After the FCC spent several years wrestling with regulations to implement the law,[169] Congress changed the statute. The new law banned all obscene and indecent interstate telephone communications made for commercial purposes—that is, to earn a profit. This prevented adults as well as children from having access to dial-a-porn services.

In *Sable Communications of California, Inc. v. FCC,* the Supreme Court found the law constitutional in banning obscene telephone communications, but unconstitutional regarding indecent content.[170] The Court rejected an argument that a national ban on obscene communications meant dial-a-porn services would have to comport with the least tolerant community's standards. The *Miller v. California* decision requires prurient interest and patent offensiveness to be assessed based on contemporary community standards. The Court said it had not found that variable community standards in other federal laws banning obscenity made those laws unconstitutional.

But the law's indecency restriction could not withstand a strict scrutiny analysis. Strict scrutiny requires the government to have a compelling reason to regulate expression and, if it does, to impose a regulation limiting speech as narrowly as possible. Congress had a compelling interest in protecting children from dial-a-porn, the Court said. But the law was not the most narrowly tailored way to accomplish this purpose because it prevented adult access to protected expression in order to keep children away from inappropriate content. There were other ways to accomplish the purpose, the Court said. For example, a dial-a-porn service could issue identification numbers to adults who wanted them. Then the service would allow calls only from adults with proper numbers. Also, a dial-a-porn service could scramble its messages, making them available through a descrambler that could be purchased only by adults with identification numbers. When Congress adopted a law protecting dial-a-porn services using those methods, but banning all other indecent telephone communications with minors, a federal district court upheld the statute.[171]

SUMMARY

THE SUPREME COURT UPHELD A CONGRESSIONAL mandate that the National Endowment for the Arts must consider "general standards of decency and respect for the diverse beliefs and values" when making monetary grants to arts organizations. The music recording industry adopted a voluntary labeling system to make parents aware of content not appropriate for minors. The Supreme Court has allowed cities to use zoning laws to either clump together adult establishments or disperse adult establishments throughout the city. However, governments cannot use zoning laws to prohibit adult establishments from operating in a community. The Court has ruled that companies may use telephone facilities to transmit sexually explicit content if they employ ways to ensure that only adults are using the companies' services, such as verified identification numbers. ■

Video Games and Media Violence

The Internet's pervasiveness and vast content make it a ready target for citizens and legislators who believe the media should be held responsible if they deliver speech promoting violence. At the start of the 21st century, scholars and citizens clamored for legislation and civil remedies to reduce violent crime in America. One solution, they argued, would be to regulate violent content reaching minors through the Internet, television, books, music, video games and movies.[172] Courts rapidly squelched most of these initiatives with rulings that the First Amendment protects violent expression.[173] However, some people argued that specific regulations should limit violent content in video games and Internet sites because the content is directed at and readily accessible to impressionable youngsters. For example, the two teenagers who killed fellow students and a teacher at Columbine High School in Littleton, Colo., in 1999, reportedly were avid players of violent video games.

Early in 2003, the Supreme Court refused to hear a case in which parents of three murdered girls argued that violent video games, such as "Doom," and websites that reach minors are not constitutionally protected.[174] The lower court had said that although protecting children from violent content is a legitimate government goal, it should be achieved through legislative, not judicial, action.[175]

In part, the court suggested the First Amendment protects violent content, although it does not protect obscenity. As a federal appellate court said, the concerns that "animate obscenity laws" and those that cause some people to urge limits on media violence are different.[176] The court said:

> A work is classified as obscene not upon proof that it is likely to affect anyone's conduct, but upon proof that it violates community norms regarding the permissible scope of depictions of sexual or sex-related activity. . . . Obscenity is to many people disgusting, embarrassing, degrading, disturbing, outrageous and insulting, but it generally is not believed to inflict [physical] (as distinct from spiritual) harm.[177]

However, behind moves to prevent children from seeing violent content "is a belief that violent video games cause [physical] harm by engendering aggressive attitudes and behavior, which might lead to violence," the judge said.[178] Courts have not seen that as a sufficient reason to remove First Amendment protection from violent content.

realWorld Law

Dickens v. The House of the Dead

U.S. Appellate Judge Richard Posner wrote:

> Maybe video games are different [from movies or television]. They are, after all, interactive. But this point is superficial, in fact erroneous. All literature (here broadly defined to include movies, television, and the other photographic media, and popular as well as highbrow literature) is interactive; the better it is, the more interactive. Literature when it is successful draws the reader into the story, makes him identify with the characters, invites him to judge them and quarrel with them, to experience their joys and sufferings as the reader's own. Protests from readers caused Dickens to revise *Great Expectations to* give it a happy ending. . . . Most of the video games . . . are stories. Take . . . "The House of the Dead." The player is armed with a gun—most fortunately, because he is being assailed by a seemingly unending succession of hideous axe-wielding zombies, the living dead conjured back to life by voodoo. The zombies have already knocked down and wounded several people, who are pleading pitiably for help; and one of the player's duties is to protect those unfortunates from renewed assaults by the zombies. His main task, however, is self-defense.
>
> Self-defense, protection of others, dread of the "undead," fighting against overwhelming odds—these are all age-old themes of literature, and ones particularly appealing to the young. "The House of the Dead" is not distinguished literature. . . .[1]

---

1. American Amusement Machine Association v. Kendrick, 244 F.3d 572, 577–78 (7th Cir.), *cert. denied,* 534 U.S. 994 (2001).

Concerns that violent media content has profound effects on children have not diminished, nor have worries that the mass media deliberately exploit children's fascination with violence rather than imposing effective self-regulation to prevent children's access to inappropriate violent content. A report from the Federal Trade Commission (FTC) titled "Marketing Violent Entertainment to Children," released in 2000, concludes that the motion picture, music recording and video game industries intentionally market violent content to children.[179] The FTC says children under 17 years old may easily buy recordings and video games labeled as inappropriate for children and tickets to R-rated movies, a rating indicating the film is meant for viewers 17 years old and older. Exposure to media violence tends to inure children to violence in society, make them more aggressive in their own behavior, incline them to view violence as a means to solve problems and increase their belief that the world is more violent than it in fact is, the FTC says its review of academic studies shows.

Under pressure from Congress, the FCC reviewed televised violence and its impact on children. The commission's 2007 violence report recognized that scholarly studies disagree about how media violence affects young people.[180] The FCC noted the FTC report and agreed with a 2000 U.S. Surgeon General's report that "'a diverse body of research provides strong evidence that exposure to violence in the media can increase children's aggressive behavior in the short term.'" But, the commission said, it does recognize that "'many questions remain regarding the short- and long-term effects of media violence, especially on violent behavior.'"[181] The commission's primary focus, though, was "that a significant number of health professionals, parents and members of the general public are concerned about television violence and its effects on children."[182]

The FCC did not adopt new regulations responding to those concerns. Rather, it recommended that Congress and the television industry take action. The commission said that devices currently available allowing viewers to block programming so that children could not see it, perhaps based on program ratings, likely will not solve the problem. The V-chip has only limited effectiveness, the FCC said, because fewer than half of television sets have V-chips and few viewers use the V-chips even if they are available in their sets. Similarly, cable television blocking technology is not available in more than half of television sets and is rarely used even when available. However, the commission suggested that more effective and user-friendly systems enabling viewers to block violent television content could be useful. The commission suggested Congress should develop a definition of excessively violent programming that courts could find acceptable under the First Amendment. Also, Congress could consider channeling violent television programming into certain hours when children are less likely to be watching, as is done with indecent programming. The commission urged the television industry to reduce violence in programs children likely will watch. Finally, the FCC suggested that cable and satellite providers could allow subscribers to purchase only certain, more family-friendly channels rather than having that programming included with channels containing violence.

The movie, recording and video game industries have adopted self-regulatory systems for identifying and notifying potential purchasers or their parents of sexual and violent content. The video game industry began the Entertainment Software Rating Board (ESRB) in 1994, in response to congressional moves to impose a ratings system for computer games.[183] The ratings system is voluntary for video game manufacturers, but the ESRB says it has rated more than 10,000 games manufactured by 350 companies.[184] The front of a video game package is to have a label specifying the ESRB's ratings. On the back of video game packages are more detailed descriptions, such as, "Alcohol reference—Reference to and/or images of alcoholic beverages," "Blood—Depictions of blood" and "Sexual violence—Depictions of rape or other sexual acts." A video game manufacturer may use one or more of 31 such descriptions.[185]

Ratings systems advising parents about violent or sexual content would be unnecessary if the government could ban movies, music recordings and video games containing material inappropriate for children. Of course, the government cannot simply censor movies and recordings, which have had First Amendment protection for decades. However, courts only recently have considered whether video games have constitutional protection.

Video games have communicative content and therefore have First Amendment protection, the U.S. Supreme Court ruled in 2011.[186] Courts initially said

Video Game Ratings

The Entertainment Software Rating Board (ESRB) established by the video game industry, applies the following ratings when manufacturers submit video games for the board's consideration:

- EC (Early Childhood): have content that may be suitable for ages 3 and older. Contains no material that parents would find inappropriate.

- E (Everyone): have content that may be suitable for persons ages 6 and older. Titles in this category may contain minimal violence, some comic mischief and/or mild language.

- E10+ (Everyone 10 and Older): have content that may be suitable for ages 10 and older. Titles in this category may contain more cartoon, fantasy or mild violence, mild language and/or minimal suggestive themes.

Several states have adopted laws preventing the selling or renting of violent video games to minors. But courts have consistently found that the government has failed to prove that playing such games causes psychological harm.

- T (Teen): have content that may be suitable for persons ages 13 and older. May contain violent content, mild or strong language and/or suggestive themes.

- M (Mature): have content that may be suitable for persons ages 17 and older. Titles in this category may contain mature sexual themes, more intense violence and/or strong language.

- AO (Adults Only): have content suitable only for adults. Titles in this category may include graphic depictions of sex and/or violence. Adult Only products are not intended for persons under the age of 18.[1]

---

1. ESRB Game Ratings, n.d., *available at* http://www.esrb.org/ratings/ratings_guide.jsp.

video games do not inform, that they do not communicate information.[187] In later cases, courts showed uncertainty about video games. "We cannot tell whether the video games at issue here are simply modern day pinball machines or whether they are more sophisticated presentations involving storyline and plot that convey to the user a significant artistic message protected by the First Amendment," one court said.[188] However, the Supreme Court said video games express ideas in the same ways movies and books do.[189]

Several state legislatures have claimed there are compelling reasons to prevent minors from having access to violent video games. For example, Minnesota said protecting minors' psychological well-being and safeguarding their moral and ethical development both are compelling reasons to restrict minors from purchasing or renting violent video games. In 2008, the U.S. Court of Appeals for the Eighth Circuit accepted these as compelling state interests. The court, however, said the state failed to present sufficient empirical evidence to support Minnesota's contention that violent video games cause children to suffer psychological harm.[190] Based on similar reasons, courts have invalidated laws preventing selling or renting violent video games to minors in Illinois, Louisiana, Michigan and Washington.[191]

The U.S. Supreme Court settled the issue in 2011, invalidating the California law that banned selling or renting violent video games to minors. Several speech categories, such as obscenity and incitement, are exempt from the general rule that government may not restrict expression because of its content, the Court said. But government may not add new categories of restricted speech that a legislature believes are harmful to society. That includes limiting violent expression, as California did by banning violent video game sales to minors, the Court ruled in *Brown v. Entertainment Merchants Association.*[192]

Restricting video game sales and rentals is a content-based regulation requiring a strict-scrutiny analysis, the Court said. There has to be a direct correlation between a regulation and its effectiveness in achieving a state's compelling interest. There is little evidence playing violent video games harms children psychologically or that banning their sale would protect children, the Court ruled. The Court also said the California law is underinclusive because it does not include other violent content, such as Saturday-morning cartoons. And the law is overinclusive, the Court said, because not all parents want violent video games unavailable to their children.

Is there sufficient empirical evidence to show a causal link between playing violent video games and increased violence in children? The FCC in 2010 cited a study showing "that children who spend more time playing video games are more likely to get into physical fights."[193] However, the U.S. Supreme Court asserted that studies California presented "show at best some correlation between exposure to violent entertainment and minuscule real-world effects, such as children's feeling more aggressive or making louder noises in the few minutes after playing a violent game than after playing a nonviolent game."[194]

SUMMARY

Courts find the First Amendment protects video games because the games have communicative content. State laws preventing minors from buying or renting violent video games consistently have been found unconstitutional. The video game industry has adopted a voluntary labeling system to alert purchasers and parents about the games' contents. ∎

Cases for Study

Thinking About It

The two case excerpts that follow offer the U.S. Supreme Court's definitions of obscenity and indecency. As you read these case excerpts, keep the following questions in mind:

- Is the *Miller* obscenity definition clear and easily applied?
- The *Miller* obscenity definition remains in use today. Have circumstances—technology, the public's toleration of media content—changed sufficiently that *Miller* no longer is an appropriate definition?
- In *Fox*, does the FCC clearly justify why the law forbids indecency?
- Does the ban on broadcast indecency remain appropriate for the 21st century?

Miller v. California
SUPREME COURT OF THE UNITED STATES
413 U.S. 15 (1973)

CHIEF JUSTICE WARREN BURGER delivered the Court's opinion:

. . . [Miller] conducted a mass mailing campaign to advertise the sale of illustrated books, euphemistically called "adult" material. After a jury trial, he was convicted of . . . a misdemeanor, by knowingly distributing obscene matter [and a California appellate court affirmed]. His conviction was specifically based on his conduct in causing five unsolicited advertising brochures to be sent through the mail in an envelope addressed to a restaurant in Newport Beach, California. The envelope was opened by the manager of the restaurant and his mother. They had not requested the brochures; they complained to the police.

The brochures advertise four books entitled "Intercourse," "Man-Woman," "Sex Orgies Illustrated," and "An Illustrated History of Pornography," and a film entitled "Marital Intercourse." While the brochures contain some descriptive printed material, primarily they consist of pictures and drawings very explicitly depicting men and women in groups of two or more engaging in a variety of sexual activities, with genitals often prominently displayed.

I

This case involves the application of a State's criminal obscenity statute to a situation in which sexually explicit materials have been thrust by aggressive sales action upon unwilling recipients who had in no way indicated any desire to receive such materials. This Court has recognized that the States have a legitimate interest in prohibiting dissemination or exhibition of obscene material when the mode of dissemination carries with it a significant danger of offending the sensibilities of unwilling recipients or of exposure to juveniles. It is in this context that we are called on to define the standards which must be used to identify obscene material that a State may regulate without infringing on the First Amendment as applicable to the States through the Fourteenth Amendment. . . .

II

This much has been categorically settled by the Court, that obscene material is unprotected by the First Amendment. We acknowledge, however, the inherent dangers of undertaking to regulate any form of expression. State statutes designed to regulate obscene materials must be carefully limited. As a result, we now confine the permissible scope of such regulation to works which depict or describe sexual conduct. That conduct must be specifically defined by the applicable state law, as written or authoritatively construed. A state offense must also be limited to works which, taken as a whole, appeal to the prurient interest in sex, which portray sexual conduct in a patently offensive way, and which, taken as a whole, do not have serious literary, artistic, political, or scientific value.

The basic guidelines for the trier of fact must be: (a) whether "the average person, applying contemporary community standards" would find that the work, taken as a whole, appeals to the prurient interest; (b) whether the work depicts or describes, in a patently offensive way, sexual conduct specifically defined by the applicable state law; and (c) whether the work, taken as a whole, lacks serious literary, artistic, political, or scientific value. We do not adopt as a constitutional standard the "utterly without redeeming social value" test of *Memoirs v. Massachusetts;* that concept has never commanded the adherence of more than three Justices at one time. If a state law that regulates obscene material is thus limited, as written or construed, the First Amendment values applicable to the States through the Fourteenth Amendment are adequately protected by the ultimate power of appellate courts to conduct an independent review of constitutional claims when necessary.

We emphasize that it is not our function to propose regulatory schemes for the States. That must await their concrete legislative efforts. It is possible, however, to give a few plain examples of what a state statute could define for regulation under part (b) of the standard announced in this opinion:

(a) Patently offensive representations or descriptions of ultimate sexual acts, normal or perverted, actual or simulated.

(b) Patently offensive representations or descriptions of masturbation, excretory functions, and lewd exhibition of the genitals.

Sex and nudity may not be exploited without limit by films or pictures exhibited or sold in places of public accommodation any more than live sex and nudity can be exhibited or sold without limit in such public places. At a minimum, prurient, patently offensive depiction or description of sexual conduct must have serious literary, artistic, political, or scientific value to merit First Amendment protection. For example, medical books for the education of physicians and related personnel necessarily use graphic illustrations and descriptions of human anatomy. In resolving the inevitably sensitive questions of fact and law, we must continue to rely on the jury system, accompanied by the safeguards that judges, rules of evidence, presumption of innocence, and other protective features provide, as we do with rape, murder, and a host of other offenses against society and its individual members.

Mr. Justice Brennan . . . has abandoned his former position and now maintains that no formulation of this Court, the Congress, or the States can adequately distinguish obscene material unprotected by the First Amendment from protected expression. Paradoxically, Mr. Justice Brennan indicates that suppression of unprotected obscene material is permissible to avoid exposure to unconsenting adults, as in this case, and to juveniles, although he gives no indication of how the division between protected and nonprotected materials may be drawn with greater precision for these purposes than for regulation of commercial exposure to consenting adults only. Nor does he indicate where in the Constitution he finds the authority to distinguish between a willing "adult" one month past the state law age of majority and a willing "juvenile" one month younger.

Under the holdings announced today, no one will be subject to prosecution for the sale or exposure of obscene materials unless these materials depict or describe patently offensive "hard core" sexual conduct specifically defined by the regulating state law, as written or construed. We are satisfied that these specific prerequisites will provide fair notice to a dealer in such materials that his public and commercial activities may bring prosecution. If the inability to define regulated materials with ultimate, god-like precision altogether removes the power of the States or the Congress to regulate, then "hard core" pornography may be exposed without limit to the juvenile, the passerby, and the consenting adult alike, as, indeed, Mr. Justice

Douglas contends. . . . In this belief, however, Mr. Justice Douglas now stands alone.

Mr. Justice Brennan also emphasizes "institutional stress" in justification of his change of view. Noting that "the number of obscenity cases on our docket gives ample testimony to the burden that has been placed upon this Court," he quite rightly remarks that the examination of contested materials "is hardly a source of edification to the members of this Court." He also notes, and we agree, that "uncertainty of the standards creates a continuing source of tension between state and federal courts. . . ." "The problem is . . . that one cannot say with certainty that material is obscene until at least five members of this Court, applying inevitably obscure standards, have pronounced it so."

It is certainly true that the absence . . . of a single majority view of this Court as to proper standards for testing obscenity has placed a strain on both state and federal courts. But today, for the first time since *Roth v. United States* was decided in 1957, a majority of this Court has agreed on concrete guidelines to isolate "hard core" pornography from expression protected by the First Amendment. . . .

This may not be an easy road, free from difficulty. But no amount of "fatigue" should lead us to adopt a convenient "institutional" rationale—an absolutist, "anything goes" view of the First Amendment—because it will lighten our burdens. . . .

III

. . . It is neither realistic nor constitutionally sound to read the First Amendment as requiring that the people of Maine or Mississippi accept public depiction of conduct found tolerable in Las Vegas, or New York City. People in different States vary in their tastes and attitudes, and this diversity is not to be strangled by the absolutism of imposed uniformity. As the Court made clear . . . the primary concern with requiring a jury to apply the standard of "the average person, applying contemporary community standards" is to be certain that, so far as material is not aimed at a deviant group, it will be judged by its impact on an average person, rather than a particularly susceptible or sensitive person—or indeed a totally insensitive one. We hold that the requirement that the jury evaluate the materials with reference to "contemporary standards of the State of California" serves this protective purpose and is constitutionally adequate.

IV

The dissenting Justices sound the alarm of repression. But, in our view, to equate the free and robust exchange of ideas and political debate with commercial exploitation of obscene material demeans the grand conception of the First Amendment and its high purposes in the historic struggle for freedom. . . . The First Amendment protects works which, taken as a whole, have serious literary, artistic, political, or scientific value, regardless of whether the government or a majority of the people approve of the ideas these works represent. "The protection given speech and press was fashioned to assure unfettered interchange of *ideas* for the bringing about of political and social changes desired by the people." But the public portrayal of hard-core sexual conduct for its own sake, and for the ensuing commercial gain, is a different matter.

There is no evidence, empirical or historical, that the stern 19th century American censorship of public distribution and display of material relating to sex in any way limited or affected expression of serious literary, artistic, political, or scientific ideas. On the contrary, it is beyond any question that the era following Thomas Jefferson to Theodore Roosevelt was an "extraordinarily vigorous period," not just in economics and politics, but in *belles lettres* and in "the outlying fields of social and political philosophies." We do not see the harsh hand of censorship of ideas— good or bad, sound or unsound—and "repression" of political liberty lurking in every state regulation of commercial exploitation of human interest in sex.

Mr. Justice Brennan finds "it is hard to see how state-ordered regimentation of our minds can ever be forestalled." These doleful anticipations assume that courts cannot distinguish commerce in ideas, protected by the First Amendment, from commercial exploitation of obscene material. Moreover, state regulation of hard-core pornography so as to make it unavailable to nonadults, a regulation which Mr. Justice Brennan finds constitutionally permissible, has all the elements of "censorship" for adults; indeed even more rigid enforcement techniques may be called for with such dichotomy of regulation. One can concede that the "sexual revolution" of recent years may have had useful byproducts in striking layers of prudery from a subject long irrationally kept from needed ventilation. But it does not follow that no regulation of patently offensive "hard core" materials is needed or permissible; civilized people do not allow unregulated access to heroin because it is a derivative of medicinal morphine.

In sum, we (a) reaffirm the *Roth* holding that obscene material is not protected by the First Amendment; (b) hold that such material can be regulated by the States, subject to the specific safeguards enunciated above, without a showing that the material is "utterly without redeeming social value"; and (c) hold that obscenity is to be determined by applying "contemporary community standards," not "national standards." The judgment of the Appellate Department of the Superior Court, Orange County, California, is vacated and the case remanded to that court for further proceedings not inconsistent with the First Amendment standards established by this opinion.

Vacated and remanded.

JUSTICE WILLIAM DOUGLAS, dissenting:

I

Today we leave open the way for California to send a man to prison for distributing brochures that advertise books and a movie under freshly written standards defining obscenity which until today's decision were never the part of any law.

The Court has worked hard to define obscenity and concededly has failed. . . .

Today the Court retreats from the earlier formulations of the constitutional test and undertakes to make new definitions. This effort, like the earlier ones, is earnest and well intentioned. The difficulty is that we do not deal with constitutional terms, since "obscenity" is not mentioned in the Constitution or Bill of Rights. And the First Amendment makes no such exception from "the press" which it undertakes to protect nor, as I have said on other occasions, is an exception necessarily implied, for there was no recognized exception to the free press at the time the

Bill of Rights was adopted which treated "obscene" publications differently from other types of papers, magazines, and books. So there are no constitutional guidelines for deciding what is and what is not "obscene." The Court is at large because we deal with tastes and standards of literature. What shocks me may be sustenance for my neighbor. What causes one person to boil up in rage over one pamphlet or movie may reflect only his neurosis, not shared by others. We deal here with a regime of censorship which, if adopted, should be done by constitutional amendment after full debate by the people.

Obscenity cases usually generate tremendous emotional outbursts. They have no business being in the courts. . . .

The idea that the First Amendment permits government to ban publications that are "offensive" to some people puts an ominous gloss on freedom of the press. That test would make it possible to ban any paper or any journal or magazine in some benighted place. The First Amendment was designed "to invite dispute," to induce "a condition of unrest," to "create dissatisfaction with conditions as they are," and even to stir "people to anger." The idea that the First Amendment permits punishment for ideas that are "offensive" to the particular judge or jury sitting in judgment is astounding. No greater leveler of speech or literature has ever been designed. To give the power to the censor, as we do today, is to make a sharp and radical break with the traditions of a free society. The First Amendment was not fashioned as a vehicle for dispensing tranquilizers to the people. Its prime function was to keep debate open to "offensive" as well as to "staid" people. The tendency throughout history has been to subdue the individual and to exalt the power of government. The use of the standard "offensive" gives authority to government that cuts the very vitals out of the First Amendment. As is intimated by the Court's opinion, the materials before us may be garbage. But so is much of what is said in political campaigns, in the daily press, on TV, or over the radio. By reason of the First Amendment—and solely because of it—speakers and publishers have not been threatened or subdued because their thoughts and ideas may be "offensive" to some. . . .

Fox Television Stations, Inc. v. Federal Communications Commission
613 F.3d 317 (2d Cir. 2010)

Circuit Judge Rosemary S. Pooler delivered the court's opinion:

. . . [W]e must now decide whether the FCC's indecency policy provides a discernible standard by which broadcasters can accurately predict what speech is prohibited. The FCC set forth its indecency policy in its 2001 Industry Guidance, in which the FCC explained that an indecency finding involved the following two determinations: (1) whether the material "describe[s] or depict[s] sexual or excretory organs or activities"; and (2) whether the broadcast is "patently offensive as measured by contemporary community standards for the broadcast medium." Under the policy, whether a broadcast is patently offensive depends on the following three factors: (1) "the explicitness or graphic nature of the description or depiction"; (2) "whether the material dwells on or repeats at length" the description or depiction; and (3) "whether the material appears to pander or is used to titillate, or whether the materials appears to have been presented for its shock value." Since 2001, the FCC has interpreted its indecency policy in a number of decisions, including Golden Globes Order and the orders on review here.

The FCC argues that the indecency policy in its Industry Guidance, together with its subsequent decisions, give the broadcasters sufficient notice as to what will be considered indecent. The Networks argue that the policy is impermissibly vague and that the FCC's decisions interpreting the policy only add to the confusion of what will be considered indecent.

We agree with the Networks that the indecency policy is impermissibly vague. The first problem arises in the FCC's determination as to which words or expressions are patently offensive. For instance, while the FCC concluded that "bullshit" in a "NYPD Blue" episode was patently offensive, it concluded that "dick" and "dickhead" were not. Other expletives such as "pissed off," up yours," "kiss my ass," and "wiping his ass" were also not found to be patently offensive. The Commission argues that its three-factor "patently offensive" test gives broadcasters fair notice of what it will find indecent. However, in each of these

cases, the Commission's reasoning consisted of repetition of one or more of the factors without any discussion of how it applied them. Thus, the word "bullshit" is indecent because it is "vulgar, graphic and explicit" while the word "dickhead" was not indecent because it was "not sufficiently vulgar, explicit, or graphic." This hardly gives broadcasters notice of how the Commission will apply the factors in the future.

The English language is rife with creative ways of depicting sexual or excretory organs or activities, and even if the FCC were able to provide a complete list of all such expressions, new offensive and indecent words are invented every day. For many years after *Pacifica,* the FCC decided to focus its enforcement efforts solely on the seven "dirty" words in the Carlin monologue. This strategy had its limitations—it meant that some indecent speech that did not employ these seven words slipped through the cracks. However, it had the advantage of providing broadcasters with a clear list of words that were prohibited. Not surprisingly, in the nine years between *Pacifica* and the FCC's abandonment of this policy, not a single enforcement action was brought. This could be because we lived in a simpler time before such foul language was common. Or, it could be that the FCC's policy was sufficiently clear that broadcasters knew what was prohibited.

The FCC argues that a flexible standard is necessary precisely because the list was not effective—broadcasters simply found offensive ways of depicting sexual or excretory organs or activities without using any of the seven words. In other words, because the FCC cannot anticipate how broadcasters will attempt to circumvent the prohibition on indecent speech, the FCC needs the maximum amount of flexibility to be able to decide what is indecent. The observation that people will always find a way to subvert censorship laws may expose a certain futility in the FCC's crusade against indecent speech, but it does not provide a justification for implementing a vague, indiscernible standard. If the FCC cannot anticipate what will be considered indecent under its policy, then it can hardly expect broadcasters to do so. And while the

FCC characterizes all broadcasters as consciously trying to push the envelope on what is permitted, much like a petulant teenager angling for a later curfew, the Networks have expressed a good faith desire to comply with the FCC's indecency regime. They simply want to know with some degree of certainty what the policy is so that they can comply with it. The First Amendment requires nothing less.

. . .

The FCC's current indecency policy undoubtedly gives the FCC more flexibility, but this flexibility comes at a price. The "artistic necessity" and "bona fide news" exceptions allow the FCC to decide, in each case, whether the First Amendment is implicated. The policy may maximize the amount of speech that the FCC can prohibit, but it results in a standard that even the FCC cannot articulate or apply consistently. Thus, it found the use of the word "bullshitter" on CBS's The Early Show to be "shocking and gratuitous" because it occurred "during a morning television interview," before reversing itself because the broadcast was a "bona fide news interview." In other words, the FCC reached diametrically opposite conclusions at different stages of the proceedings for precisely the same reason—that the word "bullshitter" was uttered during a news program. And when Judge Leval asked during oral argument if a program about the dangers of pre-marital sex designed for teenagers would be permitted, the most that the FCC's lawyer could say was "I suspect it would." With millions of dollars and core First Amendment values at stake, "I suspect" is simply not good enough.

With the FCC's indiscernible standards come the risk that such standards will be enforced in a discriminatory manner. The vagueness doctrine is intended, in part, to avoid that risk. If government officials are permitted to make decisions on an "ad hoc" basis, there is a risk that those decisions will reflect the officials' subjective biases. . . .

We have no reason to suspect that the FCC is using its indecency policy as a means of suppressing particular points of view. But even the risk of such subjective, content-based decision-making raises grave concerns under the First Amendment. Take, for example, the disparate treatment of "Saving Private Ryan" and the documentary, "The Blues." The FCC decided that

the words "fuck" and "shit" were integral to the "realism and immediacy of the film experience for viewers" in "Saving Private Ryan," but not in "The Blues." We query how fleeting expletives could be more essential to the "realism" of a fictional movie than to the "realism" of interviews with real people about real life events, and it is hard not to speculate that the FCC was simply more comfortable with the themes in "Saving Private Ryan," a mainstream movie with a familiar cultural milieu, than it was with "The Blues," which largely profiled an outsider genre of musical experience. But even if there were a perfectly benign way of explaining these particular outcomes, nothing would prevent the FCC from applying its indecency policy in a discriminatory manner in the future. . . .

The FCC argues that its context-based approach is consistent with, indeed even required by, *Pacifica* [Foundation]. While *Pacifica* emphasized the importance of context in regulating indecent broadcasts, it did so in order to emphasize the limited scope of its holding, finding that the particular "context" of the Carlin monologue justified an intrusion on broadcasters [sic] rights under the First Amendment. It does not follow that the FCC can justify any decision to sanction indecent speech by citing "context." Of course, context is always relevant, and we do not mean to suggest otherwise in this opinion. But the FCC still must have discernible standards by which individual contexts are judged.

The FCC assures us that it will "bend over backwards" to protect editorial judgment, at least in the news context, but such assurances are not sufficient given the record before us. Instead, the FCC should bend over backwards to create a standard that gives broadcasters the notice that is required by the First Amendment.

Under the current policy, broadcasters must choose between not airing or censoring controversial programs and risking massive fines or possibly even loss of their licenses, and it is not surprising which option they choose. Indeed, there is ample evidence in the record that the FCC's indecency policy has chilled protected speech.

For instance, several CBS affiliates declined to air the Peabody Award-winning "9/11" documentary, which contains real audio footage—including occasional expletives—of firefighters in the World Trade

Center on September 11th. Although the documentary had previously aired twice without complaint, following the [Bono, Cher and Nicole Richie decisions] affiliates could no longer be sure whether the expletives contained in the documentary could be found indecent. . . .

The FCC's application of its policy to live broadcasts creates an even more profound chilling effect. In the case of the 2003 Billboard Music Awards broadcasts, Fox had an audio delay system in place to bleep fleeting expletives. It also pre-cleared the scripts of the presenters. Richie, however, departed from her script and used three expletives in rapid sequence. While the person employed to monitor and bleep expletives was bleeping the first, the following two slipped through. Even elaborate precautions will not protect a broadcaster against such occurrences. The FCC argues that Fox should simply implement a more effective screening system, but, short of giving up live broadcasting altogether, no system will ever be one hundred percent effective. Instead, Fox may decide not to ask individuals with a history of using profanity to present at its awards shows.* But, of course, this will not prevent someone who wins an award—such as Cher or Bono—from using fleeting expletives. In fact, the only way that Fox can be sure that it won't be sanctioned by the FCC is by refusing to air the broadcast live.

This chilling effect extends to news and public affairs programming as well. Broadcasters may well decide not to invite controversial guests on to their programs for fear that an unexpected fleeting expletive will result in fines. The FCC points to its "bona fide news" exception to show that such fears would be unfounded. But the FCC has made clear that it considers the decision to apply this exception a matter within its discretion. Otherwise, why not simply make an outright news exception? . . . For instance, Phoenix TV stations dropped live coverage of a memorial service for Pat Tillman, the former football star killed in Afghanistan, because of language used by Tillman's family members to express their grief. . . . If the FCC's policy is allowed to remain in place, there will undoubtedly be countless other situations where broadcasters will exercise their editorial judgment and decline to pursue contentious people or subjects, or will eschew live programming altogether, in order to avoid the FCC's fines. This chill reaches speech at the heart of the First Amendment.

The chill of protected speech has even extended to programs that contain no expletives, but which contain reference to or discussion of sex, sexual organs, or excretion. For instance, Fox decided not to re-broadcast an episode of "That 70s Show" that dealt with masturbation, even though it neither depicted the act or discussed it in specific terms. The episode subsequently won an award from the Kaiser Family Foundation for its honest and accurate depiction of a sexual health issue. Similarly, an episode of "House" was re-written after concerns that one of the character's struggles with psychiatric issues related to his sexuality would be considered indecent by the FCC.

As these examples illustrate, the absence of reliable guidance in the FCC's standards chills a vast amount of protected speech dealing with some of the most important and universal themes in art and literature. Sex and the magnetic power of sexual attraction are surely among the most predominant themes in the study of humanity since the Trojan War. The digestive system and excretion are also important areas of human attention. By prohibiting all "patently offensive" references to sex, sexual organs, and excretion without giving adequate guidance as to what "patently offensive" means, the FCC effectively chills speech, because broadcasters have no way of knowing what the FCC will find offensive. To place any discussion of these vast topics at the broadcaster's peril has the effect of promoting wide self-censorship of valuable material which should be completely protected under the First Amendment.

For the foregoing reasons, we strike down the FCC's indecency policy. We do not suggest that the FCC could not create a constitutional policy. We hold only that the FCC's current policy fails constitutional scrutiny. . . .

---

* Indeed, there is evidence in the record that broadcasters have made personnel decisions on the basis of the FCC's indecency policy. For instance, public radio personality Sandra Loh was fired after a single use of an expletive as "a precautionary measure to show the station had distanced itself . . . in case the FCC investigates."

Chapter 13

If "piracy" means using the creative property of others without their permission . . . then the history of the content industry is a history of piracy. Every important sector of "big media" today—film, records, radio, and cable TV—was born of a kind of piracy. . . . There is piracy of copyrighted material. Lots of it. This piracy comes in many forms. The most significant is commercial piracy, the unauthorized taking of other people's content within a commercial context. Despite the many justifications that are offered in its defense, this taking is wrong. No one should condone it, and the law should stop it.

Lawrence Lessig, Harvard Law School professor[1]

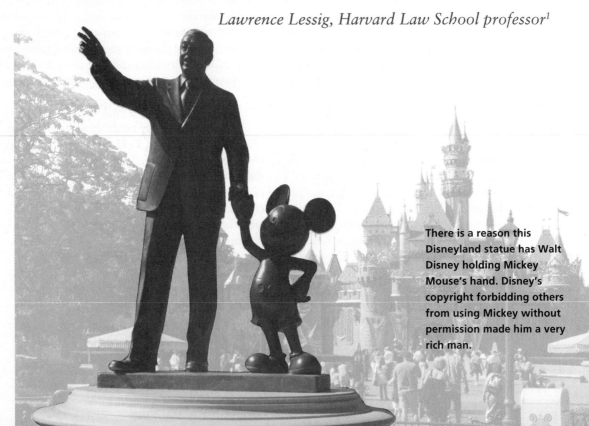

There is a reason this Disneyland statue has Walt Disney holding Mickey Mouse's hand. Disney's copyright forbidding others from using Mickey without permission made him a very rich man.

Intellectual Property

Protecting and Using Intangible Creations

Copyright

The Development of U.S. Copyright Law
The 1976 Copyright Act
Proving Copyright Infringement
Remedies for Copyright Infringement
Copyright Infringement Defense: Fair Use
Copyright, Computers and the Internet
Music Licensing
Music, the Internet and File Sharing

Trademarks

Distinctiveness Requirement
Registering a Trademark
Domain Names
Trademark Infringement
Trademark Infringement Defenses

Cases for Study

➤ *Eldred v. Ashcroft*
➤ *Metro-Goldwyn-Mayer Studios, Inc. v. Grokster, Ltd.*

Suppose . . .

. . . that a company creates a cartoon character—an anthropomorphic mouse. The company produces movie cartoons, comic books and other materials featuring the mouse. The company also allows other firms to make clothing, toys and additional merchandise using the mouse character. The mouse makes the company millions of dollars. But copyright protection on the first movie cartoon featuring the mouse is about to expire. Should courts uphold a law extending the period of copyright protection by 20 additional years so the mouse cartoons, as well as millions of other copyrighted works, will retain their copyright protection? If the law is upheld, society will not be able to freely use these copyrighted works for two more decades. Look for the answers to this question when the case of *Eldred v. Ashcroft* is discussed later in this chapter and the case is excerpted at the end of the chapter.

The law protects people's personal property. Stealing someone's car is illegal. Robbing a bank, burglarizing a house or shoplifting a book from a store is illegal. If a person writes a magazine article, it is against the law to take the manuscript without permission. Although the paper may be worth a few dollars, that is not the real concern. The law also protects what is written on the paper—the author's expression of his or her ideas. No one but the author may publish that article unless the writer consents. Nor may the article be made into a movie or used in any other way without the author's permission. The article is not personal property the way a car is. The law calls the article "intangible property." Nonetheless, copyright law gives the article legal protection.

intellectual property law The legal category including copyright, trademark and patent law.

Similarly, trademark law protects creations such as advertising slogans, movie and book titles and cartoon characters. Patent law protects inventions. Patent, trademark and copyright statutes all are categorized as **intellectual property law.** Generally, intellectual property laws—particularly patent and copyright statutes—are intended to encourage creativity. Ensuring that people will benefit financially from their creations encourages them to continue being creative. If people could use others' intellectual creations without permission, there would be no financial incentive to write, paint or invent.

Beginning in the Middle Ages, patent law prevented skilled workers—such as goldsmiths—from using other craftsmen's creations. Congress adopted the United States' current patent law in 1952, giving protection to useful, novel, "nonobvious" processes and inventions.[2] Trademarks also began in the Middle Ages—although it has been suggested that potters 3,500 years ago marked their wares—when members of a guild, an organization of artisans, used unique marks to distinguish their goods from those of other guilds. The Lanham Act, discussed in Chapter 14, is the current U.S. trademark law, intended to prevent consumer confusion about what company supplies particular goods.[3]

Copyright

copyright An exclusive legal right used to protect intellectual creations from unauthorized use.

A **copyright** is an exclusive legal right protecting intellectual creations from unauthorized use. Copyright law attempts a balancing act. The law balances the creator's right to restrict the use of his or her work against society's belief that some uses should be allowed without the creator's permission. However, achieving the balance has been a difficult task from the time the United States adopted its first copyright law in 1790.

Points of Law

The U.S. Constitution: Copyrights and Patents

The Congress shall have Power . . . To promote the Progress of Science and useful Arts, by securing for limited Times to Authors and Inventors the exclusive Right to their respective Writings and Discoveries.[1]

1. U.S. Const., art. 1, § 8, cls. 1, 8.

Copyright law encourages people to create new works by allowing them to profit from their efforts. The profits—and copyright infringement damages—may be considerable. A federal district court jury in 2010 ordered SAP, a German company, to pay Oracle, a computer software and hardware company, $1.3 billion for illegally downloading Oracle's copyrighted software and accompanying documents.[4] Copyright law also provides society with new creations—novels, paintings, motion pictures, newspapers, music—by stimulating innovation.

U.S. copyright law protects "original works of authorship."[5] Creators of novels, plays, motion pictures, musical compositions, statues and many other works own the rights to use their creations. The copyright holder has complete control over a work. Effectively, the federal copyright law creates a monopoly allowing the work's creator—the copyright holder—to say who can use the work, for what purpose and for how long. The U.S. Constitution grants creators control over their works for only a "limited time."[6] Once the limit was 28 years. Today copyright for many works lasts for the creator's life plus 70 more years. Should there be limits to this control? When should the copyright control over the work end? Should the creator and his or her heirs collect the rewards forever?[7]

Protecting creators' works meant little before development of the printing press. Reproducing manuscripts by hand was tedious. No one could steal someone else's work and transcribe enough copies to make the theft worthwhile. But the situation changed when the printing press arrived in England in the 15th century. Many copies could be printed cheaply on a press. In England, the monarchy settled the issue of who should profit: Printers would control publication, and the Crown would control printers. Authors might be paid for a manuscript, but then they dropped out of the picture.[8] Beginning in the late 1400s, the printers who owned presses were England's publishers. Thus, the freedom of the press belonged to him who owned one.

Copyright's initial purpose was not to reward creators but to prevent sedition—criticizing the king or queen. The Crown gave a group of printers, called the Stationers' Company, control over printing in mid-16th-century England. Printers had to obtain a Stationers' Company license to publish a pamphlet, a book or any other work. The license included giving the printer a right to publish the work in perpetuity. The ban on anyone else publishing the work lasted forever. The monarchy retained ultimate control over what could be published, but the Stationers' Company did the Crown's dirty work, including destroying publications the Stationers' Company had not condoned.

The license requirement ended in 1694, but the Stationers' Company did not disappear. Rather, it shifted its focus from printers to authors. The first

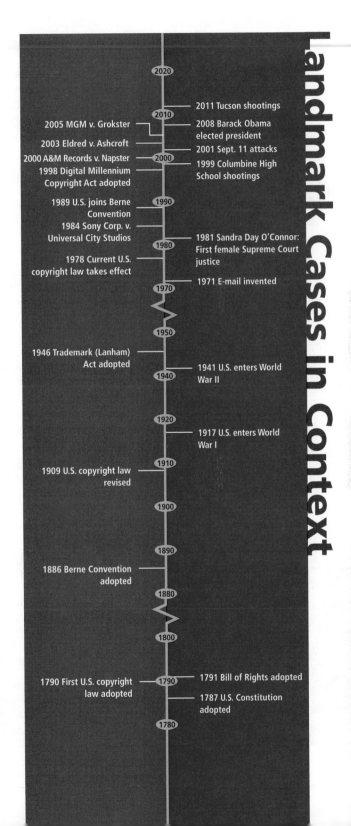

Landmark Cases in Context

- 2020
- 2011 Tucson shootings
- 2010
- 2005 MGM v. Grokster
- 2008 Barack Obama elected president
- 2003 Eldred v. Ashcroft
- 2001 Sept. 11 attacks
- 2000 A&M Records v. Napster — 2000
- 1999 Columbine High School shootings
- 1998 Digital Millennium Copyright Act adopted
- 1989 U.S. joins Berne Convention — 1990
- 1984 Sony Corp. v. Universal City Studios
- 1980
- 1981 Sandra Day O'Connor: First female Supreme Court justice
- 1978 Current U.S. copyright law takes effect
- 1970
- 1971 E-mail invented
- 1950
- 1946 Trademark (Lanham) Act adopted
- 1941 U.S. enters World War II
- 1940
- 1920
- 1917 U.S. enters World War I
- 1910
- 1909 U.S. copyright law revised
- 1900
- 1890
- 1886 Berne Convention adopted
- 1880
- 1800
- 1790 First U.S. copyright law adopted — 1790
- 1791 Bill of Rights adopted
- 1787 U.S. Constitution adopted
- 1780

Statute of Anne The first copyright law, adopted in England in 1710.

copyright law in 1710, called the **Statute of Anne**, protected authors' works[9] and granted authors copyright protection if they registered their works with the government. When the copyright period ended—after 14 years, or 28 years if the author renewed the copyright—the work went into the public domain, and anyone could use it without permission. Under the Statute of Anne, authors controlled their creations but often sold their rights to printers as a way of turning their works into ready cash.

The Development of U.S. Copyright Law

The United States followed England's lead, granting copyrights to encourage authors to create new works. The U.S. Constitution allows Congress to adopt copyright and patent laws.[10] Before the Constitution was ratified, 12 of the 13 states had passed their own copyright laws. The first Congress in 1790 adopted a law giving books, maps and charts a 14-year copyright.[11] The U.S. Supreme Court later ruled that the federal law took the place of state statutes and any common law copyright claims.[12] This decision also applies to later copyright acts, including the current one; the federal law is the country's only copyright statute.

During the 19th century, Congress amended the copyright law to protect musical compositions, photographs and paintings.[13] Congress also amended the law in 1831 and adopted a comprehensive revision in 1870.[14] The 1870 act established the Library of Congress, giving it the power to register copyrights and requiring the deposit with the library of two copies of a copyrighted work.

Berne Convention The primary international copyright treaty that many countries adopted in 1886 but that the United States adopted only in 1988.

In 1866, the Berne Convention for Protection of Literary and Artistic Works was signed by several countries in a step toward protecting works across international borders. However, the United States did not join the Berne treaty. The country was unconcerned with protecting its citizens' works overseas and did not want to protect foreign creators' works in the United States. The **Berne Convention**, though, spurred a movement for change in U.S. copyright law. This led to a major

realWorld Law

Copyright: United States Ignored the World

According to copyright lawyer David Nimmer, before the United States joined the Berne Convention in 1988, the country had "been a copyright island. . . . As long as it served American interests, U.S. copyright law did not concern itself with the waves that our statutes or rulings would set in motion outside our borders, and few ripples from abroad affected U.S. copyrights."[1]

---

1. David Nimmer, *Nation, Duration, Violation, Harmonization: An International Proposal for the United States Copyright*, 55 Law & Contemp. Probs. 211, 211 (1992).

revision of the copyright act in 1909.[15] Among other changes, the law extended copyright protection to 28 years, with a renewal period of another 28 years.

As the 20th century progressed, entertainment, news, computer and other industries pressured Congress to change the copyright law to accommodate the many technological developments that had occurred since 1909. In response, Congress adopted the Copyright Revision Act of 1976, which took effect Jan. 1, 1978. In 1988, Congress amended the 1976 act in ways that permitted the United States to join the Berne Convention, effective in 1989—more than 100 years after the treaty's initial adoption.[16]

SUMMARY

Intellectual property law includes copyrights, trademarks and patents. The United States brought copyright law from England, included in the Constitution a congressional right to adopt copyright laws and passed its first copyright statute in 1790. Congress comprehensively revised the copyright law in 1870, 1909 and 1976. The United States joined the major international copyright agreement, the Berne Convention, in 1989, 103 years after the treaty took effect. ■

The 1976 Copyright Act

After two decades of debate, lobbying, committee reports and compromise, Congress adopted the current copyright law. The act—amended several times since adoption—is the United States' copyright law. It specifies what may be protected by copyright, what rights that protection includes, any restrictions on those rights and the formalities necessary to exercise the rights.

The 1976 act was outdated almost immediately. It did not foresee the personal computer, the Internet, MP3 players, satellite-delivered television and radio signals, wireless transmissions and other new technologies. Technology moves too quickly for the law ever to fully protect media content.

Copyright law also does not completely account for another change. The statute protects creators, such as authors, composers and artists. But creators usually sell their creations—and accompanying copyrights—to corporations. For example, a writer grants the copyright of his or her novel to a publisher in return for a share of the book's sales revenue. And when people working for corporations create material as part of their employment, the corporation owns the copyright. Copyright has become an important part of the U.S. economy, and news and entertainment corporations have come to rely on it to protect their products.[17] In fact, copyright's original purpose of inspiring individuals to create may have become less important than its role in the national and international marketplace. The length of time a copyright lasts is the only important legal difference between an individual and a corporation holding a copyright.

The Works Copyright Protects The 1976 law gives copyright protection to a wide variety of works. Realizing that it could not list all possible works eligible for copyright, however, Congress provided two broad criteria, offered some examples and left it to the courts to provide more clarity. The 1976 law says that copyright protection applies to "original works of authorship" that are "fixed in any tangible medium of expression."[18] By authorship, the law does not mean only written works. Rather, Congress used the word authorship to include artists, composers, journalists, sculptors and many other creators.

A work must be substantially original to be protected.[19] Copyright law does not define "original." As one court said, "originality" simply means "a work independently created by its author, one not copied from pre-existing works, and a work that comes from the exercise of the creative powers of the author's mind."[20] A person changing four words in Shakespeare's "Macbeth" or six notes in Beethoven's "Fifth Symphony" could not successfully claim a copyright for the works. The changed play or symphony would not be substantially original. A work does not have to be of high or even average quality to qualify for copyright protection. It just must be a work no one else has created before.

A collection of previously created works can be protected if there is substantial originality in the choice or arrangement of the works.[21] The copyright law refers to this as a "compilation," such as a book consisting of selected magazine articles.[22] The statute grants a copyright to the creation of the compilation, but each work included in the collection retains its own copyright protection. However, a list of names, addresses and telephone numbers is not sufficiently original to have copyright protection. There must be originality or novelty in compiling or organizing facts.[23]

In addition to being original, a work must be fixed in a tangible medium. That is, a work must be capable of being felt or seen—words or pictures on paper, images on videotape, a quilt made of cloth, a statue made of marble, words and music on a CD. A baseball game shown on broadcast television is not fixed in a tangible medium until the broadcast is, for example, videotaped.

What works that are original and fixed in a tangible medium may be copyrighted? The 1976 copyright act lists eight categories of works eligible for protection: (1) literary works, (2) musical works, including any accompanying words, (3) dramatic works, including any accompanying music, (4) pantomimes and choreographic works, (5) pictorial, graphic and sculptural works, (6) motion pictures and other

Points of Law

An Original Creation

Writing for a unanimous U.S. Supreme Court, former Justice Sandra Day O'Connor said:

> Originality, as the term is used in copyright, means only that the work was independently created by the author (as opposed to copied from other works), and that it possesses at least some minimal degree of creativity. To be sure, the requisite level of creativity is extremely low; even a slight amount will suffice. The vast majority of works make the grade quite easily, as they possess some creative spark, "no matter how crude, humble or obvious" it might be. Originality does not signify novelty; a work may be original even though it closely resembles other works so long as the similarity is fortuitous, not the result of copying.[1]

1. *Feist Publications, Inc. v. Rural Telephone Service Co., Inc.*, 499 U.S. 340, 345 (1991).

audiovisual works, (7) sound recordings, and (8) architectural works.[24] But these categories are more illustrative than definitive. For example, software can be copyrighted, even though it is not listed among the eight categories. Designs, patterns and shapes also can have copyright protection.

The 1976 statute protects all works eligible for copyright, both published and unpublished creations.[25] Before the 1976 statute was adopted, unpublished works were protected by state common law, not the federal statute. Common law protection for unpublished works lasted forever—an unpublished work never lost its common law copyright protection.[26] Once a work was published, it came under the 1909 law, giving it protection for 28 years with renewal possible for another 28 years. The new law changed this scheme, giving unpublished creations the same protection as published works.

A work that is not original or is not fixed in a tangible medium cannot

A book's ideas about why the dirigible Hindenburg exploded in midair became the basis of the 1975 movie, "The Hindenburg," but the book's author lost a copyright infringement suit against the film's producer because history and ideas cannot be copyrighted.

be copyrighted. Neither can ideas, history or facts be copyrighted.[27] A news story reporting an automobile accident can receive copyright protection. But the underlying facts—the accident itself—cannot be copyrighted. A reporter's description of the accident is original and is fixed in a tangible medium when typed into a computer. However, the reporter may not successfully claim he or she was first on the scene and therefore no other journalist can write about the accident. Nor may a scholar write a book about a historical incident—even one that has not been described previously—and prevent anyone else from writing about the incident. An author proposed that a German crew member sabotaged the dirigible Hindenburg, causing it to explode and kill 36 people while attempting to dock in Lakehurst, N.J., in 1937.[28] Copyright protected the author's book describing his idea. But neither the facts nor the author's interpretation of the facts can be copyrighted. The author could not prevent a Hollywood studio from making a motion picture based on his idea about why the dirigible exploded.

Although copyright law does not protect news facts, one mass medium cannot persistently take information from another outlet and present the news as its own. This is called "misappropriation" or "unfair competition." Unfair competition is not a copyright infringement. Instead, it is actionable under the common law of individual states.

Nearly 90 years ago, the Supreme Court found unfair competition when one news service used information gathered by another service.[29] During World War I, British censors would not allow International News Service (INS) journalists to send war reports to the United States. Reporters for the Associated Press (AP), a competing service, were able to get their stories into the country. The INS bought copies of newspapers served by the AP, rewrote the war stories and sent them to INS papers. The AP had not copyrighted its stories, as necessary for protection under the 1909 law. But the AP sued the INS on the common law basis of unfair competition. The Court agreed with the AP. The INS profited from taking material the AP had developed through its own skill and money, the Court said. Unfair competition also could apply if a radio station consistently rewrites stories from a local newspaper and presents the stories as the station's own reporting.

The INS decision became known as the "hot news" doctrine. Today, courts find misappropriation of news when (1) a news organization spends money to gather news, (2) the information is time sensitive, (3) another person or company competing with the news organization uses that information without permission or payment, and (4) the news organization's ability to gather news is threatened by others' using the information.[30] The issue particularly arises when a website can instantaneously copy information posted on a different site.[31]

The law does not give copyright protection to words and phrases, including advertising slogans and titles of books, movies and television programs. These lack sufficient originality to qualify for copyright protection. However, a trademark can protect these creations. Also, works created by the U.S. government are not eligible for copyright protection.[32] For example, a report issued by the U.S. Department of Justice is not protected by copyright and may be used by anyone without obtaining the Department of Justice's permission.

plagiarism Using another's work or ideas without attribution.

Using someone's work without identifying the source may be plagiarism rather than a copyright violation. Plagiarism and copyright infringement have similarities and differences. **Plagiarism** commonly means using others' ideas without attribution. But when someone's work is sufficiently similar to another's creation—copying a novel's plot, using similar fictional characters or replicating another's interpretation of historical facts, for example—plagiarism becomes a copyright law violation.

Although plagiarism may not rise to the level of a copyright violation, it can have serious consequences. For example, prominent newspaper columnists and reporters, such as the Boston Globe's Mike Barnicle, have resigned or been fired after plagiarism accusations.[33] After being accused of plagiarism, a New York Times business reporter resigned in 2010, as did a reporter for the online website, The Daily Beast.[34] New York Times reporter Jayson Blair resigned in 2003 after being charged with plagiarism.[35] Best-selling authors and law school professors have been accused of plagiarism.[36] In 2009 the author of the popular book series "Conversations with God," Neale Donald Walsch, admitted that one of his website postings was very similar to another author's essay.[37] Plagiarism also violates university academic honesty policies.

AN ORIGINAL WORK FIXED IN A TANGIBLE medium may have copyright protection. This includes literary, musical, dramatic, motion picture and many other works. Ideas, history and facts may not be copyrighted. Short phrases, titles and advertising slogans may not be copyrighted. Using information from news reports without permission may be unfair competition. ■

When Copyright Takes Effect An original work automatically is copyrighted from the moment it is created and fixed in a tangible medium. The law gives immediate protection to a news story typed into a computer, a journalist's notes written on a pad of paper, a television reporter's story put on videotape and a filmed Hollywood movie. To obtain copyright protection, the creator needs no more than to fix an original work in a tangible medium. The copyright must be registered, however, before the creator may sue for copyright infringement under the federal law. Registration is discussed later in this chapter.

Copyright Ownership A work's creator owns the work's copyright—with some exceptions.[38] For example, if two people create a work, the copyright is jointly owned. That is, both creators have all the protection a copyright gives and each owns half the work. Joint ownership works the same with three or more creators.

realWorld Law

Happy Money . . . er, Birthday

Did friends and family sing "Happy Birthday to You" at your last birthday party? Did they pay royalties to Time Warner? Two Kentucky kindergarten teachers, Mildred and Patty Hill, published the melody for "Happy Birthday" in 1893 and, after legal disputes were settled, copyrighted the music and words in 1935—more than 40 years after composing the song. A division of Time Warner purchased the copyright in 1989 for an estimated $25 million. The company earns $2 million annually in royalties from "Happy Birthday." Because the song is copyrighted, restaurant servers celebrating customers' birthdays often sing something other than "Happy Birthday"—otherwise the restaurant would have to pay royalties to Time Warner. The 2004 documentary film, "The Corporation," includes a minute of silence rather than using "Happy Birthday" during a party scene. Otherwise the film producers would have had to pay thousands of dollars in royalties. "Happy Birthday to You" will not enter the public domain until at least the year 2030.[1]

1. See Eldred v. Ashcroft, 537 U.S. 186, 262 (2003) (Breyer, J., dissenting); Bonneville International Corp. v. Peters, 347 F.3d 485, 487 n.1 (3d Cir. 2003); Thomas Plotkin & Tarae Howell, *"Fair Is Foul and Foul Is Fair": Have Insurers Loosened the Chokepoint of Copyright and Permitted Fair Use's Breathing Space in Documentary Films?*, 15 Conn. Ins. L.J. 407, 416–17 (2009).

work made for hire Work created when working for another person or company. The copyright in a work made for hire belongs to the employer, not the creator.

However, when a person creates a work as part of her or his employment, the law gives the copyright to the employer.[39] If a journalist employed full-time by a television station reports a story on the evening news, the story's copyright belongs to the station, not to the reporter. The copyright law calls such a creation a "work made for hire."[40]

A work made for hire occurs in only two circumstances. First, an employee preparing a work as part of his or her regular employment will not own the copyright.[41] Instead, the employer will own the copyright. Second, and less commonly, a work may be for hire if the creator and employer agree to that in writing and if the work is specially ordered or commissioned for use in, for example, a compilation, a motion picture, a textbook or any of several other categories the law specifies.[42]

In one case, the U.S. Supreme Court listed a number of factors for courts to consider in determining whether a person acted as an employee so that the works were made for hire.[43] The case involved a nonprofit organization that asked an artist to create a sculpture. When the artist completed the work, both he and the organization claimed to own the copyright. In *Community for Creative Non-Violence v. Reid,* the Court said the organization would own the copyright only if the sculptor was the organization's employee. Finding in favor of the artist, the Court said several criteria help to determine a person's status as an employee or, instead, an independent contractor: (1) the organization's right to control how the work is accomplished, (2) who owns the equipment used to create the work, (3) where the work took place—at the organization's offices or the artist's studio, (4) who determined the days and hours the artist worked, (5) whether there was a long-term relationship between the two parties, (6) who hired any assistants the artist used and several other factors. The more the company or organization controls the factors, the more the balance tips toward the creator being an employee and the work being made for hire. When the criteria more generally favor the creator, the more likely he or she will be an independent contractor and own the work's copyright.

Under most circumstances, freelance journalists own the copyrights to their work. However, the Court's factors likely mean that a student interning at a television station or other media outlet creates works made for hire when she or he completes assignments from supervisors at the station, newspaper, advertising agency or other organization.

The copyright law allows copyright ownership to be changed by contract. A magazine may agree to purchase a story written by a freelance journalist only if the journalist agrees to transfer the copyright to the magazine. But if a famous newspaper columnist wants to own the copyrights to his or her columns, the newspaper and columnist may sign a contract to that effect. In the absence of a contract, the newspaper would own the copyrights because the columns would be works made for hire.

When a magazine or newspaper reproduces issues in, for example, CD-ROM form, the articles and pictures remain in context. A picture will be seen surrounded by the same pictures or words as in the original publication. The copyright law calls newspapers and magazines "collective works."[44] If a publication has permission to print an article or picture, the law allows it to use the work in any revision of the "collective work." Reproduction in CD-ROM form or in a coffee table book, for instance, is a revision under the copyright law. A photographer could not successfully claim copyright infringement when his pictures were included in a CD-ROM set containing each National Geographic magazine from 1888 through 1996, a federal appellate court said. "The Complete National Geographic" contained issues as they originally were published. The pictures, then, remained in context.[45]

However, contracts transferring copyrights in freelancer material to a newspaper or magazine did not explicitly transfer control to media organizations when they put their contents online. The media assumed the contracts implicitly allowed online publication under their copyright control of the collection as a whole. The media said they merely were using their copyright in the collection—each complete newspaper containing individual stories—to put the material online. But the U.S. Supreme Court disagreed.[46] In *New York Times Co., Inc. v. Tasini,* the Court said the online publication reproduced and distributed each individual article, not the newspapers as a whole. That is, the Times took articles out of context because the database contained individual articles rather than articles in the context of the original newspaper page. The freelance writers retained their copyrights in the individual articles, the Court said. If a contract between a freelancer and a newspaper did not specifically include online publications, the agreement covered only the initial publication.

SUMMARY

AN ORIGINAL WORK IS COPYRIGHTED FROM THE MOMENT it is fixed in a tangible medium. A work's creator owns the copyright to the work. However, if an employee creates a work, it is a work made for hire. The employer owns the copyright to a work made for hire in the absence of a contract stating otherwise. Courts use several criteria to determine whether a creator was an employee or independent contractor. Freelance journalists usually are considered to be independent contractors and thus own the copyrights to their work. ■

Copyright Protection The law specifies six exclusive rights copyright holders have in their works:[47]

1. *The right to reproduce the work.* No one may copy a work without the copyright holder's permission. This prevents anyone from copying the original work or copying an authorized reproduction. An original photograph may not be copied, for example, nor may anyone make a copy of the photo from a book in which it is printed. A court said a jury could find copyright infringement when a luggage store used a computer scanner to copy part of a copyrighted photograph.[48] Without permission from the

copyright holder, the store enlarged the scanned photo and displayed it on its walls.

There are exceptions to this copyright protection. The U.S. Supreme Court allowed home taping of television broadcasts for personal use.[49] Also, Congress amended the copyright act to permit making a single copy of an analog or digital recording for personal use.[50]

Congress created another exception to this right for broadcasters who transmit copyrighted material. The law permits broadcasters to make a copy, such as on videotape, if necessary to air the material. This may be to broadcast the program on a delayed basis, for example. The law calls such copies "ephemeral recordings." The recording must be destroyed within six months or placed in archives and not used on the air.[51]

2. *The right to make derivative works.* Without the copyright holder's permission, no one may use a novel as the basis of a play or make a movie from a television program. The play and movie would be derived from works that are protected by copyright. In one case, the entertainer Prince owned a copyright for a symbol used as a visual element in clothing, jewelry and other items. Another person made a guitar closely resembling Prince's symbol. A court said the guitar infringed on Prince's copyright because it was a derivative work based on a copyrighted design.[52]

3. *The right to distribute the work publicly.* The copyright owner determines when a work will be publicly distributed. For example, a television commercial may not be shown to the public until the copyright holder gives permission. In one case, a record producer included two songs in an album without the composer's permission. A record distributor then supplied copies of the album to retail stores. A court said the distributor violated the composer's right to determine if and when the copyrighted songs would be distributed.[53]

4. *The right to publicly perform a work.* This right applies to "literary, musical, dramatic, and choreographic works, pantomimes, and motion pictures and other audiovisual works."[54] This restricts anyone from showing a movie to the public, for example, without the copyright holder's permission.

5. *The right to publicly display a work.* This applies to "literary, musical, dramatic, and choreographic works, pantomimes," as does the right to publicly perform a work. But this right adds protection for "pictorial, graphic, or sculptural works, including the individual images of a motion picture or other audiovisual work."[55] Under this provision, no one may display a painting, sculpture, photograph or similar work without the copyright owner's permission.

6. *The right to transmit a sound recording, such as a CD, through digital audio means.*[56] This provision requires obtaining permission from a

recording company to play one of its recordings via the Internet, satellite radio or other digital media, including interactive services. Permission is not required to play a recording over a broadcasting station or in live performance. However, recording companies and musicians have pressured Congress to change the law. In mid-2009, key members of Congress said it was probable the law soon would require recording companies' permission to air recordings over broadcast stations as well as digital services. Recording companies likely would seek payment to grant consent.

Additionally, under U.S. copyright law, creators of certain works have what are called **moral rights.** These rights protect a work's integrity and the creator's reputation. Many European countries grant extensive moral rights.[57] For example, print authors may prevent others from falsely attributing works to the author. Also, no one may use the author's works in ways that would reflect adversely on the author's professional reputation. Some countries forbid even the owner of a copyrighted work—a painting, for example—from deforming or changing it in any way. The Berne Convention, the most important international copyright agreement, also includes a moral rights provision. The treaty protects authors' rights to "object to any distortion, mutilation, or other modification" of their works that would harm their reputations.[58]

When the United States joined the Berne Convention, effective in 1989, it had to grant some form of moral rights to copyright holders, as the treaty required. Congress adopted a very narrow moral rights provision.[59] The right applies only to certain artistic works: paintings, drawings, prints, sculptures or art photographs. The law protects single copies—an original painting or sculpture, for example—or a copy that is one of a limited number of a single work, consecutively numbered and signed by the artist. Creators have two moral rights in these works. First, they may claim authorship of a work. That is, authors may prevent having their name removed from the work and insist on having their name connected with the work when it is displayed. Also, artists may prevent having their name attached

moral rights Under U.S. copyright law, the rights of certain artists—creators of paintings, drawings, prints, sculptures and art photographs—to require that their name be associated with their works, forbid others from claiming to be creators of the works and prevent intentional harm to or modification of a work that would harm the artist's reputation.

Points of Law

Exclusive Rights in Copyrighted Works

The copyright holder with exclusive rights may:

1. Reproduce the copyrighted work in copies or phonorecords

2. Prepare derivative works based upon the copyrighted work

3. Distribute copies or phonorecords of the copyrighted work to the public by sale or other transfer of ownership, or by rental, lease or lending [except CDs and computer software]

4. Perform the copyrighted work publicly in the case of literary, musical, dramatic and choreographic works, pantomimes, and motion pictures and other audiovisual works

5. Display the copyrighted work publicly in the case of literary, musical, dramatic and choreographic works, pantomimes, and pictorial, graphic, or sculptural works, including the individual images of a motion picture or other audiovisual work, and

6. Perform the copyrighted work publicly by means of a digital audio transmission in the case of sound recordings.[1]

1. 17 U.S.C. § 106.

to a work they did not create. Second, artists have a right to prevent intentional harm to or modification of a work that would harm their reputations.[60]

Print media works, broadcast programs and motion pictures, among other creations, are not protected by the U.S. copyright law's moral rights provision. This leaves movie directors, for example, without a remedy when they believe their creations are being altered without their permission. Movie studios and directors were outraged when, beginning in 2002, companies began editing offensive language, sexual scenes and violent action out of films. The companies then sold the edited movies. The studios and directors claimed copyright infringement—that the companies made derivative works without permission by making the films into something other than the original movie.[61] While litigation between the movie makers and film editors continued, Congress adopted the Family Movie Act (FMA), part of the Family Entertainment and Copyright Act of 2005.[62] The FMA allows people to purchase and use technology that will filter from a movie the material a viewer does not want to see or hear. Specifically, the law says it is not an infringement to make "imperceptible . . . limited portions of . . . a motion picture . . . for performance in a private home."[63] The FMA does not allow sale of an edited movie without permission of the copyright holder.

The movie directors were concerned with more than derivative works being distributed without permission. They also did not want their films altered in any way. The directors wanted to defend their moral rights, an effort not possible under U.S. copyright law.[64]

Copyright Law Limitations Some protections are not absolute under U.S. copyright law. For instance, although the law says that only the creator may copy his or her work, the Supreme Court held that individuals may make videotape copies of television programs for their own use.[65] The Court said using a videotape recorder merely to shift the time a program is watched is not a copyright infringement. Congress also allowed individuals to make a copy of a recording—again, only for the individual's own use.[66] Courts have not yet decided if digital copying—using a TiVo or Replay device, for example—violates the copyright law.[67]

Libraries open to the public have a limited right to make photocopies for certain purposes.[68] Libraries may make a copy to respond to an interlibrary loan request or to replace a deteriorating copy of a work, for example.

Teachers have certain copying rights Congress did not include in the 1976 law but acknowledged in the legislative reports accompanying the statute. These reports, collectively called **legislative history**, help judges and others interpret what Congress meant by the law. A set of classroom copying guidelines applicable to not-for-profit educational institutions[69] establish copying limits that allow a teacher, no more than twice per term, to copy one chapter from a book for the teacher's own use or copy an excerpt of no more than 1,000 words or 10 percent of the book to distribute to a class. The guidelines do not include an exception for students to copy materials.

legislative history Congressional reports and records containing discussions about proposed legislation.

Copyright owners do not have the right to control individual copies of their works after distribution—with a few exceptions. A person who buys a copy of a novel may give away that book, or sell it, or rent it or throw it away.[70] The author has no right to stop the purchaser from taking any of those actions. This is called the "first-sale doctrine."[71] The copyright law says that once creators have distributed copies of a work, they no longer can regulate what happens to those copies. However, when copyright holders agree to transfer the physical object containing the copyrighted work—the book containing a novel, a videotape containing a movie, a magazine containing articles—they do not transfer any rights in the copyrighted work. The law still restricts copying the novel, making derivative works from a movie and so on. The first-sale doctrine distinguishes between the physical object and the intellectual creation itself. The doctrine does not change the copyright holder's control of the creation, only control of the object containing the creation. Courts and Congress justify the first-sale doctrine based on a preference not to limit what a person can do with her or his own property. Also, copyright law is meant to encourage people to create but also to give the public access to those creations. The first-sale doctrine allows copies to be disseminated less expensively—used books, free libraries, secondhand CDs—than if the copyright holder controlled every copy of his or her creation.

Concerns about people renting computer software or recordings, such as CDs, and then making cheap copies prompted Congress to limit the first-sale doctrine. Congress restricted rentals of recordings without the copyright holder's permission.[72] One federal appellate court ruled that the ban on renting recordings applies only to recordings of musical works but does not include recordings of audiobooks or books on tape.[73] The law also forbids renting computer software. Additionally, the law's moral rights provision limits what owners of artistic works may do with them.

The first-sale doctrine, like some other parts of the copyright law, was meant for a pre-digital world. Copyright scholar Jessica Litman says the doctrine allows the owner of a book "to sell, loan, rent or give it away" but does not allow someone receiving a "lawful digital copy to transmit it to someone else."[74] The problem is that a computer makes an additional copy of the document, which the law does not allow.

SUMMARY

A COPYRIGHT PROTECTS THE CREATOR'S RIGHT to reproduce the work, make derivative works and distribute, perform or display a work. It also protects the right to transmit a sound recording through digital audio means. U.S. law grants creators of artistic works limited moral rights, protecting a work's integrity and the creator's reputation. Individuals may make videotape copies of television programs and audiotape copies of recordings for their own personal use. The first-sale doctrine allows purchasers to dispose as they choose of objects containing copyrighted works, such as books and videotapes. However, CDs and software may not be rented. ∎

statutory damages Damages specified in certain laws. Under these laws, copyright being an example, a judge may award statutory damages even if a plaintiff is unable to prove actual damages.

Copyright Notice Until 1989, copyright could be lost if a published work did not include a copyright notice, such as "© 2010 Jane Doe." To the contrary, international copyright agreements do not require a copyright notice for a work to be protected. When the United States joined the Berne Convention, Congress changed the law so it does not require a copyright notice to be placed on works published on or after March 1, 1989.[75] The 1976 copyright act encourages including a notice, however.[76] For example, an infringer might claim she or he did not know a work was copyrighted because it did not have a copyright notice. If a court accepts that argument, the court could award a very small amount in **statutory damages,** damage amounts specified in certain laws. The copyright statute allows a court to award damages even if an infringer does not make a profit from the creator's work.[77]

Transferring Copyrights A copyright is a property right. Just like a person's automobile, a copyright can be given away, sold or leased.

Rights protected by copyright can helpfully be thought of as a bundle of sticks. Each of the rights includes a number of sticks. For example, an author writes a novel and has the right, among others, to prevent unauthorized copying. If the author sells to a publisher the right—the stick—to reproduce the novel as a hardback book, the author still has all the other copying sticks. The author may sell the paperback copying stick to another publisher. Because the author also has the sticks representing all the other copyright holder's rights, the author may sell to a film studio one of the derivative work's sticks—the right to make a movie from the novel. That still leaves the author with many other sticks. Or the author may choose to sell the whole bundle of sticks to one person or company. Then, the author has no rights remaining. Of course, each time the author sells a stick, or the whole bundle of sticks, he or she likely wants money in return. That may be a lump sum payment but often is a percentage of revenue from, for example, book sales.

Whoever buys a stick from the author then owns that right. The author no longer has any claim on the right unless a contract between the author and the buyer says otherwise. If the buyer wants to sell the right to a third person, the author cannot refuse to allow the sale unless the author has a contractual right to do so. The situation is no different from selling a car. The purchaser owns the car and can sell it to someone else without the original owner's permission.

Unlike a personal right, such as a person's reputation, a copyright does not disappear when the copyright holder dies. The copyright holder may transfer the right to someone else through a will.

The 1976 copyright law recognizes that creators often do not have equal bargaining rights with the large corporations purchasing creators' copyrights. To strike a more equal balance, the law gives creators a termination right.[78] This allows creators, or their heirs, to require the transferred rights be returned 35 to 40 years after the original transfer. This does not apply to works made for hire.

Not only may copyright holders completely transfer their rights, they may license or lease rights to another person. A license is a contract giving limited

realWorld Law

The Sonny Bono Law

Sonny Bono, formerly an entertainer and once singer-actress Cher's husband, was a member of the U.S. House of Representatives when he died in a skiing accident in 1998.

Congress named the copyright extension act in Bono's honor. His second wife, Mary Bono, who succeeded Sonny Bono as a U.S. representative and served in Congress when the copyright extension law passed, said Bono believed copyrights should last forever.[1]

Sonny Bono's connection to the entertainment industry is pertinent. Mickey Mouse's copyright protection, originally granted in 1928 when Mickey's first cartoon, "Steamboat Willie," was shown, would have expired in 2003. But the Walt Disney Company, which owns Mickey's copyright, lobbied Congress to make the copyright period longer than the 1976 Copyright Act specified. By one estimate, Disney spent more than $6.3 million persuading members of Congress to change the law. The Copyright Term Extension Act—the Sonny Bono law— protects Mickey's copyright until 2023.[2] Considering that Mickey may be worth more than $3 billion, will the Walt Disney Company be talking with Congress then?[3]

1. *See* 3 MELVILLE B. NIMMER & DAVID NIMMER, NIMMER ON COPYRIGHT § 9.01 (2010).
2. Laurie Richter, *Reproductive Freedom: Striking a Fair Balance Between Copyright and Other Intellectual Property Protections in Cartoon Characters,* 21 ST. THOMAS L. REV. 441, 451–52 (2009).
3. Joseph Menn, *Disney's Rights to Young Mickey Mouse May Be Wrong,* L.A. TIMES, Aug. 22, 2008, at A1.

permission to use a stick. For example, a photographer may license a picture to a company for use in an advertising campaign during the year 2006. The photographer has not given up any rights but, rather, retains the copyright on the picture and all the rights protected by the copyright. The agreement may give the company exclusive use of the photograph for advertising during 2006, or the photographer may retain the right to allow others also to use it.

Copyright Duration The U.S. Constitution gives Congress the right to adopt copyright and patent laws "for limited times."[79] Lobbying by corporate copyright holders—movie and television program producers, book publishers and others— convinced Congress to stretch the definition of limited times almost to the breaking point.

The 1976 copyright law gave copyright protection for the creator's lifetime plus 50 years after the creator's death with no renewal possible. The Sonny Bono Copyright Term Extension Act of 1998 extended all copyright periods by 20 additional years. For example, after the Bono Act took effect, the copyright period for works created on or after Jan. 1, 1978, became the author's lifetime plus 70 more years.[80] Works made for hire are protected for 95 years from publication or 120 years from creation, whichever is shorter.[81]

Copyright protection's duration depends on several factors. First, when the current copyright statute took effect, many works already were in the **public domain** because their copyrights had expired—such as Nathaniel Hawthorne's

public domain The sphere that includes material not protected by copyright law and therefore available for use without the creator's permission.

Points of Law

The Public Domain

Material that is no longer under copyright protection is in the public domain. Material that was never copyrighted in the first place, such as federal government publications, also is in the public domain. Such public domain material, including text, photographs, drawings and other materials, including those found on the Internet, may be used without obtaining permission. Be sure material is not protected before using it without permission. Some public domain material may contain other works that remain under copyright. And material that may no longer be under copyright protection still may be protected by trademark.

Material also may be in the public domain if a creator says it is. The federal copyright law says material that is substantially original and fixed in a tangible medium is under copyright protection when it is created. But the creator may disavow copyright protection and allow anyone to use the material without permission.

"The Scarlet Letter" and Herman Melville's "Moby-Dick." Also, some works copyrighted under the 1909 law lost protection because their creators failed to renew copyrights. The current statute did not affect works that were in the public domain on Jan. 1, 1978. Public domain works remained in the public domain.

The 1976 law also covers unpublished works, formerly given perpetual protection under state common law. The statute replaced common law protection for unpublished works and protected unpublished works for the author's life plus 70 years.

The Supreme Court in 2003 upheld the Bono Act against claims that it violates the constitutional copyright clause and the First Amendment.[82] The case arose when Eric Eldred, the owner of a website that posts public domain literature such as Nathaniel Hawthorne's "The Scarlet Letter," wanted to put a collection of Robert Frost's poems on the site. The Frost collection was due to go out of copyright and into the public domain in 1998. When Congress extended the copyright period, Eldred sued.

In *Eldred v. Ashcroft* the Supreme Court said extending the copyright period is constitutional. The creator's life plus 70 years is a limited time within the meaning of the Constitution's copyright clause, the Court said. The phrase "limited time" does not mean a fixed time. The copyright period may be flexible. Congress has the right to determine what "limited" means as long as the copyright period is not forever, the Court said. The many times Congress has extended copyright protection does not amount to forever, the Court held. However, the Court did not define "limited time," nor did it offer a test for determining what period might go beyond "limited."

Congress could justify extending the copyright period because people live longer now than when earlier laws were in force, the Court said. Also, technological changes—for example, DVDs and other digital media—make copyrighted works last longer.

The Court also rejected First Amendment arguments against the Bono Act. The Constitution's adopters knew about both the First Amendment and the copyright clause, seemingly finding no tension between the two, according to the Court. The current law balances free speech and copyright protection concerns. Original expression is protected, but ideas and facts are not. And the fair use defense, discussed later in this chapter, allows the public to use portions of copyrighted works under certain circumstances, the Court said.

Law professor Lawrence Lessig represented Eldred in the Supreme Court. After losing the case, Lessig led development of the Creative Commons, an attempt to make copyrighted material more accessible to those who want to use

realWorld Law

© 1959, King Features Syndicate, Inc.

Popeye the Sailor Man

Is Popeye Free?

Elzie Segar created Popeye the Sailor Man, a character that first appeared in a comic strip in 1929 and still is in the comic pages. Segar died in 1938. Under European Union copyright law, stating that copyright lasts for 70 years after a creator's death, Popeye entered the public domain in 2009. But only in the European Union.

Because U.S. copyright protected Popeye when the 1976 law took effect on Jan. 1, 1978, Popeye's copyright lasts in the United States until 2024, 95 years after the creator's death.

Segar's drawings may be copied without permission in Europe but not in the United States. Hearst Corporation owns Popeye's trademark, which will protect Popeye merchandise in the United States. The trademark also is protected in many other countries. Trademarked Popeye merchandise annually generates more than $2.5 billion worldwide.

---

it in their own creations. Through Creative Commons, copyright holders may license their works in whatever way they choose. As one article explains: "Advocates of Creative Commons hope to reduce the transaction costs inherent in the traditional licensing system. Creative Commons is creating a user-friendly license system that copyright owners can adopt to designate what rights they are willing to give up and under what conditions they are willing to surrender those rights."[83] Creators may register their works with Creative Commons as well as with the U.S. Copyright Office.

Registering a Copyright An original work fixed in a tangible medium has copyright protection from the moment it is created. Registration with the U.S. Copyright Office is not required for a work to be copyrighted.[84] However, if a copyright is infringed upon, the copyright holder cannot sue under the law unless the copyright has been registered.[85]

To register a copyright, the creator must complete and submit the proper form. The forms are not complex, and creators generally do not need a lawyer's help to complete them. The creator can obtain forms, instructions and other information at the Copyright Office's website (www.copyright.gov). Additionally, a $35 fee is required to register online, as the Copyright Office prefers. The mail registration fee is $50 or $65, depending on the form used. The registration process also requires submitting two copies of a published work or one copy of an unpublished work to the Copyright Office, part of the Library of Congress in Washington, D.C.[86] There are provisions for registering online-only works, daily newspapers, feature films and other works. After it receives the form, fee and copies, the Copyright Office will send a Certificate of Registration to the creator. Usually it takes four to six months for the certificate to be issued.

An author may wait until after a copyright infringement occurs before registering a copyright and bringing a lawsuit. This is inadvisable for several reasons. First, unless registration occurs before the infringement, the author cannot recover statutory damages. Nor can the court require the infringer to pay the author's attorney's fees and court costs.[87] Second, registration is the best proof of when the author created the work.[88] A court will assume that the registration certificate form accurately shows who created the work and when the work was created. If a copyright infringer claims to have created the work first, he or she bears the burden of proof to prove the claim in the face of the registration.

Registering a copyright does not mean the copyright is valid. The Copyright Office has neither the responsibility nor enough personnel to confirm that each submitted item is original. If a registered copyright is challenged, a court may find that the work does not comply with the requirements necessary to receive copyright protection. Also, the Copyright Office may refuse to register a copyright if it finds the work—such as a book title or advertising slogan—is not eligible for copyright protection.[89]

Federal authorities may bring criminal action against a copyright infringer even if the copyright has not been registered.[90]

Compulsory Copyright Licenses In cable television's infancy in the 1960s and 1970s, the Supreme Court held that cable did not infringe on anyone's copyright when it retransmitted broadcast station signals to cable subscribers.[91] The Court said retransmitting broadcast signals was not a performance under the 1909 copyright law. Therefore, cable did not need permission to send the stations' signals to its customers.

Program producers and broadcasters urged Congress to change the Court's decisions as part of the 1976 law. Congress agreed and adopted a compromise that cable system owners had reached with the producers and broadcasters.[92] The law now allows cable operators to retransmit radio and television broadcast signals without obtaining permission. In turn, cable systems must pay a compulsory fee. The fee is based on a percentage of a cable system's annual revenues and is paid to the U.S. Copyright Office. The fees then are distributed to those who hold copyrights on the programs and other material that radio and television stations broadcast.

Direct broadcast satellite (DBS) services have a similar compulsory license to retransmit broadcast signals.[93] DBS services pay royalties according to the number of subscribers they have.

SUMMARY

PROVIDING COPYRIGHT NOTICE IS NOT NECESSARY to retain protection of original material, but applying a notice provides certain rights under the copyright law. Copyrights may be given away, sold or leased.

Copyrights on works created on or after Jan. 1, 1978, last for the creator's life plus 70 years. A work made for hire lasts for 95 years from publication or 120 years from creation, whichever is shorter. Works protected under the 1909 law and still in copyright when the current law took effect are protected for 95 years from the date they first were copyrighted.

A copyright must be registered before a creator may sue for infringement under the copyright law.

A compulsory copyright license allows cable and satellite television providers to retransmit broadcast signals to their subscribers. ■

Proving Copyright Infringement

Using any part of a copyrighted work is infringement unless there is an applicable defense. A copyright owner can sue an infringer for damages, and in some cases the government may bring criminal charges.

A copyright owner first must show proof of a valid copyright—the work is original and fixed in a tangible medium. And the copyright must be registered before the copyright holder can bring a lawsuit under the federal law. If the copyright holder can prove direct copying, she or he can win the suit if the defendant has no effective defense.

More likely, the plaintiff will attempt to show that the infringer had access to the copyrighted work and the two works are substantially similar. To prove that a defendant could have been exposed to the copyrighted material, the plaintiff must show a reasonable possibility of access. Access may be inferred if the work has been widely distributed and the defendant's and plaintiff's works are very similar.[94] In one case, a composer claimed that the theme song to a James Bond film, "The World Is Not Enough," used a four-note sequence from one of his songs. The court said there was no evidence that the Bond theme composer could have had access to the plaintiff's song, which had not been generally distributed.[95]

Many courts use a two-part test to determine whether works are substantially similar.[96] First, courts apply an objective "extrinsic" test. This compares similarities between the two works' expressive qualities, such as plot, dialogue, musical notes, shapes and use of colors. If the extrinsic test shows there may be substantial similarity, the court then applies a subjective "intrinsic" test. This considers whether a reasonable person would judge the two works to be similar based on the works' concept and feel. Both parts of the test must be met if works are to be found substantially similar.

Points of Law

Infringing Copyright

A copyright plaintiff must prove:

1. The work used is protected by a valid copyright—meaning it is an original work fixed in a tangible medium.

2. The valid copyright is registered with the Copyright Office.

3. And either:

   a. There is evidence the defendant directly copied the copyrighted work, or

   b. The infringer had access to the copyrighted work and the two works are substantially similar.

The plaintiff may show the defendant knowingly aided or contributed to copyright infringement rather than being the primary infringer. The plaintiff need not show the infringement was deliberate.

James Bond, an active copyright litigant, has also been on the plaintiff's side of the courtroom. A federal district court applied the two-part test in finding that a Honda Motor Co. commercial infringed on James Bond movie copyrights.[97] The court described the ad, aired in the mid-1990s, as showing "a young, well-dressed couple in a Honda del Sol being chased by a high-tech helicopter. A grotesque villain with metal-encased arms jumps out of the helicopter onto the car's roof, threatening harm. With a flirtatious turn to his companion, the male driver deftly releases the Honda's detachable roof . . . , sending the villain into space and effecting the couple's speedy get-away."[98] Hollywood studio MGM sued Honda, claiming the commercial infringed on the studio's copyrights in several James Bond movies.

Using the extrinsic test, the court found the commercials and Bond films were substantially similar in several ways, including using "a handsome hero who, along with a beautiful woman, leads a grotesque villain on a high-speed chase," "hi-tech effects, with loud, exciting horn music in the background," "dialogues laced with dry wit and subtle humor" and "tuxedo-clad, British-looking men [who] exude uncanny calm under pressure."[99] The court also cited a number of specific aspects of the ads that seem to have been drawn directly from individual Bond films. For example, in "Dr. No" a character has metal-encased hands, and in "Moonraker" the villain, Jaws, wears oversized goggles and has metallic teeth. In the Honda ad the villain has goggles and metallic teeth.

The court also ruled that the commercials and Bond films were substantially similar under the intrinsic test: "There are many ways to express a helicopter chase scene, but only [the] Bond films would do it the way the Honda commercial did with these very similar characters, music, pace and mood. Plaintiffs are therefore likely to prevail on the 'intrinsic test.'"[100]

Some courts use an "ordinary observer" test in determining substantial similarity. This test asks if an average person would recognize one work as having been appropriated from another. For example, a beer manufacturer commissioned designs for a six-pack carrying case. The designer submitted initial drawings before the manufacturer canceled the agreement. After the beer company marketed a carrying case, the designer sued for copyright infringement. An appellate court said a jury of ordinary observers could have found the two carrying cases were substantially similar.[101]

No reasonable jury could find substantial similarities between a play and "Life," a movie starring Eddie Murphy, a federal appellate court ruled.[102] The playwright sued the movie producers and others connected with the film, claiming they infringed on the play's copyright. The playwright described his play, "No Harm, No Foul," as being about a basketball player falsely accused of rape. The player is convicted and is sentenced to picking cotton for a year, during which time he conceives many escape plans. The defendants summarized the movie script as being about two New York City residents who travel to the South and are arrested for a crime they did not commit. The New Yorkers are sentenced to life in prison. During the next 65 years they trade insults and plan ways to escape. The appellate court agreed with a federal district court that any similarities between the play and the movie were superficial. The district court said the similarities were nonprotectable ideas common to prison movies.

A plaintiff does not have to prove that a copyright infringement was deliberate. Even accidental infringement violates the law. A court may reduce statutory damages imposed on an innocent infringer, a person who unintentionally infringed on another person's copyright, and waive statutory damages completely if the innocent infringer works for a nonprofit library or public broadcaster.[103]

Contributory Infringement Nor does a plaintiff have to prove that the defendant directly infringed on copyright. Showing that the defendant knowingly aided or contributed to copyright infringement is sufficient. Although contributory infringement is not specifically banned in the copyright law, the statute implies that contributory infringement is actionable and courts long have held it actionable.[104]

Contributory infringement may be difficult to prove. Several television program producers sued Sony for making videocassette recorders (VCRs) that allowed viewers to tape copyrighted programs without permission. The producers claimed without the VCRs there could be no unauthorized copying. The U.S. Supreme Court said Sony might have known that viewers used VCRs to tape television programs. But the Court said it could be fair use to tape programs for time-shifting purposes—to watch the program later. As discussed following, fair use is a defense against a charge of copyright infringement. If time shifting is not copyright infringement, the VCRs could be used for non-infringing purposes, the Court ruled.[105]

A quarter-century after the *Sony v. Universal City Studios* case, when Cablevision Systems moved the VCR to computers and into the cable system owner's premises, a group of movie studios and broadcast and cable networks did not argue contributory infringement. Cablevision's technology allowed its cable subscribers to have Cablevision to record a program. The customer had to alert the company before a program began. The customer then could watch the program at a later time. The studios and networks argued Cablevision would directly infringe on program copyrights by making unauthorized copies on computers and publicly performing the programs when customers later watched them. In 2008 the U.S. Court of Appeals for the Second Circuit ruled that the cable customer, rather than Cablevision, copied the program. Cablevision's computers acted as a modern VCR or another kind of TiVo. Because only one customer at one time viewed the program, the program was not publicly performed, "public" being a larger group than just one customer.[106]

Those who benefit financially from copyright infringers also may be liable under copyright law. This might include a store selling pirated DVDs copied without permission of the movies' copyright holders. These are called "vicarious copyright infringers."

Finally, the U.S. Supreme Court established a third type of indirect copyright infringer. These are individuals or companies who induce or encourage others to engage in copyright infringement. In the *Metro-Goldwyn-Mayer Studios, Inc.*

v. Grokster, Ltd. decision, discussed further in the music licensing section later in this chapter, the Court held that Grokster infringed on the copyright because it knew people used its software to download music files. The Court said it did not matter that the software could be used for legal purposes because Grokster encouraged users to infringe on copyrights.[107]

Remedies for Copyright Infringement

A copyright infringement suit is a tort action—the copyright holder seeks compensation for the harm the infringer caused.[108] The plaintiff may ask for actual damages.[109] These include income the copyright holder lost and profits the infringer made due to the infringement.

Alternatively, the plaintiff may seek statutory damages. The copyright statute allows a plaintiff to ask for appropriate compensation ranging from $750 to $30,000.[110] The defendant may ask that a jury rather than a judge decide how much to award in statutory damages.[111] The amount of statutory damages awarded depends in part on the defendant's actions. If the defendant deliberately infringed on the plaintiff's copyright,[112] the court may increase the $30,000 up to a total of $150,000. A court may award as little as $200 in statutory damages if the defendant was an innocent infringer.[113] This might happen if the plaintiff did not include a copyright notice and the defendant reasonably did not know the work was protected by copyright.

A judge can award attorney's fees to the winning party in a copyright infringement suit.[114] Even the defendant may receive attorney's fees if the lawsuit had little merit. Despite First Amendment limitations on prior restraints, the copyright law allows a court to impose an injunction on works infringing on copyrights.[115] Also, unauthorized copies of recordings, such as CDs, may be seized and destroyed.[116]

The government can bring criminal charges against a person or company infringing on another's copyright.[117] Criminal charges can be brought even if the infringer did not profit from the infringement as long as the infringer received something of value, including a copyrighted work.[118] Once, the government could prosecute for stealing copyrighted material only if the theft was for commercial or private financial gain.[119] But the No Electronic Theft Act took effect in December 1997, allowing prosecution even in the absence of an infringer's profit motive.[120] In part, Congress wanted to allow criminal prosecution of people downloading many copyrighted audio and video works or making copies of copyrighted videodiscs for their own use but without permission.

SUMMARY

To prove copyright infringement, the copyright holder must show (1) she has a valid copyright, (2) the work is registered, and (3) the defendant either directly copied the work or the defendant had access to the copyrighted work and the two works are substantially similar. Many courts use a two-part test to determine whether works are substantially similar. The courts apply an objective "extrinsic" test and a subjective "intrinsic" test. Other courts ask if an average person would consider the disputed work to have been taken from the original work.

A copyright plaintiff may ask for actual damages or statutory damages. The winning party in a copyright infringement suit may be awarded attorney's fees. ∎

Copyright Infringement Defense: Fair Use

A person sued for copyright infringement might claim that the plaintiff did not file within the law's three-year statute of limitations (or five years for criminal charges against an infringer).[121] Or a defendant may argue that the copyright holder has abandoned the copyright—knowingly given up rights in the work—placing the work in the public domain.[122] The most common defense, however, is **fair use.**

Courts recognized the fair use defense long before Congress wrote it into the 1976 copyright law.[123] Courts understood that the copyright statutes—from 1790 to the present—give copyright holders the right to forbid any use of their works without permission. But what if an English teacher copies a few paragraphs from a novel for a class discussion? Or a movie reviewer on television shows 15 seconds of a film to illustrate a point about the movie? Or a comedian sings a portion of a song's lyrics before offering a parody of the composition? According to a strict interpretation of the copyright law, all these are infringements. However, courts long ago decided that these and similar uses could be fair to the copyright holder and to society. Congress agreed, and the 1976 copyright act included fair use as a defense.[124]

What is fair to the copyright holder? And what is fair to society? One judge has said that to be fair "the use must be of a character that serves the copyright objective of stimulating productive thought and public instruction without excessively diminishing the incentives for creativity."[125] Fair use is difficult to define. Deciding whether a use is fair is not an exact science. This is partly because courts do not agree what a copyright means. Is it a narrow group of rights granted to the copyright holder, allowing the public to generally use copyrighted works? Or is it an all-encompassing right, granting only narrow exceptions to the general rule that a copyright holder has nearly complete control of her work?[126]

The 1976 law set out four criteria courts use in balancing the plaintiff's rights to forbid any use of a work without permission and the defendant's right to use a portion of the work under certain circumstances:

> **fair use** A test courts use to determine whether using another's copyrighted material without permission is fair or an infringement. Fair use test is also used in trademark infringement cases.

Points of Law

Fair Use Defense

1. Why and for what purpose was the copyrighted work used without permission?

2. What was the nature of the copyrighted work that was used without permission?

3. How much and what particular portion of the copyrighted work was used without permission?

4. What effect did the unauthorized use have on the copyrighted work's market value?

(1) the purpose and character of the use, (2) the nature of the copyrighted work, (3) the amount and substantiality of the portion used, and (4) the effect on the plaintiff's potential market.

In more detail, the four criteria are

1. *The purpose and character of the use.* What did the defendant use the copyrighted material for? In determining the purpose and character of the use, courts consider several factors, including whether the use is for commercial or nonprofit purposes. The law gives examples of uses that would tilt the balance toward a fair use: criticism, comment, news reporting, teaching (including multiple copies for classroom use), scholarship and research. Other uses also may be seen as fair, such as parody.[127]

News reporting may be considered a fair use. But as with the rest of the fair use balancing test, this factor is not clear. For example, The Nation magazine used 300–400 words from President Gerald R. Ford's memoirs without the book publisher's permission. In fact, the publisher had sold Time magazine the exclusive right to run excerpts. The U.S. Supreme Court acknowledged that Ford's thoughts were news, but that alone did not make The Nation's copying fair use.[128]

In a case involving a crude cover version of a popular song, the Supreme Court considered whether a parody changes the work it mocks. Does the new work merely repeat the copyrighted material or alter it in a way that adds a new dimension?[129] The more the parody transforms the work it mimics, the more likely it is a fair use. The Court made transformativeness a key part of fair use's first element. As the Court said, fair use is more likely to be found if the new work "adds something new, with a further purpose or different character, altering the [copyrighted work] with new expression, meaning, or message."[130] A 2 Live Crew parody of Roy Orbison's song "Oh, Pretty Woman" might be fair use because it did transform the original, the Court said.[131] However, the other fair use factors also must be considered before finally concluding whether the parody infringed on the original song's copyright.

A group of students sued the company that owns Turnitin, a plagiarism detection service, claiming Turnitin copies students' written assignments by archiving them in the company's computers. A federal appellate court rejected the students' copyright infringement claim, holding that Turnitin's goal of identifying plagiarism is a transformative purpose, different from the students' objective of research and completing class assignments.[132] A different federal appellate court in 2010 barred publication of a novel portraying Holden Caulfield as 76 years old, 60 years older than he was in J.D. Salinger's "Catcher in the Rye." Holden's transformation was not enough to convince the court the new novel's author could prove fair use as a defense against copyright infringement by using Salinger's character.[133]

The "Oh, Pretty Woman" case suggests that without fair use protection society largely would be without parodies. A parody requires using enough of an original work that people can recognize it. What creator would allow a portion

2 Live Crew: Pretty or Hairy?

The First Amendment offers much protection to parody but little to the creator whose work is parodied. The creator may lose financially because her work may be parodied without permission. But as law professor L. Richard Walton wrote, "the most significant theft is not The artist's immediate profits but her dignity."[1]

Luther Campbell of 2 Live Crew wrote a parody of the classic rock song "Oh, Pretty Woman." Roy Orbison and William Dees wrote the song; Orbison's recording sold millions and remains popular. The song's music publisher, Acuff-Rose Music, Inc., of Nashville, Tenn., refused Campbell's request for permission to use parts of the song in his rap parody. He recorded the song despite the refusal—a song "about a cheating behemoth of a 'hairy woman'"—and the record sold 250,000 copies.[2] Acuff-Rose sued Campbell for copyright infringement. The U.S. Supreme Court ruled that a parody must use part of the original work or no one would know it was a parody. Campbell's fair use defense, then, won the day.

Roy Orbison

What about Orbison and Dees? As Walton wrote, "One senses the real damage . . . was to Orbison's artistic sensibilities and his dignitary rights in the original song."[3]

---

1. L. Richard Walton, *Heartbreak Hotel in B-Flat Broke: Music, Money and (Un)Fair Use*, 21 Cardozo Arts & Ent. L.J. 423, 427 (2003).
2. *Id.*
3. *Id.*

of his work to be used for a biting parody?[134] As explained in Chapter 7, a parody mimics a work and a satire uses a work to spoof a different target.

Some courts also consider whether the copyrighted material is used for productive or nonproductive purposes. News reporting is a productive use, although such use does not always justify copyright infringement. Conversely, nonproductive purposes may be found to be fair uses.[135] Making videotape copies of television programs for personal use, such as watching the program at a later time, is a fair use, the Supreme Court ruled.[136] Videotaping for personal use is similar to a teacher copying an article to help broaden her understanding of the field she teaches, the Court said.

2. The nature of the copyrighted work. This factor focuses on the work that is being used without permission. Is the copyrighted work largely creative, such as a novel or a feature film, or more informational or functional, like a scientific paper or compilation of court decisions?[137] Courts often find more copyright protection for creative works. Copying portions of factually based materials may tilt the balance toward a fair use.

Should unpublished materials be especially protected against a fair use defense? The issue arose when a court allowed J.D. Salinger, author of the novel "Catcher in the Rye" and other works, to stop distribution of an unauthorized biography including excerpts from letters Salinger wrote.[138] A federal appellate court held that unpublished materials are entitled to more protection than published works. After a series of court decisions disagreeing about protecting unpublished works, Congress amended the Copyright Act. The law now says unpublished materials are not necessarily protected if balancing all four fair use factors shows copying without permission should be permitted.[139]

3. *The amount and substantiality of the portion used.* Courts ask two questions with regard to the amount and substantiality factor. First, how much of the copyrighted work was used without permission? Courts may count how many words from a story or seconds from a videotape were used. However, courts look not only at the absolute amount taken from the copyrighted work but also at what percentage of the original was used. Taking 100 words from a 400-page novel is more likely to tilt toward a fair use than quoting 10 words from a 12-word poem. For example, without permission the cable network Court TV used a few seconds of approximately two minutes of videotape showing the beating of Reginald Denny during the 1992 Los Angeles riots. Finding this a fair use, a federal appellate court in 2002 said Court TV's use "was quite small, both in absolute terms—a few seconds at most—and in relation to the copyrighted work as a whole."[140]

The Librarian of Congress ruled in 2010 that college and university professors, film and media studies students and documentary filmmakers may use short clips from movie DVDs for criticism, commentary or even to make new, noncommercial videos.[141]

Second, what particular portion of the copyrighted work was used? Was the excerpt used without permission a very important part of the copyrighted work? Quoting from the last page of a mystery novel—the words telling who committed the murder, how and why—would tip the balance toward copyright infringement, not fair use. The balance would tip toward infringement even if only a comparatively few words—but the most important words—were quoted from the mystery novel.

The Supreme Court found this to be an essential point when it rejected The Nation magazine's fair use defense. The magazine used only about 300 words from President Ford's 200,000-word memoirs, but those were the very words explaining why Ford pardoned President Richard Nixon. The Court called this excerpt "essentially the heart of the book."[142]

Using all of a copyrighted work rarely allows a court to find fair use. However, a federal appellate court said reprinting full pictures of Grateful Dead posters and concert tickets did not preclude finding fair use when the images were scattered throughout a book in collages of images, text and graphic art. The court said the use was transformative because images were shown in reduced size and only a few unauthorized copyrighted works were published among 2,000 images.[143] Not all courts or copyright scholars would agree that reprinting an entire poster, or all of any copyrighted work, can be fair use.[144]

4. The effect on the plaintiff's potential market. Did the unauthorized copying diminish the copyright holder's likely profits from his or her creation? Giving away the end of a mystery novel might mean potential readers would not purchase the book. Because of the financial impact on a copyright holder, many courts consider this the most important of the four fair use factors.

This factor is meant to balance the adverse impact on the copyright holder against the public's benefits if use is permitted.[145] When a Kinko's store responded to professors' requests to make course packets by copying chapters from numerous books without permission, several publishers sued for copyright infringement. A court rejected Kinko's fair use defense.[146] Finding the fourth factor the "single most important" part of the fair use test, the court said:

> [T]he competition for "student dollars" is easily won by Kinko's, which produced 300- to 400-page packets including substantial portions of copyrighted books at a cost of $24 to the student. [One packet] contained excerpts from 20 different books, totaled 324 pages, and cost $21.50. While it is possible that reading the packets whets the appetite of students for more information from the authors, it is more likely that purchase of the packets obviates purchase of the full texts.[147]

SUMMARY

THE COPYRIGHT LAW SPECIFIES A THREE-YEAR statute of limitations, or five years for criminal prosecutions.

Fair use, the most common copyright infringement defense, is a four-part balancing test. Courts consider (1) the purpose and character of the use, (2) the nature of the copyrighted work, (3) the amount and substantiality of the portion used, and (4) the effect on the plaintiff's potential market. Criticism, news, scholarship and parody tend toward fair use. Using an important part of a work may suggest infringement. Harm to the plaintiff's potential profits may be the most important fair use criterion. ∎

Copyright, Computers and the Internet

Congress certainly did not anticipate computers or the Internet when it adopted the 1790 and 1909 copyright laws. Computers existed in 1976, as did the Internet in rudimentary form, but they were not part of Congress' thinking when it passed the current copyright law. Since then, Congress and the courts have struggled to apply copyright concepts and laws to computers and to the unique communications medium of the Internet.

Copyright infringement can occur on the Internet just as it can in print. Copying pictures from a magazine's website onto another website or into a class paper without permission violates the copyright law, for example.[148] More important, downloading copyrighted music or movies infringes on copyright holders' rights.

Copyright holders looked to Congress for help. Congress responded by adopting the Digital Millennium Copyright Act (DMCA) in 1998, amending the 1976 act in an attempt to bring the Internet and other digital media into the copyright law.[149] The DMCA bans software and hardware that facilitates circumventing copyright protection technology.[150] For example, the act forbids software that would disable anticopying features in a DVD player or software enabling video DVDs to be copied.[151] The DMCA also prohibits removing or changing copyright information, such as the copyright owner's name.[152]

The DMCA also dealt with concerns that Internet service providers (ISPs) could lose copyright suits based on content their users put on the ISPs' systems. One court found that an ISP violated the copyright law when its subscribers uploaded and downloaded copyrighted pictures without the ISP's knowledge.[153] Another court said a bulletin board service operator infringed on copyright when its customers used the service to trade copyrighted computer games.[154]

Technology once again ran ahead of the law. YouTube, MySpace, Veoh and other video-sharing sites allowed users to upload material copyrighted not by the users but by movie studios and television networks.

To protect ISPs and video-sharing sites, the DMCA shields them from copyright infringement claims if an ISP removes material that a copyright holder tells the website is posted without permission.[155] This is called a "takedown notice." This protection is available if a website names an agent to receive takedown requests, lets site users know of the site's copyright infringement policy and complies with takedown requests the site receives. The takedown request must clearly identify the work claimed to infringe on copyright and let the ISP know the Uniform Resource Locator (URL, or Web address) of the infringing work. An ISP need not comply with an incomplete takedown request.[156] There is no protection if the ISP knowingly transmits material that violates another's copyright. A customer cannot sue the ISP for removing material even if the customer later shows the material did not violate a copyright holder's rights.

The DMCA offers other protection to video-sharing websites when a user, rather than the site, posts copyrighted material without permission. The law refers to this as content posted "at the direction of a user." The copyright holder cannot successfully sue the site for monetary damages if the site operator did not know the content infringed on someone's copyright, did not earn money directly from the posted material and promptly complied with a takedown notice. These and the takedown protections are called "safe harbors." That is, they limit video-sharing sites' liability in copyright infringement suits.

The DMCA's safe harbors twice protected an Internet-based video-sharing service called Veoh Networks. In 2008, a federal district court said Veoh's automatically making and storing a flash file preview and screen shots when a user uploaded a file did not prevent Veoh's protection under the DMCA.[157] However, a federal appellate court said in 2007 that a Web service storing thumbnail-sized images of larger photographs infringes on a copyright holder's display right.[158] Veoh also won another 2008 case in which Universal Music Group claimed the website permitted users to upload and store UMG's copyrighted music. A federal district court ruled Veoh did not have actual knowledge that the users uploaded copyrighted music. Veoh also agreed to remove any copyrighted works when notified to do so by a copyright holder.[159] Both Veoh decisions suggest that the DMCA's safe harbors remain, even if users upload and download files containing copyrighted material.

A website or blog containing an embedded copyrighted video does not lose DMCA protection. As long as the video is a link to another site and no copy is maintained, the DMCA applies.[160]

Music Licensing

Copyrighted music is part of many media presentations. Even the print media must be concerned with music copyrights if they print song lyrics or a composition's notes.

Obtaining permission to use copyrighted music may involve many steps because there are many copyright holders. Listening to a recording means listening to two copyrighted works. First, the composition—the music and lyrics. Songs, symphonies and other musical compositions that are original and fixed in a tangible medium have copyright protection. Second, a recorded song is a sound recording—the words and music performed by musicians and embedded into a CD, DVD, audiotape or another recording medium. But there is more. Third, the CD, DVD or tape is called a "phonorecord." Phonorecords have copyright protection. Finally, permission is needed to copy a recorded composition onto film or videotape. This is called a "synchronization license."

Compositions Because compositions are protected by copyright—they are original and fixed in a tangible medium—permission is needed to use them. Composers have the right to limit public performances of their works.[161] Consent is required to broadcast or record a song, perform the song live, play a recording containing the song in many restaurants and stores, or use the song in any of numerous other ways. However, songs, called "musical works" in the Copyright Act, may be used by many people for many reasons. A composer cannot know each time a song is performed. Nor can a composer reach contractual agreements with every person who might want to perform the song—even if each of those people wants to seek permission. Instead, music publishers and most composers have music licensing organizations that represent them.

Performing rights organizations act as intermediaries between those who wish to perform copyrighted music and the songwriters and music publishing companies who want to be compensated for use of their copyrighted music. The

Points of Law

What Does "Perform" Mean?

A congressional report explains that

> a singer is performing when he or she sings a song; a broadcasting network is performing when it transmits his or her performance (whether simultaneously or from records); a local broadcaster is performing when it transmits the network broadcast; a cable television system is performing when it retransmits the broadcast to its subscribers; and any individual is performing whenever he or she plays a phonorecord embodying the performance or communicates the performance by turning on a receiving set.[1]

---

1. House of Representatives Report No. 1476, 94th Congress, 2d Session 63 (1976).

oldest performing rights organization, ASCAP (American Society of Composers, Authors and Publishers) began in 1914. In 1939, when ASCAP increased the fees broadcasters paid to play compositions on the air, radio stations organized BMI (Broadcast Music, Inc.). More recently, SESAC (once called the Society of European Stage Authors and Composers) began operations in the United States as the third performing rights organization. ASCAP and BMI each have hundreds of thousands of members and controls millions of songs. The three performing rights organizations combined distribute nearly $2 billion annually to their member composers and music publishing companies.[162] ASCAP and BMI are nonprofit organizations, while SESAC, the smallest of the three, is a profit-making company.

ASCAP, BMI and SESAC grant licenses (another word for contracts) to people, groups and businesses. The licenses give permission to perform copyrighted songs for specific purposes. In return for the licenses, the groups collect fees from the song users. The fees may be a few hundred dollars annually for a small bar that hosts live musicians to millions of dollars from a major broadcast television network. Car dealerships, miniature golf courses, nightclubs with "karaoke nights" and numerous other businesses use music—and need ASCAP, BMI and SESAC licenses.

ASCAP, BMI and SESAC licenses are for songs, not for complete works such as musical comedies, operas, operettas and motion picture scores. Permission to use these musical creations comes from the music publishers who produce the printed scores for these works.

A composer joins just one of the organizations or is represented by a music publisher that belongs to one of them. Thus, a composition is under the auspices of one performing rights organization. Most music users, then, must have agreements with each of the three groups. It is not practical for broadcast stations, for example, to play songs controlled only by ASCAP or only by BMI.

A songwriter who joins a performing rights organization does not give up his or her copyrights. They may grant performance rights themselves, even if they belong to ASCAP, BMI or SESAC. Usually, however, composers allow the organizations to represent them, ensuring that they are paid when their songs are performed.

Usually ASCAP, BMI and SESAC grant blanket licenses. These agreements give permission to perform all the songs in the organization's catalog. The organizations also grant per-program licenses allowing a broadcaster to use music in a particular program. The fees collected from these license agreements are distributed semiannually to music publishers and composers primarily based on how often their songs are played.

Performing rights organizations employees go to nightclubs, stores, radio stations and other music users to confirm that these venues have licenses. If they do not have agreements, the organizations will issue several warnings. If the warnings do not convince the music users to obtain licenses, the organizations will sue for copyright infringement.[163]

After years of ASCAP and BMI insisting that stores have licenses even to turn on a radio and play music, and of courts disagreeing, even where retail stores had amplified the music through a speaker system, Congress stepped into the dispute.[164] In the Fairness in Music Licensing Act of 1998, based on a compromise between the performing rights organizations and the business community, Congress established that certain businesses would not have to purchase licenses to broadcast music in their stores.[165] The exemption applies to retail stores with less than 2,000 square feet of space and restaurants with less than 3,750 square feet of space, if no admission is charged and the music is not played outside the establishments. Larger establishments also are exempt if they have no more than six speakers and four television sets. The Fairness in Music Licensing Act applies only to playing music through radio and television sets in businesses. It does not apply to live performances, the playing of recordings or other nonbroadcast uses of copyrighted compositions.

When a song's copyright holder allows one recording to be made of a composition, the law grants a compulsory license—also called "statutory license"—to anyone else who wants to make a recording of the song.[166] That is, the composition's copyright holder must allow others to record the song. In return, the song's copyright holder receives compensation based on the number of recordings sold. The copyright law establishes the method of compensation. The compulsory license applies only to individual songs, not to musical comedy scores, movie soundtracks, operas and similar scores. Also, the license does not allow other material to be included in the recording, such as CD-ROMs that include video images or text information. Permission to record a composition is called a **mechanical license.** The performing rights organizations do not grant these licenses. Rather, permission is obtained from a New York City nonprofit organization, the Harry Fox Agency, formed by music publishers in 1927. The right to record a composition is separate from the right to publicly perform a song, such as a radio station or a large department store playing a recording of a song.

mechanical license Permission to record a composition.

An ASCAP or BMI license allows broadcast stations to both air compositions and stream them on the station's website. SESAC charges separately for these two rights.[167]

Sound Recordings A sound recording is the series of musical or other sounds recorded on a vinyl disc, a CD, a DVD, an audiotape or some other storage medium.[168] Sound recordings are eligible for copyright protection.[169] A sound recording is not the composition, which itself is copyrighted. Rather, a sound recording is the recorded composition—the captured performance of the musical sounds and the words. Nor is a sound recording the CD or tape itself. Those are called phonorecords, and they have their own copyright protection.

A sound recording must have originality to be given copyright protection. Congress and courts suggest that originality may be found in two elements of a sound recording. First, the performers bring the composition to life. As a judge said many years ago: "A musical score in ordinary notation does not determine the entire performance. . . . In the vast number of renditions, the performer has a wide choice, depending on his gifts, and this makes his rendition . . . quite as original" as the composition itself.[170] Second, a record producer may add originality to a sound recording. A producer may choose what sounds to emphasize, edit the recording and make suggestions to the musicians.

The sound recording copyright, then, may be owned by the performers or owned jointly by the musicians and the record producer. It also is possible for a recording company to own the sound recording copyright. This may happen because of an employment situation—the producer may work full-time for a recording company—or a contractual agreement between the performers and the recording company.

In one respect, it matters little who owns the sound recording copyright. The law does not require permission to perform the sound recording.[171] A radio station may play a recording over the air without anyone's consent except the songwriter's (usually obtained through a blanket license with ASCAP, BMI or SESAC). Sound recording copyright holders have only three rights.[172] First, no one may copy the sound recording without permission. Second, consent is required to make a derivative work based on the sound recording. This right does not preclude cover records—recordings of the same song by other musicians—even if the new recording sounds exactly like the original.[173] Third, only the sound recording copyright owner may decide to publicly distribute the recording.

Copyright law prohibits digitally transmitting sound recordings without permission. This does not apply to performing a sound recording live, as a DJ might, or broadcasting it through nondigital means, as an over-the-air radio station does. The law applies only to sound recordings performed through a digital audio transmission, such as by a satellite music service or a radio station streaming its programming on a website.

Interactive services must negotiate directly with sound recording copyright holders. These are services allowing subscribers or other users to choose what artist or song will be played or to know the recordings that will be played because the service posts that information on a list. The situation differs for non-interactive services, such as webcasters. A "non-interactive" service is defined as one playing no more than two songs in a row from the same album and no more than three songs in any four-hour period from the same artist.[174] Non-interactive services obtain a statutory license. A statutory license is created by law, requires all affected copyright owners to grant the permission the license covers, and sets fees—or states how fees will be set—that are paid by copyrighted material users and then disbursed to the copyright holders. A nonprofit group the recording industry established, SoundExchange, administers the royalties. Those who use the copyrighted material may negotiate a fee with SoundExchange. If negotiations fail, users will pay royalties established by a government group, the

Copyright Royalty Board, every five years.[175] Examples of non-interactive services are Sirius-XM satellite radio and Pandora Internet radio.

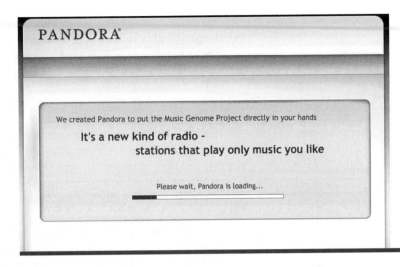

Pandora Internet Radio interface

Outside of the music context, using a small portion of copyrighted material could be considered fair use. Courts even have referred to this as "*de minimis* copying"—that is, copying so little that it is not worth a court's time to hear a copyright infringement case. But music is different. A musician borrowing a few notes from a recording is called "sampling." Two court decisions, one from the U.S. Court of Appeals for the Sixth Circuit and the other from the Ninth Circuit, suggest sampling infringes on the sound recording copyright holder's rights. In the Sixth Circuit case, a three-note, two-second guitar riff on a George Clinton, Jr., and the Funkadelics' recording was lowered in pitch, looped and extended to 16 beats. The soundtrack of the movie "I Got the Hook Up" included that sample five times. Clinton's record company sued the movie producer for using the recording without permission.[176] In the Ninth Circuit case, the Beastie Boys obtained ECM Records' permission to use a three-note sample from jazz and classical musician James Newton's recording of his song, "Choir." The Beastie Boys used the sample in the song "Pass the Mic." Newton sued for using his composition without permission.[177]

The Sixth Circuit case involved the record company's right under the copyright law to prevent copying a sound recording without the company's permission. The court said the de minimis doctrine did not apply. Essentially, not a note of a sound recording may be copied without the copyright holder's permission. The record company, in this case and in most instances, owns the sound recording copyright. The court, ruling for Clinton based on the movie's use of the sound recording, suggested it might take a different view if the composition instead of the sound recording were at issue. The Ninth Circuit did deal with the composition, not the sound recording. The Beastie Boys had ECM Records' permission to copy the sound recording but did not have permission to use the composition. But the Ninth Circuit said using a few notes of a composition does not infringe on a copyright.

Musicians Artists who perform compositions have few copyright protections. Musicians who write songs have their compositions protected by copyright. It also is possible for a performer who records a song to have the copyright on the sound recording. However, most musicians—in their roles as musicians—sign away their sound recording copyrights as part of the contracts between the artists and their recording companies. (Some artists even agree to transfer their composition copyrights to recording companies.) In one way, this is not much different from a novelist who transfers her or his copyright to a book publishing company in return for a share of the book's sales revenues. Recording artists receive a share of their recordings' sales revenues—per their contracts with their recording companies. However, many performers and some legal scholars argue that recording company contracts are unfair to recording artists.[178] One complaint is that recording companies require artists to agree that their recordings are works made for hire, giving the company complete control over the recordings. The recording artist Prince "went so far as trading in his name for an unpronounceable symbol to protest his relationship with his label at the time, Warner Brothers. During the rest of his contract with Warner Brothers, [he] took to scribbling the word 'slave' on his face during appearances."[179]

Congress has given performers one right. Making bootleg copies—audio or video recordings—of live musical performances violates the copyright law.[180] Making copies of the live recordings and selling or distributing the copies also infringes on the performers' rights.[181]

Phonorecords   When a composition is recorded, usually on audiotape, a CD or another digital device, the recording company has made a phonorecord. The 1976 law gives phonorecords copyright protection.[182]

The 1909 copyright law gave no protection to phonorecords. Congress and courts thought that if the naked eye could not see the work contained in an object, the law could not protect the object.[183] Words could be seen in a book, and drawings could be seen on paper. Copying the words or drawings infringed on the copyright. But duplicating a record was not copying because what the record contained—musical sounds—could not be seen.

Congress first protected the sound recordings contained in records and tapes in 1971.[184] In the 1976 copyright law, Congress said phonorecords—the disc, record, tape or other object containing the sound recording—have copyright protection. This means it violates the copyright law to copy or distribute a phonorecord without permission. It also is impermissible to make adaptations of the phonorecord.[185] In practice, this means a broadcast radio station only playing recordings of songs must have ASCAP, BMI and SESAC licenses but need not have recording companies' permission. However, if the station copies the recordings—while taping the radio program that includes the recordings, for example—it then must have the recording companies' permission. The recording company's permission is called a "master use license."

Synchronization Rights   If a television station uses a recording as background music, in a station promotional spot, for example, one more permission is required. The station must have the appropriate ASCAP, BMI or SESAC license and the recording company's permission to copy the sound recording and phonorecord onto videotape. But more, the station also must have a synchronization license. This allows the station to synchronize the musical work with the images

realWorld Law

Music and Politics

During political campaigns from 2008 through 2010, several musicians complained that politicians they did not support were using their songs without permission. David Byrne sued Charlie Crist, former Florida governor, for using the song "Road to Nowhere" in Crist's 2010 U.S. Senate campaign. Byrne claimed copyright infringement.[1] Jackson Browne said Sen. John McCain, the 2008 Republican presidential candidate, violated Browne's copyright by playing "Running on Empty" at campaign stops. In 2009 Browne agreed to settle a copyright infringement lawsuit he filed against McCain and the Republican National Committee.[2] The Eagles' Don Henley filed a copyright infringement suit against Charles DeVore for using two of Henley's songs in YouTube videos when DeVore ran for U.S.

Mike Huckabee, a 2008 Republican presidential candidate, is among several politicians drawing musicians' ire for using copyrighted songs without permission.

Senate as a Republican in 2009.[3] Tom Scholz, founder of the band Boston, said Republican presidential candidate Mike Huckabee used "More Than a Feeling" during campaign appearances in 2008. Huckabee's use of his song promoted ideas he disagreed with, Scholz said.[4]

Members of the band Rage Against the Machine said the U.S. Central Intelligence Agency (CIA) used their songs to torment prisoners at detention centers. They accused the CIA of loudly playing the band's music to degrade and humiliate detainees.[5]

1. Ben Sisario, *Talking Head to Campaign: That's My Song,* N.Y. TIMES, May 25, 2010, at A15.
2. *G.O.P. to Apologize to Jackson Browne,* N.Y. TIMES, July 22, 2009, at C2.
3. Greg Sandoval, *Don Henley Battles Republicans over YouTube Video,* CNET NEWS, Apr. 18, 2009, *available at* http://news.cnet .com/8301-1023_3-10222772-93.html.
4. *This Time, Without 'Feeling,'* CHI. TRIB., Feb. 18, 2008, at 36.
5. Joe Heim, *Torture Songs Spur a Protest Most Vocal: Musicians Call for Release of Records on Guantanamo Detainee Treatment,* WASH. POST, Oct. 22, 2009, at C1.

on videotape. Motion picture producers also need a synchronization license to include recorded music in movies.

Synchronization rights are needed any time a recorded composition is used in a filmed or videotaped work. Synchronization rights belong to the composer and music publisher, the company that publishes and helps publicize the song. Synchronization rights must be obtained directly from the music publisher.

Alternatives to Licensing There is a way to avoid the complexities of music licensing. There are companies that hire composers to write songs for the company and hire musicians to record those songs. The companies sell CDs and audiotapes containing the recordings. Because the company owns all the rights—for the compositions, sound recordings, phonorecords and synchronization—it can sell a complete package. The product does not include best-selling recordings of well-known songs, but it may be the easier and less expensive way to obtain music for some purposes. Firms providing these services are variously called "music library companies," "needle-drop shops" or "one-stop shops." Muzak is a well-known music library.

Music, the Internet and File Sharing

Technology continues to outpace the copyright law. For example, using the Internet and a centralized server, a company named Napster allowed one computer user to reach into another user's computer and retrieve files containing copyrighted music. Not just one computer user did this, millions did. The technology is called a peer-to-peer (P2P) network, and computer users can employ it to make unauthorized copies of sound recordings.

A federal appellate court agreed with the recording industry that Napster's operation violated the copyright law.[186] The court said Napster users infringed on copyrights by downloading software and sharing copyrighted music. Napster executives knew users were infringing on recording companies' copyrights, the court said. Napster's sole purpose was aiding copyright infringement, according to the court.

The recording industry also sued hundreds of Napster users, many of them college students, who were directly infringing on the recording companies' copyrights by copying sound recordings without permission.[187] The recording industry subpoenaed ISPs to obtain names of peer-to-peer networks users. A federal appellate court said the Digital Millennium Copyright Act did not allow using subpoenas to find names of peer-to-peer users.[188]

Responding to Napster's legal troubles, several new peer-to-peer systems appeared, most not using a central server. The recording industry continued to sue individual downloaders. A federal district court jury in 2010 awarded the recording industry $1.5 million in a case involving a woman who distributed 24 songs using the KaZaA P2P network.[189] A U.S. district court judge, also in 2010, ordered a Boston University graduate student to pay $67,500 in damages for illegally downloading and sharing 30 songs. A jury earlier had set damages in that case at $675,000.[190]

The recording and movie industries filed a copyright infringement lawsuit against two P2P networks, Grokster and Morpheus, claiming they contributed to copyright infringement by allowing their network users to illegally download copyrighted songs and movies. The U.S. Supreme Court said Grokster and Morpheus promoted and encouraged their users to violate the copyright law and therefore were themselves copyright infringers.[191] In its unanimous decision the Court said Grokster's and Morpheus' systems aided in copyright "infringement on a gigantic scale" and that "the probable scope of copyright infringement is staggering."[192] Grokster and Morpheus argued they were no more responsible for copyright infringement than was Sony for making videocassette recorders. Two decades earlier in *Sony v. University City Studios,* the U.S. Supreme Court had ruled that because VCRs had many non-infringing purposes, such as allowing a user to watch a television program at a later time, and Sony had not encouraged VCR owners to violate copyright law, Sony was not contributing to copyright infringement.[193] The Court said the difference between Sony and the file-sharing services is "inducement." Sony may have known VCRs could be used to infringe on copyright, but it did not encourage illegal copying. Grokster and Morpheus, on the other hand, aimed their services at former Napster users, did not develop filtering tools to prevent copyright infringement and sold advertising directed to people who were illegally downloading copyrighted digital content, the Court said. All this showed Grokster and Morpheus encouraged copyright infringement, or "induced" their users to illegally download protected content, according to the Court.

A federal district court shut down LimeWire, one of the last P2P services, in 2010.[194] But lawsuits have not stopped illegal file sharing. It is estimated that 95 percent of music downloads are illegal, amounting to 40 billion songs annually.[195] Considering this, the recording industry tried another tactic. It convinced Congress to have colleges and universities develop "plans to effectively combat the unauthorized distribution of copyrighted material" or risk losing federal funds.[196] School must offer students movies and music through subscription services "to the extent practicable" and prevent students from using P2P networks to obtain copyrighted material.

SUMMARY

USING COPYRIGHTED MUSIC MAY INVOLVE obtaining permission from several sources. Songwriters and music publishers usually have a music licensing organization—ASCAP, BMI or SESAC—represent them. The organizations grant licenses allowing use of compositions. Copyright holders receive compensation from the license fees.

When a composition is performed and recorded on a disc or other medium, the recorded performance is a sound recording. The disc containing the sound recording is a phonorecord. Both sound recordings and phonorecords have copyright protection, including bans on copying them without permission. However, sound recordings may be "performed" without permission. This occurs when a broadcast radio station plays a recording, for example. However, permission must be obtained to play a sound recording through a digital transmission, such as satellite radio.

Additionally, synchronization rights are required to copy a recorded composition onto videotape or film.

Some companies hire songwriters and performers to make sound recordings. These companies will sell CDs of their music and provide all necessary performance, copying and synchronization rights.

The Digital Millennium Copyright Act bans technologies that circumvent copyright protections. The law also protects Internet service providers against copyright suits if the ISP takes down material a copyright holder says is posted without permission.

The recording industry has sued Napster and others providing software that allows file sharing when the networks have been used for unauthorized copying of sound recordings. The recording industry has won some suits and lost some others. ∎

Trademarks

trademark A word, name, symbol or design used to identify a company's goods and distinguish them from similar products other companies make.

A **trademark** is a word, name, symbol or design used to identify a company's goods and distinguish them from similar products other companies make.[197] A service mark accomplishes the same purpose for services a firm provides. A trade name identifies a particular company rather than the company's product or service. Federal law also protects trade dress, which describes a product's total look, including size, shape, color, texture and graphics. The word "trademark" may be used generally to include all four of these categories. However, the law does not protect trade names or trade dress as completely as it protects the trademarks and service marks with which this section of the chapter primarily is concerned.

Companies use trademarks to advertise their products and services. Customers use trademarks to ensure they are getting the quality of goods or services they expect from a company. Trademarks are valuable. Consider the importance of McDonald's, Nike, Kodak, Kleenex and Coke as trademarks. Reaching for a soft drink, a customer does not want to have to read the small print on a can's label to confirm that a company named Coca-Cola in Atlanta, Ga., licenses the product. A customer simply wants to see the word "Coke" and know it is the product he or she wants. Coca-Cola's trademark is worth millions of dollars.

Trademarks may be considered brand names or logos. A logo is a design a company uses to identify its product. The Nike "swoosh" is an example of a logo. But in addition to words and logos, the list of what can be trademarked is lengthy: letters (CBS), numbers (VO-5), domain names (Amazon.com), slogans ("Just do it"), shapes (Coke bottle), colors (Corning Fiberglass pink insulation),[198] sounds (the roar of MGM's lion) and smells ("fresh cut grass" for tennis balls).[199]

A federal law called the Lanham Act protects trademarks that are eligible for registration with the U.S. Patent and Trademark Office.[200] The Lanham Act, as it has been amended, ensures that if a company complies with certain requirements, no other company may use a word, symbol, slogan or other such item that will confuse consumers about who supplies a particular product or service. The Lanham Act also prevents using a mark to falsely suggest a product's source even if the mark is not registered.[201]

realWorld Law

We Own That Panther!

Professional sports leagues and teams protect their trademarks because they are worth millions of dollars. The leagues' and teams' logos are used on clothing and other merchandise, in advertising for game tickets and as part of televised sports events. When a T-shirt maker puts the phrase "Who Dat," on shirts, it has used a phrase the National Football League says it has trademarked and is used by New Orleans Saints fans.[1] The words "Super Bowl" and "Olympics" also are trademarks.

Colleges also protect their trademarked logos. The University of Florida in 2010 ordered a private K–12 school to stop using an alligator as its mascot because it nearly matched Florida's Gator. The school said it could cost $60,000 to change its logo on everything from uniforms to the gym floor. Penn State told a Texas high school—1,400 miles from the university—its Cougar logo looked too much like Penn State's Nittany Lion. The University of Pittsburgh instructed a Toledo, Ohio, high school to stop using Pitt's trademarked Panther. The university and the high school both used the logo for sports teams and, more generally, to identify the schools. Using a trademark without permission for purposes similar to the trademark owner's use violates federal law.[2]

The Pittsburgh Panther mascot celebrates during a University of Pittsburgh win over Butler University in the 2011 NCAA men's basketball tournament.

1. Ken Sugiura & Michael Carvell, *In Brief*, Atl. J-.Const., Jan. 30, 2010, at 1C.
2. Adam Himmelsbach, *Colleges Fight to Keep Logos off High School Playing Fields*, N.Y. Times, Nov. 27, 2010, at A1, A3.

Distinctiveness Requirement

Distinctive words, designs or other indicators of a product's or service's origin are eligible for trademark registration.[202] The mark must distinguish one company's goods from another's. The word "popcorn" simply tells what product it is, not what company makes it. Act II indicates the popcorn comes from ConAgra. "Act II" is a distinctive term for a certain product, distinguishing it from other manufacturers' popcorn.

A trademark will be protected only if it is distinctive. There is a spectrum of distinctiveness in trademark law. The less unique a mark is—that is, the more broadly descriptive it is—the less likely that it will be eligible for trademark registration. If a mark is not sufficiently distinctive, it cannot be protected under federal law.

The most distinctive category is "fanciful marks." These are invented marks, including made-up words. A court found that Peterbilt and Kenworth are fanciful marks applied to trucks.[203]

Points of Law

Confusing?

The Lanham Act says trademark infringement occurs when a mark "is likely to cause confusion, or to cause a mistake, or to deceive as to the affiliation, connection, or association of such person with another person, or as to the origin, sponsorship, or approval of his or her goods, services, or commercial activities by another person. . . ."[1]

1. 15 U.S.C. § 1125(a)(1) (Lanham Act—U.S. trademark law).

The trucks' manufacturer sued a website operator who used the words "Peter-bilt" and "Kenworth" in the site's address without permission. The court said fanciful marks are the strongest and most distinctive trademarks possible. When a strong mark is infringed on, the court said, it becomes more likely that consumers would be confused. Therefore, the most trademark protection should be applied to fanciful marks, the court concluded. Lexus, Xerox and Exxon are examples of fanciful marks.

"Arbitrary marks," the next most distinctive category, are words that have ordinary meanings but not meanings applied to a product or service. For example, an apple is a fruit. But Apple is a trademark for computers and other products manufactured by Apple Computer, Inc. A dictionary will define the word "apple" as a fruit, but not as a computer. Numbers and letters arranged in a distinctive order may be arbitrary marks, such as BEBE for clothes[204] or V-8 for vegetable juice.[205]

"Suggestive marks" hint at a product's qualities but do not describe what the product is. One court said Coppertone, Orange Crush and Playboy are good examples of suggestive marks "because they conjure images of the associated products without directly describing those products."[206] A court held that the word "CarMax" is a suggestive mark for a used car dealership.[207] The word suggests that CarMax is involved in the automobile business but does not say the company sells used cars. A fanciful or arbitrary mark provides no hint about what a firm sells, but a suggestive mark implies its user's business. A suggestive mark requires consumers to use their imagination to discern the company's exact business.[208]

A "descriptive mark" leaves little to a consumer's imagination. The mark describes the product or service and may or may not suggest what company provided it. Many soft drink companies may use the word "refreshing" to describe their products. Generally, descriptive terms should be available for everyone's use—after all, they are words commonly used in everyday conversation. For this reason, they cannot be trademarked.

However, a descriptive mark may be a trademark if it has acquired a distinctive connection to the product for which it is used, or what courts call a "secondary meaning" beyond the word's commonly used meaning. Distinctive, arbitrary and suggestive marks do not require a secondary meaning, but descriptive marks do. To obtain a secondary meaning, the public must associate a word with a product's source. A connection with the product is not required, but a connection with the product's producer is. Courts do not agree on a test for finding a secondary meaning, but the Ninth Circuit's approach is illustrative: "(1) whether actual purchasers of the product bearing the claimed trademark associate the trademark with the producer; (2) the degree and manner of advertising under the claimed trademark; (3) the length and manner of use of the claimed trademark; and (4) whether use of the claimed trademark has been exclusive."[209]

Certain groups of descriptive words, such as geographic terms, have difficulty acquiring a secondary meaning. A geographic term cannot be a registered trademark if it only describes where the goods or services are made or offered. For example, a court refused to find that the word "Boston" had a secondary meaning in the phrase "Boston Beer."[210] Although the beer is manufactured in Boston, "Boston" means the Massachusetts city and is not connected in the public's mind with that brand of beer, the court said. The court did not allow Boston Beer to be a trademark. But 90 years ago the Supreme Court held "The American Girl" to be an arbitrary trademark for a brand of shoes because it did not suggest the shoes were made in America or even that the product was shoes.[211] A geographic term also cannot be a registered trademark if it is deceptive. For example, a ham processor located in Nebraska cannot use the term "Danish ham" as a trademark for its product.

Similarly, people's names must acquire a secondary meaning to be protected. The first names Steven and Linda, and the last names Jones and Smith, are shared by millions of people and therefore are not distinctive. In one case, Fabrikant & Sons, a jewelry company, trademarked the word "Fabrikant." Several years later, Fabrikant Fine Diamonds began business as a buyer and seller of jewelry. Both companies are located in New York City and both are owned by individuals named Fabrikant. A court ruled that Fabrikant Fine Diamonds had to either stop using the name Fabrikant or use a first name in front of the word to distinguish it from Fabrikant & Sons.[212] Otherwise the public would be confused, the court said.

Courts often consider three factors to rule in competing name cases. As one court put it, the factors are "(a) the interest of the plaintiff in protecting the good will which has attached to his personal name trademark, (b) the interest of the defendant in using his own name in his business activities and (c) the interest of the public in being free from confusion and deception."[213]

Finally, generic words will not be given trademark protection. A graham cracker manufacturer cannot use the word "cracker" as a trademark, for example. A manufacturer is not allowed to take a word commonly used to describe a product category and use it exclusively for the company's own purpose. For instance, Harley-Davidson could not use the word "hog" as a mark for its motorcycles,[214] nor could a concert promoter obtain a trademark for the term "summer jam" to advertise its summer concerts.[215]

Some marks that once were protected have become generic. This may happen when the public begins using the mark to mean a category of goods rather than a particular manufacturer's product. Thermos, cellophane, brassiere, aspirin, shredded wheat and monopoly (the board game) all once were protected copyrights that became generic words.[216] Courts ask what a word's primary significance is to the public. If the public thinks of a word as describing a class of goods—a vacuum bottle is a thermos—the word is generic and cannot be a protected mark. If the word primarily means a particular manufacturer—Xerox makes Xerox copying machines—the word will remain a trademark.[217]

Companies can take several steps to prevent a trademark from becoming generic. Among other actions, a company should select a distinctive mark, advertise the goods using both the trademark and the product's generic word (Kleenex facial tissue), use advertisements to educate the public that the product's trademark is not a generic word and use the trademark on several different products.[218]

Registering a Trademark

A history of using a distinctive mark to identify a product can give the mark protection even if it is not registered with the U.S. Patent and Trademark Office (PTO). The first person or company to use the mark owns it. State courts recognize common law rights in marks within the geographic area where the mark is used. It is not necessary to register a mark to give it common law protection. An owner of a mark protected by common law may use the symbols ™ (trademark) or ˢᴹ (service mark), but these are not recognized by statute.

Federal registration provides a mark more protection than does the common law, however. Registration is for nationwide use and lets competitors know that a company owns the mark. Registration also dates when the mark first was used if another company argues it had a prior interest in the mark. A company may use the statutory symbol for registered marks. The symbol ® or the phrase "Registered U.S. Patent and Trademark Office" is acceptable. If a registered mark is infringed on, its owner may sue in federal court. And after a company uses a registered mark for five years, there are few grounds on which the registration may be contested, providing nearly complete protection.[219]

A mark must be registered with the PTO to have statutory protection under the Lanham Act.[220] Registering a mark requires submitting to the PTO an application form, a drawing of the mark and a filing fee. If the registration is based on prior use, specimens of the use also must be submitted.

An individual or company may register a mark on either the Principal Register or the Supplemental Register. The Principal Register gives all legal rights to a distinctive mark being used in commerce.[221] The Principal Register also can be used for marks that may be used in the future. However, using the Principal Register to reserve a mark for future use does not allow a federal registration to be issued. Descriptive marks go on the Supplemental Register, with their owners hoping to move them to the Principal Register once secondary meaning has been established.[222]

Registering a mark is not the same as registering a copyright. The Copyright Office registers any material sent to it with a correct form, copies of the work and a fee. Only after registration may a copyright be challenged. The PTO, however, will not register a mark that does not qualify. The PTO will not register a mark if it is considered immoral or deceptive, includes a flag or other insignia of any country or U.S. state or city, resembles another registered mark, includes a name or other identification of a living person without the individual's consent or is only a descriptive mark without secondary meaning.

Nor will the PTO register a mark identical or similar to an existing mark. PTO examiners carefully consider each mark submitted for registration. A mark proposed for registration is published in the PTO's Official Gazette. Any company believing the mark will cause consumer confusion and harm the company's use of a similar mark may object. The PTO will resolve any objections, allowing or dismissing them. Finally, if the PTO examiner approves the mark and there are no objections, the mark is registered.

During the sixth year after registration, a mark owner must file an affidavit confirming the mark has been in continued use.[223] Marks registered before Nov. 16, 1989, were enforced for 20-year periods. Marks registered after that date have a 10-year term. Registrations may be renewed indefinitely.[224]

Trademark law's complexity means a trademark attorney needs to be involved in registering a mark. A work's creator easily can register a copyright, but registering a trademark requires expertise and experience.

Domain Names

The Internet's development caused Congress to adapt trademark law to the new technology as Congress did with copyright law. Web addresses, or domain names, have been a particular problem for trademark law. Domain names may be trademarked, although the domain name suffixes, such as .com or .org, are not considered part of a trademarked domain name. A domain name registered as a trademark is protected against infringement.

A cybersquatter is a person who claims domain names that include trademarks or famous people's names. When cybersquatting began, trademark owners often sued, frequently successfully. Congress tried to stop cybersquatting by adopting the Anticybersquatting Consumer Protection Act (ACPA) in 1999.[225] The law provides civil and criminal remedies for registering a domain name with the intention of selling it to the trademark owner. The ACPA applies to a domain name identical or confusingly similar to a trademark and to a domain name that disparages or injures a well-known trademark. A defendant must have acted in bad faith to be liable under the statute. Damages can be as high as $100,000.

In one ACPA case, a company named Spider Webs registered hundreds of domain names, including ErnestandJulioGallo.com. The Gallo winery sued. A federal appellate court held the ACPA constitutional and said the unauthorized domain name could injure Gallo's trademark.[226] Spider Webs admitted it held on to the domain name hoping the ACPA would be found unconstitutional. That showed bad faith, the appellate court said. The court upheld a $25,000 damage award and a court order preventing Spider Webs from registering any domain name that used "Gallo" or "Ernest and Julio."

Two companies might have identical or similar trademarks for two different products. The companies' domain names would be the same—chip.com for a computer chip company and chip.com for a potato chip company. Who may use the domain name? One court said trademark law takes precedence over domain registration. The court gave a disputed domain name—moviebuff—to the company that first used the mark.[227] However, if two domain names are similar but both describe the companies' products, courts may allow the firms to continue using the names. For example, the manufacturer of Beanie Babies sued a company using bargainbeanies.com as a domain name. The bargain beanies company sold used beanbag animals. A federal appellate court said preventing a firm from using a domain name describing its business would be like "forbidding a used car dealer who specializes in selling Chevrolets to mention" the car's name in the dealer's advertising.[228] The court allowed both companies to use their domain names.

Trademark Infringement

Valid trademarks are protected by the common law or federal registration. Competing marks that confuse consumers about the source of a product or service may be grounds for lawsuits. Also, marks that lessen a competing trademark's value are not permitted.

Anyone may use a protected trademark in a way that is not confusing. Including the words "Pontiac," "Tommy Hilfiger" and "Burger King" in this paragraph is not a trademark infringement. Using marks for informational purposes is a fair use. The First Amendment protects using a competitor's trademark in comparative advertising, courts have ruled.[229] However, a competitor may not alter a mark in a comparative ad. In one case, a competitor to John Deere's lawn tractor business aired a comparative ad that somewhat distorted and animated Deere's trademarked deer logo. The ad showed the deer jumping through a hoop that breaks apart, for instance. The ad diminished Deere's logo in consumers' minds, a court ruled.[230]

Four Beach Boys band members brought a trademark infringement suit against former band member Al Jardine to prevent his using the name Beach Boys Family and Friends. Pictured clockwise from far left are Jardine, Mike Love, Brian Wilson, Carl Wilson and Dennis Wilson.

Trademark infringement occurs when there is a likelihood of confusion.[231] This may occur when a company asks the PTO to register a mark. If an examiner finds that the mark will confuse consumers about a product's or service's origin, the PTO will not register the mark. The question also may arise when a company uses a mark and a competitor using a similar mark claims there will be a likelihood of confusion. A court must decide which company will be allowed to use the mark. In one case, a federal appellate court said using a singing group's name without its permission could confuse people, making them think the group sponsored a new band.[232] Al Jardine, a former member of the Beach Boys, began touring and performing as the Beach Boys Family and Friends. Using the Beach Boys' name was trademark infringement, the court ruled.

Similar—even identical—marks may not cause confusion if the goods for which the marks are used are not the same. Wendy's automobile parts may coexist with

realWorld Law

Diluting a Trademark

A federal appellate court used the famous jewelry store Tiffany's name to help explain what the word "dilution" means in trademark law:

> Suppose an upscale restaurant calls itself "Tiffany." There is little danger that the consuming public will think it's dealing with a branch of the Tiffany jewelry store if it patronizes this restaurant. But when consumers next see the name "Tiffany" they may think about both the restaurant and the jewelry store, and if so the efficacy of the name as an identifier of the store will be diminished. . . . So "blurring" is one form of dilution.
>
> Now suppose that the "restaurant" that adopts the name "Tiffany" is actually a striptease joint. Again, and indeed even more certainly than in the previous case, consumers will not think the striptease joint under common ownership with the jewelry store. But because of the inveterate tendency of the human mind to proceed by association, every time they think of the word "Tiffany" their image of the fancy jewelry store will be tarnished by the association of the word with the strip joint. So "tarnishment" is a second form of dilution.[1]

1. Ty, Inc. v. Perryman, 306 F.3d 509, 511 (7th Cir. 2002), *cert. denied*, 538 U.S. 971 (2003).

Wendy's restaurants if a court says consumers would not think the restaurant company also owns the auto parts store.

Courts use a variety of criteria to determine whether consumers likely will be confused by similar marks. These include the marks' similarities, the similarities of products or services for which the marks are used, how consumers purchase the goods (impulse buying or careful consideration), how well known the first-used mark is, actual confusion that can be proved and how long both marks have been used without confusion.[233]

Using a famous trademark in a way that disparages the mark or diminishes its effectiveness is known as "dilution." Congress adopted an antidilution statute in 1996 and revised it in 2006.[234] Dilution may happen in two ways. First, a product name similar to a well-known trademark could make the famous mark less distinctive. Consumers' attention to the famous mark could be distracted by the similar product name. The law calls this "blurring." It is whittling away a trademark's selling power. Second, a poorly made product using a name similar to a famous trademark could cause consumers to think less of the well-known mark. This is "tarnishment," linking a substandard product or one placed in an unsavory context with the famous mark.[235]

Congress revised the antidilution law in 2006 in response to a 2003 U.S. Supreme Court decision. The case involved an "adult novelties" store in Elizabethtown, Ky. The store initially opened as Victor's Secret. Victoria's Secret, which operates more than 750 retail stores and distributes 400 million catalogs annually, asked the store's owners not to use the name Victor's Secret. The owners changed the store's name to Victor's Little Secret. Victoria's Secret sued for trademark dilution. The Supreme Court said Victoria's Secret had to show that actual dilution of its trademark occurred.[236] The Court suggested that might be difficult for the large corporation to do. The Court said there is "a complete absence of evidence of any lessening of the capacity of the Victoria's Secret mark to identify . . . goods . . . sold in Victoria's Secret stores or advertised in its catalogs."[237]

Congress rejected that approach. Its antidilution law revision permitted companies with famous trademarks to show only a likelihood of dilution. The company does not have to show actual dilution of its trademarks' effectiveness. But the core of the antidilution law remains the same: A company does not have to prove it is likely consumers will be confused between a famous trademark and a similar product or service name. Rather, the company only has to show another firm's similar mark has diminished the well-known mark's distinctiveness or injured its reputation.

Nearly half the states have antidilution statutes. These laws protect dilution of all marks used in the state, not just the famous marks the federal antidilution law protects.

Several remedies are available for trademark infringement. First, a company or individual notified of an alleged infringement may voluntarily stop using the disputed mark. Second, a court may issue an order requiring the infringing company to stop using the mark. Initially, a temporary restraining order or preliminary injunction will stop the disputed mark's distribution while a court decides if infringement took place. A permanent injunction prevents the disputed mark's use forever. If a mark owner is able to prove actual consumer confusion, a court may award monetary damages against the infringer.

Trademark Infringement Defenses

The Lanham Act lists nine defenses to a trademark infringement action.[238] Most turn on disputed facts. For example, a defendant might argue that the registered trademark was obtained fraudulently or that the trademark has been abandoned and no longer is in use. A defense against trademark infringement is that the mark misrepresents a product's origin. A defendant might claim to have used and registered the mark first.

The Lanham Act also provides a fair use defense.[239] This permits using one company's trademark to describe another company's product. Courts will accept the fair use defense if the defendant used the mark to describe its goods and not as a trademark. Also, the use cannot cause customer confusion. For example, a company sold a VCR with two decks in one machine. The company called its product VCR-2. Another firm sold products to which two VCRs could be attached. This firm labeled the products' terminals VCR-1 and VCR-2. Because "VCR-2" merely described the product, a court found it a fair use of the first company's mark.[240]

Referring to the defendant's own product or service by using the plaintiff's mark without permission also may be a fair use. This may be done in comparative advertising, but it also occurs in other contexts. In one case, two newspapers used the trademarked name of a band, New Kids on the Block, to promote the newspapers' telephone polls about the band. The papers used the band's name to describe the papers' own product—the telephone poll. A court found this a fair use because the band could not be identified without using its trademarked name and the papers did not suggest that the band endorsed the poll.[241]

The antidilution law also provides a fair use exception. Using a famous trademark for comparative advertising, parody or all forms of news reporting and commentary is not an infringement.[242]

SUMMARY

A FEDERAL LAW, THE LANHAM ACT, PROTECTS trademarks from infringement. The common law protects unregistered marks within the geographic area where they are used. Marks may be words, designs, colors and other devices identifying the source of products or services. A trademark will be protected only if it is distinctive. Distinctiveness ranges from strongly distinctive to merely descriptive and generic. Merely descriptive and generic marks cannot be protected.

A mark must be registered with the U.S. Patent and Trademark Office to have protection under the Lanham Act. Registering is a complex process and marks may be rejected for a variety of reasons.

Domain names may be registered as trademarks. The federal Anticybersquatting Consumer Protection Act is intended to prevent people from claiming domain names only to sell them to companies or individuals. ∎

Cases for Study

Thinking About It

The following excerpts are from two of the three copyright cases the U.S. Supreme Court has decided in the 21st century (*New York Times Co. v. Tasini*, discussed in this chapter, is the third). As you read these case excerpts, keep the following questions in mind:

- Does the U.S. Supreme Court seem to be favoring copyright holders or users of copyrighted material?

- Do you agree with *Eldred*'s interpretation of "for a limited time" in the U.S. Constitution's copyright provision? Why?

- Do you agree with the distinction drawn in *Grokster* between that case and the *Sony* decision allowing home taping of television programs? Why?

Eldred v. Ashcroft
SUPREME COURT OF THE UNITED STATES
537 U.S. 186 (2003)

JUSTICE RUTH BADER GINSBURG delivered the Court's opinion:

This case concerns the authority the Constitution assigns to Congress to prescribe the duration of copyrights. The Copyright and Patent Clause of the Constitution, Art. I, §8, cl. 8, provides as to copyrights: "Congress shall have Power . . . to promote the Progress of Science . . . by securing [to Authors] for limited Times . . . the exclusive Right to their . . . Writings." In 1998, in the measure here under inspection, Congress enlarged the duration of copyrights by 20 years. As in the case of prior extensions, principally in 1831, 1909, and 1976, Congress provided for application of the enlarged terms to existing and future copyrights alike.

Petitioners are individuals and businesses whose products or services build on copyrighted works that have gone into the public domain. They seek a determination that the CTEA [Copyright Term Extension Act] fails constitutional review under both the Copyright Clause's "limited Times" prescription and the First Amendment's free speech guarantee. Under the 1976 Copyright Act, copyright protection generally lasted from the work's creation until 50 years after the author's death. Under the CTEA, most copyrights now run from creation until 70 years after the author's death. Petitioners do not challenge the "life-plus-70-years" time span itself. "Whether 50 years is enough, or 70 years too much," they acknowledge, "is not a judgment meet for this Court." Congress went awry, petitioners maintain, not with respect to newly created works, but in enlarging the term for published works with existing copyrights. The "limited Time" in effect when a copyright is secured, petitioners urge, becomes the constitutional boundary, a clear line beyond the power of Congress to extend. As to the First Amendment, petitioners contend that the CTEA is a content-neutral regulation of speech that fails inspection under the heightened judicial scrutiny appropriate for such regulations.

In accord with the District Court and the Court of Appeals, we reject petitioners' challenges to the CTEA. In that 1998 legislation, as in all previous copyright term extensions, Congress placed existing and future copyrights in parity. In prescribing that alignment, we hold, Congress acted within its authority and did not transgress constitutional limitations.

I

A

We evaluate petitioners' challenge to the constitutionality of the CTEA against the backdrop of Congress' previous exercises of its authority under the Copyright Clause. The Nation's first copyright statute, enacted in 1790, provided a federal copyright term of 14 years from the date of publication, renewable for an additional 14 years if the author survived the first term. The 1790 Act's renewable 14-year term applied to existing works (*i.e.,* works already published and works created but not yet published) and future works alike. Congress expanded the federal copyright term to 42 years in 1831 (28 years from publication, renewable for an additional 14 years), and to 56 years in 1909 (28 years from publication, renewable for an additional 28 years). Both times, Congress applied the new copyright term to existing and future works; to qualify for the 1831 extension, an existing work had to be in its initial copyright term at the time the Act became effective.

In 1976, Congress altered the method for computing federal copyright terms. For works created by identified natural persons, the 1976 Act provided that federal copyright protection would run from the work's creation, not—as in the 1790, 1831, and 1909 Acts—its publication; protection would last until 50 years after the author's death. In these respects, the 1976 Act aligned United States copyright terms with the then-dominant international standard adopted under the Berne Convention for the Protection of Literary and Artistic Works. For anonymous works, pseudonymous works, and works made for hire, the 1976 Act provided a term of 75 years from publication or 100 years from creation, whichever expired first.

These new copyright terms, the 1976 Act instructed, governed all works not published by its effective date of January 1, 1978, regardless of when the works were created. For published works with existing copyrights as of that date, the 1976 Act granted a copyright term of 75 years from the date of publication, a 19-year increase over the 56-year term applicable under the 1909 Act.

The measure at issue here, the CTEA, installed the fourth major duration extension of federal copyrights. Retaining the general structure of the 1976 Act, the CTEA enlarges the terms of all existing and future copyrights by 20 years. For works created by identified natural persons, the term now lasts from creation until 70 years after the author's death. This standard harmonizes the baseline United States copyright term with the term adopted by the European Union in 1993. For anonymous works, pseudonymous works, and works made for hire, the term is 95 years from publication or 120 years from creation, whichever expires first.

Paralleling the 1976 Act, the CTEA applies these new terms to all works not published by January 1, 1978. For works published before 1978 with existing copyrights as of the CTEA's effective date, the CTEA extends the term to 95 years from publication. Thus, in common with the 1831, 1909, and 1976 Acts, the CTEA's new terms apply to both future and existing copyrights.

B

Petitioners' suit challenges the CTEA's constitutionality under both the Copyright Clause and the First Amendment. . . .

II

A

We address first the determination of the courts below that Congress has authority under the Copyright Clause to extend the terms of existing copyrights. Text, history, and precedent, we conclude, confirm that the Copyright Clause empowers Congress to prescribe "limited Times" for copyright protection and to secure the same level and duration of protection for all copyright holders, present and future.

The CTEA's baseline term of life plus 70 years, petitioners concede, qualifies as a "limited Time" as applied to future copyrights. Petitioners contend, however, that existing copyrights extended to endure for that same term are not "limited." Petitioners' argument essentially reads into the text of the Copyright Clause the command that a time prescription, once set, becomes forever "fixed" or "inalterable." The word "limited," however, does not convey a meaning so constricted. At the time of the Framing, that word meant what it means today: "confined within certain bounds," "restrained," or "circumscribed." Thus understood, a time span appropriately "limited" as applied to future copyrights does not automatically cease to be "limited" when applied to existing copyrights. And as we observe, there is no cause to suspect that a purpose to evade the "limited Times" prescription prompted Congress to adopt the CTEA.

To comprehend the scope of Congress' power under the Copyright Clause, "a page of history is worth a volume of logic." History reveals an unbroken congressional practice of granting to authors of works with existing copyrights the benefit of term extensions so that all under copyright protection will be governed evenhandedly under the same regime. As earlier recounted, the First Congress accorded the protections of the Nation's first federal copyright statute to existing and future works alike. Since then, Congress has regularly applied duration extensions to both existing and future copyrights. . . .

Congress' consistent historical practice of applying newly enacted copyright terms to future and existing copyrights reflects a judgment stated concisely by Representative Huntington at the time of the 1831 Act: "[J]ustice, policy, and equity alike forbid" that an "author who had sold his [work] a week ago, be placed in a worse situation than the author who should sell his work the day after the passing of [the] act." The CTEA follows this historical practice by keeping the duration provisions of the 1976 Act largely in place and simply adding 20 years to each of them. Guided by text, history, and precedent, we cannot agree with petitioners' submission that extending the duration of existing copyrights is categorically beyond Congress' authority under the Copyright Clause.

Satisfied that the CTEA complies with the "limited Times" prescription, we turn now to whether it is a rational exercise of the legislative authority conferred by the Copyright Clause. On that point, we defer substantially to Congress.

The CTEA reflects judgments of a kind Congress typically makes, judgments we cannot dismiss as outside the Legislature's domain. As respondent describes, a key factor in the CTEA's passage was a 1993 European Union (EU) directive instructing EU members to establish a copyright term of life plus 70 years. Consistent with the Berne Convention, the EU directed its members to deny this longer term to the works of any non-EU country whose laws did not secure the same extended term. By extending the baseline United States copyright term to life plus 70 years, Congress sought to ensure that American authors would receive the same copyright protection in Europe as their European counterparts. The CTEA may also provide greater incentive for American and other authors to create and disseminate their work in the United States. . . .

In addition to international concerns, Congress passed the CTEA in light of demographic, economic, and technological changes, and rationally credited projections that longer terms would encourage copyright holders to invest in the restoration and public distribution of their works.

In sum, we find that the CTEA is a rational enactment; we are not at liberty to second-guess congressional determinations and policy judgments of this order, however debatable or arguably unwise they may be. Accordingly, we cannot conclude that the CTEA—which continues the unbroken congressional practice of treating future and existing copyrights in parity for term extension purposes—is an impermissible exercise of Congress' power under the Copyright Clause.

B

Petitioners' Copyright Clause arguments rely on several novel readings of the Clause. We next address these arguments and explain why we find them unpersuasive.

1

Petitioners contend that even if the CTEA's 20-year term extension is literally a "limited Time," permitting Congress to extend existing copyrights allows it to evade the "limited Times" constraint by creating effectively perpetual copyrights through repeated extensions. We disagree.

As the Court of Appeals observed [in this case], a regime of perpetual copyrights "clearly is not the situation before us." Nothing before this Court warrants construction of the CTEA's 20-year term extension as a congressional attempt to evade or override the "limited Times" constraint. Critically, we again emphasize, petitioners fail to show how the CTEA crosses a constitutionally significant threshold with respect to "limited Times" that the 1831, 1909, and 1976 Acts did not. Those earlier Acts did not create perpetual copyrights, and neither does the CTEA.

2

Petitioners dominantly advance a series of arguments all premised on the proposition that Congress may not extend an existing copyright absent new consideration from the author. They pursue this main theme under three headings. Petitioners contend that the CTEA's extension of existing copyrights (1) overlooks the requirement of "originality," (2) fails to "promote the Progress of Science," and (3) ignores copyright's *quid pro quo*.

Petitioners' "originality" argument draws on *Feist Publications, Inc. v. Rural Telephone Service Co.*, 499 U.S. 340 (1991). In *Feist,* we observed that "the *sine qua non* of copyright is originality," and held that copyright protection is unavailable to "a narrow category of works in which the creative spark is utterly lacking or so trivial as to be virtually nonexistent." Relying on *Feist,* petitioners urge that even if a work is sufficiently "original" to qualify for copyright protection in the first instance, any extension of the copyright's duration is impermissible because, once published, a work is no longer original.

Feist, however, did not touch on the duration of copyright protection. Rather, the decision addressed the core question of copyrightability, *i.e.,* the "creative spark" a work must have to be eligible for copyright protection at all. Explaining the originality requirement, *Feist* trained on the Copyright Clause words "Authors" and "Writings." The decision did not construe the "limited Times" for which a work may

be protected, and the originality requirement has no bearing on that prescription.

More forcibly, petitioners contend that the CTEA's extension of existing copyrights does not "promote the Progress of Science" as contemplated by the preambular language of the Copyright Clause. To sustain this objection, petitioners do not argue that the Clause's preamble is an independently enforceable limit on Congress' legislative power. Rather, they maintain that the preambular language identifies the sole end to which Congress may legislate; accordingly, they conclude, the meaning of "limited Times" must be "determined in light of that specified end." The CTEA's extension of existing copyrights categorically fails to "promote the Progress of Science," petitioners argue, because it does not stimulate the creation of new works but merely adds value to works already created.

As petitioners point out, we have described the Copyright Clause as "both a grant of power and a limitation," and have said that "[t]he primary objective of copyright" is "to promote the Progress of Science." The "constitutional command," we have recognized, is that Congress, to the extent it enacts copyright laws at all, create a "system" that "promote[s] the Progress of Science."

We have also stressed, however, that it is generally for Congress, not the courts, to decide how best to pursue the Copyright Clause's objectives. The justifications we earlier set out for Congress' enactment of the CTEA provide a rational basis for the conclusion that the CTEA "promotes the Progress of Science."

On the issue of copyright duration, Congress, from the start, has routinely applied new definitions or adjustments of the copyright term to both future works and existing works not yet in the public domain. Such consistent congressional practice is entitled to "very great weight, and when it is remembered that the rights thus established have not been disputed during a period of [over two] centur[ies], it is almost conclusive." Indeed, "[t]his Court has repeatedly laid down the principle that a contemporaneous legislative exposition of the Constitution when the founders of our Government and framers of our Constitution were actively participating in public affairs, acquiesced in for a long term of years, fixes the construction to be given [the Constitution's] provisions." Congress' unbroken practice since the founding generation thus overwhelms petitioners' argument that the CTEA's extension of existing copyrights fails *per se* to "promote the Progress of Science."

Closely related to petitioners' argument, or a variant of it, is their assertion that the Copyright Clause "imbeds a quid pro quo." They contend, in this regard, that Congress may grant to an "Author" an "exclusive Right" for a "limited Time," but only in exchange for a "Writing." Congress' power to confer copyright protection, petitioners argue, is thus contingent upon an exchange: The author of an original work receives an "exclusive Right" for a "limited Time" in exchange for a dedication to the public thereafter. Extending an existing copyright without demanding additional consideration, petitioners maintain, bestows an unpaid-for benefit on copyright holders and their heirs, in violation of the *quid pro quo* requirement.

We can demur to petitioners' description of the Copyright Clause as a grant of legislative authority empowering Congress "to secure a bargain—this for that." But the legislative evolution earlier recalled demonstrates what the bargain entails. Given the consistent placement of existing copyright holders in parity with future holders, the author of a work created in the last 170 years would reasonably comprehend, as the "this" offered her, a copyright not only for the time in place when protection is gained, but also for any renewal or extension legislated during that time. Congress could rationally seek to "promote . . . Progress" by including in every copyright statute an express guarantee that authors would receive the benefit of any later legislative extension of the copyright term. Nothing in the Copyright Clause bars Congress from creating the same incentive by adopting the same position as a matter of unbroken practice. . . .

III

Petitioners separately argue that the CTEA is a content-neutral regulation of speech that fails heightened judicial review under the First Amendment. We reject petitioners' plea for imposition of uncommonly strict scrutiny on a copyright scheme that incorporates its own speech-protective purposes and safeguards. The Copyright Clause and First Amendment were adopted close in time. This proximity indicates that, in the Framers' view, copyright's limited monopolies are compatible with free speech principles, indeed, copyright's purpose is to *promote* the creation and publication of free expression. As *Harper & Row* observed: "[T]he Framers intended copyright itself to be the engine of free expression. By establishing a marketable right to the use of one's expression, copyright supplies the economic incentive to create and disseminate ideas."

In addition to spurring the creation and publication of new expression, copyright law contains built-in First Amendment accommodations. First, it distinguishes between ideas and expression and makes only the latter eligible for copyright protection. Specifically, [federal law] provides: "In no case does copyright protection for an original work of authorship extend to any idea, procedure, process, system, method of operation, concept, principle, or discovery, regardless of the form in which it is described, explained, illustrated, or embodied in such work." As we said in *Harper & Row,* this "idea/expression dichotomy strikes a definitional balance between the First Amendment and the Copyright Act by permitting free communication of facts while still protecting an author's expression." Due to this distinction, every idea, theory, and fact in a copyrighted work becomes instantly available for public exploitation at the moment of publication.

Second, the "fair use" defense allows the public to use not only facts and ideas contained in a copyrighted work, but also expression itself in certain circumstances. [The Copyright Act] provides: "[T]he fair use of a copyrighted work, including such use by reproduction in copies . . . , for purposes such as criticism, comment, news reporting, teaching (including multiple copies for classroom use), scholarship, or research, is not an infringement of copyright." The fair use defense affords considerable "latitude for scholarship and comment."

The CTEA itself supplements these traditional First Amendment safeguards. First, it allows libraries, archives, and similar institutions to "reproduce" and "distribute, display, or perform in facsimile or digital form" copies of certain published works "during the last 20 years of any term of copyright . . . for purposes of preservation, scholarship, or research" if the work is not already being exploited commercially and further copies are unavailable at a reasonable price. Second, Title II of the CTEA, known as the Fairness in Music Licensing Act of 1998, exempts small businesses, restaurants, and like entities from having to pay performance royalties on music played from licensed radio, television, and similar facilities. . . .

IV

If petitioners' vision of the Copyright Clause held sway, it would do more than render the CTEA's duration extensions unconstitutional as to existing works. Indeed, petitioners' assertion that the provisions of the CTEA are not severable would make the CTEA's enlarged terms invalid even as to tomorrow's work. The 1976 Act's time extensions, which set the pattern that the CTEA followed, would be vulnerable as well.

As we read the Framers' instruction, the Copyright Clause empowers Congress to determine the intellectual property regimes that, overall, in that body's judgment, will serve the ends of the Clause. Beneath the facade of their inventive constitutional interpretation, petitioners forcefully urge that Congress pursued very bad policy in prescribing the CTEA's long terms. The wisdom of Congress' action, however, is not within our province to second guess. Satisfied that the legislation before us remains inside the domain the Constitution assigns to the First Branch, we affirm the judgment of the Court of Appeals.

It is so ordered.

Metro-Goldwyn-Mayer Studios, Inc. v. Grokster, Ltd.
SUPREME COURT OF THE UNITED STATES
545 U.S. 913 (2005)

JUSTICE DAVID SOUTER delivered the Court's opinion:

The question is under what circumstances the distributor of a product capable of both lawful and unlawful use is liable for acts of copyright infringement by third parties using the product. We hold that one who distributes a device with the object of promoting its use to infringe copyright, as shown by clear expression or other affirmative steps taken to foster infringement, is liable for the resulting acts of infringement by third parties.

I

Respondents Grokster, Ltd., and StreamCast Networks, Inc., defendants in the trial court, distribute free software products that allow computer users to share electronic files through peer-to-peer networks, so called because users' computers communicate directly with each other, not through central servers. The advantage of peer-to-peer networks over information networks of other types shows up in their substantial and growing popularity. Because they need no central computer server to mediate the exchange of information or files among users, the high-bandwidth communications capacity for a server may be dispensed with, and the need for costly server storage space is eliminated. Since copies of a file (particularly a popular one) are available on many users' computers, file requests and retrievals may be faster than on other types of networks, and since file exchanges do not travel through a server, communications can take place between any computers that remain connected to the network without risk that a glitch in the server will disable the network in its entirety. Given these benefits in security, cost, and efficiency, peer-to-peer networks are employed to store and distribute electronic files by universities, government agencies, corporations, and libraries, among others.

Other users of peer-to-peer networks include individual recipients of Grokster's and StreamCast's software, and although the networks that they enjoy through using the software can be used to share any type of digital file, they have prominently employed those networks in sharing copyrighted music and video files without authorization. A group of copyright holders (MGM for short, but including motion picture studios, recording companies, songwriters, and music publishers) sued Grokster and StreamCast for their users' copyright infringements, alleging that they knowingly and intentionally distributed their software to enable users to reproduce and distribute the copyrighted works in violation of the Copyright Act. MGM sought damages and an injunction.

Discovery during the litigation revealed the way the software worked, the business aims of each defendant company, and the predilections of the users. Grokster's eponymous software employs what is known as FastTrack technology, a protocol developed by others and licensed to Grokster. StreamCast distributes a very similar product except that its software, called Morpheus, relies on what is known as Gnutella technology. A user who downloads and installs either software possesses the protocol to send requests for files directly to the computers of others using software compatible with FastTrack or Gnutella. On the FastTrack network opened by the Grokster software, the user's request goes to a computer given an indexing capacity by the software and designated a supernode, or to some other computer with comparable power and capacity to collect temporary indexes of the files available on the computers of users connected to it. The supernode (or indexing computer) searches its own index and may communicate the search request to other supernodes. If the file is found, the supernode discloses its location to the computer requesting it, and the requesting user can download the file directly from the computer located. The copied file is placed in a designated sharing folder on the requesting user's computer, where it is available for other users to download in turn, along with any other file in that folder.

In the Gnutella network made available by Morpheus, the process is mostly the same, except that in some versions of the Gnutella protocol there are no supernodes. In these versions, peer computers using the protocol communicate directly with each other. When a user enters a search request into the Morpheus software, it sends the request to computers connected with it, which in turn pass the request along to other connected peers. The search results are communicated to the requesting computer, and the user can download desired files directly from peers' computers. As this description indicates, Grokster and StreamCast use no servers to intercept the content of the search requests or to mediate the file transfers conducted by users of the software, there being no central point through which the substance of the communications passes in either direction.

Although Grokster and StreamCast . . . argue that potential noninfringing uses of their software are significant in kind, even if infrequent in practice. Some musical performers, for example, have gained new audiences by distributing their copyrighted works for free across peer-to-peer networks, and some distributors of unprotected content have used peer-to-peer networks to disseminate files, Shakespeare being an example. . . .

. . . MGM's evidence gives reason to think that the vast majority of users' downloads are acts of infringement, and because well over 100 million copies of the software in question are known to have been downloaded, and billions of files are shared across the FastTrack and Gnutella networks each month, the probable scope of copyright infringement is staggering.

Grokster and StreamCast concede the infringement in most downloads, . . . and it is uncontested that they are aware that users employ their software primarily to download copyrighted files, even if the decentralized FastTrack and Gnutella networks fail to reveal which files are being copied, and when. From time to time, moreover, the companies have learned about their users' infringement directly, as from users who have sent e-mail to each company with questions about playing copyrighted movies they had downloaded, to whom the companies have responded with guidance. And MGM notified the companies of 8 million copyrighted files that could be obtained using their software.

Grokster and StreamCast are not, however, merely passive recipients of information about infringing use. The record is replete with evidence that from the moment Grokster and StreamCast began to distribute their free software, each one clearly voiced the objective that recipients use it to download copyrighted works, and each took active steps to encourage infringement.

After the notorious file-sharing service, Napster, was sued by copyright holders for facilitation of copyright infringement, StreamCast gave away a software program of a kind known as OpenNap, designed as compatible with the Napster program and open to Napster users for downloading files from other Napster and OpenNap users' computers. Evidence indicates that "[i]t was always [StreamCast's] intent to use [its OpenNap network] to be able to capture email addresses of [its] initial target market so that [it] could promote [its] StreamCast Morpheus interface to them"; indeed, the OpenNap program was engineered "to leverage Napster's 50 million user base." . . .

. . . StreamCast developed promotional materials to market its service as the best Napster alternative. . . .

The evidence that Grokster sought to capture the market of former Napster users is sparser but revealing, for Grokster launched its own OpenNap system called Swaptor and inserted digital codes into its Web site so that computer users using Web search engines to look for "Napster" or "[f]ree filesharing" would be directed to the Grokster Web site, where they could download the Grokster software. And Grokster's name is an apparent derivative of Napster. . . .

In addition to this evidence of express promotion, marketing, and intent to promote further, the business models employed by Grokster and StreamCast confirm that their principal object was use of their software to download copyrighted works. Grokster and StreamCast receive no revenue from users, who obtain the software itself for nothing. Instead, both companies generate income by selling advertising space, and they stream the advertising to Grokster and Morpheus users while they are employing the programs. As the number of users of each program increases, advertising opportunities become worth more. While there is doubtless some demand for free Shakespeare, the evidence shows that substantive volume is a function of free access to copyrighted work. Users seeking Top 40 songs, for example, or the latest release by Modest Mouse, are certain to be far more numerous than those seeking a free Decameron, and Grokster and StreamCast translated that demand into dollars.

Finally, there is no evidence that either company made an effort to filter copyrighted material from users' downloads or otherwise impede the sharing of copyrighted files. Although Grokster appears to have sent e-mails warning users about infringing content when it received threatening notice from the copyright holders, it never blocked anyone from continuing to use its software to share copyrighted files. StreamCast not only rejected another company's offer of help to monitor infringement, but blocked the Internet Protocol addresses of entities it believed were trying to engage in such monitoring on its networks. . . .

II

A

MGM and many of the *amici* fault the Court of Appeals's holding for upsetting a sound balance between the respective values of supporting creative pursuits through copyright protection and promoting innovation in new communication technologies by limiting the incidence of liability for copyright infringement. The more artistic protection is favored, the more technological innovation may be discouraged; the administration of copyright law is an exercise in managing the trade-off.

The tension between the two values is the subject of this case, with its claim that digital distribution of copyrighted material threatens copyright holders as never before, because every copy is identical to the original, copying is easy, and many people (especially the young) use file-sharing software to download copyrighted works. This very breadth of the software's use may well draw the public directly into the debate over copyright policy, and the indications are that the ease of copying songs or movies using software like Grokster's and Napster's is fostering disdain for copyright protection. As the case has been presented to us, these fears are said to be offset by the different concern that imposing liability, not only on infringers but on distributors of software based on its potential for unlawful use, could limit further development of beneficial technologies.

The argument for imposing indirect liability in this case is, however, a powerful one, given the number of infringing downloads that occur every day using StreamCast's and Grokster's software. When a widely shared service or product is used to commit infringement, it may be impossible to enforce rights in the protected work effectively against all direct infringers, the only practical alternative being to go against the distributor of the copying device for secondary liability on a theory of contributory or vicarious infringement.

One infringes contributorily by intentionally inducing or encouraging direct infringement and infringes vicariously by profiting from direct infringement while declining to exercise a right to stop or limit it. Although "[t]he Copyright Act does not expressly render anyone liable for infringement committed by another," these doctrines of secondary liability emerged from common law principles and are well established in the law.

B

Despite the currency of these principles of secondary liability, this Court has dealt with secondary copyright infringement in only one recent case, and because MGM has tailored its principal claim to our opinion there, a look at our earlier holding is in order. In *Sony Corp. v. Universal City Studios*, this Court addressed a claim that secondary liability for infringement can arise from the very distribution of a commercial product. There, the product, novel at the time, was what we know today as the videocassette recorder or VCR. Copyright holders sued Sony as the manufacturer, claiming it was contributorily liable for infringement that occurred when VCR owners taped copyrighted programs because it supplied the means used to infringe, and it had constructive knowledge that infringement would occur. At the trial on the merits, the evidence showed that the principal use of the VCR was for "time-shifting," or taping a program for later viewing at a more convenient time, which the Court found to be a fair, not an infringing, use. There was no evidence that Sony had expressed an object of bringing about taping in violation of copyright or had taken active steps to increase its profits from unlawful taping. Although Sony's advertisements urged consumers to buy the VCR to "record favorite shows" or "build a library" of recorded programs, neither of these uses was necessarily infringing.

On those facts, with no evidence of stated or indicated intent to promote infringing uses, the only conceivable basis for imposing liability was on a theory of contributory infringement arising from its sale of VCRs to consumers with knowledge that some would use them to infringe. But because the VCR was "capable of commercially significant noninfringing uses," we held the manufacturer could not be faulted solely on the basis of its distribution. . . .

In sum, where an article is "good for nothing else" but infringement, there is no legitimate public interest in its unlicensed availability, and there is no injustice in presuming or imputing an intent to infringe. Conversely, the doctrine absolves the equivocal conduct of selling an item with substantial lawful as well as unlawful uses, and limits liability to instances of more acute fault than the mere understanding that some of one's products will be misused. It leaves breathing room for innovation and a vigorous commerce.

The parties and many of the *amici* in this case think the key to resolving it is the *Sony* rule and, in particular, what it means for a product to be "capable of commercially significant noninfringing uses." MGM advances the argument that granting summary judgment to Grokster and StreamCast as to their current activities gave too much weight to the value of innovative technology, and too little to the copyrights infringed by users of their software, given that 90% of works available on one of the networks was shown to be copyrighted. Assuming the remaining 10% to be its noninfringing use, MGM says this should not qualify as "substantial," and the Court should quantify *Sony* to the extent of holding that a product used "principally" for infringement does not qualify. As mentioned before, Grokster and StreamCast reply by citing evidence that their software can be used to reproduce public domain works, and they point to copyright holders who actually encourage copying. Even if infringement is the principal practice with their software today, they argue, the noninfringing uses are significant and will grow.

We agree with MGM that the Court of Appeals misapplied *Sony*, which it read as limiting secondary liability quite beyond the circumstances to which the case applied. *Sony* barred secondary liability based on presuming or imputing intent to cause infringement solely from the design or distribution of a product capable of substantial lawful use, which the distributor knows is in fact used for infringement. The Ninth Circuit has read *Sony*'s limitation to mean that whenever a product is capable of substantial lawful use, the producer can never be held contributorily liable for third parties' infringing use of it; it read the rule as being this broad, even when an actual purpose to cause infringing use is shown by evidence independent of design and distribution of the product, unless the distributors had "specific knowledge of infringement at a time at which they contributed to the infringement, and failed to act upon that information." Because the Circuit found the StreamCast and Grokster software capable of substantial lawful use, it concluded on the basis of its reading of *Sony* that neither company could be held liable, since there was no showing that their software, being without any central server, afforded them knowledge of specific unlawful uses.

This view of *Sony*, however, was error, converting the case from one about liability resting on imputed intent to one about liability on any theory. Because *Sony* did not displace other theories of secondary liability, and because we find below that it was error to grant summary judgment to the companies on MGM's inducement claim, we do not revisit *Sony* further, as MGM requests, to add a more quantified description of the point of balance between protection and commerce when liability rests solely on distribution with knowledge that unlawful use will occur. It is enough to note that the Ninth Circuit's judgment rested on an erroneous understanding of *Sony* and to leave further consideration of the *Sony* rule for a day when that may be required.

C

Sony's rule limits imputing culpable intent as a matter of law from the characteristics or uses of a distributed product. But nothing in *Sony* requires courts to ignore evidence of intent if there is such evidence, and the case was never meant to foreclose rules of fault-based liability derived from the common law. Thus, where evidence goes beyond a product's characteristics or the knowledge that it may be put to infringing uses, and shows statements or actions directed to promoting infringement, *Sony*'s staple-article rule will not preclude liability. . . .

The rule on inducement of infringement as developed in the early cases is no different today. Evidence of "active steps . . . taken to encourage direct infringement," such as advertising an infringing use or instructing how to engage in an infringing use, show an affirmative intent that the product be used to infringe, and a showing that infringement was encouraged overcomes the law's reluctance to find liability when a defendant merely sells a commercial product suitable for some lawful use.

For the same reasons that *Sony* took the staple-article doctrine of patent law as a model for its copyright safe-harbor rule, the inducement rule, too, is a sensible one for copyright. We adopt it here, holding that one who distributes a device with the object of promoting its use to infringe copyright, as shown by clear expression or other affirmative steps taken to foster infringement, is liable for the resulting acts of infringement by third parties. We are, of course, mindful of the need to keep from trenching on regular commerce or discouraging the development of technologies with lawful and unlawful potential. Accordingly, just as *Sony* did not find intentional inducement despite the knowledge of the VCR manufacturer that its device could be used to infringe, mere knowledge of infringing potential or of actual infringing uses would not be enough here to subject a distributor to liability. Nor would ordinary acts incident to product distribution, such as offering customers technical support or product updates, support liability in themselves. The inducement rule, instead, premises liability on purposeful, culpable expression and conduct, and thus does nothing to compromise legitimate commerce or discourage innovation having a lawful promise.

III

A

The only apparent question about treating MGM's evidence as sufficient to withstand summary judgment under the theory of inducement goes to the need on MGM's part to adduce evidence that StreamCast and

Grokster communicated an inducing message to their software users. The classic instance of inducement is by advertisement or solicitation that broadcasts a message designed to stimulate others to commit violations. MGM claims that such a message is shown here. It is undisputed that StreamCast beamed onto the computer screens of users of Napster-compatible programs ads urging the adoption of its OpenNap program, which was designed, as its name implied, to invite the custom of patrons of Napster, then under attack in the courts for facilitating massive infringement. Those who accepted StreamCast's OpenNap program were offered software to perform the same services, which a factfinder could conclude would readily have been understood in the Napster market as the ability to download copyrighted music files. Grokster distributed an electronic newsletter containing links to articles promoting its software's ability to access popular copyrighted music. And anyone whose Napster or free file-sharing searches turned up a link to Grokster would have understood Grokster to be offering the same file-sharing ability as Napster, and to the same people who probably used Napster for infringing downloads; that would also have been the understanding of anyone offered Grokster's suggestively named Swaptor software, its version of Open-Nap. And both companies communicated a clear message by responding affirmatively to requests for help in locating and playing copyrighted materials.

In StreamCast's case, of course, the evidence just described was supplemented by other unequivocal indications of unlawful purpose in the internal communications and advertising designs aimed at Napster users ("When the lights went off at Napster . . . where did the users go?") Whether the messages were communicated is not to the point on this record. The function of the message in the theory of inducement is to prove by a defendant's own statements that his unlawful purpose disqualifies him from claiming protection (and incidentally to point to actual violators likely to be found among those who hear or read the message). Proving that a message was sent out, then, is the preeminent but not exclusive way of showing that active steps were taken with the purpose of bringing about infringing acts, and of showing that infringing acts

took place by using the device distributed. Here, the summary judgment record is replete with other evidence that Grokster and StreamCast, unlike the manufacturer and distributor in *Sony*, acted with a purpose to cause copyright violations by use of software suitable for illegal use.

Three features of this evidence of intent are particularly notable. First, each company showed itself to be aiming to satisfy a known source of demand for copyright infringement, the market comprising former Napster users. StreamCast's internal documents made constant reference to Napster, it initially distributed its Morpheus software through an OpenNap program compatible with Napster, it advertised its OpenNap program to Napster users, and its Morpheus software functions as Napster did except that it could be used to distribute more kinds of files, including copyrighted movies and software programs. Grokster's name is apparently derived from Napster, it too initially offered an OpenNap program, its software's function is likewise comparable to Napster's, and it attempted to divert queries for Napster onto its own Web site. Grokster and StreamCast's efforts to supply services to former Napster users, deprived of a mechanism to copy and distribute what were overwhelmingly infringing files, indicate a principal, if not exclusive, intent on the part of each to bring about infringement.

Second, this evidence of unlawful objective is given added significance by MGM's showing that neither company attempted to develop filtering tools or other mechanisms to diminish the infringing activity using their software. While the Ninth Circuit treated the defendants' failure to develop such tools as irrelevant because they lacked an independent duty to monitor their users' activity, we think this evidence underscores Grokster's and StreamCast's intentional facilitation of their users' infringement.

Third, there is a further complement to the direct evidence of unlawful objective. It is useful to recall that StreamCast and Grokster make money by selling advertising space, by directing ads to the screens of computers employing their software. As the record shows, the more the software is used, the more ads are sent out and the greater the advertising revenue becomes. Since the extent of the software's use determines the gain to the distributors, the commercial sense of their enterprise turns on high-volume use, which the record shows is infringing. This evidence alone would not justify an inference of unlawful intent, but viewed in the context of the entire record its import is clear.

The unlawful objective is unmistakable.

B

In addition to intent to bring about infringement and distribution of a device suitable for infringing use, the inducement theory of course requires evidence of actual infringement by recipients of the device, the software in this case. As the account of the facts indicates, there is evidence of infringement on a gigantic scale, and there is no serious issue of the adequacy of MGM's showing on this point in order to survive the companies' summary judgment requests. Although an exact calculation of infringing use, as a basis for a claim of damages, is subject to dispute, there is no question that the summary judgment evidence is at least adequate to entitle MGM to go forward with claims for damages and equitable relief.

In sum, this case is significantly different from *Sony* and reliance on that case to rule in favor of Stream-Cast and Grokster was error. *Sony* dealt with a claim of liability based solely on distributing a product with alternative lawful and unlawful uses, with knowledge that some users would follow the unlawful course. The case struck a balance between the interests of protection and innovation by holding that the product's capability of substantial lawful employment should bar the imputation of fault and consequent secondary liability for the unlawful acts of others.

MGM's evidence in this case most obviously addresses a different basis of liability for distributing a product open to alternative uses. Here, evidence of the distributors' words and deeds going beyond distribution as such shows a purpose to cause and profit from third-party acts of copyright infringement. If liability for inducing infringement is ultimately found, it will not be on the basis of presuming or imputing fault, but from inferring a patently illegal objective from statements and actions showing what that objective was.

There is substantial evidence in MGM's favor on all elements of inducement, and summary judgment in favor of Grokster and StreamCast was error. On remand, reconsideration of MGM's motion for summary judgment will be in order.

The judgment of the Court of Appeals is vacated, and the case is remanded for further proceedings consistent with this opinion.

It is so ordered.

Chapter 14

Our question is whether speech which does "no more than propose a commercial transaction," is so removed from any "exposition of ideas," and from "truth, science, morality, and arts in general, in its diffusion of liberal sentiments on the administration of Government," that it lacks all protection. Our answer is that it is not. . . . As to the particular consumer's interest in the free flow of commercial information, that interest may be as keen, if not keener by far, than his interest in the day's most urgent political debate. . . . Even an individual advertisement, though entirely "commercial," may be of general public interest.

U.S. Supreme Court Justice Harry Blackmun[1]

Regulators and lawmakers sometimes target tobacco advertising, with disputes often settled in court.

Advertising
When Speech and Commerce Converge

The Evolution of the Commercial Speech Doctrine

Putting the Doctrine to Work

Corporate Speech Regulation

Legislative and Agency Advertising Regulation

The Federal Trade Commission

Other Administrative Regulation

Internet Advertising

Cases for Study

➤ *Central Hudson Gas & Electric Corp. v. Public Service Commission of New York*
➤ *Lorillard v. Reilly*

Suppose . . .

. . . that just after an energy crisis, a public utility company wants to sell energy-efficient electrical appliances. It plans advertising to spread the word. The government, however, says that use of electricity should not be promoted, and it uses an existing law to prevent the ads. The utility company fights the government in court. Is the law constitutional? Or does it violate a First Amendment right to commercial speech? Should commercial speech have any First Amendment protection? Does a government interest in an issue justify the advertising regulation? Look for the answers to these questions when the case of *Central Hudson Gas & Electric Corp. v. Public Service Commission of New York* is discussed later in this chapter. The case is also excerpted at the end of the chapter.

G iven that advertising is the lifeblood for many media organizations, a legitimate issue for both the creators of ads and those who run them is whether the First Amendment protects them. For years, it was an accepted part of free speech dogma that advertising, or commercial speech, was not subject to First Amendment protection. Rather than being a core First Amendment value—as it is generally agreed that, for example, political speech is[2]—commercial speech has been viewed as lying on the fringe of First Amendment protection. Even today, commercial speech does not enjoy the same level of protection as political speech. Early in its legal history, advertising was thought to contain so little value that it deserved no First Amendment protection.

There is perhaps no better example than a 1942 U.S. Supreme Court case that started with a used submarine. A New York City entrepreneur named F.J. Chrestensen purchased a submarine from the U.S. Navy and docked it at a pier on the East River, hoping to charge people for tours on board. When Chrestensen learned that distributing handbills to advertise the venture would violate a city ordinance, he printed a protest of that law on the side of the leaflet opposite the advertisement, thinking that the inclusion of this "political speech" would immunize him from prosecution. But when told the revised handbills would still violate the ordinance, he filed suit seeking an injunction to bar interference with his attempt to distribute them. The injunction was granted, and the decision was affirmed on appeal. The U.S. Supreme Court, however, reversed. The Court viewed Chrestensen's handbill as little more than advertising and said that advertising had no First Amendment protection and therefore could be regulated. The Court acknowledged that "the streets are proper places for the exercise of the freedom of communicating information and disseminating opinion."[3] While states and municipalities may not unduly limit such communication in these kinds of public thoroughfares, the Court said, "the Constitution imposes no such restraint on government as respects purely commercial speech."[4]

The *Valentine v. Chrestensen* ruling was interpreted by many, including judges, to mean that advertising was clearly outside the scope of First Amendment protection. Over time, however, the perception and, more important, the legal status of commercial speech, changed. The prime mover in this evolution was the U.S. Supreme Court.

The Evolution of the Commercial Speech Doctrine

Courts use the term "commercial speech" to distinguish ads proposing commercial transactions from other kinds of ads—political ads or purely informational ads, for example. In this chapter, the word "advertising" is used to mean commercial speech.

In some respects, the transformation that gave advertising some First Amendment protection was initiated by *New York Times Co. v. Sullivan,* the U.S. Supreme Court's landmark 1964 libel ruling explained in Chapter 4. The case originated with a paid advertisement. Justice William Brennan's opinion for the Court began to clarify the meaning of *Chrestensen,* dispelling any suggestions that the decision had placed commercial speech outside the range of First Amendment protection: "That the Times was paid for publishing the advertisement is as immaterial in this connection as is the fact that newspapers and books are sold."[5] The Court was articulating the idea that advertising could be considered "speech" and was therefore entitled to First Amendment protection. In *Chrestensen,* the advertisement for the submarine tour did no more than propose a commercial transaction. In *Sullivan,* by contrast, the advertisement was not a commercial advertisement. Instead, it communicated information, expressed opinions and sought support "on behalf of a movement whose existence and objectives are matters of the highest public interest and concern."[6] It was paid political speech. Hints were emerging of a theory of free speech in which some kinds of commercial speech could fall within the protections of the First Amendment.

The U.S. Supreme Court took another step in acknowledging that some First Amendment protection for commercial speech may exist with a 1973 ruling.[7] While the Court affirmed the ability of governments to regulate advertising, it also suggested that (1) a First Amendment interest could be served by advertising a commercial proposal, and (2) the interest could outweigh the government's interest in regulating the advertising.[8] While the second factor was not satisfied in this case, the acknowledgment by the Court that even purely commercial advertising could contain First Amendment interests provided a significant clue regarding the direction of the development of the commercial speech doctrine.

Another step toward protection for commercial speech happened when the Court ruled that advertisements for abortion services were legal. A New York–based referral service placed ads in a weekly newspaper in Virginia. A Virginia law had made it illegal to encourage or prompt the procuring of an abortion by the sale or circulation of any publication. The publisher of the newspaper, Jeffrey Bigelow, was charged and convicted of violating that law. By the time the U.S. Supreme Court heard the appeal, it had issued its ruling in *Roe v. Wade*,[9] making most abortions legal by ruling them to be matters of personal privacy. The Court found it difficult to justify restricting advertisements for a service when the service itself was legal. Moreover, in the *Bigelow v. Virginia* case, the Court ruled that the ads in question were not purely commercial speech. Instead, like the ad in *New York Times Co. v. Sullivan*, those in Bigelow's newspaper "did more than simply propose a commercial transaction. It contained factual material of clear 'public interest.'"[10]

But the *Bigelow* Court went even further. Citing previous rulings, the Court said, "Our cases . . .

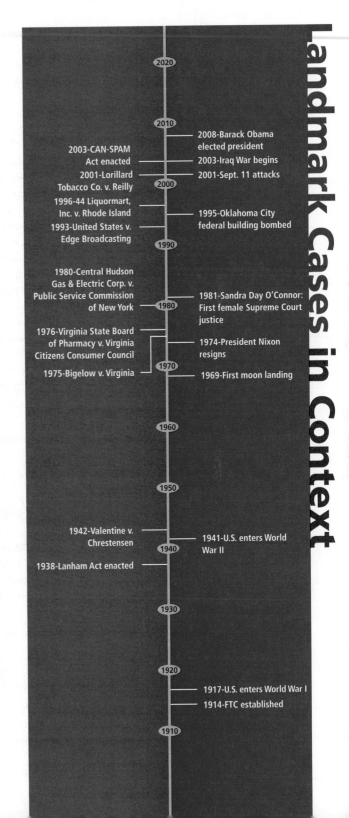

Landmark Cases in Context

- 2020
- 2010
- 2008-Barack Obama elected president
- 2003-CAN-SPAM Act enacted
- 2003-Iraq War begins
- 2001-Lorillard Tobacco Co. v. Reilly
- 2001-Sept. 11 attacks
- 2000
- 1996-44 Liquormart, Inc. v. Rhode Island
- 1995-Oklahoma City federal building bombed
- 1993-United States v. Edge Broadcasting
- 1990
- 1980-Central Hudson Gas & Electric Corp. v. Public Service Commission of New York
- 1981-Sandra Day O'Connor: First female Supreme Court justice
- 1980
- 1976-Virginia State Board of Pharmacy v. Virginia Citizens Consumer Council
- 1974-President Nixon resigns
- 1975-Bigelow v. Virginia
- 1970
- 1969-First moon landing
- 1960
- 1950
- 1942-Valentine v. Chrestensen
- 1941-U.S. enters World War II
- 1940
- 1938-Lanham Act enacted
- 1930
- 1920
- 1917-U.S. enters World War I
- 1914-FTC established
- 1910

clearly establish that speech is not stripped of First Amendment protection merely because it appears in [the] form" of paid commercial advertisements.[11] The fact that the abortion referral service ads had commercial aspects or reflected the advertiser's commercial interests, the Court said, did not negate all First Amendment guarantees.

The *Bigelow* Court specifically added that *Chrestensen* did not hold all statutes regulating commercial advertising were immune from challenges based on the First Amendment.[12] In addition, the Court noted that Justice William O. Douglas, who was on the Court for both *Chrestensen* and *Bigelow,* wrote that the former ruling was "casual, almost offhand" and that it "has not survived reflection."[13] Thus, while the Court still had not said that purely commercial speech had First Amendment protection, it clearly believed it was a mistake to view any speech that is commercial in nature as automatically lacking constitutional protection.

The next significant step in the development of a commercial speech doctrine involved a Virginia state pharmacy board rule that prohibited licensed pharmacists from advertising the price of any prescription drug. The rationale was

Points of Law

The Free Flow of (Commercial) Information

In *Virginia State Board of Pharmacy v. Virginia Citizens Consumer Council,*[1] the U.S. Supreme Court established several principles concerning advertising:

- "Freedom of speech" applies to both the speaker and recipient of information. There is a right to receive information.

- First Amendment protection had never been denied to speech merely because it was commercial. That was made clear in *Bigelow v. Virginia.*

- "[S]peech does not lose its First Amendment protection because money is spent to project it, as in a paid advertisement."

- Speech that does no more than propose a commercial transaction is not so removed from "any exposition of ideas" that it lacks all protection.

- Consumer interest in the free flow of commercial information may be as high as, if not higher than, the interest in the day's most urgent political debate. Even an individual advertisement, though entirely commercial, may be of general public interest.

- Particularly in a free enterprise economy, it is a matter of public interest that economic decisions be intelligent and well informed.

- As with other categories of speech, some forms of commercial speech may be regulated. Untruthful speech, for example, has never been protected for its own sake.

1. 425 U.S. 748 (1976).

to maintain a high degree of professionalism in the field. But the result was to prevent publication of information that would be useful to the public about prescription drug prices. A group of plaintiffs sued, arguing that the First Amendment entitles prescription drug users to receive pricing and discount information that pharmacists wish to communicate to them through advertising and other promotional means. The Court agreed, clearly establishing that commercial speech is subject to some First Amendment protection with this 1976 ruling. The degree of constitutional protection, however, is far more limited than that afforded to other categories of speech, for example, political speech. While the Court said that untruthful expression could be regulated, the law is clearly more tolerant of error and falsehood in a political context than of speech in the commercial arena.

Even with its ruling in *Virginia Pharmacy,* the Court had yet to definitively establish when, exactly, commercial speech could be regulated without offending the First Amendment. That changed with its 1980 ruling in *Central Hudson Gas & Electric Corp. v. Public Service Commission.*[14] In the midst of a nationwide energy crisis, Central Hudson was one of many utility companies in New York state that were being prevented from placing advertisements in the media that even indirectly promoted the use of electricity. The company filed suit, arguing that its First Amendment rights were being violated by the advertising ban. The case presented the Court with a conflict between two competing policy interests: the company's free speech rights on the one hand, and the government's arguably legitimate interest, on the other, in promoting the conservation of energy. To resolve the issue in this and subsequent commercial speech cases, the Court developed a test.

First, the Court reaffirmed the constitutionality of regulations forbidding untruthful and misleading advertising as well as prohibitions on ads that promote illegal products or services. If an advertisement clears that first hurdle, *Central Hudson* said, then a government regulation is constitutional only if there is a substantial state interest that justifies the regulation, the regulation directly advances that state interest, and the regulation directly advances the state interest through the least speech restrictive means possible. Applying this test to the advertising prohibition that *Central Hudson* had complained about, the Court found the ban to be unconstitutional. As lights came on across New York in the wake of the ruling, so did the decision light the way for further development of the commercial speech doctrine.

In a 1989 ruling, the Court modified the last element of its *Central Hudson* test. In *Board of Trustees of the State University of New York v. Fox,*[15] the Supreme Court backed away from the standard that an advertising regulation must advance a state

Points of Law

The Commercial Speech Doctrine

- The government may regulate advertising that is false, misleading or deceptive.

- The government may regulate advertising for unlawful goods and services.

Even truthful, honest advertising for legal goods and services may be regulated if the following conditions are met:

- The government claims a substantial state interest to justify the regulation.

- The government demonstrates that the regulation directly advances the claimed interest.

- The government shows that there is a reasonable fit between the claimed interest and the regulation.

U.S. Supreme Court Justice Clarence Thomas

interest through the "least restrictive means." Now there only has to be a "reasonable fit" between the regulation and the state interest. Justice Antonin Scalia's opinion for the Court said that while *Central Hudson* and subsequent rulings had suggested that the least restrictive means standard be used, it was not strictly required: "What our decisions require is a 'fit' between the legislature's ends and the means chosen to accomplish those ends—a fit that is not necessarily perfect, but reasonable."[16] This revision makes it easier for advertising regulations to pass the test and be ruled constitutional.

Putting the Doctrine to Work

Since the commercial speech doctrine was established, it has been the standard by which attempts to regulate advertising have been judged. As with other First Amendment areas, controversial commercial speech—that is, advertising for "vice" products—is primarily where the doctrine has been tested. Some examples follow.

Alcohol Advertising The Coors Brewing Company wanted to print the percentage of alcohol in its beer on the product label. A federal law, however, prohibited information about alcohol content appearing on product labels or in advertising. Coors challenged the law on First Amendment grounds. In defending the regulation, the federal government claimed the state had an interest in preventing "strength wars" between brewers. The law was necessary, in other words, to prevent a beer potency war among brewers that could harm society. Writing for the U.S. Supreme Court, Justice Clarence Thomas said that while there may be a substantial interest in combating any "strength wars," the challenged law did not achieve that goal. The law failed the *Central Hudson* test, the Court said, because there are "alternatives that would prove less intrusive to the First Amendment's protections for commercial speech."[17]

Alcoholic beverage advertising provided the backdrop for another commercial speech test that originated with a Rhode Island law forbidding liquor stores from advertising the price of their products. A liquor store owner believed the law to be absurd and tried to circumvent it by placing the exclamation "Wow" next to certain bargain products in his newspaper ads. The state did not find this amusing. It levied a stiff fine on the creative liquor store owner. He sued, asserting he had a First Amendment right to advertise his prices. Rhode Island relied on the *Central Hudson* test by arguing that the law advanced the government's substantial interest in promoting temperance. The state argued that if people knew about bargain prices on alcoholic beverages, consumption would increase. The U.S. Supreme Court disagreed, ruling that the state had failed to establish a causal

realWorld Law

44 Liquormart: The "Little Guy" Fights Back . . . and Wins

The man behind *44 Liquormart, Inc. v. Rhode Island* is John Haronian, the owner of that retailer. He was fed up with what he thought was an unfair state law restricting his ability to conduct business. "When you talk to the average consumer out there—the public—they can't understand why these laws are put into place," Haronian says. "They can't understand why we couldn't advertise price."

He ultimately hired Boston lawyer Evan Lawson. "The regulation didn't promote temperance at all," Lawson says. "We were fighting for the right of all consumers to have meaningful information about prices before they make a purchase. And secondly we were fighting so that people who are going to buy a product are going to get a fair price that reflects a competitive environment."

For Haronian, the case embodied basic rights. "A person has a right to know. That's all it is. A person has a right to know. It was so the public would know before they enter the store, of what they were paying for goods. That's all it meant. And all I wanted the consumer to understand was to make a decision where you're going to spend your money, not being forced to spend your money where you don't want to. In other words, have all the tools and have all the information in front of you so you can make a proper decision."

"I think what was at issue in this case," says attorney Lawson, "was how important the Court was going to see informational advertising. There are various kinds of advertising. Informational advertising—where you're providing the consumer with information about the product so that they can make a reasoned choice, so to speak—that has always had a very high value, I think, in the Court's mind, at least since it held that advertising was protected by the First Amendment."[1]

1. Joseph Russomanno, Speaking Our Minds: Conversations with the People Behind Landmark First Amendment Cases 321–22, 334, 336 (Mahwah, N.J.: Lawrence Erlbaum Associates/Taylor & Francis, 2002).

relationship between its abridgment of commercial speech and achieving its goal of temperance.[18] Withholding information from the public about the price of alcoholic beverages would not necessarily achieve the goal of decreasing drinking. The Court found the law was unconstitutional.

Tobacco Advertising Tobacco advertising first appeared in America in 1789, when the Lorillard brothers advertised their snuff and tobacco products in a New York daily newspaper. More than 200 years later, the same company was at the U.S. Supreme Court to argue its case that a Massachusetts law restricting its ability to advertise tobacco products was unconstitutional. Massachusetts had created regulations that included attempts to restrict outdoor advertising and point-of-sale ads. The outdoor advertising regulations prohibited smoke-less tobacco or cigar advertising within 1,000 feet of a school or playground. Applying the *Central Hudson* test, the Court first determined there was a legiti-mate state interest in regulating tobacco advertising: preventing minors from accessing tobacco products. Justice Sandra Day O'Connor's opinion also stated that the regulations would address that interest. However, in completing the *Central Hudson* analysis, she said there was not a reasonable fit between the regulations and the goals of the regulatory scheme. In fact, the regulations were more extensive than necessary to accomplish the stated goals.

The Court also addressed regulation of retail sales practices applied to all tobacco products. The regulations targeted cigarette machines and other self-service displays and required that certain tobacco products be placed out of the consumer's reach. The Court upheld these restrictions, reasoning that they withstood First Amendment scrutiny because the state's interest was "unrelated to the communication of ideas."[19]

This case was the latest in a series of developments aimed at protecting people—especially children—from the lure of tobacco products. Young people are thought to be especially susceptible to advertising. For example, when it was introduced in the 1990s, the cartoon character of Joe Camel was heavily criticized for its ability to tempt minors. After the introduction of the Joe Camel cartoon character, Camel cigarettes' share of the youth market rose from 4 percent to 13 percent.[20]

In 1995, President Clinton instructed the Food and Drug Administration (FDA) to "initiate a broad series of steps all designed to stop sales and marketing of cigarettes and smokeless tobacco to children." A federal district court in North Carolina ruled in 1997 that the FDA had the authority to regulate tobacco products.[21] The next year, as part of a settlement with 46 states (the other 4 states had already settled their cases), the tobacco industry agreed to discontinue billboard and transit ads and to stop using cartoon characters to promote their products.

These developments were preceded by the enactment of the Public Health Cigarette Smoking Act in 1969. One section of the act required a ban on cigarette advertising on broadcast television and radio stations. The act was challenged, but a federal court upheld the constitutionality of the law. It ruled that the free speech rights of tobacco companies were not being abridged because they still had other advertising outlets at their disposal.[22] It was a prophetic statement, since print media, billboards and other avenues were then pursued with vigor.

Gambling Advertising A case involving a ban on the advertising for a state lottery gave the Supreme Court an opportunity to address commercial speech further. A North Carolina radio station owned by Edge Broadcasting challenged a law that prohibited it and other broadcasters in the state from airing ads for any lottery. Because the station was located only three miles from the Virginia border, most of its listeners were Virginians. The station wanted to be able to run ads for the Virginia lottery. But because lotteries were illegal in North Carolina at the time, and because that state had the authority to discourage gambling, the U.S. Supreme Court upheld the constitutionality of the law. As the Court often does, it deferred to Congress' judgment in passing the challenged law. Justice Byron White wrote:

> Congress surely knew that stations in one State could often be heard in another but expressly prevented each and every North Carolina station, including Edge, from carrying lottery ads. Congress plainly made the

realWorld Law

Smoke and Mirrors: A New Era for *Central Hudson*?

The tobacco advertising ruling described in this chapter, *Lorillard Tobacco Co. v. Reilly,*[1] suggests a shift in the U.S. Supreme Court's application of the *Central Hudson* commercial speech doctrine. The issue was Massachusetts regulations directed at tobacco product advertising, both outdoor (primarily billboards) and point of sale (i.e., vending machines). Neither could be within 1,000 feet of a school or playground.

In applying the *Central Hudson* test, the Court's majority agreed that "tobacco use, particularly among children and adolescents, poses perhaps the single most significant threat to public health in the United States"[2] and that there was clear evidence of a link between advertising and an increase in the use of tobacco products by young people.[3]

But it was in applying *Central Hudson's* fourth prong that the Court's ruling turned. There was not a reasonable fit between the regulations and the state interest in reducing tobacco consumption by minors, the Court said.[4] The Court blamed the Massachusetts attorney general for not "carefully calculat[ing] the costs and benefits associated with the burden on speech imposed by the regulations."[5] In short, the 1,000-foot perimeter established by the regulations meant that in crowded urban areas where schools and playgrounds are densely clustered, the advertising in question would be effectively prohibited. In fact, Lorillard claimed the regulations would prohibit its advertising in about 90 percent of the land area in Massachusetts' biggest cities. In the Court's view, this kind of near-total ban was not the reasonable fit required by *Central Hudson*.

Another point revolves around the issue of regulating speech to protect minors and in doing so improperly restricting information adults have a right to access. While noting that "efforts to protect children from exposure to harmful material will undoubtedly have some spillover effect on the free speech rights of adults," Justice David Souter acknowledged that "finding the appropriate balance is no easy matter."[6] He believed the 1,000-foot provision of the regulations needed to be more carefully considered.

Thus, *Central Hudson's* fourth prong seems to have entered a new era. In large part, some claim, that is due to its subjective nature. As one analyst has written: "[T]he Court can use the test to defeat objectionable legislation without articulating any set of coherent limits for commercial speech doctrine. And, of course, if there is no articulable reason why commercial speech is protected, how can any regulation proscribe too much speech?"[7] The U.S. Supreme Court's ruling in *Lorillard* is excerpted at the end of this chapter.

---

1. 533 U.S. 525 (2001).
2. *Id.* at 570.
3. *Id.* at 561.
4. *Id.*
5. *Id.*
6. *Id.* at 601 (Souter, J. dissenting).
7. Charles Fischette, *A New Architecture of Commercial Speech Law,* 31 HARV. J.L. & PUB. POL'Y 663, 666–67 (2008).

commonsense judgment that each North Carolina station would have an audience in that State, even if its signal reached elsewhere and that enforcing the statutory restriction would insulate each station's listeners from lottery ads and hence advance the governmental purpose of supporting North Carolina's laws against gambling. This congressional policy of balancing the interests of lottery and nonlottery States is the substantial governmental interest that satisfies *Central Hudson*.[23]

Justice John Paul Stevens was one of two dissenters. He argued that in a nation with legal lotteries in (at that time) 34 states—and with North Carolina itself then considering adopting a lottery—the government lacked a substantial interest in trying to discourage gambling.[24]

A few years later, a group of New Orleans broadcasters challenged a regulation that banned broadcasters from airing ads for legal casino gambling. The case was distinguished from the one involving the North Carolina radio station mentioned previously. Here, even though broadcast signals from New Orleans may reach states where private casino gambling is unlawful, those signals originate from a state where gambling is legal. Justice Stevens wrote for a unanimous Court that the regulation failed the *Central Hudson* test. While there was a substantial state interest—reducing the social costs associated with gambling—the law did not advance it. Prohibiting advertising for private casinos but allowing it for other casinos (those operated by Native American tribes), as well as permitting advertising for other forms of gambling such as lotteries, only served to steer gamblers to specific outlets rather than others. Moreover, the Court said, the regulation was not as narrowly tailored as it could be.[25]

Advertising by Attorneys Though certainly not advertising for a "vice" product, lawyers advertising their services has been considered controversial. There was a time when attorneys were forbidden to advertise. State bar associations prohibited the practice, and most lawyers thought advertising was unethical or, at the very least, unprofessional. Not surprisingly, it is an issue that judges have a great interest in, given that most of them started out as practicing attorneys.[26] The U.S. Supreme Court dealt with the issue when two Arizona lawyers challenged the advertising regulation, in part on First Amendment grounds. Just one year before, the Court had ruled in the *Virginia Pharmacy* case that a law in that state to prevent unprofessional conduct among pharmacists by preventing them from advertising was unconstitutional. In the Arizona case, the Court rejected the arguments of the state bar association and ruled its regulation in violation of the First Amendment. The ruling emphasized, however, that it was stopping short of granting a blanket endorsement to attorney advertising. "Reasonable" restrictions—for example, those pertaining to false advertising—could survive First Amendment scrutiny.[27]

Corporate Speech Regulation

One way that corporations and businesses communicate with customers is through advertising. Most ads have a clear purpose: to enhance sales. Moreover, it is usually clear that when a corporation "speaks," it is advertising. Any attempt to regulate that speech is subject to the commercial speech doctrine.

But there are situations when the distinction between commercial speech and another kind of speech—political, for example—is not so clear. What happens when a business claims to have engaged in political speech? Is it possible to do so without the speech also being a form of advertising?

First, the U.S. Supreme Court has upheld the right of corporations to communicate through purely political speech. The first in this line of cases involved a bank that wanted to influence a voter referendum by communicating its viewpoint.[28] In this and subsequent cases, the Court ruled in support of the businesses and their free speech, though it narrowed its view over time.[29] This is important for corporations because political speech has more First Amendment protection than does commercial speech.

But, second, what about a more complicated situation? Suppose that a corporation wants to communicate about an issue of public importance. Is that political speech? Suppose that the communication about an issue of public importance is done in a way that would place the corporation in an improved public light, thereby potentially increasing its sales. Now is the speech commercial? This was the situation in a case that came to the U.S. Supreme Court in 2003. The corporation in question was Nike, Inc. It responded to accusations that in its overseas plants, workers were abused, made to work longer hours than the law allowed and subjected to unsafe working conditions. The communication was in the form of press releases and letters to newspapers, university presidents and university athletic directors. An activist in California, Marc Kasky, filed a claim against Nike, saying its statements were knowingly false. A trial court dismissed the case, but the California Supreme Court reversed, ruling that the speech was commercial and could therefore be punished under state false advertising and unfair competition laws. The court's rationale was threefold: (1) Nike engaged in commerce, (2) the intended audience was largely composed of potential Nike customers, and (3) the speech consisted of representations of fact of a commercial nature that were intended to maintain and increase sales of Nike products.[30] The dissenters believed that the speech was political and protected because it was in response to claims—themselves protected speech—that Nike mistreated workers.[31]

On appeal to the U.S. Supreme Court, Nike argued that its speech, even if false, was absolutely protected by the First Amendment because it was political in nature, concerning as it did discussions about factory working conditions, not commercial speech involving such things as product pricing or performance characteristics. The Court dismissed the case, stating that Kasky had not suffered sufficient injury due to Nike's speech to confer on him the **standing** required to file a lawsuit. In other words, he was not personally qualified to challenge Nike's conduct. A few months later, Nike and Kasky settled their dispute. Though some aspects were undisclosed, it was revealed that Nike paid $1.5 million to the Fair Labor Association.

Many people view this case as a lost opportunity. The Court had before it a case with which it could clarify the meaning of commercial speech. Justice Stephen Breyer was among those who believed the questions before the Court directly concerned "the freedom of Americans to speak about public matters in public debate." He went on to say that "no jurisdictional rule prevents us from deciding those questions now, and delay itself may inhibit the exercise of constitutionally protected rights of free speech without making the issue significantly easier to decide later on."[32]

standing The position of a plaintiff who has been injured or has been threatened with injury. No person is entitled to challenge the constitutionality of an ordinance or statute unless he or she has the required standing—that is, unless he or she had been affected by the ordinance or statute.

Though not a commercial speech case, 2010's *Citizens United v. Federal Election Commission*[33] is worth noting here because it addresses corporate speech regulation. The U.S. Supreme Court ruling, analyzed in Chapters 1 and 3, extended the degree to which corporations' speech has First Amendment protection.

SUMMARY

AFTER DECADES IN WHICH IT EXPRESSLY DECLINED TO GRANT First Amendment protection to commercial speech, the U.S. Supreme Court acknowledged for the first time in the 1960s that advertising can contain important information and may deserve some constitutional protection. The Court elaborated its commercial speech doctrine in the *Central Hudson* case, which established a framework to determine when an advertising regulation is constitutional. A regulation is constitutional if there is a substantial state interest, the regulation directly advances that interest, and there is a reasonable fit between the interest and the regulation. While this approach is used to evaluate any regulation, its most noteworthy applications have included those for controversial goods and services. ■

Legislative and Agency Advertising Regulation

While advertising is subject to regulation on the state level, it is the federal government that has largely assumed the responsibility. Among the reasons is the ability of ads to cross state lines. Because advertising crosses state lines, it falls under the U.S. Constitution's commerce clause. Therefore, Congress may control it—within the limits of the First Amendment.

Lanham Act A federal law that regulates the trademark registration process but that also contains a section permitting business competitors to sue one another for false advertising.

The **Lanham Act,** passed by Congress in 1938, prohibits any false or misleading description of goods, services or commercial activities in any forum, including commercial advertising or promotion.[34] Though the act was seldom used as a check on advertising initially, it eventually became the foundation for lawsuits as advertising grew and began using new techniques such as comparative advertising. For example, the assertions made in print media advertisements in the 1980s by Jartran, a truck rental company, were the catalyst for claims that they violated the Lanham Act. The ads compared Jartran's trucks with those offered by U-Haul, the market leader and Jartran's primary competition. The problem was that the ads used photographs of brand-new, shiny Jartran trucks and beaten, worn U-Haul trucks. In addition, rate comparisons were calculated unfairly for U-Haul. In the wake of the ad campaign, U-Haul profits dropped significantly while Jartran's rose. A federal court ruled that the advertisements violated the Lanham Act by being deliberately false and misleading to consumers.[35]

Advertising and Product Demand: Are They Linked?

Advertising is premised on the idea that it increases product demand. Most accept that premise, including the U.S. Supreme Court. Its interpretations of advertising regulations are conducted with that belief in mind. For example:

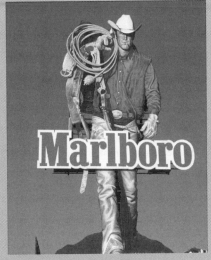

- In the *Central Hudson* case, the Court said that the utility company would not have contested the advertising ban "unless it believed that promotion would increase sales."[1]

- In its analysis of a regulation forbidding casino advertising in Puerto Rico, Justice William Rehnquist noted that when the Puerto Rico legislature passed the advertising restrictions, it believed "that advertising of casino gambling aimed at the residents of Puerto Rico would serve to increase the demand for the product advertised. We think the legislature's belief is a reasonable one."[2]

- In the *Lorillard* case concerning restrictions on tobacco advertising, the Court embraced the link between advertising and product demand, noting that the "theory" had been accepted for years.

Advertising like this for tobacco products, according to one ruling, stimulates consumer demand.

"In previous cases, we have acknowledged the theory that product advertising stimulates demand for products, while suppressed advertising may have the opposite effect. [In this case], the Attorney General cites numerous studies to support this theory in the case of tobacco products."[3]

But those outside the courts have a more mixed view as to whether advertising increases product demand. While one study led the Food and Drug Administration to observe a correlation between advertising and an increase in product demand,[4] the Reagan administration was skeptical. Douglas Kmiec of the Office of Legal Counsel said in 1986 that the administration was "not convinced that advertising leads to increased consumption."[5] The administration was therefore hesitant to support any advertising ban without a demonstrated connection.

Empirical studies have produced similarly mixed results. On the one hand, a study on cigarette advertising suggests that advertising results in increased demand and implies that the government could decrease demand by banning all forms of advertising.[6] On the other hand, a study on advertising and alcohol demand indicates a minimal effect of advertising on beverage consumption, and no increase related to beer advertising. Alcohol advertising, the study concludes, serves only to reallocate brand sales with no effect on total consumption.[7]

Does advertising increase product demand? While the jury may be out, our courts have accepted the proposition and seem to base their rulings with that in mind.

1. Central Hudson Gas & Electric Corp. v. New York Public Service Commission, 447 U.S. 557, 569 (1980).
2. Posadas de Puerto Rico Associates v. Tourism Co. of Puerto Rico, 478 U.S. 328, 342 (1986).
3. Lorillard Tobacco Co. v. Reilly, 533 U.S. 525, 557 (2001).
4. *See, e.g.,* Rosalind M. Kendellen, *The Food and Drug Administration Retreats from Patient Package Inserts for Prescription Drugs,* 40 Food Drug Cosm. L.J. 172 (1985) (showing the FDA's motivation for establishing a package insert plan for consumers).
5. 1 Antitrust & Trade Reg. Rep. (BNA) No. 1277, p. 199 (Aug. 7, 1986).
6. Barry J. Seldon & Khosrow Doroodian, *A Simultaneous Model of Cigarette Advertising: Effects on Demand and Industry Response to Public Policy,* 71 Rev. Econ. & Stat. 673 (1989).
7. Jon P. Nelson & John R. Moran, *Advertising and U.S. Alcoholic Beverage Demand: System-Wide Estimates,* 27 Applied Econ. 1225 (1995).

The Federal Trade Commission

In addition to regulating advertising through laws passed by legislatures—both federal and state—commercial speech may also be regulated at the agency level. While states may have agencies that have authority to address advertising, this primarily happens in administrative agencies at the federal level.

The U.S. Congress conferred its authority to control advertising on the **Federal Trade Commission (FTC)** when it established the agency in 1914. The FTC is an independent agency that reports to Congress on its actions. The commission is headed by five commissioners, nominated by the president and confirmed by the Senate, each serving a seven-year term. The president chooses one commissioner to act as chair. No more than three commissioners may be of the same political party.

Federal Trade Commission (FTC)
A federal agency created in 1914. Its purpose is to promote free and fair competition in interstate commerce; this includes preventing false and misleading advertising.

The primary function of the FTC is to protect consumers from unfair or deceptive practices by businesses. Over time, this has included policing advertising. Today, the FTC is the primary federal regulator of advertising. It works in conjunction with other federal agencies to execute its various functions. The commission's authority was broadened in 1938 when it was given the power to demand that advertisers substantiate the accuracy of ad claims as part of its role in detecting deception.

The FTC includes the Bureau of Consumer Protection, whose mandate is protecting consumers against unfair, deceptive or fraudulent practices. One element of this bureau is the Division of Advertising Practices. That division "is the nation's enforcer of federal truth-in-advertising laws."[36] Most recently, it has focused on the following:

Points of Law

FTC: False and Misleading Advertising

This FTC Policy Statement explains false and misleading advertising from the commission's viewpoint:

- First, there must be a representation, omission or practice that is likely to mislead the consumer.

- Second, we examine the practice from the perspective of a consumer acting reasonably in the circumstances. If the representation or practice affects or is directed primarily to a particular group, the commission examines reasonableness from the perspective of that group.

- Third, the representation, omission or practice must be a "material" one. The basic question is whether the act or practice is likely to affect the consumer's conduct or decision with regard to a product or service.[1]

1. FTC Policy Statement by Chairman James C. Miller III, Oct. 14, 1983, *available at* http://www.ftc.gov/bcp/poli cystmt/ad-decept.htm.

- Deceptive advertising of fraudulent cure-all claims for dietary supplements and weight loss products
- Deceptive Internet marketing practices that develop in response to public health issues
- Enforcement strategies for new advertising techniques and media, such as word-of-mouth marketing
- Advertising of food to children, including the impact of practices by food companies and the media on childhood obesity
- Industry practices regarding the marketing of violent movies, music, and electronic games to children
- Alcohol and tobacco marketing practices

One area where the commission distinguishes between what it will and will not pursue is "puffery." **Puffery** is defined as advertising that exaggerates the merits of products or services in such a way that no reasonable person would take the ad seriously. A former FTC commissioner described the situation as follows:

> The FTC does not pursue subjective claims or puffery—claims like "this is the best hairspray in the world." But if there is an objective component to the claim—such as "more consumers prefer our hairspray to any other" or "our hairspray lasts longer than the most popular brands"—then you need to be sure that the claim is not deceptive and that you have adequate substantiation *before* you make the claim. These requirements apply both to explicit or express claims and to implied claims. Also, a statement that is literally true can have a deceptive implication when considered in the context of the whole advertisement, even if that implication is not the only possible interpretation.[37]

The FTC at Work The FTC is made aware of potentially problematic advertisements in a variety of ways: letters from consumers or businesses, congressional inquiries, articles on consumer or economic subjects and so on. In addition, questions come from advertisers themselves who are seeking advice and want to avoid problems. Generally, FTC investigations are nonpublic to protect both the investigation and the companies involved.

Once notified, the FTC has several powers at its disposal. These powers are designed either to prevent problematic advertising before it gets to the public or to remedy ads once they have entered the public domain. Either way, the commission's measures are meant to protect the public first. But the FTC's mission, especially on the preventive side, can also be viewed as an effort to work with advertisers to ensure that they are not inadvertently doing anything improper. These FTC measures may be considered as if they are on a continuum, from most informal and least serious to official and extremely critical.

Preventive Measures First, if an advertiser wants an unofficial opinion about an ad that is being considered or is about to be placed in the media, it can request an **opinion letter** from the FTC. The advice contained in the letter does not bind the commission in any way, but it can be a quick and efficient way for businesses to avoid problems with possibly deceptive or fraudulent advertising.

Next, an **advisory opinion** typically contains more information than an opinion letter. In addition, it is more official. It is placed in the public record

---

puffery Advertising that exaggerates the merits of products or services in such a way that no reasonable person would take the ad seriously. Usually, puffery is not illegal given that a reasonable person understands the claim is not to be taken literally.

Points of Law

FTC Mechanisms

Preventive Measures

- Opinion letters
- Advisory opinions
- Industry guides
- Trade rules
- Voluntary compliance

Corrective Measures

- Cease and desist orders
- Consent orders
- Substantiation
- Litigated orders
- Corrective advertising
- Injunctions

---

opinion letter A letter requested by an advertiser from the Federal Trade Commission containing advice about an advertising technique.

advisory opinion In advertising, a Federal Trade Commission measure that suggests to an advertiser how a specific advertisement may be false or misleading and how to correct it.

and therefore holds the FTC accountable for the advice it provides. So while an advertiser may request an advisory opinion for these reasons, a disadvantage may be that these opinions tend to be harsh, thus placing a heavy obligation on the advertiser to adhere to the opinion it sought.

industry guides In advertising, a Federal Trade Commission measure that outlines the FTC's policies concerning a particular category of product or service.

The FTC will sometimes issue **industry guides.** These outline the commission's policies concerning a particular category of product or service. For example, if a situation surfaces that the FTC believes all distributors, sellers and advertisers of jewelry should be aware of, it will issue a guide for those in that industry to let them know about the policy. These guides are intended to prevent problems in the future. For example, the FTC issued an industry guide in 2009 to update its policies about advertisements that use testimonials and endorsements. These policies especially affect celebrity endorsements and directly affect the established practices of broadcasters and new media companies. These new guidelines include several provisions: First, endorsers themselves may be liable for false claims. These guidelines said the liability-dodging "results not typical" disclaimer used in many testimonial situations will no longer excuse endorsers or media companies from responsibility. The FTC guide explains:

> For broadcast advertising, the new guidelines make clear that endorsers can themselves be liable for misleading statements made during a product pitch. So a radio announcer paid to try a diet plan or some other product and to report about its results on the air needs to be sure not only that his statements are truthful, but that the "results" claimed are in line with what the advertiser can actually prove for the product through clinical study and research. The radio pitchman cannot turn a blind eye to claims that are inherently incredible. In the past, a simple disclosure that "your results may vary" or "these results are not necessarily typical" was sufficient. Today, that disclaimer is no longer enough.[38]

Second, "material connections" such as payment for the endorsement must be disclosed. Third, the guide especially focuses on "new media" and specifically mentions bloggers, social media and viral campaigns. They are warned that understanding the guidelines is vital so as not to become the target of any FTC enforcement action. Fourth, these guidelines are directed at "nontraditional" advertising, such as celebrity guest endorsers on programs or endorsements by personnel such as "on-air DJ's."[39]

trade regulation rule A broadly worded statement by the Federal Trade Commission that outlines advertising requirements for a particular trade.

Another measure the FTC may use to deal with deceptive advertising is the **trade regulation rule.** Like the industry guides, these rules are broad in scope. That is, rather than singling out a specific advertiser, they target an entire trade. The rules differ from the guides in their strength. As opposed to suggesting that a particular practice either be followed or avoided, the trade rules demand it. The benefits of the trade regulation rule include allowing the FTC, in effect, to deal with an entire group of advertisers rather than having to file separate claims against each one individually. Specific advertisers have the opportunity to challenge the rules to the commission and to appeal any FTC decision in court.

The FTC also assesses the extent to which advertisers follow laws that regulate their practices and whether consumer complaints are handled. This comes under the heading of the commission's **voluntary compliance** function. Advertisers have the opportunity to comply with complaints that the commission judges to have merit. If, for example, the commission is made aware of a problem in an advertiser's ad campaign, the commission may request that the advertiser make modifications in the ads. If that fails to occur, then the commission can resort to its corrective measures.

Corrective Measures If an advertiser is given the option to voluntarily comply with regulatory directives but fails to do so for whatever reason, the FTC may then begin executing one or more corrective measures. Among these is the **cease and desist order.** This is an order by the commission for an advertiser to stop one or more advertising practices. The order is contained within a **consent order,** an official document of the Federal Trade Commission. That order is sometimes also referred to as a "consent agreement" because representatives of both the advertiser and the FTC sign it, agreeing to its terms. In 2009, for example, the FTC made public its agreement, including a consent order, with American Nationwide Mortgage Co. In a direct mail ad campaign, American Nationwide failed to adequately disclose the terms of its mortgage offer. According to the commission's complaint, the ad stated, "30-Year Fixed. 1.95%." However, a fine-print, virtually illegible footnote at the bottom of the ad stated, "4.981% Annual Percentage Rate," and a fine-print disclosure on the reverse side of the ad stated: "Initial Annual Percentage Rate (APR) for a 30-year mortgage loan with 80% loan to value is 4.981%. Rate is fixed for 12 months and adjusts upward 7.5% of the payment amount annually for the first ten years of the loan."[40]

A consent order is for settlement purposes only. It does not constitute an admission of guilt by the advertiser. While some advertisers may be reluctant to sign such an agreement, there are practical reasons to do so. Not only is the failure to sign the agreement likely to generate negative publicity, the FTC is likely to impose severe penalties on those who do not settle. In 2010, for example, the FTC issued an agreement containing a consent order in a matter regarding Rite Aid Corporation. Rite Aid pharmacies advertised that they protect the privacy of their prescription drug customers. But after receiving complaints, the FTC concluded that Rite Aid failed, in part by discarding materials such as labels that contained personal information in unsecured, publicly accessible trash containers. The FTC's order contained specific procedures as to how Rite Aid would correct this problem. The company was also fined $1 million.[41]

Though it is usually advantageous for an advertiser to sign a consent order and follow its directives, there may be times when it chooses not to. In these situations, the FTC can issue a **litigated order.** This is an order to stop a specific advertising claim filed in an administrative court. If the court upholds the order, the advertiser may appeal to a federal court. Once the appeal process has been exhausted, failing to abide by an order's stipulations can have serious consequences, including fines of up to $10,000 per day. In a well-known case that

voluntary compliance In advertising, the opportunity granted by the Federal Trade Commission to an advertiser to abide by the FTC's rules.

cease and desist order An administrative agency order prohibiting a person or business from continuing a particular course of conduct. For example, the Federal Trade Commission may order an advertiser to cease and desist from misleading consumers with its advertising.

consent order In advertising, an agreement between the Federal Trade Commission and an advertiser stipulating the terms that must be followed to address problematic advertising; also called a consent agreement.

litigated order A Federal Trade Commission order to stop a specific advertising claim. If the order is upheld in an administrative court, the advertiser may appeal to a federal court; once the appeal process has been exhausted, failing to abide by an order's stipulations can have serious consequences, including fines of up to $10,000 per day.

ultimately contributed significantly to validating the FTC's authority, the commission tackled the advertisements for Geritol. In the 1960s, Geritol was a vitamin and iron tonic. Its advertising claimed to cure "iron poor blood" and increase the energy of its users. The commission concluded that the claims were unfounded. Fatigue, it said, stems from problems that Geritol does not help. After the company violated a cease and desist order, the FTC took action, including fining the tonic's manufacturer, the J.B. Williams Company. That company appealed.[42] After more time in the courts, a $280,000 judgment was levied against J.B. Williams.

Substantiation is a tool vital to the FTC's work and can be an element within any of its corrective measures. It gives the commission the authority to demand that an advertiser prove its claims. The FTC calls it the "science of compliance" and requires advertisers to provide "competent and reliable evidence"[43] for the claims they make. If the advertiser fails to confirm the assertions made in its advertising, the FTC then has the corroboration it needs to take additional action. This can include some of the measures described earlier, such as the cease and desist order. It can also take the form of **corrective advertising.** This measure goes well beyond requiring an advertiser to stop making particular claims. The FTC may also require the advertiser to set the record straight regarding its erroneous claims. Corrective advertising may take the form of future ad campaigns and/or other kinds of information distribution.

The first time the FTC used its corrective advertising power after it was instituted in 1971 was in a case involving the maker of Listerine mouthwash, Warner-Lambert. The FTC had stated that Warner-Lambert's advertising of Listerine had misled the public for more than 50 years by claiming that using the product helped to prevent colds and sore throats. The commission decided that corrective advertising was called for, and a federal appeals court ruled the FTC's implementation of the corrective advertising did not violate the First Amendment.[44] The court believed "Listerine's advertisements play[ed] a substantial role in creating or reinforcing in the public's mind a false belief about the product. . . . [T]his belief [would] linger on after the false advertising ceases."[45] In finding the company's advertising claims to be false, the court relied on a record of hearings that consumed more than four months and produced evidence consisting of approximately 4,000 pages of documentary exhibits and the testimony of 46 witnesses. The court also concluded that the approximately one year of required corrective advertising was not "an unreasonably long time in which to correct a hundred years of cold claims."[46] Thus, over the next year, Warner-Lambert spent $10 million on ads telling people that Listerine did not help prevent colds.

More recently, the FTC ordered the maker of Bayer aspirin to publish corrective advertising over false claims made on behalf of its product. For several years in the mid- to late 1990s, advertisements for Bayer aspirin included the claim that regular use could help save lives by reducing stroke and heart attack risk. While that is true for some people, the ads failed to mention that patients should consult a doctor before beginning to use aspirin regularly because frequent use may cause side effects. Bayer complied with the order to spend $1 million on corrective

substantiation In advertising, the authority of the Federal Trade Commission to demand that an advertiser prove the claims made in its advertisements.

corrective advertising In advertising, a requirement imposed by the Federal Trade Commission forcing an advertiser to include information in future advertisements that corrects false or misleading claims made in previous ads.

advertising and a brochure that laid out the facts more thoroughly.

The FTC's demand to "prove it" was central to its case against Tropicana's Healthy Heart orange juice. In both television and print advertising, Tropicana claimed that drinking three or more glasses per day of its product would have positive benefits such as raising levels of "good" cholesterol and lowering blood pressure. The clinical study Tropicana cited when asked to substantiate its claims did not, according to the FTC, prove the claims.[47] Because the ads were false or misleading, Tropicana was ordered to stop making the claims.

Another instrument the FTC can use is a court **injunction**. In instances when advertising is not only false or misleading but may also cause immediate harm, the FTC may seek an injunction or restraining order from a court. These orders vary somewhat

The Federal Trade Commission put the squeeze on Tropicana Products, Inc., for claims the orange juice company made in advertising.

in specifics but generally include the requirement to stop the advertising until a full hearing takes place. In late 2010, for example, the FTC filed complaints for permanent injunctions against companies accused of making unsubstantiated claims to lure consumers into paying thousands of dollars in up-front fees but failing to reduce credit card debts as promised. According to the FTC's complaints, the defendants made deceptive claims that consumers who enrolled in their programs could eliminate 30 to 60 percent of their credit card debt and be out of debt in 18 to 36 months. The defendants marketed their services via websites and television and radio ads that urged consumers to call toll-free numbers for a free consultation and to enroll in their debt relief programs. One operation claimed to use "secret programs most credit card companies won't tell you about."[48]

SUMMARY

WHILE THE COURTS ARBITRATE DISPUTES over government efforts to regulate advertising, the regulatory process begins with legislative action. For example, in 1938 the U.S. Congress passed the Lanham Act, which defines unfair and deceptive advertising. In 1914, Congress also established the Federal Trade Commission, conferring on this agency its authority to regulate advertising. While other agencies are involved, the FTC is the primary advertising regulator. The commission has several measures available to police advertising, some preventive and some corrective. Advertisers who believe the FTC unjustly levies its sanctions against them can ask a court to hear the case. ∎

Other Administrative Regulation

Though the FTC is the administrative agency that is the primary regulator of advertising, others can also become involved. The Federal Communications Commission (FCC) has the authority to deal with problematic ads in the broadcast media. The Food and Drug Administration (FDA) may also serve as a regulator of advertising for products that are within its influence, at least indirectly. In 2010, the FDA issued an Enforcement Action Plan to restrict promotion and advertising of tobacco products. The year before, Congress passed the Family Smoking Prevention and Tobacco Control Act. That law gave the FDA the authority to regulate tobacco products to protect the public health. The 2010 action plan detailed how the FDA would implement its authority, including the targeting of advertising, especially ads directed at minorities and minors.[49]

Internet Advertising

One significant factor in advertising growth is the opportunities presented by the Internet. Several factors have contributed to the growth of Internet advertising. Advertisers view it as cost effective. Although a state-of-the-art interactive website may cost a substantial sum to produce, an advertisement on the Internet may reach an audience of hundreds of thousands of users nationally, and even more internationally. Technological developments also permit advertisers to gather data on user activity that is useful for marketing purposes. Though this "data mining" method generates controversy, it enables advertisers to target ads to consumer interests. Measuring site activity is a critical issue in setting advertising budgets. From the consumer's perspective, online advertisements provide more detailed product and company information than traditional print or broadcast advertisements. They are also convenient, given that a consumer may purchase a product immediately, saving time and money. The seller's savings in overhead are passed along to consumers. Unfortunately, the instantaneous nature of Internet advertising and transactions has created a fertile field for both fraud and unwanted ads.

The FTC is central to monitoring illegal advertising practices on the Internet. The FTC enforces laws against fraudulent online advertisers just as it would against advertisers in other media. The commission's first enforcement against deceptive advertising on the Internet took place in 1994. The defendant had placed advertisements on an online service advising consumers to take what were illegal steps to repair their credit records.[50] The action was settled according to a consent decree that required the advertiser to establish a compensation fund, not to engage in future misrepresentations, to disclose future credit programs and to cooperate in FTC investigations of sellers of the credit program materials.

Another example of the FTC's role in online advertising occurred in late 2010 when a commission official testified before Congress. He said that while

realWorld Law

In the Amazon Jungle: Third Party Liability

A 2010 ruling in New York shed light on whether "third-party liability" exists in the world of Internet advertising. The case involves several online entities: Amazon, Google, Sellify, OneQuality and Cutting Edge Designs. The parent company of the online retailer OneQuality was unhappy with ads on Amazon. The ads were placed by Cutting Edge Designs. Cutting Edge was one of the millions of associate businesses that Amazon allows to link to its website.

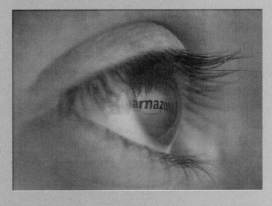

Cutting Edge had purchased keywords from Google so that when those words were searched, ads would appear accompanied by warnings such as "Beware of the SCAM Artist." Among these keywords was the name of an Amazon associate, "onequality.com." Because Cutting Edge ads appeared on Amazon, OneQuality's parent company, Sellify, contacted Amazon demanding that Cutting Edge's ads be removed. Amazon did not have the ability to remove Cutting Edge's ads but issued a warning to Cutting Edge. When there was no response, Amazon terminated Cutting Edge's associate account. Meanwhile, Sellify had sued Amazon, claiming the retail giant was responsible for Cutting Edge's problem ads. A New York court ruled that Amazon could not be held liable for the actions of a third party (Cutting Edge). Amazon did not control, nor had it partnered with, Cutting Edge simply by allowing it to become an associate. Granting permission to third parties to link to its website, the court said, does not create the kind of relationship in which Amazon could be held responsible for any Lanham Act violations by Cutting Edge. Moreover, there was no evidence showing that Amazon had induced others to believe that Cutting Edge was acting as its authorized agent.[1]

The court dismissed the case, seemingly extending the doctrine of no third-party liability to online advertising.

---

1. Sellify, Inc. v. Amazon.com, Inc., 2010 U.S. Dist. LEXIS 118173 (S.D.N.Y. Nov. 4, 2010).

---

the FTC recognizes that consumers may benefit in some ways from the practice of targeted advertising, it also supports providing consumers a "Do Not Track" option. Because the targeted advertising is invisible—accomplished with "cookies" that reveal websites a consumer visits—consumers should have a way to control it, the FTC said.[51] Very shortly afterward, Microsoft announced that it would add a cookie-blocking feature to Internet Explorer 9.[52]

Another form of online advertising comes through unsolicited, unwanted e-mail, or spam. In response to estimates that spam constituted up to 65 percent of all e-mail, public pressure increased for the government to address the problem. From the beginning of the Internet, some people believed the FTC should take an active role in overseeing advertising on the new medium. Others were reluctant to hamstring the new medium during the early stages of its development or to curtail

realWorld Law

CAN-SPAM: A Test Case

Some of the ambiguities in the CAN-SPAM (Controlling the Assault of Non-Solicited Pornography and Marketing) Act were clarified in a recent ruling. James Gordon sought damages when he sued Virtumundo, an online marketer. Gordon claimed Virtumundo violated the CAN-SPAM Act as well as several laws of Washington state. As an online marketer, Virtumundo widely transmitted e-mail advertisements and solicitations to potential customers on behalf of third-party clients. As the U.S. Court of Appeals for the Ninth Circuit said, "In the parlance of our time, they are 'spammers.'"[1]

Gordon had created several e-mail accounts, all of which received transmissions from several online marketers, including Virtumundo. At some point, he set up an automated response to all commercial e-mail sent to his accounts. He claimed the response created a binding contract through which senders agreed to stop sending e-mails or they would pay Gordon $500 for each e-mail sent after that. When the e-mails continued, Gordon sued.

After a district court ruled the case should be dismissed, Gordon appealed to the Ninth Circuit. Its ruling contains several clarifications about the CAN-SPAM Act. First, the act does not ban SPAM outright. Instead, the court said, the law "provides a code of conduct" to regulate commercial e-mail messaging practices.[2] These include prohibiting false and misleading header information, requiring the sender's postal address and notifying recipients of their option to decline future mailings.

Second, in evaluating Gordon's case, the court examined a plaintiff's standing—that is, his eligibility to file suit. The court stated that CAN-SPAM empowers the Federal Trade Commission, states attorney generals and other state and federal agencies to pursue legal actions to enforce the act's provisions.[3] It is here that the court acknowledged ambiguities in CAN-SPAM and began to determine Congress' intent. Here, the court concluded Congress wanted to limit enforcement actions to those best qualified to do so.

Still, CAN-SPAM also allows those who are providers of Internet access who are adversely affected by violation of the law to bring a civil action. The appeals court ruled that Gordon met neither standard and therefore lacked standing. The court said that while Gordon had received a large volume of commercial e-mail, that was not enough to prove he had sustained harm. The Ninth Circuit concluded that the type of harm envisioned by Congress "did not encompass the ordinary inconveniences experienced by consumers and end users."[4] The harm necessary for standing, the court said, must be beyond mere annoyance—rather, it must be "evidence of some combination of operational or technical impairments and related financial costs."[5] As the court said, despite what Gordon and like-minded anti-spam enthusiasts might believe, CAN-SPAM's purpose was not to stamp spam out of existence. In fact, the appeals court believed Gordon was seeking to use the law to "build a litigation factory for his personal financial benefit."[6] Accordingly, it ruled against him by affirming the district court's decision to dismiss his claims.

1. Gordon v. Virtumundo, 575 F.3d 1040, 1045 (9th Cir. 2009).
2. *Id.* at 1048.
3. *Id.*
4. *Id.* at 1053.
5. *Id.* at 1054.
6. *Id.* at 1067.

any of the medium's wealth of free speech opportunities. On the federal level, therefore, the adoption of any regulatory measures was undertaken cautiously.

In 2003, Congress enacted the Controlling the Assault of Non-Solicited Pornography and Marketing (CAN-SPAM) Act.[53] Under the act, Internet service providers, states attorney generals and federal agencies can pursue spammers in federal courts with criminal and civil penalties. The law prohibits the use of false header information in commercial e-mail and requires unsolicited messages to include opt-out instructions. It also provides a protection against spam containing unmarked pornographic material. Penalties for violations include up to five years imprisonment and fines of up to $6 million. In 2008, the FTC approved new rule provisions under the CAN-SPAM Act to strengthen its enforcement.[54]

Many in the technical and legal professions, however, question the federal government's ability to enforce those restrictions and have criticized the way the act supersedes stricter state laws. CAN-SPAM "is an abomination at the federal level," says Harvard law professor Lawrence Lessig. "It's ineffective and it's affirmatively harmful because it preempts state legislation."[55] A 2008 article questioned the effectiveness of CAN-SPAM over its first five years, claiming that spam not only increased significantly in volume but became more malicious by including links with viruses to infect computers.[56]

In an effort to supplement federal law, 37 states have enacted their own anti-spam regulations as of 2010.[57] One of those is Virginia, whose law targeted unsolicited commercial bulk e-mails.[58] A man once considered one of the world's most prolific spammers,[59] Jeremy Jaynes, was charged with violating that law after he sent more than 55,000 unsolicited e-mails to subscribers of America Online. In 2008, the Virginia Supreme Court overturned lower court rulings upholding Jaynes' conviction. Jaynes had challenged the Virginia law, saying that it was overbroad. The court agreed, ruling that a right to engage in anonymous speech was protected by the First Amendment. By prohibiting false routing information in the dissemination of e-mails, the law infringed on that protected right. Unsolicited noncommercial bulk e-mails were not the target of the statute and were not a focus of the problem addressed through the enactment of the Virginia law. "That statute is unconstitutionally overbroad on its face," the court said, "because it prohibits the anonymous transmission of all unsolicited bulk e-mails including those containing political, religious or other speech protected by the First Amendment to the United States Constitution."[60] The U.S. Supreme Court denied Virginia's appeal request, allowing the state supreme court ruling to stand.[61]

SUMMARY

THE GROWTH OF THE INTERNET HAS MEANT a growth in advertising on the medium. As with other media, the government monitors Internet advertising. In fact, since fraudulent and deceptive advertising is in some ways especially troublesome on the Internet, the medium receives special attention. Not only has the Federal Trade Commission dealt with what it believes to be improper advertising practices online, but so have federal and state legislators. The CAN-SPAM Act, a law designed to help prevent unsolicited e-mail messages, was passed by Congress in 2003. Its effectiveness since then, however, has been questioned. Thirty-seven states now have anti-spam laws, though a section of at least one, Virginia's, has been ruled unconstitutional. ∎

Cases for Study

Thinking About It

The two case excerpts that follow address the regulation of commercial speech and whether specific regulations are consistent with the First Amendment. The first is the U.S. Supreme Court case that established the test for answering that question. The second case, also from the U.S. Supreme Court, deals with the application of that test and represents a shift by the Court in how part of the test is evaluated. As you read these case excerpts, keep the following questions in mind:

- What are the circumstances surrounding each case?
- What is the nature of the regulations being challenged in each case?
- What is the state interest in each case? Are those interests legitimate?
- How does the *Lorillard* ruling represent a shift in the application and interpretation of the test? What is the crucial element of the test with regard to this shift?

Central Hudson Gas & Electric Corp. v. Public Service Commission of New York
SUPREME COURT OF THE UNITED STATES
447 U.S. 557 (1980)

JUSTICE LEWIS POWELL delivered the Court's opinion:

This case presents the question whether a regulation of the Public Service Commission of the State of New York violates the First and Fourteenth Amendments because it completely bans promotional advertising by an electrical utility.

I

In December, 1973, the Commission, appellee here, ordered electric utilities in New York State to cease all advertising that "promot[es] the use of electricity." The order was based on the Commission's finding that "the interconnected utility system in New York State does not have sufficient fuel stocks or sources of supply to continue furnishing all customer demands for the 1973–1974 winter."

Three years later, when the fuel shortage had eased, the Commission requested comments from the public on its proposal to continue the ban on promotional advertising. Central Hudson Gas & Electric Corp., the appellant in this case, opposed the ban on First Amendment grounds. After reviewing the public comments, the Commission extended the prohibition in a Policy Statement issued on February 25, 1977.

The Policy Statement divided advertising expenses "into two broad categories: promotional—advertising intended to stimulate the purchase of utility services . . . and institutional and informational, a broad category inclusive of all advertising not clearly intended to promote sales." The Commission declared all promotional advertising contrary to the national policy of conserving energy. It acknowledged that the ban is not a perfect vehicle for conserving energy. For example, the Commission's order prohibits promotional advertising to develop consumption during periods when demand for electricity is low. By limiting growth in "off-peak" consumption, the ban limits the "beneficial side effects" of such growth in terms of more efficient use of existing powerplants. And since oil dealers are not under the Commission's jurisdiction and thus remain free to advertise, it was recognized that the ban can achieve only "piecemeal conservationism." Still, the Commission adopted the restriction because it was deemed likely to "result in some dampening of unnecessary growth" in energy consumption.

The Commission's order explicitly permitted "informational" advertising designed to encourage "shifts of consumption" from peak demand times to periods of low electricity demand. Informational advertising would not seek to increase aggregate consumption, but would invite a leveling of demand throughout any given 24-hour period. The agency offered to review "specific proposals by the companies for specifically described [advertising] programs that meet these criteria."

When it rejected requests for rehearing on the Policy Statement, the Commission supplemented its rationale for the advertising ban. The agency observed that additional electricity probably would be more expensive to produce than existing output. Because electricity rates in New York were not then based on marginal cost, the Commission feared that additional power would be priced below the actual cost of generation. The additional electricity would be subsidized by all consumers through generally higher rates. The state agency also thought that promotional advertising would give "misleading signals" to the public by appearing to encourage energy consumption at a time when conservation is needed. . . .

II

The Commission's order restricts only commercial speech, that is, expression related solely to the economic interests of the speaker and its audience. The First Amendment, as applied to the States through the Fourteenth Amendment, protects commercial speech from unwarranted governmental regulation. Commercial expression not only serves the economic interest of the speaker, but also assists consumers and furthers the societal interest in the fullest possible dissemination of information. In applying the First Amendment to this area, we have rejected the "highly paternalistic"

view that government has complete power to suppress or regulate commercial speech. . . .

Nevertheless, our decisions have recognized "the 'commonsense' distinction between speech proposing a commercial transaction, which occurs in an area traditionally subject to government regulation, and other varieties of speech." . . . The Constitution therefore accords a lesser protection to commercial speech than to other constitutionally guaranteed expression. The protection available for particular commercial expression turns on the nature both of the expression and of the governmental interests served by its regulation.

The First Amendment's concern for commercial speech is based on the informational function of advertising. Consequently, there can be no constitutional objection to the suppression of commercial messages that do not accurately inform the public about lawful activity. The government may ban forms of communication more likely to deceive the public than to inform it, or commercial speech related to illegal activity.

If the communication is neither misleading nor related to unlawful activity, the government's power is more circumscribed. The State must assert a substantial interest to be achieved by restrictions on commercial speech. Moreover, the regulatory technique must be in proportion to that interest. The limitation on expression must be designed carefully to achieve the State's goal. Compliance with this requirement may be measured by two criteria. First, the restriction must directly advance the state interest involved; the regulation may not be sustained if it provides only ineffective or remote support for the government's purpose. Second, if the governmental interest could be served as well by a more limited restriction on commercial speech, the excessive restrictions cannot survive. . . .

The second criterion recognizes that the First Amendment mandates that speech restrictions be "narrowly drawn." The regulatory technique may extend only as far as the interest it serves. The State cannot regulate speech that poses no danger to the asserted state interest, nor can it completely suppress information when narrower restrictions on expression would serve its interest as well. . . .

In this case, the Commission's prohibition acts directly against the promotional activities of Central

Hudson, and, to the extent the limitations are unnecessary to serve the State's interest, they are invalid. . . .

In commercial speech cases, then, a four-part analysis has developed. At the outset, we must determine whether the expression is protected by the First Amendment. For commercial speech to come within that provision, it at least must concern lawful activity and not be misleading. Next, we ask whether the asserted governmental interest is substantial. If both inquiries yield positive answers, we must determine whether the regulation directly advances the governmental interest asserted, and whether it is not more extensive than is necessary to serve that interest.

III

We now apply this four-step analysis for commercial speech to the Commission's arguments in support of its ban on promotional advertising.

A

The Commission does not claim that the expression at issue either is inaccurate or relates to unlawful activity. Yet the New York Court of Appeals questioned whether Central Hudson's advertising is protected commercial speech. Because appellant holds a monopoly over the sale of electricity in its service area, the state court suggested that the Commission's order restricts no commercial speech of any worth. The court stated that advertising in a "noncompetitive market" could not improve the decisionmaking of consumers. The court saw no constitutional problem with barring commercial speech that it viewed as conveying little useful information.

This reasoning falls short of establishing that appellant's advertising is not commercial speech protected by the First Amendment. Monopoly over the supply of a product provides no protection from competition with substitutes for that product. . . .

Even in monopoly markets, the suppression of advertising reduces the information available for consumer decisions and thereby defeats the purpose of the First Amendment. The New York court's argument appears to assume that the providers of a monopoly service or product are willing to pay for wholly ineffective advertising. Most businesses—even regulated monopolies—are unlikely to underwrite promotional advertising that is of no interest or use to consumers. Indeed, a monopoly enterprise legitimately may wish to inform the public that it has developed new services or terms of doing business. A consumer may need information to aid his decision whether or not to use the monopoly service at all, or how much of the service he should purchase. In the absence of factors that would distort the decision to advertise, we may assume that the willingness of a business to promote its products reflects a belief that consumers are interested in the advertising. Since no such extraordinary conditions have been identified in this case, appellant's monopoly position does not alter the First Amendment's protection for its commercial speech.

B

The Commission offers two state interests as justifications for the ban on promotional advertising. The first concerns energy conservation. Any increase in demand for electricity—during peak or off-peak periods—means greater consumption of energy. The Commission argues, and the New York court agreed, that the State's interest in conserving energy is sufficient to support suppression of advertising designed to increase consumption of electricity. In view of our country's dependence on energy resources beyond our control, no one can doubt the importance of energy conservation. Plainly, therefore, the state interest asserted is substantial.

The Commission also argues that promotional advertising will aggravate inequities caused by the failure to base the utilities' rates on marginal cost. The utilities argued to the Commission that if they could promote the use of electricity in periods of low demand, they would improve their utilization of generating capacity. The Commission responded that promotion of off-peak consumption also would increase consumption during peak periods. If peak demand were to rise, the absence of marginal cost rates would mean that the rates charged for the additional power would not reflect the true costs of expanding production. Instead, the extra costs would be borne by all consumers through higher overall rates. Without promotional advertising, the Commission stated, this inequitable turn of events would be less likely to occur. The choice among rate structures involves difficult and important questions of economic supply and distributional fairness. The State's concern that rates be fair and efficient represents a clear and substantial governmental interest.

C

Next, we focus on the relationship between the State's interests and the advertising ban. Under this criterion, the Commission's laudable concern over the equity and efficiency of appellant's rates does not provide a constitutionally adequate reason for restricting protected speech. The link between the advertising prohibition and appellant's rate structure is, at most, tenuous. The impact of promotional advertising on the equity of appellant's rates is highly speculative. Advertising to increase off-peak usage would have to increase peak usage, while other factors that directly affect the fairness and efficiency of appellant's rates remained constant. Such conditional and remote eventualities simply cannot justify silencing appellant's promotional advertising.

In contrast, the State's interest in energy conservation is directly advanced by the Commission order at issue here. There is an immediate connection between advertising and demand for electricity. Central Hudson would not contest the advertising ban unless it believed that promotion would increase its sales. Thus, we find a direct link between the state interest in conservation and the Commission's order.

D

We come finally to the critical inquiry in this case: whether the Commission's complete suppression of speech ordinarily protected by the First Amendment is no more extensive than necessary to further the State's interest in energy conservation. The Commission's order reaches all promotional advertising, regardless of the impact of the touted service on overall energy use. But the energy conservation rationale, as important as it is, cannot justify suppressing information about electric devices or services that would cause no net increase in total energy use. In addition, no showing has been made that a more limited restriction on

the content of promotional advertising would not serve adequately the State's interests.

Appellant insists that, but for the ban, it would advertise products and services that use energy efficiently. These include the "heat pump," which both parties acknowledge to be a major improvement in electric heating, and the use of electric heat as a "backup" to solar and other heat sources. Although the Commission has questioned the efficiency of electric heating before this Court, neither the Commission's Policy Statement nor its order denying rehearing made findings on this issue. In the absence of authoritative findings to the contrary, we must credit as within the realm of possibility the claim that electric heat can be an efficient alternative in some circumstances.

The Commission's order prevents appellant from promoting electric services that would reduce energy use by diverting demand from less efficient sources, or that would consume roughly the same amount of energy as do alternative sources. In neither situation would the utility's advertising endanger conservation or mislead the public. To the extent that the Commission's order suppresses speech that in no way impairs the State's interest in energy conservation, the Commission's order violates the First and Fourteenth Amendments, and must be invalidated.

The Commission also has not demonstrated that its interest in conservation cannot be protected adequately by more limited regulation of appellant's commercial expression. To further its policy of conservation, the Commission could attempt to restrict the format and content of Central Hudson's advertising. It might, for example, require that the advertisements include information about the relative efficiency and expense of the offered service, both under current conditions and for the foreseeable future. In the absence of a showing that more limited speech regulation would be ineffective, we cannot approve the complete suppression of Central Hudson's advertising.

IV

Our decision today in no way disparages the national interest in energy conservation. We accept without reservation the argument that conservation, as well as the development of alternative energy sources, is an imperative national goal. Administrative bodies empowered to regulate electric utilities have the authority—and indeed the duty—to take appropriate action to further this goal. When, however, such action involves the suppression of speech, the First and Fourteenth Amendments require that the restriction be no more extensive than is necessary to serve the state interest. In this case, the record before us fails to show that the total ban on promotional advertising meets this requirement.

Accordingly, the judgment of the New York Court of Appeals is

Reversed. . . .

JUSTICE WILLIAM REHNQUIST, dissenting:

The Court today invalidates an order issued by the New York Public Service Commission designed to promote a policy that has been declared to be of critical national concern. The order was issued by the Commission in 1973 in response to the Mideastern oil embargo crisis. It prohibits electric corporations "from promoting the use of electricity through the use of advertising, subsidy payments . . . or employee incentives." Although the immediate crisis created by the oil embargo has subsided, the ban on promotional advertising remains in effect. The regulation was reexamined by the New York Public Service Commission in 1977. Its constitutionality was subsequently upheld by the New York Court of Appeals, which concluded that the paramount national interest in energy conservation justified its retention.

The Court's asserted justification for invalidating the New York law is the public interest discerned by the Court to underlie the First Amendment in the free flow of commercial information. Prior to this Court's recent decision in *Virginia Pharmacy Board v. Virginia Citizens Consumer Council,* however, commercial speech was afforded no protection under the First Amendment whatsoever. Given what seems to me full recognition of the holding of *Virginia Pharmacy Board* that commercial speech is entitled to some degree of First Amendment protection, I think the Court is nonetheless incorrect in invalidating the carefully considered state ban on promotional

advertising in light of pressing national and state energy needs. . . .

This Court has previously recognized that, although commercial speech may be entitled to First Amendment protection, that protection is not as extensive as that accorded to the advocacy of ideas. . . . ". . . We have not discarded the 'common-sense' distinction between speech proposing a commercial transaction, which occurs in an area traditionally subject to government regulation, and other varieties of speech. To require a parity of constitutional protection for commercial and noncommercial speech alike could invite dilution, simply by a leveling process, of the force of the Amendment's guarantee with respect to the latter kind of speech. Rather than subject the First Amendment to such a devitalization, we instead have afforded commercial speech a limited measure of protection, commensurate with its subordinate position in the scale of First Amendment values, while allowing modes of regulation that might be impermissible in the realm of noncommercial expression."

The Court's decision today fails to give due deference to this subordinate position of commercial speech. The Court in so doing returns to the bygone era . . . in which it was common practice for this Court to strike down economic regulations adopted by a State based on the Court's own notions of the most appropriate means for the State to implement its considered policies.

I had thought by now it had become well established that a State has broad discretion in imposing economic regulations. . . . The State of New York has determined here that economic realities require the grant of monopoly status to public utilities in order to distribute efficiently the services they provide, and in granting utilities such status it has made them subject to an extensive regulatory scheme. When the State adopted this scheme and when its Public Service Commission issued its initial ban on promotional advertising in 1973, commercial speech had not been held to fall within the scope of the First Amendment at all. . . .

The Court today holds not only that commercial speech is entitled to First Amendment protection, but also that when it is protected a State may not regulate it unless its reason for doing so amounts to a "substantial" governmental interest, its regulation "directly advances" that interest, and its manner of regulation is "not more extensive than necessary" to serve the interest. The test adopted by the Court thus elevates the protection accorded commercial speech that falls within the scope of the First Amendment to a level that is virtually indistinguishable from that of noncommercial speech. . . .

An ostensible justification for striking down New York's ban on promotional advertising is that this Court has previously "rejected the 'highly paternalistic' view that government has complete power to suppress or regulate commercial speech. '[P]eople will perceive their own best interests if only they are well enough informed and . . . the best means to that end is to open the channels of communication, rather than to close them. . . . '" Whatever the merits of this view, I think the Court has carried its logic too far here. . . .

While it is true that an important objective of the First Amendment is to foster the free flow of information, identification of speech that falls within its protection is not aided by the metaphorical reference to a "marketplace of ideas." There is no reason for believing that the marketplace of ideas is free from market imperfections any more than there is to believe that the invisible hand will always lead to optimum economic decisions in the commercial market. . . . Indeed, many types of speech have been held to fall outside the scope of the First Amendment, thereby subject to governmental regulation, despite this Court's references to a marketplace of ideas. . . .

I remain of the view that the Court unlocked a Pandora's Box when it "elevated" commercial speech to the level of traditional political speech by according it First Amendment protection in *Virginia Pharmacy Board v. Virginia Citizens Consumer Council*. The line between "commercial speech," and the kind of speech that those who drafted the First Amendment had in mind may not be a technically or intellectually easy one to draw, but it surely produced far fewer problems than has the development of judicial doctrine in this area since *Virginia Pharmacy Board*. . . .

The notion that more speech is the remedy to expose falsehood and fallacies is wholly out of place in the commercial bazaar, where if applied logically the remedy of one who was defrauded would be merely a statement, available upon request, reciting the Latin maxim "*caveat emptor*." But since "fraudulent speech" in this area is to be remediable under *Virginia Pharmacy Board*, the remedy of one defrauded is a lawsuit or an agency proceeding based on common-law notions of fraud that are separated by a world of difference from the realm of politics and government. What time, legal decisions, and common sense have so widely severed, I declined to join in *Virginia Pharmacy Board*, and regret now to see the Court reaping the seeds that it there sowed. For in a democracy, the economic is subordinate to the political, a lesson that our ancestors learned long ago, and that our descendants will undoubtedly have to relearn many years hence.

III

The Court concedes that the state interest in energy conservation is plainly substantial, as is the State's concern that its rates be fair and efficient. It also concedes that there is a direct link between the Commission's ban on promotional advertising and the State's interest in conservation. The Court nonetheless strikes down the ban on promotional advertising because the Commission has failed to demonstrate, under the final part of the Court's four-part test, that its regulation is no more extensive than necessary to serve the State's interest. In reaching this conclusion, the Court conjures up potential advertisements that a utility might make that conceivably would result in net energy savings. The Court does not indicate that the New York Public Service Commission has in fact construed its ban on "promotional" advertising to preclude the dissemination of information that clearly would result in a net energy savings, nor does it even suggest that the Commission has been confronted with and rejected such an advertising proposal. The final part of the Court's test thus leaves room for so many hypothetical "better" ways that any ingenious lawyer will surely seize on one of them to secure the invalidation of what the state agency actually did. . . .

Ordinarily it is the role of the State Public Service Commission to make factual determinations concerning whether a device or service will result in a net energy savings and, if so, whether and to what extent state law permits dissemination of information about the device or service. Otherwise, as here, this Court will have no factual basis for its assertions. And the State will never have an opportunity to consider the issue and thus to construe its law in a manner consistent with the Federal Constitution. . . .

It is, in my view, inappropriate for the Court to invalidate the State's ban on commercial advertising here, based on its speculation that in some cases the advertising may result in a net savings in electrical energy use, and in the cases in which it is clear a net energy savings would result from utility advertising, the Public Service Commission would apply its ban so as to proscribe such advertising. Even assuming that the Court's speculation is correct, I do not think it follows that facial invalidation of the ban is the appropriate course. . . .

For the foregoing reasons, I would affirm the judgment of the New York Court of Appeals.

Lorillard v. Reilly
SUPREME COURT OF THE UNITED STATES
533 U.S. 525 (2001)

JUSTICE SANDRA DAY O'CONNOR delivered the Court's opinion:

I

. . . In January 1999 . . . the Massachusetts Attorney General (Attorney General) promulgated regulations governing the sale and advertisement of cigarettes, smokeless tobacco, and cigars. The purpose of the cigarette and smokeless tobacco regulations is "to eliminate deception and unfairness in the way cigarettes and smokeless tobacco products are marketed, sold and distributed in Massachusetts in order to address the incidence of cigarette smoking and smokeless tobacco use by children under legal age . . . [and] in order to prevent access to such products by underage consumers." . . . The regulations place a variety of restrictions on outdoor advertising, point-of-sale advertising, retail sales transactions, transactions by mail, promotions, sampling of products, and labels for cigars.

The cigarette and smokeless tobacco regulations being challenged before this Court provide:

". . . (5) Advertising Restrictions. Except as provided in [S.21.04(6)], it shall be an unfair or deceptive act or practice for any manufacturer, distributor or retailer to engage in any of the following practices:

"(a) Outdoor advertising, including advertising in enclosed stadiums and advertising from within a retail establishment that is directed toward or visible from the outside of the establishment, in any location that is within a 1,000 foot radius of any public playground, playground area in a public park, elementary school or secondary school;

"(b) Point-of-sale advertising of cigarettes or smokeless tobacco products any portion of which is placed lower than five feet from the floor of any retail establishment which is located within a one thousand foot radius of any public playground, playground area in a public park, elementary school or secondary school, and which is not an adult-only retail establishment.". . .

Before the effective date of the regulations, February 1, 2000, members of the tobacco industry sued the Attorney General in the United States District Court for the District of Massachusetts. Four cigarette manufacturers (Lorillard Tobacco Company, Brown & Williamson Tobacco Corporation, R. J. Reynolds Tobacco Company, and Philip Morris Incorporated), a maker of smokeless tobacco products (U.S. Smokeless Tobacco Company), and several cigar manufacturers and retailers claimed that many of the regulations violate the Commerce Clause, the Supremacy Clause, the First and Fourteenth Amendments. . . .

III

A

For over 25 years, the Court has recognized that commercial speech does not fall outside the purview of the First Amendment. Instead, the Court has afforded commercial speech a measure of First Amendment protection "'commensurate'" with its position in relation to other constitutionally guaranteed expression. In recognition of the "distinction between speech proposing a commercial transaction, which occurs in an area traditionally subject to government regulation, and other varieties of speech," we developed a framework for analyzing regulations of commercial speech that is "substantially similar" to the test for time, place, and manner restrictions. The analysis contains four elements:

"At the outset, we must determine whether the expression is protected by the First Amendment. For commercial speech to come within that provision, it at least must concern lawful activity and not be misleading. Next, we ask whether the asserted governmental interest is substantial. If both inquiries yield positive answers, we must determine whether the regulation directly advances the governmental interest asserted, and whether it is not more extensive than is necessary to serve that interest.". . .

Only the last two steps of *Central Hudson*'s four-part analysis are at issue here. The Attorney General has assumed for purposes of summary judgment that petitioners' speech is entitled to First Amendment protection. With respect to the second step, none of the petitioners contests the importance of the State's interest in preventing the use of tobacco products by minors.

The third step of *Central Hudson* concerns the relationship between the harm that underlies the State's interest and the means identified by the State to advance that interest. It requires that "the speech restriction directly and materially advance the asserted governmental interest. 'This burden is not satisfied by mere speculation or conjecture; rather, a governmental body seeking to sustain a restriction on commercial speech must demonstrate that the harms it recites are real and that its restriction will in fact alleviate them to a material degree.'"

We do not, however, require that "empirical data come . . . accompanied by a surfeit of background information. . . . [W]e have permitted litigants to justify speech restrictions by reference to studies and anecdotes pertaining to different locales altogether, or even, in a case applying strict scrutiny, to justify restrictions based solely on history, consensus, and 'simple common sense.'"

The last step of the *Central Hudson* analysis "complements" the third step, "asking whether the speech restriction is not more extensive than necessary to serve the interests that support it." We have made it clear that "the least restrictive means" is not the standard; instead, the case law requires a reasonable "'fit between the legislature's ends and the means chosen to accomplish those ends, . . . a means narrowly tailored to achieve the desired objective.'" Focusing on the third and fourth steps of the *Central Hudson* analysis, we first address the outdoor advertising and point-of-sale advertising regulations for smokeless tobacco and cigars. We then address the sales practices regulations for all tobacco products.

B

The outdoor advertising regulations prohibit smokeless tobacco or cigar advertising within a 1,000-foot radius of a school or playground. The District Court and Court of Appeals concluded that the Attorney General had identified a real problem with underage use of tobacco products, that limiting youth exposure to advertising would combat that problem, and that the regulations burdened no more speech than necessary to accomplish the State's goal. The smokeless tobacco and cigar petitioners take issue with all of these conclusions.

1

The smokeless tobacco and cigar petitioners contend that the Attorney General's regulations do not satisfy *Central Hudson*'s third step. They maintain that although the Attorney General may have identified a problem with underage cigarette smoking, he has not identified an equally severe problem with respect to underage use of smokeless tobacco or cigars. The smokeless tobacco petitioner emphasizes the "lack of parity" between cigarettes and smokeless tobacco. The cigar petitioners catalogue a list of differences between cigars and other tobacco products, including the characteristics of the products and marketing strategies. The petitioners finally contend that the Attorney General cannot prove that advertising has a causal link to tobacco use such that limiting advertising will materially alleviate any problem of underage use of their products.

In previous cases, we have acknowledged the theory that product advertising stimulates demand for products, while suppressed advertising may have the opposite effect. The Attorney General cites numerous studies to support this theory in the case of tobacco products. . . .

Our review of the record reveals that the Attorney General has provided ample documentation of the problem with underage use of smokeless tobacco and cigars. In addition, we disagree with petitioners' claim that there is no evidence that preventing targeted campaigns and limiting youth exposure to advertising will decrease underage use of smokeless tobacco and cigars. On this record and in the posture of summary judgment, we are unable to conclude that the Attorney General's decision to regulate advertising of smokeless tobacco and cigars in an effort to combat the use of tobacco products by minors was based on mere "speculation [and] conjecture."

2

Whatever the strength of the Attorney General's evidence to justify the outdoor advertising regulations, however, we conclude that the regulations do not satisfy the fourth step of the *Central Hudson* analysis. The final step of the *Central Hudson* analysis, the "critical inquiry in this case," requires a reasonable fit between the means and ends of the regulatory scheme. The Attorney General's regulations do not meet this standard. The broad sweep of the regulations indicates that the Attorney General did not "carefully calculate the costs and benefits associated with the burden on speech imposed" by the regulations.

The outdoor advertising regulations prohibit any smokeless tobacco or cigar advertising within 1,000 feet of schools or playgrounds. In the District Court, petitioners maintained that this prohibition would prevent advertising in 87% to 91% of Boston, Worcester, and Springfield, Massachusetts. The 87% to 91% figure appears to include not only the effect of the regulations, but also the limitations imposed by other generally applicable zoning restrictions. The Attorney General disputed petitioners' figures but "conceded that the reach of the regulations is substantial." Thus, the Court of Appeals concluded that the regulations prohibit advertising in a substantial portion of the major metropolitan areas of Massachusetts.

The substantial geographical reach of the Attorney General's outdoor advertising regulations is compounded by other factors. "Outdoor" advertising includes not only advertising located outside an establishment, but also advertising inside a store if that advertising is visible from outside the store. The regulations restrict advertisements of any size and the term advertisement also includes oral statements.

In some geographical areas, these regulations would constitute nearly a complete ban on the communication of truthful information about smokeless tobacco and cigars to adult consumers. The breadth and scope of the regulations, and the process by which the Attorney General adopted the regulations, do not demonstrate a careful calculation of the speech interests involved.

First, the Attorney General did not seem to consider the impact of the 1,000-foot restriction on commercial speech in major metropolitan areas. The Attorney General apparently selected the 1,000-foot distance based on the FDA's decision to impose an identical 1,000-foot restriction when it attempted to regulate cigarette and smokeless tobacco advertising. But the FDA's 1,000-foot regulation was not an adequate basis for the Attorney General to tailor the Massachusetts regulations. The degree to which speech is suppressed—or alternative avenues for speech remain available—under a particular regulatory scheme tends to be case specific. . . .

In addition, the range of communications restricted seems unduly broad. For instance, it is not clear from the regulatory scheme why a ban on oral communications is necessary to further the State's interest. Apparently that restriction means that a retailer is unable to answer inquiries about its tobacco products if that communication occurs outdoors.

Similarly, a ban on all signs of any size seems ill suited to target the problem of highly visible billboards, as opposed to smaller signs. To the extent that studies have identified particular advertising and promotion practices that appeal to youth, tailoring would involve targeting those practices while permitting others. As crafted, the regulations make no distinction among practices on this basis. . . .

The State's interest in preventing underage tobacco use is substantial, and even compelling, but it is no less true that the sale and use of tobacco products by adults is a legal activity. We must consider that tobacco retailers and manufacturers have an interest in conveying truthful information about their products to adults, and adults have a corresponding interest in receiving truthful information about tobacco products. In a case involving indecent speech on the Internet we explained that "the governmental interest in protecting children from harmful materials . . . does not justify an unnecessarily broad suppression of speech addressed to adults." As the State protects children from tobacco advertisements, tobacco manufacturers and retailers and their adult consumers still have a protected interest in communication.

In some instances, Massachusetts' outdoor advertising regulations would impose particularly onerous burdens on speech. . . .

In addition, a retailer in Massachusetts may have no means of communicating to passersby on the street that it sells tobacco products because alternative forms of advertisement, like newspapers, do not allow that retailer to propose an instant transaction in the way that onsite advertising does. The ban on any indoor advertising that is visible from the outside also presents problems in establishments like convenience stores, which have unique security concerns that counsel in favor of full visibility of the store from the outside. It is these sorts of considerations that the Attorney General failed to incorporate into the regulatory scheme.

We conclude that the Attorney General has failed to show that the outdoor advertising regulations for smokeless tobacco and cigars are not more extensive than necessary to advance the State's substantial interest in preventing underage tobacco use. . . .

A careful calculation of the costs of a speech regulation does not mean that a State must demonstrate that there is no incursion on legitimate speech interests, but a speech regulation cannot unduly impinge on the speaker's ability to propose a commercial transaction and the adult listener's opportunity to obtain information about products. After reviewing the outdoor advertising regulations, we find the calculation in this case insufficient for purposes of the First Amendment.

C

Massachusetts has also restricted indoor, point-of-sale advertising for smokeless tobacco and cigars. Advertising cannot be "placed lower than five feet from the floor of any retail establishment which is located within a one thousand foot radius of" any school or playground. The District Court invalidated these provisions, concluding that the Attorney General had not provided a sufficient basis for regulating indoor advertising. The Court of Appeals reversed. The court explained: "We do have some misgivings about the effectiveness of a restriction that is based on the assumption that minors under five feet tall will not, or will less frequently, raise their view above eye-level, but we find that such [a] determination falls within that range of reasonableness in which the Attorney General is best suited to pass judgment."

We conclude that the point-of-sale advertising regulations fail both the third and fourth steps of the *Central Hudson* analysis. A regulation cannot be sustained if it "'provides only ineffective or remote support for the government's purpose,'" or if there is "little chance" that the restriction will advance the State's goal. As outlined above, the State's goal is to prevent minors from using tobacco products and to curb demand for that activity by limiting youth exposure to advertising. The 5 foot rule does not seem to advance that goal. Not all children are less than 5 feet tall, and those who are certainly have the ability to look up and take in their surroundings. . . .

Massachusetts may wish to target tobacco advertisements and displays that entice children, much like floor-level candy displays in a convenience store, but the blanket height restriction does not constitute a reasonable fit with that goal. . . . We conclude that the restriction on the height of indoor advertising is invalid under *Central Hudson*'s third and fourth prongs.

D

The Attorney General also promulgated a number of regulations that restrict sales practices by cigarette, smokeless tobacco, and cigar manufacturers and retailers. Among other restrictions, the regulations bar the use of self-service displays and require that tobacco products be placed out of the reach of all consumers in a location accessible only to salespersons. . . . Two of the cigarette petitioners (Brown & Williamson Tobacco Corporation and Lorillard Tobacco Company), petitioner U.S. Smokeless Tobacco Company, and the cigar petitioners challenge the sales practices regulations on First Amendment grounds. The cigar petitioners additionally challenge a provision that prohibits sampling or promotional giveaways of cigars or little cigars. . . .

The cigarette and smokeless tobacco petitioners contend that "the same First Amendment principles that require invalidation of the outdoor and indoor advertising restrictions require invalidation of the display regulations at issue in this case." The cigar petitioners contend that self-service displays for cigars cannot be prohibited because each brand of cigar is unique and customers traditionally have sought to handle and compare cigars at the time of purchase.

We reject these contentions. Assuming that petitioners have a cognizable speech interest in a particular means of displaying their products, these regulations withstand First Amendment scrutiny.

Massachusetts' sales practices provisions regulate conduct that may have a communicative component, but Massachusetts seeks to regulate the placement of tobacco products for reasons unrelated to the communication of ideas. We conclude that the State has demonstrated a substantial interest in preventing access to tobacco products by minors and has adopted an appropriately narrow means of advancing that interest.

Unattended displays of tobacco products present an opportunity for access without the proper age verification required by law. Thus, the State prohibits self-service and other displays that would allow an individual to obtain tobacco products without direct contact with a salesperson. It is clear that the regulations leave open ample channels of communication. The regulations do not significantly impede adult access to tobacco products. Moreover, retailers have other means of exercising any cognizable speech interest in the presentation of their products. We presume that vendors may place empty tobacco packaging on open display, and display actual tobacco products so long as that display is only accessible to sales personnel. As for cigars, there is no indication in the regulations that a customer is unable to examine a cigar prior to purchase, so long as that examination takes place through a salesperson. . . .

We conclude that the sales practices regulations withstand First Amendment scrutiny. The means chosen by the State are narrowly tailored to prevent access to tobacco products by minors, are unrelated to expression, and leave open alternative avenues for vendors to convey information about products and for would-be customers to inspect products before purchase.

IV

We have observed that "tobacco use, particularly among children and adolescents, poses perhaps the single most significant threat to public health in the United States." From a policy perspective, it is understandable for the States to attempt to prevent minors from using tobacco products before they reach an age where they are capable of weighing for themselves the risks and potential benefits of tobacco use, and other adult activities. Federal law, however, places limits on policy choices available to the States.

In these cases, Congress enacted a comprehensive scheme to address cigarette smoking and health in advertising and pre-empted state regulation of cigarette advertising that attempts to address that same concern, even with respect to youth. The First Amendment also constrains state efforts to limit advertising of tobacco products, because so long as the sale and use of tobacco is lawful for adults, the tobacco industry has a protected interest in communicating information about its products and adult customers have an interest in receiving that information.

To the extent that federal law and the First Amendment do not prohibit state action, States and localities remain free to combat the problem of underage tobacco use by appropriate means. The judgment of the United States Court of Appeals for the First Circuit is therefore affirmed in part and reversed in part, and the cases are remanded for further proceedings consistent with this opinion.

It is so ordered.

Endnotes

Chapter 1

The Rule of Law

1. Powell v. McCormack, 395 U.S. 486, 506 (1969) (citing Kilbourn v. Thompson, 103 U.S. 168, 199 (1881)).

2. Austin v. Michigan Chamber of Commerce, 494 U.S. 652 (1990); McConnell v. Federal Election Commission, 540 U.S. 93 (2003).

3. (aka McCain–Feingold), 2 U.S.C. § 441b.

4. Federal Election Commission v. Wisconsin Right to Life, 551 U.S. 449, 534 (2007) (Souter, J., dissenting).

5. Memorandum Opinion. Citizens United v. Federal Elections Commission (D. D.C. 2008), *available at* https://ecf.dcd.uscourts.gov/cgi-bin/show_public_doc?2007cv2240–39.

6. *See* DR. SEUSS, THE LORAX (1971). (Dr. Seuss is Theodore Seuss Geisel's pseudonym.)

7. Linda Greenhouse, *2,691 Decisions,* N.Y. TIMES, July 13, 2008, at WK1.

8. 5 U.S. 137, 177 (1803).

9. *See, e.g.,* Keeton v. Hustler Magazine, Inc., 465 U.S. 770 (1984) (overturning a lower court ruling dismissing a libel suit filed by a resident of New York against an Ohio corporation in a New Hampshire court). *See also* New York Times v. Sullivan, 376 U.S. 254 (1964) (in which the trial and first appeal were heard in Alabama courts).

10. Sherwin-Williams Co. v. Holmes County, 343 F.3d 383 (5th Cir. 2003); *see also* In re Condor Insurance Limited, 601 F.3d, 319 (5th Cir. 2010).

11. Young v. New Haven Advocate, 315 F.3d 256, 261 (4th Cir. 2002), *cert. denied,* 538 U.S. 1035 (2003).

12. 28 U.S.C 1292(a)(1).

13. U.S. Const. art. III, sec. 1.

14. John P. Avlon, *Is Elena Kagan a Liberal—or a Centrist?* CNN OPINION, June 30, 2010, *available at* http://www .cnn.com/2010/OPINION/06/29/avlon.kagan.centrist/ index.html.

15. The Volokh Conspiracy, *available at* http://www.volokh .com/posts/1212602633.shtml (posted Aug. 3, 2008).

16. 5 U.S. 137 (1803).

17. *See, e.g.,* Gregory A. Caldeira & John R. Wright, *The Discuss List: Agenda Building in the Supreme Court,* 24 LAW & SOCIETY REVIEW 807 (1990).

18. Lisa McElroy, *Citizens United v. TEC in Plain English,* SCOTUS BLOG, Jan. 22, 2010, *available at* http://www .scotusblog.com/2010/01/citizens-united-v-fec-in-plain-english/.

19. Adam Liptak, *Justices, 5–4, Reject Corporate Spending Limit,* N.Y. TIMES, Jan. 21, 2010, *available at* http://www .nytimes.com/2010/01/22/us/politics/22scotus.html.

20. Glenn Greenwald, *What the Supreme Court Got Right,* SALON, Jan. 22, 2010, *available at* http://www.salon.com/ news/opinion/glenn_greenwald/2010/01/22/citizens_united.

21. Samuel D. Warren & Louis D. Brandeis, *The Right to Privacy,* 4 HARV. L. REV. 193 (1890).

22. *See, e.g.,* David Ardia, *Free Speech Savior or Shield for Scoundrels? An Empirical Study of Intermediary Immunity under Section 230,* CITIZEN MEDIA LAW PROJECT BLOG, June 30, 2010, *available at* http://www.citmedialaw.org/ blog.

23. Aktepe v. United States, 105 F.3d 1400, 1402 (11th Cir. 1997) (citing Japan Whaling Ass'n v. American Cetacean Soc., 478 U.S. 221, 230 (1986)).

24. Susan Dente Ross, *Access and New Media Technology: Teleconferencing, Telecommuting, and Public Access.* In CHARLES DAVIS & SIG SPLICHAL, eds., ACCESS DENIED: FREEDOM OF INFORMATION IN THE INFORMATION AGE 65–85 (2000).

25. U.S. Const. art. VI, par. 2.

26. *See* Dept. of Justice v. Reporters Comm. for Freedom of the Press, 489 U.S. 749 (1989).

27. *See, e.g.,* Red Lion Broadcasting Co. v. FCC, 395 U.S. 367 (1969); Miami Herald Pub. Co. v. Tornillo, 418 U.S. 241 (1974).

28. Agostini v. Felton, 521 U.S. 203 (1997) (reversing Aguilar v. Felton, 473 U.S. 402 (1985)).

29. Nike v. Kasky, 539 U.S. 654 (2003).

30. Nikebiz.com, *The Inside Story Press Release: Nike Inc. and Kasky Announce Settlement of Kasky v. Nike First Amendment Case, available at* http://www.nike.com/nikebiz/news/pressrelease.jhtml?year=2003&month=09&letter=f (posted Sept. 2003).

31. Mourning v. Family Publishing Service, 411 U.S. 356, 382 (1973). *See also* Adickes v. Kress & Co., 389 U.S. 144, 157 (1970); United States v. Diebold, Inc., 369 U.S. 654, 655 (1979).

32. *See* Anderson v. Liberty Lobby, Inc., 477 U.S. 242 (1986).

33. Washington Post Co. v. Keogh, 365 F.2d 965, 968 (D.C. Cir. 1966).

34. *See* New York Times v. Sullivan, 376 U.S. 254 (1964).

35. *See, e.g.,* 44 Liquormart v. Rhode Island, 517 U.S. 484 (1996).

36. *See* New York Times v. Sullivan, 376 U.S. 254 (1964).

37. *See, e.g.,* Dan Eggen & T.W. Farnam, *More Setbacks for Campaign Finance Rules,* WASH. POST, July 15, 2010, at A17; Green Party of Connecticut v. Garfield, 2010 U.S. App. LEXIS 14248 (2d Cir. July 13, 2010); Long Beach Area Chamber of Commerce v. City of Long Beach, 603 F.3d 684 (9th Cir. 2010); SpeechNow.org v. Federal Election Comm'n, 599 F.3d 686 (D.C. Cir. 2010); Citizens United v. Federal Election Comm'n, 130 S. Ct. 876 (2010).

38. *Connecticut Campaign Finance Decisions from Second Circuit: Green Party v Garfield,* CONSTITUTIONAL LAW PROF BLOG, July 13, 2010, *available at* http://lawprofessors.typepad.com/conlaw/2010/07/connecticut-campaign-finance-decisions-from-second-circuit-green-party-v-garfield.html.

39. Michael Cummins, Citizens United *and the Roberts Court,* CAMPAIGN FOR LIBERTY, June 30, 2010, *available at* http://www.campaignforliberty.com/article.php?view=978.

40. Damon W. Root, Citizens United, *Stare Decisis, and the Chicago Gun Case,* REASON, Jan. 22, 2010, *available at* http://reason.com/blog/2010/01/22/citizens-united-stare-decisis.

41. 5 U.S. 137 (1803).

Chapter 2

The First Amendment

1. JOHN TRENCHARD AND THOMAS GORDON, CATO'S LETTERS No. 15, at 110 (Ronald Hamowy ed., Liberty Fund 1995) (1755).

2. Gitlow v. New York, 268 U.S. 652 (1925).

3. Note that even Justice Hugo Black, viewed as nearly a First Amendment absolutist, acknowledged that the authors of the First Amendment accepted some restraints on speech.

4. *See* Turner Broadcasting Sys. Inc. v. FCC, 512 U.S. 622 (1994).

5. Potter Stewart, *Or of the Press,* 26 HASTINGS L.J. 631 (1975); David A. Anderson, *The Origins of the Press Clause,* 30 UCLA L. REV. 455 (1983); M. Ethan Katsh, *Rights, Camera, Action: Cyberspatial Settings and the First Amendment,* 104 YALE L.J. 1681 (1995).

6. *See* Texas v. Johnson, 491 U.S. 397 (1989) (striking down a conviction for flag burning).

7. Nat'l Archives & Records Admin. v. Favish, 541 U.S. 157 (2004).

8. United States v. Stevens, 130 S. Ct. 1577, 1584 (2010).

9. 315 U.S. 568, 571–572 (1942).

10. John Milton, *Areopagitica* (1st ed. n.p. 1644) in GREAT BOOKS OF THE WESTERN WORLD 409 (1952).

11. JOHN LOCKE, THE SECOND TREATISE OF CIVIL GOVERNMENT (1690).

12. JEAN-JACQUES ROUSSEAU, THE SOCIAL CONTRACT (1762).

13. 4 WILLIAM BLACKSTONE, COMMENTARIES 151–52 (London: 1769).

14. *Id.*

15. FREDERICK S. SIEBERT, FREEDOM OF THE PRESS IN ENGLAND 1476–1776, at 10 (1952); LEONARD LEVY, LEGACY OF SUPPRESSION (1960).

16. Speech on the Stamp Act, House of Burgesses, Williamsburg, Va. (May 29, 1765).

17. *See, e.g.,* LEONARD LEVY, LEGACY OF SUPPRESSION (1960); LEONARD LEVY, EMERGENCE OF A FREE PRESS (1985). *But see* ZECHARIAH CHAFEE, FREE SPEECH IN THE UNITED STATES 2 (1941) (arguing that the First Amendment was designed to eliminate the law of sedition forever).

18. *See* JAMES MORTON SMITH, FREEDOM'S FETTERS (1956).

19. *See* New York Times v. Sullivan, 376 U.S. 254 (1964).

20. *See, e.g.,* JOHN STUART MILL, ON LIBERTY (1859); THOMAS I. EMERSON, THE SYSTEM OF FREE EXPRESSION (1970); ALEXANDER MEIKLEJOHN, FREE SPEECH AND ITS RELATION TO SELF-GOVERNMENT (1948); CASS SUNSTEIN, DEMOCRACY AND THE PROBLEM OF FREE SPEECH (1993).

21. *See, e.g.,* Vincent Blasi, *The Checking Value in First Amendment Theory,* 1977 AM. B. FOUND. RES. J. 521 (1977).

22. 376 U.S. 254 (1964).

23. *See, e.g.,* CATHARINE MACKINNON, FEMINISM UNMODIFIED, DISCOURSES ON LIFE AND LAW (1987); WORDS THAT WOUND: CRITICAL RACE THEORY, ASSAULTIVE SPEECH, AND THE FIRST AMENDMENT (Mari J. Matsuda et al. eds., 1993).

24. *See, e.g.,* LEE C. BOLLINGER, THE TOLERANT SOCIETY: FREEDOM OF SPEECH AND EXTREMIST SPEECH IN AMERICA (1986).

25. *See, e.g.,* C. Edwin Baker, *Scope of the First Amendment Freedom of Speech,* 25 UCLA L. REV. 964 (1978).

26. 395 U.S. 367 (1969).

27. *Id.* at 387, 389.

28. 418 U.S. 241, 256 (1974).

29. *Id.*

30. 283 U.S. 697 (1931).

31. *Id.*

32. 403 U.S. 713 (1971).

33. *Id.* at 714.

34. Nebraska Press Ass'n v. Stuart, 427 U.S. 539, 559 (1976).

35. New York Times v. Jascalevich, 439 U.S. 1317 (1978); Nebraska Press Ass'n v. Stuart, 427 U.S. 539 (1976).

36. CBS v. Davis, 510 U.S. 1315 (1994) (Blackmun, J., Circuit Justice).

37. *Id.* at 1320.

38. Zennie62, *NY times v. google, Twitter in TheFlyontheWall.com "Hot News" Case,* June 29, 2010, *available at* http://www.sfgate.com.

39. 2010 U.S. Dist LEXIS 25728 (S.D.N.Y., 2010); 2010 U.S. Dist LEXIS 45093 (S.D.N.Y., 2010); 2010 U.S. Dist LEXIS 49098 (S.D.N.Y., 2010).

40. Intern'l News Service v. Associated Press, 248 U.S. 215 (1918).

41. *Id.* at 242.

42. *Citizen Media Law Project, EFF, and Public Citizen advocate First Amendment Scrutiny in Hot News Cases,* CITIZEN MEDIA LAW PROJECT, June 22, 2010, *available at* http://www.citmedialaw.org.

43. *Id.* at 263.

44. *Id.* at 250.

45. *Google, Twitter Go to Bat for TheFlyontheWall,* REUTERS, June 22, 2010, *available at* http://www.reuters.com.

46. Sam Bayard, *New Hampshire Supreme Court Rules Website Covered by State Reporter's Privilege,* CITIZEN MEDIA LAW PROJECT, May 6, 2010, *available at* http://www.citmedialaw.org.

47. *Summary:* The Mortgage Specialists v. Implode-Explode Heavy Industries, CITIZEN MEDIA LAW PROJECT, April 1, 2009, *available at* http://www.citmedialaw.org.

48. *Court Order,* Apex Technology v. Doe, N.J. Sup. Ct., Dec. 23, 2009, *available at* http://www.programmersguild.org.

49. Eric P. Robinson, *Hate Mongers and Tunnel Rats Are Entitled to Free Speech, Too,* CITIZEN MEDIA LAW PROJECT, May 28, 2010, *available at* www.citmedialaw.org.

50. *Julius Baer Bank and Trust v. WikiLeaks,* CITIZEN MEDIA LAW PROJECT, May Feb. 18, 2008, *available at* http://www.citmedialaw.org.

51. State ex rel. Miami Publishing v. McIntosh, 340 So. 2d 904 (Fla. 1977) (adapting Nebraska Press Ass'n v. Stuart, 427 U.S. 539 (1976)).

52. Hill v. Colorado, 530 U.S. 703 (2000).

53. Burson v. Freeman, 504 U.S. 191 (1992).

54. 502 U.S. 105 (1991).

55. 502 U.S. 105 (1992).

56. United States v. O'Brien, 391 U.S. 367 (1968).

57. *Id.*

58. Ward v. Rock Against Racism, 491 U.S. 781 (1989). See also Matthew D. Bunker & Emily Erickson, *The Jurisprudence of Precision: Contrast Space and Narrow Tailoring in First Amendment Doctrine,* 6 COMM. L. & POL'Y 259 (2001).

59. Forsyth County, Ga. v. The Nationalist Movement, 505 U.S. 123 (1992).

60. Virginia v. Black, 538 U.S. 343, 365 (2003).

61. Meyer v. Grant, 486 U.S. 414 (1988).

62. *See, e.g.,* Buckley v. Valeo, 424 U.S. 1 (1976).

63. 558 U.S. 50 (2010).

64. McConnell v. FEC, 540 U.S. 93 (2003).

65. Rep. Nat'l Comm. v. FEC, 2010 U.S. LEXIS 5530 (2010).

66. SpeechNow.org v. FEC, 599 F.3d 686 (D.D.C., 2010).

67. Emily's List v. FEC, 581 F.3d 1 (D.D.C., 2009).

68. 551 U.S. 449 (2007).

69. 424 U.S. 1 (1976).

70. Ysura v. Pocatello Ed. Ass'n., 129 S. Ct. 1093 (2010).

71. 548 U.S. 230 (2006).

72. 528 U.S. 377 (2000).

73. White House, Office of the Press Secretary, *Ensuring Responsible Spending of Recovery Act Funds,* Memo for the heads of Executive Departments and Agencies, March 20, 2009.

74. 514 U.S. 334, 357 (1995).

75. *See* Talley v. California, 362 U.S. 60 (1960); Buckley v. American Const'l Law Found., 525 U.S. 182 (1999); Watchtower v Stratton, 536 U.S. 150 (2002).

76. 130 S. Ct. 2811 (2010).

77. 129 S. Ct. 1523 (2009).

78. Pleasant Grove City v. Summum, 129 S. Ct. 1125 (2009).

79. *Id.* at 1138.

80. Thomas Emerson, Toward a General Theory of the First Amendment 9 (1966). *See also* Meiklejohn, *supra* note 20.

81. *See, e.g.,* Perry v. Sindermann, 408 U.S. 593 (1972). For discussion of parallel treatment of public school students, *see* Chapter 3 and Tinker v. Des Moines Independent Community School Dist., 393 U.S. 503 (1969).

82. *See, e.g.,* Pickering v. Board of Education, 391 U.S. 563 (1968); Snepp v. United States, 444 U.S. 507 (1980); Toni M. Massaro, *Significant Silences: Freedom of Speech in the Public Sector Workplace,* 61 S. Cal. L. Rev. 1 (1987); Sissela Bok, Secrets (1993). *But see* Freedom at Risk: Secrecy, Censorship, and Repression in the 1980s (Richard O. Curry ed., 1998); Benjamin S. DuVal, Jr., *The Occasions of Secrecy,* 47 U. Pitt. L. Rev. 579 (1986); Daniel N. Hoffman, Governmental Secrecy and the Founding Fathers: A Study in Constitutional Controls (1981); Seth F. Kreimer, *Sunlight Secrets and Scarlet Letters: The Tension Between Privacy and Disclosure in Constitutional Law,* 140 U. Pa. L. Rev. 1 (1991); Kermit L. Hall, *The Virulence of the National Appetite for Bogus Revelation,* 56 Md. L. Rev. 1 (1997).

83. *See, e.g.,* United Public Workers of America v. Mitchell, 330 U.S. 75 (1947); United States Civil Service Commission v. National Association of Letter Carriers, 413 U.S. 548 (1973).

84. 547 U.S. 410 (2006).

85. Connick v. Myers, 461 U.S. 138, 146–47 (1983).

86. 547 U.S. at 422.

87. David L. Hudson, Jr., *Garcetti's Palpable Effect on Public-Employee Speech* (May 29, 2007), *available at* http://www.firstamendmentcenter.org.

88. Hague v. Committee for Industrial Organization, 307 U.S. 496, 515 (1939).

89. *See, e.g.,* Susan Dente Ross, *An Apologia to Radical Dissent and a Supreme Court Test to Protect It,* 7 Comm. L. & Policy 401 (2002); Ronald J. Krotoszynski, Jr., *Essay: Celebrating Selma: The Importance of Context in Public Forum Analysis,* 104 Yale L.J. 1411 (1995).

90. *See, e.g.,* Village of Skokie v. National Socialist Party of America, 439 U.S. 916 (1978); Hess v. Indiana, 414 U.S. 105 (1973); Brown v. Louisiana, 383 U.S. 131 (1966); Edwards v. South Carolina, 371 U.S. 229 (1963); NAACP v. Claiborne Hardware Co., 458 U.S. 886 (1982); Gregory v. City of Chicago, 394 U.S. 111 (1969); Grayned v. Rockford, 408 U.S. 104 (1972).

91. Grayned v. Rockford, 408 U.S. 104, 116 (1972); Perry Education Association v. Perry Local Educators' Association, 460 U.S. 37 (1983).

92. *See, e.g.,* Hague v. Committee for Industrial Organization, 307 U.S. 496 (1939).

93. *See, e.g.,* Greer v. Spock, 424 U.S. 828 (1976).

94. *See, e.g.,* United States v. Albertini, 472 U.S. 675 (1985); Los Angeles City Council v. Taxpayers for Vincent, 466 U.S. 789 (1984); United States v. Kokinda, 497 U.S. 720 (1990).

95. *See, e.g.,* Adderley v. Florida, 385 U.S. 39 (1966).

96. *See, e.g.,* Frisby v. Schultz, 487 U.S. 474 (1988); Madsen v. Women's Health Center, Inc., 512 U.S. 753 (1994). *But see* Scheidler v. National Organization for Women, 537 U.S. 393 (2003) (removing civil injunction on anti-abortion protesters and rejecting claim that their protests constituted illegal extortion and racketeering).

97. *See, e.g.,* Amalgamated Food Employees Union v. Logan Valley Plaza, Inc., 391 U.S. 308 (1968); Hudgens v. National Labor Relations Board, 424 U.S. 507 (1976); Prune Yard Shopping Center v. Robins, 447 U.S. 74 (1980). *But see* Lloyd Corp., Ltd. v. Tanner, 407 U.S. 551 (1972).

98. Prune Yard Shopping Center v. Robins, 447 U.S. 74 (1980).

99. *Id.* at 82 (footnote omitted).

100. *Id.* at 83 (footnote omitted).

101. *See, e.g.,* David F. Freedman, *Press Passes and Trespasses: Newsgathering on Private Property,* 84 COLUM. L. REV. 1298 (1984).

102. *See also,* Troy Ltd. v. Renna, 727 F.2d 287 (3d Cir. 1984); Flynn v. City of Cambridge, 383 Mass. 152 (1981); State v. Shack, 58 N.J. 297 (1971).

103. Glickman v. Wileman Bros. & Elliott, 521 U.S. 457, 505 n.2 (1997) (Souter, J., dissenting).

104. *See, e.g.,* Bd. of Regents of the Univ. of Wisc. v. Southworth, 529 U.S. 217 (2000); Rosenberger v. Rector & Visitors of the Univ. of Virginia, 515 U.S. 819 (1995).

105. *See, e.g.,* Grosjean v. American Press Co., 297 U.S. 233 (1936); Minneapolis Star & Tribune Co. v. Minnesota Commissioner of Revenue, 460 U.S. 575 (1983); Arkansas Writers' Project v. Ragland, 481 U.S. 221 (1987). *But see* Leathers v. Medlock, 499 U.S. 439 (1991).

106. National Endowment for the Arts v. Finley, 524 U.S. 569 (1998).

107. Island Trees Union Free School District Board of Education v. Pico, 457 U.S. 853 (1982).

108. Wooley v. Maynard, 430 U.S. 705, 714 (1977).

109. *See, e.g.,* Boy Scouts of America v. Dale, 530 U.S. 640 (2000).

110. Hurley v. Irish-American Gay, Lesbian and Bisexual Group of Boston, 515 U.S. 557, 575 (1995).

111. ITHIEL DE SOLA POOL, TECHNOLOGIES OF FREEDOM (1983).

112. *See* Lovell v. Griffin, 303 U.S. 444, 452 (1938); Burstyn v. Wilson, 343 U.S. 495 (1952).

113. Kovacs v. Cooper, 336 U.S. 77, 97 (1949) (Jackson, J., concurring).

114. Minneapolis Star & Tribune Co. v. Minnesota Commissioner of Revenue, 460 U.S. 575, 585 (1983).

115. *See, e.g.,* Red Lion Broadcasting Co. v. FCC, 395 U.S. 367 (1969).

116. *See, e.g.,* Turner Broadcasting Sys. Inc. v. FCC, 512 U.S. 622 (1994); Turner Broadcasting Sys. Inc. v. FCC, 530 U.S. 180 (1997).

117. Project for Excellence in Journalism of the Columbia University Graduate School of Journalism, *Overview.*

The State of the News Media 2005, An Annual Report on American Journalism, available at http://www.journalism.org.

118. *Id.*

119. *Id.*

120. *Id.*

121. *Id.*

122. Timothy Karr, *Big Media: The Real Elephant in the Garden,* Aug. 27, 2004, *available at* http://www.MediaChannel.org.

123. *Id.*

124. Project for Excellence in Journalism of the Columbia University Graduate School of Journalism, *Journalist Survey, The State of the News Media 2004, An Annual Report on American Journalism, available at* http://www.journalism.org.

125. 539 U.S. 654 (2003).

Chapter 3

Speech Distinctions

1. Schenck v. United States, 249 U.S. 47, 52 (1919).

2. MARGARET A. BLANCHARD, REVOLUTIONARY SPARKS 489 (1992); Margaret A. Blanchard, *"Why Can't We Ever Learn?" Cycles of Stability, Stress and Freedom of Expression in United States History,* 7 COMM. L. & POL'Y 347 (2002); Martin E. Halstuk, *Policy of Secrecy—Pattern of Deception: What Federalist Leaders Thought About a Public Right to Know, 1794–98,* 7 COMM. L. & POL'Y 51 (2002); Susan D. Ross, *An Apologia to Radical Dissent and a Supreme Court Test to Protect It,* 7 COMM. L. & POL'Y 401 (2002).

3. Vincent Blasi, *The Pathological Perspective and the First Amendment,* 85 COLUM. L. REV. 449, 450 (1985).

4. ACLU Press Release, *PATRIOT Act Fears Are Stifling Free Speech, ACLU Says in Challenge to Law,* Nov. 3, 2003, *available at* http://www.aclu.org/safefree/patriot/18418prs20031103.html.

5. Holder v. Humanitarian Law Project, 130 S. Ct. 2705 (2010).

6. Office of the Coordinator for Counterterrorism, *Foreign Terrorist Organizations,* U.S. DEPARTMENT OF STATE,

Jan. 19, 2010, *available at* http://www.state.gov/s/ct/rls/other/des/123085.htm.

7. 130 S. Ct. 2605 at *37.

8. *Id.* at *59, *63.

9. *Id.* at *69.

10. The Uniting and Strengthening America by Providing Appropriate Tools Required to Intercept and Obstruct Terrorism Act of 2001, Pub. L. No. 107–56, 115 Stat. 272.

11. USA PATRIOT Improvement and Reauthorization Act of 2005, 18 U.S.C. §2709, Pub. L. No. 109–177, 120 Stat. 192 (2006).

12. Nancy Kranich, Commentary: *The Impact of the USA PATRIOT Act on Free Expression,* Aug. 27, 2003, *available at* http://www.fepproject.org/commentaries/patriotact.html.

13. Foreign Intelligence Surveillance Act Amendments Act, P.L. 110–261 (July 10, 2008).

14. *See, e.g.,* Humanitarian Law Project v. U.S. Dept. of Justice, 352 F.3d 382 (9th Cir. 2003), *vacated and remanded,* 393 F.3d 902 (9th Cir. 2004).

15. William H. Rehnquist, All the Laws but One 224 (1998).

16. American Communications Ass'n v. Douds, 339 U.S. 332, 448–49 (1950) (Black, J., dissenting) (affirming national rule requiring union organizers to swear they have no Communist affiliations).

17. Kleindienst v. Mandel, 408 U.S. 753, 773 (1972) (Douglas, J., dissenting).

18. Chaplinsky v. New Hampshire, 315 U.S. 568, 572 (1942).

19. Schenck v. United States, 249 U.S. 47, 52 (1919).

20. *Id.*

21. *Id.*

22. Frohwerk v. United States, 249 U.S. 204 (1919).

23. *Id.* at 208–09.

24. Debs v. United States, 249 U.S. 211 (1919).

25. Abrams v. United States, 250 U.S. 626 (1919).

26. *Id.* at 628 (Holmes, J., dissenting).

27. *Id.* at 630.

28. Dennis v. United States, 341 U.S. 494 (1951); Scales v. United States, 367 U.S. 203 (1961). *See also* Whitney v. California, 274 U.S. 357 (1927); Kent Greenawalt, *Speech and Crime,* 1980 Am. B. Found. Res. J. 645 (1980).

29. Gitlow v. New York, 268 U.S. 652 (1925).

30. *Id.* at 667.

31. *Id.* at 669.

32. *Id.* at 673 (Holmes, J., dissenting).

33. *Id.* at 666.

34. Whitney v. California, 274 U.S. 357 (1927).

35. *Id.* at 377–78 (Brandeis, J., concurring).

36. *Id.* at 379 (emphasis added).

37. American Communications Ass'n v. Douds, 339 U.S. 382, 448–49 (1950) (Black, J., dissenting).

38. Dennis v. United States, 341 U.S. 494 (1951).

39. Kunz v. New York, 340 U.S. 290, 300 (1951).

40. Yates v. United States, 354 U.S. 298 (1957).

41. *See* Liezl Irene Pangilinan, Note: *"When a Nation Is at War": A Context-Dependent Theory of Free Speech for the Regulation of Weapon Recipes,* 22 Cardozo Arts & Ent. L.J. 683 (2004).

42. 395 U.S. 444 (1969).

43. *Id.* at 447.

44. *Id.* at 448.

45. Cohen v. California, 403 U.S. 15 (1971).

46. Martin H. Redish, *Advocacy of Unlawful Conduct and the First Amendment: In Defense of Clear and Present Danger,* 70 Cal. L. Rev. 1159, 1162 (1982).

47. Gitlow v. New York, 268 U.S. 652, 673 (1925).

48. 315 U.S. 568 (1942).

49. *Id.* at 571–72.

50. Terminiello v. Chicago, 337 U.S. 1, 4 (1949) (emphasis added).

51. *Id.*

52. *Id.*

53. *See, e.g.,* Gooding v. Wilson, 405 U.S. 518 (1972).

54. R.A.V. v. City of St. Paul, 505 U.S. 377 (1992).

55. 538 U.S. 343 (2003).

56. *Id.* at 394.

57. *See* Watts v. United States, 394 U.S. 705 (1969).

58. United States v. Baker, 890 F. Supp. 1375 (S.D. Mich. 1995).

59. *Id.* at 1382.

60. *Id.* at 1385.

61. *Id.* at 1390 (footnote omitted).

62. Planned Parenthood v. American Coalition of Life Activists, 290 F.3d 1058 (9th Cir. 2002), *cert. denied*, 593 U.S. 958 (2003).

63. United States v. O'Brien, 391 U.S. 367, 376 (1968).

64. Tinker v. Des Moines Indep. Community School Dist., 393 U.S. 503, 505 (1969).

65. United States v. O'Brien, 391 U.S. 367 (1968).

66. The Supreme Court has said symbolic speech exists and warrants First Amendment protection when (1) speech and action combine, (2) there is an intent to convey a message, and (3) witnesses are likely to understand that message.

67. Texas v. Johnson, 491 U.S. 397, 414 (1989).

68. Hess v. Indiana, 414 U.S. 105 (1973).

69. Mark C. Rahdert, Point of View: *The Roberts Court and Academic Freedom*, Chron. Higher Educ., July 27, 2007, *available at* http://chronicle.com/forums/index.

70. *See, e.g.,* Board of Regents v. Southworth, 529 U.S. 217 (2000); Rosenberger v. Rector of the University of Virginia, 515 U.S. 819 (1995).

71. Board of Regents v. Southworth, 529 U.S. 217, 234 n.7 (2000).

72. Widmar v. Vincent, 454 U.S. 263, 274 (1981).

73. Bethel School Dist. v. Fraser, 478 U.S. 675, 683 (1986). *See also* Edwards v. Aguillard, 482 U.S. 578, 583 (1987).

74. Tinker v. Des Moines Ind. Community School Dist., 393 U.S. 503 (1969).

75. Erwin Chemerinsky, *Students Do Leave Their First Amendment Rights at the Schoolhouse Gates: What's Left of* Tinker? 48 Drake L. Rev. 527 (2000).

76. Tinker v. Des Moines Ind. Community School Dist., 393 U.S. 503, 508 (1969).

77. *Id.* at 509.

78. *Id.*

79. *Id.* at 506.

80. Grayned v. Rockford, 408 U.S. 104 (1972).

81. 551 U.S. 393 (2007).

82. *Id.* at 2624.

83. *Id.* at 2649 (Stevens, J. dissenting).

84. Board of Educ., Island Trees Union Free School Dist. v. Pico 457 U.S. 853 (1982).

85. *Id.* at 857.

86. *Id.* at 868.

87. *Id.* at 870.

88. 478 U.S. 675 (1986).

89. *Id.*

90. *Id.*

91. *Id.* at 271.

92. *Id.* at 270–71.

93. *Id.* at 270.

94. *Id.* at 234 n.7.

95. Wooley v. Maynard, 430 U.S. 705, 714 (1977) (Burger, C.J.).

96. West Virginia State Bd. of Educ. v. Barnette, 319 U.S. 624 (1943).

97. Ambach v. Norwick, 441 U.S. 68 (1979).

98. *See, e.g.,* Epperson v. Arkansas, 393 U.S. 97 (1968); Edwards v. Aguillard, 482 U.S. 578 (1987); Pickering v. Bd. of Educ., 391 U.S. 563 (1968).

99. West Virginia State Bd. of Educ. v. Barnette, 319 U.S. 624, 633 (1943).

100. *Id.* at 642.

101. *Id.*

102. Abood v. Detroit Board of Education, 431 U.S. 209 (1977).

103. Santa Fe Independent School District v. Doe, 530 U.S. 290 (2000). *See* Elk Grove Unified Sch. Dist. v. Newdow, 542 U.S. 1, 58 (2004) (O'Connor, J., concurring) (suggesting that the First Amendment permits school practices that merely reference God and constitute "ceremonial deism").

104. Santa Fe Independent School District v. Doe, 530 U.S. 290, 309 (2000).

105. *Id.* at 324 (Rehnquist, J., dissenting).

106. Rosenberger v. Rector, 515 U.S. 819, 833 (1995).

107. *See, e.g.,* Board of Regents of the Univ. of Wisc. v. Southworth, 529 U.S. 217 (2000); Rosenberger v. Rector & Visitors of the Univ. of Virginia, 515 U.S. 819 (1995).

108. Board of Regents of the Univ. of Wisc. v. Southworth, 529 U.S. 217, 239 (2000) (Souter, J., concurring).

109. Papish v. Bd. of Curators of the Univ. of Missouri, 410 U.S. 667 (1973).

110. *Id.* at 670.

111. *Id.* at 233.

112. *Id.* at 242–43 (Souter, J., concurring).

113. Note that the Court said this public forum also enhanced the university's curricular goals, but public forum analysis typically protects precisely those types of speech that would not be embraced by the government agency providing the forum.

114. 130 S. Ct. 2971 (2010).

115. *Id.* at 2991.

116. Tinker v. Des Moines Indep. Community School Dist., 393 U.S. 503, 506 (1969).

117. 130 S. Ct. 2971, 3000 (Alito, J., dissenting).

118. Adam Goldstein, *Supreme Court's CLS Decision Sucker-Punches First Amendment,* Huff. Post, June 29, 2010, *available at* http://www.huffingtonpost.com/adam goldstein/supreme-courts-cls-decisi_b_628329.html.

119. Kincaid v. Gibson, 236 F.3d 342 (6th Cir. 2001) (en banc).

120. Hosty v. Carter, 412 F.3d 731 (7th Cir. 2005), *cert. denied,* 546 U.S. 1169 (2006).

121. *Michele Nagar Fired for Diversity's Sake,* July 22, 2004, *available at* www.campusreportonline.net/main/articles.php?id=139.

122. *SPJ Members Issue Resolution Condemning Kansas Adviser's Firing,* Oct. 6, 2004, *available at* http://www.splc.org; *SPLC Condemns Kansas State's 'Bizarre' Interpretation of the First Amendment,* July 21, 2004, *available at* http://www.splc.org/newsflash.

123. *Johnson Fired from Position of Director, Collegian Adviser,* Kan. St. Collegian, May 11, 2004, at 1.

124. *Newspaper Content Analysis Given in Reasons Not to Reappoint Collegian Adviser,* Kansas State Collegian, May 18, 2004, *available at* http://www.kstatecollegian.com/article.php?a=2141.

125. *See* Lane v. Simon, 2005 U.S. Dist. LEXIS 11330 (D. Kan. 2005), *vacated and remanded,* 2007 U.S. App. LEXIS 17814 (10th Cir., July 26, 2007).

126. *Id.*

127. *See, e.g.,* Dinesh D'Souza, Illiberal Education: The Politics of Race and Sex on Campus (1992).

128. *See, e.g.,* The Price We Pay: The Case Against Racist Speech, Hate Propaganda, and Pornography (Laura Lederer & Richard Delgado eds., 1994).

129. *See, e.g.,* Andrew Altman, *Liberalism and Campus Hate Speech,* in Campus Wars: Multiculturalism and the Politics of Difference (John Arthur & Amy Shapiro eds., 1993).

130. *See, e.g.,* Doe v. Univ. of Michigan, 721 F. Supp. 852 (E.D. Mich. 1989); UWM Post v. University of Wisc. Board of Regents, 774 F. Supp. 1163 (E.D. Wis. 1991); Dambrot v. Central Michigan University, 839 F. Supp. 477 (E.D. Mich. 1993).

131. Doe v. University of Michigan, 721 F. Supp. 852, 864 (E. D. Mich. 1989).

132. Arati R. Korwar, War of Words: Speech Codes at Public Colleges and Universities (1994); Jon B. Gould, *The Precedent That Wasn't: College Hate Speech Codes and the Two Faces of Legal Compliance,* 35 Law & Soc'y Rev. 345 (2001).

Chapter 4

Libel: The Plaintiff's Case

1. New York Times v. Sullivan, 376 U.S. 254, 270–72 (1964).

2. *See, e.g.,* Diane Leenheer Zimmerman, *Defamation in Fiction: Real People in Fiction: Cautionary Words About Troublesome Old Torts Poured into New Jugs,* 51 Brooklyn L. Rev. 355 (1985).

3. Milkovich v. Lorain Journal Co., 497 U.S. 1, 22 (1990) (Rehnquist, C.J.).

4. Rosenblatt v. Baer, 383 U.S. 75, 86 (1966).

5. Dun & Bradstreet, Inc. v. Greenmoss Builders, Inc., 472 U.S. 749, 757 (1985).

6. *See* Gavin Clark, Famous Libel and Slander Cases of History (1950).

7. M. Lindsay Kaplan, The Culture of Slander in Early Modern England 9 (1997).

8. *See, e.g.,* Norman L. Rosenberg, Protecting the Best Men: An Interpretive History of the Law of Libel (1986).

9. Van Vechten Veeder, *The History and Theory of the Law of Defamation,* 3 Colum. L. Rev. 546, 565 (1903) (quoting De Libellis Famois, 5 Co. Rep. 125 (1606)).

10. *Id.*

11. J. H. Baker, An Introduction to English Legal History 506 (3d ed. 1990).

12. 4 William Blackstone, Commentaries 152 (1979).

13. *Id.*

14. Milkovich v. Lorain Journal Co., 497 U.S. 1, 12 (1990) (Rehnquist, C.J.).

15. The Sedition Act of 1798, ch. 74, 1 Stat. 596 (1798).

16. John Marshall, *Report of the Minority on the Virginia Resolutions,* J. House of Delegates (Va.) 6: 93–95 (Jan. 22, 1799), reprinted in 5 THE FOUNDERS' CONSTITUTION 136–38 (Philip B. Kurland & Ralph Lerner eds., 1987).

17. *Id.* at 138.

18. James Madison, *The Virginia Report of 1799–1800, Touching the Alien and Sedition Laws,* reprinted in THE FOUNDERS' CONSTITUTION 141–42 (1986).

19. The expression "SLAPP" was initially coined by two University of Denver professors. *See* Penelope Canan & George W. Pring, *Studying Strategic Lawsuits Against Public Participation: Mixing Quantitative and Qualitative Approaches,* 22 LAW & SOC'Y REV. 385 (1988).

20. *See, e.g.,* Cal. Code Civ. Proc. sec. 425.16 (stating, in part, "The Legislature finds and declares that there has been a disturbing increase in lawsuits brought primarily to chill the valid exercise of the constitutional rights of freedom of speech and petition for the redress of grievances. The Legislature finds and declares that it is in the public interest to encourage continued participation in matters of public significance, and that this participation should not be chilled through abuse of the judicial process. . . . A cause of action against a person arising from any act of that person in furtherance of the person's right of petition or free speech under the United States or California Constitution in connection with a public issue shall be subject to a special motion to strike, unless the court determines that the plaintiff has established that there is a probability that the plaintiff will prevail on the claim.").

21. Reporters Committee for Freedom of the Press, Mar. 19, 2010.

22. *See, e.g.,* Whitney v. California, 274 U.S. 357, 374–77 (1927) (Brandeis, J., concurring) ("The best answer for bad speech is more speech.").

23. Admission Consultants, Inc. v. Google, Inc., N.Y.L.J., Dec. 8, 2008, p. 17, col. 1 (Sup. Ct., N.Y. Co.).

24. Lunney v. Prodigy Services Co., 94 N.Y.2d 242, 249 (1999).

25. Cubby, Inc. v. CompuServe, Inc., 776 F. Supp. 135 (1991) (holding that the ISP is not responsible for content posted).

26. Stratton Oakmont v. Prodigy Servs. Co., 23 Med. L. Rep. 1794 (N.Y. Sup. Ct., May 24, 1995) (holding that because Prodigy claimed to monitor its content, the ISP is placed in the role of publisher).

27. Zeran v. America Online, Inc., 129 F.3d 327, 330 (4th Cir. 1997).

28. Blumenthal v. Drudge, 992 F. Supp. 44 (D.D.C. 1998).

29. Google "Blogger!" terms of service (2011), *available at* http://www.blogger.com/terms.g.

30. Dimeo v. Max, 433 F. Supp. 2d 523 (E.D. Pa. 2006).

31. *Id.* at 529 (Dalzel, J.).

32. Brett Barrouquere, *Website Hit with $11M Penalty for Cheerleader Post,* WASH. POST, Aug. 26, 2010, *available at* http://www.washingtonpost.com/wp-dyn/content/article/2010/08/26/AR2010082604744.html.

33. McIntyre v. Ohio Elections Commission, 514 U.S. 334, 357 (1995).

34. Dendrite Int'l, Inc. v. John Doe No. 3, 775 A.2d 756, 760 (N.J. Sup. 2001).

35. RESTATEMENT (SECOND) OF TORTS § 564A cmt. b (1976).

36. Neiman-Marcus v. Lait, 13 F.R.D. 311, 316 (S.D.N.Y. 1952).

37. Carter-Clark v. Random House, Inc., 768 N.Y.S.2d 290, 293 (N.Y. Sup. Ct. 2003).

38. *See* RESTATEMENT (SECOND) OF TORTS § 559 (1997).

39. *See* W. PAGE KEETON ET AL., PROSSER AND KEETON ON THE LAW OF TORTS § 111, at 773–78 (5th ed. 1984).

40. *See* RESTATEMENT (SECOND) OF TORTS § 559 cmt. e.

41. *See, e.g.,* Kimmerle v. New York Evening Journal, Inc., 262 N.Y. 99 (1933).

42. Kaelin v. Globe Communications, 162 F.3d 1036 (9th Cir. 1998).

43. *Id.* at 1042.

44. RODNEY A. SMOLLA, THE LAW OF DEFAMATION § 7.10 (2d ed. 2010).

45. Cochran v. NYP Holdings, Inc., 58 F. Supp. 2d 1113, 1121 (C.D. Cal. 1998).

46. Bose Corp. v. Consumers Union, 466 U.S. 485, 487 (1984).

47. Auvil v. CBS, 836 F. Supp. 740 (E.D. Wash. 1993).

48. Auvil v. CBS, 67 F. 3d 816 (9th Cir. 1995).

49. Philadelphia Newspapers, Inc. v. Hepps, 474 U.S. 767, 776–77 (1986).

50. Liberty Lobby v. Dow Jones, 838 F.2d 1287, 1296 (D.C. Cir. 1988).

51. Masson v. New Yorker Magazine, Inc., 501 U.S. 496, 516–17 (1991).

52. Dolcefino and KTRK Television v. Turner, 987 S.W. 2d 100, 109 (Tex. Ct. App. 1998).

53. Yeakey v. Hearst Communcations, Inc., 234 P.3d 332 (Wash. App. 2010).

54. Stevens v. Iowa Newspapers, Inc., 728 N.W.2d 823 (Iowa 2007).

55. Hanash and Yousef v. WFLD, 1998 U.S. Dist. LEXIS 17738 (N.D. Ill. 1998).

56. 376 U.S. 254 (1964).

57. *See, e.g.,* Harry Kalven, Jr., *The New York Times Case: A Note on "The Central Meaning of the First Amendment,"* 1964 Sup. Ct. Rev. 191.

58. New York Times v. Sullivan, 376 U.S. 254, 272 (1964).

59. *Id.* at 270.

60. *Id.* at 266.

61. *Id.* at 279.

62. *Id.* at 270.

63. *Id.* at 278.

64. *See, e.g.,* Lawrence Friedman, American Law in the 20th Century 341 (2002).

65. Goldwater v. Ginsburg, 414 F.2d 324 (2d Cir. 1969), *cert. denied,* 396 U.S. 1049 (1970).

66. Masson v. New Yorker Magazine, Inc., 501 U.S. 496, 517 (1991).

67. Curtis Publishing Co. v. Butts, 388 U.S. 130, 158 (1967).

68. Associated Press v. Walker, 388 U.S. 130, 140 (1967).

69. *Id.* at 157–59.

70. St. Amant v. Thompson, 390 U.S. 727, 731 (1968).

71. Herbert v. Lando, 441 U.S. 153 (1979).

72. Harte-Hanks Communications, Inc. v. Connaughton, 491 U.S. 657 (1989).

73. M. Lindsay Kaplan, The Culture of Slander in Early Modern England 23 (1997).

74. Rosenblatt v. Baer, 383 U.S. 75, 85 (1966).

75. *Id.* at 86.

76. *Id.* at 87.

77. 388 U.S. 130, 163 (1967) (Warren, C.J., concurring).

78. *Id.* at 163–64.

79. Gertz v. Robert Welch, Inc., 418 U.S. 323, 345 (1974).

80. *Id.*

81. *Id.* at 344.

82. *Id.* at 345.

83. Curtis Publishing Co. v. Butts and Associated Press v. Walker, 388 U.S. 130, 163 (1967).

84. Wolston v. Reader's Digest Ass'n, 443 U.S. 157 (1979).

85. Time, Inc. v. Firestone, 424 U.S. 448 (1976).

86. Hutchinson v. Proxmire, 443 U.S. 111 (1979).

87. *Id.* at 135.

88. Chuy v. Philadelphia Eagles Football Club, 431 F. Supp. 254, 276 (E.D. Pa. 1977).

89. Renner v. Donsbach, 749 F. Supp. 987 (W.D. Mo. 1990).

90. *See, e.g.,* Williams v. Pasma, 656 P.2d 212 (Mont. 1982).

91. Gertz v. Robert Welch, Inc., 418 U.S. 323, 351 (1974).

92. *Id.* at 345.

93. Tillman v. Freedom of Information Commission, 2008 Conn. Super. LEXIS 2120, *25 (Aug. 15, 2008).

94. Dun & Bradstreet v. Greenmoss Builders, Inc., 472 U.S. 749 (1985).

95. *Id.* at 783.

96. *Id.* at 774.

97. *See, e.g.,* Brad Snyder, *Protecting the Media from Excessive Damages: The Nineteenth-Century Origins of Remittitur and Its Modern Application in Food Lion,* 24 Vt. L. Rev. 299, 325 (2000) ("The *Sullivan* case is a classic example of how punitive damages can inhibit the freedom of the press.").

98. *See* Gertz v. Robert Welch, Inc., 418 U.S. 323, 349 (1974) (endorsing the compensation of private individuals for injury to reputation for actual damages, but holding "that the States may not permit recovery of presumed or punitive damages, at least when liability is not based on a showing of knowledge of falsity or reckless disregard for the truth").

99. Randall P. Bezanson et al., Libel Law and the Press: Myth and Reality 79 (1987).

100. *See, e.g.,* Lisa Litwiller, *Has the Supreme Court Sounded the Death Knell for Jury Assessed Punitive Damages? A Critical Re-Examination of the American Jury,* 36 U.S.F.L. Rev. 411 (2002); Victor E. Schwartz, Mark A. Behrens & Joseph P. Mastrosimone, *Reining in Punitive Damages "Run Wild": Proposals for Reform by Courts and Legislatures,* 65 Brooklyn L. Rev. 1003 (1999); David Crump, *Evidence, Economics, and Ethics: What Information Should Jurors Be Given to Determine the*

Amount of a Punitive-Damage Award? 57 Md. L. Rev. 174 (1998); Susan M. Gilles, *Taking First Amendment Procedure Seriously: An Analysis of Process in Libel Litigation,* 58 Ohio St. L.J. 1753 (1998); Lyndon F. Bittle, Comment: *Punitive Damages and the Eighth Amendment: An Analytical Framework for Determining Excessiveness,* 75 Calif. L. Rev. 1433 (1987); William W. Van Alstyne, *Defamation and the First Amendment: New Perspectives: Reputation, Compensation, and Proof: First Amendment Limitations on Recovery from the Press—an Extended Comment on "The Anderson Solution,"* 25 Wm. & Mary L. Rev. 793 (1984).

101. *See, e.g.,* Brown & Williamson v. Jacobsen, 827 F.2d 1119 (7th Cir. 1987).

102. Reporters Committee for Freedom of the Press, "The First Amendment Handbook" (2011), *available at* http://www.rcfp.org/handbook/c01p10.html.

Chapter 5

Libel: Defenses and Privileges

1. Gertz v. Robert Welch, Inc., 418 U.S. 323, 339–40 (1974).

2. Moreno v. Crookston Times and McDaniel, 30 Med. L. Rep. 1208 (Minn. 2002).

3. Hurst v. Capital Cities Media, Inc., 754 N.E.2d 429 (Ill. App. 2001).

4. Weimer v. Rankin, 790 P.2d 347 (Ida. 1990).

5. *But see, e.g.,* Lee v. Dong-A Ilbo, 849 F.2d 876 (4th Cir. 1988) (ruling that the privilege does not extend to official reports issued by governments other than those in the United States).

6. Cowley v. Pulsifer, 137 Mass. 392, 394 (1884).

7. Liquori v. Republican Co., 396 N.E.2d 726, 728 (Mass. App. 1979).

8. Salzano v. North Jersey Media Group, 201 N.J. 500, 520 (2010).

9. McIntosh v. The Detroit News, Inc., 2009 Mich. App. LEXIS 128 (Jan. 22, 2009).

10. Moldea v. New York Times, 793 F. Supp. 335, 337 (D.D.C. 1992).

11. Moldea v. New York Times, 22 F.3d 310, 315 (D.C. Cir. 1994).

12. 1 Fowler V. Harper & Fleming James, Jr., Law of Torts § 5.28, at 456 (1956).

13. *See* Restatement of Torts § 606 (1938).

14. Restatement (Second) of Torts (1977) § 566, cmt. a.

15. Milkovich v. Lorain Journal Co., 497 U.S. 1, 14 (1990) (Rehnquist, C.J.).

16. *See* Gertz v. Robert Welch, Inc., 418 U.S. 323, 339–40 (1974).

17. Citizen Publishing Co. v. U.S., 394 U.S. 131, 139–40 (1969).

18. Whitney v. California, 274 U.S. 354, 375 (1927) (Brandeis, J., concurring).

19. New York Times v. Sullivan, 376 U.S. 254 (1964).

20. *Id.*

21. Ollman v. Evans, 750 F.2d 970 (D.C. Cir. 1984).

22. *Id.*

23. Janklow v. Newsweek, 788 F.2d 1300, 1305 (8th Cir. 1986).

24. Spelson v. CBS, Inc., 581 F. Supp. 1195 (N.D. Ill. 1984); Anderson v. Liberty Lobby, Inc., 746 F.2d 1563 (D.C. Cir. 1984), *aff'd on other grounds,* 477 U.S. 242 (1986); Henderson v. Times Mirror Co., 669 F. Supp. 356 (D. Colo. 1987); Dow v. New Haven Indep., Inc., 549 A.2d 683 (Conn. 1987).

25. Gertz v. Robert Welch, Inc., 418 U.S. 323, 339 (1974).

26. Milkovich v. Lorrain Journal Co., 497 U.S. 1, 4 (1990).

27. *Id.* at 1.

28. *Id.* at 18.

29. *Id.*

30. *Id.* at 21.

31. John v. Tribune Co., 24 Ill. 2d 437, 442 (1962).

32. Madison v. Frazier, 539 F.3d 646, 654 (7th Cir. 2008).

33. Missner v. Clifford, 393 Ill. App. 3d 751 (2009).

34. *See* Robert D. Sack, Sack on Defamation: Libel, Slander, and Related Problems 2–68–2–69 (1999, rev. 2008) (citations omitted).

35. Madsen v. Buie, 454 So. 2d 727, 729 (Fla. Dist. Ct. App. 1984).

36. Wampler v. Higgins, 752 N.E.2d 962 (Ohio 2001).

37. Hustler Magazine v. Falwell, 485 U.S. 46 (1988).

38. Greenbelt Cooperative Publishers Association, Inc. v. Bressler, 398 U.S. 6, 7–8 (1970).

39. *Id.* at 14.

40. Old Dominion Branch No, 496, Nat'l Assn. of Letter Carriers v. Austin, 418 U.S. 264 (1974).

41. *Id.* at 268.

42. *Id.* at 285–86.

43. Knievel v. ESPN, Inc., 223 F. Supp. 2d 1173, 1180 (2002).

44. Silberman v. Georges, 456 N.Y.S.2d 395 (1982).

45. New Times, Inc. v. Isaacks, 91 S.W.3d 844, 850 (Tex. 2002).

46. New Times, Inc. v. Isaacks, 146 S.W.3d 144 (Tex. 2004), *cert. denied,* 545 U.S. 1105 (2005).

47. Edwards v. National Audubon Society, 556 F.2d 113 (2d Cir. 1977) (ruling that "when a responsible, prominent organization . . . makes serious charges against a public figure, the First Amendment protects the accurate and disinterested reporting of those charges, regardless of the reporter's private views of their validity. . . . We do not believe that the press may be required under the First Amendment to suppress newsworthy statements merely because it has serious doubts regarding their truth."). *Id.* at 120.

48. Dan Laidman, *When the Slander Is the Story: The Neutral Report Privilege in Theory and Practice,* 17 UCLA ENT. L. REV. 74, 76 (2010).

49. McKinney v. Avery Journal, Inc., 393 S.E.2d 295 (N.C. 1990).

50. Auvil v. CBS, 140 F.R.D. 450 (E.D. Wash. 1991).

51. Cardillo v. Doubleday Co., Inc., 518 F.2d 638 (2d Cir. 1975) (ruling that the passages of a book whose authors wrote that a habitual criminal was involved in various other criminal activities did not constitute actual malice).

52. Liberty Lobby, Inc. v. Anderson, 746 F.2d 1563 (D.C. Cir. 1984), *rev'd on other grounds,* 477 U.S. 242 (1986).

53. *Id.* at 1568.

54. *Id.*

55. Logan v. District of Columbia, 447 F. Supp. 1328 (D.D.C. 1978).

56. Wynberg v. National Enquirer, Inc., 564 F. Supp. 924 (C.D. Cal. 1982).

57. *Id.* at 928 (emphasis added).

58. Masson v. New Yorker Magazine, Inc., 501 U.S. 496, 523 (1991).

59. *See, e.g.,* November v. Time, Inc., 13 N.Y.2d 175, 178 (1963) (noting that "the rule still holds that language charging a professional man with ignorance or mistake on a single occasion only and not accusing him of general ignorance or lack of skill cannot be considered defamatory on its face and so is not actionable unless special damages are pleaded.").

60. Mourning v. Family Publ'ns. Serv., 411 U.S. 356, 382 (1973). *See also* Adickes v. Kress & Co., 389 U.S. 144, 157 (1970); U.S. v. Diebold, Inc., 369 U.S. 654, 655 (1979).

61. *See* Anderson v. Liberty Lobby, Inc., 477 U.S. 242 (1986).

62. Washington Post Co. v. Keogh, 365 F.2d 965, 968 (D.C. Cir. 1966).

63. Hutchinson v. Proxmire, 443 U.S. 111, 120 n.9 (1979).

64. Anderson v. Liberty Lobby, 477 U.S. 242, 244, 256 (1986).

65. *See, e.g.,* Hustler Magazine, Inc., 465 U.S. 770 (1984) (overturning a lower court ruling dismissing a libel suit filed by a resident of New York against an Ohio corporation in a New Hampshire court). *See also* New York Times v. Sullivan, 376 U.S. 254 (1964) (where the trial and first appeal were heard in Alabama courts).

66. Young v. New Haven Advocate, 315 F.3d 256, 261 (4th Cir. 2002), *cert. denied,* 538 U.S. 1035 (2003).

67. *Id.* at 263.

68. *Id.*

69. John C. Martin, *The Role of Retraction in Defamation Suits,* 1993 U. CHI. LEGAL F. 293, 294 (1993).

70. Two states' retraction statutes apply only to newspapers. *See* Minn. Stat. Ann. 548.06 (1987); S.D. Codified Laws 20–11–7 (1995). Two others include media other than newspapers but exclude radio and television. *See* Wis. Stat. 895.05 (1998); Okla. Stat. tit. 12, 1446a.

71. Dennis Hale, *The Impact of State Prohibitions of Punitive Damages on Libel Litigation: An Empirical Analysis,* 5 VAND. J. ENT. L. & PRAC. 96, 100 (2003).

72. Boswell v. Phoenix Newspapers, Inc., 730 P.2d 186 (Ariz. 1986).

73. A.R.S. §§12–653.02 and 12.653.03.

74. ARIZ. CONST., art. 18, § 6.

75. Early v. Toledo Blade, 720 N.E.2d 107 (Ohio Ct. App. 1998).

76. Dolcefino and KTRK Television, Inc. v. Turner, 987 S.W. 2d 100 (Tex. 1998).

77. In its entirety, the column reads as follows:
    Yesterday in the Franklin County Common Pleas Court, judge Paul Martin overturned an Ohio High School

Athletic Assn. decision to suspend the Maple Heights wrestling team from this year's state tournament.

It's not final yet—the judge granted Maple only a temporary injunction against the ruling—but unless the judge acts much more quickly than he did in this decision (he has been deliberating since a Nov. 8 hearing) the temporary injunction will allow Maple to compete in the tournament and make any further discussion meaningless.

But there is something much more important involved here than whether Maple was denied due process by the OHSAA, the basis of the temporary injunction. When a person takes on a job in a school, whether it be as a teacher, coach, administrator or even maintenance worker, it is well to remember that his primary job is that of educator.

There is scarcely a person concerned with school who doesn't leave his mark in some way on the young people who pass his way—many are the lessons taken away from school by students which weren't learned from a lesson plan or out of a book. They come from personal experiences with and observations of their superiors and peers, from watching actions and reactions.

Such a lesson was learned (or relearned) yesterday by the student body of Maple Heights High School, and by anyone who attended the Maple-Mentor wrestling meet of last Feb. 8.

A lesson which, sadly, in view of the events of the past year, is well they learned early.

It is simply this: If you get in a jam, lie your way out.

If you're successful enough, and powerful enough, and can sound sincere enough, you stand an excellent chance of making the lie stand up, regardless of what really happened.

The teachers responsible were mainly head Maple wrestling coach, Mike Milkovich, and former superintendent of schools H. Donald Scott.

Last winter they were faced with a difficult situation. Milkovich's ranting from the side of the mat and egging the crowd on against the meet official and the opposing team backfired during a meet with Greater Cleveland Conference rival Metor [sic], and resulted in first the Maple Heights team, then many of the partisan crowd attacking the Mentor squad in a brawl which sent four Mentor wrestlers to the hospital.

Naturally, when Mentor protested to the governing body of high school sports, the OHSAA, the two men were called on the carpet to account for the incident.

But they declined to walk into the hearing and face up to their responsibilities, as one would hope a coach of Milkovich's accomplishments and reputation would do, and one would certainly expect from a man with the responsible poisition [sic] of superintendent of schools.

Instead they chose to come to the hearing and misrepresent the things that happened to the OHSAA Board of Control, attempting not only to convince the board of their own innocence, but, incredibly, shift the blame of the affair to Mentor.

I was among the 2,000-plus witnesses of the meet at which the trouble broke out, and I also attended the hearing before the OHSAA, so I was in a unique position of being the only non-involved party to observe both the meet itself and the Milkovich-Scott version presented to the board.

Any resemblance between the two occurrances [sic] is purely coincidental.

To anyone who was at the meet, it need only be said that the Maple coach's wild gestures during the events leading up to the brawl were passed off by the two as 'shrugs,' and that Milkovich claimed he was 'Powerless to control the crowd' before the melee.

Fortunately, it seemed at the time, the Milkovich-Scott version of the incident presented to the board of control had enough contradictions and obvious untruths so that the six board members were able to see through it.

Probably as much in distasteful reaction to the chicanery of the two officials as in displeasure over the actual incident, the board then voted to suspend Maple from this year's tournament and to put Maple Heights, and both Milkovich and his son, Mike Jr. (the Maple Jaycee coach), on two-year probation.

But unfortunately, by the time the hearing before Judge Martin rolled around, Milkovich and Scott apparently had their version of the incident polished and reconstructed, and the judge apparently believed them.

"I can say that some of the stories told to the judge sounded pretty darned unfamiliar," said Dr. Harold Meyer, commissioner of the OHSAA, who attended the hearing. 'It certainly sounded different from what they told us.'

Nevertheless, the judge bought their story, and ruled in their favor.

Anyone who attended the meet, whether he be from Maple Heights, Mentor, or impartial observer, knows in his heart that Milkovich and Scott lied at the hearing after each having given his solemn oath to tell the truth.

But they got away with it.

Is that the kind of lesson we want our young people learning from their high school administrators and coaches?

I think not.

Chapter 6

Protecting Privacy

1. Jennifer Martinez, *Internet Firms Grilled on Privacy*, L.A. Times, July 28, 2010, at B6.

2. John Schwartz, *As Big PC Brother Watches, Users Encounter Frustration*, N.Y. Times, Sept. 5, 2001, at A1.

3. U.S. Const. amend. IV.

4. U.S. Const. amend. III.

5. Julia Angwin & Tom McGinty, *Sites Feed Personal Details to New Tracking Industry*, Wall St. J., July 30, 2010, *available at* http://online.wsj.com/article/; Julia Angwin, *The Web's New Gold Mine: Your Secrets*, Wall St. J., July 30, 2010, *available at* http://online.wsj.com/article/; Jennifer Valentino-DeVries, *Lawsuit Tackles Files That 'Re-Spawn' Tracking Cookies*, Wall St. J., July 30, 2010, *available at* http://blogs.wsj.com/digits/2010/07/30/.

6. *See, e.g., In re* Doubleclick Inc. Privacy Litation, 154 F. Supp. 2d 497 (S.D.N.Y. 2001).

7. Jordan Robertson, *What Your Phone App Doesn't Say: It's Watching*, San Jose Mercury News, July 30, 2010.

8. Jennifer Martinez, *Lawmakers Grill Internet Firms over Privacy Protections*, L.A. Times, July 28, 2010, at B6.

9. Brad Stone, *Twitter Settles F.T.C. Privacy Case*, N.Y. Times, June 25, 2010, at B4.

10. *100 Million Facebook Users' Information Published on Web*, Star-Ledger (Newark, N.J.), July 30, 2010, at 10.

11. Ostergren v. Cuccinelli, 615 F.3d 263 (4th Cir. 2010).

12. Jessica Rich, Federal Trade Commission, Deputy Director of Consumer Protection, *Protecting Youths in an Online World*, testimony before U.S. Senate Committee on Commerce, Science and Transportation, Subcommittee on Consumer Protection, Product Safety, and Insurance, July 15, 2010, *available at* http://www.ftc.gov/os/testimony/os/testimony/100715tooptestimony.pdf.

13. Declan McCullagh, *FTC Says Current Privacy Laws Aren't Working*, CNet News, June 22, 2010, *available at* http://news.cnet.com/8301–13578_3–20008422–38.html.

14. Nick Bilton, *Price of Facebook Privacy? Start Clicking*, N.Y. Times, May 13, 2010, at B8.

15. Jeffrey Rosen, *The End of Forgetting*, N.Y. Times Magazine, July 25, 2010, at 32.

16. City of Ontario v. Quon, 130 S. Ct. 2619 (2010).

17. O'Conner v. Ortega, 480 U.S. 709 (1987).

18. Ray Lewis, Comment: *Employee E-mail Privacy Still Unemployed: What the United States Can Learn from the United Kingdom*, 67 La. L. Rev. 959 (2007).

19. Smyth v. Pillsbury Co., 914 F. Supp. 97, 101 (E.D. Pa. 1996).

20. 50 U.S.C. §§ 1804(a)(7)(B), 1823(a)(B) (2003).

21. The "First Amendment has a penumbra where privacy is protected from governmental intrusion." Griswold v. Connecticut, 381 U.S. 479, 482 (1965).

22. Griswold v. Connecticut, 381 U.S. 479 (1965).

23. U.S. Const. amend. V.

24. Griswold v. Connecticut, 381 U.S. 479.

25. Eisenstadt v. Baird, 405 U.S. 438 (1972).

26. Roe v. Wade, 410 U.S. 113 (1973).

27. Lawrence v. Texas, 539 U.S. 538 (2003).

28. 18 U.S.C. § 2710.

29. For example, California, Connecticut, Delaware, Iowa, Maryland, Minnesota, New Hampshire, New York and Rhode Island. *See* James P. Nehf, *Incomparability and the Passive Virtues of Ad Hoc Privacy Policy*, 76 U. Colo. L. Rev. 1, 9 n.39 (2005).

30. Lane v. Facebook, Inc., 2010 U.S. Dist. LEXIS 24762 (N.D. Cal., Mar. 17, 2010); Lane v. Facebook, Inc., 2009 U.S. Dist. LEXIS 103668 (N.D. Cal., Oct. 23, 2009).

31. Jeffery A. Smith, *Moral Guardians and the Origins of the Right to Privacy*, 10 Journalism & Comm. Monographs 65 (Spring 2008).

32. Samuel D. Warren & Louis D. Brandeis, *The Right to Privacy*, 4 Harv. L. Rev. 193 (1890).

33. Warren and Brandeis rested their contention on an English case, Prince Albert v. Strange, 64 Eng. Rep. 293 (V.C. 1848), on appeal, 64 Eng. Rep. 293 (1849). But not until 2001 did English courts explicitly recognize a right to privacy. See Douglas v. Hello! Ltd., [2001] W.L.R. 992, 1033, para. 110 ("We have reached a point at which it can be said with confidence that the law recognizes and will appropriately protect a right of personal privacy.") (per Sedley, L.J.).

34. *See* Don R. Pember, Privacy and the Press (1972).

35. William L. Prosser, *Privacy*, 48 Cal. L. Rev. 383 (1960).

36. N.Y. Civil Rights Law §§ 50–51.

37. Restatement (Second) of Torts § 6521.

38. *See, e.g.,* RESTATEMENT (THIRD) OF UNFAIR COMPETITION § 46, cmt. d (right of publicity limited to "natural persons").

39. RESTATEMENT (SECOND) OF TORTS, § 652E, cmt. b, illus. 1.

40. Spahn v. Julian Messner, 233 N.E.2d 840 (N.Y. 1967).

41. Colorado, Florida, Massachusetts, Minnesota, Missouri, New York, North Carolina, North Dakota, Ohio, South Carolina, Texas, Virginia and Washington do not accept the false light tort. Under its privacy statute, New York allows suits very much like a false light action. *See* Denver Publishing Co. v. Bueno, 54 P.3d 893 (2002); Charmaine West v. Media General Convergence, Inc., 53 S.W.3d 640, 644–45 (Tenn. 2001).

42. Solano v. Playgirl, Inc., 292 F.3d 1078, 1082 (9th Cir.), *cert. denied,* 537 U.S. 1029 (2002).

43. *See, e.g.,* Diane Leenheer Zimmerman, *False Light Invasion of Privacy: The Light That Failed,* 64 N.Y.U. L. REV. 364 (1989).

44. See RESTATEMENT (SECOND) OF TORTS § 652E.

45. *Id.* at § 652I, cmt. c.

46. *Id.* § 652D, cmt. a.

47. *See, e.g.,* Solano v. Playgirl Inc., 292 F.3d 1078 (9th Cir.), *cert. denied,* 537 U.S. 1029 (2002).

48. *See, e.g., id.*

49. *See, e.g.,* Eberhardt v. Morgan Stanley Dean Witter Trust FSB, 2001 U.S. Dist. LEXIS 1090 (N.D. Ill. 2001).

50. Brauer v. Globe Newspaper Co., 217 N.E.2d 736 (1966).

51. Howard v. Antilla, 294 F.3d 244 (1st Cir. 2002).

52. Peterson v. Grisham, 594 F.3d 723 (10th Cir. 2010).

53. Moriarty v. Greene, 732 N.E.2d 730 (Ill. App. Ct. 2000).

54. Fanelle v. LoJack Corp., 2000 U.S. Dist. LEXIS 17767 (E.D. Pa. 2000).

55. Kelson v. Spin Publications, Inc., 1988 U.S. Dist. LEXIS 4675 (D. Md. 1988).

56. Peoples Bank & Trust Co. v. Globe International, 978 F.2d 1065 (8th Cir. 1992), on remand, Mitchell v. Globe International Publications, Inc., 817 F. Supp. 72 (W.D. Ark.), *cert. denied,* 510 U.S. 931 (1993).

57. Time, Inc. v. Hill, 385 U.S. 374 (1967).

58. Cantrell v. Forest City Publishing Co., 419 U.S. 245, 247–48 (1974).

59. State courts or federal courts applying state law to follow *Gertz* rather than *Hill* and *Cantrell,* thus not requiring private false light plaintiffs to prove actual malice, include Alabama, Delaware, Kansas, Utah, West Virginia and the District of Columbia. MEDIA LAW RESOURCE CENTER, MEDIA PRIVACY AND RELATED LAW 2007–2008 (2007).

60. State courts or federal courts applying state law to follow *Hill* and *Cantrell* rather than *Gertz,* thus requiring private false light plaintiffs to prove actual malice, include Arkansas, California, Connecticut, Florida, Georgia, Illinois, Indiana, Iowa, Kentucky, Maine, Michigan, Mississippi, Montana, Nebraska, Nevada, New Jersey, Oklahoma, Oregon, Pennsylvania, Tennessee and Washington. *Id.* at 788–90.

61. William L. Prosser, *Privacy,* 48 CAL. L. REV. 383, 389 (1960).

62. *See* HARVEY L. ZUCKMAN ET AL., MODERN COMMUNICATIONS LAW 357–61 (1999).

63. *See id.* at 360–61 (1999).

64. *E.g.,* Veilleux v. NBC, 206 F.3d 92, 134 (1st Cir. 2000), said opinion could be a false light defense, while Boese v. Paramount Pictures Corp., 952 F. Supp. 550, 558–59 (N.D. Ill. 1996), said opinion is not a false light defense.

65. *See* HARVEY L. ZUCKMAN ET AL., MODERN COMMUNICATIONS LAW 351–52 (1999).

66. Hilton v. Hallmark Cards, 599 F.3d 894, 899 (9th Cir. 2010).

67. MEDIA LAW RESOURCE CENTER, *supra* note 59.

68. RESTATEMENT (THIRD) OF UNFAIR COMPETITION § 46.

69. Some states, such as Georgia, New Jersey and Utah, and the U.S. Court of Appeals for the Second Circuit have decided by common law that the right of publicity survives after death. Statutes in 10 states say the same. Some states, such as Illinois and Ohio, and the U.S. Courts of Appeals for the Sixth and Seventh Circuits, say by common law that the right of publicity ends when a person dies. Five states agree by statute: Arizona, Massachusetts, New York, Rhode Island and Wisconsin.

70. By statute: California, Florida, Illinois, Indiana, Kentucky, Nebraska, Nevada, Ohio, Oklahoma, Pennsylvania, Tennessee, Texas, Virginia, Washington. By common law: Connecticut, Georgia, Michigan, New Jersey, Utah. J. THOMAS MCCARTHY, THE RIGHTS OF PUBLICITY AND PRIVACY §§ 9:20–9:39 (2010).

71. *Id.* § 9:18. For example, Virginia limits the right of publicity to 20 years after a person's death, Indiana and Oklahoma allow the right to last 100 years after a person's death, and Nebraska has no stated duration. *Id.*

72. N.Y. Civil Rights Law §§ 50–51.

73. Roberson v. Rochester Folding Box Co., 64 N.E. 442 (N.Y. 1902).

74. J. THOMAS MCCARTHY, THE RIGHTS OF PUBLICITY AND PRIVACY § 1:16 (2010).

75. Pavesich v. New England Life Insurance Co., 50 S.E. 68 (1905).

76. Haelan Laboratories, Inc. v. Topps Chewing Gum, Inc., 202 F.2d 866 (2d Cir. 1953).

77. See MCCARTHY, supra note 74, §§ 1:27, 4:7.

78. See, e.g., Dalbec v. Gentleman's Companion, Inc., 828 F.2d 921 (2d Cir. 1987).

79. Cohen v. Herbal Concepts, 482 N.Y.S.2d 457 (1984).

80. Shamsky v. Garan, Inc., 632 N.Y.S.2d 930, 934 (Sup. 1995).

81. See MCCARTHY, supra note 74, § 3:7.

82. Abdul-Jabbar v. General Motors Corp., 85 F.3d 407 (9th Cir. 1996).

83. Prudhomme v. The Procter & Gamble Co., 800 F. Supp. 390 (E.D. La. 1992).

84. Tin Pan Apple, Inc. v. Miller Brewing Co., 737 F. Supp. 826 (S.D.N.Y. 1990).

85. Onassis v. Christian Dior, 472 N.Y.S.2d 254 (Sup. Ct. N.Y. Co. 1984).

86. Allen v. National Video, Inc., 610 F. Supp. 612 (S.D.N.Y. 1985).

87. Allen v. Men's World Outlet, Inc., 679 F. Supp. 360, 362 (S.D.N.Y. 1988).

88. Midler v. Ford Motor Co., 849 F.2d 460 (9th Cir. 1988). A federal district court denied Midler punitive damages, but the jury awarded $400,000 in compensatory damages. The Ninth Circuit affirmed. Midler v. Young & Rubicam, Inc., 944 F.2d 909 (9th Cir. 1991), cert. denied, 503 U.S. 951 (1992).

89. 849 F.2d at 463.

90. Waits v. Frito-Lay, Inc., 978 F.2d 1093, 1097 (9th Cir. 1992).

91. White v. Samsung Electronics America, Inc., 971 F.2d 1395 (9th Cir. 1992), cert. denied, 508 U.S. 951 (1993).

92. William L. Prosser, Privacy, 48 CAL. L. REV. 383, 401 n.155 (1960).

93. Wendt v. Host International, Inc., 125 F.3d 806 (9th Cir. 1997), cert. denied, 531 U.S. 811 (2000).

94. Norm and Cliff Cheered by Lawsuit, CHI. TRIB., June 22, 2001, at C2.

95. See, e.g., Cardtoons, L.C. v. Major League Baseball Players Assoc., 95 F.3d 959 (10th Cir. 1996).

96. MCCARTHY, supra note 74, § 4:46 (2010).

97. The Romantics v. Activision Pub., Inc., 574 F. Supp. 2d 758 (E.D. Mich. 2008).

98. RESTATEMENT (THIRD) OF UNFAIR COMPETITION § 49, cmt. d.

99. ETW Corp. v. Jireh Publishing, Inc., 332 F.3d 915, 924 (6th Cir. 2003).

100. Messenger v. Gruner + Jahn Printing & Publishing, 727 N.E.2d 549 (N.Y. 2000, 208 F.3d 122 (2d Cir. 2000) (vacating district court decision based on New York Court of Appeals decision), cert. denied, 531 U.S. 818 (2000).

101. Toffoloni v. LFP Pub. Group, 572 F.3d 1201 (11th Cir. 2009).

102. Zacchini v. Scripps-Howard Broadcasting Co., 433 U.S. 562 (1977).

103. C.B.C. Distribution and Marketing, Inc. v. Major League Baseball Advanced Media, L.P., 505 F.3d 818 (8th Cir. 2007), cert. denied, 128 S. Ct. 2872 (2008).

104. See Mark S. Lee, Agents of Chaos: Judicial Confusion in Defining the Right of Publicity-Free Speech Interface, 23 LOYOLA L.A. ENT. L. REV. 471, 488 (2003).

105. Haelan Laboratories, Inc. v. Topps Chewing Gum, Inc., 202 F.2d 866, 868 (2d Cir.), cert. denied, 346 U.S. 816 (1953).

106. Cardtoons, L.C. v. Major League Baseball Players Association, 95 F.3d 959, 962 (10th Cir. 1996).

107. Id. at 969.

108. Id. at 976.

109. Factors Etc., Inc. v. Pro Arts, Inc., 579 F.2d 215 (2d Cir. 1978); Brinkley v. Casablancas, 438 N.Y.S.2d 1004 (App. Div. 1981); Titan Sports, Inc. v. Comics World Corp., 870 F.2d 85 (2d Cir. 1989).

110. Paulsen v. Personality Posters, Inc., 299 N.Y.S.2d 501 (Sup. Ct. 1968); Montana v. San Jose Mercury News, Inc., 40 Cal. Rptr. 2d 639 (Ct. App. 1995).

111. Rogers v. Grimaldi, 875 F.2d 994, 999 (2d Cir. 1989).

112. Mattel, Inc. v. MCA Records, Inc., 296 F.3d 894 (9th Cir. 2002), cert. denied, 537 U.S. 1171 (2003).

113. Parks v. LaFace Records, 329 F.3d 437, 442 (6th Cir. 2003), *cert. denied*, 540 U.S. 1074 (2003).

114. *See* Campbell v. Acuff-Rose Music, 510 U.S. 569 (1994); Pierre N. Leval, *Toward a Fair Use Standard*, 103 HARV. L. REV. 1105, 1111 (1990).

115. Comedy III Productions, Inc. v. Gary Saderup, Inc., 106 Cal. Rptr. 2d 126 (Cal. 2001).

116. For a thorough and critical discussion of the Three Stooges decision, *see* F. Jay Daugherty, *All the World's Not a Stooge: The "Transformativeness" Test for Analyzing a First Amendment Defense to a Right of Publicity Claim Against Distribution of a Work of Art*, 27 COL. J. L. & ARTS 1 (2003).

117. Comedy III Productions, Inc., 106 Cal. Rptr. 2d at 140.

118. Winter v. DC Comics, 69 P.3d 473 (Cal. 2003).

119. *Id.* at 478 (*quoting* Comedy III Prods., Inc. v. Gary Saderup, Inc., 106 Cal. Rptr. 2d at 140 (2001)).

120. ETW Corp. v. Jireh Publishing, Inc., 332 F.3d 915 (6th Cir. 2003).

121. Kirby v. Sega of America, Inc., 50 Cal. Rptr. 3d 607 (Ct. App. 2006).

122. Doe v. TCI Cablevision, 110 S.W.3d 363 (Mo. 2003), *on remand*, Doe v. McFarlane, 207 S.W.3d 52 (Mo. Ct. App. 2006).

123. Seale v. Gramercy Pictures, 949 F. Supp. 331 (E.D. Pa. 1996), *aff'd without opinion*, 156 F.3d 1225 (3d Cir. 1998).

124. Rosemont Enterprises, Inc. v. Random House, Inc., 294 N.Y.S.2d 122 (Sup. 1968), *judgment aff'd*, 301 N.Y.S.2d 948 (App. Div. 1969).

125. *See, e.g.,* Tyne v. Time Warner Entertainment Co., 336 F.3d 1286 (11th Cir. 2003).

126. Guglielmi v. Spelling-Goldberg Productions, 603 P.2d 454 (1979); Taylor v. National Broadcasting Co., Inc. 22 Media L. Rep. 2433 (Cal. Supp. 1994).

127. Spahn v. Julian Messner, Inc., 233 N.E.2d 840 (N.Y. 1967), appeal dismissed 393 U.S. 1046 (1969).

128. Booth v. Curtis Publishing Co., 223 N.Y.S.2d 737 (N.Y. Sup. Ct.), *aff'd*, 228 N.Y.S.2d 468 (1962).

129. Cher v. Forum International, 692 F.2d 634 (9th Cir.), *cert. denied*, 462 U.S. 1120 (1983).

130. Schifano v. Greene Country Greyhound Park, Inc., 624 So. 2d (Ala. 1993).

131. Netzer v. Continuity Graphic Associates, Inc., 963 F. Supp. 1308 (S.D.N.Y. 1997).

132. Pooley v. National Hole-in-One Association, 89 F. Supp. 2d 1108 (D. Ariz. 2000).

133. RESTATEMENT (SECOND) OF TORTS § 652B.

134. MEDIA LAW RESOURCE CENTER, MEDIA PRIVACY AND RELATED LAW 2007–2008 (2007).

135. Webb v. CBS Broadcasting Inc., 2009 U.S. Dist. LEXIS 38597, at *9 (N.D. Ill., May 7, 2009).

136. *See, e.g.,* Broughton v. McClatchy Newspapers, Inc., 588 S.E.2d 20 (N.C. App. 2003).

137. Boring v. Google Inc., 362 Fed. Appx. 273 (3d Cir. 2010).

138. Hill v. Colorado, 530 U.S. 703 (2000).

139. Diane Leenheer Zimmerman, *I Spy: The Newsgatherer Under Cover*, 33 U. RICH. L. REV. 1185, 1185 (2000).

140. California Civil Code § 1708.8.

141. Shulman v. Group W Productions, Inc., 74 Cal. Rptr. 2d 843, opinion modified, 1998 Cal. LEXIS 4846 (Cal. 1998).

142. United States v. Maldonado-Norat, 122 F. Supp. 2d 264 (D.P.R. 2000).

143. Le Mistral, Inc. v. Columbia Broadcasting System, 402 N.Y.S.2d 815 (1978).

144. Medical Laboratory Management Consultants v. American Broadcasting Cos., Inc., 306 F.3d 806, 819 (9th Cir. 2002).

145. Belluomo v. KAKE TV & Radio, Inc., 596 P.2d 832 (Kan. App. 1979).

146. Machleder v. Diaz, 538 F. Supp. 1364 (S.D.N.Y. 1982).

147. Zimmerman, *supra* note 139, at 1185, 1190.

148. Desnick v. American Broadcasting Companies, 44 F.3d 1345 (7th Cir. 1995).

149. Baugh v. CBS, Inc., 828 F. Supp. 745, 756 (N.D. Cal. 1993).

150. Carter v. Superior Court of San Diego County, 2002 Cal. App. Unpub. LEXIS 5017 (Ct. App. 2002).

151. Dietemann v. Time, Inc., 449 F.2d 245, 249 (9th Cir. 1971).

152. *Id.*

153. *See* John J. Walsh et al., *The Constitutionality of Consequential Damages for Publication of Ill-Gotten Information*, 4 WM. & MARY BILL RTS. J. 1111, 1137–40 (1996).

154. Shulman v. Group W Productions, 74 Cal. Rptr. 2d 843, 870 (Cal. Ct. App. 1998).

155. Medical Laboratory Management Consultants v. American Broadcasting Companies, Inc., 30 F. Supp. 2d 1182 (D. Ariz. 1998), *aff'd on other grounds,* 306 F.3d 806 (9th Cir. 2002).

156. Sanders v. American Broadcasting Companies, 978 P.2d 67, 74 (Cal. 1999).

157. RESTATEMENT (SECOND) OF TORTS § 652D.

158. Michaels v. Internet Entertainment Group, 5 F. Supp. 2d 823, 842 (C.D. Cal. 1998).

159. Brents v. Morgan, 299 S.W. 967 (Ky. Ct. App. 1927).

160. J. THOMAS MCCARTHY, THE RIGHTS OF PUBLICITY AND PRIVACY § 5:70 (2008). Alaska, Indiana, Nebraska, New York, North Carolina, North Dakota, Virginia and Wyoming have not yet recognized the private facts tort by statute or common law. Oregon recognizes the private facts tort only when the defendant causes the plaintiff some injury beyond hurt feelings.

161. *See, e.g.,* Jones v. U.S. Child Support Recovery, 961 F. Supp. 1518 (D. Utah 1997). A debt collection agency sent a WANTED poster to the employer of a divorced parent who was behind on child support payments.

162. *See, e.g.,* Y.G. v. Jewish Hospital of St. Louis, 795 S.W.2d 488 (Mo. Ct. App. 1990). A couple, pregnant with triplets after an in vitro fertilization process, were invited to and attended a social gathering for couples who were part of a hospital's in vitro program. The hospital promised there would be no publicity. However, a television station reporting team was at the gathering, photographing and trying to interview the couple. The couple's pictures were part of the station's television report. The couple had not told anyone they were part of the in vitro program.

163. *See, e.g.,* Baugh v. CBS, Inc., 828 F. Supp. 745 (N.D. Cal. 1993). Without permission, a television program taped and showed the aftermath of a domestic violence incident.

164. *See, e.g.,* Michaels v. Internet Entertainment Group, 5 F. Supp. 2d 823, 842 (C.D. Cal. 1998). Musician Bret Michaels brought a private facts suit against an Internet adult entertainment company for distributing a videotape showing Michaels and actress Pamela Anderson Lee having sex. Michaels and Lee made the tape, which an unknown person apparently stole and sold to the Internet company.

165. Winstead v. Sweeney, 517 N.W.2d 874 (Mich. Ct. App. 1994).

166. Daly v. Viacom, Inc., 238 F. Supp. 2d 1118 (N.D. Cal. 2002).

167. Zieve v. Hairston, 598 S.E.2d 25 (Ga. App. 2004).

168. *See* Robert C. Post, *The Social Foundations of Privacy: Community and Self in the Common Law Tort,* 77 CAL. L. REV. 957, 983–984 (1989).

169. RESTATEMENT (SECOND) OF TORTS § 652D, illus. 10.

170. *Id.* cmt. c.

171. *See* M.G. v. Time Warner, Inc., 107 Cal. Rptr. 2d 504, 511 (Cal. App. 2001).

172. Sandler v. Calcagni, 565 F. Supp. 2d 184 (D. Me. 2008).

173. *See, e.g.,* Sipple v. Chronicle Publishing Co., 201 Cal. Rptr. 665, 668–69 (Cal. App. 1984).

174. RESTATEMENT (SECOND) OF TORTS § 652D, cmts. g & h.

175. The Restatement also adopted the test. *Id.* cmt. h.

176. Virgil v. Time, Inc., 527 F.2d 1122 (9th Cir. 1975), *cert. denied,* 425 U.S. 998 (1976).

177. Virgil v. Sports Illustrated, Inc., 424 F. Supp. 1286 (S.D. Cal. 1976).

178. Shulman v. Group W Productions, 955 P.2d 469, 488 (Cal. 1998).

179. Michaels v. Internet Entertainment Group, Inc., 5 F. Supp. 2d 823 (C.D. Cal. 1998).

180. Diaz v. Oakland Tribune, 188 Cal. Rptr. 762 (1983).

181. RESTATEMENT (SECOND) OF TORTS, § 652D, requires the private facts to be disseminated "to the public at large, or to so many persons that the matter must be regarded as substantially certain to become one of public knowledge."

182. *See* Patrick J. McNulty, *The Public Disclosure of Private Facts: There Is Life After* Florida Star, 50 DRAKE L. REV. 93, 100 (2001).

183. See Beaumont v. Brown, 257 N.W.2d 522, 531 (Mich. 1977), *overruled in part on other grounds,* Bradley v. Saranac Board of Education, 565 N.W.2d 650 (1997).

184. Johnson v. K Mart Corp., 723 N.E.2d 1192 (Ill. Ct. App. 2000).

185. Robert C. Ozer, P.C. v. Borquez, 940 P.2d 371 (Colo. 1997).

186. Florida Star v. B.J.F., 491 U.S. 540, 541.

187. *See id.* at 536–37.

188. 491 U.S. 524 (1989).

189. Bowley v. City of Uniontown Police Dept., 404 F.3d 783 (3d Cir.), *cert. denied,* 546 U.S. 1033 (2005).

190. 420 U.S. 469 (1975).

191. Oklahoma Publishing Co. v. District Court, 430 U.S. 308 (1977).

192. Smith v. Daily Mail, 443 U.S. 97 (1979).

193. 532 U.S. 514 (2001).

194. *See, e.g.,* Carafano v. Metrosplash, 207 F. Supp. 2d 1055 (C.D. Cal. 2002), *aff'd on other grounds,* 339 F.3d 1119 (9th Cir. 2003).

195. Green v. CBS Inc., 286 F.3d 281 (5th Cir.), *cert. denied,* 537 U.S. 887 (2002).

196. *See, e.g.,* United States v. Smith, 992 F. Supp. 743 (D.N.J. 1998).

197. *See, e.g.,* Doe v. New York City, 15 F.3d 264 (2d Cir. 1994).

198. *See,* Green v. Chicago Tribune Co., 675 N.E.2d 249 (Ill. App. Ct. 1996), appeal denied, 679 N.E.2d 379 (Ill. 1997).

199. Sidis v. F-R Publishing Corp., 113 F.2d 806 (2d Cir.), *cert. denied,* 311 U.S. 711 (1940).

Chapter 7

Emotional Distress and Physical Harm

1. Bruce W. Sanford & Bruce D. Brown, *Hit Man's Miss Hit,* 27 N. Ky. L. Rev. 69, 71 (2000).

2. A jury awarded McDonald's drive-through customer Sheila Liebeck $2.7 million in punitive damages after she spilled hot coffee onto her lap. An appellate court reduced the award to $480,000. *See* Andrew Tilghman, *Lawsuit Juries Harder to Find,* Hous. Chron., Feb. 14, 2004, at A1.

3. Restatement (Second) of Torts § 46 (1965), cmt. j.

4. *See, e.g.,* Gouin v. Gouin, 249 F. Supp. 2d 62 (D. Mass. 2003).

5. *See* Charles E. Cantu, *An Essay on the Tort of Negligent Infliction of Emotional Distress in Texas: Stop Saying It Does Not Exist,* 33 St. Mary's L.J. 455, 458 (2002).

6. Cox Newspaper L.P. v. Wooten, 59 S.W.3d 717 (Tex. Ct. App. 2001).

7. Idema v. Wager, 29 Fed. Appx. 676 (2d Cir. 2002).

8. *See, e.g.,* Nancy Levit, *Ethereal Torts,* 61 Geo. Wash. L. Rev. 136 (1992).

9. *Id.*

10. Restatement (Second) of Torts § 46 (1965).

11. *See, e.g.,* Covey v. Detroit Lakes Publishing Co., 490 N.W.2d 138, 144 (Minn. Ct. App. 1992).

12. *See* Pierce v. Clarion Ledger, 236 Fed. Appx. 887, 889 (5th Cir. 2007).

13. Restatement (Second) of Torts § 46 (1965).

14. *Id.* cmt. d.

15. *Id.*

16. Lin v. Rohm & Haas Co., 293 F. Supp. 2d 505, 522 (E.D. Pa. 2003), *quoting* Hunger v. Grand Cent. Sanitation, 670 A.2d 173, 177 (Pa. Super. Ct. 1996).

17. Showler v. Harper's Magazine Foundation, 222 Fed. Appx. 755 (10th Cir.), *cert. denied,* 552 U.S. 825 (2007).

18. Riley v. Harr, 292 F.3d 282 (1st Cir. 2002).

19. *Id.* at 299.

20. Alvarado v. KOB-TV, L.L.C., 493 F.3d 1210, 1222 (10th Cir. 2007).

21. Hatfill v. New York Times, 532 F.3d 312 (4th Cir.), *cert. denied,* 129 S. Ct. 765 (2008).

22. *See* Scott Shane & Eric Lichtblau, *New Details on F.B.I.'s False Start in Anthrax Case,* N.Y. Times, Nov. 26, 2008, at A23.

23. Best v. Malec, 2010 U.S. Dist. LEXIS 58996 (N.D. Ill., June 11, 2010).

24. Armstrong v. H & C Communications, 575 So. 2d 280 (Fla. App. 1991).

25. *Id.* at 281.

26. *Id.* at 282.

27. *Id.*

28. KOVR-TV, Inc. v. Superior Court, 37 Cal. Rptr. 2d 431 (Cal. App. 1995).

29. Roach v. Stern, 675 N.Y.S.2d 133 (1998).

30. Esposito-Hilder v. SFX Broadcasting, Inc., 665 N.Y.S.2d 697 (1997).

31. Estate of Duckett v. Cable News Network, 2008 U.S. Dist. LEXIS 88667 (M.D. Fla., July 31, 2008), *quoting* Williams v. City of Minneola, 575 So. 2d 683, 691 (Fla. Ct. App. 1991).

32. Ruffin-Steinback v. Depasse, 267 F.3d 457 (6th Cir. 2001).

33. RESTATEMENT (SECOND) OF TORTS § 46(1).

34. Catsouras v. Department of California Highway Patrol, 181 Cal. App. 4th 856 (Cal. App. Ct. 2010), *rev. denied,* 2010 Cal. LEXIS 3456 (Cal., April 14, 2010).

35. 376 U.S. 254 (1964).

36. Hustler Magazine, Inc. v. Falwell, 485 U.S. 46 (1988).

37. *See* RODNEY SMOLLA, SMOLLA AND NIMMER ON FREEDOM OF SPEECH § 24.10 n.2 (2010). *See also* RODNEY A. SMOLLA, JERRY FALWELL V. LARRY FLYNT: THE FIRST AMENDMENT ON TRIAL (1988).

38. Falwell v. Flynt, 797 F.2d 1270 (4th Cir.), *rehearing en banc denied,* 805 F.2d 484 (4th Cir. 1986).

39. Hustler Magazine v. Falwell, 485 U.S. 46 (1988).

40. *See, e.g.,* Neilson v. Union Bank of Cal., N.A., 290 F. Supp. 2d 1101, 1142 (C.D. Calif. 2003).

41. *See, e.g.,* Nelson v. Harrah's Entertainment Inc., 2008 U.S. Dist. LEXIS 46524 (N.D. Ill., June 13, 2008).

42. *See* Camper v. Minor, 915 S.W.2d 437, 440 (Tenn. 1996).

43. *Id.*

44. *See, e.g.,* Boyles v. Kerr, 855 S.W.2d 593 (Tex. 1993).

45. *See, e.g.,* Johnson v. Ruark Obstetrics and Gynecology Associates, 395 S.E.2d 85 (N.C. 1990).

46. RESTATEMENT (SECOND) OF TORTS § 436A.

47. Doe v. American Broadcasting Companies, Inc., 543 N.Y.S.2d 455 (N.Y. App.), *appeal dismissed,* 549 N.E.2d 480 (N.Y. 1989).

48. Sleem v. Yale University, 843 F. Supp. 57 (M.D.N.C. 1993).

49. Hyde v. City of Columbia, 637 S.W.2d 251 (Mo. Ct. App. 1982).

50. Times-Mirror Co. v. Superior Court, 244 Cal. Rptr. 556 (Cal. Ct. App. 1988).

51. FEDERAL TRADE COMMISSION, VIOLENCE IN MEDIA REPORT i–ii (2000).

52. *See generally* John Charles Kunich, *Shock Torts Reloaded,* 6 APPALACHIAN J.L. 1 (2006); John Charles Kunich, *Natural Born Copycat Killers and the Law of Shock Torts,* 78 WASH. U.L.Q. 1157 (2000).

53. Zamora v. Columbia Broadcasting System, 480 F. Supp. 199, 200 (S.D. Fla. 1979).

54. *Id.* at 201, 205.

55. Olivia N. v. National Broadcasting Co., 126 Cal. App. 3d 488 (1981).

56. Sanders v. Acclaim Entertainment, Inc., 188 F. Supp. 2d 1264 (D. Colo. 2002).

57. James v. Meow Media, Inc., 300 F.3d 683 (6th Cir. 2002), *cert. denied,* 537 U.S. 1159 (2003).

58. *Id.* at 693.

59. Eimann v. Soldier of Fortune Magazine, Inc., 880 F.2d 830, 832 (5th Cir. 1989), *cert. denied,* 493 U.S. 1024 (1990).

60. Norwood v. Soldier of Fortune, Inc., 651 F. Supp. 1397 (W.D. Ark. 1987).

61. *Id.* at 1403.

62. Eimann v. Soldier of Fortune Magazine, Inc., 880 F.2d 830, 834 (5th Cir. 1989), *cert. denied,* 493 U.S. 1024 (1990).

63. *Id.* at 834.

64. Braun v. Soldier of Fortune Magazine, Inc., 968 F.2d 1110 (11th Cir. 1992), *cert. denied,* 506 U.S. 1071 (1993).

65. *Id.* at 1115.

66. Winter v. G. P. Putnam's Sons, 938 F.2d 1033 (9th Cir. 1991).

67. McCollum v. CBS, Inc., 249 Cal. Rptr. 187 (Cal. App. 1988).

68. *See* April M. Perry, Comment: *Guilt by Saturation: Media Liability for Third-Party Violence and the Availability Heuristic,* 97 NW. U.L. REV. 1045, 1055–56 (2003).

69. Watters v. TSR, Inc., 904 F.2d 378 (6th Cir. 1990).

70. David A. Anderson, *Incitement and Tort Law,* 37 WAKE FOREST L. REV. 957 (2002).

71. 395 U.S. 444, 447 (1969) (per curiam).

72. 414 U.S. 105 (1973) (per curiam).

73. Anderson, *supra* note 70 at 957, 985.

74. Byers v. Edmundson, 712 So. 2d 681 (La. App. 1998), *cert. denied,* 526 U.S. 1005 (1999).

75. Byers v. Edmundson, 826 So. 2d 551 (La. App. 2002).

76. Herceg v. Hustler Magazine, 814 F.2d 1017 (5th Cir. 1987), *cert. denied,* 485 U.S. 959 (1988).

77. Yakubowicz v. Paramount Pictures Corp., 536 N.E.2d 1067 (Mass. 1989).

78. Rice v. Paladin Enterprises, Inc., 128 F.3d 233 (4th Cir. 1997), *cert. denied,* 523 U.S. 1074 (1998).

79. *Id.* at 244.

80. Martin Garbus, *State of the Union for the Law of the New Millennium, the Internet, and the First Amendment,* 1999 Ann. Surv. Am. L. 169, 173–74.

81. Wilson v. Midway Games, Inc., 198 F. Supp. 2d 167 (D. Conn. 2002).

82. Weirum v. RKO General, Inc., 123 Cal. Rptr. 468 (1975).

83. 47 U.S.C. §§ 230 (c)(1), (e)(3).

84. Doe v. MySpace, Inc., 528 F.3d 413 (5th Cir.), *cert. denied,* 129 S. Ct. 600 (2008).

85. Doe II v. MySpace Inc., 175 Cal. App. 4th 561 (Calif. Ct. App. 2009), *rev. denied,* 2009 Cal. LEXIS 10656 (Calif., Oct. 14, 2009).

86. Doe IX v. MySpace, Inc., 629 F. Supp. 2d 663 (E.D. Tex. 2009).

87. Fair Housing Council of San Fernando Valley v. Roommates.com, LLC, 521 F.3d 1157 (9th Cir. 2008).

88. *See, e.g.,* GW Equity LLC v. Xcentric Ventures LLC, 2009 U.S. Dist LEXIS 1445.

89. Gibson v. Craigslist, Inc., 2009 U.S. Dist. LEXIS 53246 (S.D.N.Y., June 15, 2009).

90. Barnes v. Yahoo!, Inc., 570 F.3d 1096 (9th Cir. 2009), *on remand,* 2009 U.S. Dist. LEXIS 116274 (D. Or., Dec. 8, 2009).

91. Wildmon v. Berwick Universal Pictures, 803 F. Supp. 1167 (D. Miss. 1992), *aff'd without opinion,* 979 F.2d 21 (5th Cir. 1992).

92. Savage v. Pacific Gas and Electric Co., 26 Cal. Rptr. 2d 305 (Cal. Ct. App. 1993).

93. Caine v. Duke Communications, International, 24 Media L. Rep. 1187 (C.D. Calif. 1995).

94. Doe 2 v. Associated Press, 331 F.3d 417 (4th Cir. 2003).

95. Brandt v. The Weather Channel, Inc., 423 F. Supp. 2d 1344, 1345–46 (S.D. Fla.), *aff'd without opinion,* 204 F.3d 1123 (11th Cir. 1999).

Chapter 8

Newsgathering

1. Branzburg v. Hayes, 408 U.S. 665, 728 (1972).

2. *Id.* at 684 (1972).

3. *See, e.g.,* Cohen v. Cowles Media Co., 501 U.S. 663, 669 (1991) ("generally applicable laws do not offend the First Amendment simply because their enforcement against the press has incidental effects on its ability to gather and report the news").

4. Potter Stewart, *Or of the Press,* 26 Hastings L.J. 631, 636 (1975).

5. *See, e.g.,* Matthew D. Bunker, Sigman L. Splichal & Sheree Martin, *Triggering the First Amendment: Newsgathering Torts and Press Freedom,* 4 Comm. L. & Pol'y 273 (1999). Erwin Chemerinsky, *Protect the Press: A First Amendment Standard for Safeguarding Aggressive Newsgathering,* 33 U. Rich. L. Rev. 1143 (2000).

6. Branzburg v. Hayes, 408 U.S. 665, 681 (1972).

7. Chemerinsky, *supra* note 5 at 1143, 1145.

8. *Id.* at 1158.

9. Bunker et al., *supra* note 5 at 273, 296–97.

10. *See, e.g.,* Michael W. Richards, *Tort Vision for the New Millennium: Strengthening News Industry Standards as a Defense Tool in Lawsuits over Newsgathering Techniques,* 10 Fordham Intell. Prop. Media & Ent. L.J. 501, 505 (2000) ("The plaintiffs' bar has increasingly taken notice of this trend as challenges to newsgathering techniques become a new arena for attacks on investigative work."). *See also,* Lyrissa Barnett Lidsky, *Prying, Spying, and Lying: Intrusive Newsgathering and What the Law Should Do About It,* 73 Tul. L. Rev. 173, 202 (1998) (noting a "disturbing trend in newsgathering law [where] plaintiff's lawyers [see] the difficulty in establishing a viable claim for defamation, invasion of privacy, or intentional infliction of emotional distress based on newsgathering practices, [and] press[] other tort theories into service").

11. Pell v. Procunier, 417 U.S. 817 (1974) (emphasis added).

12. Huchins v. KQED, 438 U.S. 1 (1978).

13. *See* Pell v. Procunier, 417 U.S. 817 (1974) and Saxbe v. Washington Post, 417 U.S. 843 (1974).

14. *See, e.g.,* Miller v. NBC, 187 Cal. App. 3d 1463, 1480 (1986): "The essence of the cause of action for trespass is an 'unauthorized entry' onto the land of another."

15. LeMistral, Inc. v. CBS, 402 N.Y.S.2d 815, 815 (1978).

16. *Id.* at 816.

17. Florida Publishing Co. v. Fletcher, 340 So. 2d 914 (Fla. 1976).

18. Miller v. NBC, 187 Cal. App. 3d 1463, 1489 (1986).

19. *Id.* at 1488.

20. *Id.* at 1492 (quoting Dietemann v. Time, Inc., 449 F.2d 245, 249 (1971)).

21. *Id.* at 1493.

22. "At trial, Paul Berger was acquitted of federal charges of violating laws protecting eagles and found guilty of misdemeanor use of a pesticide." Nancy L. Trueblood, Comment: *Curbing the Media: Should Reporters Pay When Police Ride-Alongs Violate Privacy?* 84 MARQ. L. REV. 541, 560 n.131 (2000).

23. Berger v. Hanlon, 129 F.3d 505 (9th Cir. 1997), *withdrawn,* 188 F.3d 1155 (9th Cir. 1999) (affirming the district court's decision in part, reversing in part, and remanding in part, complying with the Supreme Court's opinion in Hanlon v. Berger, 526 U.S. 808 (1999)). *See* Trueblood, *supra* note 22 at 541, 560.

24. Hanlon v. Berger, 526 U.S. 808 (1999).

25. 129 F.3d 505, 510 (9th Cir. 1997).

26. *Obituaries,* ST. PETERSBURG (FLA.) TIMES, Apr. 20, 2003, at 21A.

27. Wilson v. Layne, 526 U.S. 603, 607 (1999).

28. *Id.* at 611 (1999).

29. *Id.*

30. *Id.* at 613.

31. *Id.*

32. *Id.*

33. *Id.* at 614.

34. *See, e.g.,* Shulman v. Group W Productions, Inc., 18 Cal. 4th 200 (1998) (ruling that outfitting a nurse with a wireless microphone then videotaping her rescue of two people in an overturned automobile at the bottom of an embankment, then broadcasting the tape, constituted intrusion).

35. Greg Braxton, *Producers Say Ruling Won't Affect Shows; "COPS" and Others Claim Privacy Issues Are Already Addressed,* L.A. TIMES, May 26, 1999, at F4.

36. Galella v. Onassis, 353 F. Supp. 196 (S.D.N.Y. 1972).

37. Galella v. Onassis, 487 F.2d 986 (2d Cir. 1973).

38. Wolfson v. Lewis, 924 F. Supp. 1413 (E.D. Pa. 1996).

39. *Id.* at 1435.

40. *Id.* (emphasis added).

41. Cal Civ. Code § 1708.8.

42. *See* Clay Calvert & Robert D. Richards, *The Irony of News Coverage: How the Media Harm Their Own First Amendment Rights,* 24 HASTINGS COMM. & ENT. L.J. 215, 218 (2002) (stating that the federal anti-paparazzi legislation was not passed "because no further Diana-like tragedies have occurred, and because it turned out that the initial media-created perception that members of the paparazzi were culpable for Diana's death was simply wrong"). *See also* Andrew D. Morton, *Much Ado About Newsgathering: Personal Privacy, Law Enforcement, and the Law of Unintended Consequences for Anti-Paparazzi Legislation,* 147 U. PA. L. REV. 1435 (1999).

43. *See generally* Jane Kirtley, *It's the Process, Stupid: Newsgathering Is the New Target,* COLUM. JOUR. REV. (Sept./Oct. 2000). "New and more intrusive methods of newsgathering, often involving electronic equipment such as video cameras and recording devices, became commonplace. Reporters and their editors, eager to feed the appetite of a voyeuristic public, assumed that the First Amendment would allow them to do anything they wished to get a story. They couldn't have been more wrong." *Id.*

44. Food Lion, Inc. v. Capital Cities, Inc./ABC, 964 F. Supp. 956, 959 (1997).

45. *Id.* "The duty of loyalty recognized in this case requires an employee to use her efforts, while working, for the service of her employer. The jury found that each of the producers violated this duty by failing to make a good faith effort toward performing the job requirements of her employer Food Lion as a result of the time and attention she was devoting to her investigation for ABC and by performing specific acts on behalf of ABC which proximately resulted in damage to Food Lion." *Id.*

46. Food Lion, Inc. v. Capital Cities, Inc./ABC, 964 F. Supp. 956, 959 (1997).

47. *Id.*

48. *See, e.g.,* Neil Hickey, *Climate of Change: Everybody Is More Careful Than They Used to Be,* COLUM. JOUR. REV., Sept./Oct. 2000, at 52; Jane Kirtley, *Don't Pop That Cork: The Food Lion Verdict Was Hardly a Total Victory for the News Media,* AMER. JOUR. REV., Jan./Feb. 2000, at 84; Jim Moccou, *Newsgathering Tactics on Trial,* EDITOR & PUBLISHER, Dec. 18, 1999, at 18; Russ W. Baker, *Damning Undercover Tactics as "Fraud": Can Reporters Lie About Who They Are? The Food Lion Jury Says No,* COLUM. JOUR. REV., Mar./Apr. 1997, at 28; Russ W. Baker, *Truth, Lies, and Videotape: "PrimeTime" Live and the Hidden Camera,* COLUM. JOUR. REV., July/Aug. 1993, at 25.

49. Food Lion, Inc. v. Capital Cities, Inc./ABC, 194 F.3d 505, 526 (1999) (Niemeyer, J., dissenting).

50. According to one of the attorneys involved, ABC's bill from one of the law firms handling the appeal only was in the "six figures" (personal communication).

51. *Hidden Cameras, Hard Choices,* "Primetime Live" (Feb. 12, 1997). After the trial portion of the case, ABC's "Primetime Live" broadcast interviews with members of the jury. One juror said that on a scale of 1-to-10, with 10 being the worst, ABC's wrongdoing was a 10. "Because the—the girls were telling stories to get into a man's personal business, and they even made up stories to get in." This same juror said she wanted the punitive damages levied against ABC to be $1 billion. *Id.*

52. Special Force Ministries v. WCCO Television, 584 N.W. 2d 789 (Minn. 1998).

53. Veilleux v. NBC, 8 F. Supp. 2d 23, 30 (D. Me. 1998).

54. Veilleux v. NBC, 206 F.3d 92, 105 (1st Cir. 2000).

55. Nancy Garland, *Settlement Reached in "Dateline" Suit,* BANGOR DAILY NEWS, Sept. 1, 2000.

56. Cohen v. Cowles Media, 501 U.S. 663 (1991).

57. Cohen v. Cowles Media, 479 N.W.2d 387 (Minn. 1992).

58. *See* Reporters Committee for Freedom of the Press, *A Practical Guide to Taping Phone Calls and In-Person Conversations in the 50 States and D.C.* (2003), *available at* http://www.rcfp.org/taping. This section draws from the Reporters Committee's excellent guide to state and federal recording laws.

59. Interviews with jurors after the trial support this notion. One juror said: "The verdict didn't say anything about hidden cameras. It was the way they got in." *See* Hidden Cameras, Hard Choices, "Primetime Live" (Feb. 12, 1997).

60. Cal. Penal Code § 632.

61. *Id.* at § 632(a).

62. Deteresa v. ABC, 121 F.3d 460, 463 (9th Cir. 1997).

63. *Id.* at 465.

64. 18 U.S.C. §2510(1).

65. *See, e.g.,* Rafe Needleman & Felisa Yang, *Internet Calling: What It Is,* CNET.com, May 6, 2005, *available at* http://reviews.cnet.com/4520–9140_7–5131539–1. html; *Howstuffworks: How VoIP Works,* n.d., *available at* http://computer.howstuffworks.com/ip-telephony.htm.

66. 18 U.S.C. §2510 (2002) (defining the "aural transfer" that occurs in wire communication as "a transfer containing the human voice at any point between and including the point of origin and the point of reception.").

67. 18 U.S.C. §§ 2701–2711 (2000).

68. Eric Koester, *VoIP Goes the Bad Guy: Understanding the Legal Impact of the Use of Voice over IP Communications in Cases of NSA Warrantless Eavesdropping,* 24 J. MARSHALL J. COMPUTER & INFO. L. 227, 234 (2006).

69. Reporters Committee, *supra* note 58.

70. *Id.*

71. *Id.*

72. 18 U.S.C. § 2511(2)(d).

73. *See* Use of Recording Devices in Connection with Telephone Service, 2 F.C.C.R. 502 (1986).

74. *See id.*

75. 47 C.F.R. § 73. 1206.

76. Bartnicki v. Vopper, 532 U.S. 514, 518–19 (2001).

77. 18 U.S.C. § 2511(1)(c).

78. Bartnicki v. Vopper, 532 U.S. 514, 525 (2001).

79. *Id.* at 527 (citation omitted).

80. *Id.* at 534, 535.

81. Jessup-Morgan v. America Online, Inc., 20 F. Supp. 2d 1105 (E.D. Mich. 1998).

82. 18 U.S.C. § 2510(2), 2511(1)(a), (c), (d).

83. Bowens v. Aftermath Entertainment, 254 F. Supp. 2d 629 (E.D. Mich. 2003), 2004 U.S. Dist. LEXIS 5320 (E.D. Mich. Mar. 24, 2004) (motion granted, claim dismissed, sanctions disallowed), 364 F. Supp. 2d 641 (E.D. Mich. 2005) (summary judgment granted).

84. Sigma Delta Chi v. Speaker, Maryland House of Delegates, 310 A.2d 156 (Ct. App. Md. 1973).

85. *Id.* at 8.

86. *See also,* RONALD L. GOLDFARB, TV OR NOT TV, TELEVISION JUSTICE, AND THE COURTS 56–95 (1998).

87. City of Oak Creek v. Ah King, 436 N.W.2d 285 (Wisc. 1989).

88. *See* Reporter's Committee for Freedom of the Press, *Department of Defense Memo: Interaction with the Media,* July 2, 2010, *available at* http://www.rcfp.org/newsitems/docs/20100910_105806_dod_memo_2.pdf.

89. *See, e.g.,* Thom Shanker, *Defense Secretary Tightens Rules for Military's Contact with News Media,* N.Y. TIMES, July 3, 2010, at 7.

90. Nation Magazine v. U.S. Department of Defense, 762 F. Supp. 1558 (S.D.N.Y. 1991); JB Pictures v. Department of Defense, 21 M.L.R. 1564 (D.D.C. 1993).

91. Flynt v. Rumsfeld, 180 F. Supp. 2d 174 (D.C. Cir. 2002).

92. Gina Lubrano, *Who Paid for the Media in Iraq?*, SAN DIEGO UNION-TRIBUNE, June 23, 2003, at B-7. *See also* Jack Shafer, *Full Metal Junket: The Myth of the Objective War Correspondent*, SLATE, Mar. 5, 2003, *available at* http://slate.msn.com/id/2079703.

93. Blaine Harden & Dana Milbank, *Photos of Soldiers' Coffins Revive Controversy*, WASH. POST, Apr. 23, 2004, at A10.

94. 20 U.S.C. § 1232g. (The nickname "Buckley Act" refers to the U.S. senator who introduced the bill, James Buckley of New York.)

95. *See* 34 C.F.R. § 99.3.

96. Red & Black Publishing Co. v. Board of Regents, Univ. of Georgia, 427 S.E.2d 257 (Ga. 1993); John Doe v. Red & Black Publishing Co., 437 S.E.2d 474 (Ga. 1993).

97. Red & Black Publishing Co. v. Board of Regents, 427 S.E.2d 257 (Ga. 1993).

98. United States v. Miami University, 294 F.3d 797 (6th Cir. 2002).

99. 18 U.S.C. §§ 2721–25.

100. Reno v. Condon, 528 U.S. 141 (2000).

101. 18 U.S.C.A. § 1801.

102. Letter from James Madison to W. T. Barry (Aug. 4, 1822), in 9 THE WRITINGS OF JAMES MADISON, 1819–1836 at 103, 103 (Galliard Hunt ed. 1910).

103. *See, e.g.*, MARTIN, SHANNON E., FREEDOM OF INFORMATION: THE NEWS THE MEDIA USE (2008).

104. Dep't of the Air Force v. Rose, 425 U.S. 352, 361 (1976).

105. *See e.g.*, Mark Carreau, *Another Shuttle, Another Breach*, HOUSTON CHRON., July 9, 2003, at A1; John Schwartz & Matthew L. Wald, *Earlier Shuttle Flight Had Gas Enter Wing on Return*, N.Y. TIMES, July 9, 2003, at A14; Ralph Vartabedian, *E-Mail to Columbia Discounted Danger*, L. A. TIMES, July 1, 2003, at A12; and Lee Hockstader, *Release of Challenger Tape Ordered*, WASH. POST, July 30, 1988, at A8.

106. 5 U.S.C. 552(f)(1).

107. *See* Kissinger v. Reporters Comm. for Freedom of the Press, 445 U.S. 136, 156 (1980). *But cf.* United States v. Clarridge, 811 F. Supp. 697 (D.D.C. 1992) (holding that the Tower Commission was an "agency" for purposes of 18 U.S.C. § 1001). Compare Meyer v. Bush, 981 F.2d 1288 (D.C. Cir. 1993) (holding that FOIA does not reach President's Task Force on Regulatory Relief, comprising vice president and certain cabinet members) and National Security Archive v. Archivist of the United States, 909 F.2d 541 (D.C. Cir. 1990) (holding that FOIA does not reach Office of Counsel to President) and Rushforth v. Council of Economic Advisers, 762 F.2d 1038 (D.C. Cir. 1985) (holding that FOIA does not reach CEA) and Pacific Legal Found. v. Council on Envtl. Quality, 636 F.2d 1259 (D.C. Cir. 1980) (holding that FOIA does not reach CEQ) with Energy Research Found. v. Defense Nuclear Facilities Safety Bd., 917 F.2d 581 (D.C. Cir. 1990) (holding that Board is agency for purposes of FOIA and Sunshine Act). The Sunshine Act incorporates the FOIA's definition of "agency."

108. Goland v. CIA, 607 F.2d 339, 345 (D.C. Cir. 1978). In Forsham v. Harris, 445 U.S. 169, 178 (1980), the Supreme Court declared that Congress "did not provide any definition of 'agency records.'"

109. Forsham v. Harris, 445 U.S. 169, 183 (1980).

110. *Id.* at 178.

111. *Id.* at 184.

112. Washington Post v. U.S. Dept. of State, 632 F. Supp. 607 (1986).

113. Note: *A Control Test for Determining "Agency Record" Status Under the Freedom of Information Act*, 85 COLUM. L. REV. 611, 616 (1985).

114. *See, e.g.*, Note: *The Definition of "Agency Records" Under the Freedom of Information Act*, 31 STAN. L. REV. 1093, 1093 (1979); Note: *What Is a Record? Two Approaches to the Freedom of Information Act's Threshold Requirement*, 1978 B.Y.U. L. REV. 408, 408; Nichols v. United States, 325 F. Supp. 130, 134 (D. Kan. 1971), *aff'd on other grounds*, 460 F.2d 671 (10th Cir.), *cert. denied*, 409 U.S. 966, 34 L. Ed. 2d 232, 93 S. Ct. 268 (1972).

115. Goland v. CIA, 607 F.2d 339 (D.C. Cir. 1978).

116. *Id.* at 347.

117. Reporters Committee for Freedom of the Press, *How to Use the Federal FOIA Act*, n.d., *available at* http://www.rcfp.org/foiact/index.html.

118. Reporters Committee for Freedom of the Press, *FOI Letter Generator*, n.d., *available at* http://www.rcfp.org/foi_letter/generate.php.

119. David Cuillier, *Honey v. Vinegar: Testing Compliance-Gaining Theories in the Context of Freedom of Information Laws*, 15 COMM. L & POL'Y 203–29 (2010).

120. DAVID CUILLIER & CHARLES N. DAVIS, THE ART OF ACCESS: STRATEGIES FOR ACQUIRING PUBLIC RECORDS (2010). *See also* http://www.theartofaccess.com.

121. Reporters Committee for Freedom of the Press, *Citizens Group Wins FOIA Battle with Nuclear Agency*, n.d., *available at* http://www.rcfp.org/newsitems/index. php?i=4891.

122. *See Memorandum for Heads of All Federal Departments and Agencies* (Oct. 12, 2001) from Atty. Gen. John Ashcroft, *available at* http://www.usdoj.gov/foia/011012 .htm: "I encourage your agency to carefully consider the protection of all such values and interests when making disclosure determinations under the FOIA. Any discretionary decision by your agency to disclose information protected under the FOIA should be made only after full and deliberate consideration of the institutional, commercial, and personal privacy interests that could be implicated by disclosure of the information. . . . When you carefully consider FOIA requests and decide to withhold records, in whole or in part, you can be assured that the Department of Justice will defend your decisions unless they lack a sound legal basis or present an unwarranted risk of adverse impact on the ability of other agencies to protect other important records."

123. New Attorney General FOIA Memorandum Issued, Oct. 15, 2001, *available at* http://www.fas.org/sgp/foia/ ashcroft.html.

124. *See, e.g.,* Mark Fitzgerald, *The War of Fog in D.C.,* EDITOR & PUBLISHER, Apr. 7, 2003, at 16.

125. *See, e.g.,* Brett Strohs, *Protecting the Homeland by Exemption: Why the Critical Infrastructure Information Act of 2002 Will Degrade the Freedom of Information Act,* 2002 DUKE L. & TECH. REV. 18 (2002).

126. Memorandum for the Heads of Executive Departments and Agencies, White House news release, Jan. 23, 2009, *available at* http://www.whitehouse.gov/the_press_office/ FreedomofInformationAct/.

127. US Agencies Are Still Slow to Open Files, Boston Globe, Mar. 15, 2010, at 2.

128. *See* Exec. Order No. 12958, § 4.2 (b), *available at* http:// www.fas.org/sgp/bush/drafteo.html.

129. CIA v. Sims, 471 U.S. 159, 183 (1985).

130. Dep't of the Air Force v. Rose, 425 U.S. 352, 369–70 (1976).

131. Chrysler v. Brown, 441 U.S. 281, 292 (1979).

132. Russell v. Dep't of the Air Force, 682 F.2d 1045, 1048 (D.C. Cir. 1982).

133. Department of the Interior and Bureau of Indian Affairs v. Klamath Water Users Protective Association, 532 U.S. 1, 7 (2001), quoting Department of Air Force v. Rose, 425 U.S. 352, 361 (1976).

134. Cochrane v. U.S., 770 F.2d 949, 956 (11th Cir. 1985).

135. *See* U.S. Dep't of Justice v. Reporters Committee for Freedom of the Press, 489 U.S. 749 (1989).

136. Dep't of Justice v. Reporters Committee for Freedom of the Press, 489 U.S. 749, 765 (1989).

137. National Archives and Records Administration v. Favish, 541 U.S. 157 (2004).

138. *Id.* at 173.

139. Department of Justice v. Reporters Comm. for Freedom of the Press, 489 U.S. 749, 773 (1989).

140. Federal Communications Commission v. AT&T Inc., 131 S. Ct. 1177 (2011).

141. Electronic Freedom of Information Act Amendments of 1996, Pub. L. No. 104–231, § 1–12, 110 Stat. 3048 (1996).

142. General Accounting Office Briefing to the Senate Committee on Governmental Affairs, Government Paperwork Elimination Act, August 8, 2001, *available at* http://www.gao.gov/new.items/d011100.pdf. *See* also Electronic Government: Selection and Implementation of the Office of Management and Budget's 24 Initiatives, GAO-03–229, Nov. 22, 2002.

143. TPS, Inc. v. Dept. of Defense, 330 F.3d 1191 (9th Cir. 2003).

144. *See, e.g.,* Arkansas Freedom of Information Act, *available at* http://www.foiarkansas.com/1010/1010foia.html.

145. Electronic Records: Management and Preservation Pose Challenges, GAO-03–936T, July 8, 2003.

146. Some studies indicate that FOIA use is very low among journalists. *See, e.g.,* Heritage Foundation, *Media Center Study Finds Little FOIA Use by Journalists,* Dec. 1, 2001, *available at* http://www.heritage.org/Research/ Reports/2001/12/Media-Center-Study-Finds-Little-FOIA-Use-by-Journalists (showing that only 5% of FOIA requests came from journalists).

147. Haw. HB 2002, § 2.

148. Del. Code Ann. tit. 29, § 10001.

149. Ill. Rev. Stat. ch. 116, ¶201.

150. T.C.A. § 10–7-301 (6).

151. Shabazz v. Campbell, 63 S.W.3d 776 (Tenn. Ct. App. 2001).

152. Daxton R. "Chip" Stewart, *Let the Sunshine In, or Else: An Examination of the "Teeth" of State and Federal Open Meetings and Open Records Laws*, 15 COMM. L. & POL'Y 265, 307–8 (2010).

153. 5 Ill. Comp. Stat. 140/1–1.

154. They are Arkansas, Connecticut, Maine, Missouri, North Dakota, South Carolina and Virginia.

155. The Michigan Open Meetings Act and Freedom of Information Act, *available at* http://www.legislature.mi.gov/documents/Publications/OpenMtgsFreedom.pdf.

Chapter 9

Reporter's Privilege

1. Branzburg v. Hayes, 408 U.S. 665, 709–10 (1972).

2. Record at 1279, Cohen v. Cowles Media Co. (No. 90–634) (testimony of Bernard Casserly, characterizing the use of confidential sources as "a way of life in the profession of journalism.").

3. *See, e.g.,* Brief of Petitioner, Cohen v. Cowles Media Co., 501 U.S. 663 (1990) (No. 90–634). One of the best known examples of investigative journalism, The Washington Post's uncovering of the Watergate scandal, was driven by a confidential source the reporters dubbed "Deep Throat." *See* BOB WOODWARD, THE SECRET MAN: THE STORY OF WATERGATE'S DEEP THROAT (2005).

4. Record at 694, Cohen v. Cowles Media Co. (No. 90–634) (testimony of Arnold Ismach).

5. U.S. v. Bryan, 339 U.S. 323, 331 (1950).

6. Branzburg v. Hayes, 408 U.S. 665, 710 (1972) (Powell, J., concurring).

7. *See, e.g.,* Nathan Swinton, *Privileging a Privilege: Should the Reporter's Privilege Enjoy the Same Respect as the Attorney-Client Privilege?*, 19 GEO. J. LEGAL ETHICS 979 (2006).

8. *See generally* David Rudenstine, *A Reporter Keeping Confidences: More Important Than Ever*, 29 CARDOZO L. REV. 1431 (2008).

9. Branzburg v. Hayes, 408 U.S. 665, 710 (1972) (Powell, J., concurring).

10. *Id.* at 674.

11. *Id.* at 709.

12. *Id.* at 710.

13. *Id.* at 725.

14. *Id.*

15. *Id.,* quoting Time, Inc. v. Hill, 385 U.S. 374, 389 (1967).

16. *Id.* at 739.

17. *Id.* at 743.

18. *See Paying the Price: A Recent Census of Reporters Jailed or Fined for Refusing to Testify*, n.d., *available at* http://www.rcfp.org/jail.html. *See also* Ross E. Milloy, *Writer Who Was Jailed in Notes Dispute Is Freed*, N.Y. TIMES, Jan. 5, 2002, at A8 (detailing Leggett's incarceration and release). *See, e.g.,* Edmond J. Bartnett, *Columnist Loses in Contempt Case*, N.Y. TIMES, Oct. 1, 1958, at 30 (explaining the jailing of reporter Marie Torre for refusing to disclose a source of information).

19. Tracy Benton, *Taricani Found Guilty of Contempt*, PROVIDENCE JOURNAL, Nov. 19, 2004, at A1.

20. Pam Belluck, *Reporter Who Shielded Source Will Serve Sentence at Home*, N.Y. TIMES, Dec. 10, 2004, at 28.

21. *In re* Grand Jury Subpoenas, No. 01–20745 (5th Cir. Aug. 17, 2001) (unpublished) (per curiam).

22. *In re* Grand Jury Subpoenas, No. 01–20745, at 4.

23. *Id.*

24. *Id.* at 8–9.

25. Branzburg v. Hayes, 408 U.S. 665, 706 (1972).

26. *In re* John Doe Grand Jury Investigation, 410 Mass. 596, 598 (1991).

27. Castellani v. Scranton Times, 956 A.2d 937 (Pa. 2008) (emphasis added).

28. *Id.*

29. *See, e.g.,* New Jersey's shield law, which protects "any news or information obtained in the course of pursuing [the journalist's] professional activities whether or not it is disseminated." N.J. Stat. § 2A:84A-21.

30. *See, e.g.,* Delaware's shield law: "A reporter is privileged in an adjudicative proceeding to decline to testify concerning the source or content of information that he or she obtained within the scope of his or her professional activities if the reporter states under oath that the disclosure of the information would violate an express or implied understanding with the source under which the information was originally obtained or would substantially

hinder the reporter in the maintenance of existing source relationships or the development of new source relationships." 10 Del. C. § 4322.

31. *See, e.g.,* United States v. Lloyd, 71 F.3d 1256 (7th Cir. 1995) (finding that a district court did not abuse discretion in quashing subpoena in criminal case); LaRouche v. NBC, 780 F.2d 1134 (4th Cir. 1986) (finding that a lower court correctly applied privilege when it quashed subpoenas for journalists in libel case); United States v. Caporale, 806 F.2d 1487 (11th Cir. 1986) (recognizing qualified privilege in criminal case); Zerilli v. Smith, 656 F.2d 705 (D.C. Cir. 1981) (recognizing existence of federal privilege in a civil case in which journalists were not parties); Miller v. Transamerican Press, Inc., 621 F.2d 721 (5th Cir. 1980) (finding that journalists have a First Amendment privilege, although it is not absolute); United States v. Cuthbertson, 630 F.2d 139 (3d Cir. 1980) (stating that federal privilege exists in both civil and criminal cases); Silkwood v. Kerr-McGee, 563 F.2d 433 (10th Cir. 1977) (recognizing privilege and finding that documentary filmmaker could assert it); Cervantes v. Time, Inc., 464 F.2d 986 (8th Cir. 1972) (determining that a magazine could assert privilege in a libel case); Bursey v. United States, 466 F.2d 1059 (9th Cir. 1972) (finding that newspaper employees could assert privilege to quash grand jury subpoenas); Baker v. F & F Investment Co., 470 F.2d 778 (2d Cir. 1972) (recognizing privilege in civil case). *But see* In re Grand Jury Proceedings, 810 F.2d 580 (6th Cir. 1987) (denying existence of any First Amendment privilege for journalists).

32. *See, e.g.,* O'Neill v. Oakgrove Construction, Inc., 71 N.Y.2d 521 (1988).

33. Zurcher v. Stanford Daily, 436 U.S. 547, 563–64 (1978).

34. *Invading the Newsroom,* N.Y. Times, July 29, 1980, at A14.

35. 42 U.S.C. § 2000aa.

Chapter 10

The Media and the Courts

1. Sheppard v. Maxwell, 384 U.S. 333, 362 (1966).

2. *See, e.g.,* http://www.courttv.com/trials/peterson.

3. *See, e.g.,* Meredith Diane Lett et al., *Examining Effects of Television News Violence on College Students through Cultivation Theory,* 21 Comm. Res. Rep. 39 (2004);

Kimberly Gross & Sean Aday, *The Scary World in Your Living Room and Neighborhood: Using Local Broadcast News, Neighborhood Crime Rates, and Personal Experience to Test Agenda Setting and Cultivation,* 53 J. Comm. 411 (2003); Daniel Romer et al., *Television News and the Cultivation of Fear of Crime,* 53 J. Comm. 88 (2003).

4. Estes v. Texas, 381 U.S. 532 (1965).

5. *The Pulitzer Prizes, 1963 Winners, available at* http://www.pulitzer.org/awards/1963.

6. Patton v. Yount, 467 U.S. 1025 (1984).

7. Sheppard v. Maxwell, 384 U.S. 333 (1966).

8. *Id.* at 340.

9. Interactive Media Lab, *Sheppard v. Maxwell* (1966), College of Journalism and Communications, University of Florida, *available at* http://iml.jou.ufl.edu/projects/Spring01/Woell/Sheppard.html.

10. Mu'Min v. Virginia, 500 U.S. 415 (1991).

11. Batson v. Kentucky, 476 U.S. 79 (1986); J.E.B. v. Alabama, 511 U.S. 127 (1994).

12. *See, e.g.,* Don J. DeBenedictis, *The National Verdict,* A.B.A. J., Oct. 1994, at 52, 54 (citing poll finding 86 percent of those people questioned thought media had some effect on trial fairness); Edith Greene, *Media Effects on Jurors,* 14 Law & Human Behav. 439, 448 (1990).

13. United States v. Koubriti, 305 F. Supp. 2d 723 (E.D. Mich. 2003).

14. *See, e.g.,* United States v. Shryock, 342 F.3d 948 (9th Cir. 2003), *cert. denied,* 541 U.S. 965 (2004).

15. Tex. Crim. Proc. Code Ann. § 35.29 (1994).

16. Sheppard v. Maxwell, 384 U.S. 333, 342 (1966).

17. 129 S. Ct. 2252, 2263, 2255 (2009).

18. *Id.* at 2265.

19. Republican Party of Minn. v. White, 536 U.S. 765 (2002).

20. *Id.* at 787.

21. Gannett v. DePasquale, 433 U.S. 368 (1979).

22. *Id.* at 378.

23. 433 U.S. 368, 383 (1979).

24. *Id.* at 415, 423.

25. 448 U.S. 555 (1980).

26. *Id.* at 569.

27. *Id.* at 581.

28. *Id.* at 575.

29. Globe Newspaper v. Superior Court, 457 U.S. 596 (1982).

30. *Id.* at 606.

31. Press-Enterprise (I) v. Superior Court, 464 U.S. 501 (1984); Press-Enterprise (II) v. Superior Court, 478 U.S. 1 (1986).

32. Press-Enterprise (II) v. Superior Court, 478 U.S. 1, 9 (1986).

33. *See, e.g., In re* Globe Newspaper Co., 920 F.2d 88 (1st Cir. 1990).

34. Press-Enterprise (I) v. Superior Court, 464 U.S. 501, 510 (1984).

35. ABC Inc. v. Stewart, 360 F.3d 90 (2nd Cir. 2004).

36. Hollingsworth v. Perry, 130 S. Ct. 705 (2010).

37. Lisa Leff, *Court Won't Order California Officials to Appeal Ruling That Struck Down Gay Marriage Ban,* L.A. TIMES, Sept. 8, 2010, *available at* http://www.latimes.com/sns-ap-us-gay-marriage-tria1,0,3059623.story.

38. 130 S. Ct. 721 (2010).

39. *Id.* at 722.

40. *Id.* at 725.

41. *In re* Intel Corp. Microprocessor Antitrust Litigation, Consolidated Action: Motion to intervene for purpose of unsealing judicial records and for partial reassignment, C.A. No. 05–441-JJF (D. Del. Aug. 21, 2008).

42. AMD v. Intel Corp., 2006 U.S. Dist. LEXIS 72722 (D. Del. Sept. 26, 2006).

43. Intel Corp. v. AMD, 524 U.S. 241 (2004).

44. Greg Sandoval & Declan McCullagh, *Judge Seals Courtroom in MPAA DVD-copying Case,* CNET NEWS, April 24, 2009, *available at* http://news.cnet.com/8301–13578_3–10227195–38.html. *See also* RealNetworks Response to RealDVD Preliminary Injunction Ruling, Aug. 11, 2009, *available at* http://www.realnetworks.com/pressroom/releases/2009/realdvd_initial_ruling.aspx.

45. Butterworth v. Smith, 494 U.S. 624 (1990).

46. Kent v. United States, 383 U.S. 541, 556 (1966).

47. *In re* Gault, 387 U.S. 1, 33, 36–37 (1967).

48. Smith v. Daily Mail, 443 U.S. 97, 107 (1979).

49. Kristin N. Henning, *Eroding Confidentiality in Delinquency Proceedings: Should Schools and Public Housing Authorities Be Notified?* 79 N.Y.U. L. REV. 520 (2004). States that presumptively close juvenile proceedings are Alabama, Alaska, the District of Columbia, Illinois, Kentucky, Massachusetts, Mississippi, New Jersey, New York, Oklahoma, Rhode Island, South Carolina, Tennessee, Vermont, West Virginia, Wisconsin and Wyoming.

50. Robert E. Shepherd, *Collateral Consequences of Juvenile Proceedings: Part II, Media Exposure,* 15:3 CRIM. JUST MAG. (2000), *available at* http://www.abanet.org/crimjust/juvjus/cjmcollconseq1.html.

51. Henning, *supra,* note 49. States with presumptively open proceedings are Arizona, Arkansas, Colorado, Florida, Iowa, Kansas, Maryland, Michigan, Montana, Nevada, New Mexico, North Carolina, Ohio, and Washington. States with open proceedings for children over a certain age or charged with certain offenses are California, Delaware, Georgia, Hawaii, Idaho, Indiana, Louisiana, Maine, Minnesota, Missouri, North Dakota, Pennsylvania, South Dakota, Texas, Utah and Virginia.

52. Juvenile Courts and Juvenile Offenders, Juvenile Justice Act of 1977, Rev. Code Wash. (ARCW) § 13.40.140 (2004).

53. New World Communications of Ohio, Inc. v. Geauga County Court of Common Pleas, Juvenile Division, 734 N.E.2d 1214 (Ohio 2000).

54. Howard Snyder and Melissa Sickmund, *Juvenile Offenders and Victims: 2006 National Report,* Nat'l Center for Juv. Just. & U.S. Dept. of Justice, Office of Juv. Just. & Delinquency Prevention (March 2006), *available at* http://www.ojjdp.ncjrs.gov/ojstatbb/nr2006/.

55. *Id.*

56. Nat'l Dist. Attorneys Assoc., *Rape Shield Summary Chart* (January 2010), *available at* http://www.ndaa.org/ncpa_state_statutes.html.

57. *See, e.g.,* Colorado Rape Shield Law § 18–3–407 (2)(a).

58. Ariz. Rev. Stat. § 13–1421.

59. Mu'Min v. Virginia, 501 U.S. 1269 (1991).

60. Butterworth v. Smith, 494 U.S. 624 (1990).

61. Sheppard v. Maxwell, 384 U.S. 333, 350, 362 (1966).

62. 427 U.S. 539 (1976).

63. United States v. Noriega, 917 F.2d 1543 (11th Cir. 1990).

64. *Id.*

65. United States v. Noriega, 752 F. Supp. 1032 (S.D. Fla. 1990).

66. United States v. Cable News Network, 865 F. Supp. 1549 (S.D. Fla. 1994).

67. Phil Kloer, *On Television, CNN Retreats, Airs Admission of Guilt*, ATL. J.-CONST., Dec. 20, 1994, at D8.

68. Seattle Times v. Rhinehart, 467 U.S. 20 (1984).

69. Chandler v. Florida, 449 U.S. 560 (1981).

70. La Monica Everett-Haynes, *Experts Evaluate the 'New Media' and Courts*, UNIV. OF ARIZ. NEWS, Sept. 9, 2008, *available at* http://uanews.org/node/21471.

71. C. Danielle Vinson & John S. Ertter, *Entertainment or Education: How Do Media Cover the Courts?* 7 HARV. INT'L J. PRESS/POLITICS 80 (2002).

72. *See* Rule 2.450, Rules of Judicial Administration, Florida Rules of Court (2008); Florida v. Palm Beach Newspapers, 395 So. 2d 544 (1981).

73. Re: WLBT-TV, 905 So. 2d 1196, 1199 (Miss. 2005).

74. Rule 1.150, California Rules of Court (2008).

75. NATHAN BRAVERMAN, et al., REPORT OF THE COMMITTEE TO STUDY EXTENDED MEDIA COVERAGE OF CRIMINAL TRIAL PROCEEDINGS IN MARYLAND, Feb. 1, 2008.

76. James Podgers, *Social Media Is New Norm, But Courts Still Grappling with Whether to Let Cameras In*, ABA J., Aug. 8, 2010, *available at* http://www.abajournal.com/news/article/social_media_is_norm_but_courts_still_grappling_with_whether_to_let_cameras/.

77. Associated Press, *Kan. Reporter Gets OK to Use Twitter to Cover Federal Gang Trial*, Mar. 6, 2009, *available at* http://www.firstamendmentcenter.org/news.aspxid=21329&SearchString=media.

78. Dana Liebelson, *Judge Approves Web Coverage of Hearing*, Reporters Committee for Freedom of the Press, Jan. 16, 2009, *available at* http://www.rcfp.org/newsitems/index.php?i=9903.

79. Associated Press, *1st Circuit Won't Allow Song-Swapping Hearing to Be Webcast*, Apr. 17, 2009, *available at* http://www.firstamendmentcenter.org/news.aspxid=21491&SearchString=media; RIAA v. Tenenbaum Verdict, LAW & FINANCE MANAGEMENT CHANNEL, Aug. 10, 2009, *available at* http://lawfinancechannel.squarespace.com/law-finance-channel/2009/8/10/riaa-v-tenenbaum-verdict.html.

80. Greg Sandoval, *RIAA Suffers Big Setback in Tenenbaum Case*, CNET NEWS, July 9, 2010, *available at* http://news.cnet.com/8301-31001_3-20010164-261.html.

81. Leanne Italie, *Divorce Lawyers: Facebook Tops in Online Evidence*, SAN JOSE MERCURY NEWS, July 2, 2010, *available at* http://www.siliconvalley.com/the-valley/ci_15429107.

82. Amer. Assoc. for Justice, *Texts and "Tweets" by Jurors, Lawyers Pose Courtroom Conundrums*, 45:8 TRIAL NEWS & TRENDS (August 2009), *available at* http://www.justice.org/cps/rde/xchg/justice/hs.xsl/10049.htm.

83. Laurie Sullivan, *Courtroom Bans on Social Media Spreading Across United States*, ONLINE MEDIA DAILY, Mar. 10, 2010, *available at* http://www.firstamendmentcoalition.org/2010/03/courtroom-bans-on-social-media-spreading-across-united-states/.

84. Federated Pub., Inc. v. Kurtz, 615 P.2d 440 (Wash. 1980).

85. Federated Pub., Inc. v. Swedberg, 633 P.2d 74 (Wash. 1981). *cert. denied*, 456 U.S. 984 (1982).

86. 435 U.S. 589 (1978).

87. *Id.* at 608–11.

88. IND. CODE § 5–15–3-3, § 5–14–3-4 (West 1998).

89. KAN. STAT. ANN. § 45–217(e)(2)(A) (1997).

90. *See* Nast v. Michels, 730 P.2d 54 (Wash. 1986).

91. State ex rel. Cincinnati Enquirer v. Winkler, 101 Ohio St. 3d 382 (2004).

92. Copeland v. Copeland, 966 So. 2d 1040 (La. 2007).

93. President Barack Obama, Exec. Order: Review and Disposition of Individuals detained at the Guantanamo Bay Naval Base and Closure of Detention Facilities, Jan. 22, 2009, *available at* http://www.whitehouse.gov/the_press_office/ClosureOfGuantanamoDetentionFacilities/.

94. Ginnie Graham, *Courts Keeping Cases Secret*, TULSA WORLD, Aug. 10, 2008, *available at* http://www.tulsaworld.com/news/article.aspx?articleID=20080810_11_A1_hDistr562350.

95. Doe v. C.A.R.S. Protection Plus Inc., 543 F. 3d 178, *cert. denied*, 129 S. Ct. 576 (2008).

96. *Id.* at 179.

97. Kathleen Cullinan, *Newspaper Asks Supreme Court to Review Secret Docket*, Reporters Committee for Freedom of the Press, Oct. 14, 2008, *available at* http://www.rcfp.org.

98. *Sealed Cases in Federal Courts*, Federal Judicial Center, Oct. 23, 2009, *available at* ftp.resource.org/courts.gov/fjc/sealset3.pdf.

99. Open the Government, *2008 Secrecy Report Card*, n.d., *available at* http://www.openthegovernment.org/otg/SecrecyReportCard08.pdf.

100. United States v. Reynolds, 345 U.S. 1 (1953).

101. Glenn Greenwald, *Obama Wins the Right to Invoke 'State Secrets' to Protect Bush Crimes,* SALON, Sept. 8, 2010, *available at* http://www.salon.com/news/opinion/glenn_greenwald/2010/09/08/obama.

102. Charlie Savage, *Court Dismisses a Case Asserting Torture by CIA,* N.Y. TIMES, Sept. 8, 2010, *available at* http://www.nytimes.com/2010/09/09/us/09secrets.html?_r=1&hp.

103. *In re:* Sealed Case, 494 F.3d 139 (App. D.C. 2007).

104. Martha Wade Steketee & Alan Carlson, *Developing CCJ/COSCA Guidelines for Public Access to Court Records: A National Project to Assist State Courts,* State Justice Institute, Oct. 18, 2002, vi, *available at* http://www.courtaccess.org/modelpolicy/18Oct2002FinalReport.pdf; Alan Carlson & Martha Wade Steketee, *Public Access to Court Records: Implementing the* CCJ/COSCA Guidelines *Final Project Report* (2005), *available at* http://www.ncsconline.org/WC/Publications/Res_PriPub_PubAccCrtRcrds_FinalRpt.pdf.

105. U.S. Courts, Judicial Privacy Policy Page: Privacy Policy, n.d., *available at* http://www.privacy.uscourts.gov/b4amend.htm.

106. Steketee & Carlson, *supra* note 104 at 7.

107. Florida Star v. B.J.F., 491 U.S. 524 (1989).

108. *Id.*

109. C. Danielle Vinson & John S. Ertter, *Entertainment or Education: How Do Media Cover the Courts?* 7 HARV. INT'L J. PRESS/POLITICS 80 (2002).

110. Beth Givens, *Public Records on the Internet: The Privacy Dilemma,* Privacy Rights Clearinghouse, Apr. 19, 2002, *available at* http://www.privacyrights.org/ar/onlinepubrecs.htm.

111. Samuel Warren & Louis D. Brandeis, *The Right to Privacy,* 4 HARV. L. REV. 193 (1890).

112. Final Report Minn. Sup. Ct Advisory Committee and Order on Rules of Public Access to Records of the Judicial Branch. Minn Court Rules: Record Access Rules Order No. C4–85–1848, Minn. Statutes.

113. *Developing CCJ/COSCA Guidelines for Public Access to Court Records: A National Project to Assist State Courts,* State Justice Institute, Oct. 18, 2002, *available at* http://www.courtaccess.org/modelpolicy/18Oct2002FinalReport.pdf.

114. Department of Justice v. Reporters Committee, 489 U.S. 749 (1989).

115. General Rule 31, adopted Oct. 7, 2004, by the Washington Supreme Court. *See* http://www.courts.wa.gov/newsinfo/?fa=newsinfo.pressdetail&newsid=484.

Chapter 11

Electronic Media Regulation

1. Mark A. Conrad, *The Demise of the Fairness Doctrine: A Blow for Citizen Access,* 41 FED. COMM. L.J. 161, 184 (1989) (quoting radio talk by Mark Fowler).

2. Pub. L. 262, 36 Stat. 629.

3. *See* THOMAS G. KRATTENMAKER, TELECOMMUNICATIONS LAW AND POLICY 3–4 (1994).

4. Pub. L. 264, 27 Stat. 302.

5. United States v. Zenith Radio Corp., 12 F.2d 614 (N.D. Ill. 1926).

6. *Id.*

7. Pub. L. 69–632, ch. 169, 44 Stat. 1162.

8. Federal Radio Comm'n v. Nelson Bros., 289 U.S. 266 (1933).

9. Ch. 652, 48 Stat. 1064.

10. Pub. L. No. 98–549, 98 Stat. 2779.

11. 47 U.S.C. §§ 151, 303(g); *see* National Association of Broadcasters v. FCC, 740 F.2d 1190 (D.C. Cir. 1984).

12. 47 U.S.C. § 153(6).

13. 47 U.S.C. § 605.

14. Joseph Burstyn, Inc. v. Wilson, 343 U.S. 495, 503 (1952).

15. National Broadcasting Co. v. FCC, 319 U.S. 190 (1943).

16. 395 U.S. 367 (1969).

17. Miami Herald Publishing Co. v. Tornillo, 418 U.S. 241 (1974).

18. 319 U.S. 190 (1943).

19. FCC v. League of Women Voters, 468 U.S. 364, 376 n.11 (1984).

20. FCC v. Pacifica Foundation, 438 U.S. 726 (1978).

21. *See* Robinson v. American Broadcasting Co., 441 F.2d 1396, 1399 (6th Cir. 1971).

22. *See, e.g.,* 47 U.S.C. §§ 302(a), 307(d), 309(a) and 316(a).

23. 47 U.S.C. § 326.

24. 47 U.S.C. § 315.

25. *See, e.g.,* 47 C.F.R. 73.1940.

26. Paramount Pictures Corp., 3 F.C.C.R. 245, 246 (Mass Media Bureau 1988).

27. *Id.*

28. Time-Telepictures Television, 17 F.C.C.R. 16273 (2002).

29. Multimedia Entertainment Inc., 9 F.C.C.R. 2811 (Political Programming Branch 1994).

30. Infinity Broadcasting, 18 F.C.C.R. 18603 (Media Bureau 2003).

31. Arkansas Educational Television Commission v. Forbes, 523 U.S. 666 (1998).

32. 47 U.S.C. § 315(b).

33. 47 U.S.C. §§ 317, 507.

34. Becker v. FCC, 95 F.3d 75 (D.C. Cir. 1996).

35. Farmers Educational and Cooperative Union v. WDAY, Inc., 360 U.S. 525 (1959).

36. 47 U.S.C. § 312(a)(7).

37. CBS v. FCC, 453 U.S. 367 (1981).

38. *Id.* at 387–88.

39. Radio-Television News Directors Association v. FCC, 229 F.3d 269 (D.C. Cir. 2000).

40. 47 U.S.C. § 399.

41. Federal Communications Commission v. League of Women Voters, 468 U.S. 364 (1984).

42. 47 U.S.C. § 315(3e)(1).

43. McConnell v. Federal Election Comm'n, 540 U.S. 93 (2003) (ruling on challenges to Pub. L. No. 107–155, 116 Stat. 81).

44. 26 U.S.C. § 527.

45. Kate Phillips, *Settlements Including Fines Are Reached in Election Finance Cases of Three Groups,* N.Y. TIMES, Dec. 14, 2006, at A38.

46. Children's Television Act, Pub. L. 101–437, 104 Stat. 996.

47. 47 C.F.R. § 73.520, 73.671.

48. Children's Television Programming, 6 F.C.C.R. 7199 (1990).

49. Viacom International, Inc., 19 F.C.C.R. 20802 (2004) (Enforcement Bureau).

50. International Family Entertainment, Inc., 19 F.C.C.R. 20789 (2004) (Enforcement Bureau).

51. Children's Television Programming, 6 F.C.C.R. 2111 (1991); Children's Television Programming, 6 F.C.C.R. 5093 (1991).

52. Children's Television Programming; Revision of Programming Policies for Television Broadcast Stations, 11 F.C.C.R. 10660 (1996).

53. *FCC Approves Transfer of Univision Communications Inc.,* 2007 FCC LEXIS 2345 (March 27, 2007).

54. 47 C.F.R. § 73.671(c)(5).

55. 21 F.C.C.R. 1106519 (2006); F.C.C.R. 22943 (2004).

56. Children's Television Report and Policy Statement, 50 FCC 2d 1, 13–14 (1974).

57. Children's Television Programming; Revision of Programming Policies for Television Broadcast Stations, 11 F.C.C.R. 10660, 10730 (1996).

58. 47 C.F.R. § 73.1211.

59. United States v. Edge Broadcasting, 509 U.S. 418 (1993).

60. Saga Communications of Arkansas, LLC, 23 F.C.C.R. 6927 (Audio Division 2008).

61. Greater New Orleans Broadcasting Association, Inc. v. United States, 572 U.S. 173 (1999).

62. 47 C.F.R. § 73.1216, n.1(a).

63. 47 C.F.R. § 73.1217.

64. Ch. 287, 37 Stat. 302, 308.

65. Ch. 169, 44 Stat. 1162, 1172.

66. 47 U.S.C. § 325(a).

67. *See* Justin Levine, *A History and Analysis of the Federal Communications Commission's Response to Radio Broadcast Hoaxes,* 52 FED. COMM. L.J. 273, 277–79 (2000); HADLEY CANTRIL, THE INVASION FROM MARS (1940).

68. *See, e.g.,* Tim Crook, *The Psychological Power of Radio,* n.d. *available at* http://www.irdp.co.uk/hoax.htm.

69. *See* Justin Levine, *A History and Analysis of the Federal Communications Commission's Response to Radio Broadcast Hoaxes,* 52 FED. COMM. L.J. 273, 280–87 (2000).

70. *Id.* at 289–305.

71. 47 C.F.R. § 73.1217.

72. *See* Levine, *supra* note 57, at 313.

73. Great Lakes Broadcasting, 3 F.R.C. Ann. Rep. 34 (1929).

74. Editorializing by Broadcast Licensees, 13 F.C.C. 1246 (1949).

75. *Id.* at 1257–58.

76. Red Lion Broadcasting Co. v. FCC, 395 U.S. 367, 391 (1969).

77. Miami Herald Pub. Co. v. Tornillo, 418 U.S. 241 (1974).

78. Syracuse Peace Council, 2 F.C.C.R. 5043 (1987).

79. Syracuse Peace Council v. FCC, 867 F.2d 654 (D.C. Cir.1989), *cert. denied,* 493 U.S. 1019 (1990).

80. *See, e.g.,* Editorial: *A Muse Unplugged,* N.Y. Times, Oct. 8, 2007, at 18.

81. Radio-Television News Directors Ass'n v. FCC, 229 F.3d 269 (D.C. Cir. 2000).

82. 47 U.S.C. § 399; FCC v. League of Women Voters, 468 U.S. 364 (1984).

83. 47 U.S.C. § 317.

84. 47 U.S.C. § 508.

85. 47 C.F.R. § 73.1212.

86. *See* Devin Kosar, Note: *Payola: Can Pay-for-Play Be Practically Enforced?,* 23 St. John's J.L. Comm. 211, 220–22 (2008).

87. *See* Chuck Philips, *Clear Channel Fined Just $8,000 by FCC for Payola Violation,* L.A. Times, Oct. 20, 2000, at C1.

88. *See* Jeff Leeds & Louise Story, *Radio Payoffs Are Described as Sony Settles,* N.Y. Times, July 26, 2005, at A1.

89. *See, e.g.,* Citadel Broadcasting Corp., 22 F.C.C.R 7856 (2007).

90. Univision Radio, Inc., 2010 FCC LEXIS 4600 (July 26, 2010).

91. *See* Clay Calvert, *What Is News? The FCC and the New Battle over the Regulation of Video News Releases,* 16 CommLaw Conspectus 361, 370 (2008).

92. Sonshine Family Television, Inc., 22 F.C.C.R. 18686 (2007).

93. Comcast Corp., 22 F.C.C.R. 17474 (2007); 22 F.C.C.R. 17030 (2007).

94. Use of Video News Releases by Broadcast Licensees and Cable Operators, 20 F.C.C.R. 8593 (2005).

95. Sponsorship Identification Rules and Embedded Advertising, Notice of Inquiry and Notice of Proposed Rule Making, 23 F.C.C.R. 10682 (2008).

96. 47 U.S.C. § 301.

97. 47 U.S.C. § 309(j); 47 C.F.R. §§ 73.5000–73.5009; Competitive Bidding Order, 13 F.C.C.R. 15920 (1998).

98. 47 U.S.C. §§ 308(b), 319(a).

99. 47 U.S.C. § 310(b).

100. 47 U.S.C. § 308(b).

101. *See* Character Qualifications in Broadcast Licensing, 5 F.C.C.R. 3252 (1990); Character Qualifications in Broadcast Licensing, 102 F.C.C.2d 1179 (1986).

102. 47 U.S.C. § 308(b).

103. 47 C.F.R. § 73.3555(a).

104. 47 C.F.R. § 73.3555(e); Consolidated Appropriations Act of 2004, Pub. L. No. 108–199, § 629, 118 Stat. 3, 99.

105. 47 C.F.R. § 73.3555(b); Review of the Commission's Regulations Governing Television Broadcasting, 14 F.C.C.R. 12903, 12907–8 (1999).

106. 47 C.F.R. § 73.3555(c).

107. Consolidated Appropriations Act of 2004, Pub. L. 108–199, § 629, 118 Stat. 3, 86ff.

108. 2006 Quadrennial Review, 23 F.C.C.R. 2010 (2008).

109. *See, e.g.,* Metro Broadcasting, Inc. v. FCC, 497 U.S. 547 (1990).

110. *See, e.g.,* Adarand Constructors, Inc. v. Pena, 515 U.S. 20 (1995); Lamprecht v. Federal Communications Commission, 958 F.2d 382 (D.C. Cir. 1992).

111. Promoting Diversification of Ownership in the Broadcasting Services, 23 F.C.C.R. 5922 (2007).

112. 2002 Biennial Regulatory Review, 18 F.C.C.R. 13620, 13627 (2003), *aff'd in part and remanded in part,* Prometheus Radio Project. v. Federal Communications Commission, 373 F.3d 372 (2004), *cert. denied,* 545 U.S. 1123 (2005).

113. *See, e.g.,* Fox Television Stations, Inc., FCC 08–277 (Dec. 22, 2008).

114. 47 U.S.C. § 399B.

115. 47 U.S.C. § 399b(a).

116. Commission Policy Concerning the Noncommercial Nature of Educational Broadcasting Stations, 7 F.C.C.R. 827 (1992).

117. *See* Minority Television Project, Inc., 19 F.C.C.R. 25116 (2004).

118. 47 U.S.C. § 396(g)(1)(A).

119. Accuracy in Media, Inc. v. FCC, 521 F.2d 288 (D.C. Cir. 1975), *cert. denied,* 425 U.S. 934 (1976).

120. FCC v. League of Women Voters of California, 468 U.S. 364 (1984).

121. *Id.* at 402.

122. Muir v. Alabama Educational Television Commission, 688 F.2d 1033, 1036 (5th Cir. 1982).

123. National Farmworkers Service Center, Inc., 25 F.C.C.R. 7486, 7488 (2010).

124. Reexamination of the Comparative Standards for Noncommercial Educational Applicants, 16 F.C.C.R. 5074 (2001), *aff'd,* American Family Ass'n v. FCC, 365 F.3d 1156 (D.C. Cir. 2004); 47 C.F.R. § 73.7003.

125. *See* James C. Goodale, All About Cable § 1.02 (2011).

126. Frontier Broadcasting Co., 24 F.C.C. 251 (1959).

127. Carter Mountain Transmission Corp., 32 F.C.C. 459 (1962), *aff'd,* 321 F.2d 359 (D.C. Cir. 1963), *cert. denied,* 375 U.S. 951 (1963).

128. United States v. Southwestern Cable Co., 392 U.S. 157 (1968).

129. 47 U.S.C. § 224.

130. Pub. L. No. 98–549, 98 Stat. 2779.

131. Pub. L. No. 102–385, 106 Stat. 1460.

132. Pub. L. No. 104–104, 110 Stat. 56.

133. Turner Broadcasting System v. FCC, 512 U.S. 622 (1994).

134. Denver Area Educational Telecommunications Consortium, Inc. v. FCC, 518 U.S. 727 (1996) (plurality opinion).

135. *See* United States v. Playboy Entertainment Group, Inc., 529 U.S. 803 (2000).

136. 512 U.S. 622 (1994).

137. Turner Broadcasting System v. FCC, 520 U.S. 180 (1997).

138. 518 U.S. 727 (1996) (plurality opinion).

139. *Id.* at 743.

140. 529 U.S. 803 (2000).

141. 47 U.S.C. § 561.

142. 47 U.S.C. § 542.

143. 47 U.S.C. § 544.

144. 47 U.S.C. § 546.

145. 47 U.S.C. § 537(e).

146. Alliance for Community Media v. FCC, 529 F.3d 763 (6th Cir. 2008), *cert. denied,* 129 S. Ct. 2821 (2009).

147. Nat'l Cable & Telecommunications Ass'n v. FCC, 567 F.3d 659 (D.C. Cir. 2009).

148. Implementation of Section 621(a)(1), 22 F.C.C.R. 5101 (2007).

149. Comcast Corp. v. FCC, 579 F.3d 1 (D.C.Cir. 2009); 240 F.3d 1126 (D.C. Cir. 2001).

150. Time Warner Entertainment Co. v. United States, 211 F.3d 1313 (D.C. Cir. 2000), *cert. denied,* 531 U.S. 1183 (2001).

151. 47 U.S.C. § 533(a).

152. 47 U.S.C. §§ 571, 573.

153. Implementation of the Child Safe Viewing Act; Examination of Parental Control Technologies for Video or Audio Programming, 24 F.C.C.R. 11413, 11438 (2009).

154. 47 U.S.C. §§ 534 (commercial stations), 535 (noncommercial stations).

155. 520 U.S. 180 (1997).

156. 391 U.S. 367 (1968).

157. Cablevision Sys. Corp. v. FCC, 570 F.3d 83 (2d Cir. 2009), *cert. denied,* 130 S. Ct. 3275 (2010).

158. 47 U.S.C. § 531.

159. *See, e.g.,* Denver Area Educational Telecommunications Consortium, Inc. v. FCC, 518 U.S. 727, 761–62 (1996).

160. Time Warner Entertainment Co. v. FCC, 93 F.3d 957 (D.C. Cir. 1996).

161. 47 U.S.C. § 532.

162. Leased Commercial Access, 12 F.C.C.R. 5267 (1997); *see also* Leased Commercial Access, 23 F.C.C.R. 2909 (2007).

163. Value Vision International, Inc. v. FCC, 149 F.3d 1204 (D.C. Cir. 1998).

164. 47 U.S.C. §§ 531(e) (public access), 532(c)(2) (leased access).

165. 47 C.F.R. §§ 76.92, 76.94.

166. 47 C.F.R. § 76.5(j).

167. 47 C.F.R. § 76.101.

168. 47 C.F.R. § 76.111.

169. 47 U.S.C. § 548(b).

170. 47 C.F.R. § 76.1001.

171. Development of Competition and Diversity in Video Programming Distribution and Carriage, 8 F.C.C.R. 3359 (1993).

172. Cablevision Sys. Corp. v. FCC, 597 F.3d 1306 (D.C. Cir. 2010).

173. 47 U.S.C. § 533(f)(1)(B).

174. 47 C.F.R. § 76.504.

175. 47 U.S.C. § 551.

176. Annual Assessment of the Status of Competition in the Market for the Delivery of Video Programming, 19 F.C.C.R. 1606 (2004).

177. National Association of Broadcasters v. FCC, 740 F.2d 1190 (D.C. Cir. 1984).

178. Pub. L. No. 102–385, § 25, 106 Stat. 1460.

179. Daniels Cablevision, Inc. v. United States, 835 F. Supp. 1 (D.D.C. 1993).

180. Application of Network Non-Duplication, Syndicated Exclusivity, and Sports Blackout Rules to Satellite Retransmissions of Broadcast Signals, 15 F.C.C.R. 21688 (2000), modified by 17 F.C.C.R. 20693 (2002).

181. Direct Broadcast Satellite Public Interest Obligations, 13 F.C.C.R. 23254 (1998); 47 C.F.R. § 100.5.

182. Direct Broadcast Satellite Public Interest Obligations, 19 F.C.C.R. 5647 (2004).

183. Satellite Home Viewer Improvement Act, Pub. L. No. 106–113, § 1001–1012, 113 Stat. 1501. The act was upheld in Satellite Broadcasting and Communications Association v. FCC, 275 F.3d 337 (4th Cir. 2001), *cert. denied*, 536 U.S. 922 (2002).

184. Satellite Television Extension & Localism Act of 2010 (STELA), Pub. L. 111–175, 124 Stat. 1218.

185. Carriage of Digital Television Broadcast Signals, 23 F.C.C.R. 5352 (2008).

186. *See* Broadcast Signal Carriage Issues, 16 F.C.C.R. 16544 (2001); Good Faith Negotiation and Exclusivity, 16 F.C.C.R. 15599 (2001); Broadcast Signal Carriage Issues, Retransmission Consent Issues, 16 F.C.C.R. 1918 (2000).

187. *See* Katie Hafner & Matthew Lyon, Where Wizards Stay Up Late: The Origins of the Internet 103–36 (1996).

188. *See Internet Corporation for Assigned Names and Numbers*, n.d., *available at* http://icann.org/; ICANN Watch, *ICANN for Beginners*, n.d., *available at* http://www.icannwatch.org/icann4beginners.shtml.

189. Appropriate Framework for Broadband Access to the Internet over Wireline Facilities, 20 F.C.C.R. 148653 (2005).

190. 47 U.S.C. § 154(i).

191. United States v. Southwestern Cable Co., 392 U.S. 157 (1969); United States v. Midwest Video Corp., 406 U.S. 649 (1972) (*Midwest I*); United States v. Midwest Video Corp., 440 U.S. 689 (1979) (*Midwest II*).

192. National Cable & Telecommunications Assoc. v. Brand X Internet Services, 545 U.S. 967 (2005).

193. 47 U.S.C. §§ 201–209, 251(a)(1).

194. High-Speed Access to the Internet over Cable and Other Facilities, 17 F.C.C.R. 4798 (2002).

195. Broadband Industry Practices, 223 F.C.C.R. 13028 (2008).

196. Comcast Corp. v. FCC, 600 F.3d 642, 644 (D.C. Cir. 2010).

197. In the Matter of Preserving the Open Internet, 25 F.C.C.R 17905 (2010).

198. Reno v. American Civil Liberties Union, 521 U.S. 844 (1997).

199. Pub. L. No. 104–104, Title V, §§ 501–561, 110 Stat. 56, 133–43 (codified at 18 U.S.C. §§ 1462, 1465, 2422 and at scattered sections of 47 U.S.C.).

200. *Id.* at 869.

201. *Id.* at 853.

202. *Id.* at 870.

203. Miller v. California, 413 U.S. 15 (1973).

Chapter 12

Obscenity, Indecency and Violence

1. Jacobellis v. Ohio, 378 U.S. 184, 197 (1964) (Stewart, J., concurring).

2. Erznoznik v. City of Jacksonville, 422 U.S. 205 (1975).

3. Cohen v. California, 403 U.S. 15 (1971).

4. *See, e.g.,* Shannon Creasy, Note & Comment: *Defending Against a Charge of Obscenity in the Internet Age: How Google Searches Can Illuminate Miller's "Contemporary Community Standards,"* 26 Ga. St. U. Rev. 1029, 1031 (2010).

5. *See, e.g.,* Cass R. Sunstein, Democracy and the Problem of Free Speech 210–26 (1993).

6. *See, e.g.,* Marianne Wesson, *Girls Should Bring Lawsuits Everywhere . . . Nothing Will Be Corrupted: Pornography as Speech and Product,* 60 U. Chi. L. Rev. 845 (1993).

7. *See, e.g.,* Catharine Mackinnon, Only Words (1993).

8. American Booksellers Association, Inc. v. Hudnut, 771 F.2d 323, *aff'd without opinion,* 475 U.S. 1001 (1986).

9. Regina v. Butler, [1992] 89 D.L.R. 4th 449 (Canada); *see also* Little Sisters Book and Art Emporium v. Canada (Minister of Justice), [2000] 193 D.L.R. (4th) 193 (Canada).

10. *See, e.g.,* Creasy, *supra* note 4.

11. *See* MARGARET A. BLANCHARD, REVOLUTIONARY SPARKS: FREEDOM OF EXPRESSION IN MODERN AMERICA (1992).

12. An Act for the Suppression of Trade in, and Circulation of, Obscene Literature and Articles of Immoral Use, ch. 258, § 2, 17 Stat. 598, 599 (1873).

13. Congress amended the Comstock Act in 1876. Amendment to the Comstock Act, ch. 186, § 1, 19 Stat. 90.

14. L.R. 3 Q.B. 360, 371 (1868).

15. United States v. One Book Called "Ulysses," 5 F. Supp. 182, 184, 185 (S.D.N.Y. 1933), *aff'd,* United States v. One Book Entitled "Ulysses" by James Joyce, 72 F.2d 705 (2d Cir. 1934).

16. 18 U.S.C. §§ 1460–1470.

17. 18 U.S.C. §§ 1470, 2252B; 47 U.S.C. §§ 223(d), 231.

18. Roth v. United States, 354 U.S. 476, 489 (1957).

19. Miller v. California, 413 U.S. 15 (1973).

20. *Id.* at 22.

21. Roth v. United States, 354 U.S. 476, 487 n.20 (1957).

22. Smith v. United States, 431 U.S. 291, 305 (1977); Hamling v. United States, 418 U.S. 87, 104–5 (1974).

23. Jacobellis v. Ohio, 378 U.S. 184 (1964).

24. Ward v. Illinois, 431 U.S. 767 (1977).

25. Mishkin v. New York, 383 U.S. 502, 508–9 (1966).

26. United States v. Thomas, 74 F.3d 701 (6th Cir.), *cert. denied,* 519 U.S. 820 (1996).

27. Ashcroft v. American Civil Liberties Union, 535 U.S. 564, 597 (2002) (Kennedy, J., concurring in the judgment).

28. *Id.* at 590 (Breyer, J., concurring in part and concurring in the judgment).

29. *Id.* at 586–89 (O'Connor, J., concurring in part and concurring in the judgment).

30. United States v. Kilbride, 584 F.3d 1240 (9th Cir. 2009).

31. United States v. Little, 365 Fed. Appx. 159 (11th Cir. 2010).

32. Miller v. California, 413 U.S. 15, 25 (1973).

33. Jenkins v. Georgia, 418 U.S. 153 (1974).

34. *Id.* at 160.

35. Ward v. Illinois, 431 U.S. 767 (1977).

36. *Id.*

37. A Book Named John Cleland's Memoirs of a Woman of Pleasure v. Attorney General of Massachusetts, 383 U.S. 413 (1996).

38. Pope v. Illinois, 481 U.S. 497 (1987).

39. Luke Records, Inc. v. Navarro, 960 F.2d 134 (11th Cir.), *cert. denied,* 506 U.S. 1022 (1992).

40. Butler v. Michigan, 352 U.S. 380, 383 (1957).

41. *Id.*

42. Ginsberg v. New York, 390 U.S. 629 (1968).

43. United States v. Williams, 553 U.S. 285, 288 (2008). The federal law is the Protection of Children Against Sexual Exploitation Act, 18 U.S.C. § 2252.

44. *See* 18 U.S.C. §§ 2251–2252, 2256.

45. 458 U.S. 747 (1982).

46. *Id.* at 758.

47. 18 U.S.C. §§ 2251(a), 2252(b)(4), 2256(8).

48. 18 U.S.C. § 2256(2)(A).

49. John A. Humbach, *'Sexting' and the First Amendment,* 37 HASTINGS CONST. L.Q. 433, 446 (2010).

50. United States v. Knox, 32 F.3d 733, 737 (3d Cir. 1994), *cert. denied,* 513 U.S. 1109 (1995).

51. *Id.*

52. United States v. Matthews, 209 F.3d 338, 345 (4th Cir.), *cert. denied,* 531 U.S. 910 (2000).

53. Ashcroft v. Free Speech Coalition, 535 U.S. 234 (2002).

54. THE NAT'L CAMPAIGN TO PREVENT TEEN AND UNPLANNED PREGNANCY, SEX AND TECH: RESULTS FROM A SURVEY OF TEENS AND YOUNG ADULTS 1 (2008), *available at* http://www.thenationalcampaign.org/sextech/.

55. Humbach, *supra* note 49.

56. Mary Graw Leary, *Sexting or Self-Produced Child Pornography? The Dialog Continues—Structured Prosecutorial Discretion within a Multidisciplinary Response,* 17 VA. J. SOC. POL'Y & L. 486 (2010).

57. A.H. v. State, 949 So. 2d 234 (Fla. Dist. Ct. App. 2007).

58. Osborne v. Ohio. 495 U.S. 103 (1990).

59. *See* Humbach, *supra* note 49, at 434.

60. Miller v. Mitchell, 598 F.3d 139 (3d Cir. 2010); *see* Catherine Arcabascio, *Sexting and Teenagers: OMG R U Going 2 Jail???,* 16 RICH. J.L. & TECH. 10 (2010).

61. Nathan Koppel & Ashby Jones, *Are "Sext" Messages a Teenage Felony or Folly,* WALL ST. J., Aug. 25, 2010, at D1.

62. Stanley v. Georgia, 394 U.S. 557 (1969).

63. *Id.* at 550.

64. 18 U.S.C. § 2252A; Osborne v. Ohio, 495 U.S. 103 (1990).

65. Osborne v. Ohio, 495 U.S. 103 (1990).

66. Joseph Burstyn, Inc., v. Wilson, 343 U.S. 495 (1952).

67. Times Film Corp. v. City of Chicago, 365 U.S. 43 (1961).

68. Freedman v. Maryland, 380 U.S. 51 (1965).

69. Pub. L. No. 91–452, 84 Stat. 922 (1970), codified at 18 U.S.C. §§ 1961–1968 (as amended by USA-Patriot Act of 2001, Pub. L. No. 107–56, § 813, 115 Stat. 272, 382).

70. *See* Teresa Bryan et al., *Racketeer Influenced and Corrupt Organizations,* 40 AM. CRIM. L. REV. 987 (2003).

71. Alexander v. United States, 509 U.S. 544 (1993).

72. 18 U.S.C. § 1464; 47 C.F.R. § 73.3999.

73. 18 U.S.C. § 1464.

74. FCC v. Pacifica Foundation, 438 U.S. 726, 739 (1978).

75. *Id.* at 740.

76. *Id.* at 727.

77. Enforcement of Prohibitions Against Broadcast Indecency, 8 F.C.C.R. 704, 705 n.10 (1993).

78. Fox Television Stations, Inc. v. Federal Communications Commission, 613 F.3d 317 (2d Cir. 2010).

79. Pub. L. 69–632, ch. 169, § 29, 44 Stat. 1162 (1927); Ch. 652, § 326, 48 Stat. 1064 (1934).

80. 18 U.S.C. § 1464.

81. 47 U.S.C. § 503(b)(1)(D).

82. *See, e.g.,* Sable Communications of California, Inc. v. FCC, 492 U.S. 115, 126 (1989).

83. 47 U.S.C. § 326.

84. *See, e.g.,* Application of The Jack Straw Memorial Foundation for Renewal of the License of Station KRAB-FM, Seattle, Wash., 21 Rad. Reg. 2d (P&F) 505 (1971).

85. Sonderling Broadcasting Corp., 41 F.C.C.2d 777, 782 (1973), *aff'd,* Illinois Citizens Comm. for Broadcasting v. FCC, 515 F.2d 397 (D.C. Cir. 1974).

86. Pacifica Foundation, 56 F.C.C.2d 94 (1975) (the words, as listed in the FCC's decision, are "shit, piss, fuck, cunt, cocksucker, motherfucker, and tits").

87. Citizen's Complaint Against Pacifica Found. Station WBAI (FM), N.Y, N.Y., 56 F.C.C.2d 94 (1975).

88. 438 U.S. at 750.

89. *Id.*

90. Federal Communications Commission v. Pacifica Foundation, 438 U.S. 726 (1978).

91. Pacifica Foundation, Inc., 2 F.C.C.R. 2698, 2699 (1987).

92. *In re* Infinity Broadcasting Corp. of Pennsylvania, 2 F.C.C.R. 2705 (1987) (*Infinity*); *In re* Pacifica Foundation, Inc., 2 F.C.C.R. 2698 (1987); *In re* Regents of the University of California, 2 F.C.C.R. 2703 (1987); New Indecency Enforcement Standards to Be Applied to All Broadcast and Amateur Radio Licensees, 62 Rad. Reg. 2d (P & F) 1218 (1987).

93. New Indecency Enforcement Standards to Be Applied to All Broadcast and Amateur Radio Licensees, 2 F.C.C.R. 2726 (1987). The D.C. Circuit upheld the FCC's more expansive indecency definition. Action for Children's Television v. FCC, 852 F.2d 1332 (D.C. Cir. 1988) (ACT I).

94. FCC v. Pacifica Foundation, 438 U.S. 726, 772 (1978).

95. *Id,* at 8002–3.

96. *In re* Complaints Against Various Broadcast Licensees Regarding Their Airing of the "Golden Globe Awards" Program, 19 F.C.C.R. 4975 (2004).

97. *In re* Complaints Regarding Various Television Broadcasts Between February 2, 2002 and March 8, 2005, 21 F.C.C.R. 2664 (2006).

98. *See* Fox Television Stations, Inc. v. Federal Communications Commission, 613 F.3d 317, 322 (2d Cir. 2010).

99. *Id.* at 322.

100. Complaints Against Various Television Licensees Concerning Their February 1, 2004, Broadcast of the Super Bowl XXXVIII, 19 F.C.C.R. 19230 (2004).

101. CBS Corp. v. FCC, 535 F.3d 167, 174 (3d Cir. 2008), *vacated and remanded,* 129 S. Ct. 2176 (2009).

102. FCC v. CBS Corp., 129 S. Ct. 2176 (2009).

103. FCC v. Fox TV Stations, Inc., 129 S. Ct. 1800 (2009).

104. Complaints Regarding Various Television Broadcasts, 21 F.C.C.R. 2664 (2006), *modified,* 21 F.C.C.R. 13299, 13327 (2006).

105. *In re* Complaints Against Various Television Licensees Regarding Their Broadcast on November 11, 2004, of the ABC Television Network's Presentation of the Film "Saving Private Ryan," 20 F.C.C.R. 4507 (2005).

106. Complaints Regarding Various Television Broadcasts, 21 F.C.C.R. 2664 (2006), *modified,* 21 F.C.C.R. 13299, 13327 (2006).

107. See *id.;* Evergreen Media Corp. of Chicago, 6 F.C.C.R. 5950 (Mass Media Bureau 1991).

108. ABC, Inc. v. FCC, 2011 U.S. App. LEXIS 72 (2d Cir., Jan. 4, 2011).

109. 47 C.F.R. § 73.3999.

110. Action for Children's Television v. FCC, 58 F.3d 654 (D.C. Cir. 1995) (*en banc*), *cert. denied,* 516 U.S. 1043 (1996) (ACT III).

111. New Indecency Enforcement Standards to Be Applied to All Broadcast and Amateur Radio Licensees, 62 Rad. Reg. 2d (P & F) 1218 (1987).

112. Action for Children's Television v. FCC, 852 F.2d 1332 (D.C. Cir. 1988) (ACT I).

113. Pub. L. No. 100–459, § 608, 102 Stat. 2186, 2228.

114. Enforcement of Prohibitions Against Broadcast Indecency in 18 U.S.C. § 1464, 5 F.C.C.R. 5297 (1990).

115. Action for Children's Television v. FCC, 932 F.2d 1504 (D.C. Cir. 1991) (ACT II), *cert. denied,* 503 U.S. 913 (1992).

116. Public Telecommunications Act of 1992, Pub. L. No. 102–356, § 16(a), 106 Stat. 949.

117. Enforcement of Prohibitions Against Broadcast Indecency in 18 U.S.C. § 1464, 8 F.C.C.R. 704 (1993).

118. Action for Children's Television v. FCC, 58 F.3d 654 (D.C. Cir. 1995), *cert. denied,* 516 U.S. 1043 (1996) (ACT III).

119. Federal Communications Commission, FCC V-Chip Task Force Releases Updated Survey on the Encoding of Video Programming, 2000 FCC LEXIS 143 (2000).

120. Implementation of Section 551 of the Telecommunications Act of 1996; Video Programming Ratings, 13 F.C.C.R. 8232, 8237 (1998).

121. See Classification and Rating Administration, Questions & Answers: Everything You Always Wanted to Know about the Movie Rating System, n.d., *available at* http://www.filmratings.com/questions.htm.

122. Cruz v. Ferre, 755 F.2d 1415 (11th Cir. 1985), citing FCC v. Pacifica Foundation, 438 U.S. 726 (1978).

123. *See, e.g.,* Community Television of Utah, Inc. v. Roy City, 555 F. Supp. 1164 (D. Utah 1982); Home Box Office, Inc. v. Wilkinson, 531 F. Supp. 987 (D. Utah 1982).

124. 47 U.S.C. § 532(h) (franchising authorities may prohibit leased access programming that is "obscene or is in conflict with community standards in that it is lewd, lascivious, filthy or indecent, or is otherwise unprotected by the Constitution of the United States"); 47 U.S.C. § 544(d)(i) (franchising authorities may require a franchise to prohibit obscene or "otherwise unprotected" programming); 47 U.S.C. § 558 (franchising authorities may enforce state or local laws forbidding obscenity and "other similar laws").

125. 47 U.S.C. § 544(d)(2).

126. Various Complaints Against the Cable/Satellite Television Program "Nip/Tuck," 20 F.C.C.R. 4255, 4255 (2005), quoting Violent Television Programming and Its Impact on Children, Notice of Inquiry, 19 F.C.C.R. 14394, 14403 (2004).

127. Denver Area Educational Telecommunications Consortium, Inc. v. FCC, 518 U.S. 727 (1996) (ruling on Pub. L. No. 102–385, § 10, 106 Stat. 1486).

128. 47 U.S.C. § 531(e).

129. Telecommunications Act of 1996, Pub. L. 104–104, §§ 504, 505, 110 Stat. 136.

130. Implementation of Section 505 of the Telecommunications Act of 1996, 12 F.C.C.R. 5212 (1997).

131. United States v. Playboy Enterprises, Inc., 529 U.S. 803 (2000).

132. Dan Thang Dang, *Cell Phone the Newest Frontier for Porn,* BALTIMORE SUN, Feb. 19, 2004, at 9D.

133. *See* generally Amitai Etzioni, *Do Children Have the Same First Amendment Rights as Adults? On Protecting Children from Speech,* 79 CHI.-KENT L. REV. 3 (2004).

134. Pub. L. No. 104–104, § 502, 110 Stat. 56 (1996) (codified at 47 U.S.C. §§ 223(a)(1)(B)(ii), 223(d)).

135. 521 U.S. 844 (1997).

136. *Id.* at 877.

137. Pub. L. No. 105–277, §§ 1401–6, 112 Stat. 1681 (codified at 47 U.S.C. § 231).

138. American Civil Liberties Union v. Reno, 31 F. Supp. 2d 473 (E.D. Pa. 1999).

139. American Civil Liberties Union v. Reno, 217 F.3d 162 (3d Cir. 2000).

140. Ashcroft v. American Civil Liberties Union, 535 U.S. 564 (2002).

141. American Civil Liberties Union v. Ashcroft, 322 F.3d 240 (3d Cir. 2003).

142. Ashcroft v. American Civil Liberties Union, 542 U.S. 656 (2004).

143. American Civil Liberties Union v. Gonzales, 478 F. Supp. 2d 775 (E.D. Pa. 2007).

144. American Civil Liberties Union v. Mukasey, 534 F.3d 181 (3d Cir. 2008), *cert. denied,* 129 S. Ct. 1032 (2009).

145. American Civil Liberties Union v. Ashcroft, 322 F.3d 240, 268 (3d Cir. 2003).

146. Mukasey v. ACLU, 129 S. Ct. 1032 (2009).

147. Pub. L. 104–208, 110 Stat. 3009.

148. 47 U.S.C. § 2256(8)(B), (D).

149. Ashcroft v. Free Speech Coalition, 535 U.S. 234 (2002).

150. Pub. L. 108–21, §§ 102–601, 117 Stat. 650.

151. United States v. Williams, 553 U.S. 285 (2008).

152. Pub. L. No. 106–554, 114 Stat. 2763A-335 (2000).

153. 539 U.S. 194 (2003).

154. United States v. American Library Association, 539 U.S. 194 (2003).

155. *See* Elizabeth Megen Ray, Comment: *"I May Not Know Art, But I Know What I'll Pay For": The Government's Role in Arts Funding Following* National Endowment for the Arts v. Finley, 2 U. PA. J. CONST. L. 497 (2000).

156. Pub. L. No. 101–121, 103 Stat. 741.

157. 20 U.S.C. § 954 (d)(1).

158. National Endowment for the Arts v. Finley, 524 U.S. 569 (1998).

159. *See* Adam L. Fernandez, Comment: *Let It Be: A Comparative Study of the Content Regulation of Recorded Music in the United States and the United Kingdom,* 21 PENN. ST. INT'L L. REV. 227, 240 (2002).

160. Recording Industry Association of America, *Tools for Parents and Educators* (2006), *available at* http://www.riaa.com.

161. Recording Industry Association of America, *Parental Advisory* (2006), *available at* http://www.riaa.com/parentaladvisory.php.

162. City of Renton v. Playtime Theatres, 474 U.S. 41 (1986).

163. *See, e.g.,* Arcara v. Cloud Books, Inc., 478 U.S. 697 (1986); Young v. American Mini Theatres, 427 U.S. 50, 71, n.34 (1976).

164. Barnes v. Glen Theatre, Inc., 501 U.S. 560, 566 (1991).

165. City of Erie v. Pap's A.M., 529 U.S. 277 (2000); Barnes v. Glen Theatre, Inc., 501 U.S. 560 (1991).

166. City of Los Angeles v. Alameda Books, Inc., 535 U.S. 425 (2002).

167. *See* Ashley C. Phillips, Comment: *A Matter of Arithmetic: Using Supply and Demand to Determine the Constitutionality of Adult Entertainment Zoning Ordinances,* 51 EMORY L.J. 319, 320–21 (2002).

168. City of Renton v. Playtime Theatres, 474 U.S. 41, 47–48 (1986).

169. *See* Sable Communications of California, Inc. v. FCC, 492 U.S. 115, 120–23 (1989).

170. 492 U.S. 115 (1989).

171. Dial Information Services Corp. v. Thornburgh, 938 F.2d 1535 (2d Cir. 1991), *cert. denied,* 502 U.S. 1072 (1992).

172. *See, e.g.,* Amitai Etzioni, *Porn Blocking Law Should Be Scrapped,* BROWARD DAILY BUS. REV., Mar. 19, 2003, at A7; James v. Meow Media, 300 F.3d 683 (6th Cir. 2002), *cert. denied,* 537 U.S. 1159 (2003).

173. *See, e.g.,* American Amusement Machine Association v. Kendrick, 244 F.3d 572 (7th Cir.), *cert. denied,* 534 U.S. 994 (2001).

174. James v. Meow Media, 300 F.3d 683 (6th Cir. 2001), *cert. denied,* 537 U.S. 1159 (2003).

175. James v. Meow Media, Inc., 90 F. Supp. 2d 798 (W.D. Ky. 2000).

176. American Amusement Machine Association v. Kendrick, 244 F.3d 572, 575, 575 (7th Cir.), *cert. denied,* 534 U.S. 994 (2001).

177. *Id.* at 574.

178. *Id.* at 575.

179. Federal Trade Commission, *Marketing Violent Entertainment to Children: A Review of Self-Regulation and Industry Practices in the Motion Picture, Music Recording & Electronic Game Industries* (2000).

180. 22 F.C.C.R. 7929 (2007).

181. *Id.* at 7938, quoting *Youth Violence: A Report of the Surgeon General* (2001), at Appendix 4-B.

182. *Id.* at 7938.

183. *See* William Li, Note: *Unbaking the Adolescent Cake: The Constitutional Implications of Imposing Tort*

Liability on Publishers of Violent Video Games, 45 Ariz. L. Rev. 467 (2003).

184. *About ESRB,* n.d., *available at* http://www.esrb.org/about.asp.

185. *ESRB Game Ratings,* n.d., *available* at http://www.esrb.org/esrbratings_guide.asp.

186. Brown v. Entertainment Merchants Ass'n, 2011 U.S. LEXIS 4802 (June 27, 2011).

187. *See, e.g.,* America's Best Family Showplace Corp. v. New York City, 536 F. Supp. 170, 172 (E.D.N.Y. 1982).

188. Rothner v. City of Chicago, 929 F.2d 297, 303 (7th Cir. 1991).

189. Brown, 2011 U.S. LEXIS 4802, at *5-6.

190. Entertainment Software Assoc. v. Swanson, 519 F.3d 768 (8th Cir. 2008).

191. *See* Gregory Kenyota, Note: *Thinking of the Children: The Failure of Violent Video Game Laws,* 18 Fordham Intell. Prop. Media & Ent. L.J. 785, 786 n.7 (2008).

192. Brown, 2011 U.S. LEXIS 4802, at *13.

193. Empowering Parents and Protecting Children in an Evolving Media Landscape, 24 F.C.C.R. 13171, 13181 (2010).

194. Brown, 2011 U.S. LEXIS 4802, at *24.

Chapter 13
Intellectual Property

1. Lawrence Lessig, Free Culture 53, 62 (2004).

2. 35 U.S.C. §§ 101–03, 112.

3. 15 U.S.C. §§ 1051–1127.

4. Verne G. Kopytoff, *Rival Ordered to Pay Oracle over $1 Billion,* N.Y. Times, Nov. 24, 2010, at A1.

5. 17 U.S.C. § 102(a).

6. U.S. Const., art. I, § 8, cl. 8.

7. *See* Paul Goldstein, Copyright's Highway: From Gutenberg to the Celestial Jukebox 30 (rev. ed. 2003).

8. *Id.*

9. 8 Anne, C. 19 (1710).

10. U.S. Const., art. I, § 8, cl. 8.

11. Act of May 31, 1790, ch. 15, 1 Stat. 124.

12. Wheaton v. Peters, 33 U.S. 590 (1834).

13. Act of Feb. 3, 1831, 4 Stat. 436 (musical compositions); Copyright Act of 1865, 13 Stat. 540 (photographs); Act of July 8, 1870, 16 Stat. 212 (paintings).

14. Act of July 8, 1870, ch. 230, 86–111, 16 Stat. 198, 212–216.

15. Pub. L. No. 60–349, 35 Stat. 1075.

16. Berne Convention Implementation Act of 1988, Pub. L. 100–568, 102 Stat. 2853.

17. 17 I. Fred Koenigsberg, Commentary: *Overview of Title 17, Copyrights,* available at LEXIS, 17 US NITA PREC 101 (2010).

18. 18 U.S.C. § 102(a).

19. *See* Burrow-Giles Lithographic Co. v. Sarony, 111 U.S. 53 (1884).

20. Boisson v. Banian, Ltd., 273 F.3d 262, 268 (2d Cir. 2001).

21. *See, e.g., id.;* American Dental Association v. Delta Dental Plans Association, 126 F.3d 977 (7th Cir. 1997).

22. 17 U.S.C. § 103.

23. Feist Publications, Inc. v. Rural Telephone Service Co., Inc., 499 U.S. 340 (1991).

24. 17 U.S.C. § 102(a).

25. 17 U.S.C. § 301.

26. *See* Wheaton v. Peters, 33 U.S. 591 (1834).

27. *See* 17 U.S.C. § 102(b).

28. Hoehling v. Universal City Studios, Inc., 618 F.2d 972 (2d Cir. 1980), *cert. denied,* 449 U.S. 841 (1980).

29. International News Service v. Associated Press, 248 U.S. 215 (1918).

30. National Basketball Ass'n v. Motorola, Inc., 105 F.3d 841, 845 (2d Cir. 1997).

31. *See, e.g.,* Barclays Capital Inc. v. Theflyonthewall.com, Inc., 700 F. Supp. 2d 310 (S.D.N.Y. 2010).

32. 17 U.S.C. § 105.

33. *See* Mark Jurkowitz, *Barnicle Resigns After New Questions on Reporting,* Boston Globe, Aug. 20, 1998, at A1; Dan Barry et al., *Correcting the Record: Times Reporter Who Resigned Leaves Long Trail of Deception,* N.Y. Times, May 11, 2003, at A1; *Writer Admits Plagiarism,* N.Y. Times, Aug. 24, 2004, at C9.

34. Clark Hoyt, *Journalistic Shoplifting,* N.Y. Times, Mar. 7, 2010, at WK10.

35. JAYSON BLAIR, BURNING DOWN MY MASTER'S HOUSE: MY LIFE AT THE NEW YORK TIMES (2004).

36. *See* Ralph Blumenthal & Sarah Lyall, *Repeat Accusations of Plagiarism Taint Prolific Biographer*, N.Y. TIMES, Sept. 21, 1999, at A1; Jacques Steinberg, *New Book Includes Passages from Others*, N.Y. TIMES, May 31, 2003, at B9; Sara Rimer, *When Plagiarism's Shadow Falls on Admired Scholars*, N.Y. TIMES, Nov. 24, 2004, at B9.

37. *See* Motoko Rich, *An Essay Wasn't His, Author Now Concedes*, N.Y. TIMES, Jan. 7, 2009, at C1, 7.

38. 17 U.S.C. § 201(a).

39. 17 U.S.C. § 201(b).

40. 17 U.S.C. §§ 101, 201.

41. Community for Creative Non-Violence v. Reid, 490 U.S. 730 (1989).

42. 17 U.S.C. § 101.

43. Community for Creative Non-Violence v. Reid, 490 U.S. 730.

44. 17 U.S.C. § 201(c).

45. Greenberg v. National Geographic Society, 533 F.3d 1244 (11th Cir.), *cert. denied*, 129 S. Ct. 727 (2008).

46. 533 U.S. 483 (2001).

47. 17 U.S.C. § 106.

48. Silberman v. Innovative Luggage, Inc., 2003 U.S. Dist. LEXIS 5420 (S.D.N.Y. Apr. 3, 2003).

49. Sony Corp. of America v. Universal City Studios, Inc. 464 U.S. 417 (1984).

50. Audio Home Recording Act of 1992, Pub. L. No. 102–563, 106 Stat. 4244 (codified at 17 U.S.C. §§ 1001–1010).

51. 17 U.S.C. § 112(a).

52. Pickett v. Prince, 207 F.3d 402 (7th Cir. 2000).

53. Ortiz-Gonzalez v. Fonovisa, 277 F.3d 59 (1st Cir. 2002).

54. 17 U.S.C. § 106(4).

55. 17 U.S.C. § 106.

56. Digital Performance Right in Sound Recordings Act, Pub. L. No. 104–39, 109 Stat. 336, as amended by Digital Millennium Copyright Act, Pub. L. 105–304, 112 Stat. 2860.

57. *See* 4 MELVILLE NIMMER & DAVID NIMMER, NIMMER ON COPYRIGHT § 8D.01[A] (2010).

58. Berne Convention, art. 6bis(1).

59. Visual Artists Rights Act, Pub. L. No. 101–650, § 601, 104 Stat. 5089.

60. 17 U.S.C. § 106A.

61. Clean Flicks of Colo., LLC v. Soderbergh, 433 F. Supp. 2d 1236 (D. Colo. 2006).

62. Pub. L. No. 109–9, 119 Stat. 218 (2005) (codified at 17 U.S.C. §§ 408, 506(a) and 18 U.S.C. § 2319).

63. 17 U.S.C. § 110(11).

64. *See* Jacob Armstrong, *FECA Matter: An Epic Copyright Infringement Trial, Congressional Interference, and the Diminution of Moral Rights in the United States of America*, 7 J. MARSHALL REV. INTELL. PROP. L. 376 (2008).

65. Sony Corp. of America v. Universal City Studios, Inc. 464 U.S. 417 (1984).

66. 17 U.S.C. § 1008.

67. *See, e.g.,* Paramount Pictures Corp. v. RePlayTV, 298 F. Supp. 2d 921 (C.D. Cal. 2004).

68. 17 U.S.C. § 108.

69. *See* R. S. TALAB, COMMONSENSE COPYRIGHT: A GUIDE FOR EDUCATORS AND LIBRARIANS (2d ed. 1999).

70. 17 U.S.C. § 109(a).

71. The Supreme Court provides a brief history and interpretation of the first-sale doctrine in Quality King Distributors, Inc. v. L'Anza Research International, Inc., 523 U.S. 135 (1998).

72. 17 U.S.C. § 109(b)(1)(A); Computer Software Rental Amendments, Pub. L. No. 101–650, tit. viii, 104 Stat. 5089, 5134–35; Record Rental Amendment of 1984, Pub. L. No. 98–450, 98 Stat. 1727.

73. Brilliance Audio, Inc. v. Haights Cross Communictions, Inc., 474 F.3d 365 (6th Cir. 2007).

74. Jessica Litman, *Billowing White Goo*, 31 COLUM. J.L. & ARTS 587, 594 (2008).

75. Berne Convention Implementation Act of 1988, Pub. L. 100–568, 102 Stat. 2853.

76. 17 U.S.C. § 401.

77. 17 U.S.C. § 401(c).

78. 17 U.S.C. §§ 203(a), 304(c).

79. U.S. CONST. art I, § 8, cl. 8.

80. 17 U.S.C. § 302(a).

81. 17 U.S.C. § 302(c).

82. 537 U.S. 186 (2003).

83. Lynn M. Forsythe & Deborah J. Kemp, *Creative Commons: For the Common Good?*, 30 U. La Verne L. Rev. 346, 347–48 (2009).

84. 17 U.S.C. § 408(a).

85. 17 U.S.C. § 411(a).

86. 17 U.S.C. §§ 407, 408(b).

87. 17 U.S.C. § 412.

88. 17 U.S.C. § 410(c).

89. 37 C.F.R. § 202.1.

90. 17 U.S.C. § 411.

91. Teleprompter Corp. v. Columbia Broadcasting System, 415 U.S. 394 (1974); Fortnightly Corp. v. United Artists Television, Inc., 392 U.S. 390 (1968).

92. 17 U.S.C. § 111.

93. 17 U.S.C. § 119; Satellite Home Viewer Improvement Act of 1999, Pub. L. No. 106–113, §§ 1001–1012, 113 Stat. 1501.

94. *See, e.g.,* Cottrill v. Spears, 87 Fed. Appx. 803 (3d Cir. 2004), *amended,* 2004 U.S. App. LEXIS 10773 (3d Cir. June 2, 2004).

95. Fogerty v. MGM Group Holdings Corp., 379 F.3d 348 (6th Cir. 2004), *cert. denied,* 543 U.S. 1120 (2005).

96. *See, e.g.,* Cavalier v. Random House, 297 F.3d 815 (9th Cir. 2002); Leigh v. Warner Brothers, 212 F.3d 1210 (11th Cir. 2000).

97. Metro-Goldwyn-Mayer, Inc. v. American Honda Motor Co., 900 F. Supp. 1287 (C.D. Cal. 1995).

98. *Id.* at 1290.

99. *Id.* at 1298.

100. *Id.* at 1299.

101. Atkins v. Fischer, 331 F.3d 988 (D.C. Cir. 2003).

102. Hudson v. Imagine Entertainment Corp., 128 Fed. Appx. 178 (2d Cir. 2005), *aff'd* Hudson v. Universal Pictures, 2004 U.S. Dist. LEXIS 11508 (E.D.N.Y., Apr. 29, 2004), *cert. denied,* 547 U.S. 1070 (2006).

103. 17 U.S.C. § 504(c).

104. *See, e.g.,* Kalem Co. v. Harper Brothers, 222 U.S. 55 (1911) (producer of infringing film violated copyright law although movie theaters, not producer, showed film to public); 17 U.S.C. §§ 106, 501(a).

105. Sony Corp. of America v. Universal City Studios, Inc. 464 U.S. 417 (1984).

106. Cartoon Network LP v. CSC Holdings, 536 F.3d 121 (2d Cir. 2008), *cert. denied,* 129 S. Ct. 2890 (2009).

107. Metro-Goldwyn-Mayer Studios, Inc. v. Grokster Ltd., 545 U.S. 913 (2005).

108. *See* 17 U.S.C. § 501(b).

109. 17 U.S.C. § 504(b).

110. 17 U.S.C. § 504(c)(1); *See* Digital Theft Deterrence and Copyright Damages Improvement Act, Pub. L. No. 106–160, 113 Stat. 1774.

111. Feltner v. Columbia Pictures Television, Inc., 523 U.S. 340 (1998).

112. 17 U.S.C. § 504(c)(2).

113. *Id.*

114. 17 U.S.C. § 505; *See* Fogerty v. Fantasy, Inc., 510 U.S. 517 (1994).

115. 17 U.S.C. § 502.

116. 17 U.S.C. § 509.

117. 17 U.S.C. § 506.

118. 17 U.S.C. § 101 (definition of "financial gain").

119. 17 U.S.C. § 506(a).

120. Pub. L. No. 105–147, 111 Stat. 2678.

121. 17 U.S.C. § 507.

122. *See, e.g.,* Dam Things from Denmark v. Russ Barrie & Co., 290 F.3d 548, 560 (3d Cir. 2002).

123. *See* Pierre N. Leval, *Toward a Fair Use Standard,* 103 Harv. L. Rev. 1105, 1105 (1990).

124. 17 U.S.C. § 107.

125. Leval, *supra* note 123, at 1110.

126. *See, e.g.,* Jessica Litman, *Billowing White Goo,* 31 Colum. J.L. & Arts 587, 596 (2008).

127. Campbell v. Acuff-Rose Music, Inc., 510 U.S. 569, 578 (1994).

128. Harper & Row Publishers, Inc. v. Nation Enterprises, 471 U.S. 539 (1985).

129. *See* 4 Melville Nimmer & David Nimmer, Nimmer on Copyright § 13.05[A][1] (2010).

130. Campbell v. Acuff-Rose Music, Inc., 510 U.S. at 579.

131. Campbell v. Acuff-Rose Music, Inc., 510 U.S 569 (1994).

132. A.V. v. iParadigms, 562 F.3d 630 (4th Cir. 2009).

133. Salinger v. Colting, 607 F.3d 68 (2d Cir. 2010).

134. *See* NIMMER & NIMMER, *supra* note 129, at § 13.05[C][1].

135. See *id.* at § 13.05.

136. Sony Corp. of America v. Universal City Studios, Inc. 464 U.S. 417 (1984).

137. *See* 4 MELVILLE NIMMER & DAVID NIMMER, NIMMER ON COPYRIGHT § 13.05[A][2] (2010).

138. Salinger v. Random House, Inc., 811 F.2d 90 (2d Cir. 1987), *cert. denied*, 484 U.S. 890 (1988).

139. 17 U.S.C. § 107; Pub. L. No. 102–492, 106 Stat. 3145.

140. Los Angeles News Service v. CBS Broadcasting, Inc., 305 F.3d 924, 940 (9th Cir.), *amended*, 313 F.3d 1093 (9th Cir. 2002).

141. Benny Evangelista, *Consumers Can Now Pass Go, Collect Any App*, S.F. Chron., July 27, 2010, at D1.

142. Harper & Row, Publishers, Inc. v. Nation Enterprises, 471 U.S. 539, 566 (1985).

143. Bill Graham Archives v. Dorling Kindersley Ltd., 448 F.3d 605 (2d Cir. 2006).

144. *See, e.g.,* Paul Goldstein, *Fair Use in Context*, 31 COLUM. J.L. & ARTS 433, 442 (2008).

145. *See* NIMMER & NIMMER, *supra* note 129, at § 13.05[A][4] (2010).

146. Basic Books, Inc. v. Kinko's Graphics Corp., 758 F. Supp. 1522 (S.D.N.Y. 1991).

147. *Id.* at 1534.

148. *See, e.g.,* Playboy Enterprises, Inc. v. Russ Hardenburgh, Inc., 982 F. Supp. 503 (N.D. Ohio 1997).

149. Pub. L. 105–304, 112 Stat. 2860.

150. 17 U.S.C. § 1201.

151. *See, e.g.,* 321 Studios v. Metro Goldwyn Mayer Studios, Inc., 307 F. Supp. 2d 1085 (N.D. Cal. 2004).

152. 17 U.S.C. § 1202.

153. Playboy Enterprises, Inc. v. Frena, 839 F. Supp. 1552 (M.D. Fla. 1993).

154. Sega Enterprises, Ltd. v. Maphia, 857 F. Supp. 679 (N.D. Cal. 1994).

155. 17 U.S.C. § 512(c).

156. Perfect 10, Inc. v. Google, Inc., 2010 U.S. Dist. LEXIS 75071 (C.D. Cal., July 26, 2010).

157. Io Group, Inc. v. Veoh Networks, Inc., 586 F. Supp. 2d 1132 (N.D. Cal. 2008).

158. Perfect 10 Inc. v. Amazon.com, Inc., 508 F.3d 1146, 1159–60 (9th Cir. 2007).

159. UMG Recordings, Inc. v. Veoh Networks, Inc., 620 F. Supp. 2d 1081 (C.D. Cal. 2008).

160. Perfect 10 Inc. v. Amazon.com, 508 F.3d at 1160–61.

161. 17 U.S.C. § 106(4).

162. John Bowe, *The Copyright Enforcers*, N.Y. TIMES MAGAZINE, Aug. 8, 2010, at 38.

163. *Id.*

164. *See, e.g.,* Twentieth Century Music Corp. v. Aiken, 422 U.S. 151 (1975); Edison Stores v. BMI, 954 F.2d 1419 (8th Cir. 1992).

165. Pub. L. 105–298, § 201, 112 Stat. 2827 (1998).

166. 17 U.S.C. § 115.

167. David Oxenford, *Steps to Legal Streaming* (August 2010), *available at* http://www.broadcastlawblog.com.

168. 17 U.S.C. § 101.

169. 17 U.S.C. § 102(a)(7).

170. Capitol Records, Inc. v. Mercury Records Corp., 221 F.2d 657, 664 (2d Cir. 1955) (L. Hand, J., dissenting).

171. *See* 17 U.S.C. § 106(4).

172. 17 U.S.C. § 114(b).

173. *See, e.g.,* Lieb v. Topstone Industries, Inc., 788 F.2d 151, 153 (3d Cir. 1986).

174. 17 U.S.C. § 114(j)(13); *see* Arista Records, LLC v. Launch Media, Inc., 578 F.3d 148 (2d Cir. 2009).

175. *See* Oxenford, *supra* note 167.

176. Bridgeport Music, Inc. v. Dimension Films, 410 F.3d 792 (6th Cir. 2005).

177. Newton v. Diamond, 388 F.3d 1189 (9th Cir. 2004), *cert. denied*, 545 U.S. 1114 (2005).

178. *See, e.g.,* Scott T. Okamoto, Comment: *Musical Sound Recordings as Works Made for Hire: Money for Nothing and Tracks for Free*, 37 U.S.F.L. REV. 783 (2003).

179. Phillip W. Hall, Jr., *Smells Like Slavery: Unconscionability in Recording Industry Contracts*, 25 HASTINGS COMM. & ENT. L.J. 189, 190 (2002).

180. 18 U.S.C. § 2319A. *See* United States v. Moghadam, 175 F.3d 1269 (11th Cir. 1999).

181. 17 U.S.C. § 1101.

182. 17 U.S.C. § 106.

183. *See* White-Smith Music Publishing Co. v. Apollo Co., 209 U.S. 1 (1908).

184. Sound Recording Amendment, Pub. L. 92–140, 85 Stat. 391 (1971).

185. 17 U.S.C. § 106(1), (2), (3).

186. A&M Records, Inc. v. Napster, Inc. 239 F.3d 1004 (9th Cir. 2001).

187. *See* Jeremy Paul Sirota, Note: *Analog to Digital: Harnessing Peer Computing,* 55 Hastings L.J. 759, 769 (2004).

188. Recording Industry Association of America, Inc. v. Verizon Internet Services, Inc., 351 F.3d 1229 (D.C. Cir. 2003), *cert. denied,* 543 U.S. 924 (2004).

189. Mark Stodghill, *Jury Says Brainerd Mom Owes $1.5 Million to Record Companies,* Duluth News Trib., Nov. 3, 2010, *available at* http://www.duluthnews tribune.comevent/article/id/183069.

190. Jonathan Saltzman, *Judge Slashes Downloading Penalty,* Boston Globe, July 10, 2010, at A1.

191. Metro-Goldwyn-Mayer Studios, Inc. v. Grokster Ltd., 545 U.S. 913 (2005).

192. *Id.* at 922, 940.

193. Sony Corp. of America v. Universal City Studios, Inc. 464 U.S. 417 (1984).

194. Tim Arango, *Judge Tells LimeWire, the File-Trading Service, to Disable Its Software,* N.Y. Times, Oct. 27, 2010, at B3.

195. John Bowe, *The Copyright Enforcers,* N.Y. Times Magazine, Aug. 8, 2010, at 38, 42.

196. Higher Education Opportunity Act, 20 U.S.C. § 1161r; *see* Lyombe Eko, *American Exceptionalism, the French Exception, Intellectual Property Law, and Peer-to-Peer File Sharing on the Internet,* 10 J. Marshall Rev. Intell. Prop. L. 94, 134–35 (2010).

197. 15 U.S.C. § 1127.

198. Qualitex Co. v. Jacobson Products Co., Inc., 514 U.S. 159 (1995).

199. *See* Jerome Gilson, Trademark Protection and Practice § 10A.09[5] (2010).

200. 15 U.S.C. § 1051 *et seq.*

201. 15 U.S.C. § 1125(a).

202. 15 U.S.C. § 1052.

203. PACCAR, Inc. v. TeleScanTechnologies, L.L.C., 319 F.3d 243 (6th Cir. 2003).

204. Bebe Stores, Inc. v. May Dep't Stores Int'l, 313 F.3d 1056 (8th Cir. 2002) (per curiam).

205. Standard Brands, Inc. v. Smidler, 151 F.2d 34 (2d Cir. 1945).

206. Sara Lee Corp. v. Kayser-Roth Corp., 81 F.3d 455, 464 (4th Cir. 1996).

207. Circuit City Stores Inc. v. CarMax Inc., 165 F.3d 1047 (6th Cir. 1999).

208. *See* Gilson, *supra* note 199, at § 2.04[1] (2010).

209. Japan Telecom, Inc. v. Japan Telecom of America, Inc., 287 F.3d 866, 873 (9th Cir. 2002).

210. Boston Beer Co., L.P. v. Slesar Brothers Brewing Co., Inc., 9 F.3d 175 (1st Cir. 1993).

211. Hamilton-Brown Shoe Co. v. Wolf Brothers & Co., 240 U.S. 251 (1918).

212. M. Fabrikant & Sons, Ltd. v. Fabrikant Fine Diamonds, Inc., 17 F. Supp. 2d 249 (S.D.N.Y. 1998).

213. Gilson, *supra* note 199, at § 2.08[1] (2010).

214. Harley-Davidson, Inc. v. Grottanelli, 164 F.3d 806 (2d Cir. 1999).

215. Small Business Assistance Corp. v. Clear Channel Broadcasting, Inc., 210 F.3d 278 (5th Cir. 2000).

216. *See* Sung In, Note: *Death of a Trademark: Genericide in the Digital Age,* 21 Rev. Litig. 159 (2002).

217. *See, e.g.,* George K. Chamberlin, *Annotation: When Does Product Mark Become Generic Term or "Common Descriptive Name" So as to Warrant Cancellation of Registration of Mark,* 55 A.L.R. Fed. 241 (2004).

218. *See* Gilson *supra* note 199, at § 2.02[6] (2010).

219. 15 U.S.C. § 1115(a), (b).

220. 15 U.S.C. § 1051.

221. 15 U.S.C. §§ 1052, 1072, 1115.

222. 15 U.S.C. § 1091.

223. 15 U.S.C. § 1058.

224. 15 U.S.C. § 1059.

225. Pub. L. 106–113, 113 Stat. 1536.

226. E. & J. Gallo Winery v. Spider Webs Ltd., 286 F.3d 270 (5th Cir. 2002).

227. Brookfield Communications, Inc. v. West Coast Entertainment Corp., 174 F.3d 1036 (9th Cir. 1999).

228. Ty, Inc. v. Perryman, 306 F.3d 509, 513 (7th Cir. 2002), *cert. denied,* 538 U.S. 971 (2003).

229. *See, e.g.,* Triangle Publications v. Knight-Ridder Newspaper, Inc., 626 F.2d 1171 (5th Cir. 1978).

230. Deere & Co. v. MTD Products, Inc., 41 F.3d 39 (2d Cir. 1994).

231. 15 U.S.C. § 1114(1).

232. Brother Records Inc. v. Jardine, 318 F.3d 900 (9th Cir.), *cert. denied,* 540 U.S. 824 (2003).

233. *See* Applicant of E. I. DuPont de Nemours & Co., 476 F.2d 1357, 1361 (C.C.P.A. 1973).

234. 15 U.S.C. §§ 1125(c), 1127.

235. ANNE GILSON LALONDE ET AL., GILSON ON TRADEMARKS § 5A.01[5], [6].

236. Moseley v. V Secret Catalogue, Inc., 537 U.S. 418 (2003).

237. *Id.* at 434.

238. 15 U.S.C. § 1115(b).

239. 15 U.S.C. § 115(b)(4).

240. *In re* Dual-Deck Video Cassette Recorder Antitrust Litigation, 11 F.3d 1460 (9th Cir. 1993).

241. New Kids on the Block v. News American Publishing, Inc., 971 F.2d 302 (9th Cir. 1992).

242. 15 U.S.C. § 1125(c)(3).

Chapter 14

Advertising

1. Va. State Board of Pharmacy v. Va. Citizens Consumer Council, 425 U.S. 748, 762, 763, 764 (1976).

2. *See, e.g.,* ALEXANDER MEIKLEJOHN, FREE SPEECH AND ITS RELATION TO SELF-GOVERNMENT (1948).

3. Valentine v. Chrestensen, 316 U.S. 52, 54 (1942).

4. *Id.*

5. New York Times v. Sullivan, 376 U.S. 254, 266 (1964).

6. *Id.*

7. Pittsburgh Press Co. v. Pittsburgh Commission on Human Relations, 413 U.S. 376 (1973).

8. *Id.* at 389.

9. Roe v. Wade, 412 U.S. 113 (1973).

10. Bigelow v. Virginia, 421 U.S. 809, 822 (1975).

11. *Id.* at 817.

12. *Id.* at 820.

13. *Id.*

14. 447 U.S. 557 (1980).

15. 492 U.S. 469 (1989).

16. *Id.* at 480.

17. Rubin v. Coors Brewing Co., 514 U.S. 476, 490 (1995).

18. 44 Liquormart, Inc. v. Rhode Island, 517 U.S. 484, 507 (1996).

19. Lorillard Tobacco Co. v. Reilly, 533 U.S. 525, 569 (2001).

20. *Id.* at 558.

21. Coyne Beahm, Inc. v. FDA, 966 F. Supp. 1374 (M.D.N.C. 1997).

22. Capital Broadcasting Co. v. Mitchell, 333 F. Supp. 582 (D.D.C. 1971).

23. United States v. Edge Broadcasting, 509 U.S. 418, 428 (1993).

24. *Id.* at 441.

25. Greater New Orleans Broadcasting Assn., Inc. v. U.S., 527 U.S. 173 (1999).

26. *See, e.g.,* Bates v. State Bar of Arizona, 433 U.S. 350 (1977). "We recognize, of course, and commend the spirit of public service with which the profession of law is practiced and to which it is dedicated. The present Members of this Court, licensed attorneys all, could not feel otherwise and we would have reason to pause if we felt that our decision today would undercut that spirit." *Id.* at 368.

27. Bates v. State Bar of Arizona, 433 U.S. 350 (1977).

28. First National Bank of Boston v. Bellotti, 435 U.S. 765 (1978).

29. *See, e.g.,* Federal Election Commission v. National Right to Work Committee, 459 U.S. 197 (1982); Federal Election Commission v. National Conservative Political Action Committee, 470 U.S. 480 (1985); Federal Election Commission v. Massachusetts Citizens for Life, Inc., 479 U.S. 238 (1986); and Austin v. Michigan State Chamber of Commerce, 494 U.S. 652 (1990).

30. Kasky v. Nike, Inc., 45 P.3d 243, 258 (Cal. 2002).

31. *Id.* at 263.

32. Nike, Inc. v. Kasky, 539 U.S. 654, 667 (2003) (Breyer, J., dissenting).

33. 130 S. Ct. 876 (2010).

34. 15 U.S.C. 1125, § 43 (a)(1)(A)(B).

35. U-Haul International, Inc. v. Jartran, Inc., 793 F.2d 1034 (9th Cir. 1986).

36. The Division of Advertising Practices, n.d., *available at* http://consumerprotection.uslegal.com.

37. Roscoe B. Starek, III, *Myths and Half-Truths About Deceptive Advertising,* address to the National Infomercial Marketing Association, Oct. 15, 1996, available at www .ftc.gov/speeches/starek/nima96d4.htm.

38. *Id.*

39. *Three Home Loan Advertisers Settle FTC Charges; Failed to Disclose Key Loan Terms in Ads,* Federal Trade Commission: Jan. 8, 2009, *available at* http://www.ftc.gov/ opa/2009/01/anm.shtm.

40. *Id.*

41. *Rite Aid Settles FTC Charges That It Failed to Protect Medical and Financial Privacy of Customers and Employees,* FTC News Release, July 27, 2010 (http:// www.ftc.gov/opa/2010/07/riteaid.shtm).

42. U.S. v. Williams, Co., 498 F.2d 414 (2d Cir. 1975).

43. Lesley Fair, *Substantiation: The Science of Compliance,* n.d. , *available at* http://business.ftc.gov/documents/ substantiation-science-compliance).

44. Warner-Lambert Co. v. FTC, 562 F.2d 749 (1977), *cert. denied,* 435 U.S. 950 (1978).

45. *Id.* at 762.

46. *Id.* at 764.

47. In the Matter of Tropicana Products, Inc., Federal Trade Commission Complaint, Docket No. C-4145 (2005), *available at* http://www.ftc.gov/os/caselist/0423154/05082 5comp0423154.pdf).

48. *FTC Charges Marketers with Making Unsubstantiated Claims That They Could Eliminate Consumers' Debt,* Dec. 2, 2010, *available at* http://www.ftc.gov/opa/2010/12/ffdc .shtm

49. *Enforcement Action Plan for Promotion and Advertising Restrictions,* FDA, Oct. 2010, *available at* http://www.fda.govdownloads/TobaccoProducts/ GuidanceComplianceRegulatoryInformation/UCM227882 .pdf).

50. FTC v. Corzine, No. Civ.-S-94–1446 (E.D. Ca. 1994).

51. *FTC Testifies on Do Not Track Legislation,* Dec. 2, 2010, *available at* http://www.ftc.gov/opa/2010/12/dnttestimony .shtm).

52. *Microsoft Adds "Do Not Track" Option to Internet Explorer 9,* NPR, Dec. 8, 2010, *available at* (http://www .npr.org/blogs/alltechconsidered/2010/12/09/131914019/ microsoft-ads-do-not-track-option-to-internet-explorer-9).

53. 15 U.S.C. §§ 7701–7713 (2004).

54. *FTC Approves New Rule Provision Under the CAN-SPAM Act,* Federal Trade Commission, May 12, 2008, *available at* http://www.ftc.govopa/2008/05/canspam. shtm.

55. Amit Asaravala, *With This Law, You Can Spam,* Wired News, Jan. 23, 2004, *available at* http://www.wired.com/ news/business/0,1367,62020,00.html?tw=wn_story_ related.

56. Carolyn Duffy Marsan, *CAN-SPAM: What Went Wrong?* Network World, Oct. 6, 2008, *available at* http://www .networkworld.com/news/2008/100608-can-spam.html.

57. These states are Alaska, Arizona, Arkansas, California, Colorado, Connecticut, Delaware, Florida, Georgia, Idaho, Illinois, Indiana, Iowa, Kansas, Louisiana, Maine, Maryland, Michigan, Minnesota, Missouri, Nevada, New Mexico, North Carolina, North Dakota, Ohio, Oklahoma, Pennsylvania, Rhode Island, South Dakota, Tennessee, Texas, Utah, Virginia, Washington, West Virginia, Wisconsin and Wyoming.

58. Va. Code Ann. § 18.2–152.3:1.

59. *See Virginia: Spam Law Struck Down on Grounds of Free Speech,* N.Y. Times, Sept. 13, 2008, at A17.

60. Jaynes v. Commonwealth of Virginia, 276 Va. 443, 464 (2008), *cert. denied,* 129 S. Ct. 1670 (2009).

61. Virginia v. Jaynes, 129 S. Ct. 1670 (2009).

Glossary

A

absolute privilege A complete exemption from liability for the speaking or publishing of defamatory words of and concerning another because the statement was made within the performance of duty such as in judicial or political contexts.

actual malice In libel law, a statement made knowing it is false or with reckless disregard for its truth.

ad hoc balancing Making decisions according to the specific facts of the case under review rather than more general principles.

administrative law The orders, rules and regulations promulgated by executive branch administrative agencies to carry out their delegated duties.

admonitions Judges' instructions to jurors warning them to avoid potentially prejudicial communications.

advisory opinion In advertising, a Federal Trade Commission measure that suggests to an advertiser how specific advertisement may be false or misleading and how to correct it.

affirm To ratify, uphold or approve a lower-court ruling.

all-purpose public figure In libel law, a person who occupies a position of such persuasive power and influence as to be deemed a public figure for all purposes. Public figure libel plaintiffs are required to prove actual malice.

amicus brief A submission to the court from an amicus curiae, or "friend of the court," an interested individual or organization who is not a party in the case.

appellant The party making the appeal; also called the petitioner.

appellee The party against whom an appeal is made.

appropriation Using a person's name, picture, likeness, voice or identity for commercial or trade purposes without permission.

artistic relevance test A test to determine whether the use of a celebrity's name, picture, likeness, voice or identity is relevant to a disputed work's artistic purpose. It is used in cases regarding the infringement of a celebrity's right of publicity.

as applied A phrase referring to interpretation of a statute on the basis of actual effects on the parties.

B

Berne Convention The primary international copyright treaty that many countries adopted in 1886 but that the United States adopted only in 1988.

black-letter law Formally enacted, written law that is available in legal reporters or other documents.

bootstrapping In libel law, the forbidden practice of a defendant claiming that the plaintiff is a public figure solely on the basis of the statement that is the reason for the lawsuit.

burden of proof The requirement for a party to a case to demonstrate one or more claims by the presentation of evidence. In libel law, for example, the plaintiff has the burden of proof.

C

categorical balancing The process through which courts reach judgments by weighing different broad categories, such as political speech, against other categories of interests, such as privacy. The rules may be applied in later cases with similar facts.

cease and desist order An administrative agency order prohibiting a person or business from continuing a particular course of conduct. For example, the Federal Trade Commission may order an advertiser to cease and desist from misleading consumers with its advertising.

child pornography   Any image showing children in sexual or sexually explicit situations.

chilling effect   The discouragement of a constitutional right, especially free speech, by any practice that creates uncertainty about the proper exercise of that right. civil contempt Acts, generally outside the courtroom, that defy court orders or obstruct court proceedings, such as failure to comply with a subpoena to appear in court; sometimes called "indirect contempt."

clear and present danger   Doctrine establishing that restrictions on First Amendment rights will be upheld if they are necessary to prevent an extremely serious and imminent harm.

commercialization   The appropriation tort used to protect people who want privacy.

common law   Unwritten, judge-made law consisting of rules and principles developed through custom and precedent.

Communications Decency Act (CDA)   The part of the 1996 Telecommunications Act that largely attempted to regulate Internet content. The CDA was successfully challenged in *Reno v. ACLU* (1997).

compelling interest   A government interest of the highest order, an interest the government is required to protect.

concurring opinion   A separate opinion of a minority of the court or a single justice agreeing with the majority opinion but applying different reasoning or legal principles.

conditional (or qualified) privilege   An exemption from liability for repeating defamatory words of and concerning another because the original statement was made within the performance of duty such as in judicial or political contexts; usually claimed by journalists who report statements made in absolutely privileged situations; this privilege is conditional (or qualified) on the premise that the reporting is fair and accurate.

consent order   In advertising, an agreement between the Federal Trade Commission and an advertiser stipulating the terms that must be followed to address problematic advertising; also called a consent agreement.

constitutional law   The set of laws that establish the nature, functions and limits of government.

contempt of court   Any act that is judged to hinder or obstruct a court in its administration of justice. For example, journalists may be cited for contempt of court for refusing to disclose information.

content-based laws   Laws enacted because of the message, the subject matter or the ideas expressed in the regulated speech.

content-neutral laws   Laws that incidentally and unintentionally affect speech as they advance other important government interests.

Continuance   Postponement of a trial to a later time.

copyright   An exclusive legal right used to protect intellectual creations from unauthorized use.

corrective advertising   In advertising, a requirement imposed by the Federal Trade Commission forcing an advertiser to include information in future advertisements that corrects false or misleading claims made in previous ads.

criminal contempt   Conduct in or near a court that willfully disregards, disobeys or interferes with the court's authority; sometimes called "direct contempt."

D

damages   Monetary compensation that may be recovered in court by any person who has suffered loss or injury. Damages may be compensatory for actual loss or punitive as punishment for outrageous conduct.

defamation   A false communication that harms another's reputation and subjects him or her to ridicule and scorn; incorporates both libel and slander.

defendant   The party accused of violating a law, or the party being sued in a civil lawsuit.

deference   An act in which courts give weight to the judgment of expert administrative agencies or legislative policies and strategies.

demurrer   A request that a court dismiss a case on the grounds that although the claims are true they are insufficient to warrant a judgment against the defendant.

de novo   Literally, "anew" or "over again." On appeal, the court may review the facts de novo rather than simply reviewing the legal posture and process of the case.

deposition   Testimony by a witness conducted outside a courtroom and intended to be used in preparation for trial.

designated public forum   Government spaces or buildings that are available for public use (within limits).

discovery   The pretrial process of gathering evidence and facts. The word also may refer to the specific items of evidence that are uncovered.

discretion   The authority to determine the proper outcome.

dissenting opinion   A separate opinion of a minority of the court or a single justice disagreeing with the result reached by the majority and challenging the majority's reasoning or legal basis.

distinguish from precedent   To justify an outcome in a case by asserting that differences between that case and preceding cases outweigh any similarities.

doctrines   Principles or theories of law (e.g., the doctrine of content neutrality).

Driver's Privacy Protection Act   Federal legislation that prohibits states from disclosing personal information that drivers submit in order to obtain drivers' licenses.

due process   Fair legal proceedings. Due process is guaranteed by the Fifth and Fourteenth Amendments to the U.S. Constitution.

E

Electronic Freedom of Information Act (EFOIA)   A 1996 amendment to the Freedom of Information Act (FOIA) that updates the act by including electronically stored information and subjecting it to the FOIA's provisions.

emotional distress   Serious mental anguish.

en banc   Literally, "on the bench" but now meaning "in full court." The judges of a circuit court of appeals will sit en banc to decide important or controversial cases.

equity law   Law created by judges to apply general principles of ethics and fairness, rather than specific legal rules, to determine the proper remedy for legal harm.

establishment clause   The portion of the First Amendment that prohibits government from setting up an official religion or passing laws that favor a specific religious doctrine.

executive orders   Orders from a government executive, such as the president, a governor or a mayor, that have the force of law.

experience and logic test   A doctrine that determines the presumptive openness of judicial proceedings on the basis of their history and the role openness plays in assuring the credibility of the process.

F

facial challenges   A broad legal claim based on the argument that the challenged law or government policy can never operate in compliance with the Constitution.

facial meaning   The surface, apparent or obvious meaning of a legal text.

fact finder   In a trial, a judge or the jury determining which facts presented in evidence are accurate.

fair comment and criticism   A common law privilege that protects critics from lawsuits brought by individuals in the public eye.

fair report privilege   A privilege claimed by journalists who report events on the basis of official records. The report must fairly and accurately reflect the content of the records; this is the condition that sometimes leads to this privilege being called "conditional privilege."

fair use   A test courts use to determine whether using another's copyrighted material without permission is fair or an infringement. Fair use test is also used in trademark infringement cases.

false light   A privacy tort that involves making a person seem in the public eye to be someone he or she is not. Several states do not allow false light suits.

Family Educational Rights and Privacy Act (FERPA)   A federal law that protects the privacy of student education records. The law applies to all schools that receive funds under an applicable program of the U.S. Department of Education; FERPA gives parents certain rights with respect to their children's school records; these rights transfer to the student when he or she reaches the age of 18 or attends a school beyond the high school level.

Federal Communications Commission (FCC)   An independent U.S. government agency, directly responsible to Congress, charged with regulating interstate and international communications by radio, television, wire, satellite and cable. The FCC was established by the Communications Act of 1934; its jurisdiction covers the 50 states, the District of Columbia and U.S. possessions.

Federal Radio Commission (FRC)   A federal agency established by the Federal Radio Act in 1927 to oversee radio broadcasting. The FRC was succeeded by the Federal Communications Commission in 1934.

Federal Trade Commission (FTC)   A federal agency created in 1914. Its purpose is to promote free and fair competition in interstate commerce; this includes preventing false and misleading advertising.

federalism   A principle according to which the states are related to yet independent of each other, and related to yet independent of the federal government.

fiduciary relationship   A legal duty or responsibility one party owes to another when the parties are in certain relationships with each other.

fighting words   Words not protected by the First Amendment because they cause immediate harm or illegal acts.

for-cause challenge   In the context of jury selection, the ability of attorneys to remove a potential juror for a reason the law finds sufficient, as opposed to a peremptory challenge.

forum shopping   A plaintiff choosing a court in which to sue because he or she believes the court will rule in the plaintiff's favor.

franchise   A contract or agreement between a government, usually a city, and a cable system operator.

franchise fees   The charges cable companies pay to franchising authorities for the right to use public rights-of-way.

franchising authority   The governmental unit granting a franchise to a cable system operator; usually a city, but may also be a state or county.

Freedom of Information Act (FOIA)   The 1966 act that provides for making information held by federal government agencies available to the public, provided that the information sought does not fall within one of nine exempted categories.

G

gag orders   A nonlegal term used to describe court orders that prohibit publication or discussion of specific materials.

generally applicable law   A law that is enforced evenly, across the board. Within First Amendment contexts, it is the idea that the freedom of the press clause does not exempt journalists and news organizations from obeying laws.

Government in the Sunshine Act   Sometimes referred to as the Federal Open Meetings Law, an act passed in 1976 that mandates that meetings of federal government agencies be open to the public unless all or some part of a meeting is exempted according to exceptions outlined in the law.

grand jury   A group summoned to hear the state's evidence in criminal cases and decide whether a crime was committed and whether charges should be filed; grand juries do not determine guilt. A grand jury may be convened on the county, state or federal level; with 12 to 23 members, grand juries are usually larger than trial juries.

H

habeas corpus   A court order requiring the government to present a detained person to the court and to show legal grounds for the person's detention.

hate speech   A category of speech that includes name-calling and pointed criticism that demeans others on the basis of race, color, gender, ethnicity, religion, national origin, disability, intellect or the like.

heckler's veto   A First Amendment concept that generally favors the right of an orderly speaker over the right of an offended or antagonized member of the audience.

Hicklin rule   A rule taken from a mid-19th-century English case and used in the United States until the mid-20th century that defines material as obscene if it tends to corrupt children.

holding   The decision or ruling of a court.

I

impanel   To select and seat a jury.

important government interest   An interest of the government that is substantial or significant (i.e., more than merely convenient or reasonable) but not compelling.

incorporation   The Fourteenth Amendment concept that most of the Bill of Rights applies equally to the states.

indecency   A narrow legal term referring to sexual expression inappropriate for children on broadcast radio and television.

industry guides   In advertising, a Federal Trade Commission measure that outlines the FTC's policies concerning a particular category of product or service.

injunction A court order prohibiting a person or organization from doing some specified act.

innocent construction Allegedly libelous words that are capable of being interpreted, or construed, to have an innocent meaning are not libelous, so long as that interpretation is a reasonable one.

intellectual property law The legal category including copyright, trademark and patent law.

intentional infliction of emotional distress Extreme and outrageous intentional or reckless conduct causing plaintiff severe emotional harm; public official and public figure plaintiff also must show actual malice on defendant's part.

intermediate scrutiny A standard applied by the courts to the review of laws that implicate core constitutional values; also called heightened review.

intrusion upon seclusion Physically or technologically disturbing another's reasonable expectation of privacy.

involuntary public figure In libel law, a person who does not necessarily thrust himself or herself into public controversies voluntarily but is drawn into a given issue.

J

judicial review The power of the courts to determine the meaning of the language of the Constitution and to assure that no laws violate constitutional dictates.

jurisdiction The geographic or topical area of responsibility and authority of a court.

L

Lanham Act A federal law that regulates the trademark registration process, but that also contains a section permitting business competitors to sue one another for false advertising.

laws of general application Laws such as tax and equal employment laws that fall within the express power of government. Laws of general application are generally reviewed under minimum scrutiny.

legislative history Congressional reports and records containing discussions about proposed legislation.

libel per quod A statement whose injurious nature requires proof.

libel per se A statement whose injurious nature is apparent and requires no further proof.

libel-proof plaintiff A plaintiff whose reputation is deemed to be so damaged already that additional false statements of and concerning him or her cannot cause further harm.

limited-purpose public figure In libel law, those plaintiffs who have attained public figure status within a narrow set of circumstances by thrusting themselves to the forefront of particular public controversies in order to influence the resolution of the issues involved; this kind of public figure is more common than the all-purpose public figure.

litigated order A Federal Trade Commission order to stop a specific advertising claim. If the order is upheld in an administrative court, the advertiser may appeal to a federal court; once the appeal process has been exhausted, failing to abide by an order's stipulations can have serious consequences, including fines of up to $10,000 per day.

lowest unit rate The maximum rate a broadcaster or cable system may charge a politician for advertising time during the 45 days before primary elections and the 60 days before general elections.

M

mechanical license Permission to record a composition.

memorandum order An order announcing the vote of the Supreme Court without providing an opinion.

modify precedent To change or revise rather than follow or reject precedent.

moot Word used to describe a case in which the issues presented are no longer "live" or in which the matter in dispute has already been resolved; a case is not moot if it is susceptible to repetition but evading review.

moral rights Under U.S. copyright law, the rights of certain artists—creators of paintings, drawings, prints, sculptures and art photographs—to require that their name be associated with their works, forbid others from claiming to be creators of the works, and prevent intentional harm to or modification of a work that would harm the artist's reputation.

motion to dismiss   A request to a court for a complaint to be rejected because it does not state a claim that can be remedied by law or because it is legally lacking in some other way.

N

negligence   Generally, the failure to exercise reasonable or ordinary care. In libel law, negligence is usually the minimum level of fault a plaintiff must prove in order to receive damages.

negligent infliction of emotional distress   Owing a duty to a plaintiff, breaching that duty and causing the plaintiff severe emotional harm.

neutral reportage   In libel law, a defense accepted in some jurisdictions that says when an accusation is made by a responsible and prominent organization, reporting that accusation is protected by the First Amendment even when it turns out the accusation was false and libelous.

nonduplication rules   FCC regulations requiring cable systems not to carry certain programming that is available through local broadcast stations.

nonpublic forum   Government-held property that is not available for public speech and assembly purposes.

Notice of Proposed Rule Making   A notice issued by the FCC announcing that the commission is considering changing certain of its regulations or adopting new rules.

O

O'Brien test   A three-part test used to determine whether a content-neutral law is constitutional.

opinion letter   A letter requested by an advertiser from the Federal Trade Commission containing advice about an advertising technique.

originalists   Supreme Court justices who interpret the Constitution according to the perceived intent of its framers.

original intent   The perceived intent of the framers of the First Amendment. The concept of original intent guides contemporary First Amendment application and interpretation.

original jurisdiction   The authority to consider a case at its inception, as contrasted with appellate jurisdiction.

originalist   Supreme Court justices who interpret the Constitution according to the perceived intent of its framers.

overbroad law   Law that violates the principles of precision and specificity in legislation.

overrule   To reverse the ruling of a lower court.

overturn precedent   To reject the fundamental premise of a precedent.

P

patently offensive   Term describing material with hard-core sexual conduct.

PEG access channels   Channels that cable systems set aside for public, educational and government use.

per curiam opinion   An unsigned opinion by the court as a whole.

peremptory challenge   During jury selection, a challenge in which an attorney rejects a juror without showing a reason. Attorneys have the right to eliminate a limited number of jurors through peremptory challenges.

plagiarism   Using another's work or ideas without attribution.

plaintiff   The party who files a complaint; the one who sues.

'political questions'   Questions that the courts will not review because they are either outside the jurisdiction of the court or they are not capable of judicial resolution; an issue that can and should be handled more appropriately by another branch of government.

pornography   A vague—not legally precise—term for sexually-oriented material.

precedent   Case judgment that establishes binding authority and guiding principles for cases to follow on closely analogous questions of law within the court's jurisdiction.

predominant use test   In a right-of-publicity lawsuit, did the defendant use the plaintiff's name or picture more for commercial purposes or protected expression.

Premptory challenge   During jury selection, a challenge in which an attorney rejects a juror without showing a reason. Attorneys have the right to eliminate a limited number of jurors through peremptory challenges.

prior restraint   Action taken by the government to prohibit publication of a specific document or text before it is distributed to the public; a policy that requires government approval before publication.

private facts   The tort under which media are sued for publishing highly embarrassing private information that is not newsworthy or lawfully obtained from a public record.

private figure   In libel law, a plaintiff who cannot be categorized as either a public figure or public official. Generally, a private figure is not required to prove actual malice in order to recover damages, but merely negligence on the part of the defendant.

probable cause   The standard of evidence needed for an arrest or to issue a search warrant. More than mere suspicion, it is a showing through reasonably trustworthy information that a crime has been or is being committed.

promissory estoppel   A legal doctrine requiring liability when a clear and unambiguous promise is made and is relied on, and injury results from the breaking of the promise.

proximate cause   Determining if it is reasonable to conclude the defendant's actions led to the plaintiff's injury.

prurient interests   Lustful thoughts or sexual desires.

public domain   The sphere that includes material not protected by copyright law and therefore available for use without the creator's permission.

public figure   In libel law, a plaintiff who is in the public spotlight, usually voluntarily, and must prove the defendant acted with actual malice in order to win damages.

public forum   Government property held for use by the public, usually for purposes of exercising rights of speech and assembly.

public record   A government record, particularly one that is publicly available.

puffery   Advertising that exaggerates the merits of products or services in such a way that no reasonable person would take the ad seriously. Usually, puffery is not illegal given that a reasonable person understands the claim is not to be taken literally.

Q

quash   To nullify or annul, as in quashing a subpoena.

R

radio frequencies   The part of the electromagnetic spectrum used to send information, such as voice and pictures.

rational review   A standard of judicial review that assumes the wisdom of reasonable legislative or administrative enactments and applies minimum scrutiny to their review.

reasonable person   The law's version of an average person.

reckless   Word used to describe actions taken with no consideration of the legal harms that might result.

remand   To send a case back to a lower court for further action.

reporter's privilege   The concept that reporters can keep information such as source identity confidential. The idea is that the reporter-source relationship is similar to doctor-patient and lawyer-client relationships.

restraining order   A court order forbidding the defendant from doing a specified act until a hearing can be conducted.

retraction statutes   In libel law, state laws that limit the damages a plaintiff may receive if the defendant had issued a retraction of the material at issue. Retraction statutes are meant to discourage the punishment of any good-faith effort of admitting a mistake.

retransmission consent   Part of the federal cable television law allowing broadcast television stations to negotiate.

ride-along   A term given to the practice of journalists and other private citizens accompanying government officials—usually those in law enforcement or other emergency response personnel—as they carry out their duties.

right of publicity   The appropriation tort protecting a celebrity's right to have his or her name, picture, likeness, voice and identity used for commercial or trade purposes only with permission.

rule of law   The framework of a society in which preestablished norms and procedures provide for consistent, neutral decision making.

S

safe harbor policy   An FCC policy designating 10 p.m. to 6 a.m. as a time when broadcast radio and television stations may air indecent material without violating federal law or FCC regulations.

search warrant   A written order issued by a judge, directed to a law enforcement officer, authorizing the search and seizure of any property for which there is reason to believe it will serve as evidence in a criminal investigation.

Sedition Act of 1798   Federal legislation under which anyone "opposing or resisting any law of the United States, or any act of the President of the United States" could be imprisoned for up to two years. The act also made it illegal to "write, print, utter, or publish" anything that criticized the president or Congress. The act ultimately was seen as a direct violation of the First Amendment and expired in 1801.

seditious libel   Communication meant to incite people to change the government; criticism of the government.

sequestration   The isolation of jurors to avoid prejudice from publicity in a sensational trial.

serious social value   Material cannot be found obscene if it has serious literary, artistic, political or scientific value determined using national, not local, standards.

shield laws   State laws that protect journalists from being found in contempt of court for refusing to reveal a source.

single publication rule   A rule that limits libel victims to only one cause of action even with multiple publications of the libel, common in the mass media and on websites.

slander per quod   A spoken statement whose injurious nature requires proof.

slander per se   A spoken statement whose injurious nature is apparent and requires no further proof.

SLAPP (strategic lawsuits against public participation)   Libel suits whose purpose is to harass critics into silence, often to suppress those critics' First Amendment rights.

sound-alike   Someone whose voice sounds like another person's voice. Sound-alikes may not be used for commercial or trade purposes without permission or a disclaimer.

spectrum scarcity   The limitation that arises because only a certain number of broadcast radio and television stations in a geographical area may use the spectrum without causing interference with other stations' signals. Spectrum scarcity is the primary reason courts give for allowing Congress and the FCC to regulate broadcasters.

standing   The position of a plaintiff who has been injured or has been threatened with injury. No person is entitled to challenge the constitutionality of an ordinance or statute unless he or she has the required standing—that is, unless he or she had been affected by the ordinance or statute.

stare decisis   Literally, "stand by the previous decision."

Statute of Anne   The first copyright law, adopted in England in 1710.

statutory construction   The review of statutes in which courts determine the meaning and application of statutes. Courts tend to engage in strict construction, which narrowly defines laws to their clear letter and intent.

statutory damages   Damages specified in certain laws. Under these laws, copyright being an example, a judge may award statutory damages even if a plaintiff is unable to prove actual damages.

statutory law   Written law formally enacted by city, county, state and federal legislative bodies.

strict liability   Liability without fault; liability for any and all harms, foreseeable or unforeseen, which result from a product or an action.

strict scrutiny   A test for determining the constitutionality of laws restricting speech, under which the government must show it has a compelling interest at stake that is advanced by the least restrictive means available.

subpoena   A command for someone to testify in court.

substantiation   In advertising, the authority of the Federal Trade Commission to demand that an advertiser prove the claims made in its advertisements.

summary judgment   The quick resolution of a legal dispute in which a judge summarily decides certain points and issues a judgment dismissing the case.

summons   A notice asking an individual to appear at a court. Potential jurors receive such a summons.

symbolic expression   Action that warrants First Amendment protection because its primary purpose is to express ideas.

T

textualists   Judges—in particular, Supreme Court justices—who rely exclusively on a careful reading of legal texts to determine the meaning of the law.

time/place/manner (TPM) laws   A First Amendment concept that laws regulating the conditions of speech are more acceptable than those regulating content; also, the laws that regulate these conditions.

tort A private or civil wrong for which a court can provide remedy in the form of damages.

tortious newsgathering The use of reporting techniques that are wrongful and unlawful and for which the victim may obtain damages in court.

trademark A word, name, symbol or design used to identify a company's goods and distinguish them from similar products other companies make.

trade regulation rule A broadly worded statement by the Federal Trade Commission that outlines advertising requirements for a particular trade.

traditional public forum Lands designed for public use and historically used for public gathering, discussion and association (e.g., public streets, sidewalks and parks). Free speech is protected in these areas.

transformativeness test A test to determine whether a creator has transformed a person's name, picture, likeness, voice or identity for artistic purposes. If so, the person cannot win a right-of-publicity suit against the creator.

true threat Speech directed toward one or more specific individuals with the intent of causing listeners to fear for their safety.

U

underinclusive A First Amendment doctrine that disfavors narrow laws that target a subset of a recognized category for discriminatory treatment.

USA PATRIOT Act The Uniting and Strengthening America by Providing Appropriate Tools Required to Intercept and Obstruct Terrorism Act of 2001. Passed in the wake of the Sept. 11 attacks, the act was designed to give law enforcement agencies greater authority to combat terrorism.

V

vague laws Laws that either fail to define their terms or use such general language that neither citizens nor judges know with certainty what the laws permit or punish.

variable obscenity A concept that sexually-oriented material would not meet the definition of obscenity if distributed to adults but would be found obscene if distributed to minors.

venire Literally, "to come" or "to appear"; the term used for the location from which a court draws its pool of potential jurors, who must then appear in court for voir dire. Thus, a change of venire means a change of the location from which potential jurors are drawn.

venue The locality of a lawsuit and of the court hearing the suit. Thus, a change of venue means a relocation of a trial.

viewpoint-based discrimination Government censorship or punishment of expression based on the ideas or attitudes expressed. Courts will apply a strict scrutiny test to determine whether the government acted constitutionally.

voir dire Literally, "to speak the truth"; the questioning of prospective jurors to assess their suitability.

voluntary compliance In advertising, the opportunity granted by the Federal Trade Commission to an advertiser to abide by the FTC's rules.

W

work made for hire Work created when working for another person or company. The copyright in a work made for hire belongs to the employer, not the creator.

Wiretap Act A federal law initially passed in 1968 to protect the privacy of phone calls and other oral conversations. It has been amended and updated several times, largely to keep up with the changing communications landscape. The law makes it illegal to intercept, record, disseminate or use a private communication without one party's permission. The consenting person has to be a party to the conversation. Tapping into other people's phone calls violates the wiretap law. The federal wiretap law allows the government to bring criminal charges and those whose privacy was violated to sue for civil damages.

writ of certiorari A petition for review by the Supreme Court of the United States; *certiorari* means "to be informed of."

Z

Zapple rule A political broadcasting rule that allows a candidate's supporters equal opportunity to use broadcast stations if the candidate's opponents' supporters use the stations.

Recommended Readings

1. The Rule of Law

Bingham, Tom. *The Rule of Law*. New York & London: Penguin Global (2010).

Casper, Gerhard. *Separating Powers: Essays on the Founding Period*. Cambridge, Mass.: Harvard University Press (1997).

Cass, Ronald A. *The Rule of Law in America*. Baltimore: Johns Hopkins University Press (2001).

Clouatre, Douglas. *Presidents and Their Justices*. Lanham, Md.: University Press of America (2011).

Raz, Joseph. *The Authority of Law*. New York: Oxford University Press (1979).

Scarry, Elaine. *Rule of Law, Misrule of Me*n. Boston: MIT Press (2010).

Tamanaha, Brian Z. *Law as a Means to an End: Threat to the Rule of Law*. New York: Cambridge University Press (2006).

Toobin, Jeffrey. *The Nine: Inside the Secret World of the Supreme Court*. New York: Doubleday (2007).

2. The First Amendment

Amar, Akhil Reed. *The Bill of Rights: Creation and Reconstruction*. New Haven, Conn.: Yale University Press (2000).

Chafee, Zechariah. *Free Speech in the United States*. Cambridge, Mass.: Harvard University Press (1941).

Fish, Stanley. *There's No Such Thing as Free Speech, and It's a Good Thing, Too*. New York: Oxford University Press (1994).

Friendly, Fred. *Minnesota Rag: Corruption, Yellow Journalism, and the Case that Saved Freedom of the Press*. Minneapolis: University of Minnesota Press (reprint ed. 2003).

Pasley, Jeffrey L. *"The Tyranny of Printers": Newspaper Politics in the Early American Republic*. Charlottesville, Va.: University of Virginia Press (2001).

Pool, Ithiel de Sola. *Technologies Without Boundaries: On Telecommunications in a Global Age*. Cambridge, Mass.: Harvard University Press (1990).

Rudenstine, David. *The Day the Presses Stopped: A History of the Pentagon Papers Case*. Berkeley, Calif.: University of California Press (1996).

Sunstein, Cass R. *Democracy and the Problem of Free Speech*. New York: Free Press (1993).

Sunstein, Cass R. *A Constitution of Many Minds: Why the Founding Document Doesn't Mean What It Meant Before*. Princeton, N.J.: Princeton University Press (2009).

Zick, Timothy. *Speech Out of Doors: Preserving First Amendment Liberties in Public Places*. New York: Cambridge University Press (2009).

3. Speech Distinctions

Bollinger, Lee C. & Geoffrey R. Stone (eds.). *Eternally Vigilant: Free Speech in the Modern Era*. Chicago: University of Chicago Press (2002).

Chang, Nancy. *Silencing Political Dissent: How Post-September 11 Anti-Terrorism Measures Threaten Our Civil Liberties*. New York: Seven Stories Press (2002).

Cleary, Edward J. *Beyond the Burning Cross: The First Amendment and the Landmark R.A.V. Case*. New York: Random House (1994).

Cohen-Almagor, Raphael. *The Scope of Tolerance: Studies on the Costs of Free Expression and Freedom of the Press*. New York: Routledge (2006).

Finan, Christopher M. *From the Palmer Raids to the Patriot Act: A History of the Fight for Free Speech in America*. Boston, Mass.: Beacon Press (2007).

Foster, James. *Bong Hits 4 Jesus: A Perfect Constitutional Storm in Alaska's Capital*. Fairbanks, Alaska: University of Alaska Press (2010).

Freeberg, Ernest. *Democracy's Prisoner: Eugene V. Debs, the Great War, and the Right to Dissent.* Cambridge, Mass.: Harvard University Press (2008).

Lewis, Anthony. *Freedom for the Thought That We Hate: A Biography of the First Amendment.* New York: Basic Books (2010).

Shiell, Timothy. *Campus Hate Speech on Trial.* Lawrence, Kan.: University of Kansas Press (2d ed. 2009).

Stone, Geoffrey R. *Perilous Times: Free Speech in Wartime from the Sedition Act of 1798 to the War on Terrorism.* New York: W. W. Norton (2004).

New York Times v. Sullivan, 9 VAND. J. ENT. & TECH. L. 551 (2007).

Kirchmeier, Jeffrey L. *The Illusion of the Fact-Opinion Distinction in Defamation Law,* 39 CASE W. RES. 867 (1989).

Laidman, Dan. *When the Slander Is the Story: The Neutral Report Privilege in Theory and Practice,* 17 UCLA ENT. L. REV. 74 (2010).

Rothfeld, Charles. *The Surprising Case Against Punitive Damages in Libel Suits Against Public Figures,* 19 YALE L. & POL'Y REV. 165 (2000).

Sack, Robert D. *Protection of Opinion Under the First Amendment,* 100 COLUM. L. REV. 294 (2000).

4. Libel: The Plaintiff's Case

Bernstein Ellen., *Libel Tourism's Final Boarding Call,* 20 SETON HALL J. SPORTS & ENT. L. 205 (2010).

Forde, Kathy Roberts. *Literary Journalism on Trial: Masson v. New Yorker and the First Amendment.* Amherst, Mass.: University of Massachusetts Press (2008).

Lewis, Anthony. *Make No Law: The Sullivan Case and the First Amendment.* New York: Random House (1991).

McNamara, Lawrence. *Reputation and Defamation.* New York: Oxford University Press (2007).

Milo, Dario. *Defamation and Freedom of Speech.* New York: Oxford University Press (2008).

Sack, Robert D. *Sack on Defamation: Libel, Slander, and Related Problems.* New York: Practicing Law Institute (4th ed. 2010).

Schachter, Madeleine & Joel Kurtzberg. *Law of Internet Speech.* Durham, N.C.: Carolina Academic Press (3d ed. 2008).

Smolla, Rodney A. *The Law of Defamation.* St. Paul, Minn.: West Group (2d ed. 2010).

Solove, Daniel J. *The Future of Reputation: Gossip, Rumor, and Privacy on the Internet.* New Haven, Conn.: Yale University Press (2007).

5. Libel: Defenses and Privileges

Ehrenfeld, Rachel. *A Legal Thriller in London,* NEWSWEEK, June 7, 2010, at 12.

Elder, David A. *Truth, Accuracy and "Neutral Reportage": Beheading the Media Jabberwock's Attempts to Circumvent*

6. Protecting Privacy

Cate, Fred H. *The Privacy Problem: A Broader View of Information Privacy and the Costs and Consequences of Protecting It.* Nashville, Tenn.: First Amendment Center (2003).

Friedman, Lawrence M. *Guarding Life's Dark Secrets: Legal and Social Controls over Reputation, Propriety, and Privacy.* Stanford, Calif.: Stanford University Press (2007).

Jasper, Margaret C. *Privacy and the Internet: Your Expectations and Rights under the Law.* N.Y.: Oxford University Press (2009).

Klosek, Jacqueline. *The War on Privacy.* Westport, Conn.: Praeger (2007).

Osorio, Andrew. Note, *Twilight: The Fading of False Light Invasion of Privacy,* 66 N.Y.U. ANN. SURV. AM. L. 173 (2010).

Rosen, Jeffrey. *The Unwanted Gaze: The Destruction of Privacy in America.* New York: Random House (2000).

Solove, Daniel J. *Privacy, Information, and Technology.* New York: Aspen Pub. (2009).

Solove, Daniel J. *Understanding Privacy.* Cambridge, Mass.: Harvard University Press (2008).

7. Emotional Distress and Physical Harm

Anderson, David A. *Incitement and Tort Law,* 37 WAKE FOREST L. REV. 957 (2002).

Calvert, Clay. *War, Death, Politics and Religion: An Emotionally Distressing Amalgamation for Freedom of Speech and the Expression of Opinion,* 30 WHITTIER L. REV. 207 (2008).

Gilles, Susan M. *"Poisonous" Publications and Other False Speech Physical Harm Cases*, 37 WAKE FOREST L. REV. 1073 (2002).

Kunich, John Charles. *Shock Torts Reloaded*, 6 APPALACHIAN J.L. 1 (2006).

Malloy, S. Elizabeth Wilborn. *Taming Terrorists But Not "Natural Born Killers,"* 27 N. KY. L. REV. 81 (2000).

Smolla, Rodney. *Deliberate Intent: A Lawyer Tells the True Story of Murder by the Book*. New York: Crown Pub. (1999).

Smolla, Rodney. Jerry Falwell v. Larry Flynt: *The First Amendment on Trial*. New York: St. Martin's Press (1988).

Volokh, Eugene, *Freedom of Speech and the Intentional Infliction of Emotional Distress Tort*, 2010 CARDOZO L. REV. DE NOVO 300.

Wood, L. Lin & Corey Fleming Hirokawa. *Shot by the Messenger: Rethinking Media Liability for Violence Induced by Extremely Violent Publications and Broadcasts*, 27 N. KY. L. REV. 47 (2000).

8. Newsgathering

Bezanson, Randall P. *How Free Can the Press Be?* Urbana, Ill.: University of Illinois Press (2003).

Birkinshaw, Patrick. *Freedom of Information: The Law, the Practice, and the Ideal*. Charlottesville, Va.: Michie (3d ed. 2008).

Cuillier, David & Charles N. Davis, *The Art of Access: Strategies for Acquiring Public Records*. Washington, D.C.: CQ Press (2011).

Davis, Charles N. & Sigman L. Splichal (eds.). *Access Denied: Freedom of Information in the Information Age*. Ames, Iowa: Iowa State University Press (2000).

Klosek, Jacqueline. *The Right to Know: Your Guide to Using and Defending Freedom of Information Law in the United States*. Santa Barbara, Calif.: Praeger/ABC-CLIO (2009).

Melanson, Philip H. *Secrecy Wars: National Security, Privacy, and the Public's Right to Know*. Washington, D.C.: Brassey's (2001).

Montgomery, Bruce P. *The Bush-Cheney Administration's Assault on Open Government*. Westport, Conn.: Praeger (2008).

Stewart, Daxton R. *Let the Sunshine In, or Else: An Examination of the "Teeth" of State and Federal Open Meetings and Open Records Laws*, 15 COMM. L. & POL'Y 265 (2010).

9. Reporter's Privilege

Berger, Linda L. *Shielding the Unmedia: Using the Process of Journalism to Protect the Journalist's Privilege in an Infinite Universe of Publication*, 39 HOUSTON L. REV. 1371 (2003).

Eliason, Randall D. *The Problems with the Reporter's Privilege*, 57 AM. U.L. REV. 1341 (2008).

Elrod, Jennifer. *Protecting Journalists From Compelled Disclosure: A Proposal for a Federal Statute*, 7 N.Y.U. J. LEG. & PUB. POL'Y 115 (2003/2004).

Pearlstine, Norman. *Off the Record: The Press, the Government, and the War over Anonymous Sources*. New York: Farrar, Straus and Giroux (2007).

Pracene, Ulan C. (ed.). *Journalists, Shield Laws, and the First Amendment: Is the Fourth Estate under Attack?* New York: Novinka Books (2005).

Rothenberg, Elliot C. *The Taming of the Press:* Cohen v. Cowles Media Company. Westport, Conn.: Praeger (1999).

Rudenstine, David. *A Reporter Keeping Confidences: More Important Than Ever*, 29 CARDOZO L. REV. 1431 (2008).

Toland, Carol J. Comment: *Internet Journalists and the Reporter's Privilege: Providing Protection for Online Periodicals*, 57 KAN. L. REV. 461 (2009).

Ugland, Erik. *The New Abridged Reporter's Privilege: Policies, Principles, and Pathological Perspectives*, 71 OHIO ST. L.J. 1 (2010).

10. The Media and the Courts

Alexander, S. L. *Media and American Courts: A Reference Handbook*. Santa Barbara, Calif.: ABC-CLIO (2004).

Bruschke, Jon & William E. Loges. *Free Press vs. Fair Trials: Examining Publicity's Role in Trial Outcomes*. Mahwah, N.J.: Lawrence Erlbaum Associates (2004).

Bybee, Keith (ed.). *Bench Press: The Collision of Courts, Politics and the Media*. Stanford, Calif.: Stanford University Press (2007).

Fox, Richard & Robert W. Van Sickel. *Tabloid Justice: Criminal Justice in an Age of Media Frenzy*. Boulder, Colo.: L. Rienner (2001).

Giles, Robert & Robert W. Snyder (eds.). *Covering the Courts: Free Press, Fair Trials & Journalistic Performance*. New Brunswick, N.J.: Transaction Pub. (1999).

Haltom, William & Michael McCann. *Distorting the Law: Politics, Media, and the Litigation Crisis.* Chicago: University of Chicago Press (2004).

Phillipson, Gavin. *Trial by Media: The Betrayal of the First Amendment's Purpose,* 71 LAW & CONTEMP. PROB. 15 (2008).

Scherer, Mark R. *Rights in Balance: Free Press, Fair Trial, and Nebraska Press Association v. Stuart.* Lubbock, Tex.: Texas Tech University Press (2008).

Thaler, Paul. *The Spectacle: Media and the Making of the O.J. Simpson Story.* Westport, Conn.: Praeger (1997).

11. Electronic Media Regulation

Black, Sharon K. *Telecommunications Law in the Internet Age.* San Francisco: Morgan Kaufmann Pub. (2002).

Carter, T. Barton, et al. *The First Amendment and the Fifth Estate: Regulation of Electronic Mass Media.* New York: Foundation Press (7th ed. 2008).

Creech, Kenneth. *Electronic Media Law and Regulation.* Boston: Focal Press (5th ed. 2007).

Dominick, Joseph R., et al. *Broadcasting, Cable, the Internet, and Beyond: An Introduction to Modern Electronic Media.* Boston: McGraw Hill (6th ed. 2008).

Lipschultz, Jeremy Harris. *Free Expression in the Age of the Internet: Social and Legal Boundaries.* Boulder, Colo.: Westview Press (2000).

Scott, Michael D. *Scott on Multimedia Law.* New York: Aspen Publishers (2008).

Slotten, Hugh Richard. *Radio's Hidden Voice: The Origins of Public Broadcasting in the United States.* Urbana, Ill.: University of Illinois Press (2009).

Sterling, Christopher N. & John Michael Kittross. *Stay Tuned: A History of American Broadcasting.* Mahwah, N.J.: Lawrence Erlbaum Associates (3d ed. 2002).

Travis, Hannibal. *The FCC's New Theory of the First Amendment,* 51 SANTA CLARA L. REV. 417 (2011).

12. Obscenity, Indecency and Violence

Collins, Ronald K. L. & David M. Skover. *The Trials of Lenny Bruce: The Fall and Rise of an American Icon.* Naperville, Ill.: Sourcebooks MediaFusion (2002).

Corcos, Christine A. *George Carlin, Constitutional Law Scholar,* 37 STETSON L. REV. 899 (2008).

Fairman, Christopher M. *Fuck: Word Taboo and Protecting our First Amendment Liberties.* Naperville, Ill.: Sphinx Pub. (2009).

Heins, Marjorie. *Not in Front of the Children: "Indecency," Censorship and the Innocence of Youth.* New Brunswick, N.J.: Rutgers University Press (2007).

Jasper, Margaret C. *The Law of Obscenity and Pornography.* New York: Oxford University Press (2009).

Lipschultz, Jeremy Harris. *Broadcast and Internet Indecency: Defining Free Speech.* New York: Routledge/Taylor & Francis (2008).

MacKinnon, Catharine A. *Women's Lives, Men's Laws.* Cambridge, Mass.: Belknap Press of Harvard University Press (2005).

Saunders, Kevin W. *Saving Our Children from the First Amendment.* New York: New York University Press (2003).

Wood, Janice Ruth. *The Struggle for Free Speech in the United States, 1872–1915: Edward Bliss Foote, Edward Bond Foote, and Anti-Comstock Operations.* New York: Routledge (2008).

13. Intellectual Property

Fishman, Stephen. *Copyright and the Public Domain.* New York: Law Journal Press (2009).

Goldstein, Paul. *Copyright's Highway.* Stanford, Calif.: Stanford University Press (2d ed. 2003).

Johns, Adrian. *Piracy: The Intellectual Property Wars from Gutenberg to Gates.* Chicago: University of Chicago Press (2009).

Krikorian, Gaëlle, & Amy Kapczynski, eds. *Access to Knowledge in the Age of Intellectual Property.* New York: Zone Books (2010).

Lutzker, Arnold P. *Content Rights for Creative Professionals: Copyrights and Trademarks in a Digital Age.* Boston: Focal Press (2003).

Netanel, Neil. *Copyright's Paradox.* New York: Oxford University Press (2008).

Samuels, Edward B. *The Illustrated Story of Copyright.* New York: Thomas Dunne Books/St. Martin's Press (2000).

14. Advertising

Baker, C. Edwin. Nike v. Kasky *and the Modern Commercial Speech Doctrine: Paternalism, Politics, and Citizen Freedom: The Commercial Speech Quandary in* Nike, 54 Case W. Res. 1161 (2004).

Bennigson, Tom. Nike *Revisited: Can Commercial Corporations Engage in Non-Commercial Speech?* 39 Conn. L. Rev. 379 (2006).

Bhagwat, Ashutosh. *A Brief History of the Commercial Speech Doctrine (With Some Implications for Tobacco Regulation)*, 2 Hastings Sci. & Tech. L.J. 103 (2010).

Fischette, Charles. *A New Architecture of Commercial Speech Law*, 31 Harv. J.L. & Pub. Pol'y 663 (2008).

Kuhne, Cecil C. III. *Testing the Outer Limits of Commercial Speech: Its First Amendment Implications*, 23 Rev. Litigation 607 (2004).

Moore, Roy L. *Advertising and Public Relations Law*. New York: Routledge (2011).

Ortiz, Nicholas A. *Consumer Speech and the Constitutional Limits of FTC Regulations of "New Media,"* 2010 Colum. Bus. L. Rev. 936.

Smolla, Rodney A. Nike v. Kasky *and the Modern Commercial Speech Doctrine. Afterword: Free the Fortune 500! The Debate Over Corporate Speech and the First Amendment*, 54 Case W. Res. 1277 (2004).

Strasburger, Victor C., et al. *Children, Adolescents, and the Media*. Los Angeles: Sage (2d ed. 2009).

Photo Credits

1 The Rule of Law

Page 2: Wade Payne/AP Images for AT&T

Page 14: Justices Roberts, Thomas, Ginsburg, Breyer, Alito, Sotomayor, and Kagan: Steve Petteway, Collection of the Supreme Court of the United States

Page 14: Justice Scalia: Molly Isaacs, Collection of the Supreme Court of the United States

Page 14: Justice Kennedy: Robin Reid, Collection of the Supreme Court of the United States

Page 22: The National Archives

Page 30 (top): Used by permission of Chris Elliott

Page 30 (bottom): MIKE SEGAR/Reuters/Corbis

2 The First Amendment

Page 48: AP Photo/Kathy Willens

Page 52: AP Photo/Dennis Cook

Page 56: AFP/Getty Images

Page 62: AP Photo

Page 70: Photo by Alex Wong/Getty Images

3 Speech Distinctions

Page 98: Photo by David Leeson/Image Works/Image Works/Time Life Pictures/Getty Images

Page 107: © Bettmann/CORBIS

Page 113: Photo by Charles Ommanney/Getty Images

Page 121: ©Clay Good/ZUMA

Page 123: © Bettmann/CORBIS

4 Libel: The Plaintiff's Case

Page 138: © Bettmann/CORBIS

Page 143: AP Photo/Lawrence Jackson

Page 156: AP Photo/MJ Schear, file

Page 162: Originally published in the New York Times March 29, 1960

Page 165 (top): Photo by Kim Komenich/Time Life Pictures/Getty Images

Page 165 (bottom): AP Photo/Wesley Wong

5 Libel: Defenses and Privileges

Page 186: The Plain Dealer/Landov

Page 192: State Historical Society of Iowa, Iowa City—Ms178 Orville and Jane Rennie Collection

Page 196 (left): Photo by Francis Miller/Time Life Pictures/Getty Images

Page 196 (right): AP Photo/Pablo Martinez Monsivais

Page 205: AP Photo/Brett Cooomer, File

Page 208: reprinted with permission of Rachel Ehrenfeld

6 Protecting Privacy

Page 222: TIM SLOAN/AFP/Getty Images

Page 232: AP Photo/Tina Fineberg

Page 236: Ralph Crane/Time Life Pictures/Getty Images

Page 240: Photo by Ronald C. Modra/Sports Imagery/Getty Images

Page 242: AP Photo/Jake Bacon

Page 243: http://FunnyOrDie.com/m/194t

Page 246: © Bettmann/CORBIS

Page 248: PAUL J. RICHARDS/AFP/Getty Images

Page 249: AP Photo/Dave Weaver

Page 250: Reprinted by permission of Jireh Publishing and Rick Rush, www.RickRushArt.com

7 Emotional Distress and Physical Harm

Page 278: © Bettmann/CORBIS

Page 284: Paul Drinkwater/NBCU Photo Bank via AP Images

Page 286: Photo by Jamie McCarthy/WireImage

Page 287: Used by permission of Joseph Russomanno
Page 290: Hustler magazine, LFP Publishing Group, LLC
Page 295: Getty Images
Page 299: © ROBERT ERIC/CORBIS SYGMA
Page 302: Reprinted with permission of Paladin Press

8 Newsgathering

Page 320: Photo by MPI/Getty Images
Page 324: © Julie Dermansky/Corbis
Page 330: © Bettmann/CORBIS
Page 345: Photo by Jill Carroll Collection/Getty Images
Page 355: Memo excerpt from, "Interrogation of al Qaeda operative" by Jay S. Bybee, Assistant Attorney General, OLC to John Rizzo, Acting General Counsel of the Central Intelligence Agency. August 1, 2002. Can be found online at: http://s3.amazonaws.com/propublica/assets/missing_memos/OLCfinalRedact_01-08-02.pdf
Page 356: AP Photo/Seth Wenig, File
Page 360: © Mike Stewart/Sygma/Corbis
Page 367: NICHOLAS KAMM/AFP/Getty Images

9 Reporter's Privilege

Page 380: AP Photo/Pablo Martinez Monsivais/File
Page 384: AP Photo/Dennis Cook
Page 386: AP Photo/Victoria Arocho
Page 390: Photo by Stefan Wermuth-WPA Pool/Getty Images
Page 396: AP Photo/Benjamin Sklar

10 The Media and the Courts

Page 420: AP Photo/Nick Ut
Page 424: © Bettmann/CORBIS
Page 426: © Bettmann/CORBIS
Page 427: AP Photo/Lawrence Jackson
Page 438: Photo by Issac Brekken-Pool/Getty Images

11 Electronic Media Regulation

Page 474: Photo by Jason Andrew/Getty Images
Page 476: © Hulton-Deutsch Collection/CORBIS

Page 480: Rock Creek Ventures (www.rock-creek-ventures.com)
Page 491: AP Photo/Dario Lopez-Mills
Page 494: Jonathan Alcorn/Bloomberg via Getty Images
Page 500: AP Photo/Kathleen Beall
Page 505: Steve Petteway, Collection of the Supreme Court of the United States
Page 514: Photo by Daniel Acker/Bloomberg via Getty Images

12 Obscenity, Indecency and Violence

Page 528: AP Photo/David Phillip, File
Page 530: © Larry Lee Photography/CORBIS
Page 534: © Bettmann/CORBIS
Page 539: © John Springer Collection/CORBIS
Page 543: The National Campaign to Prevent Teen and Unplanned Pregnancy
Page 549: Margaret Norton/NBCU Photo Bank via AP Images
Page 551: AP Photo/Ron Edmonds, File
Page 569: AP Photo/Paul Sakuma

13 Intellectual Property

Page 578: Photo by Barry King/WireImage
Page 585: © Bettmann/CORBIS
Page 597: Image by MGM Studios/Courtesy of Getty Images
Page 605: © Neal Preston/CORBIS
Page 613: http://www.pandora.com/
Page 615: AP Photo/Alex Brandon
Page 619: Photo by Nick Laham/Getty Images
Page 624: AP Photo

14 Advertising

Page 640: Photo by Piotr Malecki/Getty Images
Page 646: MANDEL NGAN/AFP/Getty Images
Page 653: © Carl & Ann Purcell/CORBIS
Page 659: © David Brabyn/Corbis
Page 661: Danny Lawson/PA Wire URN:10021624 (Press Association via AP Images)

Text Credits

4 Libel: The Plaintiff's Case

Page 143: Joseph A. Russomanno and Kyu Ho Youm, "The '60 Minutes' Controversy: What Lawyers Are Telling the News Media," *Communications and the Law* 18 (Sept. 1996): 65–91. Reprinted with permission.

5 Libel: Defenses and Privileges

Pages 196–197: Joseph Russomanno, *Speaking Our Minds: Conversations with the People Behind Landmark First Amendment Cases* (Mahwah, N.J.: Lawrence Erlbaum Associates, 2002), 92, 115. Copyright 2002 by Taylor & Francis Group LLC - Books. Reproduced with permission of Taylor & Francis Group LLC - Books in the format Other book via Copyright Clearance Center.

6 Protecting Privacy

Page 257: Joseph Russomanno, *Speaking Our Minds: Conversations with the People Behind Landmark First Amendment Cases* (Mahwah, N.J.: Lawrence Erlbaum Associates, 2002), 146. Copyright 2002 by Taylor & Francis Group LLC - Books. Reproduced with permission of Taylor & Francis Group LLC - Books in the format Other book via Copyright Clearance Center.

7 Emotional Distress and Physical Harm

Page 289: Joseph Russomanno, *Speaking Our Minds: Conversations with the People Behind Landmark First Amendment Cases* (Mahwah, N.J.: Lawrence Erlbaum Associates, 2002), 179, 188. Copyright 2002 by Taylor & Francis Group LLC - Books. Reproduced with permission of Taylor & Francis Group LLC - Books in the format Other book via Copyright Clearance Center.

9 Reporter's Privilege

Page 399: Joseph Russomanno, *Speaking Our Minds: Conversations with the People Behind Landmark First Amendment Cases* (Mahwah, N.J.: Lawrence Erlbaum Associates, 2002) 204–205, 220, 239. Copyright 2002 by Taylor & Francis Group LLC - Books. Reproduced with permission of Taylor & Francis Group LLC - Books in the format Other book via Copyright Clearance Center.

12 Obscenity, Indecency and Violence

Page 532: Cass R. Sunstein, *Democracy and the Problem of Free Speech* (New York: The Free Press, 1993): 216, 217, 219. Reprinted with permission.

Page 533: Nadine Strossen, "A Feminist Critique of 'The' Feminist Critique of Pornography," *Virginia Law Review* 79 (August 1993): 1099, 1111–1112. Copyright 1993 by Virginia Law Review. Reproduced with permission of Virginia Law Review in the format Other book via Copyright Clearance Center.

Page 559: Joseph Russomanno, *Speaking Our Minds: Conversations with the People Behind Landmark First Amendment Cases* (Mahwah, N.J.: Lawrence Erlbaum Associates, 2002), 423, 434. Copyright 2002 by Taylor & Francis Group LLC - Books. Reproduced with permission of Taylor & Francis Group LLC - Books in the format Other book via Copyright Clearance Center.

13 Intellectual Property

14 Advertising

Case Index

Page numbers in bold indicate excerpted cases. Boxes and notes are indicated by *b* or *n* following the page numbers. Alphabetization is letter-by-letter (e.g., "Newton" precedes "New York City").

A

A&M Records, Inc. v. Napster, Inc., 719*n*186

Abbott v. State, 115*b*

ABC, Inc. v. FCC, 713*n*108

ABC, Inc. v. Stewart, 704*n*35

Abdul-Jabbar v. General Motors Corp., 692*n*82

Abood v. Detroit Bd. of Educ., 683*n*102

Abrams v. United States, 106, 682*nn*25–27

Accuracy in Media, Inc. v. FCC, 708*n*119

ACLU; Reno v., 148, 151*b*, 517, 518*b*, 519, 557, 557*b*, 713*nn*138–139

Action for Children's Television v. FCC, 712*n*93, 713*n*110, 713*n*112, 713*n*115, 713*n*118

Adarand Constructors, Inc. v. Pena, 708*n*110

Adderley v. Florida, 680*n*95

Adickes v. Kress & Co., 678*n*31, 688*n*60

Admission Consultants, Inc. v. Google, Inc., 685*n*23

Agostini v. Felton, 678*n*28

A.H. v. State, 711*n*57

Aktepe v. United States, 677*n*23

Albertini; United States v., 680*n*94

Alexander v. United States, 712*n*71

Allen v. Men's World Outlet, Inc., 692*n*87

Allen v. National Video, Inc., 692*n*86

Alliance for Cmty. Media v. FCC, 709*n*146

Alvarado v. KOB-TV, LLC, 695*n*20

Amalgamated Food Employees Union v. Logan Valley Plaza, Inc., 680*n*97

Ambach v. Norwick, 683*n*97

AMD v. Intel Corp., 437, 704*n*42

American Amusement Mach. Ass'n v. Kendrick, 567*b*, 714*n*173, 714*nn*176–178

American Booksellers Ass'n, Inc. v. Hudnut, 710*n*8

American Broad. Cos.; Doe v., 696*n*47

American Civil Liberties Union v. Ashcroft, 713*n*141, 714*n*145

American Civil Liberties Union; Ashcroft v., 711*nn*27–29, 713*n*140, 714*n*142

American Civil Liberties Union v. Department of Defense, 362*b*

American Civil Liberties Union v. Gonzales, 714*n*143

American Civil Liberties Union v. Mukasey, 714*n*144

American Civil Liberties Union v. Reno, 710*n*198

American Commc'ns Ass'n v. Douds, 682*n*16, 682*n*37

American Dental Ass'n v. Delta Dental Plans Ass'n, 715*n*21

American Family Ass'n v. FCC, 709*n*124

American Library Ass'n; United States v., 561, 714*n*154

America's Best Family Showplace Corp. v. New York City, 715*n*187

Anderson v. Gannett Co., 230*b*

Anderson v. Liberty Lobby, Inc., 678*n*32, 687*n*24, 688*n*61

Arcara v. Cloud Books, Inc., 714*n*163

Arista Records, LLC v. Launch Media, Inc., 718*n*174

Arkansas Educ. Television Comm'n v. Forbes, 707*n*31

Arkansas Writers' Project v. Ragland, 681*n*105

Armstrong v. H & C Commc'ns, 695*nn*24–27

Ashcroft v. *See name of opposing party*

Ashwander v. TVA, 42

Associated Press v. Canterbury, 365*b*

Associated Press v. Walker, 686*nn*68–69

Associated Press; Doe 2 v., 697*n*94

Atkins v. Fischer, 717*n*101

AT&T; FCC v., 701*n*140

Austin v. Michigan State Chamber of Commerce, 39–44, 677*n*2, 720*n*29

Auvil v. CBS, 685*nn*47–48, 688*n*50

A.V. v. iParadigms, 717*n*132

B

Bailey; State v., 427*b*

Baker v. F & F Inv. Co., 703*n*31

Baker; United States v., 682*nn*58–61

Barclays Capital v. TheFlyontheWall.com, 64–66, 715*n*31

Barnes v. Glen Theatre, Inc., 714*nn*164–165

Barnes v. Yahoo!, Inc., 697*n*90

Bartnicki v. Vopper, 71*b*, 268, 339–340, 699*n*76, 699*nn*78–80

Basic Books, Inc. v. Kinko's Graphics Corp., 718*nn*146–147

Bates v. State Bar of Ariz., 720*nn*26–27

Batson v. Kentucky, 703*n*11

Baugh v. CBS, Inc., 693*n*149, 694*n*163

Beaumont v. Brown, 694*n*183

Bebe Stores, Inc. v. May Dep't Stores Int'l, 719*n*204

Becker v. FCC, 707*n*34

Belluomo v. KAKE TV & Radio, Inc., 693*n*145

Berger v. Hanlon, 698*n*23

Best v. Malec, 695*n*23

Bethel Sch. Dist. v. Fraser, 119*b*, 122–123, 683*n*73

Bigelow v. Virginia, 643–644, 644*b*, 720*nn*10–13

Bill Graham Archives v. Dorling Kindersley Ltd., 718*n*143

B.J.F. v. Florida Star, 266–267

Blumenthal v. Drudge, 685*n*28

Board of Educ., Island Trees Union Free Sch. Dist. v. Pico, 683*nn*84–87

Board of Regents of the Univ. of Wis. Sys. v. Southworth, 119*b*, 681*n*104, 683*n*70, 683*nn*107–108

Board of Tr. of the State Univ. of N.Y. v. Fox, 645

Boese v. Paramount Pictures Corp., 691*n*64

Boisson v. Banian, Ltd., 715*n*20

Bonneville Int'l Corp. v. Peters, 587*b*

Booth v. Curtis Publ'g Co., 693*n*128

Boring v. Google, Inc., 693*n*137

Bose Corp. v. Consumers Union, 685*n*46

Boston Beer Co. v. Slesar Bros. Brewing Co., 719*n*210

Boswell v. Phoenix Newspapers, Inc., 688*n*72

Bowens v. Aftermath Entm't, 699*n*83

Bowley v. City of Uniontown Police Dep't, 695*n*189

Boyles v. Kerr, 696*n*44

Boy Scouts of Am. v. Dale, 681*n*109

Brandenburg v. Ohio, 108–109, 117, 298–299, 301, 302*b*, 312–317

Brandt v. The Weather Channel, Inc., 697*n*95

Branzburg v. Hayes, 383–386, 387*b*, 389, 390–392, 391*b*, 394–395, 394*b*, **405–417**, 414, 697*nn*1–2, 697*n*6, 702*n*1, 702*n*6, 702*nn*9–14, 702*n*25

Brauer v. Globe Newspaper Co., 691*n*50

Braun v. Soldier of Fortune, 297, 696*nn*64–65

Brents v. Morgan, 694*n*159

Bridgeport Music, Inc. v. Dimension Films, 718*n*176

Brilliance Audio, Inc. v. Haights Cross Commc'ns, Inc., 716*n*73

Brookfield Commc'ns, Inc. v. West Coast Entm't Corp., 720*n*227

Brother Records Inc. v. Jardine, 720*n*232

Broughton v. McClatchy Newspapers, Inc., 693*n*136

Brown v. Entertainment Merchants Ass'n, 715*n*186, 715*n*189, 715*n*192, 715*n*194

Brown v. Louisiana, 680*n*90

Brown & Williamson v. Jacobsen, 687*n*101

Bryan; United States v., 415, 702*n*5

Buckley v. American Constitutional Law Found., 151*b*, 680*n*75

Buckley v. Valeo, 73–74, 679*n*62

Burrow-Giles Lithographic Co. v. Sarony, 715*n*19

Bursey v. United States, 703*n*31

Burson v. Freeman, 679*n*53

Burstyn v. Wilson, 681*n*112

Butler v. Michigan, 711*nn*40–41

Butterworth v. Smith, 704*n*45, 704*n*60

Byers v. Edmundson, 696*nn*74–75

C

Cable News Network; United States v., 704*n*66

Cablevision Sys. Corp. v. FCC, 709*n*157, 709*n*172

CACI v. Rhodes, 173*b*

Caine v. Duke Commc'ns, Int'l, 697*n*93

Caldwell v. United States, 406, 414, 416

Campbell v. Acuff-Rose Music, Inc., 289*b*, 693*n*114, 717*n*127, 717*nn*130–131

Camper v. Minor, 696*nn*42–43

Cantrell v. Forest City Publ'g Co., 234–235, 691*n*58

Caperton v. Massey Coal Co., 428

Capital Broad. Co. v. Mitchell, 720*n*22

Capitol Records, Inc. v. Mercury Records Corp., 718*n*170

Caporale; United States v., 703*n*31

Carafano v. Metrosplash, 695*n*194

Cardillo v. Doubleday Co., 688*n*51

Cardtoons, L.C. v. Major League Baseball Players Ass'n, 692*n*95, 692*nn*106–108

C.A.R.S. Protection Plus Inc.; Doe v., 454, 705*nn*95–96

Carter v. Superior Ct. of San Diego County, 693*n*150

Carter-Clark v. Random House, Inc., 685*n*37

Carter Mountain Transmission Corp., 709*n*127

Cartoon Network LP v. CSC Holdings, 717*n*106

Castellani v. Scranton Times, 702*nn*27–28

Catsouras v. Department of Cal. Highway Patrol, 696*n*34

Cavalier v. Random House, 717*n*96

C.B.C. Distrib. and Mktg, Inc. v. Major League Baseball Advanced Media, L.P., 692*n*103

CBS v. Davis, 679*nn*36–37

CBS v. FCC, 707*nn*37–38, 712*n*101

Central Hudson Gas & Elec. Corp. v. Public Serv. Comm'n of N.Y., 641, 645–647, 649*b*, 650, 652, 653*b*, **664–670**, 671–674

Cervantes v. Time, Inc., 703*n*31

Chandler v. Florida, 445, 705*n*69

Chaplinsky v. New Hampshire, 52, 110, 114*b*, 682*n*18

Charmaine West v. Media Gen. Convergence, Inc., 691*n*41

Cher v. Forum Int'l, 693*n*129

Cherry v. Des Moines Leader, 192*b*

Children's Television Programming, 707*n*48, 707*n*51

Christian Legal Soc'y v. Martinez, 126–127, 129*b*

Chrysler v. Brown, 358, 701*n*131

Chuy v. Philadelphia Eagles Football Club, 686*n*88

CIA v. Sims, 701*n*129

Circuit City Stores Inc. v. CarMax Inc., 719*n*207

Citadel Broad. Corp., 708*n*89

Citizen Publ'g Co. v. United States, 687*n*16

Citizen Publ'g Co. v. Miller, 199*b*

Citizens United v. Federal Election Comm'n, 2, 5, 17, **38–44**, 72–73, 74*b*, 652, 677*n*5, 678*n*37

City of. *See name of city*

Clarridge; United States v., 700*n*107

Clean Flicks of Colo., LLC v. Soderbergh, 716*n*61

Coalition to Protest the Democratic Nat'l Convention v. City of Boston, 81*b*

Cochran v. NYP Holdings, Inc., 685*n*45

Cochrane v. United States, 701*n*134

Cohen v. California, 109–110, 682*n*45, 692*n*79, 710*n*3

Cohen v. Cowles Media Co., dba Minneapolis Star & Tribune Co., 306, 398, 400, **417–419**, 697*n*3, 699*nn*56–57, 702*nn*2–4

Columbia Ins. Co. v. Seescandy.com, 151*b*

Comcast Corp., 709*n*149

Comcast Corp. v. FCC, 710*n*196

Comedy III Prods., Inc. v. Gary Saderup, Inc., 693*n*115, 693*n*117, 693*n*119

Community for Creative Non-Violence v. Reid, 588, 716*n*41, 716*n*43

Community Television of Utah, Inc. v. Roy City, 713*n*123

Complaints Against Various Broad. Licensees Regarding Their Airing of the "Golden Globe Awards" Program, In re, 712*n*96

Complaints against Various Television Licensees Concerning Their February 1, 2004, Broad. of the Super Bowl XXXVIII, 712*n*100

Complaints Against Various Television Licensees Regarding Their Broad. on November 11, 2004, of the ABC Television Network's Presentation of the Film "Saving Private Ryan, In re, 712*n*105

Complaints Regarding Various Television Broad., 712*n*104, 713*n*106

Complaints Regarding Various Television Broad. Between February 2, 2002 and March 8, 2005, In re, 712*n*97, 712*n*104

Condor Ins. Ltd., In re, 677*n*10

Connick v. Myers, 680*n*85

Conradt v. NBC Universal, 284*b*

Convertino v. United States Dep't of Justice, 365*b*

Copeland v. Copeland, 705*n*92

Corzine; FTC v., 721*n*50

Cottrill v. Spears, 717*n*94

Covey v. Detroit Lakes Publ'g Co., 695*n*11

Cowley v. Pulsifer, 687*n*6

Cox v. Louisiana, 81*b*

Cox v. New Hampshire, 81*b*

Cox Broad. Corp. v. Cohn, 223, 267, **270–273**

Cox Newspaper L.P. v. Wooten, 695*n*6

Coyne Beahm, Inc. v. FDA, 720*n*21

Cruz v. Ferre, 713*n*122

Cubby, Inc. v. CompuServe, Inc., 685*n*25

Curtis Publ'g Co. v. Butts, 169–170, 181–182, 686*n*67, 686*n*83

Cuthbertson; United States v., 703*n*31

D

Dalbec v. Gentleman's Companion, Inc., 692*n*78

Daly v. Viacom, Inc., 694*n*166

Dambrot v. Central Mich. Univ., 684*n*130

Dam Things from Denmark v. Russ Barrie & Co., 717*n*122

Daniels Cablevision, Inc. v. United States, 710*n*179

Debs v. United States, 682*n*24

Deere & Co. v. MTD Prod., Inc., 720*n*230

Dendrite Int'l, Inc. v. John Doe No. 3, 685*n*34

Dennis v. United States, 682*n*28, 682*n*38

Denver Area Educ. Telecomms. Consortium, Inc. v. FCC, 81*b*, 505, 555–556, 709*n*134, 709*n*159, 713*n*127

Denver Publ'g Co. v. Bueno, 691*n*41

Department of Defense v. American Civil Liberties Union, 362*b*

Department of Justice v. Reporters Comm. for Freedom of the Press, 33, 457–458, 677*n*26, 701*n*136, 701*n*139, 706*n*114

Department of the Air Force v. Rose, 700*n*104, 701*n*130

Department of the Interior & Bureau of Indian Affairs v. Klamath Water Users Protective Ass'n, 701*n*133

Desnick v. American Broad. Co., 693*n*148

Deteresa v. ABC, 699*nn*62–63

Dial Info. Servs. Corp. v. Thornburgh, 714*n*171

Diaz v. Oakland Tribune, 694*n*180

Diebold, Inc.; United States v., 678*n*31, 688*n*60

Dietemann v. Time, Inc., 693*nn*151–152, 698*n*20

Dimeo v. Max, 685*nn*30–31

Doe v. *See name of opposing party*

Dolcefino & KTRK Television, Inc. v. Turner, 686*n*52, 688*n*76

Doubleclick Inc. Privacy Litig., In re, 690*n*6

Douglass v. Hustler Magazine, Inc., 233*b*

Dow v. New Haven Indep., Inc., 687*n*24

Drew; United States v., 300*b*

Dual-Deck Video Cassette Recorder Antitrust Litig., In re, 720*n*240

Duckett, Estate of v. Cable News Network, 695*n*31

Dun & Bradstreet, Inc. v. Greenmoss Builders, Inc., 684*n*5, 686*nn*94–96

E

E. & J. Gallo Winery v. Spider Webs Ltd., 719*n*226

Early v. The Toledo Blade, 688*n*75

Eberhardt v. Morgan Stanley Dean Witter Trust FSB, 691*n*49

Edge Broad.; United States v., 707*n*59, 720*nn*23–24

Edwards v. Aguillard, 683*n*73, 683*n*98

Edwards v. National Audubon Soc'y, 202–203*b*, 688*n*47

Edwards v. South Carolina, 680*n*90

Ehrenfeld v. Mahfouz, 208*b*

Eimann v. Soldier of Fortune Magazine, Inc., 296, 696*n*59, 696*nn*62–63

Eisenstadt v. Baird, 690*n*25

Eldred v. Ashcroft, 587*b*, 596, **628–633**

Elk Grove Unified Sch. Dist. v. Newdow, 683*n*103

Emily's List v. FEC, 680*n*67

Energy Research Found. v. Defense Nuclear Facilities Safety Bd., 700*n*107

Entertainment Software Ass'n v. Swanson, 715*n*190

Epperson v. Arkansas, 683*n*98

Erie, City of v. Pap's A.M., 714*n*165

Erznoznik v. City of Jacksonville, 710*n*2

Esposito-Hilder v. SFX Broad., Inc., 695*n*30

Estes v. Texas, 423, 703*n*4

ETW Corp. v. Jireh Publ'g, Inc., 692*n*99, 693*n*120

Euclid v. Ambler Realty Co., 550*b*

Evans v. The Sandersville Georgian, Inc., 199*b*

Ex parte. *See name of party*

F

Factors Etc., Inc. v. Pro Arts, Inc., 692*n*109

Fair Housing Council of San Fernando Valley v. Roommates. com, LLC, 697*n*87

Falwell v. Flynt, 696*n*38

Fanelle v. LoJack Corp., 691*n*54

Farmers Educ. & Coop. Union v. WDAY, Inc., 707*n*35

FCC v. *See name of opposing party*

Federal Election Comm'n v. *See name of opposing party*

Federal Radio Comm'n v. *See name of opposing party*

Federated Publ'ns, Inc. v. Kurtz, 705*n*84

Federated Publ'ns, Inc. v. Swedberg, 705*n*85

Feist Publ'ns, Inc. v. Rural Tel. Serv. Co., 584*b*, 631, 715*n*23

Feltner v. Columbia Pictures Television, Inc., 717*n*111

Ferber v. New York, 541

First Nat'l Bank of Boston v. Bellotti, 720*n*28

Florida v. Palm Beach Newspapers, 705*n*72

Florida Publ'g Co. v. Fletcher, 697*n*17

Florida Star v. B.J.F., 261*b*, 456, 694*nn*186–188, 706*nn*107–108

Flynn v. City of Cambridge, 681*n*102

Flynt v. Rumsfeld, 700*n*91

Fogerty v. Fantasy, Inc., 717*n*114

Fogerty v. MGM Group Holdings Corp., 717*n*95

Food Lion, Inc. v. Capital Cities, Inc./ABC, 331, 332*b*, 333–335, 698*n*44, 698*nn*46–47, 699*n*49

Forsham v. Harris, 700*nn*109–111

Forsyth County, Ga. v. The Nationalist Movement, 679*n*59

44 Liquormart, Inc. v. Rhode Island, 647*b*, 678*n*35, 720*n*18

Fox Television Stations, Inc., 708*n*113

Fox Television Stations, Inc.; FCC v. (2009), 551, 712*n*103

Fox Television Stations, Inc. v. FCC (2010), 529, 571, **575–577**, 712*n*78, 712*nn*98–99

Frazier v. Boomsma, 242*b*

Freedman v. Maryland, 712*n*68

Free Speech Coalition; Ashcroft v., 560, 711*n*53, 714*n*149

Frisby v. Schultz, 81*b*, 680*n*96

Frohwerk v. United States, 682*nn*22–23

Frontier Broad. Co., 709*n*126

FTC v. *See name of opposing party*

G

Galella v. Onassis, 698*nn*36–37

Gannett v. DePasquale, 433, 703*nn*21–24

Garcetti v. Ceballos, 77

Gault, In re, 704*n*47

Gertz v. Robert Welch, Inc., 170, **180–185**, 214–216, 219–221, 235, 686*nn*79–82, 686*nn*91–92, 686*n*98, 687*n*1, 687*n*16, 687*n*25

Gibson v. Craigslist, Inc., 697*n*89

Ginsberg v. New York, 541, 711*n*42

Gitlow v. New York, 106, 678*n*2, 682*nn*29–33, 682*n*47

Glickman v. Wileman Bros. & Elliott, 681*n*103

Globe Newspaper Co. v. Superior Ct., 434, 704*nn*29–30

Godbehere v. Phoenix Newspapers, 233*b*

Goland v. CIA, 700*n*108, 700*nn*115–116

Goldwater v. Ginsburg, 686*n*65

Gooding v. Wilson, 682*n*53

Gordon v. Virtumundo, 662*b*

Gouin v. Gouin, 695*n*4

Grace; United States v., 81*b*

Grand Jury Proceedings, In re, 702*nn*21–24, 703*n*31

Grand Jury Subpoenas, In re, 387*b*

Grayned v. Rockford, 680*nn*90–91, 683*n*80

Greater New Orleans Broad. Ass'n, Inc. v. United States, 61, 720*n*25

Great Lakes Broad., 707*n*73

Green v. CBS Broad., Inc., 269*b*, 695*n*195

Green v. Chicago Tribune Co., 695*n*198

Greenbelt Coop. Publ'rs Ass'n, Inc. v. Bressler, 687*nn*38–39

Greenberg v. National Geographic Soc'y, 716*n*45

Green Party of Conn. v. Garfield, 678*n*37

Greer v. Spock, 680*n*93

Gregory v. City of Chi., 680*n*90

Griswold v. Conn., 690*n*22, 690*n*24

Grosjean v. American Press Co., 681*n*105

Guglielmi v. Spelling-Goldberg Prods., 693*n*126

GW Equity LLC v. Xcentric Ventures LLC, 697*n*88

H

Haelan Labs., Inc. v. Topps Chewing Gum, Inc., 692*n*76, 692*n*105

Hague v. Committee for Indus. Org., 680*n*88, 680*n*92

Hamilton-Brown Shoe Co. v. Wolf Bros. & Co., 719*n*211

Hamling v. United States, 711*n*22

Hanash & Yousef v. WFLD, 686*n*55

Hanlon v. Berger, 327, 698*nn*23–24

Harley-Davidson, Inc. v. Grottanelli, 719*n*214

Harper & Row Publ'rs, Inc. v. Nation Enters., 717*n*128, 718*n*142

Harte-Hanks Commc'ns, Inc. v. Connaughton, 686*n*72

Hatfill v. New York Times, 695*n*21

Hazelwood v. Kuhlmeier, 119*b*, 124, 128

Henderson v. Times Mirror Co., 687*n*24

Herbert v. Lando, 686*n*71

Herceg v. Hustler Magazine, 696*n*76

Hess v. Indiana, 299, 301, 680*n*90, 683*n*68

Hicklin; Regina v., 533–535

Hill v. Colorado, 70*b*, 255, 679*n*52, 693*n*138

Hilton v. Hallmark Cards, 691*n*66

Hoehling v. Universal City Studios, Inc., 715*n*28

Holder v. Humanitarian Law Project, 101, 103*b*, 681*n*5

Hollingsworth v. Perry, 704*n*36

Hosty v. Carter, 684*n*120

Howard v. Antilla, 691*n*51

Howell Educ. Ass'n v. Howell Bd. of Educ., 365*b*

Huchins v. KQED, 697*n*12

Hudgens v. National Labor Relations Bd., 680*n*97

Hudson v. Imagine Entm't Corp., 717*n*102

Hudson v. Universal Pictures, 717*n*102

Humanitarian Law Project v. U.S. Dep't of Justice, 682*n*14

Hurley v. Irish-American Gay, Lesbian & Bisexual Group of
Boston, 681*n*110

Hurst v. Capital Cities Media, Inc., 687*n*3

Hustler Magazine v. Falwell, 198, 279, 287*b*, 288, 289*b*, 290,
309–311, 687*n*37, 688*n*65, 696*n*36, 696*n*39

Hutchinson v. Proxmire, 686*nn*86–87, 688*n*63

Hyde v. City of Columbia, 696*n*49

I

Idema v. Wager, 695*n*7

Immuno AG v. Moor-Jankowski, 199*b*

Infinity Broadcasting, 707*n*30, 712*n*92

In re. *See name of party*

Intel Corp. v. AMD, 704*n*43

Intel Corp. Microprocessor Antitrust Litig., In re, 704*n*41

International Family Entm't, Inc., 707*n*50

International News Serv. v. Associated Press, 679*n*40,
715*n*29

Io Group, Inc. v. Veoh Networks, Inc., 718*n*157

Island Trees Union Free Sch. Dist. Bd. of Educ. v. Pico,
681*n*107

J

Jacobellis v. Ohio, 710*n*1, 711*n*23

James v. Meow Media, Inc., 696*nn*57–58, 714*nn*174–175

James B. Beam Distilling Co. v. Georgia, 18*b*

Janklow v. Newsweek, 687*n*23

Japan Telecom, Inc. v. Japan Telecom of Am., Inc., 719*n*209

Japan Whaling Ass'n v. American Cetacean Soc'y, 677*n*23

Jaynes v. Commonwealth of Va., 721*n*60

J.E.B. v. Alabama, 703*n*11

Jenkins v. Georgia, 711*nn*33–34

Jessup-Morgan v. America Online, Inc., 699*n*81

Jews for Jesus v. Rapp, 230*b*

John v. Tribune Co., 687*n*31

John Doe Grand Jury Investigation, In re, 702*n*26

Johnson v. K Mart Corp., 694*n*184

Johnson v. Ruark Obstetrics & Gynecology Assocs., 696*n*45

Jones v. U.S. Child Support Recovery, 694*n*161

Joseph Burstyn, Inc. v. Wilson, 712*n*66

K

Kaelin v. Globe Commc'ns, 685*n*42

Kalem Co. v. Harper Bros., 717*n*104

Kasky v. Nike, Inc., 720*nn*30–31

Katz v. United States, 275

Keeton v. Hustler Magazine, Inc., 677*n*9

Keller v. Electronic Arts, Inc., 249*b*

Kelson v. Spin Publ'ns, Inc., 691*n*55

Kent v. United States, 704*n*46

Kilbourn v. Thompson, 677*n*1

Kilbride; United States v., 537*b*, 711*n*30

Kimmerle v. New York Evening Journal, Inc., 685*n*41

Kincaid v. Gibson, 127, 684*n*119

Kirby v. Sega of Am., Inc., 693*n*121

Kissinger v. Reporters Comm. for Freedom of the Press, 700*n*107

Kleindienst v. Mandel, 682*n*17

Knievel v. ESPN, Inc., 688*n*43

Knox; United States v., 711*nn*50–51

Kokinda; United States v., 81*b*, 680*n*94

Koubriti; United States v., 703*n*13

Kovacs v. Cooper, 681*n*113

KOVR-TV, Inc. v. Superior Ct., 695*n*28

Kunz v. New York, 682*n*39

L

Ladue, City of v. Gilleo, 71*b*

Lake v. City of Phoenix, 367*b*

Lamprecht v. Federal Commc'ns Comm'n, 708*n*110

Lane v. Facebook, Inc., 690*n*30

Lane v. Simon, 684*n*125

LaRouche v. NBC, 703*n*31

Lawrence v. Texas, 690*n*27

League of Women Voters; FCC v., 706*n*19, 707*n*41,
708*nn*82–84, 708*nn*120–121

Leased Commercial Access, 709*n*162

Leathers v. Medlock, 681*n*105

Lee v. Dong-A Ilbo, 687*n*5

Leigh v. Warner Bros., 717*n*96

LeMistral, Inc. v. Columbia Broad. Sys., 693*n*143, 697*nn*15–16

Lemon v. Kurtzman, 119*b*

Liberty Lobby, Inc. v. Anderson, 688*nn*52–54

Liberty Lobby, Inc. v. Dow Jones, 685*n*50

Lieb v. Topstone Indus., Inc., 718*n*173

Lin v. Rohm &Haas Co., 695*n*16

Liquori v. Republican Co., 687

Little; United States v., 711*n*31

Lloyd; United States v., 703*n*31

Lloyd Corp. v. Tanner, 680*n*97

Logan v. District of Columbia, 688*n*55

Long Beach Area Chamber of Commerce v. City of Long Beach, 678*n*37

Lorillard Tobacco Co. v. Reilly, 649*b*, 653*b*, 664, **670–675**, 720*nn*19–20

Los Angeles, City of v. Alameda Books, Inc., 714*n*166

Los Angeles City Council v. Taxpayers for Vincent, 680*n*94

Los Angeles News Serv. v. CBS Broad., Inc., 718*n*140

Lovell v. Griffin, 681*n*112

Luke Records, Inc. v. Navarro, 711*n*39

Lunney v. Prodigy Servs. Co., 685*n*24

M

Machleder v. Diaz, 693*n*146

Madison v. Frazier, 687*n*32

Madsen v. Buie, 687*n*35

Madsen v. Women's Health Ctr., 81*b*, 114*b*, 680*n*96

Maldonado-Norat; United States v., 693*n*142

Marbury v. Madison, 3, 5, 6, 16–17, 36–37, 38, **44–47**

Massachusetts Citizens for Life, Inc.; Federal Election Comm'n v., 720*n*29

Masson v. New Yorker Magazine, Inc., 165*b*, 686*n*51, 686*n*66, 688*n*58

Matera v. Superior Ct., 394*b*

Mattel, Inc. v. MCA Records, Inc., 692*n*112

Matter of. *See name of party*

Matthews; United States v., 711*n*52

McCollum v. CBS, Inc., 696*n*67

McConnell v. Federal Election Comm'n, 73, 74*b*, 677*n*2, 680*n*64, 707*n*43

McFarlane; Doe v., 693*n*122

McIntosh v. The Detroit News, Inc., 687*n*9

McIntyre v. Ohio Elections Comm'n, 75, 685*n*33

McKinney v. Avery Journal, Inc., 688*n*49

Medical Lab. Mgmt. Consultants v. American Broad. Cos., 693*n*144, 694*n*155

Memoirs v. Massachusetts, 572

Menotti v. City of Seattle, 81*b*

Messenger v. Gruner + Jahn Printing & Publ'g, 692*n*100

Metro Broad., Inc. v. FCC, 708*n*109

Metro-Goldwyn-Mayer Studios, Inc. v. American Honda Motor Co., 717*nn*97–100

Metro-Goldwyn-Mayer Studios, Inc. v. Grokster, Ltd., 601, **633–639**, 717*n*107, 719*nn*191–192

Meyer v. Bush, 679*n*61, 700*n*107

M. Fabrikant & Sons, Ltd. v. Fabrikant Fine Diamonds, Inc., 719*n*212

M. G. v. Time Warner, Inc., 694*n*171

Miami Herald Publ'g Co. v. Tornillo, 60–61, 482, 678*n*27, 706*n*17, 708*n*77

Miami Publishing, State ex rel. v. McIntosh, 679*n*51

Miami Univ.; United States v., 700*n*98

Michaels v. Internet Entm't Group, Inc., 694*n*158, 694*n*164, 694*n*179

Midler v. Ford Motor Co., 692*nn*88–89

Milkovich v. Lorain Journal Co., 187, **218–221**, 684*n*3, 685*n*14, 687*n*15, 687*nn*26–30

Milk Wagon Drivers Union of Chi. v. Meadowmoor Dairies, 114*b*

Miller v. California, 530*b*, 535, 536–541, 536*b*, 540*b*, 558, 565, **571–574**, 710*n*203, 711*n*32

Miller v. NBC, 697*n*14, 697*nn*18–21

Miller v. Transamerican Press, Inc., 703*n*31

Miller v. United States, 387*b*

Miller v. Mitchell, 711*n*60

Milligan, Ex parte, 104*b*

Minneapolis Star & Tribune Co. v. Minnesota Comm'r of Revenue, 681*n*114

Minority Television Project, Inc., 708*n*117

Mishkin v. New York, 711*n*25

Missner v. Clifford, 687*n*33

Mitchell v. Globe Int'l Publ'ns, Inc., 691*n*56

Mobilisa, Inc. v. John Doe 1 and The Suggestion Box, Inc., 151*b*

Moghadam; United States v., 718*n*180

Moldea v. New York Times, 687*nn*10–11

Montana v. San Jose Mercury News, Inc., 692*n*110

Moreno v. Crookston Times & McDaniel, 687*n*2

Moriarty v. Greene, 691*n*53

Morse v. Frederick, 120–121, 129*b*

Moseley v. V Secret Catalogue, Inc., 720*nn*236–237

Mourning v. Family Publ'g Serv., 678*n*31, 688*n*60

Muir v. Alabama Educ. Television Comm'n, 708*n*122

Mukasey v. ACLU, 714*n*146

Multimedia Entm't Inc., 707*n*29

Mu'Min v. Virginia, 703*n*10

Musumeci v. U.S. Dep't of Homeland Sec., 343*b*

MySpace, Inc.; Doe v., 697*n*84

MySpace, Inc.; Doe II v., 697*n*85

MySpace, Inc.; Doe IX v., 697*n*86

N

NAACP v. Claiborne Hardware Co., 114*b*, 680*n*90

Nast v. Michels, 705*n*90

National Archives & Records Admin. v. Favish, 701*nn*137–138

National Ass'n of Broadcasters v. FCC, 710*n*177

National Basketball Ass'n v. Motorola, Inc., 715*n*30

National Broad. Co. v. FCC, 482, 706*n*15

National Cable & Telecomms. Ass'n v. Brand X Internet Servs., 710*n*192

National Cable & Telecomms. Ass'n v. FCC, 709*n*147

National Conservative Political Action Comm.; Federal Election Comm'n v., 720*n*29

National Endowment for the Arts v. Finley, 681*n*106

National Farmworkers Serv. Center, Inc., 709*n*123

National Right to Work Comm.; Federal Election Comm'n v., 720*n*29

National Sec. Archive v. Archivist of the U.S., 700*n*107

Nation Magazine v. U.S. Dep't of Defense, 700*n*90

Near v. Minnesota, 61–62

Nebraska Press Ass'n v. Stuart, 442–444, 452, 679*nn*34–35, 679*n*51

Neilson v. Union Bank of Cal., N.A., 696*n*40

Neiman-Marcus v. Lait, 685*n*36

Nelson v. Harrah's Entm't Inc., 696*n*41

Nelson Bros.; Federal Radio Comm'n v., 706*n*8

Netzer v. Continuity Graphic Assocs., Inc., 693*n*131

New Kids on the Block v. News Am. Publ'g, Inc., 720*n*241

New Times, Inc. v. Isaacks, 688*nn*45–46

Newton v. Diamond, 718*n*177

New York City; Doe v., 695*n*197

New York Times Co. v. Google, 679*n*38

New York Times Co. v. Jascalevich, 679*n*35

New York Times Co. v. National Aeronautics & Space Admin., 359*b*

New York Times Co. v. Sullivan, 58, 139, 160–164, 163*b*, 166–171, 173*b*, 175, **178–180**, 181–185, 193, 197, 207, 219, 287*b*, 288, 310–311, 642–643, 677*n*9, 678*n*34, 678*n*36, 679*n*19, 684*n*1, 686*nn*58–63, 687*nn*19–20, 688*n*65, 720*n*5

New York Times Co. v. Tasini, 589, 628

New York Times Co. v. United States, 49, 62–64, 63*b*, **89–92**

Nichols v. United States, 700*n*114

Nike, Inc. v. Kasky, 678*n*29, 721*n*32

Nixon v. Shrink Mo. Gov't PAC, 75

Nixon v. Warner Commc'ns, 452

Noriega; United States v., 704*nn*63–65

Norwood v. Soldier of Fortune, Inc., 296–297, 696*nn*60–61

November v. Time, Inc., 688*n*59

O

Oak Creek, City of v. Ah King, 699*n*87

O'Brien; United States v., 49, 69, 72, 89, **92–96**, 116–117, 511, 679*nn*56–57, 683*n*63, 683*n*65

O'Connor v. Ortega, 275–277, 690*n*17

Oklahoma Publ'g Co. v. District Ct., 695*n*191

Old Dominion Branch No. 496, Nat'l Ass'n of Letter Carriers v. Austin, 688*n*40–42

Olivia N. v. National Broad. Co., 696*n*55

Ollman v. Evans, 177, 193–195, 196–197*b*, 198, 201, **213–218**, 220, 687*nn*21–22

Onassis v. Christian Dior, 692*n*85

One Book Entitled "Ulysses" by James Joyce; United States v., 711*n*15

O'Neill v. Oakgrove Constr., Inc., 703*n*32

O'Neill v. City of Shoreline, 367*b*

Ontario, City of v. Quon, 225–226, **273–277**, 690*n*16

Ortiz-Gonzalez v. Fonovisa, 716*n*53

Osborne v. Ohio, 711*n*58, 712*n*65

Ostergren v. Cuccinelli, 690*n*11

P

PACCAR, Inc. v. TeleScanTech., LLC, 719*n*203

Pacifica Found., In re, 712*n*86, 712*n*92

Pacifica Found.; FCC v., 548–549, 549–550*b*, 555, 558, 559*b*, 575–576, 706*n*20, 712*nn*74–76, 712*n*91, 712*nn*94–95

Pacific Legal Found. v. Council on Envtl. Quality, 700*n*107

Papish v. Board of Curators of the Univ. of Mo., 126, 683*nn*109–112

Paramount Pictures Corp., 707*nn*26–27

Paramount Pictures Corp. v. RePlayTV, 716*n*67

Parks v. LaFace Records, 693*n*113

Patton v. Yount, 703*n*6

Paulsen v. Personality Posters, Inc., 692*n*110

Pavesich v. New England Life Ins. Co., 271, 692*n*75

Payton v. New York, 372

Pell v. Procunier, 697*n*11

Pennekamp v. Florida, 385*b*

People Bank & Trust Co. v. Globe Int'l, 691*n*56

Perfect 10 Inc. v. Amazon.com, Inc., 718*n*156, 718*n*158, 718*n*160

Perry v. Sindermann, 680*n*81

Perry Educ. Ass'n v. Perry Local Educators' Ass'n, 680*n*91

Peterson v. Grisham, 691*n*52

Philadelphia Newspapers, Inc. v. Hepps, 685*n*49

Pickering v. Board of Educ., 680*n*82, 683*n*98

Pickett v. Prince, 716*n*52

Pierce v. Clarion Ledger, 695*n*12

Pittsburgh Press Co. v. Pittsburgh Comm'n on Human Relations, 720*nn*7–8

Planned Parenthood v. American Coal. of Life Activists, 683*n*62

Playboy Enters., Inc. v. Frena, 718*n*153

Playboy Enters., Inc. v. Russ Hardenburgh, Inc., 718*n*149

Playboy Enters., Inc.; United States v., 505–506, 709*n*135, 713*n*131

Pleasant Grove City v. Summum, 76–77, 680*nn*78–79

Pooley v. National Hole-in-One Ass'n, 693*n*132

Pope v. Illinois, 540, 711*n*38

Posadas de P.R. Assocs. v. Tourism Co. of P.R., 653*b*

Powell v. McCormack, 677*n*1

Preserving the Open Internet, In the Matter of, 710*n*197

Presley v. Georgia, 437

Press-Enterprise (I) v. Superior Ct., 434*b*, 435, 456, 704*n*31, 704*n*34

Press-Enterprise (II) v. Superior Ct., 434*b*, 435, 435*b*, 456, 704*nn*31–32

Prometheus Radio Project, v. Federal Commc'ns Comm'n, 708*n*112

Prudhomme v. Procter & Gamble Co., 692*n*83

Prune Yard Shopping Ctr. v. Robins, 82–83, 680*nn*97–100

Q

Qualitex Co. v. Jacobson Prods. Co., 719*n*198

R

Radio-Television News Directors Ass'n v. FCC, 519–520, 707*n*39, 708*n*81

Randall v. Sorrell, 74

R.A.V. v. City of St. Paul, 111–112, 114*b*, 682*n*54

Recording Indus. Ass'n of Am., Inc. v. Verizon Internet Servs., Inc., 719*n*188

Red & Black Publ'g v. Board of Regents, Univ. of Ga., 700*nn*96–97

Red Lion Broad. Co. v. FCC, 60, 475, 482, 496–497, **519–524**, 526, 678*n*27, 681*n*115, 707*n*76

Reed; Doe v., 75

Regents of the Univ. of Cal., In re, 712*n*92

Regina v. *See name of opposing party*

Regina v. Butler, 177*n*9

Renner v. Donsbach, 686*n*89

Reno v. Condon, 700*n*100

Reno v. *See name of opposing party*

Renton, City of v. Playtime Theatres, 714*n*162, 714*n*168

Republican Nat'l Comm. v. FEC, 680*n*65

Reynolds; United States v., 705*n*100

Rice v. Paladin Enters., Inc., 302*b*, **311–319**, 696*nn*78–79

Richmond Newspapers Inc. v. Virginia, 434, 459, **467–473**

Riley v. Harr, 695*nn*18–19

Riley v. National Fed'n of the Blind of NC, 71*b*

Roach v. Stern, 695*n*29

Roberson v. Rochester Folding Box Co., 692*n*73

Robert C. Ozer, P.C. v. Borquez, 694*n*185

Robinson v. American Broad. Co., 706*n*21

Roe v. Wade, 70*b*, 643, 690*n*26, 720*n*9

Rogers v. Grimaldi, 247–248, 692*n*111

The Romantics v. Activision Pub., Inc., 692*n*97

Rosemont Enters., Inc. v. Random House, Inc., 693*n*124

Rosenberger v. Rector & Visitors of the Univ. of Va., 681*n*104, 683*n*70, 683*nn*106–107

Rosenblatt v. Baer, 684*n*4, 686*nn*74–76

Roth v. United States, 535, 540, 573–574, 711*n*21

Rothner v. City of Chi., 715*n*188

Rubin v. Coors Brewing Co., 720*n*17

Ruffin-Steinback v. Depasse, 696*n*32

Rumsfeld v. Forum for Academic & Institutional Rights, Inc., 129*b*

Rushforth v. Council of Economic Advisers, 700*n*107

Russell v. Department of the Air Force, 701*n*132

S

Sable Commc'ns of Cal., Inc. v. FCC, 565, 712*n*82, 714*nn*169–170

Saga Commc'ns of Ark., 707*n*60

St. Amant v. Thompson, 686*n*70

Salinger v. Random House, Inc., 718*n*138

Salinger v. Colting, 718*n*133

Salzano v. North Jersey Media Group, 687*n*8

Sanders v. Acclaim Entm't, Inc., 696*n*56

Sanders v. American Broad. Cos., 694*n*156

Sandler v. Calcagni, 694*n*172

Santa Fe Indep. Sch. Dist. v. Doe, 683*nn*103–105

Sara Lee Corp. v. Kayser-Roth Corp., 719*n*206

Savage v. Pacific Gas & Elec. Co., 697*n*92

Scales v. United States, 682*n*28

Scheidler v. National Org. for Women, 680*n*96

Schenck v. Pro-Choice Network of W. N.Y., 105, 114*b*

Schenck v. United States, 681*n*1, 682*nn*19–21

Schifano v. Greene Country Greyhound Park, Inc., 693*n*130

Schill v. Wisconsin Rapids Sch. Dist., 365*b*

Schneider v. New Jersey, 81*b*

Seale v. Gramercy Pictures, 693*n*123

Sealed Case, In re, 706*n*103

Seattle Times v. Rhinehart, 705*n*68

Sega Enters., Ltd. v. Maphia, 718*n*154

Sellify, Inc. v. Amazon.com, Inc., 661*b*

Shabazz v. Campbell, 702*n*151

Shack; State v., 681*n*102

Shamsky v. Garan, Inc., 692*n*80

Sheppard v. Maxwell, 422, 424–426, 426*b*, 428–429, 441, 451, **459–466**, 703*n*1, 703*nn*7–9, 703*n*16, 704*nn*61–62

Sherwin-Williams Co. v. Holmes County, 677*n*10

Showler v. Harper's Magazine Found., 695*n*17

Shryock; United States v., 703*n*14

Shulman v. Group W Prods., 693*n*141, 694*n*154, 694*n*178, 698*n*34

Sidis v. F-R Publ'g Corp., 695*n*199

Sigma Delta Chi v. Speaker, Md. House of Delegates, 699*nn*84–85

Silberman v. Georges, 688*n*44

Silberman v. Innovative Luggage, Inc., 716*n*48

Silkwood v. Kerr-McGee, 703*n*31

Simon & Schuster v. Crime Victims Bd., 68

Sipple v. Chronicle Publ'g Co., 694*n*173

Skokie, Village of v. National Socialist Party of Am., 680*n*90

Sleem v. Yale Univ., 696*n*48

Small Bus. Assistance Corp. v. Clear Channel Broad., Inc., 719*n*215

Smith v. Daily Mail, 695*n*192, 704*n*48

Smith v. United States, 711*n*22

Smith; United States v., 695*n*196

Smyth v. Pillsbury Co., 690*n*19

Snepp v. United States, 680*n*82

Snyder v. Phelps, 287*b*

Solano v. Playgirl, Inc., 691*n*42, 691*nn*47–48

Sonderling Broad. Corp., 712*n*85

Sonshine Family Television, Inc., 708*n*92

Sony Corp. of Am. v. Universal City Studios, Inc., 628, 636–639, 716*n*49, 716*n*65, 717*n*105, 718*n*136, 719*n*193

Southwestern Cable Co.; United States v., 709*n*128, 710*n*191

Spahn v. Julian Messner, Inc., 691*n*40, 693*n*127

Special Force Ministries v. WCCO Television, 699*n*52

SpeechNow.org v. Federal Election Comm'n, 680*n*66

Spelson v. CBS, Inc., 687*n*24

Standard Brands, Inc. v. Smidler, 719*n*205

Stanley v. Georgia, 544–545, 712*nn*62–63

State v. *See name of opposing party*

State ex rel. *See name of party*

Stern v. Cosby, 205*b*

Stevens v. Iowa Newspapers, Inc., 686*n*54

Stevens; United States v., 6*b*, 678*n*8

Stratton Oakmont, Inc. v. Prodigy Servs. Co., 685*n*26

Sweezy v. New Hampshire, 415

Syracuse Peace Council v. FCC, 708*nn*78–79

T

Talley v. California, 680*n*75

Taylor v. National Broad. Co., 693*n*126

TCI Cablevision; Doe v., 693*n*122

Teleprompter Corp. v. Columbia Broad. Sys., 717*n*91

Terminiello v. Chicago, 111, 682*nn*50–52

Texas v. Johnson, 99, 117, **131–133**, 678*n*6, 683*n*67

Texas Beef Group v. Oprah Winfrey, 156*b*

Thomas; United States v., 711*n*26

Thornhill v. Alabama, 81*b*

321 Studios v. Metro Goldwyn Mayer Studios, Inc., 718*n*151

Tillman v. Freedom of Info. Comm'n, 686*n*93

Time, Inc. v. Firestone, 686*n*85

Time, Inc. v. Hill, 234–235, 691*n*57, 702*nn*15–17

Times Film Corp. v. City of Chi., 712*n*67

Times-Mirror Co. v. Superior Ct., 696*n*50

Time-Telepictures Television, 707*n*28

Time Warner Entm't Co. v. FCC, 708*n*150, 709*n*150, 709*n*160

Tinker v. Des Moines Indep. Cmty. Sch. Dist., 119–120, 119*b*, 131, **133–137**, 680*n*81, 683*n*64, 683*n*74, 683*nn*76–79, 684*n*116

Tin Pan Apple, Inc. v. Miller Brewing Co., 692*n*84

Toffoloni v. LFP Pub. Group, 692*n*101

Too Much Media v. Hale, 396*b*

TPS, Inc. v. Department of Defense, 701*n*143

Treasury Employees v. Von Raab, 275

Triangle Publ'ns v. Knight-Ridder Newspaper, Inc., 720*n*229

Tropicana Prods., Inc., Matter of, 721*n*47

Troy Ltd. v. Renna, 681*n*102

Turner Broad. Sys., Inc. v. FCC, 71*b*, 505, 511, **524–527**, 678*n*4, 681*n*116, 709*n*133, 709*n*137

Twentieth Century Music Corp. v. Aiken, 718*n*164

2THEMART.COM; Doe v., 151*b*

Ty, Inc. v. Perryman, 625*b*, 720*n*228

Tyne v. Time Warner Entm't Co., 693*n*125

U

U-Haul Int'l, Inc. v. Jartran, Inc., 721*n*35

UMG Recordings, Inc. v. Veoh Networks, Inc., 718*n*159

United Public Workers of Am. v. Mitchell, 680*n*83

United States v. *See name of opposing party*

Universal Commc'n Sys., Inc. v. Lycos, Inc., 149*b*

University of Mich.; Doe v., 684*nn*130–131

Univision Radio, Inc., 708*n*90

U.S. Civil Serv. Comm'n v. National Ass'n of Letter Carriers, 680*n*83

U.S. Dep't of Justice v. Reporters Comm. for Freedom of the Press, 360, **374–379**, 701*nn*135

UWM Post v. University of Wisc. Bd. of Regents, 684*n*130

V

Valentine v. Chrestensen, 642, 644, 720*n*3

Value Vision Int'l, Inc. v. FCC, 709*n*163

Varian Med. Sys., Inc. v. Delfino, 150*b*

Veilleux v. NBC, 691*n*64, 699*nn*53–54

Viacom Int'l, Inc., 707*n*49

Village of. *See name of village*

Virgil v. Time, Inc., 694*n*176

Virginia v. Black, 114*b*, 679*n*60

Virginia v. Jaynes, 721*n*61

Virginia State Bd. of Pharm. v. Virginia Citizens Consumer Council, 644*b*, 645, 650, 668–669, 720*n*1

W

Waits v. Frito-Lay, Inc., 692*n*90

Wampler v. Higgins, 687*n*36

Ward v. Illinois, 711*n*24, 711*nn*35–36

Ward v. Rock Against Racism, 70*b*, 679*n*58

Warner Lambert Co. v. FTC, 721*nn*44–46

Washington Post Co. v. Keogh, 678*n*33, 688*n*62

Washington Post Co. v. United States Dep't of State, 700*n*112

Watchtower v. Stratton, 680*n*75

Watters v. TSR, Inc., 696*n*69

Watts v. United States, 114*b*, 682*n*57

Webb v. CBS Broad. Inc., 693*n*135

Weimer v. Rankin, 687*n*4

Weirum v. RKO Gen., Inc., 697*n*82

Wendt v. Host Int'l, Inc., 682*n*93

West Va. State Bd. of Educ. v. Barnette, 683*n*96, 683*nn*99–101

Wheaton v. Peters, 715*n*12, 715*n*26

White v. Samsung Elecs. Am., Inc., 692*n*91

White-Smith Music Publ'g Co. v. Apollo Co., 719*n*183

Whitney v. California, 107, 682*n*28, 682*nn*34–36, 685*n*22, 687*n*18

Widmar v. Vincent, 683*n*72

Wildmon v. Berwick Universal Pictures, 697*n*91

Williams v. Pasma, 686*n*90

Williams; United States v., 711*n*43, 714*n*151, 721*n*42

Wilson v. Layne, 321, 327–329, **370–373**, 698*nn*27–33

Wilson v. Midway Games, Inc., 697*n*81

Winstead v. Sweeney, 694*n*165

Winter v. DC Comics, 693*n*118

Winter v. G. P. Putnam's Sons, 696*n*66

Wisconsin Right to Life; Fed. Election Comm'n v., 73, 677*n*4

WLBT-TV, In re, 705*n*73

Wolfson v. Lewis, 698*nn*38–40

Wolston v. Reader's Digest Ass'n, 686*n*84

Wooley v. Maynard, 681*n*108, 683*n*95

Wynberg v. National Enquirer, Inc., 688*nn*56–57

Y

Yakubowicz v. Paramount Pictures Corp., 696*n*77

Yates v. United States, 682*n*40

Yeakey v. Hearst Commc'ns, Inc., 686*n*53

Y.G. v. Jewish Hosp. of St. Louis, 694*n*162

Young v. American Mini Theatres, 714*n*163

Young v. New Haven Advocate, 677*n*11, 688*nn*66–68

Ysursa v. Pocatello Educ. Ass'n, 680*n*70

Z

Zacchini v. Scripps-Howard Broad. Co., 246, 692*n*102

Zamora v. Columbia Broad. Sys., 294, 696*nn*53–54

Zenith Radio Corp.; United States v., 706*nn*5–6

Zeran v. America Online, Inc., 149*b*, 685*n*27

Zerilli v. Smith, 703*n*31

Zieve v. Hairston, 694*n*167

Zurcher v. Stanford Daily, 402–403, 403*b*, 703*n*33

Subject Index

Page numbers in italics denote photos/illustrations. Boxes, maps, figures, and notes are indicated by *b, m, f,* and *n,* respectively, following page numbers. Alphabetization is letter-by-letter (e.g., "Courtroom" precedes "Court system").

A

Abbott, Walter C., Jr., 115*b*
ABC (television network)
    face-to-face recording, 336
    fraud and misrepresentation claim against, 330–333
    intrusion claim against, 256
    retransmission, 510, 510*b*
ABC Family Channel, 491, 510*b*
Abdul-Jabbar, Kareem, 240, *240*
Abortion rights, 66, *70*, 70*b*, 114–115
Abrams, Floyd, 403*b*
Abrams, Jacob, 106
Absolute privilege
    defined, 190
    false light, 236
Abu Ghraib prison photos, 362*b*
Academic freedom, 118. *See also* Universities
Access to court records, 452–458
Access to military operations, 343–345
Access to records, 345–348. *See also* Freedom of Information
    Act of 1966
Access to trials. *See* Trials, access to
ACPA (Anticybersquatting Consumer Protection Act of
    1999), 623
Actual damages, 175
Actual malice, 164–174
    advertising, 178–180
    all-purpose public figures, 170, 180–185
    bootstrapping, 171
    criminal libel, 176–177
    defined, 161, 164
    elements of, 164*b*
    intentional infliction of emotional distress, 288–290,
        309–311
    involuntary public figures, 172

knowledge of falsity, 164–166, 164*b*
limited-purpose public figures, 170–172
losing public-figure status, 172
nature of statement, 174
private figures, 172–174
public officials, 168–169
reckless disregard for truth, 166–168, 167*b*
Adams, John, 57
Aday, Sean, 703*n*3
Ad hoc balancing, 52
Administrative law
    advertising, 660–663
    creation of, 20
    defined, 20
    internal agency rules and procedures, 357
    notice of proposed rule making, 479
    rules, 26
Admonitions, 425–426
Adult programming, 505–506
Adult stores
    secondary effects of, 564
    zoning restrictions and, 563–564
Advanced Micro Devices, 437
Advertising, 640–675. *See also* Legislative advertising
        regulation; Programming and advertising regulations
    administrative regulation, 660–663
    alcohol, 646–647
    appropriation, 251–252
    attorneys, 650
    broadcast regulation, 484–498
    Central Hudson test, 645–646, 649*b*, 664–670
    commercial speech doctrine, 642–646, 644–645*b*
    corporate speech regulation, 3, 17, 38–44, 74*b*, 650–652
    corrective, 655*b*, 658
    elections, 72–75
    false and misleading, 52, 654*b*

Advertising *(cont.)*
  FCC, regulation by, 660
  gambling, 648–650
  Internet, 660–663
  libel and, 160–164, *162*, 178–180
  political ads, 72–75, 243*b*
  product demand and, 653*b*
  puffery, 655
  targeted, 660–661
  tobacco, 647–648, 649*b*, 670–675
Advisory opinions, 655–656, 655*b*
Afghanistan, 344
Afghanistan war, 390*b*
Agencies, 350
AIDS, 265
Alcindor, Ferdinand Lewis ("Lew"), 240, *240*
Alcohol and advertising, 646–647
Alito, Samuel, *14*
  conservative votes and, 13, 13*b*
  on law school denial of funding to student religious group,
    127
Allen, Thad, 324*b*
Allen, Woody, 240
All-purpose public figures and libel, 170, 180–185
Altman, Andrew, 684*n*129
Ambler, Eric, *236*, 236*b*
American Center for Democracy, 208*b*
American Coalition of Life Activists (ACLA), 114–115
American Jurisprudence 2d, 32
American Library Association, 122*b*
American Revolution, 55
American Society of Composers, Authors and Publishers
    (ASCAP), 610, 614
America Online (AOL), 148, 149*b*, 340
Amicus curiae and amicus briefs, 10
Anderson, David, 298, 678*n*5, 696*n*70, 696*n*73
Animal cruelty, depictions of as speech, *6b*, 51
Ann-Margret, 539
Anonymous juries, 428
Anonymous posters on Web, 65, 398*b*
Anonymous speech, 75, 151*b*, 152, 152*b*
Anthrax letters, 283–284, 395*b*
Antiabortion protests, 66, *70*, 70*b*, 114–115
Anticybersquatting Consumer Protection Act of 1999
    (ACPA), 623

Anti-SLAPP state statutes, 144–146, 144*b*
Anti-Terrorism and Effective Death Penalty Act, 103*b*
Antiwar t-shirts and soldiers' names, 242*b*
AOL (America Online), 148, 149*b*, 340
AP (Associated Press), 64, 166, 307, 324*b*, 586
Appellants, 31
Appellate courts, 10–12, 11*f*, 11*m*
  amicus briefs and amicus curiae, 10
  certiorari, 12
  concurring opinions, 11
  de novo review, 10
  dissenting opinions, 11
  due process, 10
  en banc, 10
  levels, 10
  majority decisions, 11
  plurality decisions, 11–12
  process, 15*f*
  remand, 12
  writ of certiorari, 12
Appellate process, 15*f*
Appellees, 31
Appropriation, 237–244
  antiwar t-shirts and soldiers' names, 242*b*
  artistic relevance test, 247–248
  artistic works, 246–251
  commercialization, 237*b*, 238–239, 241*b*
  consent, 252
  damages, 244
  defenses, 244–253
  defined, 228*b*, 237
  First Amendment, 246–251
  identity, 241–244
  incidental use, 252
  likeness, 239–240
  media ads, 251–252
  name, 239–240
  newsworthiness, 245–246
  plaintiff's case, 239–244
  public domain, 246
  publicity, right of, 237*b*, 238–239, 691*n*70
  Rogers test, 247–248, 250
  sound-alikes, 240–241
  transformativeness test, 248–250, 249*b*
  voice, 240–241

Arbitrary marks, 620
Arcabascio, Catherine, 711*n*60
Ardia, David, 677*n*22
Aristotle, 4, 5*b*
Armstrong, Jacob, 716*n*64
Arthur, John, 684*n*129
Article I courts, 8*t*
Artistic relevance test, 247–248
Artistic works
    appropriation and, 246–251
    obscenity and, 533
    public funding of, 562–563
    sexual expression in, 530, 533
ASCAP (American Society of Composers, Authors and
        Publishers), 610, 614
Ashcroft, John, 354, 428, 628–633, 701*n*122
Assange, Julian, 390*b*
Assembly, freedom of
    First Amendment protection of, 21
    public forums, 78–84, 80*b*
Associated Press (AP), 64, 166, 307, 324*b*, 586
AT&T records, 361
Attorneys and advertising, 650
Authorship and copyright law, 584–586
Autoerotic asphyxiation and incitement, 299
Avara, Mary, 544*b*

B

Bad-tendency standard, 106
Baker, C. Edwin, 679*n*25
Baker, J. H., 684*n*11
Baker, Meredith, 480*b*
Baker, Russ W., 698*n*48
Ballot issues, 490
Banned books, 121–122, 122*b*
Barbie dolls, 247
Barnes, Cynthia, 304
Barry, W. T., 700*n*102
Baseball cards, 246–247
Bayard, Sam, 679*n*45
Beach Boys, 624, 624
Beeson, Ann, 101
Behrens, Mark A., 686*n*100

Belushi, John, 388*b*
Bench-bar-press guidelines, 451–452, 451*b*
Benton, Tracy, 702*n*19
Bergen, Candice, 539, 539
Berne Convention for Protection of Literary and Artistic
        Works, 582–583, 582*b*, 591, 594
Best, Eran, 285
Bezanson, Randall P., 686*n*99
Bigelow, Jeffrey, 643
Billings Gazette, 398*b*
Bill of Rights, 21, 22*b*, 106, 323. *See also specific amendments*
Biographies, 251
Bipartisan Campaign Reform Act of 2002 (BCRA), 12, 72
Bittle, Lyndon F., 687*n*100
Black, Hugo
    on clear and present danger, 107
    on restraints on speech, 678*n*3
Black, Robert, 296
Black, Sandra, 296
Black-letter law, 19, 24
Blackmail, 52
Blackmun, Harry
    on advertising as speech, 640
    on bench-bar-press guidelines, 452
    on indefinite delay of news broadcast, 64
    on trial closure, 434
Blackout rules, 510*b*, 512, 514
Black Panther Party, 251
Blackstone, William, 54–55, 141–142, 678*nn*13–14,
        684*nn*12–13
Blair, Jayson, 716*n*35
Blanchard, Margaret A., 681*n*2, 711*n*11
Blasi, Vincent, 679*n*21, 681*n*3
Blogs, 393, 396*b*. *See also* Internet
Bly, Nelly, 256
BMI (Broadcast Music, Inc.), 610, 614
Bock, Carey, 150*b*
Bok, Sissela, 680*n*82
Bollinger, Lee C., 679*n*24
Bong Hits 4 Jesus, 120, *121*, 129*b*
Bono, 550, *551*
Bono, Sonny, 595*b*
Books. *See also titles and authors of specific books*
    banned, 121–122, 122*b*
    reviews of, 191

Booth, Shirley, 251

Bootstrapping, 171

Bork, Robert, 197*b*

Bose Corp., 157

Boston University, 450

Boyle, Paul, 390*b*

BP oil spill, 324*b*

Brandeis, Louis, 677*n*21, 690*n*32, 706*n*111
   on clear and present danger, 107
   on holding and expressing opinions, 193
   on prior restraints, 65
   on right to privacy, 228, 238, 457

Brandenburg, Clarence, 108

Brandenburg/Hess test, 108–109, 108*b*, 117, 299–301, 311–319

Branzburg test, 383–386, 384*b*, 405–417

Braverman, Nathan, 701*n*75

Braxton, Greg, 698*n*35

Breach of contract, 305–306, 306*b*

Brennan, William
   on advertising as speech, 642
   on libel standard and public figures, 138, 161, 163, 168
   on offensive protest, 117
   on Sedition Act, 57

Breyer, Stephen, *14, 505*
   on cable television and First Amendment rights, 505, 556
   on community standards and Internet speech, 538
   on media coverage of trials, 426
   swing votes and, 13
   on wiretapping, 340

Bright-line distinctions, 59

Broadband Internet, 516

Broadcast Music, Inc. (BMI), 610, 614

Broadcast regulation
   advertising, 484–498. *See also* Advertising
   broadcast licensing, 499–502
   children's programming, website addresses displayed during, 493
   core programming, 492–493
   DBS, 482, 508, 514–515, 598
   editorials, 490
   electromagnetic spectrum, 482, 483*b*, 503
   electronic media regulation, 481–482. *See also* Electronic media regulation
   equal opportunity, 484

hoaxes, 495–496, 496*b*

Internet, 482

licensing, 499–502

local radio station ownership, 501*b*

low-power radio and television, 482

noncommercial broadcasting, 501–502

payola, 497

political broadcasting, 484, 485*b*

programming, 484–498. *See also* Programming and advertising regulations

public interest standard, 482–484

reasons to regulate, 481–482

satellite radio, 482

spectrum scarcity, 482, 483*b*, 503

VNRs, 497, 498

website addresses displayed during children's programming, 493

Zapple rule, 490

Brown, Bruce D., 695*n*1

Brown & Williamson Tobacco Co., 143*b*

Browne, Jackson, 615*b*

Bryan, Teresa, 712*n*70

Bryant, Paul "Bear," 166

Buckley Act of 1974, 346

Bundled political contributions, 75

Bunker, Matthew D., 679*n*58, 697*n*5, 697*n*9

Burden of proof, 146, 159*b*

Bureau of Consumer Protection, 654

Burger, Warren, 434

Burnett, George, 166

Burning protests
   cross-burning, 52, 111
   draft card burning, 92–96, 116–117
   flag burning, 67, 98–99, 117, 131–133
   symbolic speech, 116–117

Bush, George W.
   executive orders, 20
   Patriot Act reauthorization and, 102
   reelection of, 490

Business reputation, 157

Butler University, 619*b*

Butts, Wally, 166

Byrne, Brendan, 388*b*

Byrne, David, 615*b*

C

Cable Communications Policy Act of 1984, 504, 511
Cable modems, 516
Cable Television Consumer Protection and Competition Act of 1992, 504, 512–513, 514
Cable television regulation, 503–509
  access requirements, 511–512
  adult programming, 505–506
  blackout rules, 510*b*, 512, 514
  CATV, 503
  channel capacity, 512–513
  content-specific, 505–506
  development of, 503–506
  electronic media regulation, 503–509. *See also* Electronic media regulation
  federal cable laws, 504
  First Amendment rights, 505–506
  franchising, 506–508
  indecency, 555–557
  microwave transmissions, 503
  must-carry rules, 505, 509–511, 514
  MVS, 508
  nonduplication rules, 512
  ownership, 508
  PEG access channels, 511–512, 555–556
  pole rules, 504
  programming, 509–514
  P2P applications, 516
  retransmission consent rules, 509–511, 510*b*
  sales of cable systems, 507
  sharing programs and channel capacity, 512–513
  strict scrutiny, 506
  subscribers' privacy, 513
  syndicated exclusivity rules, 512
Cablevision Systems, 510*b*, 601
CACI International, 173*b*
Caldeira, Gregory A., 677*n*17
Calvert, Clay, 698*n*42, 708*n*91
Cameras
  in courtrooms, 440*b*, 440*m*, 446*b*, 448–449, 448*b*
  in private places, unauthorized use of, 335*b*
Campaign financing, 2, 3, 17, 38–44, 72–75, 74*b*
Campbell, Luther, 605*b*

Campus Security Act of 1990, 346
Campus speech codes, 128–130
Canan, Penelope, 685*n*19
CAN-SPAM (Controlling the Assault of Non-Solicited Pornography and Marketing Act of 2003), 662–663, 662*b*
Cantrell, Margaret, 234–235
Cantril, Hadley, 707*n*67
Cantu, Charles E., 695*n*5
Carlin, George, 548, 549–550*b*
Carlson, Alan, 706*n*104, 706*n*106
"Carnal Knowledge" (film), 539, *539*
Carneal, Michael, 295–296
Carreau, Mark, 700*n*105
Carroll, Jill, *345*
Carter, Jimmy, 489
Case law
  analysis of, 35
  briefing of, 35–36
  common law rule of law, 35
  concurring opinions, 11
  dissenting opinions, 11
  en banc opinions, 10
  facts, 34–35
  history, 35
  holding, 34
  issue identification, 34
  per curiam opinions, 15
  reading of, 34–35
  rule of law, 35
Case process, 27–31
  appellants, 31
  appellees, 31
  civil suits, 28–29, 31
  complaints, 28
  criminal matters, 27–28
  defendant, defined, 28
  demurrer, 29
  discovery, 29
  dismissal, 29
  grand juries, 27
  motion to dismiss, 29
  path of lawsuits, 28*f*
  peremptory challenges, 29, 430
  plaintiff, defined, 28

Case process *(cont.)*
  probable cause, 27
  settlement, 29
  standing, 651
  strict liability, 28, 29
  subpoena, 29, 30*b*
  summary judgment, 31–32, 206–207
  summons, 28, 429
  tort, defined, 28, 29
  venire, 29, 429, 430
  venue, 29, 425, 430
  voir dire, 29
"Catcher in the Rye" (Salinger), 604
Categorical balancing, 51–52, 100
Catholic Church, 53
CATV (Community antenna television), 503
CBS (television network)
  BP spill, access to Gulf site, 324*b*
  chilling effect, 143*b*
  Fourth Amendment rights, violation of, 327–329
  public record of private facts, 268
  reasonable time for federal candidates, 489
  retransmission, 510
  trade libel claims, 157
  wardrobe malfunctions, 480, *528*, 550–551
CBS Radio, 497
CDA. *See* Communications Decency Act of 1996
CD-ROMs and copyright law, 588–589
Cease and desist orders, 655*b*, 657
Ceballos, Richard, 77
Celebrities and libel, 170
Cell phones and pagers, 222
  government employees, privacy rights of, 225–226, 273–277
  privacy concerns, 226*b*
  sexting, 543–544
  smart phone applications, 224
Censorship
  books and public schools, 121–122, 122*b*
  of films, 544*b*, 545
  First Amendment, 61–66
  of Internet, 557*b*
  prior restraints and, 61–66, 62–63*b*, 65*b*
Censorship boards, 544*b*, 545
Central Hudson test, 645–646, 649*b*, 664–670
Central Intelligence Agency (CIA), 351, 356–357, 615*b*

Certiorari, 12
CFAA (Computer Fraud and Abuse Act), 300*b*
Chafee, Zechariah, 678*n*17
Challenger space shuttle, *320*, 359*b*
Challenges for cause, 29, 430
Chamberlin, George K., 719*n*217
Channel capacity, 512–513
Chaplinsky, Walter, 110
Checks and balances, 20
Chemerinsky, Erwin, 127*b*, 683*n*75, 697*n*5, 697*nn*7–8
Cheney, Richard, 344
Cher, 251–252, 550
Cherry Sisters, 192*b*
Child Online Protection Act of 1998 (COPA), 558–560
Child pornography, 52, 541–544
Child Pornography Protection Act of 1996 (CPPA), 542, 560–561
Children
  programming for, 491–493
  transmission of obscenity to, 557–558
  violent programming and, 293–294, 566–570
  website addresses displayed during programming for, 493
Children's Internet Protection Act of 2000 (CIPA), 561
Children's Television Act of 1990, 491
Chilling effect
  CBS and tobacco story, killing of, 143*b*
  defined, 102
  fleeting-obscenity rule, effect of, 551
  libel suits, threat of, 144
  New York Times v. Sullivan, effect of, 163*b*
  PATRIOT Act and, 102–103
  Sedition Act and, 144
  vague laws and, 6*b*
Chrestensen, F. J., 642
Christian Dior clothing, 240
Christian Legal Society, 126
Chronicle of Higher Education, 347
Chrysler Corp., 357–358
CIA (Central Intelligence Agency), 351, 356–357, 615*b*
CIPA (Children's Internet Protection Act of 2000), 561
Citadel Broadcasting, 497
Citizens United, 3, 17, 38–44, 74*b*
City parks and monuments, 76
Civil contempt of court, 385*b*, 431
Civil suits, 28–29
  appellants, 31

appellees, 31

complaints, 28

defendant, defined, 28

demurrer, 29

discovery, 29

dismissal, 29

motion to dismiss, 29

path of lawsuits, 28f

peremptory challenges, 29, 430

plaintiff, defined, 28

settlement, 29

strict liability, 28, 29

subpoena, 29, 30b

summary judgment, 31–32, 206–207

summons, 28, 429

tort, defined, 28, 29

venire, 29, 429, 430

venue, 29, 425, 430

voir dire, 29

Civil War, 343

CJOG (Coalition of Journalists for Open Government), 353b

Clark, Gavin, 684n6

Clark, Tom, on prejudicial publicity, 420

Clear and present danger test, 105–108

Clear Channel Broadcasting, 480, 497

Clery Act of 1990, 346

Cleveland Plain Dealer, 234–235

Clinton, Bill, 360, 360–361, 648

Clinton, Hillary, 3, 360

Clyburn, Mignon, 480b

CNN (cable network), 327, 443, 507

Coalition of Journalists for Open Government (CJOG), 353b

Codes and codification, 21, 23–24

Cohen, Dan, 398–400, 399b, 417–419

Cohen, Paul Robert, 109

Cohn, Martin, 270–273

Cole, David, 103b

Colgate, Samuel, 533

Colleges. See Universities and colleges

Collins, Richard, 107

Columbine High School (Littleton, Colorado), 295, 566

Comcast Corp., 498, 510, 516

Commerce Clause, 66–67

Commercialization, 237b, 238–239, 241b

Commercial speech doctrine, 642–646, 644–645b

Common law

  defined, 19

  libel and English common law, 141–142, 158

  reading case law, 34–35

  as source of law, 24–26, 35

Communications Act of 1934

  adoption of, 478

  enforcement of, 479

  FCC creation, 478

  hoaxes, 495

  indecency, 546, 547

  Internet regulation, 515

  public interest standard, 482–484

  Section 312, 489, 490, 514

  Section 315, 484, 487b, 489, 514

  spectrum users, 482, 483b, 503

Communications Decency Act of 1996 (CDA)

  Internet and First Amendment, 517–518

  Internet indecency, 559b

  ISPs as vendors, 148

  libel and online publishers, 149b

  minors, transmission of obscenity to, 557–558

  third parties, protection of, 303–305

  unconstitutionality of, 24

Communist Party, 106–107

Community antenna television (CATV), 503

Community standards and Internet speech, 538

Compelled speech, 84, 124

Compelling interests, 67

Compositions, 609–611

Compulsory licenses and copyright law, 598

Computer Fraud and Abuse Act of 1986 (CFAA), 300b

Computer records, 362–363

Computers

  copyright law, 607–609

  privacy rights, 222, 224, 225

Comstock, Anthony, 533–535, 534, 534b

Comstock Act of 1873, 533

Concurring opinions, 11

Conditional privilege, 190

Conference of Chief Justices, 455

Conference of State Court Administrators, 455

Confidential sources

  breaking promises to, 398–404, 399b, 417–419

  protection of, 393b

Congressional Record, 349

ConnectU, 437

Conrad, Mark A., 706*n*1

Consent

  appropriation, defense to, 252

  intrusion, defense to, 256

Consent orders, 655*b*, 657

Conspiracy of intellect, 52*b*

Constitution, U.S.

  Article I, 8*t*

  Article III, 7, 8*t*

  First Amendment, 48–96. *See also* First Amendment

  Third Amendment, 223–224, 227

  Fourth Amendment

    public employees, privacy rights of, 226, 273–277

    search warrants, 327–328*b*, 327–329, 370–373, 400

    text of, 223

  Fifth Amendment, 227

  Sixth Amendment, 422, 430, 432–445

  Fourteenth Amendment, 106, 227

  amendment of, 5, 21

  Bill of Rights, 21, 22*b*, 106, 323

  branches of government, 20, 21*b*

  checks and balances, 20

  Commerce Clause, 66–67

  copyrights, 9, 580*b*

  due process, 10, 106

  Establishment Clause, 125

  facial challenges, 4, 6*b*

  original intent, 50

  patents, 580*b*

  political questions, 20

  privacy protection and, 227

  separation of powers, 17, 20

  speedy trial right, 430

  state constitutions vs., 20–21

  Supremacy Clause, 23

  vague laws, 4, 6*b*

Constitutions, 19, 20–21. *See also* Constitution, U.S.

Consumer Protection Bureau, 654

Consumer Reports, 157

Contemporary prior restraints, 61–66, 62–63*b*, 65*b*

Contempt of court

  blogging and, 396*b*

  civil, 385*b*, 431

criminal, 385*b*, 432

  defined, 431

  reporters and subpoenas, 395*b*

Content-based laws and regulations, 67–68

Content-neutral laws, 66, 68–72, 339–340

Contests, 493–495, 494*b*

Continuance, 425, 430

Contracts, 305–306, 306*b*

Contributory infringement, 601–602, 633–639

Controlling the Assault of Non-Solicited Pornography and Marketing Act of 2003 (CAN-SPAM), 662–663, 662*b*

Cookies on computers, 224, 661

COPA (Child Online Protection Act of 1998), 558–560

Copps, Michael, 480*b*

"COPS" (television series), 329

Copyright Act of 1976

  authorship, 584–586

  enactment of, 583

  limitations, 592–593

  musical works, 609–611

  notice, 594

  originality, 584–586, 584*b*

  ownership, 587–589

  protection rights, 589–592

  timing of protection, 587

  transfer of copyright, 594–595

  works protected by, 584–586

Copyright law, 9, 580–618, 580*b*, 628–639. *See also* Copyright Act of 1976

  amount and substantiality of portion used, 606–607

  authorship, 584–586

  CD-ROMs, 588–589

  compulsory licenses, 598

  computers and Internet, 607–609

  copyright, defined, 580

  derivative works, 590, 591*b*

  development of, 582–583

  duration, 595–597, 628–633

  fair use defense, 603–607, 603*b*, 626–627

  federal courts, 9

  first-sale doctrine, 593

  free speech, 66

  infringement, 599–603. *See also* Infringement

  Internet regulation, 607–609

  joint ownership, 587–589

legislative history, 592

limitations, 592–593

moral rights, 591

music licensing, 609–616. *See also* Music licensing

nature of copyrighted work, 605–606

notice, 594

originality, 584–586, 584*b*

ownership, 587–589

plagiarism, 586

potential market, effect on, 607

protection rights, 589–592, 591*b*

public display, 590, 591*b*

public distribution, 590, 591*b*

public domain, 595–596, 596*b*, 628–633

public performance, 590, 591*b*, 610*b*

registration, 597–598

remedies for infringement, 602

reproduction rights, 589–590, 591*b*

satire and, 604–605

Sonny Bono Copyright Term Extension Act of 1978,
     595, 595*b*

sound recording transmission, 590–591, 591*b*

statutory damages, 594

timing of protection, 587

transfer of copyrights, 594–595

use, purpose, and character of, 604–605

works made for hire, 588

works protected by, 584–586

Copyright Office, 597–598

Core programming, 492–493

Cornell Legal Information Institute, 33

Corporate speech regulation, 3, 17, 38–44, 74*b*, 650–652

Corporation for Public Broadcasting (CPB), 501–502

Corpus Juris Secundum, 32

Corrective advertising, 655*b*, 658

Cosby, William, 55

Court access and closure, 435–445, 455–456

Court dockets, 453–454

Court of Military Appeals, U.S., 8*t*

Court of Veterans' Appeals, U.S., 8*t*

Court records
   access to, 452–458
   constitutional access, 452–453
   court access rules, 455–456
   court dockets, 453–454

electronic access to, 456–458
   state secrets, 454–455
   statutory access, 452–453

Courtrooms and cameras, 440*b*, 440*m*, 446*b*, 448–449, 448*b*

Courtroom Sciences (Dr. Phil's company), 156*b*

Court system, 7–16
   amicus briefs and amicus curiae, 10
   appellate courts, 10–12. *See also* Appellate courts
   de novo review, 10
   district courts, 9
   due process, 10
   en banc, 10
   establishment of, 7
   federal, 7–9, 8*t*, 11*b*
   intermediate scrutiny, 69, 70–71*b*
   juries, 9. *See also* Juries and jurors
   jurisdiction, 7–9. *See also* Jurisdiction
   media, 420–473. *See also* Media and courts
   rational review, 67
   state, 8*t*
   strict scrutiny review, 66–68, 67*b*, 117, 340, 506
   Supreme Court, 12–13. *See also* Supreme Court, U.S.
   trial courts, 9

Court TV, 606

Covert recording, 335–343. *See also* Newsgathering
   broadcasting recorded telephone calls, 339–341
   face-to-face recording, 335–336
   in-state telephone calls, 337
   interstate telephone calls, 337–339

Cowles Media Co., 417–419

Cox Broadcasting Corp., 270–273

CPB (Corporation for Public Broadcasting), 501–502

CPPA (Child Pornography Protection Act of 1996), 542, 560–561

Craigslist, 304

Creasy, Shannon, 710*n*4, 711*n*10

Creative Commons, 596–597

Credit card debt reduction programs, advertising of, 659

Credit reports, 174

Crews, Timothy, 388*b*

Crime and criminal cases
   case process, 27–28
   grand juries, 27
   reporting and crime rates, 425*b*

Criminal contempt of court, 385*b*, 432

Criminal libel, 176–177

Crist, Charlie, 615*b*

Crook, Tim, 707*n*68

Cross-burning, 52, 111

Crum, Bartley, *107*

Crump, David, 686*n*100

"Cuidado con el Angel" (telenovela), *491*

Cuillier, David, 700*nn*119–120

Cullinan, Kathleen, 705*n*97

Cummins, Michael, 678*n*39

Curry, Richard O., 680*n*82

Cutting Edge Designs, 661*b*

Cyberbullying, 300*b*

Cybersquatting, 623

D

Dalglish, Lucy, 30*b*

Damages
  actual, 175
  appropriation, 244
  defined, 143
  exemplary, 176
  libel, 175–177
  presumed, 175
  punitive, 175–176
  special, 175
  statutory, 594

Data mining, 660

"Dateline," 284*b*, 334

Daugherty, F. Jay, 693*n*116

Davis, Charles N., 700*n*120

Davis, David, 104*b*

DBS (Direct broadcast satellite service), 482, 508, 514–515, 598

DEA (Drug Enforcement Administration), 455

DeBenedictis, Don J., 703*n*12

Debs, Eugene, 106

Defamation, 52, 54, 65, 140, 154–157. *See also* Libel

Defendants, defined, 28

Defense Department (DOD), 62, 343–344, 362*b*

Deference, 26

Delgado, Richard, 684*n*128

Demurrer, 29

Denny, Reginald, 606

De novo review, 10

Depositions, 168

Derivative works, 590, 591*b*

Descriptive marks, 620

Designated public forums, 79, 80*b*. *See also* Forums

Des Moines Leader, 192*b*

Desnick, J. H., 256, 257*b*

DeVore, Charles, 615*b*

DHS (Homeland Security Department), 20, 324*b*

Dial-a-porn, 565

Diana, Princess of Wales, 255, 330

Diaz, Toni, 264–265

DiCaprio, Leonardo, *295*

Digital Millennium Copyright Act of 1998 (DMCA),
  608–609, 616

Dilution of trademark, 625, 625*b*

Direct broadcast satellite (DBS) service, 482, 508, 514–515, 598

Direct right of appeal, 12

Discovery, 29, 168

Discretion, 4

Discrimination
  government funding and, 83
  sexual discrimination, 532
  viewpoint-based, 111–112

Dish Network, 510*b*

Dismissal of cases, 29

Disney, Walt, *578*

Disruptive speech, 98–137
  Brandenburg/Hess test, 108–109, 108*b*, 117, 299–301,
    311–319
  campus speech codes, 128–130
  clear and present danger test, 105–108
  compelled speech, 84, 124
  court tests to protect, 105–109
  current standard, 112
  educationally inappropriate content in public schools, 121–124
  fighting words, 52, 110–111, 111*b*, 656
  government slogans, 124
  hate speech, 111–112, 128–130
  heckler's veto, 127*b*
  ideological orthodoxy in public schools, 124
  incitement test, 108–109, 108*b*, 117, 299–301, 311–319
  incorporation doctrine, 106
  intimidation and threats, 112–115
  national security, 100–105. *See also* National security
  offensive content in public schools, 121–124

protests, 116–117, 119–121, 133–137

public schools and, 52, 118–130, 119*b*, 133–137

religion in public schools, 125

speech assaults, 109–116

terrorist groups, 101–102, 103*b*

tranquility, protection of, 100–105

true threats, 52, 112–115, 115*b*

underinclusiveness, 111

viewpoint-based discrimination, 111–112

wiretapping, 104, 337–341

Dissenting opinions, defined, 11

Distinctiveness requirement, 619–621

Distributors of libel, 147–152

District courts, 9

DMCA (Digital Millennium Copyright Act of 1998), 608–609, 616

Dockets, 453–454

Doctrines as sources of law, 19–20

DOD (Defense Department), 62, 343, 344, 362*b*

Dodge, William, Jr., 533

DOE (Education Department), 346, 347, 498

DOJ (Justice Department), 104, 374–379

Domain names, 515, 623–624

"Doom" video game, 556

Douglas, William, on commercial speech doctrine, 644

Downloading and file sharing, 616–617

Draft card burning, 92–96, 116–117

Drennan, John, 30*b*

Drew, Sarah and Lori, 300*b*

Driver's Privacy Protection Act of 1994, 347

Drudge, Matt, 148, 393

"The Drudge Report," 148

Drug Enforcement Administration (DEA), 455

D'Souza, Dinesh, 684*n*127

Due process, 10, 106

"Dungeons and Dragons" (game), 297

Duty of care, 291

DuVal, Benjamin S., Jr., 680*n*82

Dymtryk, Edward, *107*

E

EA (Electronic Arts), 249*b*

Economic advantage, interference with, 306–307

ECPA (Electronic Communications Privacy Act of 1986), 339–341

Editorials, 490

Educational values. *See* Schools; Universities

Education Department (DOE), 346, 347, 498

EFOIA (Electronic Freedom of Information Act of 1996), 351, 362–363

Ehrenfeld, Rachel, 208*b*

Eko, Lyombe, 719*n*196

Eldred, Eric, 596, 628–633

Election advertising and financing, 3, 17, 38–44, 72–75, 74*b*. *See also* Campaign financing

Elections Campaign Act of 1971, 73

Electromagnetic spectrum, 482, 483*b*, 503

Electronic access

to court records, 456–458

to trials, 445–451

Electronic Arts (EA), 249*b*

Electronic Communications Privacy Act of 1986 (ECPA), 339–341

Electronic Freedom of Information Act of 1996 (EFOIA), 351, 362–363

Electronic Frontier Foundation, 30*b*, 33

Electronic media regulation, 474–527

broadcast regulation, 481–482. *See also* Broadcast regulation

cable television, 503–509. *See also* Cable television regulation

DBSs, 482, 508, 514–515, 598

FCC, 478–480. *See also* Federal Communications Commission

Internet regulation, 515–518, 607–609. *See also* Internet

Elliott, Christopher, *30*, 30*b*

Ellsberg, Daniel, *62*

E-mail

commercial bulk e-mail regulation, 663

privacy, 661–663, 662*b*

public employees' e-mail, 365*b*

threats via, 115*b*

Embedded journalists, 344–345

Emerson, Thomas I., 679*n*20, 680*n*80

EMI, 497

Emotional distress, 279–293

defined, 280

incitement, 298–303. *See also* Incitement

intentional infliction of emotional distress, 280, 282–291, 283*b*, 309–311

negligent infliction of emotional distress, 280, 291–293, 292*b*

Emotional distress *(cont.)*
    suits, development of, 280–282
    tort law, expansion of, 307–308
En banc opinions, 10
English common law and libel, 141–142, 158
Entercom, 497
Entertainment Software Rating Board (ESRB), 568, 569*b*,
        715*nn*184–185
Entine, John, 257*b*
Equal opportunity, 484
Equity law, 19, 24
Erickson, Emily, 679*n*58
Ertter, John S., 705*n*71, 706*n*109
Espionage Act of 1917, 105
ESPN (television network), 504, 507, 510*b*
ESRB (Entertainment Software Rating Board), 568, 569*b*,
        715*nn*184–185
Establishment Clause, 125
Estes, Billie Sol, 423–424, *424*
Eszterhas, Joe, 234–235
Ethics
    advertising by attorneys, 650
    Aristotle on, 5*b*
    bench-bar-press guidelines, 451–452, 451*b*
Etzioni, Amitai, 713*n*133, 714*n*172
Evans, Josh, 300*b*
Evans, Rowland, Jr., *196*, 196–197*b*, 213–218
Everett-Haynes, La Monica, 705*n*70
Exclusivity rules, 512
Executive orders, 20, 26–27
Exemplary damages, 176
Experience and logic test, 435
Extortion, 52

F

FAA (Federal Aviation Administration), 324*b*
FACA (Federal Advisory Committee Act of 1972), 365
Facebook, 225, 264*b*, 367*b*, 437, 449
Face-to-face recording, 335–336
Facial challenges, 4, 6*b*
Facial meaning, 23
Fact finder, defined, 232
Fair, Lesley, 721*n*43

Fair comment and criticism, 191, 192*b*
Fair Labor Association, 651
Fairness doctrine, 496–497, 519–524
Fairness in Music Licensing Act of 1998, 611
Fair report privilege, 188–190, 188*b*
Fair trials, 422–429
Fair use
    amount and substantiality of portion of copyrighted work
            used, 606–607
    copyright infringement and, 603–607, 603*b*, 626–627
    defined, 603, 603*b*
    Lanham Act, 626–627
    nature of copyrighted work, 605–606
    potential market effect, 607
    purpose and character of use, 604–605
    trademark infringement and, 626–627
False advertising, 52, 654*b*
False light, 229–237, 691*n*41
    absolute privilege, 236
    defenses, 231*b*, 235–236
    defined, 228*b*, 229
    elements of claim, 231*b*
    falsity, 231–232
    fault, 234–235
    fiction, 233–234
    Florida's rejection of, 230*b*
    highly offensive standard, 232–234
    identification, 152–153, 231
    implication, 233*b*
    opinion, 193–195, 236
    plaintiff's case, 231–235
    positive misinformation, 236*b*
    privacy, 229–237, 691*n*41
    publication, 231
    truth, 236
False pretenses, 256–258, 257*b*
Falsity
    false light, 231–232
    implication and innuendo, 159
    knowledge of, 164–166, 164*b*
    libel, 157–158
    substantial truth, 158
Falwell, Jerry, 288–290, *290*, 309–311
Family Educational Rights and Privacy Act of 1974 (FERPA), 346
Family Entertainment and Copyright Act of 2005, 592

Family Movie Act of 2005 (FMA), 592

Family Smoking Prevention and Tobacco Control Act of 2009, 660

Fanciful marks, 619–620

Farber, Myron, 388*b*

The Fat Boys, 240

Fault and libel, 160–164, 172–174, 234–235

Favish, Allan, 360–361

FBI (Federal Bureau of Investigation), 283–284, 360, 374–379

FCC. *See* Federal Communications Commission

FDA (Food and Drug Administration), 648, 660

FEC (Federal Election Commission), 75, 490

Federal Advisory Committee Act of 1972 (FACA), 365

Federal Aviation Administration (FAA), 324*b*

Federal Bureau of Investigation (FBI), 283–284, 360, 374–379

Federal cable laws, 504

Federal Communications Commission (FCC)
    administrative law, creation of, 20
    advertising regulation by, 660. *See also* Advertising
    broadcasting of recorded telephone calls, 339–341
    broadcast licensing, 499–502
    chair appointment, 480*b*
    creation of, 478
    electronic media regulation, 478–480. *See also* Electronic media regulation
    fairness doctrine, 496–497, 519–524
    First Amendment, 524–527. *See also* First Amendment
    fleeting-obscenity rule, 551
    indecency, defined, 547, 575–577
    Internet regulation, 515–517. *See also* Internet
    interstate telephone calls, recording of, 337–339
    notice of proposed rule making, 479
    "The Phone Rule," 339
    radio broadcast regulation, 60, 476
    reduction of commissioners, 479*b*
    telephone calls, recording of, 337–341

Federal courts, 7–9, 8*t*, 11*f*, 11*m*

Federal Election Commission (FEC), 75, 490

Federalism, 20

Federal Open Meetings Law, 364–365

Federal preemption, 23–24

Federal Radio Act of 1927, 547

Federal Radio Commission (FRC), 478

Federal Trade Commission (FTC)
    administrative law, creation of, 20
    advisory opinions, 655–656, 655*b*
    cease and desist orders, 655*b*, 657
    computer privacy, 222, 224, 225
    consent orders, 655*b*, 657
    corrective advertising, 655*b*, 658
    corrective measures, 655*b*
    false and misleading advertising, 654*b*
    industry guides, 655*b*, 656
    injunctions, 655*b*, 659
    legislative advertising regulation, 654–659
    litigated orders, 655*b*, 657
    mechanisms, 655*b*
    opinion letters, 655, 655*b*
    preventive measures, 655*b*
    substantiation, 655*b*, 658
    trade regulation rules, 655*b*, 656
    violent content marketed to children, report on, 293–294, 567
    voluntary compliance, 655*b*, 657

Fellini, Federico, 247

"Female Forces" (TV show), 285

FEPP (Free Expression Policy Project), 102–103

Fernandez, Adam L., 714*n*159

FERPA (Family Educational Rights and Privacy Act of 1974), 346

Fiction
    false light and, 233–234
    Internet and, 113
    libel in, 153–154, 153*b*

Fiduciary relationship, 307

Fifth Amendment, 227

Fighting words, 52, 65*b*, 110–111, 111*b*

File sharing and music, 616–617

Films, censorship of, 544*b*, 545

Financial records, 361

Finding law. *See* Research sources

Findlaw, 33

Fines for refusing to reveal sources, examples of, 388*b*

Finkelstein, Howard, 232

First Amendment, 48–96
    ad hoc balancing, 52
    appropriation, 246–251
    blackmail, 52
    bright-line distinctions, 59
    cable television regulation, 505–506

First Amendment *(cont.)*

categorical balancing, 51–52, 100

censorship, 61–66

child pornography, 52

compelling interests, 67

contemporary prior restraints, 61–66, 62–63*b*, 65*b*

content-based laws and regulations, 67–68

content-neutral laws, 66, 68–72, 339–340

corporations, rights of, 3, 17, 38–44

court scrutiny of laws affecting, 66–72

cross-burning, 52, 111

defamation, 52, 54

disruptive speech in public schools, 52, 118–130, 133–137

draft card burning, 92–96, 116–117

Establishment Clause, 125

extortion, 52

false advertising, 52

FCC and, 524–527

fighting words, 52, 65*b*, 110–111, 111*b*

flag burning, 67, 98–99, 117, 128–130

freedom of assembly, 21

freedom of press, 48–96

freedom of speech, defined, 60*b*

free speech, value of, 58–59*b*

general application laws, 83, 400

government speech, 76–78

hate speech, 111–112, 128–130

important government interests, 69

incorporation doctrine, 106

individual liberty, 58*b*

intermediate scrutiny, 69, 70–71*b*

Internet and CDA, 517–518

interpretation of, 50–53

limited government power, 58*b*

media content determinations, 59–61

media emergence, convergence and consolidation, 85–88

media types and regulatory differences, 86–88

news broadcast, indefinite delay of, 64

O'Brien test, 69, 70*b*, 511

obscenity, 52. *See also* Obscenity and indecency

offensive speech, 109–110

original intent, 50

origins of, 53–57

perjury, 52

political contributions, 72–75, 74*b*

political speech, 52, 72–78

prior restraints, 61–66, 62–63*b*, 65*b*

privacy rights, 17

private facts, 266–269. *See also* Private facts

rape victims' names, publication of, 266–267, 270–273, 441

rational review, 67

rights under, 21

seditious libel, 55, 57, 143–144

seditious speech, 52

self-government, 58*b*

strict scrutiny, 66–68, 67*b*, 117, 340, 506

students, applicability to, 118

summary judgments, 31–32

symbolic speech, 67, 69, 116–117, 131–133

text of, 50

theory, foundations of, 53–57

TPM (time/place/manner) laws, 68

true threats, 52, 112–115, 115*b*

truth, attainment of, 59*b*

vague laws, 4, 6*b*

values, 57–61

video games, 568–570

wiretapping, 104, 337–341

work product, 77

First Amendment Center, 33

First Amendment Law Review, 33

First-sale doctrine, 593

Fish and Wildlife Service (FWS), 327

Fitzgerald, Mark, 701*n*124

527 groups, 490

Flags

burning, 67, 98–99, 117, 131–133

saluting, 124

Flaherty, Robert, 30*b*

Flickr, 264*b*

Florida's rejection of false light, 230*b*

Florida Star, 266–267

Flynt, Larry, 278, 288–290, 289*b*, 344

TheFlyontheWall (website), 64–65

FMA (Family Movie Act of 2005), 592

FOIA. *See* Freedom of Information Act of 1966

Folgers coffee, 240

Food and Drug Administration (FDA), 648, 660

Food Lion grocery chain, 330–333, 332*b*

For-cause challenges, 430

Forcible overthrow of government, 65*b*

Ford, Gerald, 262, 604, 606

Ford Motor Co., 241

Foreign Intelligence Surveillance Court, 453

Foreign libel judgments, enforcement of, 208*b*

Foreseeability, 295–297

Forsythe, Lynn M., 717*n*83

"48 Hours" (television series), 268

Forums, 78–84

  city parks and monuments, 76

  designated public forums, 79, 80*b*

  government speakers and virtual forums, 83

  limited/designated public forums, 80*b*

  monuments in city parks, 76

  nonpublic forums, 79, 80*b*

  private property as public forum, 81–83

  public forums, 71*b*, 78–84, 80–81*b*

  public schools as limited public forums, 118

  shopping centers, privately-owned, 81–83

  traditional public forums, 79, 80*b*

  universities as limited public forums, 118, 125–126

  virtual, 83

Forum shopping

  defined, 9

  libel and jurisdiction, 207–209, 208–209*b*

Foster, Lisa, *360*

Foster, Vince, *51, 360*, 360–361

Fourteenth Amendment, 106, 227

Fourth Amendment

  public employees, privacy rights of, 226, 273–277

  search warrants, 327–328*b*, 327–329, 370–373, 400

  text of, 223

Fowler, Mark, 474, 479*b*, 483

FOX (television network), 329, 510, 510*b*

Franchise fees, 507

Franchises, 506–508

Frank, Jerome, 239

Fraser, Matthew, 122–123

Fraud and misrepresentation, 307, 330–334

Frazier, Dan, *242, 242b*

FRC (Federal Radio Commission), 478

Frederick, Joseph, 120

Freedman, David F., 681*n*101

Freedom Forum, 33

Freedom of assembly

  First Amendment protection of, 21

  public forums, 78–84, 80*b*

Freedom of Information Act of 1966 (FOIA)

  Abu Ghraib prison photos, 362*b*

  agency, defined, 350

  agency memos, 358

  basic tenets of, 349*b*

  computer records, 362–363

  corporate privacy not protected, 361

  denying access to records, 346

  e-mail, 365*b*

  exemptions, 353–362, 354*b*

  financial records, 361

  geological data, 362

  internal agency rules and procedures, 357

  law enforcement records, 359–361, 374–379

  national security, 356–357

  newsgathering, 349–364. *See also* Newsgathering

  obtaining records under, 351–353

  personal privacy, 359

  public interest vs. privacy interest, 51

  public records, 365*b*

  redacted document released under, *355*

  requests, responsiveness to, 353*b*

  statutory exemptions, 357

  trade secrets, 357–358

Freedom of press, 48–96. *See also* First Amendment

Freedom of speech, 48–96. *See also* First Amendment

Free Expression Policy Project (FEPP), 102–103

Free Flow of Information Act (proposed), 392

Freeman, George, 145*b*

Friedman, Lawrence, 686*n*64

Frischling, Steve, 30*b*

FritoLay, 241

Frohwerk, Jacob, 105–106

FTC. *See* Federal Trade Commission

FWS (Fish and Wildlife Service), 327

FX (FOX station), *555*

G

Gadahn, Adam, *56, 56b*

Gag orders, 425, 441–444

Galanter, Yale, *438*

Galella, Ron, 329–330

Gambling, advertising and, 648–650

Games, 297

GAO (General Accounting Office), 363

Garbus, Martin, 697n80

Garland, Nancy, 699n55

Gaston Gazette, 398b

Gates, Robert, 343

Geisel, Theodore Seuss, 677n6

Genachowski, Julius, 480, 480b

General Accounting Office (GAO), 363

General application laws, 83, 400

General Electric, 87

Generic words, 621

Geological data, 362

Gibson, Calvin, 304

Gilles, Susan M., 687n100

Gilson, Jerome, 719n199, 719n208, 719n213, 719n218

Ginsburg, Ralph, 164

Ginsburg, Ruth Bader, 14
    on law school denial of funding to student religious group,
        126–127
    liberal-leaning moderate on Court, 13, 13b

Gitlow, Benjamin, 106

Givens, Beth, 706n110

"Golden mean," 4

Goldfarb, Ronald L., 699n86

Goldman, Ronald, 336

Goldstein, Paul, 715nn7–8, 717n144

Goldwater, Barry, 164

Goodale, James C., 709n125

Google, 65, 148, 224, 254–255, 337

Gordon, Thomas, 678n1

Gore, Al, 563

Gore, Tipper, 563

Gould, Jon B., 684n132

Government
    branches of, 20, 21b
    checks and balances, 20
    government speakers and virtual forums, 83
    important interests, 69
    limited power, 58b
    self-government, 58b
    separation of powers, 20
    slogans, 124

Government employees, privacy rights of, 225–226,
    273–277, 365b

Government in Sunshine Act of 1976, 364–365

Government slogans, 124

Government speech, 76–78, 83

Governors State University, 128

Grace, Nancy, 286, 286–287

Grand juries
    case process, 27
    defined, 27
    juries and jurors, 27
    reporter's privilege and, 383, 405–417. See also Reporter's
        privilege

Grasso, Gabriel, 438

Gray, Larry, 296

Greenawalt, Kent, 682n28

Greene, Edith, 703n12

Greenhouse, Linda, 5

Greenwald, Glenn, 706n101

Grenada, 344

Griffin, Oscar, Jr., 423–424

Grisham, John, 232, 232

Grokster, Ltd., 616–617, 633–639

Gross, Kimberly, 703n3

Group identification in libel, 153

H

Hafner, Katie, 710n187

Hale, Dennis, 688n71

Hall, Kermit L., 680n82

Hall, Phillip W., Jr., 718n179

Halstuk, Martin E., 681n2

Hamilton, Alexander, 55

Hamowy, Ronald, 678n1

Hansen, Chris, 284, 284b

"Happy Birthday" (song), 587b

Harassment, 329–330

Hardcore, Max, 538

Harden, Blaine, 700n93

Haronian, John, 647b

Harper, Fowler V., 687n12

Harrelson, Woody, 299

Harris, Eric, 295

Hate speech, 111–112, 128–133

Hatfill, Steven J., 283–284, 395*b*

Hayes, John P., 402–417

HBO (Home Box Office), 504, 512, 555

Health and Human Services Department, 347

Health Insurance Portability and Accountability Act of 1996 (HIPAA), 347

Hearn, John Wayne, 296

Heckler's veto, 127*b*

Henley, Don, 615*b*

Henning, Kristin N., 704*n*49, 704*n*51

Henry VIII, 53

Henry, Patrick, 55

Hess, Gregory, 298–299

Hickey, Neil, 698*n*48

Hicklin rule, 533–534, 534*b*

High-definition signals, 515

Highly offensive standard, 232–234

Hill, Henry, 68

Hilton, Paris, 237, 243, 243*b*, 420

Hindenburg, 585, *585*

HIPAA (Health Insurance Portability and Accountability Act of 1996), 347

"Hit Man: A Technical Guide for Independent Contractors" (book), 300, *302*, 302*b*, 311–319

HIV/AIDS, 265

Hoaxes, 495–496, 496*b*

Hockstader, Lee, 700*n*105

Hoffman, Daniel N., 680*n*82

Holiday magazine, 251–252

Holmes, Oliver Wendell
   on clear and present danger test, 98, 105, 106
   on fair report privilege, 190

Home Box Office (HBO), 504, 512, 555

Homeland Security Act of 2002, 354

Homeland Security Department (DHS), 20, 324*b*

Honda Motor Co., 600

Honest Leadership and Open Government Act of 2007, 75

Horn, Lawrence, 302*b*

Horn, Mildred, 302*b*

Horn, Richard, 455

Hot news doctrine, 64–65

"The House of the Dead" (video game), 567*b*

House Un-American Activities Committee, *107*

Howard, Robert, 231–232

Huckabee, Mike, *615*, 615*b*

Hudson, David L., Jr., 680*n*87

Hughes, Howard, 251

Hulon, Willie, 56*b*

Humanitarian Law Project, 101–102, 103*b*

Humbach, John A., 711*n*49, 711*n*59

Hundt, Reed, 480*b*

Hunt, Galliard, 700*n*102

Hurtful speech, 287*b*

Hustler Magazine, 233*b*, 288–290, 289*b*, 309–311, 344

Hyperbole, 198–200

I

ICANN (Internet Corporation for Assigned Names and Numbers), 515

iChat, 337

Identification as element of libel, 152–153, 231

Identity and appropriation, 241–244

Ideological orthodoxy in public schools, 124

Imminent lawless action, 301

Impartiality
   judges, 428
   jurors, 422–423, 436*b*

Impartial jurors, 426–428

Implication and innuendo, 159

Important government interests, 69

In, Sung, 719*n*216

Incidental use and appropriation, 252

Incitement, 298–303
   Brandenburg/Hess test, 108–109, 108*b*, 117, 299–301, 311–319
   imminent lawless action, 301
   intention to incite, 299–301, 311–319
   likelihood of lawless acts, 301–303
   prior restraint, 65*b*

Incorporation doctrine, 106

Indecency. *See* Obscenity and indecency

Indian Affairs Bureau, 358

Individual liberty, 58*b*

Industry guides, 656, 656*b*

Infringement
   contributory, 601–602, 633–639
   copyright law, 599–603

Infringement *(cont.)*
   defenses to, 603–607, 626–627
   fair use, 603–607, 603*b*, 626–627
   parody, 604–605, 605*b*
   plaintiff's case, 599*b*
   proof of, 599–603
   remedies, 602
   satire and, 604–605
   trademarks, 624–626
   VCRs, 601
Injunctions
   FTC use of, 655*b*, 659
   hot news, delay of distribution, 64–65
   Internet, free speech on, 64–65
   as prior restraint, 62
   WikiLeaks case, 63*b*, 65
Innocent construction as defense to libel, 195–197
Innuendo and implication, 159
INS (International News Service), 586
"Inside Edition" (television series), 330
In-state telephone calls, recording of, 337
Intel, 437
Intellectual property, 578–639
   copyright, 9, 580–618, 580*b*, 628–639. *See also* Copyright
     law
   defined, 580
   patents, 580*b*
   Statute of Anne, 582
   trademarks, 618–627. *See also* Trademarks
Intentional infliction of emotional distress,
     282–291, 283*b*
   actual malice, 288–290, 309–311
   defined, 280
   hurtful speech, 287*b*
   intentional or reckless action, 288–290
   outrageousness, 283–288
Interference with economic advantage, 306–307
Interior Department, 358
Intermediate scrutiny
   defined, 69
   First Amendment, 69, 70–71*b*
   government employees, 71*b*
   private media and property, 71*b*
   public forums, 71*b*
   symbolic conduct, 71*b*

International News Service (INS), 586
Internet, 515–518
   advertising, 660–663
   bloggers and shield laws, 393, 396*b*
   broadband, 516
   broadcast regulation, 482
   cable modems, 516
   censorship, 557*b*
   Communications Act of 1934, 515
   community standards and, 538
   copyright law, 607–609
   cybersquatting, 623
   data mining, 660
   development of, 86
   domain names and trademarks, 515, 623–624
   electronic media regulation, 515–518
   e-mail, 661–663, 662*b*
   FCC and, 515–518
   fiction, 113
   file sharing, 616–617
   First Amendment status, 517–518
   indecency, 557–561, 559*b*. *See also* Obscenity and
     indecency
   intrusion and, 254. *See also* Intrusion
   ISPs, 148, 303–305, 340, 516–517, 608–609
   jurisdiction over disputes, 9, 9*b*
   libel on, 9, 148–152, 149–150*b*
   music, file sharing and, 616–617
   obscenity, 535, 537*b*. *See also* Obscenity and
     indecency
   prior restraints, 64–65
   privacy-proof plaintiffs, 264*b*
   P2P applications, 516, 616–617, 633–639
   as public forum, 81*b*
   regulation, 515–518, 607–609
   spam, 661–663, 662*b*
   targeted advertising, 660–661
   trademarks and domain names, 623–624
   true threats and, 113
   video blogging, 396*b*
   video sharing sites, 608–609
   website addresses displayed during children's
     programming, 493
   wiretapping and, 340
World Wide Web, 86, 515

Internet Corporation for Assigned Names and Numbers (ICANN), 515

Internet service providers (ISPs), 148, 303–305, 340, 516–517, 608–609

Interstate telephone calls, recording of, 337–339

Interviews. *See* Newsgathering

Intimate facts, 260–262

Intimidation and threats, 112–115

Intrusion
    claim against ABC network, 256
    consent to, 256
    defenses, 256–259
    defined, 228*b*
    false pretenses and, 256–258, 257*b*
    Internet and, 254
    methods of, 254
    newsworthiness, 258–259
    paparazzi, 255, 329–330, 331*b*
    privacy and, 253–259
    private property and, 254–255
    reasonable person standard for, 253
    seclusion and, 253
    by trespass, 255*b*

Involuntary public figures and libel, 172

Iraq, 344–345

Isaacman, Allan, 289*b*

ISPs. *See* Internet service providers

J

Jackson, Janet, 480, *528, 550–551*

Jackson, Michael, 422

Jail time for refusal to reveal sources, examples of, 388*b*

James, Fleming, Jr., 687*n*12

"James Bond" (film), 599

Jardine, Al, 624, *624*

Jaynes, Jeremy, 663

Jena six, *427, 427b*

"Joe Camel" advertising, 648

"John Doe" lawsuits, 151–152*b,* 152

Johnson, Bruce E.H., 145

Johnson, Gregory, *98, 99,* 117, 131–133

Johnson, Ron, 128

Joint ownership of copyright, 587–589

Joyce, James, 534

Judges
    impartiality of, 428
    selection of, 8*t*

Judicial review, 16–19. *See also* Standards of review

Juries and jurors
    anonymous juries, 428
    bias, 424–425
    bias and pre-trial publicity, 436*b,* 459–466
    challenges for cause, 29, 430
    grand juries, 27
    impaneling, 430
    impartial jurors, 422–423, 426–428, 436*b*
    juror admonition, 431
    juror sequestration, 425, 431
    jury selection, 429–430
    peremptory challenges, 29, 430
    pre-trial publicity, 424–425, 436*b,* 459–466
    summons, 429
    trial courts, 9
    venire, 29, 429, 430
    venue change, 430
    voir dire, 29

Jurisdiction, 7–9
    defined, 7
    forum shopping, 9, 207–209, 208–209*b*
    Internet disputes, 9, 9*b*
    libel, 9, 207–209, 209*b*
    original, 12
    tests, 9*b,* 208*b*
    U.S. Supreme Court, 12

Justice Department (DOJ), 104, 374–379

Justice Management Institute, 457

Justices of U.S. Supreme Court, 14*b. See also specific justice by name*

Juveniles. *See* Children

K

Kaelin, Brian "Kato," 155

Kagan, Elena, 13, 13*b,* 14

Kalven, Harry, Jr., 163*b,* 686*n*57

Kansas State University, 128

Kaplan, M. Lindsay, 684*n*7, 686*n*73

Karr, Timothy, 681n122

Kasky, Marc, 29, 651

Katsh, M. Ethan, 678n5

KaZaA, 450, 616

Keeton, W. Page, 685n39

Keller, Sam, 249b

Kemp, Deborah J., 717n83

Kennedy, Anthony, 14

    on community standards and Internet speech, 538

    conservative votes and, 13, 13b

    on falsity and libel, 166

    on Internet as public forum, 81b

Kennedy, Caroline, 330

Kennedy, John, Jr., 330

Kennedy, Peter, 334

Kenny, Robert, 107

Kenyota, Gregory, 715n191

Kerry, John, 490

Kirtley, Jane, 433b, 698n43, 698n48

KKK (Ku Klux Klan), 108, 113, 298

Klebold, Dylan, 295

Kloer, Phil, 705n67

Kmart, 265

Kmiec, Douglas, 653b

Knowledge of falsity, 164b

Koenigsberg, I. Fred, 715n17

Koester, Eric, 699n68

Korwar, Arati R., 684n132

Kosar, Devin, 708n86

Kranich, Nancy, 682n12

Krattenmaker, Thomas G., 706n3

Kreimer, Seth F., 680n82

Kristof, Nicholas, 283–284

Krotoszynski, Ronald J., Jr., 680n89

Ku Klux Klan (KKK), 108, 113

Kunich, John Charles, 696n52

Kurdistan Workers Party (PKK), 102, 103b

Kurland, Philip B., 685nn16–17

L

Laidman, Dan, 688n48

Lalonde, Anne Gilson, 720n235

Lanham Act of 1946, 619b, 622, 626–627, 652

Lardner, Ring, Jr., 107

LawCrawler, 33

Law enforcement records, 359–361, 374–379

Law review articles, 33

Laws of general application, 83

Lawsuit process. See Case process

Leahy, Patrick, 208b

Leaks, 65, 390b

Leary, Mary Graw, 711n56

Lederer, Laura, 684n128

Lee, Mark S., 692n104

Lee, Pamela Anderson, 264

LegalTrac, 33

Leggett, Vanessa, 388b

Leggett, Virginia, 389

Legislative advertising regulation, 652–659

    corrective measures, 657–659

    FTC, 654–659

    preventive measures, 655–657

Legislative history and copyright law, 592

Leibowitz, Jonathan, 222

Lerner, Ralph, 685nn16–17

Lessig, Lawrence, 578, 596–597, 663, 715n1

Lett, Meredith Diane, 703n3

Letters to editors, 198, 199b

Leval, Pierre N., 693n114, 717n123, 717n125

Levine, Justin, 707n67, 707nn69–70, 707n72

Levit, Nancy, 695n8

Levy, Leonard, 678n15, 678n17

LexisNexis, 33

Li, William, 714n183

Libel (defenses and privileges), 186–221

    absolute privilege, 190

    conditional privilege, 190

    court filings, reporting from, as defense, 190

    fair comment and criticism, 191, 192b

    fair report privilege, 188–190, 188b

    innocent construction, 195–197

    jurisdiction, 207–209, 208–209b

    letters to editors, 198, 199b

    libel-proof plaintiffs, 204–206, 205b

    neutral reportage, 201–203b

    opinion, 193–195, 236

    parody, 154, 198–200

    qualified privilege, 190

    responsible reporting, 211–212

    retractions, 210–211

rhetorical hyperbole, 198–200
satire, 154, 198–200
single-mistake rule, 206
single publication rule, 203–204
statutes of limitations, 209–210, 210*m*
summary judgment, 206–207
wire service defense, 202–203, 202*b*
Libel (plaintiff's case)
    actual malice, 164–174. *See also* Actual malice
    advertising, 160–164, *162*, 178–180
    all-purpose public figures, 170, 180–185
    burden of proof, 146, 159*b*
    business reputation, 157
    contemporary issues, 146
    criminal, 176–177
    current trends, 145*b*
    damages, 175–177
    defamation, 52, 54, 140, 154–157
    "defamation by implication," 159
    defined, 142*b*
    distributors of libel, 147–152
    elements of case, 146–160, 147*b*, 152*b*, 167*b*, 170*b*
    falsity, 157–158. *See also* Falsity
    fault, 160–164, 172–174, 234–235
    fiction, identification of libel in, 153–154, 153*b*
    group identification, 153
    history of libel, 140–146
    identification, 152–153, 231
    implication and innuendo, 159
    Internet, 9, 148–152, 149*b*, 150*b*
    involuntary public figures, 172
    jurisdiction, 9, 207–209, 208–209*b*
    libel tourism, 208*b*
    limited-purpose public figures, 170–172, 170*b*
    losing public-figure status, 172
    nature of statement, 174
    online publishers, 149–150*b*
    private figures, 172–174
    publication, 147–152
    public figures, 169–170, 180–185
    public officials, 168–169
    republication, 147
    reputation, 142*b*, 157
    slander vs., 140*b*
    statement of fact, 147
    substantial truth, 158

    trade libel, 157
    unknown publishers of, 151–152*b*, 152
    vendors and distributors, 147–152
Libel per quod, 155
Libel per se, 154–155
Libel-proof plaintiffs, 204–206, 205*b*
Libel tourism bill, 208*b*
Liberty, 58*b*
Libraries, as designated public forums, 79
Library of Congress, 582, 597
Licenses and licensing
    broadcast licensing, 499–502
    compulsory licenses and copyright law, 598
    mechanical licenses, 611
    music licensing, 609–616. *See also* Music licensing
    politics and music licensing, 615*b*
Lichtblau, Eric, 695*n*22
Lidsky, Lyrissa Barnett, 697*n*10
Liebelson, Dana, 705*n*78
Life (movie), 600–601
Life magazine, 234, 258
Likeness, appropriation of, 239–240
LimeWire, 617
Limited government power, 58*b*
Limited public forums. *See also* Forums
    defined, 80*b*
    public schools as, 118
    universities as, 118, 125–126
Limited-purpose public figures and libel, 170–172, 170*b*
Litigated orders, 655*b*, 657
Litman, Jessica, 593, 716*n*74, 717*n*126
Little, Paul, 538
Litwiller, Lisa, 686*n*100
Local radio station ownership, 501*b*
Local standards, 535, 536–538, 537*b*
Locke, John, 54, 678*n*11
Locy, Toni, 395*b*
Lohan, Lindsay, *420*
London, Jack, 199
Lorain Journal, 218–221
Lorillard Tobacco Co., 647, 649*b*, 670–675
Lotteries, 493–495
Louisville Courier-Journal, 405–417
Love, Mike, *624*
Low-power radio or television, 482

Lubrano, Gina, 700*n*92
Lyon, Matthew, 710*n*187

M

MacKinnon, Catharine, 531, 679*n*23, 710*n*7
Made for hire works, 588
Madison, James, 144, 348, 685*n*18, 700*n*102
Majority decisions, 11
Major League Baseball Players Association, 246
Malcolm, Janet, 164, 164*b*
Malice. *See* Actual malice
Mapplethorpe, Robert, 562
Marconi, Guglielmo, 476, 476
Markey, Edward, 324*b*
Marlboro cigarette advertising, *640, 653b*
Marshall, John, 144, 685*nn*16–17
Martin, John C., 688*n*69
Martin, Shannon, 700*n*103
Martin, Sheree, 697*n*5, 697*n*9
Mascots, 619*b*
Massaro, Toni M., 680*n*82
Masson, Jeffrey, 164–166, 164*b*
Mastrosimone, Joseph P., 686*n*100
Matera, Dary, 394*b*
Matsuda, Mari J., 679*n*23
Mauro, Tony, 446*b*
Maxwell, E. L., 459–466
Maynard, George, 84
McCain, John, 243*b*, 615*b*
McCain-Feingold Act of 2002, 72
McCarthy, J. Thomas, 692*n*74, 692*n*77, 692*n*81, 692*n*96, 694*n*160
McChrystal, Stanley, 343
McDowell, Robert, 480*b*
McGraw, Phil, 156*b*
McNealy, Scott, 222
McNulty, Patrick J., 694*n*182
McNulty, Paul, 56*b*
Mechanical licenses, 611
Media and courts, 420–473
   admonitions, 425–426
   anonymous juries, 428
   bench-bar-press guidelines, 451–452, 451*b*

broadcasting and recording, 445–451
challenging closure, 440
constitutional and statutory access to courts, 452–453
contempt, 431–432
content determinations, 59–61
continuance, 425, 430
court access rules, 455–456
court closure, 435–445, 440
court dockets, 453–454
court records, access to, 452–458
crime reporting, 425*b*
electronic access to court records, 456–458
electronic access to trials, 445–451. *See also* Trials, access to
fair trials, 422–429
gag orders, 425, 441–444
history of media, 85–88
impartial judges, 428
impartial jurors, 422–423, 426–428
juror admonition, 431
juror sequestration, 431
jury selection, 429–430
juveniles, protection of, 439, 441, 447*b*, 447*m*
media effects, 423–426
media types and regulatory differences, 86–88
newer technologies, 449–450, 450*b*
new venire, 430
open trials, 433–434*b*, 433–435, 438*b*, 467–473
prejudicial speech, 422–429
prosecutor prejudice, 427*b*
protective orders, 437
rape victims, protection of, 266–267, 270–273, 441
recording and broadcasting, 445–451
remedies to prejudice, 429–432
search warrants, 327–328*b*, 327–329, 370–373, 400–403
state secrets, 454–455
student newspapers, 123–124
super-sealed cases, 454
trials, access to, 432–445. *See also* Trials, access to
venue, change of, 425, 430
Media Law Reporter, 32
Media Law Resource Center, 145*b*, 450*b*
Media violence, 303*b*, 566–570
Medical records, 347
Meetings, access to, 364–365, 368–369, 368*b*
Meier, Megan, 300*b*

Meiklejohn, Alexander, 679*n*20, 680*n*80, 720*n*2

Memorandum orders, 15

Metadata subject to FOIA requests, 367*b*

Meta-Index for Legal Research, 33

MGM, 600

Miami University of Ohio, 347

Michaels, Bret, 264

Mickey Mouse, *578*

Microsoft, 224, 661

Microwave transmissions, 503

Midler, Bette, 240–241

Milbank, Dana, 700*n*93

Military

    access to operations of, 343–345

    recruiting on campuses, 129*b*

    recruitment, obstruction of, 65*b*

    tribunals, 104*b*

Military troop information, 65*b*

Milkovich, Michael, *186,* 194–196, 218–221

Mill, John Stuart, 679*n*20

Miller, Judith, *380,* 387–388*b,* 389

Miller, Marvin, *536b,* 571–574

Miller beer, 240

Miller test, 535–541, 571–574

Milligan, Lambden P., 104*b*

Milton, John, 54, 678*n*10

Minneapolis Star & Tribune Co., 417–419

Minnesota Daily, 388*b*

Minors. *See* Children

Misrepresentation, 307, 330–334

Moccou, Jim, 698*n*48

Modems, cable, 516

Mohamed, Binyam, 455

Monuments, 76

Moore, Sara Jane, 260

Mootness, 12

Moral rights and copyright law, 591

Morgan, J. P., 533

Morpheus, 616–617

"Mortal Kombat" (video game), 301, 567*b*

Morton, Andrew, 698*n*42

Motion Picture Association of America (MPAA), 554

Motion to dismiss, 29

MoveOn.org, 490

Movies

    censorship, 544*b,* 545

    rating system, 544*b,* 567

MTV (television network), 504

Multichannel video service (MVS), 508

Murdoch, Rupert, *500, 500b*

Murphy, Eddie, 600

Musical works, 609–611

Music licensing, 609–616

    alternatives to, 615–616

    compositions, 609–611

    file sharing and, 616–617

    Internet and, 616–617

    mechanical licenses, 611

    musicians, 613–614

    phonorecords, 614

    politicians using songs without permission, 615*b*

    sound recordings, 611–613

    synchronization rights, 609, 614–615

Must-carry rules, 505, 509–511, 514

Musumeci, Antonio, 342*b*

Muzak, 616

MVS (Multichannel video service), 508

MySpace, 264*b,* 300*b,* 304, 608

N

Names

    anonymous juries, 428

    anonymous speech, 151–152*b,* 152

    appropriation, 239–240

    domain names, 515, 623–624

    rape victims' names, publication of, 266–267, 270–273, 441

    soldiers' names and antiwar t-shirts, 242*b*

Napster, 616

NASA, 359*b*

National Association of Broadcasters, 554

National Association of Theater Owners, 554

National Audubon Society, 202–203*b*

National Cable Television Association, 554

National Center for State Courts, 457

National Endowment for the Arts (NEA), 83, 562–563

National Examiner, 155

National Football League, 512

National Nuclear Security Administration (NNSA), 352–353

National Parent Teacher Association, 563

National Public Radio (NPR), 501

National security
  FOIA and, 356–357
  newsgathering and, 356–357
  protection of, 100–105
  threats to, 101–104

"Natural Born Killers" (movie), 299

NBC (television network), 87, 284*b*, 334, 510

NEA (National Endowment for the Arts), 83, 562–563

Near, Jay, 61–62

Nebraska Press standard, 442*b*

Negligence
  defined, 160
  foreseeability, 295–297
  physical harm, 294–295
  proof of, 168, 172–174
  proximate cause, 297, 297*b*

Negligent infliction of emotional distress, 291–293
  defined, 280
  duty of care, 291
  plaintiff's case, 292*b*

Nehf, James P., 690*n*29

Neiman-Marcus, 153

Nelson, Bill, 324*b*

Net neutrality, 516

Neutral reportage, 201–203*b*

News broadcast, indefinite delay of, 64

News Corp., 510*b*

Newsgathering, 320–379
  access to meetings, 364–365
  access to records, 349–364
  agency memos, 358
  cameras in private places, states that forbid unauthorized use of, 335*b*
  computer records, 362–363
  confidentiality, breaking promises of, 398–404, 399*b*, 417–419
  covert recording, 335–343
  denying access to records, 345–348
  driver's information, 347
  federal wiretap law, 337–341
  financial records, 361
  FOIA, 349–364
  fraud and misrepresentation, 330–334

  geological data, 362
  harassment, 329–330
  internal agency rules and procedures, 357
  law enforcement records, 359–361
  medical records, 347
  military operations, access to, 343–345
  national security, 356–357
  newsroom searches, 401–402
  noncovert recording, 341–342
  one-party states for consent to recording interview, 336
  personal privacy, 359
  pitfalls, 323–334
  "pool reporting," 344
  Privacy Protection Act of 1980, 402–403
  protections, 348–369
  recording private conversations, states requiring consent for, 336*b*
  ride-alongs, 326–329, 328*b*, 329*b*
  search warrants, 327–328*b*, 327–329, 370–373, 400–403
  state open-records laws, 365–368
  statutory exemptions, 357
  student records, 346–347
  tape recording laws by state, 338*m*
  tortious newsgathering, 330
  trade secrets, 357–358
  trespass, 325–329
  two-party states for consent to recording interview, 336
  video voyeurism, 348

Newspapers. *See* Media and courts; Newsgathering

Newsroom searches, 401–402

Newsweek, 194

Newsworthiness
  appropriation, 245–246
  intrusion, 258–259

New Yorker Magazine, 164, 164*b*

New York State Open Meeting Law, 368*b*

New York Times
  anthrax letters, 283–284, 395*b*
  book review not defamatory, 191
  BP spill, access to Gulf site, 324*b*
  Challenger shuttle explosion, 359*b*
  chilling effects and, 163*b*
  civil rights advertorial, 160–164, 178–180
  Pentagon Papers, 24, 62, 63*b*, 89–92
  WikiLeaks, 63*b*

New York University (NYU), 196–197*b*

Nicholson, Jack, 539, *539*

Nickelodeon (television network), 490, 507

Nike, 29, 651

Nimmer, David, 582*b*, 716*n*57, 717*n*129, 718*n*134, 718*n*137, 718*n*145

Nimmer, Melville, 716*n*57, 717*n*129, 718*n*134, 718*n*137, 718*n*145

9/11 terrorist attacks, 102, 354

Nintendo Wii, 494*b*

"Nip/Tuck" (TV program), 555

Nixon, Richard, 62, 234, 452, 606

NNSA (National Nuclear Security Administration), 352–353

No Electronic Theft Act of 1997, 602

No Harm, No Foul (play), 600–601

Noncommercial broadcasting, 501–502

Noncovert recording, 341–342

Nonduplication rules, 512

Nonpublic forums, 79, 80*b*. *See also* Forums

Noriega, Manuel, 443

Northwest Airlines, 30*b*

Norwood, Norman, 296

Notice and copyright, 594

Notice of proposed rule making, 479

Novak, Robert, *196*, 196–197*b*, 213–218

NPR (National Public Radio), 501

NYU (New York University), 196–197*b*

O

Obama, Barack
    on corporate political contributions, 74*b*
    FCC chair appointment, 480*b*
    FOIA policy, 354–356, *356*, 362*b*
    political ads against, 243*b*
    secrecy surrounding accused terrorists, reduction of, 453
    Twitter fake user alleging to be, 224
    WikiLeaks, condemnation of, 63*b*

O'Brien, David Paul, 68–69, 92–96, 116–117

O'Brien test, 69, 70*b*, 511

Obscenity and indecency, 528–577
    adult stores and zoning restrictions, 563–564
    artistic works, 533

    broadcast indecency, 547–553
    cable indecency, 555–557
    channeling broadcast indecency, 552–553
    child pornography, 541–544
    definition of indecency, 547
    dial-a-porn, 565
    enforcing obscenity laws, 541–546
    First Amendment and, 52
    fleeting-obscenity rule, 551
    Hicklin rule, 533–534, 534*b*
    indecency, 531, 546–554, 575–577
    Internet indecency, 557–561, 559*b*
    Internet regulation, 535, 537*b*
    local standards and prurient interests, 535, 536–538, 537*b*
    Miller test, 535–541, 571–574
    minors, transmission of obscenity to, 557–558
    nudity on television, 552
    obscenity, 532–535
    obscenity, defined, 518, 530*b*
    offensive speech, 109–110
    Oversight Monitoring Board, 554
    Pacifica test, 548–549
    patently offensive material, 517–518, 538–540
    pornography, 531, 532–533*b*, 541–544, 565
    possession of obscene material, 544–545
    procedural protections, 545
    publications, 65*b*
    public funds for pornographic art, 562–563
    recording labels, 563
    safe harbor policy, 552–553
    secondary effects of adult stores, 564
    serious social value, 540
    sexting, 543–544
    SLAPS test, 540*b*
    telephone indecency, 565
    television program ratings, 553*b*, 554, 568
    TV Parental Guidelines, 554
    variable obscenity, 541
    v-chips, 554, 568
    zoning to restrict adult stores, 563–564

O'Connor, Sandra Day, *113*
    on burden of proof regarding falsity, 158
    on commercial speech doctrine, 647
    on community standards and Internet speech, 538

O'Connor, Sandra Day *(cont.)*
  on corporate political contributions, 74*b*
  on originality and copyright, 584*b*
  on true threats, 113
Offensive content. *See also* Obscenity and indecency
  highly offensive standard, 232–234
  patently offensive material, 517–518, 538–540
  in public schools, 121–124
Offensive speech, 109–110
"Oh, Pretty Woman" (song), 604, *605, 605b*
Ohio State University, 347
Okamoto, Scott T., 718*n*178
Oklahoma City bombing, 149*b*
Oldsmobile, 240, *240*
Ollman, Bertell, 196–197*b*, 213–218
Ollman test, 193–195, 194*b*, 196–197*b*, 198, 220
Onassis, Jacqueline Kennedy, 240, 329–330, *330*
One-party states for consent to recording interview, 336
Online Defamation Limited Liability Act. *See* Communications
    Decency Act of 1996
Online publishers and libel, 149–150*b*
Open government laws, 348–349
Open-records laws, 75, 365–368
Open the Government, 455
Open trials
  interest in, 433*b*
  presumption of, 433–435, 434*b*, 438*b*, 467–473
Opinion as defense to libel, 193–195, 236
Opinion letters, 655, 655*b*
Opinions, court
  concurring, 11
  dissenting, 11
  en banc, 10
  per curiam, 15
"The Oprah Winfrey Show," 156*b*
Oracle (computer company), 580
Orbison, Roy, 604, *605, 605b*
Orders
  cease and desist orders, 657
  consent orders, 657
  executive orders, 20, 26–27
  gag orders, 425, 441–444
  litigated orders, 657
  memorandum orders, 15

protective orders, 437
  restraining orders, 24, 441–442
Oren, Michael, 127*b*
Original intent, 50
Originalists, 17
Originality and copyright law, 584–586, 584*b*
Original jurisdiction, 12
Osbourne, Ozzy, 297
Outrageousness, 283–288
Overbroad laws, 4–5, 6*b*
Oversight Monitoring Board, 554
Overturning precedent, 25–26, 38–47
Oxenford, David, 718*n*167, 718*n*175

P

Pacifica Foundation, 548–549
Pacifica test, 548–549
Pagers and cell phones, 222, 224, 225–226, 226*b*, 273–277
Paladin Enterprises, 311–319
Paladin Press, 300–301
Panama, 344
Pandora Internet Radio, 613, *613*
Pangilinan, Liezl Irene, 682*n*41
Paparazzi, 255, 329–330, 331*b*
Paramount Pictures, 299–300
Parental Advisory labels, 563
Parents Against Tired Truckers (PATT), 334
Parents Music Resource Center, 563
Parks, Larry, *107*
Parks, Rosa, 248, *248*
Parks and monuments, 76
Parody
  copyright infringement and, 604–605, 605*b*
  libel and, 154, 198–200
  satire vs., 289*b*
Passage of time, 169, 172, 268–269
Patent and Trademark Office, 622–623
Patently offensive material, 517–518, 538–540
Patents, 580*b*
Patriot Act. *See* USA PATRIOT Act of 2001
PATT (Parents Against Tired Truckers), 334
Pavesich, Paulo, 239

Payola, 497–498

PBS (Public Broadcasting Service), 501

Peer-to-peer (P2P) applications, 516, 616–617, 633–639

PEG access channels, 511–512, 555–556

Pember, Don R., 690n34

Penn State, 619b

Pentagon Papers, 24, 62, 63b, 89–92, 340

Pentagon terrorist attack, 102

Per curiam opinions, 15

Peremptory challenges, 29, 430

Perjury, 52

Perry, April M., 696n68

Perry, James Edward, 300–301, 302b

Persian Gulf War (1991), 344

Personally identifiable information, 346

Personal privacy, 359

Phelps, Fred, 287b

Phillips, Ashley C., 714n167

"The Phone Rule," 339

Phonorecords, 614

Photobucket, 264b

Physical harm, 293–298
  foreseeability, 295–297
  negligence, 294–295
  proximate cause, 297

Picketing at marine funerals and hurtful speech, 287b

Pittsburgh Panther, 619

PKK (Kurdistan Workers Party), 102, 103b

Plagiarism, 586

Plaintiffs, 28

Plame, Valerie, 387b

Playboy magazine, 233b

Plurality decisions, 11–12

Podgers, James, 701n76

Pole rules, 504

Political ads, 72–75, 243b
  music licensing for, 615b

Political broadcasting, 484, 485b

Political contributions, 72–75, 74b

Political ideology of U.S. Supreme Court, 12–13

Political questions, 20

Political speech, 52, 72–78

Pollack, David, 150b

Pooley, Dan, 252

"Pool reporting," 344

Popeye the Sailor Man, 597, 597b

Pornography, 531, 532–533b, 541–544, 562–563, 565

Post, Robert C., 694n168

Powell, Lewis
  on holding and expressing opinions, 186, 193
  on libel and limited-purpose public figures, 170
  on newsgathering, 320, 322
  on reporter's privilege, 380, 384, 386

Precedent
  defined, 4, 5
  distinguishing from, 25
  majority decisions as, 11–12
  modification of, 25
  overturning, 25–26, 38–47

Predominant use test, 250–251

Preemption, federal, 23–24

Prejudice, remedies to, 429–432

Prejudicial speech, 422–429

Preponderance of evidence, 28, 177

Presley, Eric, 437

Press-Enterprise test for court closure, 434–435, 435b, 456

Presumed damages, 175

Pre-trial publicity, 424–425, 436b, 459–466

"Primary Colors" (novel), 154

Primary sources of law, 32

"PrimeTime Live" (TV show), 256, 257b, 330–333

Principal Register of trademarks, 622

Pring, George W., 685n19

Prior restraints, 61–66, 62–63b, 65b

Prisoners and prisons
  hostages held by escaped convicts, suing for untrue story of
    events, 234
  investigation criticizing prison conditions, 209
  media access to, 325, 403b
  petitions to U.S. Supreme Court, 14

Privacy
  appropriation, 237–244. See also Appropriation
  cable television subscribers, 513
  cell phones and pagers, 222, 225–226, 226b, 273–277
  e-mail, 661–663, 662b
  facts, 259–262, 260b. See also Private facts
  false light, 229–237, 691n41. See also False light
  intrusion, 253–259. See also Intrusion

Privacy *(cont.)*
   law, development of, 228–229
   personal privacy, 359
   protection of, 222–277
   public vs., 269*b*
   right to, 17
   sources of protection, 227–228
   torts related to, 228*b*
Privacy Act of 1974, 345–346
Privacy interest vs. public interest, 51
Privacy-proof plaintiffs, 264*b*
Privacy Protection Act of 1980, 402–403, 403*b*
Private facts, 259–262, 260*b*
   defined, 228*b*, 259
   First Amendment defense, 266–269
   intimate facts, 260–262
   lawfully obtained, 267–268
   legitimate public concern, 262–269
   publicity and, 265
   public records and, 261*b*, 268
   public significance, 266–267
   time, passage of, 268–269
Private figures and libel, 172–174
Private media and property, 71*b*
Private property, 71*b*
   exclusion rights, limits on, 81–83
   intrusion and, 254–255
   as public forum, 81–83
Privileges
   absolute privilege, 190
   conditional privilege, 190
   fair report privilege, 188–190, 188*b*
   false light, 236
   qualified privilege, 190
   reporter's privilege, 380–419, 399*b*. *See also* Reporter's
     privilege
Probable cause, 27
Product demand and advertising, 653*b*
Profanity, 122–123, 248, 550–551, 575–577
Programming and advertising regulations, 484–498. *See also*
   Advertising
   ballot issues, 490
   broadcast editorials, 490
   cable television regulation, 509–514
   candidates' supporters, 489–490

   censoring not permitted, 488–489
   children's programming, 491–493
   contests, 493–495
   fairness doctrine, 496–497
   federal candidates, reasonable time for, 489
   527 groups, 490
   hoaxes, 495–496, 496*b*
   legally qualified candidates, 484–485
   lotteries, 493–495
   lowest unit rate, 487–488
   political broadcasting, 484
   recordkeeping, 490
   section 315, invocation of, 486
   sharing programs and channel capacity, 512–513
   sponsor identification, 488, 497–498
   stations or cable systems, use of, 485
   use rule, exceptions to, 485–486
   website addresses displayed during children's programming,
     493
Promissory estoppel, 400
Proof, burden of, 159*b*
Propaganda videos, 56*b*
Proposed rule making, notice of, 479
Prosecutorial Remedies and Other Tools to End the Exploita-
   tion of Children Today Act of 2003 (Protect Act), 561
Prosecutor prejudice, 427*b*
Prosser, William, 228, 235, 242, 690*n*35, 691*n*61, 692*n*92
Protective orders, 437
Protests
   burning, 116–117. *See also* Burning protests
   disruptive speech, 119–121, 133–137
   in public schools, 119–121, 133–137
Proximate cause, 297, 297*b*
Prudhomme, Paul, 240
Prurient interests, 535, 536–538
P2P applications, 516, 616–617, 633–639
Public, educational or governmental (PEG) access channels,
   511–512, 555–556
Publication of libel, 147–152
   republication, 147
   unknown publisher, 151–152*b*, 152
   vendors and distributors, 147–152
Public Broadcasting Service (PBS), 501
Public display and copyright law, 590, 591*b*
Public distribution and copyright law, 590, 591*b*

Public domain, 246, 595–596, 596b, 628–633
Public figures and libel, 169–170
    actual malice, 169
    all-purpose public figures, 170, 180–185
    involuntary public figures, 172
    losing public-figure status, 172
    nature of statement, 174
    public officials, 168–169
    university professors, 172
Public forums, 71b, 78–84, 80–81b. *See also* Forums
Public Health Cigarette Smoking Act of 1969, 648
Public interest standard, 51, 482–484
Publicity, right of
    appropriation, 237b, 238–239, 691n70
    biographies, 251
    death, survival of, 691n70
    defined, 238
    predominant use test, 250–251
    Rogers test, 247–248, 250
Publicity vs. private facts, 265
Public officials and libel, 168–169
Public performance and copyright law, 590, 591b, 610b
Public places, video of, 342b
Public records, 261b, 266, 268, 269b, 350. *See also* Freedom of
    Information Act of 1966
    e-mail as, 365b, 367b
    metadata, 367b
    social media websites as, 367b
Public schools. *See* Schools
Public Service Commission of New York, 664–670
Puffery, 655
Punitive damages, 175–176

Q

Qualified privilege, 190
Quashing subpoenas, 382

R

Rachel, Irving, *107*
Racketeer Influenced and Corrupt Organizations Act of 1970
    (RICO), 545

Radio Act of 1912, 476–477, 495
Radio Act of 1927, 478, 482–483, 495
Radio regulation
    broadcast regulation, 60, 476
    local radio station ownership, 501b
    low-power radio, 482
    payola, 497
    satellite radio, 482
    station ownership, 501b
    talk shows, 173b
Rage Against the Machine (band), 615b
Rahdert, Mark C., 683n69
Rape victims' names, publication of, 266–267, 270–273, 441
Rational review, 67
Ratzenberger, John, 242–243
Ray, Elizabeth Megen, 714n155
RCFP (Reporter's Committee for Freedom of the Press). *See*
    Reporter's Committee for Freedom of the Press
Reagan, Ronald, 479b
RealDVD, 437
Reasonable doubt, 28, 177
Reasonable person standard, 253
Reckless acts, 280, 288–290
Reckless disregard for truth, 166–168, 167b
Recording
    covert, 335–343
    face-to-face, 335–336
    noncovert, 341–342
    private conversations, states requiring consent for, 336b
    of telephone calls, 337–341
Recording Industry Association of America (RIAA), 450, 563
Recording labels and Parental Advisory labels, 563
Records, access to, 345–348. *See also* Freedom of Information
    Act of 1966
"Red flag" words, 154
Redish, Martin H., 682n46
Red Lion Broadcasting Co., 519–524
Referendum supporters, disclosure of, 75
Refusal to reveal sources, 388b
Registration
    of copyrights, 597–598
    of trademarks, 622–623
Rehnquist, William
    on cameras in court, 448
    on civil liberty, 104, 682n15

Rehnquist, William *(cont.)*
   on Establishment Clause, 125
   on opinion as defense to libel, 195
Reilly, Thomas F., 670–675
Religion in public schools, 125
Religious student groups at state law school, 126
Remand, 12
Remedies
   for copyright infringement, 602
   to prejudice, 429–432
Rendition program as state secrets, 455
Reporter's Committee for Freedom of the Press (RCFP)
   bullying subpoenas, 30*b*
   criminal libel laws, 176
   FOIA online use guide, 351
   FOIA requests, 360, 374–379
   telephone calls, recording of, 337
   website, 33
Reporter's privilege, 380–419, 399*b*
   Branzburg test, 383–386, 384*b*, 405–417
   confidential sources, breaking promises to, 393*b*, 398–404,
      399*b*, 417–419
   contempt of court, 395*b*
   defined, 382
   denial of, 394*b*
   fines for refusing to reveal sources, examples of, 388*b*
   grand juries and, 383, 405–417
   jail time for refusing to reveal sources, examples of, 388*b*
   shield laws, 390–393, 391*b*. *See also* Shield laws
   subpoenas, 395*b*
Reproduction rights and copyright, 589–590, 591*b*
Republication of libel, 147
Reputation and libel, 142*b*, 157
Research sources, 32–33
   American Jurisprudence 2d, 32
   Congressional Record, 349
   Cornell Legal Information Institute, 33
   Corpus Juris Secundum, 32
   LexisNexis, 33
   Library of Congress, 582, 597
   Media Law Reporter, 32
   Westlaw, 33
Responsible reporting, 211–212
Restraining orders, 24, 441–442

Retractions, 210–211
Retransmission consent rules, 509–511, 510*b*
Reviews of books, 191
Revolutionary Communist Youth Brigade, 99
Reynolds, Robert, *123*
Rhetorical hyperbole, 198–200
Rhodes, Randi, 173*b*
RIAA (Recording Industry Association of America), 450, 563
Richards, Michael W., 697*n*10
Richards, Robert D., 698*n*42
Richie, Nicole, *550*
Richmond Newspapers, 467–473
RICO (Racketeer Influenced and Corrupt Organizations Act of
   1970), 545
Ride-alongs, 326–329, 327–329*b*
Ripeness, 12
Rite Aid Corporation, 657
Ritter, Carol, 433
Roberson, Abigail, 238
Roberts, John, *14*
   on cameras in court, 448*b*
   on campus speech, 120–121
   conservative votes and, 13, 13*b*
   on donations to terrorist organizations, 103*b*
   on picketing at military funerals, 287*b*
Roberts Court and move to the right on free speech, 129*b*
Robinson, Eric P., 679*n*49
Rogers test, 247–248, 250
Rolling Stone magazine, 343
Roman Catholic Church, *53*
Romer, Daniel, 703*n*3
Rosen, Jeffrey, 225
Rosenberg, Norman L., 684*n*8
Ross, Susan Dente, 677*n*24, 680*n*89, 681*n*2
Rossen, Robert, *107*
Rousseau, Jean-Jacques, 54, 678*n*12
Rudenstine, David, 702*n*8
Ruffin, David, 287–288
Rule of law, 2–7
   Aristotle and, 4, 5*b*
   case law, 35
   common law, 35
   defined, 4
   discretion, 4

facial challenges, 4, 6*b*

interpretation of law, 18*b*

overbroad law, 4–5, 6*b*

precedent, 4, 5, 11–12, 38–47

stare decisis, 4, 5, 24–25

vague laws, 4, 6*b*

Rush, Rick, 250

Rutland Herald, 388*b*

S

Sack, Robert D., 687*n*34

Safe harbor policy, 552–553

St. Paul Pioneer Press, 399*b*

Sales of cable systems, 507

Salinger, J. D., 604

Salisbury, Bill, 399*b*

Salt, Waldo, *107*

Same-sex domestic partners, state referendum on, 75

Same-sex marriage, court trial on California ballot measure
banning, 436–437

Samsung Electronics, 241

Sandoval, Greg, 705*n*80

Sanford, Bruce, 278, 695*n*1

Sanger, Michael, 150*b*

Satellite radio, 482

Satellites, 482, 508, 514–515, 598

Satire

copyright infringement and, 604–605

libel and, 154, 198–200

parody vs., 289*b*

Saturday Evening Post, 166

The Saturday Press, 61–62

Savage, Michael, 296–297

Scalia, Antonin, *14*

on anonymous speech, 152

on commercial speech doctrine, 646

conservative votes and, 13, 13*b*

on interpretation of law, 18*b*

on libel, 197*b*

on libel-proof plaintiff doctrine, 204

originalists and textualists, 17

on public park monuments, 76

Scheff, Sue, 150*b*

Schenck, Charles, 105

Scholz, Tom, 615*b*

Schools

disruptive speech, 52, 118–130, 119*b*, 133–137

educationally inappropriate content in, 121–124

high schools distinguished in treatment from universities,
118–119, 119*b*, 125–126

ideological orthodoxy in public schools, 124

as limited public forums, 118

offensive content in, 121–124

religion in, 125

student newspapers, 123–124

symbolic protests in, 119–121, 133–137

Schumer, Charles, 390*b*

Schwartz, Victor E., 686*n*100

Scott, Adrian, *107*

Scripps-Howard Broadcasting Co., 273–277

Scrutiny. *See* Intermediate scrutiny; Strict scrutiny

Search warrants, 327–328*b*, 327–329, 370–373, 400–403

Seclusion, intrusion upon, 253

Secondary effects of adult stores, 564

Secondary sources of law, 32

Sedition Act of 1798, 57, 104, 144, 163*b*

Seditious libel, 55, 57, 143–144

Seditious speech, 52

Segar, Elzie, 597*b*

Self-government, 58*b*

Separation of powers, 17, 20

September 11, 2001 terrorist attacks, 102, 354

Sequestration, 425, 431

Serious social value, 540

Serrano, Andres, 562

Service marks, 618

SESAC (Society of European Stage Authors and Composers),
610, 614

Settlements

case process, 29

of libel claims, 145*b*

Sexting, *543*, 543–544

Sexual assault victims' names, publication of, 266–267,
270–273, 441

Sexual discrimination, 532

Shafer, Jack, 700*n*92

Shane, Scott, 695n22

Shapiro, Amy, 684n129

Shepherd, Robert E., 704n50

Sheppard, Sam, 424–425, 426, 426b, 459–466

Shield laws

    anonymous posters on news websites, 398b

    confidential sources, protection of, 393b

    defined, 392

    example, 391b

    Internet bloggers, 393, 396b

    reporter's privilege, 390–393

    state shield laws, 391–392b, 397b

    what is covered, 394–395

    who is covered, 393–394

Shopping centers, privately-owned, 81–83

Showtime, 555

Sickmund, Melissa, 704nn54–55

Siebert, Frederick S., 678n15

Simon & Schuster, 68

Simpson, O.J., 155, 336, 438, 438b

Sinclair, Upton, 256

Single-mistake rule, 206

Single-publication rule, 203–204

Sipple, Oliver, 262

Sirius-XM satellite radio, 514, 613

Sirota, Jeremy Paul, 719n187

Sixth Amendment, 422, 430, 432–445, 437

"60 Minutes," 143b, 157, 168

Skype, 337

Slander compared to libel, 140b

Slander per quod, 157

Slander per se, 155, 157

SLAPP lawsuits, 144–146, 144b

SLAPS test for obscenity, 540b

Slogans, 124

Smallheer, Susan, 388b

Smartphones. See Cell phones and pagers

Smith, Anna Nicole, 205b

Smith, Cathy, 388b

Smith, James Morton, 678n18

Smith, Jeffery A., 690n31

Smith Act of 1940, 107

Smolla, Rodney A., 329b, 685n44, 696n37

Snyder, Albert, 287b

Snyder, Brad, 686n97

Snyder, Howard, 704nn54–55

Socialist Party, 105, 106

Social media websites as public records, 367b

Social Security numbers, 224, 346, 347, 457

Society for the Suppression of Vice, 533

Society of European Stage Authors and Composers (SESAC), 610, 614

Society of Professional Journalists (SPJ), 128, 440, 440b

Socrates, 140

Sola Pool, Ithiel de, 681n111

Soldier of Fortune Magazine, 296–297

Sonny Bono Copyright Term Extension Act of 1978, 595, 595b

Son of Sam, 68

Sony BMG, 497

Sotomayor, Sonia, 12, 13b, 14

Sound-alikes and appropriation, 240–241

SoundExchange, 612–613

Sound recordings

    defined, 611–613

    transmission and copyright law, 590–591, 591b

Sources of law, 19–27, 20b

    administrative rules, 26. See also Administrative law

    case law, 34–35. See also Case law

    common law, 24–26, 35. See also Common law

    constitutions, 19, 20–21. See also Constitution, U.S.

    deference, 26

    doctrines, 19–20

    equity law, 19, 24

    executive orders, 20, 26–27

    precedent, distinguishing from, 25

    precedent, modification of, 25

    precedent, overturning, 25–26, 38–47

    primary sources, 32

    secondary sources, 32

    statutes, 21, 23–24. See also Statutory law

    Supreme Court, 12–16. See also Supreme Court, U.S.

Souter, David, 14

    on cameras in court, 448b

    on campaign spending, 3

    on community standards and Internet speech, 538

    on government speech doctrine, 76

    on public park monuments, 76

Spahn, Warren, 230, 251

Spam e-mail, 661–663, 662b

Special damages, 175

Spectrum scarcity, 482, 483b, 503

Speech, chilling effect on, 102, 143b, 163b

Speech, types of
  animal cruelty, depictions of, 6b, 52
  anonymous speech, 75, 151–152b, 152
  campus speech, 125–128
  commercial speech, 644–645b
  compelled speech, 84, 124
  corporate speech, 3, 17, 38–44, 74b, 650–652
  disruptive speech, 98–137. *See also* Disruptive speech
  government, 76–78
  hate speech, 111–112
  offensive, 109–110
  political speech, 52
  prejudicial speech, 422–429
  seditious speech, 52
  speech assaults, 109–116
  symbolic speech, 67, 69

Speedy trial right, 430

SPJ (Society of Professional Journalists), 128, 440, 440b

Splichal, Sigman L., 697n5, 697n9

Sponsor identification, 488, 497–498

Sports Illustrated magazine, 263

Sports teams, 619b

Stamp Act of 1765, 55

Standards of review
  de novo review, 10
  intermediate scrutiny, 69, 70b, 71b
  judicial review, 16–19
  rational review, 67
  reasonable person standard, 253
  strict scrutiny review, 66–68, 67b, 117, 340, 506

Standing, 651

Stanford Daily, 401–402

Stanford University, 401–402

Star Chamber, 141, 144b

Stare decisis, 4, 5, 24–25

Starek, Roscoe B., III, 721nn37–38

Starr, Kenneth, 197b

State constitutions, 20–21

State courts, 8t

State laws
  anti-SLAPP laws, 144–146, 144b
  open-records laws, 365–368
  recording private conversations, states requiring consent for, 336b
  shield laws, 391–392b, 397b
  tape recording laws by state, 338m
  unauthorized use of cameras in private places, 336b

Statement of fact, 147

State open-records laws, 365–368

State secrets, 454–455

Statute of Anne, 582

Statutes of limitations, 209–210, 210b

Statutory damages and copyright law, 594

Statutory law
  codes and codification, 21, 23–24
  construction and facial meaning of, 23
  defined, 19
  enactment of, 23b
  federal preemption, 23–24
  judicial review, 23–24

Steketee, Martha Wade, 706n104, 706n106

Stephenson, Randall, 2

Stern, Howard, 286, 480

Stern, Howard K., 205b

Stevens, John Paul, 14
  on commercial speech doctrine, 650
  on disclosure of records pertaining to private citizens, 360
  on Internet and First Amendment rights, 517–518, 518b
  liberality of, 12
  on political contributions, 73
  retirement of, 12
  on students' freedom of speech, 121

Stewart, Clarence "C.J.," 438b

Stewart, Daxton R. "Chip," 702n155

Stewart, Martha, 436

Stewart, Potter, 52, 384
  on fair trial right, 433–434
  on freedom of press, 50, 52b, 678n5
  on newsgathering, 322, 697n4
  on pornography, 528
  on reporter's privilege, 384–385

Stone, Oliver, 299

Stored Communications Act, 337

Strategic Lawsuits Against Public Participation (SLAPP), 144–146, 144*b*

Strict liability, 28, 29

Strict scrutiny, 66–68, 67*b*, 117, 340, 506

Strohs, Brett, 701*n*125

Strossen, Nadine, 533*b*

Student Press Law Center, 33, 127, 128

Students. *See* Schools; Universities

Subpoenas

  on blogging, 396*b*

  bullying, 30*b*

  contempt of court, 395*b*

  defined, 29

  quashing of, 382

  reporter's privilege, 395*b*

Substantial truth and falsity, 158

Substantiation, 655*b*, 658

Suggestive marks, 620

Sullivan, L. B., *138,* 160–161, 178–180

Sullivan, Laurie, 705*n*83

Sulzberger, Arthur, Jr., 387*b*

Summary judgment, 31–32, 206–207

Summons, 28, 429

Sunstein, Cass, 532*b*, 679*n*20, 710*n*5

Super-sealed cases, 454

Supplemental Register of trademarks, 622

Supremacy Clause, 23

Supreme Court. *See* Supreme Court, U.S.

Supreme Court, U.S., 8*t*

  appellate process, 15*f*

  certiorari, 12

  conservative votes and, 12–13

  court system and, 12–13

  direct right of appeal, 12

  establishment of, 7

  granting review, 14

  interpretation of law, 18*b*

  judicial review, 16–19

  jurisdiction, 12

  justices of, 14*b. See also specific justice by name*

  memorandum orders, 15

  mootness, 12

  oral arguments, audio recordings of, 448

  originalists, 17

  original jurisdiction, 12

  per curiam opinions, 15

  political ideology, 12–13

  prisoners, petitions from, 14

  reaching decisions, 14–15

  sources of law, 12–16. *See also* Sources of law

  textualists, 17

  writ of certiorari, 12

Supreme Court Review, 163*b*

Swift Boat Veterans for Truth, 490

Swinton, Nathan, 702*n*7

Symbolic conduct, 71*b*

Symbolic protests

  draft card burning, 92–96, 116–117

  flag burning, 67, 98–99, 117, 131–133

  in public schools, 119–121, 133–137

Symbolic speech, 67, 69, 116–117, 131–133

Synchronization rights, 609, 614–615

Syndicated exclusivity rules, 512

T

Talab, R. S., 716*n*69

Talen, "Reverend Billy," *48*

Talk radio, 173*b*

Targeted advertising, 660–661

Targeted advertising on Internet, 660–661

Taricani, Jim, *386, 388b,* 389

Tax Court, U.S., 8*t*

Taylor, Elizabeth, 205–206, 251

Telecommunications Act of 1996, 148, 504

  CDA, 24, 516

  PEG content and indecency, 555–556

Telenovelas, *491*

Telephone regulation

  broadcasting recorded telephone calls, 339–341

  indecency, 565

  in-state telephone calls, 337

  interstate calls, 337–339

  recording of calls, 337–341

Television program ratings, 553*b*, 554, 568

Television regulation

  cable television regulation, 503–509. *See also* Cable television regulation

CATV, 503
  low-power television, 482
  program ratings, 553*b*, 554, 568
The Temptations, 287–288
Tenenbaum, Joel, 450
Terrorist attacks, 56*b*, 102, 149*b*, 354
Terrorist groups, material support of, 101–102, 103*b*
Texas Beef Group, 156*b*
Text messages, 225–226, 273–277
Textualists, 17
Third Amendment, 223–224, 227
Third parties, protection of, 303–305
Third-party liability and Internet advertising, 661*b*
Thomas, Carleen, 537–538
Thomas, Clarence, *14, 646*
  on commercial speech doctrine, 646
  conservative votes and, 13, 13*b*
  on true threats, 113
Thomas, Robert, 537–538
Threats. *See* True threats
Three Stooges, 248–249
Tilghman, Andrew, 695*n*2
Timberlake, Justin, *528,* 550–551
Time, Inc., 234
Time/place/manner (TPM) laws, 68
Time Warner Cable, 510, 510*b*, 512, 587*b*
Titanic tragedy, 476
TiVo, 592, 601
Tobacco and advertising, 647–648, 649*b*, 670–675
"To Catch a Predator" (TV series), 284*b*
Tortious newsgathering, 330
Torts. *See also* Intentional infliction of emotional distress;
    Libel; Negligence; Negligent infliction of emotional
    distress
  defined, 28, 29
  expansion of law, 307–308
TPM (time/place/manner) laws, 68
Tracking devices on computers, 224
Trade dress, 618
Trade libel, 157
Trademarks, 618–627
  arbitrary marks, 620
  cybersquatters, 623
  defined, 618, 619*b*

descriptive marks, 620
dilution, 625, 625*b*
distinctiveness requirement, 619–621
domain names, 623–624
fair use, 626–627. *See also* Fair use
fanciful marks, 619–620
generic words, 621
infringement, 624–626
infringement defenses, 626–627
mascots, 619*b*
Principal Register of, 622
registration, 622–623
service marks, 618
suggestive marks, 620
Supplemental Register of, 622
trade dress, 618
Trade names, 618
Trade regulation rules, 655*b*, 656
Trade secrets, 357–358
Traditional public forums, 79, 80*b*. *See also* Forums
Tranquility, protection of, 100–105
Transfer of copyright, 594–595
Transformativeness test, 248–250, 249*b*
Transportation Security Administration (TSA), 30*b*, 226
Treason, 56*b*
Trenchard, John, 678*n*1
Trespass
  intrusion by, 255*b*
  newsgathering and, 325–329
Trial courts, 9
Trial publicity, 436*b*
Trials, access to, 432–445
  court access rules, 455–456
  experience and logic test, 435
  Nebraska Press standard, 442*b*
  open trials, 433–435, 434*b*, 438*b*, 467–473
  Press-Enterprise test for court closure, 434–435, 435*b*, 456
  restraining orders, 24, 441–442
Tribunals, military, 104*b*
Tropicana Products, Inc., *659*
Trueblood, Nancy L., 698*nn*22–23
True threats
  defined, 113
  disruptive speech, 52, 112–115, 115*b*

True threats *(cont.)*
  via email, 115
  First Amendment, 52, 112–115, 115*b*
  Internet and, 113
Truth
  attainment of, 59*b*
  false light, 236
  reckless disregard for, 166–168, 167*b*
  substantial, 158
TSA (Transportation Security Administration), 30*b*, 226
Turner Broadcasting System, 524–527
TV Parental Guidelines, 554
Twist, Tony, 250
Twitter, 65, 224, 264*b*, 449–450
2 Live Crew, 604, 605*b*
Two-party states for consent to recording interview, 336

U

"Ultimate Mortal Kombat 3" (video game), 567*b*
"Ulysses" (Joyce), 534
Underinclusiveness, 111
Universal Declaration of Human Rights, 17
Universal Music Group (UMG), 497, 609
Universal Pictures, 87
Universities and colleges
  academic freedom, 118
  campus press and publications, 127–128, 401–402
  campus recruiting, 129*b*
  campus speech, 125–128
  as designated public forums, 79
  as limited public forums, 118, 125–126
  plagiarism and, 586
  professors and status as public figures, 172
  student records, privacy of, 346–347
  trademarked logos of, 619*b*
University of Alabama, 166
University of Florida, 619*b*
University of Georgia, 166, 346
University of Maryland, 196–197*b*
University of Michigan, 113
University of Mississippi, 166

University of Pittsburgh, 619*b*
University of Wisconsin, 126
Univision, 493
Unknown publishers of libel, 151–152*b*, 152
USA Network, 87
USA PATRIOT Act of 2001, 102–103, 226, 346
USA Today, 498
U2, 550

V

Vague laws, 4, 6*b*
Valentino, Rudolph, 251
Van Alstyne, William W., 687*n*100
Van Ness, Christopher, 388*b*
Variable obscenity, 541
Vartabedian, Ralph, 700*n*105
V-chip, 554, 568
VCRs (Videocassette recorders), 601
Veeder, Van Vechten, 684*nn*9–10
Veilleux, Raymond, 334
Vendors
  ISPs as, 148
  publication of libel and, 147–152
Venire, 29, 429, 430
Venue, 29, 425, 430
"Venus de Milo" statue, *530*
Veoh Networks, 608–609
Viacom Inc., 551
Victoria's Secret, 625–626
Video blogging, 396*b*
Videocassette recorders (VCRs), 601
Video games, 249*b*
  "Doom," 556
  First Amendment protection of, 568–570
  ratings, 569*b*
  violence of, 301, 566–570, 567*b*
Video news releases (VNRs), 497, 498
Video of public places, 342*b*
Video Privacy Protection Act of 1988, 228
Video sharing websites, 608–609
Video Voyeurism Prevention Act of 2004, 348

Vietnam War
  government cover-up and, 168
  Pentagon Papers, 24, 62, 63*b*, 89–92, 340
  protest over, 68–69, 119–120, 133–137
  television coverage of, 344
Viewpoint-based discrimination, 111–112
Vinson, C. Danielle, 701*n*71, 706*n*109
Violence
  content marketed to children, FCC report on, 293–294, 567
  media-inspired violent acts, 303*b*
  media violence, 566–570
Virgil, Mike, 263
Virtual forums, 83. *See also* Forums
VNRs (Video news releases), 497, 498
Voice and appropriation, 240–241
Voice over Internet Protocol (VoIP), 337
VoIP (Voice over Internet Protocol), 337
Voir dire, 29, 437
Voluntary compliance, 655*b*

W

Waits, Tom, 241
WALE-AM hoax, 496*b*
Walker, Edwin, 166–167
Wall Street Journal, 500*b*
Walsch, Neale Donald, 586
Walsh, John J., 693*n*153
Walt Disney Co., 510*b*
Walton, L. Richard, 605*b*
Wardrobe malfunctions, 480, *528*, 550–551
"The War of the Worlds" (Wells), 495
Warren, Earl
    on Constitution, U.S., 2
    on libel standard and public figures, 169
Warren, Samuel, on privacy rights, 228, 238, 457, 677*n*21, 690*n*32, 706*n*111
Washington Post, 24, 89–92
Watchdog function of press, 163–164, 284*b*
Watergate scandal, 452, 606
The Weather Channel, 307–308
Website addresses displayed during children's programming, 493

Weir, Dominic, 260–261
Welles, Orson, 495
Wendt, George, 242–243
Wesson, Marianne, 710*n*6
Westboro Baptist Church, 287*b*
Westlaw, 33
White, Byron
    on actual malice standard in libel, 166
    on commercial speech doctrine, 648–649
    on falsity and libel, 164*b*
    on general application laws, 400
    on newsroom searches, 401–402
    on reporter's privilege, 384, 393
White, Vanna, 241, 242, 243
Whitney, Anita, 107
Wichita Eagle, 397*b*
Wigand, Jeffrey, *143*, 143*b*
WikiLeaks, 63*b*, 65, 390*b*
Wildmon, Donald, 306
Williams, Armstrong, 498
Wilson, Brian, *624*
Wilson, Carl, *624*
Wilson, Charles H., 370–373
Wilson, Dennis, *624*
Winfrey, Oprah, 156*b*
Winter, Edgar, 249
Winter, Johnny, 249
Wireless Ship Act of 1910, 476
Wire service defense, 202–203, 202*b*
Wiretap Act, 337
Wiretapping, 104, 337–341
Wisconsin Right to Life (WRL), 73
Wolf, Joshua, 388*b*, 396, 396*b*
Woods, Tiger, 250, *250*
Woodward, Bob, 702*n*3
Work product and First Amendment, 77
Works made for hire, 588
World Trade Center terrorist attacks, 102, 354
World Wide Web. *See* Internet
Wright, James, 388*b*
Wright, John R., 677*n*17
Writ of certiorari, 12
WRL (Wisconsin Right to Life), 73

X

XM Radio, *514*

Y

Yahoo, 304
Yale University, 292–293
YMCA, 533
YouTube, *264b*, 608

Z

Zacchini, Hugo, 245, *246*, 273–277
Zamora, Ronny, 294
Zapple rule, 490
Zenger, John Peter, 55
Zeran, Kenneth, 149*b*
Zimmerman, Diane Leenheer, 684*n*2, 691*n*43, 693*n*139, 693*n*147
Zoning to restrict adult stores, 563–564
Zuckman, Harvey L., 691*n*62, 691*n*65